Volume I

EMPIRE FOR LIBERTY

"... Such an Empire for Liberty as She

Thomas Jefferson in a letter

EMPIRE for

The Genesis and Growth of the

DUMAS MALONE
COLUMBIA UNIVERSITY
and UNIVERSITY OF VIRGINIA

•

BASIL RAUCH
BARNARD COLLEGE
COLUMBIA UNIVERSITY

has never surveyed since the Creation."

to James Madison, April 27, 1809

LIBERTY

United States of America

VOLUME ONE
To 1865

APPLETON-CENTURY-CROFTS, Inc.
New York

PICTURE CREDITS

ABBREVIATIONS
LC—*Library of Congress;* N-YHS—*New-York Historical Society;* NYPL—*New York Public Library.*

END PAPERS: front, *NYPL;* back, *Courtesy of the Mabel Brady Garvan Collection, Yale University Art Gallery.*

Insert, PART I: 1 top, *William L. Clements Library, University of Michigan,* 1 bottom, *Michigan Tourist Council.* 2 top, *LC,* 2 bottom, *Philadelphia Museum of Art.* 3 top, *Virginia Chamber of Commerce,* 3 bottom, *H. F. du Pont Winterthur Museum.* 4 top, *Metropolitan Museum of Art,* 4 bottom, *NYPL.*

Insert PART II: 1 top, *Historical Society of Pennsylvania,* 1 bottom, *Culver Service.* 2 & 3, *Courtesy of the Yale University Art Gallery.* 4 top, *NYPL,* 4 bottom, *LC.*

Insert PART III: 1 top & center, *N-YHS,* 1 bottom, *Museum of Fine Arts, Boston.* 2 top, *N-YHS,* 2 bottom, *LC.* 3, *Culver Service.* 4 bottom, *NYPL.*

Insert PART IV: 1, *Historical Society of Pennsylvania.* 2 top, *N-YHS.* 3 top, *N-YHS,* 3 center & bottom, *Collection of the Corcoran Gallery of Art.* 4 top, *Baltimore and Ohio Railroad,* 4 bottom, *State Historical Society of Wisconsin.* 5 top right, *Valentine Museum,* 5 bottom, *N-YHS.* 6-7, *The Butler Institute of American Art.* 8, *Peabody Museum of Salem, Mass.*

Insert PART V: 1 top & bottom, *Brown Brothers.* 2, *Collection of City Art Museum of St. Louis.* 3, *LC.* 4 top, *American Museum of Photography,* 4 bottom, *N-YHS.*

Insert PART VI: 1 top, *Brown Brothers,* 1 bottom, *National Archives.* 2 top left & 2 top right, *LC,* 2 bottom right, *National Archives.* 3, *Department of the Army.* 4 top, *National Archives,* 4 bottom, *LC.*

To

the students we have been privileged to teach —at Columbia, Barnard, Yale, the University of Virginia, the United States Naval Academy, and elsewhere—*we gratefully dedicate this book.*

PREFACE

THIS HISTORY OF THE UNITED STATES AND ITS PEOPLE HAS GROWN OUT OF our study and our teaching of American history in college and university. We believe that if history is to come alive in the minds of readers it must be presented primarily as a story. Therefore, this work is predominantly narrative in form. Within the inexorable limits of space, we have tried to do justice to all the important aspects of American history—political, economic, constitutional, diplomatic, social, religious, artistic, and intellectual.

In the process of selection, we have laid emphasis on two themes of special interest today. The course of world affairs in our century has magnified the importance of American foreign policy, and in this work we have emphasized the history of United States international relations. In response to the crucial importance of ideology and movements of thought in our time, we have also given special attention to these. But we do not forget that the American story is one of human beings rather than impersonal forces. We have paid special attention to the people and their leaders in all fields at each stage.

We are wedded to no single thesis, knowing of none by which the whole of our history can be adequately explained. But we do see, as a thread running through the entire fabric, the idea of the free individual. And we believe that, with occasional exceptions, an "Empire for Liberty" comprises the ambition that Americans have had for their expanding society.

The word "empire," as used by Thomas Jefferson in the quotation on our title-page, connotes no exploitation of subject regions on this continent or anywhere else. Its meaning has been newly illustrated by the admission of Alaska and Hawaii as full-bodied members of the Union of self-governing states. The vision of a better life for every human being, with faith that it would result from maximum liberty compatible with public order, inspired all the most fruitful public and private actions of Americans from the beginnings of English settlement. If this vision was temporarily blurred after the Civil War, it has gained renewed life because of events in the twentieth century, especially the rise of totalitarianism in the world.

The threat to the free individual that is implicit in the consolidating tendencies of our generation, both at home and abroad, intensifies the need to grasp the meaning of the American experience. Americans and all others who believe that man fulfills himself in conditions of political, social, economic, and cultural freedom should understand that American history is less important as a success story in material terms than as a struggle to fulfill human potentiality. The authors will be grateful to readers who accept this work as an effort to contribute to such understanding.

*   *   *   *   *

Our thanks are due to all those who have helped us through the years to understand our country better—especially to the host of scholars who have enlarged knowledge and increased understanding. That roll is much too long to call. More immediately we owe particular thanks for critical comments on large portions of this large work to Professors Gerald S. Brown of the University of Michigan, Chilton Williamson and Virginia Harrington of Barnard College, John L. Mundy of Columbia University, C. Vann Woodward of the Johns Hopkins University, and John M. Blum of Yale University. Dr. Miles S. Malone of Phillips Academy, Andover, read and commented on the whole work; in addition he rendered special service with respect to the maps and appendices. Miss Ruth Douglas Keener, besides doing much skillful editing, deserves chief credit for the selection of illustrations. The index was prepared by Mrs. Grace Parker. Virtually the entire manuscript was copied by Miss Lucille Ogden. Our publishers have co-operated most generously with us towards completion of the book and at all times have given us the best of counsel.

Since the labor and judgment of both authors have gone into all parts of this work, no precise apportionment of responsibility between them is possible. In the full meaning of the term this is a joint product. We have put far more time and labor into it than we expected; but, now that the task is done, we realize that in restudying and resurveying the whole of our country's past we have enjoyed a very great experience. We hope that this book will serve as an invitation to others to explore that past and share that experience.

D. M.
B. R.

CONTENTS

Part II: Beginnings of the Republic, 1763-1789

Part III: Establishing the Republic, 1789–1815

Part IV: Nationalism, Sectionalism, and Democracy, 1815-1841

Part VI: The Civil War, 1861-1865

MAPS and CHARTS

Annand

Pacific
Ocean

Miles
0   600

Miles
0   100

PHYSIOGRAPHIC

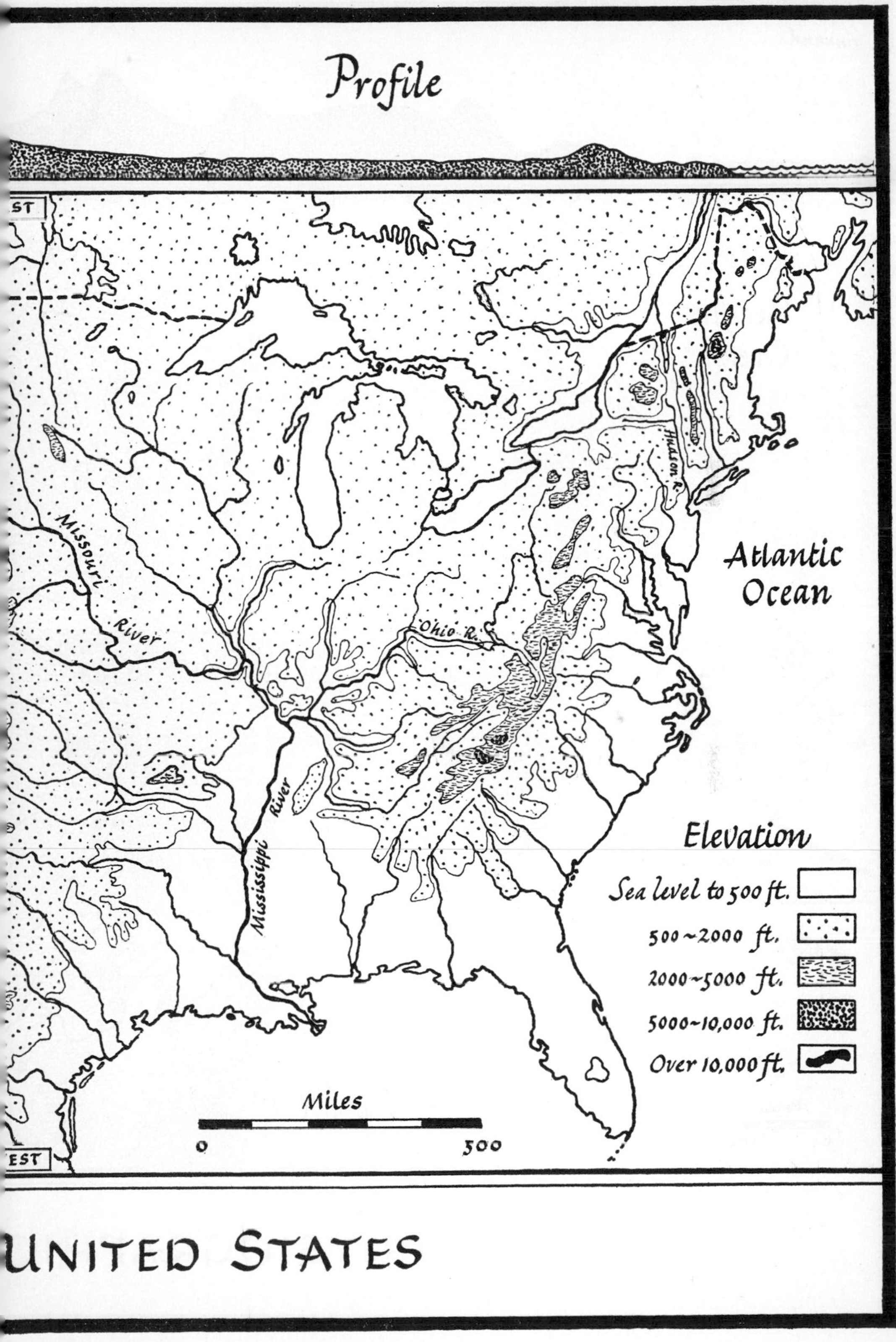

Profile

ST

EST

Missouri River

Mississippi River

Ohio R.

Hudson R.

Atlantic
Ocean

Elevation

Sea level to 500 ft. ☐

500~2000 ft.

2000~5000 ft.

5000~10,000 ft.

Over 10,000 ft.

Miles

0   500

UNITED STATES

Part I

COLONIAL FOUNDATIONS
TO 1763

CHAPTER 1

European Backgrounds

THE MIGRATION OF EUROPEANS TO AMERICA WAS ONE of the greatest folk movements of human history. In the vast and rich new land mankind was given a fresh chance to create on this planet a civilization more nearly like its dreams. Men of all sorts and conditions sought to seize upon unparalleled opportunities for more abundant life, and their continuing efforts comprise the essence of the American story. The desire to create a new and better society has been a leading motivating force in American history from the beginning. It is necessary, however, to inquire why Europeans left their homes and began to come to the New World at a particular period of time. At least one "discovery of America" was made long before the birth of Columbus, but this did not result in permanent trans-Atlantic settlements.

Iceland, a steppingstone to America on the northerly sailing route, has been occupied by Europeans since the seventh century, A.D. Irish immigrants lived there first in small numbers. The boldness of the Irish in going as far as Iceland can be related to the burst of creative energy in many aspects of life that characterized the Ireland of this period, when the rest of western Europe slept in the Dark Age between the breakup of the Roman Empire and the rebirth of civilization in the later Middle Ages. But the Irish did not now venture farther westward.

Scandinavians, thrust out to sea by the inhospitable nature of their rugged peninsula, became the greatest voyagers of the Dark Age. In the ninth century they pushed the Irish out of Iceland and made that island their base for voyages to Greenland. Eric the Red founded Brattahlid on the west coast of Greenland in the tenth century. In the year 1000, which some Europeans feared would witness the end of the world, Leif Ericsson or Leif the Lucky, son of Eric the Red, touched the coast of the North American continent, though scholars cannot agree just where. He was pleased with what he saw, and called the country Wineland the Good.

About a dozen years later, Thorfinn Karlsefni tried to found a colony

3

on the coast where wild grapes grew. He and his little band lived for
more than a year at a spot which may have been on the banks of the
Saint Lawrence River. Indians, whom the Norsemen called Skrellings,
were unfriendly, and the colonists left. But the experiences of Ericsson
and Karlsefni were not forgotten. Their stories were repeated among their
descendants from generation to generation and written down in the four-
teenth century. Scandinavians from time to time voyaged to the remembered coast. It is possible that English fishermen, who sailed to the Grand
Banks off Newfoundland years before the first English colony was established in America and who sometimes went ashore, had learned the way
from the Scandinavians. Yet nothing permanent resulted from the Scandinavian voyages, for the settlement at Greenland disappeared.

The "rediscovery" of America by Columbus on October 12, 1492, might
have been just as indecisive as the adventure of Leif the Lucky, had not
Europe undergone revolutionary changes which made the settlement of a
new hemisphere a practical, almost a necessary, enterprise.

The Commercial Revolution

When Leif stepped ashore at Wineland the Good, and for several centuries thereafter, European society was organized to suit the requirements
of an inefficient agricultural economy. Farming methods were primitive
and did not produce enough food to support any considerable increase
in population, or to free more than a tiny privileged minority from
subsistence labor. There was little trade, since local agricultural groups
did not depend on it for the necessities of life, and almost all effective
political authority was in the hands of local landowners or feudal lords.
Religious activity was international in scale and directed from Rome for
all Christendom, but efforts to create a parallel political organization in
such experiments as the Holy Roman Empire were, on the whole, a
failure. The Church itself supported agriculture as a way of life more
conducive than trade to Christian virtue.

Successful military chiefs in the Middle Ages made themselves and their
heirs lords of the lands they conquered. These lords with bands of fighting
men provided armed protection to those who worked the land as serfs.
The serf, unlike a slave, enjoyed rights, chiefly security under the lord in
his tenure of his strips of land; but it was the lord who interpreted the
rights and duties of all within his domain, and he was often undisposed
to heed the injunctions of any higher religious or political authority.

Every manor and castle with the serfs' huts around it tended to be an
independent community. Artisans produced rudimentary manufactured
articles, and little contact with the outside world was necessary. A priest
in charge of spiritual life was likely to be the only person who could read
and write. Monasteries and cathedral towns were often centers of learning

and art, but they were organized much like the manors, with serfs to till the land and an abbot or bishop as both the secular and spiritual head of the community.

The most striking feature of medieval society was its immobility. It was virtually impossible for anyone to escape the social status and occupation of his parents unless he entered the ranks of the clergy. Freedom of opportunity to better one's condition, or, in the phrase of the sociologist, vertical mobility, an outstanding characteristic of modern American society, was practically nonexistent. Medieval society—hierarchical, authoritarian, and hereditary—seemed frozen in a rigid mold. Yet no sooner was medieval order victorious over the chaos created by the destruction of the Roman Empire by barbaric invasions than the system began to yield, little by little, to forces of change. Barely perceptible in the eleventh century, these forces steadily accelerated the dissolution of medieval society and substituted the forms of life that we call modern. By the sixteenth century, change had progressed far enough to release the extraordinary energies which transplanted European civilization to America.

One of these great changes was the Commercial Revolution. It did not put an end to agriculture as the occupation of the great majority of Europeans. That was left for the later Industrial Revolution to accomplish. But trade and banking became dominant forms of economic activity in addition to agriculture.

Trade had not entirely died out in Europe after the dissolution of the Roman Empire. The use of money for exchange gave way to simple barter of one local product for another. Market days and fairs were customary occasions when surrounding farmers brought their small surpluses of products to a village to exchange them with their neighbors. Towns grew up around such markets, and their year-round population slowly increased. Artisans, whose craft skills created demand for their wooden, metal, leather, or glass wares, set up shops. Officials, notaries, and innkeepers thrived by serving the needs of the market. Merchants bought the surplus of one town and its surrounding countryside and carried it to another for sale at a profit. Prosperous merchants accumulated their profits in the form of gold and loaned it out at interest to lesser merchants, to lords and kings, and even to the Popes of Rome. The Church rule that interest was usury and a sin, because money cannot "breed" money, was relaxed when churchmen realized that trade redounded to the common advantage and that lenders must be compensated for their risk.

The merchants and artisans of the medieval towns fought hard to free their communities from the control of their lords with their incessant demands for soldiers and taxes. Town leaders demanded the right to govern their communities independently in ways conducive to commercial prosperity. They asserted the right to make a serf who escaped from the land and sought refuge and a better livelihood inside the town walls a *freeman* of the town.

The growth of trade and the towns introduced a new factor of vertical mobility into medieval society. Craft artisans banded together in guilds to protect the price and quality of their products. The merchants' guild effectively governed the town. Trade with other towns and distant lands loosed the bonds of superstition and ignorance among townsmen sooner than among country people. The beginnings of technological improvements of manufacturing processes were conducive to scientific advance. The medieval towns, step by step, won their fight for freedom against the lords of the land and became centers of wealth, power, and culture.

In some parts of Europe, especially in the areas of modern Italy and Germany, towns became so powerful that they dominated the surrounding countryside. They developed into city-states, and partly for this reason, Italy and Germany did not become national states until the nineteenth century was well advanced. In other parts of Europe, however, especially in England and France, kings found willing allies in the towns in their struggles to suppress the local princes and nobles and unify their kingdoms under strong central governments.

During the Crusades of the twelfth and thirteenth centuries, generations of warriors from the castles of Europe found in the Near East spicy foods, silken garments, gorgeous tapestries, art and architecture which made their own lives seem tasteless and rude, almost barbaric. When they returned, they were dissatisfied with the productions of Europe. Merchants eagerly invaded Eastern markets to buy the products which the wealthy of Europe demanded.

The self-sufficiency of the manor gave way to dependence on towns and merchants. In England many of the serfs were freed to starve or find work in the towns as best they could while their lands were enclosed for sheep pastures and the wool was sold abroad. Elsewhere serfs were encouraged to raise crops that could be sold, as the lords demanded gold with which to buy luxuries. Serfs were, therefore, transformed into tenants, and diversified farming was increasingly replaced by the production of staples.

Trade by barter gave way to the use of money. Merchants organized trade routes and merchant-bankers financed manufacturers to swell their stocks. They invented basic devices of modern business, such as the chartered company and the letter of credit. They ruled cities, became the paymasters of armies, raised up kings, and patronized artists and scholars. Rightly they were called *merchant-princes*.

By the end of the fifteenth century the Commercial Revolution had progressed far enough to permit daring new ventures beyond the boundaries of Europe and the Near East. Merchant-adventurers and ambitious governments sent ships into the seven seas to discover new supplies of goods Europe wanted and new markets for European productions. The search for gold and silver was especially keen because Europe produced almost none, and its trade with the Orient drained accumulated stores of the precious metals to the East. European merchants became impatient with the cumbersome method of trading with the Orient through middlemen, each of whom made his own profit. They resented the trade monopoly of the Italian city-states. Besides that, an old route through Constantinople was less profitable after 1453 when the city was conquered by the Turks. The hope of breaking the monopoly of the Italian cities led to a search for a new route to the Orient and the "rediscovery" of America.

The event was an incident in the world-wide quest for trade and gold. The Commercial Revolution had introduced a dynamic factor into European society, and the transplanting of European civilization to America, though not wholly attributable to it, was one of its results.

The Rise of National Monarchies

A second great change which helps to explain the settlement of America occurred in the political organization of the western European peoples. The fifteenth century witnessed in Spain, France, and England the rise of national governments controlled by absolute monarchs. Monarchical government in which the king personally wields ultimate power has in our century passed from the European scene. But nationalism has steadily increased in force until today it is perhaps the most important single determinant of society. It deserves particular attention by Americans because, although they have rejected monarchy, they have adopted nationalism with little modification.

After the breakup of the Roman Empire, Europeans dreamed of some day restoring such a universal government with its many advantages of peace, law, and unity for the known portion of humanity. The Church of Rome adapted to religious purposes the universal organization of the Empire, and to some extent it succeeded in encouraging a single law for Christendom, but Europeans were unable to achieve political unity or peace.

In the later Middle Ages a new principle of political organization emerged. It was in a sense a compromise between the localism under which men suffered and the universalism of which they dreamed. This was the principle of nationalism. It meant the political organization under one central government of people speaking the same language, occupying a particular geographic area, sharing a common historical tradition and a common destiny. Individuals were ready to serve this new order, co-operating to create a coherent economic system, and tending towards religious unity or, in the nineteenth and twentieth centuries, agreeing upon tolerance of religious differences. Nationalism was slow in growth, often involving civil war before a country accepted it, and it has assumed protean forms, but we may detect its earliest beginnings in the very system of feudalism it destroyed.

Increasingly during the Middle Ages, feudal lords allied themselves to each other in bonds of fealty under which the one gave service, military and financial, and the other gave protection against enemies. Intermarriage among the nobility of Europe, and ownership by one family of widely scattered lands and castles, strengthened these ties. It often happened that one lord was linked to dozens of others, to some of whom he gave service, while from others he received protection. These alliances by no means united contiguous geographic areas, but the convenience of such contiguity created a steady tendency towards the amassing of holdings in one region. Furthermore, feudal lords who claimed kingship struggled to bind all the lords of their kingdom, and even other kings, in personal fealty to themselves. At the same time, the Commercial Revolution encouraged larger political units.

In the climactic wars of the Middle Ages two tendencies were visible. First, the attempts of kings to subject distant kingdoms to their rule failed. Thus the Hundred Years' War of the English kings to make good their claim to rule France resulted in defeat and the political independence of both countries. Second, the attempts of kings to subject the lords of their own kingdom to their rule succeeded, notably in Spain, France, and England.

In Spain, the struggle took the form of centuries-long wars of Spaniards to expel the Moors, and this resulted in a high degree of political and religious unity among all Spaniards. Feudal lords consented to the leadership of their local monarchs, and the famous marriage of Ferdinand of Aragon and Isabella of Castile united under one dynasty the last two separate Spanish kingdoms. Success against the Moors followed. They were finally defeated in 1492, the very year of Columbus's first voyage. In that year also, Ferdinand and Isabella expelled the Jews from Spain. A powerful kingdom emerged, intolerant of racial or religious differences from the Spanish Catholic norm, experienced in war and arrogant with power, ready for new adventures to spread Spanish Catholic civilization to new lands, and eager to gather riches from them to pay for the wars and bring luxury to the rather barren Spanish Peninsula.

In France, free of alien intruders like the Moors, national unity was achieved less dramatically and less quickly but nonetheless surely. The French feudal aristocracy was particularly factious and only the most skillful king could hold the lords in check. Francis I was such a king. Early in the sixteenth century he achieved so much authority that France seemed about to rival Spain in capacity for national enterprise beyond her borders. But a succession of weak kings after Francis allowed the

ploitation. The Dutch organized a rich trade in spices with the East Indies, and established their rule over many of those islands, but their larger ambitions were frustrated by the weakness of their position in Europe. Portugal opened up new trade routes from which stronger countries chiefly profited. England, the last comer in the race for power through trade, and the least rigid in her mercantile regulations, was nevertheless the most successful of all. Why this should have been true will become clear later in our study.

At this point we can safely say that the political and economic energies of the new national monarchies in western Europe, which emerged from feudalism during the fifteenth century, help to explain why the isolation of the Western Hemisphere since the dawn of time was suddenly and irrevocably destroyed in 1492.

THE RELIGIOUS REVOLUTION

We should commit a serious historical error if we were to read our own preoccupations with politics and economics into the minds of our ancestors and minimize that aspect of life which they regarded as most significant of all: the effort to know and obey God's will. For Europeans of the fifteenth century this all-important effort was unthinkable without the aid of the One, Holy, Roman, Catholic, and Apostolic Church. The Church provided not only certitude of knowledge of God and his Divine Plan for mankind, but also rules of conduct and sacramental means guaranteed to provide the obedient soul with eternal happiness. The Pope of Rome was Vicar of Christ on earth, administering the temporal power and the spiritual treasury of grace which Jesus had entrusted to Peter for the comfort and salvation of humanity. The authority of the Pope, and therefore of God, reached down along the descending levels of the Church hierarchy of cardinals, archbishops, bishops, and abbots into every hamlet of Europe in the person of the local priest. It was an impressive structure, this international organization and hierarchy, wealthy and powerful in temporal things beyond lords and kings, yet still more wealthy and powerful in the realm of the spirit, because it held the keys to Heaven and Hell for all humanity. It controlled minds as well as souls, bodies as well as minds. Its power, the reflection on earth of the Divine Will, was all-pervasive: in art and science as well as theological and philosophical speculations; in the processes of governments as well as the conduct of serfs; in daily life as well as Sunday religious service and the myriad festivals of the saints in Heaven.

The Church used its vast power and wealth in many beneficent ways. It fostered art, architecture, and learning, so that the high medieval culture emerged from the semibarbarism that followed the fall of the Roman Empire. It ministered to the sick and the poor, so that the monasteries and houses of charity of medieval Europe performed some of the functions which private charity and governmental assistance perform in modern society. It tempered the barbarism of the early invading hordes and the cruelties of the powerful with the Christian law of love. It mitigated the pride and bitterness of caste by preaching that, in the eyes of God and the Church, lord and serf were equally destined for eternal glory. It even reduced the scourge of war occasionally by invoking the "Truce of God." Most important of all, the Catholic Church held before men's eyes a spiritual vision of Divine Order and noble destiny for man which redeemed the sorrows and futilities of this world. Through Christ, the Church conquered death itself.

The Church claimed that its civilizing and spiritualizing mission justified the obedience and material support it demanded from the mighty and the humble. Europeans for the most part responded willingly to its demands. Here and there a recalcitrant king or a doubting reader of the Bible challenged the authority of the Church and pointed to abuses of its power. But the Church resisted the argument that abuses by its ministers justified rejection of its authority, regarding it as heresy and a threat to its mission. It did not claim that its officials were never sinners, but it denied that their sins justified overthrow of their authority. Pious churchmen called for reform *within* the Church.

Corruption grew among the clergy during the later Middle Ages in some proportion to the ever-increasing wealth of the Church; and, more and more, men questioned the divinity of an institution that seemed so obviously temporal in its interests. Laymen, gaining in instruction, became ambitious for equality with the clergy. The lowest serf compared his own hunger and rags with the luxurious life of the fat prelate wrapped in furs and supping on rare food and wine. Ambitious kings looked enviously at vast lands engrossed by the Church and at its chests of gold and jewelry which yielded no increment to the wealth and power of their kingdoms. Particularly they resented the huge quantities of precious metals which the Church drew to Rome from every domain in Europe that imported them. Also, the Pope was a rival temporal king among kings, as well as spiritual Vicar of Christ, and the loyalty he claimed from all Christians he sometimes used to further the interests of his temporal kingdom, so that other kings found their subjects divided in their loyalty. The popes seemed to chaffer in the marketplace for gold; to play chess in the power politics of Europe with kings as pawns and the unfair advantage of hidden armies of loyal subjects inside every kingdom; to relish the vices and luxuries of the ancient Roman emperors; and their claim to be the surrogates of Jesus Christ fell into disrespect.

Prior to the sixteenth century, the Church put down religious rebellions by force, and for centuries more it continued to use force against them. But on October 31, 1517, a German monk named Martin Luther raised a banner of revolt which the Church could not suppress. On that day, Luther nailed to the church door in Wittenberg his famous Ninety-five Theses opposing doctrines and practices of the Church. Millions rallied to the standards of Luther and other reformers until North Europe, after more than a century of ferocious religious wars, established its religious freedom from Rome.

Luther protested against the sale of indulgences, which are remissions of temporal punishment after death for sins. He proposed a doctrine which deprived the Church of most of its function as intermediary between God and man. The essence of this was that men could achieve salvation by faith without works. By "works" he meant chiefly the sacraments which the Catholic Church claimed were essential to salvation and which could be administered by its priests alone. Luther reduced the number of sacraments from seven to two, baptism and communion, and reduced the importance even of these. He abolished monastic orders and the celibacy of the clergy. For a time he attempted to win the approval of Church authorities for his doctrines, but when they refused, he denied the authority of the Pope. A large part of Germany and all of Scandinavia quickly adopted Lutheranism. Princes and kings were particularly enthusiastic. They found in the new doctrines justification for depriving the Church of Rome of its possessions and power in their domains. They established new churches which took on the character of national institutions.

Lutheranism was conservative in comparison with new revolts which followed—especially the Peasants' Revolt of 1525 in Germany. This was directed against the land-owning aristocracy and both Catholicism and Lutheranism; and it coupled economic and political radicalism with extreme religious individualism. Martin Luther supported the violent suppression of the Peasants' Revolt, and the "radical sects" were persecuted by both Lutherans and Catholics. In the seventeenth century, some of the German sectarians found refuge in America, particularly in William Penn's tolerant colony of Pennsylvania where they still maintain their beliefs and unique social customs. Lutheranism itself as a state church never found a habitation in the New World, but in later generations it appeared there, in one form or another, among immigrants from Germany and Scandinavia.

In Switzerland a revolt broke out which had great significance for America. Ulrich Zwingli in 1527 repeated Luther's action and went farther. He abolished all ritual and attributed only symbolic meaning to the sacraments. Religious war broke out in Switzerland and Zwingli was killed in 1533, but a Frenchman, John Calvin, carried on the work in Geneva, which became the capital from which revolt spread far and wide. In 1536 Calvin published *The Institutes of the Christian Religion,* the manual on which all subsequent varieties of Calvinism were based.

The chief doctrine of Calvin was predestination, according to which God had determined from the beginning of time which human souls were destined for Heaven and which for Hell. This denied free will to human beings. But even though his doctrine meant that nothing could be done to change one's ultimate fate, Calvin taught that a devout and virtuous life was a visible sign that God had "elected" an individual for Heaven. Calvinism therefore led its adherents to engage in continuous self-examination and rigorous self-improvement, in the hope that one might discover that he belonged to the elect rather than the damned.

The question of the individual's election was important not only to himself but also to his co-believers because of the system of church organization that Calvin established. The local congregation with its minister was the sole structure. It was controlled, not by the whole congregation, but only by those who were thought to be elect in co-operation with the minister who was the final judge. Later in New England, participation in government was also restricted to church members, that is, the elect led by the clergy.

Calvinism was a harsh but powerful creed. It spread rapidly into France, where its adherents were called Huguenots, into The Netherlands (Dutch Reformed Church), into Scotland (Presbyterians), into England and the English colonies in America (Puritans—Congregationalists), and elsewhere. Worldly pleasure, even of sorts that others regarded as innocent, Calvinists rigorously forbade to themselves and their neighbors because they regarded it as a visible sign of an unregenerate heart. Outwardly and inwardly, the Calvinist was severe and somber—in keeping with his vision of God as an unpropitiable and inflexible Master. Some historians believe that the Protestant religions in general and Calvinism in particular reflected the new economic system of merchant-capitalism. They point out that the individual responsibility of the Protestant for his religious life parallels the individual enterprise of the capitalist, and that codes of religious ethics which imposed thrift and sobriety were better suited to a rising capitalism than the tolerance of human weakness characteristic of Roman Catholicism.

However that may be, it seems clear that the Protestant Revolution contributed to the growth of nationalism and to the expansion of European powers overseas. This can be seen not only in countries where Protestantism was successful, but also in France and Spain, where the Catholic Counter-Reformation defeated Protestantism. With the spread of revolt, the Catholic Church organized a defensive campaign against it. Many of the abuses of which reformers complained were stopped. The Society of Jesus, or Jesuit Order, made up of devoted "Soldiers of Christ," was founded by Ignatius Loyola of Spain in 1540 to combat heresy by militantly propagating the Catholic faith. It sought new converts for the Church everywhere in the world, to compensate, as it were, for losses in Europe. The colonial enterprises of France and Spain were partially designed to further such missionary work. The Counter-Reformation also inspired international and civil wars against Protestantism.

These wars, which ended only with the Peace of Westphalia in 1648, while they were mainly religious, also strengthened nationalism in Europe. Kings exploited the religious fervor of their subjects in order to advance their personal and national interests against rival monarchs, so that sometimes Catholic governments fought Catholic governments. At the same time, monarchs strove to put down religious dissent within their territories, in order to add religious unity as an element of national strength to political unity. At the end of the Thirty Years' War, which involved practically all of Europe, the peacemakers in 1648 turned to a principle other than religion as a basis for peace. This principle was nationalism, which dictated boundaries roughly corresponding to those of Europe today. Each ruler was permitted to determine for himself the religion which should be supported by his government and imposed on his subjects. Thus nationalism triumphed while the religious issue was compromised. Thenceforth religion, when it played a political role at all, was subordinated to the power of the nation-state.

The case of England was special in many respects, but there, too, nationalism triumphed over the Universal Church. The refusal of the Pope to annul the first marriage of King Henry VIII and the favors shown by the popes to rival kings led Henry to put through Parliament in 1534 the Act of Supremacy, which denied the authority of the Pope and made the King head of the English Church. This permitted Henry to appropriate to his own uses the vast lands and wealth of the monasteries. He distributed much of the land to faithful supporters of the Tudor dynasty, especially merchants, thereby creating a new aristocracy loyal to the Crown and the nation and further undermining divisive feudalism. At the outset the Anglican Church did not differ doctrinally from Roman Catholicism. Bishops became the effective leaders of the hierarchy, and for this reason the Church came to be called Episcopalian in the United States after the achievement of independence.

Lutheranism and Calvinism as well as radical sectarianism won many adherents in England in the sixteenth century, and they sought to reform or overthrow the Anglican Church as they did the Roman Catholic Church elsewhere. Queen Elizabeth, the last Tudor, temporarily settled the issue in favor of national peace by according, in 1558, a degree of tolerance to doctrinal differences within the Church of England. After her death in 1603, the Stuarts of Scotland came to the English throne, and critics and opponents of the Established Church were persecuted. James I and his son, Charles I, believed in their Divine Right to rule and the duty of the people and Parliament to obey in secular as well as religious matters. Many of the English settlers in America, especially the Puritans of the Great Migration to New England during the decade beginning in 1630, were motivated by a desire to escape the Stuart tyranny.

In 1642, civil war broke out in England between the Royalists, or Cavaliers, and the Parliamentary Party, or Roundheads. The landowning noblemen and "High Church" Anglicans supported the King. Parliament drew its strength from the rural gentry, merchants, and artisans of the towns, who were Puritan or Congregationalist Calvinists; from the Presbyterian Calvinists who were strong in Scotland; and from many more radical varieties of dissenters. Oliver Cromwell organized the "Ironsides," an army fired with religious zeal, and easily overcame the King's forces In 1649, Charles I was convicted of treason and executed. Oliver Cromwell became Lord Protector—in effect, dictator. When he died the English people and Parliament were ready to accept promises by the exiled son of Charles I that he would rule with due respect for Parliament. He was invited to the throne as Charles II in the Restoration of 1660, and for twenty-five years ruled England on the Tudor model.

His brother and successor, James II, threatened to restore Catholicism and reassert the old Stuart claims to rule by Divine Right. Parliament deposed him and made his daughter, Mary, with her husband, William of Orange, joint sovereigns. Parliament passed in 1689, and the monarchs of England thereafter adhered to, the several acts that constituted the "Glorious Revolution." These acts included a Bill of Rights, an Act of Toleration applying to all Protestants, and in general allowed the growth of the authority of Parliament to rule England. This settlement was the foundation of an era of religious and civil peace within England which persists to our day and is unrivaled in modern history.

Most of the English colonies in America were founded during the troubled seventeenth century. Unlike the Spanish and French colonies, the English settlements as a group were heterogeneous in the religious composition of their populations, and they enjoyed in varying degree the privileges of self-government. These circumstances were peculiarly favorable to the growth of free institutions in English America. The Religious Revolution which Luther launched led Spain and France to build in America new strongholds of the old Catholic faith, but in one or another of the English colonies an adherent of any Christian religion might find a haven.

THE INTELLECTUAL AWAKENING

The Intellectual Awakening of the fifteenth and sixteenth centuries also helps to explain the European expansion. In general, the mind of man was freed from control by religious and political authority and men set out to discover the truth about humanity, society, nature, and the universe, guided solely by observation and individual reasoning power. The Renaissance, that is, the revival of ancient Greek and Roman learning and arts, began in Italy in the thirteenth century and spread throughout Europe. It created the intellectual climate in which modern science and culture were born.

At first the scholars and artists of the Renaissance did not challenge the authority of Church or State. Indeed, the great thirteenth-century theologian Saint Thomas Aquinas reconciled pagan philosophy, especially that of Aristotle, and Catholic faith. Some of the popes and many feudal lords and kings were patrons of the new learning and art. But the thrill of rediscovering ancient culture led bold thinkers to add new discoveries of their own by questioning accepted notions and following the dictates of observed fact and reason, and these discoveries sometimes required the defiance of religious and political authority.

Such a discovery was made by Nikolaus Copernicus (1473-1543), a Pole or German who lived in Italy. He conceived that the earth was a planet revolving around the sun. His proofs of this heliocentric theory were inadequate, and he hesitated to publish them, but his hypothesis upset the accepted view, derived from the Greek philosopher Ptolemy, that the earth was the center of the universe. The implication of the Ptolemaic view that man, the highest form of life on earth, was the most important entity in the universe, fitted well the Christian view that man was God's climactic creation and the special object of his Divine Plan. The heliocentric view seemed to undermine these foundations of Christian faith. The Copernican hypothesis was partially proved by the Italian mathematician and astronomer Galileo Galilei (1564-1642), but the Roman Catholic Inquisition required him to deny its truth.

In Protestant England scientific advance was not restricted. Issac Newton in his *Principia* of 1687 established the laws of physics which were accepted by scientists until further discoveries partially modified them in the twentieth century. The English also excelled in the invention of practical applications of scientific principles in devices and machinery which helped them to lead the world in efficiency of industrial production. The English colonies were the heirs of English science. In Benjamin Franklin they produced an experimental scientist capable of advancing human knowledge, especially in the field of electricity, and Americans eventually equalled the British in practical inventions.

The same pattern may be observed in the history of the social sciences. The application of reason to the laws of human society was encouraged by the rediscovery of ancient writers and reached a culmination in the work of the Englishman, John Locke (1632-1704). Rationalist social scientists believed that government, economics, and all social institutions were, or should be, subject to natural law in the same manner as the physical universe. Locke declared that natural law and human reason justified the

Glorious Revolution of 1688. His theories were applied even more rigorously by the authors of the American Declaration of Independence in the next century.

As Europeans came to make empirical science the sole criterion of truth and to subject all aspects of reality to human reason, they turned to the exploration of the surface of the earth in order that it, too, might yield its secrets. The great explorers provided experimental proof of the hypothesis that the earth was round. The fifteenth and later centuries saw a long procession of such "experimenters" set sail from Europe to seas and shores unknown. The thirst of these explorers for knowledge, far surpassing that of the Scandinavians of earlier centuries, would not be satisfied until every foot of the globe was studied and charted. Thus it was that the "rediscovery" of America became an incident of the Intellectual Awakening.

The revolutionary ferment of Europe, which began in the thirteenth century and touched all phases of economic, political, religious, and intellectual life, is the essential explanation of the settlement of America.

CHAPTER 2

Continental Powers
and the New World

THE AGE OF DISCOVERY WHICH BEGAN IN THE FIFTEENTH century has gone on until brave men have reached the poles and scaled the earth's highest mountains in the twentieth. Furthermore, the discoveries and explorations of the fifteenth and sixteen centuries ushered in a new and unparalleled era of trade and settlement which is best summed up by the phrase, the expansion of Europe. The process of expansion whereby a small and relatively impotent continent achieved undisputed world leadership continued for upwards of four centuries, until the great powers fell to fighting among themselves in 1914. Australia and New Zealand were eventually colonized by the British, while Asia was penetrated by Europeans and parts of Africa were settled by them; but the conquest and colonization of the Americas comprise the most significant phase of European expansion. For long generations the star of empire was brightest in the West, and the struggle for position there was a major element in the conflicts among European nations, at least until the winning of independence by the United States. Even after the republics of North and South America were established, they carried on European languages and civilization, modified though these were by New-World conditions. Viewed in the world setting these countries were outposts of Europe, and their colonial history is a part of European history.

We must lay chief emphasis on England, but other nations of the Old World played an even more conspicuous part in the early saga of discovery, exploration, and conquest. In a brief survey of their accomplishments it is impossible to do justice to the bold mariners who braved the perils of vast and unknown waters, to the explorers who treaded the trackless forests and overcame the mountains, to the conquerors who invaded and took over the fastnesses of ancient Indian potentates, to the

19

traders who plied the seas. These audacious men were seeking treasure, to be sure, but they faced incalculable dangers in the name of national patriotism and their holy religions; and, despite the many stains of cruelty on their records, they were heralds and pioneers of European civilization.

PORTUGAL

Prince Henry of Portugal (1394-1460), called "The Navigator," was the precursor of the Age of Discovery. His chief accomplishment was a series of voyages, led by himself or navigators he had trained, along the uncharted western coast of Africa. In his career may be observed the transition of Europe from medieval to modern interests. He began as a religious crusader conquering the infidels of Africa; he ended as a political and economic imperialist expanding the power and wealth of the Portuguese monarchy. He advanced the science of navigation and European knowledge of geography as means to religious and secular triumphs.

Portugal was in a strategic position for such adventures in the fifteenth century when Spain was still partially occupied by the Moors. Prince Henry was zealous to win new territory for Christendom, and the popes issued Bulls calling upon the kings of Christendom to help Portugal in holy war against the African Muslims. But rising nationalism was fast destroying the ardor of kings for international religious crusades, and Henry received no help. His capture of Ceuta in North Africa was a national victory for Portugal. He conquered the Atlantic islands—Madeira, Cape Verde, and the Azores—and became more and more interested in a plan of empire for his country. The gold and slaves of Africa tempted him to send his navigators down along the coast of the unexplored continent.

After Henry's death, Portuguese navigators continued to lead Europe in explorations. In 1488, Bartholomew Diaz sailed around the Cape of Good Hope. India lay ahead, and Vasco da Gama in 1498 reached that fabled land. But by this time Spain, newly unified and triumphant over the Moors, had superseded Portugal as the leading promoter of explorations. The Portuguese navigator Magellan was in the employ of Spain when he set out to circumnavigate the globe in 1521. Portugal during her brief era of glory had won footholds overseas which she retained as trading posts, and the Pope awarded her a monopoly over the southern sea route to India and title to Brazil, but she was unable to compete with the more powerful Atlantic monarchies for the chief prizes.

SPAIN

Columbus

Jealousy of Portuguese achievements incited Ferdinand and Isabella of Spain to surpass them. The Genoese trader and navigator Christopher Columbus gave them their opportunity. Almost every aspect of Columbus's early career is in dispute, but this much may be fairly stated: he was learned in the geographical knowledge of his time and his determination to extend it was of heroic proportions. He knew the earth was round, he was familiar with Atlantic wind currents, and he was an expert navigator. He may have known of the voyages of the Scandinavians beyond Iceland and he was certainly well acquainted with the explorations of the Portuguese. He made an inspired guess on the basis of fragmentary knowledge that new lands existed westward beyond the Azores. Whether he expected to find "unknown" lands or Cypangu (Japan) and Cathay (China) is in doubt. But it cannot be doubted that he possessed the mentality and character of a "modern" man—persistence in the study of available facts, boldness in projecting startling hypotheses, and determination to subject his dreams to the test of evidence.

Besides this, Columbus was persuasive in argument and skilled in leadership. He offered his enterprise to one sovereign after another, promising them glory, gold, and converts. Finally the Spanish monarchs financed the speculation. They made him commander of a fleet comprising the *Niña, Pinta,* and *Santa Maria,* vessels about 75 feet long, well equipped and manned. They sailed from the Spanish port of Palos on August 3, 1492. It was an easy voyage, marred only by a mutiny on October 10 which Columbus quelled by promising to turn back after three days more. At two o'clock on the morning of October 12 the *Pinta* sighted San Salvador, now called Watling Island, one of the Bahamas. After exploring several islands and erecting a fort on Hispaniola (now Haiti and Santo Domingo or Dominican Republic) and leaving a small garrison there, Columbus returned to Spain, where he and his men were greeted with excitement and joy.

Another Genoese, John Cabot, was employed by King Henry VII of England and made two voyages to America in 1497 and 1498, but nothing came of them except an English "legal" title to North America. England was not yet ready for overseas expansion. But Spain was ready. The voyage of Columbus was a national enterprise and it was made to serve the national interest.

The Spanish monarchs provided Columbus with seventeen vessels for a second voyage to establish Spanish rule firmly in the West Indian islands. The garrison at Hispaniola had been wiped out by Indians. Co-

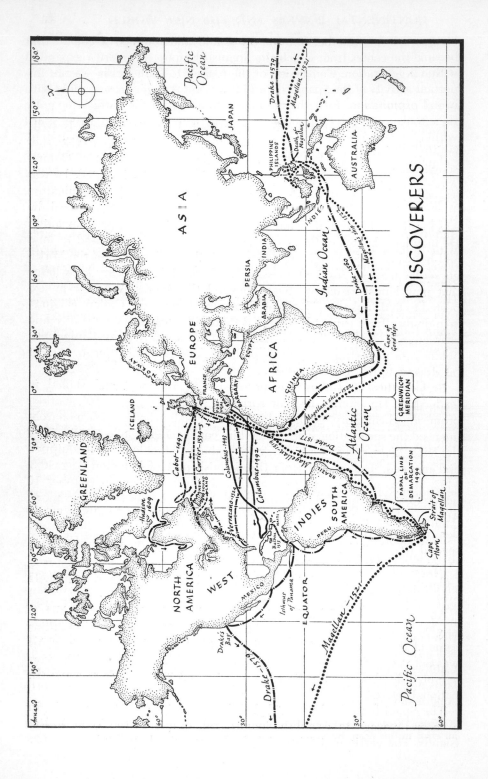

DISCOVERERS

lumbus selected another site on the island and founded a colony that became the center from which the Spanish Empire in America expanded within a generation. Conversion of the natives to Catholicism was an important activity of the Spaniards, and it was not thought incompatible with brutal exploitation. First the Spaniards traded with the natives for gold, then took it by force, and finally drove them to labor in mines until within a few years the Indians of all the islands were exterminated by cruelty, overwork, and European diseases. Then slave-hunting expeditions sought new supplies of labor for the islands on the mainland of South America, and African Negro slaves were bought from the Portuguese.

Spanish colonists were largely unemployed veterans of the Moorish wars who regarded work in the mines and on the land as beneath their dignity. A system of *encomiendas,* comparable to European feudal estates, with Indians as serfs and Spaniards as lords of the land, was gradually developed. Columbus died in obscurity in Spain after a fourth voyage to America, but his work was carried on by *adelantados* and *conquistadores.* His family relinquished to the Crown his claims to hereditary authority over America. Everywhere in the New World governors appointed by Spain followed the explorers and conquerors. As viceroys and captains-general they exercised the absolute authority of the Crown.

Conquest and Colonization

Puerto Rico, Jamaica, Cuba, and other islands were quickly conquered and colonized. Cattle ranches and sugar and cotton plantations flourished. But the Indians' stories of untold wealth in gold, of natural marvels and great cities, led one expedition after another to the mainland. Juan Ponce de Leon discovered and named Florida in 1513 while searching for a legendary spring that would restore youth to the aged. Vasco Núñez de Balboa with several hundred Indians and Spaniards searched for the fabulous Inca Empire of Peru. He crossed the Isthmus of Panama and, "silent, upon a peak in Darien,"[1] saw and named the Pacific Ocean in 1517, only to be put to death by a rival adventurer.

Hernando Cortés with 550 Spaniards found in Mexico the advanced civilization of the Aztecs and vast quantities of gold. Some of the Indians greeted him as their legendary "Fair God" and helped make him in 1521 master of an empire. By 1535, Francisco Pizarro had conquered the equally rich empire of the Incas in Peru. Tales of more rich cities and civilizations led intrepid explorers into the territory from present South Carolina to California, but they found nothing to match Mexico and Peru. The Spaniards never established more than weak frontier outposts along the North American Gulf Coast and westward into New Mexico and California. They

---

[1] From Keats's sonnet "On First Looking into Chapman's Homer." Keats made an error in this poem by naming Cortés as the discoverer of the Pacific.

concentrated their efforts in Central and South America, where, by the middle of the sixteenth century, Spanish civilization and Christianity flourished over the ruins of the Indian states. The Portuguese had won a foothold in Brazil, and in 1580 Philip II succeeded to the thrones of both Spain and Portugal, so for a brief era Spanish glory was unrivaled. The Philippines had been conquered by the Spaniards after Magellan's discovery. The wealth of the Orient as well as of the New World made Spain perhaps the richest empire yet known on earth.

The Spaniards were the first of the modern empire builders and their methods provide a norm with which other imperial systems may be compared. From such comparisons explanations may be drawn in answer to the significant question, why the Spanish Empire, at first so brilliantly successful, lost first place in less than two centuries to the British Empire, that seemingly haphazard creation of latecomers.

The foundations of the Spanish imperial system were Bulls issued in 1493 by the Spanish Pope Alexander VI. In them the authority of the Papacy gave sanction to a division of the whole world into Spanish and Portuguese spheres of influence. Portugal was dissatisfied with its share and Spain consented in the Treaty of Tordesillas in 1494 to a Line of Demarkation running north and south 370 leagues west of the Azores, so that Portugal could enter Brazil. But the Papal Bulls of 1493 had established several great principles. These were: (1) that discovery of non-Christian lands gave legal title to those lands to the Christian sovereign whose agents or subjects discovered them; (2) that the subjects of other sovereigns were forbidden to enter territory legally held by a Christian prince; and (3) that the trade of a colony was an absolute monopoly of its mother country. The other maritime governments paid no attention to Papal Bulls which would have excluded them forever from colonial power. Francis I of France, when he sent Jacques Cartier to the Saint Lawrence, told Spain he wanted to see "Adam's will to learn how he had partitioned the world."

England flouted the Bulls even before Henry VIII displaced the Pope as head of the English Church, and after that event competition with Spain was stimulated by religious rivalry. But Spain proceeded to build her empire on the principle of absolute monopoly. To its political and economic control was added the absolute authority of the Crown of Spain over the religious institutions of the colonies when the Pope conveyed to it the *patronato real*. Under this power of royal patronage the King of Spain controlled all ecclesiastical appointments and benefices in the empire and enjoyed the power of taxation over Church properties. He could even prevent papal orders from being promulgated in the empire by the clergy. In return for these extraordinary privileges, the Spanish Crown had responsibility for the conversion of the natives to Catholicism and the general welfare of religion.

Thus no limit was placed on the authority of the Spanish monarchs in their overseas domain. The Council of the Indies was established in Spain in 1524 to rule the colonies in the name of the king. It made laws, appointed governors and officials, heard cases as the court of final appeal, and supervised the economic life of the colonies. This latter function was the special province of the *Casa de Contratación,* an agency in Spain subordinate to the Council of the Indies. The Casa managed the trade of the empire as a monopoly of the Crown, with the particular purpose of making it yield maximum profits in gold and silver. No Spanish merchant could do business with the colonies except through the Casa and under its rules. No colonial merchant could deal with any other Spanish colony or with any foreign colony or nation—only with Spain, and in Spain only with the Casa. Virtually all colonial activities, personal as well as economic, political, and religious, were heavily taxed for the benefit of the Crown. No share in government was allowed the Spanish settlers in the colonies, and much less did the bulk of the population, Indian serfs or Negro slaves, enjoy power. In the course of time, corruption and inefficiency mitigated the rigors of Spanish rule, but they only substituted other evils.

The great purpose of the Spanish colonial system was to provide the Crown with the wealth in the literal form of gold and silver which spelled luxury and power. Spain might have used this wealth as capital to establish industries at home and supply the colonies with the manufactures they needed. Instead, such manufactures were purchased in northern Europe, where industries consequently thrived on the Spanish market. The Spanish government also wasted the wealth of America on wars intended to make it supreme in Europe—an ambition which was rudely shattered by the destruction of the Armada in 1588. The English even dared to rob Spain of her American profits by attacks on fleets carrying gold in the Spanish Main.

Strength and Weakness of the Spanish System

Spain was a modern power insofar as the country was united under a powerful centralized government, and the life-blood of her empire was trade, regulated according to mercantilist principles. But in most other respects Spain and her empire were medieval. Social organization was even more rigidly defined by hereditary class and caste distinctions in the colonies than at home. The Reformation was countered in the colonies as at home by the Inquisition, which forcefully stamped out heresy, and by the Jesuits, so that Catholicism was at least outwardly strengthened in the process. Although two universities were founded at Mexico City and Lima, Peru, at an early time, the intellectual life of the colonists was subject to censorship in order to prevent infiltration of modern thought. In all that pertained to political and economic freedom, the colonies were equally excluded from participation in modern developments. The wealth of the Indies slipped through Spanish fingers, leaving hardly a trace beyond the transitory luxuries of the few. Within a century after the voyages of Columbus, the Spanish Empire had passed its apogee.

For three more centuries Spain gave ground slowly before the incursions of rival empires and revolts of its subjects, until in 1898 in the Spanish-American War Cuban rebels and the United States delivered the *coup de grâce*. If one chief reason for the failure of the Spanish colonial system can be detected, it is that it stifled rather than encouraged the participation of the colonial peoples in the development of modern social, economic, political, and religious institutions. Nevertheless, the positive gifts of Spain to the Empire, especially in the fields of religion, literature, language, and art, brought millions out of barbarism and remain today as a precious heritage of their descendants in Latin America.

FRANCE

The exciting news of gold in the world that Columbus had discovered acted like a magnet in drawing adventurers of all the Atlantic states across the ocean. Fishermen frequently sailed from France and England to the Grand Banks of Newfoundland, where nets were rarely pulled in empty. French sea dogs raided Spanish settlements and waylaid gold fleets during the years after the conquests of Mexico and Peru. Papal Bulls, the Ten Commandments, and Spanish power were all inadequate to protect the Spanish monopoly of the New World.

Early Explorers

France soon sent the explorers de Gonneville and Verrazano to search out a suitable place for permanent French settlement. Francis I decided that the St. Lawrence River might be a Northwest Passage to the Orient, and in any case was the route to a fabled interior kingdom rich in diamonds and gold. He sent Jacques Cartier on three voyages in 1534, 1535, and 1541. On the third trip, Cartier built a fort on the site of modern Quebec, established a colony, and set out to find the mythical kingdom. Within a year the whole venture was abandoned and the French returned home. The enormous debts Francis I bequeathed to his successors and the civil wars in the kingdom postponed the building of a French empire.

But the claim by discovery and exploration was not forgotten. In better times, during the truce between Huguenots and Catholics under the Edict of Nantes, King Henry of Navarre granted in 1603 to a Huguenot nobleman, Sieur de Monts, feudal and trading rights to a vast strip of North

America lying between the 40th and 46th parallels. This overlapped territory that England claimed and began to settle a few years later. The Anglo-French rivalry for empire in North America was one of the causes of a series of great wars during the next two centuries.

Samuel de Champlain (1567-1635) was an outstanding empire builder of his time. He was a tireless explorer who penetrated the interior of North America and, when too old to go himself, sent young men into the forests and along the lakes and rivers until Frenchmen had traversed the whole area from the Saint Lawrence River to present-day Minnesota and Missouri. Champlain was a diplomat who organized alliances between the King of France and the Algonquin-Huron Confederation of Indian tribes. He helped these tribes expel the Iroquois from the Saint Lawrence Valley and thereby secured a monopoly of the rich fur trade for France. The King of France gave monopoly rights over the fur trade to other favorites, but Champlain and de Monts ignored the royal decree and re-established a colony at Quebec which became the headquarters of the trade in treasured beaver skins. Champlain ruled over savage Indians and hardy Frenchmen until he died in 1635.

The fur trade gave France a source of American wealth less spectacular but more enduring than the gold of the Spanish Empire. The wearing of fur was a sign of wealth and dignity in all Europe. Kings, nobles, and merchant princes paid well for furs trapped by Indians and sold in Quebec for knives and trinkets. The fur trade largely determined the character of the French Empire in America. Because the Indians performed the main task of providing the pelts, French rule over them was benevolent and hardly disturbed the Indians' way of life. The French carried on agriculture only in a limited strip of land on the banks of the Saint Lawrence. There *habitants* tilled the soil as virtual serfs of feudal landholders and created a reproduction of the rural life of old France which has persisted to this day.

In 1632, the first Jesuit missionaries reached Quebec. They were fearless and tireless in the work of exploring the continent and converting the Indians. Thus the Counter-Reformation won new adherents for Catholicism in North America to make up for Protestant inroads in Europe. France might have built a Catholic-Indian empire in the vast region of the Mississippi Valley and the Great Lakes but for the failure of her Indian allies to withstand the Iroquois. The Five Tribes of the Iroquois Confederation—the Mohawks, Oneidas, Onondagas, Cayugas, and Senecas—living then in the present area of New York State, formed ties with Dutch traders at Albany, and later with the English, which made them more than a match for the Algonquin-Huron Confederation. The Iroquois wars, beginning in 1642, disrupted the fur trade and led King Louis XIV to strengthen French rule in America.

Building an Empire

Coming to the throne in 1661, Louis XIV consolidated his absolute rule at home and at the same time made himself personal master over New France. In this work he was influenced by the mercantilist ideas of his principal minister, Colbert. Canada was converted into a royal colony ruled by an *intendant* who exercised the authority of the king in America. The first intendant, Jean Talon, invaded the Iroquois country and defeated the Five Tribes in 1666. Then he reorganized French relations with the Algonquin-Huron tribes whom the Iroquois had scattered as far west as Minnesota, and regularized the fur trade to provide maximum profits for France. In 1673, the Jesuit priest Jacques Marquette and Louis Joliet discovered the upper Mississippi River. Talon's successor, Louis Count de Frontenac, and the explorer Sieur de La Salle, boldly planned to build a string of forts along an interior route that would tie the Saint Lawrence to the Mississippi. La Salle built forts along the route as far as the Illinois River, then he went to France and organized an expedition to invade the Spanish Empire to the south and establish a fort at the mouth of the Mississippi River. He was killed in 1684 by his own followers when they failed to find the difficult entrance to the "Father of Waters." But France was deeply committed now to the struggle for empire in North America.

In 1689, Louis XIV refused to recognize William of Orange as King of England. This was the starting point of four wars between England and France which had for their greatest prize supremacy in the whole of North America. As the fortunes of war favored now one, now the other of the two great contenders, there hung in the balance not merely the question of which Old World monarchy should rule the new continent, but whether it should be held in fief for the Indians and the fur trade, or should be settled by farmers seeking homes in the wilderness.

The Dutch

In the sixteenth century, the kings of Spain ruled The Netherlands by virtue of dynastic marriages. But Calvinism won over a large part of the Dutch people, they were jealous of their ancient rights of self-government, and Spanish religious and military rule were severe. Revolt followed revolt, until the Dutch finally won their independence in 1648 and established a republic ruled by the States General (parliament), and the eldest male of the House of Orange as hereditary *statthalter*. England had helped the Dutch against Spain, and after the defeat of the Spanish Armada the Dutch exploited their excellent geographic position to build an overseas trading empire. The Dutch Calvinist merchants and sailors made up in vigor and persistence what their country lacked in power to compete with the Spanish and the Portuguese. The Dutch East India Company, founded in 1602, was granted extensive political, military, and trade rights. It expelled the Portuguese from much of their East Indian empire and became the chief purveyor of spices to Europe. The Dutch West India Company, founded in 1621, was granted similar powers over American and African trade. Within a few years the Dutch gained a foothold on the coast of Brazil, several West Indian islands, including St. Eustatius and Curaçao, and founded New Amsterdam on the island of Manhattan. Thus the Dutch Republic boldly challenged Portugal, Spain, and England for trade and empire.

New Netherland

Henry Hudson was looking for a shorter route to Asia when, in 1609, he sailed up the majestic American river that bears his name. The Dutch West India Company founded New Amsterdam as a trading post in 1624 and this became the governmental seat of the colony of New Netherland. From this center, Dutch settlements spread eastward into Connecticut and Long Island, northward along the Hudson River, westward into New Jersey, and along the lower Delaware River. But the Dutch had now committed themselves to imperial enterprises so farflung that they could not conduct all of them effectively. They were chiefly interested in Oriental trade and neglected American ventures in favor of the East Indies. Nevertheless, the settlements they made in the present area of the United States were destined to leave a permanent impress upon the country. Dutch architecture provided excellent models for American builders. Dutch tolerance quickly fixed the cosmopolitan character of life on Manhattan Island, where languages, peoples, and religions mingled in carefree confusion. The neat husbandry and solid business methods of the Dutch, their love of plain comfort and domesticity, entered into the American heritage.

In spite of the advanced self-governing character of the Dutch at home, no popular representation was allowed in the government of the New Netherland colony. A governor and council appointed by the Dutch West India Company had sole authority. The governors, such as Wouter van Twiller, Willem Kieft, and Peter Stuyvesant, were regarded as petty tyrants. They mishandled relations with the Indians. The company imposed a feudal land system on the rich Hudson Valley which remained as a relic of medievalism until long after the American Revolution. Anyone who would settle fifty families of tenants at his own expense was granted a large tract of land with rights as *patroon* over the tenants. The patroons exercised political, judicial, and economic authority in their domains. Vast quantities of the best land were kept out of cultivation because the patroons could not attract many farmers to work under this archaic system.

Peter Stuyvesant, the last Governor (1647-1664), injured the commercial prosperity of New Amsterdam by ending the free-trade policy which had promised to make the settlement the headquarters of American commerce. He antagonized the burghers of the town by violating the company's grant to them of self-governing privileges. He imprisoned many who objected to his tyranny. A small Swedish settlement on the Delaware River was taken over by the Dutch, but in the east the English settlers came in such numbers that the Dutch were pushed back. The authorities in Massachusetts in 1659 encouraged migration to the Hudson Valley and sanctioned an English post near Poughkeepsie to attract the Iroquois trade. The Dutch West India Company went bankrupt when its invasion of Brazil failed and it could not support New Amsterdam against the English.

Yielding To The English

After the Spanish danger receded, the English and the Dutch had fallen out. Through the seventeenth century they fought several wars. These ended in 1674. The Statthalter William III of Orange married the daughter of James II of England in 1677, thus paving the way for his accession to the English throne in 1689. The Netherlands retained much of her eastern Empire, but the English in 1664 pushed her out of New Netherland and renamed the colony New York. Weakened by neglect and misrule, it was surrendered by Peter Stuyvesant to an English expedition without a blow.

The English used their victory wisely. The Dutch colonists transferred their loyalty to England and remained an important, even dominant element in the population long after they were outnumbered by English newcomers. The patroons emerged as a provincial aristocracy whose daughters' hands were eagerly sought in marriage by the English merchants of New York City. The Dutch origins of names famous in later American history—such as Schuyler, Van Buren, Vanderbilt, and Roosevelt—attest the enduring importance of the Dutch contribution to American civilization.

❊   ❊   ❊

Trade, religion, and national power were the chief incentives leading Portugal, Spain, France, and The Netherlands to explore and colonize the New World. Portugal, Spain, and France successfully established colonies organized on absolutist and monopolistic principles. Native populations and Negro slaves performed the hard labor of winning wealth for European settlers, who were exploited in turn for the benefit of their mother countries. It hardly entered the minds of Portuguese, Spaniards, and Frenchmen that the destiny of America might be to give Europeans, much less other peoples, a chance to build societies on any other model than one determined for them by the kings of Europe. The opportunity they perceived in America was for kings and their governments to realize their dreams of wealth and power. Consequently, absolutism and monopoly were imposed on the colonies even more harshly than at home.

The official motives of the English government in its colonial policy were not greatly different from those of the continental governments. England attempted to establish an economic monopoly over her American colonies according to the Spanish norm. But the English Crown lacked money to finance colonial enterprises, and had to make concessions to the private groups who did finance them. More important, the traditions and institutions of the English people favored a degree of personal liberty and self-government unknown in Portugal, Spain, and France. In practice, the English government permitted its American colonists wide latitude in economic, political, and religious matters. Thus it became possible for the English colonies to serve not the interests of the king so much as the interests of the colonists themselves. Finally, these colonists carried to America visions of an ideal society far different from the societies the other powers created there.

CHAPTER 3

Early English Settlements:
Virginia and Maryland

THE ENGLISH RESPONSE TO THE DISCOVERY OF AMERICA
was suggested by Sir Thomas More in his famous book *Utopia*, published
in the sixteenth century. Utopia was an ideal society on an island in the
New World and it has given its name to all such visionary schemes. But
some of the most important features of social organization in Utopia that
seemed impossible dreams then are commonplaces of American life now.
Such were the nine-hour working day, inventions to save labor, city planning, free and compulsory education, intellectual and religious freedom,
and, most significant of all, government by representatives chosen by the
citizens.

Englishmen were not content to dream about a better and happier
society. They founded one colony after another in America to carry into
practice one scheme or another for attaining it. The states of the Union
and the federal government itself are practical applications of the utopian
dream of freedom and self-government, and Americans to this day consider it their birthright to criticize public evils and devise improvements
which will bring the ideal society a little closer to realization. The peculiar
English and American combination of social vision and common-sense
practicality underlies the whole course of American history.

SIXTEENTH-CENTURY ENGLAND

At the beginning of the century, England was poor and weak. Henry
VIII built up the Royal Navy in order to protect the homeland from
invasion and the colonies from imperial rivals. To encourage the merchant
class which supported him against unruly nobles, Henry, in the middle of
the century, chartered the Muscovy Company to trade with Russia. This

was a joint-stock company of a type that was destined to play a large role in English colonization. Membership in such a company could be obtained by contributing a sum of money for the purchase of stock, and the members organized themselves as a self-governing body. The company exercised authority outside the kingdom, chiefly economic but also political, which was bestowed by the king in a "charter of privileges." Profits from the business activities were distributed among the members in proportion to their ownership of stock. It can be readily seen that such an organization was an ancestor of the modern business corporation, but its importance goes far beyond the business field. The practice of self-government and the exercise of political authority by companies chartered to colonize America provided experience which led directly to the organization of governments on the same principles.

Rivalry with Spain

England prospered during the sixteenth century in part because the gold of Mexico and Peru was used by Spain to buy English woolens and other products. Also, the religious quarrels between Catholic Spain and the Protestant England of Queen Elizabeth gave English seadogs an excuse to capture treasure ships before they arrived in Spain. When Francis Drake dropped anchor at London with a cargo of Spanish gold, Good Queen Bess paid him the signal honor of visiting him aboard his ship, where she knighted him—and shared his treasure.

Englishmen took over the external trade of their kingdom which had formerly been in the hands of foreigners. Daring English traders even invaded the commerce of foreign empires, as John Hawkins did when he carried African slaves to Spanish America in defiance of the Papal Bull and the laws of Spain and Portugal. The ideal of economic self-sufficiency appealed greatly to Englishmen. Colonies able to provide not only gold but also the commodities that England had to import, such as tar and timber for shipbuilding and all kinds of semitropical products, and capable of buying English manufactures in exchange, were essential to the developing English scheme of self-sufficiency. Besides this, Protestantism could be strengthened by extending it to colonies and thereby limiting the expansion of Catholicism. Thus dreams of national power, national wealth, and national religious security all entered into the creation of an English empire in America.

Spain had no intention of allowing the bold English heretics to destroy her monopoly in the New World. Spurred on by the semipiratical raids of the seadogs, Spain organized the Invincible Armada for the invasion and conquest of England. When the 132 Spanish ships, carrying 3165 cannon and thousands of soldiers, stood in the English Channel in 1588, the future of America hung in the balance. But the seamen of England rallied to the national defense, the Royal Navy was expanded by numerous ships faster and more skillfully managed than the clumsy Spanish galleons, and, under the leadership of Drake, Hawkins, and Howard, the Spaniards were defeated and their proud vessels scattered. A storm off the Hebrides completed the destruction of the Armada, and England was delivered. The joy and patriotic fervor of Englishmen knew no bounds. Their new-found greatness manifested itself exuberantly in literature, notably in the immortal works of William Shakespeare. It also expressed itself in colonial enterprises.

ENGLAND TURNS TO AMERICA

Up to the time of the Armada, English explorers, beginning with John Cabot, had been chiefly concerned with finding a passage through or around America to the Orient. In 1576, Sir Martin Frobisher thought his expedition to find a Northwest Passage was successful when he entered the region of Hudson Bay. Sir Humphrey Gilbert in 1583 laid claim to Newfoundland in the name of the Queen. In 1600, the East India Company was chartered, and it eventually controlled most of the trade of India, paving the way for that country's addition to the British Empire. Richard Hakluyt and others compiled accounts of English voyages which were exceedingly popular reading matter in Elizabethan England. But attempts at English settlement in America in the sixteenth century were not successful. Sir Walter Raleigh, under a patent from the Queen, claimed all North America north of Florida, named it Virginia in honor of his sovereign, and in 1585 planted two colonies on the sands of Roanoke Island, in what is now North Carolina. The first group of colonists went back to England after a year, and the second had mysteriously disappeared without a trace when ships returned to America in 1590.

In 1603, Elizabeth died. Her successor, the Stuart James I, made peace with Spain, thus releasing English soldiers and sailors for American adventures. The business of capturing Spanish treasure ships now declined, and merchants sought other outlets for their venture capital. Thousands of English farmers had been thrown off the land by Enclosure Acts which joined tillage tracts into sheep meadows to provide wool for the textile industry. The Elizabethan Poor Law of 1601 had made such unemployed "sturdy beggars" the charges of the local parishes, which were anxious to get them off their hands. England, suddenly at peace, found herself suddenly overpopulated. Poor families begged for employment for their hands and rich men sought employment for their capital. At the same time, Puritans and Dissenters feared the High-Church Anglicanism of the Stuarts, which seemed but a disguise of Roman Catholic leanings and, worst of all, friendliness to the great enemy of the English patriots—Spain. Furthermore, the Stuarts—James I and his son Charles I

—seemed bent on destroying the ancient rights and privileges of Englishmen, particularly the powers and privileges of Parliament. When the House of Commons adopted the Great Protestation of 1621, including the assertion, "That the liberties, franchises, privileges, and jurisdictions of Parliament are the ancient and undoubted birthright and and inheritance of the subjects of England," the King tore the page from the journal, dissolved Parliament, and imprisoned its leaders.

With the King riding roughshod over his subjects, it seemed to many Englishmen that escape to the New World was the only chance to secure their freedom from Stuart tryanny. Yet it must be realized that the very willingness of the Crown to allow rebellious subjects to go to America was in sharp contrast to the Spanish requirement that none should go to America except Spaniards of proved loyalty and religious orthodoxy. The English settlements in America were unique in that they were largely populated by the poor and the rebellious who were determined to create a society designed for their own well-being rather than the mere aggrandizement of their monarch. The first permanent settlement, however, at Jamestown in 1607, was made under the auspices of a company of merchants and other adventurers whose motives were patriotic as well as commercial.

THE FOUNDING OF VIRGINIA

The King, on April 10, 1606, issued a patent authorizing two companies to set up colonies in what was known as Virgina—the region between the 34th and 45th parallels of latitude, that is, between the Cape Fear River and the present site of Bangor, Maine. The London Company was to begin settlement in the southern part of the territory, the Plymouth within the northern. The specific lands granted were to center in the first seat of settlement in each instance, extending 50 miles north and south along the coast and 100 miles inland. The charter provided that the companies should elect resident councils to govern each colony. A Royal Council in England, appointed by the king, was placed over the resident councils to supervise them in the national interest. This contained persons identified with the companies. Also, the rights of the colonists as Englishmen were guaranteed. Colonists of Spain and France were considered to be outside the law and subject to the arbitrary rule of their kings. But in the charter of the Virginia companies, all "liberties, franchises, and immunities" enjoyed by Englishmen at home were guaranteed to English settlers and their children in America. Among such rights were trial by jury, habeas corpus, and the ownership and inheritance of land. At the same time, the colonies were placed outside the kingdom for purposes of customs duties and in the matter of representation in Parliament.

Jamestown

Members of the companies subscribed money to finance the settlements. The charters enjoined the duty of converting the natives to Christianity, and it was hoped that gold might be found. In spirit the companies were intensely patriotic, but their major immediate purpose was to establish a profitable trade in fish and furs. Only the London Company concerns us here. On December 20, 1606, it sent three ships, the *Susan Constant,* the *Goodspeed,* and the *Discovery,* with 144 men under the command of Captain Christopher Newport, on the southerly route to America. After sailing among the West Indies, the ships entered Chesapeake Bay on April 26, 1607. They were instructed to settle on the river which seemed most likely to afford a Northwest Passage, and away from the coast for security against the Spaniards. Therefore the ships entered the river that was named the James, and on May 24 the site of Jamestown was chosen. Thirty-nine men had died on the long voyage. The survivors built a fortified enclosure for a church and houses and set about exploring the low and heavily wooded country.

These first Englishmen to establish a permanent settlement in America had more liking for adventure than for labor and hardships. They hoped for quick riches by barter with the Indians or the discovery of gold, and they became unruly when threatened by starvation and disease in this rich but untamed land. One mutiny was put down only by executing its leader, Captain George Kendall, and all but thirty-eight men died before the year had ended. Supply ships from England, a new group of immigrants that included more craftsmen and laborers, and the firm rule of Captain John Smith, who became president of the Resident Council in September 1608, saved the colony. The redoubtable Captain put all hands to work and threatened to send shirkers into the forest to starve.

The zeal and intelligence of the leaders of the company in England ensured the endurance of the little settlement. They studied the weaknesses of the venture and worked hard to correct them. They decided that the secret of success was not quick riches, but a stable life for families tilling the soil. Sir Edwin Sandys, an able member of the Royal Council, obtained in 1609 a new charter from the King which enlarged the bounds of the colony to include Chesapeake Bay and gave the officers of the company greater control over the government of the colony. Sir Thomas Smith, an outstanding businessman who was highly experienced in commerce and government, became treasurer and head of the company and he supervised its affairs with skill. A great public campaign was opened to obtain subscribers and settlers. One circular declared that the objects of the company were to spread the Gospel, "to plant an English nation" in America, and to establish a trade which would secure Englishmen from being "eaten out of all profits" by foreigners. Enthusiasm ran high. Guilds and clergymen joined in supporting a heroic new effort. Purchasers of stock were promised their pro-rata share of "Golde, Silver and other mettals or treasure, Pearles, Precious Stones or any kind of wares or Merchandizes, commodities or profits whatsoever." Enough money was raised to outfit nine ships and about a thousand immigrants. In money and in human life the cost of this patriotic enterprise was high.

The company had decided to make Lord De la Warre "Lord Governor and Captain General of Virginia" as a virtual dictator. Sir Thomas Gates went out in May 1609 with the first expedition as De la Warre's deputy. A hurricane forced Gates's ship to Bermuda but the others reached Jamestown, and Captain John Smith gave way reluctantly to Captain George Percy as head of the Resident Council. Disease and Indian attacks quickly played havoc with the newcomers. There followed the grim "Starving Time," which every colony in America seemed fated to endure until the skills and organization necessary to establish a colony were at length attained. By the end of the next winter less than half of the colonists were alive, and these were famished and beseiged by Indians. Gates arrived from Bermuda in May 1610, but when food for only sixteen days remained, the settlers boarded ship for Newfoundland where they hoped for help from fishermen.

Jamestown was abandoned in June 1610, and the fleeing ships were some miles down the river when they met a fleet under the command of Lord De la Warre, with reinforcements and supplies from England. Gates and his men turned about and the whole company reoccupied Jamestown. The Starving Time was past. De la Warre returned to England in March 1611, but Sir Thomas Dale, Sir Thomas Gates, and Captain Samuel Argall successively ruled the colony and placed it on a permanent footing. Settlements on more healthful sites than the one at Jamestown were founded, peace was established with the Indians, and artisans and farmers were more numerous among new immigrants. The rulers of the colony were harsh, but they had to gain some security before they could allow much freedom.

In 1612, Sir Thomas Smith and his associates obtained another revision of the charter, which proved to be the final one. This now gave title to Bermuda. Soon transferred to a subsidiary company, Bermuda was permanently occupied by the English from this time on. Also, the company gained full control of the Royal Council. The affairs of Virginia were completely under the company hereafter until 1624, when the royal period began.

Virginia under the Company

Sir Thomas Dale in 1613 introduced a new land system of great significance for the future of English colonization. Up to this time, the company had retained title to the land, agricultural products were placed in the common storehouse, and supplies were distributed among the colonists according to need with little regard to the labor individuals performed. Dale allotted to every man three acres which he might cultivate for himself in return for a fixed annual payment of produce as rent to the company. Thus an incentive was provided for the individual colonist to work hard. John Rolfe in 1612 began experiments to raise tobacco for export which met with great success. Encouraged by the opportunity to make private profits, the colonists turned eagerly to tobacco production. In 1617, £20,000 worth was sent to England. The economic foundations of Virginia were being firmly laid in smoke.

Sir Edwin Sandys realized that the colony could be rapidly populated only if immigrants were granted an opportunity to own land outright. Beginning in 1618, the company offered fifty acres to anyone who bought a share of stock in the company. Land was also granted to the Church of England for the support of parish churches and clergymen, and to a college which the company hoped to found. Finally, the famous "headright" system was adopted, whereby the company granted fifty acres of land for every person transported to America. An individual could collect a headright for himself and also one for every member of his family or servant he brought with him. Thus an Englishman of small means could transform himself into a landowner in America, and a person of means might establish a large plantation.

Sandys and his associates showed far-sighted statesmanship. They gave up the search for immediate profits for the company in order to create a prosperous colony based on private ownership and private profits which, in time, would redound to the benefit of England and its merchant class as a whole. Moreover, the headright system, which persisted and was afterwards extended to other colonies, facilitated the development of a society composed of self-reliant freemen in sharp contrast to the feudal system of Spanish America. By 1618, however, the Company was heavily in debt. In an effort to recover their losses, members of the company now joined with outsiders to form subsidiary associations and engage in particular enterprises which might be profitable. A number of great plantations, modeled on the English village and its outlying lands, were established or projected by associations of adventurers and planters who received patents from the company. The Pilgrims who ended up at Plymouth had set out to establish one of these Virginia plantations. Other associations were formed to engage in manufactures, but the cultivation of tobacco superseded all other activities.

The anxiety of Sandys to make Virginia attractive to the best type of settler was responsible for the first institution of popular self-government in America. Colonists complained of the tyrannical practices of their rulers, particularly Captain Samuel Argall, and the company in reply bestowed a Charter of Grants and Liberties in 1618. This de-

clared that Virginia should be constituted a "free popular state," and
that no government should be imposed on the colonists without their
consent. A new governor, Sir George Yeardley, was sent out with the
charter in 1619 and instructed to call a general assembly of the
planters every year. Each "corporation" in Virginia, that is, each settlement, hundred, and plantation, was permitted to elect two burgesses as
delegates to the assembly, for the purpose of doing "those things as might
best tend to their good."

Yeardley called the first meeting of the famous Virginia House of
Burgesses in July 1619. He proclaimed the annulment of "cruell lawes"
established by his predecessors, and declared that henceforth Virginia
would be ruled by the "free lawes" that prevailed in England. Elections
for the House of Burgesses were extraordinarily democratic, even servants
and youths of seventeen years taking part. When the twenty-two burgesses
met in the church of Jamestown, no other colony in the Western Hemisphere could match Virginia's progress towards that ideal society of
which Sir Thomas More had dreamed. The experience of Englishmen
in their ancient Parliament in London and, more directly, the experience
of the colonists with the corporation form of business organization, had
provided excellent training. The burgesses immediately organized themselves on the pattern of the House of Commons and proceeded to enact
laws for the government of the colony and draw up petitions to the
company for the enlargement of their sphere of power. One of these
petitions resulted in an important concession by the company in 1621
that none of its orders should be carried out unless it was approved
by the House of Burgesses.

The company had now divested itself of a large share of its political
as well as economic reason for existence, and several difficulties hastened
its dissolution. The first of these involved the new staple crop of tobacco.
The craze for smoking the "sotweed" created a great market in England
and Europe. Many moralists, led by King James I, spoke out violently
against the habit of "drinking" smoke, but their efforts seemed only to
popularize it. The English government imposed a heavy import duty
on Virginia tobacco and forbade the colonists to export it to any other
country, in return for which cultivation of the plant was forbidden in
England. Also, the right to import tobacco was granted by the King to
his favorites as a monopoly privilege. The situation was made worse
when Sandys obtained for the company a monopoly contract to import
tobacco into England, because this contract promised a large share of
the profits to the King and various officials. The leaders of the company
fell to wrangling, Sandys was defeated, and the tobacco contract was
dissolved. Henceforth, tobacco could be imported by anyone into England upon payment of a duty. The English market was protected and

the situation was favorable to the Virginia colonists, but the greatest potential source of profit to the company had been lost.

Meetings of the company in London became contests between embittered factions. Meanwhile, in 1622, a large number of the Virginia colonists were massacred by the Indians, and many of the company's properties, including experimental factories, were destroyed. King James became convinced that the company had mismanaged its affairs, and it was true that defenses had been neglected in favor of the universal cultivation of tobacco. The King moved through his Privy Council to take control of Virginia. Leaders of the company attempted to raise the issue in Parliament but James denied Parliament's authority and was upheld by the courts. The company was dissolved by court order and Virginia became a royal colony in 1624. The new King, Charles I, appointed a governor and council to rule under royal instructions. The colonists preferred this to the company's rule, and were gratified to find that their legislature and local courts of law were not disturbed under the new regime.

Life in the First Colony

Thus Virginia evolved into the first royal colony in America while enjoying a high degree of self-government. Immigration proceeded apace, yet it never caught up with the demand for labor on the tobacco plantations. Indentured servants provided the bulk of the labor supply until the last quarter of the seventeenth century, when Negro slaves were imported in increasing number from Africa. During the middle of the century, as many as 1500 indentured servants came to Virginia every year. They usually had volunteered to serve a master from two to seven years in return for transportation and an "outfit" of clothing and equipment. Then, at the end of their term, they became free citizens, and, obtaining land of their own on easy terms, they often rose rapidly in the social and economic scale.

This transformation of poor Englishmen into landowners enjoying political privileges set a pattern which was to give special character to life in the English colonies. The number of immigrants who belonged to the families of the English nobility was negligible. The first "ruling class" in Virginia as elsewhere in the English colonies was chiefly composed of members of the merchant and yeoman farmer classes who had enough money to bring servants with them and obtain large tracts of land. They formed the "plantation aristocracy" of the new colony, and some Cavaliers joined them later, but their ranks were continually swelled by "new men" rising in the social scale.

Not all of the immigrants came to Virginia and the other colonies voluntarily. English judges sentenced criminals to transportation to

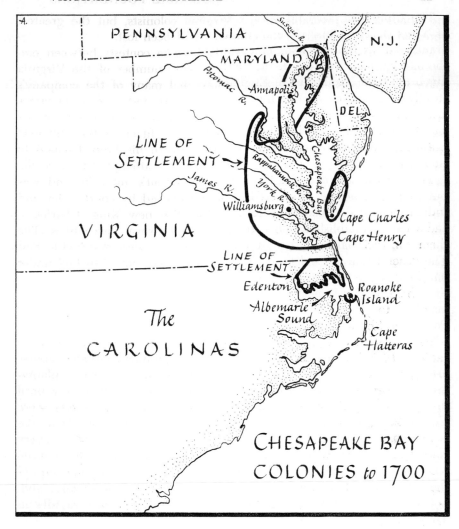

America and overseers of the poor got rid of their charges in the same way. Parliament sometimes banished political offenders to the colonies. Poor children were sent over, as were women to provide wives for the settlers. Prisoners of war, especially Irish, were sometimes transported. Illegal methods of populating the colonies were also used: kidnappers "crimped" the unwary and shipped them off in virtual slavery. The vast majority of involuntary immigrants were unfortunate rather than vicious, and they generally turned into excellent citizens in the New World. As the English poet and divine, John Donne, said, colonization was "not only a spleen to drain ill humours of the body, but a liver to breed good blood."

The Church of England was early established as the state church of Virginia. Provisions were made for its support by means of land grants and tax funds. As settlement advanced along the rivers and into the interior, parishes were defined and placed in charge of clergymen in much the same manner as in England itself. But conformity was never strictly enforced, even after the House of Burgesses in 1642 passed a law to expel dissenters from the colony. The need for settlers and laborers was too compelling for landowners to support any effective campaign against members of dissenting sects or even against clergymen who ministered to them.

The worst hazard of life in the low-lying Tidewater areas was malaria, but when quinine was discovered it helped to mitigate the scourge. The Indian menace declined after several bloody outbreaks. The company had tried to establish friendly relations with the natives and to pay them for their lands, although their legal title was never admitted. The general rule in English as in Spanish America was that any Christian king whose subjects seized territory belonging to infidels acquired title thereby. For some years trouble was avoided in Virginia by the marriage to John Rolfe of Pocahontas, daughter of the Indian Chief Powhatan. She warned the colonists of impending attacks by her tribe. After her father died, his brother Opechancanough led the fearful massacre of 1622. This caused the company to import antiquated weapons, armor, and artillery from the Tower of London, and these medieval arms were employed with great effect in the American wilderness, so that thereafter, except for one uprising in 1644, Virginia was very little troubled by the natives.

The Spanish claimed as their own the lands on which the first English colony in America was established, and they went so far as to send reconnoitering expeditions to Jamestown. But they were convinced that the colony would fail for lack of gold or silver mines, and they would not risk another war with England over territory that seemed so useless. They remained a potential threat, however, and actually the boundary between Spanish and English territory in North America remained in dispute for two centuries, being inherited and finally settled by the United States. France claimed territory indefinitely southward from the Saint Lawrence region, and for a time there were French settlements at Mt. Desert in the present state of Maine. But Sir Samuel Argall wiped these out, and after 1616 Virginia felt secure for some years against the French.

By establishing and maintaining this first colony, the English became successful contenders in the contest of European powers for imperial position in America. According to Spanish standards, Virginia was a useless possession, requiring backbreaking labor of white men and yielding little wealth to the mother country. The population was a "foul brood

of heretics," undisciplined and ambitious for personal rather than imperial gain. Even in imperial terms, however, the English had followed
wise policy. Time was to show that the institutions of self-government
and private ownership of readily available land were more productive
of wealth and human happiness than was the system of absolutism and
feudalism that Spain brought to the Western World.

Maryland

The colony of Maryland began, not under the auspices of a trading
company, but of a proprietor. Its political, economic, and social system proved to be much the same as in Virginia. Maryland was originally the feudal domain of a noble Catholic family. George Calvert,
Lord Baltimore, obtained in 1632 from King Charles I a grant of
nearly ten million acres lying between the Potomac River and the
40th parallel of north latitude. He and his heirs were created "Absolute Lords and Proprietaries" with power to make, with the consent
of the freemen, any laws that were consonant with the laws of England.
They were empowered to make grants for subordinate feudal manors,
to fix rents and levy duties and taxes. In return, the King received two
Indian arrows annually in token of feudal service. The Calverts were
poor and hoped to make their fortune in America and also to establish a
haven for Catholics. The proprietors encouraged Protestants as well to
settle in their domain, realizing that Catholics wishing to migrate were
not numerous enough to build up the colony.

On the death of George Calvert in 1632, the year of the grant to him,
his son Cecil became Lord Baltimore, and the latter appointed his
brother, Leonard, Governor of Maryland. Several hundred colonists of
various faiths voyaged to the Chesapeake in 1634 aboard the *Ark* and
the *Dove*. Catholics chiefly settled around Saint Mary's, Protestants in
and around Providence, later called Annapolis. Immigration proceeded,
and soon the Tidewater region was dotted with tobacco plantations.
The Marylanders learned the technique of successful colonization from
the Virginians and suffered relatively few hardships. All the settlers were
tenants of the Calverts. Some, mostly Catholics, were granted manorial
privileges and great tracts of land. These men farmed their lands with
tenants of their own and servants, and paid quitrents to Lord Baltimore.
Yeoman farmers leased land from the proprietor, used their own labor
supplemented sometimes by that of a few servants, and also paid quitrents.

The Lords Baltimore drew up the laws for their colony and sent them
to a representative assembly of the freemen for approval. From the beginning the Assembly asserted its right to introduce laws. The officeholders, unlike the population, were in majority Catholics, but they

were jealous of the proprietors' pretensions to absolute power. The Assembly enacted a law of religious toleration in 1649, which gave assurance to Protestant immigrants that they would not be persecuted, and many Puritans answered the invitation. Englishmen in Maryland, especially the Protestant majority, continued to challenge the absolute authority of their feudal Catholic rulers, and sporadic civil conflicts marked the history of the colony. The Puritans of Maryland won power for a time during the rule of Oliver Cromwell in England. They did not hesitate to persecute Roman Catholics and to repeal the Act of Toleration in 1654. With the Restoration in 1660, the Calverts regained control and established an uneasy peace. More important than religious disputes in causing unrest in Maryland was the unwillingness of yeoman farmers to pay their quitrents—small money payments representing a commutation of feudal dues and services which were payable to the proprietor by freeholders. Like other frontiersmen in America, they believed they had a God-given right to absolute ownership of the land they cleared and farmed. Despite its proprietary form, Maryland became another nursery of individual freedom, and another school of self-government.

Negro Slavery in the Tobacco Colonies

The supply of indentured servants from England proved insufficient to meet the demand for labor on the expanding Tidewater tobacco plantations of Virginia and Maryland. The theory that England was overpopulated, which had impelled the first colonial settlements, gave way in the 1660's to the opposite view that the mother country was suffering from a shortage of labor. Epidemics of the plague wiped out a sizeable fraction of the poorest classes in England, the shortage of labor sent wages skyrocketing, and loud complaints were made against the draining of artisans and farmers to America. One of the acts of King Charles II after he came to the throne was to charter the Royal African Company to invade and monopolize the slave trade of Portugal. Subsequently, by the *Assiento* (1713), Spain granted Englishmen the privilege of selling African slaves into the Spanish Empire. The trade in slaves to the English colonies was even more lucrative, and it solved their labor problem at the cost of fastening on English America its most inhuman institution.

The usual justification for slavery at the time was that it permitted the conversion of the Africans to Christianity and their general advancement in civilization. But the slave trade, conducted by means of warfare and the corruption of African tribal life, frustrated the development of native civilization in Africa. Also, it killed off many more Negroes than those who were submissive and healthy enough to survive the infamous "middle passage" to America, and the cruel "breaking-in" process which made them amenable to disciplined labor.

Chattel slavery as a legal institution was established in the English colonies almost by accident. Such a form of servitude was unknown in English law. The first Negro slaves in the mid-seventeenth century were regarded as servants who would normally obtain their freedom after a term of labor. But they had no indentures to present to a court to prove their right to freedom, and the temptation to hold them and their children in bondage was too strong for the labor-hungry planters to resist. Late in the seventeenth century large numbers of slaves were brought into the colonies and their status was fixed in codes of laws passed by provincial legislatures. The standard slave codes in English colonies were more severe than among the Spanish and Portuguese, insofar as they left the slaves with no rights against their masters which could be enforced at law. The typical slaveowning planter of Tidewater Virginia and Maryland was kind and patriarchal towards his human chattels, particularly towards those who served him personally, but he was greatly interested in "getting a crop," and he generally left the field hands to the mercies of overseers, who were notoriously brutal as a class.

The introduction of Negro slaves had the effect of expanding the large plantation system. The best Tidewater tobacco lands in Maryland and Virginia came under the ownership of great planters who used gangs of slaves to work them. Small farmers who could not afford to buy slaves found it hard to compete for good land or to sell tobacco as cheaply as the large planters. Many of them eventually turned westward to the Piedmont region, the foothills of the Blue Ridge Mountains, though even there the lands were often opened up first by planters. Lesser men tended to engage in diversified agriculture on family farms similar to those in the northern colonies. In Tidewater a plantation aristocracy grew up. The culture and way of life of the English country gentry were taken as models by this new colonial class. Replicas of English country homes were built along the rivers, sons were educated in England, ships brought the latest English books and fashions to the planters' own wharves and took away the tobacco crop, and hospitality was dispensed lavishly.

For the owner of thousands of acres and dozens or hundreds of slaves, whose father in many cases had left England a poor man, America had indeed proved to be the land of promise. Along with relative ease and luxury, however, went a high sense of social and political responsibility, which was well exemplified in the next century by George Washington, Thomas Jefferson, and other leaders. Public life was considered the proper career for the masters of great plantations, and they schooled themselves in the law. The planters dominated the Virginia and Maryland legislatures and they strengthened their position as a privileged class by statute. Laws of primogeniture and entail were intended to secure family position in future generations, but they were of much less importance in the New World than the Old because of the abundance of land. The apportionment of seats in the lesislatures gave disproportionate representation to the older counties, and this became an increasing grievance as population grew to the westward. On the foundation of Negro slave labor, a society was erected in the tobacco colonies which seemed to be divided into castes, and certainly was divided between slave and free. But the large area of unoccupied land offered real opportunity to poor oottlors and servants whose indentures had run out, and society remained fluid to a degree that was not matched in Europe.

CHAPTER 4

The New England Colonies

THE COLONY OF VIRGINIA WAS IN MOST RESPECTS A reproduction of English society and institutions—more flexible in offering greater opportunity to the poor and more rigid in that it was based on a staple agricultural economy and eventually on Negro slavery. New England, on the other hand, became in the seventeenth century the seat of a series of experiments in the establishment of colonial societies on original patterns—according to specifications which were found by religious enthusiasts in the Bible. These zealots were in varying degrees rebels against the Church of England, and nothing distinguished English colonial policy from that of the other European powers more than the toleration, even the encouragement, of the rebellious utopian experiments that were carried on by the Pilgrims of Plymouth, the Puritans of Massachusetts Bay and Connecticut, and the Baptists of Rhode Island. At the beginning religious and social idealism were virtually unalloyed by commercialism in these colonies.

THE PILGRIMS

In the same year, 1607, that the first settlers sent by the London Company arrived at Jamestown, the Plymouth Company sent out two vessels with 120 men to establish a colony in the northern section of the vast region then called Virginia. These men reached the coast of Maine in August, entered the Sagadahoc (Kennebec) River and built a fort on its banks. Gardens were planted and trade was opened with the Indians for furs. But all the difficulties that beset Jamestown, except fevers, were encountered by the settlers in Maine, and no strong leadership or aid from England carried the colony through the first severe winter. The factious settlers returned home before the year was out. The timber and furs and fish of the district attracted numerous expeditions during the following years. Fishermen sometimes stayed ashore through

47

the winters, and trading posts were maintained on the rivers. New England was not an unknown territory when the Pilgrims arrived at Plymouth in 1620.

The Pilgrims were Separatists, believing that salvation could be attained only outside the Church of England, and followers of the Brownist principle of church organization. The Brownists abolished all officialdom and authority in religion except what was set up by a voluntary association of individuals who "covenanted" together. A clergyman held office only by consent of the members of the covenanting body, and Brownists would not recognize any office or organization above that of minister. This extremely democratic religious policy made Brownists anathema to conservatives of all faiths. One such congregation of Scrooby, Nottinghamshire, fearing persecution after an investigation by Anglican authorities, fled in 1609 from England to Holland, where religious eccentricity was tolerated. Led by their minister, John Robinson, a graduate of Cambridge University, they settled in Leyden and for a decade were quite content.

They were simple folk, intent on pursuing godliness, modest in behavior, mild and kindly even to adherents of other faiths. Personal holiness and virtue were the extent of their ambition in this world. But as time passed they saw that their children were losing their English speech and, what was worse, were failing in piety and turning to dissolute ways. They feared that Spain would resume her rule of Holland and that they would be thrown into the torture rooms of the Inquisition. Meanwhile, they found in this placid and tolerant society no real opportunity to advance their vision of the Kingdom of Christ on earth. The community in its little meeting-house in Bell Alley carefully debated the best course. They felt that God called them to the New World, but they lacked money, powerful friends, experienced leaders—everything that seemed necessary for the dangerous adventure.

Leaders of the Virginia Company of London, who were casting about for groups to swell the population of their colony, decided that the Leyden Separatists were likely material. Their religious radicalism could be overlooked in favor of their willingness to work. Thomas Weston organized a stock company subordinate to the Virginia Company to use a land patent the parent company gave to him and associated capitalists. A generous offer was made to the Leyden group. They should go to Virginia not as employees of the company, but as stockholders, partners, and freemen. Those who could not afford to pay for stock would receive one share in consideration of their labor. For seven years all the products and property of the colony would be owned in common, then a general distribution among stockholders in America and in England would take place. A group of workmen from London, some of them artisans and the others servants of the company, would be added to the Leyden farmers and craftsmen.

The Leyden flock divided on the question of accepting the offer. Many were fearful that persecution would meet them in the Anglican colony of Virginia. A minority dwelt hopefully on the possibility that they might maintain their identity in America as an independent civil and religious community. After prolonged negotiations and debate, thirty-five "saints" from the Leyden minority joined sixty-six "strangers" from London to make the memorable voyage in the *Mayflower* from Plymouth, England, in September 1620.

Immediately the passengers elected one of the Leyden men, John Carver, as their Governor. The ship was overcrowded and scurvy broke out because of poor diet. Yet only one passenger died on the way, and two children were born, who were given the names Oceanus and Peregrine. On November 9, Cape Cod was sighted. This was recognized as being outside the boundaries of the parent Virginia Company, but the passengers were sick, winter was at hand, and the possibility of establishing an independent Separatist community far from Jamestown was inviting. On November 11, anchor was dropped in the harbor of present-day Provincetown inside the tip of the Cape. A better site was found across Massachusetts Bay on the mainland where Indians, recently ravaged by an epidemic, had abandoned their cultivated land. The strangers were threatening to strike out for themselves on the argument that the site was outside the jurisdiction of the company. Therefore the saints, before going ashore, drew up a compact of agreement that laws consented to by the majority would be accepted as binding by all, and Carver was confirmed as Governor to rule the community ashore. This *Mayflower* Compact is ever memorable as a primitive American constitution of self-government. It was no sudden invention: the Brownist practice of church government by covenant and the stock-company practice of self-government by shareholders were both familiar to the saints and strangers of the Plymouth colony. But these religious and economic precedents were now extended to cover political government by compact, and this was a new thing in the world.

On Christmas Day, 1620, the little band began to build their first house, and they labored through the winter despite scanty food, sickness, and the death of half the company including Governor Carver. William Bradford was elected in his place. The survivors refused to give up, for, as Bradford later wrote in his history of the colony, "they knew they were pilgrimes, and looked not much on those things, but lift up their eyes to the heavens, their dearest cuntrie." In the spring, the Indian Squanto showed them how to plant maize, the New World corn which, by the abundance of its yield, saved many an American colony and frontier settlement from starvation. Each man built his own house along a street running up the hill from the harbor and planted his own garden behind his house, while a stockade surrounded the whole. On the hill a meeting-house was built with a flat roof where six cannon were mounted. This building, where religious services and town meetings were held, was at the same time a fort to defend the Pilgrims' experiment in freedom against all enemies—a fitting symbol of Plymouth Colony.

In the fall of 1621, the ship *Fortune* with supplies and new immigrants arrived. A good harvest was gathered, turkeys and deer were shot, and a feast of Thanksgiving was celebrated for three days, with the Indian chief Massasoit and ninety aborigines as guests. The remarkable industry of the settlers produced a valuable cargo of oak timbers and beaver furs to be sent home in the *Fortune*. The colony survived, although it grew slowly and contained only 300 settlers after ten years.

In 1627, to prevent distribution of the property of the colony among the shareholders, including those in England, Governor Bradford and seven Pilgrims bought out the London shareholders and distributed the land and cattle among the residents of Plymouth. Thus in this colony, as at Jamestown, individual ownership succeeded the joint-stock system. Gradually offshoots of the Plymouth settlement were established in the surrounding country, but Plymouth never became large enough to rival the later Puritan settlement at Boston.

Charles M. Andrews, the New England historian, has declared: "The Pilgrim Fathers stand rather as an emblem of virtue than a moulding force in the life of the nation." Their simplicity in faith, heroism in labor, and innovation in political self-government have made them spiritual ancestors of the American people. Their form of government was demo-cratic, although they retained one of the minor social distinctions of England, that between "master" and "mistress," and "goodman" and "good-wife." Education was not particularly valued by them. They found in the Bible all their learning, and they read the Bible not for insight into problems of theology, which did not interest them, but for encouragement of plain virtue. While they were mildly disposed towards other faiths, they did not believe in religious freedom within their own community. When a clergyman of the Church of England, the Reverend John Lyford, came to Plymouth to administer the sacraments to those desiring them, he was tried and driven out of the colony.

In practice the government was under the control of Governor Brad-ford, who was annually re-elected twenty-nine times, and his council of assistants, who were also elected by the freemen. After ten new towns had been settled, the meeting of all the freemen gave way in 1643 to a representative assembly with two delegates from each town elected by its freemen. Bradford and his successors tried to obtain a charter from the Crown legalizing their government as a separate colony, but they failed. In 1691, Plymouth was annexed to Massachusetts. Thereafter the Pil-

grims suffered some loss of religious independence. They were forced
to pay for the support of Puritan clergymen, although they continued
for many years to maintain their own clergy as well. Eventually they lost
their identity as a distinct element in Massachusetts. Nevertheless, the
Pilgrim practice of government by consent of the whole people and the
direct election of governors left a permanent imprint on American history.
The simple heroism and idealism of the Pilgrim Fathers was never forgotten by succeeding generations, and certain episodes in their quiet
history, such as the story of Priscilla and John Alden, became part of the
folklore of the American people.

THE PURITANS

New England might have become the domain of a landed aristocracy
if the plans of Sir Ferdinando Gorges had succeeded. He obtained control
of the Virginia Company of Plymouth, and, after the failure at Sagadahoc,
spent a fortune on numerous expeditions to the New World. In 1621, he
obtained from the King a new patent authorizing him and forty other
noblemen and landed gentlemen to incorporate themselves as the Council
for New England and to take over the territory of the Virginia Company
of Plymouth. Grandiose plans were drawn to divide the land among
baronies, lordships, and manors, whose owners should enjoy feudal
privileges, the whole to be ruled by an autocratic governor and a bishop.
Visible in the scheme was the purpose of Royalists to recover in the New
World some of the position they were losing in England.

The Council began to issue patents to settlers of a very different character from the pious and sober Pilgrims. Probably Captain Wollaston
held such a patent when he led a party of several gentlemen and many
servants to the present site of Braintree, Massachusetts, twenty-five miles
from Plymouth. One of the group was Thomas Morton, Gent., a lawyer
and a singularly gay fellow. He named the settlement Merry Mount and
organized scandalous revels in the wilderness, as if to torment the neighboring Pilgrims. For days on end drinking and dancing around a maypole,
dalliance with Indian women, and feasting occupied Morton and his
crew. A rimester like any other English gentleman of the day, Morton
composed ribald jests in verse at the expense of the pious Pilgrims.
In 1628, goaded by his trade in guns with the Indians, as well as mortified
by his impious revels, the Pilgrims sent Captain Miles Standish to disperse
the settlement. Morton surrendered and returned to England. Merry
Mount provided a glimpse of the future New England if the plans of the
aristocratic Council had succeeded. But the only direct effort of the
Council to settle the country, an expedition under Sir Ferdinando's son
Robert to the present site of Weymouth in 1622, failed within six months.
The profit and aggrandizement of a few provided no sufficient incentive

NEW ENGLAND COLONIES to 1700

to the settlers who had to do the work and endure the hardships of a new colony.

As in the case of Plymouth, so in the founding of the Massachusetts-Bay Colony, a religious ideal provided the impulse for colonization that proved successful. The Puritans were Calvinists who wished to reform the Church of England, to "purify" it of all relics of Roman Catholicism in ritual and organization. They were scandalized by the frivolity and corruption of the Anglican clergy and wished to carry the Reformation to its logical conclusion. They did not lose hope that they might succeed without disloyalty to the King and the Establishment until King Charles I and Bishop Laud tried to purge the church of Lutheran and Calvinist elements. Clergymen of Puritan tendency were silenced and deprived of their incomes; Puritan writings were burned; and in many parishes the Word of God was preached only secretly by "lecturers" who were subject to punishment. Under these circumstances, the professions of loyalty to the Established Church by the Puritans who migrated to New England were only nominal; in practice they became Separatists.

Many merchants and landowners of England turned to Puritanism during the 1620's and 1630's, and even some members of the nobility were sympathetic. Plain fashions in dress were an outward expression of the strict morality that Puritans opposed to the frivolities and luxuries of the nobility and court. Thrift and careful attention to money-making, so long as wealth was justly acquired and used, had a significance for Puritans that went beyond their ordinary meaning: material success and possession of the economic virtues encouraged the Puritan to believe that God had ordained him for Heaven. Puritans looked upon the absolutist tendencies of Charles I as more dangerous to their faith than the persecutions of Laud himself, because Laud was only an instrument of the King. Many leading Puritans began to dream of a City of God in the American wilderness, where they could escape the authority of the King and establish a commonwealth ruled by the elect according to God's design.

The project seemed hopeless so long as Gorges and the Council for New England reserved the territory for Royalists and Anglicans. But Puritan leaders of exceptional intelligence outwitted the Council. A group of Dorchester men with Puritan tendencies attempted in 1623 to establish a fishing station at Cape Ann under patent of the Council. The project did not prosper, and the remnant of settlers under the leadership of Roger Conant moved to Salem. Conant appealed to friends in London to save the experiment by obtaining aid from such men as wanted a religious refuge. A number of Puritans of wealth, who had friends among the nobility, obtained from the Council a charter to establish the New England Company and settle territory between the Merrimac and Charles Rivers. John Endicott was sent over in 1628 as Governor of the struggling Salem community. He was ordered to make preparations for a great enterprise that was forming in the minds of the outstanding Puritans of England.

The Massachusetts-Bay Colony

With the help of the Earl of Warwick and other sympathetic noblemen, the Puritan leaders in 1629 by a shrewd maneuver obtained from King Charles I a charter granting to a new corporation, the Massachusetts-Bay Company, the land patent of the New England Company. This charter violated the rights of the Council for New England, not only in giving the new company land rights, but also in granting it political authority to govern its territory. In many respects the new

charter was irregular, and the Puritans concluded that they could ensure
the success of their scheme only if the officials of the company moved
with the charter itself to America. Then neither king nor company could
interfere with them. The Puritans would make the charter into the constitution of a self-governing holy commonwealth. This audacious scheme
they carried out with efficiency and dispatch. The strange sequel was the
establishment of an independent religious and political community in
America by the very party to which Charles would yield nothing at
home. Apparently the King was willing to see the Puritans of England
weakened by a mass migration.

The Puritans poured their money into the new enterprise. Hundreds,
eventually thousands, sold their properties in England and moved to
America with many things—such as fine silver and furniture, ample
provisions and tools—that earlier settlers had lacked. The region of East
Anglia, the "Cradle of Puritanism," yielded many migrants, most eminent
of them being John Winthrop, lord of the manor of Groton, lawyer,
matriculate of Trinity College, Cambridge, and justice of the peace, who
was elected Governor of the company before it moved to America.
Landed gentry, well-educated professional men and ministers, and successful merchants were numerous in the Great Puritan Migration of the
1630's. In their combination of intelligence, knowledge of the world and
its business, classical and professional education, theological preoccupations, religious and social idealism, and wealth, perhaps no colony in
the world's history could match the settlers of Massachusetts-Bay.

Seventeen vessels sailed to New England in 1630, among them the
Arabella carrying Governor Winthrop and the charter, and for thirteen
years each summer saw another fleet cross the ocean. Charlestown was
the first site of the government, but settlers quickly scattered throughout
the Boston region and established towns. Clergymen were numerous
among the migrants and became the unofficial rulers of each community
and of the colony as a whole. Winthrop had promised before he left
England that the colony would not set up a church separately from the
Church of England. But it was a "purified" Church he had in mind, and
these Puritans recognized no authority over them but God.

The churches and the town and colony governments of Massachusetts-
Bay were organized according to a Puritan addition to Calvinist doctrine that differed very little from the covenant idea of the Separatists.
The Puritans as Calvinists retained the important distinction between
the elect and the damned. They admitted that in individual cases it
was not always possible to detect in a virtuous life and material success
the "outward signs" whereby God's elect manifested their heavenly
destiny. Therefore they recognized two covenants: the invisible Covenant
of Grace, which joined God with his saints and was known only to Himself; and the visible Covenant of the Church, which was composed of

those who by outward signs seemed destined for Heaven and therefore entitled to join in the government of the Church as full-fledged members with voting power. In early Massachusetts others might, indeed they must, support the Church and attend its services, but they stood anxiously outside the circle of the elect, without a voice in the government of the Church or in determining their own admission to its Covenant.

Massachusetts is often called a theocracy because Church members, led by their ministers, effectively ruled in the civil as well as the religious sphere. But the Puritan theologians recognized a third or Civil Covenant, between political officials with Church members who had a vote in their election, and the people as a whole. Therefore the political government was theoretically distinct from the religious, even though, in practice, the will of the clergy became the law of the colony. Formerly, "freemen of the company," that is, stockholders, had elected officials. In Massachusetts a transformation took place in 1631 whereby the elect of God acquired the privilege of freemen. Under this dispensation there was a rough correspondence between social and economic position on the one hand, and political and religious position on the other. Massachusetts was very far from being a democracy, a form of government for which the Puritans could find no authority in the Bible. It was a religious oligarchy.

The unprecedented transformation of the Massachusetts-Bay Company into the government of the religious commonwealth of Massachusetts occurred in the following way. The charter called for elections by the freemen of the company of a governor, deputy governor, and court of eighteen assistants or magistrates. The freemen were to meet in general court, or legislative assembly, four times each year. Very few of the settlers were stockholders of the company. Therefore, in order to fulfill the requirements of the charter, Winthrop called a mass meeting soon after he arrived, and asked all those who wished to be freemen to raise their hands. This informal procedure, however, opened the possibility that some who were not in sympathy with the religious aims of the leaders might gain influence in the government. At a general court in May 1631, it was voted that Winthrop should continue as governor. He thereupon required all who wanted to qualify as freemen to take an "ironclad oath" that none but Church members would be "admitted to the freedom of this body politicke." Thenceforth a freeman was not necessarily a stockholder of the company but a person recognized in his congregation as one of the elect of God.

At first Winthrop and the magistrates tried to rule arbitrarily. They distributed lands and settled issues in their own way. But when they laid taxes on the towns without their consent, a "revolt" occurred which ended in concessions by Winthrop and led to the establishment of a representative form of government. It was decided in 1634 that the freemen of each town should elect delegates to represent them in meetings of the General Court, and that this body should have legislative authority. The freemen retained their right to elect the governor and magistrates by direct vote. They celebrated their victory over Winthrop by electing Thomas Dudley as Governor. Ten years later the question whether the governor and magistrates could veto an act of the deputies was settled by decision against the veto. Gradually a system evolved which added an important precedent to the one already set by the establishment of the House of Burgesses in Virginia: a governor who received office by direct election.

The rule of the Massachusetts oligarchy was continually opposed by settlers who were excluded from church membership; it was fought outright by sectarians of other faiths; and sometimes even the elect resisted leadership which they found arbitrary and autocratic. Furthermore, the Puritan oligarchs allowed to grow up almost unnoticed a form of local government, the town meeting, which was purely democratic.

The town system originated in the method of distributing land. A group of settlers, usually numbering about sixty, could obtain from the government a land grant for a new town amounting to 36 square miles on the western fringe of settlement. At a suitable location in the new tract a village was laid out. Common lands, pasture and woodlot, were set aside and each head of family received a village plot for his house and a share of the surrounding farm lands. Thus each family started out on a roughly equal economic footing with its neighbors. A meeting-house to serve as church and town hall was erected on the village green. At least once a year all the property owners of the town met to vote on all matters of local interest, including education and defense, and to elect selectmen and other town officials. Thus the legislative authority was vested in virtually the whole body of citizens. The chief concerns of a farming population were local, and the town meeting was a democracy for which perhaps there had been no precedent since that of Athens in the fifth century, B.C. It developed a citizenry that was skilled in self-government and jealously watchful of the rights of the people. The New England town meeting was one of the seedbeds of modern American democracy.

The method of town settlement was conducive to religious unity. So long as the population of the town clustered in medieval style around the village green, the minister could handily control his flock. Later in the seventeenth century, settlers tended to live on their farms rather than in the village, and this removal from the guardian eye of the minister helped to undermine the authority of the Puritan oligarchy. Still to this day, the New England village of simple but comely houses drawn up in friendly ranks around the village green and dominated by the church spire is a symbol of equalitarianism, as well as a masterpiece of town planning.

Next to religion, education was of highest importance to the Puritans. Many of the leaders were graduates of Emmanuel College, Cambridge. They were determined that their children in America should not be deprived of educational opportunity, and that new generations of learned clergymen to lead the people should be assured. Moreover, the Puritans were concerned that everyone should be able not only to read the Bible but to interpret it with some of the subtle insight of the Calvinist theologian. They were not "primitive" Christians. They believed that learning, like wealth, was a sign of God's grace. In 1647, the General Court decided that in order to foil "that old deluder Satan," who wished to deprive men of knowledge of the Scriptures, each town of fifty households must provide a teacher of reading and writing for its children, and each town of a hundred must also provide a Latin grammar school. This was the first American law establishing a free public school system.

To provide training for the ministry, the General Court in 1636 established Harvard College, the first institution of higher learning in the present territory of the United States. Harvard offered the same course of instruction as Oxford and Cambridge universities. Scholarships were provided for talented poor boys, and tuition payments were often made in farm produce. Most of the graduates entered the ministry and were called to frontier towns, where as teachers and preachers they set remarkably high cultural standards for New England. It was not unknown for a farmer graduate of a Latin grammar school to prepare his boy for Harvard in Hebrew, Latin, Greek, and mathematics in the kitchen of their remote farm home. New England Puritanism is a chief source of the modern American ideal of some education for all and advanced education for the talented without regard to wealth.

The Great Migration ended when the success of the Puritan Party in England in 1646 removed the religious incentive for migration. Later immigrants were less homogeneous in character. Many of them came to New England without sympathy for the rule of the Puritan clergy and magistracy, and they helped to overthrow it. In the meantime, the rigidity of the oligarchy resulted in the founding of a new colony, Rhode Island, by refugees from religious tyranny.

RHODE ISLAND

Roger Williams, the founder of Rhode Island, was a minister and a graduate of Pembroke College, Cambridge, who came to New England in 1631. He was a theologian and political scientist far in advance of his time. He carried the revolutionary doctrines of seventeenth-century England to their logical "modern" conclusions. He would not compromise his theories in favor of "practical necessities," therefore he was execrated

as a troublemaker. But his successful experiment in state-building proved
that he was also gifted in practical affairs.

Williams refused a pulpit in Boston because he regarded the nominal
loyalty of the Puritan Church to the Anglican as dishonest. The Salem
church members were more sympathetic to Separatism and made Williams
their pastor. From the Salem church he launched bitter attacks against
the Puritan unity of Church and State, which he called a heinous mixture of "Christ and the World together." He demanded, not toleration of
religious differences, because toleration implied superiority in one religion
and inferiority in others, but the treatment of all religions as equal by
the civil government. Thus he anticipated the modern American solution
of the relations between Church and State. Another of his sins was that
he denied the right of white men to take Indian lands. His diatribes were
too much for the Salem congregation, so, undaunted, he separated
from it and conducted religious meetings for a handful of adherents in
his own house. In 1635, the General Court banished the rebel. Williams
planned to lead a group of his followers to Narragansett Bay. The magistrates tried to arrest him, but he escaped through the woods, deep in
winter snow, to Rhode Island, where the Indians befriended him. Then
he set about drawing up a form of government for a new colony (1636)
according to his principles of religious liberty.

At this time the methods of the Puritan leaders were under attack
in England. Pointed questions were asked as to whether the charter
justified their independent and despotic course; the Bay Colony was
in danger from the French and Indians; and, worst of all, the Antinomian
heresy was winning converts in Boston and threatening to destroy the
theological unity of the commonwealth. The leader of the Boston heretics
was Anne Hutchinson, the mother of fourteen children and possessor
of a brilliant mind and fearless character, who refused to follow the
Puritan prescription that a woman should obtain her ideas of God
"from the contemplation of her husband's excellencies." She organized
a group of followers to whom she preached in her home that the Puritans
were guilty of "legalism," that is, they mistook outward signs for evidence
of inward grace. She denied the validity of the Church Covenant with
its requirement that "works" (the performance of prescribed religious
duties) must precede admission to membership in the Church. She
taught that the Covenant of Grace comprised all believers, that each
individual need only listen to the inner voice of God to be saved. This
doctrine, called Antinomianism, threatened to destroy the theological
foundations of the Puritan Church since it wiped out the distinction
between the elect, who were entitled to leadership, and the rest of
mankind, who were required to obey. It even threatened to make
ministers unnecessary altogether. It was similar to the doctrines of
Quakers, Anabaptists, and all the radical Pietist sects. It became danger-

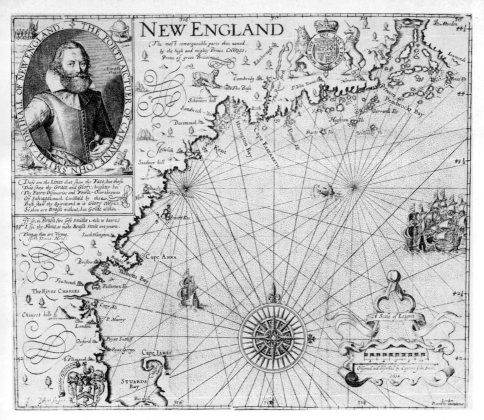

CAPTAIN JOHN SMITH'S MAP OF NEW ENGLAND, 1614. This early drawing of the northeastern coastline, printed in *A Description of New England* (1616) and later works of the doughty Captain, did much to establish the name of the region.

FORT MICHILIMACKINAC. First built by the French explorer, Cadillac, on the Straits of Michigan in 1695.

The grace and serenity of colonial architecture belied the youthfulness of the country

St. Michael's, Charleston, South Carolina, 1752. The dominating steeple of this beautiful white church is thought to be an adaptation of that of St. Martin's-in-the-Fields, London.

A Pennsylvania-Dutch Kitchen: Lebanon County, 1752. A restoration showing the typical household articles and decorative skills of the sturdy German settlers.

A Virginia Mansion: Carter's Grove, near Williamsburg. One of the finest Georgian houses, notable for its interior as well.

A New Jersey Dining Room: Cumberland County, 1725. The elegance of domestic life among well-to-do colonists is reflected in this museum setting.

BENJAMIN FRANKLIN

1706-1790

Portrait by Duplessis

A benign portrait of the most famous of colonial Americans at his peak as a Revolutionary diplomat.

COLUMBIA COLLEGE, NEW YORK (established as KING'S COLLEGE, 1754). The original part of the building was erected 1756-1760 and the wings added later.

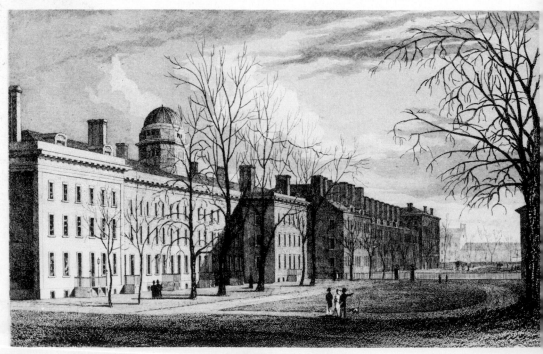

ous to the rule of the oligarchy when it was embraced by a large share of the Boston church members, including the Reverend John Wheelright and Governor Vane.

The issue was settled in the fiercely contested elections of 1637. Vane was defeated, though by rather high-handed methods. A meeting of ministers followed and, after twenty-four days of theological debate, 82 heresies were condemned. The leading heretics were then banished. Anne Hutchinson was subjected to a theological "trial." When she declared that her doctrines were "an immediate revelation" by God, she was banished on the ground that, since Puritanism was itself a revelation by God, contrary doctrines must be inspired by Satan. The Puritan commonwealth was strengthened by this purge of heretics and faced its external enemies with greater unity. But tyranny was also confirmed as the method of obtaining unity. The oligarchy went to even greater excesses against Quakers—adding to the penalties whippings, mutilations, and death for those who returned after banishment. The mass of settlers gave in to apathy as the safest attitude towards religious matters. In the long run this undermined the rule of the oligarchy as effectively as opposition.

In the Rhode Island of Roger Williams, seekers of liberty found a refuge. Anne Hutchinson and many other exiles from Puritan wrath joined him there. Williams bought land from the Indians and divided it among the settlers. They erected a government under a compact that it should have jurisdiction only over political matters and should do nothing to coerce any individual's conscience. Liberty of religion was extended to non-Christians, and one of the first Jewish communities in America was subsequently established at Newport. Williams lived up to his own principle of absolute religious freedom. He opposed the Quakers in theological matters but invited them to dwell in safety in his colony.

The Rhode Island settlements prospered by means of farming and raising cattle. Williams obtained from Parliament in 1644 a charter legalizing "Providence Plantations" as a separate and self-governing colony. An extremely democratic system of government left legislative authority largely in the hands of town meetings, while the central executive officers, a president and four assistants, were elected by freemen of the towns. In 1663, King Charles II confirmed the charter of Rhode Island, and it remained in force until 1842. Its longevity constitutes a remarkable tribute to the advanced character of the ideas of Roger Williams.

Rhode Island attracted all manner of heretics and discontented elements from Europe and other colonies. Dissensions naturally resulted from the heterodox character of the people, and the little haven of individualism seemed to conventional observers of the seventeenth century a nest of anarchy. Neighboring colonial governments looked upon Rhode Island as an eyesore and in petty ways persecuted its inhabitants when they came within reach. But the experiment weathered all trials and stood as a first proof that separation of Church and State, absolute religious freedom, and democracy might be the guiding principles of a successful body politic. Roger Williams was an idealist who brought his dream to realization in America.

CONNECTICUT

Rhode Island, Connecticut, and New Hampshire were all early offshoots of the settlements in Massachusetts. They illustrated a rule of American expansion: as soon as one district was settled, discontented elements with hope in their hearts to improve their economic, social, political, and religious condition set forth into the wilderness to settle new areas. Fur traders often acted as the scouts for such movements. They spied out new territories and brought back reports of fertile lands. Trading posts became the sites of towns and the trails of traders through the forests became roads of migration.

The Connecticut River Valley is the most fertile strip of land in New England. The Dutch of New Amsterdam in 1633 established a trading post, the "House of Good Hope," near the site of Hartford. Indians carried news of this "invasion" to the English at Plymouth and Massachusetts-Bay. Soon English traders had posts on the river north and south of the Dutch. News of level fields and deep soil excited settlers who were discouraged by the thin, stony soil of eastern Massachusetts. The territory was claimed by both the Massachusetts-Bay Company and by Lord Saye and Sele and Lord Brooke by patent from the Crown. The latter sent over from England in 1635 John Winthrop, Jr., as "Governor of the river Connecticut" and surrounding areas. Young Winthrop and a group of wealthy Puritans built a fort at the mouth of the river and this became the center of Saybrook plantation.

The Reverend Thomas Hooker and his congregation at Newtown (Cambridge), Massachusetts, saw in Connecticut an opportunity. They were orthodox Puritans, and claimed that they wished to emigrate only to find better land, but they also had in mind independence from the Massachusetts oligarchy and a freer system of government. They sold their homes to immigrants from England and set out for the Promised Land on foot, driving their cattle before them. This first mass migration in American history set the pattern for many a future trek.

Hooker and his followers founded Hartford. Other groups from Massachusetts founded Wethersfield and Windsor. In 1637, the three settlements, ignoring the claims of Massachusetts and the backers of Saybrook, organized the self-governing colony of Connecticut. The form of government was an imitation of the Massachusetts system, with one important difference: church membership, that is, "election" by God, was not required in order to enjoy the right to vote for civil officials. In 1639, a constitutional convention in Hartford drew up the Fundamental Orders of Connecticut, the first American constitution providing in detail a form of government. Its authors had been inspired by a famous sermon in which Hooker declared that the power of government resides in the people. Still Connecticut was not a democracy, because religious orthodoxy, adherence to Calvinistic Christian belief, was required of voters. Hooker's colony stood somewhere between the conservatism of Massachusetts-Bay and the radicalism of Rhode Island.

The Connecticut settlements prospered from the fur trade and farming. Fearful lest Connecticut depart too far from strict Puritanism, the Reverend John Davenport in 1638 led a band of settlers to found New Haven on Long Island Sound. Theophilus Eaton, a former London merchant, shared the leadership, and New Haven became an important trade center. Davenport organized a government even stricter than that of Massachusetts. Nothing but Old Testament precedent was respected. Such an English right as trial by jury, which was recognized in Massachusetts, was denied in New Haven. For generations after its removal to the town in 1703 Yale College (founded in 1701) continued the tradition of outdoing Boston itself in Puritan orthodoxy. But the Connecticut River towns refused to be swallowed up by orthodox New Haven. In 1662, they applied to the King for a charter recognizing their government. John Winthrop, Jr., supported the petition and it was shortly granted. New Haven and its surrounding settlements were then placed under the government defined by the Fundamental Orders. Thus Connecticut was firmly established as a third self-governing colony in New England.

New Hampshire and Maine

Settlers in present-day New Hampshire and Maine did not so easily escape the control of Massachusetts. The Council for New England granted these territories to Sir Ferdinando Gorges and Captain John Mason. They divided the area between themselves, Gorges taking Maine and Mason New Hampshire. But they were not successful in colonizing their domains. Actually, the first settlements were made by sundry unauthorized groups, some of them refugees from Massachusetts. The Antinomian Reverend John Wheelright and a handful of followers founded Exeter, New Hampshire, in 1638. The coastal towns of Portsmouth, Dover, and Rye were founded by English Anglicans. The settlers set up their own government on lines very similar to that of Rhode Island. But in 1641 Massachusetts took advantage of the Civil War in England to extend its rule over New Hampshire. After the Restoration, the New Hampshire towns reasserted their independence and in

1679 obtained a charter as a royal province, under which they were ruled by an elected legislature and a governor appointed by the king. Massachusetts won a complete victory in quarrels over Maine, which was ruled from Boston until 1820.

Indian Wars

Within a few years after the first settlements on the coast of New England, the Massachusetts-Bay Colony had shown marked expansive power. The rapid advance of settlement struck fear and dismay into the hearts of the Indians of the region. The Puritans, unlike the Pilgrims and Roger Williams, did not repay the Indians for their friendly advances and indispensable aid to the first settlers. The Puritans professed the aim of converting the Indians to Christianity, but harshness stemmed from the conviction that only they themselves had truth, all differences from them being the product of Satan which the "saving remnant," God's chosen few, must destroy. Consequently, their conduct towards the original occupants of the land was marked by extreme brutality. They tried to enslave Indians and force them to labor, but the proud redmen, bred to hunting and fighting, looked upon ordinary labor as women's work and would not submit to it. The view became common among the settlers that Indians were children of the devil, wherefore the part of virtue required their extermination. The Reverend John Eliot believed that Christ intended even Indians to be saved, and he did what he could to convert them and save them from the wrath of the colonists as well as that of God. But the government of Massachusetts-Bay refused to admit that Indians held any legal title to the land, and this made conflict inevitable.

The Pequots were the weakest of the New England tribes. They had been defeated by the Iroquois and pushed into a narrow strip of land along the Mystic River where they were flanked by the Rhode Island and Connecticut settlements. They killed a Boston trader in 1636. The Massachusetts authorities sent an expedition to burn their villages, and the Pequots in desperation declared war. In 1637, Captain John Mason led a small force in a surprise attack and not only defeated the Pequot warriors but also massacred all their women and children, wiping out the tribe.

Other tribes waged sporadic warfare against the frontier settlements. To strengthen measures against them, and also against the French in the North and the Dutch in the West, the Puritan colonies in 1643 organized the New England Confederation. This was the first attempt of American colonies to unite, and their motive, defense against external dangers, inspired all subsequent attempts. A board of commissioners was established to concert measures of defense. Quarrels among the colonies over boundaries and runaway servants were also dealt with by the commissioners.

Settlers in Connecticut wanted the confederation to expel the Dutch from New England, but Massachusetts refused to take part in such a war. The Dutch were nevertheless eliminated as trade rivals by the English conquest of New Netherland in 1664 and its conversion into the royal province of New York. The French were pushing westward from the Saint Lawrence into the Great Lakes country, and New England was temporarily spared trouble from that quarter. But the Indian tribes of New England, harried by the rapid establishment of tier after tier of towns, decided to meet unity with unity. With them the question was not merely that of holding on to their lands. Fur traders had given them guns and "firewater," and such products of civilization made them dependent on the whites. Settlers who followed the fur traders attempted to withhold guns and rum from the Indians. The Indians chose to fight rather than allow themselves to be disarmed preliminary to the seizure of their lands. Thus it was that they fought for the products of the civilization that destroyed their own way of life.

King Philip, sachem of the Wampanoags who lived east of Rhode Island, refused to accept a disarmament treaty offered by the Plymouth and Boston authorities, and his warriors raided the Plymouth frontier in 1675. This might have remained a local affair, but Massachusetts-Bay seized the opportunity to strike a blow at Rhode Island and gain control of lands in that neighborhood by sending an army against the Narragansett tribe. This invasion led all the New England tribes to unite under the leadership of King Philip. The bloodiest war of New England's history followed. Exposed frontier towns like Deerfield, Massachusetts, were raided, and each side massacred men, women, and children and burned villages without mercy. A Massachusetts army of a thousand men destroyed the Narragansett tribe by slaughtering all of its members except some warriors who escaped to the frontier. The whole belt of English settlements beyond the seacoast was practically deserted and Boston prepared fortifications in fear of the other tribes.

Victory by the whites was almost accidental. In 1676, they followed up a local success by burning Indian cornfields in the Connecticut Valley. The main body of Indian warriors suddenly gave up the fight because they feared starvation the next winter. They were easily driven into the mountains of New Hampshire, and King Philip was captured and shot. Indians remaining within reach were slaughtered or sold into slavery, their lands being awarded to veteran soldiers. Massachusetts and Connecticut agreed to establish a ring of frontier posts beyond their limits of settlement, and local Indians never again menaced the advance of this frontier. The New England Confederation, having served its purpose, fell into disuse.

Codfish and Witches

After 1650, New England grew prosperous. Its economy was based on the fur trade, forest products, agriculture, and the codfish which were caught in huge numbers and exported—especially to the Catholic countries of Europe. Shipbuilding thrived as trade grew with all parts of America and Europe, and eventually with Africa as the slave traffic developed. Fisheries, shipbuilding, and commerce were the chief sources of New England's prosperity, but even the farmers eked out a fair living from the less stony fields. Diversified crops for subsistence were the standard practice, and surplus wheat, corn, pork, and beef were sold for export. The forests yielded timber to the farmer who turned woodsman during the winter months. Farmers learned to make most of their own tools and clothing, built neat houses and good barns with the help of neighbors, and saved their money for the essential imports and a few luxuries.

In the coastal towns, merchants who acted as middlemen between the interior and the far ports of the world began to grow rich. They invested surplus capital in ships and extended loans to less fortunate businessmen. These merchant-shipowner-bankers became a new aristocracy, living in beautiful houses furnished with imported luxuries. They rivaled the Puritan clergy in influence and power. Luxury for the few did not contradict Puritan principles. In fact, it was provided for in Massachusetts laws which authorized laces, ribbons, and ornaments for the upper class and forbade them to the "meaner sort." But in the later seventeenth century, Puritan gentlemen took up such an English court fashion as the full-bottomed, curled, and perfumed wig, and this was eloquent of the worldliness that came with prosperity. Contacts with the outer world through trade broadened the Puritans' outlook and made the ideal of an isolated wilderness Zion seem provincial. Ministers preached in vain against the growing indifference to religion. The oncoming generation that had been born in America had not the zeal of their fathers who had known persecution for Christ's sake in England.

At the frontier, too, the original zeal was dying. This was due in part to a change after 1650 in the system of town settlement. Anxiety to speed the process of settlement in order to erect barriers against the Indians led the General Court to grant towns to speculators and absentee owners who promised to finance actual settlers. Such proprietors held the best lands for themselves, to be sold later at a profit. Proprietors were careless of the religious orthodoxy of the settlers, and the western towns became hotbeds of heresy. Quakers, Antinomians, Baptists, Anabaptists, and members of many other sects found refuge at the frontier in Massachusetts as elsewhere in America, and as they grew in numbers they built up rough democracies which struggled, sometimes violently, against the rule of the conservative East.

Still the Puritan stamp on New England was so firm that it was modified only in the course of many generations by growing worldliness, religious dissent, and democracy. The "New England conscience," famous for its habit of anxious examination of personal morals—those of neighbors as well as self—and insistence on righteousness, were perhaps the most enduring Puritan legacies. Long after the Massachusetts oligarchy had been overthrown, New England continued to live by high standards of personal probity. The Puritan ideal of self-improvement was also a peculiarly valuable bequest because it included the ideal of mental culture and learning. In Boston it was necessary for a gentleman to be more than wealthy; he had to be educated, preferably at Harvard. Conversely, the person of talent, although he might lack wealth and family position, was honored in New England as nowhere else in America.

Hysteria in Salem

The darker side of Puritanism, its harshness towards dissent, produced its own corrective. The excesses of the oligarchy in the last decades of the seventeenth century produced a reaction which contributed greatly to its overthrow. This is the broad meaning of the notorious witch trials at Salem and elsewhere in 1692. This episode must be placed against the background of the political and religious situation of the time. The oligarchy was under attack from England and from "unruly spirits" in the colony. Indifference to religion was perhaps the most effective weapon of Satan against God's commonwealth. The clergy turned to desperate measures to revive the zeal of the fathers in the hearts of the sons. In sermons they insisted that hell-fire awaited their listeners. Poetry was enlisted in the cause. Michael Wigglesworth's terrifying epic of the Last Judgment, *The Day of Doom* (1662) became the most popular poem in New England, and children were required to memorize its stanzas, including one in which the doctrine of infant damnation was moderated only by God's assurance that unbaptized infants would be allowed to enter "the easiest room in hell." Increase Mather in his *Essay for the Recording of Illustrious Providences* (1684) gave examples to prove that God and Satan daily intervened in New England, and that Satan sent demons who functioned in the persons of witches to corrupt Zion.

The literature of superstition caught hold of people's imaginations, as it did in Europe at this time. Even in easy-going Virginia, "witches" were persecuted, although none was executed. In Europe and England, executions were common. That Massachusetts-Bay fell victim to the mania is not surprising in view of its attempt to apply literally the injunctions of the Old Testament. "Thou shalt not suffer a witch to live" was incorporated in the colony's "Body of Liberties." Mistaking public fascination by the literature of superstition for religious sentiment, the Puritan clergy strengthened the potion. Cotton Mather, son of Increase, took accused witches into his house for observation, and published his horrendous findings in *Memorable Providences Relating to Witchcrafts and Possessions* (1689).

Public hysteria followed. The pattern of demagogic appeals to fears, resulting in mob action against the innocent, was to be repeated often enough in American history, and in this early case the responsible officials of the government satisfied the mob's demands for blood. Harmless eccentrics, especially old women, were targets of weird accusations. The clergy, led by the Mathers, urged the courts to speed trials and execute ruthless punishments. Reasonable rules of evidence went by the board. Refusal to confess guilt was regarded as proof that Satan possessed the accused. Hundreds were jailed, many were hanged, and one person was pressed to death in medieval style. Even those of high standing in the community were not exempt, and it was this perhaps that gave rise to doubts among the leaders. The panic subsided quickly in 1693. Judge Samuel Sewall publicly confessed error and repentance for his part in the trials. An eminent merchant, Thomas Brattle, spoke out boldly against the ignorance of the clergy. The clergy in general refused to recant, and they never fully recovered from the blow to their prestige.

Strangely, the Mathers themselves did as much as anyone to rout superstition and promote scientific studies in New England. Cotton Mather advocated inoculation for smallpox and was persecuted for his advanced views. In 1682, Increase organized a scientific society in Boston. He made reports to the Royal Society of Science in London and was elected a member. Learned men of New England studied the new physics of Sir Isaac Newton, and such influences destroyed superstition and substituted a rational view of nature. Thus the Puritan devotion to learning corrected Puritan religious extremism. The decisive blow that overthrew the oligarchy, however, did not come from inside the colonies but from England, in the course of a general organization of the Empire.

CHAPTER 5

Organization and Development of the Empire

THE FOUNDING OF THE ENGLISH COLONIES IN THE FIRST half of the seventeenth century was a rather haphazard affair. No over-all plan for an empire existed, and the promoters and settlers were allowed almost free rein in carrying out their ideas. The first colonies received no aid from the home government beyond permission to settle on land claimed by the Crown. The grants and charters were issued carelessly, the same land was sometimes bestowed on half a dozen persons and companies, and this caused endless trouble. Neglected by their home government in a period of domestic conflicts in England, and dependent on their own plans and efforts for success, the settlers soon showed a spirit of self-reliance and independence.

But in 1660 the English government began to show an interest in organizing the patchwork of colonies into a coherent system and planning a centralized empire. The government of Charles II sought to assert the royal prerogative in many spheres and adopted to some extent the absolutist doctrines of the French government which the King had learned to admire during his exile in France. Thus the Restoration of the Stuarts led to an attempt by England to install a mercantilist colonial system modeled in certain respects after the policies of Spain and France. English merchants and economists had advocated a consistent colonial policy since early in the century. A few general measures had been enacted by Parliament, but the policy was not adequately implemented by laws and administrative agencies until Charles II took power.

Merchants and officials saw definite benefits which a mercantilist empire would bring to England. The money now paid to Scandinavia for naval stores, to Portugal and the Dutch for spices, to the French for wine, might be kept in English hands if the colonies could be encouraged to produce these and other commodities that were now imported.

English manufactures would thrive if the colonists were forbidden to buy foreign articles. English trade would increase if the colonies were forced to send all their produce to England, not only what England consumed but also what foreign countries would buy; it should be handled by English merchants and carried in English ships. All this would make England richer and more powerful in peace and in war. The colonies would gain some advantage, but not to the injury of the mother country: they should exist not for the benefit of their inhabitants but for the greater wealth, power, and glory of the Empire in general and the mother country in particular. Such a program had important political implications for the colonies, because self-willed proprietors, local legislatures, and charter governments could not be allowed to interfere with imperial regulations.

The program also involved strategic considerations which led to planned extensions of settlement in America. For defense against Spain, buffer colonies were established in the Carolinas between Virginia and Spanish Florida. New Netherland was taken from the Dutch to unify control of the coast. New Jersey, Pennsylvania, and Delaware were settled to complete the occupation of territory from north to south. The abortive Dominion of New England was organized to strengthen northern defenses against France. All the new colonies were handed over to proprietors who, it was hoped, would carry out imperial policy more faithfully than companies with privileges of self-government.

The program had material value for the colonies in that it encouraged certain types of economic prosperity, furthered the expansion of settlement, and strengthened colonial defenses. English imperialism and mercantilism were never worked out with the logical and oppressive rigor of the French or Spanish system. The English colonists for a century shared in the patriotic elation of membership in a great new empire. But the program nevertheless contained germs of trouble because the English colonists were even more devoted to unlimited mastery of their own fate than they were to imperial glory.

THE NAVIGATION ACTS

In 1651, a Navigation Act had been passed by the Cromwellian government, chiefly to drive Dutch shipowners out of the English carrying trade. This was confirmed by the Act of 1660, under the Restoration, and supplemented by the Act of 1662. These laws forbade the bringing of cargoes to England from Asia, Africa, or America in foreign ships, and the taking of European cargoes to America in the ships of any nationality except England or the European country that produced the cargo. The laws created business for the English merchant marine, including American-owned vessels. They strengthened the English Navy, which could draw in time of need upon the merchant fleet for trained sailors and on the shipyards for warships. Another part of the Act of 1660 was directed at the colonies as sources of raw materials. Enumerated commodities— sugar, tobacco, ginger, indigo, and dyewoods to begin with—might be shipped from a colony only to England or some other English colony. Rice, naval stores, and other articles were added later. Thus tobacco planters could not sell to Europe directly, but only to English middlemen who took a profit when they resold to Europe. At first, the banning of Dutch ships and the closing of Dutch markets worked a hardship on Virginians, but this law forbade the growing of tobacco in England and the purchase there of tobacco grown in non-English colonies, so that a market was assured to the American planters. This market grew and English taste to this day is for pure "Virginia" tobacco.

In 1660, mercantilist purposes became clearer when the King created a planning committee best known as the Lords of Trade and afterwards superseded (1696) by the Board of Trade. Its duties were to supervise the trade of the Empire and to recommend laws and policies to Parliament and the Privy Council.

The Navigation Act of 1663, called the Staple Act, regulated imports into the colonies just as the Act of 1660 had regulated their exports. Colonists were forbidden to buy European products directly, with a few exceptions, such imports being required to pass through England and the hands of English middlemen. The profit taken by the latter and increased shipping costs raised the prices colonists had to pay for European goods. This provision was intended to create a lower relative price for English manufactures in the colonies so that England would benefit either way: if the colonists bought European products, English merchants profited; if they wished to buy more economically, English industry could grow. The English government, unlike the French and Spanish, did not intend to obtain revenue for itself from foreign goods sold to its colonies, hence it allowed drawbacks or rebates of duties when European goods were sent from England to America. The Navigation Act of 1672 was designed to prevent evasion of the Act of 1660. It required that a duty—the so-called "plantation duty"—be paid on the enumerated commodities before they left the colonies unless the ship captain gave financial surety that he would not evade the law by carrying cargo to some other country than England. Customs collectors were sent to America to enforce the laws. Further administrative machinery was set up later by the summarizing Act of 1696.

The Americans, by illicit trade with the foreign West Indies and other devices, generally avoided the injuries the Navigation Acts might do them, while taking full advantage of the favorable clauses of the laws. In New England especially, the colonists opposed the efforts to subordinate their interests to imperial aims, and they gave the customs collectors a hard time. From the imperial point of view this opposition was one of the evil effects of the self-governing institutions which had taken root in the colonies. The English government concluded that if colonial economic life was to be made subordinate to England, then political institutions must be made subservient to the home government. This led to drastic action on one side and strong resentment on the other.

New Proprietary Colonies

The Restoration government's regulations of trade were paralleled by its encouragement of new settlements. We have already seen that New Netherland was taken from the Dutch in 1664 and developed as a prosperous colony. The purpose of gaining tighter hold on the American colonies was apparent in the grant to the Duke of York, brother of King Charles II, as proprietor of the regions claimed by the Dutch. It was he who had organized the expedition of 1664. New Netherland was renamed New York for him, and he furthermore made subgrants of New Jersey to John Lord Berkeley and Sir George Carteret, and of the Dutch and Swedish settlements in what is now the state of Delaware to the Penn family.

New Jersey

Proprietors were entitled to rule in any way that did not conflict with English law, and their motive was usually the simple desire to obtain revenue from land sales, quitrents, and taxes. But they found it expedient to make many concessions in order to attract settlers. Berkeley and Carteret in 1665 provided for freedom of conscience, a representative assembly, and cheap land in their "Concessions and Agreements." In 1674, Berkeley sold his share in New Jersey to Quaker proprietors who presently added William Penn to their number. This part became known as West Jersey, while Carteret held East Jersey. On his death in 1680, his heirs sold this also to Quakers, including Penn. The latter's influence was visible in further concessions to settlers. In 1701, the two districts were united as a royal colony, but proprietors continued to hold land rights, and confusions of title vexed New Jersey until all vestiges of the proprietors' rights were abolished in the American Revolution. New Jersey lacked a favorable seacoast for trade. Small farming prospered, but the cream of its economic prosperity was drained off to New York in the northeast and Philadelphia in the west.

The Carolinas

Rational planning for the organization of the Empire was more fully carried out by the founding and settlement of Carolina. The area between

Virginia and Florida invited the erection of a buffer colony to protect the English settlements from the Spanish in the far south. It was believed that the semitropical products of the region would be ideally suited to mercantilist aims because they would not compete with English crops and would enable the home country to stop buying such produce from foreign countries. A group of courtiers saw in this situation an opportunity to make themselves lords of profitable estates, and Charles II was pleased to encourage their devotion to aristocratic principles as well as imperial interests. In 1663, he granted to a group of eight, including Sir Anthony Ashley Cooper (later Earl of Shaftesbury), the Earl of Clarendon, the Duke of Albemarle (General Monck), and other outstanding nobles, the region between Virginia and the present northern boundary of Florida, and westward to the "South Seas." Sir Anthony Ashley Cooper commissioned John Locke to draw up the Fundamental Constitutions for the colony in 1669.

This document was a strange mixture of feudalism and utopianism, reflecting the hope of the Restoration era that aristocracy and colonial profits were not incompatible. It called for a fantastic hierarchy of ranks with proportionate land holdings, ranging from palatines (the proprietors) in England to freeholders in the colony with the 50-acre share required for voting, and in between were landgraves, *caciques,* and lords of manors. The bulk of the population would be nonvoting tenants, serfs, and slaves. The hierarchical experiment never got started. Tenants and serfs were unavailable. No manors were erected and the few landgraves and caciques that were created died out. After more normal settlement had begun, the proprietors modified Locke's scheme (1682) but the colonial assembly would have none of it.

So many small farmers and runaways from indentured service had already settled in the region of Albemarle Sound below the Virginia line that the proprietors recognized the area in 1691 as the separate province of North Carolina. The relatively inaccessible Albemarle district became a region of tobacco culture, but its agriculture was on a lesser scale than in Virginia. The Cape Fear district in the present state of North Carolina was settled in the early eighteenth century, and Wilmington became an important port for naval stores. The inland country became the home of small farmers with strong dislike for the slave-owning aristocracies and the religious and political institutions of their neighbors to the north and south. As early as 1677, settlers in the Albemarle region staged a revolt against the proprietors known as "Culpeper's Rebellion," and a century later the "regulators" in the Piedmont carried on the tradition of hostility to authority. North Carolina was the Rhode Island of the South, the least aristocratic and most individualistic colony of the region.

The coastal area of South Carolina was extremely well suited to staple productions. The Lords Proprietors sent out an expedition of Englishmen

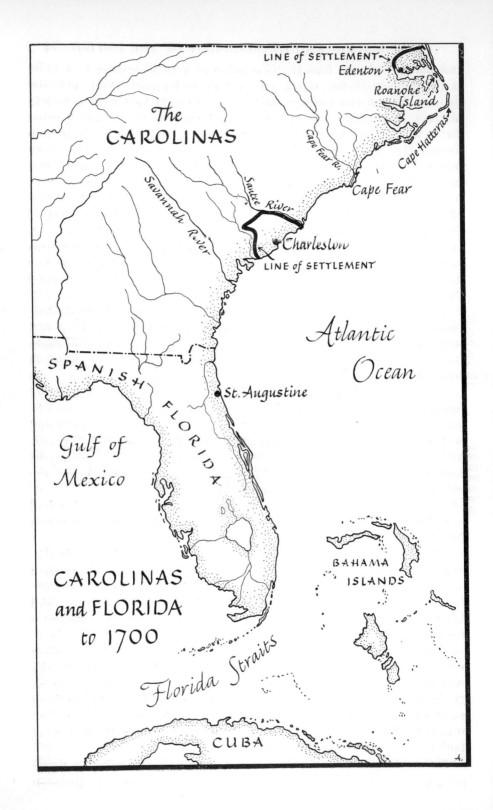

LINE of SETTLEMENT
Edenton →

Roanoke
Island

Cape Hatteras

The
CAROLINAS

Cape Fear R.

Sautee River

Cape Fear

Savannah River

Charleston

LINE of SETTLEMENT

Atlantic

Ocean

SPANISH FLORIDA

St. Augustine

Gulf of
Mexico

CAROLINAS
and FLORIDA
to 1700

BAHAMA
ISLANDS

Florida Straits

CUBA

A.

and Barbadians who founded Charlestown (later Charleston) in 1670, at the junction of two rivers, which were named the Ashley and the Cooper. After a considerable period of experimentation with a variety of crops, rice, which was afterwards supplemented by indigo, became the basis of South Carolina's prosperity and of her plantation system. French Huguenots added their admirable qualities to the population before the end of the century. The excellent harbor of Charlestown invited trade and shipping, while along the coastal inlets and rivers huge plantations were built up. Connections with the West Indies were close, and Negro slaves were probably introduced from Barbados in the first year of settlement; they were specially useful in this climate and economy. By the end of the seventeenth century, Negroes outnumbered whites, as they continued to do until recent times. As in Virginia and Maryland, landowners who could afford to buy slaves engrossed the best lands and made themselves into a plantation aristocracy before the middle of the eighteenth century. Merchants invested their profits in plantations, and in South Carolina a fusion of merchants and landowners produced a ruling aristocratic class which was less challenged by small farmers through the generations than the comparable group in Virginia was.

The original proprietors of Carolina had lost interest when the colony failed to provide quick profits for themselves. They made little effort to carry out Locke's plans and allowed the settlers to establish a legislature which was only nominally subordinate to a governor appointed by the proprietors. Quarrels between settlers and proprietors resulted in the conversion of the grant into two royal provinces, South Carolina in 1721 and North Carolina in 1729. The Anglican Church was established in both of them, firmly in South Carolina where the Huguenots generally joined it, and rather feebly in North Carolina, where radical sectarians found refuge from other colonies.

North Carolina was afterwards described as "the valley of humility between two mountains of conceit." The planting aristocracies of Virginia and South Carolina were similar in many respects, but they were differentiated by the fact that the latter colony had an urban center, Charleston, to which wealthy landholding families escaped from their plantations during the summer malaria season. There in the course of time they built town houses surpassing in luxury anything in America and supported a social season which was a provincial replica of fashionable life in London. If the Virginia planters took the English country gentry as their models, the South Carolinians looked to the English capital and nobility for their pattern. They assumed the style and prerogatives of an ordained ruling class. Despite the collapse of Locke's fantasy, aristocracy was more real in South Carolina than in any other English colony on the mainland. The sense of public responsibility which so strikingly characterized Virginia's planters in the eighteenth century and bore such rich fruit in later statesmanship, was less keen among the leading South Carolinians. They were notable in colonial times as patrons of the arts, but were little concerned with education beyond providing schools or tutors for their own children and sending them to England for higher education. Their responsibility to protect the frontier against Spain and the Indians was fairly easily discharged, and after 1733, when Georgia was founded, that colony assumed the burden. Secure and prosperous, the planters who flourished amid the luxuriant vegetation of the Low Country did reflect the aristocratic-utopian hopes of the founders. Only enterprising men could have established and maintained an English society in this far-southern region, but their historic role was to be predominantly, and in the end passionately, conservative.

Pennsylvania

Visions and results of another sort marked the founding and early history of Pennsylvania. Charles II in 1681 granted to William Penn the vast and fertile region between New York and Maryland. Its indefinite boundaries led to endless disputes. The charter made Penn and his heirs proprietors, but the increased tendency towards imperial control was shown in the requirement that Penn enforce the Navigation Acts and submit to the Privy Council all laws passed in his colony. The new colony would fill the gap between northern and southern settlements and complete England's control of seacoast and frontier from New England to Florida. Troubles with proprietors made the English government reluctant to create another colony of this sort. It did so only because William Penn skillfully exploited the indebtedness of the House of Stuart to his eminent father, Admiral Sir William Penn, for whom the new colony was named.

No colony represented more faithfully than Pennsylvania the ideals of a single man. Penn had been expelled from Christ Church College, Oxford, for his nonconformist religious opinions, and he was afterwards converted to Quakerism, the most radical religion of the period. George Fox, the great founder of the Quakers (more properly called the Society of Friends), rejected all external authority, even that of the Bible, over the individual conscience. The individual was responsible only to the voice of God speaking to his soul. Every man was his own priest, as is exemplified perfectly in the religious services of the Friends; these consist merely of meeting together to listen to whatever persons feel impelled by the Inner Voice to say. The merciful and loving Jesus of the New Testament, rather than the angry and vengeful Jehovah of the Old Testament dominates the Quaker spirit. Nevertheless, the latter-day notion that the Friends were invariably meek and mild is incorrect: the early members of the group earned the name "Quakers" by their outlandish manner of preaching, and they were aggressive and fearless in proclaiming their doctrine to hostile audiences. In deliberate defiance of the Puritans, Quakers sought martyrdom by shouting anathemas on the streets of Boston. Thousands of them were imprisoned in England during the first years after the Restoration, but they could not be crushed.

William Penn dreamed of a colony in America where not only Quakers but members of any faith might enjoy religious and political liberty. In 1669, while imprisoned in the Tower of London for writing one tract, he composed another and more famous one, *No Cross, No Crown*. The next year he was tried for preaching, but the jury freed him. He made missionary journeys into the German Rhineland, where he met radical sectarians of similar views and broadened his conception of a colony to include the idea of refuge for the persecuted of all nations. That such a man should have obtained from Charles II the grant of Pennsylvania to try out his unorthodox scheme is a tribute not only to his power of persuasion but also to the basic tolerance of the English government, even under the Stuarts.

His proprietary grant was not quite virgin territory in 1682 when Penn arrived in the ship *Welcome*. Fur traders and farmers were scattered here and there. Swedes, Finns, and Netherlanders lived on the lower banks of the Delaware River and small groups of Englishmen could also be found. The Three Lower Counties (later the state of Delaware) were most thickly settled. Penn took charge of the existing settlements there, though his title to the government was uncertain. Penn's first Frame of Government for his province (April 25, 1682) asserted the "native goodness" of all men, and he established the most liberal form of government to be found in any proprietary colony except the one in West Jersey for which he was also responsible. Penn or his deputy was governor, but the members of the Governor's Council as well as the Assembly were elected by the freemen. All Christians were guaranteed liberty of religion, and all settlers were assured of the fullest measure of English personal liberties. Penn, like Roger Williams, recognized the Indians' ownership of the land. He treated them as brothers and in a series of treaties established peaceful relations which long continued.

Penn conducted a vast international publicity campaign to attract settlers to his "Holy Experiment." It was immediately successful in bringing to his province Welsh and Germans (who settled Germantown), besides many Englishmen. Palatine Germans and Scotch-Irish poured in during the early decades of the eighteenth century and moved on to the fertile lands of the interior. Pennsylvania became the country's first "melting pot." The American of mixed ancestry emerged as a notable type in this "keystone" colony, which had a strategic location in relation to the expansion of the frontier. From the Swedes and Finns the settlers

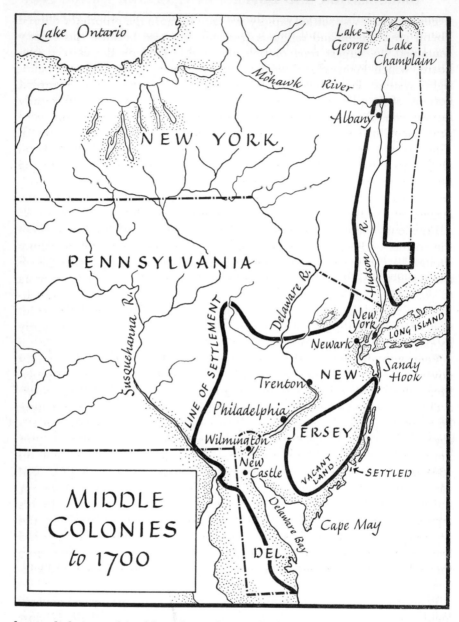

Lake Ontario

Lake George   Lake Champlain

Mohawk River

Albany

NEW YORK

PENNSYLVANIA

Susquehanna R.

Delaware R.

Hudson R.

LINE OF SETTLEMENT

Trenton

Philadelphia

Wilmington

New Castle

NEW

JERSEY

New York

Newark

LONG ISLAND

Sandy Hook

VACANT LAND

SETTLED

Delaware Bay

Cape May

DEL.

MIDDLE
COLONIES
to 1700

learned the art of building log cabins. These strong, cheap houses were
ideally suited to the requirements of frontiersmen. They sprouted
wherever trees grew in America and became a symbol of pioneer life.
Penn laid out Philadelphia, the "City of Brotherly Love," between the
Delaware and the Schuylkill rivers in a rectangular pattern which became the model for planning many later American towns and cities.

Pennsylvania was settled rapidly not only because the proprietor offered liberal government and religious freedom, but also because this colony contained the largest tract of rich and arable land on the eastern seaboard, which Penn offered to the poorest comer under a 50-acre headright system. Penn furthermore paid little attention to mercantilist notions of proper colonial economic activities. He encouraged family farms raising diversified food crops. Soon the farmers of Pennsylvania were producing surpluses of corn, wheat, pork, and beef which they exported. This colony became the granary of the British West Indies. Penn also offered great estates to those who could afford to buy land, but the family farm became the typical unit. Many craftsmen came to Pennsylvania, and trade and shipbuilding thrived. Philadelphia became the largest city in the country by the time of the Revolution.

Freedom, bountiful resources, and hard work by plain people were the secrets of Pennsylvania's success. Still the anomaly that this colony should be the private possession of one man led to disputes between Penn and the settlers. The efforts of the proprietor and his descendants to collect quitrents caused much trouble, especially among the Scotch-Irish on the frontier. The issue was finally settled only after the Revolution when the state government cancelled the claims of the Penn family by paying the heirs a lump sum.

Penn was absent from the colony between 1684 and 1700. His deputy governors lacked his great tact and got embroiled with the Assembly. Meanwhile, the overthrow of the Stuarts in England placed Penn under a cloud because of his intimate associations with them, and for a time he went into hiding. In 1689, William and Mary made Pennsylvania a royal province in line with the general program for the Empire. But Penn succeeded in making his peace with the new monarchs and in 1694 regained ownership of the colony. In 1700, he returned to Pennsylvania, hoping to stay and enjoy the splendid estates he had built for himself, but soon he returned to England to defend his rights. In his famous Charter of Privileges (1701) he modified and liberalized the government, making the Council appointive but merely advisory and leaving the unicameral legislature virtually supreme. At the same time the suffrage was extended and a separate legislature was promised Delaware.

Penn paid most of the administrative expenses of the provincial government and of his incessant efforts abroad in the colony's behalf. He lost heavily by his Holy Experiment. During his last years he spent time in debtors' prison in London. The people of Pennsylvania showed little practical appreciation for what he did for them, but he did not much complain when, after having encouraged the spirit of liberty among the colonists, he himself was made to feel its pinch.

Pennsylvania became a colony that was formally proprietary but almost wholly self-governing, the well-to-do Quakers being generally in effectual control. Neighboring colonies resented the liberties of her people, especially because settlers left other colonies to share them and because the pacifist Quakers did little to co-operate in wars against the Indians and the French. Imperial regulations were mostly ineffective in Pennsylvania. The people of the colony were guilty both of refusing "to gird on the carnal sword" and of harboring pirates as "honest men for bringing money into the country and encouraging trade." Bitter controversies raged in the Assembly between the proprietors' supporters and the antiproprietary party. The latter usually won.

Pennsylvania developed not only a rich mixture of ethnic and religious groups but also diverse social experiments and the most advanced scientific learning in eighteenth-century America. Crimes statutorily punishable by death in England were sharply reduced in number in Pennsylvania. The Quakers' humanitarian idealism was early expressed in such institutions as hospitals and orphanages. They were the first Americans to raise their voices loudly in protest against slavery. Education was provided publicly or privately for most children. Classical learning was not scorned, but emphasis was laid on the useful arts. Penn suggested that the old and the new in education might be combined by writing textbooks for mechanics in Latin! The colony gave land and liberty to many experimenters (chiefly from Germany) in austere religious and social doctrines: Mennonites and Moravians, Dunkards, Ephratists, River Men, the Society of the Woman in the Wilderness, the New Mooners, and many others.

Excellent education in the useful arts and crafts provided a foundation for advances on the frontiers of science. It was in this congenial environment that Benjamin Franklin of Boston found scope for his astonishing array of talents. The second generation of Quakers with growing prosperity relaxed their fathers' fanaticism and learned to indulge a decent appreciation of worldly pleasures, but they rarely lost their lofty ethical idealism, so that Quaker integrity and benevolence are bywords to this day. If liberty, plenty, progress, and civic virtue were tests, Pennsylvania was indeed the land of promise that its swelling crowds of immigrants sought. No colony was more directly responsible than Penn's for the character of later American life and institutions.

The West Indies

Georgia was founded in 1733 by James Oglethorpe for a combination of imperial and philanthropic purposes somewhat comparable to Penn's. It was the last new colony to be established on the mainland and will be described in the next chapter. Meanwhile, expansion and organization of colonies in the West Indies had proceeded on the same principles as those governing the mainland to form one integrated empire. The Bermuda Islands had been settled as early as 1612, and various adventurers and proprietors competed with Frenchmen for possession of islands of the Lesser Antilles which the Spaniards left unguarded. Cromwell was responsible for the addition of Jamaica (1655) to the English holdings. Prosperous English colonies developed on Barbados, Trinidad, St. Kitts, and other smaller islands. The rich soil and numerous Negro slaves were engaged in the production of sugar cane and other tropical or semitropical crops. Colonial Americans often combined holdings in both the mainland and the islands. Islanders developed their own assemblies with due care for the rights of Englishmen. West Indian settlements became important for New England traders, who found there a valuable market for foodstuffs from the continental colonies to feed the slaves, and ready cargoes of molasses to distill into rum in New England. Exchanged for Negroes in Africa, this became the key of the famous triangular routes. To maintain their trade with the British West Indies the Americans struggled persistently long after the Revolution. For England, the islands were more valuable than the northern mainland colonies because their products and needs fitted perfectly into the mercantilist system. For the planters, whether they lived in the islands or spent their profits on luxury in London, the West Indies were utopian. Negro slavery was more extensive and probably more exploitative than on the mainland. Americans hoped that the British islands would join them in revolt against the mother country in 1776, but contented planters and a population chiefly composed of slaves discouraged such a possibility.

THE RESTORATION AND THE GLORIOUS REVOLUTION

The organization and growth of the empire did not proceed without severe strains. These resulted from both internal colonial and external English causes. Culpeper's Rebellion in North Carolina has been mentioned. A similar but much more important outbreak occurred in Virginia exactly a hundred years before the Declaration of Independence.

"Bacon's Rebellion"

After the Stuart Restoration of 1660, Sir William Berkeley, the royal Governor of Virginia, took advantage of reaction in England to impose arbitrary rule. In the 1670's, overproduction of tobacco resulted in the collapse of prices, and Indian troubles contributed greatly to popular unrest. Berkeley refused to take strong measures to protect frontier settlements against Indian massacres, and the frontiersmen thought it was because he feared Indian reprisals against his personal fur-trade interests. The settlers decided in the spring of 1676 to take matters into their

own hands. They organized a little army, chose as their commander
Nathaniel Bacon, a planter and member of the Council well noted
for his popular sympathies, and defeated the Indians. Furious at this
assertion of provincial self-reliance, Berkeley sought to arrest Bacon,
but support of the rebels was so widespread that he reluctantly consented to call an election for a new Assembly. Before this could convene, Bacon, still without commission from the lordly Governor, attacked
the Indians again. When he came to Jamestown he was denied a seat
in the Assembly and seized by Berkeley, but, being finally released,
he escaped to lead a body of irate supporters back with him. The
Governor was now forced to grant him a military commission, and
reform measures were voted by the Assembly, but civil strife was renewed when the obdurate Governor proclaimed Bacon a rebel. In the
course of the confused conflict Berkeley had to flee to the Eastern
Shore of the Chesapeake, but he returned while Bacon was away on
another Indian expedition. Bacon then marched on Jamestown, which
he burned, and again forced the Governor to flee.

The rebellion suddenly collapsed when Bacon died in October 1676.
It was most notable as a violent colonial conflict with stupid and tyrannical English authority, anticipating the greater one a century later.
Berkeley executed remaining leaders of the rebellion, going to such
extremes that Charles II is reported to have exclaimed: "That old fool
has killed more men in that naked country than I have done for the
murder of my father." A more moderate governor was sent out to take
Berkeley's place, and the victory of Parliament in the Glorious Revolution of 1688 strengthened the position of the Virginia House of Burgesses.
Largely controlled by the eastern planting gentry, this became a great
arena of peaceful opposition to the governors.

Discontent in Maryland

In Maryland the frontiersmen had more serious grievances than in
Virginia, and anti-Catholic sentiment increased with the growth of
Protestant settlement. Josias Fendall, formerly Governor of the province,
led abortive revolts against the proprietary rule of the Calverts and in
1681 he was banished. Associated with him was John Coode, an adventurer who later seized upon the opportunity provided by the Glorious
Revolution. When the Maryland officials in 1689, more Jacobean than
the English Parliament, refused to recognize William and Mary as their
new monarchs, Coode led a band of militiamen of the "Protestant Association" to the provincial capital, St. Mary's, and seized the government.
He called together an assembly that petitioned the King to make Maryland a royal province. The King did so in 1691, and within a few years
the Church of England was established in the province and the capital

moved to Annapolis, a Protestant settlement. When the Calverts were finally restored as proprietors in 1715, after they had become Anglican, the Maryland legislature had entrenched itself sufficiently so that the proprietors were unable to assert much authority. But in Maryland as in Virginia, legislative powers were exercised chiefly by the eastern planters.

New England against the Stuarts

Stuart reaction reached its American climax in New England. Economically, that region was relatively unimportant to mercantilists because few of its products were useful to the Empire. Indeed New England and to some extent the middle colonies were economically dangerous to the success of mercantilism, because in their energetic search for prosperity they embarked on manufacturing and agricultural activities that competed directly with those of the mother country. The New England colonies furthermore developed religious and political institutions which were highly distasteful to Royalists. The Puritan oligarchs defiantly refused to tolerate Anglicans after the Restoration. Their governments, especially that of Massachusetts-Bay, promised to perpetuate in America the anti-Royalist principles which had been overcome in England with the collapse of the Commonwealth. Massachusetts showed dangerous "imperialist" tendencies of her own by absorbing New Hampshire and Maine. New Haven harbored the regicide judges, Whalley and Goffe, whom the agents of Charles II hunted in order to punish them for the execution of his father. In 1662, after a year of obedience to a royal order that persecution of Quakers be stopped, Massachusetts-Bay re-enacted its law inflicting corporal punishment on them. Royal commissioners in 1665 reported to England the many contumacies of the Puritan colonies, and the King commanded that representatives come to England to answer charges, but the General Court refused to send them.

During the desperate fighting of King Philip's War, (1675-1676) New England was not harassed by the home government, but in 1676 a new royal agent, Edward Randolph, reported damning evidence that Massachusetts failed to enforce the Navigation Acts, executed English subjects for their religious views, denied the right of appeal to the Privy Council, and refused the oath of allegiance. Further hostile reports stressed the colonists' defiance of the Navigation Acts. In 1679, a royal commission separated New Hampshire from Massachusetts, and proceedings in the Court of Chancery resulted in 1684 in the annulment of the charter of Massachusetts-Bay on the grounds that it had been stretched out of all recognition and violated.

There was much evidence for these charges. But the remedies devised by imperial planners under James II, who ascended the throne in 1685 and attempted to revive the Divine-Right rule of his ancestors, bore hard on the rights and liberties of colonists in new ways, even while the severities of Puritan rule were being mitigated. Imperial planners designed a consolidation of all the northern colonies from Pennsylvania to New England for better military defense and enforcement of the Navigation Acts, calling this the Dominion of New England, and sent out Sir Edmund Andros in 1686 to organize it and be Governor of Massachusetts, Maine, and New Hampshire. Andros incorporated Rhode Island and assumed the government of Connecticut as well, although the charter was successfully withheld from him in the famous episode of the Charter Oak. Andros gave the Americans a sharp experience of reactionary government. He abolished assemblies, violated charters when courts were too slow, demanded payment of quitrents by freeholders, suppressed town meetings, levied taxes without consent, and forced Puritans to turn over church buildings to Anglicans. All this paralleled and exceeded the rigors of the rule of James II in England itself. Revolt stirred in the colonies and at home.

The Revolution of 1688

When a son was born to James's second wife, Parliament in 1688 deposed the King rather than permit his Catholic son to become ruler of England, and invited his first wife's Protestant daughter, Mary, and her husband, William of Orange, to take the throne. The new monarchs were required to give consent to the rule of Parliament and to a comprehensive Bill of Rights which codified the traditional rights and liberties of Englishmen. This Glorious Revolution, the turning point in the history of English liberty and self-government, was entirely peaceful in England, but in America some violence occurred as the colonists eagerly exploited events at home to overthrow James's agents in America.

In Massachusetts, armed rebels jailed Andros and sent him and his councilors to England for trial. In New York a popular leader named Jacob Leisler seized control of the government. The Dominion of New England collapsed and the various colonies re-established their self-governing bodies. The Mathers and other Puritan leaders struggled to recover the old charter of Massachusetts-Bay, but the new Parliamentary government of England had no more taste for Puritan than for Stuart tyranny. A new charter made Massachusetts a royal colony in 1691. Its Governor was appointed by the Crown, the General Court elected a council, and both were subject to the governor's veto. Most significant, the religious qualification for voting was abolished and a property qualification substituted. Appeals were allowed from the colonial government to the Privy Council and royal review of legislation was provided. Plymouth Colony and Maine were recognized as parts of Massachusetts-Bay. The new charter broke the hold of the Puritan oligarchy, which was already losing its grip as a result of its excesses, the witchcraft trials having been the latest. Connecticut and Rhode Island, however, were allowed to retain their old charters and elect their own governors. In New York a royal governor reasserted control and Leisler was hanged.

The Glorious Revolution greatly advanced liberty and self-government in America as well as in England. John Locke's treatise *Of Civil Government,* which asserted the compact theory of government to justify as legal the overthrow of Stuart tyranny and the assertion of popular and parliamentary rights, became a handbook of colonial rights. The example of Parliament's triumph in England was used by Americans to justify claims of authority by their own legislatures. Such claims obviously contained the seeds of American opposition not only to royal prerogative but also to Parliament's authority to legislate for the Empire. But these seeds did not sprout so long as imperial regulations did not impinge too severely on colonial development. The events of 1688-1689 actually resulted in a new fervor of American pride in and loyalty towards the mother country because she now stood with the Bill of Rights, which applied to Americans as well as Englishmen, as the most sturdy protector of human liberty in the world.

The new government of England furthermore expressed the economic ambitions of colonists as well as Englishmen. After 1689, the pursuit of wealth superseded the pursuit of salvation as the chief purpose of government. The reduction of Puritan power in New England and the indifference of Anglicans elsewhere removed religion from the center of politics. The colonies entered a long period of internal peace, territorial expansion, and economic and cultural growth. Rich opportunities for the acquisition of wealth were left open by the mercantile system; colonists seized these and did not very much object to, although they often evaded, new measures for the consolidation of imperial control. In 1697, a system of Vice-Admiralty Courts was set up in America to enforce the Navigation Acts, as part of the machinery created by the Act of 1696. Obedience to the rule that no colonial law or policy should contradict English law or policy was strengthened by requiring all acts of colonial assemblies to be submitted to the newly-established Board of Trade for recommendation to the Privy Council for approval or "disallowance." Litigants in colonial courts were encouraged to appeal to the Privy Council for review of judicial decisions. The Board of Trade was continually active in surveying colonial affairs, drawing up instructions for the guidance of colonial officials and making recommendations on imperial policy and legislation.

The most important new laws forbade the colonies to develop manufactures which would compete with English factories and forbade them to depreciate the value of money. These measures came chiefly in the eighteenth century and completed the organization of the Empire. As the colonies entered a Golden Age of maturity and prosperity, few could foresee that the very growth of local liberty and wealth in the American colonies, despite the consolidation of imperial control, was creating foundations for the overthrow of British rule.

CHAPTER 6

Colonial Life in the Eighteenth Century

EXPANSION AND GROWTH WERE THE KEYNOTES OF colonial life in the eighteenth century. Between 1700 and the outbreak of the American Revolution the population grew, as the result of a high birth rate and immigration, from about a quarter of a million to about two and a half millions. During the seventeenth century little more than the seacoast and the shores of tidal rivers had been settled. By the time of the Revolution, the wider belt of territory between Tidewater or Low Country and the Appalachian range was filling with farms, and hardy traders and pioneers were pushing through gaps in the mountain barrier into the vast and fertile lands beyond. At the same time, coastal towns grew into thriving little cities, and interior settlements, especially those located at the fall line of the rivers, became important trade centers. Lacking agricultural machinery, the family farm of the eighteenth century was still small and methods of transportation were still primitive. The pioneer wagon, covered or uncovered, was not developed until late in the century. Meanwhile, the fortunate went on horseback into the new and trackless country while the others went on foot, often pushing crude and heavy-laden carts by hand.

SETTLING THE OLD WEST

During the seventeenth century, the eastern seaboard itself was a frontier territory. By trial and error the settlers acquired the techniques which made for success. They learned the peaceful and violent methods of handling the Indians, the ways of the fur trade, the forest arts of hunting, building log cabins, and preparing timber for market, skills in growing crops suited to the new land, and the business of marketing American products abroad. They learned how to attract immigrants by propaganda and by offering land and liberty to all comers. Negro slaves were coming to be used, however, to fill out the labor force when freemen found working for others unattractive. In the eighteenth century these techniques were used to conquer the next belt of territory, the "Old West." Explorers entered the wilderness and were followed in rapid order by fur traders, cattle drovers, pioneer settlers who cleared the fields, and farmers who raised crops for subsistence and for market. Organized government, churches, schools, and towns created civilization where Indians and wild animals had roamed.

The Southern Region: Georgia

This general pattern of frontier development was not invariable. In Virginia, for example, the work of pioneering was often performed by an overseer and a gang of slaves whom a planter had sent ahead to prepare for his occupancy lands that he had acquired by grant from the Governor and Council. The southern Piedmont was settled before the less hospitable hills of the North. Forts were built at the falls of the rivers, and from them exploring parties and fur traders moved into the wooded hills. A new chapter in the settlement of Virginia was started in the second decade of the eighteenth century during the governorship of Alexander Spotswood. He pacified the Piedmont Indians and led a party of explorers whom he called the "Knights of the Golden Horseshoe" into the beautiful Shenandoah Valley. There English from the East were to mingle with Scotch-Irish and Germans who came down from Pennsylvania. Spotswood had some success in his efforts to check the monopolizing of great tracts of lands by individuals who held them for speculative purposes, and to aid actual settlers in the outlying regions, though he gained large holdings for himself while Governor. He became embroiled with the Council, through which lands were granted and which consisted of wealthy planters. He vainly sought to remove from that body William Byrd, second of the name in Virginia, a great landowner and the elegant master of Westover. The greatest estate in the province was that of Lord Fairfax, in form a proprietorship which dated back to the time of Charles II. This extended from the Potomac to the Rappahannock rivers, covering what was known as the "Northern Neck." Here the lord proprietor granted the lands, and here were the homes of the Lees and George Washington. Among other great Virginia landholders were various Carters and Randolphs. Besides the acres they planted in tobacco, they characteristically had great holdings in the West. In the Carolinas, also, huge western grants were made to influential eastern planters, and Maryland's relatively narrow strip of western land was settled much as Virginia's was.

The speculator with his agents had much to do with the settlement of every new American frontier. The headright system, like the later Homestead Act, was to some extent nullified by the favoritism that provincial governments showed to influential persons. Farmers who improved their lands, only to find that these had been granted to speculators, staged a continual fight for their rights, which were often, so far as legal title went, more shadowy than those of the speculator. Out of this sort of struggle grew much of the antagonism between West and East. Some grantees attempted to hold their land while tenants farmed it, but slaves were the only laborers who could not easily avoid working for others. Inefficient surveying and overlapping grants vexed the actual settlers. The farmer who followed the pioneer had to pay for his title, sometimes several times over.

In the southern Piedmont the frontier did not advance in the orderly manner of New England, where as a rule a new tier of four-square townships was opened only when the preceding tier was settled. Large counties were the standard political units of the South, and farms were laid out in helter-skelter fashion. The scattered population was not unified by such an institution of local self-government as the New England town meeting. The backwardness of education among the people as a whole may be largely attributed to geographical conditions and to the intense individualism that prevailed in the region.

The western area of South Carolina was the scene of a long contest between French, Spanish, and English forces. The Indians were allied to one or another and the frontier was in turmoil. In the midst of the Natchez War (1729-1739) between the French and a coalition of Indian tribes fighting for the English, the colony of Georgia was founded to protect the southern frontier and at the same time to provide homes for debtors and other unfortunate persons. James Edward Oglethorpe, a wealthy young Englishman who has been aptly described as an "Imperial Philanthropist," obtained in 1732 a charter permitting him and others as trustees to settle the region between South Carolina and Spanish Florida, and he personally established the first settlement at Savannah. He built a ring of forts around it and at his instance the trustees forbade slavery in the colony, prohibited liquor to prevent traders from giving it to the Indians, and limited farms to 50 acres to insure compact settlement. The English government helped finance the Georgia enterprise for imperial purposes, and wealthy associates helped in the work for philanthropic reasons. The colony was made a proprietary domain under the trustees for twenty-one years, after which it was to revert to the Crown as a royal province. The paternalistic regime was exceedingly unpopular and it actually ended in 1751, a little ahead of time, after the trustees had been forced to repeal the liquor and slavery prohibitions, to relax the land laws, and finally to grant the settlers an assembly. The colony continued to be an expense to the British government almost until the

Revolution. It soon lost its character as a refuge for the unfortunate, but it served a real imperial purpose as a military outpost. Most of the present state of Georgia was still occupied by Indians, but a plantation economy like that of South Carolina developed in the coastal region around Savannah.

The Middle Colonies: Germans and Scotch-Irish

In the middle colonies, westward expansion was hindered by the mountain barrier which runs closer to the seacoast there than elsewhere. New York's great route through the Appalachians by way of the Hudson and Mohawk rivers was long closed to settlers by the refusal of fur-trading interests, with headquarters at Albany, to allow farmers to move into the western domain where Indians trapped and traded. Furthermore, the English who succeeded to Dutch rule maintained the patroon system and extended the similar English manorial system to the whole Hudson Valley. Huge speculative holdings were common. But farmers refused to work as tenants on the great Dutch and English estates, some of which were millions of acres in extent, and the fertile land was idle. In this situation the English government decided to take a hand.

Certain German Protestants, who had suffered religious persecutions and fallen into extreme poverty as a result of the devastating Thirty Years' War, were eager to go to America, and immigration and shipping companies began to make a business of organizing migration. The English government sent out a small party of Palatine Germans in 1708 to found the town of Newburgh on the Hudson. The next year thousands of Palatines descended on London, where the army housed them in tents while ships were made ready. Groups were dispatched to various colonies, the largest number to New York. They were settled in camps along the Hudson and fed at government expense while they produced naval stores. The enterprise was not a success and was abandoned in a few years. The Germans, who were allowed to go where they pleased, promptly defied the Albany traders and moved into the Mohawk Valley. Soon a line of neat German villages and thrifty farms pointed the way to New York's great and fertile interior valleys, though the full settlement of that region was delayed because of the Indians. Afterward the main movement of the Germans was into Pennsylvania, where they came to be called incorrectly the Pennsylvania Dutch (from *Deutsch*, meaning German), and through that province into western Maryland and the Valley of Virginia, whence they proceeded southward into the Carolinas and the eastern part of what is now Tennessee.

Proprietors' rights were largely ignored in New York and Pennsylvania. Settlers simply squatted on the land and defied the authorities to dislodge them. Out of their practice they boldly rationalized the theory of "squatters' rights." The Scotch-Irish were especially aggressive in advocating and practicing this doctrine. These hardy people were mostly Lowland Scots who had been sent to northern Ireland in the seventeenth century to subdue the Irish and create a Protestant counterweight to the native Catholic population. In Ulster they learned how to clear their fields and produce a crop while fighting off marauding Irish tribesmen. Despite their services to the English government, the Scots in Ireland were not allowed to prosper. Between 1665 and 1699, a series of laws restricted their trade; Presbyterians were placed under civil and religious disabilities in 1704; and the rents on their lands were increased a few years later. Stubborn in their determination to make their way in the world and full of hatred for England, the Scotch-Irish migrated to America in such numbers that they constituted about one-eighth of the population by the time of the Revolution and were the largest non-English group.

At first they thought that Calvinistic New England would be a congenial place to settle. The Puritans were willing enough to send the rough newcomers to the frontier as Indian fighters, and a number of them settled in New Hampshire and western Massachusetts and all along the northern border, as the town names show. But the land was poor, the Puritans forced them to support the established Congregational Church, which varied in organization from their Presbyterianism, and their turbulent ways and strange accents made them unpopular. The main stream of Scotch-Irish migrants turned to Pennsylvania. There they moved into mountain valleys, westward of the Germans. Thence many of them went southwards through the Great Valley of Virginia to settle the back country of the southern colonies. John C. Calhoun and Andrew Jackson were of this stock.

The Scotch-Irish defied landowners and rent collectors. They said it was "against the laws of God and nature, that so much land should be idle while so many Christians wanted it to labor on to raise their bread." They fought Indians with righteous zest and had little respect for the laws of England or of its colonies. No group was more nearly unanimous in support of the American Revolution or provided a larger percentage of tough fighters for Washington's Army. While they advanced the frontier in many colonies with unexampled vigor, the Scotch-Irish by no means abandoned their Calvinist love of learning. Wherever they went they established church schools and in 1726 they founded at Neshaminy, Pennsylvania, the famous Log College to provide training for the ministry. Classical learning was maintained in these frontier institutions, but the special genius of the Scotch-Irish was for practical affairs. In time their businessmen, lawyers, engineers, politicians, and soldiers displaced Quakers and other groups as leaders of the middle colonies. In every colony that had a frontier they strengthened the radical party in opposition to eastern as well as English rule, in favor of western farmers' rights and the overthrow of established churches. They typified the spirit of the Old West.

New Jersey and Delaware were hemmed in by other colonies and produced no important frontier development. Conflicting proprietary grants in New Jersey troubled that colony. It attracted a bewildering variety of settlers from Europe, England, and other colonies, who united only in demanding freemen's rights against remnants of the proprietors' authority. Agriculture, whaling, and trade thrived. The present area of Delaware was claimed by William Penn, and the Privy Council gave him the right to appoint a governor in 1703. Its people won a separate legislative assembly in 1704 and later made good their independence from Pennsylvania by the indirect method of declaring their independence from England. Delaware developed a placid rural economy and way of life which was little disturbed until the great industrial activities of the du Pont family in the nineteenth and twentieth centuries transformed it.

New England

In New England, the Old West was the hill country of New Hampshire, Vermont, and western Massachusetts. The downfall of the Puritan oligarchy at the end of the seventeenth century and the rise of a rich merchant class in the seacoast towns transformed the New England method of frontier settlement. Towns were still laid out in neat tiers and the town meeting persisted as a democratic instrument of local government, but land speculators skimmed rich profits from the work of the settlers. The colonial governments began in the 1720's to create new towns for the benefit of promoters, who were usually merchants looking for investments. Often the promoters established sawmills and other improvements in new town sites, gave away the first lots to settlers who would build roads, and then sold the remaining lots at enhanced prices. The worst evil of the new system came from the influence of absentee owners during the period of settlement. The speculative fever also created new towns faster than settlers could fill them, resulting in a weak frontier line and poor communications. The system gave rise to a bad situation in the present area of Vermont, which both New York and New Hampshire claimed. Governor Benning Wentworth of New Hampshire began in 1749 to give town sites in the "New Hampshire Grants" to speculators—reserving 500 acres in each for himself. Settlers found their titles disputed by agents of New York, and organized the famed "Green Mountain Boys" to fight off the Yorkers. Like the inhabitants of Delaware, the Vermonters tried to secure their independence from neighboring colonies by declaring independence from England, but the stratagem did not work so well. They were kept waiting for admission to the Union until 1791.

The New England pioneers rapidly penetrated the Berkshire hills and threatened to spill over into New York. The tenant farmers of the Hudson Valley welcomed them, hoping that the New England colonies might annex the region and make them owners of the farms they tilled, but the New York authorities obtained a Crown decree fixing the eastern boundary of New York 20 miles east of the Hudson River. Thwarted there, the New Englanders moved northward into Maine, New Hampshire, and Vermont. Some Connecticut groups also found outlets for the land fever of speculators and settlers in the Wyoming Valley of Pennsylvania.

Frontier radicalism was nourished in New England as elsewhere by the excesses of Eastern speculators. The frontiersmen became impatient of all law, restless in the search for independence which seemed to require remoteness from other settlers, supremely self-reliant and contemptuous of anything hinting of personal subservience, and equally fearless in facing the dangers and hardships of the forest and man-made dangers to their liberty and independence. In the Old West, cut off from Europe and the seacoast, the American as a new type of humanity first took form. Compounded of many nationalities, dependent on nothing but his axe and his gun, capable of turning his hand to anything from making his own clothes to building a house, given to hard drinking and wild, exaggerated humor, distrustful of theory but quick to invent and adopt new practical devices, intensely optimistic, fierce in enmity and generous in friendship, the Westerner was certain that he was indeed "nature's nobleman." He created in his own image a distinctive American civilization which was a mixture of European inheritances and frontier influences.

THE BROADENING ECONOMY

Commerce

Throughout the eighteenth century the eastern seaboard maintained closer contacts with Europe than with the new settlements in the western hills. Colonial merchants sometimes were agents of English mercantile houses, but as profits accumulated in colonial hands independent capitalists often took over the business of the colonies with the mother country. A favorite form of investment was in ships. Trade and shipping prospered as a result of rising prices for colonial produce in Britain and Europe. Higher prices directly affected the West Indies and the southern colonies, which produced the sugar, molasses, tobacco, rice, indigo, and other staples most in demand abroad. But the merchants, shipowners, and

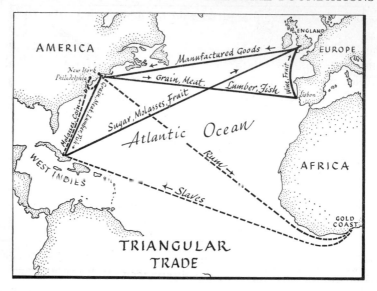

TRIANGULAR
TRADE

manufacturers of the northern colonies quickly learned how to obtain a share of the prosperity of their neighbors.

West Indian molasses was brought into the northern colonies and manufactured into rum. Parliament in 1733 passed the Molasses Act, imposing a prohibitory duty on foreign molasses and sugar, but the law was commonly violated in order to bring in the cheap products of the French and Spanish West Indies. Rum was carried from the New England ports to Africa where it was exchanged for slaves. The slaves were sold into the West Indies and southern plantations, where cargoes of molasses or other staples were taken aboard, thus completing the triangular trade on which colonial as well as English merchants grew rich.

Baltimore was founded in 1729 and became a leading site of water-powered mills which ground wheat into flour for sale to the West Indies, England, and Europe. Philadelphia remained pre-eminent in the grain and meat trade, while New York was the chief purveyor of furs to the world. The coast of New England from Connecticut to Maine was dotted with busy seaports. Fish and forest products were the chief articles of New England commerce, but the aggressive Yankee businessman followed his keen scent for profits into many a trade, triangular and quadrangular, which employed his ships and capital. The rice and indigo of South Carolina flowed through Charleston, making it the leading southern port, but in Tidewater Virginia and Maryland ships came up to the wharves of the plantations and the planters dealt directly with English factors or northern merchants, hence there were hardly any towns.

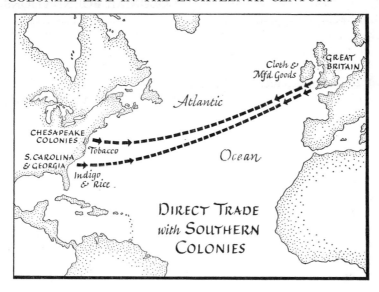

Crafts and Skills

Economic freedom in the colonies was considerably achieved in spite of imperial mercantilist laws. This was chiefly because of the ease of acquiring land and the laxity of English law enforcement. The prosperity of American trade, partially conducted in violation of English law, encouraged manufactures. Back-country conditions encouraged mechanical ingenuity and widespread cultivation of craft skills. "Kitchen manufactures" of tools, cloth, furniture, leather goods, and many other things thrived from the beginning. The English government forbade the emigration of skilled artisans with their tools to America, but they came anyway.

In America every farmer and his family practiced many crafts and American industry grew out of this vast reservoir of skills. Textile production was the earliest important manufacture. The governments of New England early encouraged sheep-raising by tax exemptions, special pasture privileges, and prohibitions against killing ewes. At first all the work of shearing the sheep, cleaning the wool, carding, combing, spinning, dyeing with the juices of plants, and weaving the cloth was performed by hand, much of it by the women and children. By 1700, New England was self-sufficient in the coarser grades of woolen cloth. In the other colonies woolen manufactures were also common, while linen made from flax and cotton goods were also produced. The textile industry was one of the first to be moved out of the kitchens into specialized mills. By the middle of the eighteenth century the most skillful craftsmen were spending their full time in performing one or more of the processes for their neighbors, and from this system factory production gradually grew.

Manufactures of wood had a similar history. At first every settler turned his hand to carpentry and the fashioning of tools and furniture. Wooden tools were almost universal except for axes and tips of plows. Wooden pegs substituted for nails and mauls for hammers. Sturdy furniture in simplified imitation of the Jacobean styles of England was one of the earliest and best products of American craft. In the eighteenth century the carpenter's trade became important as a special vocation. Ship-carpenters were the earliest professionals, and their skill advanced so rapidly that along the seacoast houses and furniture like the "Cape Cod cottage" and the "captain's chair" were often built according to sea-going techniques. While the wealthiest began to insist on mansions of brick, which was sometimes even imported from abroad, and a few, especially in eastern Pennsylvania and among the Dutch in New York, built with stone, the characteristic building material in early America was wood. In forest clearings the log cabin became standard. Prosperous farmers and most townsmen built with boards supplied by local sawmills. The most pretentious of these houses displayed wooden imitations of current European styles of ornament. The typical "architect" of the colonial period was a carpenter with a well-thumbed European builder's manual.

Ships were the greatest of the colonial manufactures of wood and in this craft New England, with ample timber, numerous craftsmen, and maritime ambitions, surpassed the other colonies. Governor Winthrop had the first American ship, the *Blessing of the Bay*, built in 1631. After 1700, the numerous shipyards of the New England towns, some of them far inland on rivers, not only supplied local owners but sold ships to the other colonies, England, and Europe. During the colonial period it was the cheapness of materials that gave American shipyards their advantage; but superiority of design and construction maintained it. The middle colonies had some success in shipbuilding, but the southern colonies failed to develop or attract shipwrights despite bounties.

Iron manufacture was the first metal trade practiced in British America. The need for tools, kettles, and hardware stimulated many efforts to exploit the readily available deposits of bog-iron. In this, too, New England excelled. The first American furnace for smelting iron ore and forge for beating it into hardness and fashioning useful shapes were erected at Lynn, Massachusetts, in 1643. In the seventeenth century, Connecticut vied with Massachusetts in developing iron industries, but by 1750 Pennsylvania had won the supremacy which she has never lost. The chief product of the mills was bar iron and steel which was distributed to local blacksmiths for working into finished articles. Few families by the end of the colonial period could afford to buy much domestic metalware because even the simplest nail required special forging of the head to the shank. An iron kettle, iron plow-point, an iron axe head, and the indispensable gun were the extent of the average farmer's metal equipment.

American skill was notably displayed in the development of the Pennsylvania rifle, later called the Kentucky rifle, from a German prototype.
Its elongated barrel was the secret of the frontiersman's famous accuracy
in bringing down game or more formidable quarry. New England ingenuity survived Pennsylvania's supremacy in heavy metal manufacturing,
as it retained its lead in the production of hardware. The scarcity of
metal was solved in the case of clockworks by the ingenious use of wood.
By the middle of the century, other metals than iron were coming to be
used. Lead for bullets and pewter was scarce and mostly imported, as
was silver for the advanced craftsmen—like Jeremiah Dummer, John
Coney, and Paul Revere. The future of metallurgical industries in America
was visible, however, by the end of the colonial period in the fact that
in 1775 the colonies produced one-seventh of the world's pig and bar iron.

Sawmills using the straight saw, and grist mills whose stones were
turned by oxen or by water-wheels, were the most common colonial
"factories." Sawyers and millers were the first manufacturers in every
new settlement. Rum distilleries were probably the most profitable of all
colonial factories. Shoemaking which many farmers practiced in the
kitchen was gradually developed into a specialized trade. In the Old
West, home processing of grain into whiskey and of wood into potash and
pearl ash solved the problem of poor roads by reducing bulky materials
to forms which justified costly transportation.

Dominance of Merchants

Manufacturing, whether at home or in specialized mills and shops, remained throughout the colonial period subordinate to the merchant. No
manufacturer produced enough to undertake distribution himself beyond
his own locality. Interchange of goods between localities was in the hands
of merchants who bought the productions of many localities and sold
them elsewhere in the colonies or abroad. The most successful merchants
made their headquarters in the seaports of the northern colonies. They
owned their own ships to ply the coasts and rivers and cross the ocean,
and even functioned as bankers, extending loans at interest to lesser
merchants and to manufacturers. Their strategic position enabled them
to dictate low prices to the farmers and millers from whom they bought
and high prices to consumers. Engrossing the markets, that is, establishing monopoly control by encompassing the total supply of a particular
commodity, although forbidden by English law which colonial governments frequently affirmed, became a common practice.

From Massachusetts to Pennsylvania the merchants dominated colonial
society. Their influence was felt in the South, which developed no strong
merchant class of its own, although it accounted for more than two-thirds
of all colonial exports and imports. The northern merchants were them-

selves subordinate to English merchants, for whom they often acted as American agents. Some English mercantile houses specialized in the southern trade and sent ships with English goods direct to the wharves of Tidewater plantations and picked up cargoes of tobacco. The northern merchant possessed market power of his own, but the southern planter could not avoid dependence on northern or English middlemen.

The consequence was that the northern merchant outranked all other Americans in ready wealth and steadily made headway even against his English competitors. By developing intercolonial trade, encouraging manufactures, invading the southern market, and ingeniously exploiting loopholes in the imperial trade walls, notably the triangular routes to the West Indies and Africa, he emerged as the controlling figure in the American economy. But at the end of the seventeenth century the English government began a new series of attempts to restrict the growth of American mercantile independence.

CULTURAL DEVELOPMENTS

Rising prosperity after 1700 was accompanied by a new emphasis on worldly culture. Northern merchants and southern planters enjoyed comfortable living and cultivated the arts and graces. Rows of elegant mansions in the port cities, and plantation houses matching the splendor of English manors, were visible symbols of economic status. While the poorest family used homemade pine furniture, American cabinet makers learned to reproduce for richer clients the mahogany styles of England in native cherry, and the wealthiest imported the original articles. Fine silverware, porcelain, and glass displaced for the few the woodenware and pewter of common use. It became possible for a painter to support himself in America by turning out portraits of colonial worthies which bespoke wealth and status in the glow of silken garments, the pride of facial expressions, and the softness of hands.

Education

Mental cultivation was an ideal with more than ornamental meaning for the colonial merchants and planters. They collected libraries of ancient classics, the latest English publications, and a growing number of colonial imprints. In education the northern colonies maintained the lead which Massachusetts had early won. William and Mary College (1693) at Williamsburg, the capital of Virginia, whose reconstruction in our day provides an image of the golden age of the colonies, remained the only southern institution of higher learning during the colonial period. Yale College (1701) was followed by the College of New Jersey at Princeton (1746), which provided Presbyterian seminary training for the

Scotch-Irish in succession to their Log College. The University of Pennsylvania, nonsectarian, was founded in 1749 and King's College (now Columbia University) in 1754 as an Anglican institution. The Baptists educated their ministers at the College of Rhode Island (now Brown University), founded at Providence in 1764, and the Dutch Reformed Church established Queen's College (now Rutgers University) in 1766. Even the wild frontier of New Hampshire was provided with a college, Dartmouth at Hanover, established in 1769, partially for the benefit of Indian youths. Wealthy colonists, Southerners especially, went to England for professional education in law or medicine or for broadening travel. The latest fashions in ideas, the arts, and amusements quickly found their way to America, and little courts in imitation of the royal court clustered around the colonial governors. Frosty religious attitudes towards the theater, dancing, and other frivolities gradually melted in the face of the worldliness that accompanied growing wealth. Gambling, horse racing, and tavern drinking were popular diversions indulged in by those who could not as well as by those who could afford them.

Religion

The religious fervor of the earliest settlers gave way along the seaboard to decorous forms of worship and relative indifference, especially among the southern planters. The latter maintained nominal adherence to the Anglican faith as a kind of civil responsibility. The spiritual quality of the Anglican clergymen was not high. In Virginia they became famous for short and pallid sermons and long bouts of worldly diversion. They entered into the gay round of fox hunting, horse racing, and hospitality with the planters. Frontiersmen who liked their religion hot resented the attempt to make them help pay for the support of the Anglican establishment. All the Anglican churches in America belonged to the diocese of London, and the highest American official was a commissary of that diocese. Earnest Anglicans tried to improve the discipline and organization of the American clergy by asking the English government to create independent dioceses in the colonies, but local Anglicans as well as dissenters feared that it would lead to heavier taxes and successfully opposed the reform. The Anglican Society for the Propagation of the Gospel conducted missionary campaigns among the Indians and the colonists, but they were not so successful as dissenting evangelical preachers in arousing religious enthusiasm.

In New England increasing worldliness did not so easily overcome the religious spirit. The Puritan or Congregational Church remained the established Church everywhere except in Rhode Island, and dissenters were made to pay taxes for its support. There was a tendency among preachers to temper the rigors of Calvinism in favor of the mental comfort of their wealthier listeners, but it was dramatically reversed by the "Great Awakening." This religious revival got under way in several northern colonies in the 1720's and 1730's. Eventually it touched all the colonies and all the diverse religious groups in them with the exception of the negligible number of Roman Catholics. It caused splits in the older churches between enthusiasts and conservatives and led ultimately to the organization of a bewildering variety of new sects. The Great Awakening was a reaction against moderation and intellectualism in religion. Polite sermons by educated preachers failed to satisfy the mass of colonists, and they turned to preachers who excited their emotions. Revivalism was institutionalized and became a permanent feature of American religion.

The first great leader of the Awakening was Jonathan Edwards, a graduate of Yale and the Congregational minister of Northampton, Massachusetts. A famous revival began there in 1734 under his preaching. Edwards was a prose artist, something of a mystic, and an extremely eloquent orator. The tendency of his preaching was to strengthen the Calvinist conception of predestination and yet to encourage all men to behave as if they were elect by renouncing sin and striving to believe they were granted a share of Divine Grace. Edwards' evocations of the tortures of the damned made his hearers roll on the floor in physical agonies, but he thrilled them with hope that they might yet be saved, and the experience of conversion became the core of revivalist religion. His influence reached far beyond his parish by means of such publications as *A Faithful Narration of the Surprising Work of God in the Conversion of Many Hundred Souls in Northampton* (1737), which was widely reprinted in America and Europe. Revivalism spread like wildfire along the Atlantic seaboard and into the West during the following years. It was taken up by lay preachers, hysterics, and charlatans, as well as by many a sincere minister of the older churches. Conservative clergymen and their calmer followers held fast, and Edwards himself was eventually deprived of his pulpit. But in a series of penetrating theological works he developed a modification of Calvinism which placed emphasis on the capacity of every man for holiness and communication with God. He was the founder of the New England or Edwardean theology, which gave a new lease of life to Calvinism.

In England, John Wesley strove to bring invigorating emotionalism into the Anglican Church, and the movement he founded succeeded in turning large numbers away from their complacent religious leaders into the separate "Low Church," "Chapel," or "Methodist" communions. Wesley's English movement ultimately resulted in the Methodist Church in America, but its organization was long delayed. George Whitefield, sent out to preach in Georgia, was fired by Edwards' example, and in 1739 began his amazing career as itinerant revivalist preacher throughout the

American colonies. With Whitefield the Awakening literally burst forth from the churches, because no building could accommodate the crowds he drew. He could make himself heard by 20,000 people, could preach two sermons in one day, and ride many miles to repeat the performance the next day. Even the skeptical Benjamin Franklin could not withstand the eloquence of Whitefield. He went to hear him out of curiosity, decided presently that he might contribute a few coppers to the inevitable collection plate, and ended by pouring out the entire contents of his purse.

The Baptists and the "New Light" Presbyterians were the chief beneficiaries of the Great Awakening. These groups made conversion of sinners their chief objective, the revival meeting their chief technique, and extreme democracy their system of church government. In the East revivalism had less permanent importance than in the Old West. There it became not only the central religious activity but also an important means of social expression, mitigating the loneliness of frontier life and uniting the settlers in opposition to the established and more decorous religions of the seaboard. The broadest meaning of the Great Awakening is that it inaugurated the process whereby the conditions of American life which were conducive to individualism invaded the sphere of religion.

In the East a few of the most advanced minds developed religious attitudes precisely the opposite of emotional revivalism. They were influenced to move towards rationalism in religion by the rise of scientific inquiry into the laws of nature, heralded by the career of Sir Isaac Newton. The theology of Christianity became less important in their minds than the study of nature as a means of understanding God, "the Great Artificer." They rejected miracles and certain other articles of orthodox faith as superstitions based on ignorance of the immutable laws of nature. They conceived of God, not as a person intimately concerned with the doings of men, but as a "force," the "prime mover," more or less identical with the created universe. Such attitudes of the Age of Enlightenment gave moral and spiritual impetus to learning, particularly in the fields of the sciences, but they tended to reduce church-going to a rather empty formality. In extreme form these attitudes led to the rationalist, unorthodox religion of Deism. Many of the most intelligent colonists, including such later leaders as Benjamin Franklin and Thomas Jefferson, turned to rationalism in religion. Perhaps the best proof of their faith in reasonableness is that they did not personally break with the institutions of orthodoxy or attack the beliefs of others. But they strongly opposed the political claims of certain religious groups. The impulse that later resulted in the complete separation of Church and State was shared by seaboard intellectuals and frontier revivalists.

Rise of the Press

While science was displacing theology as the absorbing concern of the best-educated Americans, the press to some extent displaced the pulpit as the chief vehicle of popular education. The schools and colleges clung to older and safer notions, but the book and periodical press spread among Americans the latest and most dangerous political and philosophical ideas, imported and domestic. Without the growth of the press in the seaboard cities during the earlier eighteenth century, it is difficult to imagine that the Revolution, which required unity of minds and hands scattered along thousands of miles of coast and frontier, could have succeeded.

During the seventeenth century, colonial printing presses had turned out little besides religious works. The prolific and pedantic writings of the Mathers dominated the output of the most active printing center, Boston and Cambridge. The first attempt to establish an American newspaper in 1690 in Boston failed after the first issue because it displeased the authorities, but the Boston postmaster, John Campbell, successfully published the *Boston News-Letter,* beginning in 1704. The *Boston Gazette,* which began publication in 1719, was printed by James Franklin, half-brother of Benjamin. Two years later, James launched the *New England Courant,* in which certain of the traditional practices of American journalism were tried out. This newspaper promised "to entertain the town with the most comical and diverting incidents of human life," and it grievously offended the Puritans not only by its levity but by its severe attacks on the Mathers, Harvard College, and the Assembly. Young Ben Franklin served as printer's devil and writer for this paper, but he soon decided to go to Philadelphia to make his own way in its freer atmosphere. There he became printer-in-chief to the American people, disseminating books, tracts, almanacs, and periodicals, many of them written by himself, which made his presses the greatest engines of humorous common sense and political and scientific enlightenment the colonies possessed.

By 1765, there were twenty-five newspapers in the colonies. A famous victory for freedom of the press had been won in New York in 1735. John Peter Zenger was a Palatine German and the publisher of the *New York Weekly Journal,* which he made an organ of the popular opposition to the "court" party around the Governor. He published criticisms and jibes against Governor William Cosby which would not be considered remarkable if, today, they were directed against a President of the United States. But the colonies, like England, had severe libel laws and Cosby threw Zenger into prison. For many months the editor conducted his paper from a cell. His trial aroused excitement throughout the colonies. The great lawyer Andrew Hamilton of Philadelphia defended Zenger, arguing that the editor was innocent of libel because his criticisms of the Governor were true. Chief Justice De Lancey pronounced the English principle that anything "scandalous and ironical" was a libel even if it *was* true. Thus the issue was clearly joined on the question whether the press was free to print the truth. The verdict of the jury was that Zenger was not guilty of libel and he went free. This did not prevent further suppression of the freedom of the press before and after the Revolution, but it was a precedent of great importance which eventually prevailed.

CHAPTER 7

Colonial Politics
and a Cycle of Wars

JUST AS MERCANTILIST REGULATIONS MODIFIED BUT did not prevent independent economic growth in the English colonies, so the efforts of the Crown to systematize political administration were partially defeated by the lusty growth of colonial political skill and institutions. War usually requires a higher degree of centralized administration than peace, but even the participation of the colonies in four major wars against European powers, beside endemic war against the Indians, did not greatly alter colonial or imperial political development until after 1763. Internal colonial forces rather than any external influences were the chief source of political development. The character, ambitions, and ideals of the people provided the main explanation of colonial politics.

COLONIAL POLITICAL INSTITUTIONS

The type of colonial government favored by England after 1689 was the royal province. This form of government was not conducive to the establishment of new colonies, because it offered no incentives to competent leaders to risk investments of time and money. Therefore, almost all the colonies were founded by business companies holding charter privileges or by individual proprietors who received royal grants. It was after colonies had been successfully established that the English authorities wanted to transform them into royal provinces in order to gain more direct control over the policies and acts of their governments. Yet charters and royal grants were respected as vested rights in English law, and they could not be extinguished without court proceedings in which the government or some other suitor could show substantial cause why the Crown should be permitted to revoke them. The consequence was that not all the colonies were converted into royal provinces. Connecticut and Rhode Island kept their charters to the end and Maryland, Pennsylvania, and Delaware retained the proprietary form.

Governors

The essential distinctions among these three forms—charter or corporate, proprietary, and royal—lay in the degree of local self-government. All three were subject to the requirement that no colonial act should contravene English law, and to the review of their legislation by the Board of Trade, with the possibility of royal disallowance. The Privy Council was the highest court of appeal. A more immediate means of preventing undesired action by a colonial government, including action which did *not* contravene English law, was to install a Crown-appointed governor who was subject to instructions from the home government and armed with veto power over the colonial legislature. The royal governorship was the essential institution that differentiated the eight royal provinces from the proprietary and charter colonies. Governors were elected in Rhode Island and Connecticut, and in the proprietary colonies were chosen by the proprietor. In practice, after the Glorious Revolution, the proprietary governors were generally less severe than the royal because they learned from experience that the home government was eager to take advantage of disorder in proprietary colonies and convert them into royal provinces. Similarly, the charter governments of Connecticut and Rhode Island learned to avoid giving too much temptation to the English authorities. They retained their unusual rights of self-rule by keeping out of controversy.

Besides holding the veto power over the legislatures, the governors were the chief executives of the provinces. In the performance of their executive functions they were aided by a council, which was appointed except in Massachusetts, where it was elected by the lower house of the legislature. The council also served as an upper house of the legislature. It represented a cross between the Privy Council and the House of Lords in England, but in practice it often was hand in glove with the lower house of the assembly, which by the eighteenth century won the right to initiate legislation. Inasmuch as the governor himself was generally dependent on legislative grants or taxes for his salary, powers over local taxation and appropriations were crucial, and the assemblies had both powers. The threat of withholding his salary whipped many a governor into compliance even in matters over which the assemblies had no formal authority. In time of war the English government commonly laid requisitions on the colonies and these, too, were dependent on the consent of the assemblies. The power of the purse in the hands of the colonies caused the home government itself normally to exercise moderation in dealing with them. Today the exclusive right of the United States House of Representatives to initiate money bills is an inheritance of the most potent of all colonial legislative rights.

Bribery and corruption were common among government officials in eighteenth-century England and Europe and the system was not much criticized there. Public offices were handed out as favors without much regard for training or competence, and it was considered a normal exercise of privileged status for an administrator to enrich himself. But in America the corruption of royal officials was more palpable than in England, because many of them so obviously detested the colonies and accepted these offices only as a means of extracting plunder to take home. Furthermore, in the colonies, even the wealthiest classes identified themselves with other Americans as against court favorites from abroad. Some royal officials were able and honest, but criticism of most of them for their arrogance and malpractices was common throughout the colonial period.

Assemblies

The assemblies were generally made up of the leading men of each colony—as defined in terms of education, wealth, and social standing. In no colony was the franchise universal, but the ease of satisfying the property qualification for the vote—generally a 50-acre freehold, or a town lot with a structure on it, or property worth £40 or £50—was such that ordinarily only slaves, servants, tenants, and some artisans were disfranchised, besides young men who had yet to make their way. Large landowners were the earliest typical legislators. With the rise of trade and professional classes in the eighteenth century, lawyers became the typical representatives, though often they were also large landowners, especially in the southern colonies. Most lawyers identified their interests with the merchants or planters, but a few derived from their legal study doctrines of liberty which transcended class interests. Such "radicals" were the outstanding champions of colonial rights against royal privilege. The leaders of the last colonial generation of legislators were generally lawyers or planters versed in the law, and they became leaders of the Revolution. There has probably never been a revolution that displayed more legal and political skill, and this was a direct result of the long experience and training in self-government afforded by the colonial assemblies.

Political parties as such did not exist in colonial times, though factions were common. Voters and legislators grouped themselves around individuals without creating any permanent extragovernmental organization. Nevertheless, the germs of political parties were present in divisions created by issues, and as all issues tended to boil down to the one between colonial rights and English authority, with the great majority of assmbly-men on the side of colonial rights, governors had to contend with legis-latures controlled by what amounted to an opposition "party." The two were fairly evenly matched, the governor holding negative powers of veto and of dissolution, the colonials having power to frustrate the governor by refusing funds. But the governors were more reluctant to use their powers than the assemblies, so that prior to 1763, with minor exceptions, the assemblies made good their claim to sole jurisdiction over internal taxation and built up by steady accretions their authority over executive functions, such as the appointment of administrative offi-cials and control of the militia and armaments.

While the perennial struggle between governor and assembly was an excellent school of politics for the colonials, it also established a tradition of competition between the two branches of government which persists in the United States today and greatly differentiates American govern-ment from the English Parliamentary model. During the colonial period a lesser party division existed between representatives of the wealthier East and those of the newly settled West. The royal governors sometimes favored the East against the "leveling" demands of the West, and when such an alignment occurred the Westerners could easily be outvoted be-cause representation of their districts lagged far behind the actual growth of population.

The Rights and Liberties of Englishmen

The judicial systems of the colonies were modeled on those of England. In small matters justice was administered by local justices of the peace, as by the county courts of Virginia. More important civil and criminal cases were tried in courts presided over, as a rule, by judges appointed by the governors. In Virginia the Council served as the highest court, though the great landholders on it were not necessarily lawyers. Appeals from these courts could be taken to the Privy Council in England, but this arduous and expensive procedure was not practicable for the ordinary citizen. The English common law, which is the body of decisions in former cases used as precedents in later ones, prevailed in the American courts except where it was superseded by specific legislation, colonial or Parliamentary. English judicial process, including arrest only by war-rant, the right of accused to a writ of habeas corpus, the right to a trial by jury, and the right to present and to examine witnesses, besides the rule of assumed innocence until guilt is positively proved, also obtained in the colonies. In no sphere of government were English institutions more directly or more advantageously transplanted in America and better maintained after the Revolution. Nor was any other English action more conducive to revolution than the interference after 1763 with colonial judicial procedure.

Conflict between the colonies and the mother country was inherent in the original guarantee that Englishmen in the colonies would enjoy all the rights and liberties of Englishmen at home, on the one hand; and on the other the presence of colonial legislatures which, despite their real powers, were not autonomous but subject to the will of the home government. The colonists admitted at most that they owed obedience to the English government only in external affairs such as imperial trade regulations. They tended to avoid even this admission by claiming that their legislatures had the same power that the Glorious Revolution won for Parliament. That same Revolution, however, was cited by Englishmen as making Parliament the sole ultimate lawgiver in all matters whatsoever for the whole empire. This conflict remained insignificant so long as neither side was impelled to test its theory in practice. Such impulsions first became visible in new mercantilist regulations of the eighteenth century, and then in Parliamentary enactments that went beyond mercantilist principles and sought to make the colonies help pay for wars.

New Mercantilist Regulations

When colonial manufactures for export became possible, England forbade the development of those colonial industries which would compete with established English industries. Thus the Woolens Act of 1699 forbade the sale of colonial woolen textiles in any market outside the colony of manufacture. This affected Ulster in Ireland much more than the American colonies. The Hat Act of 1732 forbade the colonists to make hats out of beaver fur in shops employing more than a limited number of apprentices, or to export their products. The Iron Act of 1750 encouraged the export to Britain of colonial pig and bar iron, but forbade further colonial investment in manufacture of semifinished or finished products. The obvious purpose of these laws was to protect British industries by forcing the colonists to send raw materials to the mother country and buy back the manufactured articles. Their immediate effect was not very oppressive, but for the future the colonists were discouraged from developing large-scale industries in forbidden fields. The English laws against American manufactures, like so many others, were considerably violated as illegal factories sprang up.

The Money Question

English mercantilists held one trump card: control over the coinage of money. The over-all purpose of mercantilism was to make the colonial economy a source of English wealth which could be collected in bullion,

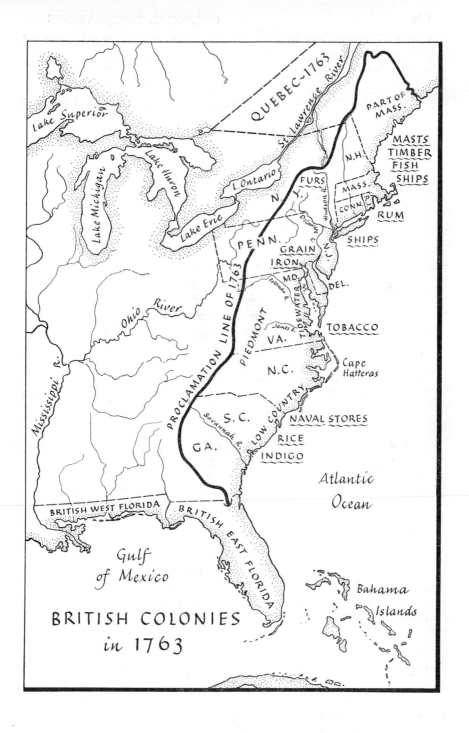

BRITISH COLONIES
in 1763

Lake Superior

Lake Michigan

Lake Huron

L. Ontario

Lake Erie

QUEBEC-1763

St. Lawrence River

PART OF
MASS.

N.H.

MASTS
TIMBER
FISH
SHIPS

N. Y.

FURS

MASS.

CONN.

Hudson R.

RUM

Delaware R.

PENN.

SHIPS

GRAIN

IRON

MD.

DEL.

Ohio River

Mississippi R.

PROCLAMATION LINE OF 1763

PIEDMONT

Potomac R.

TIDEWATER

James R.

VA.

TOBACCO

N. C.

Cape
Hatteras

S. C.

LOW COUNTRY

Savannah R.

NAVAL STORES

GA.

RICE

INDIGO

Atlantic
Ocean

BRITISH WEST FLORIDA

BRITISH EAST FLORIDA

Gulf
of Mexico

Bahama
Islands

and at the same time to prevent the diminution of the Empire's supply of gold and silver. Therefore, the export of specie from the Empire was prohibited. The creation of a balance of trade with the colonies favorable to the mother country was not difficult. Even in the eighteenth century the colonies were frontier communities, producing chiefly raw materials for export; they were in great need of basic manufactures such as cloth, tools, glass, and cutlery, and were desirous of improving their standard of living by importing articles of luxury. England was the greatest European producer of the first class of goods, and the Navigation Acts effectually cut off colonial imports from her competitors except by smuggling, which went on, especially with Holland. The northern colonies produced little that was sent directly to England. How could they make up the difference between the value of the goods they exported and that of their imports? It was done by means of the favorable trade to Spain, Portugal, the Wine Islands and the West Indies in fish, lumber, foodstuffs, and slaves. The colonials were paid considerable sums in Spanish silver dollars and Portuguese gold pieces, which could then be sent to England to meet their unfavorable balances with the mother country.

But as the business of the colonial community grew, the need appeared for a domestic circulating medium—a money supply within the colonies. Lacking this, all local trade had to be carried on by barter, and the settlement of debts for services or loans was exceedingly difficult. The colonies had no supplies of precious metals, and England made no attempt to create a colonial currency. The Spanish and Portuguese coins might have supplied this need, but the continuous adverse balances with England acted as a siphon to draw them off. The colonists cast about for some way of discouraging the export of foreign coins to England. The first such effort was in Massachusetts, where foreign silver was melted down and recoined as the "pine-tree shilling" which contained less silver than the English shilling, and would therefore be undesirable for payments to England and remain in the colony. The home government attacked this as a depreciation of the currency and made it one of the charges that led to loss of the Massachusetts charter. Unable to create currencies of their own in this fashion, the colonies then had recourse to another stratagem: they overvalued foreign coins in terms of English money. Thus, while in England the Spanish dollar was valued at 4s.6d., in New York by act of the legislature it was valued at 8s., and in Pennsylvania at 7s. The theory was that this gave the Spanish dollar a greater purchasing power in the colony, and that people would therefore prefer to spend it at home rather than to send it to pay for purchases in England. This was not satisfactory to the English government, and in 1704 a royal proclamation, later embodied in an act of Parliament, officially set the rates at which foreign coins would be accepted. However, the act allowed the colonies to accept foreign coins at one-third more than the rate in Britain, and coins circulating at this rate came to be called "proclamation money." In spite of this concession colonies which had set a higher rate continued by various subterfuges to violate the law.

Financing Colonial Wars

The outbreak of the wars with the French created a new problem, that of financing colonial expeditions. There was not much free capital which might support a bond issue, and it was as impracticable in the eighteenth as in the twentieth century to equip and pay military expeditions on a pay-as-you-go basis out of current taxes. The New England colonies, which were the chief participants in the early colonial wars, therefore resorted to paper money issues which were made legal tender within the particular colony. The laws always established a definite period during which the money was to be accepted (or "current") and levied additional taxes, which should be sufficient to redeem and retire it at the end of the period of currency. The paper money, however, turned out to be not only an excellent method of financing war, but a welcome addition to the circulating medium, hence the practice was continued in peace times and imitated between 1700 and 1760 by all the colonies. The last to follow suit was Virginia, which did not resort to paper until the French and Indian War put her under a heavy burden of expense.

The colonies did not all manage their paper issues wisely. Western Europe had had very little experience with this kind of currency. In England none was issued by the government and bank notes were not legal tender. Some depreciation of colonial paper resulted when, because of inexperience, the times of redemption were extended over too long a period. The taxes were often insufficient to redeem the issues, and the money was allowed to circulate beyond its period of currency instead of being called in and destroyed. Many of the later issues were based not only upon taxes but also upon "land-banks," that is, they were issued directly to farmers on their lands as security. It was difficult to force farmers to pay either interest or principal promptly, particularly since the legislators and the sheriffs were mostly farmers themselves. New England was the worst offender in this respect.

In Massachusetts, when the earliest issue had depreciated beyond cure, it was stabilized at a fraction of its face value. A new issue was called "new tenor" as against the "old tenor." When this second issue in turn depreciated it became, by the same process, "middle tenor," and a third issue of "new tenor" was made. Thus within the same colony three kinds of paper money circulated. One can easily imagine the difficulties which this practice created in business as well as the continuous inflation which it represented. When the farmers in western Massachusetts proposed to set up a private land-bank, the eastern merchants appealed to England

and obtained a ruling that the South Sea Bubble Act of 1720, which had been directed at speculative excesses, forbade land-banks. In 1751, Parliament passed a law forbidding the New England colonies to make any further issues of legal-tender paper money.

The British government had made an earlier attempt to restrict the issues of paper money by instructing the royal governors to veto acts which did not levy adequate taxes to redeem the notes or which extended the period of currency beyond five or ten years. But the governor often found it easier to disregard his instructions than to oppose a determined legislature which could and did refuse to pay him his salary unless he approved the paper-money bills. The British merchant did not suffer from colonial monetary experiments as long as the debts due him were payable in England at sterling rates, and normally this was the case. But he encountered trouble when he had to collect his debts *in America,* through resident agents, who might be compelled to accept either specie at the overvalued rate or legal-tender paper. This was the situation in Virginia where, by the middle of the eighteenth century, English and Scottish tobacco merchants had established resident "factors" or agents. The "Virginia merchants" in London, joined by their colleagues in Liverpool and Glasgow, made representations to the Board of Trade and their protest eventually resulted in 1764 in the extension of the Act of 1751 to all the colonies. Since business in the colonies was in the doldrums after the French and Indian War, the deflationary effect of the Currency Act of 1764 was resented by merchants as well as farmers.

American farmers have usually suffered under burdens of debt—partly because of their willingness to mortgage their farms in the hope that the value of their land will rise—and schemes to inflate the currency and cheapen credit have generally appealed to them. English laws against such schemes were responsible for some of the eagerness with which the western regions embraced the Revolution in 1776. Eastern businessmen found these laws useful insofar as they protected colonial creditors, and harmful insofar as they protected English creditors. For them, the solution of the currency problem lay in the overthrow of English rule and the administration of "hard-money" policies by American authorities for the benefit of American creditors. What had been a three-cornered struggle over currency in the colonial period was reduced by the Revolution to a two-sided conflict which long persisted.

Growth of the Spirit of Independence

By the middle of the eighteenth century the businessmen of the seaports were beginning to rival their English competitors and to reach out for the trade, manufacturing, and financial independence which would permit them to take the lead in the exploitation of American resources. The rise of business activity gave employment to lawyers, who were displacing the clergy as the intellectual leaders of the middle and New England colonies and becoming effective mouthpieces of American interests in opposition to British rule. In the cities the ranks of artisans rapidly swelled. Everywhere planters, farmers, frontiersmen, businessmen, clergymen, editors, lawyers, and artisans thought of themselves as Americans, and became hypersensitive to any encroachment on their traditional liberties. They chafed at anything that implied colonial inferiority; and without quite formulating the thought, they were moving inexorably towards the creation of a new society, distinctively American in that it was freer (if slavery be overlooked) and more diverse in racial and religious composition than any Old World society. Long before the American Revolution began, as John Adams said, it occurred in the hearts of men.

COLONIAL WARS

Many settlers had come to America in order to escape the interminable wars of Europe. This was literally true of Quakers and other religious pacifists. The majority of settlers were not pacifists, but they were isolationists in the sense that they wanted to avoid embroilments in international politics and wars which did not concern them. They largely agreed with the statement of Increase Mather: "There never was a generation that did so perfectly shake off the dust of Babylon, both as to ecclesiastical and civil constitution, as the first generation of Christians that came into this land for the gospel's sake." The colonists felt themselves to be as remote from Europe spiritually as they were in fact remote from it geographically.

From the very beginning, however, Americans were willing to fight when they believed that their interests required it. Conflict with the Indians turned the mass of colonists into militiamen at a time when wars in Europe were still fought by professional soldiers. Americans also recognized their obligation to support England against European rivals. Their support was desultory during the Anglo-Dutch Wars of the seventeenth century. But during the seventy-five years beginning in 1689, England fought France in a series of four wars for world supremacy, and the interest and obligation of the colonists led them to take an increasingly important part in these. If Americans were to protect their settlements and push them into the mountains and beyond, they would have to fight France as well as the Indians.

Intermittent Imperial Wars, 1689-1748

Close ties between the English colonists and the Iroquois Confederation for a time protected the frontiers of New York and Pennsylvania, but late in the seventeenth century the Spaniards in the South and the French

north of New England waged sporadic warfare against the English settlements. King William III organized the Grand Alliance of European
powers to thwart the ambitions of Louis XIV and this led to warfare in
Europe and America. French raiding parties attacked frontier towns in
New England, pushing back the line of settlement, and French privateers
attacked colonial fishermen and traders. New Englanders organized an
expedition that captured Port Royal, Nova Scotia, in 1690, but another
expedition under Sir William Phips attempted to take Quebec and failed.
What was known in America as King William's War (1689-1697) ended in
a draw. Port Royal was returned to the French, and this seeming neglect of
colonial interest gave a foretaste of grievances to come.

Spain was on the French side during the next three wars. Thus the
colonists were faced with a threat from both south and north. The War of
the Spanish Succession (1702-1713), called Queen Anne's War in America,
began in Europe when Louis XIV placed his Bourbon grandson on the
throne of Spain. The French in Canada and Louisiana were now united
with the Spaniards in Florida against the English settlements. South
Carolina begged England for help, as did Massachusetts, but they were
left to protect themselves as best they could while England spent her resources in Europe. The middle colonies, protected by the Iroquois, tried
to preserve "neutrality." Spaniards attacked Charleston and South Carolinians attacked Pensacola, with Indian tribes changing sides indiscriminately, and there was no decisive result. Massachusetts was pushed back
along the frontier, while her troops again captured Port Royal and another expedition against Quebec failed. The peace treaty established
British authority over the Hudson Bay country, Acadia, and Newfoundland. France kept Cape Breton Island, where Louis XIV built the
great fortress of Louisbourg, and this French stronghold was a gun
cocked at New England. Britain's chief prize in the Treaty of Utrecht
(1713) was the "*Assiento* Privilege" of selling slaves into the Spanish
Empire.

During the generation of peace before the outbreak of the third war
in 1744, the English colonies experienced their most rapid expansion of
population and wealth. Their ability to wage war increased accordingly,
and so did their desire that colonial interests should not be neglected by
the mother country. England's violations of Spanish colonial trade monopoly and Spanish retaliations led in 1739 to the War of Jenkins' Ear.
An expedition against Cartagena on the Gulf of Darien, Colombia, under
Admiral Edward Vernon, which included among colonial volunteers
Lawrence Washington, brother of George, was a disastrous failure. On
the other hand, General Oglethorpe successfully defended the southern
frontier against Spanish attacks. Meanwhile, France became engaged in
the War of the Austrian Succession on the continent of Europe, and in
1744 she joined Spain in fresh hostilities against the British. The American

phase of the conflict is known as King George's War (1745-1748). The greatest of colonial military enterprises was the Massachusetts expedition that captured Louisbourg in 1745. Governor Sir William Shirley brilliantly organized this and it was commanded by a Maine fish and lumber merchant, William Pepperell, who was knighted for his success. The amphibious expedition was remarkable chiefly for unorthodox tactics derived from Indian warfare, which confused and frightened the French. But by the Treaty of Aix-la-Chapelle in 1748 the British returned Louisbourg to France in exchange for Madras in India. That the home government should barter away New England's great victory for the sake of gains in remote India infuriated the Americans, and they were only partially conciliated by England's payment to Massachusetts of the cost of the expedition. It was a meaningful lesson of the subordination of colonial to imperial interests.

The Final Struggle with the French

Before the French and Indian War began in 1754, the expansion of the frontier produced a significant change in strategy. During the first three wars, the colonists had fought defensively on the frontier and offensively at sea. Now the strategy was reversed. As the colonies breached the Appalachian walls and looked beyond into the great valley of the Ohio, they believed that their destinies drew them westward, and both sides prepared to fight for the interior of the continent as the greatest prize in the world. France sent expeditions into the Ohio country to confirm her claims and to build a string of forts which should effectively hold the English colonists east of the mountains. Since Virginia claimed a large part of the Ohio Valley, Governor Dinwiddie took the lead in the attempt to expel the French from the rich interior. In 1753, he sent George Washington, a young surveyor who had already shown singular qualities of leadership and character, to protest to the French commander on the Ohio that he had invaded English ground. This action having no effect, the Governor gave Washington a company of militia to try other means. But the French had already built Fort Duquesne at the strategic site of modern Pittsburgh, and a militia company was no match for them. At Great Meadows, Washington fired on a French force, killing the commander and twenty men. Then he hastily threw up a log stronghold, and correctly named it Fort Necessity. Trapped by superior French forces, he was forced to surrender on July 4, 1754. But he and his company had fired the first shot of a world war which ended with the practical destruction of France as a colonial power in America.

For the English colonists the issue was between expansion beyond the mountains, with all that portended for the future of the American people, or subordination to the absolutist and Catholic French monarchy they hated. English liberty and the opportunity to create a successful new society on that foundation would not be easily surrendered by Americans. A danger signal to them was the growing success of the French in winning away from the British their traditional Iroquois allies who held the key to the defenses of the middle colonies. The Board of Trade in London ordered the Governor of New York to call a conference of commissioners from all the colonies and make a treaty with the Iroquois chiefs. The result was the Albany Congress of June 1754.

Albany Congress

This Congress of delegates elected by the colonial assemblies was the first instrument of continental union in American history. Just as the regional New England Confederation had been organized in the seventeenth century to protect those colonies against external dangers, so the Albany Congress was called to protect the thirteen colonies, and defense against foreign danger continued thereafter to be a leading motive for the creation of a central government. It was Benjamin Franklin who saw most clearly the implications of the Albany Congress. When he was elected delegate of Pennsylvania, he published in his *Gazette* a warning that the French were full of confidence because the English colonies would never "agree to any speedy and effectual measures for our common defense and security." He printed a cartoon which provided a slogan later for the Revolution: a picture of a snake cut into bits with the caption, "Join or Die." At Albany, Franklin offered his famous "Plan of Union."

This would have divided political authority between a new central body and the thirteen local governments. The central body would be composed of an executive, the president-general, appointed by the Crown; and a legislature, the Grand Council of representatives chosen by the assemblies in proportion to the taxes paid by them into the general treasury. This government would have control over relations with the Indians; power to make war and peace with them and to raise armies and navies; power to regulate new settlements; and power to levy taxes, particularly customs duties. These are roughly the chief spheres of federal authority as afterwords defined, with the addition of foreign relations. Franklin was ahead of his time. The British government objected to the Plan as giving too much control to the colonists, while the colonists held that it took too much power away from their assemblies. These refused to adopt it, though it had been approved by the Congress. The Albany Congress accomplished little beyond inconclusive attempts to win over the Iroquois to the English cause and recommendations that the colonies see to their defenses.

Fighting on the Frontier

The thirteen colonies, although they were eager to defeat France in the West, fell into petty bickering over the distribution of the burdens of war. Assemblies refused to vote taxes or raise military forces unless the governors gave in on points of authority, and only four colonies contributed their full quota of militiamen. The British sent over two regiments of regulars under General James Braddock to help the colonies, and he put George Washington on his staff. In the summer of 1755, Braddock led his forces against Fort Duquesne but, through incompetence, he allowed them to be trapped and routed and was himself mortally wounded. This left the Virginia frontier exposed. Governor Dinwiddie made Washington, aged twenty-three, commander-in-chief of the Virginia militia, and he fought a disheartening war against heavy odds—but learned the art of defensive holding operations which he used to great effect in a later war.

The New York frontier was defended chiefly by William Johnson, a great landowner of the Mohawk Valley whose beautiful Georgian house and stone fort still stand. Johnson was an expert diplomatist who was able to hold enough Indians in support of the British to fend off a French invasion at Lake George in September 1755. But the French held on to Crown Point on Lake Champlain and built a powerful new strong point at Fort Ticonderoga. All along the frontier the Indians, egged on by the French, raided settlements and massacred with great daring and savagery, while fear gripped the colonies and England. This prompted revenge on the fifteen thousand French settlers of Nova Scotia (Acadia) who were expelled and scattered throughout the English colonies. Only those who reached Louisiana were able to recreate a community life, and their descendants, the "Cajuns," have retained their own language and customs to this day.

The Seven Years' War

From these beginnings in America, the war spread in 1756 throughout the world and it lasted long enough to be called the Seven Years' War. Prussia was allied with Great Britain, and France won strong allies in Austria, Russia, and Spain. In America and elsewhere, British fortunes soon ebbed. The Earl of Loudoun was appointed military commander in America, but he proved dilatory, and the French General Montcalm advanced southward to Lake George while reinforcements from Europe strengthened his rear. The British lost Calcutta in India; Frederick the Great of Prussia was defeated by the French and Austrians; and an English army was surrendered to the French by King George's son, the

Duke of Cumberland. Then in 1757 William Pitt (the elder) became head of the British ministry in circumstances and with results not dissimilar to the assumption of power by Winston Churchill in 1940.

Pitt believed that America should be the main theater of war, that if the French could be expelled from Canada and the West, British power would henceforth be securely based on a rich and expanding North American Empire. He subsidized Frederick the Great to keep the French occupied in Europe, used the navy to control the seas and cut French communications, and concentrated the military strength of Great Britain in America. He appointed General Jeffrey Amherst commander in America, with James Wolfe brigadier general under him. In 1758, with Admiral Boscawen, they captured Louisbourg. Colonel Dudley Bradstreet and a small army of New Englanders marched westward and broke French communications at the exit of the Saint Lawrence from Lake Ontario. General Forbes and Washington captured Fort Duquesne, henceforth named Pittsburgh for the Prime Minister. Even greater successes were won that same year by Clive in India and Frederick the Great in Europe. In 1759, the first British Empire reached its zenith. Victory after victory brought Britain closer to ruling the world than any power in modern times. The greatest of these victories was the capture of Quebec, on which Pitt, true to his strategy, had concentrated Britain's main offensive effort.

Victory over the French

The plan against Quebec called for co-ordination between Wolfe's forces, moving by water up the Saint Lawrence, and Amherst's forces, moving north by lakes and land. Amherst captured Crown Point and Ticonderoga but got no farther. Nevertheless, Wolfe pressed on and, after two failures in flank attacks, deployed troops above Quebec on the Plains of Abraham and won the city with one volley. He himself was killed but he knew the victory was his before he died. Montreal surrendered the next year, and the French Empire in North America was truncated. The Indian allies of the French in the West rebelled against their fate in the Conspiracy of Pontiac (1763) to no effect.

Great Britain might have gone on to further conquests, but the new King, George III, who was jealous of Pitt, dismissed him and made peace by giving up some of the fruits of victory. For a while it was even thought that Canada might be returned to France in exchange for the sugar island of Guadeloupe in the West Indies. France was allowed to give Louisiana to Spain in payment for her support, but Britain took over the Floridas, all French claims in North America east of the Mississippi, all of India, and lesser positions elsewhere—emerging as the greatest empire since ancient Rome. During these triumphant years, industrial machines increased in England to supply textiles for her expanding markets, so that British industrial supremacy came to match political supremacy.

Americans rejoiced with the mother country in outbursts of loyalty and congratulation. Well they might, because it was English power as well as colonial effort that had won for the colonists a degree of security and scope for expansion equal to their most ambitious dreams. But the problems of victorious peace are often more difficult than those of war, and King George III, after the peace treaty, threw away even more of what Pitt had won for him than he had in the treaty itself. He lost the loyalty of his American subjects by the ineptness of his statesmanship in organizing the peace.

Part II

BEGINNINGS OF THE REPUBLIC
1763-1789

CHAPTER 8

The Colonies and the Empire

1763-1774

THE DECADE AFTER THE TREATY OF 1763 WAS MARKED by a succession of controversies between the British colonies in North America and the home government, the cumulative effect of which was to create a crisis in the Empire. Reduced to simplest terms, this continuing conflict was one between local and imperial interests. Victory over the French brought Great Britain to heights of national power and prestige never before reached by a modern European country, but it also imposed on the nation unexampled responsibilities and burdens. The efforts of British statesmen to work out the problems of empire were often bungling and shortsighted. No peace-time minister showed genius at all comparable to that of William Pitt as War Minister, and the policies of the government, instead of being based on a long-range imperial plan, were largely improvised to meet immediate needs and problems. The successive ministers were very conscious of the political and financial situation in England, but were appallingly ignorant of American sentiment and attitudes.

To Americans it seemed that the triumph over the French had removed from them the chief threat to their physical security and the major external obstacle to their future development. By the same token, they felt far less dependent on the mother country than previously. To Americans, victory implied enlarged opportunity, not increased responsibility; their spirit was one of growing self-reliance and impatience with restraint. They were undisposed to share the burden of empire, and were jealous of their own political rights and liberties. Under these circumstances some conflict of interest between the home government and the outlying provinces was to be expected. The times called for farsighted statesmanship in high places and an unusual degree of tactfulness if the vast British Empire was to be preserved.

American patriots afterwards laid on the King the major blame for dissolution of the colonial empire. They were incorrect in thinking of him as another Stuart tyrant, for that he did not try to be. King George III came to the throne in 1760 as a young man determined to play a larger part in government than his Hanoverian predecessors had done. But he worked within the framework of the system which had been developed in the years since the Stuarts had been overthrown. When he became King, the Whigs, inheritors of the Glorious Revolution and champions of Parliament against the royal prerogative, had long been supreme, but they were split into factions, rallying round individual leaders in the hope of jobs. George himself played the patronage game and gathered a following called "the King's Men," becoming a powerful political leader. With this nucleus in Parliament he maneuvered to gain a majority for ministers of his own liking, and in the end he created a new party. The term "Tory" came to be applied to this, but he and his following accepted the old Whig idea of the supremacy of Parliament. What George III sought was personal control over the ministry and Parliament. His motives were not unworthy, for he entertained elevated ideals of the public good, but he made himself largely responsible for the policies which eventually cost him part of his empire.

In 1761, the ministry of William Pitt gave way to that of Lord Bute, and in 1763 the latter was succeeded by the ministry of George Grenville, who as Chancellor of the Exchequer and leader of the Commons was directly responsible for the hated Stamp Act. Beginning in July 1765 the ministry of the Marquis of Rockingham was in office less than a year. After that the Rockingham Whigs, more nearly than any other group, constituted the party of the Opposition. They objected to the personal power of the King, which was clearly established by 1770 when Lord North became First Lord of the Treasury, but it must not be supposed that the Whigs as a group supported the American patriots in their resistance to Parliament. Men like John Adams and Thomas Jefferson called themselves Whigs, and William Pitt was like them in his emphasis on the ancient liberties of Englishmen and his belief in the restraint of government by law, but he was a lonely political figure in this period. Furthermore, he valued empire far more than the American patriots did. Edmund Burke castigated British policy on many occasions, but he avoided the theoretical issue of Parliamentary supremacy and argued in terms of expediency. A few men who were regarded as extremists, like John Wilkes and Dr. Richard Price, supported American principles of liberty whole-heartedly; but the net effect of the astuteness of the King in identifying his own cause with that of Parliament was to leave American champions of human rights and self-government with only slight support in English political circles.

THE PROCLAMATION OF 1763 AND THE WESTERN QUESTION

The ineptness of the King and his ministers played a larger part in bringing on the American Revolution than any conscious attempt to destroy the liberties of the colonists. Coupled with ineptness, however, was a failure to perceive that the colonies were rapidly maturing, that their interests and ambitions could not be safely ignored, that their growing society could not be hemmed in. The Americans believed that the expulsion of the French was their victory as much as the mother country's. The West, they felt, was their prize. The powerful impulse to expand was shared alike by the newest immigrant from the Old World who was looking for cheap land, the small farmer who wanted the chance to pull up stakes and move to new land any time he felt like it, and the members of organized land companies who were looking for new domains of profit in the vast interior. An open road to the West was perhaps the most important single ingredient of the American dream.

To policy-makers in England, viewing the problems of the empire as a whole and particularly aware of immediate British interests, it seemed, however, that there was now good reason to delay the development of the country beyond the mountains. Previously, the actual occupation of outlying regions by bona-fide settlers had strengthened the hands of the British in their conflict with the French, but the threat of French rule there was now removed. The Indians, to whom promises had been made, were restive; and the fur trade offered the prospect of great profit, which British merchants might richly share. It was to the interest of fur-traders and their backers in the home country to keep the unsettled western country as a reserve for the Indians, and some regulation of the trade with them was necessary to prevent their ruthless exploitation and demoralization. In England it seemed that, for a variety of reasons, the situation called for tighter imperial control of the American West.

At the same time the colonists, who were so eager to surge westward, were increasingly unwilling to accept limitations on individual freedom and determined to maintain the largest possible local control of matters regarded by them as domestic. Certain of the colonies, notably Virginia, had strong claims to western lands based on original charters, and wanted to extend their own jurisdiction over the interior. If it was to the interest of fur-traders to leave the Indian country a wilderness, both land companies and prospective settlers wanted it opened up. Any sort of centralized control of the Indian trade was objectionable to certain irresponsible traders, as it was in general to colonial governments. In this welter of conflicting interests it would have been exceedingly difficult

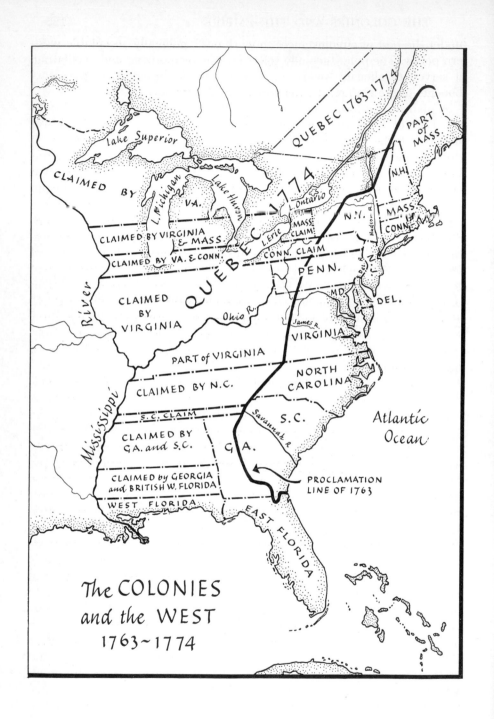

The COLONIES and the WEST 1763~1774

under the best of circumstances to work out a generally acceptable western policy. The policy actually followed was temporizing and vacillating; it served to alienate American opinion without bringing compensatory benefits to the empire, the fur-traders, or the Indians.

A plan for western policy was submitted to the King in June 1763 by the Earl of Shelburne, as President of the Board of Trade. This was intended to be temporary and did not pretend to be comprehensive. It drew a line along the Appalachians beyond which settlement was forbidden, but this took account of existing settlements. Before this plan was accepted, news reached England of Pontiac's Conspiracy, which had begun in May and clearly showed that there was a real problem of defense against the Indians. While this dangerous revolt was still in process, Shelburne was succeeded by the Earl of Hillsborough. His modifications of the earlier proposals were incorporated in the Proclamation of October 7, 1763, which announced among other things the erection of the distinct governments of Quebec, East Florida, and West Florida. This proclamation drew a line of demarcation along the crest of the Appalachian highlands beyond which lands should not be granted; it did not allow for existing settlements further to the westward, and it ordered the frontiersmen to withdraw. Trade with the Indians was permitted under a license system.

The next major step in the development of British western policy was the attempt to regulate trade with the Indians, under the Plan of 1764. Control was placed in the hands of the Indian superintendents, Sir William Johnson in the North and John Stuart in the South, and an elaborate system of trading centers was set up. The complicated scheme proved unenforceable, and it was specially resented by the governments of the southern colonies. The policy had to be modified so as to leave trade more under local control. Meanwhile, the land companies brought great pressure to bear on the home government and this caused the Proclamation Line of 1763 to be moved westward, following the negotiation of treaties with the Indians under the leadership of the superintendents. The best-known of these was the Treaty of Fort Stanwix (1768), which left parts of southwestern New York and northwestern Pennsylvania in Indian hands but from Fort Pitt set the boundary at the Ohio River. This was supplemented on the south by the Treaty of Lochaber (1770) and a survey which carried the line roughly to the Kentucky River, satisfying some but by no means all of the ambitions of the Virginians. The period after 1768 was marked by great pressure on the home government by the various land companies for grants or the renewal of old grants, by much activity on their part in "buying" land from the Indians beyond treaty lines, and by a considerable increase in settlement on the frontier. In the colonies impinging on the West, however, it was believed that imperial restrictions were designed to protect Indians and fur-traders and constituted a hindrance to settlers. Meanwhile, there was enough vacillation in imperial policy to create a situation of uncertainty if not one of chaos.

At the end of the decade of western policy which began with the Proclamation of 1763 came the Quebec Act of 1774. Designed to reconcile the conquered French Canadians to English rule, this made concessions to them which now seem statesmanlike: religious freedom to them as Roman Catholics, and the establishment of legal and political institutions in the French tradition. But to the Protestant colonists, living under English law, these provisions smacked of "Popery" and amounted to the recognition of the rival French Catholic civilization which they had fought to hold at bay. Worse still, all the territory west of the mountains as far south as the Ohio River was annexed to Quebec. There was a clause saying that the claims of other colonies should not be prejudiced, but the Americans believed that the hated French were now privileged to expand southward into the very domain from which they had been expelled. The chief prize of victory in the war was being awarded to the losers. In the same year, 1774, new and stricter regulations for the granting of lands were announced. It was to these that Jefferson referred when he spoke in the Declaration of Independence of "raising the conditions of new appropriations of lands." By 1776, revolution seemed necessary for a number of reasons, but one of the most important of these was to regain for British Americans the fruit of the French and Indian War—the West.

THE STAMP ACT AND THE TAXATION QUESTION

The Americans, by their resistance to taxation, played a part in the defeat of the original plans of the home government for the West. The war itself had more than doubled the national debt of Great Britain, which now amounted to about £130 million; and the sudden expansion of the empire greatly increased the regular military and administrative expenses. Annual costs in America which were borne by the British government had increased several times beyond the prewar figures and stood at nearly £500,000. The American colonies were direct beneficiaries of the victory over the French. British officials and Parliament thought it was only fair that the Americans should share some of the costs, and such men as Benjamin Franklin did not object to the principle.

But Americans pointed out that they too had incurred debts connected with the war, and that their local governments were already taxing them heavily to pay these. Furthermore, American commerce paid English port duties into the British Treasury, and British businessmen profited greatly by that commerce. If the British government had cautiously avoided the appearance of seeking new sources of revenue in America, and had realized more fully on the old ones, probably nothing more than normal grumbling would have resulted. But Americans were eager to seize any opportunity to call revenue measures "unconstitutional," and when the British government gave them one, the natural dislike of taxes gave force to outcries against infringements of colonial rights.

Enforcement of the Trade Laws

George Grenville, Chancellor of the Exchequer, decided that the laws which were originally devised in the spirit of mercantilism to regulate colonial trade should be extended so as to produce revenue. The customs service in America cost more than the duties the officials collected. In mercantilist theory this was not illogical, because the purpose of the laws was to prevent foreign commodities from entering the colonies. In line with this purpose, the tax that American distillers were supposed to pay on molasses imported from non-British sources was prohibitory. Everyone knew that the law of 1733 did not actually prevent the importation of foreign molasses, great quantities of which were smuggled into the colonies. Toward the end of the French and Indian War the British government made vigorous efforts to enforce the law and provoked a controversy over writs of assistance. These were general warrants issued by courts to enforcement officers, permitting them to invade premises and make arrests without the traditional warrant specifying the premises, the persons, and the reasons. James Otis, an eloquent Boston lawyer, opposed writs of assistance so vehemently in the courts that John Adams described him as a "flame of fire." Facing the realities of colonial evasion and opposition, Grenville now concluded that if the tax were reduced from 6d. to 3d. per gallon and the efficiency of the customs service were increased at the same time, the molasses trade could be brought into legal channels and made to pay a revenue into the Treasury.

This meant that Britain would abandon the mercantilist purpose of the original tax on molasses and substitute a tax for revenue such as had never before been applied to any important item of colonial commerce. Grenville was incautious enough to admit his purpose in the Act, generally called the Sugar Act, which he put through Parliament in 1764. The preamble stated that new regulations should be established "for improving the revenue of this Kingdom." The law cut in half the duty on molasses and placed additional duties on luxuries such as sugar, wine, coffee, and silk. It was believed that the lower duty on molasses would not discourage distillers of rum from importing it, while higher duties on articles of consumption would not prevent the wealthier classes from buying foreign luxuries. The latter reasoning also lay behind a provision of the law that the drawbacks, or refunds, of duties paid on European articles re-exported from England to the colonies, should stop. The law provided new methods of enforcement to stop smuggling. Not only were customs officers required to stay at their posts, but jurisdiction over smuggling cases was given to the Admiralty Courts. The Admiralty Courts had been established to hear only cases involving maritime affairs, outside the boundaries of any particular colony. To give these courts jurisdiction over customs cases seemed to be an invasion of the colonies' traditional right to reserve local affairs to the jurisdiction of their local courts. Their own courts used juries; the Admiralty Courts did not.

Thus the Americans could find several grounds for the claim that the Revenue Act of 1764 was "unconstitutional," that is, contrary to the former practice. The most important of these was that it asserted the power of the British government to impose "taxation without representation" insofar as this was a revenue act rather than merely one in regulation of commerce. Protests were widespread, but Grenville ignored the outcry he had caused and proceeded to violate colonial rights more grievously.

Failure of the Stamp Tax

This violation was by means of the Stamp Act of 1765. The notorious measure provided that revenue stamps must be bought at prices from a half penny to a pound and affixed to all public or semipublic papers, including bonds, notes, legal documents, newspapers, pamphlets, advertisements, and so forth. This was an "internal" tax, since it drew revenue from transactions taking place entirely inside the colonies rather than transactions across their boundaries, such as trade. Cases involving violations of the Act were also placed under the jurisdiction of the Admiralty Courts, although Americans were appointed as agents to administer the law. The revenue thus raised was to be spent in the colonies to pay for their defenses. Formerly the British government had tapped "internal" sources of revenue in the colonies by laying requisitions on the colonial governments and had left to their assemblies the decision how these should be raised—or, indeed, whether they should be paid at all. Often the assemblies had failed to meet requistions, and the Stamp Act was designed to bypass these legislative bodies and reach directly into the pockets of the colonists.

Probably no law in American history produced such violent opposition as the Stamp Act. The law bore hardest on those people who were most able to make their opposition known and felt: lawyers and journalists. Businessmen everywhere were faced with the prospect of paying a fee on every operation of theirs that involved papers. A wave of resentment united the colonists as never before. Clergymen took up the cause and sounded blasts against the law from their pulpits. Legislatures and town meetings adopted blistering resolutions. Soon action superseded words and mobs took vengeance on British officials. Merchants formed nonimportation associations committed to a boycott of British goods. Bands of "Sons of Liberty" were formed to prevent enforcement of the Stamp Act.

Patrick Henry in Virginia and Samuel Adams in Massachusetts took the lead in stirring up opposition by means of inflammatory oratory and other forms of agitation.

Trade with Great Britain fell to a fraction and the colonists refused to pay their debts to creditors in England. The Massachusetts Assembly called a congress in New York to organize opposition on a continental scale and delegates from nine colonies met in October 1765. This was the first organization initiated by the colonists themselves to unite the country. The Stamp Act Congress adopted resolutions denouncing the law as an unprecedented and unconstitutional invasion of the rights and liberties of the colonists. Some leaders proposed the more radical doctrine that their "natural rights" were violated. They saw that the ambiguous nature of the British constitution made it possible to answer their legal argument by pointing out that Parliament was itself the court of last authority on the limits of its powers, that the Stamp Act itself became a valid precedent and part of the British constitution by virtue of its enactment. The doctrine of natural rights appealed to an authority presumed to be higher than any man-made law *or* constitution, namely, the law of nature. According to philosophers such as John Locke, natural rights, including the right of self-government, were inherent and inalienable. But few colonists were ready as yet to appeal to a doctrine containing implications beyond the immediate issue. They clung to the argument that the British constitution had been violated. They were not represented in Parliament, therefore that body had no right to impose an internal tax on them.

To this, British officials answered that the colonists were *virtually* represented in Parliament. They meant that every British *interest* was represented there, even though every geographic district in England or the colonies was not. Many of the new industrial districts of England, such as Manchester and Birmingham, were not directly represented in Parliament until the Reform Act of 1832. Instead, many "rotten boroughs" with little or no population were entitled to seats, and these were controlled by single individuals or handfuls of great landowners. But the Americans had become accustomed to a system of representation based on geographic districts rather than interests, and the corrupt English system of the day seemed a poor substitute for it. They rejected the doctrine of virtual representation. At the same time, they knew that if the colonies were given seats in Parliament their few representatives would be easily outvoted. Hence they made no serious demand for representation in the English legislature, demanding instead that sole jurisdiction over internal taxation be returned to their own assemblies.

More effective than American arguments was the American boycott of English business. In a curious way the doctrine of virtual representation was shown to have some validity, because English businessmen insisted that Parliament repeal the Stamp Act before they were ruined by the colonists' boycott. William Pitt denied that Parliament had the right to take the money of the Americans "out of their pockets without their consent," but he believed that Parliament had absolute authority over colonial trade and manufactures. If, he said, the colonists violated a law against manufacturing, Britain should send men-of-war to bombard their cities. Benjamin Franklin, who was serving in England as the agent of several colonial assemblies, testified with great effectiveness before the House of Commons, urging repeal of the Stamp Act on grounds of common sense, and his published testimony attracted wide attention.

The Grenville ministry was dismissed in July 1765, though not because of American affairs. A ministry under Lord Rockingham, which Pitt refused to join, succeeded; and this remained in office until June 1766. In March of that year Parliament passed the Declaratory Act, in which it asserted its authority over the colonies "in all cases whatsoever," and then repealed the Stamp Act, which was manifestly unenforceable and to which British merchants had strongly objected. The Declaratory Act passed the Commons without a division and the Lords with virtually no opposition, showing that opinion in regard to the *right* to tax was practically unanimous in Parliament. On the other hand, the repeal of the Stamp Act, on grounds of expediency, was debated bitterly. The phrase "in all cases whatsoever," in the Declaratory Act, was a pointed repetition of the terms of the Act of 1719 in which Parliament had made Ireland totally subservient to it, but most Americans ignored the ominous language. They celebrated the repeal of the Stamp Act with balls, toasts, and fireworks. Gratitude inspired protests of loyalty to King and Parliament, "the Guardians of the English Nation." The Virginia House of Burgesses carefully entered in its journal a statement of colonial rights in flat contradiction of the Declaratory Act, and then allowed matters to "remain in status quo."

THE TOWNSHEND ACTS

Matters might have remained there but for several circumstances. The problem of raising revenue remained. The Stamp Act had only caused further drain on the British Treasury to pay for the unused stamps and useless administrative expenses. King George turned to William Pitt, called the "Great Commoner" but now raised in rank to Earl of Chatham, to head a government which should unite the King's Men and the old Whigs. Chatham was more sympathetic to the American defense of ancient English liberties than any other Parliamentary leader, but he was ill and anxious to avoid responsibility. The showy new Chancellor of the Exchequer, Charles Townshend, assumed the effective leadership. He was no friend of American rights. He devised a scheme to reduce the taxes on English landowners, reduce the costs of military defenses in the colonies, and raise new revenues from colonial trade. These measures, he hoped, would end the deficit.

The scheme was clever. Townshend had no respect for the argument that internal taxes were unconstitutional, but he tried to get around that issue by laying import duties on the colonists' purchases of English paint, lead, paper, and tea. Such duties might masquerade as "external taxes," but when the colonists admitted Parliament's right to impose external taxes they meant taxes to regulate trade rather than to raise revenue. John Dickinson of Pennsylvania pointed out this important distinction in his influential *Letters of a Pennsylvania Farmer* (1768). The Townshend duties, he declared, were of the revenue sort and beyond the power of Parliament. Townshend's scheme also aimed to reduce the power of the colonial legislatures by paying the salaries of governors, administrative officials, and judges out of the money collected under the new import duties. Writs of assistance were provided for, and new Vice-Admiralty Courts were set up to help enforce payment of the duties. These measures were regarded in the colonies as encroachments on American rights and liberties, and as a clear sign that the home government was determined to subordinate these to imperial control.

The Townshend Acts threw the colonies again into turmoil. The English government suspended the New York Assembly when it refused to comply with all the requirements of a law which quartered English soldiers in the homes of colonists when public quarters were not available. The General Court of Massachusetts sent a letter to the other legislatures protesting against the Townshend Acts. When it refused to withdraw the letter it was dissolved, as were the Virginia and New York legislatures for receiving the letter. These high-handed actions by the English government showed that the narrow issue of taxation involved the much greater issue of colonial self-government.

Merchants once more turned to a boycott of English imports. It became a patriotic thing to establish colonial manufactures of textiles and paper, and tea drinking was foresworn. Customs officers were mobbed, and when disorder reached a certain stage in Boston, two regiments of red-coated British regulars were quartered on the town. The citizenry resented their presence and on the night of March 5, 1770, bloodshed resulted. Bystanders watching a detachment of troops passing through the streets tossed a few snowballs, along with insults, and the troops, who were getting tired of abuse, were ordered to fire and killed four citizens. This was the "Boston Massacre." It was seized upon by agitators like Samuel Adams who raised a fearful clamor and indulged in vast exaggeration. The trial of the soldiers, at which John Adams bravely appeared for the defense, resulted in the acquittal of all except two, who were branded on the hand, but the regiments were removed to Castle William in Boston harbor to prevent further trouble. Lesser incidents occurred in other colonial towns. The opposition to the Townshend Acts, however, was not as widespread as opposition to the Stamp Act, and it made much less impression on British merchants.

The Chatham ministry gave way to that of the Duke of Grafton (1768-1770), and then Lord North became head of the government in 1770. He yielded to colonial opposition because he believed that duties on English imports into the colonies only defeated the imperial interest in building up such trade. He repealed all the Townshend duties except the one on tea. The tax of 3d. per pound on tea was retained in order to maintain the principle of Parliament's authority to legislate for the colonies "in all cases whatsoever." Once more the government conceded the substance of colonial demands while denying the principle on which they rested. Conservative-minded Americans were inclined to accept Lord North's concessions as a victory and ignore the theoretical issue. A few years of quiet followed. Customs duties were collected efficiently and smuggling virtually stopped. In spite of this, prosperity increased. Men like Benjamin Franklin were satisfied.

A more radical group of American leaders were unwilling to accept peace on these terms. To them the vital issues were the preservation of the historic rights, privileges, and immunities of Englishmen which had been promised them in their first charters, and the maintenance of at least the degree of political self-government they had already attained. As Thomas Jefferson, one of the younger patriots, saw it, an admission by the Americans that they held their political existence at the will of Parliament would be a surrender of common sense. He and other bold thinkers were approaching a position which was irreconcilable with views of the British constitution generally held in England. Lord North said the language of America was this: "We are subjects of the King; with Parliament we have nothing to do." Even as a Tory he could accept no such doctrine, and the Whigs as a group could not, because of their historic emphasis on the authority of Parliament even over the King. Many Americans were willing to dodge the question of ultimate authority, but to more radical leaders it seemed a betrayal of liberty to accept substantial concessions from Parliament and ignore what they regarded as violations of principle. They saw grave danger of the eventual loss of personal freedom and self-government if the colonists were lulled to complacency.

Committees of Correspondence

Such radicals as Samuel Adams and Dr. Joseph Warren of Boston and Patrick Henry of Virginia worked hard to overcome the complacency of Americans during the three years of calm that followed Lord North's concessions. In this period was created a form of organization which later became a prime instrument of revolution in America, France, and elsewhere. The "committees of correspondence," were more or less clandestine bodies which met regularly and organized propaganda and other activities. Unity of mind, swiftness of communication, and consistent work to arouse and lead the populace were their objectives. Town committees were started in Massachusetts, and provincial committees were afterward set up in Virginia and elsewhere. By 1773, the leaders had created a continental organization with local branches in all the colonies. Governors could not destroy these by dissolving the colonial legislatures.

The committees would not allow Americans to forget their grievances. Documents setting forth colonial claims were widely circulated, and evidence of British designs for the future was exaggerated into condemnations of the present course of British officials. For example, private letters from Governor Hutchinson of Massachusetts to friends in England were obtained by Benjamin Franklin and made public by the committees. In one of these Hutchinson had written that English liberties must be diminished in Massachusetts if the Empire was to be preserved. For this, the General Court voted Hutchinson's impeachment. Franklin, although he had not supported the American radicals, was publicly excoriated in the House of Commons for his part in the affair and was called "a Skunk, or American Pole Cat." It is said that the wise and witty Doctor did not again put on the suit of clothes he wore on that day until the day in 1782 when he signed the treaty in which Great Britain acknowledged American independence. Even religious groups, especially the Congregationalists and Presbyterians, were organizing committees of correspondence to unite the colonists against the Church of England and the proposed creation of an American bishopric. The Americans had become highly sensitive to even the smallest threats to their liberties. The English themselves were noted the world over for their stiff-necked jealousy of their rights. In this respect the colonists had now become more English than the English.

THE BOSTON TEA PARTY

The East India Company held the monopoly of English trade with the Orient, and the officials of the company acted as Crown agents to govern India. By and large they were a corrupt and brutal group who plundered the people of India and the company alike. In 1773, the company was close to bankruptcy, while mismanagement had left millions of pounds of tea and other goods to spoil in its warehouses. A disaster to it would injure its English shareholders and the Bank of England, cause a loss of revenues to the English Treasury, and endanger Britain's rule in India. The company's directors feared that the government would seize the occasion to strip it of its authority in India. The American colonists were themselves partly to blame for the company's plight because they had cut down their consumption of taxed tea, but they felt that the validity of their own charters would be injured if the company's charter were violated, therefore they supported it against the government. Lord North made no attempt to violate its charter, but his program of aid resulted in an affront to the Americans more severe than if he had wiped out the company. He thought the Americans could be bribed into drinking the tea of the East India Company if its price were lowered more than enough to compensate for the duty of 3*d*. per pound. He was warned that Americans treasured principle more than they liked cheap tea, but he would not believe it.

The Tea Act of 1773 was therefore intended to bail the East India Company out of some of its difficulties. The company was granted permission to sell tea directly to American consumers without regard for the old Navigation Act which had required it to be sold to English dealers, who had sold it in turn to American merchants. The company was given a monopoly over the tea trade in America. No American merchant was allowed to deal in the article and no American tea-drinker could buy it from any other source. The savings which the company could effect by eliminating the profits of middlemen allowed it to offer its tea to consumers at a lower price, even after the duty was paid, than that of any smuggled tea. It was a neat scheme to make Americans swallow their principles with their drink.

The granting of monopoly rights to private interests in one part of the Empire over consumers in another part was not unprecedented, but such a monopoly had never been given to a single person or company by the English government, although this was the common practice of the French and Spanish governments. The English were now trying to play economic favorites in the Continental style. It seemed to Americans that if their wants as consumers could be exploited by Britain in favor of a monopolistic system, their position as freemen would be deeply undermined. The Tea Act of 1773 directly affected both smugglers and legitimate merchants and threw them both on the side of the radicals and the committees of correspondence. In Boston smuggling was prevented by the presence of a naval squadron, but the ports of New York and Philadelphia were still fairly open. The first outcries against the Tea Act were raised in the latter two cities, led by the smugglers. But merchants in all lines quickly followed suit as they saw the menace of monopoly to all trade.

Company tea was shipped into the colonies in huge quantities. Those willing to taste it found that the leaves were rotten from storage. The East India Company was accused of planning to take over monopolistic control of all American business and make itself ruler of the land. But, "Thank God," John Dickinson said, "we are not sepoys, nor Marattas, but British subjects." He urged night watchmen to call out, as they made their rounds, "Beware of the East India Company!" Everywhere drinkers of tea were warned that it would ruin their health, destroy American prosperity, and wipe out American liberty. One warning stated: "Do not suffer yourself to sip the accursed, dutied stuff. For if you do, the devil will immediately enter into you, and you will instantly become a traitor to your country."

The colonists feared that feminine love of tea would make Lord North's diabolical scheme a success. Englishmen congratulated themselves that they had found in the colonial women a weakness easy to exploit. It was said that even the New Englanders could not boycott the tea because, for all their noise against Britain, they were a henpecked lot at home. But American women gave up the brew, turning to coffee and unpalatable but untaxed substitutes. To make sure that the boycott would be effective, the Sons of Liberty busied themselves tracing every sale of tea and rallying public pressure against the purchasers. The boycott was soon so complete that in most of the colonies agents of the company resigned their jobs, the governors refused to support the company, and ships loaded with tea returned to England. But in Boston the situation was exceptional in several respects. The Sons of Liberty were strong and well-organized, while Governor Hutchinson was determined to stand fast against the opponents of the Act. The agents of the company refused to resign and received the protection of the Governor in Castle William. Three tea ships lay in the harbor under the protection of British warships. Citizens met at Faneuil Hall and petitioned the Governor to allow these to return to England. Later, on that same night of December 16, 1773, three bands of fifty men each, disguised as "Mohawks," went aboard the ships and dumped the tea into the harbor.

The identity of the men was kept secret, although evidence suggests that Samuel Adams and John Hancock were among them, and the rank and file were doubtless recruited from among the Sons of Liberty. The Boston Tea Party gave the signal for similar parties in other ports during the following year. Nothing could be done to prevent this violence because the populace was too strongly in favor of it. The disappearance of tea from the American market was complete. It did not reappear until after the Revolution, and by that time Americans had developed a taste for coffee as their favorite beverage which they have never lost. The radicals justified the violence, under the "great law of nature and reason" that every society has a right to defend itself from ruin and tyranny without regard to statutes.

The British view was different. All England was excited. It was evident that the colonial governors had lost control of the situation, and legal action against participants in "tea parties" seemed futile because American juries would be composed of patriots. "Hypocritical bandits" was one of the kinder descriptions of the colonials in the English press. Lord North was confused. Who could have foreseen that the Americans would oppose so violently the sale of tea at cheap prices? Even the Earl of Chatham said the Boston Tea Party was "certainly criminal." Sentiment was general that, since individuals could not be punished, the colonies as a whole must be. Lord North said that the quarrel was no longer about taxation; the question was whether the mother country had any authority whatever over the "haughty American republicans." He did not give in to demands that Boston, that nest of "puritanical rebels," should be taught a lesson by the hanging of a hundred of its inhabitants, but he decided on a policy of punishment that had precisely the opposite effects from those he intended.

King George III supported Lord North, saying they must "master" the Americans. Thus by 1774 the British attempt to reorganize the Empire developed into a contest of wills between the colonists and the home government. No responsible Americans yet spoke of independence as a desirable outcome of this struggle. But they had seen in specific issues a threat to all their liberties and the British government had made claims, chiefly in the Declaratory Act, which were subversive of colonial liberty in all spheres. The colonists had opposed particular acts of the British government with a violence which seemed to Englishmen excessive, but which was in fact proportionate to the sweeping claim of the British government to authority over the colonies "in all cases whatsoever."

CHAPTER 9

Towards American Independence, 1774-1776

GOVERNMENTS ARE OFTEN CONFRONTED BY THE NECESSITY of choosing between dread alternatives: they must either press their official authority to an ultimate test, thereby risking failure, or compromise theoretical authority for the sake of immediate peace and order, thereby risking ultimate loss of authority. Between 1763 and 1773, the British government wavered between the two poles of the dilemma. It compromised on immediate issues by repealing the Stamp Act and most of the duties imposed by the Townshend Acts. On the other hand, it made broad and provocative assertions of theoretical authority and refused to yield on the specific issues of writs of assistance and the tax on tea. After the Boston Tea Party, the government turned to the policy of making an ultimate test of its claims to authority over the colonies. This fateful decision made impossible the solution of the problem of imperial control by adjustment, mutual accommodation, and compromise. It gave the Americans no third choice between subordination and independence.

THE COERCIVE ACTS

Lord North's decision to punish Boston for the sins of the "Mohawks" was based on a fatal misjudgment. He thought that by singling out Boston he could divide the colonies. He believed that if Boston was forbidden to function as the trade center of New England, merchants of other ports, eagerly snatching the opportunity to steal her markets, would refuse to support the little city in her struggle with the home government. Ignorance of the temper of the patriots from Maine to Georgia, and cynicism regarding their motives and their ability to see beyond immediate interests, could not have been more complete. Instead of giving accurate information, the governors and other royal officials appear to have told the British authorities what they wanted to hear.

Lord North introduced in Parliament in March 1774 the Boston Port Bill. It required the city to pay the East India Company for the tea that the "Indians" had destroyed, and also the customs duty on it. Until the citizens paid these costs British men-of-war would close the port to all shipping. The bill passed Parliament without difficulty, the members evidently accepting North's assurances that Boston would be isolated and quickly repent.

News of the Port Act, which was to go into effect June 1, reached Boston early in May, and the Committee of Correspondence went into prompt action. In preparation for such an emergency, a system of rapid communication with committees in other towns had been established. Paul Revere rode express to New York and Philadelphia with appeals for aid, and other riders fanned out into the interior and down along the seaboard. The gist of the appeal was that Boston must be supported by all the colonies, else the British government, successful in this place, would bring to heel one by one the other ports that had offended the East India Company, and soon the liberties of all could be destroyed with ease.

The argument was convincing to patriots everywhere. George Washington asked whether Americans should "supinely sit and see one province after another fall prey to despotism?" Sympathy for Boston was specially pronounced in Virginia. Late in May the House of Burgesses passed resolutions, "cooked up" by a little group of fervid patriots that included Patrick Henry and Thomas Jefferson. These called for a day of fasting and prayer on the day that the Port Bill was to become effective. The royal Governor, Lord Dunmore, dissolved the House of Burgesses as a result, but on June 1 a group of the "late" burgesses, including Washington, marched solemnly to Bruton Church in Williamsburg and heard a proper sermon. Elsewhere in the colonies on that day shops were closed by merchants, flags were hung at half-mast, and copies of the law were burned. Far from increasing divisions among the colonies, the strong exercise of British authority encouraged them to forget former suspicions of Puritan cant and city mobs and to regard the Bostonians as martyrs on the altar of liberty. The Virginia resolutions spoke of "our sister colony of Massachusetts Bay."

Among the patriots, however, there were differences of opinion about the precise steps to be taken in the effort to secure a redress of grievances. Samuel Adams and the Boston Committee, representing chiefly the artisan class rather than merchants, asked that an absolute boycott be imposed against all British trade (exports as well as imports) by all the colonies. Merchants elsewhere, especially in Philadelphia and New York, feared that such an extreme measure would ruin them; and in the South, there was doubt about the wisdom of forbidding exports—on which the prosperity of the planters depended and which were the only means whereby they could pay their honest English debts. Hence the suggestion, made in several quarters, that a general congress of colonial representatives be called for purposes of consultation and joint action met the favor of conservatives and came to be accepted by patriots everywhere. The Bostonians pointed out that such a body might obtain repeal of the Port Act too late to save them from starvation. The other colonists thereupon donated food in such quantity that the residents of the blockaded city were reported to be "as sleek and round as robins." During the summer plans went forward for a congress, which at the suggestion of Massachusetts was to be held in Philadelphia. Meanwhile, the British government by further extreme action played into the hands of the radicals.

Lord North made another error of judgment. He decided that he could divide the radicals of Boston from the conservatives by further coercion. He would do this by reorganizing the government of the province so as to place power in the hands of "respectable characters" who, he felt sure, would rally loyally to the support of Great Britain. He put three laws through Parliament in May 1774. The Massachusetts Government Act provided that members of the upper branch of the legislature should no longer be elected by the lower house but be appointed by the king; that the royal governor should appoint and could remove all judges of the lower courts; and that town meetings could be called only at the pleasure of the governor. The Administration of Justice Act provided that soldiers and officials accused of abuses could be tried in England or other colonies rather than in Massachusetts. The Quartering Act provided that troops should be quartered in the homes of citizens whenever public order required their presence in a particular area. These laws, together with the Boston Port Act, were what the colonists called the "Coercive" or "Intolerable" Acts.

The Massachusetts Government Act was resented most bitterly of all because it showed that the British government was willing to take legislative authority away from the people and place it in the hands of the king. Far from weakening the radicals, the new laws strengthened them. Many conservatives who had belittled charges directed against British intentions now concluded that the government would not hesitate to destroy American liberty utterly. Strongly supported by public sentiment, the Boston Committee of Correspondence took over the leadership of the populace. Outside Boston, British authority ceased to exist and committees of correspondence and town meetings ruled Massachusetts. Mobs of farmers outdid the Boston Sons of Liberty in violence against Crown officials. The latter found it best to give up exercise of their offices and flee to the protection of the troops in Boston. In all the colonies, the worst predictions of the radicals seemed about to come true and the ranks of the patriots swelled as fear and loathing of British tyranny mounted.

The Quebec Act, to which we have already referred in connection with the land question, was not a punitive measure inspired by the Boston Tea Party, but it was tossed into the colonial caldron in June. It was regarded as proof of a plan to raise up forces of French Popery against English Protestantism and to turn over the continent to them. The favors offered to the French Canadians in that law contrasted ominously with the injuries visited on the English colonists and infuriated the latter. In fact an argument used in England in favor of the Quebec Act was precisely that it would check the "fierce fanatic spirits in the Protestant colonies." This threat against all thirteen of the colonies roused frontiersmen and farmers to support the radicals of the seaport towns and cities. The laws of May and June 1774, which became known before the Continental Congress assembled in the autumn, greatly increased the likelihood that that body would be captured by the advocates of resistance, not conciliation.

THE FIRST CONTINENTAL CONGRESS

The body of somewhat more than fifty men, representing all the continental colonies except remote Georgia, who met in Carpenters' Hall, Philadelphia, during the months of September and October 1774, is remembered as the first American Congress in a long and continuing series. It was a convention of patriots which assumed the right to speak for the colonies as a whole. Occasionally, in later months, a former member of this historic body slipped over the line into the group designated as Tories or Loyalists; but, if John Adams can be believed, Tories were despised by this gathering "like spiders, toads, and snakes." The delegates had been chosen by the legislatures in some instances, and by revolutionary or at least extralegal bodies in others—but in nearly all cases the processes of selection were orderly. In Virginia, for example, the delegates were elected by a provincial convention, which had been called by former members of the dissolved assembly and amounted to another House of Burgesses. There was less regularity in some other places, notably in New York where sentiment was specially confused, but as a rule the patriots gained control of existing political machinery where they could, and when blocked by royal officials they created new machinery of the sort they were accustomed to. Meanwhile, committees of correspondence operated with great effectiveness behind if not on the scene. The colonists were realizing on their long training in self-government.

The Earl of Chatham called this Congress "the most honorable Assembly of statesmen since those of the ancient Greeks and Romans." Various shades of opinion were represented among the members—the term "radical" being commonly applied by writers to those who most strongly favored resistance, and "conservative" to those most hopeful of conciliation. From the heated scene of Boston came Samuel Adams, who was unsurpassed in "popular intrigue" but whose single-minded devotion to the cause of colonial rights was unmarred by considerations of personal gain or glory. From the same colony came his distant kinsman John Adams, a stocky and forthright man who was such a pillar of strength in the next few years that he was described as "Atlas" and "Colossus." He himself thought the delegates from Virginia the most spirited and consistent of any that were present. Those who had most to say in public were Patrick Henry and Richard Henry Lee, sometimes described as the American Demosthenes and Cicero, both of whom were radical. Peyton Randolph, a large and genial man from their province, presided over this body with dignity and firmness, as he did over the House of Burgesses at home. Although modest George Washington was no speechmaker, he gained everybody's confidence, and if he was not one to favor reckless measures, few men perceived the essence of this conflict so clearly.

Though Christopher Gadsden, an aristocrat of South Carolina, had a record of opposition to British policy that was not unworthy of comparison to Samuel Adams's, the attitude of the other Southern delegations was less certain than that of Virginia. The rest of the New Englanders were expected to support Massachusetts, while the deputies from the Middle Colonies comprised the most doubtful group of all. John Jay of New York, a bright young lawyer and an excellent speaker, was a man of conservative temper, and it was in his province that opinion was most divided. Benjamin Franklin had not yet returned from Europe to Pennsylvania, and John Dickinson from that colony was regarded as a moderate, while Joseph Galloway, speaker of the Pennsylvania House of Representatives, was probably the outstanding conservative in the Congress. Charles Thomson, reputed to be "the Sam Adams of Philadelphia," was elected secretary, much to Galloway's chagrin, and became the permanent holder of that office. Some of the differences of opinion among these leaders persisted, but in 1774, facing a common external danger, they succeeded in maintaining a high degree of unity, which was a notable achievement in itself. The Massachusetts men worked quietly in private while Southerners took the lead in public. The early actions of the Continental Congress followed the logic of events that were skillfully exploited, and a policy of resistance was agreed to before the more conciliatory members could effectively object.

Resistance but Not Rebellion

The delegates had little more than opened their sessions and decided that each colony should have an equal vote, when they were disturbed by reports that British General Gage was bombarding and burning Boston. These rumors were proved false but they created great sympathy, along with fear and indignation. Meanwhile, the proscribed town meetings of Massachusetts had organized the Suffolk County Convention, and the strong "Resolves" of this extralegal but representative body were brought speedily to Philadelphia by Paul Revere. These called for the making of military plans against possible British forays from Boston, and for the imprisonment of every official of "the present tyrannical and unconstitutional government" if any patriot leader should be seized. More to the point, however, were the resolution that the Coercive Acts should not be obeyed, the proposal that trade relations with Great Britain should be severed, and the announced determination to act only on the defensive.

Less than two weeks after the Congress held its first session, the delegates adopted by unanimous vote a resolution approving the action of their countrymen of the Massachusetts-Bay, and they published this along with the Suffolk Resolves. John Adams described the day of that vote (September 17) as the happiest of his life, and he was now convinced that America would support Massachusetts or perish with her. The die was cast for resistance to British policy, and Boston was assured that she would not stand alone so long as her conduct remained defensive. Also, Congress soon went on record as favoring the suspension of commercial intercourse. The agreement not to import or consume British goods was unanimous, and nonexportation was approved in principle before the end of the month, though there was sharp conflict on this latter question and it was not finally settled until the famous "Association" was adopted toward the close of the session (October 20, 1774).

In the meantime, while committees were busily at work on statements of colonial rights and the infringement of them, conservative Joseph Galloway introduced (September 28) a "Plan of Union" between Great Britain and the colonies which would have patched things up much too tightly for the radicals. This called for a President General to be appointed by the King, and a Grand Council to be chosen by the various colonial legislatures, which, as an inferior and distinct branch of the British legislature, was to govern the colonies in conjunction with the latter. The assent of both this continental colonial body and Parliament would be necessary to give validity to laws. According to the Plan, local and internal affairs would be left to the existing colonial governments, but it sounded like a scheme of consolidation, not a guarantee of ancient liberties. Furthermore, an important purpose of Galloway was that the Congress, after adopting his Plan of Union, should avoid provocation of the mother country while negotiating with her about it. That is, he would decline to share in resistance to the Coercive Acts.

Galloway himself believed that his Plan was favored by all the most loyal and the wealthiest Americans, and that it was opposed by "Congregational and Presbyterian republicans," bankrupts, and hopeless debtors to British merchants. He connected the radicalism of the New Englanders and the Scotch-Irish frontiersmen with their religious doctrines, and attributed that of the Southern planters to their debts. Like most simple ascriptions of motive, this represented a distorted view. Yet Galloway was not far from wrong about the groups that were most opposed to his proposals, and it is to his credit that he himself recognized the need for unity and allowed debate of his Plan to be postponed. Actually it failed little of adoption when it came up later, but ultimately the radicals caused it to be repudiated wholly and expunged from the records.

Thus the control that the advocates of resistance had gained at the beginning was reasserted and maintained. Moderate counsels prevailed, however, when Congress came to a statement of aims and grievances. It seemed wise strategy to object only to British actions since 1763 and to urge a return to the relatively mild system of mercantilism that was in operation before that date. By this time some outstanding patriots—including James Wilson of Pennsylvania, Thomas Jefferson, and John Adams—had taken the position in their writings that Parliament had no authority whatever over the colonies and that the tie with the mother country was only in the person of the King. While admitting that the colonists had acquiesced in the control of commercial matters by Parliament, they denied both the historical justification and practical need for it. The status they sought was closely akin to that of a member of the (British) Commonwealth of Nations today, but such a solution of the imperial problem would have been opposed in England by those who feared the growing personal power of the King. The Congress did not take this position regarding the nature of the Empire for important practical reasons. The Earl of Chatham had warned the Americans that they could expect no support from Whigs if they did not admit the authority of Parliament to regulate imperial affairs, including external commerce. So long as the patriots continued to hope for redress of grievances, it was the part of wisdom to maintain harmony with the English political leaders who might influence the government to repeal offensive measures.

In the dignified Declaration they adopted on October 14, the delegates acknowledged the practical necessity of Parliamentary acts in regulation of external commerce and announced their "cheerful consent" to the operation of these. At the same time they solemnly asserted their rights—based on "the immutable laws of nature, the principles of the English constitution, and the several charters or compacts"—and specified the infringments on these in acts of Parliament since 1763. They could not submit to these acts, they said, and, pending a revision of them and a restoration of the former state of happiness and prosperity, they were resolved to enter into a nonimportation, nonconsumption, and nonexportation agreement. This they did in the "Continental Association," which they adopted the following week. The agreement with respect to exports was not to become effective for almost a year, and a concession had to be made in the case of rice, but this was a long step toward an absolute boycott of British trade and the establishment of colonial union. The mood of self-sacrifice found further expression in the resolution to discourage horse racing, gambling, cockfighting, shows, and all forms of expensive entertainment. Enforcement of the measures was not left to merchants, but to local committees authorized by the Congress. As events soon showed, these were dominated by radicals and were exceedingly effective. Congress had forged a strong weapon of defense and retaliation.

It did not close the door to conciliation, however, for this body also addressed a petition to the King. In this the delegates assured their "Most Gracious Sovereign" of the loyalty of the colonists, blamed "designing and dangerous men" in the British government for colonial oppression, and begged him to check those men and thus restore harmony in the Empire. The adoption of the petition to the King was a victory for the moderate and conservative patriots, and it gave George III an excellent opportunity to draw them away from the radicals by concessions. But the stubborn monarch had already decided on a policy of rule or ruin. In September he had said that "the colonies must either submit or triumph," that "there must always be one tax to keep up the right," and that as such he approved of the tea duty. By November he had declared that the New England governments were now in a state of rebellion, and that blows must decide whether they were subject to England or independent. If the radicals consented to petition the King solely as a tactical maneuver to demonstrate that reconciliation was impossible, nothing could have suited their purpose better than the King's decision to concede nothing and decide the issue by arms. King George III himself made American independence the only alternative to complete submission.

Critics and opponents of the ministry in Parliament would not support the patriots' contention that the Declaratory Act was unconstitutional, but Lord Chatham proposed that the British troops be removed and that the government should return to the old system of obtaining revenues for imperial expenses by requisitioning the colonies and leaving it to their legislatures to decide how the money should be raised. Edmund Burke went further. He asked for repeal of the Coercive Acts and denial of the jurisdiction of the Admiralty Courts over "internal" cases. These proposals were supported by only a minority in Parliament, but Lord North decided that before the government could safely adopt the King's policy of testing the issue by arms, a last effort should be made to satisfy the opposition and unify the country by making a conciliatory offer of his own. He also hoped that such an offer might win over New York and break the unity of the colonies. Therefore the Prime Minister, early in 1775, introduced in Parliament a "Conciliatory Resolve." It did not repudiate the principle of the Declaratory Act but promised that Parliament would refrain from exercising its authority to tax any colony that taxed itself sufficiently to fulfill requisitions made by Parliament. This would only change the method of collecting internal taxes, and no mention was made of the other grievances of the colonies beyond tax matters. Slight as the concession was, it was bitterly opposed in Parliament by the King's Men. On a plea for unity, the House of Commons passed the measure. This gesture would have seemed meaningless to the patriots in any case, and, actually, news of it reached America one day after the King's policy of force had resulted in the battles of Lexington and Concord on April 19, 1775.

LEXINGTON AND CONCORD

Recourse to arms had been decided upon by the Continental Congress only as a defensive measure. But the patriots had their own definition of what would constitute defense, namely, resistance to any attempt by the British troops in Boston to check the quasi-revolutionary activities of the patriots. The Continental Association, as administered by the radicals in Massachusetts and elsewhere, had taken on some of the character of a revolutionary government. Agents of the Association enforced the boycott with great energy, inspecting the affairs of businessmen and the customs offices, going into offices and kitchens to enforce the rules, and supervising their communities in order to impose a Spartan regime in private and public life. Loyalists cried in alarm that the authority of the legislatures was usurped and the mild rule of Parliament replaced by the tyranny of mobs. Names of violators of the Association were published in the press; and when publicity did not bring obedience, tar and feathers were used in some localities. Rarely if ever have Americans submitted to a stricter regulation of their daily lives.

The aim of the Association was to force by economic measures a peaceful capitulation by the British government. This policy may be regarded as a primitive example of what the twentieth century calls "economic sanctions." But powerful governments, such as that of Great Britain then, are indisposed to yield to economic pressure so long as they see—or think they see—a possibility of easy victory in shooting war. The situation in Boston was ready-made for an appeal to arms. The population offered no resistance when regiments occupied the town, but they made life as difficult for the soldiers as they could, refusing to provide quarters for them or to sell supplies to them. The troops on their part heightened the tension by licentious behavior, robbery, and violence—their offenses being multiplied and exaggerated in the propaganda of the Committee of

Correspondence. Clergymen hurled anathemas against Lord North and handed out arms to their congregations. Massachusetts patriots urged the other New Englanders to join them in raising an army of 18,000 men. Though companies of "minutemen" were organized and military stores were collected, the leaders still clung to the policy of purely defensive action.

The position of the British troops in Boston became humiliating. They were virtually under siege, and their chief function seemed to be the protection of refugee British officials and American Loyalists. Taunts were thrown at General Gage and Major Pitcairn that if they dared venture into the countryside, the minutemen would hustle them back with musket bullets. Pitcairn, in March 1775, nevertheless led a contingent to Salem without incident. British regulars were contemptuous of the New England militiamen. They lacked all the obvious military qualifications except one which European military theory of the time held in low esteem: the ability of the individual musketman to take aim at a particular target and hit it.

As the spring of 1775 advanced, the patriot cause was suffering. Congress had been torn by demands to exempt the staples of certain colonies from the rules against exportation, and the New York Assembly refused to approve the Association, although local committees enforced its provisions. Loyalists took heart and conservative patriots urged the provincial assemblies to send more petitions to the King. Those of Georgia and New York did so. Lord North was hopeful that his Conciliatory Resolve would divide the colonies, and General Gage decided that a march into the countryside was all that was needed to discourage and scatter the overblown rebels. It was his duty to enforce the Coercive Acts. He received orders to arrest Hancock and Sam Adams, who were in the neighborhood of Lexington, and spies informed him that the minutemen were collecting powder at Concord. The General decided to make a careful demonstration of authority by marching to Lexington and Concord.

British "aggression" outside Boston, the arrest of patriot leaders who were guilty only of supporting their rights as freeborn Englishmen, and the confiscation of means of defense which the militia system entitled citizens to possess—these were precisely what the radicals hoped would rouse Americans to their danger. The Boston Sons of Liberty and Committee of Correspondence had established close co-operation with patriots of the countryside. Their spies and watchers foiled Gage's plan for Major Pitcairn to slip from Boston secretly with a detachment of troops. The moment Pitcairn set out, Paul Revere saw the signal-light in the tower of Old North Church and rode express to Concord, giving warning to the patriot leaders at Lexington and rousing the farmers as he went. His cry in the night was not extemporized; it sounded the determined plan of the patriots to fight defensively if the British gave cause.

When Pitcairn and his company of infantry marched into Lexington in the dawn of April 19, 1775, a company of minutemen faced them across the village green. Who fired first is to this day uncertain, although patriot propaganda left no doubt that the redcoats did. The point is of no importance because the British sally was the sort of "aggression" to which Congress had authorized resistance, and the minutemen had mobilized in order to resist it. Eight of the embattled farmers were killed on the Lexington green, then the minutemen scattered. American farmer-soldiers were not accustomed to volleys fired from the hip by neat ranks of disciplined professionals. But they were trained in hunting and Indian fighting, and while the redcoats marched on to Concord the minutemen took up the positions of sharpshooters, behind stone walls along the road and under any cover that offered.

At Concord a company of minutemen made a stand at the bridge and the British detachment turned to march back. Pitcairn failed to find either Hancock or Adams and destroyed only part of the military stores. On the return march, the troops received the aimed fire from cover of farmers who had rallied from miles around. The British, who would not break ranks, lost more than 200 men in killed and wounded. The minutemen closed in behind the column and took up positions around Boston, holding it under seige against another sally. Before he heard the clash of resounding arms, Patrick Henry in Old Saint John's Church, Richmond, had already pronounced his most famous words: "Give me liberty, or give me death!" Events had now proved that Americans would fight for their liberties against the Coercive Acts, though their attitude toward a struggle for full independence remained a question.

The story of "the shot heard round the world," accumulated lurid details in the telling. Major Pitcairn's soldiers were said to have butchered men, women, and children and devastated the countryside. The British and Loyalists also invented atrocities on the part of the minutemen, accusing them of scalping, cutting off noses and ears, and gouging out eyes like Indians or devils. The patriots had the better of the contest of propaganda because their superior communications enabled them to get their story to the public first, and also because, atrocities aside, none could deny that the British had provoked the fight and that American "peasants" had put the British regulars to flight. The latter fact was especially important in both its immediate and long-range effects: it buoyed the hopes of the patriots and encouraged them to rely too much on undisciplined militia.

Conservative talk of conciliation was drowned out. New York, the weakest link in the patriot chain, became stronger when it went over to the radicals. Association committees ruled the colony. They confiscated

British supplies intended for the troops in Boston, took over the customs-house, and frightened the British garrison of New York City into going aboard warships in the harbor. Loyalists were silenced. Everywhere in the colonies, militia companies began to prepare for war. Guns and equipment in the King's arsenals were seized. Even Quaker Philadelphia turned warlike and mustered military escorts for the delegates of the Second Continental Congress. This body held its first session early in May while the echoes of the shots fired at Lexington and Concord still lingered.

THE SECOND CONTINENTAL CONGRESS

The Second Congress met in the State House in Philadelphia (later Independence Hall) rather than in Carpenters' Hall. In effect it was a continuation of the first and had much the same membership. Peyton Randolph presided over it until he was called home, and his successor in the chair was a new member, John Hancock of Massachusetts. His successor as a delegate from Virginia did not arrive until after the Congress had been about six weeks in session. This was Thomas Jefferson, a tall, sandy-haired young planter, already noted for his zealous patriotism and his "happy talent for composition." If he was to become the most famous penman of this body, Dr. Benjamin Franklin was its most renowned elder statesman. Just returned from England, where he had served as a colonial agent until he despaired of conciliation, the most famous of living Americans contributed his immense prestige to the cause of the patriots and his intimate knowledge of English and European politics to their councils.

If an appeal to arms and the God of Hosts was all that was now left to the defenders of colonial rights, as Patrick Henry had said, the first task of the Congress was to deal with military matters, and the odds against the colonists necessitated the maintenance of unity. The provisions for a Continental Army and the selection of a commander-in-chief were the most important early actions. John Adams of Massachusetts, where the seat of the trouble was, showed political wisdom in recommending George Washington of Virginia for the supreme command. Colonel Washington, who had resigned his commission in considerable dissatisfaction toward the end of the French and Indian War, and had devoted himself assiduously to his extensive private affairs until the controversy with the mother country aroused him, had never wavered in his support of colonial rights from the time of the Stamp Act onward. His determination to resist tyranny by force, if need be, was suggested by his appearance at the sessions of Congress in uniform. About this time he wrote: "Unhappy it is . . . that the once-happy and peaceful plains of America are either to be drenched with blood or inhabited by slaves. Sad alternative! But can a virtuous man hesitate in his choice?" He was a fine figure of a man at the age of forty-three, and he inspired the confidence of all by his good sense, balanced judgment, and irreproachable character. Later events were to show that the choice of him was little less than providential, and men hoped from the beginning that the unanimity of it was prophetic.

French secret agents were present in Philadelphia and held out the prospects of aid from England's historic enemy, but acceptance of it would have amounted to a denial of the avowed purposes of the present conflict. From being a struggle for the restoration of rights it would have become a movement for national independence. At this time Congress summed things up in a "Declaration of the Causes and Necessity of Taking up Arms" (July 6, 1775), to which Jefferson made important contributions though it was chiefly the work of John Dickinson. The potentialities of the situation were set forth in a rather boastful passage:

> Our cause is just. Our union is perfect. Our internal resources are great, and, if necessary, foreign assistance is undoubtedly attainable. . . .

Independence, itself, was mentioned as a threat in a passage which perhaps protested too much:

> We mean not to dissolve that union which has so long and so happily subsisted between us. Necessity has *not yet* driven us into that desperate measure. . . . We have not raised armies with ambitious designs of separating from Great Britain, and establishing independent states. . . .

Why, then, did Congress raise an army? The answer rang clear:

> For the preservation of our liberties, being with one mind resolved to die free men rather than live slaves.

The logic of its position forced Congress to assume some of the legislative and executive powers of a revolutionary government. To meet the expenses of the Continental Army, for example, it printed paper money, violating thereby one of the central prohibitions of the old Empire. Benjamin Franklin saw clearly the implications of the situation and eagerly embraced them by drawing up "Articles of Confederation and Perpetual Union—" in effect, the constitution of an American republic. But, strictly speaking, Congress was nothing more than a body of delegates—each of whom could act only on instructions from his colonial assembly or the extralegal body that had supplanted it. Thirteen revolutions were required before the delegates to Congress could be instructed to cap the movement with a national Declaration of Independence. In each colony a struggle occurred between militants and conservatives for control of local affairs. Antagonisms between West and East, and between merchants on one side and radical artisans and small farmers on the other, came to the fore in many of these local struggles. Economic lines were less sharply drawn in the South than in the North. In general, however, conservatives saw that not only English rule, but also their own position in society was endangered, and they hesitated. While the issue of these conflicts remained in doubt, Congress was disposed to evade the full revolutionary implications of its own actions.

Franklin's plan of union was not debated by Congress except privately, and John Dickinson obtained approval of a petition to the King. No answer to the petition of the First Congress had been received, and there was no chance whatever that Britain would accept anything less than submission to the Declaratory Act, but the militant radicals themselves admitted that it was wiser to move slowly towards independence so that it might be achieved in unity. Dickinson's petition was duly sent, but stirring new events had intervened and the King really had to answer the patriots who fought at Bunker Hill.

Civil War in the Empire, 1775

That fight (June 17, 1775) was technically a defeat for the raw militiamen, but they won a victory in terms of the damage they did the redcoats. After Lexington and Concord, motley American forces rapidly gained numbers around Boston. In June they occupied the Charlestown peninsula, entrenching themselves on Breed's Hill and the more elevated Bunker Hill behind it. From these positions cannon could command the city and harbor of Boston. Instead of cutting the Americans off by utilizing their sea force and seizing the narrow neck of land behind them, the British foolishly made a succession of direct attacks. Eventually they took both positions, amid scenes of carnage that were not exceeded in the entire Revolution. Among the American losses was General Joseph Warren, and among the British was Major Pitcairn. The redcoats marched up the slope in long close-order lines, the front rank stopping every few feet to fire a volley. The Americans held their fire against the enemy until they could "see the whites of their eyes," and at this highly effective range their muskets took terrific toll, but the next British line filled the gaps and moved forward. The Americans finally withdrew only when they ran out of ammunition. The British losses were so heavy that the victory had no savor. General Gage wrote to his government that the spirit and conduct of the Americans were far superior to what they had shown in former years when fighting for the king. The ministry decided that the war must be prosecuted to victory, and that conciliation would now be regarded as an admission of defeat.

General Washington heard reports of Bunker Hill while en route to his new command. He incorporated the New England troops in the Continental Army, set up his headquarters in Cambridge, and embarked on the long and disheartening task of welding short-term recruits and raw militia into an effective force. That a Virginian should be accepted as commander of New Englanders was itself an important demonstration of unity. Washington's personal qualities of absolute integrity, firmness, administrative skill, and infinite patience overcame the Yankees' suspicion of the gentleman planter; and from this time forward the colonial cause centered on him.

The organization of the Continental Army under Washington was final proof to the British that they faced not merely the armed "peasants" of New England, but the united thirteen colonies. In May 1775, Ethan Allen and the Green Mountain Boys had surprised and captured the forts at Crown Point and Ticonderoga. These positions were strategic keys to Canada and to unity between New England and the other colonies. Ethan Allen's feat, and the decision of Congress to retain the forts, signified the continental aims of the Americans. Thus when Dickinson's "olive-branch" petition arrived in England, it was accompanied by news that civil war on a continental scale had started in the Empire. The King refused to receive the petition. Instead, on August 23, 1775, he issued a "Proclamation of Rebellion" declaring all the colonies to be in a state of revolt. Thirty thousand British troops and three major generals were sent to put down this rebellion and mercenaries were hired from German princes.

By the time that news of the Proclamation reached Philadelphia in November, Congress had authorized the invasion of Canada. Congress had addressed friendly invitations to the Canadians to join the thirteen colonies to no effect. Canadians had been satisfied by the Quebec Act of 1774 and they were suspicious of the Protestant English colonists who had so recently inveighed against their religion and their laws. After capturing Montreal, brave General Richard Montgomery joined his forces with those of the valiant General Benedict Arnold before Quebec, but there the combined bodies of raw militiamen were defeated, Montgomery being killed. To the British the futile invasion seemed an overt aggression.

Meanwhile, Congress had answered the Proclamation of Rebellion by opening negotiations with France for aid. It appointed Benjamin Franklin, John Adams, and three others to a "Secret Committee of Correspondence." Within six months, King Louis XVI and his ministers had decided to encourage the rebels by supplying munitions from the royal arsenals and all kinds of stores. The fictitious Hortalez et Compagnie was the channel through which aid flowed to the Americans while France was maintaining technical neutrality. During the next few years, all but a small fraction of Washington's munitions came from France, and without them the American cause could not have been sustained. The French government did not render this aid because it loved liberty or Americans. Many Frenchmen—including powerful personages, leading writers, and the philosophers of the Enlightenment—idealized the American cause almost beyond recognition. But this did not influence officials like the

Comte de Vergennes, the Foreign Minister, who reasoned that France could regain her rightful place as the leading power in Europe by helping to destroy British sources of wealth in America.

Congress, in December 1775, authorized a Continental Navy and issued letters of marque and reprisal to American shipowners. A large share of the American merchant fleet was converted into armed vessels entitled under international law to prey on British commerce. The privateers did their work well, and the prizes, which were divided among owners and crew, were so rich that they laid the foundations of new fortunes and attracted recruits to man the vessels to the detriment of the Continental Army. The French government allowed American privateers to use French ports so that they could waylay British ships within sight of English shores.

By the end of 1775, Congress had shown that it was willing to accept the King's definition of its actions as rebellion, and that it would prosecute war aggressively, assuming all the powers necessary for the tasks at hand. Nevertheless, the delegates hesitated even to debate the question of independence. Positions taken in the war of propaganda were partly responsible. The Americans had claimed that they were resisting only the unjust measures of a corrupt and tyrannical Parliament and that their loyalty to the King was unimpaired. The radicals found they had done too good a job of distinguishing between the King and his government. British accusations bore heavily on the theme that they were plotting independence, and denials by Americans made it awkward for them to perform an about-face. During the winter of 1775-1776, therefore, the patriots stood in a political no-man's-land: they were breaking their ties with the mother country and yet were unready to advance towards independence.

THE DECLARATION OF INDEPENDENCE

The radicals had relied time and again on events to force the more reluctant patriots to take forward steps, and they were rarely disappointed. In December 1775, Parliament forbade all trade and contact between British subjects and the American colonists. This was called by the Americans the "Act of Independency," and they asked why Americans should maintain a connection the British government had broken.

Paine and Common Sense

In January 1776, a powerful assault on that connection was launched by Thomas Paine, who was not afraid of the word "independence." His pamphlet, *Common Sense*, turned American eyes to a strange new destiny outside the British Empire. Paine was an Englishman of ardent libertarian principles. As an excise officer, he had tried to organize his fellow officials so as to gain an increase in salary. Expelled from the service, he came to America as the land of promise in 1774. Throwing himself into the radical movement, he became its most extreme and skillful propagandist. He believed that the war required a supreme effort which the people would not make so long as they were told that "Good King George" would protect their liberties against Parliament inside the Empire. The Americans needed, Paine believed, a stirring "war aim," and an end to delusions that a middle way could be found between independence and slavery.

In *Common Sense*, Paine attacked the King in unheard of terms. The "Royal Brute," he wrote, was a "hardened, sullen-tempered Pharaoh" who by corruption had gained control of Parliament and the ministry. From attacking George III, Paine went on to attack the institution of monarchy as an absurd form of government. One honest man was worth "all the crowned ruffians that ever lived." Monarchs derived their power from the crimes of robber barons. Paine appealed to a law superior to the British constitution, the law of nature, to discredit all government as "a badge of lost innocence," and monarchy as the most unnatural form of government. Furthermore, it was unnatural that an island should govern a continent. Such a connection exposed Americans to economic exploitation and costly involvements in European politics and wars. This philosophy of natural rights was the "common sense" of Paine's title and it seemed to Americans very good sense. In ringing words he called for a declaration of independence in order that Americans might set up their own government according to the laws of nature.

Modern political science has rejected the notion of natural-rights philosophers that primitive society was, in Paine's words, a "bower of paradise" which the institution of government had destroyed. But the doctrine seemed very plausible to Americans who had been advancing for generations on the frontier and whose individual liberties had been interfered with by autocratic British power. Eighteenth-century philosophy encouraged Americans to glorify the simplicity of American life and to regard the influence of decadent Europe as the serpent in their earthly paradise. Paine's amazing eloquence made the ideas of philosophers, which were already current in enlightened circles, understandable and convincing to the mass of Americans. At a critical moment of indecision in the struggle against Great Britain, he reminded them of their opportunity to create an ideal society and summoned them to seize it.

> O! ye that love mankind! Ye that dare oppose not only the tyranny but the tyrant, stand forth! Every spot of the old world is overrun with oppression. Freedom hath been hunted around the Globe. Asia and Africa have long expelled her. Europe regards her as a stranger and England hath given her warning to depart. O! receive the fugitive and prepare in time an asylum for mankind.

Loyalists answered *Common Sense* by pointing to Paine's exaggerated indictment of the British constitution, but he had carried the debate beyond the point where the virtues of the British constitution mattered. The authority of the "rotten old state" of England over American freemen must be destroyed. Freedom had been snuffed out in one European country after another: in Corsica at the hands of the French; in Sweden, where despotism succeeded constitutional rule; in Poland, which was being divided among neighboring tyrants. Americans must act in time, as John Dickinson now said, against this "damn'd conspiracy of Kings and Ministers." Paine's pamphlet was read and talked about everywhere. It served to abolish hesitation and confusion, brought over many converts to the patriot cause, and emboldened the radicals to make independence their public goal.

Growth and Triumph of the Spirit of Independence

Defense against British encroachments on American liberty gave way during the spring of 1776 to positive assertion of what Americans could hope for if the British tie should be destroyed. Paine's vision of an asylum of freedom was made specific in the writings and speeches of the radicals. American trade might be expelled from the protected British market, but under American laws of free trade merchants could invade the markets of the world. Relieved of obedience to the Quebec Act of 1774, pioneers could invade the vast trans-Allegheny country and create a rich and powerful empire for liberty. Independence would give Americans control over their foreign relations and, as Benjamin Franklin said, prevent Englishmen from dragging them into "all the plundering wars, which their desperate circumstances, injustices, and rapacity, may prompt them to undertake." Furthermore, independence would open the highest positions in society to merit. Thus not only political liberty, but economic and social freedom and opportunity in a rich and powerful republic would follow in its train.

In these terms, the issue of independence was debated publicly for the first time in Congress in January 1776. The issue split the delegates into two camps, and on the first trial vote the radicals lost. A mistaken rumor concerning royal instructions to General Sir William Howe and Admiral Sir Richard Howe, when they took command over the British forces, strengthened the conservatives in Congress. The two Howes had refused to accept the command unless the King would also authorize them to enter into peace negotiations. George agreed, and rumors of this made American conservatives argue that conciliation was still possible and that the question of independence should meanwhile be shelved. But once more the folly of George III came to the aid of the radicals: he had instructed the Howes to make no peace with the rebels on terms of American

SUPPLEMENT to the PENNSYLVANIA JOURNAL,
EXTRAORDINARY.

PHILADELPHIA, *May 19, 1766.*

This Morning arrived Capt. WISE, in a Brig from POOL in
8 Weeks, by whom we have the GLORIOUS NEWS of the

REPEAL OF THE STAMP-ACT,

As paſſed by the *King, Lords* and *Commons.* It received
the ROYAL ASSENT the 18th of March, on which we moſt
ſincerely congratulate our Readers.

An Act to repeal an Act made in the laſt Seſſion of Parliament, entituled, *An Act for granting and applying certain
Stamp Duties, and other Duties,* in the British *Colonies and
Plantations* in America, *towards further defraying the Ex-
pences of defending, protecting and securing the same; and
for amending such Parts of the several Acts of Parliament,
relating to the Trade and Revenues of the said Colonies and
Plantations, as direct the Manner of determining and re-
covering the Penalties and Forfeitures therein mentioned.*

BOSTON MASSACRE, 1770. *Engraving by Paul Revere.* This
exaggerated representation served as a constant reminder of
British "tyranny" to the hundreds of colonial Americans who
pinned it up in their kitchens.

DECLARATION OF INDEPENDENCE. *Detail from painting by John Trumbull.* The members of the Committee—John Adams, Roger Sherman, Robert R. Livingston, Jefferson, and Franklin—face the President of the Congress, John Hancock. At his side the Secretary, Charles Thomson, is standing.

GEORGE WASHINGTON

1732-1799

Portrait by John Trumbull

In this painting of Washington at the Battle of Trenton,
his heroic stature, both physical and spiritual, is eloquently
suggested by the artist.

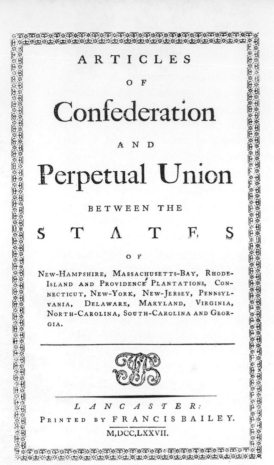

ARTICLES
OF
Confederation
AND
Perpetual Union
BETWEEN THE
S T A T E S
OF
NEW-HAMPSHIRE, MASSACHUSETTS-BAY, RHODE-
ISLAND AND PROVIDENCE PLANTATIONS, CON-
NECTICUT, NEW-YORK, NEW-JERSEY, PENNSYL-
VANIA, DELAWARE, MARYLAND, VIRGINIA,
NORTH-CAROLINA, SOUTH-CAROLINA AND GEOR-
GIA.

LANCASTER:
PRINTED BY FRANCIS BAILEY.
M,DCC,LXXVII.

ARTICLES

OF CONFEDERATION

Title page from the proposal
distributed to the 13 original
states in 1777.

THE HORSE "AMERICA" THROWING HIS MASTER. *An Englis*
cartoon, 1779. This shows Lord North, British Prime Minister
brandishing a whip of swords while a Frenchman rushes by in
the background.

liberty within the empire. Only surrender and submission would be acceptable, and the King's wish that the Americans should be chastised before they were offered even these peace terms was also embodied in the commanders' instructions.

While the conservatives in Congress imposed delay, the individual colonies proceeded to establish independent governments. In the Carolinas the patriot cause was weakened by suspicions of the frontiersmen that the seaboard Whigs would use their power against Western interests. In North Carolina bitter memories survived from the "Regulators' War" of 1770. But in March 1776 the North Carolina legislature instructed its delegates in Congress to vote for independence, and the erstwhile Regulators of the western counties turned to the support of the patriot cause. In Pennsylvania the Scotch-Irish frontiersmen joined city artisans in favor of independence. Germans were on the whole indifferent to the issue, while the dominant group of wealthy Quakers was pacifist and conservative. Frontiersmen and artisans overthrew the proprietary government and, under the leadership of Franklin and Paine, set up the most radical of all the new state governments. The Pennsylvania delegates were then instructed to vote for independence. In most colonies radicals seized the opportunity of leading the struggle against Britain in order to install more democratic local governments. Conservatives were constrained to go along rather than yield control of the revolutionary movement completely to them. Loyalists were proscribed and their property in many states was confiscated. When General Gage evacuated Boston he carried more than a thousand of them into exile, and Loyalists elsewhere were forced to seek the protection of British warships.

While the radicals in Congress waited for instructions in favor of independence to accumulate, they pointed the way to it by several important actions. In March, the Secret Committee of Correspondence sent Silas Deane as diplomatic agent to Vergennes. In April, Congress opened American ports to trade with all nations except Great Britain, thus overthrowing the mercantile system. In May, Congress advised the colonies to suppress every vestige of British authority within their borders and to establish governments whose authority would be derived solely from the people.

Then, on June 7, 1776, Richard Henry Lee of Virginia, following instructions from his province, moved: "That these United Colonies are, and of right ought to be, Free and Independent States." The phrasing of the motion shows that the radicals presented independence as an accomplished fact which Congress should merely ratify. Nevertheless, the debate was bitter when the question at length came up for decision. The final action concealed evidence of opposition, since the rule of procedure was that the vote of each colony was cast in accordance with the position of the majority of its delegates. The sentiment of individuals was not unanimous. The New York delegation was uninstructed and abstained from voting, though they afterwards acceded. After considerable maneuvering all the other colonies supported Lee's motion on July 2, 1776. This was the day that John Adams expected to be commemorated by succeeding generations as the day of deliverance, but the formal adoption of the entire document which we call the Declaration, including Lee's resolution, occurred on July 4, and that has always been regarded as the birthday of the American Republic.

The document had already been drafted by a committee consisting of Thomas Jefferson, John Adams, Benjamin Franklin, Roger Sherman, and Robert Livingston, of whom the three first were the active members. They set forth the causes which impelled Congress to this "mighty resolution." The youngest member of the committee except Livingston and its most eloquent writer, Thomas Jefferson, actually made the draft and it was not subjected to enough changes to invalidate his acknowledged claim to the authorship of the most famous American state paper.

The Meaning of the Declaration

The Declaration of Independence is one of the great generative documents of modern world history. It inspired emulation in every subsequent democratic movement from the French Revolution of 1789 to the recent upsurges of the Hindus and Moslems of India and the peoples of the former Dutch East Indies. This is because Jefferson, correctly reflecting dominant patriot opinion in 1776, did not rest the case for independence on the specific grievances of the colonists but on general philosophic principles. These principles were the common heritage of English and French thinkers of the seventeenth and eighteenth centuries and they had already been incorporated in the Virginia Declaration of Rights, but Jefferson gave them their classical expression:

> We hold these truths to be self-evident, that all men are created equal, that they are endowed by their Creator with certain unalienable Rights, that among these are Life, Liberty and the pursuit of Happiness. That to secure these rights, Governments are instituted among Men, deriving their just powers from the consent of the governed, That whenever any Form of Government becomes destructive of these ends, it is the Right of the People to alter or to abolish it, and to institute new Government, laying its foundation on such principles and organizing its powers in such form, as to them shall seem most likely to effect their Safety and Happiness.

These phrases are immortal because they make the people, and the people's will, the sovereign determinant of public polity. Probably nothing in the political literature of the world has been fought over more than the words: *all men are created equal.* Men of conservative persuasion, even Americans, have time and again dismissed these words along with other expressions in the Declaration as "glittering generalities," since human beings are obviously endowed with unequal abilities. But other Americans have appealed—successfully on the whole—to this principle of the Declaration on the ground that men are endowed with equal legal and political rights, regardless of their personal inequalities. It is in this sense that Jefferson's famous dictum has been given force by subsequent American development. When he announced it, glaring contradictions existed in the society about him, most obviously in the matter of chattel slavery. He had placed in his original draft an indictment against King George for furthering the slave trade. Southern and New England delegates had struck it out, but, like Jefferson, most of the patriots, Southern as well as Northern, regarded slavery as an evil which would presently be abolished. The Declaration lighted a beacon that searched out the darker corners of American society and led reformers to wage war against whatever could not bear the light. The question whether its "truths" were indisputable "facts" is of little importance compared with the influence of the Declaration itself in converting its principles into realities.

Jefferson altered the standard trinity of rights, derived from John Locke—"life, liberty, and property"—into the seemingly less materialistic "life, liberty, and the pursuit of happiness." The last phrase, however, was assumed by him and everybody else to include the right to own property, and the full establishment of this was a recognized motive, as it was one of the important fruits, of the Revolution.

Equality before the law and the right to life, liberty, and property were not very startling conceptions in 1776. Jefferson's assertion of the right of revolution was more notable. John Locke had formulated it *after* the Glorious Revolution as a rationalization of what Parliament had done, but Parliament itself had never admitted that it acted other than conservatively to protect the English constitution from royal "rebels." For a government to assert the right of revolution seemed to invite anarchy. Here, however, the invitation was to establish self-government, and the American patriots were determined to make their new governments genuinely responsive to the popular will and therefore secure against popular rebellion. Their success in this respect was so great that no aspect of the American political system has been more striking than its durability. Yet citizens of the United States have generally been sympathetic with political revolts against tyrannical rule elsewhere—such as those against the Spanish and Portuguese governments, leading to the establishment of the independent Latin-American republics.

Highly significant among the principles of the Declaration was the idea of government by compact. Here there could be no dispute about the correspondence of practice to theory: the organization of a government by free association of the governed and the formulation of a contract between them and their political authorities which the latter must obey even more strictly than the people. This was no more than a repetition on the national level of what had been said and done by Americans for a century and a half on the local levels. It was the long and successful experience of Americans in organizing government by compact that made this central theme of the Declaration the most "self-evident" of all the principles.

Jefferson placed specific grievances in a subordinate position in the Declaration, and offered them in deference to the proposition that, although the right of revolution against tyranny was inherent, prudence dictated that "governments long established should not be changed for light and transient causes." He recited a long and rather tendentious "train of abuses and usurpations . . . all having in direct object the establishment of an absolute Tyranny over these States." Leading the list were instances of interference with colonial legislatures and the judicial process. "Imposing taxes on us without our Consent" was one of the counts in the indictment, but mercantilist laws were not mentioned. The Quebec Act of 1774 was condemned as a scheme to introduce absolute rule into the colonies. Chiefly the grievances related to direct attacks on American liberty and self-government. King George III was blamed for them all, and Parliament was referred to only by implication.

> He [the King] has combined with others to subject us to a [Parliamentary] jurisdiction foreign to our constitution, and unacknowledged by our laws; giving his assent to their pretended acts of legislation.

This was not an accurate description of the relations between the colonies and Parliament during the years prior to 1763; and those once-amicable relations were now forgotten while the full-blown radical theses were advanced that Parliament held no rightful authority over the colonies, and that the King had forfeited his authority by abusing it.

Beyond all considerations of advantage in propaganda, the sweeping assertion of absolute popular sovereignty in the Declaration of Independence caused the document to mark a watershed in human history. It was flung into a era dominated by absolute monarchs, and it has by no means lost its point in a twentieth-century world which totalitarian governments threaten to dominate. It was primarily an act of faith by the immortal signers that if peoples were free to create their own governments, they would create governments that would guarantee freedom, and subsequent history has largely justified this faith.

Most Americans greeted the Declaration of Independence with joyous enthusiasm. Copies of it were sped to every city and village for public reading and celebration. The "Liberty Bell" in the Pennsylvania State House rang out, and it was echoed in belfries across the land. The Phrygian cap worn by liberated Greek slaves, the liberty pole, the American eagle, and a great variety of designs for an American flag replaced the old royal symbols. Conservative patriots joined the radicals in hailing independence, but with certain reservations. Some hoped it might merely be used as a bargaining point to win reconciliation with Britain. Some were firmly opposed to any movement to carry into practice the advanced principles of the Declaration. Like John Dickinson, who enlisted as a private in Washington's army after losing the fight in Congress against independence, many conservatives would defend American liberty against Britain, but they would also oppose in varying degree the growth of popular rule in America.

During the long war that followed, conservatives often feared that the Loyalists were right in their contention that British rule was the only alternative to mob rule. Some radicals made no secret of their purpose to make the revolution a fight against planter and merchant aristocracies as well as against Great Britain. It was an uneasy alliance between divergent groups that fought for American independence, and their contentions foreshadowed a large part of subsequent American history: on the one side to carry out the "principles of 1776"; on the other to embalm these in a document of purely antiquarian interest. The central idea in this revolt was the attainment of self-government, and the almost-deified leader of it was George Washington, an aristocratic planter and relatively conservative in his social ideas, who yet recognized the necessary sovereignty of the people and aimed at justice to all human beings. Men supported him irrespective of classes. Its spiritual prophet was Thomas Jefferson, and through the years the democratization of society has proceeded—too slow for some and too fast for others—in the spirit of the great Declaration.

CHAPTER 10

The American Revolution

REVOLUTION HAS BECOME ALMOST A CHARACTERISTIC institution of modern civilization. In modern times, revolutions have not been confined to *coups d'état* or palace revolutions, which affect little more than the personnel of governments. Forms of government have been overthrown and new forms substituted, in what may be called political revolutions. Occasionally whole classes of a population have lost their economic, social, and political positions and society has assumed new class configurations. Such social revolutions are typified by the French Revolution of 1789 and the Russian Revolution of 1917.

No economic or social class was dispossessed by the American Revolution. The wealthiest classes produced the most conspicuous Loyalists and many individual Loyalist merchants and landowners were proscribed, but they suffered for their opinions and actions, not for their class affiliations. Patriot merchants and landowners were often strengthened in their economic positions. The American Revolution did level downwards the social and political status of the wealthier classes at the same time that it raised the poorer classes to something approaching equality with the rich in everything but riches, and it widened opportunity for any man to achieve wealth and other forms of distinction. Therefore, it may well be called a *democratic* revolution insofar as it accelerated that process of equalizing rights and access to privileges which marked the American adventure from the beginning and continues to mark it. Social revolutions have often eventuated in abiding political tyranny, and this above all differentiates them from the American Revolution, which did nothing of the sort. This was predominantly a political revolution. As such, it had a double aspect: a colonial people overthrew the rule of their mother country; and the subjects of a king overthrew the institution of monarchy and made themselves citizens of a federated republic which they erected in its place.

The various aspects of the American Revolution may be subsumed under the single word, freedom: freedom of the whole people to advance their individual social, economic, political, and cultural ambitions; freedom of a colonial people to govern themselves; freedom from hereditary monarchs and nobles in a republic; freedom even for local self-government within a federal frame. Pre-eminently a *liberating* movement, it is distinctive if not unique among the major revolutions of world history. It produced no guillotine, no program of "revolutionary justice" carried to the point of tragic bloodshed. The respect for individual rights which was an impelling motive with the patriots at the outset was not violated by immoderate reprisals against even the enemies of the revolution. There were numerous confiscations and many Loyalists left the country, but perhaps no revolution of comparable scope ever abided by its first principles more faithfully. This was partly because it had high-minded leaders, partly because the Americans until very recently had enjoyed a large degree of freedom and self-government in a land of unexampled opportunity. After they had cut the tie with the mother country their main task was to maintain or develop their institutions, and there was relatively little that they wanted to destroy.

The War: Character and General Conditions

The indubitable fact of American moderation in revolutionary action has led to the growth of a legend that the War of Independence was an Arcadian affair consisting of gentlemanly jousts in picturesque costumes, shadowed only by the sufferings of Washington's Army at Valley Forge. Actually it was a grim conflict and long drawn out. Both sides began the war with the thought that victory would be quick and easy, and both sides were slowly disabused. The Americans depended for victory chiefly on geography. They controlled the huge territory from Canada to Florida and from the mountains to the ocean. British troops might install themselves at one point or another but they could not control more territory than they actually occupied, and Britain simply could not support an army large enough to occupy any considerable portion of the American domain.

American geographic reasoning was basically sound and Washington's strategy was dominated by it. Nevertheless, enthusiastic patriots underestimated the time and positive military effort that would have to be spent before the stubborn government of King George would admit the impossibility of conquering America. After the first few months Washington himself did not make that mistake. He struggled manfully to convince Congress and the states that positive effort and planning for a long war were necessary.

The optimism of the early days was shown by the fact that the first Continental soldiers were enlisted for terms of only a few months. This optimism was modified but it persisted in dangerous degree. State governments refused to conscript soldiers or to order their militia to co-operate with Washington's troops except when danger inside their own boundaries threatened. Americans preferred militia service: a few days or weeks of fighting on home grounds in good weather, with wives and mothers handy to cook good meals, and then back to the farm for the harvest. The Continental Army was made up largely of the more ardent patriots and it also had a good share of homeless adventurers. Even so, the turnover was enormous. After 1776, the total number of Continental soldiers was usually less than 5000, yet several hundred thousand men (and a few women) served at one time or another.

To make a disciplined and skilled army of maneuver out of these materials was a task requiring supreme talents, and the patriot cause miraculously found these in George Washington. If too much is not made of Washington's occasional and usually justifiable bursts of tremendous rage, and of a sensitiveness to criticism which he generally transmuted into patience, no weakness can be found in the man. In the darkest days the Army, and the Revolution itself, had little else to sustain them besides his character, but that turned out to be enough. Congress failed to provide even the minimum of support in money, equipment, or direction. At times it seemed ready to give Washington sole authority in the government as it gave him sole responsibility. The marvel is that his republicanism was proof against the temptation to follow the easy pattern of many another revolutionary military leader in similar circumstances, and make himself dictator. Several times in his life Washington had "Napoleonic" opportunities; but there is no evidence that he even saw them as such, much less that he considered grasping them. Conservative though he was in social philosophy, his faith in the people was simple and complete.

It is notable that Washington never blamed his soldiers for their shortcomings—their lack of discipline, their desertions and quasi-mutinies. He blamed Congress while deferring to it, and, even more fundamentally, he blamed the lack of centralized constitutional authority in the government. But even while he saw the long-term need for a strong government and wrote endless begging letters to Congress and local authorities pointing out the desperate needs of the moment, Washington made no apologies but compelled himself and his ragged, hungry followers to endure all in the solid faith that if the Continental Army, no matter how much it retreated or how small it shrank, could somehow remain an army "in being," victory one day was sure.

Fortunately for the United States, Britain found no leader, political or military, for her war in America of a stature remotely comparable to George Washington. Indeed, her noblest political leaders, as British historians proudly affirm, were in opposition to the King's American policy, and many an outstanding army officer resigned his commission rather than fight against American liberty. Nor did the British population as a whole respond to the war. Enlistments in the army were at low ebb and the King was forced to hire German mercenaries. Many American Loyalists joined the British Army and they fought more avidly than the English or German troops. The Loyal Greens, Tory Rangers, and other regular and irregular regiments perpetrated the worst atrocities of the war, including the Wyoming Massacre in Pennsylvania. There is some truth in the statement that the American Revolution was a civil war in which the King's party at home and in America faced the opponents of royal power in both countries. The American Loyalists, even with British support, were nowhere able to control territory in America unless a major British force was present. But the Opposition in Britain was strong enough to force a change in government after six years of war of attrition that had brought nothing but useless local victories and the defeat of two British armies.

The worst disadvantage of the British was the distance at which this war of extensive conquest had to be fought. Troops and supplies had to be transported across 3000 miles of ocean. Such an operation strained the capacity of the slow ships of the period, and American privateers multiplied the difficulty. Added to this was the fact that the three most important maritime powers besides Britain—France, Spain, and The Netherlands—entered the war against her while the other European powers joined a hostile "League of Armed Neutrality" and faced her by 1780 with a world-wide conflict in which she had no allies. Heavily opposed at home, attempting to conquer a distant enemy-controlled continent and hold off all Europe, King George III finally gave up. There is poetic if not literal truth in the story that it was the American hornet's nest that drove him insane.

THE WAR: FIRST PHASE, 1776-1778

Time and again Washington avoided the ultimate test of arms by tactics of retreat, and he was wise in so doing, but he knew that retreat never won a war. Bunker Hill had been lost in June 1775, but Washington seized an equally good vantage point on Dorchester Heights and set up cannon capable of bombarding the British troops in Boston. As a result, General Sir William Howe ordered Boston evacuated on March 17, 1776. Washington marched to New York the portion of his soldiers who were willing to go. Howe waited at Halifax for his brother, the Admiral, to arrive with reinforcements. In July, the combined British forces entered New York harbor and full-fledged war was imminent, though the Howes asked first to parley. Congress designated Benjamin Franklin to meet them at Staten Island. Since he was instructed to negotiate on no basis except American independence, and the Howes had nothing to offer except clemency to the rebels if they surrendered, there was no negotiation. Washington's untrained troops were outnumbered almost two to one, but he decided to fight, partly because a demonstration would support the New York patriots in their struggle with Loyalists.

Long Island to Valley Forge

The American regiments on Long Island, outflanked as a result of faulty intelligence, were dangerously defeated there on August 27, 1776, but retreated skillfully to Manhattan after a disappointing performance in the field. General Howe landed on the southern tip of the island, occupied New York, and forced Washington to retreat to Harlem Heights, where he won a minor victory in September before retreating further. It was about this time that Nathan Hale was hanged by the British as a spy after uttering words that were cherished by American patriots ever afterward: "I only regret that I have but one life to lose for my country." If this was not the darkest hour of the Revolution, as it has been called, it was probably the most confused period of Washington's leadership; he seemed to be groping in a fog. After an engagement at White Plains, which was a defeat though costly to the enemy, he retreated into New Jersey. The American forces were dangerously dispersed. Fort Washington on the Hudson, which was not evacuated in time, was taken by direct British assault, and Fort Lee across the river was abandoned with the loss of precious stores. These events fitted nicely into the British strategic plan, which was to sever the colonies by effecting a meeting between troops under Sir Guy Carleton moving down the waterways from Canada, and the Howes in New York. This might have succeeded at this time had not Benedict Arnold, who had retreated after the failure of the Canadian expedition, fought a masterful naval action against Carleton on Lake Champlain in October, so that the latter gave up for that year (1776) and returned north.

The British pursued Washington across New Jersey. His forces had already dwindled alarmingly because of desertions and the expirations of enlistments. The terms of so many others were to run out by the end of the year that it looked as though he would soon be without an army. Congress forsook Philadelphia for Baltimore. In the middle of December, Major General Charles Lee, who was extremely critical of Washington and had delayed bringing up his forces to join the commander-in-chief, was captured by a British patrol through his own imprudence. The game appeared to be nearly up when Washington executed a brilliant counterstroke. From his encampment in Pennsylvania on the west side of the Delaware, he took his troops in small boats back across the river—now floating with ice—and captured nearly a thousand surprised Hessians at Trenton the day after Christmas. Washington himself said, "this is a glorious day for our country." General

Lord Cornwallis was immediately dispatched with what seemed an overwhelming force to capture the "Old Fox," but the Americans evaded the main body, handily defeated a detachment at Princeton in January, and then retired to the hills at Morristown to make winter quarters. The men who had been induced to stay a little beyond their term soon departed, and the British could hardly have known how weak Washington was. As a result of his brilliant campaign they abandoned most of New Jersey, and before summer fresh enlistments had swelled his little army.

The British plan for the year 1777 was still to effect a union between the forces in Canada, which were to be led by Burgoyne in this invasion, and those in New York. But first General Howe was to move on Philadelphia. Luckily for the Americans, the co-ordination of the widely separated British land and sea forces was imperfect. There was no good way to prevent Howe from attaining his immediate objective. Early in the summer, availing himself of sea power and considerably mystifying his foes, he took most of his forces toward Philadelphia by way of the Chesapeake Bay and head of the Elk River, thus avoiding the forts on the Delaware. Washington placed his army in Howe's path at Brandywine Creek southwest of Philadelphia, but, partly because of the failure of his intelligence, suffered a defeat (September 11, 1777). The British occupied Philadelphia and Congress fled to York, Pennsylvania. Noting that the forces of the enemy were divided, Washington tried desperately in October to match the stroke he had made at Trenton, but his operations at Germantown were too complicated, a fog handicapped his movements, and a near-victory was turned into a defeat. He was unable to retrieve his fortunes before he made winter quarters at Valley Forge, some twenty miles from Philadelphia. He had maintained his army, which was the most important thing, and it was there that he really trained it, but his prestige was dimmed at just the time that other military leaders were gaining bright laurels.

Burgoyne's Surrender

In the North, a decisive and almost incredible victory was won at Saratoga. "Gentleman Johnny" Burgoyne led upwards of 7000 troops south from Canada in leisurely fashion and took Ticonderoga on July 6, 1777. The loss of the cannon and ammunition there was serious for the Americans but Burgoyne was already oversupplied with both. He and his officers, including Baron Riedesel, the genial commander of the German mercenaries, would not sacrifice their comfort for the sake of speed, and the ponderous invading army proceeded through the forests at a snail-like pace. They ran out of supplies and the farmers of New England and New York were given time to rally. Militiamen harried Burgoyne's troops, built roadblocks, destroyed bridges and cornfields,

and drove away cattle. The British at length reached Fort Edward, but Burgoyne hesitated to cross the Hudson at Saratoga and push on to Albany without sufficient supplies. He sent a motley detachment of British, Indian, Tory, and German troops under Colonel Baum, who spoke no English, to capture supplies in Bennington, Vermont.

The stroke was intended to win by surprise, but the German and British troops wore cumbersome and dazzling European uniforms. Unable to hide, they made excellent targets for militiamen as they crashed through the forests. The Green Mountain Boys rallied near Bennington, and General John Stark took command. "Wherever the King's forces point," Burgoyne complained, "militia, to the amount of three or four thousand assemble in twenty-four hours." Burgoyne had the support of the Six Nations of the Iroquois Confederation to offset the rebel militia; but he was appalled by the savagery they directed against Loyalists as well as patriots, and he lost their support when he insisted on civilized restraints. Meanwhile, their atrocities had excited the Americans to fever pitch. The wily Yankees played upon the British conviction that Loyalists would rally in force wherever British troops appeared. On his march to Bennington, Colonel Baum handed out arms freely to Green Mountain Boys who asked for them. When a large party asked for admission into his lines as Loyalists, he instructed his outposts to welcome them. Once inside, the Yankees opened fire, rushing up to the mouths of cannon to pick off artillerymen. In a mountain pass west of Bennington, Baum's forces were practically destroyed (August 16, 1777) and he himself was mortally wounded.

Part of the British plan was for Colonel St. Leger to proceed eastward from Fort Oswego on Lake Ontario, whither he had come from Canada by water, and to join Burgoyne, but he was held up by the stubborn defense of Ft. Stanwix, to which he was forced to lay siege. General Herkimer and his militia were ambushed when they sought to relieve the fort and forced to retire after heroic fighting. But when Benedict Arnold led troops into the Mohawk Valley against St. Leger, the latter, deserted by his Indian allies, gave up the siege of Fort Stanwix (August 24) and retreated. Both of Burgoyne's flanks were exposed by these American successes at Bennington and Stanwix. His Indian allies deserted him, and the Canadians, losing interest in fighting Britain's battles, took off for home. Burgoyne had no reason to expect aid from Howe, who had to contend with Washington's army, and that British general had turned southward to Philadelphia when things seemed to be going well in the North. Meanwhile, the mutual suspicions of Yorkers and New Englanders, on which the British had depended to weaken patriot opposition, were dissipated when Congress gave command in the North to General Horatio Gates. The New Englanders regarded General Philip Schuyler as a "damned Dutch aristocrat," and they were unjust to his real achievements, but they rallied with enthusiasm to Gates. New Englanders swarmed in from the east, American forces from the Mohawk Valley moved into positions on Burgoyne's west flank, and General Washington spared a few Continental troops who came up from the South. General Clinton, left in New York with a small body of troops, attempted to come to Burgoyne's relief, but he was too late.

Incapable of imagining defeat, General Burgoyne courageously moved across the Hudson and attempted to break out of the American ring near Saratoga. The Americans held firm. In the fighting at Freeman's Farm and Bemis Heights, Benedict Arnold particularly distinguished himself. Sharpshooters picked off officers in the British camp; food supplies ran low; and champagne parties for the officers' ladies gave way to hospital duties for them. The Americans repelled assaults on their lines and poured ceaseless fire into the British camp. In October, Burgoyne, who now had bullet holes in his gorgeous uniform, asked for surrender terms. Then the onlookers witnessed the extraordinary spectacle of British troops stacking their arms in front of American rebels while the band played "Yankee Doodle," and this was duly reported to the incredulous world. A goodly number of British aristocrats and a dozen members of Parliament were bagged. Burgoyne at dinner with Gates proposed a toast to George Washington. Released on parole to return to England, the defeated General did his utmost to dispel the myth that Americans would not fight. Although Englishmen were loath to believe that Burgoyne's conduct of the campaign had not been at fault, the French accepted Saratoga as proof that the American cause was worth backing to the limit. For this reason, the victory is rightly called the turning point in the War for Independence.

THE FRENCH ALLIANCE

Prior to Saratoga, French aid to the American cause was tendered cautiously under cover of neutrality and in fear that a victorious Britain would turn on France. Silas Deane, agent of Congress in France since the spring of 1776, was privately welcomed by officials there and was allowed to fit out American privateers in French ports. King Louis XVI himself had little interest in the American cause, but his foreign minister, Vergennes, worked with such enthusiasts as the playwright Caron de Beaumarchais to send aid to America. In September 1776, Congress sent Arthur Lee and Benjamin Franklin to join Deane as commissioners, hoping to obtain public recognition of American independence. Franklin was now seventy years old and famous in Europe as a scientist and philosopher, but his greatest achievements still lay ahead. In France he was lionized by the sophisticated as the apotheosis of the "natural man" —simple and wise, virtuous and witty. The New World sage carefully cultivated his popularity for its value to his country. Throwing away his powdered wig, he wore a frontiersman's fur cap—and the French ladies promptly imitated his romantic headgear with a hair-do *à la Franklin*. His portrait appeared everywhere, the worlds of fashion and learning vied for his company, and crowds followed him wherever he went. Franklin's head was not turned, but he clothed his extraordinary diplomatic skill in the modest benevolence of the true "friend of man."

More than diplomatic skill was needed to bring the French monarchy to a public alliance with the American enemies of monarchy. The treasury was approaching that depleted state which precepitated the Revolution of

1789. Recognition of American independence would inevitably bring war with Great Britain. French officials fearsomely studied the chances and refused to go beyond secret aid until they got news of Burgoyne's surrender. Then Franklin made a master stroke. The events at Saratoga caused the government of Lord North to consider making concessions in order to end the American rebellion. His offer amounted to that complete self-government within the empire which patriots had asked for prior to 1776, but now it was too late. Congress had firmly instructed Franklin to accept no terms short of British recognition of American independence. Nevertheless, he entered into negotiations with a British agent and carefully implanted the idea among French officials that their great opportunity to disrupt the British Empire would be lost if they did not hurry to offer attractive terms.

Thus Franklin devised the diplomatic strategy which was to be used by the American government in many later situtaions. This was to exploit the disunity and rivalries of the European powers by threatening to throw America's weight onto one side or another, as circumstances dictated, in order to obtain advantage for the United States. It seemed to Vergennes that a reunion of Britain and her former colonies would result in an assault on France which would strip her of the remnants of her empire in the West Indies. If, on the other hand, France combined with the United States against Great Britain, success in establishing American independence seemed quite likely. American trade would be diverted from England to France, the United States would become a strong economic and political support of France, and that country could reassert its supremacy on the continent of Europe. These were the arguments that Vergennes urged on his King, and the young and weak-willed Louis XVI succumbed to them. His Finance Minister, Turgot, warned him that war with Britain would ruin his government, but the King dismissed Turgot and plunged ahead. It was a decision that was vital for the American cause and suicidal for the French monarchy.

France was bound in the Bourbon Family Compact of 1761 to make war only in company with Spain, and she needed the help of the Spanish Navy if her own fleet was to avoid quick defeat by that of the British. But the Spanish government of Charles III was fearful that a successful American republic would seize possessions of Spain in the New World and give encouragement to rebels in her colonies. Vergennes offered Gibraltar and the Floridas to Spain, and did not hesitate to bait the hook with promised territory between the Appalachians and the Mississippi River—thus indicating the dangers to the United States which accompanied its entry into the game of European power politics. Still Charles III hesitated to embrace the cause of rebellion against monarchy, so Vergennes went ahead without Spain.

He wanted a binding commitment from the United States to be

France's permanent ally in return for recognition and large-scale military aid. Congress hesitated to make a permanent alliance in order to win the independence which was intended to sever America from European leading strings, but the practical necessities of the moment prevailed, and instructions were sent to the commissioners to give Vergennes what he wanted. At its inception, American foreign policy was geared to participation in European politics to whatever extent might be necessary to secure American interest, without regard for isolationist preferences.

The Treaties of 1778

Accordingly, on February 6, 1778, Franklin, Deane, and Lee signed two treaties with the government of Louis XVI. The first was a treaty of recognition, amity, and commerce. In it France recognized the independence of the United States of America and agreed with this new sovereign power on terms of commercial co-operation and international law. Each government accorded to the other "most-favored-nation" status, that is, granted to its shipping and trade the most favorable terms accorded to any other power. Liberal rules of international law were adopted in conformity with the "Plan of 1776" which Congress had drawn up for incorporation in all American treaties. These rules were adapted to the situation of governments having small navies but large merchant marines. They affirmed that in wartime neutral-owned ships might carry belligerent-owned cargoes of noncontraband and be immune from capture by any enemy ("free ships make free goods"); and that contraband be defined narrowly to exclude naval stores, food, clothing, and money, leaving little but arms and ammunition subject to capture when carried on a neutral ship. In the current situation the French and the Americans wanted neutrals like the Dutch to carry supplies for them, and the Franco-American rules contradicted those favorable to a big-navy power which Britain followed. The American Plan of 1776 contained the seeds of a world-wide alliance of maritime powers against Great Britain, and the French treaty was its first fruit.

The other treaty was one of permanent military and political alliance, the only treaty of the sort that the United States signed until after the Second World War. Both governments agreed to wage war against Great Britain until American independence was assured; to conclude no separate truce or peace with Great Britain; and to guarantee each other's possessions in America "forever against all other powers." In the territorial provisions, France showed that it was not recovery of her empire in North America that she sought: if Canada were wrested from Great Britain, it should become part of the United States, and France could acquire only such West Indian Islands as might be taken from the

enemy. Thus the risk of the return of French power to the northern and
western frontiers of the United States was guarded against. Vergennes believed that the erection of an independent republic in North America was
enough to strengthen France by weakening Britain.

The terms of the French treaties were amazingly favorable to the
young and struggling republic. Only the clause making the alliance
permanent could be construed as disadvantageous, because it might lead
the United States into some future war on the French side when American interests would demand neutrality or opposition. But the makers of
American foreign policy in 1778 considered this risk preferable to that
of defeat in the current war. In January, Lord North had introduced in
Parliament his bills granting self-government within the Empire to the
Americans, and these were passed early in March. Franklin had incited
the two greatest powers in the world to compete for American friendship. Their offers raced across the Atlantic, and the patriots in and out
of Congress did not hesitate. In 1775, they might have accepted "dominion status" but now they chose independence. Carping voices were raised
that the French Alliance would bring absolute monarchy and popery to
crush American freedom, and there was plentiful irony in the spectacle
of Louis XVI embracing American radicals as his "very dear great friends
and allies." But the patriots rejoiced over the Alliance as a brilliant
American diplomatic victory.

After signing the treaties, the American commissioners were publicly
received by Louis XVI in a brilliant court ceremony, and the king sent
Conrad Gérard as his minister plenipotentiary to the United States.
Congress, mightily impressed, tried to receive him with fitting ceremony.
It also attempted as a body to carry on negotiations with him, but the
impracticality of a legislature's assuming the functions of a foreign office
soon led to the creation of an executive Committee for Foreign Affairs to
conduct day-to-day business under the supervision of Congress. The
actions of Gérard and of his successor, La Luzerne, showed that the
French government intended to make the United States a satellite serving
French interests. They did their best to take control of American foreign
relations away from Congress and turn it over to Vergennes, and succeeded to the extent that Congress instructed its commissioners in France
to subordinate themselves to the French Foreign Office. Fortunately,
Franklin and his colleagues did not obey these instructions.

The aid France now sent to America was extremely generous. Direct
loans provided almost the only hard money Congress had to bolster up
issues of Continental paper. Many French officers with the connivance of
their government had already volunteered for service in America. While
most of them only sought high rank and pay, a few, notably the gallant and
idealistic if vainglorious young Marquis de Lafayette, were genuinely
devoted to the patriot cause. Now the French government ordered its

military and naval forces to join the war. In March 1778, while France was still at peace with Britain, the French fleet under command of the Count d'Estaing and carrying 4000 soldiers sailed out of the Mediterranean and across the Atlantic to deliver a blow against the British naval and land forces at Philadelphia. France and Britain formally declared war in June 1778.

Isolation of the British

The Spanish government resented the French violation of the Family Compact. Charles III decided that it would be wise to prolong the war and thereby weaken the Americans, and that Spain might, without joining them, go to war against Britain in order to win Gibraltar and other positions. Spain made a few secret loans to the United States under cover of personal favors to American agents, but would not hear of recognizing American independence. She extorted from France extraordinary terms which were incorporated in the secret Convention of Aranjuez in April, 1779. The most important provision was that France would continue fighting until Britain gave up Gibraltar to Spain. Since the United States was committed to France to make no separate peace, this meant that the Americans, without knowing it, were now committed to fight until Spain won the rock of Gibraltar.

All Europe seemed ready to seize the opportunity of Britain's embarrassment in America to settle old scores with the mistress of the seas. The Dutch built up a booming trade with the United States by way of their Caribbean island of St. Eustatius. Under protection of their neutral flag, and of a special Anglo-Dutch agreement on the principle "free ships make free goods," the Dutch carried an enormous quantity of supplies of all kinds to the little island, where they were transferred to ships which ran them into American ports. The British government decided that war with the Dutch was preferable to toleration of this trade, and therefore declared war in December 1780. The Dutch government was only slightly more sympathetic with the American cause than the Spanish government, but Dutch bankers made loans to the United States which kept the American government afloat when French loans gave out. In October 1782, when peace was at hand, the Dutch government entered into a treaty with the United States which recognized the independence of the latter and contained liberal trade provisions, the second such treaty in American history.

Meanwhile, no less an autocrat than Catherine the Great of Russia turned to harry Britain and thus to aid the American rebels. In 1780, she organized the "League of Armed Neutrality," comprising all the remaining maritime powers of Europe. This League threatened to use force to protect neutral shipping against the British fleet. It adopted the principles of the American Plan of 1776 and faced Britain with the possibility of war with all Europe unless she permitted neutrals freely to carry cargoes owned by Americans or other enemies. Vergennes saw the League as an instrument conducive to the recovery of French power in Europe and encouraged it accordingly, just as he had incited the Dutch to offend Britain to the point of war.

Thus the American Revolution was utilized by the European Powers to further their own ends. They aided the American cause in varying degree in order to pull Great Britain down from the world supremacy she had won in 1763. The American War became almost a sideshow in the struggle of Europe to re-establish the balance of power. The scheme of Vergennes to displace Britain on the continent of Europe was remarkably successful. By 1780, Britain was fighting with her back to the wall. The necessity to protect shipping and possessions in the seven seas overextended the British Navy, and it lost control of the English Channel for the first time in a century. The raids on the English coasts by the intrepid John Paul Jones were an evidence of this.

It was scarcely possible for Americans to win the war without the direct and indirect aid of the European Powers. The gamble of rebellion had been premised on calculations of such aid, and American diplomacy was exerted to widen the breach between Britain and her rivals. The Republic in its infancy was entangled in the politics of the Old World, and accepted all the attendant risks in order to attain the great goal of freedom.

YEARS OF TRIAL, 1778-1779

The surrender of Burgoyne at Saratoga was of little help to General Washington during the winter of 1777-1778. General Howe established his forces pleasantly in Philadelphia, where a good share of the people of wealth and fashion welcomed them. The officers were feted in a gay round of dinners, balls, and theatricals. Farmers of the surrounding countryside eagerly carried provisions into the city in exchange for hard money. General Howe had hit upon the comfortable strategy of waiting for starvation and disaffection to defeat Washington's Army.

Ordeal in the East

The strategy was not at all unreasonable. Washington fixed on Valley Forge as winter quarters because it was within striking distance of Philadelphia, and he hoped to maintain a menacing attitude towards Howe's Army, but the condition of his troops became so pitiful that he could do no more than hold a remnant together. The soldiers had literally worn out their clothing in the summer campaign; some huddled naked in dugouts, while others stood guard or gathered firewood in the snow without shoes or shirts. Officers of high rank used scraps of blankets for clothing. Farmers scorned Continental paper money and refused to bring food into the camp. Some of the troops starved, many more died of disease, and hundreds deserted.

What had happened to the patriot cause that its champions were subjected to such horrors? The ineffectiveness of Congress and the agencies it had created, and its inability to coerce the states to meet requisitions, were part of the answer. Equally or more important was the unwillingness of civilians to sacrifice opportunities for private gain in a time of low public credit and skyrocketing prices. While the Army starved and froze, food and clothing sought more promising markets.

The troops at Valley Forge felt themselves neglected by Congress and abandoned by the people at large. One soldier wrote: "Poor food— hard lodging—Cold Weather—fatigue—Nasty Cloaths—nasty Cookery— Vomit half my time—smoak'd out of my senses—the Devil's in it—I can't Endure it—Why are we sent here to starve and freeze?" Vermin invaded the camp. General Anthony Wayne forced himself to visit every hut of his troops once a week, and often wished he had neither sight nor hearing. An impetuous fighter, "Mad Anthony" Wayne preferred a hopeless attack on the British to inaction. But the troops lacked arms as well as shoes, and they could not even attack enemy foraging parties. The miracle of Valley Forge was that a remnant of the soldiers remained loyal and justified Washington's iron determination to hold out, to maintain an army at all costs.

The soldiers did more than hold out. Tried and toughened, they became the nucleus of a new army. General von Steuben, a Prussian volunteer, was appointed adjutant general and whipped this ragged remnant into a disciplined fighting force. He applied Prussian drill techniques, which he wisely accommodated to the temper of the Americans. He said that in the Prussian army a soldier obeyed orders without question. But in the American army he was obliged to say to a soldier, "This is the reason why you ought to do that," and then the soldier did it. Steuben was a remarkable combination of slave driver and democrat, and the men learned from him the arts of drill, tactics, and maneuver. Seldom before or since have American soldiers risen more nobly to the challenge sounded by Tom Paine in the first of his *American Crisis* pamphlets:

> These are the times that try men's souls. The summer soldier and the sunshine patriot will, in this crisis, shrink from the service of their country; but he that stands it *now*, deserves the love and thanks of man and woman. Tyranny, like hell, is not easily conquered; yet we have this consolation with us, that the harder the conflict, the more glorious the triumph.

Washington himself came through the winter strengthened by adversity. The "Conway Cabal" attempted to displace him as commander-in-

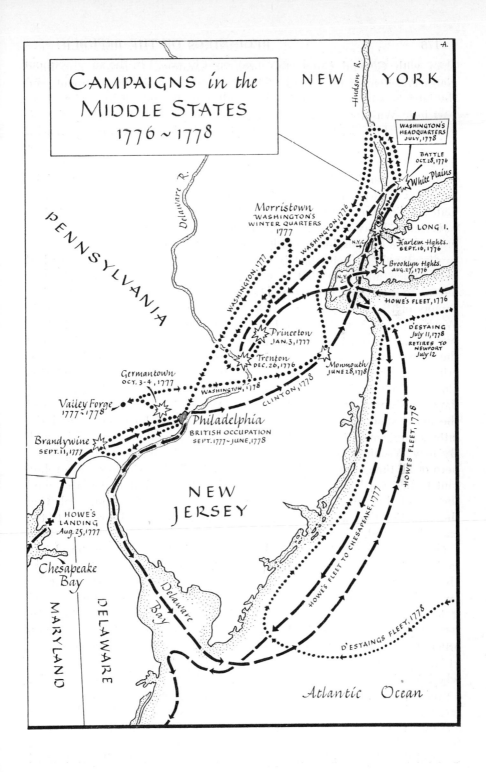

CAMPAIGNS in the
MIDDLE STATES
1776 ~ 1778

NEW YORK

PENNSYLVANIA

Delaware R.

Morristown
WASHINGTON'S
WINTER QUARTERS
1777

WASHINGTON 1777

WASHINGTON 1776

WASHINGTON'S
HEADQUARTERS
JULY, 1778

BATTLE
OCT. 28, 1776

White Plains

LONG I.

N.Y.C.

Harlem Hghts.
SEPT. 16, 1776

Brooklyn Hghts.
AUG. 27, 1776

N.Y.C.

HOWE'S FLEET, 1776

D'ESTAING
July 11, 1778
RETIRES TO
NEWPORT
July 12

Princeton
JAN. 3, 1777

Trenton
DEC. 26, 1776

Monmouth
JUNE 28, 1778

CLINTON, 1778

Germantown
OCT. 3-4, 1777

Valley Forge
1777 ~ 1778

WASHINGTON, 1778

Philadelphia
BRITISH OCCUPATION
SEPT. 1777 ~ JUNE, 1778

Brandywine
SEPT. 11, 1777

HOWE'S FLEET, 1778

NEW
JERSEY

HOWE'S FLEET TO CHESAPEAKE 1777

HOWE'S
LANDING
Aug. 25, 1777

Chesapeake
Bay

Delaware Bay

MARYLAND

DELAWARE

D'ESTAINGS FLEET, 1778

Atlantic Ocean

chief with General Gates, the hero of Saratoga. Congress appointed Gates President of the Board of War, an embryo War Department, and the intrigue was carried on in his behalf, whether or not he had a direct part in it. Washington's defeats could be compared unfavorably with his glorious victory, and some Congressional leaders were unduly fearful that the Commander-in-Chief would turn into a military dictator. Thomas Conway, a former French officer of Irish birth whose promotion to major general had been opposed by Washington but was voted by Congress anyway, made insolent references to the latter in a letter to Gates which seems to have been destroyed. Conway was reported to have said: "Heaven has determined to save your country or a weak general and bad counselors would have ruined it." Gates's bungling efforts to disentangle himself—first by saying that the letter from Conway had been stolen and then that it was forged—and Washington's vigorous letters to him and Congress discredited him. Towards spring, when rumors of the "plot" became widespread, there was a sharp reaction in Washington's favor. The people and Congress rallied to him and Gates was soon removed to a subordinate command. The selfless patriotism of the Commander-in-Chief was all but universally appreciated, and his critics were helpless in the face of his enormous prestige and popularity. Conway's loose talk was not wholly quieted until summer. Then he was dangerously wounded in a duel with General John Cadwalader, one of the many staunch supporters of Washington, and he soon begged the latter's forgiveness. "You are in my eyes the great and good man," he said. By now Washington had become to nearly all Americans the greatest hero of all time, and this view of him persisted. Doctrinaires were reluctant to believe that a republic has need of heroes; but it was the good fortune of the American Republic to find one who, far from exploiting the adulation that was accorded him, made it a source of strength to the cause he served.

One day in the spring of 1778, Washington's Army was mustered into ranks to hear the news of the French Alliance, and broke into hoarse cheers. The British authorities relieved the gouty General Howe at his own request and gave his command to Sir Henry Clinton, who assumed it in May with orders to evacuate Philadelphia. This he did in June, setting out for New York by land with a long baggage train. Washington ordered an attack on the slow-moving British at Monmouth Courthouse in New Jersey. He entrusted the advance corps to General Charles Lee, who had recently entered into ambiguous relations with the enemy while a prisoner of war. Almost before the action began, that officer ordered a retreat. Then occurred perhaps the most famous instance of Washington's loss of temper. A French officer said later: "I saw for the first time what fury was, because anything more appallingly terrible than the face of General Washington when he appeared on the scene and galloped toward

Lee, I have never seen, nor has any one else. It was like the God of Battles intent to kill or destroy." Washington called Lee a coward, thundered a volley of oaths at him, and set about reorganizing the lines. They held, but during the night the British went on toward New York and the attack could not be renewed. A court-martial found Lee guilty on several counts, including disobedience to orders. At Monmouth Court-house Washington saved the newly trained American Army from disaster, and he claimed a victory, but the losses were about even.

Clinton was in New York when a French fleet under d'Estaing approached. The latter, hesitating to force his way into the harbor against Lord Howe's warships, turned instead to Rhode Island. Washington was thus disappointed, as he was several times thereafter, in his hope of co-operating by land with the French in an attack on Clinton. In Newport, the British had developed a strong naval base. New England militiamen under General John Sullivan flocked to attack this by land in support of d'Estaing, but delays that were caused by the difficulties of co-ordination gave time for Lord Howe, whose fleet had been reinforced, to sail from New York to Newport. Before the French could give battle, a storm separated the two fleets and d'Estaing then took his ships to Boston. "Heroes of Flight" was what Sullivan's disgusted troops called them. In the fall, the French fleet went to the West Indies. It damaged the British there, but the first results of Franco-American military co-operation were slight indeed. The New Englanders gave up the attack on Newport, and Washington ended the year (1778) in camp at White Plains, New York—where he had been two years before, when the British were in Manhattan. After all his maneuvering he was back where he had started.

The War in the West

A notable success in the West was achieved in 1778-1779 by Lieutenant-Colonel George Rogers Clark and a body of Virginia frontier militia. They floated down the Ohio past the mouth of the Tennessee, marched overland to the Mississippi, and captured the fort of Kaskaskia in July 1778. Clark then took possession of Cahokia, farther up the river, and extended his authority to Vincennes on the Wabash—the whole region being organized as the county of Illinois, State of Virginia. But Lieutenant Governor Henry Hamilton of Detroit, notorious on the frontier as the "hair-buyer," recaptured Vincennes, and Clark performed his greatest exploit when he and his little band marched heroically across the drowned lands in the dead of winter and took it back in February 1779. They also took Hamilton, who was sent as a prisoner to Williamsburg. Thus Americans fought for and won territory which had been forbidden them by the British legislation of 1774. There is no record, however, that the victories of Clark and his men were used by the commissioners in the final peace negotiations as arguments for American possession of the West. Nor did Clark himself accomplish his full purpose—to destroy the Indian menace at its source by capturing the British posts, whence the Indians were incited. He was never able to take Detroit, the main enemy post.

At about this time the British were making a special effort to enlist Indian allies. This was not in the spirit of the Howe brothers but it was in that of Lord George Germain, who was directing military affairs in England, and of the commissioners who bore Lord North's conciliatory proposal to America in June 1778, and were infuriated when Congress would neither receive nor discuss it. Lord Carlisle, the head of the commission, urged his government to wage a war of extermination against the rebels; and he issued a proclamation threatening the Americans with burning and pillaging—in modern terminology, with total war. Whigs in Parliament expressed horror when scalping knives appeared on the lists of army supplies, but the ministry asserted that if it did not hire the savages, the Americans would. Generally speaking, the Indians fought on the British side because the rewards were greater. In 1778 and 1779, the frontier was terrorized by Indian raiding parties in which Loyalists strongly participated. Colonel John Butler, a Tory, was the leader in the Wyoming Massacre in Pennsylvania in the summer of 1778; and his son Walter joined hands with the Mohawk chief Joseph Brant in the Cherry Valley Massacre in New York State in the fall. An expedition led by General John Sullivan in 1779 wreaked terrible vegeance on scores of Indian villages in New York, but it did not fully accomplish its purpose since it never reached Fort Niagara, the real seat of the trouble, and Brant continued to harass the frontier.

*　*　*

So far as the main forces were concerned, the war in 1779 degenerated into raiding. Washington strengthened his defenses on the Hudson, particularly at West Point, guarding against the old British plan of dividing the rest of the states from New England. Fortifications were started by him at Stony Point and constructed at Verplanck's Point. Clinton seized both of these points in a sudden rally, but did not succeed in drawing the "Old Fox" from his lair. Washington's plan was to take them back, and this was admirably executed by General Anthony Wayne with troops drawn from the new Light Infantry who were well trained in bayonet fighting. More prophetic were the British raids to the south, in which use could be made of sea power. Such a raid toward the end of 1778 led to the capture of the port of Savannah. An ill-co-ordinated Franco-American attempt to recapture the city failed in the following autumn. Washington continued to hope that his Army and the French Navy could engage in a successful joint operation against Clinton in New York, but for the time being he had to content himself with watchful waiting.

LAST PHASES OF THE WAR, 1780-1781

Meanwhile, in England, Lord North became disgusted with the whole enterprise of the war and begged his King to relieve him of office, but George III saw the triumph of the Whigs as the only alternative to North's ministry and forced him to carry on. The King now tortured himself with fears that England faced ruin and the loss of all her colonies —which would be followed by invasion by the French and Spanish and defeat in the home islands. These nightmares steeled him to continue the struggle in the face of rising opposition. As if to give support to his fears, the Irish, feeling themselves even worse victims of British tyranny than the Americans, raised claims and an army ominously like those of the American patriots. The North ministry quickly made concessions to them, including some relaxation of restraints against Irish industry and Roman Catholicism, but this liberalism only resulted in riots in England itself by Protestants who raised the cry: "No Popery!" One mob forced the members of Parliament to barricade themselves and maltreated members of the ministry.

These "Lord George Gordon Riots," so named after their Scottish leader, exposed rotten features of the English society of the era. The bitter poverty of London slum dwellers led them to turn political demonstrations into wild uprisings for bread and plunder, and fires were set all over London. After the rioters with great difficulty had been put down, the Americans were blamed: it was said that Dr. Franklin's agents were the instigators. Franklin had indeed hoped for a liberal reform or revolutionary development in England, but the riots actually put an end to attempts by responsible Whigs to reform the government, and fear of mob rule strengthened the King's hand. He was able to win the elections of 1780 for his supporters in time-honored fashion by paying out huge sums of money and dealing out plums on the civil list.

King George came through the crisis of 1780 strengthened in his determination to win the war. During that year and the early part of the next, American fortunes declined to their lowest point since the weeks before Trenton. Clinton followed up the allied failure at Savannah by taking the garrison from Rhode Island and sailing with a strong force to South Carolina. In May, he took Charleston and all the American forces with it. He returned to New York with part of his Army, leaving Lord Cornwallis in charge. There were many Loyalists in the Carolinas, but there were also patriot bands under such leaders as Sumter and Marion. These harassed the British regulars and waged bitter civil war against the Loyalists.

Treason and Mutiny

This was the year of Benedict Arnold's treason. Offended because Congress failed to take him at his own high estimate, Arnold, as military governor of Philadelphia after Howe's departure, turned to luxurious living, spurred on by his extravagant young wife, Peggy Shippen, and was eager to cut a wide social swath among the Loyalists of the Quaker City. Desperate for money, and resentful because of a reprimand which was recommended by a court-martial as a result of his irregularities, he turned to the British. He had been giving military information to them for some time when, in order to increase his value, he had himself appointed commander of West Point so that he could sell this key fortification to the British along with his own honor.

Clinton was wary and demanded first-hand evidence from Arnold that he would indeed betray West Point. He sent his aide, Major André, up the Hudson to meet Arnold behind the American lines. André's ship was forced by American fire to return without him and, unluckily for the gay and witty Major, he was carrying incriminating papers and wearing a disguise instead of his uniform. Attempting to return by land, he was captured and executed as a spy. Arnold heard of his capture in the nick of time and escaped to New York. The British did not like him and paid him less than he wanted, but he got a brigadier general's commission and more than £6000 altogether. The Americans had prided themselves on the purity and faithfulness of their leaders, and Arnold's treason was a severe blow to their morale, but fortunately he had no confederates. The patriots burned him in effigy and it was commonly said that no man since Judas Iscariot had earned such black hatred.

Mutiny broke out in the Continental Army a few months after Arnold's treason, though the events were not connected. The underlying reason for the revolt was that the soldiers, largely because of the ineptitude and impotence of Congress, were ill-clad and badly fed and had been long unpaid in a time of spiraling inflation and apparent civilian plenty. The immediate occasion for the mutiny of the Pennsylvania Line, which began on New Year's Day, 1781, and was followed by that of the New Jersey Line, was a dispute over the terms of their enlistment. The regulars claimed that they had signed for only three years, not for the duration, and that they were being held too long. They defied their officers and shed some blood. Clinton sent spies among them and they demonstrated their patriotism by delivering these over for execution. A committee of Congress patched things up with the Pennsylvanians, and the mutiny of the Jerseymen collapsed after a couple of the leaders faced a firing squad. Congress blamed the states for the trouble, but both Congress and the states now bestirred themselves. Conditions were

distinctly improved by summer, thus facilitating Washington's Yorktown
campaign.

From Camden to Yorktown

Meanwhile, there had been major disaster and minor success in the
South, where the war was especially exhausting and destructive. Congress
gave General Gates command of the Southern Department, and he had
an army composed chiefly of militia to employ against the ruthless Cornwallis. In August 1780, Gates's forces were disastrously defeated at
Camden, South Carolina, and the fame of the victor of Saratoga was
sadly dimmed. On Washington's recommendation, he was replaced by
General Nathanael Greene, who organized a new army and waged a
damaging campaign. Employing guerilla tactics, the Americans won minor
victories at King's Mountain (October 6, 1780) and Cowpens (January
17, 1781). Cornwallis moved on into North Carolina, nevertheless, and
appeared to have maneuvered Greene out of the state when the latter
turned and made a stand in March at Guilford Courthouse. He is said
to have made a bargain with his militiamen, who were the butt of jokes
and complaints at this stage, that they should fire two volleys before they
ran away. Cornwallis made Greene retreat but the British casualties
were so great that the victory was worthless. Cutting in behind the Earl,
Greene set out to reconquer the Carolinas, which he did with considerable
success, while Cornwallis plunged into Virginia, creating consternation as
he went.

Washington's own state, to which he never showed any favors, was
now governed by Thomas Jefferson, who had more than his share of
troubles as a war governor. Virginia had been largely denuded of troops
in order to reinforce Gates, who had been defeated, and Greene, who
for reasons that seemed sufficient had turned the other way. The state
was drained of supplies and its treasury was empty. It was practically
defenseless, and in a condition bordering on exhaustion. Clinton had
already dispatched Arnold to this region which was so accessible by sea,
and the latter had conducted a slashing raid before retiring to the coast.
He had afterwards been reinforced by General William Phillips, who
had surrendered with Burgoyne but had been exchanged. Cornwallis
set out to link his forces with theirs and, after devastating the countryside,
to proceed to a seaport whence, as he thought, the transporation of his
troops to New York would be easy. Besides militiamen, only small forces
under Lafayette and Steuben opposed him. He inflicted damage chiefly
by means of raids, the most famous of which was that of Tarleton. This
dashing horseman sought to capture the state legislators, who were in
Charlottesville since Richmond was untenable, and Governor Jefferson
at nearby Monticello. He did not have the satisfaction of catching them,

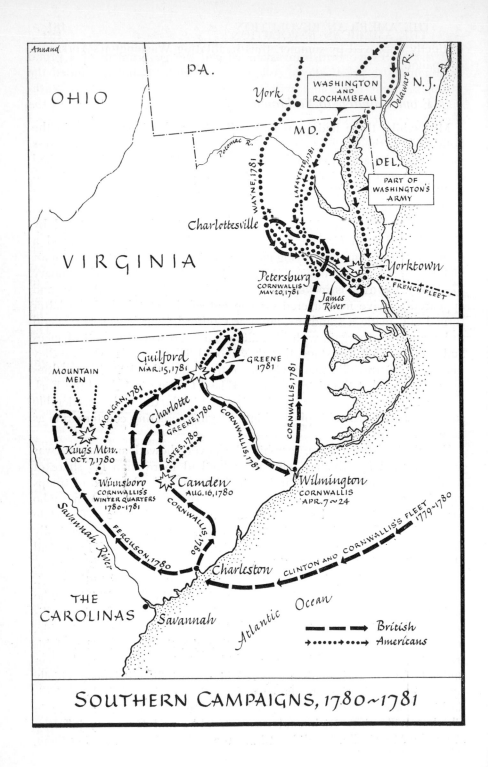

Annand

OHIO

PA.

VIRGINIA

York

WASHINGTON
AND
ROCHAMBEAU

MD.

Potomac R.

DEL.

N.J.

Delaware R.

PART OF
WASHINGTON'S
ARMY

WAYNE, 1781

LAFAYETTE, 1781

Charlottesville

Yorktown

Petersburg
CORNWALLIS
MAY 20, 1781

*James
River*

FRENCH FLEET

MOUNTAIN
MEN

Guilford
MAR. 15, 1781

GREENE
1781

MORGAN, 1781

Charlotte

GREENE, 1780

CORNWALLIS, 1781

CORNWALLIS, 1781

King's Mtn.
OCT. 7, 1780

GATES, 1780

Winnsboro
CORNWALLIS'S
WINTER QUARTERS
1780-1781

Camden
AUG. 16, 1780

Wilmington
CORNWALLIS
APR. 7~24

Savannah River

CORNWALLIS, 1780

CORNWALLIS, 1780

FERGUSON, 1780

CLINTON AND CORNWALLIS'S FLEET
1779~1780

Charleston

THE
CAROLINAS

Savannah

Atlantic Ocean

British

Americans

SOUTHERN CAMPAIGNS, 1780~1781

but the successive British invasions caused the government of a proud commonwealth practically to collapse. Meanwhile, Lafayette eluded the stronger enemy forces and, with General Anthony Wayne, whom Washington had ordered to join him, harassed Cornwallis until at length the Earl arrived at Yorktown, a small port on a deep river near the coast and a safe enough place while the British ruled the sea.

For months Washington had been hoping and planning for a major operation in conjunction with his allies, and French military aid was now available. On a trip to France, from which he returned in the spring of 1780, Lafayette had convinced Vergennes, who had begun to lose interest in this interminable American war, that France must give substantial military and naval aid if the Allies were ever to win it; and in the following summer the Comte de Rochambeau had arrived in Newport with more than 5000 troops. But the French fleet that brought this army was soon bottled up in Newport by the British. One element necessary to victory was lacking—French naval superiority. This was supplied a year later by De Grasse for a brief period that proved long enough, but the aid did not come at the place that Washington had expected. The operation he had in mind was against Clinton in New York, and until the last minute that General expected a move against him. The thought was natural enough, since the forces of Washington and Rochambeau were joined above New York in the summer of 1781. But Cornwallis had got himself into a position which was untenable without naval support, and Washington learned that De Grasse was making for the Chesapeake. Therefore, he quickly and skillfully adjusted his long-cherished plans to a new situation. Instructing Lafayette to keep Cornwallis on the peninsula, deceiving Clinton to the last, and keeping his own troops in ignorance of their destination, he set them moving southward late in August, while Rochambeau's regulars closely followed.

The operations of the Allies were conducted with clocklike precision, while the enemy were confused and baffled. About the time that the ragged Continentals and the white-coated French left Philadelphia, after a review before Congress which gratified the members of that body, the British Admiral Graves sighted De Grasse's ships in the Chesapeake. He engaged them indecisively, and then, discovering that the arrival of the French fleet from Newport had further increased the odds against him, he sailed back to New York. De Grasse, now in full command of the situation, transported most of the Allied troops down Chesapeake Bay, and on September 28 they began the siege of Yorktown. With a large body of Virginia militia that had recently been assembled, the American forces somewhat outnumbered the French, and together they outnumbered the forces of Cornwallis two to one. Clinton organized a relief expedition but it did not actually put to sea until October 19, the day that the unfortunate Earl surrendered.

For the second time an army of British regulars laid down its arms in America. On this momentous occasion the redcoats marched between the French regulars, resplendent in the white dress uniform of the Bourbons, and the Continental Army, which could muster only enough uniforms for the front rank, while the rear ranks stood in rags. Many of the British pretended that they surrendered only to the French, but their own bands played "The World Turned Upside Down" and the French played the rebel "Yankee Doodle."

The news of the surrender at Yorktown came like a stroke of lightning in England. Lord North staggered as if he had been hit. Yet in a military sense the Franco-American victory need not have ended the war. Britain could have looked upon it as a defeat in one campaign and proceeded to mount another. George III, Lord North, and many a Tory leader found it impossible to believe that Britain had lost a war, but the events at Yorktown convinced many others of the correctness of the opposition's view that this war had been a mistake from the beginning. Yorktown turned out to be the last battle primarily because it produced a revulsion in British public opinion that brought another political group to power. A secondary reason was the European situation, which American diplomats skilfully exploited.

PEACE AND INDEPENDENCE

During the winter of 1781-1782, the King and his ministry gradually lost control of Parliament. The landed gentry who had hoped to make Americans pay for the Seven Years' War were disgusted by the redoubling of the national debt; Gibraltar was under siege by the Spaniards; the British Navy had lost control of the West Indies; and even in India, British rule was threatened. It seemed the part of wisdom to make peace in order to avoid complete loss of the British Empire. In February 1782, the Opposition won a majority in Parliament for a motion to make no further effort to reduce the Americans to obedience. Burke, Charles James Fox (who liked to compare the King to Satan), and others now worked to make Yorktown a lever to push the King's Men out of power. George III was forced to allow Lord North to resign in March, and then the Whig Rockingham formed a new government. Later in the year, after Rockingham's death, Shelburne, a follower of the late Earl of Chatham, became head of the ministry. It was his government that made the peace.

In the month of April 1782, Admiral Rodney showed that Britain was far from beaten in the war. He returned to the West Indies and in the Battle of Saints' Passage completely defeated De Grasse. In India also, Britain by the close of the year had put an end to the French threat and the siege of Gibraltar was raised by a relief expedition. In America, strong British forces still controlled New York and Charleston, while there was serious discontent in Washington's unpaid army. In these circumstances, Britain would accept no dictated peace. The new British government set about making peace with the Americans as a positive strategy to divorce the United States from France and re-establish political and economic ties with the former colonies. The Whigs had a normal English fear for the safety of their country in the face of a Europe united against it.

It mattered little to them whether they treated with France or with the United States. In the spring of 1782, they approached the two governments separately, offering peace to each at the price of breaking with the other. Vergennes refused to treat for the United States, but he encouraged Franklin to negotiate separately with the British, on the understanding that no final terms would be agreed upon without French consent.

The Negotiations

The peace commissioners appointed by Congress were Franklin, John Adams, John Jay, Jefferson (who did not serve) and John Laurens (who served very briefly). Instructions from Congress, dated June 1781, had too trustfully imposed on them subservience to the French government regarding terms of settlement. The Americans did not hesitate to disregard their instructions. The canny Franklin saw an interesting opportunity in the situation: by holding out to Britain the possibility of a postwar alliance he might obtain excellent territorial and other terms. He even proposed that Canada be given to the United States as proof of "sweet reconciliation," a gesture which would help the American people forget the cruelties of Great Britain. Beyond that, Franklin dreamed of a pact between Britain, the United States, and France which should substitute arbitration of disputes for wars and give the world a new era of peace.

About the time that Shelburne emerged as chief minister, John Jay returned to Paris from a fruitless mission to Spain, where he had conceived a profound distrust of Vergennes. Jay had some inkling of the French Minister's actual plan to favor Spain in a peace settlement and prevent the United States from gaining sufficient territory to grow powerful and free herself from French leading strings. Jay learned that the French planned to draw the western boundary of the United States at the Alleghenies, thus depriving the Republic of one of its chief goals in the struggle with Great Britain. Vergennes would turn over the West to Spain to compensate for her disappointments elsewhere. Jay, who was equally suspicious of Great Britain, disrupted the delicate machinery of Franklin's plans, and insisted that Britain recognize the independence of the United States before any discussions began—because Vergennes tolerated British references to the United States as "colonies," if for no other reason. Then Jay learned of a secret French mission to London and decided that his country was about to be betrayed by its ally. He gained the support of John Adams against what they considered the complacency of Dr. Franklin with respect to the French.

Vergennes certainly betrayed the spirit of the alliance by telling Shelburne that France would consent to unfavorable British terms for the United States. Jay insisted that he be allowed to deal directly and secretly with the British in order to avert disaster, and Franklin consented. Jay forced the British to recognize American independence prior to negotiations. Shelburne squirmed, hoping to retrieve some sort of Anglo-American federation from the ruins of empire. Still he saw an opportunity to drive a wedge between the French and the Americans, and he agreed, therefore, to extremely generous terms. The Americans signed "Preliminary Articles of Peace" with Great Britain on November 30, 1782. These were virtually unchanged in the final treaty. When Vergennes protested at the failure of the Americans to consult him, Franklin pointed out that they had not made a separate peace and hinted that the British hoped to divide the allies, wherefore he prayed Vergennes to keep their "little misunderstanding" secret. Franklin had already asked for another French loan—and got it. Vergennes, after all, was eager to bring pressure on Spain to make peace without Gibraltar, and the action of the Americans gave him a convenient argument. The diplomacy of Franklin, Jay, and Adams was brilliantly successful in exploiting the rivalries of the European Powers for American advantage. The final treaty was signed with the full approval of France on September 3, 1783, the same day on which that country, Spain, and The Netherlands signed peace treaties with Great Britain.

The Settlement

The United States was the only winner in this settlement of a world war. Besides formally recognizing the independence of the new Republic, the British agreed to magnificent boundaries: the Mississippi River in the West, the Spanish Floridas in the South, and roughly the present boundary in the North. The United States had by no means established its right to the great western territory by force of arms. Britain, France, and Spain all came to regret the territorial terms of the treaty, and time and again they tried to prevent the United States from filling up its giant-sized boots. But they were no better united afterward than in 1783.

Other articles of the peace treaty by their very generosity also gave trouble in the future. Britain recognized the "liberty" of Americans to fish in Canadian waters and they were also to be allowed to dry and cure their fish on certain shores. Debts owed by Americans to British merchants when the Revolution began were made collectible, inasmuch as the treaty promised that the creditors should "meet with no lawful impediment" to their collection. The British also felt that they must do something for the American Loyalists, almost 100,000 of whom had been exiled, otherwise British subjects would hesitate to support the Crown elsewhere in the Empire. After bitter quarrels, the Americans agreed that persecutions should stop and that Congress should "earnestly recommend" to the states that they restore confiscated property of Loyalists who had not borne arms. Both the articles on debts and Loyalists were compromises: Congress could not force the states to act, and the British knew it.

In only one respect did the treaty fail seriously to satisfy American hopes. No commercial arrangements were incorporated in it. Therefore, the young nation was shut out of its formerly protected British market and carrying trade. Americans soon realized that the imperial mercantile system had given their commerce many advantages. The closing of the British West Indies to American shipping was the most serious blow.

France, Spain, and The Netherlands in their treaties with Great Britain obtained practically nothing tangible in return for their war efforts. The French government was content to win greater prestige in the councils of Europe, although the cost of the American adventure was so great that it led to bankruptcy and a revolution which drew some of its inspiration from the American example. The Spanish government regarded this Republic with the utmost suspicion and set out to protect its colonies from the bad example and the expansionist hunger of the North Americans. Yet the suspicion of the Spanish brought them no more safety than French infatuation brought them. The Dutch were not afraid of republics, and they loaned the new government money at excellent rates of interest. But eventually—in the mid-twentieth century—the peoples of Indonesia demanded independence from The Netherlands on the American model.

Many Englishmen regarded the Treaty of Paris of 1783 as the death warrant of their country's greatness. The British negotiators had given away an empire without obtaining any guaranteed compensations such as Franklin had held out in his plan for "sweet reconciliation." The Franco-American Alliance was still in force. Americans, on the other hand, were astonished at the liberality of the boundary terms and objected only to the promises on behalf of Loyalists and debtors. Congress contentedly overlooked the commissioners' disregard of its instructions and ratified the treaty. Rightly, Americans regarded it as the birth certificate of a new nation pledged to principles of liberty and self-government more advanced than any in the world.

Rejoicing over victory and peace did not last long, however. Washington fondly believed, when he resigned his commission as Commander-in-Chief and said his moving words of farewell to his brother officers, that he and every citizen could now return to the simple enjoyment of the fruits of freedom and peace. But soon the condition of the country made it seem exceedingly doubtful that the great experiment could long endure. The main difficulty was that Americans had modified their society in various democratic ways without as yet establishing a government capable of protecting it against chaos at home and enemies abroad.

CHAPTER 11

The Internal Revolution
1776-1786

INDEPENDENCE FROM THE MOTHER COUNTRY WAS THE chief objective and main result of the American Revolution. But many peoples in the world's long history after achieving political independence have lost it by lapsing into anarchy; or, by submitting to dictatorship, they have lost their freedom as individuals. No sooner did the Americans decide to throw off external rule than they were faced with the crucial internal question: Independence for what? Whose notion of the good society should prevail in the new nation? Closely associated with the radicalism which won the vote for independence in the first place was a thoroughgoing plan for the reconstruction of American society on decentralized and democratic lines. Carried far enough, this program contained dangers of anarchy. At the other extreme, certain conservatives, while going along with the radicals in favor of independence after July 4, 1776, cried out against their domestic program and worked to install in America a replica of British society on centralized and aristocratic lines. Carried far enough, this program contained dangers of new tyranny.

The special character of American history derives from the remarkable answer it gave to the radical-conservative conundrum. During the Revolution, democratic features of the radical program were installed, but social anarchy was avoided; conservatism afterward came to power but dictatorship was avoided, and the constructive features of the federal system were permanently established. The Republic is not the creation of any one segment of the American people nor of any one political faction or philosophy. It is a joint result of the labors and dreams of individuals, groups, classes, and parties that were often bitterly opposed to one another in their own times. The Founding Fathers pointed the way to fruitful reconciliation by joining popular rights to nationalism, freedom to security, liberty to order.

STATE CONSTITUTIONS AND BILLS OF RIGHTS

The radicals of 1776 stood for independence, popular rights, and state rights. They opposed compromise with Great Britain, aristocracy, and centralized power. Their program was supported by small farmers and frontiersmen of the outlying regions in the various states, by a number of liberal southern planters, by artisans and occasional merchants of the northern cities, and by a fraction of the educated professional classes everywhere—especially lawyers and dissenting clergymen. The radicals demanded independence in order to secure popular American rights; the British had centralized authority in order to suppress those rights; therefore, logic seemed to require the radicals to oppose centralization of government and to place all power in local governments even after British rule was abolished. Furthermore, this logic coincided with the current view of the philosophers of the Enlightenment that government was evil in proportion as it was distant from the people themselves; therefore, local government was less to be feared as the potential enemy of the people than central government.

Fortified by experience, logic, and philosophy, the radicals strengthened local government and jealously fought off "encroachments" of the Revolutionary central government, which actually was feeble. In the state governments they distinguished between the executive and judicial powers, which were in their view engines of tyranny, and the legislative power, which was in closest contact with the people and therefore most trustworthy. Even within the legislature they drew a distinction between the upper house, traditionally a more aristocratic body close to the executive and sharing some of its functions, and the lower house, the voice of the people. In the thirteen new state governments and the independent republic of Vermont, the courts were hedged about with restrictions and narrow jurisdictions fixed by the constitutions and legislatures; practically everywhere the governor was deprived of veto power over legislation; the upper houses of the legislatures were either abolished as in Pennsylvania or were made subordinate and given little more than advisory functions, while the true seat of power was lodged in the lower houses. These generally held the sole authority to initiate legislation; they held the purse strings in tight rein; they dominated the governors and in many respects the courts. They appointed, instructed, and removed the delegates of the states to the central Congress.

Government by the legislature was no more efficient in the Revolutionary states than in the Confederation; and step by step in later years the states modified their constitutions, distributing legislative authority between two houses and governmental authority among an independent legislature, independent executive, and independent judiciary. In the states as in the federal government, the dilemma between inefficiency on the one hand and potential tyranny on the other was eventually resolved by "separation of powers" among the three branches, and "checks and balances" in the relations of each to the other two. This gradual development within the states was not a defeat for the radicals. Rather, it resulted from their own recognition that a popularly elected executive was as trustworthy as a popular legislature in guarding the people's liberties, and sometimes more so. Furthermore, an independent judiciary could safeguard individuals when legislature and executive faltered. Thus each of the states eventually worked out its own marriage between popular rights and effectiveness in government.

The original state constitutions contained Bills of Rights which, along with the Declaration of Independence, were the charters of modern democracy in America. The Virginia Declaration of Rights (June 12, 1776) is the most famous of these, because it served as a model for many of the others and was typical of all of them. It was largely the work of George Mason, an aristocratic planter of liberal philosophic leanings who asserted the equal freedom of men and stated their inherent rights in much the same way that Jefferson did in the Declaration of Independence. In the Virginia document, magistrates were described as the servants of the people in whom all power is vested, and hereditary privilege was explicitly denied. The right of suffrage was claimed for "all men having sufficient evidence of permanent interest with and attachment to the community." These words were not interpreted in Virginia as requiring the lowering of the property qualifications for voters, but actually these were not high, and in the country generally the tendency was to reduce them. The Virginia Declaration of Rights circumscribed the judicial process with guarantees which became standard for state and federal courts: the right of the accused man to be confronted by accusers and witnesses; speedy trial before an impartial jury; moderate bail; no cruel and unusual punishments; no general warrants for search or arrest. It also called for freedom of the press, subordination of military to civil authority, and freedom of religion.

The Bills of Rights of other states added to the Virginia list freedom of speech, assembly, and petition; the right to a writ of habeas corpus, so that an accused person could not be held in prison without trial; prohibition of ex-post-facto laws (laws which are retroactive with respect to liability for punishment); narrow definitions of treason so that it could not be charged against a peaceable critic of government or its officials; prohibition of uncompensated governmental seizure of private property; and various other refinements of individual liberties and governmental restrictions. Vermont was unique in granting the suffrage to all adult males without property qualifications. The thirteen states generally made property qualifications for officeholders higher than those for voters. Most states also required religious tests for office holding which were acceptable only to Protestant Christians. The original constitutions were not fully democratic in the modern sense, but their tendency was unmistakably in the direction of political democracy. They provided foundations of fuller liberty and broader democracy than any in the world, foundations on which future generations could readily build.

Contrary to later American practice, the very first state constitutions were not framed by conventions that had been elected for that express purpose, though the desirability of this procedure, in order that the constitutions should be based indisputably on the popular will, had been recognized by Thomas Jefferson and others. The idea was expressed effectively by the citizens of the little town of Concord, Massachusetts; and the procedure they recommended was actually followed in their state, thus setting an American pattern. The legislature of Massachusetts asked the people to give it authority to draw up a new constitution, but the people of Concord in town meeting took the position that a legislature which should itself be the servant of the constitution was not a proper body to frame it, since the power to create implied the power to destroy. Therefore, they demanded that the people of the state should elect representatives to a special constitutional convention, and that the product of this convention should be submitted to the people themselves for ratification. Thus the sovereign people would become the direct source of supreme law. In its essentials this procedure was followed not only by Massachusetts, but afterwards by other states, by the federal government, and by many other governments in the world. This plan displayed the genius of the American people in devising practical solutions for theoretical problems. Besides providing means whereby the people could enforce their claim of government by compact, it showed how the right of revolution should be channeled into peaceful processes of change. At any time that the people, in Abraham Lincoln's words, "shall grow tired of their form of government," they can either amend it or demand a new constitutional convention. If one considers that the American people have now for almost two centuries been creating, amending, and re-creating their state and central governments, one can appreciate the stupendous value of the constitutional procedure which assumed characteristic form toward the end of the American Revolution.

The original state constitutions were the first in world history to put fully into practice the important distinction between fundamental law and statute law. This is the distinction that is referred to when it is said that the Americans were the first people to live under comprehensive *written* constitutions. The British "unwritten constitution" consists of a complex of traditions and Parliamentary statutes. Traditions may be undermined and Parliament may repeal its own statutes. Control of Parliament gives the British people indirect control over their constitution, but the American people, more suspicious of officeholders, have preferred to write out the charters of fundamental law and place them beyond reach of anyone but themselves. The statutes enacted by legislatures and the actions of officials must conform to the mandates and prohibitions of the fundamental law or they are null and void. "Judicial review," that is, the power of courts to compare the acts of citizens and governments, including statute laws, with the terms of constitutions, was incorporated in some of the original constitutions and implied in others. Judicial review was an American adaptation of the British practice of "disallowance" of colonial statutes, and this power of the courts has given rise to abuses and objections. But the people, first and last, are sovereign, and the governments which they have erected under written constitutions are their servants.

EXTENSIONS OF INDIVIDUAL FREEDOM

Religion

A considerable number of special privileges, hitherto legalized and enjoyed by particular groups, were destroyed by the revolutionary generation as being incompatible with the principles of the Bills of Rights. Among major objects of attack were the established churches. The Anglican Church held a privileged position in Georgia, South Carolina, North Carolina, Virginia, Maryland, and part of New York. The Congregational Church was established in Massachusetts, Connecticut, and New Hampshire. In all these states, the favored church was supported by public taxes, while Presbyterians, Baptists, Quakers, and other dissenting sects were discriminated against in various ways. The view of Roger Williams, that absolute separation of Church and State and equal freedom for all religions were required by the dignity of the individual's conscience, made little headway until revolutionary agitation against British rule turned men's minds against the Anglican Church as its handmaiden.

Until this time the ideal of complete religious freedom had been most nearly realized in Rhode Island and in the middle colonies and states, especially Pennsylvania, where diversity had long been tolerated. President John Witherspoon of the Presbyterian College of New Jersey at Princeton, a signer of the Declaration of Independence, was an ardent advocate of the Roger Williams doctrine, and he turned out many a graduate like James Madison who carried his views into a state legislature.

The successful but often difficult fight for the disestablishment of the Anglican Church can be illustrated by developments in Virginia, where Madison in the next decade carried on the work that was so conspicuously begun by Thomas Jefferson in this one. During the Revolution the General Assembly relieved dissenters from taxes in support of the Established Church, but it left unsettled the question whether the various Christian sects should be supported by a general assessment of the people or by wholly voluntary contributions. At this time Jefferson drafted his Bill for Establishing Religious Freedom, which was finally passed in 1785 through the efforts of Madison, while the author himself was serving as American Minister in France. The chief significance of this famous Bill, which Jefferson ranked next to the Declaration of Independence among his memorable achievements, was that it made the separation between Church and State complete and religious freedom absolute. It asserted unequivocally the principle which became orthodox American doctrine, that the State should neither support nor oppose any religious group, and that freedom of religious profession and practice should extend, not merely to Protestant sects and Christian groups, but to all forms of religion whatsoever. As a declaration of the religious and intellectual freedom of the individual this is an ineffaceable landmark in the history of human liberty. Not until a number of years after its adoption, however, did the last vestiges of the Anglican establishment disappear in Virginia. Questions regarding church properties long persisted, and so did the memories of this bitter conflict.

In other states the Anglican Church was disestablished with less difficulty before the end of the war, and most observers agreed that the new dispensation was beneficial to it in the long run. Reorganized as the Protestant Episcopal Church, it acquired an independent hierarchy of bishops which had been denied it while it was subordinated to the diocese of London. Deprived of tithes and dependent upon the voluntary support of their communicants, the Episcopalian clergy showed marked improvement as moral and intellectual leaders over the easy-going parsons of old. Furthermore, the Episcopalians adopted a constitution which reflected the democratic tendencies of the period by according to the laity much more authority within the Church than the Anglican laity enjoyed. This church gained independence and a higher degree of religious leadership by losing its special privileges and becoming truly American.

The Roman Catholic Church also benefitted from the Revolution. In Maryland, where it was strongest, its clergy and communicants helped gain religious freedom for all churches. The Carrolls, the most eminent Catholic family in America, produced a signer of the Declaration of Independence, Charles Carroll of Carrollton, and the first American Roman Catholic Bishop, John Carroll, whose diocese of Baltimore included the whole United States. The American Church had been subordinate to the vicar apostolic of London prior to 1776, and French Catholics attempted to take over the London vicar's function; but on petition of the Maryland clergy, Pope Pius VI created an independent hierarchy for the United States. The notable part played by American

Catholics, especially those of Irish origin, in the Revolution, and their
numerical weakness, early established among them a tradition of loyalty
to the free institutions of the new Republic as their best safeguard in a
predominantly Protestant society.

The Congregational establishments in New England were not particularly affected by the Revolution. Their clergy were in the forefront
of patriotic action and could not easily be attacked as enemies of liberty.
But an entering wedge had opened a small crack between Church and
State in Massachusetts. Dissenters were forced to pay a tax to support
religion, but their money was paid over to dissenting clergymen. During
the next two generations, orthodox Calvinism steadily lost its hold on the
minds of even the Congregational clergy and the numerical strength of
dissenting groups steadily increased until, in 1833, the last link between
Church and State in America was severed in Massachusetts.

The drive for religious freedom resulted not only in the separation of
Church and State and the independence of American churches from
European national churches but also in a splintering of religious bodies
which has been equally characteristic of the American religious scene.
Freedom for any self-organized group to obtain recognition as a church
encouraged a luxuriant growth of sectarianism. The very multiplication of
sects is evidence that freedom of conscience was really achieved. Rationalist faiths such as Deism flourished among Americans educated in the
science of Newton and the philosophy of the Enlightenment. Freemasonry
claimed a large percentage of the Founding Fathers. Indeed, some conservatives interpreted the American Revolution as a plot hatched in the
secret councils of foreign and American Masons. Many of the New England intelligentsia began to turn to unorthodox varieties of religion such
as Universalism and Unitarianism. Among the frontiersmen and isolated
settlers of the West, revivalism soon fastened fundamentalist doctrines
on the minds and emotions of perhaps a majority of Americans. But an
uncountable number simply ignored religion, while a few professed positive atheism. It seemed to many observers that the American Revolution
harvested its worst fruits in infidelity and the mutiplication of sects; they
were certain that political anarchy must follow upon such a breakdown
of religious controls. But Americans as a whole reveled in religious
pluralism and regarded the individual freedom it signified as a reason
for loyalty to their government, the protector of the inviolate human conscience. Nothing in the young Republic was more striking than the successful demonstration in practice of the paradox of political unity through
religious freedom and diversity.

Freedom of Enterprise

Just as the citadels of religious privilege were undermined by the
Revolutionary generation, so certain forms of economic privilege were

weakened or destroyed. The right to acquire and possess wealth was not under attack. On the contrary, this right was demanded in 1776 by the American revolutionaries as against monopolistic, feudal, and monarchical economic privileges of the old regime. As a result of the American Revolution, freedom of enterprise, that is, the equal opportunity of any individual to engage in any economic activity he chooses in order to amass wealth, and to hold onto his wealth or dispose of it as he pleases, became a living reality in America to a greater degree than before. Mercantilist restrictions were destroyed. The King's prerogative in Crown lands and in such matters as his claim to the best timber anywhere for the uses of the Royal Navy was abolished.

Yet overthrow of British rule was not sufficient to establish economic liberty within the states. Vestiges of feudal privilege survived in several of them, and these were immediately under attack. Most archaic, although not actually very important, were primogeniture and entail, which Jefferson opposed strongly. Under the Virginia law of primogeniture, the whole estate of a landowner who died intestate was inherited by his eldest son. Laws of entail in Virginia and elsewhere permitted a propertied person to forbid the alienation or division of his estate for many generations after his death, and often were an embarrassment to living owners. The tendency of both primogeniture and entail was to "freeze" property in the hands of a hereditary aristocracy. Economic mobility was furthered by their abolition, and the attainment of wealth made easier for the many.

Quitrents were a common lien on land titles, especially in the proprietary colonies, and they too were abolished. Land titles in "fee simple," that is, absolute ownership in return for the original purchase price, became the rule in all the states as had been the case in most of New England from the beginning. In the Hudson Valley remnants of manorial privileges over tenants were retained by the descendants of the patroons until well into the nineteenth century, but this was exceptional. In the Old World and in Spanish America, land was prized not only because it produced wealth but because it bestowed family distinction and privileges upon the owners. This idea was present in the southern states and persisted to some extent, but the American land system increasingly tended to take on a capitalistic rather than feudal character. Land became one more commodity available for speculation, with easy transfer of ownership and quick improvement or loss of fortune by persons to whom land ownership had formerly been denied.

The confiscation of Loyalist estates by the state governments had an important influence upon economic opportunity. Many of these were sold for the benefit of state treasuries without regard to social policy, but legislatures often broke them up into small parcels for sale at public auction or for gifts to veteran soldiers, thus strengthening the bias of the American land system towards small-scale and widespread land ownership. Furthermore, the state governments were liberal in handing out Crown lands and other wild lands to settlers. Easy access to land caused property qualifications for voting in an overwhelmingly agrarian country to be relatively insignificant as restrictions on democratic suffrage. Only after industrialism had created a large propertyless class of laborers did property qualifications assume a strongly undemocratic character, and then they were all abolished in the states.

The Antislavery Movement and Humanitarianism

Slavery was an institution that contradicted the liberal aspirations of the American Revolution, as the English were particularly fond of pointing out. But the British government had been the first obstacle to American efforts to check the development of the institution. Colonial laws against the slave trade had often been disallowed by the Privy Council because they would destroy the business of the British-owned Royal African Company. Sentiment against this traffic was specially strong in Virginia, and the most conspicuous patriot leaders there—including Washington, Jefferson, and Patrick Henry—deplored the institution. The radicals met their toughest domestic opposition when they attacked the labor system which seemed essential to staple production on large plantations. But few supporters of slavery advanced any argument except expediency, and it was generally assumed that the institution would presently be abolished everywhere. Meanwhile, the Revolutionary generation took action which was considerably responsible for the later fact that slavery became a minority interest in the Union.

The first attack was made against the most vicious branch of the commerce in human beings, the slave trade with Africa. The Continental Congress banned this in the course of its economic warfare against the mother country. But when Congress threw open American ports to world trade, Yankee shipowners seized the opportunity to gather in the profits of the slave trade as one more blessing of the new order. Some planters, especially those of South Carolina and Georgia, were eager to purchase fresh supplies of laborers, and it was this combination of shipping and planting interests that prevented condemnation of the trade in the Declaration of Independence, as was desired by Jefferson. Reformers thereupon turned to the states for action. Most of the states, including Virginia, prohibited the trade outright, but in the far South taxes or temporary prohibitions represented the maximum of attainment in this period and even these measures were circumvented.

Jefferson hoped that gradual emancipation could be started in Virginia, with the aid of the young men "who had sucked in the principles of liberty as it were with their mother's milk." But it was easier to reconcile practice with libertarian ideals in the North, where slaves were few because of economic conditions. Vermont, not yet a state, had already abolished slavery outright in its constitution (1777); and Pennsylvania, where the earliest antislavery society had been organized, chiefly by Quakers, provided for gradual emancipation before victory over the British had been won. In Massachusetts, where slavery had existed merely as usage without express enactment in law, it came to an end in 1783 as the result of a judicial decision which now seems extraordinarily symbolic. In the case of Quock Walker, the Supreme Judicial Court declared a slave free because the constitution of Massachusetts stated that all men are free and equal and that every subject is entitled to liberty In Virginia, liberal George Wythe had similar ideas, but he was confronted with the fact that in his state the slaves constituted approximately 40 per cent of the population. Other northern states in which the proportion of slaves was higher than in Massachusetts while far lower than in the South, adopted schemes of gradual emancipation, though in New York and New Jersey there was delay in putting these into operation. In general, the difficulties in overcoming this obstacle to the triumph of the revolutionary principle of freedom were in proportion to the size of the problem, that is, to the number of slaves.

In the South, where the vast majority of the bondsmen were, there was reluctance to face the heavy financial loss, the probable disruption of the labor system, and the problem of future social relations that were involved in emancipation. Hence the reformers were checked in all the states below Pennsylvania. Nevertheless, gains were made in the liberalization of slave codes and in legalizing voluntary manumission. It seemed to many leaders that slavery was becoming unprofitable on worn-out tobacco lands, and they looked for the ultimate extinction of slavery by the operation of economic forces such as had caused its decline in the North. Planters like George Washington and Thomas Jefferson searched for new crops, and were hopeful that Southern agriculture would develop along the lines of the diversified-crop and family-farm economy of the North, as it showed signs of doing in this period. Washington willed that his slaves be freed after his wife's death. Other slaveowners made similar provision and more would have done so but for the fact that, under existing laws and customs, the status of freedmen was uncertain and often unhappy. A large number of planters, especially in Virginia, were infused with the humane spirit of the eighteenth-century Enlightenment. It was the invention of the cotton gin and the unexpectedly profitable employment of slave labor in cotton culture that defeated their hopes of the extinction of human bondage in all parts of America through the operation of economic forces. Baffled though Jefferson was throughout his public life in his efforts to reach a solution of this problem which would be acceptable to the electorate, he struck some long-range blows against the extension of slavery in this period. A provision which he drew in 1784 anticipated the prohibition of slavery in the territory northwest of the Ohio in the Ordinance of 1787. Also, his efforts at this time and later in behalf of small farmers were an indirect blow at slavery, since it did not thrive among them.

If the reformers of the Revolutionary decade achieved only limited success in the movement against slavery, they won other victories. A barbarous relic of the past was the penal code under which death was meted out for many minor crimes which today receive short prison sentences or the attentions of social workers and psychiatrists. The legislatures generally mitigated the severity of the penal code. This was particularly true in the matter of capital punishment, which was ultimately restricted by most of the states to the two crimes of murder and treason. The "crime" of failing to pay a debt remained punishable by imprisonment until well into the nineteenth century.

The American Revolution gave impetus to humanitarianism in many spheres. Private societies by the dozens were organized to improve the condition of the poor and extend a helping hand to the sick, the insane, the lame, and the blind. Individualism bore a double fruit in creating respect for the unfortunate as human beings and the determination of more fortunate people to organize themselves for the amelioration of social evils. Such voluntary organizations became characteristic of the American scene. Charity as imposed by religious injunction and directed towards good works was gradually supplemented by secular humanitarianism imposed by the natural-rights doctrine and directed towards reform of social institutions as the best method of regenerating humanity.

THE CULTURAL REVOLUTION

Education

The passion for improvement also touched cultural life in the young Republic. The war temporarily eclipsed higher education, but peace brought an upsurge of interest and rapid progress. The name of King's College in New York City was changed to Columbia College and it reopened in 1784 under the philosopher-president, William Samuel Johnson. The removal of the Virginia capital from Williamsburg to Richmond (1780) was a blow to the old College of William and Mary, but generally the prewar institutions flourished. The churches energetically established new colleges, such as the Presbyterians' Hampden-Sydney (1782) in Virginia, significantly named for seventeenth-century English champions of principles for which Americans had been fighting, and Dickinson College at Carlisle, Pennsylvania (1783); the Episcopalians' St. John's of Annapolis, Maryland, and the College of Charleston in South Carolina; and the

Roman Catholics' (Jesuit) Georgetown College in 1789. Such church colleges were not new in principle, for they were in the tradition of Harvard, William and Mary, Yale, and Princeton. Within a generation they were to be balanced by nonsectarian and tax-supported state universities, which were anticipated by some in this era. After the Revolution the classics continued to form the core of college curricula, but some republicans regarded classical education as an aristocratic relic which should give way to utilitarian subject matter. Others believed that the old curricula produced enlightened minds as well as gentlemen. They fought a bitter rear-guard battle against the utilitarians, and won an uneasy compromise in the "liberal arts" curriculum which persisted for generations.

In education as in so many spheres of American life, the new order of things encouraged experimentation; and the result was a rich variety of institutions—private and public, religious and nonsectarian—reflecting the diverse philosophies of a free people and meriting for American society the significant adjective, "pluralist." The local and state governments, churches and schools, businesses and clubs, humanitarian and propaganda societies in all their bewildering variety—all of them organized by the people themselves and devoted to the destruction of old evils and the creation of a better day for somebody or everybody— clearly show that a major consequence of the American Revolution was the unprecedented release of the energies and creative imagination of a people.

Literature

As individualists, Americans believed that the ultimate test of a society was the quality of the human beings it produced. In public life they could point to the simple greatness of George Washington, Benjamin Franklin, and other heroes of the era of Independence. But they also thirsted for heroes of art and science. Noah Webster sounded the call in 1783: "America must be as independent in literature as she is in politics, as famous for arts as she is for arms." But periods of public crisis are not the best times for cultivation of the quiet artistic ideals, and American society had to outgrow colonialism and frontier conditions before it could produce an important culture. Noah Webster himself admitted that homely spadework was necessary before his call would be answered by the appearance of American genius: his masterpiece was his famous spelling book and school reader for the grounding of millions of American children in literature.

American poets of the Revolutionary generation made manful efforts to answer Webster's call, but their verse, while it dealt with American subjects, followed the models of Augustan English poetry. Still it is a fact that the imagery of the American Revolution, like much of its doctrine, was derived from classical sources. Therefore it was not meaningless when Francis Hopkinson wrote an elaborate classical allegory, *The Temple of Minerva*, as a tribute to George Washington in 1781. Hopkinson tried to "Americanize" allegory in his later ballad celebrating the adoption of the federal Constitution, called "The New Roof: A Song for Federal Mechanics":

> Come muster, my lads, your mechanical tools,
> Your saws and your axes, your hammers and rules;
> Bring your mallets and planes, your level and line,
> And plenty of pins of American pine:
> For our roof we will raise, and our song still shall be,
> Our government firm, and our citizens free.

In general, classical models were followed by those writers who were conservatives in politics and fearful that the American Republic would become the playground of the mob. Thus the first American school of writers, the "Hartford Wits," loved to pillory democracy in such "Roman" satires as *The Anarchiad* (1786). Political radicals, on the other hand, found among the Indians models of natural virtue unalloyed by European aristocratic decadence. The meaning of the conflict is apparent in the names of veterans' organizations: the Society of the Cincinnati was founded for ex-officers and their eldest sons; but veterans in New York and other cities who had been common soldiers, and feared the Cincinnati as an entering wedge of hereditary aristocracy, named their organization the Sons of Saint Tammany in honor of a legendary Indian Chief.

Philip Freneau, "the Poet of the American Revolution," was the most talented exponent of political radicalism in the literature of the period. As a student at Princeton he distinguished himself in poetry, and his fiery love of liberty drew him into political writing during the Revolution. His capture and imprisonment in a notorious British prison ship embittered him against England. Next to Paine's his pen was the most effective one on the patriot side. After the war he devoted himself to writing realistic and humorous poems descriptive of American life and saturated with love of the common man. He echoed Noah Webster's demand for cultural independence from England:

> Can we ever be thought to have learning or grace,
> Unless it be sent from that damnable place?

Domestic conservatism was another target of Freneau's flaming hatred. He declared literary war against the Hartford Wits and afterward became the most effective early newspaper polemicist of the Jeffersonian party.

It was not a time conducive to poetry. The greatest literary achievement of the period occurred on the lower level of political prose. In this field the electric style of Thomas Paine has perhaps never been surpassed. Political pamphlets and newspapers offered by far the liveliest reading matter available to the public. But American drama was born shortly after the Revolution and was to some extent an answer to the demand for a native literature. Puritan objections to the theater as a glamorizer of sin were disappearing. Productions of English and European comedies and tragedies, usually by English touring companies, became frequent in the leading seaports during the later eighteenth century. The first play by an American to be acted publicly was Thomas Godfrey's *The Prince of Parthia,* produced in Philadelphia in 1767. This was a tragedy imitative of the Elizabethan English model. The issues of the Revolution were dramatized by no less a person than General Burgoyne, whose farce *The Blockade* lampooned the Boston patriots, and by an anonymous American who defended the patriots and lampooned the British in *The Blockheads.* The English dramatist Sheridan provided the model for the first American comedies.

Nevertheless, Royall Tyler's *The Contrast,* first produced in New York in 1787, contained fresh and rollicking characterizations of American types. This famous comedy dramatized the contrast between decadent English foppery and pure, plain Americanism. It created the immortal stock character, Jonathan, ancestor of Brother Jonathan and Uncle Sam. Tyler's Jonathan is a sturdy New England rustic, canny as well as naïve, honest and self-reliant. He learns through absurd experience not to ape English manners and morals; "If this is the way with your city ladies," Jonathan concludes, "give me the twenty acres of rock, the Bible, the cow, and Tabitha, and a little peaceable bundling." *The Contrast* was very popular and inspired many imitations. It illustrated the saving humor with which Americans could look at their present predicament of political independence and cultural immaturity. William Dunlap, the most successful early theatrical producer and a playwright as well, presented Shakespeare to American audiences more often than the work of any other playwright. He helped overcome the danger that in the longing for cultural independence Americans would neglect their great English inheritance.

The Arts

The rage for improvement and cultural independence produced a first generation of great American painters. In 1770, John Trumbull in his master's oration at Yale prophesied that Americans would overcome the British in the arts as well as by arms because they loved liberty and educated the whole people. He called for "some new Apelles" to paint the American scene, and his summons was answered by an astonishing group of painters. Benjamin West, a Pennsylvania Quaker, was acclaimed in London in 1771 for his *Death of General Wolfe,* and he accepted the post of Historical Painter to the King of England, but he did not forget his native land or its aspirations. In 1772, he explained to Englishmen that his painting, *Penn's Treaty with the Indians,* signified the conquest of a people without sword or dagger—a pointed rebuke to the British government's method of dealing with Americans. West established a school in London in which most of the leading American painters for two generations found encouragement.

John Singleton Copley of Boston was perhaps the greatest of the American "old masters." He painted New England patriots and Loyalists with impartial skill in his Beacon Hill studio until the oncoming war led him to follow West abroad. Sir Joshua Reynolds greeted him as unequaled among English painters. Critics still quarrel over the question whether Copley's work, like that of many other expatriate American artists, gained more in European refinement than it lost in native vigor as a result of his departure. Charles Willson Peale was content to commit his career to America because, as an ardent democrat, he noted that Americans had a growing taste for the arts "and are becoming more and more fond of encouraging their progress." After the Revolution, Peale painted its heroes and taught his chidren to paint. When George Washington granted him sittings, four painting Peales went to work on what the son Rembrandt Peale called "that dismal countenance." Rembrandt afterwards found a more congenial subject in the philosopher-democrat, Thomas Jefferson.

Gilbert Stuart became the most popular of all the portrait painters but his most famous work fell in a later period. Meanwhile, John Trumbull of Connecticut, a relative of the writer of the same name, claimed the title of "Painter of the Revolution." He served in Washington's Army long enough to witness and paint events from Bunker Hill to Trenton. In England, Trumbull was jailed in reprisal for the arrest of Major André, but West and Copley obtained his release. He made many portraits from life for his famous *Declaration of Independence.* For many years he toiled at heroic canvases celebrating battles and political events of the Revolution and he succeeded in fixing in American minds his rather romantic images of those events.

Emergent English romanticism dominated the Revolutionary genera-tion of American painters, but in architecture English models gave way to a classicism believed to be more suited to the requirements of a libertarian republic. Thomas Jefferson, an amateur architect of great talent, was most responsible for the new trend in American building, especially public building. Thomas Paine challenged all imitation as un-worthy of America, writing, "I have no notion of yielding the palm of the United States to any Grecians or Romans that were ever born." But

Jefferson followed the Italian and classical Palladio in believing that rules of good design were based on the laws of nature, and was convinced that temples erected by Romans to their gods were fit abodes for republican heroes. When he was minister to France after the American Revolution Jefferson gazed at the Maison Carrée in Nîmes "like a lover at his mistress," and he adapted this Roman temple to the needs of Virginia. The state capitol at Richmond was the result, and presently Roman and Greek temple forms complete with porticoes dotted the cities and the countryside in America.

Science

Jefferson was particularly interested in architecture because of its usefulness in a growing country, and he was glad to avail himself of the best classical and modern European models. He was also eager to draw on the science of other countries, and his own services, while minister in France, in sending home to the savants of the young republic information about the latest discoveries and inventions have caused him to be described as America's "scientific scout." This was in the spirit of the American Philosophical Society, founded in Philadelphia years before by Franklin, of which he was a member. The American Academy of Arts and Sciences in Boston, to which he also belonged, began its long and honorable history in 1780. Franklin's scientific pre-eminence in America was unchallenged until his death (1790); and next to him in scientific esteem was probably David Rittenhouse, the Philadelphia mathematician and astronomer.

Jefferson won his scientific fame chiefly as a naturalist, and his *Notes on Virginia,* first published in Paris in 1785 in a private edition, was destined to become the most famous American scientific work of the period. Described at the time as "a most excellent natural history not merely of Virginia but of North America and possibly equal or superior to that of any country yet published," it was notable not only for its scientific spirit but also for its patriotic fervor. While critical of certain institutions of his own state, including slavery and an insufficiently representative government, Jefferson sought to demonstrate that neither animal nor human life had degenerated in the New World, as certain French naturalists had rudely asserted, and he waxed eloquent in defense of the character of the Indians. Besides giving a large amount of accurate information, this informal and unpretentious scientific work defended the honor of human nature, challenged the doctrine of human inequality, and glorified the American philosophy of freedom. In its combination of universality and Americanism it was in the spirit of the Declaration of Independence.

Whether the civilization of the United States was more derivative than native at this stage is an idle question. Cultural independence had certainly not been achieved along with political, and without a doubt the American experiment had drawn profitably upon the whole heritage of Western civilization. But the citizens of this new country were doing their best to subject every item of that heritage to critical examination, aiming to reject what was outworn and to adapt to their purposes what was usable. At no other time in human history, probably, did a people ever set out so consciously to establish a civilization which should be, not rootless, but superior to its roots.

CHAPTER 12

The Confederation, 1781-1789

THE YEARS IMMEDIATELY FOLLOWING THE REVOLUTION and preceding the inauguration of President Washington were designated as the "critical period" of American history by the popular historian John Fiske. Writing a century later, Fiske held that the failure of the government the radicals had created in the Confederation brought on economic and political chaos and threatened the Republic with dissolution. The crisis, he believed, was surmounted only because conservatives succeeded in strengthening the central government by means of the Constitution of 1787, which went into effect two years later.

This interpretation gained wide acceptance and still persists to some degree, but in our century more careful historians have toned it down. In the light of present knowledge it would be foolish to say that the economic depression after the war was caused by the Articles of Confederation and cured by the Constitution; and it now seems that the dangers of domestic anarchy were exaggerated, though the perils of the international situation were not. The Articles of Confederation reflected the fears of a strong central government and reliance on the states that generally characterized the radicals, while the adoption of the Constitution of 1787 marked a conservative reaction. But we can now perceive the continuity of development and appreciate the extraordinary way in which these struggles were resolved in a new and better synthesis. Government under the Confederation was clearly inadequate in the domestic and even more in the international field, yet by its real services as well as its manifest failures it prepared the way for the better government and more perfect Union that followed.

GOVERNMENT UNDER THE ARTICLES

The American Republic, born on July 4, 1776, did not acquire a written constitution until March 1, 1781, when the Articles of Confederation were proclaimed. This was only six or seven months before the surrender of Lord Cornwallis at Yorktown brought the Revolution to a virtual end as a military conflict. All of the states except Connecticut and Rhode Island, which continued under their old charters after deleting references to the British Crown, had adopted constitutions by that time. Yet the famous resolutions of Richard Henry Lee, on June 7, 1776, called not only for a declaration of independence but also for the preparation of a plan of confederation. A committee for this purpose was promptly set up, under the chairmanship of John Dickinson of Pennsylvania, but independence was declared before his draft of "Articles of Confederation and Perpetual Union" was reported, and no action was taken on it that summer. To sever the tie with the mother country by resolution was far easier than to create a government that would be acceptable to thirteen different states then in the process of assuming full authority within their own borders. Young Edward Rutledge of South Carolina probably voiced the opinion that was dominant among all groups of patriots when he wrote: "I am resolved to vest the Congress with no more power than is absolutely necessary, and, to use a familiar expression, to keep the staff in our own hands." That is just what the states did—as long as possible.

Not until November 15, 1777, were the Articles formally adopted by Congress and submitted to the states. The struggle among the delegates had centered on the questions of the basis of voting, contributions to expenses, and common control of western lands. It was chiefly the last of these that delayed ratification. Most of the states ratified rather promptly, however, and long before the most reluctant of them, Maryland, gave her formal consent, Congress was guiding itself by the provisions of the Articles.

The general character of the Union is revealed at the very beginning of the document. This was to be a "confederacy," called "The United States of America," and consisting of states whose "sovereignty, freedom, and independence" were retained. The Confederation was described as "a firm league of friendship" for common defense and security, and in practice it was certainly much more like a league of nations than a union of the people. It worked best in times when there was fullest recognition of common danger.

To us it seems that the first central government was badly out of balance: framed in a time of reaction against executive power, it consisted of only a legislative body. Yet, in the light of historic developments elsewhere and particularly in England, it is clear that a legislature clothed with sufficient authority could have eventually created an adequate administrative and judicial system. The major fault was not so much that of imperfect form as of insufficient power. Congress was not authorized to set up a federal judiciary, beyond admiralty courts, and the administration of justice throughout the land was necessarily left to state and local courts. But Congress, in the effort to perform the limited functions that were committed to it, did create agencies and departments such as now fall within the executive branch of the government, and the services of these deserve more credit than they have generally received.

The chief sphere in which power was granted Congress was that of foreign relations. Only Congress could make war and peace, send and receive ambassadors, make treaties and alliances, and exercise maritime jurisdiction. In 1781, Congress created a Department of Foreign Affairs and elected Robert R. Livingston of New York as its first Secretary. He was succeeded after an interim by John Jay (1784), who performed the duties of this important office until Thomas Jefferson took them over in 1790 in President Washington's government. Early in 1781, Congress also set up a War Department under a single head—General Benjamin Lincoln in the first place. General Henry Knox assumed the office in 1785, held it throughout the rest of the Confederation's life, and was appointed Secretary of War by Washington.

The Department of Finances, established in the same year as the two others, was the most important of all during the administration of it by Robert Morris (1781-1784); he was even described as "pecuniary dictator." His views dominated Congress but that body had only limited authority to transmit to him. It lacked the power to tax, which the states had kept for themselves after denying it to the British government; and an amendment to the Articles which would have permitted a tax of 5 per cent on imports (called the Impost of 1781) was defeated in 1782 by Rhode Island. Congress could make requisitions on states for money, as it could for soldiers, but had no means of enforcement. It also lacked any authority over commerce. It could borrow money, emit bills of credit (paper money), and regulate coinage, weights, and measures. The adoption of the dollar and the decimal system of coinage, which was one of the constructive actions of the Confederation, came late in its life and was owing to Thomas Jefferson rather than to Robert Morris. It was on the recommendation of the "Financier," however, that Congress overcame its constitutional scruples and chartered the Bank of North America (1781). Morris expected this private institution to perform valuable services to the government, as it did, but it was too small and limited to serve Hamilton's purposes when he became Washington's Secretary of the Treasury. Morris, who was a very controversial figure, retired in the autumn of 1784, and financial matters were afterwards administered by a Board of Treasury.

Even in its own procedure Congress was hampered and at times gravely embarrassed by constitutional requirements. The equality of the states was assured by the provision that each state, large or small, would have one vote. Each state must send at least two and might send as many as seven delegates, and none of the important powers of Congress could be exercised without the favorable votes of at least nine states. But it frequently happened that fewer than nine states had two delegates present. For just this reason the ratification of the peace treaty with Great Britain was so long delayed that the formal notice reached England several weeks after the time limit had expired. Fortunately, the British made no point of the American failure to comply with the conditions. Unanimous action by all the delegations in Congress and agreement by all the states were necessary for the adoption of any amendment to the Articles. As the fate of the Impost of 1781 showed, the Articles were practically unamendable. This was a fatal weakness, for no unchangeable instrument of government can endure.

The Articles imposed co-operation among the states only to the extent usually required of sovereign governments entering into treaty relations. Each state gave full faith and credit to the public records, acts, and judicial proceedings of all the others; they were required to extradite criminals; and the citizens of one state were entitled to all the privileges and immunities granted in the several states. The Articles contained no bill of rights to prevent the central government from infringing on the rights of individuals, because the Confederation was created by and acted upon the state governments, not the individual citizens. The whole document was in effect a bill of *state* rights, and in practice Congress was like the central committee of a league, attempting to win the voluntary co-operation of the constituent nations. This has been aptly described as "government by supplication."

Creation of the National Domain

In one respect the Confederation turned out to be more than a league of sovereign states. It began to resemble a nation when it acquired title to a national domain. This was created from western lands to which certain states had claims resting on original charters. Maryland had no claims, and she refused to ratify the Articles of Confederation unless other states should give up their exclusive claims and turn them over to the central government. This was a reasonable attitude, because otherwise a few of the states would become so rich and powerful as to overawe the others—a situation with which modern planners of world government are quite familiar. The astonishing thing is that the states with claims did what the others asked, and their willingness to sacrifice particular interests to the common good attested their national patriotism.

Early in 1780, New York led the way in surrendering claims, saying that her action was designed "to accelerate the federal alliance." Actually, her claims were not strong. Virginia was the crucial state, for by charter she had the oldest and strongest claim to western lands, and she was much the largest by any reckoning. On September 6, 1780, Congress strongly recommended to the states that they make "a liberal surrender of their territorial claims," and at the same time it urged Maryland to ratify the Articles. Two Virginians, Joseph Jones and James Madison, then made proposals which were embodied by Congress in an important resolution on October 10: namely, that the ceded lands should be disposed of for the "common benefit" of the United States and be "settled and formed into distinct republican states, which shall become members of the federal union, and have the same rights of sovereignty, freedom and independence, as the other states." This was to be the basic principle of American expansion across the continent, and the formal recognition of it was a momentous act.

Meanwhile, another condition of cession was in the minds of leading Virginians, before they would yield an empire. Various speculative companies had acquired title to western lands from the gullible Indians, and there was fear that Congress, where these companies were very influential, might yield to their schemes. Jefferson in particular urged that the western lands be kept open on the most liberal terms for bona-fide settlers, especially small farmers; and Virginia in her own constitution had forbidden private purchases from the Indians.

By a resolution of January 2, 1781, the General Assembly of the Old Dominion, "for the sake of the public good," ceded to the general government all the territory northwest of the Ohio. The validity of this cession was contingent on the ratification of the Articles of Confederation by all the states (that is, by Maryland), and it was based on the expectation that similar cessions would be made by all the other states with claims to vacant territory. The resolution provided that in this area all deeds or grants from the Indians made for the benefit of private persons should be declared null and void. This ruled out the speculative companies. The Virginians also required that certain lands north of the Ohio be reserved for bounties to soldiers. While this offer was "not precisely conformable to the recommendations of Congress," the Marylanders decided to ratify the Articles.

When the Articles were proclaimed on March 1, 1781, the country finally had a constitution, but Congress was slow to accept the magnificent offer of the Virginians. This was chiefly because the land companies brought so much pressure that Congress would not consent to ignore their titles. It was not until 1783 that a committee of Congress worked out a compromise. Though an explicit annulment of the claims of the land companies was avoided in this proposal, the General Assembly of Virginia accepted it after making further provision for bounty lands to soldiers. What the Virginians reserved was a district between the Scioto and Little Miami rivers (shown on maps generally as the Virginia Military Reservation), and some 150,000 acres opposite Louisville for George Rogers Clark, "Conqueror of the Northwest" and his men. The deed of cession was presented to Congress by the Virginia delegation, headed by Jefferson who was now back in legislative harness. After considerable backing and filling Congress accepted it. It was signed on March 1, 1784, and the public domain may be said to date from then.

Other states followed the pattern that had now been set. The cession by Connecticut is of special interest, for she retained the lands below Lake Erie known as the Western Reserve. The southernmost states were slower in acting, but during the life of the Confederation it gained control of the region northwest of the Ohio. It was now more than the sum of thirteen sovereign states, for it held territory in its own name and began to administer this in the interest of all the American people.

CHARTERS FOR THE WEST

Next to winning independence, the government of the Confederation achieved its greatest success in formulating policies for the settlement and political development of the West. The relative failure of Congress in dealing with the Indians beyond the mountains was another count in the indictment of it by advocates of a stronger central government, but it set patterns for the future in its provisions for land sales and territorial government.

Ordinance of 1784

The Congressional leader who had the greatest faith in western frontiersmen and pioneers and the clearest vision of the future of the West was Jefferson, who started the Ordinance of 1784 on its legislative course. As chairman of a committee to prepare a plan of temporary government for the national domain he made a report immediately after Congress accepted the Virginia cession. Congress embodied in law its basic principle: that new states should be formed from the national domain and be admitted to the Union on an equal basis with the original members. Though imperial in size, the American Republic was not to be like the old British Empire in form or spirit. It was to be an expanding Union of self-governing commonwealths joined as a group of peers.

Unlike the more famous Ordinance of 1787 which superseded it, the Act of 1784 provided for the future government of all the territory that should be ceded by the states—that is, the region south as well as north of the Ohio. All of this was to be "forever" a part of the Confederation, and if Jefferson had had his way slavery would have been forbidden in the whole of it after 1800. Congress struck out the clause prohibiting the enlargement of the area of slavery, along with one forbidding hereditary titles. Also dropped were the polysyllabic names which Jefferson originally suggested for certain of the prospective states, though his Michigania and Illinoia afterward reappeared in the less classical rendering of Michigan and Illinois. The members of the committee were thinking of at least fourteen future states, even though there were only thirteen in the existing Union, and this is one measure of their audacity, for their own eastern states would be outnumbered. Provision was made for three stages of government in the West, and for self-government at every stage. First, the settlers in any one of these areas could adopt the constitution and laws of any one of the old states; this temporary government would continue until there were 20,000 free Inhabitants, when they might frame a permanent government; and when there were as many inhabitants as in the least numerous of the original states of the Union they should be admitted as full partners. The idea of successive stages of government in the new regions persisted, but later acts did not allow self-government so soon.

This act of 1784 never went into effect, since it was contingent on the cession of all claims in the West by the old states, and its democratic provisions were never tested. Another member of the committee, David Howell of Rhode Island, well expressed the faith these men had in the "Western World." He said: "As a source of future population and strength, it is a guaranty of our independence. As its inhabitants will be mostly cultivators of the soil, republicanism looks to them as its guardians." But the Western World also opened an amazing financial prospect to the government. "It is equal to our debt," Howell said. Jefferson favored the most liberal of land policies—even to the giving of land away; but the treasury of the Confederation clamored for money and everybody recognized that Congress must gain some revenue from sales.

Land Ordinance of 1785

The Land Ordinance of 1785 required the division of all these public lands into townships 6 miles square, each consisting of thirty-six sections of 640 acres. One fortunate provision was that a section in each township should be set aside for education. The minimum lot was a section and the minimum price was $1.00 per acre. In requiring preliminary survey and providing for orderly sales of large blocks of land, the law was closer to the New England practice than to the more individualistic and less orderly Southern custom. Under the latter a settler could purchase a warrant, pick out his own land, and have it surveyed afterwards. The Southern practice was better adapted to frontier conditions and the law of 1785 was not encouraging to small, independent farmers. A section of 640 acres was more than a single family needed and the price of $640 was beyond the reach of the average settler. It is no wonder that the trend in later years was to

SURVEYS of NORTHWEST TERRITORY 1785

Lake Erie

Maumee R.

PA.

Connecticut Reserve

41° N. LATITUDE

Fort Steuben

The Seven Ranges

Wheeling

Scioto Co. Lands

Lancaster

Ohio Company Lands

Marietta

Virginia Military Reserve

Chilli-cothe

Gallipolis

North Bend

Symmes Purchase

Gr. Miami R.

Little Miami R.

Columbia

Cincinnati

Ohio River

Limestone

KY.

VA.

Scioto R.

Muskingum R.

Ohio R.

SYSTEM of PUBLIC LANDS SURVEY ~ 1796

6 Miles

6	5	4	3	2	1
7	8	9	10	11	12
18	17	16	15	14	13
19	20	21	22	23	24
30	29	28	27	26	25
31	32	33	34	35	36

6 Miles

Township

640 Acres ~ 1 Mile Square

Half ~ section
320 acres

Quarter-section
160 acres

Half ~ quarter section
80 acres

Quarter-Quarter section
40 acres

1 Mile

Whole Section

reduce the size of the minimum purchase, nor is it surprising that under this law many became squatters on unsurveyed lands. Sales were by auctions, which were held regularly in the East. This provision favored large operators, who could buy whole townships and then parcel them out at a profit in small lots.

The treaties of Ft. Stanwix, Ft. McIntosh, and Ft. Finney gained important concessions from the Indians in the years 1784-1786, and the work of surveying was initiated under Thomas Hutchins, Geographer of the United States, in what became known as the Seven Ranges (beginning at the Pennsylvania line where it cut the Ohio River). But the surveying was necessarily slow and the Indian menace had not lifted. The first land auctions in 1787 brought the Treasury only about $175,000 in depreciated currency. Meanwhile, squatters were crossing the Ohio, asserting their right to take up vacant lands and establish their own governments. Troops vainly sought to displace them, and even George Washington described them as "banditti."

A group of speculators saw in this confused situation in the Northwest a great financial opportunity. Veterans of the Revolution had been paid off in Continental certificates of indebtedness which the government would accept for land but were otherwise almost worthless. General Rufus Putnam and other New England officers formed the Ohio Company, sold stock to veterans for their certificates, and proposed to Congress that it sell the company a giant tract at a few cents per acre, payable in certificates. Then the company could reap rich dividends by selling small plots. This was not according to the Land Ordinance of 1785. A shrewd lobbyist, the Reverend Manasseh Cutler, made the proposal to Congress. He found Congress little interested until William Duer, Secretary of the Board of Treasury which handled land sales, organized a group, including Congressmen who could not legally buy public land, into the Scioto Company; for this Cutler agreed that the Ohio Company would make purchases. Thereupon, with the authorization of Congress, the Board of Treasury sold more than 1.5 million acres to the Ohio Company at some 8 cents per acre, and gave it option on an even larger tract, which was destined for the Scioto Company. These lands lay between the Seven Ranges and the Virginia Military Reserve and bordered on the Ohio River.

Northwest Ordinance of 1787

Out of this sordid deal there emerged, very like a phoenix, the great Northwest Ordinance of 1787. Cutler told Congressmen that the company could not attract many settlers into the wilderness unless they were assured of the security of property in this lawless region. Congressmen knew that not only speculative interests but great national issues hinged upon western policy. From Vermont, which was a *de facto* republic threatening to rejoin the British Empire, to Tennessee (then a part of North Carolina), where John Sevier and others had set up the "State of Franklin," the West was seething with discontent and filled with the spirit of independence. On the other hand, conservative Easterners were certain that the wild frontiersmen could not be trusted to rule themselves and that, if they were granted equal statehood, radical Western farmers would soon control the central government and discriminate against Eastern interests. Congress had debated the issue for years; now in the summer of 1787 it quickly passed the Northwest Ordinance.

This was the most important law enacted by the government of the Confederation. Like the Ordinance of 1784, it provided for territories to become states by passing through three stages, but full self-government could be attained in only the last of these. The new system was colonial up to a point and then it became republican. In the first stage Congress would exercise authority through its own appointees—a territorial governor, a secretary, and three judges. When the adult male population reached 5000, the territory would enter the second stage; then the settlers would elect their own legislature to share control with a council of five appointed by the governor and Congress. This legislature could send a delegate to Congress who could speak but would have no vote. When the population reached 60,000 the territory could enter the final stage by framing a constitution and applying to Congress for admission to the Union on an equal footing with her older sisters.

Full statehood thus became a goal to be attained, but it was a sure one. Meanwhile, the individual settlers were granted protection against arbitrary power by a bill of rights. Among other things they were guaranteed freedom of religion, habeas corpus, jury trials, and security of contracts. Historically, the abolition of slavery was one of the most important features of the law but, unlike Jefferson's Ordinance of 1784, this law extended to only the region northwest of the Ohio. It also differed from the earlier act in that it provided for a smaller number of states in this region—not less than three nor more than five. In the course of time Ohio, Indiana, Illinois, Michigan, and Wisconsin were carved out of the Northwest Territory. The political provisions of the Ordinance were re-enacted by the federal Congress after the Constitution superseded the Articles of Confederation and this famous act provided precedents for later territorial legislation in other regions. Indeed, this American law offered a technique for the peaceful evolution of colonial areas into self-governing republics anywhere and set a model for the future liquidation of world empires.

Westerners were not entirely satisfied with it at the time. They detected Eastern fear and conservatism in several of its provisions: the entire lack of self-government during the first stage, property qualifications for voters (50 acres) and legislators (200 acres), and the inconveniently large size of the prospective states. But these objections dissolved as population grew and promises were kept. Settlers moved into the Northwest Territory in swelling numbers. Despite its speculative character, the Ohio Company proved to be paternalistic in practice, and Marietta, which was established by it on the river in 1788, was a transplanted New England village with all that this implied in architecture, education, and religion. Conditions were less happy in other places, but Ohio eventually became a territory unto itself and, early in the next century, a state. As one trans-Appalachian territory after another was set up and state after state was admitted in good faith, the West and particularly the Northwest became the most nationalistic of regions. The original states had created the federal government, but that federal government created the western states; it was the source and protector of their rights and privileges. These settlers were not primarily New Englanders or Virginians or Ohioans; they were first of all Americans.

THE ECONOMIC PROBLEM

While the Northwest Ordinance was a great achievement, it had little immediate effect in enhancing the prestige of the feeble government of the Confederation. By the date of its passage the general economic situation, which had been at its worst about 1786, was improving, but this was harder to see then than now. The difficulties of the previous years were unforgettable. The economic problem had touched all levels of private and public affairs. Debt and bankruptcy haunted farmers, planters, merchants, state governments, and the Congress of the Confederation. This state of affairs can be attributed to the fact that the artificial economy of wartime was followed by stagnation in time of peace, and that inflation gave way to deflation. More specifically, the new international situation was unfavorable to American commerce, and in a time of heavy debts and taxes there was an appalling shortage of currency which served to restrict if not to paralyze all forms of economic activity. The conflicting interests of debtors and creditors underlay the political struggles of the time. The attainment of general prosperity was contingent on the opening of markets and the creation of a sound and sufficient currency. The government of the Confederation has been blamed too much for a situation which could hardly have been escaped by any government, but unhappily its powers were unequal to either of these remedial tasks. Also, they were beyond the power of any single state.

During the war there had been an abnormal military market, along with risky but profitable foreign commerce. Prices rose because of the large emissions of paper money and certificates of indebtedness by Congress and the state governments, and because of the activities of speculators and profiteers. But war prosperity quickly collapsed after the peace treaty of 1783. The prewar channels of commerce with the West Indies were closed, the French withdrew special privileges they had granted during the war, and the British imposed on American commerce such restrictions as they chose, being confident that they would get whatever trade they wanted. Independence carried with it a considerable degree of commercial isolation at first, and a major task of diplomacy was to provide ways of escape from this.

American merchants aggressively searched out new markets. In 1784 and 1785, for example, they opened trade with China. But these processes were slow, and not until the end of the period of Confederation did New England traders begin to pick up furs in the Pacific Northwest, take them to China, and barter them for Oriental products. Salem traders were making fabulous profits from this sort of business within a generation, but in the years just after the Revolution the region that suffered most from the depression was commercial New England. The most violent conflicts between creditors and debtors occurred there, for the merchants were hard pressed and the farmers were distressingly short of money. The southern planters and farmers suffered less, partly because the foreign demand for their staples reasserted itself, partly because they were better treated by their state governments.

The most difficult domestic problems of this time of depression were those of debts, taxes, and the currency—which were inseparable. Despite the virtual repudiation of the paper money by which the Revolution had been so largely financed, both the state governments and the Confederation emerged from the war in debt. The foreign debt of the Confederation need not concern us here, for the interest on part of it was paid well enough to maintain credit in the Dutch money market, and it was not now or ever a real political issue. The domestic debt of the Confederation was estimated by Alexander Hamilton as amounting in 1790 to about $42 million, including interest. Roughly speaking, it consisted of loan-office certificates, given in return for actual loans, and a variety of certificates of indebtedness for supplies and services. This paper had greatly depreciated but it circulated as a sort of currency. The loan-office certificates had generally come into the hands of northern merchants and financiers, while the certificates of indebtedness were more widely scattered. Since Congress had no power to tax it could not well take in and pay off this paper in a period of depression, or even pay the promised interest.

At the end of the period the state debts came to about half as much as the domestic debt of the Confederation. The states had the power to tax and they employed it in the postwar years. This was chiefly to pay interest charges, which consumed a very large part of state incomes. But, to cite a conspicuous example of successful state financing, Virginia paid off a large portion of the principal of her debt—especially the part of it which consisted of military certificates issued to soldiers. These certificates were exchanged for western lands (of which Virginia still had a plentiful supply) and were accepted in payment of taxes, then destroyed.

The great problem of individuals everywhere was to find something with which to pay taxes and private debts. Paper money had been repudiated at the close of the war, and in the course of trade specie had been drained abroad. The supply of money was disproportionately small in view of the resources of the country, and it was inadequate to the needs of the people. Farmers were at a special disadvantage, for such wealth as they had was in things not money. It is no wonder, therefore, that a clamor arose from farmers and debtors generally for new issues of paper money, for "tender acts" requiring creditors to accept land and produce in payment of debts, and for "stay laws" on collections. Men could be thrown into jail for debt, and they were in many places. On the other hand, farmers and debtors could gain control of state legislatures in a self-governing society.

By 1786, when the politico-economic struggle reached its crisis, seven states had adopted some form of paper money, though the conditions and fortunes of the emissions varied considerably. In South Carolina, where merchants backed an inflationary move and the large planters acceded to it, the paper money did not depreciate. It was also a recognized success in New York for a time, but it depreciated badly in North Carolina, where creditors bitterly opposed it, and that state was the most extreme case—next to Rhode Island.

Long noted for individualism, "Little Rhody" now provided conservatives with a flagrant example of the perils of popular rule. The farmer-debtor group came into full legislative control and translated its extreme demands into law. The paper money which was issued could be borrowed by debtors on easy terms and in theory creditors were forced to accept it. As a result some of the latter fled the state before their debtors while others refused to accept payment. This led to the famous case of Trevett vs. Weeden (1786), which the Supreme Court of the state dismissed on grounds of lack of jurisdiction while expressing the opinion that the act forcing creditors to accept paper money was unconstitutional. The judges were dismissed by the legislature, but in the end the law was repealed. By going to such extremes the farmer-radicals had played into the hands of the merchant-conservatives.

Shays's Rebellion

The most bitter of all these struggles between debtors and creditors occurred in Massachusetts, ending in the famous Shays's Rebellion. This was an instance of resort to violence by debt-ridden farmers who had failed to impose their wishes on the legislature. Massachusetts had tried to reduce her debt too fast and had not allowed enough for depreciation under the existing circumstances; the tax laws were weighted against the farmers; taxes were much higher than elsewhere in New England; and courts were harsh against debtors. This was all in the interest of the creditors, who were not only opposed to any form of relief but favored a deflationary policy which worsened the plight of debtors. Discontent was rife in the western part of the state where farmers comprised a more important segment of the population than along the coast, and when the legislature adjourned in July 1786 without taking any relief actions, meetings of protest were held in Worcester and Hatfield. These advocated an issue of paper money while condemning the political authorities. Violent action followed. Mobs prevented the meetings of courts in Northampton, Worcester, Great Barrington, and elsewhere. Captain Daniel Shays, a veteran of the Revolution, appeared as a leader of the insurgents in late September, when his followers confronted a body of militia in Springfield. The court sat, nonetheless, and the insurgents disbanded until their hopes of peaceful reform vanished; then the movement became an armed rebellion. Governor James Bowdoin, a merchant, declared the insurgents outlaws, and General Benjamin Lincoln was appointed by the legislature to suppress them. Shays's band was finally routed at Petersham; he fled to Vermont, and, although pardoned, he did not return to Massachusetts. This ignorant man believed that he was fighting the Revolution all over again and did not doubt that his method as well as his cause was just. The government of Massachusetts wisely refrained from reprisals and a few laws were passed that limited court actions against debtors.

The reverberations of Shays's Rebellion were very important. It frightened conservatives and moderates everywhere in the Union. George Washington wrote: "There are combustibles in every state which a spark might set fire to. I feel infinitely more than I can express for the disorders which have arisen. Good God! Who besides a Tory could have foreseen, or a Briton have predicted them?" This fear turned some conservatives to dreaming of an American monarchy as the only safe solution. At just this time, Jefferson, now in Europe and disliking kings more than ever since he had seen them in action, asserted that there was far more disorder in monarchial France than republican America. But he was too far away to have immediate influence on American opinion, and he was under no illusions about the Confederation. All conservatives agreed that Congress was helpless to solve the economic problem, and that restraint should be placed on the states in money matters. A central government which should have power to place the country's currency and public credit on a solid footing seemed to conservatives a minimum necessity if the country's economy was to be saved from ruin and its political institutions saved from rebels.

Still it is true that by 1787 some of the cause for conservatives' fears had disappeared. The defeat of Shays discredited violence as a means of redress. The vast majority of Americans, including radicals, accepted the peaceful processes of petition and election as making rebellion unnecessary and wrong. By 1787, deflation had run its course and prosperity was on the way. The movement for a stronger central government was supported chiefly by merchants and creditors, but certain of the outstanding leaders of the movement, notably James Madison, cannot be identified with creditor interests. Such leaders could see in the international situation a reason to strengthen the central government which, if less emotionally compelling than fear of internal revolt and control of states by radicals, was even more urgent.

FOREIGN AFFAIRS UNDER THE CONFEDERATION

Commercial Helplessness

The economic problem was itself inseparable from the foreign problem. The American economy was predominantly extractive. Products of the sea, the forests, and the fields had to be sold abroad for consumption or processing, and manufactured articles had to be imported if American prosperity was to be achieved. But trade had to be carried on in a world of powerful and predatory economic empires with which the government of the Confederation was inadequate to cope. Americans no longer enjoyed the privileges and protection that went with membership in the British mercantilist empire, and Britain herself now waged economic war against the young republic. William Pitt, a convert to the free-trade principles of Adam Smith, proposed to Parliament in 1783 that trade relations with the United States be reorganized on a basis of complete equality, but mercantilists and Tories would not so easily forgive the ungrateful Americans. Their views were summed up by Lord Sheffield in his influential pamphlet, Observations on the Commerce of the United States (1784). Sheffield argued that it was unnecessary to make any concessions to American trade, because this would be forced back into British channels anyway. At the moment he was right, and his views prevailed.

Refusing to enter into any commercial agreement whatever with the

United States, the British government proceeded to regulate American trade unilaterally by acts of Parliament and Orders in Council precisely as if the states were still colonies. Indeed, many of the regulations were more severe than before. American wheat, for example, was now excluded from the British market by prohibitive duties—the "Corn Laws," which were not repealed until 1846. Most injurious was the exclusion of American products from the British West Indies, which had formerly absorbed great quantities of American provisions. Britain was now determined to give her loyal colonies, particularly Canada, the benefit of markets the disloyal colonies had formerly enjoyed. The few articles which Americans could sell to British colonies had to be carried in British ships. This provision fully accorded with current mercantilist practice, but it was to the disadvantage of Americans in the carrying trade, especially New Englanders. American vessels were allowed to carry American cargoes to the British Isles, but they had to pay higher fees than British ships.

John Adams, after serving with Franklin and Jefferson on a commission to negotiate commercial treaties in Europe which had very slight success, was sent to England in 1785 as the first minister of the United States to that country, while Jefferson succeeded Franklin as minister to France. In England, Adams was practically ignored and sometimes snubbed. As told in his family, the story was that King George, at a public reception, turned his back on him and Jefferson, who was visiting him at the time. American merchants spoke threateningly of retaliations against British commerce and action was taken by some of the states, but Lord Sheffield had correctly foreseen that the Confederation could not impose a uniform policy on the thirteen sovereign commonwealths. Each could establish its own tariff laws, and, far from uniting for defense against British policy, they proceeded to use their power over interstate and foreign commerce to wage economic war against each other and to compete against each other for crumbs from the British table. When Adams asked British officials to negotiate a commercial treaty, the nearest thing to an answer that he got was a jibe that it would require not one but thirteen treaties.

In the Old World, British merchants alone offered long-term credits to Americans. By resuming in this respect the practices of colonial times they further exploited American weakness: American merchants could not resist the temptation to go ever more deeply into debt in order to obtain the British goods the American consumers needed. Hard money drained out of the United States into British hands even more rapidly after the Revolution than before, and rosy dreams of fruitful economic independence turned to fear of commercial bankruptcy. Some far-sighted Englishmen saw that a prosperous and solvent America would be a far better customer, but Tory mercantilism and vindictiveness were the bases of British policy.

Far-sighted Americans, on the other hand, saw that only a central government with exclusive authority over interstate and foreign trade could make equitable commercial arrangements with Great Britain and the other maritime powers. The United States already had a commercial treaty with France (1778) and the politeness with which Jefferson was received in that country contrasted sharply with the rudeness of British officials to him and Adams. Despite the weakness of his bargaining position, he gained some concessions from the French by patient negotiation. But, like every other leader concerned with the conduct of foreign affairs, he was convinced of the absolute necessity of strengthening national authority and power in this sphere.

More than commerce was involved. The inability of the Confederation to control the states' conduct toward foreign powers threatened to destroy the political as well as the economic independence of the United States. The three great imperial governments—Great Britain, Spain, and France—had no intention of allowing the parvenu republic to become genuinely independent and powerful within the generous boundaries of the peace treaty.

British Troops on American Soil

On April 8, 1784, the day before George III solemnly proclaimed ratification of the Treaty of 1783 and enjoined his subjects to obey it, his Secretary of State for Home Affairs secretly ordered the military governor in Quebec to ignore it and maintain British troops on American soil south of the Great Lakes. The British sought to retain control over the fur trade for the benefit of Canadian traders and their British backers, and to maintain alliances with the Indian tribes of the region who would serve as buffers against the expansion of American settlement beyond the mountains. The British had made promises to the Indians and feared that failure to keep these would provoke attacks on Canada. Also, they wanted to be in position to fall heir to the territory of the Old Northwest in case the young republic should collapse. The excuse made by them for retaining the posts in violation of the treaty was that the American states had committed prior violations by refusing to live up to the promises regarding debts and Loyalists. The American Secretary of Foreign Affairs, John Jay, was so disgusted with the states that he indiscreetly let it be known that he regarded the excuse of the British as valid. This made the latter all the more complacent and immovable. Congress was in no position to do anything about the gravest problem that an independent government can face—the presence of a foreign power on its own soil.

Spain and the Mississippi River

In the Southwest, the Spanish government compromised American independence even more seriously. Spain had signed no treaty with the United States and did not recognize its ownership of trans-Appalachia. Because of deep-seated fear of American freedom and expansion as threats to their own empire, Spanish officials determined to hem in the dangerous republic east of the mountains. The British-American Treaty of 1783 had designated the 31st parallel as the southern boundary of the United States, but Spain refused to be bound by this because the boundary of West Florida (now returned to Spain) had been more than one hundred miles further north when Britain had owned it (1763-1783). Spain also claimed territory as far north as the Tennessee River on grounds of military operations during the war. Beyond the Tennessee, Spain bought the loyalty of Indian tribes and bribed American settlers who were anxious to obtain the right to ship their produce to the depots of New Orleans. Thus Spain made American ownership of the whole territory south of the Ohio River a dead letter, and the promising settlements of Kentucky and Tennessee were in danger of becoming Spanish colonies.

The great geographic determinant of Western history was the Mississippi River. In 1780, John Jay wrote: "The Americans, almost to a man, believed that God Almighty had made that river a highway for the people of the upper country to go to sea by."

In 1784, Spain closed the Mississippi to American shipping. At the same time, certain favored Americans were given special permission to carry cargoes to New Orleans as a demonstration of the advantages of loyalty to Spain. Settlers were more inclined, however, to open the river by conquering New Orleans than by knuckling under to the Spanish dons. British agents talked to them about a British protectorate. George Washington traveled through the West and concluded that the settlers stood "as it were upon a pivot. The touch of a feather would turn them any way." But the majority hated both Spain and Britain and asked only that the American government should protect them from both and, most important, secure for them the right to navigate the great river.

During the war, Spain had temporarily relaxed her mercantilist restrictions against American trade, and this trade was a source of hard money, which was sorely needed. Don Diego de Gardoqui arrived in 1785 as Spanish minister empowered to negotiate a treaty, but he was forbidden by his government to concede navigation of the Mississippi. Congress at the same time forbade John Jay to negotiate a treaty which did *not* include the navigation right. The United States could obtain no trade concessions from Spain without virtually surrendering the Southwest to her. Caught in this dilemma, Jay gave in to the demands of Eastern merchants.

He and they induced Congress to change his instructions in 1786 and permit him to trade off navigation rights in return for commercial concessions.

News of this raised a fearful clamor in the West. Westerners threatened to join England or Spain or, better still, to organize an expedition down the river to exterminate the Spaniards. Southern states with western interests opposed the treaty, and without them a vote of nine states for ratification by Congress was impossible. Therefore Jay was forced to allow the negotiations to collapse. This experience led directly to the provision in the Federal Constitution of 1787 that a two-thirds vote by the Senate is necessary for approval of a treaty. The Jay-Gardoqui negotiations left behind them a heritage of western suspicion of the East, and at the time they nakedly exposed the impotence of the Confederation in the face of the Spanish threat.

Attitude of the French

The French menace was less immediate and less open. The Americans had abundant reason to be grateful to France for past services. The kingdom was still the ally of the republic and, in the opinion of Jefferson who was minister at the Court of Versailles (1785-1789), was still its surest friend. That was not much to say but it was something. At this time the French had no designs on American territory, but they were also allied with Spain and mindful of her interests. They valued the United States as a makeweight against the British, and the great foreign minister Vergennes had intervened in the Revolution for just that reason, but he had no desire for the young country to pursue a genuinely independent course and become too strong to manage. He counted on its being a satellite of France.

The official French attitude in the 1780's was reflected in a consular convention which Vergennes and Franklin negotiated in 1784, in fulfillment of a provision of the treaty of amity and commerce of 1778. This granted to French consuls in the United States privileges and powers which amounted to extraterritorial jurisdiction—that is, the authority of officials to administer the laws of their own country in another country. This may be reciprocal in form but when one country is far stronger than the other it is not reciprocal in fact. These provisions were incompatible with American sovereignty and constituted a threat against political independence. Congress, following the advice of John Jay, did not ratify this convention. Jefferson negotiated a new convention with Montmorin, the successor of Vergennes, and, without endangering the official friendship with France, managed to get rid of all the features of extraterritoriality but one: French consuls in the United States were given jurisdiction in civil cases arising there between French citizens, while the Ameri-

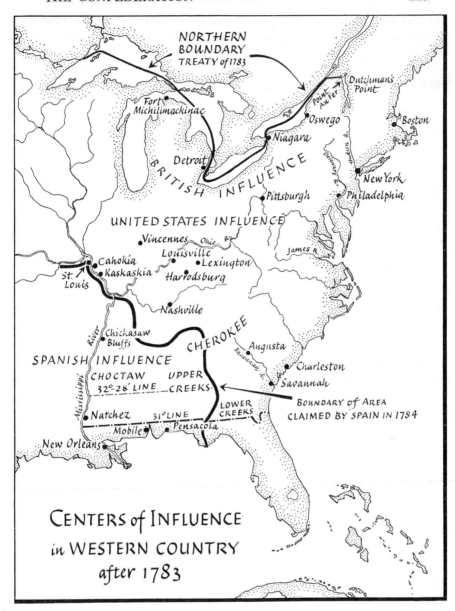

CENTERS of INFLUENCE in WESTERN COUNTRY after 1783

can consuls were given this authority in connection with Americans in France. Also he got the convention limited to twelve years. Jay recommended the ratification of this convention as a practical necessity. Actually it was the first international agreement approved by the United States Senate (1789), but in this concession of a degree of infringement on sovereignty it reflected American weakness under the Confederation.

In the 1780's the European powers did not expect or want the American experiment in revolution, liberty, and self-government to be successful. The state of American foreign relations offered the strongest of all arguments in favor of a new constitution. But the foreign and domestic problems were inseparable. A prosperous economy required a sound currency, the vitalization of public credit, and central control over interstate and foreign commerce; and all of these were prerequisite to the gaining of full independence from powers of the Old World which were not friendly to liberty.

CHAPTER 13

The Constitution of 1787

THE MEN WHO CREATED THE CONSTITUTION AND brought about its adoption had to overcome vast difficulties and their success still seems surprising. This constitutional movement as a whole has been described as a conservative revolution, in contrast to the radical revolution of 1776, but the most notable fact about it and the most wonderful is that the needs of the hour were met by the appeal of wise men to reason, rather than by the recourse of violent men to force. The leaders who met in the Federal Convention sought and found a middle way between anarchic localism and centralized tyranny; and as the Declaration of Independence voices a devotion to liberty which is characteristically American, the Constitution typifies American political realism and ability to compromise. There is no necessary conflict between these two great charters; and the Constitution, like the Declaration, was a supreme expression of the American mind.

THE FEDERAL CONVENTION

The members of the Congress, as James Madison said, had kept the Confederation afloat by working constantly at the pump, not by stopping the holes in the vessel. They were aware of the leaks, but all their efforts to render the ship seaworthy "had been frustrated by the selfishness or perverseness of some part or other of their constituency." Rhode Island, a "perverse sister," had blocked the Impost of 1781; and New York defeated the one of 1783 after a three-years' delay. The commercial state of New York was profiting greatly from the tariff duties she had imposed in her sovereign right and was disposed to grant no income from that source to Congress. Thus the effort to gain for the Confederation an independent income was a failure. An amendment granting Congress power to regulate foreign and interstate trade was debated in that body in 1784-1785, and this was defeated despite the provision that the duties would actually go to the states in which they were collected.

In the summer of 1786, a Congressional committee headed by James Monroe proposed amendments to the Articles which would have given Congress reasonable assurance of financial support and authority to regulate commerce, along with certain fresh powers to maintain full representation of the states and thus be able to carry on business. These amendments might have alleviated the most grievous ills of the immediate situation, but the legislative body never got around to passing them, and, judging from past experience, the states would not have accepted them if it had. The chances of any sort of constitutional change at the initiative of Congress had reached the vanishing point. Therefore, those who wanted change, whether great or small, centered their hopes in the winter of 1786-1787 on a movement which originated outside of the existing central government.

Preliminaries

The Convention in Philadelphia in the summer of 1787 was the consequence of two earlier interstate meetings of limited scope, the very inadequacy of which caused discerning men to conclude that a continental convention with broad purposes was necessary. The first of these two meetings was a very small one. In the summer of 1784, James Madison, who had completed a three-year tour of duty in Congress and was now an active member of the Virginia House of Delegates, made a motion in that body which led to the appointment of commissioners, including himself, to confer with representatives of Maryland about the navigation of the Potomac. This was a matter close to the heart of Washington, who lived on the banks of that river, and the deliberations took place in March 1785 at his hospitable home—which he described as a "well resorted tavern." Since Governor Patrick Henry forgot to inform Madison of the meeting he was not there, but an agreement was reached and he handled this interstate compact in the Virginia Assembly.

The Mount Vernon Conference, as this was called, dealt successfully with certain matters of commerce relating to two states, but Madison clearly saw that interstate and foreign trade could be effectively regulated only by the central government. The Virginia Assembly agreed (January 21, 1786) to a resolution which he drafted and John Tyler introduced, inviting all the states to send representatives to a commercial conference. The Annapolis Convention of September 1786 resulted.

Most of the states named deputies, but only a dozen men attended and they represented only five states. Madison, the moving spirit, gained powerful support from Alexander Hamilton, who came down from New York and drafted the address which was the only tangible result of the three-days' session. This went beyond commercial questions. It called upon all the states to appoint special commissioners to devise provisions which would render the Constitution "adequate to the exigencies of the Union." These proposals were to be reported to Congress and if approved by that body they were then to be referred to the states and confirmed by all of them. This little group of men made the specific suggestion that the meeting should be in Philadelphia on the second Monday in the following May.

Half a dozen states appointed delegates without waiting for Congressional action. Virginia was the first, and her action was made all the more impressive by the selection of George Washington to head her distinguished delegation. Madison induced him to accept. New Jersey, Pennsylvania, North Carolina, Delaware, and Georgia followed; and on February 21, 1787, Congress passed a resolution making the call for the Convention official. Congress admitted that there were "defects" in the Confederation and recognized that a convention was probably the best means of "establishing in these states a firm national government." The language itself was significant, and the changes were afterwards rung on the word "national." The Convention was to revise the Articles so as to render them "adequate to the exigencies of government and the preservation of the Union," and it was to report to Congress and the various legislatures.

The passage of this resolution encouraged other states to act. Shays's Rebellion had just occurred in Massachusetts, and this accelerated the movement for a stronger government. One New England state had no share whatsoever in these developments, however: Rhode Island stuck to her independent course and was never represented in the Convention. All the other states sent delegates, though those from New Hampshire did not arrive until the sessions were half over, because her government had trouble finding the money for their expenses.

The Federal Convention met in the Pennsylvania State House, where the Declaration of Independence had been adopted. On May 25, when at length a majority of the states were represented, the meeting was organized by the unanimous election of George Washington as president. The rules of procedure were that all voting should be by states, as in Congress, and that a majority of the states present would be sufficient to decide any question. But for the first provision the meeting would have broken up, and without the second very little would have been accomplished. With only slight interruption, the daily sessions continued until September 17, when the engrossed Constitution was signed in the names of all the states present by all of the delegates present except three.

This close approximation of unanimity is something to marvel at. It could hardly have been attained if the proceedings had not been strictly secret, and if these men had not been wholly free to change as well as to speak their minds. This secrecy was deplored by some leaders who were not there, Jefferson for instance, but it now seems exceedingly fortunate that the delegates did not have to talk and vote in the glare of publicity. Some fifty-five men attended the meetings at one time or another, but the average number present was only about thirty. This group was more like a large committee than a modern legislative body.

An "Assembly of Demigods"

Two of the leading statesmen of the day whose names are inseparable from the Declaration of Independence—Thomas Jefferson and John Adams—could not share in the making of the Constitution since they were on missions abroad. Writing from Paris to his friend Adams in London, Jefferson described this Convention as an "assembly of demigods." George Washington, now at the peak of popularity, came as near being a demigod in the eyes of his countrymen as any American who ever lived, and the prestige which he contributed to this gathering was an indispensable factor in its success. Second only to him in American esteem, and second to no one in world-wide reputation, was Benjamin Franklin, now eighty-one years old but still wise and witty. Nobody else who was there matched these two in fame then or afterwards, but James Madison and Alexander Hamilton stand very high on any list of American immortals. Madison, who was now thirty-six, was personally unimpressive but by common consent he was the most effective member of this body. On the other hand, Hamilton, who was even younger, played no important part. Outvoted by his two colleagues from New York, he attended relatively few sessions and his advice was little heeded.

Much more important was James Wilson of Pennsylvania, a nearsighted Scot whose national vision was far-reaching. Gouverneur Morris from the same state, a gallant with a shrunken arm and wooden leg, was one of the most brilliant of all the delegates though distrusted by some, and he left his mark on the language of the Constitution. Other men who made distinct contributions, when the time came for compromise, were Roger Sherman and Oliver Ellsworth of Connecticut; and John Rutledge of South Carolina was one of the more useful members. Governor Edmund Randolph of Virginia and George Mason, author of the Virginia Declaration of Rights, belong on any list of distinguished and influential delegates, even though they declined to sign the Constitution in the end, along with Elbridge Gerry of Massachusetts. Some of the delegations were mediocre; but almost all of these representatives had held important offices in their own communities and most of them had served at some time in Congress. They were men of large experience in state and Continental affairs and above all things they were practical.

In his notable book, *An Economic Interpretation of the Constitution of the United States* (first published in 1913), Charles A. Beard laid great emphasis on the identification of these men with the propertied class, especially the creditor class, and on the lack of representation of the small farmers and artisans. It is unquestionably true that the delegates belonged to the upper economic group from which the political leaders of the time were almost invariably drawn. The same can be said of most of the signers of the Declaration of Independence. It is also true that they were opposed to the sort of policies that had been carried through the legislature of Rhode Island by the debtor-farmers and had been championed by Daniel Shays and his followers in Massachusetts. The delegates had no sympathy with what they supposed to be an attempt to abolish private and public debts by legislative action or, worse still, by physical revolt. It would be a great mistake, nevertheless, to assume that everybody who was against Shays and the states' paper money was thinking solely or primarily of the particular interests of the creditor class. If we make a sharp distinction, as Beard did, between real property (such as land) and personalty (in some sort of paper), the southern planters were chiefly concerned about the former, and, despite some holdings of state and Continental paper, they were more often debtors than creditors. Special concern for the commercial and creditor groups was best exemplified in this period by Hamilton, who was of little influence in the Convention though of vast importance later. The dominant spirit of that body can be best ascertained by reading the mind of Madison. In financial matters he was characteristically conservative, he was strongly opposed to any form of repudiation, and to a notable degree he spoke for the general interest which comprehended all classes.

Madison held no securities which stood to appreciate in value by the establishment of a strong central government, and he had a conspicuous record as a defender of the rights of all men as individual human beings. It was he who carried through the Virginia Assembly, in Jefferson's absence abroad, the latter's notable revisal of the state's laws and, most particularly, the famous bill for establishing religious freedom. He deserved a lion's share of credit for the "philosophical legislation" of Virginia which won the admiration of enlightened liberals on both sides of the Atlantic. At the same time he was a political and economic realist. No leader of his day appreciated more fully than he that political conflicts more often arise from economic causes than any other; and he described this clash of interests so well that his words have been endlessly quoted. He recognized rich and poor, creditors and debtors, a landed interest, a manufacturing interest, a mercantile interest, a moneyed interest, along with many others; and he saw in the regulation of these the major task of government. But, unlike Hamilton, he did not believe in the dominance of the few over the many; and, unlike Karl Marx, he did not believe in the dominance of the many over the few. He believed that these various conflicting interests would balance each other off and cancel each other out sufficiently to avoid injustice, and his hope lay in the diversity of a large country. At this stage of his career he was specially fearful of what was afterward called the "tyranny of the majority," and he saw a dangerous possibility of this in state actions against private property. But he was not thinking of one kind of property in preference to another, and his record showed that he was concerned to protect religious as well as economic minorities. He contributed signally to American political philosophy by preaching the blessings of diversity; and if his thought is hard to grasp when stated abstractly it has been illustrated a thousand times in the history of his country. His chief conviction was that tyranny has been rare where interests have been many and no one of them has been able to gain predominance.

One of Madison's colleagues in the Convention said that he was always the best informed delegate on any point that came up in debate. This was no accident. Ever the scholar in politics, he had prepared himself fully and specifically for this occasion. His special preparations, which extended over a period of at least two years, were greatly facilitated by the books his friend Jefferson sent him from Europe. These enabled him to make a particular study of ancient and modern confederacies, and it was in the light of historical as well as personal experience that he viewed the existing American Constitution and perceived its "mortal ills." The simplest statement of the purposes he brought to Philadelphia is that he wanted this Confederacy to be transformed into a nation.

One can argue endlessly about what constitutes a nation, but the extreme alternatives which these men faced can be stated simply. On the one hand was a group of virtually independent states and on the other a consolidated republic in which the states would virtually disappear. Madison was looking for middle ground which would "support a due supremacy of the national authority, and leave in force the local authorities so far as they can be subordinately useful." It was characteristic of him to seek a working balance and to oppose most strongly the evils which were greatest at a particular time. He talked a good deal about the rights of the states in later years, but his chief concern now was to reduce centrifugal forces and to strengthen the central authority of the republic.

Extreme advocates of national authority were relatively unimportant in the Convention and the most extreme group of all was without a voice. There were in the country old army officers, members of the Society of the Cincinnati, who would have liked to establish a military dictatorship and make George Washington the King. But for Washington's own absolute refusal, such a movement might have gained great headway while the Confederation was faltering. In 1787, however, representatives of this point of view were conspicuously absent from the Convention, just as the farmer-debtors were.

FRAMING THE CONSTITUTION

The Virginia Plan

A few days after the Convention was organized, Edmund Randolph presented to it on behalf of the entire delegation from his state a set of fifteen resolutions comprising what is known as the Virginia Plan. After introducing the resolutions on May 29, Randolph withdrew the first of them the next day. This had implied that a mere correction of the Articles of Confederation would be sufficient. The three resolutions that he offered in place of the first on May 30 stated forcefully that a mere "federal" Union would not be sufficient, and that a "national" government, consisting of a *supreme* legislature, executive, and judiciary, should be created.

The Virginia Plan provided the basis of discussion in the Convention for more than two weeks, and not until June 15 was it challenged as a whole. It called for a central government with three branches. A legislature in two houses was recommended, along with a national executive and national judiciary. This was to be a new government in structure. But the three branches lacked the degree of mutual independence that was finally granted them, since the legislature would have elected the executive and the judges. The best clue to the nationalism of the Virginia Plan is to be found in its provisions for representation. Here, also, is the best explanation of the lengths to which Madison was willing to go in granting authority to the legislature. He was willing to trust it if it could be based on the sovereignty of the whole people. The crucial resolution was the one calling for representation in the legislature in proportion to quotas of contributions or to free population. This struck directly at the equality of the states in voting, which was the fundamental principle of the Confederation and had made it a league rather than a nation.

The injustice of the existing situation was obvious to the Virginians, whose state had no more voice in Congress than Delaware though it was believed to have sixteen times as many people. More than the interests of particular states was involved; this was a question of the basis of representative government. Should the basis be the states as governments (meaning in practice the legislatures) or the states as people? The Virginia Plan called for the election of the members of one house of the central legislature by the people and for the election of the members of the other by the first house from nominees of the state legislatures. The lower, popularly-elected house was to be the most important part of the central structure. Furthermore, the final resolution called for the submission of the new Constitution to conventions which were "expressly chosen by the people." The whole new structure was to be grounded on popular approval. This recognition of popular sovereignty is the more significant because of the antidemocratic reaction of the times.

The Virginia Plan appealed to states with a relatively large population or with such a large area that they might expect to be populous in the future; and when the Committee of the Whole approved the three-fifths rule for slaves the principle of proportionate representation in both houses of Congress became generally acceptable to the Southern states. But the fears of the small Northern states were rising. Quite clearly they were going to have a much smaller share in the new government than they had had in the Confederation, and they became increasingly reluctant to surrender the principle of state equality. Some of their delegates were now arguing that, if proportionate representation should obtain, the only fair procedure would be to throw all the states into "hotchpotch" and redivide them so as to make them equivalent in size. Representatives of the large states, such as Virginia and Pennsylvania, described this proposal as wholly impracticable, but they could not properly object to the request of certain small states for delay in order that they might present a plan of their own.

The New Jersey Plan

The plan that William Paterson of New Jersey offered on June 15 called merely for a strengthening of the Confederation without changing its character as a league of states centering on Congress. Additional powers were given that body to raise revenue, control commerce, and make requisitions on the states. There was to be an executive, consisting of more than one person and elected by Congress, and a judiciary without inferior courts and with only appellate jurisdiction. The strongest of the resolutions provided that acts of Congress and treaties should be the "supreme law" of the states and that the various state courts should be bound by them. This sweeping assertion of national authority afterwards got into the Constitution, but in the New Jersey Plan it was coupled with a government which was structurally weak and could never have been truly representative. The fatal flaw of the Plan lay in its basic assumption that the states were governments first of all, rather than people, and that they were equal in authority in the Union.

In the course of the discussion of the New Jersey Plan, Alexander Hamilton expressed his unfavorable opinion of it in no uncertain terms, and at the same time manifested his dissatisfaction with the Virginia Plan. His alternative proposals were not offered to the Convention; he merely read them and gave them to Madison to file. It was fortunate for his public popularity that his speech and proposals were not published until long after his death and that only a few of his contemporaries knew how doubtful he was of the success of the American Republic. The

British government was the best in the world, he believed, and the only one that united "public strength with individual security." He wanted a new American government, with decisive powers and complete sovereignty, but he was not one to stress the sovereignty of the people. He spoke of the "amazing violence and turbulence of the democratic spirit," and, while approving the election of members of the House of Representatives by popular vote, he wanted the Senate, as well as the Executive, to be chosen by electors one or two removes from the populace and to hold office for life, thus serving as a barrier against pernicious innovations after the manner of the House of Lords. Not only did he favor a President for life; he favored giving this officer a full veto over all laws passed by Congress and the right to appoint all the governors of states, who should have a similar authority over the actions of state legislators. This would have been consolidation with a vengeance, and if it was not monarchical in name it was almost that in spirit.

Hamilton's antidemocratic sentiments were undoubtedly approved by some members of the Convention, but not even he thought it feasible to set up as consolidated a system as he favored in theory. Nor were many delegations now satisfied with the sort of federation the New Jersey Plan would have maintained. Consequently, when the matter was put to a vote in the Committee of the Whole on June 19, the amended Virginia Plan was preferred to the one Paterson had submitted. Strong opposition to proportionate representation in both houses of Congress continued, however. The feeling in late June and early July was so intense that some delegates believed the Convention to be on the verge of dissolution, and Benjamin Franklin proposed that the sessions be opened with prayer for Divine assistance.

The Great Compromise

A committee containing a representative of each state recommended what has come to be known as the Great Compromise of the Constitution, and after the working out of certain details it was formally adopted on July 16. The crucial feature of this was the concession to the small states of an equal vote in the Senate. The provision for representation in the lower House was essentially the same as had already been agreed to: namely, representation was to be based on the respective numbers of inhabitants, slaves being counted as three-fifths. The provision that direct taxes should be apportioned on the same basis may be regarded as a concession by the Northern states, since it assured the Southerners that slaves would not be taxed as such. Part of the proposal was that money bills should originate in the House of Representatives and not be amendable by the Senate, though they might be rejected. Madison correctly judged this concession meaningless, and in the end the

Senate was left as free to amend money bills as any others. It was generally believed, nonetheless, that the House would be the more important legislative branch. The number of representatives from each state was specified in the first instance, and there was a good deal of guesswork in the absence of precise information about the population; but provision was made for an enumeration within three years of the first meeting of Congress and within every ten years thereafter.

On the other hand, the concession of state equality in the Senate made it impossible for that body to be genuinely representative of the American people. The convention at a later time made this situation irremediable: in the Article of the Constitution dealing with Amendments it include the specific declaration that no state may be deprived of its equal suffrage in the Senate without its own consent. Thus the Great Compromise based the membership of the legislative branch of the government on geography as well as population and imparted to Congress a federal as well as a national character. Some of the leading delegates, like Madison, and some of the largest states, like Virginia and Pennsylvania, opposed this settlement, but they came to recognize it as the necessary price of Union. After the Great Compromise, a report got into a newspaper that a proposal had been made to give the name "Unanimity Hall" to the room where the Convention was meeting. From this time on, the small states were more eager than the large ones to strengthen the central government, realizing that they would have a larger share in it than was warranted by their population or their wealth.

The Federalism of the Constitution

One of the most important of the questions which were still unsettled when the Committee on Detail was elected was that between an enumeration of the powers of the central government and a general grant of power. On this point the states had been evenly divided and the alignment was not determined by their size. As the problem was finally worked out, the central government was to be one of specified powers and functions but the scope and exercise of these were broadened by certain general expressions, chiefly the "general welfare clause" and the "necessary and proper clause." Also, a whole group of powers formerly exercised by states and falling mostly in the fiscal and commercial fields were to be explicitly denied the states. There remained, however, a very large residue of powers that were neither granted the central government nor denied the states, and by necessary implication these remained with the latter or the people. This was not explicitly stated in the Constitution drafted in Philadelphia, but the Tenth Amendment (1791) soon made that point entirely clear.

The Fathers had arrived at a dual system. This involved not merely the division of the field of government in a large country through force of practical necessity, but also the recognition in principle of both the general idea of the Union and the local idea of the individual state. The Union and the states were coexistent, and neither was at the mercy of the other. Expounding the Constitution a few weeks after the Convention, Madison said that it was neither national nor federal but a "composition of both." It was on a fresh pattern which was neither that of a league nor a consolidated republic. Conceivably it might veer in either direction and the draftsmen regarded excessive localism as the more immediate danger, but they sought to strike a balance and show the middle way. A fresh term was needed to describe their point of view, and the one most commonly employed in the next few years was "federalist." Like many other terms, this one was eventually abused by politicians, but through the generations it has been used to designate the basic American doctrine as embodied in the Constitution, and federalism is perhaps the most important American contribution to political science.

The Presidency

In the course of time the Presidency came to be regarded as a major contribution to the instrumentalities of government. There was little dispute in the Convention about the desirability of making the chief executive an important officer, but the question of his election proved difficult and was not settled until the last weeks. So long as the original proposal that he be elected by the legislature was agreed to, the general feeling was that he should have a rather long term and be ineligible for re-election. That is, he should be under no temptation to cater to Congress after he was elected. As the Convention went on, important delegates like Madison and James Wilson came to prefer his election by the people, directly or indirectly. The electoral system, which Wilson proposed, was designed to render the President independent of the legislative department from the very beginning and to vest his election in a group of qualified men who were selected for this express purpose.

The electors were to be chosen in any way that the legislatures of the various states should direct, and it was presumed that they would follow their own judgment in voting. They came to follow party judgments rather than personal opinions after parties arose, and in the course of time they were chosen everywhere by popular vote. According to the original system, each elector was to vote for two men, one at least of whom must be an inhabitant of another state. The man receiving the largest vote, if a majority, was to be President and the next man Vice-President. In case no one had a majority, the House of Representatives was to choose from the five highest on the list, voting by states. Time proved this system to be impracticable and it was changed by amendment. The term of the President was now set at four years and no limit was imposed upon his re-election. The number of electors from any state was to equal the whole number of Senators and Representatives from the state. The original system permitted adjustment to later democratic developments, and it could be rightfully said in later years that Presidents went into office with a mandate from the people, but the electoral system perpetuated the inequities of the Great Compromise. In the choice of a President the small states were to have a disproportionate voice, as they were to have in Congress.

Provision for Ratification

In form, the provision for the adoption of the Constitution was revolutionary. The delegates had set out to amend the Articles of Confederation, and the specified procedure was for amendments to be agreed to in Congress and afterwards confirmed by the legislatures of all the states. But, following the proposal in the Virginia Plan, the Convention decided that this new instrument should be ratified by conventions, not legislatures, and that it should go into effect when ratified by nine states among the states so ratifying. One reason for this disregard of the express requirements of the Articles was that unanimous ratification was doubtful or likely to be long delayed, and that conventions were more likely to ratify than legislatures, since the latter had a vested interest in state authority and would be reluctant to surrender any part of it. Also, there was an important philosophical reason. It was believed by many at this time, following the example of Massachusetts, that a convention chosen by vote of the electorate for a specific purpose was the fullest possible expression of the people's will; and, as Madison expressed it, a major difference between a nation and a league was that the former rested on the people, not on the state governments.

The American people were divided by state lines, however, and the precise language of the Preamble—"We the People of the United States" —was somewhat fortuitous. It would have been more accurate to say: "We the people of New Hampshire, Massachusetts," and so on. But nobody knew at the time what nine states would ratify first, and it would have been improper to list one that declined to ratify. The general expression in the Constitution voiced a hope rather than a reality: it was the desire of the Fathers that the new instrument should be based on the will of the sovereign people as a whole. Not all of the people voted then, to be sure, but the Constitution left requirements for the suffrage precisely where they were already—that is, in the hands of the states. It is worthy of note that no property qualifications were imposed on the holders of federal office under the proposed new government.

RATIFICATION

Some months after the Federal Convention adjourned, Madison described the Constitution as "the best that could be obtained from the jarring interests of states, and the miscellaneous opinions of politicians"; and Benjamin Franklin at the time sagely remarked that another convention could not be expected to produce a better one. This was the almost unanimous opinion of the delegates who had struggled with these problems for so many weeks. But Congress and the states had not had the benefit of these secret deliberations and the new charter of government now had to withstand public scrutiny. At the outset George Washington had issued a grave exhortation: "Let us raise a standard to which the wise and honest can repair. The event is in the hands of God." The Fathers of the Constitution did not content themselves with reliance on Divine Providence, however. They conducted a vigorous campaign for ratification and this was a major reason why the work of their hands was accepted.

The Convention sent the Constitution to Congress, then sitting in New York, with the recommendation that it be submitted to conventions in the various states, as specified in the document. On September 28, Congress, by unanimous vote of the states present, resolved to follow the prescribed procedure. In view of the sweeping changes in the government that were proposed, and the revolutionary nature of the provisions for ratification, this docility may seem surprising. But most of these men recognized the seriousness of the public situation, and sentiment favorable to the proposed plan of government increased when a dozen members of the Convention who were also regularly elected delegates to Congress came from Philadelphia to New York and joined the latter body. Conspicuous among these was Madison, who strongly defended the Convention against the charge that it had exceeded its instructions. A contradiction might be perceived in the instructions themselves, he said, since it was not possible to set up a "*national* and *adequate*" government merely by altering the Articles of Confederation. The essence of his argument was that the end justified the means, and the judgment of posterity has been that it did, especially since the means themselves were reasonable and peaceful. As Thomas Jefferson said a little later, the United States had set the world the admirable example of "changing a consitution by assembling the wise men of the State, instead of assembling armies."

Madison attributed the forbearance of the public to the "irresistible conviction" that it would be absurd to subject the fate of twelve states to "the perverseness or corruption of the thirteenth." The necessity of waiving the requirement of unanimity was generally conceded; and even those members of Congress who were turning against the Constitution, like Richard Henry Lee of Virginia, thought that the only proper procedure was to refer it to the states. The state legislatures, except for that of Rhode Island, accepted the recommendation and called specially-elected ratifying conventions, without insisting on their own right under the Articles to do the ratifying or the rejecting. This was a constitutional revolution and some have even described it as a *coup d'état*.

The ratification campaign represented a triumph of organization and skillful political management. The supporters of the Constitution, now called Federalists, were united while its various foes were divided; and the former, having seized the initiative, proceeded to keep it. During the winter of 1787-1788 and the succeeding spring and summer, eleven of the states accepted the Constitution. North Carolina, where the Anti-Federalists gained control, deferred decision, and Rhode Island did not act at all in this period. The remaining eleven commonwealths may be divided into three groups in the order of ratification:

(1) Delaware, Pennsylvania, New Jersey, Georgia, and Connecticut. These five states ratified in December and January. Their action was prompt, either because of the absence of effective opposition or the desire to forestall it. The vote in the conventions of Delaware and New Jersey was unanimous, and apparently it was in Georgia. It was two-to-one in Pennsylvania and more than three-to-one in Connecticut. The procedure in Pennsylvania was regarded by a vocal minority as hasty and high-handed and the vote may not have been a true index of the opinion of the electorate; but with this possible exception the Federalist sentiment in these five states was overwhelming. Furthermore, these early actions imparted to the movement for the Constitution a momentum it never lost.

(2) Massachusetts, Maryland, South Carolina, and New Hampshire (February 6—June 21, 1788). In Maryland and South Carolina, where action was very deliberate, the vote left no doubt of the overpowering strength of Federalist opinion. Massachusetts and New Hampshire were in very doubtful case, however, and the acceptance of the Constitution by the former by a close vote was accompanied by the strong recommendation of specific amendments. In many quarters, opponents of the Constitution were urging that another federal convention be called to consider amendments. The result of this would have been to throw the country back into the chaos of doubt from which it was emerging, and the specification by individual states of particular amendments as an absolute condition of ratification would have resulted in vast uncertainty and confusion. The example of Massachusetts in attaching recommendations rather than conditions to her act of ratification was followed by several other states. Ratification by New Hampshire was decisive, since she

was the ninth state and the establishment of the new government was thus assured. This government could hardly have hoped to endure, however, without further accessions.

(3) Virginia and New York (June 26 and July 26, 1788). Because of their size and geographical position these were key states, and the most severe battles occurred within them. Ratification was by a close vote in each case, at the end of a long campaign. The famous series of essays called *The Federalist* arose out of the conflict in New York and was employed very effectively there and in Virginia.

The heroes of the ratification fight in Virginia and New York were Madison and Hamilton, and in each instance the opposition was led and symbolized by the most popular political figure in the state—Patrick Henry in Virginia and Governor George Clinton in New York. With Henry, whose power lay in his voice and not his pen and who appeared in this conflict primarily as a localist, was ranged George Mason, who strongly criticized the new Constitution for its omission of guarantees of individual freedom. He had declined to sign it chiefly for this reason, and he also thought it went too far in the direction of consolidation. The position of Richard Henry Lee was strikingly like that of Mason. Before the end of 1787, Lee published his *Letters of the Federal Farmer*, which became a sort of textbook of the opposition. In New York, in September of the same year, Clinton, under the pseudonym "Cato," began a series of newspaper articles against the Constitution. His grounds of opposition, like those of Patrick Henry, appear to have been chiefly local; he did not want his strategically-placed state to be absorbed into a stronger Union.

The Federalist *Papers*

Realizing the difficulties of the situation in New York, Hamilton conceived the idea of a series of articles in which the Constitution should be thoroughly expounded. He himself did not think that document went far enough in granting power to the central government, but he was determined that it should be adopted and he brought to his self-imposed task unexcelled powers of exposition and persuasion. About a month after Clinton's first article appeared, Hamilton published his first as "Publius." He had gained the promise of assistance from John Jay, who was specially competent in the field of foreign relations, but that gentleman fell ill after doing four numbers and was able to do only one more. Under these circumstances Hamilton turned to Madison, who was in New York as a delegate to Congress and remained there through the winter. The result was one of the most fruitful collaborations in American history. *The Federalist* consisted of 85 numbers altogether, the last appearing in a newspaper in May 1788. All were signed "Publius" and it now appears that Hamilton wrote 59 of them, Jay 5, and Madison 29. The series was published almost immediately in book form, and competent contemporary judgment of it is reflected in the statement of Jefferson that it was "the best commentary on the principles of government which was ever written." More particularly, it was a commentary on the proposed government for the United States, written for the very practical purpose of gaining support for it.

Though they followed the orderly plan which Hamilton had formulated, the authors worked independently and the views of the two main ones were not identical. They were in complete agreement about the value of union, the gross inadequacy of the Confederation, and the necessity of adopting the Constitution. But the differences between them that had appeared in the Convention were reflected here in a difference in emphasis. Hamilton sought to show the necessity of a government "*at least equally energetic with the one proposed*," and quite obviously he would have preferred one that was considerably more energetic. To Madison fell the appropriate and congenial task of describing the actual problems that the Convention had faced, of showing the "*conformity of the proposed Constitution to the true principles of republican government*," and of defining the system of checks and balances which had been designed to prevent tyranny. In describing the operations of the new government, he dealt primarily with the House of Representatives, while Hamilton dealt with the Senate, the Executive, and the Judiciary.

Hamilton exercised considerably more restraint than he had in the Convention, but in these pages as elsewhere he appears as a major prophet of national power. Madison was closer to the spirit of the Convention itself, and he convincingly answered the criticisms of the proposed government as a "consolidation." He was setting the stage for his coming duel with Patrick Henry. The best-remembered characterization of the Constitution by that rural orator is that it "squinted" toward monarchy, and there was this special reason why Madsion should emphasize its republican form and character. Like other American political experiments, it rested on "the capacity of mankind for self-government," he said. His definition of republican government was destined to become a classic, and he gave as clear a statement as has ever been made of the extent to which the government of the United States was to be national on the one hand and federal on the other.

Virginia and New York

The Federalist served as a textbook for one side in the debate in Richmond—the greatest debate of them all. Madison had succeeded in wooing Edmund Randolph back to the side of the Constitution, partly by appealing to his distrust of Patrick Henry—a distrust which was shared by

Madison himself and Thomas Jefferson. The latter was outside this particular fight and Washington was not there. Edmund Pendleton and young John Marshall battled for the Constitution, while George Mason and James Monroe were against it. But the main antagonists were Henry and Madison: eloquence was matched and finally borne down by patient argument and explanation. The final vote was 89 to 79. It was the hardest fight and the greatest victory of Madison's long and useful life.

In Virginia as elsewhere the opponents of the Constitution could not agree on their objections. One that is specially worthy of note, however, was to the control of commerce by the Union. The fears that were now being expressed harked back to the old negotiations of John Jay about the navigation of the Mississippi. The danger that this might be surrendered in the interest of the Northern commercial states was specially alarming to representatives of the Kentucky counties, and despite Madison's own clear record on the issue these fears could not be wholly dissipated. A majority of the delegates were convinced that the proper procedure was to ratify first and amend afterwards. The Virginia convention recommended to the consideration of the first Congress a bill of rights in twenty parts, and a score of amendments to the body of the Constitution. The first of the latter, like the First Amendment proposed by Massachusetts, called for an explicit statement that the powers not specifically delegated to Congress should be retained by the states. Basic guarantees of individual liberty and this degree of protection of the rights of the states were expected of the new government, though not made an express condition of ratification. There was another expectation in the minds of the Virginians—that George Washington would be the first President—and this reconciled many opponents of the Constitution to the decision in its favor.

It has been estimated that when the New York convention first assembled, from two-thirds to three-fourths of its members were opposed to ratification, though sentiment in New York City was strongly favorable. Under the leadership of Hamilton the Federalists fought a delaying action, and the conventions in New Hampshire and Virginia acted favorably in the meantime. Hamilton was skillful in maneuver and powerful in debate, and eventually a favorable vote of 30 to 27 was attained. The convention affirmed what amounted to a bill of rights, put on record its own interpretation of certain phrases in the Constitution, and proposed a set of amendments. It assumed that there would be another federal convention, and the next legislature of the state actually called on the first Congress under the Constitution to summon one. No doubt the Federalists had concluded that any sort of ratification was better than none.

A few days after New York finally acted, North Carolina adopted a Declaration of Rights and proposed twenty-six amendments to the

Constitution, but neglected to ratify that document. One of her delegates in the Congress of the Confederation wrote to another of his country-men sarcastically: "It appears that North Carolina has at length thrown herself out of the Union, but happily she is not alone; the large, upright and respectable State of Rhode Island is her associate."

To the Congress of the Confederation it now appeared that the Constitution had been ratified, but this body delayed proclaiming that event because the delegates could not agree just where the new govern-ment should get started. They finally concluded to follow the path of least resistance and leave it in its present seat, which happened to be New York. Not until September 13 did the old Congress resolve that the new one should meet on the first Wednesday in March 1789, following the choice of electors in January and their assembling to vote for the Presi-dent in February.

The Bill of Rights

The most serious and general objection to the new Constitution was its lack of a bill of rights. Early in the first session of the first Congress, Madison introduced one, and as passed by both houses this consisted of twelve amendments. Two of these, dealing with the membership of Congress and the pay of Congressmen, were never ratified by the states but the ten others were. Proclaimed in 1791, they have ever since been regarded as virtually a part of the original Constitution. They begin with the guarantee that Congress shall make no law respecting an establish-ment of religion, or prohibiting the free exercise thereof; and they end, in the Tenth Amendment, with the express declaration that undelegated powers, not prohibited to the states, are reserved to the states or to the people. All ten are restrictions on the federal government, not the indi-vidual state governments. They were regarded as the honest fulfillment of a tacit pledge and they served to make the Constitution the guardian of liberty as well as the instrument of power.

This action was in direct response to public opinion, but there was no popular referendum on the Constitution at any time—just as there was none on the Declaration of Independence. Judging from the popular vote for delegates to the various conventions, the sentiment of the voters in several of the states that ratified the document in 1787-1788 was adverse or doubtful in the first instance. It should be borne in mind, also, that in practically all cases the suffrage was considerably restricted. Thus the movement for the Constitution, like that for independence from the mother country, was the work of a minority. Considering the times, this was not at all surprising, and both movements must be judged at last by their purposes and fruits.

In the ratification fight the lines of cleavage were not always clear but they tended to coincide with those of economic interest. The groups which had been specially imperiled under the Confederation, or were specially conscious of their peril—merchants and creditors generally—tended to favor the Constitution, which provided safeguards for their property against state actions. The two states which had been most conspicuous in connection with paper money and the relief of debtors, North Carolina and Rhode Island, did not ratify until after the new government had been set up; and opposition was most manifest among small farmers and debtors. By and large, the coastal and commercial districts favored the Constitution, while the back country tended to oppose it. But there was good reason to hope that all groups would prosper in a more perfect Union.

The Success of the Constitution

Within a remarkably short time after the Constitution became effective, opposition to it almost wholly ceased, and as soon as national political parties appeared they vied with each other in avowing their devotion to what was already becoming a sacred document. It has been said that the Americans enthroned it in place of a king; and from the presidency of George Washington until the present day the common assumption among them has been that their country has enjoyed the best of all forms of government. How can we explain the extraordinary success and popularity of the charter which issued from a closed room in Philadelphia and over the merits of which men had so fiercely battled?

The immediate success of the first administration under the Constitution was owing to various personal, political, and economic factors which appeared in happy combination. But full credit must be given the Fathers for their great skill in correcting the structural ills of the Confederation, which they understood so well from personal experience. The Union now had a government which could really function.

Unlike the Articles of Confederation, the Constitution did not contain the expression "perpetual Union," and dissolution was to be threatened a number of times before the supreme threat of the 1860's. We may now wonder why the Fathers did not speak more categorically on this point, but it was a sign of their practical wisdom that they did not deal in absolutes or peer too far into the distant future. By necessity as well as choice they set up a dual rather than a consolidated system: while declaring the supremacy of the laws of the United States they divided sovereignty between the Union and the individual commonwealths, leaving an unexplored borderland; and they left a host of unanswered questions to the arbitrament of time. Extending central authority as far as they safely could by specific grant, they made undefined general grants which could form the basis for expanding power, if there should be later need for it and if circumstances should permit its growth.

It is because of this capacity for growth and adjustment to changing circumstances that the Constitution has endured from the age of the stagecoach and post rider to that of the airplane and atomic power. By means of general expressions, such as the "elastic"' and "necessary and proper" clauses, the Fathers made it possible for the enumerated powers of Congress to be expanded. They did not anticipate the interpretation that Abraham Lincoln would give to his war powers, but they made the President the commander-in-chief of the armed forces. They could hardly have foreseen the full development of the doctrine of judicial review under Chief Justice Marshall and his successors, but they made the Constitution and the laws and treaties of the United States the supreme law of the land, and extended the judicial power to all cases arising under these.

While the *powers* of the new government proved to be flexible, the Fathers imparted a certain rigidity to the governmental *structure* which has characterized it ever since. They made provision for precise terms of office and tried to draw a sharp line of demarcation between the branches of the United States government. Thus they made it difficult to assign responsibility for public acts and made conflict between the branches almost inevitable. The conflict between Congress and the President runs through the whole of American political history, and it has caused many thoughtful Americans to long for a more unified and responsible government like that of England. But in their age of absolute monarchs in Europe and highhanded local legislatures in America, the framers of the Constitution sought to make tyranny difficult if not impossible. To them, as to Montesquieu, there were three distinct types of power—legislative, executive, and judicial—and the junction of these spelled tyranny. Efficiency may be hard to attain under the American system of divided authority and responsibility, but in our own age, when totalitarianism threatens all mankind, we can be grateful that we have been so well guarded against consolidated despotism.

The Constitution was least effective when it departed furthest from past experience and relied most on theory. If the separation of powers and system of checks and balances are not a case in point, the electoral system surely is. This novel device was a practical failure; and despite its modification by the Twelfth Amendment and the later practice of choosing electors by popular vote within each state, it remains as a sort of vermiform appendix in the constitutional system.

Other unfortunate features of the Constitution may be attributed to the necessity for compromise. The concession of equality of the states in the Senate, wholly without regard to population, is one of them; and this inequity is perpetuated also in the electoral system. The three-fifths ratio for slaves, without which the southern states would probably not have agreed to the Constitution, was destined to cause much future trouble. Mention may also be made of the denial to Congress of the right to prohibit the foreign slave trade for twenty years, which was balanced at the time by the concession to the northern states that navigation laws could be passed by a majority rather than a two-thirds vote.

It has sometimes been argued that amendment of the Constitution was made too difficult, and it is a fact that after the adoption of the Twelfth Amendment in 1804, there was no other until 1865. This led to the saying that a war is required to amend the Constitution. But the process was far easier than it had been under the Articles of Confederation. No state can be deprived of its equality in the Senate without its own consent, however, and a combination of sparsely settled states can block changes in the government even though an overwhelming majority of the whole people may regard these as imperative. This is a fault of the dual system which was otherwise particularly adapted to the American situation. A division of authority between states and nation is essential to the American system, and the provision for the admission of new states permitted the indefinite expansion of the Union.

The Constitution cannot be properly described as what Gladstone called it, "the greatest work that was ever struck off at a given time by the brain and purpose of man." Nor can one justly claim that since 1789 the people of United States have lived under the best of all possible governments. But within the framework which the experienced statesmen of 1787 set up it has been possible for a great nation to develop and for a diverse people to enjoy a fuller measure of freedom, prosperity, and happiness than has generally been offered mortal men in older countries. The Fathers had an uncommon measure of wisdom and they builded even better than they thought. The enduring Republic is their living monument.

Part III

ESTABLISHING THE REPUBLIC
1789-1815

CHAPTER 14

Launching a New Government 1789-1793

THE FIRST CONGRESS UNDER THE CONSTITUTION WAS supposed to convene in New York on March 4, 1789, but it was April 1 before the House of Representatives attained a quorum. Without waiting for a quorum the Senate chose a temporary presiding officer, whose constitutional function it was to open the electoral votes. John Langdon of New Hampshire opened them on April 6 in joint session, announcing that George Washington had been unanimously elected President and that John Adams of Massachusetts, with the next highest vote, had been elected Vice-President.

The long-time secretary of the Continental Congress, Charles Thomson, had the honor of conveying the news to Mount Vernon, where the President-elect was immersed in spring. It took Thomson a week to get there, and a couple of days later Washington started northward. Friends and admirers addressed him in Alexandria and Baltimore; he was given a public banquet in Philadelphia; he passed through a triumphal arch at Trenton; he was received by the president and faculty of the college at Princeton; he crossed the Hudson in a specially constructed barge, rowed by thirteen pilots; and on April 23 he reached New York. John Adams had already taken his seat and started presiding over the Senate.

A week after Washington's arrival he was inaugurated in Federal Hall, in the presence of both houses of Congress, the occasion being marked by severe simplicity. He took the oath at the hands of Chancellor Livingston of New York on the gallery outside the hall; then he stepped back inside and delivered the first Inaugural Address, never taking his eyes off his paper. "This great man was agitated and embarrassed more than ever he was by the leveled cannon or pointed musket," said one Senatorial observer. His delivery was halting, but the first President inspired confidence throughout the land as the new government slowly got under way.

The United States under Washington

The territory of the Republic, as defined by the Treaty of 1783, was not fully under American control in the spring of 1789, and a major task of the new government was to enter into undisputed possession of the whole of it. On the north the country extended to British North America and on the south to Spanish Florida, but in each case the boundary line was uncertain. Furthermore, the British still had posts in the Northwest and both they and the Spaniards were conniving with the Indians. The western boundary was the Mississippi, but the Spaniards controlled the mouth of that mighty stream and had not conceded to Americans its free navigation.

All of the eleven states that Washington presided over at first were along the coast, though there were considerable settlements beyond the mountains and below the Ohio. North Carolina ratified the Constitution in 1789 and Rhode Island in the next year, restoring the original thirteen. Three other states joined the Union in the eighteenth century: Vermont (1791), Kentucky (1792), and Tennessee (1796).

Considering the area, the population of the country was small, and it is hard for present-day Americans to realize how sparse and widespread it was. Figures become reasonably full and reliable at just this time, for the first census was that of 1790. The total population in 1790 was about 4,000,000, which was not much more than that of the city of Chicago in the middle of the twentieth century. Slightly more than a fourth of the people were in New England; about the same number were in the middle states, from New York through Delaware; and almost a half were in the southern states, from Maryland through Georgia. Even without her Kentucky counties, Virginia was the largest state in area and much the largest in population. Massachusetts, which then included Maine, was second in population, being followed by Pennsylvania and North Carolina. New York, the future Empire State, was fifth. There is much political significance in the fact that Virginia remained the first state until 1820, when she was passed by New York.

There were slaves in all the states except Massachusetts and Vermont, and the proportion of slaves and free Negroes to the total population was about one to five. This was considerably higher than it was in the middle of the next century, after the tide of European immigration became a flood. In the southern states the proportion was about one to three, about the same as in the 1850's.

In the 1790's the American people were overwhelmingly rural. In-

cluding its suburbs, the city of Philadelphia had somewhat more than 42,000 inhabitants, while New York on the island of Manhattan had 33,000. According to the census, Boston had 18,000 people, Charleston a few more than 16,000, and Baltimore 13,500. These were the major marts of commerce but the vast majority of the people were agricultural, living on farms or in small towns.

The English (including the Welsh) comprised some 60 per cent of the white population, and the British group as a whole (including the Scotch and Irish) constituted more than three-fourths. The term "Irish" was then loosely applied to both the Ulstermen or Scotch-Irish, who were really Scottish, and their traditional foes from present-day Ireland. The latter were chiefly to be found in Pennsylvania and the southern states. The Murphy family was more numerous in North Carolina than elsewhere, while few of the name were as yet in New York and New England. The Scots and Scotch-Irish together were the largest single ethnic group after the English, but they were followed closely by the Germans, who comprised about a twelfth of the total white population. The Irish proper, the Dutch, and the French together were only a little more than that.

The practice of Anglicizing non-British names had long been going on. In part this was a mere matter of practical convenience, but the process also reflected the dominance of the English tradition in American society. While some advocates of cultural independence resented this, there was in certain quarters a notable recrudescence of pro-British sentiments in the 1790's. It colored domestic politics and entered into the struggle over foreign policy.

THE FIRST PRESIDENT AND HIS COURT

It has been said that if George Washington should return to earth and not look like the portrait of him by Gilbert Stuart, he would be regarded as an imposter. Everybody would expect him to look just as he does on a dollar bill or a postage stamp. To most of his countrymen today he is a familiar picture, but his lineaments are frozen; he is a statue, a monument, a name; unlike Lincoln he seems unreal as a human being.

His face though not handsome was strong; he was tall and well-proportioned; he had great physical strength and endurance, and he was one of the greatest horsemen of his age. At fifty-seven he believed that he had passed his prime, and actually he had more illness during his first term as President than he had ever had in a comparable period. But he was still a strong and commanding figure. As Abigail Adams said, he looked and acted more like a king than George III.

Everybody stood in some awe of him. It is said that he never smiled during the American Revolution, and those who had witnessed his rare displays of wrath agreed that he was terrifying when aroused. But readers of his letters can find some smiles in them, along with many signs of thoughtful kindness. He was never an autocrat, and the pre-eminent quality of his mind was justness. He lacked the solid learning of John Adams, the brilliant audacity of Hamilton, the rich versatility of Jefferson, but, as a noted Frenchman described him during the Revolution, he was a "perfect whole." The mature judgment of Jefferson on him was expressed in strikingly similar language: "On the whole his character was, in its mass perfect, in nothing bad, in few points indifferent; and it may be truly said, that never did nature and fortune combine more perfectly to make a man great." He had no temperamental weakness, seemingly, except extreme sensitivity to criticism, and he made on his contemporaries an ineffaceable impression of high character, sound judgment, and devoted patriotism.

Washington's unusual personal qualifications were enormously enhanced by the symbolic character he had assumed in the minds of his countrymen. During the Revolution he had come to be regarded as the personal embodiment of the American cause. He justified the new Constitution in the minds of many, and in practically all minds he symbolized the Union. That he was unanimously elected in the first place surprised no one; his unanimous re-election in 1792 was a more notable fact but even that was largely taken for granted. Until that time at least he was regarded as indispensable, and in the whole of American history that record is unique.

Since Washington brought dignity and prestige to the new office of President merely by occupying it, there was no point in trying to embellish his title. Yet, in the Senate, John Adams proposed that he be addressed as "His Highness the President of the United States and Protector of Their Liberties." This title, which smacked of royalty, was strongly opposed in the House, and the eventual decision was to designate the Chief Executive simply as the President of the United States. From that day to this he has been addressed simply as "Mr. President." The victory went to the advocates of republican simplicity, but talk about regal forms and monarchical tendencies persisted through the decade. Some of the talk was demagoguery, and at this distance the issue seems unreal, but the people of that time did not know how things were going to turn out. In their world, kingdoms were the rule and a republic was the very rare exception.

To Thomas Jefferson, then in Paris, where he had had abundant opportunity to see monarchy at work, it seemed that his old friend Adams had made himself ridiculous, and in this connection he repeated Franklin's famous characterization of that gentleman: "always an honest man, often a great one, but sometimes absolutely mad." Nobody thought that the President wanted to be a king, but the episode injured Adams, who became both a symbol of formalism and a comic figure. Somebody dubbed that robust patriot "His Rotundity." Aware that he would have to create precedents, Washington had asked suggestions of several men about desirable social policy. In reply Adams had this to say about the presidency:

> The office, by its legal authority, defined in the Constitution has no equal in the world, excepting those only which are held by crowned heads; nor is the royal authority in all cases to be compared to it. . . . If the *state and pomp* essential to this great department are not, in a good degree, preserved, it will be in vain for America to hope for consideration with foreign powers.

Washington was entirely too well-balanced a mind to hold with such an extreme emphasis, but he wanted things to be done with a propriety and dignity that would redound to the credit of the country, and he established a formal court the like of which never surrounded another President. His weekly levees for men, on Tuesdays from three to four, were stiff affairs. But the President was fastidiously polite to everybody, and if he did not bend easily it was not because of pride of office. Mrs. Washington's levees on Fridays for both sexes were more brilliant; and no doubt many a lady and her gallant rejoiced in the thought that this Court was not unlike that of England. The Washingtons were more in character as hosts at the dinners they gave regularly. These were bountiful repasts in the best tradition of generous hospitality.

In social matters Washington set a precedent which his successors, including John Adams, did not maintain. But democratic diatribes on the formalities of these early years were not warranted by the facts. Good social form is not incompatible with republican self-government, and Washington, great gentleman that he was, properly sought to maintain it. If there were dangers to popular rights in these early years, they did not lurk in the presidential drawing room; and if there were some absurdities there, these were unimportant.

The Organization of the New Government

Indispensable as the first President was as a symbol, the carrying of the Constitution into effect was most dependent, at the outset, on the actions of the first Congress. The House of Representatives was the dominant branch, as had been expected, and Madison was the most conspicuous leader in that body at first, as he had been in the Federal Convention. Also, he was on terms of intimacy with Washington.

The most immediate need was for revenue and everybody expected this to come chiefly from duties on imports, which Congress was now empowered to impose. The first tariff act (July 1789) also had some moderate protective features. One sharply disputed question was whether there should be discrimination against countries that did not have commercial treaties with the United States. Madison favored this but Congress disapproved it. Congress did discriminate against foreign shipping in favor of American, however. Tariff duties were reduced on goods imported in American vessels, and the latter were subjected to considerably lower tonnage duties in ports than were imposed on foreign ships. These provisions worked to the distinct advantage of the American carrying trade, which had suffered grievously after the Revolution, and this enjoyed a notable revival during the decade. Also, the actions with respect to revenue had an almost immediate effect in improving American credit abroad.

The Judiciary Act of September 1789 provided for a Supreme Court consisting of a chief justice and five associates, and for circuit and district courts. Late in September, John Jay became the first Chief Justice, but it was some time before the federal judiciary had much to do. The Congressional acts creating the first executive departments were of much more immediate importance.

What the President most needed to gain full respect for his office was not pomp but power and the means to use it. The foundations of presidential power were laid in Article II of the Constitution, but this contains no details of organization. Three departments were provided for during the summer of 1789—State, the Treasury, and War. To head the first of these, Washington appointed Thomas Jefferson, then minister to France, who did not assume his duties until March 1790; in his place John Jay, who had been Secretary for Foreign Affairs under the Confederation and had little to do as Chief Justice, served temporarily. Alexander Hamilton assumed the Secretaryship of the Treasury in September, and Henry Knox, formerly Secretary of War under the Confederation, took over the same office in the new government. Edmund Randolph of Virginia became Attorney General, but he was only the legal adviser of the government on part time.

In the debates on these departments, Madison led the successful fight to make the heads responsible to the President rather than to Congress. Had this crucial question been decided the other way, the President could not have been the real master of his own household, and the executive branch could hardly have been co-ordinate with the legislative as the framers of the Constitution had intended. The expectation was that the department heads would act only in the President's name and would be his assistants. In Washington's first administration his assistants did a large amount of paperwork, but everything was supposed to clear through him and be subject to his approval. This included correspondence. At first Washington conferred with his department heads individually, and when he wanted several opinions he generally asked for them in writing. He was the hub of the wheel, for the departments radiated from him and he supplied unity through his own person. It would be hard to name a President who was a more diligent and effective administrator. He was industrious, prompt, and systematic; he did not spare himself and, without being autocratic, he was exacting of his subordinates. He wanted to gain respect for the new government by making it a good one, and he set a pattern of good administration which persisted through a generation.

It was expected that the Department of the Treasury would be closer to the legislature than the others. Direct reports to Congress were expected from the Secretary. As the law read, he was to "digest and prepare" plans regarding revenue and the public credit, and it was well understood that these were to be presented in writing, not in person, but in a special sense he had access to Congress. The Secretary of State, on the other hand, was expected to be specially close to the President and to have official dealings with Congress only through him. Washington was well informed about foreign affairs and had definite ideas about them, as he did about military affairs. He knew much less about fiscal matters and felt it necessary to give more rein to Hamilton than to Jefferson and Knox.

Hamilton had administrative abilities of the highest order, and in a very short time he built up a departmental organization that dwarfed the others. In his opinion, "most of the important measures of every government are connected with the Treasury," but some critical observers attributed this unparalleled growth to his personal desire for power. He had to gain Washington's consent to legislative proposals but not that of his fellow Secretaries. Circumstances had combined to give Hamilton an unusual opportunity. Yet his vigorous actions and distinguished though controversial public services were no mere accident of circumstance. They were the expressions of his constructive mind, his bold nature, and his particular variety of nationalistic philosophy.

HAMILTON AND HIS FINANCIAL POLICIES

Alexander Hamilton, now in his early thirties, was born on the island of Nevis in the British West Indies and came to New York as a youth to pursue his education and seek his fortune. The success that he achieved must be attributed chiefly to his own talents and energies. His marriage to Elizabeth Schuyler, daughter of General Philip Schuyler, allied him as a young man with an aristocratic family, but his ambition never ceased to drive him onward. He was briefly a student at King's College (afterward Columbia) and his precocious mind enabled him to gallop through his courses, but his intellectual interests were far more limited than those of Franklin and John Adams and Jefferson. Concentrating on law, finance, and government, he was masterful in those fields, and he might have become a great military commander had circumstances permitted. As an aide to Washington during the Revolution he gained the confidence of the General which was such an important factor in his later career. Though highly effective in paperwork in headquarters, he chafed under it and eventually resigned as aide, after an altercation with Washington which the General forgave but which revealed the impetuosity of Hamilton's nature. Finally getting an opportunity in the field, he performed brilliantly, emerging from the war as a lieutenant colonel and with a reputation for great personal courage. After that he practiced law and did magnificent service in the fight over the ratification of the Constitution.

His influence had been slight in the framing of the Constitution, because most of his colleagues thought he went to extremes in his advocacy of a powerful national government. He wanted the President to serve for life and would have liked to reduce the states virtually to provinces or departments. Many leaders of the time were dubious of political democracy, but Hamilton was conspicuous in his distrust of popular rule. It cannot be proved that he ever described the people as a "great Beast," but there is significance in the fact that the saying has been so often attributed to him. He had little faith in ordinary human beings and believed that either force or interest was necessary to cement the government. In the light of the later success of political democracy in the United States, his philosophy seems cynical, and undoubtedly he liked to exercise power and sought it for himself. But he also coveted it for his country, believing that without it the new nation would succumb to internal dissension or external force. At a time when the Republic was emerging from a condition of weakness, he performed an invaluable service in helping to make it strong. This he did, in the first place, by making it solvent.

Establishing the Public Credit

The responsible leaders of the time were generally agreed on the necessity of establishing the public credit, but Hamilton was notable for the scope of his proposals. His policies were unfolded in his successive reports to Congress. These were presented in response to requests from that body, but he did not follow Congress; he induced it to follow him. The first Report on the Public Credit was presented on January 9, 1790. This was followed, about a year later (December 14, 1790), by the Report on a National Bank. A year after that he submitted (December 5, 1791) a Report on Manufacturing; and at the end of his service as Secretary of the Treasury he presented a second Report on the Public Credit (January 1795). Viewed together, these great state papers present a unified policy. Besides establishing the credit of the new government, this policy was designed to provide for the financial needs and further the economic growth of the country. Hamilton gained his strongest support from the commercial and the rising financial groups, who benefitted most directly from his measures. There was no industrial group of any consequence as yet, and his proposals for manufacturing had little immediate result. He was most opposed by the agricultural groups—to whose interests he was relatively indifferent.

In his first Report on the Public Credit, Hamilton recommended that the entire national debt, foreign and domestic, be funded at face value with arrears of interest, and that the federal government assume the debts of the various states, which had been largely contracted during the War for Independence. These proposals generally go by the names of Funding and Assumption.

There never was serious question about the part of the national debt that was owed abroad, amounting to about $12 million. The domestic national debt, which he estimated as amounting to about $42 million, involved more difficult problems. Most of this consisted of certificates of indebtedness, which are not to be confused with the virtually repudiated Continental currency or bills of credit. These certificates had been issued at various times during and after the Revolution; they had passed from hand to hand and had depreciated to the point that Hamilton himself said they might have cost a present owner no more than 15 or 20 per cent of their face value. Yet he wanted to redeem all of them at par, with interest, and he saw no practicable way to distinguish between original and present holders.

So great was the concern of most members of Congress for the sanctity of contracts that there was no serious objection to his recommendation, except on the ground of injustice to the original holders. Madison, the leading critic of the plan, agreed that there must be no repudiation, but proposed that present holders be paid at the current market price and that original holders receive the balance. His motion was defeated in the House, partly on grounds of impracticality. Speculators who now owned many of the certificates therefore stood to profit enormously, and a cry was soon raised against them, but there could be no possible doubt that the credit of the government was going to be firmly established.

Hamilton's recommendation that the federal government assume the state debts ran into much greater difficulty. There was no contractual obligation in this case, but he argued that the state debts had been incurred in a common cause, that they could be provided for in a more orderly and effective way on one plan, rather than on many, and that this action would increase national unity. Some people opposed it on just the ground that it would strengthen the general government and weaken the states by extending the financial sphere of the former, but attitudes were chiefly determined by the advantages and disadvantages to particular states. Virginia and most of the southern states had already paid off a considerable share of their debt, though South Carolina had not, while Massachusetts and Connecticut stood to gain from assumption. A further consideration was that most of the paper representing the southern debt had fallen into the hands of northern financiers and speculators, some of whom had acquired it recently in anticipation of the rise in values that would follow federal action.

The proposals of Hamilton served to draw a line of division between those states and groups that were almost wholly agricultural and those that were relatively more commercial and financial. The former had the greater voting strength and the result was that Assumption was defeated

in a test vote. A period of mutual recrimination ensued and the business
of Congress was at a standstill. The Secretary and his warmest supporters
insisted that Funding and Assumption were inseparable, and for a time
his whole program was imperiled. This was the situation in the spring
of 1790, soon after the arrival of Thomas Jefferson at the seat of government.

The major objection of Madison and Jefferson to the Assumption proposal was that, in its original form, it was disadvantageous to their state
of Virginia by not allowing credit for payments already made on its debt.
Meanwhile, another question was pending in which they had more immediate interest: the residence of the federal government. The location
of the capital seemed more important in those days of difficult transportation than it does now, and there was keen rivalry between the localities that were regarded as possible contenders. The President had set
his heart on a Potomac site, and his fellow Virginians shared his feeling.

Finding his financial program blocked, Hamilton asked Jefferson to
use his influence with the Southerners in Congress. In response to this
appeal Jefferson brought the Secretary and Madison together for conference. Then a bargain was worked out. Hamilton agreed to a modification of the precise terms of the Assumption bill to make it less unfavorable
to Virginia—by specifying the amount to be assumed from each state
instead of lumping the existing state debts. Madison agreed to moderate
his opposition, and one or the other of them suggested that the permanent seat of the government be on the Potomac. This was to be the sugar-
coating of what many Virginians and Southerners would still regard as a
bitter pill. Two Congressmen with districts on the Potomac were approached by Jefferson, and the Assumption proposal was adopted by a
narrow margin. The Residence Bill, as enacted with Hamilton's co-operation, prescribed that the seat of the government should be for ten years
in Philadelphia (1790-1800), and on the Potomac permanently after that.
Senator William Maclay from the backwoods of Pennsylvania found con-
solation in the thought that the removal of the government to the Potomac
might "give a preponderance to the agricultural interest." Jefferson himself never regretted the residence decision, but he afterwards reproached
himself for having helped Hamilton consolidate his power and become
invincible.

The Bank and the Constitution

When Hamilton presented to Congress his second great Report (December 5, 1790), the federal government had moved from New York to
Philadelphia. In this strong and luminous paper he recommended the
establishment of the Bank of the United States. His purposes were to
facilitate the operations of the Treasury, to strengthen the central gov-

ernment, and at the same time to provide more adequately for the financial needs of the country. There were only three banks in the republic—in Boston, New York, and Philadelphia—and each of these had been chartered by a state. The institution he proposed was to be chartered by the federal government and make reports to it, but it was to be "under a *private* not a *public* direction," and was expected to pay profits to its stockholders. Three-fourths of the capital of $10 million might be subscribed by individuals in United States securities, and the government itself was to subscribe $2 million. The Bank was to receive the government deposits, which it could lend out at interest like any other deposits, and was to have authority to issue notes redeemable in specie, which were to be legal tender.

Hamilton thus maintained the initiative by making another bold and constructive proposal and he won a quick victory in the Senate. The chief practical objection raised then in the House of Representatives was that the government would be conferring more benefits on private stockholders than it would receive. The Secretary's plan was welcomed by holders of government securities and by commercial groups, who warmly approved his efforts to make credit more available for expanding business enterprise. Provision was eventually made for branch houses of the Bank, but Hamilton was opposed to these at first and he was charged with ignoring agricultural interests. Farmers required longer credit than this bank could be expected to provide, and suspicion of the rising commercial and financial groups was growing in agricultural districts, especially in the South. This suspicion was coupled with increasing fear of the extension of federal power and distrust of Hamilton, who seemed to be concentrating this power in his own department.

To a greater extent than hitherto, his critics now resorted to constitutional arguments. In the House of Representatives these were advanced most conspicuously by Madison, who asserted that the Federal Convention had rejected a proposal that Congress be empowered to grant charters of incorporation. He claimed, furthermore, that the ratification of the Constitution had been brought about by one set of arguments, while the government was now being administered on another. This was another way of saying that Hamilton as an administrator was trying to establish the sort of centralization that he had vainly advocated at the Federal Convention. There was considerable historical ground for Madison's arguments, but they were unavailing. The bank bill was adopted in the House by a majority of nearly two to one, early in February 1791. "Congress may go home," wrote Senator William Maclay in his Journal. "Mr. Hamilton is all-powerful, and fails in nothing he attempts."

The signature of the President was necessary, however, and Washington was much disturbed by the arguments of Madison, on whom he had long relied in constitutional matters. Therefore, he referred the bill to the

Attorney General, Edmund Randolph, for examination, and he was more confounded when that high official also declared it unconstitutional. Then he passed it on to Jefferson, who took the same position. The President referred these two adverse opinions to Hamilton; and, while waiting for that Secretary's reply, he had Madison draft a veto message in case this should be needed.

It is the opinion of Jefferson, which he drew in skeletonized form for Washington's convenience, that later generations of Americans have regarded as the classic statement of the doctrine of strict construction of the Constitution. He had taken no public stand against the bank bill, but he did not like it and by this time Hamilton had aroused the deep distrust of this lifelong champion of the freedom of the individual, who coupled a fear of governmental power with his faith in human beings. He regarded laws in general and constitutions in particular as "shields against tyranny"; and, while an advocate of the periodical revision of constitutions in the light of experience, he tended to be strict in his interpretation of their provisions while they were still in force.

His argument was based on the sound premise that the federal government under the Constitution is one of enumerated powers, all others being reserved to the states, as is specifically stated in the Tenth Amendment. "To take a single step beyond the boundaries thus specially drawn around the powers of Congress," he said, "is to take possession of a boundless field of power, no longer susceptible of any definition." In the powers specifically enumerated, he could not find the authority to incorporate a bank and to grant it powers historically belonging to the states, nor could he find it in either of the general phrases—the "general welfare" or the "necessary and proper" clauses, both of which he construed rigidly. Alarmed by the extreme claims of national power that had been made by some supporters of the bank bill, he was trying to find a safeguard against the dangers he perceived. He properly contended that large extensions of power should not be made on grounds of minor convenience, but he ran into the insuperable difficulty of finding an unvarying formula which would not put the government in a strait-jacket. In practice, Jefferson himself was not as inflexible as he seemed here, and this abbreviated opinion gives little inkling of his recognition of the necessity of growth and change. He believed that the reserved rights of the states were invaded in this instance. Nevertheless, he said that unless the President's mind was tolerably clear that the bill was unauthorized by the Constitution, "a just respect for the wisdom of the legislature would naturally decide the balance in favor of their opinion."

Hamilton labored on his answer until the last moment, and the lengthy paper that he presented to the President is one of the ablest that he ever wrote. Jefferson's argument in a nutshell was that the Constitution literally meant what it said, and the task of the Secretary of the Treasury was to demonstrate that it meant more than it seemed to. Basing his argument on the sovereignty of the United States within the sphere allotted to it by the Constitution, he proclaimed principles of liberal construction that have gone ringing down the generations. In his opinion, every power vested in the government carries with it the right to employ all means that are requisite and fairly applicable. These means he called "implied powers." In stating his own position with respect to implied powers, he practically took out of the mouth of Madison words that the latter had used a few years earlier, and he chided Jefferson for his extremely restrictive use of terms. Hamilton admitted that there is always chance of error and abuse when the literal meaning of terms is departed from, but he pointed out at the same time that a rigid adherence to the letter of its powers would paralyze the movements of any government. In his opinion, the bank that was proposed had a natural relation to the enumerated powers of collecting taxes, regulating trade, and providing for the common defense, and the bill was therefore constitutional.

Washington was sufficiently persuaded to give the benefit of doubt to Congress and sign the bill. This marked the highest point of Hamilton's success as a constructive statesman. It seemed to a number of his fellows at the time that he was interpreting the Constitution to suit himself and was wielding national power in behalf of the few rather than the many. But the First Bank of the United States justified its creation by its career as a financial institution (1791-1811). Though it did not do much for the agricultural population, it served business interests well. It was of great help to the government, but was not administered as a political institution. It was not subservient to Hamilton even when he was at the height of his influence. The constitutional arguments that he presented in 1791 were not then made public, any more than Jefferson's were, but they were afterward taken up by Chief Justice John Marshall; and to most later commentators it has seemed that Hamilton laid the philosophical foundation for a genuinely effective national government, armed with powers that time has proved to be indispensable.

Within the period of only a little more than a year after he submitted his first Report on the Public Credit, he had won clear title to fame as a master-builder. Until the end of the century this man of small stature, bold imagination, and imperious will was to remain a political Colossus, but his lust for power and lack of restraint were eventually to prove his undoing, and his days of great national achievement were soon past.

HAMILTON AGAINST HIS CRITICS

In the second half of Washington's first term the beginnings of an opposition party could be seen. At this stage it was an informal political grouping rather than an organized party, and it was derided by Hamilton's partisans as a faction. Its members described themselves as republicans, generally without a capital letter, and claimed to carry on the Whig tradition of the American Revolution, characterizing their opponents as monarchists or Tories. They could not properly be called Anti-Federalists since they were not against the Constitution, nor were they against Washington. They objected to certain ideas of John Adams that they labeled as aristocratic, but most of all they were against Hamilton, refusing to recognize him as the embodiment of the government. Out of these quarrels there grew the American two-party political system, which had been quite unforeseen by the framers of the Constitution.

Jefferson and the Opposition

Madison continued to be the most prominent public critic of Hamilton, and he did more than anybody else to organize the opposition to him, but it was Thomas Jefferson who came to be regarded as its personification. He and the Secretary of the Treasury were incompatible in personality and antithetical in philosophy, and he became the historic symbol of anti-Hamiltonianism primarily because of what he stood for and the kind of man he was.

The Secretary of State, who was forty-seven when he took office and considerably older than Hamilton, was undistinguished in physical appearance and had none of the characteristics that we commonly associate with successful politicians, except a marked talent for friendship. At the first meeting he seemed shy, and although an unusually facile writer he had no gift for public speech. His distinguished public services had been rendered primarily to the causes of freedom and equality of opportunity. He had left his mark on history chiefly as a legislator, and his experiences as governor of his own state during the Revolution had accentuated his distaste for personal controversy. In temperament and tastes this amiable man of learning and reason presented a sharp contrast to his ambitious, aggressive, and sometimes ruthless colleague, the Secretary of the Treasury. He was like Hamilton in his unusual capacity for work, however, and he could become passionately aroused in behalf of causes that he regarded as fundamental. Then his language often became extravagant.

He was relatively uncritical of Hamilton's financial policies at the outset. He had strongly urged that adequate provision be made for the foreign debt, and he had no sympathy whatever with repudiationists. At the same time, he was fearful of the growth of public debt and detested all forms of speculation. It seemed to him that Hamilton was extravagant in his policies and played into the hands of manipulators. His own major interest was in agriculture, though he had done much for commerce. He was opposed to the encouragement of manufacturing in

America, because he anticipated ill effects on the human beings laboring in it, and he saw no need to cater to the rising financial class. He viewed all these economic matters as a conservative who sought to maintain old values, and he now sounds rather like an old-fashioned farmer. He followed the philosophy of laissez-faire and was against the granting of special favors to anybody.

It seemed to him that Hamilton was building for his department and himself a "phalanx" within Congress. This was not in accord with Jefferson's conception of the separation of powers between the executive and the legislative branches, and he had occasion for personal annoyance when Hamilton's followers blocked measures bearing on foreign affairs and favored by the Secretary of State. The movement, which Madison had revived, to discriminate against the commerce of countries not having treaties with the United States was checked at approximately the same time that the Bank measure received Washington's approval. Furthermore, the Secretary of State now had good reason to be suspicious of his colleague's intimacy with George Beckwith, the unofficial British representative.

Jefferson was in close touch with Madison and other Virginians opposed to the policies of the Secretary of the Treasury, but the direct part he played in organizing the opposition was exaggerated by Hamilton's partisans and has often been overemphasized by historians. In the summer of 1791, when Hamilton's success was at full tide, Jefferson and Madison made a vacation trip from Philadelphia to Lake George and back through New England. Hamilton and his friends scented in this trip a political plot to unite northern and southern opponents of the Secretary of the Treasury. No doubt the two Virginians talked politics in the course of their journey, but their predominant purpose was to enjoy a holiday.

More important in the growth of the movement against Hamilton was the establishment in Philadelphia (October 31, 1791) of the *National Gazette,* under the editorship of the talented Philip Freneau. Hamilton had his own organ in Philadelphia, the *Gazette of the United States.* This was edited by John Fenno, for whom he raised money and to whom he gave government printing. Freneau was not the only journalist who spoke for the "republican interest" in this period, but he was the most effective. He had been at Princeton with Madison, and it was this old friend who persuaded him to set up a paper in Philadelphia. Former associates in New York provided the financial backing, while Jefferson gave him the vacant post of translator in the Department of State— a part-time job paying $250 a year. This action was the ground for the later charge of Hamilton that Jefferson had hired Freneau to vilify him. Freneau proved to be a fiercely independent editor who was much more extreme in his republican ideas than Madison or Jefferson.

By the spring of 1792, the *National Gazette* was filled with sharp criticisms of the Secretary of the Treasury and his "system." Hamilton seemed more vulnerable than he had previously, for a stock-market panic now followed a period of delirious speculation. The most conspicuous victim of the panic was William Duer of New York, a former Assistant Secretary of the Treasury and friend of Hamilton's whose fantastic career as a promoter and speculator in government securities brought him at last to debtor's prison. Hamilton suffered some discredit from these events, and he was publicly charged by Freneau with responsibility for the rise of speculation, while his "paper system" was sharply attacked in Congress. But his supporters could point to the continuing prosperity of the country as a whole, and it was a matter of more immediate concern to him that his special relationship with the legislative department was strongly challenged, for that was a blow at his power in Congress.

The specific question was whether Congressional requests for information should continue to go straight to him or should go to him through the President, as was the case with requests to the Secretaries of State and War. He won what he regarded as a vote of confidence on this issue, but these proceedings convinced him that Madison, co-operating with Jefferson, was the head of a faction hostile to him and his administration and "subversive of the principles of good government." He identified opposition to his policies and official conduct with opposition to the administration as a whole and sought to stamp it as "subversive." Within the executive branch he identified unity with his own virtual ascendancy, and by summer he concluded that Jefferson must be driven out.

Outbreak of a Feud

Unknown to Hamilton, Jefferson had announced to Washington his intention of retiring at the end of the presidential term. But Washington's idea of the best way to maintain the unity of the country was to keep within his official family representatives of different regions and opinions, and he continued to hope that the Secretary of State would stay. Jefferson, like Madison, was urging the President to stand for re-election. "North and South will hang together," he said, "if they have you to hang on." At the same time he was describing to his chief the causes of public discontent as he interpreted them.

Later in the spring (May 23, 1792) he sent to Washington a paper he had drafted, containing twenty-one "objections" that had been raised against the Treasury "system." Some of these were reported on hearsay and some were stated in extreme language. Jefferson did not advocate the overthrow of the Hamiltonian financial structure, since he believed that would be contrary to public faith. He wanted to check the movement toward arbitrary power which, in his eyes, Hamilton represented.

Concluding that these objections required an answer, Washington sent a copy of them to Hamilton toward the end of the summer, without naming the source. Hamilton immediately recognized it, however, and the document was fuel for the fire that was already blazing. In a newspaper communication signed "T. L." (July 25, 1792) he had charged Jefferson with hiring Freneau to revile the government.

Freneau vigorously asserted his independence and even swore to an affidavit absolving Jefferson, but Hamilton continued the attack on the editor as "the faithful and devoted servant of the head of a party." He was really gunning for the Secretary of State. By referring to certain episodes in Jefferson's career he tried to create the impression that his colleague was hostile to the Constitution and honorable provision for the public debt, and he asserted that the trend of Jefferson's doctrines was toward discredit, disorder, and disunion. After writing half a dozen pieces, he took time out to prepare for Washington a long and powerful reply to the twenty-one "objections."

Hamilton's defense of his financial policies satisfied Washington as to their soundness. What the troubled President feared most was disunity, and he regarded Jefferson's fears of tyranny as largely unwarranted. He himself disliked political criticism of any department of the government in newspapers, and most of all he disliked dissension in his own official family. He valued both Hamilton and Jefferson in their respective fields and saw no way to replace either one of them. Therefore, he now appealed to them in almost identical language to restrain themselves for the sake of the Union. In replying to these moving words, however, each of the rivals described his position and spelled out his indictment in more personal terms. Objective judgment of this feud is exceedingly difficult even now, but one person whom everybody can sympathize with is George Washington.

The battle behind the scenes was indecisive. Jefferson strongly reiterated his determination to retire, while saying that he would certainly not meddle in legislative matters now since he had never done so—except in the case of the bargain over Assumption and Residence which he so deeply regretted. The same could be said for newspaper controversy, into which he did not enter. He left no doubt, however, that he distrusted and detested Hamilton. Hamilton, on the other hand, claimed that he was the deeply injured party and, while admitting that he had had a part in the newspaper attacks on his colleague, he claimed that it was impossible for him to desist as yet.

He wrote at least a dozen more communications to the papers and these surpassed in fury those that had preceded them. He sought to display Jefferson as "the intriguing incendiary, the aspiring, turbulent competitor," comparing the supposedly modest philosopher to Caesar and Catiline. Following a common practice of his time, Hamilton wrote under a series of pseudonyms—"T. L.," "An American," "Amicus," "Catullus," "Scourge." The style and language of these pieces were not those of the superb opinion on the constitutionality of the Bank and the great reports on the public credit; they were those of the scurrilous journalists of the time, and they revealed the lack of self-control which Hamilton showed even more conspicuously later in his famous letter on President John Adams.

The defense of Jefferson by his friends was conducted on a higher plane. James Monroe, now in the Senate, and Madison provided the main reply. The account of the establishment of Freneau's *National Gazette* left some questions unanswered, but the discussion of Jefferson's attitude toward the Constitution and the debt was thoroughly convincing, and on the last day of the year 1792 they had the last word. The result of Hamilton's direct attacks on his colleague was not to drive the latter from an office he already wanted to relinquish, but to build him up in the public mind as an opponent. Hamilton did more than anybody else to make Jefferson the popular symbol of the opposition to himself.

The Virginians against Hamilton

The outcome of the second presidential election, in 1792, was the same as that of the first one. Washington, who was finally induced to serve again, received all the electoral votes, while John Adams was continued as Vice-President. Governor George Clinton of New York received the second vote of the electors from his own state and Virginia. Madison and Monroe were trying to forge an alliance with opponents of Hamilton in New York, though Jefferson believed that Adams deserved the vice-presidency on the grounds of long and honorable service to his country. Most people still regarded the two highest offices as nonpartisan, but the growth of republican sentiment was reflected in the Congressional elections.

The old Congress lasted until March 1793, however, and in this body Hamilton won a significant personal victory on the eve of Washington's second inauguration. The fight centered in successive resolutions introduced in the House by William Branch Giles of Virginia, a pugnacious debater. Giles was strongly supported by Madison on the floor, and had the spiritual support of James Monroe and John Taylor of Caroline, the two Senators from the Old Dominion, as well as that of Jefferson. The move against Hamilton can be best described as an assault from Virginia, and it reflected the intense hostility in that agricultural state to the Secretary of the Treasury and all his works. It began with a legitimate request for information about certain financial transactions of the Treasury, particularly loans made under authority of acts of Congress. Hamilton resented this request as an intended reflection on his official integrity, which it certainly was in part. There was some justification for the charge that this imperious young man had thrown a cloud of confusion over his complicated operations. He responded with a barrage of communications that revealed anew his extraordinary capacity. It does not appear that he had done anything injurious to the nation, but in his handling of certain foreign loans he seems to have gone somewhat beyond the authority given him by Congressional act.

Apart from partisanship, the point at issue was the discretion that might be allowed the administrative officer in cases of appropriation. Hamilton insisted that, in the public interest, he must be allowed latitude, while his critics argued for executive conformity to the exact letter of the law. This was another dispute over liberal and strict construction. The immediate question was whether or not Hamilton should be rebuked for specific actions as head of the Treasury and for his alleged disregard of Congress. The key resolutions of Giles were defeated by a vote of more than two to one, practically all of the Virginians voting consistently with the minority.

The Hamiltonians afterwards overstated the case when they laid chief blame on Jefferson for this attack, but they were wholly correct in identifying him with it in spirit. He did not instigate it or direct its course, but no doubt he was consulted and he probably drew a draft of the final resolutions—thus departing from his avowed policy of not intermeddling with legislative matters. He believed that Hamilton had exceeded his authority and took the extreme position that the Secretary of the Treasury should be removed from office. His own explanation of the defeat of the Giles Resolutions was that a third of the House was made up of "bank directors and stockjobbers" who acknowledged Hamilton as their chief, and that another third voted in ignorance or blind partisanship.

His charge that there was a "corrupt squadron" has often been dismissed as a partisan exaggeration, and if it be regarded as a reflection on the moral standards of a third of the members of the House it was clearly unjustified. But there can be no question of the great influence of the security-holding interests in politics at this time—when government paper comprised a far larger share of all investments that it ever has since then. Hamilton had carried out his avowed purpose of attaching powerful groups to the new government by ties of financial interest, and he had the strong support of representatives of these groups when he was attacked. Also, he had increasingly aroused the fears of countrymen like Jefferson and John Taylor of Caroline, who were old-fashioned in financial matters and abominated the speculation in government paper which Hamilton condoned. In later years, former President John Adams reinforced their judgment when he said: "The Funding and Banking systems, which are the work of the Federalists, have introduced more corruption and injustice, for what I know, than any other cause."

The Virginians had chosen their immediate issue unwisely and had weakened their case by carrying it to extremes. The Secretary of the Treasury could not be successfully challenged on mere grounds of fiscal administration, and this intemperate attack turned out to be a boomerang. His victory enabled him to regain ground he had lost by his own intemperate attacks on the Secretary of State, and at the end of Washington's first term his dominance of domestic politics was reaffirmed. He concerned himself greatly with foreign affairs, also, but he could not dominate them while Jefferson remained in office.

CHAPTER 15

The New Republic and the Old World, 1789-1793

During the first generation of government under the Constitution, foreign relations assumed an importance in American affairs that was not to be approximated until the World War of 1914 ushered in a new era of global conflict and revolution. The scant respect in which the nations of the Old World held the young Republic at the outset was indicated by the scarcity of foreign representatives at its seat. When Jefferson became Secretary of State the emissaries of other governments could have been numbered on the fingers of one hand, and only one of them had a higher rank than that of *chargé d'affaires*. The mighty Empire of Great Britain was wholly without official representation. The foreign problems that Washington's administration inherited from the Confederation had been compounded by the weakness of that government and were accentuated by the continuing tendency of the powers to think of the American states in colonial terms—that is, as fair prey for imperial exploitation. Furthermore, the rivalry of the chief powers, Great Britain and France, constituted a continuing threat to genuine American independence, which required that the young Republic avoid being drawn into either orbit. Another grave danger was that the balance of power between Great Britain and Spain on the North American continent might be upset. The friendship of France, which had no possessions there at that time, could be very useful in this connection. The entire international situation demanded skillful diplomacy on the part of a weak nation.

Jefferson and His Foreign Policies

The first department to be created by act of Congress was that of Foreign Affairs. The name was changed to Department of State soon afterward when certain domestic functions were added to it, giving it even greater dignity and scope, and it has always been the ranking executive department. The Secretary of State was the agent of the President in promulgating laws and issuing commissions and in corresponding with states and territories. Also, he was the official record keeper of the administration and handled copyrights and patents. Yet Jefferson built up no large administrative department, as Hamilton did in the Treasury.

For the conduct of foreign affairs Jefferson was the most experienced man available, since John Adams was now Vice-President, John Jay was Chief Justice, and Franklin soon died. During Jefferson's five years abroad (1784-1789) he had observed Old-World diplomacy at first hand, and had viewed the political systems of Europe with a critical and discerning eye. No American public man of his day was more appreciative of the learning and arts of the Old World, or did quite so much to enable his own countrymen to share their rich fruits. The books and architectural drawings that he sent home, and his lifelong correspondence with European scientists and philosophers, demonstrated his attitude. He had become deeply attached to France and greatly admired her culture. He was delighted with the manners of the French; he relished their cooking and their wines, continuing to order these for himself and his friends— including George Washington—after he got home; and above all things he envied them their music. But he saw nothing in the political institutions of France or her neighboring countries that Americans should emulate, and much that they should consciously avoid. Fully grasping the realities of the power politics of Europe, he believed that the best hope for the young republic lay in the rivalry of the powers, and he hoped to play one against the other in order to gain advantages for the United States.

Consistency in methods cannot be expected of anyone who must adjust himself to the shifting currents of international affairs, but Jefferson was notable in the clearness with which he perceived and the consistency with which he pursued his major objective. This was simply the completion and the maintenance of American independence. On the economic side, he wanted to relieve American external commerce of the obstacles imposed on it by the restrictions of other nations, but he could do little along this line while Secretary of State, and his other immediate objectives now seem more important. These may be summed up under two heads. (1) He wanted to gain for the Republic at the earliest possible moment full possession of its territories, now encroached on by the British and Spanish, and to assure the free navigation of the Mississippi River, which he regarded as indispensable to the retention of the western settlements in the Union. (2) He sought for his country the highest degree of freedom of action that was consonant with existing treaty obligations to France, without subservience to any power.

He was friendly to the French as long as he could be, not merely because they had been friendly to him personally or because he loved their culture and was stirred by their Revolution, but because they had shown far more friendliness to the United States than any other power had, and because he saw no real conflict of interest between these two countries. He was under no illusions about the reasons for past actions of the French; he knew that they valued the United States as a makeweight against the British. He valued them for precisely the same reason, being convinced that the British continued to be the greatest foes of American independence. In his dealings with the latter he manifested a spirit of passionate American patriotism and argued his cases against them like a lawyer for the prosecution. Toward the Spanish he was more bellicose. This was partly because Spain, as a declining power, was more likely to yield to threats; partly because Jefferson believed that the rapidly increasing Westerners could and very probably would attack New Orleans if their desires were not attained by negotiation.

Nootka Sound

His objectives, attitudes, and methods were revealed early in his Secretaryship in connection with the Nootka Sound Affair (1790). The Spanish had seized some British ships in Nootka Sound on the remote Pacific Northwest Coast; and the British, fully realizing Spanish weakness, took this favorable occasion to demand not only an indemnity but a recognition of their rights to trade and settlement on the Pacific Coast. For a time war was threatened and into this France, who was still allied with Spain, might be drawn. If so, the question was whether or not the United States, under the terms of the Treaty of 1778 with France, would be involved. Actually, the affair resulted in a resounding diplomatic victory for the British, since the French declined to support the Spanish and the latter backed down.

Jefferson's greatest fear was that, if war should break out, the British would seize Louisiana and the Floridas from Spain. Since the British controlled Canada on the north and ruled the Atlantic on the east, they would then surround the United States, and he believed they would extinguish the country's independence. If anything would justify American entrance into a general war, he believed that the seizure of these Spanish possessions would. Yet he was fully aware of the advantages of neutrality and hoped by diplomatic means to keep war away from the North American continent. Furthermore, he wanted to seize this favorable opportunity to gain concessions for the United States from one or the other of the conflicting powers.

He was willing to bargain with either Great Britain or Spain. To the former he would have offered neutrality at a price—fair observance by the British of the terms of the Treaty of 1783 and assurance that they would not conquer territory adjacent to the United States. If Britain should refuse, he hinted that the United States might join her enemies. At the same time, he was prepared to hold over the heads of the Spanish the veiled threat of co-operation with the British, as well as that of action by the irate Westerners. But he also offered Spain neutrality for a price: relinquishment to the United States of territories east of the Mississippi. To sweeten the pill, he would guarantee Spanish territories west of the river.

These measures failed because the threatened war between Great Britain and Spain did not occur, but they provided strategy for future reference and proved that Jefferson was ready to favor or oppose any European power for the sake of American advantage. If he was anti-British during most of his public career it was only because he saw in the policies of the old mother country the greatest international danger faced by the young nation. While Secretary of State he had only slight success in his vigorous efforts to effect a modification of British policies, chiefly because the realistic Britishers saw no need for favors to the United States. Furthermore, they knew that his colleague Hamilton supported them in their position.

BRITISH RELATIONS, 1789-1792

Official relations between the governments of the United States and Great Britain were not established until Washington's first term was more than half over. Before Jefferson became Secretary of State, Gouverneur Morris was sent by Washington on an informal mission to England; he was expected to find out what he could about British intentions, and he was provided by the President with proper credentials. But George Beckwith, a young man who flitted between England, Quebec, and the United States (1789-1791), picking up information for the British, had no credentials of any sort. Very properly, Washington would have nothing to do with him; but Beckwith established friendly relations with Hamilton, and the President condoned the latter's conversations with the young Britisher in the hope that something could be learned from them. It is now known from Beckwith's despatches that he connected Hamilton with the "party of the British interest." When Jefferson assumed office in the spring of 1790, he declined to receive an unaccredited representative of a foreign power; and he dated the beginnings of his own breach with Hamilton from the time that he first became aware of his colleague's continued intimacy with Beckwith. Hamilton had revealed to the young Britisher, and therefore to the high officials in London, that he himself favored a different policy from that of the Secretary of State.

The Commercial Question

Differences between Hamilton and Jefferson on commercial policy became clear in the winter of 1790-1791. Jefferson correctly concluded that the British would agree to no treaty of commerce but expected to leave themselves entirely free to impose restrictions on American trade with themselves and their possessions, being confident that the Americans would have to put up with these. As he judged the existing situation, in which about 90 per cent of American commerce had returned to British channels, the only weapon that could be effectively employed against them, and the only threat that might cause them to be more amenable in other and even more important matters, was legislative action against their valuable commerce with the United States. Therefore, he approved the policy of "discrimination."

It might just as well be called a reciprocity policy, since the proposed action against nations not having commercial treaties with the United States was expected to lead to further treaties, based on considerations of mutual advantage. The immediate target, however, was British commerce, and the most immediate effect would be a reduction in British imports. The Secretary of the Treasury counted on the revenue from tariff duties in carrying out his financial program and wanted no decline in British imports. On these financial grounds he opposed this move against the British.

Early in 1791, anti-British sentiment became vocal in Congress. Through the efforts of Madison, a strong bill that had been drawn in imitation of the British navigations laws was favorably reported by a committee of the House. Its opponents, inspired by Hamilton, expressed strong fears that it might lead to war, while its advocates scouted these fears. The wisdom of the policy was never tested and the measure itself was sidetracked, but the mere threat produced some result as the British government decided to send a minister to the United States. The instructions to him left no doubt that his major object was to be the prevention of action against British commerce. Thus it appears that the weapon of retaliatory legislation was the only one in the American arsenal that the British really feared. There would have been dangers in wielding it in 1791, when Hamilton's financial system would have suffered from even a temporary loss of revenue; and perhaps it would have been better never to use it except as a threat. But the fact remains that the foreign policy of the Secretary of State was subordinated in this instance to the financial policy of the Secretary of the Treasury, and that Hamilton deprived his colleague of the best available weapon. Also, he further revealed to the British the sharp division within the administration on the question of foreign policy, and deepened the impression of American weakness they already had.

The Infractions of the Peace Treaty

The first British minister to the United States, George Hammond, aged twenty-eight, arrived in Philadelphia in the autumn of 1791. Soon thereafter the dangerous situation in the Northwest was strikingly illustrated by General St. Clair's defeat (November 4, 1791) by the Indians—whom the British were thought to be supporting. At this psychological moment Jefferson pressed on Hammond the American charge that the British had violated Article VII of the treaty of peace, by which they had agreed to remove their troops from all parts of the United States with all convenient speed, and not to take away American slaves or any other property. Compensation for the lost property in slaves was little more than a talking point with Jefferson. The crucial matter was the presence of British troops on American soil, infringing on the sovereignty and endangering the security of the nation. Supporting his allegations with documents, he challenged Hammond to present the British case in turn.

The British contention was that the Americans had violated Articles IV, V, and VI of the treaty. These stipulated that there should be no lawful impediment to the recovery of previously contracted debts, that Congress should recommend to the states that they make provision for the restitution of the confiscated property of Loyalists and British subjects, and that there should be no future confiscations or prosecutions against such persons. Hammond, who had rather indiscriminately collected the names of about a hundred state legislative acts and court cases, believed that these provided overwhelming proof of American infractions of the treaty; and, following his own instructions from home, he asserted that the British had suspended execution of Article VII because of these previous American violations. That is, the Americans had not only offended but had offended first.

Jefferson collected pertinent materials from the various states with the thoroughness of a scholar and marshalled his arguments with the skill of a great lawyer. Regarding the confiscation of Loyalist property, he showed that many of the actions complained of had taken place before the treaty of peace, and that the acts passed since the treaty related to confiscations made during the war, not after it. As to the restitution of Loyalist property, all that Congress had promised to do, or was constitutionally able to do, was to make recommendations to the states. Such recommendations had been made in good faith, he said, and had been complied with to a greater degree than had actually been expected.

The question of the debts of individual Americans to British creditors was more difficult. Jefferson found on careful examination that relatively few states had imposed legal impediments to the collection of these debts. Congress, moreover, had asked for the repeal of all such measures. What was even more important, treaties superseded the laws of the states under the Constitution, the courts were open, and debts were in process of settlement. Some states had tried to retard the execution of this article of the treaty, but Jefferson found justification for them in the far more serious infraction of the treaty by the British in retaining the Northwest posts, claiming that the British breach of contract came first in point of time.

He asserted that the British government, unlike Congress, had not acted in good faith, correctly concluding that the claim of the previous American infraction of the treaty, as advanced by Hammond, was only a pretext for a policy that was predetermined. The reasons for this policy—in terms of relations with the Indians, control of the fur trade, and the retention of a position in the Northwest—may have seemed sufficient to British officials while the survival of the American Republic was uncertain, but the policy was incompatible with a full recognition of American independence and sovereignty. While overzealous at times in defending his own countrymen, Jefferson made his main point that the prime responsibility for the nonexecution of the treaty was British, and the total impact of his superb paper was terrific.

By any standard that can properly be applied it was an official expression of American policy. Jefferson not only submitted it in draft to Madison and Edmund Randolph but also to Hamilton, and he took advantage of some suggestions of the latter. Washington approved the document as a whole. Hammond rushed to Hamilton as soon as he got Jefferson's "stunning reply." He maintained as intimate relations with the Secretary of the Treasury as Beckwith had, and continued to identify him with the "party of the British interest." According to Hammond's despatches to his home government, Hamilton now lamented the "intemperate violence" of his colleague and stated that Jefferson's paper did not really represent the position of the United States.

It would have been strange if the British officials at home had not interpreted this report to mean that there was no real reason for them to be troubled. Hammond referred Jefferson's paper to them, but they did not reply to it. The international situation changed for the worse before the year was out, and that made them all the more disposed to procrastinate. But they certainly had little reason to respect a government whose Secretary of the Treasury intrigued in secret with a representative of a foreign power to defeat the policy of the Secretary of State and President.

The United States and the French Revolution

The French Revolution, which was destined to shake the Western World, had been going on since the beginning of Washington's first administration, but the course of events in France raised no critical questions of American policy until after Washington's second inauguration. Meanwhile, American interest in French affairs had steadily increased, and some alarmed voices had been heard above the chorus of general approval.

The attitude of the President himself during the first phase of the Revolution is significant. A few weeks after the fall of the Bastille (July 14, 1789), he received from his young friend, the Marquis de Lafayette, the key to that dismantled fortress and described it as "the token of victory gained by liberty over despotism." This prudent man feared that the reformers in France might proceed too fast, as did Jefferson, who was there as the American minister until he sailed home in the autumn; but both of them believed that the French were moving in the right direction. There was little bloodshed, and by adopting the Declaration of the Rights of Man and of the Citizen they seemed to be following the American example. Jefferson put the matter thus: "The appeal to the rights of man, which had been made in the United States, was taken up by the French, first of the European nations."

In Jefferson's judgment the French were not yet prepared for full self-government, and while he was in France he urged Lafayette to aim at a limited monarchy rather than a republic. His own basic opinions about American relations with Lafayette's country were reached before the Revolution and were independent of it. The monarchy was still absolute when he concluded that the maintenance of friendship with France would be to the interest of the United States. His foreign policy was based on his appraisal of the international struggle for power, not on his judgment of French political institutions. Nevertheless, as a philosopher and a human being he greatly rejoiced that the French were now following the Americans on the road toward individual freedom and self-government, and as a statesman he believed that the relations between the two countries would be all the friendlier for that reason.

This was the preponderant American opinion until 1793, when the situation was enormously complicated by world war and the Revolution fell into its bloodiest excesses; but before that date certain American leaders and groups had become alarmed. A conservative reaction had followed the American Revolution, but just as that was a relatively mild revolution the reaction was not extreme, and it led to constructive results in the Constitution. The conservative spirit persisted in many American minds, and as the French Revolution became more drastic there was a revulsion against revolutionary change, in the name of order and tradition.

In the English-speaking world, the classic figure in counterrevolutionary thought was Edmund Burke, who fired an opening salvo in his *Reflections on the Revolution in France* (1790). This was answered in a few weeks by Thomas Paine in the first part of *The Rights of Man*. Paine, whose writings had done so much to precipitate the American Revolution, linked the French Revolution with it. He dedicated the first part of his famous work to George Washington. Paine was an American citizen but he was living in England at this time. Though he was not yet attacking the English government and constitution as severely as he did later, he had joined battle with Burke in the realm of ideas. Thus the issue was drawn between order and tradition on the one hand, and revolutionary change in behalf of human rights on the other.

In the United States, meanwhile, John Adams had made himself a major spokesman of antirevolutionary thought. His *Discourses on Davila* had begun to appear in a newspaper, though this work was much too ponderous for the popular taste and publication was discontinued. It was hard to understand just what Adams was saying but he sounded aristocratic, and he was arrayed on the side opposite Paine when the first part of *The Rights of Man* was published in America in 1791. The publicizing of Jefferson's private endorsement of the work, and his implied criticism of Adams, served to align the Secretary of State in the public mind with the revolutionists and against the traditionalists. Americans generally viewed with satisfaction the progress of the French in the struggle for human rights; in most quarters they hailed Paine and criticized John Adams. Even Hamilton admitted that the episode contributed to the latter's unpopularity. At the same time it served to build up Jefferson in the public mind as a champion of humanity.

During the year 1792, when Jefferson and Hammond were engaged in their diplomatic duel and the feud between Hamilton and Jefferson burst into the newspapers, American sentiment continued to be strongly favorable to France and her Revolution, despite the fact that the tempo of revolution was accelerated and that there was more solid ground for the fears of disquieted conservatives. War broke out between France on the one hand and Austria and Prussia on the other in the spring of 1792. The external foes of France were antirevolutionary, and King Louis XVI was deposed in August on the strong supposition that he was conspiring with them. Gouverneur Morris, the American minister in France, whose indiscreet expression of antirevolutionary sentiments greatly embarrassed his own government, recognized that the question had resolved itself into a choice between an absolute monarchy and a republic. His own sympathies were with the former, but a republic was soon set up, with the accompaniment of considerable bloodshed. Meanwhile, attacks on propertied and religious groups had increased, and these excited in many American minds new fears of "leveling" and atheism.

As distant spectators of the European war, most Americans were still strongly pro-French in sentiment, and they greeted the establishment of the French Republic with great enthusiasm. In the *National Gazette,* Philip Freneau hailed in verse the triumph of freedom, and others confidently predicted that in all Europe the "Reign of Despotism" would not survive the eighteenth century. Even Hamilton admitted that American opinion strongly supported the establishment of a republican government in France, and Jefferson, letting his enthusiasm run away with him, stated that 99 per cent of the American citizens did. In his extreme old age, when he could look back on the full course of the Revolution and the many years of war that followed it, he concluded that his original judgment that the French were not yet ready for a republic was the right one. But at the beginning of the year 1793 he said, in an extravagantly worded private letter: "The liberty of the whole earth was depending on the issue of the contest, and was ever such a prize won with so little innocent blood." John Adams, always more skeptical than his optimistic friend Jefferson, proved to be the better prophet. He was already convinced that the accession to power of each successive revolutionary group would be marked by the destruction of its predecessor, and that force would prevail in the end.

This turned out to be a different sort of revolution from the one that Adams and Jefferson promoted in their own country in 1776. This was partly because it was directed against far greater evils, and in a society untrained in self-government tended toward excess; and partly because the French Revolution was more endangered from without. It was under conditions of external danger that the French deposed their King. They executed him early in 1793, and within a matter of weeks were involved in war with the British, the Dutch, and the Spanish. These events and circumstances had a marked effect on American opinion and forced on the government of the United States grave decisions.

American Neutrality, 1793

Americans learned of the execution of King Louis XVI about the middle of March; and the report of war between France and Great Britain was received in April. The news of the execution of the King, who had been so often referred to in diplomatic communications as the "best and greatest friend" of the United States, shocked Americans, who had already been grieved by reports of the imprisonment of a true friend, the Marquis de Lafayette. Opinions varied but the most prevalent one, probably, was that the success of the new French Republic was

still greatly to be desired, deeply as the circumstances were to be regretted.

Formulating a Policy

Congress was not in session and the President had gone home to Mount
Vernon, expecting to remain a month. The Secretary of State, who had
relieved Washington's mind by informing him of his own decision to
remain in the government a little longer, was still in Philadelphia. After
hearing the news from abroad, the President came back to the seat of
government as fast as he could and, on April 22, 1793, he issued the
Proclamation of Neutrality, which was destined to serve as a guidepost
of American foreign policy for more than a century. This he did on
the unanimous recommendation of his department heads. For several
months he had been consulting them as a group about foreign affairs.

The spread of the European conflict to include the British meant that
war would now be waged on the Atlantic and in the Caribbean, and that
American commerce would be affected. That was not the worst of the
situation, however. The United States was bound by treaty to France.
The entrance of Spain into the war against France a few weeks later
complicated things further, for her shift to the British side upset the
balance of power on the North American continent by allying the
two empires that maintained troops on United States soil. There were
dangers in an American policy of complete isolation, but these were not
so grave or so immediate as those of involvement in the war, and all
the members of the Cabinet wanted to stay out of it. Indeed, a policy
of neutrality had been anticipated by tentative instructions that Jefferson
had already sent to American representatives abroad.

While there was basic agreement within the government as to national
policy, there was considerable difference of opinion about desirable procedure, and a sharp conflict in attitudes toward the war itself. Hamilton
was an outspoken admirer of British political institutions and social
organization, and he had no sympathy whatever with the ideas that
had been loosed by the French Revolution. He would have liked to see
the French monarchy restored, and his heart was with the counter-
revolutionaries. He was convinced that peace with Great Britain was
necessary for the continued success of his financial system. The danger in his attitude lay in the possibility that he would go so far in his
efforts to conciliate the British that he would risk an outright break with
France.

Jefferson, besides being very conscious of the value of French friendship and more fearful than Hamilton of British dominance, had become
increasingly convinced of the bearing that the success of the French
Republic had on that of the American experiment in republican self-

government. He feared that the counter-revolutionary tide might engulf his own country, and he regarded the enemies of France as "conspirators against human liberty." He could not be indifferent to the outcome of a struggle between republicanism and monarchy which, as he correctly perceived, had world-wide implications. Nevertheless, he was convinced that the United States must play a neutral role in order to survive. He believed the nation could gain more for itself and serve the cause of liberty best by keeping out of this conflict, while maintaining an attitude of benevolence towards France.

Washington differed from his two chief lieutenants in being more moderate and better balanced than either one of them. He had no such admiration of England as Hamilton's, no such love for France as Jefferson's; and this practical man was disposed to minimize the conflict of ideologies. He wanted to keep wholly out of foreign squabbles and believed that nothing less than "imperious necessity" should occasion a breach between the United States and any European nation. On grounds of prudence, if for no other reason, he believed in *real* neutrality.

Chief credit for the promptness in issuing the Proclamation belongs to Hamilton and the President. There was no precedent for a presidential action, and the power to declare war was expressly assigned to Congress by the Constitution. Jefferson raised the question, therefore, whether the President by declaring "no war" would not be infringing on the prerogatives of Congress and limiting its future freedom of action. Hamilton was characteristically impatient with such scruples and Jefferson yielded this point, recognizing that the calling of Congress would have created unnecessary excitement and that Washington had no thought of infringing on the freedom of action of that body when it should meet.

Also, Jefferson saw advantages in delay, since he was hoping to exploit the situation by exacting from the British some concessions as the price of neutrality. From what we now know, however, it seems most unlikely that they would have conceded anything, and Hamilton's judgment that the dangers of the hour would brook no delay appears to have been correct. The pressing danger was that some Americans might enter into privateering or other unneutral activities and unwittingly involve the country. As Jefferson himself put the matter, citizens must be reminded that they were not free "to take side with either party and enrich themselves by depredations on the commerce of the other."

As a concession to Jefferson, the word "neutrality" was not used in the brief Proclamation, which was drafted by Edmund Randolph. This stated that the duty and interest of the United States required "friendly and impartial" conduct toward the belligerent powers, and exhorted and warned the citizens to avoid any actions tending to contravene such disposition. From the beginning everybody called it a Neutrality Proclamation, and it was welcomed as an assurance of the peace that everybody wanted, though some questioned the President's authority to issue it and a good many people wondered how this action could be reconciled with treaty obligations to France. The Cabinet took up that question promptly, and the ensuing debate between Hamilton and Jefferson behind the scenes may be compared to the one on the constitutionality of the Bank. The outcome was just the reverse, however, for Washington accepted Jefferson's interpretation.

French Relations and Fair Neutrality

All of the high executive officials recognized that the treaty of alliance and the treaty of amity and commerce with France, both of which dated back to the American Revolution, might prove embarrassing and limit the freedom of action that they all wanted for their own country. But Hamilton was much more alarmed than Jefferson. The Secretary of the Treasury, scenting grave and immediate danger, proposed a very simple solution of the problem. He would declare the treaties void, or at least suspended, on the ground that they had been made with a royal government no longer in existence. Furthermore, he argued that France was the aggressor in this war and had issued a general invitation to revolution and insurrection, while the alliance with the United States was wholly defensive. In his interpretation of the war he closely followed the British line, he strongly implied that he preferred a monarchical to a republican form of government, and he seemed willing to flout past international commitments for reasons of mere national convenience.

Jefferson had no difficulty in demolishing this extreme position. In the paper that he submitted to Washington (April 28, 1793) he showed that he was as anxious as Hamilton that his own country should escape embarrassment, but he could not agree that one nation is relieved of its treaty obligations to another because of a change in the form of the latter's government. He reasserted the principle on which the American republic had been founded, namely, that any country has a right to form whatever sort of government it likes. Believing that the people not the government constitute a nation, he regarded the treaties as still binding. He recognized the right of a nation to annul a treaty under circumstances of extreme and imminent danger, but such circumstances he did not now perceive.

Specifically, the provisions of the treaties that might cause embarrassment were: (1) the guarantee of French possessions in the New World, that is, the remnant of the French West Indies; (2) the promise to admit the prizes of France to American ports and to deny this privilege to her enemies; (3) the promise that enemy privateers should not be fitted out in American ports, which might be interpreted by the French as granting them this privilege. As to the first of these, Jefferson doubted if the

French would ever invoke the guarantee, since the United States could not possibly defend the French West Indies. As to the second, he saw no reason for the British to object, since they had incorporated similar provisions in their own treaties. As to the third, there was no need to accept the hypothetical French interpretation and he was opposed to doing so, since that would be unneutral. Events were soon to show that difficulties were to center on this third question, but Jefferson stood his ground on that against the French, and his guess that the other two would cause no trouble was borne out. Washington was warranted in accepting this interpretation of American obligations on practical as well as theoretical grounds. If a middle course of genuine independence was to be followed, there was no point in escaping from the embrace of France to fly to the arms of Great Britain.

Further problems were raised by the approach of a new French minister, Edmond Charles Genêt, known as "Citizen Genêt," who represented the French Republic not the King. Washington had already decided to receive him and the Cabinet approved this decision, but Hamilton wanted some reservations about the applicability of the treaties to be expressed. His argument was that non-renunciation of the treaties and unqualified reception of the French minister would be interpreted as siding with France. Jefferson said that nothing of the sort would be implied, but that positive action against the treaties and the minister would unquestionably be interpreted as favoritism to Great Britain and an insult to France. Washington agreed with him.

Even more important than the announcement of the policy of neutrality was the interpretation and application of it, and the chief burden of this fell inevitably on the Secretary of State. The American people were by no means impartial in spirit. As spectators of the European conflict they took sides violently, and their attitudes toward the official policy of the nation were strongly colored by emotions. At first, anti-British sentiment increased. About six weeks after the Proclamation, Jefferson said in a private letter to James Monroe: "The war between France and England seems to be producing an effect not contemplated. All the old spirit of 1776 is being rekindled." Though he was pleased at this, he realized that it would complicate his own official problems. "I wish we may be able to repress the spirits of the people within the limits of a fair neutrality," he said.

There was considerable difference of opinion as to what constituted "fair neutrality." While Jefferson was convinced that Washington would do his best to hold the balance even, he was equally convinced that Hamilton would try to tilt it in the British direction. In view of his own sentiments, it was ironical that his chief difficulties as an official arose from French actions. It was to the irrepressible emissary Genêt that he set forth the "twin principles" of neutrality, as he understood them.

The first and most obvious of these was the *right* of a neutral nation to prevent a warring power from infringing on its sovereignty; the second was the *duty* of a neutral country to prohibit actions that would injure one of the belligerents. The policy that he thus defined was notable for its express recognition of positive obligations, and it set a high standard of conduct for the young republic. A quarter of a century later, George Canning said in the British House of Commons: "If I wished for a guide in a system of neutrality, I should take that laid down by America in the days of the Presidency of Washington and the secretaryship of Jefferson, in 1793." Even in 1793 British officials admitted in private that the American policy was administered in a spirit of commendable fairness. They got more from the Secretary of State than they had anticipated, while Genêt got less than he had expected from an ally.

An Envoy Causes Trouble

Citizen Genêt had been ejected from the court of Catherine II of Russia because of his revolutionary sentiments. He was a well-educated man and an excellent linguist, but what most commended him to the group then in the ascendancy in France, the Girondists, was his ardor. French diplomacy entered a new phase when the Girondists imparted to it missionary zeal. Genêt was expected to be an evangel to the American people; he was to ring the changes on the beautiful words—liberty, equality, and fraternity—while assiduously seeking to advance the interests of a warring nation. He was instructed to observe diplomatic forms, however, and many of his troubles can be attributed to his failure to do so. He landed in Charleston on April 8, 1793, but more than five weeks passed before he presented his credentials in Philadelphia. Meanwhile, on the soil of a foreign country, he freely engaged in independent political and military actions of a grave nature, putting his own interpretation on his country's rights.

Genêt reached the American shore before the issuance of the Proclamation of Neutrality, which he did not anticipate, and he received a friendly reception, Governor William Moultrie of South Carolina being especially cordial and co-operative. The general object of his mission was to identify the United States as much as possible with the French cause, but he had other purposes that were more specifically related to the war. One of these was to use the United States as a vantage point for privateering against British commerce, while another was to send expeditions against the Spanish in Florida and Louisiana. In Charleston he commissioned privateers, which were largely manned by American citizens, and he later boasted that, while minister, he sent out fourteen vessels that took eighty prizes. During his stay in Charleston he set plans afoot for an expedition against Florida, and he left these in charge of the

French consul, Citizen Mangourit, whom he described as an excellent patriot. He hoped to get advance payments on the American debt to France to support his anti-Spanish designs, including an expedition against Louisiana under George Rogers Clark, which he worked on after arriving in Philadelphia.

Genêt himself described his journey northward as an "uninterrupted succession of civic fetes" and his entrance into Philadelphia as a "triumph of liberty." He went overland through the interior, instead of by water, hoping to stir up enthusiasm among the liberty-loving people in the back country, and unquestionably he did so. But he was wholly incorrect in believing that sentiment was against the policy of neutrality. Furthermore, as a foreign diplomat he could not escape the necessity of dealing with the designated officials of the nation. He had a polite but cool reception from Washington and did not find Jefferson demonstrative, though he made a favorable first impression on that apostle of freedom. Jefferson was glad for the Republican Party to benefit from any enthusiasm that Genêt might generate, but as a friend of France he tried to restrain the fiery young Frenchman, and as a responsible official he resisted the actions of his that were incompatible with the policy of the government and dangerous to the safety of the country.

At this time relations between the United States and Spain were strained, and in June the Cabinet believed that war was likely. Jefferson was less suspicious of Genêt's anti-Spanish design than of any other. He wrote a letter of introduction to Governor Shelby of Kentucky for André Michaux, who was going there "in pursuit of objects of natural history." The scientific project unquestionably interested Jefferson, but he also had reason to believe that Michaux had a place in Genêt's plans. Jefferson reminded the French minister that Kentuckians would suffer extreme legal penalties if they attacked Louisiana from American soil, but said that, apart from this consideration, he did not care what insurrections should be excited in Louisiana. In this matter Jefferson was neither neutral in spirit nor discreet in language, but he coveted the mouth of the Mississippi for the United States, not France. He afterward sent warnings to the Governor of Kentucky and other officials, and saw that the forms of neutrality were observed. A further reason for the failure of Genêt's plans against the Spanish was his inability to get advance payments on the debt of the United States to France from Hamilton.

Genêt's actions with respect to prizes and privateers created more difficult and vexatious problems than his designs against Spain did. According to the treaty the French had the right to bring prizes into American ports, and the frigate L'Embuscade brought one to Philadelphia before Genêt himself got there. This was the British merchant ship Grange, whose arrival created great excitement. The enthusiasm of French sympathizers was short-lived, however, since the capture had been made in

Delaware Bay—that is, in American waters—and the restoration of the vessel was promptly ordered. This was a clear case of infringing on American sovereignty, but other cases were more difficult in the lack of a precise statement of the extent of American maritime jurisdiction. It was in the autumn of 1793 that the historic three-mile limit was set. This was supposed to represent the furthest range of a cannon ball. Other difficulties arose when the French set up consular courts in the United States to try prize cases, instead of letting them be handled by American tribunals. Genêt's contention was that the French had the right to do what they pleased with prizes after they brought them in, but the United States could not tolerate such an infringment on its sovereignty, Genêt never backed down, but by means of warnings and threats the government succeeded in deterring the consuls. The worst offender, Vice-Consul Duplaine in Boston, was dismissed.

The recruiting of American sailors for purposes of privateering was forbidden by the United States government, but the latter suffered a rebuff in its effort to punish such enlistment. Gideon Henfield, an American serving on a French privateer, was arrested and tried before the United States Circuit Court sitting in Philadelphia. The jury acquitted him despite the evidence and the judge's charge that the service was punishable. This verdict was acclaimed by Freneau's *National Gazette* and other Republican papers. It strengthened Genêt's delusion that the people were for him even though the government was against him. He continued to arm and outfit privateers, despite the express prohibition of such action, and by midsummer his relations with the high officials reached the breaking point.

The Downfall of Genêt

The most notorious case was that of the *Little Democrat*. When the French captured this former British merchantman (then the *Little Sarah*) the vessel was already partly armed. After she had been further armed and equipped as a privateer in Philadelphia she was about to put to sea when the state and federal authorities were apprised of the situation, at a time when Washington was out of town. Genêt flew into a "great passion" when interviewed by Alexander J. Dallas, secretary of Governor Mifflin of Pennsylvania, threatening an appeal from the President to the people. He was also furious when Jefferson talked with him. Though the vessel dropped a little way down the Delaware River, she did not actually put to sea until after Washington got back (July 11) and took matters in hand. The question was what means the government should or could employ to stop her. Hamilton and Knox favored forcible action, arguing that if there were none the British would have just cause for war. Jefferson opposed such action on the practical ground that it would be ineffective and because he believed that it would bring on war with France, while the failure to employ force would not bring on war with Great Britain. Washington followed Jefferson's judgment, and Genêt merely received a letter telling him that he was expected to detain the vessel. This he did not do. The British, convinced by now of the sincerity of the American government in the matter of neutrality, took the position that the United States had been forced to submit to an indignity because of lack of military preparation. Thus the war threat lifted but Genêt had sealed his doom as an accredited representative.

His private threat to appeal from Washington to the people was brought into the open by Hamilton in the first of a newspaper series signed "No Jacobin" (July 31, 1793), and the public rallied to the support of their President against a foreigner. Meanwhile, there was agreement within the government that Genêt's recall must be requested. Jefferson found it impossible to deal with such an incorrigible person; and he was convinced that Genêt was endangering the neutrality policy, playing into the hands of the pro-British faction, and seriously injuring the Republican interest. As an official, a patriot, and a Republican he wanted to get rid of the French emissary, but at the same time he wanted to reduce the risk of a break with France. Hamilton had informed Hammond that a breach was likely, and he and Knox wanted the request for Genêt's recall to be peremptory. But Washington caused more prudent counsels to prevail. Jefferson dispatched to France a letter which constituted a full exposé of Genêt's conduct and was all the more effective because of its extensive quotation of the emissary's intemperate language. At the same time a clear distinction was drawn between the American attitude toward this envoy and toward the French nation. Genêt was replaced by Fauchet. Rather than risk the chance of death at the hands of the Jocobins now in power in France, he remained in the United States, where he married the daughter of Governor Clinton of New York and lived to a ripe old age. The French government had found Gouverneur Morris as unpalatable as the American officials had found Genêt, and he was replaced in 1794 by James Monroe. These actions on both sides of the Atlantic were favorable to the preservation of American neutrality.

The Success of the Policy

While the incident of the *Little Democrat* was the most flagrant and notorious case of defiance of the government in its efforts to carry out the policy of neutrality, there were many other cases, some of them involving the British and many of them complicated by legal uncertainties. Jefferson, who was overwhelmed by the burden of administering the policy, suggested the reference of disputed questions to the judiciary; and in midsummer, on behalf of the government, he submitted to the Supreme

Court twenty-nine questions, most of which were actually formulated by Hamilton. Chief Justice Jay and his associates set a negative precedent when they declined to pass on these. Soon thereafter the members of the Cabinet themselves drew up a set of rules respecting belligerents, and, for this and other reasons, relatively few difficulties about armed vessels arose afterward.

Viewed as a whole, the neutrality policy of 1793 was not only wise; it was conscientiously and successfully administered. Whether it was more endangered by the British and their partisans on the right, or the French and their zealots on the left, will always be a matter of some dispute; but the government managed to pursue the safe middle course amid strong and changing currents of public opinion. Since Genêt was such a sensational figure, there is danger of overestimating his influence on these. The popular effects of his mission, seem to have been at first a stimulation of enthusiasm for France, but later the accentuation of a reaction against her.

The year 1793 was marked by the organization of numerous Democratic or Democratic-Republican societies, and Genêt has often been held responsible for these. The most famous of them, the Democratic Society of Pennsylvania in Philadelphia, was organized about July 4; and it was regarded as the parent organization because it sent out a circular urging the formation of such societies in all parts of the country. These were nuclei for the Republican or Democratic-Republican Party, and more than forty of them were established during the decade, especially in 1793 and 1794. Unquestionably they were stimulated by the enthusiasm for the French Revolution, but these clubs went back in spirit to the American Revolution, and in form to English models as well as French. The claim that they were mere replicas of the Jacobin clubs of France was a partisan exaggeration. They tended to be centers of pro-French sentiment, nevertheless, and intemperate comments on the policy of the government emanated from them, as they did from papers like the *National Gazette.* Philip Freneau now showed how much more extreme he was than his supposed patron, for he continued to support Genêt long after Jefferson found the Frenchman unendurable and urged in private that Republicans disentangle themselves from the wreckage he had wrought.

The rage for Genêt and France and the French Revolution seems to have been greatest in Philadelphia, and John Adams in an extravagant utterance of later years said that only the yellow fever in that city saved the President from the madmen. This fearful epidemic reached its height in September and lasted until frost, paralyzing the operations of the government and carrying off some of the most ardent Republicans. It caused the demise of the *National Gazette,* though not of Freneau himself. The statement of John Adams was proof that there was hysteria on both sides. Essentially the reaction against Genêt was patriotic. It was skillfully exploited by Hamilton to the discredit of the Democratic societies, of the party identified with them, and to some extent of Jefferson. The Secretary of the Treasury remained the chief power in national politics and soon had no rival within the government. After Jefferson relinquished the Secretaryship of State at the end of the year, Washington found it much harder to preserve the balance and maintain a middle course.

CHAPTER 16

Hamilton in the Ascendant 1794-1796

GEORGE WASHINGTON WAS RELUCTANT TO RECOGNIZE the existence of parties, and the high appointments he made on Jefferson's retirement reflected his continuing desire to maintain a balance of opinion within the administration. While the neutrality policy was being carried into effect there was a large area of general agreement, but in cases of disagreement Secretary of War Knox nearly always supported Hamilton against Jefferson. Attorney General Edmund Randolph wavered between the two sides. He succeeded to the Secretaryship of State, and although this makeshift appointment was satisfactory to neither Washington nor Jefferson, Randolph was not regarded by either of them as a partisan of the Secretary of the Treasury. Neither was William Bradford of Pennsylvania, an old college friend of Madison's at Princeton who was named Attorney General in place of Randolph. More significant still was the appointment of James Monroe, a strong Republican partisan, to replace the counterrevolutionary Gouverneur Morris as minister to France. But Hamilton soon gained a control over foreign policy that approximated his dominance in the domestic field. This was specially reflected in the field of British relations. It has been said that Jay's Treaty might just as well be called Hamilton's Treaty.

Hamilton retired from the Secretaryship of the Treasury early in 1795, being succeeded by his assistant, Oliver Wolcott, Jr., of Connecticut, who saw eye to eye with him in all political matters and constantly availed himself of his advice. Knox retired a few weeks earlier and was succeeded as Secretary of War by Timothy Pickering, then of Pennsylvania but more closely identified with Massachusetts, a Federalist of the most extreme sort. In the summer of that year Edmund Randolph resigned the Secretaryship of State under confused circumstances which were exploited by Wolcott and Pickering to his political ruination, and the latter succeeded him. Meanwhile, Monroe let his zeal run away with him in France, and in 1796 he was recalled. Except for the negotiations with Spain, into which partisanship did not enter, foreign matters came to be dominated by persons who followed Hamiltonian lines.

British Relations: Jay's Treaty

Despite the satisfaction of the British with the policy of neutrality, Anglo-American relations sharply deteriorated in the winter of 1793-1794 for two main reasons. The situation in the Northwest had grown more critical, and in the course of the war between the British and the French the former took drastic action against American commerce.

In the Northwest the American position was one of great danger after St. Clair's defeat in the autumn of 1791. That demonstration of American weakness emboldened the Indians and gave new life to the British plan to create an Indian buffer state, which would have deprived the republic of all its lands north of the Ohio and a big slice of territory in western and northern New York. No responsible American statesman could consider such dismemberment, and a British proposal to mediate between the United States and the Indians was received coldly. But, while biding their time, the British from their seats in the newly created provinces of Lower and Upper Canada and their posts in American territory supported the Indians in their determination to maintain possession of their lands. A peace conference between American commissioners and western Indians on the northern shore of Lake Erie in the summer of 1793 failed completely, because of utter inability to agree on a boundary line. Colonel John Graves Simcoe, whose anti-American zeal exceeded that of his superiors in England, was now Lieutenant Governor of Upper Canada. A new American military expedition, commanded by "Mad" Anthony Wayne, had winter quarters in 1793-1794 at the site of St. Clair's defeat, and Simcoe strengthened an old fort at the Rapids of the Maumee to protect Detroit, which he believed to be Wayne's objective. Meanwhile, the Governor General of Canada, Lord Dorchester, in a violent speech to a delegation of western Indians (February 10, 1794), predicted war between the United States and Great Britain, after which the Indians might draw any boundary line they liked. News of this provocative speech reached Congress when that body was already seething with resentment because of British actions on the seas.

Infringements by a belligerent on neutral commerce that was thought to benefit the enemy might have been expected in a desperate war and, up to a point, might have been endured. The British were determined to take full advantage of their seapower by driving French shipping from

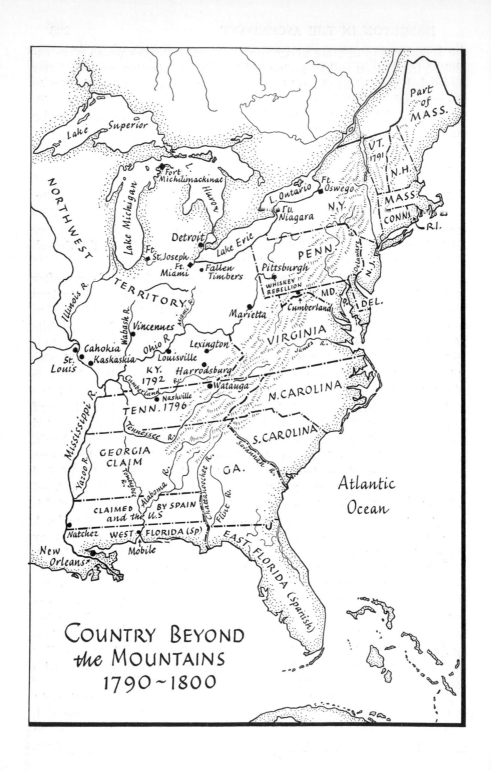

Part
of
MASS.

Lake Superior

NORTHWEST

Lake Michigan

L. Huron

Fort
Michilimackinac

VT.
1791

N.H.

L. Ontario   Ft.
Oswego

MASS.

Detroit

Ft.
Niagara

N.Y.

CONN.

R.I.

St. Joseph
Ft.
Miami   • Fallen
Timbers

Lake Erie

PENN.

Pittsburgh

Delaware R.

N.J.

Illinois R.

TERRITORY

Marietta

WHISKEY
REBELLION

MD.

O.

DEL.

Cumberland

Wabash R.

Vincennes

Ohio R.

Lexington

Miami R.

VIRGINIA

James R.

Cahokia

Louisville

St.
Louis   • Kaskaskia

KY.
1792   Harrodsburg
R.

Cumberland R.

• Watauga

N. CAROLINA

Nashville

TENN. 1796

S. CAROLINA

Mississippi R.

Tennessee R.

Savannah R.

GEORGIA
CLAIM

GA.

Atlantic
Ocean

Yazoo R.

Coosa R.

Alabama R.

Chattahoochee R.

Flint R.

CLAIMED   BY SPAIN
and the U.S

Natchez   WEST   FLORIDA (Sp)

EAST

Mobile

FLORIDA (Spanish)

New
Orleans

COUNTRY BEYOND
the MOUNTAINS
1790~1800

the seas and preventing its replacement by neutral shipping to their own disadvantage. Furthermore, they interpreted international law according to their own interests. Denying the validity of the principle incorporated by the United States in all its commercial treaties, that free ships make free goods, they asserted the right to take enemy-owned noncontraband goods from neutral-owned ships, and they defined contraband (which everyone agreed could be confiscated even if neutral-owned on a neutral ship) as anything that might aid their enemy, including food. By the Provision Order, issued in England in June 1793 and reported in America late in the summer, naval officers were instructed to bring into British ports neutral vessels carrying food to French ports. Compensation might be had for this, however. They revived the "Rule of 1756," whereby Britain had asserted that trade forbidden in time of peace might not be permitted in time of war (like non-French carrying of sugar from the French West Indies to France). The British policy came to a climax in an order of November 1793 that practically forbade all neutral commerce with the French islands and went far beyond the Rule of 1756. This order was enforced with extreme harshness and without advance notice. Several hundred American ships were detained, while their crews sweated in prison, and many ships were confiscated. The order was soon modified, but news of these ruthless actions created a wave of indignation. Even Hamilton described the order as "atrocious."

Jefferson contributed to anti-British feeling shortly before leaving office by submitting his long-deferred report on commerce (December 16, 1793). It described prewar conditions only, but this able statement of the treatment of American commerce by the various nations was anti-British; and the diplomatic correspondence that was submitted to Congress left no possible doubt of the British policy of obstruction and delay. Jefferson again recommended a policy of discriminatory legislation, and Madison shortly reintroduced the resolutions that the Secretary of the Treasury had caused to be deferred two years before. What with the reports of happenings in the Caribbean and of Dorchester's tirade in the Northwest, the anti-British feeling swelled into a tide which no one could stem. There was talk of sequestering debts to British creditors, and a temporary embargo was declared. Not since the American Revolution had the United States and Great Britain seemed so near to war, though the excitement was chiefly on the American side of the Atlantic.

Hamilton and his partisans executed a flank movement in the effort to preserve the peace. A group of Federalist Senators proposed to Washington that a special envoy be sent to England to negotiate a settlement of the various points at issue between the two countries. This proposal was accepted, but the suggestion that Hamilton be that envoy met with such violent Republican disapproval that it was dropped, and the choice fell on John Jay, who was highly acceptable to the British. Some questioned the propriety of sending the Chief Justice on such a mission, but there could be no question of the dignity of the appointment or of the experience of the appointee.

The Fruits of Jay's Mission

Jay's negotiations with Lord Grenville, the British Secretary of State for Foreign Affairs, extended over several months and the two men signed a treaty on November 19, 1794. Now that the secret archives have been opened up, we are in better position than his contemporaries were to perceive the weakness of Jay's bargaining position. The British knew that he was disposed to accept their contention about the reasons for retaining the western posts rather than that of Jefferson. To all practical purposes he got his instructions from Hamilton, and that anxious advocate of Anglo-American peace revealed to the British minister Hammond at the outset that the American interpretation of international law would not be seriously advocated, though compensation would be sought for the highhanded actions in the West Indies. Hamilton also secretly let the British government know that the United States would not join the Baltic countries in a convention of armed neutrality. The British may not have taken the threat of joint neutral action very seriously, but the treaty signed by Jay after Hamilton gave away his hand was far less favorable to the United States than the draft he had obtained earlier.

The treaty reached Philadelphia in March 1795 after Congress had adjourned, and Washington and Secretary of State Randolph did not like it. It was presented to the Senate in special session in June and discussed behind closed doors. After the elimination of Article XII, providing for limited commerce with the British West Indies but imposing at the same time intolerable restrictions on certain American exports, it was accepted by a bare two-thirds majority. The Senators agreed to keep the terms of the treaty secret, but the French minister caused an extract from it to be published and Senator Stevens Thomson Mason of Virginia released the whole of it. Then the storm broke. Nobody seemed to like the treaty except Hamilton and those closest to him, and he was stoned while making a speech in defense of it. Jay was hanged in effigy, but the main responsibility was unquestionably Hamilton's. Meanwhile, the British had issued another offensive provision order, and Washington hesitated to complete the ratification. He finally yielded to Federalist pressure and attached his signature, having concluded that he had no choice but to make the best of a bad situation.

Contemporary discussion of Jay's Treaty was highly colored by political partisanship but upon its face the settlement looked like a bad bargain. The chief American gain was the agreement of the British to give up the Northwest posts, but they did not agree to discontinue relations with

Indians on the American side of the line, and in return for their physical withdrawal from the posts, the United States government assumed the debts to the collection of which legal obstacles had been imposed by states. One wonders why Jay, the head of the federal judiciary, virtually conceded that serious obstacles to the collection of the debts to English merchants existed when the courts were open to them and decisions upholding British rights under the Treaty of 1783 were to be expected. The Americans also gained the right to appeal to a commission for compensation for shipping losses, and, as things turned out, they got more compensation than the government finally paid in settlement of the debts; hence this was not as great a blow to the pocketbook as had been expected. A principle which was to prove exceedingly important in Anglo-American relations was established by the provision for the settlement of these matters, and of northern boundary questions, by referring them to commissions for arbitration, though the significance of this precedent was not fully recognized at the time. In terms of trade, the only American gain was the opening up of the East Indies.

Besides the assumption of the debts, the price that the Americans paid for a formal settlement with the British was: (1) acceptance of virtually all British interpretations of international law, and (2) a ten-year guarantee against tariff and tonnage discrimination, with the right on the part of the British to levy countervailing duties. It seemed to his critics that Jay had surrendered neutral rights that Americans had long contended for and had bartered away a part of the economic independence of his country. Furthermore, the gains in the Northwest seemed less important than they would have a few months earlier, since the situation there had vastly improved as a consequence of Wayne's victory over the Indians at the battle of Fallen Timbers (August 20, 1794). This was followed a year later by the Treaty of Greenville, by which the western Indians ceded large areas in the present state of Ohio and acknowledged the exclusive protection of the United States. Finally, there was a serious question what effect the treaty would have on relations with France. If the French believed that the United States was being drawn into the British orbit, in violation of the terms or spirit of the treaties of 1778, they might be expected to raise strenuous objection. Thus there would be an increase in danger from that quarter. The strongest argument in favor of Jay's Treaty was that it preserved peace between the United States and Great Britain, with whom war would have been disastrous. Some interpreters of these events have taken the position that almost any treaty was better than none. But this one certainly did not amount to a full recognition of American independence, and even after allowance is made for partisan exaggeration the price of the settlement with England appears to have been unnecessarily high.

The partisan struggle by no means ended when the Senate accepted the treaty. The House of Representatives was called on to make the appropriations necessary to carry it into effect, and heated debate ensued. Important constitutional questions were involved and the alignment on these tended to be partisan. Washington assumed that Congress was obligated to pass the necessary legislation, and by refusing to submit Jay's instructions and other papers relating to the negotiations he upheld the prerogatives of the President and Senate in connection with treaties. The House, while finally voting for the appropriations by a majority of three (April 30, 1796), refused to concede the inevitability of such enabling legislation. According to this historic precedent, the House has the right to block any treaty that requires money or other enabling legislation, but out of respect for the constitutional treaty-making authority it has never exercised this right; instead, it has used it only to win influence in foreign relations.

THE RUIN OF EDMUND RANDOLPH

At the time of Edmund Randolph's appointment one of his friends expressed the fear that he had placed himself on a bed of thorns. Nobody would have found the Secretaryship of State a cozy berth at this juncture, and Randolph's character and circumstances were calculated to make him particularly uncomfortable. His entire public career showed him to be a man of vacillating judgment; and for a variety of reasons, including the long illness of his wife, he was in constant financial difficulty. His position in the administration was anomalous. He was a lifelong friend of Washington, to whom he was intensely loyal, and he had tried to keep himself uncommitted in the partisan struggles of the day. His personal associations were more with the Republicans than the Federalists, however, and he never enjoyed the confidence of the British Minister, George Hammond. Randolph thought it wise and proper to show good will to Fauchet, the new French minister, and went out of his way to be friendly. He was indiscreet at times, though hardly as indiscreet as Hamilton was in talking with Hammond.

Randolph's part in the negotiations with the British was merely nominal, and Jay adopted a patronizing tone toward him. He was in Washington's confidence, however, during the troubled weeks following the receipt of the treaty in America, and he defended it to Monroe, who was getting embarrassing questions from the French. In the summer of 1795, the Secretary of State advised Washington not to sign the treaty until the British had done something about the latest provision order, and while this question was still in the air Hammond intervened.

Hamilton was no longer Secretary of the Treasury, but his successor, Oliver Wolcott, Jr., had inherited his intimacy with Hammond. By that time, Timothy Pickering was Secretary of War in place of Knox. It was to

*The diverse but complementary
talents of these three dynamic
men molded the character of the
new Republic.*

THOMAS JEFFERSON

1743-1826

Portrait by Rembrandt Peale

Third President
of the United States

JOHN ADAMS

1735-1826

*Portrait by Asher B. Durand
after original by Gilbert Stuart*

Second President
of the United States

ALEXANDER HAMILTON

1755(?)-1804

Portrait by John Trumbull

Secretary of the Treasury
1789-1795

James Madison

1751-1836

Portrait by Asher B. Durand

Fourth President of the United States
in old age

The Capitol in Washington, before 1814. *Drawing attributed to B*jamin *H. Latrobe.* In this early view a wooden corridor connects Senate and House wings.

War of 1812: Battle of Lake Erie. Forced to abandon the *Lawrence*, the central ship, Commodore Perry continued the battle from the *Niagara*, right, and won a great victory.

THE VIRGINIA STATE CAPITOL, RICHMOND. Designed by Thomas Jefferson in 1786 after the Maison Carrée at Nîmes. It has been termed the first monument of the classical revival in America.

FULTON'S STEAMBOAT. A French lithograph of the vessel as enlarged and rebu

Wolcott that Hammond delivered an intercepted dispatch from Fauchet to the French government, and after seeing this, Washington yielded to the pressure of Pickering and Wolcott and signed the treaty. Several days later he allowed them to confront Randolph with the dispatch unexpectedly and to charge the Secretary of State with what amounted to treason. Confused and outraged, Randolph immediately resigned.

The dispatch referred to "overtures" made by Randolph at the time of the "Whiskey Rebellion," when the federal government was being defied in western Pennsylvania because of the excise tax. It mentioned civil war in the United States and the possible use of French money, intimating that certain "pretended patriots" had their price. The construction placed by Pickering and Wolcott on this was that Randolph solicited a bribe from Fauchet to further "civil war" in the French interest. But Randolph got from Fauchet, who was then on the point of sailing for France, what amounted to a full exoneration. Though Randolph had suggested early payments to Americans who were selling flour to France, he had sought no bribe, and he really wanted to *prevent* the "civil war" which he believed the *British* were fomenting. But the circumstances were confused, and some of Randolph's comments on the pro-French and pro-British factions were indiscreet and lent themselves to misinterpretation.

His own "vindication," which was published with badly translated documents a few weeks later, served to confuse the situation further. The net result was that an unwarranted partisan charge was perpetuated not only through the lifetime of the victim, who suffered further persecution, but until our own time, when at last its falsity has been fully demonstrated. The immediate result was that the Hamiltonian Federalists now became wholly dominant in the government. Randolph's place was given to the bitterly partisan Timothy Pickering, and he was succeeded as Secretary of War by James McHenry of Maryland, who gave allegiance to Hamilton.

JAMES MONROE AND FRENCH RELATIONS

Monroe arrived in France in August 1794, several weeks after Jay got to England. The two missions provide a striking illustration of the division of American counsels and policies at a time when the Western World was the scene of a duel between the two chief powers. On the one hand, Jay, instructed by Hamilton, yielded too much to the British; and on the other, Monroe, instructed by Randolph, manifested American friendship for France too exuberantly. Monroe's appearance at the outset before the National Convention, the governing body of France after the fall of Robespierre, was well calculated to advertise the friendship between the two countries, and this was dramatically sealed when he was kissed on both cheeks by the presiding officer. His actions and his overenthusiastic speech were not in the tradition of diplomacy, and in due course he was rebuked by Edmund Randolph for his excess of zeal. In emphasizing American friendliness, however, and seeking to overcome the bad impression left by Gouverneur Morris, this inexperienced diplomat was following Randolph's instructions; and he performed his functions diligently during the months before he got news of Jay's Treaty. As he was instructed to do, he assured the French that Jay had been forbidden to do anything contrary to the American treaties with France and continued to minimize the significance of the negotiations.

He knew nothing about these negotiations except what he learned from Randolph, for Jay haughtily refused to inform him of the provisions of the treaty while it was still unratified. The American government seemed to be following the policy of not letting the left hand know what the right hand was doing. After he learned the terms that Jay had accepted, Monroe was deeply embarrassed, since he regarded the treaty as a slap in the face of the French and thought of himself as an unwitting instrument in deceiving them. His resentment was not unnatural but his comments in letters that he sent home lent color to the charge that his sympathies with the French had led him to oppose the policy of the administration. It would have been better for him personally if he had offered his resignation at this juncture.

After the text of the treaty got out and the French interpreted it as a betrayal, Monroe was in an impossible situation. Matters became critical early in 1796, after the Directory was established in France and, under more orderly domestic conditions, greater attention was paid to American affairs. The Directory decided to send a special envoy to the United States, who would recall Adet (Fauchet's successor), announce the end of the Franco-American treaties, and then withdraw. Such a severance of relations might have gratified Hamilton and Pickering, but it was not to be supposed that it would have pleased Washington, and in the eyes of Monroe and the Republican leaders as a group it would have been positively disastrous. Monroe successfully argued against this drastic action, which would naturally be interpreted as the prelude to war, but in his anxiety to forestall it he was guilty of grave impropriety. In a letter to the French Minister of Foreign Affairs he said: "Left to ourselves, everything will I think be satisfactorily arranged and perhaps in the course of the present year." The French interpreted this as a reference to the presidential election of 1796 and the probable victory of the Republican Party. Far from being dissuaded from interference in American domestic affairs, through Adet they actually worked against the Federalists in the election. We now know more about what was going on than George Washington did; but by the summer of 1796 he was dissatisfied with Monroe, and Pickering had already decided to replace him with a Federalist. That decision did not become effective until several months later, and its results were part of the heritage that Washington transmitted to his own successor. Monroe became another casualty of the international strife that imperiled the independence of his country and beclouded its domestic problems. He was not ruined, as Edmund Randolph was, nor was he hung in effigy like John Jay, but as a public man he was badly injured.

SPANISH RELATIONS AND PINCKNEY'S TREATY

The settlement with Spain was the most important diplomatic achievement of the Washington administration. Political partisanship did not enter into it appreciably, and credit for it must be given to several men. Jefferson was its architect, though he had been out of office nearly two years when it was effected. In the spring of 1792, following his recommendation, William Short had been sent from The Hague to join the American *chargé*, William Carmichael, in Madrid, and Jefferson had briefed them well. The spread of the European war and the unexpected alignment of Spain with Great Britain destroyed the hope of immediate results, but success came in 1795, the year the Spanish broke away from their temporary alliance, made peace with France, and got ready for war with Britain. They were alarmed by Jay's negotiations and apprehensive of an Anglo-American alliance, specially fearing direct action against Louisiana by American frontiersmen backed by British power. So the situation now opened which Jefferson had hoped for. The United States could, as he said, "drive in the nail," that is, demand a high price from Spain for *not* joining Britain against her.

Short and Carmichael had been vainly arguing and kicking their heels in the antechambers of the Spanish court. The credit for speeding the negotiations into a decisive phase belongs to Edmund Randolph, who found out that the Spanish were willing to expedite matters if a minister of appropriate splendor were sent. Randolph tried to induce Jefferson to assume this role, but the former Secretary of State had no intention of leaving his new-found freedom in the country for thankless public service, and he claimed that he was suffering from rheumatism anyway. In the autumn of 1794 the appointment finally went to Thomas Pinckney, the American minister in Great Britain, a moderate Federalist and a South Carolina aristocrat, who had all the desired personal qualifications and conducted himself with dignity and skill. Guiding himself by the original instructions from Jefferson and refusing to agree to any alliance or guarantee of Spanish territories, he was firm at the crucial moments and achieved complete success. The agreement goes by the name of the Treaty of San Lorenzo or Pinckney's Treaty (1795).

By this treaty Spain finally agreed to the southern boundary of the United States at the thirty-first parallel of latitude, recognized the free navigation of the Mississippi, and granted the right of deposit at New Orleans to American shippers for three years with the promise of renewal. In direct contrast to the treaty with Great Britain, both parties promised to restrain the Indians in their own territories. Furthermore, neutral rights were defined according to the historic American contention, which Jay had yielded to the British. The treaty was so favorable that it was unanimously approved by the Senate. Important territorial questions were left to the future, but since Spain was a declining power the growing republic could afford to be patient. The treaty marked a long step toward the attainment of full independence. Since the Republic had now established its claim to sovereign rights in the Southwest, and British garrisons in the Northwest were removed under Jay's Treaty, the prospect of retaining in the Union the western settlements was greatly brightened. Western discontent was stilled by diplomatic action that removed its causes.

THE "WHISKEY REBELLION"

The resistance of the farmers in the Monongahela country of Pennsylvania to the federal excise tax on whiskey was an expression of western discontent with eastern policy which assumed the form of a local conflict with national authority. The "Whiskey Rebellion" came to a head in the late summer of 1794, when Jay had been several months in England, Monroe had recently arrived in France, and Pinckney had not yet set out for Madrid, but its political reverberations lasted through the election of 1796, at least. The trouble rose in a region where the distillation of whiskey on farms was more important in the local economy than anywhere else in the United States. Roughly speaking, this was the settled part of Pennsylvania beyond the Alleghenies. Pittsburgh, then a village with about 1000 residents, was the metropolis of the region, but the disaffection was greatest to the southward, especially in Washington County. Not only was whiskey a product of relatively great value and small bulk which could be carried across the mountains to the East for sale; it was a medium of exchange among people who saw hardly any money from one end of the year to the other. The salaries of church ministers were often paid in Monongahela rye whiskey, and the use of it was virtually universal. Part of every farmer's crop was turned into whiskey at his or a neighbor's still, and the beverage flowed like water. This was scarcely an earthly Paradise, however, for these people were generally poor, and the ready flow of alcoholic spirits in this frontier society was a substitute for a good diet and warm shelter.

In Pennsylvania, previous taxes on spirituous liquors had generally been imposed only when these were sold, and the tax could be passed on to the purchaser. Hostility to any sort of tax on commodities was traditional in America, and these western farmers, who were generally at loggerheads with the easterners in their own state, held all excisemen in contempt and often treated them very roughly. The federal tax of 1791, which was somewhat reduced in 1792, fell on the product of all stills, even those that produced whiskey chiefly for barter or personal use. Almost to a man the farmers thought it unjust to be taxed on their grain when, instead of eating it, they drank it.

The tax was proposed by Hamilton in order to provide for the costs of assuming the state debts, in which these frontier farmers were not at all interested, and it was adopted because nobody could think of a good alternative. The various officials received a percentage of the collections, and this arrangement did not endear them to the taxpayers. The larger and more commercial stills were in a better position than the small ones to pass the tax on to the consumer, and the spirit of resistance was strongest among the poorer farmers. They resented the inquisitorial methods of the officials and took special exception to the requirement that excise cases should be tried in the federal court in far away Philadelphia. Popular sentiment against the law was so strong that only the boldest of men dared support it. The two Democratic societies in the region did not create the opposition, for it was already tremendous when they were established in 1794, but they served as centers of disaffection.

A conference of protesters against the tax was held in Pittsburgh in August 1792. Besides drawing up a remonstrance to Congress, these men set up Committees of Correspondence after the manner of the patriots in the American Revolution, and, what was more alarming, they adopted resolutions against excise officers that amounted to defiance. Albert Gallatin of Fayette County afterwards bemoaned the fact that he signed these. At this time Hamilton believed that the employment of military force by the government was warranted, but the President thought it sufficient to issue a strong proclamation. It was signed by Jefferson as Secretary of State, who persuaded Washington to omit a phrase implying that the excise law was necessary. Later in private he described the tax as "infernal," but he did not countenance defiance of public authority. Things quieted down for some months after the proclamation, but all the stills were not registered by June 1, 1793, as they were supposed to be, and the attempt to serve legal processes in the following summer brought on open conflict. By that time the law had been changed so as to make excise cases cognizable in state courts when parties to them lived at a distance, but writs were nevertheless issued under the old law. Certain critics of Hamilton in the West saw in this procedure clear proof that he welcomed a test of strength and really wanted to provoke a crisis.

A crisis came when the United States marshal, who was seeking to serve processes, and General John Neville, federal inspector of the trans-Allegheny counties of Pennsylvania, were fired on. Neville's country house near Pittsburgh was burned and both men were held captive, though both

escaped. The efforts of Hugh Henry Brackenridge, a Princeton graduate and wise and humane lawyer, to stay the tide of passion was unavailing, and in August, at Braddock's Field, there was a muster of armed
men, variously estimated as from 1500 to 7000 in number. But they were
divided in mind, and the tide of resistance soon began to ebb. Meanwhile,
there was rioting elsewhere, in states as far away as South Carolina, and
revenue officers were subjected to some manhandling.

Hamilton, more convinced than ever that force must be employed,
wrote a series of newspaper essays under the *nom de plume* "Tully,"
and said that the question was whether there should be government or
no government. Though more reluctant to employ coercion, Washington
agreed that the situation endangered the government, and on August 7,
1794, he issued a proclamation to the governors of Pennsylvania, New
Jersey, Maryland, and Virginia which caused them to call out the militia
of those states. Meanwhile, he sent into the Monongahela country commissioners who tried to get pledges of submission in return for pardon
for past offenses. They believed that the majority wanted to submit but
were intimidated by a violent minority. Toward the end of September
some 12,000 militiamen began to move. Washington visited them briefly
and Hamilton accompanied them at his own request. Under the command
of Governor "Light-Horse" Harry Lee of Virginia, the army proceeded to
Pittsburgh without meeting any opposition. Hamilton was conspicuous throughout the operations, and his critics accused him of highhand-
edness in the investigations he conducted. A small detachment of soldiers
remained in the region all winter, and in Philadelphia trials dragged on
through the year 1795. A number of arrests had been made but evidence
of treason was hard to get, and only two men, both of them unimportant,
were convicted. Washington pardoned both of them.

Many poor men suffered hardship, but the bill of costs was smaller
than Hamilton would have been willing to assume in order to uphold the
majesty of the law and demonstrate the power of the federal government.
Hardly a voice was raised in the eastern settlements in defense of the
rebels, though some people thought that they should have been charged
with riotous conduct rather than treason, and that this ostentatious display
of force against them bordered on absurdity. In his address to Congress
in November 1794, the President condemned the "self-created societies"—
meaning the Democratic societies, which were now being blamed by the
Hamiltonians for all this trouble. Seeking to identify themselves with
the forces of law and order, the Federalists threw the Republicans on
the defensive, just as they had done a year earlier in connection with
Genêt. The Republicans continued to insist, however, on the constitutional right of free men to organize for political purposes and, if they
should see fit, to criticize the government. There was no necessary choice
between anarchy and tyranny, and most people wanted neither, but the

lines of future political conflict were being drawn and, through force of circumstances, Washington was identified more than ever with the Hamiltonians.

WASHINGTON'S FAREWELL ADDRESS

The Constitution did not prescribe the number of terms a President might serve, but George Washington limited himself to two and thus started a tradition. In 1796, at the age of sixty-four he regarded himself as an old man and was pathetically eager to go home. He was surprised and deeply pained by the partisan spirit that had manifested itself during the last two or three years. He wrote Jefferson in 1796 that "truth and right decisions" had been his "sole objects" during the time they served together. "I was no party man myself," he said, "and the first wish of my heart was, if parties did exist, to reconcile them." He was always disturbed by any criticism of the government, but not until the time of Genêt was much criticism directed against him personally. Attacks on the President himself increased after that, especially in connection with Jay's Treaty. Washington, who was an exceedingly sensitive man and had naturally interpreted his unanimous re-election as proof that all groups were behind him, writhed under them. He wrote Jefferson that he had been described "in such exaggerated and indecent terms as could scarcely be applied to a Nero, a notorious defaulter, or even a common pickpocket."

The first President did not recognize that abuse is one of the perquisites of that office. Nor did he realize the inevitability of his becoming a target of the Republicans when they came to believe that his administration had become a Hamiltonian preserve. But personal attacks on the revered President often turned out to be boomerangs. In his own state the opponents of Jay's Treaty overreached themselves, and they were wisely admonished by Jefferson to avoid direct reference to the President. Even in the heat of partisan conflict Washington continued to be a cherished symbol of national unity, and he still had reason to think of himself as the President of all the people and all the states when he released his Farewell Address. The document was unique, just as his position was.

Washington, who had no more confidence in his ability as a writer than in his judgment of constitutional questions, had turned to James Madison in 1792, when he was contemplating retirement at the end of one term, and had asked this friend to prepare an address for him. He told Madison what to say, however, and Madison sought not only to present Washington's ideas faithfully but also to employ his customary language. In 1796, the President resurrected this document and, being now on much less intimate terms with Madison, he asked Hamilton to prepare a draft along the same lines. Hamilton drew a fresh paper, but Washington took this in hand, restored some things from Madison's draft and reworked others according to his own notion. This case presents no close parallel to modern ghost-writing, for the paper clearly reflects Washington and his philosophy, and in it one can hear his very accents. Though always referred to as an address, it was not spoken to any group of auditors. Washington published it in the *American Daily Advertizer* of Philadelphia (September 19, 1796). As news, the most important thing in it was the announcement that the President intended to retire, but time has proved that the passages dealing with foreign relations were most memorable.

Characteristically, Washington urged his countrymen to pursue a course of national independence. He deplored passionate attachment or antipathy to any foreign country and warned against foreign influences in American affairs. He may have been thinking at this time of the French minister Adet, who was intriguing against him, but his warning could have been directed equally well against the activities of the British minister, George Hammond. In regard to foreign nations, he recommended as a rule of conduct that the United States have as few *political* connections with them as possible. He recognized that existing engagements must be kept, and he did not recommend the repudiation of the French treaties. He did not want to extend these engagements, however, and he advised his countrymen to steer clear of permanent alliances. He urged that the United States keep out of European affairs, which were of only remote interest to Americans. This it could do because of the detached and distant situation of the country, and he urged that it avail itself of its unusual advantages.

The significance of these recommendations did not lie in their novelty, for they were a natural outgrowth of the neutrality policy of 1793. The importance of the pronouncement lay in the fact that it was made by such a man at such a time. Inevitably it came to be regarded as a classic statement of American policy, and it served as a guidepost for a century and more—until the situation of the United States ceased to be "detached and distant," and from being a weakling the nation had become a major power.

Washington's eulogy of the Union is less often referred to, and he could not speak with the eloquence of Webster or Lincoln, but a generation that recognized the supremely important part he had played in creating the Union must have been impressed by his sensible arguments and moved by his simple expression of devotion. No one saw more clearly than he the ease and the danger of appeal to local interests, and he spoke for a genuine nation that should comprehend and advance the interests of all. It is doubtful if he fully perceived the basis of economic conflict, but he clearly foresaw the danger of conflict between regions in a large country. The worst of all parties, in his opinion, were those based on geography, for they endangered the Union. His words of warning could have been read to advantage in the 1850's.

There is little of lasting value, however, in his other reflections on political organizations, even though some of these attracted great attention at the time. He again condemned the Democratic societies, without mentioning them by name, believing that their real design was to interfere with regular governmental procedure under the constituted authorities. "They serve to organize faction," he said, and to him "party" was just another name for faction. He feared that the public councils would be distracted and the public administration enfeebled by the spirit of party. He did not value the services of voluntary organizations in the political education of a people, and had no conception of the legitimate function of political opposition as subsequently recognized in the United States and Great Britain. Even under a system of popular elections, the sort of unitary government that Washington favored had greater dangers of tyranny than this broadly patriotic and genuinely untyrannical man perceived. He was unwittingly arguing the case for the Federalists, who were seeking to identify the government with themselves and to label opposition to their policies as factious if not positively subversive. But the fact that certain passages in his Farewell Address lent themselves to partisan interpretation does not destroy the appeal of that document as a whole to the entire American people. Few men have ever worn the mantle of authority more modestly or more conscientiously than the first American President, and after serving his country well he issued a noble valedictory which still moves the hearts of men.

THE ELECTION OF 1796

In 1796, when for the first time there was a contest for the office of President, party presidential candidates were informally agreed upon by small groups of leaders. The Federalist group was dominated by Hamilton, while the Republican group consisted of Congressional leaders like Madison and Albert Gallatin of Pennsylvania, who had now admitted Senator Aaron Burr of New York to their councils. But the choice of the President and Vice-President lay with the electors, who were generally chosen by the state legislatures, and nobody could be entirely sure how they would vote. Furthermore, the provision that each elector should vote for two men lent itself to intrigue in behalf of one or the other of the two men who had been informally designated as candidates of the party.

Washington expected Vice-President John Adams to be promoted to the first office, and the strength of Adams's claim could not be denied. Despite the unpopularity he had gained by his emphasis on ceremonies and his admitted distrust of the populace, he had a large following in New England and his distinguished services to the cause of American independence were by no means forgotten. Hamilton was idolized by a small and powerful group, but he had created too many enemies and had too little popular appeal to be seriously considered as a candidate. He was the major Federalist planner and organizer, however, and he had long had serious reservations about Adams. A man of notably independent spirit, the latter was not only fearful of popular rule but also of the rising financial group to whom Hamilton catered. He regarded certain policies of the Treasury as extravagant and detested the speculation to which they had given rise, and he was much more sympathetic than Hamilton with farmers. Furthermore, while extremely critical of the French Revolution, Adams was not disposed to support the British. He was often exceedingly indiscreet in public, but in reality he was a much more moderate Federalist than Hamilton and stood between the latter and Jefferson in both economic and political philosophy. Also, he still regarded Jefferson as a friend and he disliked Hamilton.

The former Secretary of the Treasury agreed that the Federalists must support Adams as a matter of political necessity, but he chose the other man who should be backed by the party. General Thomas Pinckney of South Carolina, who had distinguished himself in the Spanish negotiations, was himself less extreme than Hamilton, but this Southern aristocrat would balance the ticket from the geographical point of view and Hamilton really preferred him to Adams. The effort to gain a full vote for Pinckney from the northern electors was properly suspected by Adams as a scheme to enable the South Carolinian to run ahead of him, and the seeds of dissension within the party that were sown at this time bore bitter fruit before the next four years were over.

On the other side of the fence, the Republican leaders realized from the first that Jefferson was the only candidate with whom they could hope to succeed. His consent was not asked, through fear of refusal. In private he had expressed his strong disapproval of Jay's Treaty and he had been consulted regarding party policy in connection with it, but he was surprisingly indifferent to the outcome of this particular election and was criticized by his supporters for his inactivity. Burr was designated as his running-mate, but nobody seems to have expected the New Yorker to get many electoral votes. As things turned out, he got only one in Virginia to Jefferson's twenty, nearly all of the others going as a compliment to Samuel Adams.

While the principals were silent in the campaign, a battle of words was waged furiously in the newspapers, which descended to new depths of bad taste. Perhaps the lowest point was reached in the attacks on Washington by Benjamin Franklin Bache, grandson of the famous Franklin and editor of the Philadelphia *Aurora*, the most conspicuous Republican paper at the seat of government since the suspension of Freneau's *National Gazette*. He published an abusive open letter of Thomas Paine to Washington, in which the former described the latter as "treacherous in private friendship" and "a hypocrite in public life." On Washington's retirement, after the battle was really over, Bache expressed national rejoicing that the name of the first President had ceased to give "currency to political iniquity, and to legalize corruption." These words have gained an unenviable immortality in the literature of political abuse. The verbal assaults on John Adams are not so well remembered. He was attacked not only for his "monarchical" and "aristocratic" doctrines, but even for his legal defense of the British soldiers after the Boston Massacre, which was one of the bravest actions of his entire life. Scurrility was no monopoly of Republican editors, and in bulk the attacks on Jefferson probably outweighed those on anybody else. Not only did the Federalist press describe him as a disorganizer and a Francophile; the scandal-mongers probed the events of his governorship of Virginia during the Revolution and made charges of personal cowardice which were wholly without foundation but which haunted him throughout the rest of his public life. He was attacked, also, for his religious views and charged with being an infidel and atheist. The first presidential contest was one of the dirtiest on record.

The vote was very close: Adams got 71 electoral votes to Jefferson's 68; Pinckney received 59 and Burr 30. Adams got no votes in the West and practically none south of Maryland, while Jefferson got none north and east of Pennsylvania. The Republican victory in Pennsylvania was significant, though the margin was very small, and the political skill of Aaron Burr had not yet sufficed to carry the Hamiltonian citadel of New York. The Federalists bettered their situation in Congress, gaining a small majority in the House where they had been slightly in the minority.

The French minister, Adet, intrigued against the Federalists in this election—against Washington until Adet learned he would retire and then against Adams. No connection between Adet and the responsible Republican leaders has been established, but anti-Federalist arguments of his may have got into Republican papers and been bandied about in Democratic societies. He may have supposed that certain official actions of his would intimidate voters, though Genêt's experience should have shown him that their effect would be just the opposite. On October 27, 1796, he announced that the French would treat the commerce of all neutral powers as the latter permitted the British to do, and a couple of weeks later he announced the suspension of his functions. This breach in diplomatic relations did not really occur, however, until after Adams was inaugurated; and in the meantime Adet, in a letter to the authorities at home, gave his mature impression of Jefferson, in whose interest, presumably, he had been intriguing. Jefferson feared France less than

England, Adet said, but he might change his opinion tomorrow. He admired much that the French had done in their revolution, but he was first of all an American and could not be a true friend of France. "An American is the born enemy of all the peoples of Europe," said the minister. He did not have it quite right, however, for the enmity of Jefferson was not to the people but the governments of Europe.

The incompatibility of the original electoral system with party government was now shown, since the vice-presidency fell to Jefferson as the second man. To his intimate friends the Virginian manifested great relief that he had escaped the first office and that his old friend Adams, his senior in years and in public life, had been preferred. It seemed to him that foreign affairs had not worn so gloomy an aspect since the conclusion of peace with the British in 1783. At a time when parties were still fluid and the office of President was not yet identified with party leadership, he wished his old comrade and recent rival well, but he correctly foresaw that honest John Adams would fall into a sea of troubles.

CHAPTER 17

The End of Federalist Control 1797-1801

JOHN ADAMS SERVED ONLY ONE TERM AS PRESIDENT and almost the whole of it fell in a time of external danger. Diplomatic relations were suspended with France, then the most terrifying power in the world, and there were naval hostilities between the two countries from 1798 until the very end of his administration. At home the close division of political opinion was indicated by the narrowness of Adams's victory—three electoral votes. Within the ranks of the Federalists themselves there was a division between the more moderate group, which was practically unorganized, and the more extreme and closely knit group, often designated as the High Federalists, of whom Hamilton was the undisputed leader. The High Federalists richly capitalized on the break with France and the perfervid patriotism it aroused, but in the end Adams defied them, returning to the policy of genuine neutrality and splitting the party as a result.

Naval and military developments caused an increase in the national debt and the imposition of fresh taxes. The High Federalists aroused fears in many minds that they were promoting war at the expense of economic groups, especially farmers, who stood to gain nothing from it. More notorious were the actions against the foreign-born and the infringements on individual liberties under the Alien and Sedition Acts. The essential purpose of these was to crush the political opposition, and this repressive policy has remained through the years a supreme American example of the arrogance of power. Jefferson and Madison, in their reaction against the tyranny of the central government, went so far in the assertion of the rights of states that they were charged by their foes with the promotion of disunion.

Adams did not initiate the policy of repression, but he was identified with it by its victims; and his wise actions in the foreign field came too late to do him much good in the election of 1800. The Republicans were able to capitalize on the reaction against the extreme policy of the government. The American people had not become pro-French or disunionist, but a neutral foreign policy and moderate domestic policy were preferred in most parts of the country. Whereas the Federalists had identified themselves in policy with the interests of a relatively small economic group, the Republicans appealed to farmers everywhere, to most of the plantation interests of the South, and to the plain people in the cities—especially in New York and Philadelphia. This powerful combination was destined to endure and to make impossible the return of the Federalists to power.

The political conflict was reflected in the realm of thought and here, also, public opinion took a course between the two extremes. Ideas of political liberty persisted, despite the excesses and perversions of the French Revolution. The antireligious doctrines of the age had conspicuous American devotees, but, by and large, Americans viewed them with disfavor. Meanwhile, they clung to conventional modes in literature and turned to classic forms in the arts. Cultural independence of the Old World still lay in the distant future.

John Adams and His Political Surroundings

The second President, who was in his sixty-second year and still vigorous when inaugurated, was a man of strong mind and forceful personality. Yet he had about him until almost the end of his term a Cabinet that took orders from Hamilton and represented the extreme wing of the Federalist party when his own philosophy was more moderate. Timothy Pickering—harsh, humorless, and efficient in small things—remained as Secretary of State; Oliver Wolcott, Jr., continued to run the Treasury in loyalty to its first head; and James McHenry was in the Department of War, relying on Hamilton for the advice he sorely needed. Not until the Department of the Navy was created in 1798 and Benjamin Stoddert was appointed as its head did Adams have a Cabinet officer of his own choosing. He never did rid himself of Wolcott, and not until his last year in office did he oust Pickering and McHenry, who had proved to be his secret enemies. The retention of such men by Adams now seems surprising, but when he took office no tradition had been established that would have led the department heads to present their resignations voluntarily, and he regarded his administration as a continuation of Washington's. There was a strong strain of suspiciousness in Adams's nature, but his personal vanity could be appealed to. This patently honest and deeply patriotic man was no kind of a politician and did not inspire the loyalty he deserved. He wanted to be an independent President, and eventually he became one, but when we look back on him the main impression he gives is that of extreme loneliness.

At the beginning he consulted Jefferson about foreign affairs and it is conceivable that between them some sort of bipartisan policy could have been worked out. But the Cabinet did not like these consultations, and circumstances soon made the Vice-President the target of fresh partisan attacks. A few weeks after the inauguration, a private letter that Jefferson wrote the previous year to Philip Mazzei, an Italian friend who had once been a neighbor of his in Virginia but had returned to Europe, was published in America. Describing the political scene in vivid but exaggerated language, Jefferson referred to men who were "Samsons in the field and Solomons in the council," but whose heads had been shorn by "the harlot England." This was interpreted as an allusion to Washington and aroused a tempest of indignation. Jefferson afterward said in private that he was actually referring to the Society of the Cincinnati, but no explanation was offered or would have been accepted at the time. He was regarded in Federalist circles as a maligner of the national Hero and an apologist for the despised French. He found presiding over the Senate a more painful task than he had expected. This was particularly the case from 1798 onward, and by that time the political indifference he had shown in the last election had given way to determination to encompass the defeat of an administration whose policies he disapproved.

Throughout his presidency, Adams was away from Philadelphia a great deal, partly because of his wife's health. He left routine affairs to his subordinates to a greater extent than Washington had done, and he made no particular effort to mobilize his own supporters. The relatively small commercial and financial groups that constituted Hamilton's clientele, along with a few great southern planters, would never have been sufficient to carry the country. Adams's appeal was broader but either he did not know how to realize on the strength of his position or did not think it incumbent on him to do so. He had no spokesman for the administration in Congress, while Hamilton maintained close contact with leading members and influenced the course of legislation considerably more than he did. He was not the author of the domestic policies that the opposition party most objected to, and he may not have realized how repressive and unrepresentative some of them were, even when he accepted them.

The domestic policy of the High Federalists was justified by them on grounds of foreign danger, and few administrations have been so dominated by foreign affairs as was that of Adams. He was widely experienced in his field, and in it the unpolitical President, after facing for long months perplexities which would have baffled the wisest of statesmen, performed his most signal services.

The XYZ Affair and Undeclared War with France

The recall of James Monroe, who sympathized with the French in their resentment at Jay's Treaty, was decided on in the summer of 1796. He was informed of it in November by the man appointed to succeed him as minister, General Charles Cotesworth Pinckney of South Carolina, brother of Thomas Pinckney. But the French Directory, while praising Monroe, declined to receive Pinckney until there had been some "reparation" for their alleged injuries, and this refusal became known in America shortly after Adams's inauguration.

Adams decided to send a commission to treat with the French, and even thought of putting Jefferson on it, but both of them concluded that it would be improper for the Vice-President to leave the country. The Cabinet agreed to the commission after Hamilton had advised them that it would be a good political move. Pinckney had been forced to leave France but he was still abroad and an obvious choice. The other two members were John Marshall of Virginia, who was just coming into prominence as a Federalist in a state where they were scarce, and Elbridge Gerry of Massachusetts, a close friend of Adams who was not regarded as a party man though he was strongly anti-British. No valid objection to this commission could be raised by the friends of France.

Appointed in June 1797, Marshall and Gerry were in Paris with Pinckney in September, but the commissioners were never officially received. They had some talk with Talleyrand, the Minister for Foreign Affairs, and more with secret intermediaries who later became known in the United States as X, Y, and Z. The negotiations did not even get started and, in April 1798, Marshall embarked for America. Pinckney remained in France because of the illness of his daughter, while Gerry, with whom Talleyrand had offered to treat alone and who believed that his withdrawal would mean war, remained. Gerry was severely criticized at home for this action, but Adams defended him. Before Marshall returned, Adams had communicated to Congress a recent declaration of the Directory foreshadowing more severe treatment of American commerce and had announced that there was no reason to hope for the success of the commission. Therefore, he said, the country must put itself in a state of defense. He kept back the communications at first, but when the Republicans demanded them and were joined by the High Federalists, after the latter had gained an inkling of their contents, he revealed the "XYZ" dispatches and confounded the friends of France.

The most startling disclosure was that of a proposal by "X'" that the United States provide a *douceur* of some $250,000 as a preliminary to negotiations. Holdups of this sort by French officials were not uncommon in this period, and even the British government paid bribes for treaties, but Pinckney gained a place for himself in history by saying, "No! No! Not a sixpence." The chief popular hero, however, was Marshall, who got home after the dispatches had been published and was feted and toasted everywhere. This affair was a turning point in his career, for he had gained the strong approval of John Adams and become a national figure overnight. At a dinner to him in Philadelphia, which was attended by many dignitaries, one of the toasts was: "Millions for defense but not a cent for tribute." It was in this time of patriotic fervor that Joseph Hopkinson wrote the song, "Hail Columbia!"

The President assumed such a bellicose tone in his replies to various addresses to him that even Hamilton thought him indiscreet. The High Federalists as a group, however, were pleased with Adams. Meanwhile, the Republicans were discredited to an even greater degree than they had been at the height of the Genêt affair. If the French were trying to drive a wedge between the American people and the government, as the Federalists claimed, they had adopted the worst possible method. Actually, they had made friendship for France seem incompatible with American patriotism. The attitude of the Directory toward the American commissioners was one of contemptuous disregard, and its bullying tactics were those of men intoxicated with new-found power. But the French did not want war with the United States, and the stories in circulation about their intention to invade the country were fantastic.

Neither France nor the United States ever declared war, but Congress suspended commerce with France and French possessions, and by provisions for the armed protection of American shipping it authorized what amounted to defensive war on the seas. Furthermore, Congress declared the treaties with France abrogated, though these did not provide for such unilateral action. This was less than hot war and more than cold war, so perhaps it may be described as warm. In 1798, however, Congress was operating in a heated atmosphere and the High Federalists took control of the situation.

Navy and Army

Adams himself had been an advocate of preparedness from the beginning of his term, but the moderate Federalists and the Republicans had prevented effective action previous to the revelation of the XYZ dispatches. Meanwhile, Hamilton had formulated a full program of defense, and the actions that Congress now took were closer to his line than to that of Adams. That body made larger provision for an army than the President thought necessary and gave him fewer ships than he wanted. More than any other man he deserves credit for the creation of the Navy, though technically this began with the act of 1794, which authorized the

construction of a few frigates at a time of trouble with the Barbary
pirates. But work on these had been suspended, and it was in Adams's
term that the *Constellation,* the *Constitution* ("Old Ironsides"), and the
President were constructed. Also, the Department of War was divided in
1798 and the Department of the Navy created. It was well administered
by Benjamin Stoddert and acquitted itself very creditably. While the
British ships-of-the-line kept the heavily armed French ships off the seas,
the American frigates with other smaller vessels made themselves very
useful in protecting American commerce against French raiders, though
the total of losses considerably exceeded American prizes. The frigates
generally got the better of French warships of their own class in such
actions as there were, and their successes were hailed with much enthusiasm.

In general the Republicans were small-navy men and, being fearful of
a standing army, they would have relied on the militia. The High Federalists under the prompting of Hamilton emphasized the importance of an
army and were less interested than Adams in the Navy—not because of
indifference to commerce but because of their reliance on the British.
Opposition to the Navy was strongest in the purely agricultural districts
in the South and West, the costliness of it being specially objected to,
and the increase in taxation because of the policy of naval and military
preparedness lost to the Federalists in 1800 considerable support they
had received four years earlier.

The naval policy of the government was wise, but the military emphasis
of the High Federalists seems much less justifiable. The authorized
strength of the regular Army (13,000) was never attained—whether this
was because of the incompetence of Secretary McHenry or the indifference of Adams, who cared little for military preparation except for its
diplomatic and political effect. But critics of the government could say
that it was creating a standing army for purposes of domestic repression
or for offensive actions of some sort in connection with the British. At
this time Francisco de Miranda was trying to interest both British and
Americans in his schemes for revolt in South America against Spain, and
Hamilton was sympathetic, though that adventurous statesman was
more interested in action against Florida and Louisiana to begin with,
and, while he would have welcomed British connivance, he did not go
so far as to favor an open British alliance. At all events, the military policy
was suspect, and a character of high comedy was imparted to it by
the controversy over rank in which Hamilton was the central figure.

Washington was nominated for the chief command, and a cry of exultation was raised at the news that the national hero would emerge from
retirement in this time of emergency. Secretary McHenry bore him his
commission, along with a list of possible appointees as major general or
brigadier general. Hamilton's name was on it but did not stand first.

Washington drew up his own list on which Hamilton appeared as Inspector General and presumably second in rank to the Commander-in-Chief. Other major generals, with Hamilton, were the former Secretary of War, Henry Knox, and Charles Cotesworth Pinckney, and among the brigadier generals was William S. Smith, son-in-law of Adams. Adams submitted this list to the Senate for confirmation, but Secretary of State Pickering by secret intrigue prevented the approval of Smith, and there was a tempest in the teapot when Knox, who had outranked Hamilton in the Continental Army and was considerably his senior in years, refused to serve below him. Adams supported Knox at first, but Washington himself refused to serve unless Hamilton were second in command, and under the pressure of High-Federalist opinion the President yielded, still smarting from the rejection of his son-in-law. In view of Washington's age, Hamilton would have been the actual commander in case of war, and if he had been in position to make his dreams of southern conquest come true he might perhaps have become an American Napoleon. But Adams had the last laugh, for there was no war and the inspector general had very slight opportunity to exercise his unquestionable military talents and realize on his vaulting ambitions.

The Alien and Sedition Acts

The perfervid patriotism that was aroused by the XYZ dispatches and the extreme partisanship of the group in power reached a climax in the laws known collectively as the Alien and Sedition Acts. This restrictive and repressive legislation was similar to legislation in this decade in England, which was faced with far greater and more immediate danger from the French. The partisanship which sought to identify Federalism with patriotism cannot be justified, but the psychological conditions under which the effort was made can be understood by any generation that has faced the fact or the terrifying threat of war. In 1798, James Madison made this melancholy comment: "Perhaps it is a universal truth that the loss of liberty at home is to be charged to provisions against danger real or pretended from abroad."

The responsible public officials of that time are blameable for letting their emotions obscure their judgment, but they must be blamed far more for seizing this opportunity to translate their prejudices and partisan purposes into restrictive and oppressive laws. The first of this set, the Naturalization Law, was an expression of hostility to the foreign-born and an incident in the long conflict between newcomers and old settlers. Sentiment against recent immigrants was specially strong in New England, and was generally characteristic of Federalists because the newcomers tended to become Republicans. Congressman Albert Gallatin of Pennsylvania, who was Swiss by birth, had become the leader of the opposition in the House after the retirement of Madison from that body, and he was a special object of Federalist dislike. Some members of the ruling group favored the exclusion of the foreign-born from public office, and some went so far as to urge that they be excluded from citizenship. The law of 1798 extended the time required for naturalization from five to fourteen years and prescribed the registration of aliens. The latter provision was regarded by immigrants as insulting, and the law as a whole was obviously designed to decrease the Republican vote. It was repealed after that party came into power, but the New England Federalists clung to their antiforeign policy and thus made it practically inevitable that the immigrants should join the other political camp.

Two other laws dealt with foreigners. The Alien Enemies Act, calling for the removal of persons of that description in case of war, need not concern us since there was no war. The Alien Act authorized the President to order from the country all aliens judged by him to be "dangerous to the peace and safety of the United States." This law was objected to as a grant of arbitrary power to the Executive. Leading Republicans believed that it was directed against men of learning and radical political views like the eminent English chemist and Unitarian minister, Joseph Priestley, who had retired to the Pennsylvania countryside but was being hounded by the Federalist press, and the French philosopher Volney, who was then in the United States but soon sailed away. A good many people departed through fear, but Adams never availed himself of the authority granted him. Hamilton condemned him for his lack of energy and wanted him to deport certain Republican editors. By its own terms the law expired in two years.

Most notorious of all was the Sedition Act, which not only forbade conspiracy, but "false, scandalous and malicious" writing or utterances against the government, the President, or Congress tending to bring any of them into contempt or disrepute. The measure was justified by its advocates on the ground that the opposition press was scurrilous, as it unquestionably was. But the much more numerous Federalist papers were also ill-mannered toward their rivals, and the enforcement of the law showed beyond any doubt the purpose of the party in power to silence criticism of the policies of the government and muzzle the Republicans, at the expense of freedom of speech and the press. Hamilton objected to the bill in an earlier and even more extreme version as inexpedient but he was sympathetic with its purposes, and the only important Federalist with a clear record of opposition to it was John Marshall. Adams was not conspicuously active in connection with it, but uncomplimentary remarks about him wounded his vanity, while naturally incensing his wife Abigail, and he condoned a punitive policy. The major executive agent in the enforcement of the Sedition law was the bitterly vindictive Timothy Pickering, who was ever on the lookout for evil-doers.

Altogether, about fifteen persons were indicted, and ten were found guilty. All were Republicans and most of them were editors. The most cherished object of Federalist wrath was Benjamin Franklin Bache, editor of the *Aurora*, whose Republican partisanship was extreme and to whom neither the person of George Washington nor a confidential public document had any sanctity. He was indicted for libel by a federal court before the Sedition law went into effect, but death stopped his pen before the trial. One of the most conspicuous victims of the Act was Thomas Cooper, an intimate friend of Joseph Priestley, and a man of learning who delighted in controversy. He served a prison sentence for written remarks about John Adams that were highly uncomplimentary but certainly not subversive. Matthew Lyon of Vermont differed from the others in that he was a Congressman. This rough Democrat, who spat in the face of Roger Griswold of Connecticut after being insulted by that Federalist in the House and who afterwards repelled Griswold's cane with firetongs, was re-elected to Congress while serving his prison term. Least attractive of the victims was the unscrupulous journalist James Thomson Callender, the greatest scandalmonger of his day, whose venom was eventually felt by Jefferson as it had been by Hamilton. As a person he did not deserve much sympathy, but he commanded a great deal because of the political aspect of his trial and the bullying tactics of Justice Chase, who also hurled insults at counsel and alienated the bar. The high-handed conduct of federal judges in these trials, coupled with their practice of delivering political harangues in charges to grand juries, strengthened the impression that the entire machinery of the central government was being employed in the interest of a party and as an instrument to repress liberty. This effort to proscribe a major political group and destroy political opposition is without parallel in American national history, and no other period can be more fittingly described as a reign of terror.

The Kentucky and Virginia Resolutions

At the session of Congress following the passage of the Alien and Sedition laws there was a Federalist proposal that they be printed for general distribution, but after a Republican amendment had been offered to print the Constitution of the United States with them the idea was abandoned. The most doubtful of them from the constitutional point of view was the Sedition Act. If the Supreme Court had formally ruled on this before its expiration on March 3, 1801, probably that Federalist body would have upheld it; but if the law had been declared unconstitutional, the judiciary would have assumed the role of protector of basic individual liberties, as guaranteed by the Bill of Rights, and there would have been no occasion for Jefferson and Madison to appeal to the states as they did in the Kentucky and Virginia Resolutions.

Two sets of resolutions were adopted by the legislature of Kentucky, one in 1798 and the other in the next year. Jefferson was the author of the first set, though his name was not made public; and the second set followed his plan, though he did not write them. The somewhat milder resolutions of the General Assembly of Virginia in 1798 were the work of Madison, who also drew the little-noticed Virginia Report of 1800, the most carefully worded of them all and the best statement of the mature Republican position. The main purpose of the earlier and more famous resolutions was political: they were designed to arouse public sentiment against the Alien and Sedition Acts and to preserve a political party which the government was trying to extinguish. But Americans of a later generation, who were struggling over the issue between nationalism and state rights, viewed the Resolutions out of context and regarded their general constitutional arguments as the most significant thing about them. In a nutshell, these arguments were: that the government of the United States originated in a compact between one state and the others; that acts going beyond the delegated powers were void; and that an individual state had the right to judge of the infractions of its own powers and of the means of redress that it would employ. It will be recalled that the doctrine of judicial review was not yet firmly established, though leading Federalists hoped it would be.

Later commentators were to say that here were the seeds of nullification—the word, meaning the voiding of a federal law by a state, was actually used in the second set of Kentucky Resolutions—and that this was a formulation of the divisive philosophy of state rights. Never again did Jefferson go so far in the direction of state rights as he did in his correspondence with Madison at this time, and it is doubtful if ever again he felt more uncertain of the persistence of the Union. Yet the resolutions expressed devotion to the Union, and the mode of redress that was recommended fell far short of nullification. A single state was to protest to Congress, and to appeal to other states to do likewise.

The responses of other states to the appeal from Virginia and Kentucky were largely determined by the politics of the situation. The Resolutions were disapproved in Northern states where the Federalists were in the ascendant, and in the replies the federal judiciary, which was then thoroughly partisan, was usually pointed out as the proper authority for the judgment of constitutional questions. In Southern states where the Republicans were still in control or relatively strong there was no formal disapproval of the Resolutions but they alarmed and repelled a good many moderates. The Republicans as a group approved of the protest against the Alien and Sedition Acts, but except in two states they did not commit themselves to any specific precedure.

Historical judgment on the Kentucky and Virginia Resolutions, like the contemporary judgment, can be divided. They were in the state-rights tradition which the New Englanders took up divisively in the next decade and the South Carolinians carried to the last extreme in nullification and secession. But if the emphasis is laid on the specific evils that these resolutions protested against, they were in the tradition of human rights and civil liberties which has persisted since the Declaration of Independence.

The Settlement with France

The man who stopped the High Federalists was not Jefferson but John Adams. He ordered a retreat from the extreme and untenable position they had taken in the foreign field. At the height of the excitement over the XYZ Affair he stated that no minister would be sent to France without assurances that he would be received as befitted the representative of "a great, free, powerful, and independent nation"; but, resisting later pressure from the Cabinet, he refused to say that he would not send one at all. By January 1799, he learned in a roundabout way that Talleyrand was willing to meet the conditions he had prescribed. William Vans Murray, the American minister at The Hague, transmitted a letter that the French Foreign Minister had written him, and Murray's judgment that Talleyrand meant what he said was supported by John Quincy Adams, son of the President and then American minister to Prussia. Meanwhile, word had come to America through informal channels that the French had undergone a change of heart. They had been impressed by the naval activities and military preparations of the United States, and were becoming fearful of an Anglo-American alliance such as Timothy Pickering favored. Already there was considerable naval cooperation between Great Britain and the United States, and the French did not want this to be formalized and extended. Their own naval defeat by Lord Nelson in the Battle of the Nile was sobering, as was the news of American opinion they had received from persons friendly to France —like the poet Joel Barlow and Dr. George Logan, who aroused the ire of the Federalists by engaging in a personal mission to France. This occasioned the "Logan Act" (1799), forbidding unauthorized activities of the sort. Talleyrand, who took a more realistic view of the situation in the New World than the Directors and who had his eye on Florida and Louisiana, had brought those indifferent officials around to a friendlier and wiser attitude.

Adams, on his part, was trying to be realistic. Believing that peace between the two countries was desirable, the President, without consulting Pickering and others in his own Cabinet who thought otherwise, nominated William Vans Murray to be minister to France and threw the High Federalists into consternation. Even those of them that had not advocated a declaration of war or a British alliance knew that, despite losses, commerce brought high profits under existing conditions and that they themselves had attained political dominance because of the war scare. They were not disposed to surrender these advantages and let the scepter of power slip from their hands. Furthermore, they could not admit good faith on the part of the French without eating their own words. Talleyrand was still a "shameless villian" to Pickering.

Most of the Eastern ultras were blind to the rising opposition to war policies outside of commercial circles, but some of them, including Hamilton, saw that they could not openly oppose Adams in his effort to remove the war threat, and they adopted the tactics of delay. On protests from the Senate, the President agreed to appoint a commission of three instead of a minister, and this eventually consisted of Murray, Chief Justice Oliver Ellsworth of Connecticut, and William R. Davie of North Carolina. Also, Adams agreed to seek more specific assurances from the French. These were received in the summer of 1799, but Pickering was in no hurry to draft the instructions for the commissioners, and by various pretexts he and his fellows prolonged the delay. After receiving a warning from Secretary Stoddert that there was a conspiracy to defeat his purposes, the President finally despatched the commissioners in November. They would have had an easier time if they had sailed sooner, for Napoleon had become First Consul before their arrival. His absence in Italy held things up, and he was a tough man to deal with anywhere.

From April 1800 through September the negotiations dragged on, and at length the commissioners concluded that they could not carry out their instructions—to secure indemnity for French spoilations of American commerce (from 1793 onward) and to gain formal release from treaty obligations. They made a temporary settlement, whereby commercial relations were restored and both the treaties and the claims of indemnity were suspended. The settlement which was finally ratified by both countries in 1801 was, in effect, a trade. The United States surrendered the claims for indemnity and France surrendered the treaties. Thus the Franco-American alliance was formally ended, peace was restored, and the United States returned to a policy of neutrality.

The wisdom of Adams in putting his country back on the road to true national independence now seems unquestionable, but the political results of his actions were not to his advantage. His own party split while the commissioners were still in France, and the High Federalists never forgave him. In an extravagant statement in later years he said that there would have been a unanimous vote against the Federalists in the Presidential election if he had not sent the commissioners, but the fact is that the opposing party won it anyway. His own motives were not partisan; they were in the fullest sense patriotic, and the settlement with France for which he was almost wholly responsible fittingly crowned his career as a statesman. Again the Atlas of the American Revolution was a great patriot and a great man.

THE ELECTION OF 1800-1801

The extreme Federalists could not afford to break openly with Adams at the time that he dispatched the commissioners. He was a fiercely independent character when aroused, and if his prerogatives as President in the conduct of foreign affairs were too much encroached upon, it was not unthinkable that he might resign the office, turn it over to Vice-President Jefferson, and denounce his opponents within his own party. The possibility of such a development was reported by the British minister. Furthermore, as the election year came around, it appeared that Adams had much more popular backing than any other Federalist. The Federalist leaders decided, therefore, to support him and Charles Cotesworth Pinckney for the two highest offices, and adopted the tactics of seeking equal electoral support for them, hoping that Pinckney (who was not a party to the scheme) would come in ahead.

Soon after this decision was reached in Congressional caucus in May 1800, Adams acted decisively to clear his cabinet of his enemies. Secretary of War McHenry tendered his resignation on request, and when Secretary of State Pickering refused to resign the President dismissed him. The purge stopped short of the Treasury, where Wolcott remained, but Adams secured a loyal and unusually able aide in the person of John Marshall, who resigned from Congress and took Pickering's place. This Virginian was strongly opposed to the disunionist tendencies that he perceived in the Kentucky and Virginia Resolutions and he was regarded as a Federalist of the school of Washington, who had strongly approved his candidacy for Congress.

Adams had strengthened his official family, but he had again defied the High Federalists, and he proceeded to inveigh against a "damned faction" and a "British faction" with characteristic brusqueness. Hamilton's actions in the late summer and autumn of 1800 provide a striking illustration of his proneness to overreach himself, but they can be explained, perhaps, as the result of his growing conviction that Adams was gaining ground within the party. Hamilton printed for circulation among Federalist leaders an exceedingly intemperate letter concerning the public conduct and character of Adams, and this inevitably fell into the hands of an eager Republican journalist who printed it again for all the world to see. The ostensible purpose of this extraordinary document was to explain the reasons for the equal support of Pinckney and Adams by the Federalists, but in stating these Hamilton admitted his preference for Thomas Pinckney in 1796 and Charles Cotesworth Pinckney in 1800 and framed an indictment of Adams which no irresponsible journalist of the opposition would have been likely to surpass. Hamilton described him as a man of eccentric and sublimated ambition, of unbounded vanity and a jealousy that was capable of discoloring every object. In a word, Adams was unfit to be President. To Thomas Cooper, emerging from the prison to which he had been committed because of less severe condemnation of Adams, it naturally seemed that Hamilton, more than anybody else, deserved to be tried under the Sedition Act. Even his warmest admirers deplored the imprudence of the most brilliant of all the Federalists, and some of them lamented that he had impaired his own usefulness.

During the presidential campaign the Republicans made the most of Federalist dissensions. There was little dissension in their own ranks, for their support of Jefferson was inevitable. Aaron Burr of New York was chosen as his running mate by the party Congressional caucus. He balanced the ticket from a geographical point of view, and there could be no possible doubt of his political skill. Republican success in the state election in New York, assuring control of the legislature and the choice of Republican electors, was a major reason for success in the nation.

Presidential nominations were made by Congressional caucuses in 1800, but there were no official party platforms. The constitutional provision that electors might be chosen in such ways as state legislatures should prescribe led to considerable maneuvering in these bodies, and the tendency was to adopt provisions favorable to the party in power in the state. Because of elements of irregularity in the choice of electors, the electoral vote was a far less accurate gauge of public opinion than it is today, and a much better index was provided by the Congressional elections. In these the Republicans won 65 seats to 41 for their opponents, showing beyond doubt that they had become the majority party.

Republican Party discipline had embarrassing results, for both Jefferson and Burr got 73 electoral votes. Surprisingly, discipline was almost as effective on the Federalist side: Adams got 65 votes and Pinckney 64, only an elector from Rhode Island declining to support them equally. The Federalists carried all of the New England states, along with New Jersey and Delaware. They divided the electoral vote of Pennsylvania and Maryland, and had a third of the electors from North Carolina, while all the rest of the country was Republican.

The Twelfth Amendment to the Constitution (1804), providing that the electors cast separate ballots for President and Vice-President, made impossible another such tie as the one between Thomas Jefferson and Aaron Burr. In 1801, the tie was resolved by the constitutional means already prescribed. The decision had to be made by the House of Representatives, voting by states, and a majority of all the states was necessary for an election—that is, 9 out of 16. The matter was necessarily referred to the old Congress, since the new one would not come in before March 4, when a new President was supposed to be inaugurated. The decision was not finally reached until February 17, 1801, and for a time it looked as though no one would be legally authorized to succeed John Adams.

The reason for the stalemate was that the Federalists supported Burr —partly because Jefferson had long been the most conspicuous object of their partisan hostility, and partly because some of them hoped that they could make a deal with the crafty New Yorker. For thirty-five ballots, Jefferson had 8 votes and Burr had 6, while two states cast no vote since their delegations were evenly divided. The jam was finally broken on the initiative of James A. Bayard of Delaware, who concluded that if there was to be a President it would have to be Jefferson. He could not persuade any of his fellow Federalists to vote for their arch-enemy, but the Federalist representatives from the two divided states (Vermont and Maryland) agreed not to vote at all, thus permitting the Republicans in these delegations to cast ballots for Jefferson. Other Federalists abstained except those from the four other New England states, who supported Burr to the bitter end.

Hamilton was frantic with fear, because he hated and distrusted Burr far more than he did Jefferson. Now he showed that he was more realistic than other leaders of the High Federalists. He still thought Jefferson "a contemptible hypocrite," but he regarded him as incorruptible, while he was convinced that Burr was both corrupt and unscrupulous. He did not view Jefferson as "an enemy of the power of the Executive," and believed that his zeal for France would cool. "To my mind," he wrote, "a true estimate of Mr. Jefferson's character warrants the expectation of a temporizing rather than a violent system." The arguments of Hamilton made no impression on the New England Federalists, and while they may have affected Bayard and other more moderate men, they were probably not the main factor in his case. It was claimed in later years that certain promises were made to Bayard on behalf of Jefferson, chiefly with respect to removals from office and fiscal policy. There is no reason to believe that Jefferson authorized any promises, but no one who really knew him would have expected him to follow a drastic policy in either case. At the end, there were wild charges on both sides about breaking up the Union, but Bayard concluded that the best way to avoid this was to let the majority party have the man of their choice. Thus the spirit of moderation triumphed over extreme partisanship.

Reasons for Federalist Defeat

Federalist dissension entered into their defeat in the election of 1800 —not in causing the Federalist electors to split their votes between Adams and Pinckney, but in raising doubts about the ability of a sharply divided party to conduct the government. The extreme policies of the Hamiltonian group had alienated many moderates. The repressive and nativistic policy that was symbolized by the Alien and Sedition Acts repelled many who persisted in thinking that America was a refuge for the oppressed and the home of personal freedom. These individuals could give ready allegiance to Jefferson, who stood as the antithesis to consolidation and tyranny.

In many places, especially in inland districts, reaction against the taxes that had been imposed because of naval and military preparations was an even more decisive factor. A direct tax of 1798 on lands and houses was a particular occasion of discontent, and in certain German counties of eastern Pennsylvania that had previously been Federalist (Northampton, Bucks, and Montgomery) it led, in the next year, to what is known as the Fries Rebellion. Raising the cry, "dämm de President, dämm de Congress, dämm de Aristokratz," the farmers threatened the tax officials until their resistance was put down by United States troops after a proclamation by the President. The leader, John Fries, was tried and sentenced to death. Adams pardoned him, over the protests of the High Federalists, but these counties went Republican afterward. On economic grounds the policy of the government offered little to back-country farmers, and the tobacco planters of the South suffered from the sharp decline of prices that followed the severance of trade with France.

Northern commercial districts, on the contrary, prospered greatly under the abnormalities of the times, and the high interest on new government loans was welcomed in financial circles. This was the policy of Wolcott and Hamilton, which Adams objected to, and the Republicans made a good deal of it in the campaign. The Federalist hold on New England can be considerably explained on the ground that governmental policy was specially favorable to commercial interests, but there were important religious reasons. The dominant Congregational clergy regarded Jefferson as their enemy and viewed the Republicans as the party of disorder and infidelity.

Near the end of 1799, George Washington died at Mount Vernon in his sixty-eighth year, and soon thereafter he was described by "Light-Horse" Harry Lee as "first in war, first in peace, and first in the hearts of his countrymen." The death of the nation's hero grieved an entire people but it cast a special pall over the spirits of the Federalists, and this was not lifted when, as one century ended and another began, the second President made his exit from public life. But to the enthusiastic supporters of the third President it seemed that the gloomy night had fled and the reign of terror ended. Soon they sang:

> Rejoice! Columbia's sons, rejoice!
> To tyrants never bend the knee,
> But join with heart, and soul, and voice,
> For JEFFERSON and LIBERTY.

THE CULTURE OF THE YOUNG REPUBLIC

The political struggle between Federalists and Republicans involved a struggle in the realm of the mind. The conflict of ideas that accompanied the French Revolution and the European war was reflected in the United States and served to intensify domestic political quarrels. The battle was also waged in other fields and it was specially bitter in religion.

Religion and Philosophy

The American response to Thomas Paine's book, *The Age of Reason* (1794), deserves particular consideration. In this the author of *The Rights of Man* made a frontal attack on all organized religion, denounced all forms of clerical tyranny, argued that reason alone should govern belief, and asserted that Deism was the only rational religion. Paine expressly stated that he believed in God, but he said, "My own mind is my own church." To the great body of church members he seemed a religious anarchist.

In the United States the various governments were crystallizing a unique relationship between Church and State in which government would not support or oppose any religion but would stand aside from all religious questions and institutions. The advocates of this system were not opponents of organized religion. Most of them were Protestant Christians who believed that true Christianity would best thrive if left to private initiative. In Europe, on the other hand, and especially in France, advocates of the separation of Church and State seemed intent on destroying organized Christianity. Paine's *Age of Reason* gave great impetus to Deism, not as a private faith tolerant of other faiths, but as a militant corollary of the fight for political liberty. Militant Deism had already been propounded in America by Ethan Allen, the Green Mountain rebel, in his *Reason the Only Oracle of Man* (1784), which was bitterly attacked by the orthodox clergy led by Timothy Dwight. The Frenchman Volney's *Ruins: Or A Survey of the Revolution of Empires* (1791) provided new ammunition for the Deists. But Paine's book reached more people. Blind Elihu Palmer, a graduate of Dartmouth and a former Baptist minister, John Fitch, and others proceeded to organize Deistic "churches" such as the Society of Ancient Druids, and to publish *The Temple of Reason* and other periodicals.

This movement reached its climax in the later 1790's and, while it influenced only a small minority, it frightened conservatives into such counterblasts that its net result was to discredit moderate as well as extreme versions of the philosophy of rationalism. Jefferson was a special sufferer from this reaction. The attitude toward him was reflected in the words of a Connecticut minister after the election of 1796. He prayed for President-elect Adams and then said: "O Lord! Wilt Thou bestow upon the Vice-President a double portion of Thy grace for *Thou knowest he needs it.*" In 1800, there was a widely-believed report in New England that Jefferson would confiscate all Bibles if elected, and the story is that many of these sacred books were hidden in wells. Actually, the only sort of religion he opposed was political religion, and what he believed in was complete religious freedom. It was in 1800, in a private letter to Dr. Benjamin Rush that he said: "I have sworn on the altar of God eternal hostility against every form of tyranny over the mind of man." His election did not stem the rising tide of religious conservatism, and his religious liberalism was a greater political liability in the nineteenth century than it had been in the eighteenth.

Another conflict of ideas centered in the doctrine of environmentalism, which had been advanced by English and French philosophers. In this view, not Divine decree or even physical heredity accounts for the differences among individuals, classes, and races, and between the sexes, so much as differences of environment and opportunity do. The political consequences of this philosophy were decisive. John Adams denied that attempts to improve the condition of less-favored portions of humanity could help them, while Thomas Jefferson affirmed the truth of environmentalism, particularly with respect to the virtuous influences of rural as compared with urban life. The environmental theory of human nature found in the works of John Locke, Helvétius, Rousseau, Condorcet, Godwin, and Mary Wollstonecraft was naturalized in America during this generation and provided philosophic foundations for new waves of social reformism in the next. The most significant reforms eventually occurred in education because it offered the readiest means of improving the condition of every individual. Detailed plans for the education of the whole people were proposed by Jefferson and Benjamin Rush among others, but cost and conservative opposition postponed action.

Books and Newspapers

In literature the spokesmen of optimism, democracy, and reform won the battle against pessimistic conservatism. The Hartford Wits lost their position of literary leadership except as the die-hard Timothy Dwight continued to fulminate against all forms of infidelity to the "standing order." One of their leading poets, Joel Barlow, who in 1786 had collaborated with John Trumbull and Lemuel Hopkins in *The Anarchiad,* a satire on the radicals, turned to enthusiasm for the French Revolution in his ominous *Advice to the Privileged Orders* (1792) and became an ardent Jeffersonian. The outstanding writer of the new generation, Charles Brockden Brown, was a forthright radical throughout his short life and used his novels as vehicles for reformist doctrine. He appealed to popular tastes for Gothic horrors and Richardsonian sentiment, while teaching liberation by reason from superstition in *Wieland* (1798) and democratic idealism in *Arthur Mervyn* (1799). His tract *Alcuin* (1798) struck a blow for women's rights with the environmentalist argument that subjection by men rather than innate inferiority prevented their development as the intellectual and moral equals of men. Royall Tyler in his novel *The Algerine Captive* (1797) satirized the shortcomings of the new republic, defending Federalism. An even balance between the present weaknesses of raw democracy and future hopes was achieved by Hugh Henry Brackenridge in his most popular novel, *Modern Chivalry* (1792).

Less important as literature but more important in popular influence were novels, plays, and histories which celebrated American experience in terms of simple patriotism. The most famous of such works was Mason L. Weems's *Life of Washington* (1800). "Parson" Weems had been a militant Deist, but in his book he pictured the Father of His Country as a sort of substitute deity—as a paragon of talents and virtues which, for all the imaginary incidents Weems used to bludgeon home his point, Washington very nearly was. The colossal sale of the book during the next generations fixed him permanently among the first of American folk heroes.

But book sales were trifling in comparison with the circulation of newspapers. The American, as an English visitor remarked, was "a newspaper-reading animal." The party battles between Federalists and Republicans gave new excitement to the press, and grandiose European events on which the fortunes of the American republic largely depended were thoroughly reported. The first American daily, *The Pennsylvania Packet and Daily Advertiser* had been founded in Philadelphia in 1784. By 1815, there were over thirty dailies. Chiefly political in subject matter, the newspapers were almost all party organs. Political leaders often took the initiative in founding or supporting papers to make sure that their views on all questions reached the public. Reference has already been made to such outstanding Philadelphia papers as the Federalist *Gazette of the United States,* edited by John Fenno, the Republican *National Gazette* of Philip Freneau, and the *Aurora* edited successively by Benjamin F. Bache and William Duane. Equally notorious with these men was the Federalist William Cobbett, publisher of *Porcupine's Gazette,* who returned to England in 1800 after Benjamin Rush won a libel suit against him growing out of his attacks on that doctor's treatment of yellow fever. After their defeat in the election, Alexander Hamilton and other Federalists in 1801 founded the *New York Evening Post,* most eminent of all newspapers of the time, which presently shed its Federalism and turned to support the Democracy.

Architecture and Art

Jefferson had initiated a Roman revival in architecture when he found the Maison Carrée at Nîmes a perfect model for a republican temple and recommended it for the capitol of his state of Virginia. In 1791, President Washington asked Major Pierre Charles L'Enfant, who had served under him as an engineer in the Revolution, to submit a plan for the federal city. Although L'Enfant soon quarreled with Washington and Jefferson and was dismissed, and his plan was variously modified and violated, his conception still governs the city of Washington. Basically the plan combines the four-square grid of workaday streets with superimposed diagonal avenues radiating from circles and squares, which provide grand vistas and invite ceremonial processions reminiscent of ancient Rome. The plan matched in splendor the vision of the Founders and, like the Constitution itself, it required the labor of many decades, involving many a setback and unforeseen alteration, before the reality lived up to the promise.

The story of the design and construction of the capitol typified the whole. William Thornton, an amateur in architecture, won the original competition with a design to which his successor, Stephen Hallet, added a Roman rotunda and dome flanked by wings for the Senate and House of Representatives. After much quarreling and less construction, President Jefferson in 1803 appointed his friend, Benjamin Henry Latrobe, a professional architect and innovator of the Greek Revival, to revise the plans. Latrobe believed that Greece had proved the compatibility of art and democracy and therefore provided more suitable models of architecture than the corrupted taste of the Roman Empire. He added Greek details and delighted Jefferson by substituting tobacco leaves and corn cobs for the Corinthian acanthus. The present dome—in some eyes disproportionately large—was completed only in the last days of the Civil War, an event which President Lincoln regarded as symbolic of the restoration of the Union.

Charles Bulfinch of Boston shared with Latrobe the honor of establishing architecture as a profession. His masterpiece was the Boston State House (completed in 1800) whose gilded dome dominates Beacon Hill. In the 1790's, he introduced the restrained elegance of Roman interior and exterior ornament which the Brothers Adam had made fashionable in England. This was the basis of the "Federal" style which expressed the aristocratic aspirations of the wealthiest Americans and was used for expensive residences.

American painting gradually freed itself from dependence on its original headquarters in the London studio of Benjamin West. Gilbert Stuart's innumerable portraits of Washington were British in inspiration, but the family of painting Peales in the new century drew increasingly upon American interests in nature and realistic portraiture. Sculpture was an art for which native traditions of woodcarving provided excellent beginnings. The ships' figureheads of William Rush, such as *The Genius of the United States* and *Nature*, both of which were installed on warships, fully displayed artistic intention and achievement. But Samuel McIntire, talented architect and decorator who rebuilt his native Salem, Massachusetts, in Federal style, tried to sculpture freestanding figures in wood without great success; and even the greater success of the Skillins family of Boston did not earn for them commissions in Washington. Jefferson was determined that the carvings and sculptures of the capitol should be in stone and believed that only Europeans had mastered that medium. He had already encouraged the French sculptor Houdon to create his masterly series of statues and busts of George Washington and other Americans; now for the capitol he organized the "Italian invasion" of sculptors and put them to work on American eagles and sundry classical allegories. The polished perfection of the Italian school dominated American sculpture for two generations, while the sturdy tradition of artisan-carvers in wood was all but lost.

The taste of the founding generation of Americans, whether Federalists or Republicans, was determined by European standards and haunted by ancient Greece and Rome. To modern tastes the work of the period is too subservient to its models and too pretentiously idealistic for high regard. It was as if the founders enlisted older cultures to sanction their experiment so long as its success remained problematical. The generation after 1815, no longer doubtful of success, took up more boldly the endless task of defining the cultural identitfy of the new society.

CHAPTER 18

Jeffersonian Liberalism
1801-1805

WHEN THOMAS JEFFERSON WAS INAUGURATED AS THE third President of the United States in 1801, the population of the country, which had risen considerably above the five million mark, was about a third greater than it had been when he became Washington's Secretary of State in 1790. Only one new state, Ohio, was admitted during his administration of eight years, but the most notable external fact about his presidency was the doubling of the area of the republic by the purchase of Louisiana. In political history he is also notable as the founder of what came to be called the "Virginia Dynasty," for his lieutenants James Madison and James Monroe succeeded him in the presidency and served eight years each. His election has long been regarded as a turning point, and he himself described it as a "revolution." It is proper to ask, therefore, what important changes his political victory really brought about.

The election of the leading opponent of the Federalists unquestionably marked the resumption of the historic American trend toward political democracy. But if this be measured in terms of universal suffrage and the participation of the people in the operations of the government, the movement assumed much greater momentum after Jefferson's day, reaching its climax in the presidency of Andrew Jackson. The Republican victory represented the triumph of the principle of majority rule, but Jeffersonian democracy was evolutionary rather than revolutionary; it was a rising tide rather than a tidal wave.

Jefferson's election has often been interpreted as a victory for state rights, but a more accurate statement is that it marked a reaction against the consolidating tendencies historically associated with the name of Hamilton. Actually, the strongest state-rights tendencies of the era now

332

dawning were to be manifested in New England, among foes of the administration. This is not surprising, for, as a rule, localism and separatism characterize minority groups. Also, there is a common tendency for the party in power to move in the direction of consolidation and centralization. It is a notable fact that among the Jeffersonians this tendency was resisted. As a result, the aggrandizement of national power was relatively slight during the early years of the Republican ascendancy. What there was came largely through the expansion of territory and the exigencies of international affairs.

The victory may be rightly regarded as one of agriculture over the Hamiltonian type of capitalism, though it was followed by no extreme actions. Jefferson did not overthrow the Federalist fiscal structure, and he was forced in the end to recognize the importance of industry, along with agriculture and commerce. But he did not grant industry and finance any favors, and his heart remained with the small farmers. To them he always tried to open the door of opportunity, and with them he would have filled the land. Furthermore, he and his successors created a political tie between the South and West (along with the urban masses in the East) which prevented the full triumph of business until after the Civil War.

The election marked the definite emergence of recognized political parties. The right of political opposition was vindicated by it, and Jefferson's victory was a landmark in the history of free speech. The downfall of the Federalists was owing to many causes besides their efforts to prevent criticism of the government by means of the Sedition Act, but there were important implications in the fact that the party responsible for that notorious measure was defeated. Furthermore, even though this need not be called a revolution, there was a change in the ruling group—the first since the establishment of the new government under the Constitution. This change was not so much to leaders of a different personal type, as to leaders and policies more representative of the people as a whole.

Finally, the accession of Jefferson had great significance in the world situation. In Europe the political trend had been and continued to be reactionary. Out of the chaos created by revolutionary developments in France, repressive governments, even despotisms, emerged in the Old World. This reaction was felt in the United States, and in the perspective of history the chief significance of Jefferson's career as a national political leader, perhaps, is that he checked it. He was the chief magistrate of the American Republic at a time that William Pitt governed Great Britain and Bonaparte ruled France. In an era of war and repression, he rededicated his own country to the sacred cause of freedom and gave the United States the most liberal government in the world. It was fortunate that such a leader appeared at such a time, but the outcome was not owing to him alone. A far higher degree of freedom was possible in remote

America than in war-infested Europe. Jefferson's task as President was to preserve his country and expand its liberties.

The Beginning of the Jeffersonian Regime

Jefferson was not the first President to serve in the new Federal City of Washington, which was really a straggling village, for John Adams spent several unhappy months in it. He was the first to be inaugurated there, and that was fitting, for as Secretary of State he had been the chief agent of the President in the planning and development of the new capital.

The executive mansion was unfinished when John and Abigail Adams arrived and remained unfinished during Jefferson's presidency. It was merely a big box and a rather cheerless place. The proportions of the White House were good, but there were no porticoes as yet, no walls, no garden. After the widower President moved in, from Conrad's boarding house on Capitol Hill where he had been living unpretentiously, he rattled around in its emptiness. Only the north or Senate wing of the original capitol was ready, though the south wing was above ground. Temporarily, the House of Representatives sat in a brick building, called "the oven." Pennsylvania Avenue was a morass, and not until 1805 did an inaugural procession go down it. If Jefferson wanted a rural capital for his rural republic he unquestionably had one. There was plenty of opportunity here to vent his enthusiasm for the future, and he believed that he was embarking on an experiment.

He charted his course in the Inaugural Address he delivered in the crowded Senate chamber. He spoke in so low a tone that few people could hear him, but from that day till this, people have turned to this brief speech as the most convenient single expression of his political philosophy and public aims.

Since this was the first instance in American national history when the party of the opposition had been victorious in a presidential election, his immediate purpose was to reassure his recent opponents. But he spoke to all later Americans when he announced as a sacred principle that, "though the will of the majority is in all cases to prevail, that will, to be rightful, must be reasonable; that the minority possess their equal rights, which equal laws must protect, and to violate which would be oppression." To him the recent political conflict was a contest of opinion. Such contests are inevitable in a free society, and they lie at the base of the party system. "But every difference of opinion is not a difference of principle," he said. "We have called by different names brethren of the same principle. We are all republicans—we are all federalists." He was using the political terminology of the day, but in effect he said that when the real test comes "we are all Americans." Also, he spoke for the ages when he proclaimed that "error of opinion may be tolerated where reason is left free to combat it," and when he designated the free American system of self-government as "the world's best hope." These words were destined to live long. Abraham Lincoln echoed them in a time of grave civil conflict when he spoke of "the last best hope of earth."

The new President's more specific description of his policies and the functions of the government was directed to the conditions of his own time. There is enduring value in his claim that, in the end, a self-governing republic is stronger than any despotism, but much of his language sounds negative to any modern ear. The sum of good government, he said, is this: "a wise and frugal government, which shall restrain men from injuring one another, shall leave them otherwise free to regulate their own pursuits of industry and improvement, and shall not take from the mouth of labor the bread it has earned." There seems to be nothing here but the police power and laissez faire. Alexander Hamilton had a much more positive conception of the functions of the federal government. Jefferson spoke of the encouragement of agriculture and of commerce "as its handmaid," without mentioning industry; and he promised support of the state governments "in all their rights," as the most competent administrators of domestic matters.

In his eyes the major task of the federal government was to administer foreign affairs, and by announcing the policy of "no entangling alliances" he kept himself in the tradition of the Neutrality Proclamation and went even farther than Washington's warning in the Farewell Address against *permanent* alliances. In external relations he had never taken such a negative position as in the domestic field; and, when actually in authority, he had to disregard some of the theoretical limitations which he had set for the government during the years he was in opposition. The popularity of his rather negative political philosophy in his own time was chiefly owing to its suitability to existing conditions. After Hamilton's great work had been done there was no crying need for a forceful government in the domestic sphere. What most people wanted was freedom to take advantage of the vast opportunities of the country, without fear or favor, and this is what Jefferson sought to guarantee them. To him the strength and glory of the Republic would lie in the character and achievements of its citizens. The thought of fashioning an instrument of national power to achieve great social ends lay far in the future.

The Triumvirate

Next to the President himself, the most important members of the executive department were James Madison, the Secretary of State, and Albert Gallatin, the Secretary of the Treasury, who in conjunction with Jefferson constituted a triumvirate. Madison, now fifty-one, was a wizened little man who dressed soberly but was a good story-teller in private. Because of his long political and personal intimacy with Jefferson and his conspicuous past services to his country and party his appointment was inevitable; and because of the close attention which all the Presidents of this era gave to foreign affairs, their policy was in reality a joint policy. Dolly Payne Madison, who was friendly to everybody, was a great social asset to her husband and to the President, whom she generally served as official hostess.

Gallatin was now forty-one. His Swiss birth and French accent had been much ridiculed by the Federalists and he had never been one who cared greatly for conventional social life. From the time that he left behind him his aristocratic background in Geneva at the age of nineteen, he had lived mostly in the backwoods of Pennsylvania. Shortly before his marriage to Hannah Nicholson of New York, he had complained to her of his "anti-Chesterfieldian awkwardness in mixed companies" and told her she must polish his manners. He was a man of real personal distinction, however, and no one could question his grasp of finance.

Henry Adams has described these three men as the most aristocratic of democrats. Aristocratic they all were in origin, but as a friendly observer, Margaret Bayard Smith, said in this first year: "Never were there a plainer set of men, and I think I may add a more virtuous and enlightened one, than at present form our administration."

Jefferson was now fifty-eight. He was a gourmet and a connoisseur and he surrounded himself with books and pictures, but habits of sartorial indifference and social informality had settled upon him. Federalist newspapers never ceased ridiculing the "corduroy small-clothes, red-plush waistcoat, and sharp-toed boots with which he expressed his contempt for fashion"; and the yarn stockings and slippers down at the heel which a British envoy described have gained immortality in sober works of history. To hostile commentators these things seemed a sign of democratic affectation, the purpose of which was predominantly political. But if he looked like a tall, large-boned farmer, that was just what he was and wanted to be. As President he was just the sort of man that he was at Monticello and dispensed the same sort of hospitality. He had company for dinner—at 3:30 o'clock—every day; the food was plentiful and excellent, and the informal host put his guests at ease.

The President's style of living and entertaining was not unsuited to the rural capital of a rural republic. Yet, just as John Adams had rendered himself rather ridiculous when he urged that the President be surrounded with pomp and ceremony, Jefferson made himself a ready target when, as the presiding philosopher, he drew up democratic rules of etiquette and sought to solve the problems of precedence by the principle of "pell-mell." The carrying of this principle into effect almost created an international incident in the case of the British minister, Anthony Merry, whose wife was overlooked in the scramble at a dinner party. The Spanish minister, the Marques de Yrujo, who also had his grievance, joined with the Britisher in protestation without avail. Writing to his friend William Short, Jefferson said in 1804: "the principle of society with us, as well as of our political constitution, is the equal rights of all; . . . Nobody shall be above you, nor you above anybody, pêle-mêlc is our law." He exaggerated equality to the point of making it rather absurd, but he served to establish a tradition of relative simplicity in official American society.

REPUBLICAN ADMINISTRATION

Jefferson fully shared George Washington's conviction that the government would gain respect and confidence by deserving it. No less than their Fedcralist predecessors the Jeffersonians emphasized good administration. Throughout his public career Jefferson himsclf found administrative detail boring, but by any standard he was an efficient man and he was appallingly systematic. Also, he was fortunate in having in his Secretary of the Treasury a man of genius comparable to that of Hamilton. Gallatin worked closely with Congress as Hamilton had done but was less high-handed toward the legislators, as his institution of the annual Treasury report clearly showed. In the House of Representatives when the Federalists were in power he had been chiefly responsible for the establishment of the famous Committee on Ways and Means, and he was not one to disregard Congressional prerogatives in financial matters.

Gallatin's most conspicuous early achievement was the reduction of the national debt, along with and in spite of the abolition in 1802 of the unpopular excise taxes—including that on whiskey. This reduction was accomplished in some part by economies in administration and, to a greater extent, by decreases in expenditures for the army and navy. One of the results of the latter policy was the unpreparedness of the country for war, but Jefferson believed that the United States could avoid entanglement in European conflict. During his first term his optimism was warranted, and his later foreign policies at least postponed the evil day of war. Meanwhile, despite the unexpected expenses of the Louisiana Purchase and the minor Barbary wars, and despite the loss of revenue occasioned by the Embargo of 1807, the policy of economy was conspicuously successful. By 1810, the national debt, which had been $80 million when Gallatin come into office, had been reduced by more than one-third, and during his first years the showing was a good deal better. This action was in accord with the philosophy of the President, who had long ago questioned the right of one generation to burden another by transmitting to it a vast load of public debt, and it fulfilled the promise of his inaugural.

The success of the economy program redounded to the popularity of the government. It also made possible the more positive program which was signalized by the Louisiana Purchase of 1803, and it led Jefferson himself to suggest in his second term that the surplus revenue might be applied, by constitutional amendment, to internal improvements and education within the states. He was flexible in his economic policy, while retaining his constitutional scruples. Gallatin had fewer of the latter and he was the most important early exponent of internal improvements at national expense. The program—dealing with roads, canals, and rivers—which he presented to the Senate in 1808 in a notable report, showed that he matched Hamilton in constructive imagination as in financial management.

The Republicans had inveighed against executive encroachments during their years in the opposition, and had emphasized the prerogatives of the legislative branch of the government. As Hamilton had perceived, however, Jefferson himself was no believer in a weak executive and an omnipotent legislature. At the very beginning of Washington's administration Madison had contributed signally to the creation of the executive departments and their subordination to the President, rather than to Congress, and Jefferson as Secretary of State had organized one of these. As President, he fully maintained the prestige and authority of his high office. Because of his constitutional scruples, however, and because of his temperament, he relied on indirect methods in dealing with Congress and sought to avoid any appearance of dictation. His abandonment of the practice of delivering Presidential messages in person was partly owing to his personal dislike for public speaking, but also it was in line with this policy. The chief institutional developments which marked his administration were the establishment of the floor leader in the House of Representatives as the recognized spokesman of the President, and the growth of the party caucus as a policy-making body. While Jefferson was charged by his foes with being a secret dictator, and was sometimes sharply opposed by dissenters among the Republicans themselves, he was more skillful than Hamilton, who angered many men by his imperiousness and officiousness. Jefferson was equalled in party leadership by few of his successors, and perhaps has never been surpassed.

As the first President whose advent marked a change in parties, he had to grapple with the question of the relation between political affiliation and appointment to public office. The Federalists had come to have a practical monopoly of the public service, and they aroused the indignation of the Republicans by creating new offices during their last months in office and filling these with Federalists. The most flagrant example was provided by the "midnight judges," whose commissions were signed at the last hour. Thus twenty-four justices of the peace for the District of Columbia were appointed for five years—that is, they were protected until after another presidential election.

Jefferson cautiously worked out a policy of removal. This applied first to classes of officers the validity of whose appointment seemed doubtful —holders of offices created at the last moment or men appointed by Adams after his defeat was known. One of these cases—that of Chauncey Goodrich, collector at New Haven, whom Adams had appointed about two weeks before the end of his own term—aroused considerable talk and gave Jefferson the occasion to set forth his position and, unwittingly, to coin an epigram. He removed Goodrich and appointed a Republican, Samuel Bishop. Afterward he asked his critics: "If a due participation of office is a matter of right, how are vacancies to be obtained? Those by death are few; by resignation none." In shorter and more pointed form the saying is: "Few die; none resign."

Having restored the balance in a couple of years, he ceased making removals. In the course of time, Republicans came to dominate the public service just as the Federalists had done, but the policy was acceptable to the country and there was no lowering of standards. It has sometimes been said that Jefferson introduced the "spoils system," but the expression itself dates from the Age of Jackson, and it was not until then that the public service was really "politicized." There was more ground for the charge that Jefferson was hostile to the federal judiciary.

THE REPUBLICANS vs. THE JUDICIARY

The struggle between the victorious party and the judiciary, which ran through Jefferson's presidency, raised crucial questions about the relations of the co-ordinate branches—the executive, legislative, and judicial— and at several points it took on the form of a political duel between the President and his distant kinsman, the Federalist Chief Justice John Marshall. There was extreme partisanship on both sides which has served to discredit both parties at the bar of history, but the predominant judgment of the country then was essentially the same that it was more than a century later, when Franklin D. Roosevelt challenged the Supreme Court. Judges deserve rebuke when they play politics or arrogate to themselves unwarranted powers, but the executive and legislature deserve defeat when they make political attack on the independence of the judiciary.

The Federalists dominated the courts, as they had the civil service, and the judges had tended to identify opposition to the administration in power with opposition to the government itself and to the Constitution. The Sedition Act had been enforced by the federal courts in an extremely partisan manner. Also, the Federalist judges had shown little regard for the sovereignty of the state governments. Thus in the case of Chisholm vs. Georgia (1793), when the State of Georgia refused the summons of the United States Supreme Court to appear before it and defend itself against

Chisholm's claim to compensation under the Treaty of 1783 for property confiscated by the state during the Revolution, judgment was entered against the state government by default. State sovereignty is incompatible with such compulsion. The fears aroused by this decision led to the adoption of the Eleventh Amendment to the Constitution (1798), which forbids suits in the federal courts by citizens of other states or nations against state governments without the consent of the latter. This was a victory for state rights against consolidating tendencies, but the federal judiciary continued to be an agency for the establishment of national supremacy.

The Federalists gained more by a fortunate accident than by their deliberate action. The development of judicial power in the next generation is inseparable from the career of John Marshall, who was appointed Chief Justice by President Adams on January 20, 1801, following the resignation of Oliver Ellsworth and the declination of John Jay. He remained in office until 1835. The significance of Marshall's appointment was not fully realized at first, and the resentment of the Republicans was directed more strongly against the Judiciary Act of 1801, which has been aptly described as "the last word in the Federalist system." By means of it the defeated party had sought to maintain itself, irrespective of the popular will, in the least changeable branch of the government.

On practical grounds there were good reasons for a reorganization of the federal judiciary, and changes were suggested by Adams a good many months before he lost the election. The existing law (that of 1789, modified in 1793) provided for a Supreme Court, district courts, and circuit courts. The latter had no distinct set of judges, but consisted in each instance of a district court judge and a justice of the Supreme Court, who was thus required to ride the circuit—like a "traveling postboy," as one complained. In those days of slow and uncomfortable transportation this degree of travel imposed a hardship on elderly men. Furthermore, a justice might be required to consider on appeal cases on which he had already sat in a circuit.

The most important feature of the new act was the creation of sixteen circuit court judges. Adams named only Federalists to the new posts, and in some instances men who had been defeated for re-election to Congress were appointed to vacancies. Another provision of the law was that, beginning with the next vacancy, the Supreme Court itself should be reduced from six justices to five—thus depriving Jefferson of that potential appointment. Though the law had many merits it was inopportune and partisan. The Republicans, still smarting under the partisan administration of the Sedition Act, were determined to repeal it.

This they did, following Jefferson's suggestion, at the first session of the new Congress. In the course of the debate the Federalists said much about the "right" of the new judges to their offices, and charged that this Republican move was an attack on the independence of the judiciary and a preliminary to the overthrow of the Constitution. But the act of repeal (March 1802), restoring the old court system, accorded with dominant political opinion. It was carried by a strict party vote, and a supplementary measure provided that the Supreme Court should meet but once a year, beginning in February. The result was that the Supreme Court would be delayed at least nine months in passing on this particular piece of legislation. Actually, the justices signified their acceptance of the *fait accompli* by resuming their functions as circuit riders, and, a little later, they did so by formal action (in the case of Stuart *vs.* Baird, March 2, 1803). The first round in the struggle between the Jeffersonians and the judiciary had been won by the former, but the latter's turn came at the next session of the Supreme Court in the historic case of Marbury *vs.* Madison.

Marbury vs. Madison

One of the minor "midnight" commissions was that of William Marbury as a justice of peace of the District of Columbia. It was not delivered by Adams's acting Secretary of State, who was no other than John Marshall; and the new Secretary of State, Madison, was instructed not to deliver it, since Jefferson adjudged the appointment to be illegal or unwarranted. He reappointed a number of these justices of the peace but Marbury was not one of them. This became a *cause celèbre* because Marbury applied to the Supreme Court under the Judiciary Act of 1789 for a writ of mandamus, that is, a writ commanding the Secretary of State to deliver the commission. The application involved the Chief Justice in a dilemma. A decision in favor of Madison would have strengthened the executive in its battle with the judiciary and given comfort to his detested political foes, whereas a decision in favor of Marbury would have been unenforceable, since the executive would ignore it and no force belongs to the judiciary. Marshall's decision has been described by a sympathetic biographer as a piece of "perfectly calculated audacity," and by more critical authority as a "partisan coup."

On the merits of the case he decided in effect for Marbury, holding that the latter had a right to his commission and that it was the duty of Madison to deliver it. Thus the Chief Justice lectured the executive branch about the performance of its duties. He then proceeded to declare that the Supreme Court could nevertheless do nothing, since a writ of mandamus could not issue from that body. Such a power had been conferred on it by act of Congress, to be sure, but Section 13 of the Act of 1789 was unconstitutional, he said, since the definition of the original jurisdiction of the Supreme Court in the Constitution did not extend that far. By denying to his Court a lesser power, which would have been useless to him under the circumstances, Marshall asserted the transcendent power of declaring an act of Congress unconstitutional.

The main objection to Marshall's decision at the time was not that the Supreme Court had invalidated a minor section of an act of Congress. It was that the Chief Justice had invaded the executive sphere by telling the President and Secretary of State what their duty was. Jefferson believed that he had the right to decide on questions of propriety and constitutionality in the exercise of his executive functions. Thus, believing the Sedition Act to be unconstitutional, he regarded himself as bound not to execute it. The co-ordinate branches of the government were meant to be checks on each other, he said, but he saw no warrant for making the judiciary a "despotic branch." What he feared was judicial supremacy, and there were times in the later history of his country when this became a real danger. But through the years the American ideal became clearer —a government of laws not men—and the independent judiciary has seemed the safest and most impartial interpreter of these laws and the Constitution.

Impeachments

Since federal judges were appointed for life, they could not be held accountable at the polls, and the only available weapon against bad behavior was impeachment. The Jeffersonians resorted to impeachment in the pathetic case of a district judge of New York, John Pickering, who was wholly incapacitated for office because of insanity and drunkenness. He was charged with high crimes and misdemeanors, so as to meet the constitutional requirements, and was removed by a partisan vote. The proceedings against Justice Samuel Chase of the Supreme Court were marked by ineptitude, but he himself arouses little sympathy. The grievances against Chase went back to his conduct of trials under the Sedition Act, but the immediate occasion for action against him was provided by a highly indiscreet charge he made to a grand jury in Baltimore in May 1803. In this he attacked constitutional proposals in Maryland and universal suffrage, saying that this pointed the way toward "mobocracy"; and it was said that he violently attacked the administration. His impeachment by the House of Representatives resulted from this, though the trial before the Senate did not actually occur until the beginning of the year 1805, after Jefferson's triumphant re-election, the vote on Chase being taken only a few days before his second inauguration.

This action was distinctly partisan, and the more extreme Republicans justified it on partisan grounds. One of them, William Branch Giles of Virginia, asserted that impeachment was no more than "an inquiry by the two houses of Congress, whether the office of any public man might not be better filled by another." In other words, the object of such maneuvers was to wreak venegance on political foes and give offices to good Republicans. More moderate and more philosophical Republicans were unwilling to go that far, however, and the division of opinion in the dominant group proved a fatal weakness. The charges comprised all the complaints against Chase, and there was a majority vote against him on some articles, but the constitutional requirement of two-thirds was met in no instance. The major weakness of the case lay in the fact that the genuine grievances against Chase did not amount to high crimes and misdemeanors. He deserved rebuke but not conviction.

This round in the fight went against the Republicans. Jefferson himself declared that impeachment was a farce which would not be tried again, and he kept on lamenting through the years that the independence of the judges was really independence from public opinion. They represented to him the stubborn changelessness of the Federalist Party. But the proceedings against Justice Chase, besides revealing the necessary limitations of impeachment in the American system, did have a sobering effect on the manners and utterances of politically-minded judges. They restrained their partisanship much more after this, though the conduct of Chief Justice Marshall in the Burr trial did not provide a good example. That trial constituted the final round in Marshall's open duel with the President.

Freedom and Slander

In the philosophy of Jefferson, the freeing of the individual citizen to the fullest possible degree in all departments of life was fully as important as the attainment of popular rule, and to him freedom of the mind and freedom of speech were basic in human progress. It is in this sense that his philosophy can best be described as "liberal." He was still devoted to the ideals that he had inherited from the Enlightenment of the Eighteenth Century. There was irony, therefore, in his inability to check the rising tide of intellectual reaction and in his own grievous suffering from the freedom of the press.

In the sphere of religion certain tendencies that are commonly described as "liberal" continued in some quarters. At Harvard, the election of Henry Ware as Hollis Professor of Divinity (1805), after several years of controversy, signalized the defeat of the conservative Calvinists and the victory of the Unitarians in that historic seat of learning. But this period of religious revivalism throughout the country was marked by the rapid growth of the more evangelical Presbyterians, the Baptists, and the Methodists, all of whom tended toward religious orthodoxy. In the West and South these developments brought no political disadvantage to Jefferson as yet, since he was still remembered as the champion of freedom for dissenting sects against the old Church establishments. In New England, also, the dissenting religious groups who were warring against the privileged Church in such states as Massachusetts and Con-

necticut tended to be Jeffersonian, despite the growing conservatism of
the public in religious matters. The latter was well exemplified at Yale
College, where President Timothy Dwight had for some years been waging vigorous and successful warfare on "infidelity."

To the New England Congregational clergy, who were still closely
allied with the civil rulers, Jefferson's religious views and attitudes provided an inviting target. He avoided all public reference to his own religious opinions, believing that these were wholly a private matter.
Nominally he remained an Episcopalian, but he was essentially a Deist,
though not at all militant, and in everything except name he was a
Unitarian. During his first term he gave a handle to his critics by his
public attitude toward Thomas Paine, who returned to America in 1802
and remained in the country until his death seven years later.

Paine had expressed the wish that if Jefferson should have occasion
to send a frigate to France, he would give him the opportunity of returning by it. Jefferson offered him passage on the *Maryland,* expressing
the hope that Paine would find the Americans "returned to sentiments
worthy of former times" and that he might live long to continue his "useful labors" (March 18, 1801). This was a gracious offer, to which Paine's
past services to the cause of American independence and universal human freedom may have entitled him, but he was now better known as
the writer of an extremely abusive letter against George Washington and
as the author of *The Age of Reason,* which was regarded by practically
all the churches in the United States as a direct attack on them. He
came by a private vessel, not in an American warship, but the President
got the full discredit for the original invitation. Paine gave further fuel
to partisan wrath when he published a series of letters *To the Citizens
of the United States and Particularly to the Leaders of the Federalist
Faction* (1802-1805). During his last years he lived in poverty as a social
outcast, and in death he was denied burial in consecrated ground.

Jefferson's personal sufferings from abuses of the freedom of the press
can best be illustrated by his experiences with James Thomson Callender,
one of the conspicuous victims of the Sedition Act. Few sufferers under
that law deserved less consideration, but President Jefferson pardoned
him and remitted his fine. Impatient at the slight delay in the repayment
of his fine and resentful because of his failure to receive any political reward, Callender turned on his distinguished patron. Dipping his pen in
filth, he filled the columns of the *Richmond Recorder* (1802-1803) with
charges against Jefferson of financial impropriety and gross personal immorality. The wholly unwarranted but lingering tradition that the master
of Monticello had a slave mistress may be traced back to this vindictive
scandalmonger, who so signally illustrated the abuses of freedom. The
Federalist press gleefully took up his charges, coupling them with others
that had already been aired in the campaign of 1800. Even after Jeffer-

son's re-election the chorus of abuse continued. Early in 1805, in the House of Representatives of Massachusetts, a motion to dismiss the printers of the House for publishing libels on the President in the *New-England Palladium* was defeated. The application of libel laws, *after* the event of defamation, was not contrary to the philosophy of Jefferson, but neither at this time nor any other did he himself resort to this sort of legal action.

During his presidency he went through a sharp revulsion of feeling toward the press. He had once said that if he had to choose between a government without newspapers, and newspapers without a government, he would prefer the latter—assuming that people were sufficiently educated to read and understand them. His private correspondence shows, however, that at this stage he was deeply conscious of the unreliability of the press and appalled by the public appetite for defamation. The doctrine of freedom greatly needed supplementation by that of responsibility. There was no revival of the Sedition Law, and, as Jefferson stated in his second inaugural, his re-election attested the success of the experiment "whether freedom of discussion, unaided by power, is not sufficient for the propagation and protection of truth." He believed that experience had proved that a pure and scrupulous government could not be written down by falsehood and defamation.

He never fully recovered his earlier enthusiasm for newspapers, and in his later life he reported that he had turned with relief from them to the ancient classical writers. Some years after his retirement, however, he said: "When the press is free, and every man able to read, all is safe." By and large, his entire career may be described as a successful experiment in freedom. But his triumph in 1804, when he got 162 electoral votes to 14 for Charles Cotesworth Pinckney of South Carolina, the Federalist candidate, gaining the votes of all the states except Connecticut and Delaware and two electors from Maryland, can also be attributed to other causes. The main one was the Louisiana Purchase.

CHAPTER 19

Expansion and Domestic Faction, 1803-1809

Most of Jefferson's presidency and practically the whole of his successor's was set against the background of general European war, the reverberations of which were felt throughout the Atlantic world. The Treaty of Amiens, which brought a cessation of hostilities between Napoleon and the British, was signed in the autumn of 1801. For a couple of years there was a lull, but the titanic conflict was resumed in May 1803 and it continued practically without intermission until the final downfall of Napoleon toward the end of Madison's presidency.

From France, the chief warring country of Europe, President Jefferson gained a magnificent prize in the immense province of Louisiana. But in his second term, when the commerce of the young American Republic was caught in the cross fire, he suffered his greatest discomfiture in the ill fate of his embargo. In his conduct of foreign affairs he was motivated by the strong desire to keep his own country out of this world conflict in which, as he believed, it had no real concern, and to gain for it time to realize on its great potentialities. His greatest triumph, the Louisiana Purchase, redounded chiefly to the advantage of settlers in the West, which as he clearly foresaw was destined to become the heart of the American agricultural empire. By all rights he should be the patron saint of the Mississippi Valley. His foreign policy, though flexible in many ways, had one fixed point. As Secretary of State he was anxious to procure and as President he was determined to maintain the free navigation of the Mississippi, being convinced that this was necessary to retain the trans-Alleghany settlements in the Union.

His western policy could be properly described as nationalistic, but it was also infused with concern for the individual settlers and it turned out

346

to be good politics. Nothing showed more clearly the blindness and un-teachableness of the Federalist leaders than their indifference and opposition to western development. The President, both as a politician and a national statesman, was looking to the future, while they were looking to the past. Writing to his successor shortly after his retirement, Jefferson described the expanded American nation of his dreams as such an "empire for liberty" as had not been seen since the creation. This was the transcendent American dream, and nobody did more than he to translate it into reality.

The Men of the Western Waters

When Jefferson was inaugurated in 1801 there were still only two states beyond the mountains, Kentucky and Tennessee, but the population of both of these had trebled since the census of 1790 and both were destined to double in the next decade. The reference to these people as "men of the western waters" was proper, since they were dependent on the waterways for their major transportation. The course of commerce in this growing inland empire was inevitably southward.

In the region above the Ohio in the old Northwest Territory, settlement had been slower than below that river, chiefly because of the presence of the Indians, but the tide really began to flow after the Treaty of Greenville (1795) opened up most of the present state of Ohio. By 1798, Ohio had been granted a territorial government of her own, and in 1800 Congress passed the Harrison Land Act, which served to encourage small settlers as compared with speculative companies, even if Federalist conservatism prevented its being as liberal as the frontiersmen wanted. The price of land remained at $2 an acre as it had been in 1796, but as small a tract as 320 acres could now be bought and only a fourth of the purchase money had to be paid in cash, four years' credit being allowed for the balance. The law was liberalized by the Republicans in 1804, when the minimum was reduced to 160 acres, the credit feature being retained. In 1800, Indiana became a separate territory under the governorship of William Henry Harrison; and in 1802 a convention in Ohio, authorized by Congress, voted almost unanimously for statehood.

The Jeffersonians supported and the Federalist leaders tended to obstruct these measures, but the net result was to facilitate settlement and add another state to the Union in 1803. One important early region of settlement was the Western Reserve centering on Cleveland, and here, as in the still earlier settlement at Marietta, New England influence was strong; but the leadership of the new territory and state was predominantly Southern and most of the settlements were contiguous to the Ohio and its tributaries. In politics, Ohio was Republican, just as Kentucky and Tennessee were; and her trade also had to flow southward with the currents of the rivers. To all these people it was vital that the gate at New Orleans should not be locked.

In the region south of Tennessee, settlement had been delayed by dangers from the Indians and by grave uncertainties about boundaries and land titles. The Treaty of San Lorenzo in 1795 had fixed the southern boundary of the United States at the 31st parallel of latitude, but the Spanish did not withdraw from the southern sector until 1798, and even then the Americans were cut off from the Gulf of Mexico by Spanish West Florida. The territory of Mississippi was established in 1800 in the region between the 31st parallel and the state of Tennessee, but the state of Georgia, which laid claim to it by virtue of its colonial charter, did not formally yield title to the federal government until 1802, and the story behind that cession suggests the turmoil and feverish speculation which accompanied the early development of the Old Southwest.

In the year 1795, by means of the infamous Yazoo Act, the state of Georgia sold to four companies the greater part of the land now comprised in the states of Alabama and Mississippi. The price, less than a cent and a half per acre, was absurdly low, and the act was passed under conditions of notorious corruption. The indignant citizenry rose up in protest, and the next legislature promptly rescinded the action. Sobered and ashamed, the officials of the state acquiesced in the action of Congress in creating the Mississippi Territory, while not yet surrendering the claims of Georgia, and then they negotiated with the federal government a settlement of the long-standing dispute. This was effected in 1802, the boundaries of Georgia being then drawn as they are today and the state being granted $1.25 million. One of the provisions of this settlement, by which the federal government agreed to extinguish as soon as possible the Indian titles within the state, was the occasion of much subsequent controversy. The Georgians afterward claimed that the process of abolishing Indian titles and opening the way to settlers proceeded more rapidly in the ceded territory than in Georgia itself. Not until the presidency of Andrew Jackson were the Indians expelled from Georgia, which, by accident of circumstances, retained certain frontier characteristics considerably longer than younger states like Kentucky and Tennessee.

The episode has significance in later constitutional history, for claimants to land titles in Mississippi Territory, on the basis of purchases from the defunct companies before the rescinding of the Yazoo Act, continued to besiege the federal courts. In the case of Fletcher vs. Peck (1810) Chief Justice Marshall upheld the sanctity of the contract, regardless of the corruption and the later rescinding action. In order to meet this legal situation, Congress (1814) voted $5 million to reimburse the purchasers. Marshall had taught a hard lesson in responsibility to voters and legislators while giving assurance to businessmen that henceforth a legislative grant would be deemed as binding as a contract between private parties.

THE LOUISIANA PURCHASE

The Spanish, who had received Louisiana from the French as a reward for their services in the Seven Years' War and had been in possession for a generation, found the province a financial burden and recognized that their own tenure was precarious. As American settlement continued to grow along the western waters, hardy frontiersmen might surge down the great river and take over the port of New Orleans. Also, in the changing pattern of international affairs there was always the possibility that the Americans would team up with the British, from whom the Spanish, in the settlement after the American Revolution, had repossessed themselves of the Floridas. Thus the Spanish Court was not averse to the suggestion that they return Louisiana to the French, who would be much better able to hold it. That was just the reason why the prospective transfer aroused alarm in the minds of American leaders. Far from being a declining power, France was the most powerful and aggressive nation in the world.

The Treaty of San Ildefonso, whereby Louisiana was retroceded by Spain to France, in return for a duchy on the banks of the Italian River Arno to be provided for the Duke of Parma, son-in-law of the Spanish King, was signed on October 1, 1800, but the transfer was delayed for several years and the agreement was not officially announced. In 1801, rumors of the retrocession became persistent. Robert R. Livingston, the new minister to France who sailed in October, was instructed to do his utmost to prevent the cession if it had not occurred and to preserve the free navigation of the Mississippi in any case. He was also to inquire into possibilities of the purchase of the Floridas.

It was the land east not west of the Mississippi that the administration was interested in, and Jefferson himself described the situation vividly and concisely in a letter to Livingston. He believed that the cession by Spain to France included Florida as well as Louisiana and that the crisis created by it would require a complete reversal of his own preferred foreign policy. Hitherto this had been guided by the conviction that France was the natural friend of the United States, whereas Great Britain was a natural rival and at times even an enemy.

> There is on the globe one single spot, [he said] the possessor of which is our natural and habitual enemy. It is New Orleans, through which the produce of three-eighths of our territory must pass to market, and from its fertility it will ere long yield more than half of our whole produce and contain more than half of our inhabitants. France placing herself in that door assumes to us the attitude of defiance. . . . The day that France takes possession of N. Orleans fixes the sentence which is to restrain her forever within her low water mark. It seals the union of two nations who in conjunction can maintain exclusive possession of the ocean. From that moment we must marry ourselves to the British fleet and nation. (April 18, 1802)

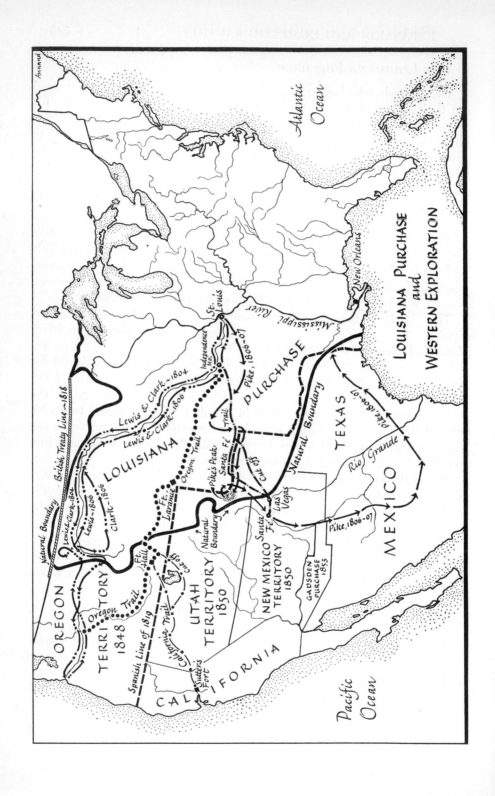

LOUISIANA PURCHASE and WESTERN EXPLORATION

Later in the same year (October 16, 1802) the Spanish Intendant, still in authority in Louisiana, announced the closure of the Mississippi. This action was not owing to the French, but most Americans thought it was and it seemed to mark the realization of their worst fears. Early in 1803 there was bellicose talk in Congress, and soon thereafter James Monroe was sent to France as a special minister to reinforce Livingston. He was authorized to offer $10 million for New Orleans and West Florida, but before he got to France Livingston had been offered the whole province of Louisiana. The famous bargain was concluded by him and Monroe. The cost went 50 per cent beyond instructions, since it came to $15 million including claims, and there was considerable uncertainty as to just what the Americans had purchased. But it was a noble bargain by any reckoning and the real question has always been, why Napoleon offered it, thus relieving President Jefferson of the necessity of "marrying the British fleet and nation."

Napoleon's larger plan to restore the French colonial empire had included the acquisition of Florida, but his blandishments were unavailing in this regard and the Spanish Court would not yield. In the meantime a disaster had befallen him in Santo Domingo. That highly profitable sugar island was central in the colonial scheme, and a major step in the Napoleonic program had been the putting down of the rebellion of the noted Negro leader, Toussaint Louverture. Louverture was captured by Napoleon's brother-in-law, General Leclerc, but the latter and his army were destroyed by the rebellious Negroes and by yellow fever. The death of Leclerc was known in Paris in January 1803, and Napoleon is then reported to have said, "Damn sugar, damn coffee, damn colonies." By this time the conqueror of the continent of Europe had had enough of this distant overseas venture.

If he was to renew his duel with the British, he wanted no rupture with the United States, and American resentment at the closing of the Mississippi by the Spanish Intendant had given him fair warning. What, then, should he do with Louisiana? By selling it to the United States he could at least get some money out of it; and, what was more important, he could check the growing rapprochement between the Americans and the British, and create for his hated enemy a powerful future rival. This reversion to the earlier French foreign policy of Vergennes was not without important fruitage in his own time. When the United States finally became involved in the European struggle in the War of 1812 it was as an opponent of Great Britain. The immediate gain of Napoleon was slight. The money acquired by the transaction was actually spent in preparations for the abortive invasion of England. But he did something to restore the balance of power, and the United States was the major beneficiary of his action.

Questions and Consequences

The predominant contemporary opinion was that the acquisition of Louisiana, by treaty with France, was the most fortunate event in American history after the adoption of the Declaration of Independence and the Constitution. But the transaction aroused grave constitutional questions. In the Constitution there is no specific grant of power to acquire territory, and Jefferson, who much preferred a safe and precise construction to one that was dangerous and indefinite, suffered many qualms. While convinced that ratification of the treaty was imperative and that delay would be perilous in dealing with as shifty a ruler as Napoleon, he would have preferred that official sanction for this unexampled action should be given in the form of a constitutional amendment. His friends and advisers, Gallatin in particular, did not share his scruples and he yielded to them, trusting that the good sense of the country would correct the possible future ills resulting from this precedent. He may be praised for political realism even if blamed for theoretical inconsistency. Certain Federalist leaders, who now advanced arguments of strict construction against the treaty, were fully as inconsistent as he.

The chief argument was not so much over the power of the government to acquire territory as over the incorporation of new territory in the Union, and the speedy admission of the inhabitants to the rights of citizenship, as provided for in one article of the treaty. Opposition to this was based primarily on political and sectional grounds. A few went so far as to urge that the acquired territories of the United States be held in a dependent status and comprise a sort of colonial domain, but the New England Federalists were chiefly motivated by fear lest, in an expanding Union, their own position would become increasingly subordinate. Fisher Ames of Massachusetts, though he could not bring himself to accept extreme strict construction, was alarmed by this huge addition of territory, saying "we rush like a comet into infinite space." Jefferson himself was not disposed to hurry the peopling of the trans-Mississippi region. He would have been content to leave most of it as an Indian sanctuary for the present, transferring to it the tribes still east of the Mississippi. But the doubling of the size of the United States threatened an ultimate change in the character of the Union, and it is no wonder that some of the Easterners were frightened.

Despite all these forebodings, enthusiasm for the treaty was so great that its ratification was inevitable. The power of the federal government to acquire territory, either by conquest or treaty, was affirmed by Chief Justice Marshall in 1828 (American Insurance Company vs. Canter), thus setting to rest for all time that question. The incorporation of this territory assured the future material greatness of the United States, but the great controversy over the extension of slavery came to a head in this region. It is one of the ironies of history that, in the end, the greatest difficulties arising from the enlargement of the Union came not to New England but to the South. It would be an exaggeration to say that the new Empire for Liberty inflicted a death blow on the doctrine of strict construction, for that doctrine was by no means dead. It would be nearer the truth to say that it made inevitable the triumph of the nationalist spirit, the eventual victory of the North, and the abolition of slavery. All that lay in the future. At the time the brilliance of the diplomatic achievement silenced the voice of fear almost everywhere and brought the President to the height of his popularity.

Another set of problems arose from the uncertainties about the boundaries of the purchase. In the treaty the province of Louisiana was described as having "the extent that it now has in the hands of Spain, and that it had when France possessed it." Napoleon made the sale before the property was turned over to him, and it had actually been in the hands of the French only a few days when they transferred it to the United States. Most modern scholars interpret the wording of the treaty as meaning that the territory acquired by the United States east of the Mississippi included only the island of New Orleans and the swamps below it, agreeing with the Spanish contention that West Florida began at the Iberville River. The western boundary of Louisiana was not yet defined, and when eventually drawn (1819) it excluded Texas, but the province included the valley of the Missouri and extended westward to the Rockies.

In view of the original American purpose to get land east rather than west of the Mississippi, perhaps it is not surprising that the envoys, taking advantage of the vagueness of the description of the territory, persuaded themselves that it really included the part of West Florida that had been administered by the Spanish in conjunction with Louisiana. There was practical reason for this rationalization since this district cut off the Mississippi Territory from New Orleans, which the Americans could approach only by the river. Livingston soon claimed that the eastern boundary was really the Perdido River, where the present state of Florida begins, and his interpretation proved irresistible. It was elaborated by Monroe in a memoir, taken up by Jefferson, and accepted as the official position. Certain provisions of the Mobile Act of 1804 were based on these territorial assumptions, but under the force of Spanish protests the administration backed down, and then dispatched Monroe to Spain on what proved to be a futile mission. Despite cajoleries and threats, Jefferson was unable to convince or overawe the Spanish and the disputed region remained nominally in their hands until Madison's presidency, when it was seized. American settlers had overrun parts of it by that time. The present state of Florida was acquired by treaty a little later (1819).

Exploring the Inland Empire, 1803-1807

The desire of the administration to possess the Gulf Coast arose from immediate considerations of commerce and national safety. The uses of the vast trans-Mississippi region north of the present state of Louisiana lay in a more distant future. Yet Jefferson had long been eager to learn more about this unknown country and, several months before it was ceded to the United States, he gained from Congress secret authority for a small expedition to explore the Missouri River "even to the Western Ocean." To head this he appointed his secretary, Captain Meriwether Lewis, a native of Jefferson's home county who had long panted to do this sort of thing. Lewis chose as his associate William Clark, recently a lieutenant in the army but called "captain" on this expedition. He was a younger brother of George Rogers Clark and was known among the Indians as "Red Head." By the time the expedition actually started up the Missouri in the spring of 1804, Louisiana was unquestionably American, hence the camouflage with which the President had originally obscured the project had become unnecessary.

Jefferson believed that the Missouri, with possibly a single portage to the headwaters of the Columbia, offered a better line of navigation from the Pacific Northwest than the one the British followed in the frozen North. He wanted to open up new routes for traffic with the Indians and hoped to tap the fur trade, but his specific instructions to the explorers show his great concern for the expansion of knowledge about his country and continent. He asked suggestions about scientific objects from leading members of the American Philosophical Society, and had Lewis visit some of them. The main object was to explore and chart the waterways, but the Indians, the soil and face of the country, the flora and fauna, the mineral resources and climate—all these were to be observed.

The story of the Lewis and Clark expedition comprises one of the most exciting, heroic, and significant episodes in the saga of western exploration. The leaders had been instructed to be friendly toward the natives, and the only serious skirmish was on the way back. This was peaceful penetration. After Lewis had spent the winter of 1803-1804 on the Illinois side of the Mississippi near St. Louis, he was joined by Clark at St. Charles, a little to the west. Then, proceeding up the river, they came to the Mandan region in what is now North Dakota in the fall and spent the winter in the fort they built there. In the spring of 1805, they were guided to the end of navigation by a French Canadian and his Indian wife, Sacagawea, carrying her infant strapped on her back. This woman of the Shoshones, who secured from relatives the horses on which the white men crossed the continental divide, rendered services which have been honored by more memorials, it is said, than have been erected to any other American of her sex. Coming at length into the Clearwater Valley, the explorers floated down the Columbia to the sea, which they reached in November 1805. They built Fort Clatsop near Astoria, spent the winter there, and started back for the East in the spring of 1806, arriving at St. Louis in September. The party divided on the return trip and thus explored additional tributaries of the Missouri.

Jefferson received "with unspeakable joy" the news of the arrival at St. Louis. The expedition had not shown that the line of the Missouri provided as easy access to the far Northwest as he had thought, and the details of geographical and other scientific information which the explorers had set down were not immediately available, since the history of the expedition was not published until 1814 and the journals remained in manuscript for generations. But time has heavily underlined the President's quiet statement that Lewis and Clark and their brave companions by their arduous service deserved well of their country.

Other expeditions of the time were less successful. A couple of attempts to explore the Red River to its source in what is now the Panhandle of Texas failed because of Spanish opposition. Lieutenant Zebulon M. Pike did not really get to the source of the Mississippi on his expedition of 1805-1806, though at the time both he and the President thought he did. He made a more famous expedition in 1806-1807, from St. Louis to the Colorado country, where his name survives in Pike's Peak. Besides exploring the upper reaches of the Arkansas, he descended the Rio Grande, became a captive of the Spanish at Santa Fé, and finally got back to the United States through northern Mexico and Texas. Jefferson fathered all these explorations, gaining Congressional support for them. Exploration died down after Pike's Colorado expedition, partly because of the absorption of the public mind in foreign questions.

FACTION AND CONSPIRACY, 1804-1807

The Louisiana Purchase served to check separatist tendencies among Westerners by giving them an assured outlet for their produce, but it seemed to many Federalist leaders that this immense accession of territory had upset the balance of power between the North and South, increased the "overbearing influence" of Virginia, and threatened to make the West dominant in the future. They were slow to perceive the import of the vast northern reaches of the new domain, which were destined to strengthen the position in the Union of the northern system of family farms, and they feared the political complexion of such new states as would be carved out of the northwestern wilderness and prairie.

These fears continued to be most pronounced in New England. It seemed that Jefferson and his minions were creating a new national geography and politics to convert the land of the Puritans into a peninsula remote from the center of the country and excluded from the national councils. Thus the minds of the high priests of New England Federalism turned to the idea of a separate northern confederacy.

Toward the end of 1803, Senator Timothy Pickering of Massachusetts, writing privately, made a grave prediction: "There will be—and our children at farthest will see it—a separation." Early in 1804 he and other conspirators were seeking to hasten the day. Among these were Congressman Roger Griswold and Senator Uriah Tracy of Connecticut, and Senator William Plumer of New Hampshire. Disunionist spirit was weak among the rank and file, however, and the Sage of New England Federalism, George Cabot of Massachusetts, believed that separation would be impracticable until there was a stronger and more flagrant cause—such as a war with the British, "manifestly provoked by our masters." He believed that democracy would proceed from bad to worse, until intolerable ills would generate their own remedies. This was essentially the position of Hamilton, now in private life in New York, who grew even more alarmed when the conspirators turned to that "Mephistopheles of politics," Aaron Burr. They felt they had to, because of the centrality of his state in a future northern confederacy, and if he did not definitely agree to their plans they were disposed to rely on his vague assurances.

Burr and Hamilton

Vice-President Burr had become a man without a party. The attempt to defeat the will of the Republicans by electing him as President instead of Jefferson in 1801 had not been forgotten or forgiven; he had been ignored in the distribution of patronage in New York; and he was wholly out of favor with the dominant Clintons and Livingstons in his own state. Nonetheless, he aspired to the governorship and was put forward for it by a caucus of his friends in February 1804, just a week before he was dropped as a vice-presidential candidate in favor of Governor George Clinton. He got a great deal of Federalist support in the final voting, but Hamilton had prevented his formal endorsement by the leaders and he lost the election. Hamilton had no intention of letting Burr become the recognized leader of the northern Federalists. Besides personal motives there were public ones. He regarded Burr as a dangerous man, not fit to be entrusted with high office, and held "a still more despicable opinion of him." These comments got into a letter written by another, and this letter got into print. They were the occasion of the most famous duel in the history of the Republic.

Burr's not unnatural demand for a retraction was handled badly by Hamilton. His reply was evasive and its closing words practically invited the challenge which eventually came, despite a belated statement that his remarks were political not personal. There was a romantic streak in Hamilton and he was highly sensitive about his own honor. Also, he believed that his political hopes would be forever dashed if he now appeared before the public as a coward. He was intrepid in spirit and, at last, he had to pay the costs of recklessness. He stated that he intended to reserve his first fire and perhaps he had some thought that his antagonist might pause and reflect, but Burr was in dead earnest.

Early in the morning of July 11, 1804, Hamilton and Burr with their seconds and Dr. David Hosack crossed the Hudson from Manhattan to a spot under the Palisades at Weehawken in New Jersey. When the moment came, two shots rang out. Whether or not Hamilton's was unintentional, as he and his second claimed, it was harmless, while Burr's inflicted a mortal wound. Hamilton died after hours of agony. His funeral was accompanied by minute guns which were answered by foreign warships in New York harbor, and even followers of Aaron Burr now did him honor. The excesses which had marred his genius and hastened his end were forgotten. Friends rallied to the support of his impoverished family. He had gained no personal advantage from the huge financial operations he had carried on, and he died in virtual bankruptcy. It was power he had craved, not money.

Appalled by the fate of the most brilliant of the Federalists, though his counsel had been heeded little in recent years, the New England conspirators abandoned Burr. In effect they adopted Cabot's policy of waiting for a time of trouble before assailing the Union. This came in 1812 during "Mr. Madison's War." Burr meanwhile found New York and New Jersey too hot for him, but nothing ever came of his indictment for murder and he served out the remaining months of his term as Vice-President, presiding with notable impartiality over the impeachment trial of Justice Chase and delivering, on March 2, 1805, a moving valedictory. He had begun to weave a web of intrigue which confounded the administration and has never ceased to fascinate and baffle the historians. In the next two years he appeared more than ever as an adventurer, and he was looking to the great West as the orbit in which his star would yet rise to glory. Also, he looked to foreign powers, making proposals to the British and the Spanish and seeking money from both of them.

Burr's Expedition and Trial

Perhaps no one will ever know precisely what this brilliant and reckless man was planning during that last winter in Washington and during the two trips to the West that he made in 1805 and 1806-1807. Was he trying to promote the secession of the western states with British and Spanish aid? If so, he did not pick an appropriate time, since the worst fears of the Westerners had been calmed by the Louisiana Purchase. Was he planning an attack on Mexico, which might or might not have as its first step the seizure of New Orleans? There was plenty of anti-Spanish feeling in the West, but he could hardly have expected the Spanish themselves to aid him in his efforts to exploit it. Was he merely interested in establishing a settlement on the Washita River in Louisiana Territory, as he stated publicly? The project of a settlement appears to have been a blind to more ambitious plans, the precise de-development of which was contingent on circumstances. Burr seems to have dreamed, at least, of a new empire stretching from the Ohio to Panama, which he should rule as emperor; and his apparent intention was to do whatever he could get away with.

While he was still in office Burr contrived to make President Jefferson himself unwittingly serve his interests by extending the functions of his chief fellow conspirator, General James Wilkinson, to include the governorship of Louisiana. Jefferson was unsuspicious of Wilkinson, though we now know that for years that grand rascal had taken pay from the King of Spain while commanding the American army in the West. Adventurous frontiersmen like Andrew Jackson, whom Burr visited in Tennessee, were charmed by the elegant Eastern duelist. The vague prospects of conquest which Burr held out were alluring to many volatile Westerners, and he himself appears to have been deluded by the enthusiasm which he evoked. His wealthiest adherent was Herman Blennerhasset, an Irish exile who had set up a feudal domain on an island in the Ohio River near Marietta. There the expedition started which Burr himself joined at the mouth of the Cumberland and recruits were picked up as they went along. In the winter of 1806-1807, Burr and some sixty followers dropped down the Ohio and the Mississippi in flatboats on one of the wildest enterprises of the wild West's history.

Federal District Attorney Joseph Daveiss of Kentucky had tried to obtain an indictment against Burr for raising armed forces to break up the Union and wage war against Spain, but successive grand juries had cleared him. Though informed by Daveiss of Burr's highly sus-picious activities, President Jefferson was strangely quiescent until the traitorous Wilkinson double-crossed his fellow conspirator. On receipt of Wilkinson's message, charging that Burr designed a descent on Mexico and auxiliary revolt of the Orleans territory, Jefferson issued (November 27, 1806) a proclamation which led to the arrest of Burr. After clearing himself before another grand jury in Mississippi Territory, he fled toward Mobile but was apprehended. On March 30, 1807, he was brought before Chief Justice Marshall in Richmond, Virginia.

Burr's trial, which began in May 1807 and lasted into September, excited much attention at the time because of its political implications, and it also had great constitutional significance. In fact, it was the most important judicial proceeding against treason in American national history. The ironies of the situation were extreme. The Chief Justice of the United States presided over the Circuit Court in the Virginia state capitol. A couple of years earlier Vice-President Burr had himself presided over the impeachment trial of a Justice of the United States Supreme Court. Now the President publicly declared that Burr's guilt was beyond doubt and did everything in his power to procure the conviction of his former colleague. John Marshall, on the other hand, was a bitter political foe of Jefferson and eager to discredit him. The trial amounted to a political duel between the absent President and the adroit and persuasive Burr, who headed his own counsel; it also amounted to a duel between the Chief Executive and the Chief Justice.

The degree to which political partisanship entered into Marshall's rulings is a matter of opinion, but undoubtedly he made conviction impossible by his rigid interpretation of the constitutional definition of treason—"levying war against the United States or adhering to their enemies, giving them aid and comfort"—and of the constitutional requirement of "two witnesses to the same overt act." Rejecting the common-law doctrine which he seems to have accepted previously, Marshall ruled that the procurer of treason was not a traitor unless he had participated personally in the overt act—in this case the assemblage at Blennerhasset's Island. There seemed little doubt of Burr's responsibility for this assemblage, but even if it were shown to be treasonable he was not physically present at that place on the specified date. Hedged about with Marshall's strict instructions, the jury returned their verdict that Burr was not proved guilty by the evidence submitted to them. From the point of view of the prosecution and the President the trial was a fiasco, but it created a precedent against any loose interpretation of treason for political purposes and for the protection of the individual against any easy charge of this capital crime. This strict construction and emphasis on individual rights by Marshall was in the Jeffersonian tradition. His pronouncements in the Burr trial are a main reason why the United States government has so rarely brought charges of treason against citizens and has turned to the milder charge of sedition, even in wartime, to protect itself against subversion and internal enemies.

These events strengthened the position of the judiciary as the safeguard and recourse of persons subjected to possible executive persecution. Marshall issued a subpoena requiring President Jefferson to present certain documents bearing on the case; but this effort, which carried with it dangerous implications of judicial supremacy and executive subservience, was defeated. Jefferson ignored the subpoena, though he sent documents to the District Attorney. His action established a valuable precedent that the President is not subject to court proceedings short of the constitutional provision of impeachment.

Burr and his associates went scot free but he was disgraced. He fled in disguise from angry mobs to Europe and spent most of his remaining years in exile. Unfortunately, the spirit of separatism which he had thought to exploit did not wholly vanish from the country with him. Within a decade it showed itself again among the Federalists in New England.

The Navy and the Barbary Pirates

Part of the continuing grievance of influential New Englanders against the President arose from the belief that he was indifferent to their sea-going commerce and to the Navy which was supposed to protect it. The extent of the Navy, said Jefferson to John Adams long afterward, "must be governed by circumstances." Since he came into office as an advocate of economy and the European wars were approaching a lull, circumstances were unfavorable to a continued development of the Navy along the lines that John Adams and Secretary Benjamin Stoddert had laid down. The new policy was determined, not by the new Secretary, Robert Smith of Maryland, but by the President and the Secretary of the Treasury.

Gallatin had been a major critic of Federalist naval policy. In Congress he had said: "I had conceived it would have been our object to have become a happy and not a powerful nation, or at least noway powerful except for self-defence." He was not concerned to develop an instrument of national power and, like Jefferson, he had a passion for economy and peace. His protesting voice had been drowned by the clamor which the naval warfare with France had aroused in 1798, but now his influence was determinative. During the last year of the Adams administration more than $3 million had been appropriated for the Navy alone. Gallatin wanted to keep the entire expenditure of the government below that figure, leaving more than twice that sum for the reduction of the national debt. In the year 1802, expenditures for the Navy fell below a million dollars, but the economy policy had to be modified to some degree soon after that because of trouble with the Barbary powers in the Mediterranean.

These piratical states—Algeria, Tripoli, Tunis, and Morocco—had long been a scourge of commerce, and the young American government had fallen into the prevailing practice of buying them off. The Treaty of 1795 with Algeria not only called for the costly ransom of American prisoners, but even for the payment of annual tribute. The latter feature of this treaty made it unique in the history of American relations with other countries. The treaty with Tripoli about a year later was less costly but by means of it, also, the United States bought an uncertain peace. This cost about $107,000, whereas the one with Algeria cost $642,000, besides the provision for annual tribute in the form of naval stores. The Pasha of Tripoli, disgruntled that he had not gained more, repudiated the treaty in February 1801 and demanded a large flat payment and tribute. In May, he declared war, chopping down the flagstaff at the American consulate. The Pasha misunderstood the new American President, however, for Jefferson's pacific intentions had never extended to the Barbary pirates. Throughout his public career he had taken the position that payments to these brigands of the sea were futile, and that they understood no language but that of force. He ordered Commodore Richard Dale to the Mediterranean, and that officer proceeded to blockade Tripoli. These actions constituted an interference with Morocco also, and its Sultan declared war in the summer of 1802. This trouble was short-lived, however. Commodore Edward Preble was sent to the Mediterranean with another squadron and the Sultan decided to renew the Treaty of 1786 without change.

The Tripolitan War

The war with Tripoli continued. It was marked by sad mishaps, the chief of which was the grounding of the frigate *Philadelphia* and the capture of Captain Bainbridge and his crew (October 31, 1803). They were held prisoners for more than a year and a half, and were deeply chagrined when the Tripolitans salvaged the abandoned vessel. The later destruction of the *Philadelphia* by Americans under the leadership of Stephen Decatur (February 16, 1804) was the most spectacular feat of the war. Direct assaults on Tripoli failed, and the naval blockade was the most effective operation. It was directed at first by Preble and afterwards by Samuel Barron. Another spectacular American enterprise was carried out under the leadership of William Eaton, consul at Tunis, who got hold of Hamet, elder brother of the Pasha and a claimant to the throne, and marched across the Libyan desert and captured Derne (April 1805). Eaton was bitter when Tobias Lear, consul-general at Algiers, negotiated a treaty with the Pasha.

Agreed to on June 4, 1805, this was favorable, as treaties with the Barbary states went. The United States paid $60,000 on the exchange of prisoners and this amounted to ransom; tribute was not mentioned but in practice each new consul made a present according to ancient custom. The Pasha had granted better terms than to any other nation and had promised to protect American rights in the future. The Bey of Tunis made peace about the same time. Trouble with Algeria flared up in 1807 but simmered down, and it was clear that the United States had taken the lead among the nations against the practice of tribute and ransom and had succeeded in curtailing it. After the War of 1812 the United States finally settled matters. The treaty with Algeria that was concluded in the summer of 1815 completely abolished ransom and tribute, and in the following years of peace the practice ceased.

The story of the Barbary Wars contains rich materials for comic opera, but they served as a training school for the Navy. One of their bad immediate effects lay in the fact that, when they were over, Jefferson's enthusiasm turned to gunboats, which had proved useful in the shallow waters off North Africa. These would serve to defend American harbors, he believed. Through the years all manner of fun has been poked at Jefferson's gunboats. These were generally about 50 feet long, fitted with oars and sails, armed with one or two small cannon, and manned by crews of twenty or more. In the year 1807, the bulk of the naval appropriations went to gunboats, which could not possibly protect commerce on the high seas and had no purpose except that of protection against actual invasion. But this policy of the landlubber President, besides having the merit of relative inexpensiveness, was part of his larger policy of passive resistance coupled with economic coercion, and it must be judged as a phase of that. Naval force had to be used against the piratical Tripolitans, but in his opinion the struggle for naval power against the great warring nations of Europe was hopeless, and the ultimate salvation of American commerce lay in keeping it at home for a time. He sought to use it as a weapon of coercion by withholding it from countries which, he believed, could not do without it.

The Embargo

The embargo of 1807-1809 may be described in modern terms as a unilateral attempt to secure redress of grievances, without recourse to war, by imposing "economic sanctions" on offending nations. It failed to its immediate purpose to force the fiercely contending European powers to respect American rights, and it brought Jefferson to a nadir of unpopularity at home. Given the circumstances of American weakness on the one hand and the strength and desperation of the British and French on the other, the chance of the success of this daring experiment in statecraft may seem to have been slight. Furthermore, the philosopher President failed to anticipate the unwillingness of many Americans, especially those dependent on foreign trade, to sacrifice short-term gains for the sake of a noble goal and a larger national purpose. Thus the embargo reveals Jefferson at the highest point of his idealism and the lowest point of his political realism.

As the responsible head of a neutral country in a time of international conflict he faced dread alternatives. Submission to the infringements on

American rights seemed intolerable; diplomacy had failed; and war, for which the country was unprepared, would have thrown the weight of the United States on the French side, since the British monarchs of the sea were the chief offenders against American rights and interests. Ostensibly, economic sanctions were directed against both the rival powers and fell within the historic pattern of American neutrality. Jefferson deserves credit for his attempt to find an alternative between war and submission, and if the course of events served to align the United States against the British in the world conflict this was not because he liked Napoleon.

That wily ruler had dropped Louisiana into the American lap in order to remove a motive for the United States to join Great Britain when France renewed her attack. Futhermore, he hoped to bring the United States as a friendly neutral into French service and thus revive the policy of Vergennes and Genêt. During the first stage of the Napoleonic Wars, from 1803 to 1805, American shipping and trade thrived and neither belligerent interfered with them. The United States owned the largest neutral merchant marine. This grew still larger as American owners took over the trade with many British markets and sold food-stuffs to the continent and to colonies at high prices. It was no favoritism towards France that led American businessmen to help Napoleon, but the British understandably came to regard the United States as a virtual ally of that tyrant.

Tribulations of a Neutral

The British Navy swept the French and Spanish merchant marines from the seas, therefore France and Spain permitted American ships to engage in the trade with their West Indian possessions which was ordinarily forbidden to foreigners. Britain invoked her "Rule of 1756," that trade forbidden in peace could not be legalized in war, but American shippers ingeniously evaded this by carrying West Indian cargoes to American ports where duties were paid and the cargoes put ashore, thus "Americanizing" them; then the cargoes were reloaded, most or all of the duties were repaid to the owners, and the cargoes were carried to Europe. At first the British Admiralty Courts consented to this device of the "broken voyage," but as the aggressive Yankee skippers threatened to nullify British naval supremacy by performing all the services of the vanquished French and Spanish merchant marines, British shippers bitterly complained that the broken-voyage farce amounted to economic warfare against Britain. In July 1805, a British Admiralty court in the famous *Essex* decision declared that only payment of a bona-fide duty, without rebates, could actually "break" a voyage and "Americanize" cargoes in an American port between the West Indies and Europe.

Under this decision the British Navy immediately seized and confiscated dozens of American vessels. British warships were stationed close off American ports. In exercising their unquestioned right to stop and their claimed right to search neutral ships to determine the nature, source, and destination of cargoes, the British acted with extreme contempt for American sensibilities and delayed many ships carrying innocent cargoes by sending them to Halifax under suspicion. Numerous incidents of insult and injury irritated American pride and raised a fearful popular clamor in addition to the wails of businessmen against the *Essex* decision.

Worst of all was the British practice of impressment. A basic reason for this practice was the superior living and working conditions of sailors on American ships as compared with the vicious cat-o'-nine-tails and rotten food meted out to sailors on British vessels. Naturally many British tars deserted and enlisted for service in Yankee ships. In the desperate war against Napoleon the British government continued the age-old practice of sending press gangs through the British Isles and to sea to force men into service. It did not claim the right to impress any but British subjects, but it followed the principle of *jus sanguinis*, that blood determined nationality: "Once an Englishman, always an Englishman!" The United States, on the other hand, with its greater respect for individual rights and its need for immigrants, supported the principle of *jus solis*, that place of residence might determine nationality, that anyone might become an American citizen by residence and desire. In practice a British sailor who deserted his "floating hell" in an American port could obtain citizenship papers in about five minutes and sign up on an American ship in five minutes more. Then the United States government was bound to defend him as entitled to all the protection of the stars and stripes.

At sea British impressment officers would stop any American ship, go aboard and require the crew to line up on deck for inspection. They paid no attention to papers but usually judged a man's nationality by his accent—a peculiarly misleading test. Sometimes, when the need for men was desperate, the British used no test whatever except health and strength. The Department of State argued that the American flag protected against impressment not only American citizens, including ex-Britons who had naturalization papers, but foreigners who did not even claim American citizenship. Thus the positions of the two governments were irreconcilable. Perhaps no foreign offense against the United States before or since has stirred American anger more deeply than impressment, which seemed to deny the very right of a man to be an American, and to claim the right to condemn to British slavery anyone at all who sailed under the American flag. This was an offense not against property but against persons.

Britain as well as France was dependent on American shipping and supplies for her war effort. In order to buy in the United States, the British had to sell their own products here. In April 1806, Jefferson signed a law that authorized him to forbid importation of certain British products. He did not invoke the law but held it as a threat while instructing James Monroe and William Pinkney of Maryland to negotiate a settlement with Great Britain. They were expressly forbidden to sign a treaty that did not include a British agreement to stop impressments. The British government bowed to the threat of nonimportation to the extent of making some concessions regarding West Indian trade and offering to give an informal promise that no bona-fide American citizen would be impressed. Monroe and Pinkney violated their instructions and signed a treaty on the last day of 1806. Jefferson refused to send this treaty to the Senate. Using hindsight, some critics have argued that he should have accepted the Monroe-Pinkney Treaty and thus have avoided worse trouble that was in store. But we cannot ask of statesmen the gift of prophecy. Jefferson had sound reason to reject a treaty which would have amounted to American consent to the British practice of impressment.

The European war had now settled down to a titanic struggle between the sea, where Britain ruled unchallenged after Nelson destroyed the French and Spanish fleets at Trafalgar in October 1805, and the land, where Napoleon a month later at Austerlitz defeated the combined Russian and Austrian armies. Sea power and land power, like the whale and the elephant, could not meet for a decision, so the antagonists resorted to an economic war of attrition. Each side tried to cut off the other from outside trade and defeat its enemy by reducing it to beggary.

The United States, the leading neutral trader, was caught in the vise between the belligerents. In 1806 and 1807, Great Britain issued Orders in Council blockading the European coast and requiring neutral ships to pay English fees and licenses for the privilege of carrying a few noncontraband articles through the blockade, while Napoleon issued decrees imposing a "paper" blockade of the British Isles. Lacking a navy he enforced this by means of privateers, seizing any neutral ship that traded with Britain or even allowed itself to be searched by the British.

Meanwhile, His Majesty's frigate *Leopard* committed a grievous offense against the United States. The British government did not claim the right to board and search American naval vessels, only merchantmen in British waters and on the high seas. But when Vice-Admiral Berkeley, in command of the American station, heard that four British sailors had deserted and enlisted on the American frigate *Chesapeake*, he ordered on his own responsibility that they be taken off the American warship by force the moment that it put to sea. Suspecting nothing and unprepared for action, the *Chesapeake* stood out from Norfolk on June 22, 1807. The *Leopard* stopped the American frigate and asked to search. Commodore Barron refused. The British warship thereupon opened fire at point blank range, killing three and wounding eighteen American seamen. Barron was forced to strike his colors and submit to a boarding party that took off the four deserters.

This unparalleled attack aroused the American people to fury without distinction between Republicans and Federalists. Mobs assaulted Englishmen and called for war. But Jefferson decided merely to use the British offense, which put its government clearly in the wrong, to make Britain abandon impressment altogether. The British government was willing to make reparation for the injury to the *Chesapeake,* but refused at this time because Jefferson coupled reparation with the larger issue. The President, whose passion was peace and who wanted to side with neither of the warring powers, thereupon decided to try economic coercion against both of them. Harking back to the nonimportation, nonexportation, and nonconsumption agreements of the days before 1776, when such measures had won some concessions from the mother country, Jefferson hoped to show the world how a nation might secure its honor and interests without resort to war.

An Experiment that Failed

The noble experiment took the form of the Embargo Act of December 1807, which prohibited the export of almost all articles to any country whatever. Many American merchantmen were abroad when the law went into effect; they never returned home but continued to serve one or another of the warring powers. Other ships got away from American ports before federal agents arrived to detain them. Still others obtained papers permitting them to carry cargoes in American coastal trade and promptly sailed abroad. The ancient art of smuggling was revived, particularly along the land frontier with Canada, where drovers of wagon trains shot down federal agents. Enough American ships and supplies evaded the law to weaken its effects on the belligerents.

At the same time, the embargo was sufficiently effective to create an economic depression in the United States. Luckless ships were tied up, merchants went bankrupt, unemployment was widespread—while profits, prices of farm products, and wages fell to ruinous levels. The industrial revolution in the United States received its chief early impulse from the necessity to manufacture goods formerly imported from Britain, but this compensation for the economic ravages of the embargo was important only for the future.

What Jefferson did not understand was that American businessmen pre-

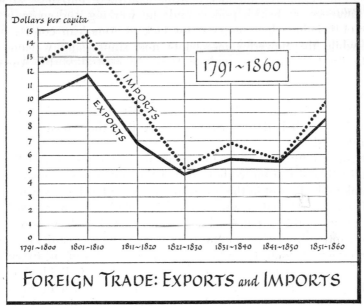

FOREIGN TRADE: EXPORTS and IMPORTS

SOURCE: Department of Commerce.

ferred the British and French injuries to American commerce to the
drastic Jeffersonian cure for them, which they likened to cutting one's
throat to cure a nosebleed. The agricultural President did not understand
that the weird manipulations of businessmen provided their own profitable cure for English and French depredations: losses by seizure of
American cargoes were more than compensated by the wartime rise in
prices for cargoes that evaded capture. Under these conditions sedate
commerce gave way to a wild speculative mania which was amply rewarded if one cargo in three reached a market. Federalists and merchants had been ready for strong measures following the *Chesapeake*
affair, but Jefferson's embargo measure seemed to them craven and
suicidal:

> Our ships all in motion,
> Once whiten'd the ocean;
>   They sail'd and return'd with a Cargo;
> Now doom'd to decay
>   They are fallen a prey,
> To Jefferson, worms, and EMBARGO.

In New England especially there was a revival of Federalism—bitter
and extremist, pro-British, anti-Southern, and anti-democratic. The South
and West, whose farmers suffered from the fall in prices, nevertheless
remained faithful to Jefferson and his experiment. The West Indies and

Newfoundland suffered for lack of American food, but these areas had small influence on British policy, and the working and manufacturing classes of Britain, which suffered for lack of American cotton, had no votes, while the powerful merchants and shipowners welcomed the opportunity to take over markets formerly controlled by Americans. Then the bumper crops of 1808 reduced British need for American food. Napoleon positively welcomed the embargo. It injured Britain more than France and besides, in April 1808, France seized all American ships and cargoes in French harbors on the pretense that they must be disguised British vessels!

Jefferson grimly held on to his policy until depression and the rising Federalist tide of resistance showed that the embargo was unenforceable and intolerable. Except in the loss of life it seemed as bad as war, without any of war's emotional compensations. It called for a negative heroism which proved galling. Jefferson had not expected such a crop of fraud and corruption, and had not foreseen that the successful operation of such a policy of control would require the exercise of arbitrary power by the government and grievous infringements on individual freedom. The "Force Act" of January 1809 was the logical result of the existing circumstances. As Gallatin saw and Jefferson had to admit, the embargo either had to be given up or be assisted by "means as strong as the measure itself." By this final supplementary measure federal collectors were authorized to seize without warrant any goods suspected of foreign destination in violation of the embargo, and these collectors were freed from legal responsibility for their actions.

Ironically, the administration invoked arbitrary powers which it itself recognized as dangerous and odious; and the New England opposition had recourse to arguments such as Jefferson and Madison had used in the Kentucky and Virginia Resolutions when protesting against the tyranny of the Alien and Sedition Acts. Timothy Pickering asked: "How are the powers reserved to the states respectively, or to the people, to be maintained, *but by the respective states judging for themselves and putting their negatives on the usurpations of the federal government?*" At this stage, also, certain New Englanders took a much longer step in the direction of nullification of a federal law than Jefferson and Madison had recommended. Early in 1809, when the Secretary of War asked the Governor of Connecticut to appoint officers of the militia with orders to aid the federal collector in enforcing the embargo, the Governor flatly refused on the ground that this measure was an unconstitutional infringement on the rights of the states, and he was strongly supported by the General Assembly.

On March 1, 1809, Congress repealed the embargo and Jefferson, with three days of his administration remaining, gave in. Thus an experiment which might have matched the Louisiana Purchase as a triumph of

Jeffersonian statecraft, seemed a disastrous failure. Yet war had been and would be avoided for five years; and the eventual repeal of the British Orders in Council, news of which came only a few days after the outbreak of the War of 1812, can be traced in part to Jefferson's policy of economic coercion.

When he left office, the failure of his campaign against the judiciary and of his attempt to find an economic substitute for war temporarily overshadowed his great success in adding an empire to the Union. But it is notable that these failures did not lead the country to return the Federalists to power in the elections of 1808. For sixteen more years the Virginian heirs of Jefferson, James Madison and James Monroe, occupied the White House and the generality of farmers and city folk clung loyally to the party organized by the Sage of Monticello. The majority of Americans recognized that he stood for human liberty and human rights. They forgave him his political failures, scorned his enemies, and revered him as the symbol of the American dream.

CHAPTER 20

The War of 1812

JAMES MADISON, THE FOURTH PRESIDENT OF THE
United States (1809-1817), had been groomed for the succession by his
friend Jefferson. He was a political scientist of great force and originality,
but his public personality was rather colorless. "Little Jemmy" was supported because the Virginians still controlled the loose alliance of southern
planters, western farmers, and northeastern city groups which comprised the Republican Party, and because he was obviously second
only to Jefferson in experience and in service to the party and the nation.
The other member of the triumvirate, Albert Gallatin, remained as Secretary of the Treasury. Madison easily met the challenge of James Monroe
in 1808, and toward the end of his first term (1811) he made his chief
Virginia rival his Secretary of State.

The eight years of this undramatic man in the presidency were more
dramatic than any previous administration. Madison was unfortunate and
seemed inept in his conduct of foreign relations and the second war
against Great Britain; but at least he delayed the outbreak of open conflict, and the failures of the war were characteristic of a young and
sprawling country which relied on crude strength without having achieved
effective military organization or developed habits of military discipline.
Despite blunders and disaffection, things turned out well in the end and
Madison closed his long and distinguished career in a glow of popular
approval. While the Federalist opposition, moving further in the direction of faction and provincialism, became impotent at last, the Republican Party emerged without loss of popular appeal as the nationalist
party. By continuing to identify the administration with expansionism
President Madison associated it with the West and with the future of a
fast-growing country; and, like President Jefferson before him, he thus
escaped from the paralysis of extreme state rights and strict construction.

DRIFTING INTO WAR AT SEA

The repeal of the embargo on March 1, 1809, was merely a sop to domestic discontent because the Nonintercourse Act was immediately substituted. This law re-established the embargo against all ports under British and French control, while freeing Americans to trade with any other ports of the world. Madison carried on the policy of economic coercion, and internal opposition to its modified form was hardly less than to the original embargo.

For a moment it seemed possible that Madison would launch his administration with a great diplomatic success. The friendly British minister, David Erskine, signed an agreement in April 1809 which made more concessions to the United States than his instructions authorized. This Erskine Agreement bound Great Britain to withdraw her Orders in Council against American shipping. As an executive agreement, the arrangement did not require approval by the Senate. Madison, unwisely taking it for granted that Canning would approve, issued a proclamation restoring intercourse with Great Britain, as he was authorized to do under the existing law. Americans were overjoyed. Hundreds of heavy-laden ships set sail for British ports. Then came the news that Canning had rejected the Agreement and recalled Erskine for violating his instructions. Overnight American joy turned to rage—against Britain for seeming perfidy, against the President for allowing himself to be duped. Madison was forced to restore nonintercourse against Britain in August 1809, but the great fleet that had got away relieved shortages in England and spoiled some of the hard-won effects of the embargo.

Anglo-American relations were further embittered by the violently anti-American conduct of Erskine's successor, Francis James ("Copenhagen") Jackson, a man notorious for his brutal treatment of the Danes. After Jackson accused the United States government of lying in the Erskine affair, Secretary of State Robert Smith refused to hold further communication with him. When Jackson's term was up, he went home and Canning refused at the time to appoint another minister.

The new Congress that met in December 1809 decided that nonintercourse, too, was a failure. On May 1, 1810, the Act was repealed by the enactment of what was known as Macon's Bill Number 2. The freeing of American commerce from legal restraint was really to the advantage of the British rather than to that of blockaded France, while the previous restrictive laws had drawn the United States unwittingly into Napoleon's continental system, which was designed to cut off trade with Great Britain. But Congress included in the new law an overly-clever fragment of the old coercive policy. France was promised that if she would withdraw her Decrees and Britain did not withdraw her Orders in Council within the three months following, the United States would restore non-intercourse with Britain. A similar promise, in reverse, was made to Britain.

This scheme to play the great powers against each other was out-witted by Napoleon, a more expert schemer. He had his Foreign Minister, the Duc de Cadore, write a letter to the American minister in France which seemed to withdraw Napoleon's Decrees against American commerce but actually would not do so until the United States should *first* obtain withdrawal of the Orders of the British or alternatively restore nonintercourse against them. The tricky wording of the Cadore Letter trapped Madision. On November 2, 1810, he issued a proclamation that nonintercourse would be restored against Britain if she did not withdraw her Orders within three months. Since there were reports that France was continuing to enforce her Decrees and confiscating American ships, Canning concluded that Madison was determined to range the United States on the French side against Britain and refused to withdraw the Orders. The British bitterly and naturally resented it when Congress on March 2, 1811, restored nonintercourse against their country.

Ten weeks later the American frigate *President* hailed at sea a British corvette, the *Little Belt;* a shot was fired by someone and both ships opened fire. The *President* made short work of the smaller British vessel. Now, too late, the British government sent a conciliatory minister, Augustus Foster, who made proper reparation for the *Chesapeake* affair. Americans were not interested. They were content with the smashing of the *Little Belt* and excited over a western movement for the conquest of Canada and of Florida. They were talking war.

THE WESTERN EXPANSIONISTS

Maritime injuries at the hands of Great Britain probably were not sufficient to create a war fever in the United States. For one thing, the section that suffered most, the Northeast, was most inclined to submit to British rule of the sea, including impressment and abuse of neutral trade, for the sake of residual profits from trade and because sentiment in that section was strongly pro-British and anti-French. Furthermore, French injuries against American trade and, what is often forgotten, French impressment of American seamen, made war against France almost as reasonable as war against Britain, but no one imagined that the young republic could take on Goliath and Samson simultaneously.

Westerners had excellent reason in the Louisiana Purchase for friendliness toward France. They had equally good and traditional reasons for hatred of Great Britain. Even after the British had abandoned the military posts on American soil following Jay's Treaty, they had not given up ambitions to dominate the American Northwest and control the fur trade. By encouraging the Indians' natural opposition to the pioneers who deprived them of their land, Britain hoped to fix bounds beyond which American settlement and power should not expand. The leadership of two Shawnees, Tecumseh and his brother the Prophet, admirably served Britain's purposes. Tecumseh was an extremely intelligent leader who saw that the white men were destroying the Indians' physical and moral health by transmitting diseases, selling whiskey, and undermining tribal religion. At the same time the whites were defeating the Indians piecemeal, tribe by tribe. The Prophet, appealing to racial pride, urged separation from the white man and revival of Indian religion and the Indian way of life. Tecumseh attempted to create a united front of all the tribes along the frontier against the encroaching pioneers. Their joint work was a remarkable effort to overcome the weaknesses and divisions of their people.

Jefferson believed that the Indians should be transformed by benevolent example into farmers who would not need as much land as they did as hunters. But during his administration federal agents speeded up the process of obtaining, by whiskey and treaty, more and more rights to the tribal lands which the deploying settlers coveted. By 1809, the message of Tecumseh and the Prophet destroyed whatever hope existed for Jefferson's agrarian vision of the Indian saved by the white man's civilization, and promised to save him by strengthening him in his own hunting civilization.

Frontiersmen generally believed that the only good Indian was a dead Indian. They were alarmed by the success of Tecumseh's revival which promised to put a stop to time-honored techniques of encroaching on Indian lands. Tecumseh and the Prophet organized a settlement in Indiana where the Tippecanoe River joins the Wabash. There redmen imbibed stern virtues uncannily like those of the white Puritans and declared that no whiskey would seduce, no treaty would dislodge them. William Henry Harrison, governor of Indiana Territory and superintendent of the Northwest Indians, made a treaty with a few unconverted Indians who pretended to have the right to sign away Tecumseh's lands. Tecumseh countered by traveling south of the Ohio to add southern tribes to his confederacy. While he was gone, Harrison with a strong force invaded the Indian country and on November 7, 1811, wiped out the village at Tippecanoe. This "battle" excited the Northwest against the British, who were accused of backing Tecumseh's confederacy with gifts of arms. "On to Canada!" was the somewhat surprising response of the northern pioneers to the news of Tippecanoe.

Pioneers south of the Ohio River were equally alarmed by Tecumseh's plan to unite all the tribes for a stand, and they similarly saw the real enemy not as the Indian but as Spain, whose policy in the American Southwest more or less duplicated Britain's policy in the Northwest.

Spain was weaker than Great Britain, her territory was more loosely held, and by 1811 pieces of it were already falling into American hands. Southwesterners nevertheless clamored that the process of expansion at Spain's expense be speeded up. They hungered for West Florida, the strip of territory from the Apalachicola River to the Mississippi lying south of the 31st parallel. It spanned the mouths of the rivers that drain to the Gulf of Mexico and the present states of Georgia, Alabama, and Mississippi, giving Spain a throttle-hold on the trade of the region, and providing pirates, Indians, and desperadoes with hideouts from which settlements to the north and shipping in the Gulf of Mexico could be harassed.

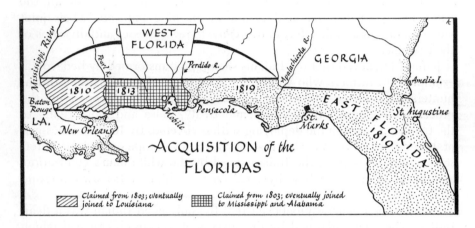

When he left office, Jefferson warned his friends that the United States must have the Floridas and Cuba. Napoleon's invasion of Spain in 1807 improved American chances. Under cover of loyalty to the displaced King Ferdinand, revolutionary juntas took charge of government in Spain's American colonies. The first and greatest of American empires was breaking up because of its inefficiency, corruption, and outmoded tyranny, as well as Napoleon's disruption of the mother country, and many Americans were determined to share in the spoils.

An advance party of American pioneers had already settled in West Florida. They were encouraged by the Madison administration to imitate the Spanish-Americans and revolt. In September 1810 they captured the Spanish fort in the colonial capital, Baton Rouge, tore down the Bourbon lily flag, and raised the flag of the Republic of West Florida containing a lone white star on a blue ground—ultraconvenient for incorporation in the flag of the United States. Then the revolutionaries applied for admission into the Union, offering the inalienable human right of revolution as expressed in the Declaration of 1776 as their legal passport. This part of West Florida was soon joined with Louisiana, which became a state in 1812. This was the first of many attempts to use revolution outside the national boundaries as a means of annexing territory to the Union.

Madison immediately proclaimed the extension of American authority over West Florida as far as the Perdido River, still basing the American claim on the Louisiana Purchase. Spain hung on to Mobile, but her weak forces were thrown out in April 1813. Lacking a force of American rebels in East Florida, Madison encouraged George Mathews, former governor of Georgia, to lead a band of invading American "insurgents" and supported them with gunboats and regular United States troops. Mathews got as far as Saint Augustine on the east coast early in 1812, then he failed and Madison repudiated him.

The Pensacola region of old West Florida and all of East Florida remained in precarious Spanish possession to inflame frontiersmen's longing. War was not declared against Spain, but that country had not, like Great Britain, given justification by maritime injuries. Furthermore, Great Britain was assiduously cultivating revolution in all Spanish America as a means of establishing for herself economic domination and political hegemony in the ancient empire of the Indies. Jefferson and many later American statesmen looked longingly at Cuba because they feared that Britain would get hold of this Gibraltar of the New World. Possession of Florida was the first step necessary to dispel such a nightmare.

In short, the magnificent meal which Jefferson had provided in Louisiana, far from satisfying the appetites of Americans, only whetted them. But if we are inclined to wonder at the gargantuan land hunger of our ancestors, we should reflect that the expansion of American liberty into empty or thinly held lands, in the face of predatory and tyrannical empires, may have been a necessary condition for its very existence.

THE "WAR HAWKS"

Expansionism, with its assertion of executive powers, cost the Jeffersonians the support of a faction which clung to the doctrine of a limited government that the Republicans had emphasized when they were in opposition to the dominant Federalists. Most bitter of these "Old Republicans" was John Randolph of Roanoke, a relative of Jefferson. Brilliant and irritating, Randolph as a member of the House refused to tolerate the devices by which his kinsman and Madison sought to gain West Florida, and extended his opposition to practically every administration measure in which he could detect a pro-French meaning, an imitation of Federalism, or a tendency towards nationalism. Stinging mockery of his fellow Virginians who compromised the old faith, as he understood it, was his chief weapon, but he and his dissident faction were powerless to move Congress. John Taylor of Caroline, chief keeper of the pure Republican doctrine, also went into opposition. But Jefferson and Madison gave the West pretty much what it wanted. Loss of the extreme state-rights faction was more than compensated by the growth of Republicanism in the West, and New England disaffection was considerably neutralized. Thus the Republican Party continued unbeatable as it sought to enlarge the country, gradually assuming the mantle of nationalism which the Federalists had discarded.

In the Congressional elections of 1810, the party won a landslide victory against the Federalists, and aggressive expansionists displaced legislators who had retreated from the costly economic warfare of the embargo to the futility of Macon's Bill No. 2. From the new states of the West and from western sections of eastern states there came to Washington in December 1811 a new generation of "buckskin statesmen," inexperienced but cocksure in their nationalism, their expansionism, and their hatred for "putrescent peace." Great Britain was their chief enemy and they gloried in the name of "War Hawks."

Men like Henry Clay of Kentucky and John C. Calhoun of South Carolina, who would dominate the political life of their sections for the next generation and grow conservative with age, were united in 1812 as belligerent nationalists. Although the War Hawks did not command a majority of the House, they managed to elect Henry Clay as Speaker, and he packed the committees with advocates of war. Fiery patriotism, revenge against Britain for outrages against the personal liberty and dignity of American citizens, contempt for the "decadent" brand of businessman's nationalism in the East, and Western brag about what mincemeat could be made of British power in Canada by a mere "frontiersmen's frolic": these were the themes of War Hawks' oratory and Western newspaper editorials.

The accusation that Clay exacted war as the price of support for Madison's renomination is false. Actually, the two, much as they differed in temperament and tone, were in close agreement on foreign policy by this time. In April 1812, Congress passed and the President signed a bill imposing a ninety-day embargo. This was not so much to renew economic coercion as to stop exports that would be useful to the prospective enemy. Late in May, the British minister conveyed to Madison and Secretary of State Monroe a message from his government which seemed to end all hope that the Orders in Council might be withdrawn. Unwilling to admit that Napoleon, too, had failed to end his restrictions of American trade, Madison on June 1 delivered a message to Congress virtually asking for a declaration of war against Great Britain.

Madison's formal accusations against Great Britain began with impressment, and the emphasis he always laid on this in negotiations shows that it was of prime importance in his own mind. His other main complaint related to the Orders in Council. Only by insinuation did he connect the British with Indian outrages against settlers in the West, and in a public statement he could not avow a desire for Canada and Florida. The House joyously responded to Madison's message by passing a resolution for war on June 4 by a vote of 79 to 49. The Senate, containing a larger Federalist contingent, delayed until June 17 and then passed a war resolution by the vote of 19 to 13. Members of the House and Senate from southern New England and the Middle States, except Pennsylvania, strongly opposed the war. Southern and Western representatives of agricultural interests voted for a war presumably fought to protect maritime interests. But the agricultural regions were the historic champions of personal liberty, their produce gave them a stake in foreign commerce, and they felt the injury of impressment more keenly than the shipowners who could easily hire other sailors to take the places of impressed men. It is impossible to separate out any one motive as *the* dominant factor, but exuberant Western nationalism undoubtedly played an important part in bringing on the war.

Although the President and Congress did not know it, a sudden turn in British policy had already eliminated a major American grievance. An Atlantic cable or radio would have almost certainly delayed and might have prevented war. The re-invocation of nonintercourse by the United States had seriously injured the business of British merchants and manufacturers. Furthermore, the government's decision to send a great expeditionary force to fight Napoleon in Spain had created a sudden need for American food and raw materials. But delays prevented Lord Castlereagh, the Foreign Secretary, from taking action until too late. On June 16, one day before the Senate passed the resolution for war, he announced that the Orders in Council would be immediately suspended in favor of the United States. Thus it may be claimed that the failure in 1812 lay not in the policy of economic coercion, but in impatience and imperfect communication. Castlereagh had removed only one main grievance, however. The problems of impressment and the Indians remained.

The American declaration of war seemed to the British a betrayal and to New England Federalists a crime. Napoleon's campaign to conquer Europe was at its climax: he invaded Russia a week later. The British were desperate and they believed that the cause of freedom in the Old World depended upon the defeat of Napoleon. For the United States to choose this moment to make war against the mother country seemed ignoble, no mere tweaking of John Bull's nose, but a stab in the back when he stood at bay. Many an American echoed the famous toast of Timothy Pickering: "The World's last hope—Britain's fast-anchored isle."

THE WAR ON LAND AND SEA, 1812-1813

British preoccupation with Napoleon made the Anglo-American war a sideshow in which military, naval, and diplomatic developments depended on the course of events in the big European tent. The boast of the

War Hawks that frontiersmen would take Canada and Florida turned out to be a dismal joke. Far from holding the offensive, the United States —on land, at sea, and in the negotiations for peace which began immediately—was thrown violently back on the defensive and had to struggle desperately to prevent utter disaster. In later years, Americans remembered the brilliant victories of their frigates in single-ship actions, although these did not prevent the overwhelmingly superior British Navy from virtually blockading the entire American coast. Also, they recalled the great victory of General Andrew Jackson against British veterans at New Orleans, although it came after peace had been signed at Ghent. But the only area where American victories affected the outcome of the war was on the northern lakes.

Military Failures

As in the Revolution the militia lacked discipline, training, and the will to fight outside their own states or districts. Jefferson, Madison, and Gallatin, fearing a standing army as a potential instrument of tyranny, had deliberately slowed the development of military power under their program of economy. Provision for additional regiments was made in 1808 and again in 1812, but when war broke out the regular army contained fewer than 7000 men, though it had an authorized strength of 35,000. Since young men preferred to serve with their local militia company or as sailors on lucrative voyages on privateers, the regular army could not obtain adequate enlistments. In 1802, President Jefferson had been authorized to establish a small corps of engineers, to be stationed at West Point and constitute a military academy. This was the beginning of the famous institution on the Hudson of which he is deemed the founder, but it was little more than a pioneer school of engineering until 1812. Then it was thoroughly reorganized but this was too late to help in the war. Military leadership in Washington was weak. President Madison had no talent for strategy; Secretary of War William Eustis inspired no confidence and resigned toward the end of 1812, to be followed by half a dozen successors. The ranking major-general, Henry Dearborn, who was placed in command of the Northeast sector, was old and soon showed himself to be incompetent.

General William Hull, the commander in the Northwest, was ordered to invade Upper Canada from Detroit without adequate forces and without regard for British troops and Indian allies in his rear. In July 1812, he entered Canada. The British General Isaac Brock was more competent than any American commander until Andrew Jackson took the field late in the war. In Canada there were about 4000 each of British regulars, Canadian regulars, Canadian militia, and Indian allies. Despite the great disparity of the populations of the United States and Canada, and the service of almost a half million American militiamen during the war, the British were able to defeat the United States on land with ease. They promptly captured Forts Michilimackinac and Dearborn (Chicago) and Brock marched westward from Niagara to Detroit, cutting off Hull, whom he summoned to surrender as an alternative to an Indian massacre. Deserted by some of his militia and cut off, Hull surrendered to Brock on August 16, 1812. The northwestern military frontier of the United States had been pushed back to the Wabash and Ohio rivers.

The crowning disgrace of the militia occurred at Niagara and at Lake Champlain. Captain John E. Wool gallantly led a few regulars across the river at Niagara and captured Queenstown Heights on October 13, 1812, but New York militia refused to follow them. Wool and his band were destroyed in sight of the mutinous New Yorkers. General Dearborn attempted in November to lead a militia force northward from Plattsburg on Lake Champlain towards Lower Canada, but after a few miles his troops also rebelled. Thus collapsed the War Hawks' plan to invade Canada in a frontiersmen's frolic.

In spite of these disasters Madison was re-elected in the fall of 1812. His victory came largely from the South and the West. He won only the frontier state of Vermont in New England, and among the Middle States only Pennsylvania by virtue of its western section. Farmer and artisan groups in New England and the Middle States whose votes Jefferson had won, abandoned Madison in 1812. Disaffection towards "Mr. Madison's War" drove New England Federalists to the edge of treason, and British collusion with them was suggested by failure to extend the blockade to the coast of Massachusetts until the war was almost ended.

Individual Victories at Sea

The gloom induced by military and political developments in the North was mitigated before the end of 1812 by events at sea. The United States possessed no ships-of-the-line (three decks of guns, the "battleships" of sailing navies), while the British had eleven in American waters. Thirty-four British frigates ("cruisers" with two decks of guns) far outnumbered American frigates. But the United States had three, the *Constitution*, the *United States*, and the *President*, which had more guns than the British frigates and more speed, by virtue of a cleaner design, than British ships-of-the-line. More important, the American crews were trained to aim their guns like sharpshooters at specific targets, whereas the British crews fired broadsides like buckshot without much aim. The American crews were volunteers, the officers were veterans of the naval wars against France and Tripoli, and all hands were determined to avenge the *Chesapeake*, while British crews were made up largely of impressed men and their officers were overconfident after the great victories of Nelson. The total

American Navy consisted of sixteen ships against ninety-seven British warships on American station, therefore the tactics of American commanders were to avoid fleet action and use their few ships as raiders in single-ship actions. They won astounding victories. The *Constitution* destroyed the *Guerrière* on August 19, 1812, and the *Java* on December 29. In November 1812, the *United States* forced the *Macedonian* to surrender. The sloop-of-war ("destroyer" with a single deck of guns) *Wasp* overcame the *Frolic,* and the *Hornet* sank the *Peacock* early in 1813.

These glorious victories enabled Americans to forget the disgraceful conduct of the militia, but they had no value beyond their effect upon morale. Most of the American warships, like hundreds of merchantmen, were tied up in port during most of the war. When the luckless *Chesapeake* accepted a British challenge to come out of Boston harbor for single-ship combat, the *Shannon* defeated her. The *President* grounded in trying to run the blockade at New York and was surrendered. The *Essex* after a gallant and successful raiding tour of the Pacific, was destroyed in Chilean waters. American privateers carried the war into European and Far-Eastern waters but their exploits served chiefly to enrich their crews. The United States had no weapons against the British blockade, which strangled American trade and enabled the enemy to invade the eastern seaboard wherever it chose.

Attempts at Negotiation

The War of 1812 might have ended in a few months but for the question of impressment. When the news of the suspension of the Orders in Council finally reached America, Secretary of State Monroe instructed the American *chargé d'affaires* in London to negotiate an armistice. The United States offered as a concession that it would prevent enlistment of British-born seamen in American ships if Britain would stop impressments. Foreign Secretary Castlereagh on August 29 rejected the offer. Next the British tried in Washington to secure an armistice without abandoning impressments, and the American government flatly refused. Britain insisted that impressment was an internal matter involving British subjects and not a question for international negotiation, while the American government insisted that it was a violation of the rights of the United States as a sovereign nation. These irreconcilable attitudes caused the war to drag on for two more years.

Meanwhile, Czar Alexander I of Russia had decided that it was to Russia's interest to end the Anglo-American conflict. The Russian "Holy City" of Moscow was captured by Napoleon in the late summer of 1812, and Alexander feared that the American war would divert the strength of his British ally from the European theaters. Also, Russia needed American trade. Therefore, the Czar proposed to the two governments that he should mediate between them in favor of peace. President Madison received the Russian proposal in March 1813 and welcomed it. By that time dreams of conquering Canada had gone glimmering; Great Britain controlled American territory in the Northwest; Napoleon's army had been destroyed in the winter retreat from Moscow; and if the French were defeated the British would be able to turn their whole weight against the United States. In his eagerness, Madison did not bother to learn whether Britain also would accept mediation. He sent Albert Gallatin and James A. Bayard, a moderate Delaware Federalist, to St. Petersburg to join John Quincy Adams, United States minister to Russia, for the purpose of negotiating there with British envoys.

Unfortunately Lord Castlereagh, suspicious of the Czar's friendliness towards the United States, refused his mediation. Castlereagh in November 1813 proposed, however, that the United States and Britain enter into direct negotiations, and Madison accepted. He ordered the three envoys in St. Petersburg to go to Ghent, Belgium, to meet British commissioners, and he sent Henry Clay and Jonathan Russell, American minister in Stockholm, to join them. Madison shrewdly named representatives of various points of view who could be relied upon to maintain particular interests and these men proved to be skillful diplomats, but they did not confront the British at Ghent until the summer of 1814.

Victory on Lake Erie

The American military situation improved in 1813, chiefly as a result of the remarkable performance of the little fresh-water navies on the Lakes. Captain Oliver Hazard Perry during the winter of 1812-1813 overcame enormous difficulties to construct a fleet of warships on Lake Erie. General Harrison attempted to retake Detroit but was beaten back. All depended on Perry's fir-built frigates and their crews of frontiersmen. On September 10, 1813, at Put-in-Bay, Perry attacked a British fleet that had been built with equal haste, and destroyed or captured all its ships. His exploit of transferring his flag, inscribed "Don't Give up the Ship," in a small boat from a shattered vessel to a sound one, and his simple report to Washington, "We have met the enemy, and they are ours," made him the hero of a classic naval tale.

Harrison then matched Perry's victory by taking Detroit and chasing General Proctor into Ontario, defeating him at the Battle of the Thames on October 5. Tecumseh was killed and his confederacy broke up. By the end of 1813, the United States controlled Lake Erie and had re-established its frontier in the Northwest. But during the same year the British retaliated against American raids across the Niagara River by capturing Fort Niagara on the American side. Undisciplined American militiamen had burned Canadian towns, including the provincial parliament buildings at York (now Toronto), and the British took revenge by inciting Indians against the American population around Niagara. A grandiose American plan to capture Montreal was easily defeated by the British.

This was the state of affairs when Madison accepted Castlereagh's proposal of direct negotiations, but it got much worse for the Americans before it got better.

THE CRISIS OF 1814

Disaster threatened the United States in the summer and autumn of 1814, when the peace commissioners were meeting at Ghent and the abdication of Napoleon and his retiremenet to Elba had brought an end, as it seemed, to the fighting in Europe. American soldiers and officers were improving in the hard school of experience, but the British were now able to send powerful reenforcements to the New World. After the bitter but indecisive Battle of Lundy's Lane at Niagara on July 25, General Prevost got ready a force, including 10,000 of Wellington's veterans, to invade the United States by Burgoyne's old route of Lake Champlain and the Hudson River. That same year the British conquered Maine as far south as the Penobscot River and established a naval base on Cape Cod; a strong British raiding force sailed directly from France to Chesapeake Bay to strike at the national capital; another force landed at Pensacola, Florida, to join Creek Indians recently defeated by General Jackson; and the most formidable expedition of all set out for New Orleans. An observer in the late summer of 1814 might easily have despaired of the continued existence of the United States as it faced invasion from north, east, and south and seemed about to break asunder from internal strain.

To top all, the British negotiators at Ghent at this moment presented the Americans with peace terms which included Canadian annexations of American territory in Maine and New York and west of Lake Superior, and also, as an indispensable condition of peace, an independent Indian state south of the Great Lakes to prevent American expansion westward and provide a buffer-state between the United States and Canada. These terms called for the loss of one-third of the territory of the United States.

If they were rejected and the many-pronged invasion succeeded—as all signs indicated it would—worse terms might obviously be expected.

Disaffection in New England

New England disaffection now reached a climax in one of the darkest periods in the history of the Republic. The policies of economic coercion as an alternative to war that were pursued by Jefferson and Madison had the important political effect of giving new life to the moribund Federalist Party. Its turn towards extreme state rights and obstructionism had

caused that staunch son of Massachusetts, John Quincy Adams, to break
with his old Federalist associates at the time of the embargo, and he
had received his recent diplomatic appointments at the hands of grateful
Republicans. He was serving his country and his section well at Ghent,
but the Federalist leaders at home achieved no such happy combination
of national and local patriotism. They opposed the war and did everything
this side of treason to hinder it. The New England people as a whole
were not extreme, but by the summer of 1813 the Federalist leaders were
back in control of all the states in that region.

The best example of official obstruction was probably provided by the
state of Massachusetts. On June 26, 1812, Governor Caleb Strong, a
consistent though not as a rule a bitter Federalist, proclaimed a public
fast shortly after the declaration of war "against the nation from which
we are descended." At the same time the House of Representatives of
the Bay State condemned the war; and toward the end of the summer
the Governor refused to comply with the request of the Secretary of War
that he call the militia into the federal service. In this action he was supported by the judges of the Supreme Court of Massachusetts, who held
that the right to determine the existence of an exigency warranting the
placing of the militia in the national service lay with the governor. They
also held that the militia could not be lawfully commanded by an officer
not of the militia. In 1827, the Supreme Court of the United States ruled,
in the case of Martin vs. Mott, that the President had the right to determine the exigency, but during the War of 1812 this matter remained in
perilous dispute. Meanwhile, voluntary enlistments in the regular army
continued, and in this respect New England showed up well.

By the summer of 1814, the region itself was gravely imperiled, for
the British were now blockading these rocky coasts and had invested a
large part of the present state of Maine. Meanwhile, the federal government had refused to maintain the Massachusetts militia unless under
federal officers, and the movement for a New England convention, which
had been long talked about, was now well under way. The success of
Federalists in the Massachusetts election of 1814 was a sign of popular
approval, since they had gone to the electorate on this issue. The actual
call for a convention was made to the other states by the legislature of
Massachusetts in October 1814. Connecticut accepted the invitation
promptly, and Rhode Island did, though with less enthusiasm. New
Hampshire and Vermont did not accept, though a few districts of these
states were represented. Thus the convention which met at Hartford on
December 15, 1814, represented southern New England and the ruling
group there. The war situation had changed much for the better by that
time, and the clearing of the skies served to moderate the temper of the
gathering.

The secrecy of the sessions of the Hartford Convention lent color to the charge of treason, but the journal which was published some years later (1823) showed that there were no grounds for this. The extremist Pickering was not there, and George Cabot, who presided, had mellowed with the years and was more willing than he had been earlier to let the world ruin itself without Federalist interference. A report, probably written by Harrison Gray Otis, the leader of the Convention, was published after adjournment. This decried indiscriminate talk of disunion and proposed, as a solution of the militia question, that the states should assume their own defense, using part of the federal taxes for that purpose. It also proposed seven amendments to the Constitution: that direct taxes and representation be proportioned to the free population; that a two-thirds vote of both houses of Congress be required for the admission of new states, for nonintercourse acts, and for a declaration of war; that embargoes be limited to sixty days; that citizens hereafter naturalized should be incapable of holding federal office; that no President should serve more than one term; and that there be no successive Presidents from the same state.

These proposed amendments amounted to a list of long-standing grievances against the "Virginia Dynasty" and its policies. The procedure was legitimate, but Americans would not soon forget that these spokesmen of the old order had taken advantage of a time of war and national danger to press their special sectional claims. The course of later events made them look ridiculous and the Federalist Party never recovered.

Even before the Hartford Convention met, the tide had already turned from the dead low of the summer of 1814, and the British terms of peace themselves helped to turn it. President Madison undiplomatically revealed them to the American public and even Federalists were appalled. Unwilling to fight for western expansion, indifferent to a war against impressment, Federalists were finally recalled to a sense of duty by the spectacle of British imperialism. Perry's slogan was broadened into "Don't Give up the Soil!" Recruits flocked to the colors, state governments invigorated defense programs, and everywhere the sentiments of 1776 were revived for a last-ditch stand.

Faltering of the British Offensive

Only a few American gunboats and a hastily-gathered body of militia were available to hold off the British expeditionary force that headed up the Chesapeake in August towards Washington. The gunboat crews resisted but the militia ran away at Bladensburg, leaving the British free to parade into Washington. In retaliation for the sacking of York, Upper Canada, they burned the executive mansion, the capitol, and other public buildings, subjecting President and Dolly Madison to the indignity of flight. While this foray had its value from the British point of view as a "lesson" to the Americans, it had no military significance. The British tried to capture Baltimore but the Maryland militia held them off and Fort McHenry withstood a naval bombardment. It was then, "in the rockets' red glare," that Francis Scott Key saw the Star-Spangled Banner "so gallantly streaming"; and, in the patriotism of his hymn, he caught the renascent spirit of 1814. The British retreated down the Chesapeake and sailed away.

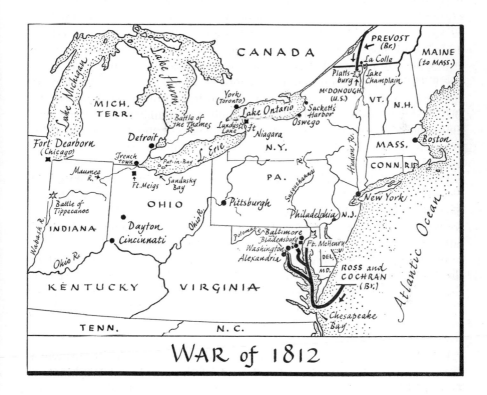

WAR of 1812

In the North, General Prevost reached Plattsburg early in September, but there a line of forts, even though undermanned, made him turn to flank them by gaining control of Lake Champlain. Commodore Thomas Macdonough had matched Perry's feat in building warships of green timbers. The British fleet attacked on September 11. Macdonough's crews laid their ships alongside the British, and by winding their anchors were able to fire broadsides from port or starboard at will. They destroyed the British fleet, and Prevost retreated to Canada. The Battle of Lake Champlain was the turning point of the war.

Now in the last days of the conflict the frontiersmen whose belligerence had done so much to initiate it finally produced in the South a victory to match their boasts. General Andrew Jackson of the Tennesseee militia was a man they would follow and one who knew how to use the harsh disciplinary methods frontier fighters respected. His crushing defeat of the Upper Creeks at Horseshoe Bend (March 27, 1814) accomplished one of the original objects of the war, and afterwards opened up vast Indian lands in the Southwest. This in itself was enough to make him a Western hero. Without orders from Washington, Jackson led a band into Florida and captured Pensacola from Indians and their British friends. Then he was ordered to New Orleans to defend it against the great expeditionary army of Sir Edward Pakenham. Inadvertently Jackson allowed the British to advance to within a few miles of the city, but Pakenham delayed his assault and gave Jackson his opportunity. He built earthworks across a strategic neck of land between the Mississippi and a swamp. On January 8, 1815, Pakenham ordered his troops to attack in close order. Laying their gun barrels between bales of cotton, the frontiersmen mowed the British down, losing only thirteen of their own number. Pakenham and more than 2000 officers and men were killed and the second and third generals in command were wounded before the victors of Europe retreated to their ships and sailed away.

Jackson's victory at New Orleans is one of the most celebrated in American military history. It had no effect on the peace treaty, which had been signed on Christmas Eve, but it indelibly impressed Americans with confidence that they were more than a match for any invaders and wiped out memories of unfortunate events on the northern frontier. Western brag was restored to prewar value and became a leading component in the ebullient nationalism of the following generation, whose greatest representative would be President Andrew Jackson.

THE TREATY OF GHENT

British territorial demands were increased over the original terms when news arrived in Europe, in October 1814, of the burning of Washington. The British commissioners at Ghent were instructed to demand more territory on the basis of *uti possidetis,* that is, Britain should receive all territory she actually occupied, and she expected to occupy a great deal. The American commissioners were ready to leave Ghent in despair when the news arrived of Macdonough's defeat of the northern invasion on September 11. Then the American diplomats complacently offered territorial terms on the basis of *status quo ante bellum.*

The British ministry now offered command to the Duke of Wellington in a new effort to invade the United States from Canada. But the wise hero of the war against Napoleon advised the ministry that British control of the Lakes was a necessary precondition of success. Since Britain lacked such control, Wellington bluntly told the government to make peace without territorial gains. Britain's greatest commander of land forces recognized the pre-eminence of sea power, and no more impressive tribute to Macdonough's victory can be imagined. The ministry decided that the war-weariness and tax-weariness of the British people forbade a new campaign on the Lakes preliminary to a new invasion of the United States. Therefore, they accepted Wellington's analysis of the situation and withdrew the demand for *uti possidetis*.

The European situation also helped the American cause. The powers which had defeated Napoleon were falling into disunity at the Congress of Vienna. Late in 1814, even before Napoleon returned from Elba to be finally defeated at Waterloo, the British government decided to liquidate the liability in America and make a quick peace. Once again dissensions in Europe strengthened the bargaining position of the United States.

The Madison administration itself had made an important contribution towards peace, in June 1814, by withdrawing its demand that Britain abandon impressment as a *sine qua non* condition. With the close of the Napoleonic wars at sea the British had stopped the hated practice and, actually, they never renewed it. Still His Majesty's government would not renounce impressment in a treaty, so the commissioners at Ghent agreed to ignore that issue and other questions of neutral rights.

The British government refused to renew without an equivalent the fishing privileges in British North American waters which had been granted the United States in the Treaty of 1783. John Quincy Adams was willing to concede renewal of the British right to navigate the Mississippi River from Canada to the Gulf, in return for renewal of New England's precious fishing privileges. But Henry Clay dreaded to face his Western constituents if he failed to push every vestige of British right out of the way of the advancing American frontier. He and Adams fought this sectional battle to a standstill. Then the astute Gallatin pointed out to the British that the American commission could not agree on the fisheries-Mississippi project and convinced them as well as his colleagues that it should be dropped from the treaty. This result was highly favorable to America because future negotiations secured the fisheries without conceding any British right south of the Canadian border. The treaty also provided for mixed arbitral commissions to settle boundary disputes in the Northeast and Northwest.

Otherwise the treaty provided simply for peace on the basis of *status quo ante bellum*. It was in the nature of an armistice, disputed questions being ignored or postponed for settlement in future treaties. Seldom has a nation recovered from disaster as swiftly as the United States between August and December of 1814, and events proved the wisdom of the commissioners. The full meaning of the Treaty of Ghent became visible only with the passage of many years. It inaugurated the era of un-challenged American security and expansion westward to the Pacific.

It marked the final acceptance of American independence by the only power in the world that was capable of destroying it.

Vocal sections of the British public were not prepared to accept the ministry's wise policy of accommodation to American long-range ambitions. The *London Times* said in an editorial: "We have retired from the combat with the stripes yet bleeding on our backs,—with the recent defeats, at Plattsburg, and on Lake Champlain, unavenged. To make peace at such a moment betrays a deadness to the feelings of honor, and shows a timidity of disposition, inviting further insult." But Napoleon's return from Elba soon justified the government's liquidation of the American war and diverted British attention back to the greater theater.

Hourly expecting news of disaster at New Orleans, the American public, early in the new year, received with unexampled joy the news of both Jackson's great victory and the signing of the Treaty of Ghent. Cities were illuminated by thousands of candles for all-night celebrations; there were parades and banquets, fireworks and endless toasts; and the pealing of bells went on for days. All this was in striking contrast to the sour public reception of the treaty in England and British North America, and it caused the "ambassadors" of the Hartford Convention—actually three men from Massachusetts—to look absurd. President Madison thankfully submitted the treaty to the Senate and it was unanimously approved. A century of world peace followed, a century that witnessed growth in American power and democracy unequalled by any people in human history.

Part IV

NATIONALISM, SECTIONALISM, AND DEMOCRACY, 1815-1841

CHAPTER 21

The Completion of Independence, 1815-1823

FOR A FEW YEARS AFTER 1815, FOREIGN RELATIONS continued to be a major preoccupation of the United States government. The classical age of American diplomacy, when the very existence of the young nation was at stake and foreign policy was necessarily dependent on the European situation, was fittingly and brilliantly closed by the work of President James Monroe (1817-1825) and his Secretary of State, John Quincy Adams. With them a generation of insecurity ended, and a new era of nationality began. In their knowledge of the ways of the Old World, their skill in diplomatic maneuver, and their devotion to the ideal of an independent republic, these two men equalled those great figures of the classical age and founders of American foreign policy, Benjamin Franklin and Thomas Jefferson. Their like was not to be seen in the land afterwards until the world crises of the twentieth century would again create the opportunity, and impose the necessity, for greatness in the conduct of American foreign relations.

The dawn of the century of peace in Europe following the Battle of Waterloo and the Congress of Vienna was the indispensable condition of the success of American diplomacy after the war. The marvel of the settlement of 1815 is that the United States emerged unharmed after taking on the most implacable of Napoleon's foes and thereby risking implication in his defeat. Henceforth the Republic did not have to risk such hairs'-breadth escapes. It could depend on peace in Europe while consolidating its own independence, and on the relative indifference of European Powers while devoting its abundant energies to the expansion of the nation.

Conventions and Agreements with the British

The Commercial Convention of 1815

No American was ever more devoted to independence and expansion than John Quincy Adams, and to him belongs the chief credit for the remarkable postwar triumphs of diplomacy which converted the "truce" of Ghent into a victorious peace. Immediately after the signing of the Treaty at Ghent, Adams, who was now Minister to the Court of St. James's, negotiated the first Anglo-American commercial treaty. Ever since the Revolution, the British had refused to make promises regarding reciprocal treatment of American trade and shipping. Perhaps the Embargo and Nonintercourse Acts won a delayed victory by teaching Britain that discriminations in tariff and tonnage duties only brought reprisals. Her policy during the new era was based on the importation of food and raw materials and the exportation of manufactured goods. A commercial treaty with the United States on the principle of reciprocity would be an essential safeguard and encouragement of increased Anglo-American trade.

Adams achieved an equitable arrangement under which each government agreed to apply to the other's goods and ships tariff and shipping rates no higher than it applied to the goods and ships of the "most-favored nation," that is, the third nation which enjoyed the most favorable terms granted to any. This Commercial Convention of June 1815 did not solve the problem of protecting American "infant industries" against British imports, but, by putting an end to the discriminations against United States trade and shipping arriving in the British Isles, it guaranteed that American merchants could sell food and raw materials there on a fair basis. The British government still refused to open the coveted West Indian trade. Consequently Adams shrewdly required that the term of the Commercial Convention be limited to four years.

The Rush-Bagot Agreement of 1817

The next step toward the achievement of permanent Anglo-American peace on the basis of mutual respect was marked by the establishment of mutual disarmament on the Great Lakes. When the war ended, Britain was building a great navy to secure supremacy along the water boundary between the United States and Canada. Congress in a postwar mood of economy refused to authorize a fleet that could match the British, and it was greatly to the advantage of both sides to avoid a naval-building race. In Parliament, however, much was heard of the necessity to prepare for another war. Minister Adams reported in 1816 that Lord

Castlereagh spoke ominously of "the great and growing military power of the United States."

President Madison and Secretary of State Monroe seized the initiative in favor of common sense and peace. They told Adams to propose mutual disarmament on the Lakes to Castlereagh. In April 1817, after Monroe had become President and before Adams had returned home to become Secretary of State, Charles Bagot, the able British minister to the United States, and Acting Secretary of State Richard Rush exchanged letters constituting an executive agreement that both governments would reduce their armed forces on the Lakes to a few revenue cutters that would be useless for war. At the British request, the Agreement was approved by the Senate so that it gained the status of a formal treaty. Later, from time to time, the principles of the Agreement were applied to the land frontier between the United States and Canada. In the end it covered the entire boundary of over 3000 miles, the longest undefended frontier in the world. With the growing Anglo-American practice of arbitration, the Rush-Bagot Agreement was far ahead of its time as a practical application of the ancient ideal that international disputes should be settled peaceably.

It is likely that without such a disarmament agreement the Canadian-American border incidents which occurred intermittently throughout the nineteenth century would have flamed into war. At the time, the Agreement signified that Great Britain, in good faith, had at last abandoned the policy of thwarting the westward expansion of the United States. Despite the recent threats of Westerners to conquer Canada, and despite the fears of the Canadians, who detected the beginning of a tendency to sacrifice their interests on the altar of Anglo-American friendship, Britain withdrew the menace of arms pointed at the American Northwest.

The Anglo-American Convention of 1818

The meaning of the Rush-Bagot Agreement was confirmed and greatly enlarged by the Convention of 1818. The British government was very anxious to renew the Commercial Convention of 1815 before it expired, and Adams exploited this anxiety after he became Secretary of State. He was unable to use the technique of exploiting divisions among the European powers to secure American bargaining advantage which had led to every previous major success in American diplomacy. But the old British contempt for "Yankee cowardice," "fir-built frigates," and "degenerate frontiersmen" had disappeared, and respect coupled with a healthy regard for the business profits of American friendship had taken its place. Only token applications of force and the threat of commercial retaliations were required to obtain a settlement of important matters on excellent terms in 1818.

A section of great importance in this treaty concerned Oregon. Just as the American negotiators of the Treaty of 1783 had reached out far beyond the frontier of settlement to secure the Old Northwest, so now the Monroe administration reached out to secure a new domain on the Pacific Coast for the future expansion of settlement.

In 1792, the crew of the Boston-owned ship *Columbia,* looking for furs, had discovered the great river which they named for their vessel and their country, thus establishing bases for the claim of the United States to the region. Thomas Jefferson had dispatched the Lewis and Clark expedition to find a virgin fur-trading area for Americans and to open up a water route to the Pacific. Other expeditions into the West found British fur traders in the North and Spanish forces in the South. In the vast region between them, American fur traders rapidly strengthened the territorial claims of the Republic.

New England ships first proved the wealth of Oregon by obtaining cargoes of furs from the local Indians, who called all white men "Bostons." One Yankee traded a rusty chisel for pelts worth $8000. The furs were carried to the Orient, to trade for tea, china, and silks, which were then sold in the United States for fantastic profits. John Jacob Astor, a German immigrant whose vision of profits matched Jefferson's continental vision of the Republic's boundaries, planned in 1810 to put the British Hudson's Bay and Northwest companies out of business by setting up a chain of fur-trading posts from the Great Lakes to the Pacific Ocean. By the summer of 1812, an expedition by sea had built a post at the mouth of the Columbia and named it Astoria, while an expedition by land discovered the best pass across the Rockies and the route later famous as the Oregon Trail. When news reached Astoria in January 1813 that war had begun and that a British warship was on the way to capture the post, Astor's partners sold out to the British Northwest Company. This was a private business exchange, but the captain of a British warship raised the Union Jack over the post and renamed it Fort George. The Madison administration, for its part, claimed in July 1815 that the provision in the peace treaty for territorial *status quo ante bellum* required that Astoria revert to the United States on the grounds that Britain held it as captured territory. The British government answered that the country around the Columbia River was part of His Majesty's dominions.

Early in Monroe's administration, Secretary of State Adams informed the British that the United States intended to retake Astoria by force, but the threat did not suffice. Therefore, in October 1817, President Monroe ordered the sloop-of-war *Ontario* to sail around the Horn with American commissioners and to expel the British from the mouth of the Columbia River. The British government then hastened to send orders that Fort George be peaceably turned over to the American commissioners. This was done in October 1818. The British thus gave up their claim to exclusive ownership of Oregon. In negotiations during 1818 the two governments agreed to postpone final settlement, meanwhile recognizing that both countries had claims to the whole area between Spanish and Russian territory. For ten years American citizens and British subjects should be free to enter, settle, and trade in the disputed region; and then the question of permanent boundaries beyond the Rocky Mountains would be reopened. The joint occupation was renewed periodically until the permanent division of 1846.

The Oregon provision was linked in the Convention of 1818 with a settlement of the boundary between the United States and Canada from the Great Lakes to the Rockies. Ignorance of geography had made earlier attempts at settlement of this boundary inoperable. Britain claimed the future bonanza wheat region of the Red River Valley in present-day Minnesota, and the United States claimed a slice of present-day Canada to the west as part of the drainage basin of the Mississippi River included in the Louisiana Purchase. These claims were evened out by agreement that the boundary should run from the Lake of the Woods along the 49th parallel to the watershed of the Rocky Mountains. In this way the Canadian border was kept above the headwaters of the Mississippi River, and Great Britain lost her right under the Treaty of 1783 to navigation of that stream. The epochal Convention of 1818 ended the story that began with the Proclamation of 1763, even as it opened a new story of consent by the Old World that the American pioneer should push on all the way to the Pacific Coast.

Settlement of the fisheries question was also obtained in the Convention of 1818. British subjects engaged in the Canadian fisheries petitioned their government to forbid the competition of Americans after the War of 1812. On the other hand, New Englanders regarded the freedom to fish inshore around the Canadian coast and to dry their catch on deserted shores as a vested interest established in colonial times and retained by revolutionary right. In spite of the failure to obtain recognition of the "right" in the Treaty of Ghent, New England fishermen returned to their accustomed grounds after the war. British warships chased them and, in the summer of 1817, an admiralty court claimed the right to confiscate any American fishing vessel caught in British North American waters. Adams found that his first job as Secretary of State was to win the codfish for Boston, as it had been the task of his father before him.

American warships were sent to protect fishing vessels entering their accustomed places. Holding out this threat of force with one hand, Adams with the other offered the British government an opportunity to negotiate. He astutely coupled the boundaries and fisheries questions with the renewal of the Commercial Convention of 1815. Britain had offered limited trade privileges in the West Indies, but in order to extort more, Congress passed the Navigation Act of 1818. This excluded British merchant ships from the trade between Britain and the United States just as the British Navigation Acts excluded American merchant ships from the British West Indian trade.

The despatch of the *Ontario* to Oregon and of other American warships to Canada and the passing of the American Navigation Act brought the British government to terms. Besides surrendering Astoria and agreeing to settlement of the northwestern boundary and joint occupation of Oregon, the British government granted Americans liberty forever to catch and dry fish along specified shores of Newfoundland, Quebec, and Labrador. In return the United States agreed to renew the Commercial Convention for ten years. Further retaliations were required before Britain in 1822 began to lower mercantilist barriers in the West Indies. Adams waged this fight throughout his eight years as Secretary of State and then for four more years as President, after which President Jackson in 1830 finally secured American privileges in the West Indies comparable to those of colonial times.

The Convention of 1818 was the first in which Great Britain treated the United States as an equal sovereign in fact as well as name. It was in reality the definitive peace settlement between the two countries. Unlike the Treaty of 1783, it was actually observed by Great Britain; unlike Jay's Treaty of 1794, it contained no terms humiliating to American sovereignty; and unlike the Treaty of Ghent it settled favorably to the United States the concrete issues in dispute. New disputes would arise between the two English-speaking nations during the next century, but without exception these would be settled peacefully according to the pattern established in 1818. True, the United States did not annex Canada and did not obtain an express disavowal of impressment. But if we remember that in the summer of 1814 it was British policy to annex northern areas of the United States to Canada and to throw an Indian state across the path of westward expansion, the territorial vista of 1818 which extended to the Pacific Coast seems a remarkable gain. As for impressment, the British abandoned the policy even though they made no promise on paper.

THE TREATY OF 1819 WITH SPAIN

In the Treaty of 1819 the United States matched with Spain in the South the settlement with Britain in the North and rounded out the permanent structure of peace. President Monroe and Secretary Adams successfully used with Spain the sort of strong methods they used against Britain. Spain was rapidly losing control over her revolted colonies in America and had already lost most of West Florida to the United States.

The proud Spaniards were faced with a choice of evils. They could refuse to settle issues and risk American intervention in behalf of the Spanish-American rebels; or they could beat a strategic retreat before the American advance into the Floridas in the hope of obtaining American abstention from aid to the rebels in the rest of the colonies.

Public sympathy for the Spanish-American revolutions was very strong in the United States. Sympathizers organized filibuster expeditions to aid the insurgents. Henry Clay led a movement in favor of open recognition of the new governments and public aid to them. Adams realized that if the United States were too slow in acting, the new republics would hasten to ally themselves economically and politically with Great Britain. But if the United States acted too soon, Spain would doubtless refuse to give way in the Floridas. Weighing these alternatives, Adams concocted the policy of postponing recognition of rebel governments until the chances of suppression by the mother country were "utterly desperate." A House resolution calling for immediate recognition of the new republics was defeated in March 1818, as a result of administration pressure.

Adams at the same time brought great pressure to bear on Spain to part with East Florida and the remainder of West Florida. An armed expedition was sent in 1817 to seize Amelia Island, near the Georgia coast, where the Spanish had lost control and pirates nested. In East Florida, the Seminole Indians, runaway slaves, and miscellaneous outlaws were accustomed to hide out between raids into the United States. Late in 1817, the Monroe administration commissioned General Andrew Jackson to punish the Seminoles and pursue them across the boundary if necessary. Jackson took on his job with gusto. Later he claimed that he received additional instructions from Monroe through Congressman Rhea that he should seize Spanish towns. He captured the military post at St. Marks in April 1818, and Pensacola a little later. He placed an American in office as Governor of East Florida and extended the revenue laws of the United States to the area. Besides punishing Indians, Jackson tried by court martial and executed two British subjects. Alexander Arbuthnot and Robert Ambrister, in order, as he wrote to the Secretary of War, to convince their government and its subjects that certain retribution awaited "those unchristian wretches who, by false promises, delude and excite an Indian tribe to all the horrid deeds of savage war." Lord Castlereagh refused to support English demands for redress because the two renegades, in his opinion, had placed themselves by their actions outside the protection of their government. Here was further evidence of Britain's new-found respect for the United States.

Henry Clay and other Congressmen castigated Jackson's bold procedures, but popular acclaim was such that resolutions condemning him were easily defeated. President Monroe and nearly all of his Cabinet members regarded Jackson's actions as unjustifiable acts of war against Spain, but Adams convinced them all that the government should support the impetuous General. Adams not only repelled Spanish demands for redress but demanded that Spain punish officials who had failed to prevent raids into the United States, and that Spain pay an indemnity for the expenses of Jackson's expedition. Otherwise, Adams hinted, American forces would have to go into Florida again, and the next time they would stay there.

Spanish officials in Florida confessed that they were unable to control the Seminoles. The home government decided, therefore, that it would be wise to sell Florida to the United States rather than risk losing it without compensation and chance a war which would range the United States on the side of the revolutionaries. Adams and Luis de Onís, the Spanish Minister, worked out treaty terms which solved problems all along the southern boundary. The United States received title to both of the Floridas and to Spain's claims to territory north of a stepped line from the Sabine River on the western border of the state of Louisiana to the 42nd parallel, and thence westward to the Pacific. In return the United States abandoned its claim to Texas based on the Louisiana Purchase and agreed to pay its own citizens claims amounting to $5 million which Spain owed them for depredations against American commerce.

This was the second United States treaty recognizing the right to expand to the Pacific Coast and the first treaty that established a transcontinental boundary. The Senate happily approved the excellent bargain in February 1819, but Spain, fearing that the United States would recognize and aid the Spanish-American rebels the moment the treaty was proclaimed in force, delayed ratification. She asked for a promise of nonrecognition, but Adams steadily refused. Finally Spain gave in and ratified, so that the treaty went into effect early in 1821.

By this time men like Henry Clay were bemoaning the loss of Texas and the "betrayal" of the Spanish Americans. After the decent interval of a year had elapsed and Spain's chances of reconquering the Spanish-American republics had become hopeless, the United States recognized them, being the first government in the world to welcome these new republics into the family of nations. As for Texas, Spanish officials in Mexico had already in 1821 granted a huge tract of land there to Moses Austin, and when the son of this American, Stephen F. Austin, began the work of settling American families, the independent government of Mexico confirmed the title. Frontiersmen thus created an American interest which would bring Texas into the Union later on.

The Adams-Onís Treaty of 1819 complemented the Convention of 1818 with Great Britain. Its substantial peaceful gains were basically a result of the determination to win security and ample boundaries which Westerners led by Andrew Jackson had proved in battle. After the Revolution, Spain had stood across the American path westward in the South just as Britain stood across it in the North. Now as a result of war and diplomacy, chiefly that of Thomas Jefferson and John Quincy Adams, both great powers had retreated. The United States had achieved security north, east, and south, and to the west there beckoned a territorial heritage for free men such as the sun had never shone upon in all man's previous history. Now Americans for the first time since 1776 could safely turn their eyes away from the Old World powers which had so persistently denied that the American experiment in liberty and self-government had a future. Now Americans could look to the West, and set about the business of building a nation whose extent and power should match the horizons of human hope. Little wonder that the new period of American history fixed the first article of American faith as simple optimism that every remaining economic, social, political, and spiritual evil could be abolished with just a little more effort on the part of the whole people and their government.

THE MONROE DOCTRINE

The Monroe Doctrine of 1823 is the symbolic capstone of the structure of security and expansion erected by the diplomatists of the classic period. The occasion for its announcement as the leading foreign policy of the United States was a final spasm in the death throes of the Old World policy of intervention in the New World. The unity of the powers, after the defeat of Napoleon and the restoration of the Bourbon government of Louis XVIII in France, contained a threat that the revolutions in America would be suppressed, just as the French Revolution had been. The Quadruple Alliance united the four victorious powers in a guarantee of the boundaries drawn by the Congress of Vienna (1815). France joined it, and the Holy Alliance united all of them except Great Britain with France in favor of monarchy and religion against republicanism and infidelity. From the point of view of American safety the disunity of the powers was desirable. Hence the refusal of Britain to join the Holy Alliance was promising, and her gradual withdrawal from the Quadruple Alliance during the years after 1815 was a boon to America. Britain controlled the seas, and she had a powerful trade interest in the independence of the American republics. These factors turned out to be fundamental reasons why the European threat against republicanism in America failed and why the United States and Great Britain slowly developed the most important friendship between two nations in modern times.

For a few years after 1815 co-operation among the European monarchs to put down rebellions succeeded. The fires of the French Revolution still smoldered among the oppressed peoples. They broke out in open rebellion after 1820 in Spain, Portugal, Naples, and Greece. The monarchs authorized Austria in 1821 to crush the Neapolitan rebels with armed force. They authorized France to invade Spain early in 1823 and place the brutal and perjured Ferdinand VII back on his throne. Then the monarchs planned a congress in Paris to authorize an expedition which would round out their victory in Spain by reconquering that country's former American colonies. Suddenly the hard-won security of the United States seemed again to be in danger. Would the monarchs stamp out the Spanish-American rebels and then hesitate to destroy the world's greatest breeding ground of republicanism?

Czar Alexander I of Russia, the leading spirit of the Holy Alliance, had shown in an imperial edict or ukase of 1821 a distinct ambition to expand Alaska. The ukase claimed that the southern boundary of Alaska lay deep in the Oregon country at the 51st parallel, and it forbade foreign ships to come closer to the Alaska shores than one hundred Italian miles, an unprecedented assertion of authority over the high seas. In July 1823, Adams, in opposition to this ukase, announced to the Russian Minister to the United States one of the great principles which was incorporated in the Monroe Doctrine a little later, namely, "that the American continents are no longer subjects for any new European colonial establishments." Britain joined the United States in opposing the Russian ukase, but the principle Adams had announced applied also to Britain, and therein is found the special character of the policy of Adams and Monroe: they were determined that the United States *alone* should repel *all* Old World interference *anywhere* in the American Hemisphere.

Britain had opposed the French invasion of Spain and was fearful lest the Bourbons would try to reconquer the former Spanish colonies. The new Foreign Secretary, George Canning, decided to make an ally of the United States. In August 1823, he proposed to Richard Rush, United States Minister in London, that the two governments join to prevent action by the European monarchs in America.

This was the offer that occasioned the announcement of the Monroe Doctrine. At first President Monroe was inclined to accept it. He asked the advice of the aged Jefferson, who replied favorably. Jefferson's advice was highly revealing. Here was the ancient leader of the anti-British party in American politics, the man who is usually considered the father of American isolationism as he was the spokesman of American independence, counseling an alliance with Great Britain such as he had been equally ready to enter into when Napoleon threatened to take over Louisiana. The seeming contradictions in Jefferson's policy can be resolved by the consideration that, while he preferred isolation, he wisely regarded both isolation and alliances as no more than alternative means to the one major goal: the security of the Republic. Therefore when a situation arose in which an isolated United States was menaced by one party of the perennially divided Old World, Jefferson was ready to embrace the opposing party even though he disliked it.

Nevertheless, Adams rejected Jefferson's advice and Canning's offer. He saw a possibility that the United States might secure all the advantages of British support while avoiding all the disadvantages. In the momentous Cabinet debates on Canning's proposed entente, the Secretary of State stood out for a unilateral announcement by the United States. For one thing, he did not want his country to "come in as a cock-boat in the wake of the British man-of-war." More important, Canning had proposed that the United States and Britain should formally promise not to annex any Spanish-American territory. The expansionist Adams refused to tie the hands of his country. If Cuba or Texas asked admission into the Union, why should the United States refuse? Adams furthermore calculated that the unity of the European allies was too shaky to support intervention in America. And even if they did intervene, Britain's interest would require the Mistress of the Seas to prevent their success.

Adams's brilliant argument convinced the President and Cabinet. Monroe decided to announce the policy in his presidential message to Congress on December 2, 1823. The "Monroe Doctrine," as the policy later came to be called, contained two warnings and two promises. The first warning stated to Britain and the Holy Allies the principle of noncolonization: that "the American continents, by the free and independent condition which they have assumed and maintain, are henceforth not to be considered as subjects for future colonization by any European powers." An important "corollary" of this principle which had already been announced by the United States in relation to Cuba was the notransfer principle—that no existing colony of one European power might be transferred to the possession of another European power. The United States, however, was left free to acquire such territories by transfer. The second warning stated to the European allies the principle of nonintervention: that "we should consider any attempt on their part to extend their system to any portion of this hemisphere as dangerous to our peace and safety." In the manner of a *quid pro quo* for these warnings, Monroe promised first, that the United States would not interfere with the existing colonies in America of any Old World power; and second, that the United States would not intervene in the internal affairs of the European powers.

Reception of the Policy

British public opinion welcomed Monroe's announcement as evidence that the United States would support Britain against the allies in case of need. But Canning had learned that the allies would not carry out the plan to reconquer Spanish America and he had led the French Ambassador to sign the "Polignac Memorandum" denying any intention of France to intervene in America. Feeling free, therefore, to concentrate on the anti-British aspect of Monroe's message, he proudly announced to Rush that Britain had no intention of accepting the noncoloniza- tion principle. Nevertheless, in Parliament Canning indicated that he welcomed the other aspects of the message. Indeed, he claimed credit for them, saying: "I called the New World into existence to redress the balance of the Old" (1826). Thus the Monroe Doctrine established an Anglo-American entente against Europe even while it warned Britain against any further expansion in America.

The continental powers were contemptuous of Monroe's declarations. They found a ridiculous gap between the vast pretensions of the United States to guard the Hemisphere and the nation's slight armed power. Not the message but the jealousies of the allies prevented their inter- vention. The Czar was most anxious to restore monarchy and religion in Spanish America, but France by the Polignac Memorandum had left him in the lurch and the other powers refused to help. In the face of the British fleet, Russia could not possibly intervene alone.

The ever-current possibility of revolution in Russia and the vast extent of her unexploited territory in Asia also led the Czar to abandon his ukase of 1821. In 1824, Adams signed a Russian-American treaty which fixed the southern boundary of Alaska at its present location, 54°–40' north latitude. This success, though not so much a result of Monroe's warning as a fortunate coincidence, strengthened the claim of the United States to Oregon and repelled an Old World scheme for territorial aggrandizement in America. Since 1823, European powers have often retreated in the Western Hemisphere: they have never advanced, and only the United States has expanded its boundaries. Whether or not the Monroe Doctrine has been the "cause" of American advance and European retreat, these were certainly purposes of Monroe and Adams.

Latin Americans were inclined to believe that Canning, rather than Monroe, had saved America from the European allies. They also recog- nized that Monroe had left the way open for the expansion of his own country and that he was primarily concerned with its interests. When Mexico and Colombia planned an expedition to free Cuba from Spain and annex it to a mainland republic, the United States government opposed the move, and this indicated that Latin-American as well as European expansion in the Hemisphere was under the ban. Colombia and Brazil proposed an alliance with the United States against Europe, but this, too, the Monroe administration opposed. Many Latin Americans came to believe that "Monroeism" was nothing more than a cover for the imperialism of the "Yankee Colossus."

The Monroe Doctrine did not displace Great Britain as the most influential power in Latin America. Only during the last generation have the unilateral and expansionist aspects of the Doctrine been abolished. Under the "Good Neighbor Policy," instituted by President Franklin D. Roosevelt in the 1930's, the United States has agreed to multilateralization of the Doctrine, repudiated expansion and intervention in Latin America, and joined in a military alliance with all the republics against aggression by American as well as non-American Powers. These actions and the displacement of Britain by the United States as the greatest Atlantic power have finally made the United States the most influential nation in the Hemisphere.

Monroe's epochal message well expresses the national mood of unbounded confidence in Americans' ability to hew their own path towards a grand destiny in defiance of the predatory and corrupt monarchs of Europe. Americans have savored the Doctrine's opposition to British ambitions in the New World while scarcely appreciating that it long depended upon the British Navy for its effectiveness against Europe. Actually, for a quarter of a century following its pronouncement, the Monroe Doctrine was remembered by few Americans. Thereafter it was invoked and applied with increasing frequency by successive administrations, and gradually it acquired a sacrosanct character, as if it were a law of nature, and a cluster of interpretations and corollaries as if it were the Constitution or a text of Holy Writ. Yet the Monroe Doctrine was only a presidential statement, lacking any character of domestic or international law prior to its incorporation in the modern Good Neighbor treaties.

With the Monroe Doctrine the United States completed the formative stage of its foreign relations. Within a decade of the Treaty of Ghent, the Republic had achieved excellent treaty relations with the Great Powers and wide boundaries. France and Spain had disappeared as menacing neighbors in the South and weak republics had taken their place. Anglo-American relations pointed towards forbearance and even co-operation. The President had proclaimed the principles of the Monroe Doctrine as a summary of what had been achieved and a portent of freedom's future. Europe, not unmindful of the two unsuccessful attempts to destroy the independence of the United States in war, did not again attempt to snuff out the flame of American liberty.

CHAPTER 22

The "Era of Good Feelings":
Nation and Sections

THE PREDOMINANT MOOD OF THE AMERICAN PEOPLE after the conclusion of the War of 1812 was one of exuberant patriotism and political unity. This was reflected in nationalistic legislation at the end of Madison's administration, in the use of the expression, "Era of Good Feelings," early in the administration of James Monroe, and in the mortal defeat of the Federalist Party, which was deemed unpatriotic and particularistic. While gaining full political independence from the Old World, the Republic was emerging from a colonial into a national economy in which domestic commerce played an increasingly important part. It would be too much to say that the Americans now turned their backs on Europe, for foreign trade was of the utmost importance to a very large number of them, but more than ever they turned their eyes and their steps westward. Furthermore, as the country grew, its component geographical regions were assuming a more distinctive character. Besides being a union of states, it was now an empire of sections, comparable in size to European countries, though the sectional boundaries were shifting and loosely drawn. Behind the façade of political unity in a one-party period, there were sharp clashes of sectional and group economic interests. These were accentuated by the economic crisis which began in 1819; and, in the struggle over the admission of Missouri at the same time, slavery became a subject of hot debate. In an era of external peace the issues of the coming generation were taking form.

THE NATIONAL POLITICAL AND ECONOMIC SCENE, 1816-1824

The Tariff Act of 1816 and the establishment of the Second Bank of the United States that year, though Republican measures, would have been fully approved by Alexander Hamilton. A few years later, when in retirement, Madison referred to the charge that the Republicans had deserted their cause and gone over to the policy of their old opponents. "But," he said, "they overlook the overbearing and vindictive spirit, the apocryphal doctrines, and rash projects, which stamped on Federalism its distinctive character; and which are so much in contrast with the unassuming and unvarying spirit which has marked the Republican Ascendancy." In the hands of Jefferson and Madison, Republicanism did escape the arrogance of High Federalism, and it was more flexible in both foreign and domestic policy. The "unvarying spirit" which Madison claimed for his party was that of devotion to the interests of the majority, not of small special classes. The actions of 1816 may have been afterwards regarded by opponents of the protective tariff and the Bank as victories for special interests, but at the time they seemed wise in view of the general economic situation.

National Legislation

The Tariff of 1816, the first in American history that was primarily designed for protection rather than revenue, was enacted in what was generally recognized as a time of emergency. The embargo and the British blockade during the war had created a sudden demand for domestic manufactures to replace formerly imported foreign articles. The result was the first burst of the American Industrial Revolution. Cotton mills multiplied so rapidly, chiefly in New England, that the number of spindles increased from 8000 in 1807 to 500,000 in 1815. Lesser advances were made in other lines of manufacturing. But immediately after the war ended, British imports began to flood the American market, threatening to overwhelm "infant industries" that ranged from the textile mills of New England to the iron foundries of Pittsburgh. It was believed that these required tariff protection. Also, it was believed that other important interests should be safeguarded. Agricultural products were not protected in this particular act to the same extent as in later ones, but hemp-growers of Kentucky and wool-growers from Vermont to Ohio were staunch and consistent supporters of the protective principle. At this time, Daniel Webster and other representatives of New England's commercial interests believed that low tariffs and a flourishing foreign trade would serve them best. On the other hand, John C. Calhoun of South Carolina favored this tariff, in view of the larger national interest. Most of the opposition to the bill came from the South, but not until the next decade did antitariff sentiment become general in that region. Sectional lines were not sharply drawn as yet on this historic issue.

The charter of the First Bank of the United States had expired in

1811, though the Secretary of the Treasury at the time, Albert Gallatin, had strongly urged that the institution be rechartered. Meanwhile, a large crop of state banks had sprung up, and in the absence of any central control the currency of the country had fallen into great disorder. During and after the war, the federal government had been embarrassed in its fiscal operations, and Madison joined with his Secretary of the Treasury, Alexander J. Dallas, in advocating a second Bank of the United States for the convenience of the government and the restoration of a sound currency. He was a hard-money man not an inflationist, and he regarded his earlier constitutional objections to such an institution as already overruled by public authority. The Supreme Court decisively affirmed the constitutionality of the Bank a little later (1819).

The new Bank was closer to the federal government than the old one had been, since five of the twenty-five directors were appointed by the President, but at the outset it was not so carefully or so conservatively administered. The liberal credit policy which its branches followed in the South and West showed that it was not unmindful of agricultural interests and the policy redounded to the Bank's popularity in those regions. But the reversal of this was one of the immediate causes of the Panic of 1819 and tended to alienate many Westerners and Southerners.

The Republican administration did not go along so readily with the policy of internal improvements, that is, the building of roads and canals at federal expense, which was especially urged by Westerners. Gallatin may be regarded as the father of the idea and Jefferson had approved it, on the understanding that an amendment to the Constitution should be passed to authorize federal action of this sort. Madison's objections were also constitutional, and he did not waive them in this case as he did in that of the Bank. In 1817, Westerners put through a bill for a large group of federal road projects but Madison vetoed it. President Monroe was rather more favorable, going so far as to sign the Survey Bill (1824), which looked toward a program of internal improvements without actually starting one. At this point the nationalism of the Virginia Dynasty became hesitant.

Leaders and Interests

The most articulate public spokesman of economic nationalism at this stage was Henry Clay of Kentucky, former leader of the War Hawks, whose program was known as the "American System." He linked together the protective tariff, the Bank, and internal improvements and continued to champion all of them vigorously for a generation. "Harry of the West" imbued his vision of the American System with an almost religious fervor, and his nationalistic spirit was most nearly matched, perhaps, by that of John C. Calhoun, who was afterwards most famous as a spokesman of the South.

These two men were Republicans, like John Quincy Adams and the other effective political leaders of the time, for the Federalist Party, though still strong in some localities, ceased to be a national institution not long after the War of 1812. The most important phase of the presidential campaign of 1816 was the struggle for the Republican nomination. It went to James Monroe, who well deserved it for past services but was objected to by many on the ground that the state of Virginia should not monopolize the presidency. Party nominees were chosen by Congressional caucus, and William H. Crawford of Georgia, Secretary of the Treasury at the very end of Madison's administration, was the most popular candidate with Congress. His failure to gain the prize may be attributed to his own vacillation and to the intrigues of Martin Van Buren of New York. Monroe received 183 electoral votes to 34 for Rufus King, who carried only the states of Massachusetts, Connecticut, and Delaware. In the next presidential election, in 1820, there was no form of opposition to Monroe, who received all the electoral votes but one that was cast for John Quincy Adams.

In the early years of the Republican Party, Monroe had seemed more partisan than either Jefferson or Madison but now, as the head of a one-party country, he sought to be conciliatory. Early in his first term (July 12, 1817) the *Columbian Centinel* of Boston, a paper which had been noted for its virulent Federalism, used the expression which has been generally attached to his administration, the "Era of Good Feelings." It was not that for long except upon the surface. Sharp clashes of economic interest appeared by the middle of his first term, and during his second term there was a scramble of personal factions out of which a new party alignment emerged.

Despite the nationalist trend of postwar legislation, constitutional arguments against the growth of national power continued and these naturally assumed a state-rights form, as they did in Monroe's own Virginia. From this time on, however, many political conflicts were in reality sectional; and the geographical regions which were assuming increased significance cut across state lines and were not recognized by the Constitution. These sections could not be definitely bounded as states can; their lines necessarily shifted in a rapidly growing country. They attained varying degrees of economic and political unity; and, having no legal existence, they garbed their claims and arguments in nationalistic or state-rights language. The great political problem of the era was to harmonize the various sectional and group interests when they were in conflict.

Prior to the commercial restrictions which accompanied the Napoleonic wars, the economy of the United States had continued to be essentially colonial. The country was still engaged primarily in the production of raw materials, shipping the excess to Europe, and receiving manufactured goods in return—much as the colonies had done under British rule. After the war the economy deserved to be called national. Raw materials (especially cotton and tobacco) continued to be shipped to Europe, and manufacturing, supported by protective tariffs, was maintained and developed, while internal commerce attained a new volume and importance. Self-sufficiency was not yet achieved and in the full sense it never was, but the movement was definitely in that direction. The United States was developing a better-rounded economy. In the Northeast, which was assuming the economic position once held by the mother country, industry and commerce were growing; the West emphasized food products and clamored for better transportation; while the South, continuing to produce staples primarily, was dependent on Northern and European manufactures, and to a considerable degree on Western food.

THE DIVIDED EAST

The East, comprising New England and the Middle States of New York, New Jersey, and Pennsylvania, was far from being a unified section. Just after the War of 1812, New England was the most homogeneous of American regions in population, but its economic interests were divided and to some extent antagonistic. Agriculture continued, especially in northern New England, but it was sharply declining while the richer lands of upstate New York and the West were being developed, and the first mill-workers were largely recruited from farmers' families. There was abundant water power which was relatively close to the sea, and the inventive and enterprising New Englanders took the initiative and gained the American pre-eminence in the textile industry. Manufacturing was gaining on commerce, which had hitherto been the major source of prosperity, but the interests of the two conflicted. The opposition of Daniel Webster to the protective tariff until 1824 and his espousal of it in 1828 was symbolic of the change in emphasis and political attitude. Also, the pessimism of that statesman at the beginning of this period was significant, and statistics of population reinforced his opinion that the region was declining in political importance. Both the West and the Middle States were growing much faster.

At the first census in 1790, Massachusetts had more people than New York. By 1820, the Bay State had been passed not only by New York but also by the young states of Ohio and Kentucky. By 1830, she had slipped behind Tennessee and was eighth in the Union. New England suffered greatly during this period from the migration of her children—chiefly to upstate New York until after the Erie Canal opened the way into the

Old Northwest—and immigrants from Europe had not yet come in sufficient number to compensate for the heavy loss. Not until after 1830 did newcomers pour through the open gates like a flood.

The Middle States had little economic unity, but by 1820 New York had gained the first rank in population and by 1830 Pennsylvania, which had always stood near the top, was firmly established in second place. New York City had gained on Philadelphia in shipping, and, even before the opening of the Erie Canal in 1825, it had become *the* American metropolis, not to be outdistanced. Upstate New York, into which New Englanders had been pouring for some time, was richly agricultural and eastern Pennsylvania was notably so. The Keystone State found compensation for relative commercial decline in the development of coal and iron. The economic interests of New York and Pennsylvania were diversified just as their people were various in origin, and these two great states were political prizes for which all groups contended. It was true until the Civil War, as indeed it was thereafter, that one or both of them was generally in the winning combination. Also, they were the breeding ground of many of the more unsavory political practices of the era. Urban machine politics were first perfected by Republicans of New York City and Philadelphia.

THE SOUTH AND THE RISE OF "KING COTTON"

The South, which became within a generation a section apart and long remained one, had an unusually homogeneous white population but no geographical unity except such as was imparted by the climate. From 1820 onward, whenever the slavery question was in the forefront of political controversy, the South was understood to consist of those states where slavery was still legal. But otherwise, in the period now being considered, Kentucky and even Tennessee were more likely to be regarded as Western than Southern. The two new Gulf states which were admitted just after the War of 1812—Mississippi (1817) and Alabama (1819)—had a distinct Western flavor but they were specially dependent on slave labor. All of the South was predominantly agricultural, but on the basis of crops an important and continuing distinction can be made between the Upper South and the Lower.

In the Upper South, which began at the Mason and Dixon line (the boundary between Pennsylvania and Maryland), the major crop in colonial times had been tobacco. By the end of the War of 1812, grain crops had infringed on this, and in many respects the agriculture of Maryland, Delaware, and northern and western Virginia resembled that of Pennsylvania. Tobacco was still cultivated in southern Virginia and North Carolina, and its area was extended westward into Kentucky and Tennessee, where the soil was fresher and richer. Hemp was an important product in Henry Clay's Kentucky, and much grain was grown in Andrew Jackson's Tennessee. These two states, which were the oldest beyond the mountains and represented a special blend of West and South, were entering the most important period of their political leadership. Meanwhile, the older states of the Upper South were losing ground. This was specially true of Virginia. The first state in population until 1820, she was displaced by New York in the census of that year, and sank to third place in 1830. She was losing her population to newer regions, much as New England was.

The most important agricultural developments of the period occurred further southward. Rice was still cultivated along the coast in South Carolina and Georgia, as long-staple cotton was, and sugar was a major crop in Louisiana, but in the Lower South short-staple cotton had usurped the throne and begun a long and fateful reign. The success story of this plant is usually thought of as beginning with the invention of the gin (1793) by a Connecticut Yankee, Eli Whitney. This permitted the extraction of the seed rapidly by machine rather than tediously by hand and encouraged more extensive production. Equally important, however, were textile inventions and developments in England and the vastly increased demand there and in New England for raw materials. The story of the rise of cotton is a chapter in the history of the Industrial Revolution. The reasons for the spread of cotton culture in the southernmost parts of the United States were chiefly climatic. The plant grows in almost any soil but it requires a long growing season and an abundance of sunshine. In times of high prices there was a tendency to stretch cotton production northward beyond its normal limits, and some cotton was raised at one time or another in all the southern states. But its permanent home was in South Carolina, Georgia, and the Gulf states. They comprised the real land of cotton.

At the end of the War of 1812, only about 150,000 bales were produced in the United States, chiefly in South Carolina and Georgia, but within a decade this yield had quadrupled, as the new lands in the Old Southwest were put into cultivation. The speed of the development was affected by the ups and downs of prices, which did not again reach the postwar peak, but until the Civil War the trend of production was upward until the figure for 1815 had been multiplied by thirty. The South had gained a virtual monopoly of one of the most prized staples in the world.

Cotton and Slavery

The spectacular rise of cotton gave a new lease on life to the institution of Negro slavery. In the Upper South, after the virgin lands had been exploited and tobacco culture began to decline, slaves tended to become a burden on their owners. Whether or not slavery would have

ELECTION DAY AT INDEPENDENCE HALL, PHILADELPHIA, *ca.* 1818. *Painting by John Lewis Krimmell.* An early, lively scene of the democratic process.

ANDREW JACKSON

1767-1845

Portrait by Asher B. Durand

"Old Hickory" on
his presidential dignity

As his enemies saw him

BORN TO COMMAND.

OF VETO MEMORY.

HAD I BEEN CONSULTED.

KING ANDREW THE FIRST.

*A famous trio of
Senatorial giants at various stages
in their long careers*

DANIEL WEBSTER

1782-1852

*Portrait by
George P. A. Healy*

HENRY CLAY

1777-1852

*Portrait by
Charles Bird King*

JOHN C. CALHOUN

1782-1850

*Portrait by
Charles Bird King*

A "Grasshopper" Engine, 1835. This was one of four locomotives that inaugurated railroad service into Washington.

Two early examples of American mechanical progress

The First Successful McCormick Reaper, 1831. *From a modern photograph.*

RALPH WALDO EMERSON

1803-1882

EDGAR ALLAN POE

1809-1849

Two of the first literary men in the United States to win world repute

CAMP MEETING IN THE WEST, 1830-1835. *Drawing by A. Rider.* Here is shown a distinctively American expression of religious fervor.

THE OREGON TRAIL. *Painting by Albert Bierstadt.* During the mid-nineteenth centu~
their livestock trailing along, continued t~

Adventurous Americans, with their families and possessions in Conestoga wagons,
trek across the continent into the Far West.

The "Dashing Wave" Passing Boston Light. One of the famous clipper ships, first built in the 1840's. These sleek vessels outsailed the new steamboats for several decades, carrying American commerce all over the world.

gradually disappeared in the old tobacco country if it had been left to itself there, is a question which no man can answer, but that was what many of the Fathers of American independence had expected. In the Lower South, Negro slave labor was regarded as indispensable in the rice and sugar districts, where crops were cultivated on a large-plantation system. Cotton thrived on small farms as well as great plantations, but this royal crop lent itself to large-scale production under the gang system even though it did not actually require it. When so much fresh land in a favorable climate became available after the War of 1812, the chief limitation on the culture of cotton was the supply of labor, and small independent farmers did not provide enough in the face of the demand.

The foreign slave trade had been abolished on January 1, 1808, by a federal law passed in the previous year. The trade had been forbidden by all the states by 1798, when Georgia legislated against it, but South Carolina reopened it in 1803 and about 40,000 slaves were imported into that state in the next five years. This action was connected with early developments in cotton culture, but among Southerners there was strong opposition to the continuance of the traffic. Besides such humanitarian motives as Jefferson expressed, there were economic and social considerations. Further importations would decrease the value of the slaves already held, and would increase the social problem and danger of revolt.

The British, who had played such an important part in the trade, abolished it in 1807, being followed in a few years by the Dutch (1814), the French (1818), the Spanish (1820), and finally the Portuguese (1830). The American law of 1807 was a mild one, imposing no severe penalties, but it was fairly effective until the high price of slaves after the War of 1812 led to an increase in smuggling. This in turn led to a strengthening of the law. In 1818, the reward to informers was increased, and in 1820 the maritime slave trade was designated as piracy and made punishable by death. So long as slavery continued as an institution in the Western World there were illicit importations, but in the United States these fell chiefly in the decade 1850-1860. A few years after the War of 1812, it seemed that the country had closed the foreign slave trade from which the maritime peoples of the Atlantic world had gained such great financial profit through almost four centuries.

Those who would procure more slaves for purposes of labor would have to draw, it seemed, on the existing American Negroes. Hence the call from the burgeoning cotton states on the old tobacco region for its surplus and the gradual weakening of resistance there. The heydey of the human traffic between the Upper and Lower South did not come until the middle of the 1830's, but not long after the Peace of Ghent, slavery, now the invaluable handmaiden of "King Cotton," began to cast an ominous shadow on the expanding American empire of freedom.

THE WEST AND THE WESTWARD MOVEMENT

The term "West" is a variable in American history, since settlement kept surging toward the sunset until it reached the Pacific and could go no farther. The West was migratory but what is meant by it here is the region beyond the Appalachian Mountains. The settlement of the lower Mississippi Valley was part of the larger westward movement. That part of the country is often called the Old Southwest. There is much stronger reason, however, to associate the oldest trans-Appalachian states, Kentucky and Tennessee, with the vigorous young society which was developing in the Old Northwest Territory, north of the Ohio River. After the War, Indiana (1816) and Illinois (1818) were admitted to the Union, and the organized territory of Michigan lay to the north of them. By 1820, Ohio, though less than twenty years old as a state, ranked fifth in population in the Union. In the whole of this vast inland region the country was growing with appalling speed.

After 1815, conditions favored the movement of settlers into the West as never before. No European power now blocked the advance of the frontiersman; and the Indian, shorn of his European allies, was helpless to halt the white invasion. Long-term mortgages and other land loans were financed by the western branches of the Bank of the United States at first, and state banks were even more eager to expand credit and the currency to meet the farmers' demands. The most crucial Western question was that of transportation.

Predominantly this was the problem of connecting the West with the East. Beyond the mountains there was no great difficulty about the southward movement of settlers and their products because of the course of the rivers; and when steamboats began to be used on western waters in 1811, four years after Robert Fulton's *Clermont* first appeared on the Hudson, it became relatively easy to go upstream. But the steamboat did not meet the problem of getting across the mountains. This occasioned the pressure for internal improvements. John C. Calhoun of South Carolina saw danger to the Republic unless it were bound together by roads and canals—the "most powerful cement" he called them. Before long it appeared that his state, blocked from the West by an unconquerable mountain barrier, could benefit little from federal internal improvements; but there was good reason for the cities of the Northeast to favor them. They would tie Western trade to their emporia and prevent it from moving exclusively down the rivers to the Gulf.

Roads and Canals

The greatest project of internal improvement in the period was the Cumberland and National Road. Private enterprise had built the first improved roads in the United States. The Lancaster Turnpike from Philadelphia to Lancaster, Pennsylvania, was their prototype. The state government chartered a private corporation in 1792 and an Englishman who was acquainted with the methods of the Scot, J. L. McAdam, directed the construction of a smooth ("macadamized") surface of crushed stone which was fairly impervious to weather and wagon wheels. Toll gates every few miles collected fees which paid profits to the private owners. Such roads were rapidly built between the main eastern centers, but many of them aroused public opposition because of exorbitant tolls and political chicanery. State governments sometimes subsidized roads into western regions within their own boundaries, but long interstate roads through difficult country were beyond the financial ability of single states.

In 1802, the federal government agreed to use some of the money derived from sales of public lands in Ohio for a road to connect that state with the Atlantic seaboard. The shortest route was one that Washington had surveyed from Cumberland on the upper Potomac to Wheeling on the Ohio River. State jealousies were temporarily overcome in 1811, and by 1818 the Cumberland Road was open to traffic. Baltimore built a turnpike to connect with the terminus at Cumberland, and Pennsylvania countered by extending the Lancaster Turnpike to Pittsburgh. New York in turn began in 1817 to build the great Erie Canal and when completed in 1825 her "water-level" route from Albany to Buffalo was the best way west.

Meanwhile, it seemed unfair that one seaboard state, Maryland, should be favored by the federal government while other states had to build their own roads. The Constitution did not specifically authorize the government to construct roads or canals, hence authority had to be found in loose construction of the interstate commerce clause. In 1817, Westerners put through Congress a bill for a large group of federal road projects, but President Madison vetoed it on constitutional grounds. President Monroe vetoed (1822) a bill authorizing tolls on the Cumberland Road to be used for its upkeep. He signed the Survey Bill in 1824, but this merely called for the preparation of a larger program of internal improvements and did not authorize any actual project. New Englanders and Southerners were predominantly against the measure. By the presidency of John Quincy Adams, who strongly favored internal improvements and had no constitutional objections to federal action, the opposition of Southerners and certain groups of Easterners had become so great that the adoption of his great plan proved impossible.

Thus the movement for the building of roads and canals by the federal government slowed down, and in the meantime individual states like New York and Pennsylvania went on with their own projects to facilitate traffic with the West. Proposals to extend the Cumberland Road as the National Road across southern Ohio, Indiana, and Illinois to Saint Louis occasioned endless wrangles in Congress. The upshot was a

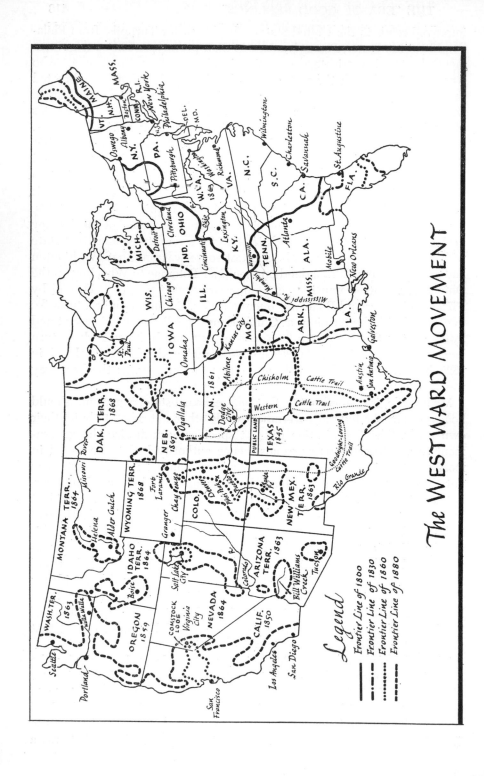

The Westward Movement

Legend

	Frontier Line of 1800
	Frontier Line of 1830
	Frontier Line of 1860
	Frontier Line of 1880

series of compromises whereby the federal government built stretches of this National Road in the 1830's, and then turned them over to the respective state governments, but the farthest it got was Vandalia, Illinois, at just about the time that Abraham Lincoln was doing odd jobs in the village of New Salem nearby. The great majority of roads and canals were built by state governments and private companies.

The Old Northwest

In the years immediately following the War of 1812 and through the 1820's, migrants to the West swarmed along the Cumberland Road, Pennsylvania's turnpike to Pittsburgh, and eventually the Erie Canal. Many from Kentucky and even from more distant Tennessee passed across the Ohio into the Old Northwest and across the Mississippi into Missouri. The general rule of settlement was that it roughly followed the parallels of latitude. The settlers in the lower halves of the states of Ohio, Indiana, and Illinois, and those in Missouri were largely of Southern origin. In the period before 1830, New Englanders were more numerous in Ohio than elsewhere in the West, but even in that state there were more people from the South and the Middle States, while Indiana and Illinois were still more strongly Southern. The greatest movement of New Englanders was after 1830, into the prairie districts which had seemed unattractive to the first settlers.

Corn to feed their families and their pigs, and pork and wheat for sale were the main crops of the farmers north of the Ohio. These crops did not invite gang labor as cotton did, and family farms were the typical units. While slave-owning planters followed and often displaced the pioneer farmers in the Old Southwest, the small farmers in the Old Northwest, and also in Kentucky and Tennessee, were soon followed by processors of various farm products. Energetic and enterprising men quickly capitalized on the advantages of processing hogs and cattle near the farms, shipping the meat to market in barrels, and of milling wheat into flour in local centers for shipment elsewhere. Cincinnati became a regional metropolis partly because of the steamboat business but chiefly because of the pork-packing industry. The "Queen of the West" was also called "Porkopolis." Progressively the West complemented diversified agriculture with diversified manufacturing, and thus tended to follow the model of the economy of the East, except for oceanic enterprises. But the flow of traffic was still chiefly southward down the rivers, and ties of kinship with the South were strong. The West was destined to become a crucial battleground in the economic and political conflicts of the generation, and the riddle of the future was whether it would ally itself with the East or South. Only when the Northwest and

Northeast were firmly tied together by railroads did the three sections of the country resolve themselves into two—North and South.

THE PANIC OF 1819

American exuberance had a rude shock in the financial crisis which began in 1818, reached its climax in 1819, and lasted for several years thereafter. This was the first of the economic depressions which occurred at fairly regular intervals in the United States until our own times. Though connected with the world situation, it was precipitated and accentuated by American actions and developments. It was a slump after a boom.

The restoration of trade with Europe had worked to the immediate disadvantage of the young manufacturers of the United States; and despite the Tariff of 1816 they had had difficulty in adjusting themselves to the situation. But there was a great boom in agriculture, resulting from an abnormal European demand for American staples which caused prices to soar. Cotton, the chief export, went to more than 30¢ a pound. Then, as a result of the great expansion of American production and the decline in European demand after supply caught up with it, agricultural prices dropped. In the year 1819, they were, in general, about half their previous maximum. There was a slump in all agricultural commodities but the heaviest blow fell on those most involved in the export trade—cotton and tobacco. Quite obviously the American economy was still dependent on the world market. Overexpansion in the United States, however, was a major factor and the panic was precipitated by actions within the chaotic banking system which amounted to a reaction against the reckless purchasing of land.

The federal government had encouraged westward migration by liberalizing the terms of sale of public lands. The law had not been changed since the Act of 1804. Under it, land could be bought at $2 per acre, the minimum quantity being 160 acres. The law was designed to facilitate purchase by actual farmers from the government land offices; and in the West and South after 1815 there was the proverbial "land-office business." The system also provided for auctions. Large purchases were made at these on a speculative basis; at the height of the boom as much as $78 per acre was bid in the Southwest. The government was a tolerant creditor, and in the year 1819 the arrears in payments on lands amounted to $22 million. Also, the government accepted the notes (paper money) of state banks in payment, though these were often not adequately backed by specie.

Western confidence in the future tended towards exaggeration. Farmers and speculators bought too much land from the government on credit and mortgaged it to the hilt to state banks, in return for paper money which had been issued in excessive quantity by those banks on the basis of assets that were difficult to liquidate. The western and southern branches of the Bank of the United States accepted the notes of state banks and loaned them money freely. State banks varied greatly in their soundness, but in general they were at their wildest in the trans-Appalachian country and in the Old Southwest, the one bank in the state of Mississippi being a notable exception. The situation in Kentucky and Alabama was particularly notorious, but throughout the newer country people were heavily in debt, while speculative mania pushed prosperity to dangerous heights of inflation.

The bubble of this western boom was pricked by the Bank of the United States, which had let itself become dangerously extended. It began in the latter months of 1818 to curtail its discounts and call on its branches for specie. Since a disproportionate part of the capital of the Bank had been drawn into the South and West, these regions were heavily involved in the process of curtailment. But the state banks could not readily pay their balances to the branches of the United States Bank and redeem their own notes in specie. They were forced to call in their own loans to farmers and speculators, often being forced to take over land which they could not sell, and soon they began to suspend specie payments. Nonetheless, many of them continued to issue their own notes, which inevitably shrank in value. Thus the finances of the country spun in a vicious circle, and the crisis soon affected all regions. Values declined even more in lands than in agricultural products, and there were foreclosures everywhere. The Bank of the United States came to own a large part of the city of Cincinnati. A common saying throughout the West and South was: "The Bank was saved and the people were ruined."

Political Effects

One of the most important consequences of this Depression was the arousing, in the West and newer parts of the South, of a spirit of hostility to banks in general and to the Bank of the United States in particular. This spirit tended to draw those regions together in common political cause. The Westerners and Southwesterners would not blame their sufferings on their own speculative fever; they blamed the Bank, now called the "Monster," whose heartless directors had transformed the institution into the servant of Eastern business, and they castigated the "Money Power." These sentiments, nourished by the long agony of the Depression, ramified into the whole complex of rebellious and reformist ideas which took shape in the movement called Jacksonian Democracy.

Losing neither their optimism nor their faith in nationalism, Westerners intensified their faith in democracy as the cure for all their woes. If the people could wrest the control of government from the hands of moneyed interests they could yet fulfill their dreams. Western state governments responded quickly to the demand for relief. Some of them defied the Supreme Court's decision in McCulloch vs. Maryland (1819) by taxing the branches of the Bank. Others evaded the constitutional provision forbidding them to issue bills of credit, an evasion which Marshall condemned in Craig vs. Missouri (1830). Westerners also turned to the federal government for relief. The Public Land Act of 1820 ended the credit system, which had resulted in the government's having to take back much of the land previously sold. The new law lowered the price of public land from $2 to $1.25 per acre and reduced the minimum size of a purchase from 160 to 80 acres. For $100 a farmer could now buy a small farm outright.

The West did not lose faith in the administration of President Monroe. He was not held responsible for the financial crisis with which his first term ended. During the next decade, however, there was increased demand for economic action on the part of the federal government. Besides the clamor for internal improvements, there was a strong movement for greater tariff protection, and this also aroused sharp political conflict. It was in connection with these clashes of interest that the new sectionalism showed itself most clearly, bringing to an end the Era of Good Feelings.

The Missouri Compromise

The Panic of 1819 sharpened the antagonism between the West and the East and tended to draw the agricultural West and South together in common hostility to the "Money Power." At just the same time a sudden eruption of the slavery question distracted the whole country and threatened a more serious antagonism between the North and the South. Then the successful solution, by compromise, of the immediate question of the expansion of slavery confirmed the hold of the Monroe administration on the voters of all sections.

Before this time slavery had not been the occasion of serious dispute between the northern and southern regions. The foreign slave trade was in process of being fully outlawed. The constitutional provision relating to slavery that bore most directly on the existing situation was the three-fifths ratio of representation, sometimes called the federal ratio. The representation of any state in the lower house of Congress was based on the number of its free inhabitants, plus three-fifths of its slaves. The free states were now forging ahead in total population and were gaining even faster in the House of Representatives, where they now had a definite majority. On the other hand, the delegation from the South was disproportionate to its free population, and the region actually had representation for its slave property. This situation vexed the Northerners, especially the New Englanders, who had suffered from political frustration since the Louisiana Purchase and who specially resented the rule of the Virginia Dynasty. Meanwhile, the admission of new free states and new slave states had been so timed that the balance between the North and South had been maintained in the United States Senate.

The tacit boundary between the two regions consisted of the Mason and Dixon Line and the Ohio River. But settlement had reached the point where Missouri, the next state to be carved out of the Louisiana Purchase, straddled the line between the free and slave states. After 1815, settlers had poured across the Mississippi and filled a wide belt along that river and also a belt westward on both sides of the Missouri River and of "Big Muddy's" tributaries—the Gasconade and the Osage. St. Louis became an important center of trade, migration, and manufacturing. Several thousand planters took their slaves into the area believing that Congress would do nothing to disturb the institution, which had enjoyed legal protection in the territory of the Louisiana Purchase under its former French and Spanish rulers. At the same time sentiment in the North was beginning to harden against slavery as a contradiction of American liberty.

In 1818, Congress received from the territory of Missouri a petition that statehood be granted. Early in the next year, during the discussion of a bill authorizing the Missourians to proceed with the drawing of a constitution, Representative James Tallmadge, Jr., of New York introduced an amendment prohibiting the further importation of slaves into the prospective state, and providing for the eventual freeing of those afterward born there. This proposal was similar to the moderate schemes of gradual emancipation which had been adopted in various northern states; but the amendment said, in effect, that Missouri could become a state only if it should present to Congress an antislavery constitution. The amendment as a whole was adopted by the House by a close vote, the representatives from the slave states being almost unanimous against it. In the Senate the two clauses were voted on separately and both were defeated, the latter overwhelmingly, sectional lines being drawn rather less sharply. During the next few months there occurred in the press and on the platform the first national popular debate on slavery. Then, at the next session of Congress, the debate was resumed in the capitol.

The Issues

Northerners did not at this time launch an attack on slaveholders, but they did publicly condemn slavery as an institution, raising the moral issue while not yet stressing it. Some of them expressed a frank hostility to Negroes as well as to slaves, and sought to preserve the interminable regions beyond the Mississippi not merely for free men but for white

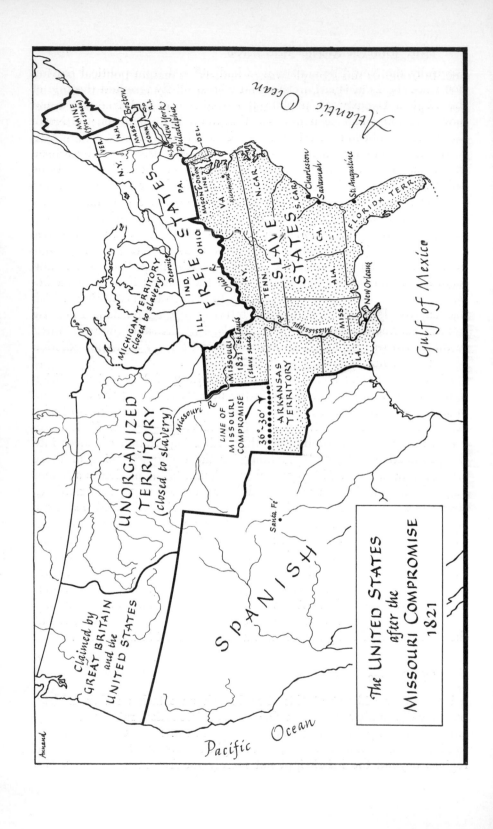

The UNITED STATES after the MISSOURI COMPROMISE 1821

men. In Congress this struggle was recognized as one for political power, as the references to the three-fifths ratio showed. Senator Rufus King of New York estimated that if this did not exist and representation were based solely on free population, the slave states would lose twenty representatives and Virginia would lose seven of her twenty-three. There was no chance to take this provision out of the Constitution, but Northerners did not want to add another state to the Southern interest, which they regarded as too great already. Federalists like King, who had New England antecedents, also saw in the Missouri dispute a particular opportunity to divorce the Southern Republicans from their Northern allies among farmers and city groups, to tie the latter to a wholly northern party, and unseat the Virginia Dynasty. Perhaps the effort to divide the Republicans was too transparent. Northern Republicans may have been lukewarm about slavery, but they were hot against "traitorous" Federalism.

In general, Southerners refused to debate the moral issues involved in slavery. Some of them, especially those from the Upper South, were ready to admit that the institution was an evil, but their major contention was that this question was irrelevant. They took their stand on the ground that Congress lacked power to impose conditions on the admission of a state. At this stage few of them denied that Congress had power over slavery in the territories. This was a question, rather, of the equality of a new state with the old ones.

One practical argument advanced by certain Southerners at this time is summed up by the pompous expression, "mitigation by diffusion"—in modern parlance, the "spread theory." Its advocates were men who clearly recognized that slavery was a problem which must eventually be solved, and who believed that it could be more easily solved if it were less concentrated. Speaking of slavery at this time, Jefferson said, "we have the wolf by the ears, and we can neither hold him, nor safely let him go."

The Southerners were aware of the struggle for political power. Already falling behind in the race for population, they wanted to attach another state to the Southern interest, and the desirability of maintaining a sectional balance in the Senate was henceforth axiomatic with them. The famous compromise with which this controversy was settled was worked out on that principle. Maine was also seeking admission to the Union, and she was coupled with Missouri. No restrictions were imposed on either, but one chose to be a free state while the other legalized slavery. It was agreed that slavery should be forever prohibited in the remainder of the Louisiana Purchase north of the parallel 36° 30'. As a political compromise this was from the Southern point of view a bad bargain, for the rest of the Louisiana Purchase above the line of 36° 30' was considerably larger than the territory below it.

The Missouri Compromise of 1820, which gained in the free states a sanctity comparable to that attaching to the Constitution, took the slavery question out of national politics until the struggle in Congress over the Gag Rule in the late 1830's and the rise of the Texas question. But, despite the confirmation of the Northern contention that Congress could prohibit slavery in the territories, that question was destined to arise again, and the moral question about slavery, once raised, would not down.

Jefferson was enjoying his peaceful retirement at Monticello when tho "momentous question" that was raised in the Missouri debates, "like a fire bell in the night," awakened him and filled him with terror. "I considered it at once as the knell of the Union," he said. "It is hushed, indeed, for the moment. But this is a reprieve only, not a final sentence. *A geographical line, coinciding with a marked principle, moral and political, once conceived and held up to the angry passions of men, will never be obliterated; and every new irritation will mark it deeper and deeper.*" John Quincy Adams, who came from the other side of the line, was equally clairvoyant. "I take it for granted," he said, "that the present question is a mere preamble—a title-page to a great, tragic volume."

CHAPTER 23

John Marshall
and John Quincy Adams

AT JUST THE TIME THAT THE UNITED STATES WAS completing political independence by winning a series of brilliant diplomatic victories, the Supreme Court was setting up the constitutional framework of the future nation by means of a series of far-reaching decisions. Chief Justice Marshall remained in office for two decades after the War of 1812, but his most important services ended in 1824. Never again after the decision in the case of Marbury *vs*. Madison (1803) did he declare an act of Congress unconstitutional, but year by year he asserted federal authority against state legislatures and state courts, while also affirming the sanctity of contracts and the rights of private property. Doctrines of state rights were soon invoked against him, however, showing that a battle still lay ahead. Marshall was charged with indifference to the economic welfare of poor men, and he was unsympathetic with the trend of his times toward political democracy. Though a friend of individual liberty, he was a conservative man in the tradition of the Federalists.

From the chaos of personal factions into which the one-party system dissolved, Andrew Jackson was emerging as the central public figure of the era. But victory went to John Quincy Adams in the presidential election of 1824, consigning the stiff New Englander to an unhappy battle of four years with the large faction that swore allegiance to the General. The political history of Adams's presidential term is a tangled tale of individual leaders and their followings and their intrigue. The tariff emerged as the most controversial issue, and it was this, rather than slavery or the reaction against the judicial nationalism of Marshall, which gave sharpest point to state-rights doctrines at that time. Meanwhile, most Americans exulted in the rising political democracy which history has connected with the name of Jackson. In the long run this was to prove the most powerful unifying force within the country.

THE NATIONALISM OF THE SUPREME COURT, 1816-1824

Marshall dominated the Supreme Court during his entire thirty-four years as Chief Justice (1801-1835). Very rarely did his opinions fail to sway the majority of the Justices, and he personally wrote almost half of the more than 1100 decisions. Appointed by a Federalist, John Adams, Marshall saw the entire remaining personnel of the Court transformed by the appointments of five successive Presidents, nearly all of whom were politically unsympathetic toward him. Newcomers, like Joseph Story who was appointed by Madison as a Republican, fell under the influence of Marshall's brilliant logic, luminous analysis, and compelling nationalism. The bar of the Court, which included such men as William Pinkney, William Wirt, Daniel Webster, Joseph Nicholson, Luther Martin, and Jeremiah Mason, attained eminence in this period. Marshall drew upon the arguments of these noted lawyers when he liked them and was stimulated by them when he did not. His decisions are singularly free of the citations culled from dusty legal tomes which make most juristic prose unreadable to the layman. As the legend runs, he used to say to his colleague: "That, Story, is the law; now you find the precedents." He was less erudite than his contemporaries, John and John Quincy Adams, Jefferson and Madison, but his mind had been nourished in the eighteenth-century school of common-sense logic and he liked general principles. His written opinions were full of both and that made them lucid and convincing.

Proclaiming National Sovereignty

Probably the most famous of his decisions in this the most fruitful period of his service was rendered in the case of McCulloch vs. Maryland (1819). In it he set forth more fully than elsewhere his philosophy of national sovereignty, while saving the Second Bank of the United States from destruction at the hands of a state legislature. This was not an isolated incident, for the action of Maryland was paralleled by that of other states during this period, chiefly in the South and West. The facts were that the Maryland legislature had imposed a tax on the notes of all banks operating within the state and not chartered by it—which meant the Baltimore branch of the Bank of the United States—and that Treasurer McCulloch of that Branch refused to pay this tax. After the state government had hauled him into its own courts and won its case, McCulloch appealed to the federal Supreme Court.

Marshall saw in the situation, in the first place, a crucial question regarding the source of federal power and authority. Counsel for Maryland claimed that the powers of the general government were delegated by the sovereign states, and "must be exercised in subordination to the states, who alone possess supreme dominion." This was in the tradition of the Kentucky and Virginia Resolutions of 1798, and by this time it was the doctrine of Old Republicans. The Chief Justice, while recognizing that the people had necessarily acted by means of state conventions, declared that, nonetheless, the Constitution and federal government proceeded directly from the people, not from the state governments. This contention about the origins of the Constitution was to be challenged many times before the Civil War, but Marshall also voiced an ideal which was to be progressively realized and eventually accepted by everybody. He said: "The government of the Union, then, . . . is emphatically and truly a government of the people. In form and substance it emanates from them, its powers are granted by them, and are to be exercised directly on them, and for their benefit."

A second and more pertinent question was whether the power to charter a national bank had been delegated to the federal government. In answering this, Marshall went straight back to the opinion of Hamilton (1791) on the constitutionality of the First Bank of the United States which he himself had summed up, along with the opposing opinion of Jefferson, in his *Life of George Washington*. Hamilton had not glorified "the people," for he distrusted them, but his argument was superb and the Chief Justice repeated it. Jefferson, as one of George Washington's advisers, had defined the "necessary and proper" clause of the Constitution narrowly, but Marshall accepted the interpretation of Hamilton and used almost the same words: "Let the end be legitimate, let it be within the scope of the Constitution, and all means which are appropriate, which are plainly adapted to that end, which are not prohibited, but consist with the letter and the spirit of the Constitution, are constitutional." Thus "liberal construction" became official American doctrine, in so far as the Supreme Court could make it so. The doctrine is liable to abuse, but an effective federal government could hardly be attained without it.

The constitutionality of the Bank having thus been affirmed, the question remained whether the State of Maryland had the right to tax it. The answer to this was decisively in the negative. Marshall said that "the power to tax involves the power to destroy." The states, he declared, "have no power by taxation or otherwise, to retard, impede, burden, or in any manner control, the operations of the constitutional laws enacted by Congress to carry into execution the powers vested in the general government." Marshall did not distinguish between state taxes designed to destroy federal functions, which was the obvious intent of the Maryland levy on the Bank, and state taxes designed only for revenue. His dictum went too far, and it has had to be limited in our own time. But no organization or property of the federal government has been subjected to state taxes since Marshall's great decision.

In deciding for the Bank, Marshall had sided with a corporation which many people now called the "Monster," but his famous decision in Gibbons *vs.* Ogden (1824) brought no comfort to would-be monopolists. In this case he ruled against a New York steamboat monopoly and gave a far-reaching interpretation of the commerce clause of the Constitution. The main facts in the case were these. Robert Fulton, builder of the pioneer steamboat, the *Clermont* (1807), had entered into partnership with the politically-powerful Robert R. Livingston to exploit the commercial possibilities of the Hudson, and Livingston had obtained from the state a twenty-year monopoly of steam-navigation rights on that river. From these partners, exclusive right to steam navigation between New York and New Jersey was secured by Aaron Ogden, and the latter sought to restrain Thomas Gibbons from engaging in such navigation. Ogden was upheld by Chancellor James Kent of New York, but Gibbons appealed to the Supreme Court, which decided unanimously in his favor.

Speaking for the Court, Marshall defined "commerce" broadly—not as traffic or mere buying and selling but as intercourse. Furthermore, he declared that commerce among the states "cannot stop at the external boundary-line of each state, but may be introduced into the interior"; and he held that the power of Congress to regulate it under the Constitution may be exercised "to the utmost." Commerce that is wholly intrastate is under state control, but whenever interstate or foreign commerce is involved, federal power can pass the borders of any state and penetrate the interior.

Under this sweeping definition, the federal government has extended its control of interstate commerce into all the states and into many spheres which were unforeseen by Marshall—such as the regulation of railroad rates and the wages and hours of labor. His decision encouraged both the expansion of private business into the national market and the regulation of business by the federal government. The first effect was immediately apparent, and steamboat companies hastened to invade waters formerly reserved by states for favored monopolists. In New York the decision was celebrated with fireworks and a great tooting of whistles by "foreign" steamboats as they churned the emancipated waters of the Hudson. But the second effect of the decision did not become apparent for several generations and it was not entirely welcome to businessmen.

The Sanctity of Contracts

Yet the growth of American business enterprises from their small beginnings in Marshall's time to their colossal later stature was enormously facilitated by his work. Besides asserting the supremacy of the federal government over the states in its allotted sphere, Marshall in another great group of decisions asserted the supremacy of the business contract over any government or individual who would violate its sanctity. In Fletcher vs. Peck (1810), a case connected with the Yazoo Claims and the state of Georgia, he had denied the right of one state legislature to void a grant of land made by a previous one, even though in this particular instance the immense grant was obtained by fraud and was overwhelmingly condemned by public opinion. Marshall has been sharply criticized for this decision, but it gave assurance that financial agreements made with governments were contracts that could be relied on. This sense of security was an essential component in the advance of American business.

In the notable case of Dartmouth College vs. Woodward (1819), the Chief Justice expanded this doctrine under much more appealing circumstances. The legislature of New Hampshire had decided that Dartmouth, which had been chartered as a private institution and was governed by a self-perpetuating private board of trustees, might conveniently be transformed into a public institution governed by the state through trustees appointed by the legislature. The existing board appealed to the federal courts on the ground that the federal Constitution forbade a state to impair the obligation of contracts. Daniel Webster, Dartmouth's most famous alumnus, serving as counsel, winsomely said that his alma mater was a small college but that there were those who loved her well. Marshall agreed that the college charter was a contract which could not be violated by the state. Just as the decision in Fletcher vs. Peck encouraged business enterprises operated for private profit, so that in the Dartmouth case encouraged privately-endowed educational and charitable institutions.

Marshall's interpretation of the contract clause of the Constitution caused him to regard as unconstitutional various state laws designed to relieve debtors and meet the problems of insolvency. In the case of Sturgis vs. Crowninshield (1819) he ruled that a state law relieving insolvents from past contracts was invalid and his decision served to limit state actions in matters of bankruptcy. But in Ogden vs. Saunders (1827), one of those rare cases in which Marshall found himself in the minority, the Court later held that a state insolvency law did not impair the obligation of *future* contracts between its citizens. A more liberal tendency had appeared in the Court, and there was more disposition to leave some leeway to the states in these matters. But in his minority opinion Marshall strongly took the position that the Constitution protected all contracts, past or future, from state legislation which impaired them in any way. When it came to financial contracts, Marshall himself was a strict constructionist, and he has been described at this stage of

his life by his chief biographer as a "supreme conservative." The trend of
the times was against him in his last years.

Protests from Virginia

Ironically enough, the most formidable attack on him was made in his
own state. The grounds of this were partly personal. There was a long-
standing feud between him and Spencer Roane, the presiding judge of
the Supreme Court of Appeals of Virginia, who presumably would have
been appointed Chief Justice of the United States instead of Marshall
if Jefferson and not John Adams had made the appointment.

The case which occasioned the controversy arose from the lands of
Lord Fairfax, the ungranted part of which the state had tried to confiscate at the close of the American Revolution, in the absence of the
Loyalist proprietor; and the Supreme Court's decision long years later
was on the fundamental ground that the action of the state was contrary
to the terms of the peace treaty with Great Britain. The Marshall family
was personally interested in the Fairfax claims, and the Chief Justice
would not sit on the case when it finally came before the Supreme Court
in 1813, but he concurred in every word of Justice Story's opinion. He
was arrayed against a popular interest in Virginia, where the original
confiscation of Tory property was widely approved, while the interest of
his own family was on the other side, and he was held responsible for
the assertion of federal jurisdiction. Justice Story asked the Virginia
Supreme Court of Appeals to execute the decision, which was a tactical
mistake. Roane and his colleagues flatly refused, declaring that the
appellate jurisdiction of the United States Supreme Court was unconstitutional. This was in 1815. The next year, in the case of Martin vs.
Hunter's Lessee, Story upheld his previous position, saying that the case
not the court gave the jurisdiction. The case started in a state court but
it bore on the question of a treaty, which was a federal matter. He was
wise enough to order a federal official to serve the writ this time, and
Roane's court was not called upon to act one way or the other.

The question of jurisdiction was again involved in the case of Cohens
vs. The State of Virginia (1821), involving fines levied by Virginia courts
on the sellers of lottery tickets. The lottery had been organized in the
District of Columbia, which was under federal control. Taking the position that there was no intention of forcing the lottery business into the
state, the Supreme Court ordered that the fines be paid. It had, however,
asserted its jurisdiction, again on the ground that the nature of the case
not the court of its origin was the determining factor.

In Virginia, meanwhile, Roane wrote a series of vehement papers
against Marshall and his judicial works. The legislature passed a resolution denying federal jurisdiction over the state courts, and an amendment

to the Constitution expressing these sentiments was drafted. Also, in the period 1820-1823, John Taylor of Caroline published three notable works in which he expounded agrarian and state-rights doctrines. More than the belligerent Roane he symbolized the Virginia trend away from centralization and against the judicial nationalism of her famous son, John Marshall.

Tall, slender, and reddish-haired like Jefferson, pure-minded and unpretentious, Taylor was the ideal picture of a republican statesman. Rarely in federal office, he was a power in state affairs, but he was most interested in farming and was a pioneer in scientific agriculture. Though a defender of slavery, he was generally a reformer in the field of local political institutions, while Marshall supported the existing order. This prolific, diffuse, and difficult writer was a foe to special privilege of any sort, and his words of warning about the rising aristocracy of "privilege and paper" were strikingly prophetic. An old-fashioned country gentleman, he distrusted bankers while John Marshall was upholding the Bank of the United States and preparing the way for the future triumphs of business. While the Chief Justice was giving national sovereignty a legal framework, Taylor saw the individual state as the only sure bulwark of the individualism which had been the dream and was now the tradition of Americans. Time was to prove that the weapon of state rights which he chose was not sufficient, but he was the guardian of the enduring values which lie at the heart of Jeffersonian republicanism.

Jefferson could not reconcile himself to the trend of Marshall's decisions. "The great object of my fear," he said in his old age, "is the Federal Judiciary. That body, like gravity, ever acting with noiseless foot and unalarming advance, gaining ground step by step, and holding what it gains, is engulfing insidiously the special governments into the jaws of that which feeds them." To him as to John Taylor, and more in his declining years than during his own presidency, the "special governments" or states were a necessary bulwark against the potential tyranny of centralization.

Marshall may have been thinking of him or John Taylor when he said this in one of his famous decisions:

> Powerful and ingenious minds, taking as postulates that the powers expressly granted to the government of the Union are to be contracted by construction, into the narrowest possible compass, and that the original powers of the states are to be retained, . . . may, by a course of well-digested, but refined and metaphysical reasoning, founded on these premises, explain away the constitution of our country and leave it a magnificent structure indeed but totally unfit for use (Gibbons vs. Ogden, 1824.).

This was an excellent description of the Chief Justice himself in reverse. His immortal service was to breathe life and vigor into the Constitution. If, in his concern for effective means of government he at times overlooked the great human and popular ends to which the Republic had long ago been dedicated, his countrymen have found a necessary supplement in the thought of Jefferson. Lincoln was true in spirit to both men when he resolved, not merely that the Union should be preserved, but that "the government of the people, by the people, and for the people should not perish from the earth."

THE ELECTION OF 1824

Three members of the Cabinet of Monroe openly aspired to the high office which he had administered so moderately and on the whole so wisely, and as candidates they were joined by Speaker Henry Clay and, last but far from least, General Andrew Jackson. Never had there been such a presidential sweepstakes, and until the very end of the race the outcome was uncertain.

William H. Crawford, the Secretary of the Treasury, who came so near the Republican nomination eight years before, was a native of Virginia who had adopted the state of Georgia. He seemed the natural heir of the Virginia Dynasty and looked like a sure winner in the Congressional caucus of the party. But in 1823 Crawford, who was a giant of a man, suffered a paralytic stroke which probably would have completely wrecked his candidacy if his physical condition had been fully known. Furthermore, and this is an important item in the history of American political institutions, the caucus system was under fire from the other candidates, who could not in this instance expect much from it, and it was now charged with being undemocratic. More than any of the others, Crawford represented the existing political order. Through thick and thin he retained the loyal support of Virginia and Georgia, and he was backed by Martin Van Buren and the Albany Regency in New York. Van Buren, the most astute political organizer of the day, saw the light and made his important alliance with Jackson after the election.

John Quincy Adams, whose superb services as Secretary of State have already been described, was a man of the highest intellectual attainments and, in the best sense of the term, a trained public servant. In this respect, more than Crawford, he was a fitting heir of the Virginia Dynasty, and, notwithstanding the nationalistic trend of his constitutional views, he was not unacceptable to some of the Old Republicans. His sure support, however, was in the Northeast, especially in his own New England. Being his father's son, he was no sort of politician, and he was relatively inactive in the canvass.

His colleague John C. Calhoun, the able and ambitious Secretary of War, was exceedingly active; and the South Carolinian, still regarded as a nationalist, had political support throughout the country. He was at least second choice almost everywhere. Before voting time he concluded that he would have to content himself with the second place, and he gained the vice-presidency by default. He was still relatively young (forty-two) and he hitched his wagon to the rising star of Andrew Jackson, not realizing that eventually the General would unhitch him.

A fourth candidate, who was to gain the reputation of being a perennial one, was Henry Clay, eloquent spokesman for the West and the American System. But this convivial and extremely popular Kentuckian was blocked by Jackson, who in common opinion was the West incarnate.

Jackson, the most commanding personality among these strong men, eventually turned out to be the best politician. At this point, however, the most natural thing to say about him is that he was the first American after George Washington who gained the highest political eminence in consequence of a military reputation. The idea of capitalizing on his fame as an Indian fighter and the victor at New Orleans was not his, but was that of a group of his friends and neighbors who comprised what is known as the "Nashville Junto." Chief among these were Senator John H. Eaton, William B. Lewis, who had served as Jackson's quartermaster in some of his Indian campaigns, and John Overton, a large Tennessee landholder who had formerly been a judge. Jackson was in his mid-fifties by the middle of Monroe's second term and in bad health. According to his wife Rachel, he had not spent under his own roof a fourth of their thirty years of married life. He would have liked to rest at the Hermitage, where he had a hundred slaves and some very fine horses, though he had ceased training them for the racetrack by now. He was conservative in his economic views, and his political mentors executed a *tour de force* when they presented him to the electorate, not only as the "Nation's Hero" but also as the "People's Friend." The former designation was wholly accurate from 1815 onward, but he had only begun to win the latter.

At this stage the "democratic" emphasis in the candidacy which his friends had imposed upon the fiery but weary General lay chiefly in the criticism they directed against the Congressional caucus. As a device for nominating presidential candidates, the caucus had been distinctly successful up to this point, judging from the caliber of the men selected, but it had ceased to be responsive to popular opinion and was largely under the control of vested political interests. Jackson was quite as ready to attack these as he was Indians or British redcoats. It may be doubted if the system of national political conventions represented an improvement in nomination machinery, and actually this did not develop until the next decade. Jackson was first presented to the country as a presidential candidate by the legislature of his own state. Other state legislatures presented him or another candidate in the same way. His crucial pre-election victory came in his endorsement by a state convention in Pennsylvania in

1823. This action occasioned the withdrawal of Calhoun, who had actually been the first candidate to oppose the caucus. Crawford, slightly improved in health, persisted in the race and won a useless nomination at the hands of a rump caucus, from which nearly all of the supporters of his rivals had abstained.

Meanwhile, there were many indications of Jackson's great public popularity. As a political legend he was still in the making, but the difficulty of electioneering against the Hero of New Orleans was quickly perceived. In 1823, his friends caused him to be elected to the United States Senate, and there, besides voting for the Tariff of 1824, he favored internal improvements. He seemed as devoted as Clay to Western interests, and he gained support in the Middle States without losing much in the South, where Calhoun was now working for him. He spoke little in the Senate but made a dignified impression in social circles, in which he was considerably lionized, and he showed none of the violence of temper he had been charged with.

The net result of all the maneuvers was that the electoral vote was split four ways among the candidates, no one of whom had a majority. Jackson led with 99 votes, being followed by Adams with 84, Crawford with 41, and Clay with 37. According to the Twelfth Amendment to the Constitution, the election then devolved upon the House of Representatives, where the three top candidates were voted for, the vote being by states. Clay, who had carried three western states, was the lowest man and dropped out. Despite the undoubted preference of the West for Jackson, Clay did what he could to throw his strength to Adams, who was elected. He explained that Jackson was only a "military chieftain"— in which he was very much mistaken.

Other factors entered into the election, such as the swing of New York to Adams by a margin of one vote in the state delegation, but not unnaturally the defeat of Jackson was blamed on the "Judas of the West," as the General himself called the Kentuckian. When Adams appointed Clay Secretary of State, the cry of "corrupt bargain" would not down; and the austere New Englander could never overcome the handicap of seeming to be an accidental President, whose election had defied the popular will and defeated the people's choice. Meanwhile the "Military Chieftain" was defiantly renominated for President by the legislature of Tennessee, and resigned the seat he had briefly held in the United States Senate.

PRESIDENT ADAMS vs. THE JACKSONIANS

Since the Monroe administration was the last for almost a century to be chiefly concerned with foreign relations, it would have been appropriate if a President principally interested in domestic affairs had been elected in 1824, as almost happened. Yet John Quincy Adams was by no means devoid of a domestic program. He was as ambitious for the internal as for the external welfare of his country, and he applied to the solution of pressing domestic problems the same high intelligence and sense of duty that he had to securing a safe, dignified, and enlarged position for the nation in the world. But, like his famous father, he lacked popularity and political sagacity. Regarded as a "President by mistake," he had no party behind him and made no effort to create one. Scorning the use of patronage to build up political support, he left opponents of his in appointive office to undermine him.

The Jacksonians spent the four years of Adams's administration making sure that there would be no mistake in 1828, and the President himself committed many tactical errors. In recommending a broad program of internal improvements, he used such strong language of loose construction as to alarm former supporters of Crawford and impel them into the Jackson camp, where Senator Van Buren was glad to welcome them; and he neglected to appeal to those local interests which are of necessary concern to politicians in a representative government. The results were that the people never understood what he wanted to do and that Congress, ignoring his recommendations, planned his defeat. More money was appropriated for roads and harbors in this administration than in any preceding one, but this redounded little to Adams's political credit and his full program never had a chance. With the mid-term election of 1826, the Jacksonians won a majority in both houses of Congress and the President was hamstrung.

The New Democracy

The highly intellectual man in the White House, who recorded his frustration in the most introspective of American political diaries, was the victim of the surging political democracy which made Jackson its beneficiary. Laws abolishing property qualifications for voting and establishing either a tax-paying qualification or manhood suffrage for white males were adopted by nearly all of the northern states and most of the southern by the next presidential election. By this continuing process the United States became the first political democracy in the modern world. Universal suffrage had been implicit in the earlier Jeffersonian movement, but in 1800 low property qualifications for voting had not seemed inconsistent with the idea of popular sovereignty for no considerable propertyless urban class existed. Now in the third decade of the century, the new factories had created the small beginnings of an industrial working class, and there was great significance in the extension of the vote to this landless group—a development which occurred in England only in 1867.

Conservatives were convinced that the result of giving the vote to citizens who had no stake in society would be demagogy and dictatorship. They believed that voters who lacked the sober stability of character presumably conferred by the ownership of property would follow the most blatant peddler of panaceas, the most reckless antagonist of wealth. A seeker for evidence that these dire prophecies were well-founded could find it in the crudity of the new generation of politicians who organized voters for Jackson, in the Jacksonian distrust of the able as well as of the rich and the well-born, and in the rough handling of delicate matters of government policy to make them yield votes—which was character-istic of most administrations during the next generation. But the Jacksonian movement also included a demand for universal education which ultimately brought dividends in intelligent use of the suffrage, and during the intervening years it was not so much the uneducated man who was glorified as the self-educated.

Jackson was the chief idol of the new democracy, and Calhoun was now ranged with him. Martin Van Buren in New York, James Buchanan in Pennsylvania, and lesser leaders in other states built up organizations pledged to the "People's Friend." For convenience we shall call these men Democrats, though the name did not become fixed until Jackson's presidency. Only "right-wing" fragments of the Republican Party remained loyal to Adams and Clay. Later they called themselves National Republicans, and in the next decade they became the Whigs. At first the two groupings were almost indistinguishable in their attitudes towards national policies. But, besides calling the Adams administration illegitimate and designating its projects as foul products of the "corrupt bargain," the Jacksonians charged it with trying to revive discredited and antidemocratic Federalism. This was a partisan exaggeration, but if the lines of descent must be drawn, the National Republicans and Whigs were the heirs of the Federalists, and the Democrats of the Jeffersonians.

The Panama Congress

Even in the field of foreign relations, where as Secretary of State he had won such acclaim, President Adams was frustrated by the vituperative partisanship of the Jackson men in Congress. His chief concern now was to counter British influence in Latin America. Canning's purpose there was to make the new republics into economic and political satellites of Great Britain. This is what Canning meant when he wrote in January 1825: "Spanish America is free, and if we do not mismanage our affairs sadly, she is English." Britain had the advantage of trade supremacy in Latin America and the prestige of having supported the revolutions more enthusiastically than the United States had. But Adams believed that his country might by a vigorous policy establish the hegemony of the United States in the Hemisphere.

When Simón de Bolívar, liberator of Spanish America, called the international Congress of Panama in 1826 to consider plans for a league to strengthen the commercial and legal positions of the new republics and to concert measures against Spain, he proposed that the British but not the United States government be asked to send representatives. Mexico and Colombia nevertheless invited the United States and Adams accepted. The prospect of the association of United States delegates with Haitian representatives or others who might not be "pure white" aroused an outcry from Southerners. In order to send delegates at all, the approval of the Congress of the United States and an appropriation were necessary. The Jackson men used the opportunity to lambast the President and Secretary of State with outlandish accusations. It was in the debate on this that John Randolph of Roanoke, who was a political eclectic, spoke of the coalition between "the Puritan and the Blackleg" with the result that he fought an absurd duel with Clay.

The mission was finally approved, but one American delegate died on the way to Panama and the other arrived only after the rather futile Congress had disbanded. The British delegation had carefully strengthened friendly ties with the Spanish-American governments; and, for a long time afterwards, diplomatic representatives of the United States cooled their heels in these courts, while all doors were open to British ministers.

The failure of Adams's plan to participate in the Panama Congress may not have altered the situation materially, but this was his first defeat in the field of foreign relations, and in bringing it about the opposition provided an unsavory example of playing domestic politics with foreign policy. The Jacksonians strengthened their hold on Southerners in this instance. Vice-President Calhoun was strongly opposed to the administration on the issue and he now drew closer to the Jackson partisans. Running with the General, he expected to be re-elected to the vice-presidency in 1828 and to succeed to the first office after the Hero should retire. He did not yet know how indestructible the Hero was.

Georgia and the Indians

Adams was also the political loser, and Jackson inevitably the gainer, from a heated controversy with respect to the Indians which had long been smoldering in Crawford's state of Georgia. Ever since Georgia ceded its western lands to the federal government in 1802, the people there had been restive because of the slow progress of the federal authorities in carrying out their promise to extinguish Indian titles in the state and thus permit land-hungry farmers to take up their lands. In their opinion the redskins were staying much too long. The controversy in Adams's administration related to the Creeks in the west of the state rather than the more civilized Cherokees. During Monroe's administration, by the Treaty of Indian Springs, which was made with a chief named William McIntosh, all the remaining Creek lands were ceded in return for lands west of the Mississippi and a considerable payment of money. This treaty was approved by the Senate, but afterwards McIntosh was shot and his actions were repudiated by other chiefs. Thereupon President Adams ordered that surveys of these lands, which were being speedily undertaken by the eager Georgians, be stopped and he had another treaty negotiated. His conduct was most honorable but this new treaty left some lands within the state to the Creeks, and the threat of Adams to use force to protect the Indians was matched by the defiance of Governor George M. Troup, a red-headed man who had for some time been aggressive in this business, gaining political strength thereby. In the end, further treaties fully extinguished the Creek titles (1826-1827), but the memory of the President's attitude remained vivid in the minds of Georgians and inevitably their thoughts and hopes turned toward the great Indian fighter, Andrew Jackson. He was just as much against the Indians as the Georgians were in the later and more famous case of the Cherokees.

THE TARIFF BECOMES A STORM CENTER

While political lines were being sharply drawn between the Adams administration and the Jacksonian opposition, sectional alignments on economic issues were assuming a more distinct pattern. The West, including Clay's Kentucky if not always Jackson's Tennessee, stood fast in support of a tariff to protect industry and agricultural products (especially wool and hemp), internal improvements at federal expense, and low prices for public lands. On the land question the Old Southwest took much the same position, but otherwise the South as a whole now tended to oppose all these policies.

As an exporting region which faced no domestic competition with its cotton and tobacco, the South needed no protection for its major staples, and it stood to lose when the tariff raised the prices of commodities that it had to buy. The Southerners could not sell all of their cotton in the United States. They had their best market in the British mills, and they saw their best interest in free trade. As for internal improvements, very few of these were being made in the South and hardly any in the South Atlantic states—largely for topographical reasons. It would have been a waste of money to try to build roads and quite impossible to dig canals through the towering mountains which blocked these states from the West. Maryland and the Potomac and western regions of Virginia were in a different case, but along the South Atlantic seaboard men argued not unnaturally that the states benefiting from internal improvements should pay for them.

On only one major economic issue, the Bank of the United States, were the South and West in basic agreement. Since the Panic of 1819 both of them opposed a Bank with credit policies that were unfavorable to farmers and favorable to Eastern business. But the Bank did not become the subject of major controversy until the 1830's. Before then the South had assumed a negative attitude on all the great economic questions of the day, and doctrines of state rights were revivified as a defense mechanism. The protection of slavery, like other Southern interests, could be best entrusted to the states, and this question loomed in the background from the Missouri debates onward.

In the East, the growth of industry was weakening the dominant position of merchants among businessmen, except in such commercial centers as New York City, and it swung votes to protective tariffs. The value of internal improvements in developing the Western market for Eastern manufactures and the Eastern market for Western food was recognized, whether these were financed by the federal government or by states. Because of the needs of the labor market, however, Eastern businessmen wanted to check the westward migration of potential mill hands, whether native-born or immigrant, and even more than Southerners they tended to oppose free-and-easy terms for the sale of public lands. The new lending policy of the national Bank perfectly suited Eastern businessmen. The newly-enfranchised factory workers were disposed to favor a generous public-land policy and they were afterward rallied against the Bank. On the great issue of the tariff, however, they stood with their employers in favoring the protection which, at least during the "infant" period of industrial development, meant jobs and high wages.

Battles of the Twenties

The clash of sectional interests became clearly visible during the tariff battles of the 1820's. Manufacturers regarded as insufficient the protective rates established in 1816, and their dissatisfaction was increased by the Depression that began in 1819. In 1820, a bill to raise the rates failed in the Senate by one vote, but an act was passed in 1824, raising the rates on cotton textiles, raw wool, hemp, iron, and other commodities. The New Englanders in Congress were fairly evenly divided. Daniel Webster opposed the bill. But the Middle States and the West strongly favored it, and they overcame the almost complete opposition of the South. Most Northern interests were satisfied by this Act, with the important exception of woolen textile manufacturers, who found the rates on raw wool increased without compensating advances in the rates on finished products. They failed in their efforts to extend to woolen cloth the "minimum principle" of valuation which had caused the duties on cheap cotton cloth to be virtually prohibitive. Cheap woolen cloth was chiefly imported for the clothing of slaves. To Southerners, this proposal was a danger signal: North and West could unite to defeat their section.

During the next few years, interested groups of manufacturers formed organizations and held conventions; and the protection argument was set forth in articles, books, and addresses. The chief nonpolitical spokesman of these views was Matthew Carey, a prominent publisher of Philadelphia, and the cause was constantly aided and abetted by Hezekiah Niles, publisher of *Niles' Weekly Register* in Washington, with whom Henry Clay was intimate.

The Tariff of 1824 was most bitterly resented in South Carolina. Dr. Thomas Cooper, president of South Carolina College, who has been termed the "schoolmaster of state rights," proclaimed free-trade doctrines in the classroom and in pamphlets at a time when Calhoun was either equivocal or silent on the subject. The local state-rights movement got under way without the Vice-President. In the legislature of 1825 strong resolutions were adopted, condemning the Tariff, the Bank, and internal improvements; and in 1827, Dr. Cooper boldly declared that it was time to "calculate the value of the Union." This fiery man of learning was in advance of local opinion and was roundly condemned by many, but in the course of the same year resolutions of the legislature asserted that internal improvements at federal expense and tariff acts for the protection of domestic manufacturing were unconstitutional. The right of a state to remonstrate against violations of the fundamental "compact" was asserted at the same time, and the idea of nullification by a state had been voiced by Robert J. Turnbull, though it was not emphasized by public men as yet.

Earlier in the same year a woolens bill had been defeated in the Senate by the vote of Vice-President Calhoun, who thus came out openly on the anti-tariff side now that the interests of his state and section so manifestly required it. In the summer a protectionist convention with a hundred delegates from thirteen states met in Harrisburg, Pennsylvania, and this recommended increases in the duties on both raw wool and woolen goods—the latter to be applied on the principle of minimum valuation, which would have the practical result of making them much greater. Such changes would serve only to increase the cost of clothing in regions that produced neither wool nor woolens.

Thus the issue was sharply joined and it put the Jacksonians in a quandary. Maintenance of the alliance between the South and West, which had been symbolized by the understanding between Calhoun and Jackson, seemed essential to victory in the presidential elction of 1828. On the other hand, while New England was conceded to Adams, the Middle States certainly were not. Pennsylvania had played a crucial role in the 1824 campaign; and Senator Martin Van Buren of New York had swung the powerful Albany Regency behind the General. Perhaps the best single explanation of the complicated political maneuvering which was carried on in Jackson's behalf in 1828 is that the bid for the Middle States and the West—especially the former—was the crux of it. It undoubtedly was in the astute mind of Van Buren, who already had the old Crawford states pretty well lined up behind his man. New England could be written off, and Jackson's popularity in the South as a slaveowning planter and Indian fighter could be relied on to keep that section sufficiently in line against the highly unpopular Adams. Jackson was being presented as all things to all men and all sections, but it seemed much more important to cater to New York and Pennsylvania than to South Carolina.

The Tariff of Abominations

According to vitriolic John Randolph of Roanoke, the main purpose of the Tariff Bill of 1828 was to manufacture a President of the United States, and the traditional opinion has been that the inner coterie of Jackson men in Congress artfully loaded it down with provisions which would in the end defeat it. That does not seem to have been the purpose of Silas Wright, a lieutenant of Van Buren's who played a major part in getting it through the House. But the Act was filled with so many contradictions and absurdities that it has been known ever since as the Tariff of Abominations. Duties on raw materials—including wool, hemp, and molasses— were high and some of them incompatible with a rational protectionist philosophy. Thus the duties were raised on coarse wool, which was much used in factories but little produced in the country. Meanwhile, the woolens schedule afforded little protection to the quality of goods produced in New England. By any interpretation the scheme was clever. If this distasteful bill were defeated by New England votes (combined with Southern), blame could be laid on the Adams group; and whether passed or not it would gain credit for the Jackson cause among Northern farmers and Middle-States manufacturers. If the plan was that it should fail, the plotters overreached themselves. The growing appetite of New Englanders for protection caused most of them to swallow the unpalatable measure as a matter of principle. Commercial interests in Massachusetts still objected, as they did in New York City, but Daniel Webster, now a convert to the protective principle, delivered the chief supporting speech in the Senate. Enough New Englanders voted for the bill, in combination with representatives of the Middle States and West, to carry it by a close vote in both houses.

The action inflamed the South Carolinians. One of them, William Drayton, moved in Congress to amend the title of the bill to read: "An act to increase the duties on certain imports, for the purpose of increasing the profits of certain manufacturers." Disunionist talk was still generally deplored, however, and the doctrine of nullification was not brought forward conspicuously until fall. The legislature did not meet until after the election, in which South Carolina and all the other southern states registered their distinct preference for Jackson over Adams. But at this time the Assembly ordered the South Carolina *Exposition and Protest* to be printed. This document was destined to historic fame as the classic statement of the doctrine of nullification—that is, that a state could annul an act of Congress deemed by it to be unconstitutional. The paper was not formally adopted and the authorship of Vice-President Calhoun was not yet make known. Behind the scenes he had taken his stand with his state—against the nation if need be—but upon the surface he was still allied with Jackson, whose views on the tariff and state rights were ambiguous.

CHAPTER 24

Jackson and Democratic Nationalism, 1828-1833

THE ELECTION OF ANDREW JACKSON IN 1828 AS PRESI-
dent has always been associated with the growth of political democracy
in the United States, and rightly so. His accession was marked by the
invasion of the White House by the populace, and of public office by
political spoilsmen. These events represented the triumph of a man, a
party, and the popular will, but for a good many months men must have
wondered if they meant anything more. The "Nation's Hero" did not
enter on his distinctive course of presidential leadership with full vigor
until he had reorganized his Cabinet, about the middle of his first term;
and not until the last year of it did the meaning of Jacksonian democracy
begin to be revealed in its fullness.

In the name of the whole people the indomitable old commander in
the White House defeated the most powerful financial institution of his
day, the Bank of the United States, which he regarded as a special and
privileged interest, inimical to the general good. Also, before this first
term was over, he checked the centrifugal localism which appeared in
South Carolina in the form of nullification, threatening to paralyze the
federal government and imperiling the Union. Democracy was his sword
in one case, his shield and buckler in the other; he could do what he did
because the people as a whole, the regnant people, were with him. His
enemies spoke of the "reign" of "King Andrew," and he was a sort of
People's King, but it seems fairer to describe his regime as one of democratic nationalism.

This was not nationalism such as had been aimed at by Alexander
Hamilton, who despised the plain people: in spirit it was distinctly Jeffersonian. It was not the judicial nationalism of John Marshall, who never
missed a chance to strike down a state; for Jackson was far from accepting
the full doctrine of judicial review and sharply challenged the Chief

Justice in behalf of a state upon occasion. It was not consolidation, for he retained much of state-rights philosophy in which he had grown up and tended to be a strict constructionist of the Constitution. He showed slight concern for political theory in itself, however. He met crises as he perceived them, relying on his own robust common sense. The vibrant national patriotism of his day was assuming the distinctively American form of unity in diversity, whether or not he fully realized it; and in his hands the powers of the presidency were wielded with unexampled vigor in behalf of what he regarded as the public good.

Personal and partisan motives can be discerned by the critic in Jackson's actions, and at times he sounded like a demagogue, but he responded to deep instincts, represented broad interests, and had the courage of his convictions. The tactics of the grim old warrior were often ruthless, but his over-all strategy was superb. His enemies were implacable in their hatred of him, but the vast majority of his countrymen rejoiced that he won his major battles.

JACKSON TAKES OVER

The campaign of 1828 was much the dirtiest since that of 1800, and for this the Adams men were quite as responsible as the Jacksonians. The General, in retirement at the Hermitage, let his partisans battle for him. One of the most gruesome documents ever circulated in an American campaign was used against him. This was the *Coffin Handbill,* referring to six militiamen who had been shot at his command during the fighting in Alabama, and it bore the heading: "Some Account of the Bloody Deeds of General Jackson." Also, old slanders on the reputation of his wife Rachel, relating to the circumstances of her marriage to him, were revived. Jackson, who was prone to personalize his politics, put the blame on Clay and even on the remote Adams. He had already killed one man and threatened others in Rachel's sacred name and he was entirely capable of doing so again, but soon there was no need for him to be her champion. She died in January 1829, taking all the joy out of his political victory.

Very little was said in the campaign about the problems of the day, including the tariff. The position of Jackson was purposely left vague by his partisans, and the main issue that got before the public was that of personalities. In a contest of that sort Jackson had no rival in his time, and he was triumphantly elected over Adams, as no doubt he would have been over anybody else. His popular majority was not overwhelming but his support was so widely distributed that he gained the electoral vote of all the states except for New England, New Jersey, Delaware, and half of Maryland. He even got one electoral vote in Maine. Calhoun was re-elected Vice-President.

When Jackson was inaugurated as the seventh President of the United States on March 4, 1829, he was sixty-one years old and a sick man. A consumptive cough often racked his tall, thin body, and splitting headaches made miserable his days and nights. But his iron will so dominated his ailments that vigor, firmness, determination, and remarkable swiftness of decision were all that even his intimate associates saw in him. Those who did not know him, especially the stiffer kind of Eastern conservative, thought of Jackson as a frontier barbarian given to savage rages—brutal, dictatorial, and vulgar. That was essentially the opinion of John Quincy Adams and, at an earlier time, of Thomas Jefferson. Yet those who knew him, even political enemies, gladly denied the legend. Though by no means a learned man, he was a very shrewd one and also a natural gentleman. His courtesy and respect for others were most notably directed towards women; and, for all his determination to down an adversary, he rarely lost his self-control. Often when he seemed to be furious he was simply putting on an act for some purpose of his own.

His friends believed that the chief source of the greatness they saw in him was his ability to grasp a situation correctly and to reach an accurate judgment at the same moment, seemingly by intuition. Action followed judgment, and then an unbreakable determination to make his action succeed. He aroused a strange combination of awe and affection in others in rough proportion to their intimacy. The word "noble" occurs with significant frequency in impressions recorded by persons who only glimpsed him in a parade as well as by those whom he admitted to closest friendship; but he was also loved by these and by millions who never saw him. Somewhere in the make-up of this white-haired veteran there persisted the magical, inexplicable gift of leadership that had made him the choice of frontier fighters for their captain and would make him the guide of the Democracy for years after he left the presidency.

Democracy Triumphant

"Frontier barbarism" was not entirely missing from the ceremonies of Jackson's inauguration. His political opponents were certain that a Jacobin revolution by savages in coonskin caps and buckskin shirts was at hand when hordes of his followers invaded Washington and made a frolic of the installation of the first President from west of the mountains. He himself was a dignified and impressive figure at his inauguration in the Senate chamber, and afterwards on the balcony, where he delivered a brief speech which satisfied the vast crowd even though they did not hear it. He had walked bareheaded to the Capitol and returned gallantly on horseback. Then the real fun began.

The picture was elaborated in great detail by grim opposition editors: the mob rushing the White House for the hero's reception; the muddy moccasins on the damask-covered chairs to give their wearers a glimpse of him; and Jackson, too courteous by far, ordering that tubs of punch be hauled out to the lawn to accommodate the overflow of thirsty guests. From this hilarious people's party the exhausted old man was glad to slip away.

The frontiersmen had not made the trip merely to get drunk on the taxpayers' punch; they were there to make sure that Democracy triumphant should yield plenty of government jobs for deserving Democrats. William L. Marcy, a leader of the New York Democracy, defending Van Buren a little later, coined the slogan of political warfare: "To the victors belong the spoils!" Jackson's victory in his first political war did result in a division of the spoils of office unparalleled since the founding of the government.

Previous Presidents had not appointed political opponents to high office, but in the lower reaches of the federal service it had been generally understood that ability and experience safeguarded tenure without regard for the way a jobholder acted at the polls. This system had the virtue of providing continuity on levels of routine administration. But from the Jacksonian point of view it was vicious because it created a caste of bureaucrats pretending to knowledge of hidden matters, panoplied by power and inaccessible to the people's will. In short, the system embodied aristocratic, Federalist principles, and it must go. Running the people's government, the Jacksonians argued, required no more than the common sense with which the common people, especially those who had voted for Jackson, were so richly endowed. Throw the aristocratic rascals out and put in plain men to do plain jobs, and government responsive to the plain people would follow. So it was done, and later administrations found the spoils system so convenient an instrument for rewarding political service and winning elections that it was applied in time to the lowliest janitors of government buildings and scrubwomen until, in the 1880's, the small beginnings of civil service reform began to correct its phenomenal abuses.

During most of Jackson's first year in office—until Congress met in December—he seemed to be occupied chiefly by matters of appointment and with a tempest in the social teapot which was occasioned by the wife of one member of his original Cabinet. The President's first official family was so unimpressive that one observer dubbed the new regime the "millenium of minnows." Secretary of State Van Buren, the "Little Magician," was no political minnow. A fastidiously dressed New Yorker, he brought sartorial splendor to a homespun administration, but he had no such intellectuality or personal distinction as Vice-President Calhoun, his rival for Jackson's favor. Most of the appointees to the first Cabinet appeared to be from the Calhoun camp.

The Secretary of War, John H. Eaton, was a Jackson man pure and simple. A few weeks before the inauguration, this old friend of the General had married with his encouragement Peggy O'Neale Timberlake, daughter of a Washington tavern keeper and widow of a Navy purser not long since deceased at sea. Eaton's relations with the lovely Peggy, at whose father's tavern he long stayed, had occasioned much talk and this did not die down with his marriage. His appointment seemed questionable to many people but not to the loyal Jackson. An extremely chivalrous man toward women, he drew an unwarranted parallel between the scandalmongers who were attacking Peggy and those who had slurred the name of his own beloved Rachel. But the Cabinet ladies and Mrs. Calhoun disdained Mrs. Eaton, as did Emily Donelson, niece of the President's dead wife who was living at the White House as its only mistress until Jackson sent her home for discipline. Jackson's determination that the tavern-keeper's daughter, now the wife of his old friend, should be accepted socially arose from the deepest emotional springs, but not even he could command the stubborn women.

The blame for the outcry against Mrs. Eaton was originally laid by Jackson on Clay and his crew. That it fell ultimately on Vice-President Calhoun, who had the misfortune to be a conspicuous figure, was largely owing to the skill with which the Secretary of State exploited the delicate situation. Van Buren, a widower without daughters, found it convenient to please his chief by befriending Mrs. Eaton. Furthermore, he convinced Jackson that the "Eaton malaria" was actually bred not on the feminine social heights of Washington but in political swamps of the South. Calhoun, so "Little Van" suggested, was determined to rule the administration or ruin it and had organized the phalanx of women to hide behind until their work would permit him to consolidate his victory. If Van Buren could destroy the alliance between Jackson and Calhoun, he had good reason to think that he would become the heir apparent.

Besides this social war and the war of intrigue for the succession there were other conflicts in Washington during the presidential novitiate of Andrew Jackson. The most important of these took the form of a constitutional debate on the relations between an individual state and the federal government. Into this Calhoun had already entered; Hayne and Webster took it up; and behind it lay conflicts of interest and struggles for power among the sections.

DEBATING THE NATURE OF THE UNION

The South Carolina *Exposition* of 1828 had appeared too late to affect the election and Calhoun's authorship was not avowed until the summer of 1831, but the widely circulated work was generally recognized as his. In this important treatise Calhoun set forth doctrines of state rights which were more extreme than those which Jefferson and Madison had expressed in the Kentucky and Virginia Resolutions. They had termed the Alien and Sedition Acts unconstitutional, as violations of the First Amendment, while Calhoun asserted the unconstitutionality of tariffs that were deliberately designed to promote particular industries rather than to produce revenue. While many people in later years denied the wisdom and the fairness of the protective system, few in our day would support Calhoun's position on constitutional grounds. A much larger number would support that of Jefferson and Madison with respect to the Sedition Act. Furthermore, Calhoun's purposes seemed more particularistic. He sought to guard the special interests of a geographical region, whereas they were trying to guard local interests everywhere and the freedom of all Americans, North and South.

There were also important differences between him and his supposed prototypes with respect to the remedies proposed in case of unwarranted federal actions. The earlier leaders were most concerned with the right of protest. The right of states to judge for themselves the mode of redress was claimed in Jefferson's Kentucky Resolutions of 1798, and the word "nullification" was used in the Resolutions of that state in the next year. But, as Madison pointed out in the 1830's, Jefferson regarded the right to revolt against intolerable oppression as a natural not a constitutional right; it had been invoked in the Declaration of Independence before there was a Constitution. Furthermore, these earlier protestors against supposed infringements of human and state rights had worked out no mechanism of defense and Madison definitely disapproved of Calhoun's.

The Doctrine of Nullification

Rejecting the doctrine of Marshall that the Union originated with the people and was their agent, Calhoun declared that it originated with the states, which retained sovereignty even though they had delegated specific powers to the federal government; and that a single state, acting through a convention specially chosen for the purpose, could annul an act of the federal government which it deemed unconstitutional. Recognizing, however, that the other sovereign states had some check on the actions of one of them, he conceded that nullifications of a federal act could be overruled by the vote of three-fourths of the states. That is, he would have reversed the process of amending the Constitution and thrown the burden of proof on the federal government. Finally, he declared that nullification was not secession, that is, a dissolution of partnership, but an instrument to prevent secession. In his hands it was that, but the doctrine of secession afterward flourished in the country of the nullifiers.

Calhoun's safeguards never got beyond the realm of theory and the dominant leaders in South Carolina were less reasonable than he. Since he did not originate the doctrine of nullification, it would be a fair description of his role to say that he elaborated and refined it and sought to guard it against abuse. Furthermore, his record shows that he did not want to use it and that in fact he was a moderating influence in the local scene. What he had sought to do with his powerful mind was to create a mechanism for the protection of a minority interest. But, as Madison pointed out, the process which Calhoun recommended could and probably would result in the ascendancy of a minority over a large majority. This was certainly not in the spirit of Jefferson, who declared that acquiescence in the will of the majority was the most vital principle of republican government. In his own thinking Calhoun had taken a lonely path; and it was a fair question then and often afterwards whether he did the cause of his beloved state more harm than good by defining her "rights" so sharply. This emphasis on action by a single state worked to the disadvantage of anyone who was trying to gain the co-operation of others on the larger stage.

Debating in the Senate

Of all the major questions of the day the one of greatest concern to South Carolina, and on which opinion was most inflamed, was that of the tariff. The issue of public lands in the West was less important, hence it seemed that a political alliance between South and West might be cemented if Southerners should support a more liberal western land policy in return for Western support of Southern tariff policy. Senator Thomas H. Benton of Missouri advocated a plan calling for a gradual reduction in the price of unsold lands that would lead finally to the free gift of those for which there were no bidders. This was known as the policy of "Graduation and Donation." On the other hand, the favored Eastern scheme for maintaining a policy of tariff protection with Western support, without endangering the labor market by lowering the price of western lands, was to distribute among the states the federal money from their sale. This policy was known as "Distribution," and it was advocated by Henry Clay, a Westerner who was always conscious of the opinions of Eastern businessmen. But Westerners like Benton were chiefly interested in lowering land prices and in December 1829 they joined with Southerners to defeat a Distribution bill.

It was at this juncture that Senator Samuel A. Foot of Connecticut stepped into the delicate web of sectional diplomacy. He offered a resolution that called for stopping surveys and limiting sales of western lands. In January 1830, this provoked a hot debate. Benton bitterly attacked Foot's resolution and the Northeastern manufacturers, charging the latter with intent to oppress and hold back the West in order to keep labor cheap, and criticizing the tariff policy which he himself had recently supported. Robert Y. Hayne, an eloquent and popular Senator from South Carolina, leaped to accept Benton's virtual invitation to a fresh alliance. He accused the Northeasterners of trying to rob the West of settlers just as they had robbed the South of its wealth through tariffs. Unity of the South and West, he declared, was necessary against their common enemy.

This was the occasion of the famous Hayne-Webster debate. Webster, who had been indifferent to his Senatorial duties of late, rushed into the breach and saved his section from the consequences of Foot's ineptitude by adroitly changing the subject. While defending New England he baited Hayne by attacking the state-rights philosophy of South Carolina, which Hayne thereupon defended, and Webster then answered him by powerful logic garbed in sonorous prose. Thus the debate was shifted to the highest level of constitutional theory. In reality Webster was speaking for New England as truly as Hayne was for South Carolina. His region had been a seat of state rights during and previous to the War of 1812, while its interests now called for a federal government that was armed with power. But his Second Reply to Hayne deserved to become a classic since events proved, and were already proving, that he spoke for the future nation. He voiced John Marshall's nationalistic philosophy with an eloquence which the Chief Justice could not muster, and his closing words were to be echoed in the speeches of thousands of schoolboys through the generations: "Liberty *and* Union, now and forever, one and inseparable." Webster was expressing an ideal, not describing an accomplishment, but ideals mold men and societies and this one has endured.

Webster had transformed the issue, so that it was no longer one between sections but between Unionism and Nullification. Foot's resolution was lost, but so was a bill offered a little later by Benton calling for Graduation and Donation. The alliance between South and West was too incomplete to offset powerful Eastern opposition. About the same time, in May 1830, Jackson vetoed a bill providing for federal participation in the building of the Maysville Road in Kentucky by a private company, on the ground that the road lay wholly within a state and that the federal government could not afford a part in it. This was the first of the vetoes of a President who used more of them than all of his predecessors together. It slanted in the direction of state rights and strict construction, marked a check in the policy of internal improvements at federal expense, and anticipated opposition to federal aid to private enterprise. But there was still the question of the tariff.

Jackson Breaks with Calhoun

In terms of sectional politics Jackson had made a concession to the South, though for some time now his mentor had been Van Buren, not

Calhoun. His constitutional views were predominantly pragmatic but there could be no possible question of his whole-hearted devotion to the Union, and his suspicions of Calhoun had been fanned by the sedulous Van Buren. By December 1829, he was fully convinced that the Vice-President was chiefly responsible for the petticoat warfare against Mrs. Eaton, and by that time the infirm old man was looking toward the useful Secretary of State as his eventual successor in the presidency. But the incident which has been most often pointed to as a public sign of a breach with the Vice-President occurred on April 13, 1830, at a dinner in celebration of the birthday of Jefferson.

The dinner was designed to associate Jeffersonian orthodoxy, as understood by the Calhoun group, with the party in power—which through the passing years was to go by the name of Democratic. The celebration was expected to have a state-rights flavor, and in general it did, but attention was afterwards directed chiefly to the "volunteer" toasts of the President and Vice-President after the innumerable prepared ones. That of Jackson has become, perhaps, his best-known saying: "Our Federal Union —It must be preserved." The words of Calhoun have become almost as famous: "The Union—next to our liberty most dear. May we always remember that it can only be preserved by distributing equally the benefits and burdens of the Union." Van Buren, who followed, drank to "mutual forbearance and reciprocal concession," thus sounding a note of conciliation.

The circumstances of this occasion were afterwards embroidered by partisan journalists and exaggerated by some of the participants themselves, but the reasons for this soon appeared upon the record. In May, Jackson sent Calhoun a letter from William H. Crawford, who had been in Monroe's Cabinet at the time of Jackson's expedition into Florida, alleging that Calhoun as Secretary of War had urged in 1818 a reprimand or punishment of the General for his conduct. Except for Adams, the Cabinet members as a group had thought Jackson's action high-handed, and Calhoun rightly suspected Crawford of a political trick. Indeed, Jackson himself had long known about Calhoun's earlier position, and the demand for an explanation at this time must have been made because the President had now decided that he did not need him. Calhoun's elaborate explanation, which would have been better left unmade, could not possibly be satisfactory, and Jackson now described him without hesitation as a traitor.

The *coup de grâce* to the Calhoun-Jackson alliance was delivered the following spring, after Van Buren had offered the President means to cure the social warfare within his Cabinet, get rid of the last trace of Calhoun influence, and reorient his administration. The Secretary of State and Eaton resigned simultaneously, in order that Jackson might call for the resignation of the remaining Cabinet members—all identified more or less with Calhoun. When Lewis Cass of Michigan succeeded Eaton as

Secretary of War, Jackson's friend and Peggy escaped from the social vendetta and the President heaved a sigh of relief. Of the new appointees, those who rendered him most signal service in later crises were Edward Livingston of Louisiana, formerly of New York, and the cadaverous-looking Roger B. Taney of Maryland, who took over the office of Attorney General. But from day to day the President relied on the counsel and help of a small informal group, known as the "Kitchen Cabinet" and much ridiculed by his political foes. The most important members of this were two unpretentious men recently come from the West: Amos Kendall, a former newspaper man who then had a minor post in the Treasury, and Francis Preston Blair, editor of the Jackson paper, the *Washington Globe.* Meanwhile, Van Buren was rewarded with the post of minister to Great Britain—on a recess appointment, since the Senate would not confirm him. It was understood that in due course he would succeed to the presidency.

The internecine war was liquidated and the administration reorganized at the cost of an irreparable breach with Calhoun and the sure loss of the political support of South Carolina. But circumstances served to isolate that state, as they had to isolate Calhoun in Washington; and Jackson actually lost little support in the South. Among the reasons for his continued appeal there were his policies with respect to the Indians and internal improvements and his attitude on the revived issue of the Bank. The latter appealed even more strongly to the plain people of the North, and their votes more than made up for losses elsewhere.

First Phase of the Bank War

The Second Bank of the United States was a private institution, though a fifth of its capital was owned by the government. By right of its charter it had certain great privileges, and in return for these it performed important public services. Besides having the deposits of the United States, generally made in the notes (paper money) of other banks which were presentable to them for payment, it had the power of issuing its own notes. Thus it could bring pressure on other banks to restrict their notes and credit policies and could regulate the currency. A major objection to it in the West and South was that it restricted credit and controlled the currency too well; state banks were much more responsive to the inflationary tendencies of new regions and the credit needs of farmers. The objections of Jackson to it, however, were chiefly based on other grounds. He was old-fashioned in his financial ideas, being suspicious of all banks and in favor of coin not paper as the basis of the circulating medium. He feared the Bank for its power. The government elected five of the twenty-five directors but did not control the institution, and in his opinion there was real danger it would control the government.

Under Nicholas Biddle, a cultivated Philadelphian who had been presi-dent since 1822, the Bank had followed a conservative policy which did not commend it to Western and Southern farmers but had gained the approval of Eastern businessmen, while Biddle had been careful to satisfy the needs and meet the convenience of the federal Treasury. Also, he performed favors for leading politicians, newspapermen, and other influ-ential persons; and at the outset he was conciliatory towards Jackson.

In his first message to Congress, the President, probably at the instiga-tion of Van Buren, had questioned both the expediency and the consti-tutionality of the Bank. Its affairs were afterwards inquired into by committees of the two houses of Congress, both of which made favorable reports. Opposition to the institution came chiefly from men who spoke for state banks and a more liberal currency and credit policy. Senator Thomas Hart Benton of Missouri, a hard-money man who had won the name "Old Bullion," was a vigorous exception. Jackson seemed more kindly toward the Bank as his first term wore on, and his battle with it was precipitated by an unnecessary challenge to him by its friends, the motives of which were predominantly political.

Not until 1836 was the charter to expire. But Henry Clay, who was now in the Senate and looking for an issue in the approaching presidential campaign, obtained Biddle's consent to the presentation of a rechartering bill early in 1832. Congress passed the bill early in the summer as Clay had been sure it would, and Jackson, who was no man to decline a chal-lenge, was presented with one. The General, sick in bed, told his political lieutenant who was just back from England: "The bank, Mr. Van Buren, is trying to kill me, *but I will kill it!*" He returned the bill to Congress with a powerful veto message which Amos Kendall, Attorney General Taney, and others helped prepare. In this he skillfully avoided the issue between the soft-money and hard-money critics of the Bank and directly appealed to the plain people of the country to help him put an end to governmental favors to the rich.

Jackson's Veto Message

This appeal was not in conflict with the philosophy of free economic enterprise with which Americans had been so long imbued, for he recog-nized the right of men of superior ability and industry to the full enjoy-ment of the property they had gained thereby.

> But [he said] when the laws undertake to add to these natural and just advantages artificial distinctions, . . . to make the rich richer and the potent more powerful, the humble members of society, the farmers, mechanics, and laborers, who have neither the time nor the means of securing like favors to themselves, have a right to complain of the injustice of their government.

According to Jackson, the Bank was a monopoly enjoying governmental favors which amounted to gifts of many millions of dollars to the private stockholders. The government was making a bad bargain, in his opinion, and the cost must come at last from the earnings of the American people. He reminded Congress of Biddle's remark, which was truthful though indiscreet, that most of the state banks existed by the forbearance of the Bank of the United States; and, bringing all his batteries into play, he denied to that institution the constitutionality which the Supreme Court had affirmed. Repudiating Marshall and Hamilton, he reverted to the position of Jefferson, denying judicial review in so far as it related to the executive and legislative departments and identifying himself with the school of strict construction. Many features of the recharter bill, he said, were not "necessary and proper" in the ordinary meaning of those words. This part of one of the most famous of all veto messages amounted to a judicial opinion handed down by the Executive.

The historic message ended with the most radical appeal to the class feeling of the poor against the rich which had yet appeared in an American public paper:

> There are no necessary evils in government. Its evils exist only in its abuses. If it would confine itself to equal protection, and, as Heaven does its rains, shower its favors alike on the high and the low, the rich and the poor, it would be an unqualified blessing. In the act before me there seems to be a wide and unnecessary departure from these just principles. . . .
>
> Many of our rich men have not been content with equal protection and equal benefits, but have besought us to make them richer by act of Congress. By attempting to gratify their desires we have in the results of our legislation arrayed section against section, interest against interest, and man against man, in a fearful commotion which threatens to shake the foundations of our Union. It is time to pause in our career to review our principles. . . .

Jackson's assertion of the competence of the Executive to judge questions of constitutionality within its own sphere did not become a significant precedent, but as a campaign manifesto the message was a sweeping success. Congress did not override the veto, the Bank became the chief specific issue in the election of 1832, and the newly-enfranchised groups of the North, led by a sprouting crop of reformers and organizers, moved towards Jackson.

Inevitably he aroused the fierce resentment of interested parties and frightened many of the conservative and well-to-do. Nicholas Biddle saw in the veto message all "the fury of a chained panther, biting the bars of his cage." To his friend Henry Clay he said: "It is really a manifesto of anarchy, such as Marat or Robespierre might have issued to the mob of the Faubourg St. Antoine." In the Senate, Webster said:

"It manifestly seeks to influence the poor against the rich. It wantonly attacks whole classes of the people for the purpose of turning against them the prejudices and resentment of other classes."

Beyond a doubt Jackson was seeking to arouse the many against the special beneficiaries of a particular institution. In actual number the latter were very few, but in the Northeast he revived and accentuated an older alignment. The cleavage between the party of Jefferson and the more prosperous economic groups in that region had seemed almost closed during the Monroe administration, but Jackson widened it into a chasm which was destined to endure long. By the same token, he strengthened his hold and that of the Democratic Party after him on the "farmers, mechanics, and laborers," to whom he specifically referred, and if they were mobilized they could easily outvote the groups he had offended.

The Nullification Crisis

The first phase of the Bank war ended when Jackson vetoed the recharter bill in the summer of 1832, and the sovereign people did not speak decisively until fall. Meanwhile, federal authority was being challenged not only in South Carolina, but also in the neighboring state of Georgia, where there was less emphasis on constitutional philosophy.

Jackson did not accept the latter challenge, which grew out of the efforts of the Georgians to extend their political authority over the Cherokee Indians and acquire their lands. With these purposes the old fighter was thoroughly sympathetic. In March 1832, Chief Justice Marshall, in the case of Worcester vs. Georgia, denied the right of the state to impose its will upon the Cherokees still within its borders, since these people were protected by treaties made with them by the United States. The President tacitly supported the state in its self-assertion and defiance. As the story runs, he said: "John Marshall has made his decision; now let him enforce it." His nationalism was pragmatic and lacked theoretical consistency. He was not disposed to press it against what he deemed to be the will of the people. He is often blamed for his indifference to the nullifying policies of Georgia, but he has generally been praised by historians for his stand against the brand of nullification which emanated from South Carolina. The latter, in his opinion, presented a much greater threat against the Union.

The national event which occasioned nullification in Calhoun's state was the passage of the Tariff of 1832. This was a more rational measure than the Tariff of Abominations and, for that reason, it was more acceptable to the groups and districts that were seeking protection. In general, high duties were imposed on goods produced in America and lower duties were now placed on noncompetitive foreign products. But the bill represented no real improvement from the Southern point of view, and when Jackson signed it in July the South Carolinians claimed that he had betrayed them. For several years they had been divided into the State Rights and Union Parties, but nobody defended the tariff and by this time the former party, which proclaimed nullificaton doctrines, was in full control, having a clear two-thirds majority in the legislature. The leaders were now poised for action, but they awaited the outcome of the presidential election.

Vice-President Calhoun sought to restrain them from precipitate action. In theory he was with them and by this time his constitutional position was generally known. President Jackson had not yet had occasion to make his position public, and the South Carolinians found encouragement in his attitude toward the Georgians, but he had already given informal warning. The nullifiers might pass resolutions to their heart's content, but if they should shed any blood in defiance of United States law, he would not hesitate to do some hanging. In view of his record, his words were in no sense humorous. In the election, South Carolina was the only southern state that did not support him. The electors there threw their votes to Governor John Floyd of Virginia, with no effect whatever on the outcome.

Challenge and Response

After the election the South Carolina legislature called a convention for the special purpose of considering the tariff, and this body adopted on November 24, 1832, the Ordinance of Nullification—a precursor of the more famous Ordinance of Secession. This declared the tariff acts of 1828 and 1832 null and void, forbade the collection of customs within the state, prohibited appeal to the United States Supreme Court in any cases arising under the Ordinance, and required a test oath of the civil and military officers of the state. Finally, it declared that any attempt to coerce the state would absolve it from all further obligations to the Union and be followed by the organization of a separate government. Nullification carried with it a direct threat of secession, which was just what Calhoun had said it was designed to prevent. Furthermore, the Ordinance contained no reference to any possibility that this action could be overruled by three-fourths of the other states—a provision which Calhoun had included in his South Carolina *Exposition*. His fellows had assumed a more intransigent attitude than his and they were more impatient. They set February 1, 1833, as the effective date, which was earlier than he liked.

If the reckless South Carolinians counted on the support of the other southern states they were doomed to disappointment. In Virginia there was general disapproval of the tariff but practically no approval of this method of combating it. The legislature of the Old Dominion formally declared that the historic Virginia Resolutions of 1798-1799 did not support the South Carolina doctrine, as had been claimed, and James Madison took the same ground. In Alabama, where the federal government was being practically defied on the Indian question at just this time, the doctrine of nullification was described as unconstitutional and revolutionary, and similar disapproval was expressed elsewhere. In constitutional philosophy South Carolina seemed to stand alone. Also, President Jackson, who had been born in that state, took positive and immediate steps to neutralize its actions. Unionists recalled these in 1860 and longed for him in place of irresolute James Buchanan—who faced, however, a more difficult situation. Jackson reinforced Forts Moultrie and Sumter in Charleston harbor, ordered federal officials to collect the customs in South Carolina as elsewhere, and deployed revenue cutters to do this off the coast if the officials on land were resisted. On December 10, 1832, the President issued a Proclamation to the people of South Carolina. With its ringing nationalism this complemented the democracy of his Bank veto message.

The President admitted the right to resist acts of the government which were "plainly unconstitutional and too oppressive to be endured." But South Carolina was claiming a different right, namely, that any one state might remain in the Union and yet be bound by no other laws than those it might "choose to consider as constitutional." Furthermore, Jackson's Proclamation declared, the Constitution expressly requires the judges in every state to be bound by that Constitution, the treaties, and the laws of the United States—"anything in the constitution or laws of any State to the contrary notwithstanding." By denying the possibility of appeal from its own Ordinance to the federal courts, South Carolina was clearly destroying the federal compact.

Under the South Carolina doctrine, said Jackson, the Union could not have survived infancy. Pennsylvania would have defied the whiskey tax, Virginia the carriage tax, the eastern states the Embargo and Nonintercourse Acts. In practice, the doctrine of a state veto would be an absurdity. The President repudiated it completely, describing it emphatically as *"incompatible with the existence of the Union, contradicted expressly by the letter of the Constitution, unauthorized by its spirit, inconsistent with every principle on which it was founded, and destructive of the great object for which it was formed."* As for secession, this might be morally justified as a revolutionary act against extreme oppression, he said, but to call it a constitutional right was to confound the meaning of terms and to declare that the United States was not a nation.

Jackson believed that those who argued that nullification might be achieved peaceably had deceived the people. They knew that only force could prevent the execution of the laws and that force would be repelled by force. Their object was disunion, he said, adding that disunion by armed force is *treason*. The fate of free government was in the balance, the world was looking on, and the Chief Magistrate could not and would not avoid the performance of his duty. Yet he would not allow any offensive act by the United States to bring down on man the primeval curse for the shedding of a brother's blood. He would, if possible, by moderate and firm measures prevent the necessity of force.

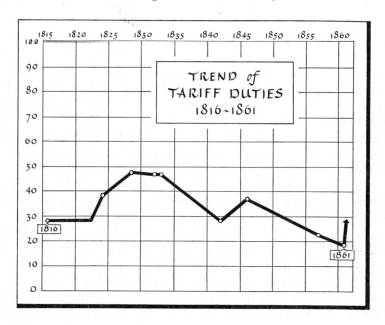

South Carolina's legislature met the challenge by raising armed forces for defense against "invasion." The Virginians did not like the threats against a sovereign state, but they sent commissioners to the rebellious commonwealth to urge moderation. Jackson talked of leading an army into South Carolina and asked Congress for a Force Act, but he also supported the attempt to compromise the tariff conflict, even though Henry Clay got a lion's share of the credit. An administration tariff bill was shelved and a proposal of Clay's was given right of way. This bill provided for a gradual reduction of all duties during the next ten years so that none would be higher than 20 per cent on July 1, 1842. The South Carolinians found that most Southern legislators were willing to support Clay's bill and, being isolated, they postponed the nullification threat and finally abandoned it. In this time of peril Senator Hayne resigned his seat to go home and become Governor, while Calhoun, resigning his position as Vice-President, succeeded to Hayne's place. He supported the compromise.

The federal government and the South Carolina Convention both reasserted their doctrinal positions while accepting the compromise Tariff Act of 1833. On March 2, Jackson signed the Tariff Act and also a Force Act authorizing him to use the Army and the Navy to collect duties if judicial process were obstructed. The South Carolina Convention repealed the Nullification Ordinance and then declared the Force Act null and void. If statesmanship consists in avoiding a fight to the finish on theoretical grounds for the sake of mutual accommodation on substance, then statesmanship had won the day.

Both sides claimed a victory, and certainly there was no acknowledgement of defeat by the nullifiers. They had proved that a single state could by threats of secession extort from the federal government the modification of a law; and, regardless of the merit of their objections to the existing tariff, this success encouraged the idea that a minority could challenge the majority. The spirit of localism continued to flourish in South Carolina, and the belief became even more firmly fixed there that loyalty to the state came before loyalty to the Union. While the nullification doctrine itself was not revived, the doctrine that secession is a constitutional right remained and grew. But most of the leaders in the state had learned that they needed support from outside their own borders, and they did not again take extreme action until convinced that other states would follow.

On the nationalist side, Jackson's Proclamation and his manifest readiness to preserve the Union by force if necessary became an unforgettable part of the historic record. His attitude aroused the enthusiasm of the vast majority of Northerners and Westerners, regardless of party, and of large groups of Southerners. Conservatives supported his nationalism, while approving radicals knew, from the Bank war if from nothing else, that his nationalism was profoundly democratic. Jackson provided average Americans with a nationalism that they liked better than that of Marshall and Webster and could more easily understand. He brought this into focus as the creed they lived by and the cause for which they would fight. South Carolina had won a compromise of the tariff, but Jackson had won the more crucial battle for national opinion.

CHAPTER 25

The Flood and Ebb of the Jacksonian Tide, 1832-1840

THE ELECTION OF 1832 REPRESENTED AN EVEN GREATER triumph for Jackson than that of 1828. It strengthened his hand against the nullifiers, and he naturally interpreted it as a full vindication of his hostility to the Bank of the United States. In the history of American political institutions it is also significant, for in the campaign presidential candidates were nominated by national party conventions for the first time. In contrast to the party caucus, which was viewed as oligarchic, the convention represented an effort to democratize party machinery. In this election and in Jackson's second term, when the opposition took on the name of Whigs, political parties and political alignments assumed a form they long maintained. There was no major regrouping until the 1850's, when sectional issues dwarfed all others.

The main controversies of the term centered on financial questions. Under the soothing operation of the compromise Tariff of 1833, nullification disappeared as an immediate issue, but the Bank war was resumed and it did not yet end, since Whig leaders continued to favor such an institution through several additional administrations. The impossibility of rechartering this particular Bank soon became apparent, however, and the more immediate problems toward the close of Jackson's presidency arose from an excess of inflated prosperity. In his own old-fashioned way the President sought to check the boom, and there is still dispute whether he did more good or harm. Recession was inevitable and Jackson's successor, Van Buren, bore the brunt of it. His unhappy administration ended with his defeat in 1840 at the hands of the Whigs, who were the rabble-rousing party in this instance. The tide of Jacksonian popularity reached its highest point early in the General's second term and it ebbed

458

somewhat before he retired to The Hermitage, but not enough to endanger Van Buren's succession. The low point was reached in the latter's defeat.

The Election of 1832: Social Unrest and Political Parties

Henry Clay, the presidential nominee of the National Republicans, had seized upon the Bank issue. His partisans printed 30,000 copies of the veto message for campaign purposes, thus revealing their colossal ignorance of the trend of the people's thinking. There was a third party in the race, the Anti-Masonic Party which nominated William Wirt, a former Attorney General of the United States. Fortunately he had no real hankering for the highest office. He got 7 electoral votes to Clay's 49 and Jackson's 217, while South Carolina's 11 went to John Floyd. The figures on the popular vote are unreliable, but the General got most of it. After the election Wirt expressed the opinion that Jackson could be President for life if he wanted to.

"Old Hickory" had lost none of his appeal as the Nation's Hero, and personal loyalty probably attached very many voters to him without much reference to specific policies of his administration. He fulfilled an often-forgotten premise of the American system of government: that the general trustworthiness of a candidate's character and the broad outlines of his political philosophy should determine the voter's choice, after which the successful candidate must exercise his own judgment as the *representative*, not merely the echo, of the electorate. In Jackson's hands the presidency attained unexampled popularity and was notably a representative institution—in the full meaning of the term. He sensed and reflected public opinion far better than his political opponents, and at the same time he aggressively exercised his executive functions and assumed leadership. The plain people rejoiced that they had found a champion and they trusted him.

By now the Jacksonians gladly called themselves Democrats. Hickory Clubs were created by enthusiasts over the country to celebrate their hero's fame and organize the vote. Beneath the manifestations upon the surface deep new currents of social unrest were flowing in national political life. These were chiefly the product of the Industrial Revolution, which seemed to challenge the adequacy of existing political arrangements and call for new ideas. A remarkable feature of Jackson's leadership was his ability to command the loyalty of clamorous new elements in spite of the fact that he did little that was specifically designed to satisfy their demands. His war against the Bank rallied the support of a bewildering variety of dissidents from the status quo. Jackson was the symbol but only to a slight extent the instrument of the rich assortment of new popular movements that are called Jacksonian Democracy. Important social and intellectual movements will be described in another chapter, while we limit ourselves here to those entering more directly into politics.

Workingmen and Politics

The granting of the vote to propertyless males differentiated the position of the American workmen from that of the Europeans of their class during the early stages of the Industrial Revolution. It is not surprising, therefore, that the first political party in the world devoted to the interests of labor appeared in the United States. This was the Workingmen's Party, which was organized in Philadelphia, New York, and other cities shortly before and during Jackson's first term. In these cities and in mill towns the growth of factories had created the first American slums. Cheap immigrant labor, which was now coming in though not yet in torrential volume, permitted employers to stretch out hours and reduce wages. Handicraft unions of skilled artisans were helpless to improve conditions, while under the factory system the ranks of the unskilled were growing.

The platforms of the Workingmen's Party show that the chief object of laborers was to achieve recognition of themselves as human beings. Mechanics' lien laws were demanded to establish the priority of laborers' claims to wages when an employer went bankrupt, the implication being that the rights of labor are human rights and are, therefore, superior to the rights of property. Abolition of imprisonment for debt was demanded on the same principle: it merely meant granting to poor men comparable consideration to that given corporate debtors by means of bankruptcy laws. The Workingmen's Party bitterly opposed the laissez-faire philosophy of employers—that labor was a commodity which must be subject to the law of supply and demand, that any form of governmental intervention in favor of the laboring class would invite economic disaster, and that the only remedy for its ills was harder work and more frugality. Terming this "irrational, antirepublican, and unchristian," the laborers blamed the poverty of the workers on the new techniques of exploitation which machinery placed in the hands of employers.

The workmen could not hope to create a national party because they were too narrowly localized in the Northeast, but by showing strength in state elections they made themselves interesting to leaders of the national parties. These could add the workingmen to their regular following by adopting specific demands of labor. In 1829, the party in New York City polled 30 per cent of the vote in local elections. After that, factions of the party heeded offers of the Democratic leaders to carry out labor reforms in return for support of Democratic candidates in state and national elections. Under this arrangement, New York passed a mechanics' lien law in 1830 and abolished imprisonment for debt. Similar developments elsewhere resulted in a nation-wide wave of prolabor reform laws in states during the following decade.

Jackson strongly appealed to workingmen by his veto message against the Bank. Labor was interested in hard money as the medium for wage payments which was least subject to depreciation in buying power, and was opposed to the paper money of both the state banks and the Bank of the United States. Jackson had not yet pressed the hard-money issue as much as he did later, but in 1832 the Workingmen's Party virtually dissolved in favor of him and the Democrats.

During his second term, Jackson ordered (1836) that the daily hours of labor in the United States Navy yards should be limited to ten. This may be regarded as the first instance of federal support of labor's demands. On the other hand, when a strike occurred among laborers building the Chesapeake and Ohio Canal, he did not hesitate to use federal troops to break it. To Jackson a strike was rebellion against proper authority. This, too, was a Jacksonian precedent in labor relations.

Anti-Masons

Another "third-party" movement appeared in the early 1830's and this was of the "crackpot" type. In 1826, a man named William Morgan had disappeared after revealing the secrets of his Freemasons' lodge. A widespread agitation against all secret societies, which were generally regarded as undemocratic, followed unproved accusations that the Masons had done away with Morgan, and it was proposed that they be outlawed. Anti-Masons saw this reform as a cure for all public ills and organized a political party to secure the remedy.

After winning victories in New York elections, the Anti-Masons devised an instrument which became an important American political institution. This was the party nominating convention, which assumed the place formerly filled by the Congressional caucus. Criticism had been leveled at the caucus because it denied the rank and file of the party a voice in the choice of candidates. The Anti-Masons saw an opportunity to stir up enthusiasm by holding a convention of delegates chosen by local groups, and arriving at the party's choices by public debate and ballot. Besides satisfying the democratic impulses of party members, such a convention would launch the party's campaign on a high tide of oratory and unity. The Anti-Masons held a national convention late in 1831, nominating William Wirt as their candidate for President. A little later in the same year the National Republicans nominated Clay in a convention. In 1832, the Democrats followed suit, and, to no one's surprise, nominated Jackson for President and Martin Van Buren for Vice-President. This Democratic Convention adopted the famous two-thirds rule in the choice of candidates, a rule suggestive of Calhoun's later theory of concurrent majorities, as in effect it gave a veto to any section commanding one-third of the delegates. In many a later Democratic Convention the majority was checked by Southern delegates, until the two-thirds rule was abandoned in 1936. After 1832, both major parties gradually institutionalized the party convention on the various electoral levels and evolved techniques of exciting the voters by colorful shenanigans.

The Whigs and "King Andrew"

The opposition party dubbed Jackson "King Andrew I," and during his second term called themselves Whigs—seeking to identify themselves with the political group, in Britain and America, historically opposed to royal power and pretensions. In reality they constituted the more conservative party, and under the leadership of Clay they were in the tradition of Hamilton except for their interest in the West. In the East, where Webster was their best-known leader, they maintained the allegiance of business interests, but they lagged behind the Democrats practically everywhere in their popular appeal and did not perfect their campaign machinery until the election of 1840, when they "out-Jacksoned" the Jacksonians.

The President himself seemed almost to have created a new "era of good feelings" when, shortly after his second inauguration, he toured New England much as Monroe had done and was greeted with vast acclaim. Even Harvard College overcame its doubts about the backwoods hero and awarded him an honorary degree, to the considerable chagrin of that learned Harvardian, John Quincy Adams. For his part, Jackson charmed those of his enemies who were brave enough to come beneath his gaze, inspiring such warm words as these written by an elderly Massachusetts Federalist, Elijah H. Mills:

> He was considered extremely rash and inconsiderate, tyrannical and despotic, in his principles. A personal acquaintance with him has convinced many who held these opinions that they were unfounded. He is very mild and amiable in his disposition, of great benevolence, and his manners, though formed in the wilds of the West, exceedingly polished and polite. Everybody that knows him loves him.

Few conservatives, however, allowed personal admiration to color their political hatred for the man who wedded nationalism to democracy, and interpreted his re-election as a command to make war against that sacred institution, the Bank of the United States.

THE BANK, THE BOOM, AND HARD MONEY

The charter of the Bank of the United States would run out in 1836 if the law were left to take its course, but the old fighter in the White House, armed with what he regarded as a mandate from the people, assumed the offensive against the "Monster" shortly after his re-election in order to consolidate his victory. He feared there might be another move to re-charter the Bank, and by now he was convinced of its unsoundness as a financial institution. Most competent observers thought him wrong on the latter point, but he had not overestimated the Bank's political power— which was his fundamental reason for opposing it.

The method he devised for weakening and decisively defeating Nicholas Biddle's establishment was to withdraw the government deposits from it. By law the Secretary of the Treasury was authorized to do this, but Jackson had to overcome stubborn resistance in his own official family. Within a period of a few months in 1833, he got rid of one Secretary of the Treasury (Louis L. McLane) by promoting him to the Secretaryship of State when Edward Livingston became Minister to France; and he quickly removed another (William J. Duane), putting in the vacant place Roger B. Taney, who as Attorney General had supported him against the Bank from the beginning. A significant aspect of these develop-ments was the assertion and full assumption by Jackson of presidential responsibility for the actions of the department heads. Early in the fall of 1833 (September 26), Taney issued an order that henceforth the public funds should be deposited in certain state banks. These were designated by critics as the "pet banks." Meanwhile, former deposits in the United States Bank were gradually withdrawn in the course of ordinary operations.

When Congress met in December, these actions and the reasons for them were reported to that body, as the law required; and the debate that was engendered there continued through this session and the next one, as it did intermittently till the end of Jackson's term. Meanwhile, Biddle had brought his financial batteries into play. Beginning in the summer of 1833, the Bank contracted its loans, thus arousing fear of a recession and bringing pressure to bear on the business community, which eventually complained. During the winter he granted personal favors to legislators. At this time Webster wrote him: "I believe my retainer has not been renewed or *refreshed* as usual. If it be wished that my relation to the Bank should be continued, it may be well to send me the usual retainers."

But it was obvious by the spring of 1834 that the Bank was waging a losing fight against the implacable President. In the Senate, it is true, Clay carried through resolutions censuring the latter for his conduct, and these remained on the record until the last weeks of the administration, when Senator Benton finally got them expunged; but the House supported Jackson, and no effective means to stay his hand could be devised by anybody. In the fall of 1834, Biddle, giving up the fight to all practical purposes, began to expand his loans in what soon developed into a boom period. When the federal charter of the Bank ran out in 1836, it got a state charter and continued to operate as a private institution in Pennsylvania.

The Flood of Speculation

The speculative mania which marked the remainder of Jackson's administration cannot be blamed primarily on the "pet banks." They were selected with considerable care and subjected to fairly stringent conditions, which were formalized by Congressional action in 1836, though inevitably there were evasions. Nor can it be blamed on any inflationary policies of the President, who was still a hard-money man. The change in the coinage ratio between silver and gold in 1834, to 16 to 1 (from 15 to 1), was designed to favor gold and increase the circulation of the soundest of all monetary mediums. This measure, which owed its success chiefly to Senator Benton, or "Old Bullion," was thoroughly approved by Jackson. But no effective agency was devised in place of the "Monster" to control the host of state banks and their loans and their myriad issues of paper money.

One traveler of the time described his experience as follows:

> At Wheeling exchanged $5.00 note, Kentucky money, for notes of the Northwest Bank of Virginia; reached Fredericktown; there neither Virginia nor Kentucky money current; paid a $5.00 Wheeling note for breakfast and dinner; received in change two $1.00 notes on some Pennsylvania bank, $1.00 Baltimore and Ohio Railroad, and balance in Good Intent shinplasters; 100 yards from the tavern door all notes refused except the Baltimore and Ohio Railroad.

This chaos created a happy hunting-ground for speculators and sharp operators as prosperity developed into a runaway inflationary boom. By January 1, 1835, the whole national debt was paid off, to Jackson's great satisfaction, but the government now faced an embarrassing problem in the growing surplus in the Treasury. The tariff, which was the chief source of the surplus, could not be touched before 1842, when the compromise provisions of 1833 would have been carried out. At this stage Westerners cared little about further reductions of the price of public lands because inflation made the price of $1.25 per acre easy to pay and aroused vast hopes of increased values. Federal internal improvements as a means of spending money were ruled out by continued Eastern opposition and Jackson's veto of the Maysville Road Bill.

The plan that Congress adopted was much closer to Henry Clay's distribution scheme than to Jackson's more conservative policy. This was a program to "deposit" the federal surplus with the state governments, under the tacit understanding that the money would never be repaid. Calling the gifts "deposits" had the advantage of avoiding delicate constitutional problems, and Jackson signed the Deposit Act in June 1836 though he had not recommended it. Senator Benton of Missouri called the procedure: "in name a deposit; in form a loan; in essential design a distribution." All surplus funds in the Treasury above $5 million on January 1, 1837, were to be divided among the states in proportion to their representation in Congress. Three out of four quarterly installments went to the states in 1837, before a turn in the economic tide caused the policy to be abandoned.

This device relieved the Treasury from the embarrassment of riches, but it stimulated the national boom by encouraging the state governments to embark on fantastic spending sprees. Imaginations already overheated by visions of canals and paved roads were crowded by dreams of railroads which should bring enormous advantages to everybody. A few states used their money wisely, but others borrowed huge sums of money on the strength of the Deposit Act and launched grandiose programs of internal improvements. State governments issued bonds and for a time speculators bid up their price wildly. The state authorities were lulled into thinking their dreams would come true and offered new issues.

The great London bank of Baring Brothers bought bonds in the United States and resold them to British investors who hardly knew the difference between federal bonds, which were as good as gold, and dubious state bonds. British investment throughout the nineteenth century substantially speeded up American industrialization and formed an important British interest on the side of peaceful relations. But the scale of investment during the middle thirties was out of all proportion to the actual progress and needs of the American economy. While borrowing increased, prices went up on both sides of the Atlantic and a mounting intoxication of prosperity seized both peoples. Wildcat banks multiplied in the South and West as state governments chartered new ones in order to sell them bonds. The banks issued paper money on the security of the state bonds and loaned the paper money back to the states as well as to land speculators. Businessmen believed that the increase in land values and the profits of transportation routes would pay huge dividends to all holders of paper securities. The federal government was sucked into the paper hurricane, since payments for public lands could be made with paper money. On this basis, land sales increased from less than $3 million in 1832 to almost $25 million in 1836.

The Specie Circular

The spiral could not move forever upwards. Since the Collapse of 1819, the business cycle had come full circle again. Bust was certain to follow boom, and the whole episode was a startling lesson in the irresponsibility of state governments and the need for some central authority to regulate the excesses of the business cycle. The eventual Crash was owing to business failures in England as well as to crop failures and other developments in America. When Jackson tried to stem the flood of speculation, his action was so rude that it accelerated the inevitable catastrophe. As a hard-money man he saw in the speculative mania proof that any kind of "paper" finance—whether federal, state or private borrowing—whether paper money of the United States Bank or state banks—was wrong, and injurious chiefly to the poorest classes. Jackson personally had been a victim of debt and had struggled for years with great probity to pay his creditors and recover solvency. He had also put the federal house in order by paying off all its debts. Now he saw the nation imprisoning itself in a colossal structure of state and private and international debt. With his usual decisiveness, he seized the handiest axe available and delivered a fearful stroke at the base of the structure. He had previously sought to restrict somewhat the receipt of state bank notes by the public-land offices; and on July 11, 1836, he issued the Specie Circular.

This was a Treasury Order instructing public land offices to accept only gold or silver in payment for public lands after August 15. Jackson tried to aim the blow chiefly at speculators and soften it for actual settlers by providing that paper money would be accepted for four more months in payment for small purchases. His broad purpose was made clear in the last paragraph of the Circular:

> The principal objects of the President in adopting this measure being to repress alleged frauds, and to withhold any countenance or facilities in the power of the Government from the monopoly of the public lands in the hands of speculators and capitalists, to the injury of the actual settlers in the new States, and of emigrants in search of new homes, as well as to discourage the ruinous extension of bank issues, and bank credits, by which those results are generally supposed to be promoted. . . .

The essence of Jacksonian Democracy was in the Specie Circular: aggressive exercise of national Executive authority in the interest of the plain people. Businessmen of the more speculative sort called Jackson a tyrant; and even Western farmers were aggrieved by his dislike for their inflationary proclivities; but most people recognized the purity of his motives.

The full effects of the Specie Circular were not felt until after Jackson had turned over the presidency to his chosen successor, Martin Van

Buren, who found in 1837 that he had acquired a panic along with Jackson's mantle. In Jackson's time people often said that his popularity would withstand anything. It had receded somewhat before he left office, but he escaped the test whether it could survive a depression while he was still in the seat of responsibility.

JACKSONIAN FOREIGN RELATIONS AND THE ADVANCING FRONTIER

The Jackson administration was far more notable in domestic than in foreign affairs, though the President's national patriotism was manifest in both spheres. He succeeded where John Quincy Adams had failed in reaching a settlement with Great Britain that fully opened the British West Indies to United States trade and shipping. In his annual message of 1830, he assured the country that the British government had shown "a sincere desire to cultivate the best relations with the United States." Smaller men in both countries continued to whip up hatred, as though they regretted Anglo-American peace, but the hero of New Orleans kept that hatchet buried.

In dealing with France, Jackson had much less reason to be conciliatory. He gained a diplomatic victory when the government of King Louis-Philippe in 1831 signed a treaty with the United States agreeing to pay 25 million francs to discharge American claims for injuries to shipping during the Napoleonic Wars. In consideration of this, duties were reduced on French wines. But the French Chamber of Deputies refused to appropriate the money, and the French Treasury defaulted on the first payment. To Jackson this was deliberate bad faith. He waited until the Deputies again met, and when they refused to act he ordered the United States Navy to prepare for action. Jackson asked Congress to authorize reprisals on French property if payment were not forthcoming, and the French Minister requested and received his passports early in 1835. Jackson's partisans enjoyed a bit of excitement over the prospect of war, but the French quickly appropriated the money with the proviso that Jackson's language to Congress be explained. In his next message to that body the President denied that he had intended to "menace or insult" France, but declared at the same time that he would never stain his country's honor by any apology. A "war of etiquette" was averted, for the French eventually accepted this statement and paid what they owed with interest.

The President engaged in a more peaceable diplomatic adventure in the Orient. In 1832, he sent Edmund Roberts, a seagoing merchant of New Hampshire, on a secret mission to negotiate treaties with the fabled kingdoms of the Far East. Roberts was unsuccessful in Cochin China because, being a good republican, he refused to kowtow to the Emperor in token of subservience. In Siam and Muscat, however, he obtained treaties which authorized American trade on favorable terms and the Senate ratified these. On a later visit Roberts died of the plague in China while on his way to open negotiations with Japan. His mission was the first chapter in the story of the diplomatic relations of the United States with the Far East, and he was a forerunner of American expansion into the Pacific.

Moving the Indians Westward

Far more important in Jackson's time was the expansion of settlement in the vast reaches of the North American continent, and this was greatly expedited by the large-scale removals of Indians from the white men's path. Statesmanship found no place for the aborigine in freedom's rapidly growing empire except on its extreme outskirts, and Jackson's concern for the "plain people" did not extend to redmen. In spirit he was one with the frontiersmen, who regarded treaties with Indians merely as successive devices for removing them, rather than with his predecessor John Quincy Adams and Chief Justice Marshall, who tried vainly to impart some sanctity to these agreements.

The policy of removing the Indians across the Mississippi River had been started, actually, in Monroe's administration, but it was implemented and vigorously carried out in that of Jackson. The Removal Act of 1830, which was occasioned by the struggle between the Georgians and the Cherokees, definitely legalized this policy, and in 1834 Indian Territory (now Oklahoma) was formally established. Jackson sought to employ methods of persuasion and thus avoid both legal appeals and recourse to force. He sent emissaries among the Indians, especially in the Old Southwest where he had won his fame as a fighter, and they negotiated nearly a hundred "evacuation treaties" by the well-known means of cajolery, bribery, and threat. The removal of the Creeks, Choctaws, and Chickasaws was effected without very great difficulty, and as a result rich new cotton lands were opened up beyond the Mississippi as well as east of it. During this time, however, the ruthless Black Hawk War was fought in the Northwest and the Seminole War began in Florida, while the Cherokees were speeded out of Georgia under distressing circumstances.

Part of the fame of the Black Hawk War (1832) came from the fact that Abraham Lincoln served in it as a volunteer and gained one of the most gratifying honors of his life when he was elected captain of his company of Illinois militiamen. Black Hawk, a chief of the Sauk tribe, technically violated a treaty whose validity he denied when he sought to repossess his fertile ancestral lands near the mouth of the Rock River. He led from Iowa a band that included women and children, claiming that his intentions were peaceful, and the fighting began when militiamen fired on a flag of truce. But he had previously been planning a confederacy against the encroaching white men and his move struck terror in Illinois. In the end he was pursued into Wisconsin, and in the Bad Axe Massacre women and children were slain along with the braves. Black Hawk himself survived and dictated an autobiography which became a classic. Following the massacre, many of the Northwestern Indians were induced to move to the Far West, and very few were east of the Mississippi at the end of Jackson's term. Settlers rushed into the undeveloped upper stretches of the Old Northwest, and in 1837 Michigan was added to the states—balancing Arkansas, which was admitted to the Union the year before. Coming out of the region covered by the Northwest Ordinance of 1787, the former was necessarily a free state; while the latter was from the Louisiana Purchase and below the line of 36° 30′ drawn by the Missouri Compromise.

In the South the Seminoles of Florida, protected by the swamps, resisted removal longer than any other tribe. War with them began late in Jackson's administration and did not end until 1842, though Chief Osceola was taken earlier, while bearing a flag of truce. The trouble with the Cherokees provided the most important Indian episode of the administration. It was peculiarly embarrassing because these people showed a special aptitude for the white man's civilization, and they appealed not to arms but to the law.

The Cherokees

The Cherokees in northern Georgia were engaged in diversified farming, cattle-raising, and such industries as spinning and weaving cotton, gristmills and sawmills. They built good houses and roads, reduced their language to an alphabet created by Chief Sequoya, published a newspaper, the *Cherokee Phoenix*, and established schools. They imitated the white man even to the extent of owning some Negro slaves. Americans had long argued that their harsh ways of dealing with the Indians were justified by the redman's refusal to abandon barbarism. The case of the Cherokees provided a test, and neither the American people nor President Jackson could meet it on high ground.

These peaceful Indians framed a constitution of the Cherokee Republic. The Georgians, who had as little forbearance and as great land-hunger as the generality of Americans and had been frustrated longer than the white men in other states, did not want this island of redmen to remain in their midst under any conditions, and the Indians had now committed the constitutional offense of erecting a government within the boundaries of a state without its consent. The discovery of gold within the "republic" brought mobs of unruly frontiersmen into the rugged Cherokee country; and the Georgia legislature extended the laws of the commonwealth to the Cherokees while denying them legal rights in cases involving white men. This action made encroachment by white men so safe that it was inevitable.

The Cherokees did not take to the warpath but used such peaceful means of redress as American civilization provided. They appealed to Congress, where they were answered by the Removal Act of 1830, and they turned to the Supreme Court, asking recognition of their rights under treaties with the federal government. But that body decided in the case of Cherokee Nation *vs.* Georgia (1831) that Indian tribes did not constitute foreign nations and therefore had no right to bring suit in a federal court. The case of Worcester *vs.* Georgia (1832) arose from the appeal of a missionary who had been imprisoned because of his failure to secure the license now required by state law for any white man residing among the Cherokees. In this instance Marshall ruled that the Cherokees were a "domestic dependent nation" enjoying the protection of the federal government, and that the state of Georgia had no right to extend its jurisdiction over them, in violation of United States treaties and federal laws. This decision was unenforceable by the Court and was virtually repudiated by the President.

Federal agents among the Cherokees exploited quarrels, practiced bribery, and persuaded a faction to sign away all the Georgia land in return for land in Indian Territory and a payment of $5.6 million. The majority rejected the agreement (the Treaty of New Echota of 1835), but gradually these Indians moved westward until finally United States troops forced the last of them to go. In far-away Concord, Ralph Waldo Emerson spoke with horror of this transaction: "Such a dereliction of all faith and virtue, such a denial of justice, and such deafness to screams for mercy were never heard of in times of peace and in the dealing of a nation with its own allies and wards since the earth was made." In Indian Territory with remarkable fortitude the Cherokees restored their uprooted civilization, little dreaming that, by a strange turn of fortune, their remote descendants would one day come into sudden riches when oil was found beneath their lands.

The human tide of frontiersmen, pioneers, and settlers surged into new river bottoms and plains of opportunity, overwhelming the redmen who dared oppose it. This tide even lapped over the international boundary line and moved into the Mexican province of Texas where some 30,000 persons of Anglo-American stock were living before the Jackson administration came to an end. President John Quincy Adams, regretting that in the Treaty of 1819 with Spain he had abandoned claim to this imperial domain, had vainly tried to persuade the government of Mexico to sell it. Jackson repeated the effort, but the question of the sale of Texas became a test of Mexican patriotism, and no Mexican administration dared attempt a deal. In 1836, the Texans, who had taken matters into their own ready hands, achieved independence under the leadership of Jackson's former comrade at arms and old friend, Sam Houston. Jackson recognized the Republic of Texas in one of his last official acts. Perhaps he would have done a good deal more if the time had been more propitious. But his main concern at the end of his term was to secure for his protegé, Martin Van Buren, succession to the presidency under favorable circumstances. He did not want to provoke a controversy over slavery or bequeath to him a foreign war.

THE END OF THE JACKSON ERA

A Democratic National Convention registered the wish of the party chief by unanimously nominating Van Buren for the presidency. The Whigs had no similar gathering, despite the precedent of the last campaign, and in the election their vote was split between three candidates: Hugh Lawson White of Tennessee and William Henry Harrison of Ohio, both of whom claimed to represent pioneer democracy just as well as Jackson had; and Daniel Webster, whose ability as a vote-getter did not match his eloquence. Van Buren won the election handily, by an electoral vote of 170 to 57, though he lost ground in both the West and the South Atlantic states.

At the age of seventy Jackson returned to The Hermitage, where he could smoke his pipe in peace during the eight years that were left to him. Unlike Jefferson, he founded no dynasty. Economic difficulties diverted attention from all other questions during Van Buren's four unhappy years in the White House and were a sufficient reason for his failure to be re-elected. Jackson's disciple Polk succeeded after another four-year interval and was distinctly in his tradition, though he lacked the public appeal which had made "Old Hickory" invincible. The Democratic Presidents after that until 1861 bore him no resemblance. By any reckoning Jackson was a strong President, but none of his successsors was, with the possible exception of Polk, until Lincoln. His record remained as an example which could be invoked and heeded, as it has been in our time, but the truth seems to be that he brought great personal power to the presidency, rather than that he greatly strengthened the office itself.

His political philosophy was so pragmatic that many have been unable to recognize it as a philosophy, and no thinker of his time ever reduced it to anything that could be called a system. Like Jeffersonianism, which had deeper intellectual roots, Jacksonianism was essentially an attitude. Jackson himself was the strong friend and dauntless champion of the plain people and the Union. Because of particular circumstances, his vigorous personality expressed itself chiefly in defensive actions—such as those against nullification and the Bank and the madness of speculation.

He fought valiantly for freedom but he was no architect of a free society like Jefferson; he was no builder of institutions like Hamilton or Marshall. But, like Washington and Jefferson before him and Lincoln after him, he has remained until this day a legend.

Jackson's Heir

After "Old Hickory's" administration, that of anybody else would have seemed an anticlimax, as Van Buren's surely did. Jackson, a Tennessee planter, had always sought to reduce the antagonism between North and South, and in his Farewell Address he warned, as Washington had, against the danger of basing party divisions on geographical distinctions. This danger grew during the term of his successor. Soon after his retirement, he spoke privately of another and more immediate conflict which he had shown no disposition to avoid. He foresaw a continued effort to make of honest laborers "hewers of wood and drawers of water to the monied aristocracy of the country through the credit and paper system." The Van Buren administration was in the democratic spirit of Jackson, and it fought the same sort of fight in the financial sphere.

Neither the new President nor his advisers believed that the federal government should act positively to alleviate bankruptcies and unemployment, or to cushion collapsing prices and markets. A policy of strict laissez-faire and nonintervention was still assumed to be the correct one in bad times as well as good. Governmental policy in the fields of banking and money did affect the private economy, but this was not as well understood then as it became in the twentieth century. Van Buren's most important domestic achievement showed no more understanding of economics than was common in his day, yet it revealed a very clear social and political orientation.

This was the Independent Treasury Act of 1840. Jackson, in his haste to destroy the second Bank of the United States, had not allowed for the possibility that the "pet" state banks in which he deposited the federal funds might turn out to be merely smaller versions of the big "Monster." The favored banks were privately controlled for private profit, after all. Some of their officers used public funds for gambling and a number of the banks defaulted in the Panic of 1837 with losses of millions of dollars to the federal Treasury. The radical wing of the Democracy in the North, particularly the "Loco-Focos" of New York, successors of the Workingmen's Party, blamed banks in general for the Depression and demanded that the government should entirely deny them the use of federal funds. Only thus, they believed, could the credit monopoly of private bankers be curbed. Van Buren called a special session of Congress in 1837 to consider his proposal that branches of the Treasury itself be established in the most important cities to receive, hold, and disburse all government money. Hamilton's and Marshall's argument, that a Bank was a "necessary and proper" means of carrying out the government's financial powers, was answered by this simple alternative.

Numerous Democrats, including the bankers who had profited by Jackson's deposits in their institutions and various advocates of "soft money," strongly opposed the Independent or Sub-Treasury Bill. Several times it was defeated in Congress before the persistence of depression and rising clamor for it secured its passage. Actually, whatever may be thought of governmental patronage of private banks, the withdrawal of federal funds from use as a basis of credit, and their "sterilization" in the public treasury, would be considered today a mistaken way to meet a depression. Banks are easy targets of unthinking anger whenever they are forced to collect loans in order to satisfy depositors' demands or go bankrupt; and the Loco-Focos were out to punish banks.

The bankers had certainly done much to excite popular hatred, and Van Buren by acting against them strengthened his hold on the plain people of the North, while offending conservative Democrats. Many of the latter abandoned his party and joined the Whigs, who proceeded after their campaign victory in 1840 to repeal the Independent Treasury Act in 1841, only to see the Democrats re-enact it in 1846. Van Buren's extension of Jackson's anti-Bank policy crystallized opposition in such a state as New York, where conservative groups elected William H. Seward as governor.

The Log Cabin and Hard Cider Campaign

The Democratic party lost the presidential election of 1840, however, not so much on issues as because of its failure to match the Whigs in "buncombe." By 1840, it seemed that the Democrats had maintained the support of the plain people in the North without losing that of Southern planters. This powerful coalition came very close to winning the election. The Whigs correctly assumed that their policies were unpopular among the masses of the people and that businessmen and conservatives generally would vote against Van Buren no matter what campaign nonsense was uttered by candidates. Therefore the Whig leaders decided to make a rousing demagogic appeal.

The Whig campaign of 1840 was something new in American national politics and, for all its wonderful jollity, it boded ill for the great experiment in democracy. Jackson and Van Buren had won the masses by organization around policies which served their interests; the Whigs would outdo the Democrats by organizing enthusiasm to distract attention from their own policies. The Federalists had gone down to defeat with anti-democratic flags flying, and had lost largely because they publicly professed their faith. The Whigs would not make that mistake.

A national Whig Convention met at Harrisburg, Pennsylvania, but could not agree on a platform, so none was offered to the voters. Nor did the Whigs dare to nominate either of their outstanding leaders, Clay or Webster, because the political principles of these men were too well known. They hit upon the hero of Tippecanoe, General William Henry Harrison, who had carried a few western states four years before. As a candidate he might win the plain people as Jackson had, without much danger that he would match Jackson's strong leadership in their favor. John Tyler of Virginia was named for Vice-President as a concession to Clay and the South. The Whig strategy in the campaign had been laid down as long ago as 1835 by the astute Nicholas Biddle:

> If General Harrison is taken up as the candidate, it will be on account of the past. Let him say not one single word about his principles, or his creed —let him say nothing—promise nothing. Let no committee, no convention, no town meeting ever extract from him a single word about what he thinks now or will do hereafter. Let the use of pen and ink be wholly forbidden.

The Democrats nominated Van Buren and adopted an elaborate platform of Jacksonian principles. But the Whigs quickly forestalled a debate on issues. Van Buren and Democratic policies were blamed for the Depression, while promises were made that the Whigs would waft away the dark clouds. In the North, they charged that the Seminole War proved the administration to be proslavery; in the South they made the refusal to annex Texas the basis of the charge that the administration was antislavery. But it was also necessary to prove that Harrison was a man of the people. A sarcastic Democrat's remark that if he were provided with a pension and a barrel of hard cider he would gladly retire to a log cabin for the rest of his days, was seized upon. The Whig orators shouted that Van Buren was a champagne-drinking aristocrat, while Harrison was a hard-cider, log-cabin Cincinnatus:

> Let Van from his coolers of silver drink wine,
>   And lounge on his cushioned settee.
> Our man on his buckeye bench can recline,
>   Content with hard cider is he!
>   The iron-armed soldier, the true-hearted soldier,
>   The gallant old soldier of Tippecanoe!

The Whig campaign became a ritualized picnic. Log cabins with cider barrels and coonskins were rolled from town to town. Even Daniel Webster found it expedient to apologize for not having been born in a log cabin. Genuine hard cider put voters in an appreciative frame of mind for Whig oratory and in good voice for song. Clay denounced the Independent Treasury as the "union of the purse and sword" which the Revolutionary Fathers had fought to sunder; and the Democrats were forced to deny that Van Buren used cologne to scent his whiskers.

"Tippecanoe and Tyler too" won a sweeping victory in the electoral college without large popular majorities. Clay and Webster were soon to be sadly surprised, for Harrison died a month after his inauguration and they could not control his successor. Nonetheless, Whig tactics had finally defeated the Jacksonians and brought an era to a close.

CHAPTER 26

Slavery Is Attacked and Defended

DURING THE DEBATE ON THE ADMISSION OF MISSOURI, Northerners in Congress had attacked slavery on moral grounds, but Southerners as a group did not then take up the moral challenge, preferring to make an issue of the equality of new states with the old. The main concern of Southerners then was to maintain the balance of political power. During the 1820's there was some philosophical defense of slavery in the Lower South, especially in South Carolina, but the great ideological controversy did not reach a climax until the 1830's, and not until then did abolitionism become an exclusively Northern movement. Before that time antislavery agitators and organizers like Benjamin Lundy and James G. Birney carried on most of their activities in the slave states; and the American Colonization Society, a moderate organization in which men from the Upper South and the Middle States were the chief participants, was in operation.

The great turning point in the history of American attitudes toward Negro slavery came in the years 1831 and 1832. In 1831, William Lloyd Garrison started the *Liberator*, proclaiming militant and uncompromising abolitionism; and the following winter, the Virginia legislature ended its greatest debate of the slavery question by doing nothing. This negative outcome amounted to the failure of the last best hope of voluntary emancipation in this important and generally moderate state, and proslavery sentiment grew there in the next decade. Meanwhile, the fear of slave revolt and of incitation from the North caused the slave states to adopt repressive measures and to limit freedom of speech. And, in response to moral censure, Southern thinkers worked out a formal philosophy in which slavery was represented as a positive good.

The struggle in the realm of ideas was reflected in Congressional debates over the right of petition, but slavery did not dominate the national stage until the question of its extension into the West again arose. Here we are concerned chiefly with the conflict of opinion.

The Turning Point in the Discussion of Slavery

In the decade after the adoption of the Missouri Compromise there were distinct signs of more positive public support of the "peculiar institution" in the Lower South. Since that region was the seat of cotton culture, which developed so rapidly after the War of 1812 with the aid of slave labor, this attitude can be attributed in part to economic reasons which did not apply to the Upper South to the same degree. At this stage, the slavery system was condemned by some Virginians because of its unprofitableness in their agriculture. But owners were not disposed to sacrifice their property, and there were other factors which affected all the southern states in rough proportion to their slave population. A major obstacle to emancipation was the social uncertainty. What should be done with the slaves if they should be freed? It was a tragedy of the antebellum period that neither in the North nor the South was a convincing answer given to that crucial question.

Free Negroes and the Colonization Movement

In the year 1830, along with about 2,000,000 slaves, there were in the United States some 300,000 free Negroes who were divided in almost equal parts between the North and South. The growth of this group had been rapid in the first two decades of the new government, 1790-1810, but the rate of increase afterward slowed down. The legal status of the free Negroes was deteriorating instead of improving. By 1830, state laws had made manumission more difficult than it was at the end of the Revolution, and privileges that had been granted freedmen had been curtailed, so that their condition was little better than that of slaves. They were obligated to no individual master, but their movements and opportunities were sharply restricted. Until the time of the Civil War their presence was unwelcome in most parts of the country and their status was considerably below that of white men, though an exception must be made in behalf of New England.

The main reason why free Negroes were not wanted in the southern states was that they were believed to constitute a danger to the slave system. But many liberal and high-minded men who favored emancipation also regarded them as undesirable members of society and were thus confronted with a dilemma. The inability of the statesmanship of the age to resolve this is well illustrated by the opinions of Jefferson, who always regarded slavery as a contradiction of the doctrine that all men have a natural right to liberty and as a denial of the dignity and sanctity of human nature. Speaking of the slaves, he said: "Nothing is more certainly written in the book of fate, than that these people are to be free." But he continued: "Nor is it less certain that the two races, equally free, cannot live in the same government. Nature, habit, opinion have drawn indelible lines of distinction between them." This melancholy judgment was echoed by Alexis de Tocqueville, the most famous foreign writer of the day on the subject of American democracy, who doubted if the white and black races would ever live together in any country on an equal footing. In the light of later events, these noted and generally liberal observers may be condemned for lack of faith, but the importance of building up the free Negroes as a transitional group was not then perceived. Most Southern and many Northern emancipationists advocated their removal from the country.

The symbol of this policy was the American Colonization Society, established on January 1, 1817, under distinguished leadership and patronage. Justice Bushrod Washington, nephew of George Washington, was the first president; and among the vice-presidents were Henry Clay, William H. Crawford, and Andrew Jackson. This was a moderate movement in which the largest part was played by the Middle States and the Upper South. In its lifetime greatest opposition to it was expressed in New England on the one hand and in South Carolina and Georgia on the other.

It operated until 1832 or 1833 in a generally favorable climate of opinion. The Colony of Liberia was established in Africa (1822) and several thousand settlers were sent there, a large number of whom died. The peak year was 1832 when there were about 800 emigrants. Emphasis was laid on the expatriation of free Negroes, but the Society also hoped to encourage emancipation and some of the settlers had been freed with a view to transportation to Africa. Soon the underlying assumption of racial inferiority was bitterly assailed by the abolitionists. The shipment of any considerable number of Negroes to the land of their forefathers would have been ruinously expensive, and by this time the slaves and freedmen as a group regarded America as their homeland and wanted to remain there. Also, in the Lower South at least, the white men believed that they could not do without them. But the colonization policy had not been discredited in the Upper South by the time of the great slavery debate in Virginia, and the proposals of emancipation which were made there were coupled with it. Also, they were made at a time of acute fear of insurrection.

Slave Revolts

Throughout the South people were aware of what had happened on the West Indian island of Santo Domingo during and after the French

Revolution. The whites and mulattoes had been massacred or expelled and the former slaves had taken over. To be sure, there was no parallel between conditions in any American state and those in the French part of Santo Domingo (Haiti), where on the eve of the French Revolution the whites and free Negroes together comprised little more than 10 per cent of the total population, but developments there continued to be held up as a terrible warning. In the American states slave revolts had been and continued to be very few. In 1822, the discovery of a projected revolt in Charleston under the leadership of a free Negro, Denmark Vesey, resulted in the deportation or hanging of about seventy conspirators. In 1829, David Walker, a free Negro from North Carolina now living in Boston and engaged in the old-clothes business, issued an appeal to the slaves who, as he believed, could and should gain their freedom by destroying their masters. Copies of *Walker's Appeal* were discovered in the hands of Negroes in Savannah in the late autumn of 1829 and were found soon afterward in several other southern states. These events created for a time a panic of fear and led to repressive legal actions. Northern whites strongly disapproved of Walker's method of solving the problem of slavery. The first number of Garrison's *Liberator* appeared on January 1, 1831. Though he claimed that his own appeal was to the conscience, not to physical force, his language was so extreme that it seemed to Southerners a call to violence. Nat Turner's Rebellion occurred in Southampton County, Virginia, in August of the same year.

This was the bloodiest of all the insurrections. Taking advantage of the absence of many of the whites, who had gone across the border into North Carolina to attend camp-meeting, Turner, hitherto a faithful slave who had come to regard himself as a prophet, led an uprising which resulted in the killing of about sixty whites, mostly women and children. Turner himself was not captured for two months, though the revolt was broken by the second day. Most of the insurgents were shot down and the rest were tried and executed, along with others who were innocent. Panic gripped the entire South, and it was weeks before the Virginians in slavery districts ceased to sleep with fear. Garrison described this as the "hour of vengeance," and declared that the insurrection was a "prelude to the deluge," but the *Liberator* had no subscribers in Virginia and did not reflect Northern sentiment. This was very sympathetic toward the Virginians, and the affair tended to solidify the whites everywhere, showing that violence of this sort served to defeat its own ends. The uprising led to further restrictive legislation throughout the South, but many Virginians were determined to do something about the disease of which it was a symptom. In the legislative session of 1831-1832 occurred the most extensive and famous of all Virginian debates of slavery, and the last one that was held in public. The state that had given to the world George

Mason's Declaration of Rights and Jefferson's Bill for Religious Freedom was erecting its last great monument to liberty of discussion.

The Virginia Debate of 1832

Much of the concern over the ills of slavery in Virginia arose from economic and social causes. Times were hard, slavery did not appear to be profitable, and there was deep anxiety over the growing preponderance of the slave population in the region east of the Blue Ridge. The whites had exceeded the blacks there in 1790, but in every decade thereafter through 1830 the latter had been in a growing majority. After Nat Turner's Rebellion, even the liberals favored temporary repressive measures for the public safety. There was talk of getting rid of the free Negroes, and of getting rid of enough, free and slave, to guarantee a white majority in the eastern as well as the western part of the state. There was also talk of general emancipation, but practically everybody believed that this would have to be coupled with a scheme of deportation.

The proposal of this sort which commanded strongest support was made by Thomas Jefferson Randolph, grandson of the late President. He proposed the submission to the voters of a plan by which all the slaves born after a specified date (July 4, 1840) should become the property of the state when they came of age; they were then to be hired out until sufficient funds had been accumulated for their removal from the United States. The impracticality of the deportation feature was recognized at the time, and neither the state treasury nor public opinion would have sustained it. For these reasons, the legislators contented themselves with declaring the existing situation an evil one and deferring further action until there could be further development of favorable public opinion.

Thus, at last, the chief significance of the debate, which lasted for two weeks in January 1832, lay in the arraignment which the Virginians themselves made of slavery. Some defended it as a positive good, while some still asserted that freedom was a natural right; but chief emphasis was laid on the injury which slavery brought to the character of the whites themselves and on the ineffectiveness of the existing economic system. In the negativeness of the outcome, this debate was typical of the more violent one which raged through the country in the next generation: evils were recognized but no acceptable solution was discovered, and victory went by default to the forces of inaction, which were afterwards solidified into reaction.

Unfortunately, the most important immediate effect of the debate was the stirring of conservatives to formulate stronger defensive arguments than the mere absence of a feasible remedy. Later in the same year, President Thomas R. Dew of the College of William and Mary made a highly significant contribution to the proslavery argument, entitled *Review of the Debate in the Virginia Legislature of 1831 and 1832.* The reform spirit, which had failed to bring about constructive action, declined thereafter. In the next few years, especially 1832-1836, the increase in the sales of slaves to the cotton region lessened the fears of Negro dominance in the East and at the same time brought money into depleted purses. Thus the Virginians, gradually overcoming their repugnance to the domestic slave trade, eased both their economic and social problem. A further reason for the quiescence of the liberals was that they were embarrassed by the abolitionist propaganda and were unwilling to be associated with it.

THE ABOLITIONIST CRUSADE, 1830-1840

Abolitionism as an organized national movement was directly inspired by the British Anti-Slavery Society, which began in 1823 and reached a climax of success ten years later when Parliament abolished slavery in the British West Indies. In certain respects American antislavery leaders availed themselves too little of the British example. They might well have given more thought and emphasis to the provisions for compensation and a temporary apprentice system which were a part of the British settlement of the slavery question. Parliament arrived at a more realistic solution of the problem than any that was ever pressed by American abolitionists.

The immediate stimulus to American abolitionism was provided by the debates on West Indian slavery in Parliament in 1830, which were much read in the United States. Among those greatly impressed by them was William Lloyd Garrison, who was then assisting Benjamin Lundy on the *Genius of Universal Emancipation* in Baltimore but who soon broke with his elder and started his own *Liberator.* Also, these debates occasioned apostles of benevolence in New York, especially the brothers Tappan, Arthur and Lewis, to move prematurely for a national organization. The American Anti-Slavery Society was established under their patronage a little later (1833); and Garrison, recently returned from a visit to England as a self-appointed representative of American abolitionism, had a conspicuous part in this. But Garrison was essentially a free-lance at all times, and he was largely responsible for the split in the Society in 1840, when the Tappans withdrew, leaving the original organization as little but a name. In that year, the Liberty Party emerged and the slavery question was henceforth enmeshed with politics, though Garrison and many others were opposed to direct political action. His own period of most significant agitation, and that of the most important activity of the national Society, fell within the 1830's.

The American roots of abolitionism, and particularly of the parts and phases of the movement that were not connected with Garrison, lay in the religious revival associated with the name of the Presbyterian evangelist, Charles G. Finney, which reached its climax in 1830. The converts of Finney went forth charged with a spirit of active benevolence which manifested itself conspicuously in abolitionism. Though sympathetic with abolition, Finney himself never made it his major business. His spirit was reflected in the crusading zeal of other men, such as the Tappans in New York and Theodore Dwight Weld, who was probably his most important convert.

Garrison and Weld

Garrison, who issued the first number of the *Liberator* in Boston on January 1, 1831, was a native of Newburyport, Massachusetts. He had emerged from poverty and had gained practically all his schooling at the printer's bench. A man of strong will and intense emotions, he identified himself utterly with the cause he championed and did not at all mind if people identified it completely with him. He was a brave man who suffered for the sake of conscience, and he showed himself to be unconquerable. Always a highly controversial figure in his own time, he is still one; but he may be regarded as a classic American example of fanaticism, which William James has described as "loyalty carried to a convulsive extreme." There was impatience, intolerance, and even cruelty in him because of his excess of devotion to his cause. The fame of the *Liberator* was less owing to its Northern supporters than to its Southern enemies. Garrison carried on a continuous campaign of denunciation against the slaveholders; and not unnaturally hatred bred hatred, while violent agitation accentuated fear.

Garrison strongly opposed the colonization policy, as the abolitionists as a group did from this time on, but he was most distinctive in his extreme emphasis on "immediatism." In the first number of his paper he said: "I shall strenuously contend for the immediate enfranchisement of our slave population." That sounded as though he believed that the slaves could all be turned into voting citizens overnight. He also said that he would not equivocate, nor excuse, nor retreat a single inch, and that he *would* be heard. He had no constructive program for the slaves who should be freed, and actually he was a philosophical anarchist, being opposed to political action. Always an independent agitator, he was personally unco-operative even within the abolitionist ranks. In the end he denounced everybody who would not echo his words of immoderation. He described the northern clergy as a "Brotherhood of Thieves" and termed the Constitution "a covenant with death and an agreement with Hell," because it left slavery as a state question. On July 4, 1854, he publicly burned a copy of that document. The chief historic significance of Garrison, besides the opposition and fear he aroused, lay in his emphasis on slavery as a moral issue. With what he regarded as a moral wrong this dauntless and implacable man could tolerate no compromise whatever. But even in the North few believed that, in a national government based upon consent, statesmanlike policies could be compounded of such untractable materials as he provided.

Among the New England abolitionists, Wendell Phillips of Massachusetts was most like Garrison in his complete identification with the cause. This high-minded man of wealth, who imperiled his superior social position by his unpopular moral crusade, was a more attractive personal figure than the editor of the *Liberator*. A younger man than Garrison, he got into the crusade later, and he gained his chief fame as an orator. He also attacked the slaveowners violently, denounced the Constitution, and valued abolition more than Union.

Theodore Dwight Weld (1803-1895) now seems the greatest of the abolitionists, though he was less widely known than Garrison since he worked behind the scenes. Moral reform can have no purer symbol than this self-effacing organizer to whom the cause was everything and personal glory nothing. He was one of Finney's converts in whom religion manifested itself in the effort for social betterment; and, far from breaking with the churches, he used the methods of personal evangelism. He himself was "converted" to abolitionism, and in turn he "converted" some of the most important leaders in the movement—such as James G. Birney, hitherto a supporter of colonization.

Commissioned by the Tappans to find a site for a seminary for Finney's converts, he selected Lane Seminary in Cincinnati. Among the students he afterwards organized a debate on slavery, destined to become famous. He aroused the ire of President Lyman Beecher and the trustees but left an indelible impress on Henry Ward Beecher and the latter's sister, Harriet Beecher Stowe. He trained a group from Lane Seminary and sent them forth as agents to win new converts to abolitionism. The regions evangelized by them became important seats of antislavery strength in later years. Later, Weld served as a power behind the legislative scenes in Washington, supplying ammunition to John Quincy Adams and others, and *Uncle Tom's Cabin* was based in part on his tract, *American Slavery As It Is*. More than any other single man, Weld was the heart and the brains of the effective abolitionist movement. He was an evangelist of reform, seeking to win hearts, and the great service that he and his converts rendered the cause was to give it a religious sanction. He sought to make abolitionism synonymous with religion, and among the evangelical sects in the North he very considerably succeeded, though he won no converts in the South.

The abolitionists designated slavery as a sin rather than a social evil, and they addressed themselves primarily to nonslaveholders. They fired inhabitants of the free states with zeal to extirpate sin from the lives of others, who lived under very different conditions and would have to face the painful task of reconstruction if the slaves should be freed. Southerners regarded them as unbearably self-righteous and Abraham Lincoln, who never lost sight of the immense practical difficulties that would be associated with emancipation, would never permit himself to be coupled with the abolitionists. Even in the North they were generally regarded as fanatics. But they gave an immoral stigma to slavery and imparted a religious sanction to Northernism. Also, they served to solidify Southern sentiment; and, since they would recognize no middle ground, they had a discouraging effect on the emancipation cause in the border states. Few have ever believed more fervently in the American dream of freedom and equality than they, but they had no part in the American tradition of political compromise and they played into the hands of the Southern extremists. Fear of abolitionism was the excuse for a great variety of repressive actions.

The South Acts against Agitators

After the outspoken debate on slavery in the Virginia Assembly in 1832 and the rise of aggressive abolitionism, the prevailing Southern policy became one of preventing all agitation of the subject. Practically all the southern states passed laws for this purpose. This was no mere matter of protecting slave property, though that motive was always present. Fears of slave revolt and consequent social revolution tended to unite the white men, whether slaveholders or not, in all regions where Negroes were numerous. At times the legislators operated in an atmosphere of hysteria, and when the tide of terror receded the states were left with a residue of laws restricting their own freedom of discussion.

A tide of terror had followed the appearance of *Walker's Appeal* in 1829. This violent pamphlet occasioned several state legislatures to forbid the introduction of literature inciting to revolt and the teaching of slaves to read and write. After Nat Turner's rebellion in 1831, new restrictions were imposed in some states on the freedom of Negroes to preach and assemble. The most intolerant period of all followed the abolitionist pamphlet campaign of 1835-1836. This literature was sent to whites, not Negroes, but it was nevertheless regarded as incendiary. In Charleston a mob took a sack of pamphlets from the post office and burned them. The federal authorities were by no means outraged by this. On the contrary, President Andrew Jackson was horrified by the "wicked procedure" of the abolitionists and believed that all good men should frown upon the circulation of their writings. Postmaster General Amos Kendall countenanced the policy of the postmaster in New York in declining to send abolitionist literature to the South. This pamphlet warfare proved generally unsuccessful even in the North, and it was at this juncture that

Theodore Dwight Weld turned back to personal evangelism and sent forth an enlarged band of missionaries to win converts in the free states.

The Southern laws which resulted from this scare were directed chiefly against persons who denied the right to own slaves or advised abolition or circulated literature urging slave revolt. They were severe in the Upper South, except in Kentucky, and even more severe in the Lower South. In practice these laws were rarely invoked, and there are indications that they were interpreted liberally in the case of Southerners, whose fundamental loyalty to their own society could be assumed. But they were a constant threat against any sort of criticism of the existing social order, and they effectively closed the South to Northern critics. "Foreign emissaries" would have been harshly treated if they had entered the region, and very wisely they stayed out.

So far as discussion of the "peculiar institution" was concerned, the freedom of the press declined after 1835 until it practically disappeared. Abolitionist editors had their troubles in the North also, the murder of Elijah Lovejoy by an Illinois mob in 1837 being a tragic illustration. The term "abolitionist" was unpopular almost everywhere and in the South it became a fighting word. A courageous Virginia editor, John Hampden Pleasants, felt compelled to issue a challenge to a younger rival when the latter applied it to him a decade later. Actually Pleasants had done little more than protest against what he regarded as hysteria, but he would not accept this epithet and died in the ensuing duel.

The fear of slave insurrection and social revolution, which hung like a cloud over Southern society in this generation, goes by the name of the "Black Terror." There was hysteria in the air at times which distorted reality, and wisdom is hard to come by when the minds of men are dominated by fear. The worst effects of these repressive measures fell upon Southerners themselves, who in their effort to assure safety lost part of their own heritage of freedom.

They gained much sympathy from other parts of the country when seeking to block the extremes of abolitionism within their own borders, but they fared worse when the fight was shifted to the national arena. A great struggle in Congress, reaching its height in the years 1836-1840, centered on the right of petition. Thousands of petitions, resulting from abolitionist zeal and relating most often to the questions of slavery in the District of Columbia and the domestic slave trade, were introduced. These were often couched in denunciatory language which aroused Southern resentment. The proslavery group secured the adoption of the so-called "Gag Rule" (1836) in the House of Representatives, requiring that all petitions and other papers on the subject of slavery or its abolition should be laid on the table automatically without further action. John Quincy Adams, who served in the House after his retirement from the presidency, gained the title "Old Man Eloquent" for his opposition to a measure which he regarded as unconstitutional; and the abolitionists saw that petitions, constantly reiterating the same themes, should continue to appear. In one period of three or four months there were enough of them to fill a large room from floor to ceiling. The Gag Rule in some form remained on the books until 1844, and Southern support of it did the section great harm. The defensive tactics of Southerners had thrown them into opposition not merely to the emancipation of the slaves and freedom of discussion in their own states, but to the liberties of their Northern countrymen.

THE PROSLAVERY PHILOSOPHY AND THE CHURCHES

Just as the efforts of Southerners to prevent agitation were directly related to their fears of slave revolt, their philosophical defense of the existing system was a response to the charges of immorality and sinfulness that had been directed against it. These charges rankled in the minds of Southerners, who were notably religious people. The desire to arrive at a philosophical and ethical justification of a system which, for a variety of reasons, they had now concluded that they could not give up, was stimulated by the Missouri debates. In the next decade the Southerners took up the moral challenge to some extent, especially in South Carolina; and in the 1830's the defense movement made strong headway in Virginia. Until the abolitionist pamphlet campaign of 1835-1836 this was largely directed to local opinion; the Southerners were trying to convince themselves. Thereafter, goaded by the abolitionists, they would have convinced the country of their rightness if they could have; but in this respect their failure was comparable to that of the abolitionists in trying to convince them of their wrongfulness.

Though the names of Thomas R. Dew, William Harper, William Gilmore Simms, James H. Hammond, and George Fitzhugh are specially associated with the proslavery philosophy, which was elaborately formulated in the generation before secession, this should not be regarded as the work of a small group. It was the fruitage of the intellect of the entire section. Statesmen developed and proclaimed it on the political front; clergymen, educators, and literary men on the social, moral, and religious fronts—at just the time that the reform spirit was burgeoning and blossoming in the North. The philosophical defense of the South in the political realm centered on an emphasis on the historic Constitution and the rights of the states that were supposed to be safeguarded by it. The classic figure here was John C. Calhoun but he was aided and abetted by a host of others. This conservative attitude toward the basic law was paralleled by a social philosophy which looked backward even farther and found its arguments in much more ancient writings. It was more than conservative; it was reactionary.

From the expressions of some of the writers who proclaimed it, it may be regarded as a repudiation of the philosophy of the Declaration of Independence; but as generally understood it represented a limitation rather than a repudiation of the historic faith and doctrine. It denied rights and opportunities to Negroes on the ground that they were distinct and inferior by nature, while affirming the political equality of white men. Thus it was fundamentally racial in its basis, though it represented an attempt to rationalize a system which was now deemed essential to Southern economic life. Negro labor was regarded as indispensable, but the free Negroes were thought to be untrustworthy and degraded. Therefore, so the white men said, there was in the South no feasible alternative to slavery.

Furthermore, the claim was made that the merits of the system were shown by its fruits. By means of slavery, savages had been lifted from barbarism to Christian civilization and they enjoyed a better situation than the free Negroes. In view of the status of the latter in nearly all parts of the country, there was point in this argument, and the Southern apologists did not fail to call attention to the plight of white industrial workers in the East and in England. As for the Southern whites, there was now a repudiation of the charges previously made in Virginia that slavery had an ill effect on their character and effectiveness. It was claimed that, far from degenerating, the white race in the southern United States had developed a unique civilization and a high degree of culture. There was more boastfulness now, and that in itself was a sign of weakness.

In their effort to find support for this social philosophy, the Southern clergymen, writers, and teachers found their greatest literary arsenal in the Sacred Scriptures. The abolitionists had turned to the Bible for texts, and the Southerners naturally did so in a time when church membership was rapidly increasing. Passages in the Old Testament sanctioning the practice of slavery in distant centuries would have been wholly unconvincing to men like Jefferson and Franklin, but the South had turned away from their religious liberalism and was little affected by that of William Ellery Channing and Emerson in New England. Southern religion had passed into what we would now call a fundamentalist phase. A biblical text was a biblical text, whether it came from Genesis or Leviticus or one of the Gospels. Southern divines pointed out that slavery was not condemned by Christ, and that the Apostle Paul actually enjoined obedience on slaves, going so far in one instance as to return a runaway slave to his master.

The Christian attitude toward slavery should have been arrived at on consideration of the spirit of Christian teachings as a whole; and the Northern divines tended to emphasize the spirit of brotherhood. The Southerners tended to be strict constructionists with respect to both the

Bible and the Constitution. But they became increasingly aware of their religious duties in human relations. Toward the end of the antebellum period, far more than at the beginning, religious leaders instructed masters in their duties and sought to carry the Gospel to the slaves.

More basic, actually, than the biblical argument was the ethnological. This was an attempt to justify on scientific grounds the concept of the natural inferiority of the Negroes which was practically universal among Southern whites and was widespread throughout the United States and the world. Inevitably the Negroes, both free and slave, were backward at that time of extremely limited opportunity; and the physical differences between them and the whites were visible to any eye. Yet, as modern anthropologists and sociologists have pointed out, it is illogical to attribute this backwardness to race and to regard color as a sign of intrinsic inferiority. The abolitionists were unrealistic in underestimating the social problems arising from the presence, side by side, of races as different in history and in external appearance as the whites and Negroes, but some of the Southern apologists went to an unbearable extreme when they denied the unity of mankind. That was too much for the Southern religious leaders. They continued to believe that God "hath made of one blood all nations of men, for to dwell on the face of the earth." The ethnological argument was the most powerful of all, and up to a point it coincided with the predominant popular opinion, but beyond that point very many would not go. There were contradictions and inconsistencies and anomalies in this racist philosophy.

Among these was miscegenation. Tocqueville is authority for the statement that there was less admixture of whites and blacks in the southern United States than in the colonies of the continental European countries, but intermixture there unquestionably was, and, as Lincoln afterward remarked, this was greater under a system of slavery than under freedom.

Division in the Churches

Nothing shows more clearly how, in this age of controversy, the union of hearts among the best of men was broken than the split in certain important churches on a North-South line. The period, 1820-1850, was one of notable increase in church membership in the South, especially among the evangelical sects—the Methodists and Baptists and certain groups of Presbyterians. In this period in Virginia, the Carolinas, and Georgia, the Baptists and Methodists increased in number at a much faster rate than the population; and the dominance of the evangelicals was as great or greater in the newer states in the interior. These sects were warmer and more democratic than the older churches, though they were less intellectual and more fundamentalist in doctrine. It was under their influence that more attention was paid to the religious life of the slaves, but a chasm opened between them and their Northern brethren. This led to a split in the largest groups, the Baptists and the Methodists. Owing to the fact that the organization of the Baptists was predominantly congregational, the split in their ranks was rather less painful and less significant. The trouble among them arose from alleged discrimination against slaveholders in connection with missionary activities, and this led to the formal withdrawal of the Southern churches and the establishment in 1845 of the Southern Baptist Convention. This is still in existence, the split never having been healed.

The Methodists were more highly organized, with bishops serving in different parts of the country, and national meetings in General Conferences. Prior to 1832, there had been a weakening of opposition to slavery within this denomination. Slavery was still regarded as an evil, but members were permitted to hold slaves. Ministers were forbidden to hold them except where the laws forbade emancipation, as they did increasingly in the southern states. With the growth of abolitionism in the North after 1832 the temper changed, but in general the church frowned on controversy and left matters to the states. As a result, some opponents of slavery in the North withdrew from membership. The controversy became acute at the General Conference of 1844, centering on Bishop James O. Andrew of Georgia, who had come into the possession of a few domestic slaves by bequest and marriage and could not emancipate them readily under existing Georgia law. The question that was raised was whether as a slaveholder he could effectively perform his episcopal functions in the free states. A motion was made that he desist from these, so long as the impediment remained, and it was carried by a vote that followed sectional lines. The Bishop himself would have been glad either to desist or to try to rid himself of the impediment, but Southern opinion would permit no action which threw upon the institution of slavery a stigma of immorality and irreligion. As a result, the Southern conferences withdrew and the Methodist Episcopal Church, South, was set up in 1846. Nearly a century was to pass before this split was healed; and in the meantime each of the sectional branches flourished the more after its separation from the other.

In a famous speech in the Senate in 1850, John C. Calhoun referred to these church affairs, pointing out that important ties of spiritual union had already been snapped because of the slavery question. He blamed it on agitation, but the situation was ominous under any interpretation. Men in the North and South could no longer understand each other, even when they used the same language of devotion.

CHAPTER 27

Jacksonian Reform Movements

A MERE CATALOGUE OF SECULAR REFORM MOVEMENTS during the Jackson era would fill many pages. They were all expressive of the expectation that humanity and society could be perfected in the United States in a prodigious hurry. In earlier decades, faith in limitless human and social improvement had been confined to a rather small class of highly educated men, of whom Benjamin Franklin and Thomas Jefferson were the archetypes, most of them rationalists in philosophy and indifferent to orthodox religion. They had accepted the responsibilities of public office in a spirit akin to *noblesse oblige*. Free political institutions were their great achievement. They hoped that within such a framework the mass of men would be encouraged to improve society and themselves, and thus bring human life closer to rational perfection.

Their faith was justified by developments in the decades following 1815. A multitude of reformers emerged, both women and men, who usually held no public office, often lacked advanced education, and were spiritually closer to evangelical religion than to rationalist philosophy. The reformer became as distinctive a type of American as the frontiersman. Democratic evangelism, the faith that a world-shaking mission beckoned America, is evident in the following passage from a manifesto written by Lyman Beecher, member of a notable family of reformers:

> . . . If it had been the design of Heaven to establish a powerful nation in the full enjoyment of civil and religious liberty, where all the energies of man might find full scope and excitement, on purpose to show the world by one great successful experiment of what man is capable, where should such an experiment have been made but in this country! The light of such a Hemisphere shall go up to Heaven, it will throw its beams beyond the

waves; it will shine into the darkness there, and be comprehended—it will awaken desire, and hope, and effort, and produce revolutions and over-turnings until the world is free. Then will the trumpet of jubilee sound, and earth's debased millions will leap from the dust, and shake off their chains, and cry, "Hosanna to the Son of David!"

So religion turned to social reform and democracy acquired religious fervor in a stupendous effort to make America, and then, by virtue of its example, the world into a paradise.

EDUCATION

If the reformers agreed on any one route to the secular paradise, it was that of education. They promptly disagreed on what should take the place of aristocratic models after these should be overthrown, but one thing they all believed: that *more* people should be educated.

This faith had been projected by the Revolutionary generation, but before 1800 little had been actually done beyond providing plans and such tools as Noah Webster's great series of textbooks. The latter enjoyed enormous popularity for almost a century. Both Americanization and secularization were apparent in the first line of his *New England Primer*, which substituted "A was an Apple Pie made by the Cook," for the tra-ditional "In Adam's Fall We Sinned All." In the twenties and thirties, the most urgent problem was to get Webster's books into the hands of every child under competent teachers. Probably a majority of Americans were illiterate. Even in New England, the compulsory common schools had been grossly neglected by the towns. Elsewhere, as a rule, charity schools offered the only chances for poor children.

Horace Mann and Educational Reform

Horace Mann of Massachusetts was the greatest spokesman of educational reform. He agitated for the appointment of a state superin-tendent of education, and occupied the office himself for eleven years after it was established in 1837. He published annual reports which were the Bible of public-school reform in all the states. Declaring that in a republic ignorance was a civic crime for which the government was re-sponsible, he and his followers proceeded to renovate every phase of educational theory and practice. Children began to be treated as human beings rather than as "limbs of Satan"; reason made headway against the rod in obtaining discipline; teachers' explanations superseded pupils' memory work; and practical knowledge of nature, technology, and so-ciety gradually displaced preceptorial dogmas. Mann warned the public in his eloquent eighth report that improved education was not only a means to the improvement of society but the only certain bulwark against the failure of the American experiment:

If we do not prepare children to become good citizens—if we do not develop their capacities, if we do not enrich their minds with knowledge, imbue their hearts with the love of truth and duty, and a reverence for all things sacred and holy, then our republic must go down to destruction, as others have gone before it.

Partly owing to Mann's efforts, the first state normal school was founded at Lexington, Massachusetts, in 1839. Samuel Read Hall had opened a private normal school in Concord, Vermont, sixteen years earlier, and its fame led to imitation in many states. A host of reformers joined the pioneers and fought in the states to improve the elementary schools and to bring every child inside their doors without distinction between rich and poor. Laborers and their unions supported the crusade, although the poor did not always favor it, while some property owners bitterly protested that their taxes should not be squandered on other people's children. To such opponents of reform the most effective answer was that the propertyless who were now entrusted with the vote must be educated or they would fall prey to demagogues who would tear down private property as well as republicanism.

The Eastern states, especially New England, produced the generative ideas of the campaign for educational reform; the Western states, lacking extremes of wealth and poverty, were quickest to adopt them; and the Southern states remained least touched by the movement until after the Civil War. By that time, all the Northern states had systems of free, compulsory, tax-supported elementary schools. In the South, planters paid for private education for their own children and had little interest in the fate of the poorer youngsters; but in the Southern cities municipal public schools became available to most white children. Free Negroes as well as slaves remained mostly illiterate. Education for them was considered dangerous to white supremacy in the South, and they suffered from discrimination in most parts of the North.

Private academies, usually religious in sponsorship, dominated secondary education and concentrated on preparation of boys for college. The idea that the states should support secondary schools was slow in winning adoption. Massachusetts once more led the way with the first high school in Boston in 1821 and a law in 1827 requiring towns with more than 500 families to provide for high schools. A high mortality rate among private academies encouraged the various state governments to take over individual institutions, but education for all qualified persons on the high school level was not provided for the whole country until the twentieth century.

During the Jackson era, a variety of experiments in what is now called progressive education were conducted by radicals, most of whose ideas came from abroad. The fountainhead of educational progressivism was Pestalozzi, a Swiss who applied the principles set forth in Rousseau's

Émile. The key to the Pestalozzian method was "naturalism." According to this view, children were naturally good and naturally talented, but their goodness and talent were frustrated by traditional education, which reflected the corruption of traditional society. If the happiness of the child could be brought about, virtue and creativity would thrive; and when enough graduates of Pestalozzian schools had filled the world, they would recreate society.

Reformers from all Europe and from America flocked to study Pestalozzi's schools in Switzerland. Robert Owen was one of them and, in the course of organizing his socialist colony of New Harmony in Indiana, he invited educational utopians to establish ideal schools there. The journey of Owen in his "boatload of knowledge" down the Ohio River in 1826 has been called the greatest cultural event of the midwestern frontier. Pestalozzism failed at New Harmony along with the whole experiment, but modifications of the Swiss system were widely adopted in the region largely through the influence of Owen's son, Robert Dale Owen.

A more consistent application of the Pestalozzian doctrine occurred in the Boston Temple School of Bronson Alcott. He surrounded pupils with works of art and beautiful furnishings. Problems of discipline were turned over to the student body for social solution, corporal punishment being forbidden. Alcott's Transcendentalist faith that evil is an illusion and his own innocent spirituality made him a model progressive teacher. In his Conversations on the Gospels, conducted by the Socratic method, he assured the children that they would find truth in their own souls and dared even to violate taboos by encouraging discussion of the mystery of the birth of Jesus. Cultivated Boston was willing to sample almost any variety of unorthodoxy except one involving sex. The Temple School closed in 1838 after two years of shocked public controversy.

Very different from Pestalozzian naturalism were the Prussian ideas which became influential in American higher education during the same period. Prussia combined exalted standards of objective scholarship and academic freedom on the university level with almost military discipline and heavy doses of nationalist propaganda on the lower levels. The regimentation of the Prussian student was firmly rejected in America, but graduates of American colleges who were ambitious to become professional scholars frequently studied in the German states, whence they brought back invigorating devotion to pure learning. Harvard was the first to benefit when George Ticknor, Edward Everett, and George Bancroft made the pioneer pilgrimages to Germany shortly after 1815 and returned to their alma mater to teach and write. Pure scholarship and academic freedom had found homes in America by the time that German militaristic nationalism destroyed them in their birthplace.

Selection and adaptation of foreign influences in education produced in America a new amalgam derived from the European extremes represented by Pestalozzism and Prussianism. "Pluralism" is the best description for the net product. Expansion of practical subjects and training in citizenship did not destroy classical learning or inhibit the growth of pure scholarship. Disciplinary methods were humanized without enthroning the child. The spread of free public education did not put an end to existing private and religious institutions or prevent the founding of many new ones. The Jeffersonian ideal of education to train an intellectual aristocracy was not abandoned in the face of the Jacksonian ideal of opening the halls of learning, like the offices of government, to all without distinction. The average quality of American education was definitely inferior to the best European standards; but in America the decisive steps were taken during the Jackson era in an unprecedented experiment to democratize education, and optimists hoped that the sacrifice of quality would be temporary.

State Universities

The highest expression of the Jeffersonian-Jacksonian amalgam was the state university, publicly controlled and financed, and open with little or no charge to all citizens of the state. The first state university to be chartered was that of Georgia, in 1785, though it was not opened until after the beginning of the next century. The University of North Carolina, though chartered a little later, began to give instruction sooner (1795). Other early state institutions of higher learning were the University of Vermont and South Carolina College, out of which the present University of South Carolina developed after the Civil War.

It was left to Jefferson to launch a broader experiment in the University of Virginia, chartered in 1819. The students had to pay fees, but the University was public in its purposes and more than a college. Jefferson himself designed the buildings as models of correct classical taste and left in this "academical village" a superb architectural monument. His purpose was to combine the traditional education of a gentleman with a love for republican institutions and a capacity to serve them. The classical curriculum was enriched by scientific and political studies under an elective system, professors were brought from abroad, and the students were granted an unusual degree of freedom. The results were not encouraging at first, for liberty became license when the high-spirited sons of planters descended on Charlottesville with Negro servants and horses. Eventually a notable honor system was developed, but the University acquired an aristocratic flavor that its Father had not intended. It could not serve as the capstone of a state system, since the state made inadequate provision for supporting schools on lower levels, so the public purposes which Jefferson had in mind and stated so prophetically were carried out more logically in the West than in his own commonwealth. The University of Michigan, authorized by the legislature of the new state in 1837 and anticipated a score of years before that, provided an admirable early example.

The Education of Women

At the beginning of the Jackson era, most parents looked upon advanced education for girls, and many even on literacy, as certain to destroy their innocence and their capacity for domestic careers. The first example of college co-education in the world occurred in Western institutions. In the East, prejudice against feminine literacy had been weakest in New England, but even there many persons believed women incapable of such studies as higher mathematics and physics, while biological and social sciences were considered injurious to feminine refinement.

Emma Hart Willard, who had educated herself in "masculine" subjects by solitary study after marriage, founded Troy Female Seminary in New York in 1821. Other women, believing it a mistake to compete with men for careers, furthered higher education in the domestic arts and sciences. Catherine Beecher founded such colleges in Hartford, Connecticut, and Cincinnati, Ohio. For the brilliant Mary Lyon this smacked too much of the despised "finishing" school for girls. She founded Mount Holyoke Female Seminary (later Mount Holyoke College) at South Hadley, Massachusetts, in 1837, modeling the curriculum on that of nearby Amherst College. The first American institution for women to bear the name college was chartered a year earlier. This was Georgia Female College at Macon (afterwards Wesleyan College). But the West nourished the most advanced experiment in higher education. Oberlin College in Ohio (1833), planned by New England reformers, opened its classes not only to women as well as men, but to Negroes as well as whites.

WOMEN'S RIGHTS

The laws inherited from England and maintained by the states after the Revolution made women minors for life. If unmarried, they were legal wards of their male relatives; if married, they were chattels of their husbands. A single woman or widow was allowed to hold property and earn a living as concessions to her abnormal position, but upon marriage the husband, while assuming responsibility for violations of law committed by his wife, acquired title to her property and earnings, and authority over her person like that of a parent over his child. A Massachusetts judge, in a fit of liberality, limited the instrument with which a husband might beat his wife to a "stick no thicker than my thumb," but other judges countenanced periodic beatings with a horsewhip.

Regardless of the law, the shortage of women in early America placed a premium on good treatment of them. Foreign visitors were astonished by the chivalry towards women. Especially among the well-to-do and in the South, women were placed on a pedestal for admiration as moral paragons whose honor must be defended against the slightest question. They were deemed superior to men in their devotion to religion, charity, and domestic glory, and too refined for the coarse masculine worlds of business, politics, social reality, and sin. Young girls were carefully trained to attract husbands by affecting weakness, ignorance, and coyness, while "strong-minded women" were travestied as freaks.

Strong-Minded Women

The Jackson era nevertheless produced a remarkable crop of strong-minded women who fought their way to improvements in the position of their sex. The spirit of the times favored them as the implications of the American Revolution were now being worked out in all areas of life. They were further stimulated by a number of English women writers who visited the United States and expressed in lectures and books disillusionment with the status of women in the land of the free. Most of all, the working equality of the sexes at the frontier, and in the new factories of the East, pointed the way to legal recognition. Among countertendencies the contemporary victory of romanticism in literature was important. The women's rights movement in America was least successful in the southern states, where the romantic novels of Sir Walter Scott were specially popular. Besides the widening of opportunities for education, the chief gain made by women was in property rights. By 1850, New York, Pennsylvania, Indiana, Wisconsin, Mississippi, and California had recognized women's right to own property after marriage. Gradually codes were altered to make women joint guardians with their husbands of their children and able to sue and be sued. Men were horrified by the demand of reformers that the drunkenness of a husband be allowed as reason for his wife to divorce him, but Indiana gave in and was followed by other states.

Lydia Maria Child in 1832 published an early comprehensive manifesto of the women's movement, entitled *History of the Condition of Women in All Ages*. Margaret Fuller, queen of all strong-minded women, published in 1845 the definitive book, *Woman in the Nineteenth Century*. In this she not only demanded complete economic, social, and political equality but shifted the blame from her own sex to men for such evils as prostitution. Embodying all that advanced women aspired to, she succeeded in making strong-mindedness seem glamorous. She had been educated by her father as a son would have been, she conducted a brilliant school-salon in Boston for aspiring and accomplished philosophers, and she won the friendship of the inner circle of New England Transcendentalists, for a time editing their rarified journal, *The Dial*. She made a happy marriage to the Italian Count Ossoli, and presented for the contemplation of women and men a career more "romantic" than that of any ethereal heroine. Her program of liberation for the sake of individual self-realization placed the women's movement on the highest plane.

Many clergymen who were liberal on other subjects used the Bible to prove that woman, created belatedly by God from Adam's rib, was ordained by Him to be a man's subordinate. On one occasion clergymen who were disrupting a women's rights convention in Akron, Ohio, were silenced by the noted Negro abolitionist, Sojourner Truth, an old woman who had been born a slave in New York. She said:

> . . . I have ploughed, and planted and gathered into barns, and no man could head me. And ain't I a woman? I have borne thirteen children, and seen them most all sold off to slavery, and when I cried out with my mother's grief, none but Jesus heard me! And ain't I a woman? Then that little man in black there, he says women don't have as much rights as men, because Christ wan't a woman. Where did your Christ come from? From God and a woman. Man had nothing to do with him!

Organizers and Reformers

While a Margaret Fuller and a Sojourner Truth from their diverse backgrounds provided arguments, other leaders proceeded in the thirties and forties to organize thousands of women and a fair sprinkling of men into strong pressure groups. The outstanding organizers were Elizabeth Cady Stanton, Susan B. Anthony, and Lucretia Mott. By the mid-forties, local women's rights societies were active, especially in the Northeast and the West. Most of the New England intellectuals, led by Emerson and William Ellery Channing, supported the women's movement, and some editors, notably Horace Greeley, aided its campaign.

In 1848, Mrs. Stanton and Mrs. Mott called a national convention at Seneca Falls, New York. The delegates adopted a Declaration of Women's Independence modeled with devastating logic on the great document of 1776: "We hold these truths to be self-evident: that all men and women are created equal. . . ." For King George as tyrant, the women substituted "*Man*." Besides demanding "the institution of a new government" by means of the repeal of all discriminatory laws, and the end of masculine monopoly of trades, professions, and business, the Convention asserted that it was the duty of the women of the country "to secure to themselves their sacred right to the elective franchise." This demand for the vote aroused serious opposition in the Convention and caused some delegates to repudiate the Declaration as too radical. Outside, it stirred up a gale of ridicule, but still the radicals persisted. National conventions were held annually except during the Civil War, when the women suspended their own demands in favor of abolition of slavery, and the historical descent of the Woman Suffrage Amendment to the Constitution (1919) from the Seneca Falls Convention is direct.

The long delay is partly explained by the special effectiveness of ridicule in this area of reform. It was easily directed against Amelia Bloomer, who found the feminine dress of the period—all whaleboned, flounced, and upholstered—a hindrance to her work as postmistress in a New York village. She invented a costume featuring a loose-fitting coat over "Turkish" trousers neatly gathered into shoe tops. The Bloomer costume and short-cut hair were affected by leading feminists until they surrendered to imputation of harem-like morals and such doggerel as this:

> Gibbey, gibbey gab,
> The women had a confab
> And demanded the rights
> To wear the tights
> Gibbey, gibbey gab.

As Miss Anthony remarked, it was impossible to win a man's attention to her argument when he was preoccupied with gazing at her clothes.

Another much-ridiculed movement was launched by Lucy Stone. A graduate of Oberlin and lecturer on abolitionism and women's rights, she and her husband signed a "Protest" immediately after their marriage. This document renounced all the laws giving the husband "injurious and unnatural superiority, investing him with legal powers which no honorable man would exercise, and which no man should possess." To symbolize her legal equality with her husband, the bride kept her maiden name, and she founded the Lucy Stoners' League to encourage other brides to follow her example. Conventional minds could not imagine a successful marriage on this basis, but Mrs. Stone combined a notable career as a reformer with a happy marriage and children.

Professional Women

It was fairly easy for women to break into the teaching profession, and by 1860 women outnumbered men in the elementary schools. The reformers made equal pay with men an important item on their agenda. School boards nevertheless continued to take advantage of the greater readiness of young women and older single women without family obligations to accept jobs at low salary. The women who invaded medicine, the law, and the pulpit had to be endowed with the pioneer's spirit and more talent than the average male competitor. One of the earliest woman graduates of an American medical college, Dr. Elizabeth Blackwell, was allowed to enter Geneva College in New York on the vote of the male students who took it as a joke. She graduated at the head of her class, founded the New York Infirmary for Women and Children in 1857 and staffed it entirely with women, headed a contingent of field nurses during the Civil War, and afterwards was the first woman to be admitted to medical practice in England. The first woman to preside in a pulpit as an ordained clergywoman was Antoinette Brown, who had found even the radical leaders of Oberlin College hard to convince that theology should not be a masculine monopoly.

By a curious paradox, the most successful women authors glorified a sentimentalized version of the romantic heroine who achieved her highest destiny in suffering self-sacrifice for her menfolk and her children. By the fifties the "Starry Sisterhood" of authors dominated the market for popular magazine verse and fiction. Mrs. Lydia Huntley Sigourney, the "Sweet Singer of Hartford," reigned supreme among them. One of them was Sara Willis Parton, who wrote as "Fanny Fern." She was the sister of Nathaniel P. Willis, editor of the profeminist *Home Journal,* and married as her third husband the eminent biographer James Parton. Her writings achieved enormous popularity, but although herself a person of notably independent spirit, she fed her readers models of retiring womanhood.

Sara Josepha Hale, editor of *Godey's Lady's Book,* combined appeals to traditional femininity—especially interest in the latest fashions—with indirect propaganda for women's rights, and was rewarded with the largest subscription list of any magazine of the period. Her brother, while studying at Dartmouth, had instructed her in every lesson as he learned it. For nearly fifty years she subtly conveyed to the readers of *Godey's* that strong-mindedness in women was fashionable, and that the right of women to equality with men was taken for granted by intelligent people. Probably in the long run she was more effective than the unconventional come-outers in converting women themselves to the cause.

LABOR REFORM AND UTOPIAN SOCIALISM

The formation of an industrial working class made Jacksonian America the laboratory of early attempts to solve the problem of the social position of labor in an industrial society. Reformist proposals were nowhere more bewildering in variety, ranging from mild economic unionism to programs for voluntary or forced social revolution. The labor problem is usually treated as a purely economic one involving material standards of living, but there is much reason for believing that the question of social status was equally or more important to the American workman.

Formerly the small scale of business enterprise had made possible personal relations between employers and employees, and there was little caste feeling on either side. No sooner had these relations begun to break down in the face of large-scale factory production, than self-appointed leaders of the working class began to advocate panaceas. The partial successes of labor groups in winning political influence have been noted in connection with the Jackson administration. The leaders were not satisfied, however, with slow gains. They championed various anti-capitalist schemes which they firmly believed would bring in the millenium. Meetings evoked endless debates among doctrinaires, including the British crusaders, Robert Dale Owen and Frances Wright. Working-men lost interest in the labor parties and they all died of factionalism by 1834.

Observing this failure, some leaders of the trade unions determined to avoid politics and panaceas and concentrate on strengthening the economic power of labor. They conducted strikes for the ten-hour day with some success. A convention of delegates of city centrals organized in 1834 the first national labor body, the National Trades Union with Ely Moore at its head. This body memorialized Congress and obtained the federal government's concession of a ten-hour day for labor, first in the Philadelphia Navy Yard in 1836, and in 1840 on all federal works.

Strikes continued to be held illegal by the courts until, in 1842, Chief Justice Lemuel Shaw of Massachusetts ruled in Commonwealth vs. Hunt that unions and strikes were not conspiracies but legitimate means to improvement of laboring conditions. This rule was gradually accepted in other states. State governments were also led to enact reforms desired by labor. The leaders of a major party, usually the Democrats, adopted one or another of labor's demands as a means of appealing for votes. The majority of American laborers were not organized in unions, much less in a labor party.

Utopian Communities

In the Jackson period impatient reformers experimented with Socialist alternatives to the capitalist system. Formerly utopian communities in America had been exclusively religious in inspiration. In the 1820's, secular utopianism based on radical social and economic philosophies came to the fore. The greatest utopian Socialist was Robert Owen, owner of textile mills in New Lanark, Scotland, who built for his workers a model com-munity and became convinced that he had found the way to release mankind from the chains of poverty and all other evils. Failing to con-vert British capitalists to his views, he determined to establish in hos-pitable America a community which should provide a model for universal imitation. Membership would be voluntary and existing governments and capitalism would not be overthrown but, so to speak, superseded as the millions would organize new communities and make old institutions empty shells. In its voluntarism and avoidance of direct action against existing institutions, utopian socialism significantly differed from the socialism of Karl Marx.

Owen bought the estate of a German Rappite, religious-communist colony at New Harmony, Indiana, in 1825, and advertised for members. The experiment got under way in an atmosphere of public good will. Daniel Webster said a good word for it. A mixture of farmers, laborers, and middle-class reformers flocked to New Harmony. But the contradiction soon appeared which dogs all socialist communities, voluntary or not. Economic success required centralized control, and the directors sacrificed for the sake of unity the democracy which they claimed would be perfected by economic co-operation. Owen found it distasteful to face the factionalism of his members and turned over management to his son, Robert Dale Owen. Workers left in disgust at the ineffectuality of the reformers and the petty tyranny of the leaders. After two years the Owens abandoned the colony and the colonists abandoned co-operation.

Frances Wright, a wealthy protegé of Lafayette, established in 1825 at Nashoba, Tennessee, a variation of Owenism designed to solve the problem of Negro slavery. Slaves were purchased and set to work on a great plantation to earn their purchase price, after which they were to be freed and the money used to buy another group. But the slaves found that petty tyranny at Nashoba was as bad as on an ordinary plantation, and that the management was worse. Fanny Wright gave up and made herself a leading trumpeter of radicalism to the American people. For a woman to mount the lecture platform, edit newspapers, and found schools was remarkable enough, but Miss Wright, short-haired, statuesquely beautiful and possessed of genuine talents, taught free thought in religion, free love, birth control, and freedom of children from parental control.

Others adopted a new variety of socialism originated by the Frenchman, Charles Fourier. He recommended that people should band together in "phalanxes" to supersede family life, build model communities rather resembling army barracks, institute a complicated system of government for themselves, and share the products of their labor. He worked out his plan in the utmost detail. It was widely propagated in the United States by Albert Brisbane in a book, *Social Destiny of Man* (1840). Some forty "phalancteries" were founded in the northern states. The most famous convert was Horace Greeley, who for a time promoted Fourierism in his *New York Tribune* along with all manner of other reformist ideas. He liked to spend his Saturday afternoons sampling socialism by pitching hay for a Fourierist community near Red Bank, New Jersey.

The most famous utopian community was Brook Farm near Boston. It was founded in 1841 by George Ripley, a Unitarian minister, and numbered Nathaniel Hawthorne, Charles A. Dana, and George William Curtis among its members. Margaret Fuller was a tempestuous visitor. It began in an arcadian atmosphere of devotion to the arts and conversation, with brief sessions of manual farm labor according to personal tastes to provide necessities. For several years the Brook Farmers represented the high noon of New England social idealism, although Emerson and Thoreau remained skeptical. Then members drifted away and an attempt to organize more strictly as a Fourierist community was cut short when a fire burned the phalanctery. Hawthorne gently satirized the experiment in a novel, *The Blithedale Romance*. Along with Brook Farm, all the Fourier communities died out by 1860. Icarian communities in Texas and Illinois on the plan set forth in Etienne Cabet's *Voyage en Icarie* fared no better. Only socialist communities with a religious basis, like the Shakers and the Mormons, not to mention Roman Catholic and Episcopalian monastic groups, enjoyed lengthy histories of success. The conclusion was inescapable that secular Americans preferred an economy salted with individualism and the stimulating mixture of rewards and risks provided by the competitive system.

Lesser forms of noncapitalist economic organization were tried, particularly by labor groups during depressions. Josiah Warren developed out of his anarchistic view of the evils of government and private ownership a program of economic co-operatives whereby labor should abolish both. Labor unions, frustrated in attempts to make gains during the Depression of 1837, turned to Warren's scheme for consumers' and producers' co-operatives. The New England Protective Union was established in 1845 to centralize purchases for retail co-operatives. Most of the co-operatives foundered for lack of capital and managerial talent; and with the revival of prosperity laborers lost interest. The Scandinavian immigrants of the Northwest turned out to be the first successful conductors of co-operatives.

The Homestead Movement

The reformist cause that won the most ardent support of American laborers during the Jackson era was the homestead movement. George H. Evans was the chief prophet of free land as the solution of laboring men's problems. An Englishman who came to the United States during the twenties, he edited a labor newspaper and emerged from the failure of the Workingmen's Party with the conviction that western land provided the means for workers to escape from the evils of industrialism. "Our refuge is upon the soil, in all its freshness and fertility—our heritage is on the Public Domain, in all its boundless wealth and infinite variety." Man, Evans argued, has a natural and unalienable right to land just as he has a right to air, water, and sunlight. The public lands should be given in family plots to the landless, who were mostly laborers, and they should be forbidden to sell or mortgage their farms. This would transform the propertyless of the next thousand years into prosperous, independent farmers.

This program elaborated Jefferson's vision of how best to build happiness in a free republic, and its popularity marked a revulsion against the first raw impact of the Industrial Revolution. Evans alone among the radical Jacksonian intellectuals found wide support among workers. Loosely organized by him as Agrarians, they formed a disruptive left wing of both major political parties and, from 1848 to 1856, the separate Free Soil Party which held the balance of power in many eastern cities.

The first Homestead Bill was introduced in Congress in 1846 by Andrew Johnson, a tailor of Tennessee who would suceed Abraham Lincoln as President, and annually thereafter the proposal was pushed in Congress. Southern opposition to the homestead movement led Northern labor to turn to abolitionism. The idea of Evans was expanded into the final slogan of the Free Soil Party: "Free Soil, Free Land, Free Labor, Free Men." Only after the Homestead Act was passed by the Republican Party of Lincoln did laborers learn that for a laborer to turn farmer more was required than free land. He needed capital for transportation, farm implements, and livestock, besides food for his family and seed for a year or more until he could bring in a good crop. Furthermore, once urbanized, people rarely wished to revert to farm life. Few natives or immigrants who took jobs in the new factories ever turned pioneers. The power of the homestead idea over the imagination of workingmen during the decades before the Civil War nevertheless helped to hold the West for free farmers against the threat of slave labor, and the homestead movement was an effective expression of labor's reformist idealism.

TEMPERANCE, HUMANITARIANISM, WORLD PEACE

Drinking in early America was probably no more common than in the countries from which Americans had migrated, with the exception that at the frontier hard liquor was a staple of diet compensating for deficiencies of food and of heat and clothing in winter. Foreign authors of travel books stressed American drunkenness as one more evidence that emigration meant degeneration. For sheer variety American intoxicants were more impressive than those of any European nation, precisely because each immigrant group added its favorite beverages to the resources of the American grog shop, and Americans developed their own varieties of whiskey. Pennsylvania rye figured in the Whiskey Rebellion of Washington's time, and the most famous corn whiskey was "bourbon" —named for a county in Kentucky. Rum never regained the position it held in colonial times, but imported wines continued in favor, while English ales gave way to German lager beer, apple cider, and domestic wines. Cheapness, however, made whiskey the almost universal drink. Some kind of alcoholic beverage was kept in supply by most families; shops and taverns in the cities and inns in the country served alcoholic drinks with or without meals; and they were an obligatory sign of domestic hospitality and of good fellowship on such occasions as ordinations, barn-raisings, and election campaigns.

American drinking increased in the early nineteenth century. The overt attack on it began in New England among preachers and reformers; it quickly extended to western areas to which New England migration was heavy, and was supported by many in the South. At first drunkenness rather than drinking was condemned. Hundreds of local temperance societies sent delegates to Philadelphia for a national convention in 1833. Out of this grew the federated American Temperance Union. Temperance publications soon outnumbered those devoted to any other reform. This cause first brought women to the lecture platform because their sufferings at the hands of drunken husbands were thought to give them a peculiar right to be heard. Children were enlisted as in the medieval crusades, the "Cold Water Army" of children staging great processions.

One group of reformers insisted on total abstinence, while conservatives held out for a campaign against distilled liquors alone, but the "teetotalers" won control of the movement by 1840. During the next decade the most sensational agitation was conducted by the Washingtonians, who were reformed drunkards. Their lurid autobiographies sometimes made drink and vice more fascinating than repulsive, but it was found that harrowing published narratives, pictures, and public interviews won larger audiences than theoretical arguments. Such eminent authors as Oliver Wendell Holmes and John Greenleaf Whittier contributed to the propaganda, but the most popular writings were heartwringing stories by Lydia Sigourney and *Ten Nights in a Bar-Room* (1854) by Timothy Shay Arthur.

Voluntary abstinence won many converts but barrooms continued to flourish, and the majority of thirsts were not slaked by cold water, fruit and root juices, or even the synthetic fizz of carbonated beverages which were invented at this time. Those who would not abstain voluntarily were clearly enslaved by the "Demon" and must be liberated by force. Neal Dow of Maine was the greatest spokesman of the early prohibition movement. In 1851, his state passed a prohibition law. Other New England states followed suit, and the western centers of New England influence became in time the chief bases of the national prohibition movement. Thus the old Puritan passion for publicly enforced righteousness found new expression.

If the wisdom of moving beyond temperance to teetotalism and beyond that to prohibition by law now seems dubious, the agitation of the Jacksonian era must be credited with a beneficial change in American attitudes towards intoxication. Formerly drunkenness had been looked upon as laughable; now it was looked upon as ill-mannered and shameful. Social disapproval turned out to be a powerful corrective. Drinking by women and children virtually ceased and in this respect Americans were well in advance of Europeans. At the same time, improved diet and heating facilities in the home reduced the need for liquor; and there was a suspicious increase in the alcohol content and popularity of "patent medicines."

Relieving the Unfortunate

Attitudes toward the insane and other unfortunates also radically changed. Formerly persons afflicted by mental illness were either thrown into prisons indiscriminately with normal persons or segregated in asylums where wardens treated them barbarously or, what was most often the case, they were left as hopeless burdens on their families. Dorothea L. Dix made herself the special champion of the insane. Her Quaker training made her sensitive to the sufferings of every class of unfortunates, and her work in the prison of Charlestown, Massachusetts, filled her with pity and indignation. She forced the public and legislators to listen to her message, and the awakening of the humanitarian conscience favored her cause. Private and public bodies reorganized existing asylums and established new ones on better principles. Such an institution as "The Retreat" in Brattleboro, Vermont, signified the new attitude in its name, and it was one of the first in the world to be founded on the principle that insanity is a disease which may be alleviated if not cured by kindness and therapy.

Ordinary prisoners and paupers also commanded the attention of Dorothea Dix and many other reformers. Such elementary improvements were won as separation of men and women prisoners, privacy in cells, abolition of the worst forms of physical punishment, and the use of constructive work as a means of rehabilitation rather than hard labor as punishment. The greatest achievement in public opinion was the popularization of the principle that a prison should be operated not merely to punish criminals but to reform them. Experiments were carried out at model prisons like that of New York at Auburn, which was studied by reformers of other states and of Europe.

Pauperism had formerly been negligible in the United States, but it grew with urbanization and, as indentured servitude fell into disuse, with the increase of penniless immigrants who became public charges. The custom of letting-out paupers to a contractor who could make a profit by neglecting his charges yielded slowly to public demands for humane treatment.

Samuel Gridley Howe, a wealthy Boston doctor, made the problems of the blind his special province. He devised means of communication for the deaf, dumb, and blind Laura Bridgman, and in 1832 founded the great Perkins Institution for the Blind. There were other expressions of the new sensitivity to suffering, but so long as most Americans lived on farms, the aged and unfortunate were mostly cared for by their families. The whole array of modern problems associated with social welfare came only dimly into view during this period.

Crusaders for Peace

Humanitarianism, like most new faiths, was subject to fanaticism. Few today would call fanatical the movements that got under way at this time to abolish capital punishment, to prevent dueling and eye-gouging matches, to prohibit cruelty to animals, cock-fighting, and animal-baiting. But hypersensitive spirits moved onwards from vegetarianism based on pity for animals to agitation against killing insects and chopping down trees because they, too, had lives and destinies to fulfill. The sentimentality that marred so much of the literature of this period had its counter part in reformist thought. Enormous energies were poured into experiments to improve man and society, and numerous visionaries roamed the land castigating old habits and calling upon the people to march forthwith into the new Jerusalem. Surprisingly few of their programs proved to be dangerous or merely absurd, and so many were usable that the history of social reform in subsequent decades amounts to little more than the effectuation of principles first pronounced in Jacksonian times.

The movement to abolish slavery, whose importance merits treatment in separate chapters, combined admirable and fanatical tendencies in a mixture more portentous for the immediate fate of the nation than any other. The movement for world peace which got under way at the same time was wholly free of fanaticism but equally portentous for the long future of the nation. Formerly action against war had been limited to individual pacifism on religious grounds among such groups as the Quakers, to the schemes of philosophers, and to the diplomacy of statesmen who did not enlist the support of the people themselves. The peace movement that originated in the United States shortly after the War of 1812 was new in that it enlisted the ideas and methods of democracy. The logic was simple and compelling: the ravages of war bear hardest on the mass of plain people, therefore a society organized by and for them must abolish war; and democratic institutions provide the technique for the just and peaceful settlement of disputes within a nation, therefore similar international institutions will serve the same function among the nations. An implied premise was that all nations must be democracies. Failing this, the democratic program for world peace has foundered time and again.

When nearly a quarter-century of world war ended in 1815, men everywhere longed to avoid a recurrence. David Low Dodge was one of many religious pacifists who saw that private protest was not enough. In August 1815, he organized the first peace society on lines suggested by Noah Worcester of New England in his book of December 1814, entitled, *The Solemn Review of the Custom of War, Showing That War*

Is the Effect of Popular Delusion, and Proposing a Remedy. The book quickly ran through five editions as people eagerly read this indictment of the wars of history and proposal for a confederation of nations and a high court of international justice. The significance of Worcester's proposal is that he saw the American compromise between state and national sovereignties as a model for relations between national governments and a new international government. The latter should enforce peace and co-operation among the nations as the American federal government did among the states; and similarly he proposed to imitate in an international government the American division of legislative, judicial, and executive powers as a safeguard against tyranny. This work continued to be influential for a century until the League of Nations and the United Nations attempted to realize his dream.

William Ellery Channing in 1815 organized the Massachusetts Peace Society. Under Worcester's editorship, this group published a periodical, the *Friend of Peace*, which urged the formation of peace societies everywhere. The technique of popular propaganda and pressure groups to secure governmental action for peace was a new thing in the world and expressed the democratic faith of the new generation.

William Ladd, a wealthy graduate of Harvard, was inspired by Worcester's writings to dedicate his life and fortune to the peace crusade. In 1828, he organized in the home of David Low Dodge the American Peace Society as a national federation of the local groups. Ladd avoided doctrinal quarrels between those who would condemn all wars and those who would make exceptions in favor of defensive wars. He invited all friends of peace to work to eliminate offensive wars first. The propaganda of the Society spread far and wide, and during the thirties peace became the passion of numerous Americans.

The Learned Blacksmith

Extremists captured control of the American Peace Society in 1837. William Lloyd Garrison and other abolitionists came out for absolute condemnation of all war; they preached moral pacifism and political anarchism. During the next years the peace crusade was saved from impotence by Elihu Burritt, Ladd's successor, and the most attractive reformer of the period. Combining a Christ-like purity of purpose with a genius for practical affairs, "The Learned Blacksmith" was a counterpart among private leaders of Abraham Lincoln among statesmen. Born to poverty in Connecticut, he apprenticed himself to the forge and educated himself in languages and history by propping his books alongside his anvil. Burritt remained all his life a workman, teaching laborers the dignity of their calling while showing how it could be combined with mental culture and civic pursuits.

His extraordinary knowledge of foreign languages and cultures led him to gain a lofty conception of the brotherhood and interdependence of all peoples. He schooled himself in practical propaganda during the Anglo-American crisis over Oregon. Burritt organized "people's diplomacy," a concert of agitation against war by crusaders in the United States and England. Leaflets called "Olive Leaves" were exchanged between the two peoples, English and American cities exchanged "Friendly Addresses," business and labor groups on both sides joined in expressions of common desire to avoid war, and mass meetings sent resolutions to the two governments demanding a peaceful settlement. Burritt edited the *Advocate of Peace and Universal Brotherhood,* acted as middleman in the international exchanges, and personally distributed propagandist literature on railroads, canals, and street corners.

It would be too much to say that the peaceful compromise of the Oregon dispute in 1846 was caused by Burritt's "people's diplomacy," but this had some effect, and it was a significant expression of the connection between democracy and peace. Burritt thereafter worked to strengthen popular international ties. He was received with enthusiasm in England and organized there the League of Universal Brotherhood. The revolutions of 1848 in their early stages manifested radical attitudes against war. Burritt quickly moved to capitalize the favorable situation by calling international peace conferences which he hoped would become instruments for the peaceful settlement of international disputes. Four international conferences of the League of Universal Brotherhood were held from 1848 to 1852 with such personages as Victor Hugo and John Bright as speakers. An American blacksmith leading the international movement which promised so much for humanity is symbolical of Jacksonian democracy.

The peace crusade temporarily failed in the general failure of the revolutions of 1848. Reaction set in when monarchs and upper classes recovered power by whipping up hatred of foreigners. Liberal nationalism went down to defeat in a new cycle of wars. The problem of slavery produced a comparable defeat in the United States. The crusaders were torn between their hatred of war and their hatred of slavery. Most of them, including Burritt, supported the Union when the war came. Theodore Parker wrote to a friend: "I think we should agree about war. I hate it, deplore it, but yet see its necessity. All the great charters of humanity have been writ in blood, and must continue to be for some centuries."

So the Civil War swallowed up another of the great Jacksonian reform movements. It would be a long day before Americans would recover the visions of Dodge, Worcester, Ladd, and Burritt and again go to work to build peace on earth.

CHAPTER 28

Cultural Achievements in a Democratic Era, 1820-1850

NO SOONER HAD EUROPEAN CONSERVATIVES GIVEN UP predicting the imminent collapse of the American Republic than they turned to equally confident predictions that it would make no notable contributions to human culture. The keynote was struck at the opening of the period by an Englishman, the Reverend Sidney Smith, in his contemptuous query of 1820: "In the four quarters of the globe, who reads an American book? or goes to an American play? or looks at an American picture or statue?" Americans eagerly accepted this challenge. Economic independence was rapidly following upon political independence. Now they set out on a still more difficult enterprise: to establish their cultural independence.

RELIGIOUS FERMENT

Until after the Civil War, religion continued to provide the dominant spiritual, intellectual, and emotional experience of most Americans. The eighteenth-century drift away from Christianity ceased. Their individualism and democracy did not lead the people away from religion; rather, the mass of them turned with intensified fervor to evangelicalism, which asserted that salvation was available for all. While the cool Unitarian of Boston shrank from the camp-meeting spirit, he agreed with the evangelicals that man and his life on earth are good, or at least may become so. The most extreme form of the old idea, the Calvinist doctrine of total depravity, gave way to extreme forms of faith in progress, human and social perfectibility, and the overwhelming supremacy of goodness. The spark of divinity in man to which every great creed has borne witness was proclaimed to be a triumphant flame.

Unitarianism and Universalism

It has been said that after the upper-class Federalists of New England had rejected the democracy of Jefferson and the French Revolution as a political faith, they accepted it as a religious faith. Unitarianism asserted that God is all love and no wrath, that man is all virtue and no sin, and that human reason is sufficient to distinguish truth from error. If revelation, miracles, and atonement were not rejected by the Unitarians, they were politely ignored. William Ellery Channing, Boston's great prophet of the new dispensation, preached that religion is no more or less than "the adoration of goodness." Whole congregations of the Episcopalian, Congregational, and Presbyterian churches went over to Unitarianism until by 1830 most of the wealthy and educated classes of New England had abandoned the old orthodoxy.

Still the moral earnestness of Puritanism persisted among the New England élite as their famous conscience continued to require untiring good works. The typical Boston capitalist was a Unitarian and a philanthropist; the typical Boston intellectual was a Unitarian and a reformer. Chilly respectability and rationality made Unitarianism unattractive to most people, but the philanthropists and reformers of Boston and its environs were accepted East and West as models of civic responsibility, personal integrity, and lofty vision. Furthermore, it was this sector of American society that produced the first great literary and cultural flowering in the Republic. The Boston influence was rejected only in the South, where it was considered synonymous with self-righteous hypocrisy.

Similar to Unitarianism in theology was Universalism, whose central dogmas were literal denial of hell and assurance of universal salvation. This genial faith spread to some extent among the farmers of New England and the West but never displaced the evangelical faiths of the majority.

Transcendentalism

The most brilliant and ardent young intellectuals of New England found Unitarianism cold to their taste. In rejecting instinct, emotion, and mysticism, Unitarianism seemed better suited to businessmen than to poets. Without reviving orthodoxy or even rejecting the basic doctrines of Unitarianism, a group of enthusiasts revolted against its prosaic attitudes and attempted to create a faith which should satisfy man's imaginative as well as his rational and ethical faculties. Led by Ralph Waldo Emerson, they asserted the transcendent reality of the supernatural and its existence in the natural. They were so far from wishing to create an organized religion that their only "church" was the short-lived Transcendental Club which met occasionally for conversational communion. The membership never numbered more than a dozen, but among those present at one or another symposium were Emerson, William Ellery Channing and his nephew William Henry Channing, Bronson Alcott, Theodore Parker, Henry David Thoreau, Nathaniel Hawthorne, Margaret Fuller, James Freeman Clarke, and George Bancroft. By their writings the influence of the Transcendentalists became nationally and internationally important. Their magazine, the *Dial*, lasted only from 1840 to 1844. Organization was not the forte of these individualists.

Transcendentalism drew upon Plato's ancient Greek and Kant's modern German philosophic idealism, the Oriental mysticism of the *Baghavad Gita*, Christian medieval mysticism, the French revolutionary thought of Rousseau, and the contemporary English literary romanticism of Wordsworth and Carlyle. The waters of all these streams were, however, mixed into a peculiarly American draught. Mystical experience had formerly been regarded as reserved for the spiritual élite, but the Transcendentalists declared that Everyman is endowed with spiritual power, and is in fact divine. By trusting his instinct he can know truth, and by acting on inspiration he can express truth, as surely as any saint. Formerly saints had been expected to purify themselves of evil and worldly dross by means of spiritual exercises; the Transcendentalists declared that evil is an illusion, that Everyman can purify himself and the world of dross by listening to and acting upon his divine inner voice. Thus these extraordinary descendants of the Puritans provided the sanction of Old-World philosophy and mysticism for the American dream of democracy.

Emerson defined the Transcendentalist as follows:

> He believes in miracles, in the perpetual openness of the human mind to the new influx of light and power; he believes in inspiration and ecstasy. He wishes that the spiritual principle should be suffered to demonstrate itself to the end, in all possible applications to the state of man.

Emerson himself did not undertake direct action for social reform, believing his mission to be that of the scholar and teacher. In his essay, "Self-Reliance," and dozens of other popular sermons which he delivered from the lecture platforms of the North, he taught the new gospel that individualism and holiness, democracy and spiritual greatness, social reform and the divine plan, were all identical. The public became deeply reverent of the Concord philosopher as its greatest teacher. If his conception of the "Over-Soul" was too Oriental for prosaic American minds, if his charge of self-reliance was distorted by some into a sanction for materialistic ruthlessness, and if his refusal to admit the reality of evil encouraged the tendency of Americans to shallow optimism, nevertheless Emerson's great influence on his countrymen was on the whole a fruitful one. His was the noblest formulation of the meaning and promise of the American experiment. Its fundamental paradox, which is so baffling to foreign observers, the juxtaposition of material preoccupations and idealism, he resolved in a synthesis of practical spirituality.

Evangelicalism

Although the New England intellectuals and the preachers of evangelical Protestantism seem at first glance to have had nothing in common, both expressed the crusading optimism of the times. Following the Great Awakening of the eighteenth century, revivalism was endemic until it became epidemic in the Great Revival of the first decade of the new century and periodically thereafter. The Baptists and the Methodists became the largest organized religions in America, expanding with the frontier. The Baptists were more given to theological controversy, insisting on adult baptism by total immersion, while the Methodists stressed the "creedless religion of the heart." Both held that any individual might find salvation by renouncing sin and submitting to Jesus. Violently emotional preaching induced the crisis of conversion, and only that kind of preaching held much meaning for frontiersmen.

The Congregational and Presbyterian churches were leaders in the effort to bring higher education and general culture to the West, but their emphasis on an educated clergy put them at a disadvantage in new districts. The Westerner was inured to a rough, lonely life of physical dangers and privations, he was highly susceptible to oratory and crowd emotions, and he responded violently to preaching of hell-fire and salvation by men like himself. Pious people who had been left behind in the East were aroused by accounts of the godless state of the West and poured out money for missionary work. Many preachers were sent from New England to follow migrants into western New York. Religious excitement became almost universal there, producing an amazing crop of new prophets, revelations, and sects and causing the district to merit the name of "The Burnt-Over Region."

The camp meeting became the most striking feature of Western religion. In a forest clearing, for days and nights without a stop, preachers spelled each other crying defiance at Satan and pleading with sinners to yield to Jesus. Whole families from miles around joined in frenzied longing for the lightning of conversion to strike them. The most popular preachers presided over scenes of mass hysteria, of weeping, screaming, writhing on the ground, and—highest sign of grace—pentecostal "speaking in tongues." Certain preachers became famous for their ability to elicit "the jerks," the "barking exercise," and "holy laughter." These were regarded as the final throes of Satan evicted from the sinner's soul.

Revivalism encouraged the subdivision of older sects and the sprouting of many new ones. Factions split away from conservative churches in favor of livelier experience. The episcopal organization of the Methodists and their reluctance to quarrel over fine points of theology preserved them from schisms better than the Baptists, whose love of theology and extreme individualism produced the bewildering variety of Hard-Shell Baptists, Soft-Shell Baptists, Particular Baptists, General Baptists, United Baptists, Primitive Baptists, Free-Will Baptists, Disciples of Christ, and others. America became the home of more different Christian sects than any other country in the world.

Millenialism and Spiritualism

Some of them were quite original, almost meriting the name of American religions. Vermont was a breeding ground of prophets and cults, but most of them moved west. The Green Mountains seemed to encourage more eccentricity than ordinary Vermonters would tolerate. William Miller, a farmer of Poultney, Vermont, calculated on the basis of hints in prophetic books of the Bible that the Second Coming of Christ would occur in 1843. His followers spread the message through the frontier country of northern New England and western New York; they even attracted great crowds in cities and built the Millenial Tabernacle in Boston. The burden of Millerite preaching was that only believers would ascend to heaven on the last day of time. When 1843 passed, the leaders confessed a slight miscalculation and named October 22, 1844, as the actual date. Excitement led in some cases to insanity and suicide. Adventists gave away all their property except white ascension robes and gathered on hilltops on the evening of October 21. Disbelievers jeered and riots occurred in several cities. The dawn of October 23 ended Millerism, but a few Adventists, while denying that the exact date could be predicted, continued to preach that the Second Coming was very near. They settled down as the Seventh Day Adventist Church.

For those who wished to penetrate the spiritual world beyond time, Spiritualism offered a technique that enthralled many Americans in the years following the Millerite disappointment. Interest in the mystical teachings of Emmanuel Swedenborg culminated in the establishment of many small churches and the conversion of educated persons as notable as the elder Henry James. More palpable communion with the other world was provided by mediums. Most famous of these were the Fox sisters, Maggie and Katie, daughters of an upstate New York farmer, who convinced many that they could communicate with sundry spirits by means of table rappings. Horace Greeley's love of new ideas overcame his skepticism; he took the Fox sisters into his home and only objected that it was boring to wait in a dark room for hours on the chance that someone's dead grandfather would make "dull music." The type of message that came from the other world ("Tell Tabitha that her dear dead Aunt Sue misses her gooseberry jell") did not disillusion believers with the glories of spiritual revelation. Nor did the admission by the Fox sisters, following a family spat, that the rappings had been produced by their double-jointed toes, make many apostates. For decades Spiritualist mediums could be found in almost every town. On a somewhat lower plane of pretension, science and pseudo-science gave birth to cults of mesmerism or hypnotism, animal magnetism, and phrenology. These raveled edges of the fabric of Jacksonian democracy suggested that optimism could conquer reason.

The Mormons

Most impressive of the new faiths was that of the Mormon Church of Latter-Day Saints. Its founder, Joseph Smith, was a homespun prophet, the movement was saturated with millenialism, and it supported the most exotic social institution imaginable—polygamy. Born in Vermont in 1808, Smith at an early age moved to Palmyra, New York, in the heart of the Burnt-Over Region. His father was indigent and his mother imbued her children with dreams of holy visions and miracles. Young Joseph became engrossed with the possibility of finding buried treasure by means of the diviner's traditional forked switch. He found a "magic peek stone" which he believed bestowed special powers on its owner. He attended revival meetings but one day Jesus and God the Father appeared to him and denounced all existing religions as false. His magic stone led him to the hiding place of "golden plates" on which were written in a strange language—translatable with the aid of two stones used as spectacles, Urim and Thummin—a tale which Smith published in 1830 as a new revelation, *The Book of Mormon*. Containing a mixture of Indian legends, religious dogma, and current economic, social, and political ideas in "biblical" language, it won converts very slowly. Joseph organized a few persons into a new church but his neighbors could not believe he was divinely chosen.

The Smith family moved to the Western Reserve in Ohio, and there the receptivity of Westerners and skilled work by several practical men, including Brigham Young, brought success. Joseph Smith was pictured as the prophet of a revived apostolic group. He ended disputes among his lieutenants by producing new revelations, decreed that converts must turn over their goods to him in favor of communism, promised that the imminent millenium would bring a division of the world's riches among the faithful, and hinted that, like the patriarchs of Israel, the elders of the new Church were entitled to a plurality of wives. Polygamy and sharp financial practices caused antagonism against the "saints," but persecution merely strengthened the faith of a hard core of followers. Smith removed his scattered bands from settled areas and organized a state of his own at Nauvoo, under charter from the government of Illinois. Prosperity and thousands of converts followed. Recruits came from as far away as England. The prophet ruled as dictator, authorized polygamy for himself and his closest associates, and proposed himself in 1844 for President of the United States.

Smith overreached himself when he attempted to acquire for himself the wife of one of his associates and violently suppressed as schismatics some who resisted him. Rumors of strange goings-on in the "City of the Saints" led to action by the Illinois authorities, but before Smith could be tried he and his brother were murdered in jail by a mob. Brigham Young made himself successor of the prophet and proved to be one of the greatest leaders of Western history. He organized the epic trek to the region of the Great Salt Lake where, despite incredible hardship, the semicommunist theocracy called the "State of Deseret" became the prosperous Zion of a hundred thousand Mormons.

After the United States acquired title to the Mormon territory in the Treaty with Mexico, Congress organized it as the Territory of Utah (1850). There followed a struggle between Young and the federal authorities which culminated in the bloodless "Mormon War" of 1858. A compromise left Young in charge of the Church, which controlled virtually all secular as well as religious affairs, while the Church recognized the authority of the federal Constitution and laws. A federal enactment against polygamy was eventually obeyed by the elders, and communism gradually gave way to private ownership of property. The Mormons remain to this day the distinctive element in the population of Utah. The extraordinary sturdiness of character of the pioneers and their descendants and their achievements in building a great state have overcome prejudices and made their checkered history a romantic memory.

The Shakers

Mormonism was the most successful of numerous Western experiments in religious communism, while the Shakers were the most prosperous and longest-lived Eastern group. Their movement was hardly distinguishable from the Society of Friends but for "agitations of the body." These induced prophetic trances and were ritualized in a sacred dance whereby worship was expressed by the body as well as the soul and sin was shaken out of both. "Mother Ann" Lee, the illiterate daughter of an

English blacksmith, after an unhappy experience of marriage joined the Shaking Quakers in 1758, experienced revelations, and made herself leader of a small group who in 1774 sought refuge from persecution by coming to the New World. The little band settled near Albany, New York, and presently made Mount Lebanon their headquarters. From there branch settlements were organized in almost every state from Maine to Kentucky. Mother Ann taught that Christ had represented only the masculine aspect of Divinity; she herself, the Second Incarnation, represented the feminine aspect. Celibacy was required of all her followers. As the sect grew, members were gathered into new "families" of ten to fifty men and women who shared ownership of worldly goods and worshipped and labored together with great devotion.

The Shakers believed that their families were the first islands of heaven on earth. Although Charles Dickens remarked that Shaker life was fearfully drab, no observer of their communities denied that they lived up to their conception of paradise as a bee-hive ruled by faith, honesty, charity, simplicity, and hard work. Competent leaders succeeded Mother Ann upon her death in 1784, many converts were won during the religious excitements of the Great Revival, and by 1830 more than a dozen prosperous communities under the benevolent dictatorship of the elders and eldresses of Mount Lebanon represented the highest achievement of Protestant monasticism in America. Their slogan, "Hands to work and hearts to God," found expression in agricultural and handicraft products, especially seeds and furniture, which were probably never matched for quality in the country. The designs of their houses, furniture, and tools were a triumph of esthetic simplicity. The virtue of their lives and the respect of their neighbors were such that a suspicious legislative committee of New York state made a report which was a vindication.

For a few years in the late thirties, the Shakers' formalized dance dissolved in a revival of pentecostal hysteria, spiritualist mediumship, gifts of song in gibberish, the climbing of real mountains to receive spiritual gifts of jewels, and exercises such as the "Midnight Cry" to worship. In later decades the Shakers became more sedate and conversions fell off. In our own time the last members of the few remaining communities are too aged to maintain the family dwellings and vast barns or to worship in the assembly halls, which, like medieval monastics, they had built for the ages.

SCIENCE AND PHILOSOPHY

While Emerson bade Americans to "hitch their wagons to the star" of idealism, President John Quincy Adams bade them to build observatories and contribute to knowledge of astronomy. "We have neither observatory nor observer upon our half of the globe and the earth revolves in perpetual darkness to our unsearching eyes," he said. Adams mourned that Americans received new discoveries "second-hand from Europe" and demanded that they return "light for light." But they did not begin to do so until the expansion of maritime commerce created a utilitarian need for accurate astronomical knowledge as an aid to navigation. Many governmental contributions to scientific knowledge resulted from the United States Exploring Expedition of 1838-1842, commanded by Lieutenant Charles Wilkes, which studied the coasts of the American hemisphere and South Atlantic and Pacific islands. Civilian geologists, biologists, ethnologists, and botanists attached to the Expedition collected materials so valuable that Congress provided for them the United States National Museum and the United States Botanical Garden. The Naval Observatory was founded in 1844 to conduct astronomical studies in aid of navigation. Perhaps the most eminent scientist in government employ during the period was a naval officer, Matthew Fontaine Maury of Virginia, a brilliant oceanographer whose studies of winds and currents pointed to more advantageous sailing routes. After the success of the Wilkes Expedition, lesser expeditions engaged in similar work, and even Matthew C. Perry's commercial-political expedition to Japan in 1852-1853 included a talented corps of scientists.

Pure Science

Federal sponsorship of pure research came about somewhat accidentally. James Smithson, an English aristocrat and scientist, decided that the rising republic of the West should become the home of scientific learning. He bequeathed in his will the princely sum of £100,000 to the federal government to be used for the advancement and diffusion of knowledge. Science seemed the best means of using the bequest, because it paid the most practical dividends. Accordingly, Congress in 1846 established the Smithsonian Institution to conduct original research and to spread knowledge by means of a library and museum. Soon the foundation became a world center of work in physics, archeology, and ethnology, and a clearing-house for knowledge in all fields. Its Early Victorian Gothic building in Washington also became a mecca of museum-goers.

Most scientists attached themselves to colleges and universities, which were rapidly expanding their instruction in the physical and biological fields. Benjamin Silliman was the greatest pioneer of scientific studies in American colleges. Early in the century he created an important place for them in the curriculum of Yale, which took leadership in supporting a faculty of scientific researchers as well as teachers. There Willard Gibbs worked as a virtual recluse, making the great discoveries in pure mathematics that lie at the basis of modern theoretical physics. Harvard and other colleges were not far behind Yale in supporting science, and new institutions like Rensselaer Polytechnic Institute and the Franklin Institute were exclusively devoted to scientific and technological studies. The *American Journal of Science,* founded in 1818 by Silliman as an organ for "original American contributions," was actually devoted to co-operation with European scientists. In 1846, the organizing work of the period was climaxed by the founding of the American Association for the Advancement of Science as the professional agency for all fields.

A strong spirit of nationalism inspired the thinking of many scientists, and more so the interest of the public. In the spirit and tradition of Jefferson's *Notes on Virginia,* American geology, flora, and fauna were glorified to refute the sneer of the Frenchman, Buffon, that nature degenerated in America. Textbooks presenting New- rather than Old-World data were enthusiastically received. By 1850, it was proclaimed with some justification that the dependence of American scientists on European teachers had ended. The work of a galaxy of American scientists was admiringly studied abroad. But the career of one of the most eminent of them, Louis Agassiz, a Swiss who came to Harvard in 1846, transcended national boundaries. He revolutionized the study of zoology from arid concern with classification to laboratory study of comparative anatomy. In geology he concentrated on the midwestern prairies and proposed the fruitful glacial hypothesis. Although his religious faith in repeated creations by God was proof against Darwin's evolutionary theory, Agassiz's researches in several respects anticipated the great Englishman's.

Medicine

Striking advances in medical science, education, and practice during this period reflected the new humanitarian concern to relieve human suffering. Public prejudice which had opposed vaccination and produced riots against lecturers on anatomy died out. Twenty-seven new medical colleges were founded between 1810 and 1840, as well as many medical journals, and in 1847 the leading professional body, the American Medical Association, was founded. Quackery was reduced by systems of state licenses for doctors and dentists, though enforcement remained lax for several generations. The *United States Pharmacopoeia,* prepared in 1802 by state medical societies, was accepted as the national authority. American technical ingenuity brought about that boon to humanity, anesthesia. Dr. Crawford W. Long of Georgia performed eight operations under ether between 1842 and 1846, though he did not publish any account of them until 1849. Dr. William T. Morton, who removed a vascular tumor in Massachusetts General Hospital in 1846 under anesthetic, was the first to publicize his discovery. The French Academy of Medicine awarded a prize for this American development.

Epidemics of cholera, typhoid fever, typhus, and smallpox grew more severe with the spread of city slums. Public-health services were quite inadequate until after the Civil War. A beginning in the knowledge of contagion was made by the eminent poet and doctor, Oliver Wendell Holmes, in his report of 1843 entitled, *Contagiousness of Puerperal Fever*. Dramatic pioneer studies of digestion were made by an alert Army doctor, William Beaumont. He induced a Canadian, Alexis St. Martin, who had suffered a wound in the wall of his stomach that healed without closing, to accompany him on duty in Michigan and Wisconsin and allow him to make prolonged observations. On these he based a revolutionary publication in 1833 on the chemistry and physiology of digestion. For every Holmes or Beaumont, however, dozens of poorly educated and occasionally unscrupulous doctors and quacks continued to practice. The public furthermore demanded panaceas, absorbed untold gallons of dubious patent medicines, which no pure-drug laws as yet prohibited, and followed fads, the most harmless of which was Dr. Graham's cure-all cracker and the most preposterous "hydropathy," the water cure for all diseases.

Science aimed to release man's mind from ignorance and his body from material want and suffering; the romantic movement in philosophy and the arts, on the contrary, aimed to free man's spirit from the limitations of rationalism and the chains of materialism. During the Jackson era both of these conflicting currents exerted profound influence on American thinking. Insofar as the conflict was resolved, it found a common denominator in the social purpose of both the scientist and the romanticist to elevate the lives of the people.

Romanticism and Utilitarianism

The philosophy of romanticism in the North superseded eighteenth-century rationalism as a source of democratic faith and inspired opposition to both Northern industrialism and Southern aristocracy, because both wage and chattel slavery frustrated the exaltation of man. The Transcendentalists erected a quasi-religion on the attitudes of romanticism. Less ecstatic were the students of philosophy who brought to America the ideas of Kant, Schelling, Fichte, and their English interpreters, particularly Samuel Taylor Coleridge. Asserting the primacy of the idea over material reality and the superiority of intuition to the rational faculty, these philosophic idealists concluded that man was supremely valuable as man without regard for class or other external circumstances. Such thinking found a ready response in America because it provided a justification of the doctrine of human equality much broader than the natural-rights philosophy of the rationalists. Its influence was felt by the people at large, however, not so much in philosophic terms as in the literature of romanticism.

A more popular formal philosophy was that of Utilitarianism, which came chiefly from England in the writings of Jeremy Bentham. In 1817, John Quincy Adams brought back from England bundles of Bentham's works which he distributed to libraries, and by 1840 an American journal, *The Diamond,* edited by Gilbert Vale in New York, was entirely devoted to the spread of Bentham's ideas. His thought was summed up in the famous slogan, "the greatest happiness of the greatest number," signifying that all human behavior, laws, and institutions should be evaluated objectively for their usefulness to the majority, granting nothing to habit, tradition, or privilege. Whatever could not meet the test should be abolished and utilitarian practices substituted. Most Americans had long been Utilitarians without knowing it, wherefore Bentham described himself to President Andrew Jackson as more of an American than an Englishman. Bentham placed greater emphasis on majority rule than on the minority rights with which the American Fathers, fearing the tyranny of majorities, had strived to reconcile it. Still Bentham's test of majority interest became a standard ingredient of American thinking. It expressed the increasingly democratic tendency of American life, and even those who spoke for minority interests were constrained to argue that they actually served the majority, if not immediately, then in the long run.

A Benthamite of this ambiguous sort was Henry C. Carey, the most eminent political economist of the period. A wealthy Philadelphia businessman and son if the distinguished publisher, Mathew Carey, he modified the systems of the English classical economists to prove that the Bank of the United States, unlimited freedom for business corporations, and protective tariffs actually served the interests of the majority of the people. In fact, they served "free trade" more effectively than the policies of laissez faire, because for Carey free trade meant freedom for businessmen to operate successfully. He presented government encouragement to private business corporations as a more effective means to group enterprise than socialism. On the other hand, Carey opposed legislation to protect labor because the profits of employers were the best guarantee that labor's status would be raised by means of higher wages. Similarly, he held that slaveowners' property in human beings should not be interfered with by government or criticized by agitators because the security of the institution would increase its profitability, and this would cause the price of slaves to rise so high that planters could no longer afford to buy them. Women, also, would achieve equality if they stopped agitating for legal protection and went to work in factories. Theoretical problems of population, wages, prices, and rents Carey solved in a way that overcame the pessimism of the English economists and pointed to hopeful consequences for the mass of humanity—always provided that government protected and encouraged property-owners while leaving others to benefit from the owners' prosperity.

His *magnum opus* was the three-volume *Principles of Political Economy,* published in 1840 and revised in 1858 as *Principles of Social Science.* He was the chief theorist of the Whig Party and later supported the Republicans. His work signified the adoption by businessmen of the goals of democracy which Hamilton had scorned. Many disciples of Carey continued his work during the next generations.

The most prevalent single idea in America during the pre-Civil War decades was that of progress. Its inevitability was accepted as an axiom. This idea had roots in the Enlightenment philosophy of natural rights. It was confirmed by Romanticism, received common-sense formulation in Utilitarianism, and was paid court by Carey. Nevertheless it was also agreed, as Albert Brisbane wrote, that nature reserved for the intelligence of human beings the noble prerogative of hastening progress. A society which was united on basic philosophic principle could nevertheless produce a babel of conflict over specific programs. Even slavery was advocated as a means to human progress and when this view met its opposite, that progress required the abolition of slavery, the conflict spread far beyond the words of philosophers.

LITERATURE

Some of the conditions necessary for the creation of a great literature were present in the United States following the War of 1812. A mood of self-confidence overcame lingering colonialism. The day when politics was the crucial interest of the nation's best minds had passed in the North, if not yet in the South. Prosperity made possible leisure and higher education for widening classes, while improvement of public education created mass hunger for stimulation by the printed word. Critical appreciation, social prestige, and fair financial rewards were accorded some of the best writers as a result of the most significant condition of all: the identity of interests and ideals between the society as a whole and some of its most talented individuals.

The Knickerbocker School

The "Knickerbocker School" of writers were the first to give evidence of the readiness of America for a mature literature. They took their name from *A History of New York by Diedrich Knickerbocker* (1809), in which Washington Irving delighted readers with urbane satire at the expense of the Dutch founders and set the tone for New York as the nation's capital of secular culture. Traveling in England and on the Continent after 1815, Irving continued to mine the vein of local lore with notable success in "Rip Van Winkle" and "The Legend of Sleepy Hollow," contained in *The Sketch Book* (1820). Irving also demonstrated in *A Chronicle of the Conquest of Granada* (1829) and *The Alhambra* (1832) that an American could use to excellent effect the materials of Europe's past. When he returned to the United States in 1832 he was greeted as the first American writer to win an international reputation. He settled down at "Sunnyside," his country house in the new romantic-Gothic style on the bank of the Hudson near Tarrytown, New York. Travels in the West resulted in books which revealed the colorful possibilities of the frontier for literature. The chief work of his later years was the *Life of George Washington,* the fifth and last volume of which was published in 1859. Irving's career as the first American professional man of letters was important evidence that the young Republic could produce and support an original artist.

William Cullen Bryant was born in Massachusetts but moved to New York in 1825, already famous for the lyric nature poems "Thanatopsis" and "To a Waterfowl." For two decades he continued to write poetry while serving as editor of the *Evening Post*. His fifty years in the latter capacity made that newspaper a leading organ of democratic influence as he abandoned the Federalism of his New England days and successively championed Jackson, the Free Soil Party, and the Republicans. "Thanatopsis" suggested the possibility of discovering in nature a better understanding of life and death than any religion offered and of achieving serenity by accepting the inviolability of every man's individual faith. When he read this poem, Richard Henry Dana, Sr., refused to believe that anyone "on this side of the Atlantic" could have written it. Bryant himself complained that Americans did not praise a thing until they saw the "transatlantic seal of approval" on it, and his own reputation verified this. His recognition as America's leading poet came only after an English edition of his poems in 1832 had been admired. Contemporary American readers found his poetry difficult; today it is read for its pleasant simplicity.

James Fenimore Cooper was not strictly a Knickerbocker; he spent most of his life in his father's village of Cooperstown, New York, and his greatest work celebrated the frontier of the Old West which had already passed. In thirty years from 1820 to his death, he wrote thirty books, including novels of the sea and of the Revolution besides his forest masterpieces, *The Last of the Mohicans, The Pathfinder,* and *The Deerslayer*. His fame was sudden and world-wide; in England he was called second only to Walter Scott. Primitivism overcome by civilization was his master-theme, treated not entirely to the advantage of the white man as compared with the Indian, and to the clear disadvantage of settled ways compared with the frontiersman's virtues, immortalized in Leatherstocking. But it was superior skill in the art of adventurous narrative that accounts for Cooper's popularity more than any philosophy. His later years were marred by angry revulsions against the new democracy, expressed in fretful attacks and bootless libel suits. He had decided that mankind needs authority more than liberty and was particularly horrified by the antirent riots of the Hudson Valley tenant farmers. Still his patriotism was passionate and his animadversions are now forgotten while his portrayals of the American struggle for civilization continue to be read, although more in foreign translation than in English.

William Gilmore Simms of South Carolina has been called the Southern Cooper; in the best-known of his many novels, *The Yemassee* (1835), he chronicled an Indian war and he depicted frontier scenes and characters with skill and power. But this prolific writer, instead of following his bent for robust realism, spent most of his vast energies glorifying the institutions and history of his native state, especially in the series of novels beginning with *The Partisan* (1835), and he never gained much of a hearing in the nation. There was no shadow of aristocratic romanticism in Augustus B. Longstreet's *Georgia Scenes* (1840), which anticipated to some degree the rollicking frontier humor of Mark Twain, but Longstreet was only incidentally a literary man and the Southern "school" of writers became increasingly sectional. Not until after the Civil War did Southern writers as a group command the attention and support of the country as a whole.

Emerson and Thoreau

Meanwhile, by 1840, Boston with Cambridge and Concord had clearly superseded New York as the literary capital of the nation. True to the Puritan inheritance, the New England Renaissance glorified moral earnestness even while it overthrew the ancestral theology; and, while both the English and the Americans found entertainment in the Knickerbockers, they found uplift in the New Englanders.

Ralph Waldo Emerson turned the gnarled sermons of his clerical forefathers into luminous essays of free, organic artistry. He knew poverty as a boy, was educated for the Unitarian ministry at Harvard, and accepted a pulpit in Boston. But, following his own prescription of self-reliance, he resigned from the ministry and, beginning with *Nature*, published in 1836, set out to deliver to a larger parish a new declaration of spiritual independence. This compound of common sense and idealism was expressed in the doctrine that the physical laws of nature and the moral law apprehended by human conscience were parallel expressions of divine unity. Emerson himself was a rare combination of shrewd Yankee and world seer; his language brought the salty New England speech into fruitful company with the vocabulary of scholarship; and his essays held all these dualities in tense suspension.

In "The American Scholar," delivered as the Phi Beta Kappa Address at Harvard in 1837, Emerson called for revolt against American intellectual and literary colonialism with such effect that James Russell Lowell called it "an event without any former parallel in our literary annals." His own career was the best answer to his call. His profound Americanism synthesized materialism and spirituality in absolute faith that the sovereign individual exercising economic, political, and spiritual liberty would justify all hopes not only by his works but as the greatest of creations—a whole man. This did not mean that Emerson did not criticize his countrymen; his faith was in their potentialities. He made himself their chief lay evangelist on the lecture platform, for forty years exhorting them to envision and fulfill their destiny. Nor was he an ordinary nationalist: following travels abroad, where he formed a notable friendship with Carlyle, Emerson wrote in *English Traits* (1856) a brilliant appreciation of British civilization. His single example did much to allay the mutual antagonism of the two peoples that lingered on after the War of 1812.

Living in Concord from 1835 until his death in 1882, Emerson the world sage was at home in the gracefully time-worn village and first among its remarkable group of literary citizens. A significant criticism of his outlook is that he was blind to the reality of evil, but this charge could not be leveled at either of his two greatest fellow-villagers, Thoreau or Hawthorne. Henry David Thoreau was called by Emerson *the* man of Concord, but he was little known during his lifetime and not so favorably then as later. With a conscience as sensitive as Emerson's, Thoreau, after graduating from Harvard, lost one teaching job because he refused to flog the pupils and gave up another because his purpose of making a living he considered unworthy. Emerson helped the younger man in writing and publishing poetry, gave him his friendship, and delighted in Thoreau's bristly independence. He tried literary life in New York under Horace Greeley's tutelage but decided that, as he told Emerson, he was made of Concord dust. Nor would he go to the "farthest Indies" by ordinary means. He walked a few miles to a woodlot of Emerson's at Walden Pond, built himself a cabin and lived there for two years. He did this in revolt against the greed and futility of conventional ways of life, and, as he wrote, "because I wished to live deliberately, to front only the essential facts of life, and see if I could not learn what it had to teach." Laborers building a railroad nearby, their bodies and minds permanently constricted by sixteen hours of toil per day for 60 cents, reminded Thoreau of what he opposed; and his intimate observations of seasons, animals, and plants, published as *Walden* (1854), recorded in prose more sinewy than Emerson's the great deal he learned of how man might live in union with nature.

This classical experiment in living Thoreau followed with an experiment in social protest against the government. As an abolitionist, he opposed the Mexican War, refused to pay his state poll tax, was arrested, and went to jail. From this experience he drew the doctrine of his essay, "Civil Disobedience," which became a guidebook of the route an individual may take when he opposes the state, and an inspiration to Mahatma Ghandi in his epochal campaign against British rule over India. An expert surveyor, Thoreau usually made his living by doing odd jobs for neighbors in Concord or making pencils for sale. Besides *Walden* only one other book was published during his lifetime, *A Week on the Concord and Merrimack Rivers* (1849). Emerson was disappointed that he was not the American scholar, great in action, he had hoped for, instead of captain of a huckleberry party. But Thoreau's protests reverberated. His last one, against the "slave power" for hanging John Brown, helped turn Massachusetts to abolitionism. After his death in 1862, further books of his essays, poems, and letters were published and his reputation slowly grew like the cairn on the bank of Walden Pond to which pilgrims from all over the world have added stones. His was the clearest of all American voices asserting the supremacy of the individual's moral imperative to dissent.

Hawthorne and Melville

Nathaniel Hawthorne created images of the evil that inheres in man rather than in society and did not pretend to exorcise it, like Emerson, or like Thoreau try to abolish it. Indeed he was unique among the New England intellectuals in adhering to the Democratic Party throughout the forties and fifties when they condemned it as the instrument of imperialism and slavery. No philosopher, he was the first American novelist to enter the highest rank of artists. His view of life was tragic and he had little faith in social reform. The fated consequence of guilt was his chief theme and his best work explored its operation among the Puritans who were his ancestors. Born in Salem, he graduated from Bowdoin College in 1825 and returned to Salem to live in seclusion and learn the craft of writing. In short tales he tried to please the taste for sentimental romance, lived for several periods in Concord among the Transcendentalists but aloof from them, and revealed his full stature only in 1850 with the publication of *The Scarlet Letter*. More than a romance, it was a profound portrayal of Puritans locked in expiatory relations to a sin. In 1851, Hawthorne published *The House of the Seven Gables,* showing Puritan guilt inherited as a family curse. European experience as United States Consul at Liverpool, an appointment Hawthorne received from his college friend, Franklin Pierce (after writing a campaign biography for him in 1852) and later as a resident in Italy, was most productively used in *The Marble Faun*. This suggests that the pagan past of the Old World also shadows its present.

Herman Melville, a New Yorker and a friend of Hawthorne, explored the power of evil in his masterpiece, *Moby Dick* (1851), in terms more universal than Hawthorne's. After voyages in the South Seas, Melville had won quick popularity with books of adventure which included reformist attacks against the misunderstanding of natives by missionaries and the brutalities of officers on warships and whalers. *Moby Dick,* however, left readers puzzled and the public indifferent until after the First World War, when the "Melville revival" placed it among the great books of all time. On its several planes it presented a mighty image of the whaling industry, a narrative of homeric chase of a legendary white whale, a drama of the humanly microcosmic crew of the whaler *Pequod,* and, in its ultimate symbolism, a tragic allegory of the enmity of nature against man. Sprawling in form and detail, and concealing its inner meanings in metaphysical imagery, totally contradictory of contemporary optimism in philosophy, *Moby Dick* was a strange production of the mid-century and earned for its author only obscurity during forty more years of life.

Edgar Allan Poe

Edgar Allan Poe was the darkest of American geniuses in private life as well as in literary creations. He identified himself with the Southern aristocracy by an exercise of imagination, and was quickly dismissed from both the University of Virginia and West Point. Dogged by poverty and tortured by alcoholism, he produced lyric poems and eerie short stories of haunting beauty and compelling power. His was the romanticism of esthetic egoism scorning social responsibility and democracy. His young bride died of consumption, and neither friends nor fame following the publication of "The Raven" in 1845 saved him from despair and early death. "The Gold Bug" and other stories turned intellectual ingenuity and grotesque emotional preoccupations to brilliant use. His poems initiated the modern school of Symbolism in which poets alienated from their societies create private mythologies. And his literary criticism was the first American attempt to judge art solely by mature artistic standards.

From Emerson to Poe this group of major writers presented in great works a spectrum of attitudes towards the eternal problems of man and society, ranging from complete acceptance and glorification of the common life of America to complete rejection of it as unredeemable except a-morally in art. With the addition of Mark Twain, who soon filled out the band with laughter, the leaders of the mid-century "renaissance" provided archetypes for many subsequent developments in American literature. It was to be expected that a maturing society should produce recollections of its past like those of Irving, Cooper, and Hawthorne, and that a radical democracy devoted to reform should evoke the protests of a Thoreau; but the optimism of Emerson and the Transcendentalists, the pessimism of Melville, and the despair of Poe, could be related to the conditions of their society only by virtue of the sunny reality of its promise which was bewilderingly offset by its equally real continuing evils.

Longfellow and Whittier

None of these greatest voices won audiences as large as those of writers whose ideas, language, and emotions were simpler. Henry Wadsworth Longfellow was the most popular of all American poets. A graduate of Bowdoin in Hawthorne's class of 1825, widely traveled in Europe, and professor of modern languages at Harvard, Longfellow's translation of Dante was scholarly, but his own poetry in sing-song rhythms made the past seem quaint, the present readily idealized, and human life ennobled by inexhaustible goodness and sweetness. His "Village Blacksmith," "Wreck of the Hesperus," "Excelsior," "Evangeline," "Courtship of Miles Standish," and "Hiawatha" were for most Americans and masses of devoted readers in England all that poetry should be. A few of John Greenleaf Whittier's poems, notably "Snow-Bound," matched Longfellow's in sweetness and popularity, but the Quaker poet spent his best energies on abolitionist propaganda and organization.

Newspapers and Magazines

Longfellow and Whittier are little read today; a host of their contemporary purveyors of sentiment are wholly unreadable. Mass literacy and the growth of the middle class during this period created a market that expanded popular literature into an industry. More than books, newspapers and magazines were relished by the new mass audience. Horace Greeley's New York Tribune, founded in 1841, was a penny paper that remained intellectually respectable, if erratic, while building a mass circulation. But most of the new "penny dreadfuls," led off by James Gordon Bennett's New York Herald, frankly cultivated readers' tastes for sensation, crime, cloying sentiment, and flamboyant patriotism. The most popular magazines maintained higher standards than the penny papers, but here, too, the cleavage between the reading material of the masses and that of the cultivated minority became apparent. The North American Review (1815-1939), the Dial (1838-1844), and the

Atlantic Monthly (founded 1857) in Boston; *Harper's Magazine* (founded 1850) and *Knickerbocker Magazine* (1833-1865) in New York; *Graham's Magazine* (1838-1858) in Philadelphia; the *Southern Literary Messenger* (1834-1864) in Richmond: these strove for and sometimes achieved the authoritative standards of the great English reviews. Indeed, these genteel magazines on the two sides of the Atlantic, led by the *North American Review* and the *Edinburgh Review,* wordily fought each other to a standstill over the question of the relative merits of British and American civilizations. The most popular American magazines, notably *Godey's Lady's Book* (1830-1898) of Philadelphia, dealt in sentimentality so pervasive that it extended to "the old home," except on a few occasions such as when the beloved Charles Dickens, following an American tour in 1842, dared to describe flaws as well as pleasant aspects of the American scene.

Historians

Most indicative of cultural maturity, perhaps, was the work and the broad popularity of a new group of American historians. George Bancroft began in 1834 to publish his eleven-volume *History of the United States* on the basis of original research made palatable to readers by his lively style and rendered inspirational by his patriotic conviction that Providence presided over the birth of the United States. William H. Prescott in his histories of the conquest of Mexico and Peru did justice to the romantic possibilities of those fabulous episodes. John Lothrop Motley's *Rise of the Dutch Republic* defined Protestantism as the impelling force of liberty; and this theme was brought closer to Americans in the work of the greatest of the classical historians—the nearly-blind Francis Parkman, who took the struggle between Britain and France for mastery of North America as his subject. Parkman injured his health after graduating from Harvard by strenuous explorations of the West, but despite invalidism began in 1851 to publish the great series of which *Montcalm and Wolfe* is the most famous. His narrative power and imaginative reach made art out of fact. These historians wrote not for students so much as for the public at large and succeeded as no historian has done since.

The Arts

Architecture

Jacksonian America produced original work in other arts. The Greek Revival in architecture was the last stage of classicism. Roman buildings now began to look pompously aristocratic to Americans and, stimulated by the Greek Revolution, they turned to the simpler forms of ancient Athens. Spurning domes, arches, and baroque details, Benjamin Henry Latrobe convinced the public that Greek temples were suitable not only for governmental and commercial buildings but even for the homes of plain citizens. Pillared and pedimented facades sprang up in cities, and in the countryside wooden replicas looked out from knolls— suggesting that republicans dwelt there as gods. Ever since, government structures have been influenced by the Greek Treasury building in Washington and banks by Latrobe's Greek Bank of Pennsylvania in Philadelphia. But for their homes Americans, except in the South, quickly tired of wooden temples, and the creative phase of the Greek Revival lasted only from about 1820 to 1840.

Then the new middle classes in the North, including prosperous farmers, turned to the more "romantic" Gothic. This style was quickly adopted also for churches. Occasional factories sported battlements, but the most striking Early American Gothic completely revolutionized domestic architecture. Carpenters learned to avoid the boredom of squat white boxes by adding whimsical wings and towers, by emphasizing verticality with battens and high, pointed window frames, and by ornamenting the exterior with wooden imitations of intricate stone carvings. Naïve approximations of Gothic gave way steadily to more authentic copies of specific medieval European buildings, the accuracy of the copy being identified with artistry. Richard Upjohn's Episcopalian Trinity Church and James Renwick's Catholic St. Patrick's Cathedral, both in New York, showed the suitability of Gothic for those traditional communions. Why Gothic should also appeal to home-builders is suggested by one client's direction to his architect to design for him "a wild sweet cottage in the country." The style satisfied current romantic naturalism. It also gave newly-prosperous families a better opportunity than the classical styles to display high-toned extravagance.

Meanwhile, these impulses found happier expression in the improvement of country estates and public gardens. The most notable landscape gardener and horticulturist of the era was Andrew Jackson Downing (1815-1852), whose work was carried on by Frederick Law Olmstead and Calvert Vaux, designers of Central Park, New York. The sculptor Horatio Greenough vigorously attacked Gothic architecture as functionally unrelated to American needs, but on country estates and in public parks romantic naturalism was more congruous with the half-tamed American landscape than the formal gardens of the classical revival were.

Sculpture and Painting

The prestige of Greek and Roman sculpture grew while that of classical architecture declined. Greenough was the first American to make sculpture his profession. In the thirties he and other American sculptors and painters went to Italy for training and some of them stayed there to do their work. Greenough executed a statue of George Washington for the national capitol which bared that Virginia gentleman's torso above a toga as if he were a Roman senator. Hiram Powers, the first American sculptor to win a European reputation, departed from his ordinary portrait busts to carve a girl in chains as a Greek slave. Her expression of sweet nobility in suffering, her nudity, and the reference to contemporary American as well as Greek slavery made this a highly controversial piece of sculpture. She was carried from city to city for exhibition throughout the North, vast crowds paid admission to see her, with separate hours for men and women viewers, and everyone had an opinion on her spiritual meaning. Marble busts of noted Americans for placement in public buildings were the chief products of scuptors' studios. In 1853, the first equestrian statue cast in the United States resulted from the return of the Democrats to power. Clark Mills' *Andrew Jackson* was placed on a rearing horse in Lafayette Square, Washington, forever raising his hat to the occupant of the White House directly opposite.

American painting during these decades was rich in accomplishment. Historical subjects continued in high favor. Emmanuel Leutze's *Washington Crossing the Delaware* and *Westward the Course of Empire Takes Its Way* apotheosized those themes, while Washington Allston led a new school of historical romanticism which dealt mostly in Biblical scenes spread across gigantic canvases. The first original American group of landscapists, called the "Hudson River School," of whom Asher Brown Durand and Thomas Cole were most celebrated, invested rugged passages of American scenery with mystical glamor. Realism also flourished, however, in the form of anecdotal genre paintings of homely scenes and incidents. George Caleb Bingham's *Jolly Flatboatmen* and William Sidney Mount's affectionate rural dramas typified the genre painters' glorification of workaday America.

Advances in technology joined with the emergence of universal literacy to create new demands, forms, and markets in the graphic arts. Cheap "chromolith" color reproductions were a marvel of the era. Currier and Ives of New York made of these a big business, putting artists to work on an assembly line and spreading millions of copies of news pictures, genre scenes, and political posters throughout the land, while the new French art of photography gradually displaced almost all other techniques of reproduction.

Music and the Theater

Music also was now organized for mass audiences. Haydn and Handel societies in the leading cities provided occasional performances of those composers' works; symphony orchestras in Boston and New York performed Beethoven between renditions of less demanding composers; choral societies became popular, especially among German immigrants; and foreign grand opera companies in New York and New Orleans performed Mozart, Weber, Bellini, and Verdi. The foundations for an independent American musical culture were laid by schools for professional training in several cities. But American compositions were not yet attempted in forms more complicated than songs elaborated from folk tunes. Stephen Foster's compositions in the 1840's and early 1850's—such as "O Susanna" and "My Old Kentucky Home"—were great favorites.

In the theater a similar pattern was discernible. European plays and actors continued to dominate the American stage, although Edwin Booth and Charlotte Cushman proved that Americans could equal the best performers of Shakespearean roles. Rivalry between partisans of American and British actors reached the pitch of riots in Astor Place, New York (1849). Twenty-two people were killed in the argument whether the Englishman William C. Macready or the American Edwin Forrest was the better Hamlet. None of the dramas or comedies of the period has survived as more than a curiosity, but in the minstrel show Americans developed a popular theatrical form exploiting native folk music and humor, especially those of the Negro. In the cities and in the hinterland, "museums" of conglomerate art, curiosities and freaks salted education with amusement. Phineas T. Barnum's American Museum, opened in New York in 1842, delighted the public with fare ranging from frank hoaxes, the dwarf General Tom Thumb, and such spectacles as "The Burning of Rome" painted on a huge moving scroll, to Jenny Lind, "The Swedish Nightingale," whose concert tour was the chief artistic event of 1850.

Lyceums and Foreign Visitors

Such museums were gradually differentiated later in the century into public collections of art and traveling circuses, while the original mixture was perpetuated in the Chautauqua movement. In the Jackson era the most important effort at adult education was the National American Lyceum. Organized in 1831 at New York, within a few years 3000 local lyceums in fifteen states offered for modest fees series of lectures on any and all subjects. Touring the lyceum circuit became a normal reward of fame in every field, and a chief source of income for writers and savants. The tremendous popularity of lyceum lectures was pointed to as evidence that the whole people would absorb culture in quick gulps.

Particularly popular as lecturers were noted Englishmen. Americans eagerly demanded to hear the truth about themselves from representatives of Old World standards and then boiled over when it was not wholly complimentary. Captain Basil Hall, Mrs. Frances Trollope, and Charles Dickens deeply wounded American sensibilities when they showed in books that on their American tours they had observed the darker as well as the brighter sides of the lusty new civilization. That their criticisms were not ineffective is clear in the popular campaign to stop the spitting of tobacco juice in public places by crying "A Trollope!" at offenders.

But one of the best books ever written on the United States, *Democracy in America* (1835), was by a Frenchman, Alexis de Tocqueville. A keen observer and student of society and government, liberal in his sympathies, Tocqueville came to America without prejudice to judge on the evidence whether it offered hope for the future of human liberty. His considered answer was optimistic even while he warned that the tyranny of the majority in the New World might be as dangerous as that of the state in the Old World. He believed that the strengthening of society and self-government which democracy achieved by opening opportunity to all citizens was paid for by the lowering of cultural values from the best aristocratic standards to a mediocre popular level. His book was accepted as a genuine aid to self-knowledge by Americans and as a guide for liberals in many countries of the world. Its popularity to this day also bespeaks the truth that during the Jackson period the main characteristics of modern America—the glories and the hazards of liberty—came fully into view.

Part V

EXPANSION AND SECTIONAL
CONFLICT, 1841-1861

CHAPTER 29

Politics and
Manifest Destiny, 1841-1848

WHEN WILLIAM HENRY HARRISON, NINTH PRESIDENT of the United States, succumbed to pneumonia on April 4, 1841, one month after his inauguration, the country found itself in an unprecedented situation. Never before had there been occasion to turn to the Vice-President, and there was considerable doubt as to the precise meaning of the constitutional provision for that officer's succession. An important precedent was established when John Tyler and Secretary of State Webster, whom Harrison had appointed, decided that the Vice-President should assume the title of President along with the powers of the office and leave the vice-presidential office vacant, rather than retain it and act as President *ad interim*. The latter course would have weakened the administration of the federal government throughout the rest of the elective term, while Tyler's precedent strengthened the American system by effecting an orderly transfer of full authority in an emergency. Nonetheless, fresh personal and political problems were inevitably created by the accession of a man who was not really the choice of his party or the people for the first office.

Because of Tyler's unwillingness to follow the lead of Henry Clay, that leader was able to carry through only part of the traditional Whig program, and the administration of "His Accidency" was marked by a chaotic situation with respect to parties. Webster remained as Secretary of State long enough to complete negotiations with Great Britain which resulted in the Webster-Ashburton Treaty. Then the lines formed for the next presidential campaign. In this the public mind was much more occupied with the question of territorial expansion than with the old financial issues between Democrats and Whigs.

The nomination of James K. Polk by the Democrats over Van Buren

535

in 1844 on an expansionist program, and his election over Clay, the Whig candidate, seemed to mark a return to nationalism of the Jacksonian sort. In fiscal policy Polk was no more in the Jackson tradition than Van Buren was; but the latter, unlike Jackson, came to be identified with Northernism on the slavery question, while Polk was another Tennessean. As for the Whigs, Clay's program was geared more than ever to the economic interests of the Northeast and Northwest; and there is considerable justification for the contention that the divisive influence of sectional conflicts could be held in check more easily by a national-minded Democratic administration than by the more class-conscious and more sectional Whigs. On the other hand, Southern influence in the Democratic Party sharply increased with the shelving of Van Buren, and rendered it suspect to reformers and many plain people in the North who had formerly rallied around Jackson.

The issue of expansion, on which Polk rode to victory and by means of which he hoped to unify the country, served also to inflame sectional antagonism because it raised a divisive question: was this to be an empire for slavery or for liberty? The annexation of Texas and the occupation of Oregon fired many American imaginations, but they also roused extremists in both the South and North. The Mexican War was favored and opposed on sectional and partisan grounds, and on both sides the national purposes of the uncommunicative and unpopular Polk were misunderstood and misinterpreted. Explosive problems about the status of the new territories arose, and these soon threatened to split the Union.

THE TYLER ADMINISTRATION, 1841-1845

John Tyler had been elected as a candidate of the Whigs, but he had opposed the only important act of President Jackson which they approved—the Force Bill against nullification. The theoretical position of this Virginian was not far from that of the Old Republicans. He promised to retain Harrison's Cabinet, headed by Webster; on the other hand, he said he would not remove any Democratic office-holder for political reasons. The Whigs controlled both houses of Congress but their majorities were not large enough to override Presidential vetoes. Factional disputes within both parties offered to any talented strategist rich opportunities for new combinations. John C. Calhoun and other Southern leaders concocted a bold plan to win Tyler away from the Whigs on all issues, and in the end they largely succeeded—in no small part because of Henry Clay's high-handedness.

Clay in the Senate had seen in Harrison's accession his long-awaited opportunity to enact his American System into law, even though it had not been an issue in the campaign. He had induced Harrison to call a special session of Congress for this purpose. When it met in June, Tyler sent it an ominously ambiguous message. Clay responded with a set of resolutions which constituted the actual platform of the Whig Party under his leadership. It called for repeal of the Independent Treasury Act, establishment of a third Bank of the United States, high tariffs, and distribution among the states of proceeds from the sales of public lands. Clay is said to have remarked of the President, "I will drive him before me." In August 1841, Tyler signed a law repealing the Independent Treasury Act, but he objected to the distribution of proceeds from land sales at a time when the Treasury was short of funds, and also because this scheme was calculated to make high tariffs necessary to fill the vacuum. Clay had to accept a compromise amendment which provided that distribution should occur only so long as tariff rates were not raised above the maximum of 20 per cent which was supposed to become effective about this time under the Compromise Tariff of 1833. When the Tariff of 1842 raised the rates to higher levels, the provisions for distribution became more meaningless than ever. The Whigs did something to satisfy the hopes roused by the log-cabin campaign, however, by attaching the Pre-emption Act to the Distribution Bill of 1841. This legalized "squatters' rights" by giving settlers who lacked title to their farms the right to buy them at the minimum price from the government instead of seeing them put up for auction to the highest bidder.

The crucial question was the Bank. Clay put a charter bill through the special session of Congress, but Tyler vetoed it on constitutional grounds. Clay steered through another measure calculated to meet the President's objections, but Tyler vetoed this in September 1841. A few days later all of the Cabinet members except Webster obeyed Clay's instructions to resign. The Secretary of State wished to show his independence of the imperious Clay and to conclude negotiations for a treaty with Great Britain. Tyler patched up a Cabinet out of Whig dissidents. His signature of the Tariff Bill of 1842, which had been passed by a strict Northern vote, enraged Southerners, and a South Carolina group wished to nullify it or even secede from the Union. The Bluffton movement, as it was called, was fully as justified as the Nullification movement had been a decade earlier, but Calhoun was playing a deeper game for larger stakes and he checked the hotheads.

The most far-sighted Southerner of his generation, Calhoun clearly foresaw that the slave states would be beaten in economic competition with the North whether they stayed in the Union or formed a separate confederacy unless they expanded the territorial scope of the "peculiar institution." Expansion of the area of slavery could more readily be achieved by the power of the existing Union than by a separate confederacy, it would serve to unite the sections behind a strong foreign policy, and would give the South its best chance to maintain its traditional influence over federal legislation. Besides, Calhoun calculated, expansion was the program on which he himself could most readily win the presidency. He bided his time while Southern anger at the failure to annex Texas mounted.

Webster finished his treaty and resigned, Clay resigned from the Senate in protest against the vetoes of his Bank bills, and the Whigs, after reading President Tyler out of the party that had elected him, fought him to a standstill. In the 1842 elections, the Whigs lost control of the House of Representatives to the Democrats. Clay in Kentucky intrigued to make himself President in 1844 on the basis of a Whig Party purged of Tyler heresies and oriented more exclusively towards the North.

He had evidently forgotten the political value of expansionism as an issue, though it had first brought him national attention before the War of 1812. Tyler by 1844 was ready to satisfy the clamor for Texas and then appointed Calhoun Secretary of State.

The situation during the later years of Tyler's tenure, when a President of one party ruled with the aid of the leaders of another party and carried out their program, is without parallel in American history. Factional disputes over domestic policies had reached a point where confusion reigned supreme. An aggressive foreign policy is the unscrupulous politician's sovereign remedy for such a situation. Calhoun was not unscrupulous and he had far more in mind than the distraction of public attention from domestic squabbles. He had in view nothing less than a permanent solution of the slavery question which should preserve the Union as well as the distinctive civilization of his beloved South.

CANADA AND THE WEBSTER-ASHBURTON TREATY OF 1842

Soon after the Texans broke away from Mexico, and while their initial move to gain admission to the United States was being blocked by opponents of Southern expansion, an insurrection in Canada (1837) led certain Northern expansionists to revive the old dream of annexing that region. It seemed to some discontented Canadians and their friends below the border only a matter of time before Canada would imitate the American example and revolt against the mother country. Then the evident success of the American experiment, the burgeoning power of the great Republic, and its roomy federal system should make annexation inevitable. So ran the argument, but events refuted it. The insurrection of 1837 proved abortive. American enthusiasts failed to understand that the Canadian rebels were a small minority of the population and the annexationists a tiny group within the minority. They organized aid for the rebellion. Volunteers, money, and supplies crossed the border, thus violating the international obligations of the United States and creating a diplomatic problem which came to a head in the *Caroline*-McLeod affair.

The *Caroline* was an American steamship on the Niagara River which Canadian rebels chartered to run volunteers and supplies from the United States. The Canadian government, late in 1837, sent troops with orders to seize the vessel on the Canadian side, but it happened to be tied up on the American side when they arrived. They crossed over, fought their way aboard, killing one man and injuring several, set fire to the ship, and cut it loose to drift burning over Niagara Falls. President Van Buren demanded reparation and apology by the British government. He was justified insofar as the violation of United States neutrality had been committed by troops of the Canadian government. American violations were committed by private citizens acting in defiance of their government's genuine efforts to control them.[1] Van Buren sent General Winfield Scott to the border and asked New York and Vermont to call out their militia. But the British government rejected Van Buren's demands and rewarded the commander of the offending Canadian troops with a knighthood.

The British remained unexcited, while Americans along the border called for revenge, "not by simpering diplomacy," as a Rochester newspaper put it, "BUT BY BLOOD." The Canadian insurrection had been put down by 1838. On the American side, tens of thousands had organized secret Hunters' Lodges, taking an oath to fight to the death to destroy British power on the continent. A few bands invaded Canada late in 1838 but were easily defeated, some of them ending up in the penal colony in Tasmania. This and Scott's work as pacificator cooled down the Hunters. Van Buren was evidently allowing the British government to neglect his demands regarding the *Caroline* incident, but an epilogue suddenly revived it. In November 1840, a Canadian, Alexander McLeod, bragged in a New York saloon that it was he who had killed the American aboard the *Caroline*. The New York authorities arrested him and charged him in a state court with murder. The British Minister demanded his release; he was told by Lord Palmerston, Foreign Secretary, that the execution of McLeod would mean war.

This was the situation when Daniel Webster became Secretary of State. The McLeod case involved foreign relations but fell within an area where the federal government had no authority. The state of New York refused to yield jurisdiction and proceeded to try McLeod. The British government ordered naval preparations and stock prices fell. Webster worked assiduously behind the scenes to prevent New York from precipitating a disaster. Fortunately the New York jury, in October 1841, accepted McLeod's plea that he had lied and his alibi that he had not been on the scene when the *Caroline* was boarded and burned. At Web-

---

[1] This distinction remained even when a Canadian ship, the *Sir Robert Peel*, caught in American waters by a band of Americans, was looted and burned to the sound of cries: "Remember the *Caroline*."

ster's request, the dangerous gap in federal authority was closed by an act of Congress which gives the federal courts appellate jurisdiction in such cases.

Meanwhile, the ancient Maine boundary dispute had become critical. Canadian lumberjacks entered the disputed area in 1839, and Maine lumberjacks then went in to slug it out. Britain wanted the area for a military road between the ice-free port of Halifax and Quebec; the men of Maine wanted the rich Aroostook Valley which today produces the country's greatest potato crops. Maine and New Brunswick called out their militia. Congress appropriated money and authorized Van Buren to raise an army. But the President sent General Scott to Maine and that respected envoy arranged a truce between the lumberjacks which kept the "Aroostook War" miraculously bloodless and gave diplomacy time to function.

A third irritant of relations between the United States and Britain arose from the illegal slave trade. The British insisted on the right to search ships flying the American flag if they were suspected of carrying slaves. National pride found this an intolerable perpetuation of practices which had led to war in 1812. In November 1841, Negroes aboard the *Creole*, an American brig engaged in the domestic slave trade between Virginia and New Orleans, mutinied, killed one passenger, took command of the ship, and sailed it to the British Bahamas. The British authorities refused to turn the slaves over to the United States Consul for repatriation; they were freed and only those found guilty of murder were punished. Outbursts over this incident were strongest in the South, but there was anger in all sections against British surveillance of American shipping.

British intrigues in Texas and their virtual domination of the Mexican government also fed American fears and anger. Wherever Americans looked—the Niagara boundary, the Maine boundary, Oregon, California, Mexico, Texas, and the high seas—they saw reason to revive their old hatred of the mother country. In the public press of both countries a verbal war embittered national feelings. Particularly offensive to Americans were the writings of British travelers who magnified the crudities and failings of the Republic.

If Webster had been a Northern expansionist or if the aggressive Palmerston had remained in office as British Foreign Secretary, the two antagonistic peoples might have been provoked into war. President Tyler wanted to turn all of Oregon north of the Columbia River over to Britain in exchange for British pressure on the Mexican government to sell California to the United States. But Webster, like most New England leaders before and after him, was disinclined to support territorial expansion on either the northern or the southern side. He was most concerned for commerce, manufacturing, and the encouragement of British investment, and believed that these interests would be best served by pacification of Anglo-American relations. A striking coincidence brought the like-minded Lord Aberdeen to office in Palmerton's place in September 1841. Aberdeen turned to Alexander Baring, Lord Ashburton, as special envoy. His banking interest as a member of the House of Baring, the chief agency for the sale of American investments to British capitalists, his American experience as agent of the House for many years, and his American wife and his admiration for Webster all suggested that friendliness, peace, and good business would triumph over all irritations.

Negotiations began early in 1842. There followed a remarkable demonstration of what diplomacy can do to settle international disputes when *both* sides are determined to reach a fair settlement. Ashburton and Webster chatted together, kept no minutes, and frankly spoke their minds. They agreed to ignore the tortured documentation of the Maine boundary dispute and fixed on a sensible compromise line, the present boundary. This gave Canada five-twelfths of the disputed territory, with room for the military road, and the United States the remainder (the best of the potato country, as it turned out), along with a scrap of land at the head of the Connecticut River and a strip north of the 45th parallel. Oddly, Webster used a "red line" map presumably marked by Franklin in 1782, which seemed to make all of the disputed area British, to convince Maine and Massachusetts that the compromise line, along with payment of $150,000 to each of the states by the federal government, was really more than they deserved; while British opponents of the settlement, headed by Palmerston, were quieted by the revelation of a map in the British archives which proved that the United States should have had all of the disputed area.

Ashburton used the word "apology" with respect to the *Caroline* affair without actually apologizing for it, and Webster was content. Similarly Webster accepted a vague promise that "officious interference" by British authorities with American vessels like the *Creole* would not recur. On the larger question of the slave trade, the British refused to abandon their claim to the right of search, but agreed that if American warships were stationed off the African coast to co-operate in suppressing the slave trade, suspected ships flying the American flag would be left for them. The system failed to work until Lincoln came to office because intervening administrations were unwilling to offend the South by maintaining the promised warships on African station. Webster and Ashburton agreed to postpone the question of Oregon.

Many an American continued to believe the statement of an Ohio newspaper that America in infancy had whipped England and in youth had whipped her again, so that it was clearly necessary that in her maturity America must whip England once more. Many Englishmen nursed the old high Tory contempt for America, expressed in rumblings that one day she must be taught her place. Probably a majority on both sides welcomed the treaty. It permanently disposed of boundary quarrels from the Rocky Mountains to the Atlantic Ocean. But rivalry in Oregon intensified after 1842; British policy in Mexico was designed to stiffen that country's resistance to American expansion; trade advantages were held out to the Texan republic in the hope that it could become a buffer against the United States; and the ink was hardly dry on the Webster-Ashburton Treaty when an incident in California prophesied things to come.

British agents in that weakly-held Mexican province were eager to annex it to Great Britain. Hearing a rumor that an American war with Mexico had started, the United States naval officer in command of Pacific forces, Commodore Thomas A. Catesby Jones, became suspicious of the intentions of British warships along the coast and decided to forestall them. He sailed into Monterey Bay, talked the Mexican authorities into surrendering, raised the United States flag over the fort on October 20, 1842, and issued a proclamation of annexation. The next day, learning that the rumor of war was mistaken, he lowered the flag. The State Department apologized to Mexico, and Lord Aberdeen instructed his agents to avoid provocation of the Americans. But the next administration in Washington went to work in earnest to secure California for the Union.

THE TEXAS QUESTION, 1822-1844

The Texan Revolution of 1836 occurred just as the controversy over slavery had reached an acute stage in the struggle over abolitionist petitions in Congress. The moral atmosphere was so heated that William Ellery Channing, noted liberal minister in Massachusetts, denounced the revolt of slaveholding Texas against Mexico as "positively criminal," and the Quaker Benjamin Lundy, in a pamphlet entitled *The War in Texas* (1836), laid down the abolitionist line of interpretation: that the events in the Southwest—colonization, revolt, and the move for annexation— were successive phases in a Southern conspiracy for the spread of slavery. Besides becoming official doctrine among abolitionists, this was taken over by many Northern sectionalists whose concern was more political than moral.

Modern historians, removed from the highly emotional atmosphere of the era, have seen no need to explain developments in Texas as the result of a "plot." The colonization of that region represented a standard drive by individual Americans who were seeking virgin lands beyond the western horizon. Actually, the chief promoter of colonization, Stephen F. Austin, was of Connecticut Yankee stock; and most of the early settlers, though naturally Southern, came from states like Tennessee and Kentucky, where slavery by no means dominated society as it did in South Carolina. Slaves never represented such a large element of the population in Texas as in the Gulf states of Alabama, Mississippi, and Louisiana. It was Mexico's misfortune that Texas, which she could neither settle with Mexicans nor defend against Americans, contained rich lands directly in the path of American frontier expansion. The Mexicans themselves believed that the influx of Americans was the result of a great conspiracy on the part of the United States government, but the migration into Texas was a folk movement. The settlement which was planted in 1822 by Stephen F. Austin was based on a legal agreement, and that conspicuously successful colonizer remained loyal to the Mexican government as long as possible.

American Settlers under Mexican Rule

Land was even cheaper in Texas than in the United States: this was the basic reason for the migration of Americans from their own country. The state of Coahuila and Texas, under Mexican authority, passed a liberal colonization law, under which a league (4428 acres) of land was made available to each married settler on easy terms for less than $200. A typical American land boom, characterized by wild speculation and a residue of solid settlement and economic progress created a Texan annex of the American wild-cat boom of the thirties. Austin became the leading *impresario* and the dominant political figure of the state of Coahuila and Texas. Though slavery was formally abolished in Mexico proper, it was permitted here under the legal fiction of "permanent indentured servants"—a fiction which did not differ greatly from Mexico's own institution of peonage. The American Protestants in Texas were forbidden to hold public worship. Austin secured their right to stay away from Catholic services, but the demand for religious equality on the American model was a basic cause of trouble between Texas and Mexico.

The vast distances in Texas, the premium that space paid to individualism, the disrespect of settlers for Mexican authority, the ease with which a poor man could become lord of a great domain and give loose rein to his every instinct, and the whole context of life exaggerated the normal phenomena of the wild American frontier and made Texas the first peninsula into that new region which earned the title of the Wild West. Suitably, Texas was the premier home of the "Arkansas Toothpick," the eighteen-inch knife invented by the Texan James Bowie, and, for the next generation, of the even more efficient six-shooter.

Private violence was common in Texas and public violence was endemic. At first rebellious spirits aimed at Austin and the state government. The most important incident, the "Fredonia Rebellion" of 1826, was put down by Austin supported by the majority of Texans who wished to make an honest effort to live under the terms of the Mexican grant. Mexicans, however, regarded such affairs as proof of a plot against their rule and linked them with American efforts to buy Texas.

Mexican government adopted the Colonization Law of 1830. It forbade further American migration into Texas, encouraged migration of Mexicans and Europeans, threw into doubt the legal status of earlier land grants, called for enforcement of Mexican laws against slavery and in favor of Catholicism, and provided for occupation of Texas by Mexican troops. Only the last provision was carried out. The law may have discouraged the immigration of more peaceful Americans, but among the adventurers who came seeking opportunity in this troubled land were Sam Houston and many another who would give Texan politics their special rambunctiousness.

Abortive revolts followed the Mexican occupation, and Mexican civil war spread to Texas. Austin supported the call for a Texas Convention to declare for General Santa Anna and petition the virtually nonexistent central government for redress of grievances. The Convention of 1832 had no success, therefore in 1833 a second Convention drew up a constitution on the model of the Massachusetts Constitution of 1780 (a copy of which was handy) and sent Austin to Mexico City to secure its acceptance. The projected state of Texas would be separate from Coahuila, and the Mexican authorities regarded this as a preliminary to separation from Mexico. The proposed arrangement would also free Texas from the provisions of the Colonization Act, recognize slavery, and permit reduction of tariff barriers impeding trade with the United States. The Mexicans rejected every demand except the one to reopen American immigration into Texas, and they threw Austin himself into jail.

Santa Anna's achievement of power in Mexico turned out to be a disaster for the Texans. He suppressed federalism (as the doctrine and practice of state rights is called in Latin America) and ruthlessly gathered power into the hands of the central government. Anti-Americanism was a chief ingredient of his policy. The *mystique* of Santa Anna's nationalism included public worship of his leg, which had been shot off, presumably in battle. It was alternately exhibited and buried with great pomp, or exhumed and thrown on a dump heap, according to the rise or fall of its former master's political fortunes. Early in 1835, Santa Anna marched an army northward, putting down federalist movements as he went and aiming for Texas as his final target. In October, a decree totally abolished self-government in the Mexican states. This justified the rebellion and brought it the support of the most stable elements among the Americans.

The Lone Star Republic

of bruary 1836, Santa Anna arrived in Texas and besieged a handful San under William B. Travis in the Alamo, the ancient mission at io. The Texans were defeated by a thousand Mexican troops and massacred. This aroused the historic cry, "Remember the Alamo," and hastened the Texan Declaration of Independence on March 2, 1836. A convention adopted a constitution patterned on that of the United States but including more specific guarantees of the rights of slaveowners. The territory of Texas was loosely defined to permit indefinite expansion westward. Sam Houston was made Commander-in-Chief of the Army of the Republic. At the Battle of San Jacinto, Houston's forces captured Santa Anna. He was released after two months on his promise that he would withdraw from Texas and support Mexican recognition of Texan independence. This was never given but Texas was now actually free, and its people avidly desired annexation by the United States.

President Jackson's public policy towards the exciting events in Texas was one of correct neutrality. But for the federal government to prevent violations of neutrality by its citizens would have required nothing short of an army big enough to patrol the whole of the long boundary and fight off armed volunteers. The Texan Revolution probably could not have succeeded without the help of individual Americans. Public opinion was the basic reason for the collapse of neutrality in practice, but the Mexicans had a just grievance and this strengthened their erroneous conviction that the United States government engineered the revolt—which was not far from the abolitionist interpretation of these events. Jackson privately sympathized with the Texans, but all that he did officially was to extend to the Lone Star Republic recognition of its independence.

In August 1837, Texas presented a formal proposal of annexation but President Van Buren, who was facing a financial crisis and did not want to add to his diplomatic and political difficulties, rebuffed it. Meanwhile, the American Anti-Slavery Society was circulating petitions which pointed out that Texas would make half a dozen states and that the annexation of this vast region would give the South dominance in the Union. These fears gave pause to many Northern politicians, just as they gave hope to Southern. In 1838, an annexation resolution that was presented in the Senate by a South Carolinian was voted down, while another that had been similarly introduced in the House was smothered by a three-weeks' filibustering speech by John Quincy Adams who was now a Representative. Soon after this the Texans withdrew their offer and turned their eyes toward Great Britain.

The question of annexation was reopened by President John Tyler, after the negotiations between Webster and Ashburton had been completed. Things had not been going well in Texas, and in 1843 do ain-Sam Houston again became president. He seems to have wanted d he tain an independent Texas, stretching all the way to the Pacif Tyler had little choice but to flirt with the British for their barn sup-was not an extremist on this issue, but he was bidding for e feared port. He was interested in California, and on national gr the growth of British influence on the North American continent. The British Foreign Minister, Lord Aberdeen, was strongly suspected of trying to gain recognition of Texan independence from Mexico, in return for which favor the Lone Star Republic would abolish slavery. An independent Texas without slavery was regarded as a danger to that institution in the South, and for that reason extremists like Robert Barnwell Rhett of South Carolina were threatening disunion if there were no annexation. Calhoun uttered no such threats but favored Tyler's policy.

The Secretary of State, Abel P. Upshur, another Virginian, negotiated a treaty of annexation at President Tyler's instigation, and to this President Houston could but agree. Fate intervened early in 1844, when Upshur, out for a Potomac cruise with a presidential party, was killed by the bursting of a cannon on the *U. S. S. Princeton.* Tyler, who had escaped injury, then asked Calhoun to become Secretary of State and complete the annexation business. In the spring, after he took office, Calhoun found in his official papers an unanswered dispatch from Lord Aberdeen, which had been transmitted by the British Minister, Richard Pakenham, and to this he replied in what is known as the "Pakenham Letter." While ostensibly disclaiming improper British designs in Texas, Aberdeen had avowed that his country desired and was constantly exerting herself to bring about "general abolition of slavery throughout the world." In reply, Calhoun analyzed British policy as designed to encircle the United States, destroy its trade, and endanger the institution of slavery to the point of servile revolt. He warned that the United States must defeat British policy in self-defense. He went so far as to launch into a spirited defense of slavery, and thus made a bad tactical mistake. When the treaty which Upshur had drafted was submitted to the Senate, the "Pakenham Letter" went with it and got into the newspapers. Calhoun's justification of slavery as morally and socially beneficial to slave and master alike was an offense to Northerners. John Quincy Adams declared that the freedom of the human race was involved in the treaty's fate. While Southern extremists shouted, "Texas or Disunion," Northern abolitionists answered with Adams that annexation itself would be a dissolution of the Union. The treaty was rejected by the Senate. But once raised the issue of annexation would not down. It was thrown into the election campaign for a decision.

THE ELECTION OF 1844 AND PRESIDENT POLK

exgon, another vast and promising region that was much talked about, both from the northern boundary of California to the southern oper of Russian Alaska at 54° 40′, and according to agreement was of both American and British settlement, pending a final drawing ing line. Postponement of this issue had been wise from the

American point of view, for possession is nine points of the law and conditions were more favorable to American than to British occupation. Settlers from the United States kept within the area of relative safety below the Columbia River, however, and the earliest considerable agricultural group was in the Willamette Valley, where the Methodist Indian mission of Rev. Jason Lee had served as a nucleus for about ten years. Best known among the pioneer missionaries was Marcus Whitman, representing the Congregationalists. In the matter of converting the Indians to Christianity a Roman Catholic, Father Blanchet, who had been appointed by the Bishop of Quebec, was the most successful. In the interest of his mission, Whitman made a heroic and well-publicized ride to the East in the winter of 1842-1843. He accompanied a party of 1000 settlers which assembled at Independence, Missouri, and proceeded during the summer to the Columbia River by the Oregon Trail. While assuring continued American possession of the country below the Columbia, this migration drew national attention to Oregon and emboldened politicians to make large territorial claims.

In 1844, expansion was a timely issue and an appealing one to the uninhibited American imagination. Majestic Oregon beckoned and mighty Texas stood waiting just outside the gate, while California seemed ripe for plucking and Cuba was only a step from the southern shore. There was talk even of Hawaii, and some enthusiasts saw no limit to the areas the United States might soon take over, though most people restricted their hopes to the continent. A New York Democratic journalist, John L. O'Sullivan, soon coined the phrase "Manifest Destiny" to replace commonplace reasons for territorial expansion and override objections to it with blind faith in its inevitability. To deny the obvious fate of the great Republic to grow greater was as foolish as to oppose a Divine Decree.

Expansion gave the Democrats a topic that seemed less divisive than domestic policies and was at least equal to the log-cabin, coonskin buncombe of the Whigs in rousing the enthusiasm of voters. It was strongly favored by Southerners and the policy as actually presented was in line with Calhoun's effort to ally the South and West. He could not be nominated, however, because he was too exclusively identified with his own section and with slavery to appeal to many Northern Democrats. Among the latter it was generally expected that Van Buren would be given another chance, but he was unpopular in the South. He sought to dodge the Texas question but at length put himself on record as opposed to immediate annexation. His nomination proved impossible under a two-thirds rule and the Convention turned on the ninth ballot to a "dark horse," James K. Polk of Tennessee, who had previously been regarded as a likely nominee for Vice-President. He had a good the Jacksonian, he could be depended upon to annex Texas political advantage of being too little known to be offensive to Northerners. The Convention adopted a platform calling for the "reannexation" of Texas and the "reoccupation" of Oregon—the idea being that the United States really owned both regions in the first place and should never have yielded any part of them. That was good politics if not good history, and expansion was presented in national rather than sectional guise. Nonetheless, effectual control of the party was passing into Southern hands, and there was tragic significance in one departure from tradition: the platform did not, as always prior to this time, include Jefferson's words in the Declaration of Independence that all men are created equal.

Sure of the South, the Democratic orators concentrated on capturing Northern voters' support with the slogan, "Fifty-four Forty or Fight!" This meant no division of Oregon with Great Britain. The Whigs nominated Henry Clay unanimously. But their platform took no stand on the Texas question and their candidate so awkwardly straddled the issue that voters on both sides of it were dissatisfied with him. Some antislavery Whigs turned to the candidate of the Liberty Party, James G. Birney, and for this reason the state of New York was won by Polk. Without it he would have lost the election. The margin was close, but the Democratic strategy of appealing to expansionists everywhere succeeded, the country's most popular politician was defeated by a colorless candidate, and Northern as well as Southern Democratic leaders thenceforth believed that Manifest Destiny was a magical formula of party unity, electoral success, and sectional peace.

The Annexation of Texas

Regarding the election as a clear mandate for expansion, Calhoun and Tyler anticipated Polk by bringing Texas into the Union. The Texans played on their fear that Great Britain would tender the republic a guarantee of independence. Mexican warnings that annexation would mean war were ignored. It was still impossible to obtain a two-thirds majority in the Senate for a treaty, therefore Tyler suggested and both Houses passed a joint resolution of annexation which required only simple majorities. The President signed the measure on March 1, 1845, three days before Polk's inauguration. Whigs argued that this procedure violated the Constitution, but the administration answered that a treaty was suitable only in relations with a continuing foreign government; annexation extinguished the independent government of Texas and future relations with a state would be a domestic matter. This argument prevailed and the precedent of annexation by joint resolution instead of was followed in the case of Hawaii in 1898.

The essential reasons for opposition to the annexation of Texas were that it would strengthen slavery in the South and increase Southern power in Washington, and that it would precipitate war with Mexico. Northern Whigs, free-soilers, and abolitionists claimed that the whole turbulent history of Texas represented a plot by the "slave power." Northerners who were conscious of the sectional struggle for power were alarmed by the provision that four additional states might be created out of Texas, with the consent of that state. These should be admitted with or without slavery as the people of each should desire, except that slavery should be prohibited in any state that might be formed north of the line drawn by the Missouri Compromise. The region of Texas, as then understood, did extend north of the 36° 30', though the boundary was afterwards drawn there (in 1850); and only one slave state below that line was ever added as a result of the annexation of Texas, since that giant never consented to her own dismemberment. To abolitionists any extension of the area of slavery was offensive. Texan boundary claims in the south and west created immediate trouble. First, they played a part in bringing on the war with Mexico, and after that they created trouble with settlers in the Santa Fé region.

The accusation of a long-range "plot" was false. The history of Texas was a natural one. The United States had postponed annexation for nine years—chiefly because of Northern objections; the Texans had established their independence fully according to normal standards of international law; nothing impeded their voluntary offer to the United States; and it was a fact that England wished to use Texas to "Balkanize" the American continent and injure the security of the United States. Equally true was President Tyler's statement: "There exists no civilized government on earth having a voluntary tender made it of a domain so rich and fertile, so replete with all that can add to national greatness and wealth, and so necessary to its peace and safety that would reject the offer." That the expansionists *wanted* war with Mexico was the falsest charge of all. Van Buren, Tyler, and finally Polk made repeated and sincere offers to settle all issues with the Mexican government on honorable and peaceful terms. The irresponsibility of Mexican officials was, however, manifest to all and when Polk judged that war was coming, he set about making a settlement with Britain of the Oregon question as a precaution against war on two fronts.

Polk and His Policies

James K. Polk was like Abraham Lincoln in at least one respect: when he became President he revealed unforeseen strength of character and powers of forceful action. He also combined boldness of plan with the in execution and a secretiveness which made his friends call him "mole." He confided only in his diary—with the result that later had tions, reading it, know him better than his contemporaries won Andrew Jackson's favor by his ardent loyalty and he considered himself Jackson's heir, but he sadly lacked the popularity of his idol and wisely denied himself ambition for a second term in office. Although his administration was remarkable for carrying out virtually the whole of the Democratic domestic and foreign program, his very success opened wide fissures in the nation which were closed only by the Civil War.

Foreign affairs commanded major attention during the Polk administration, but two notable domestic measures settled old issues in ways pleasing to Democrats generally and Southerners particularly. The Independent Treasury system was re-established in 1846. Polk named the able Robert J. Walker of Mississippi, one of the proslavery expansionists who had secured his nomination, as Secretary of the Treasury. Walker used his strategic position to frame a tariff law which reflected Southern interest in low rates and his own conviction that Britain's championship of free trade, signified by the epochal repeal of the Corn Laws in 1846, made it mandatory on the United States to join the world movement against protection. The Walker Tariff lowered the rates to approximately 20 per cent. It passed the Democratic Congress easily and Polk signed it in August 1846.

The Polk administration ignored Western demands for cheaper land or free homesteads and it did little to satisfy Western appetite for internal improvements. Government subsidies to steamship lines were granted on a large scale, but these were justified as national and even military measures, because the lines were organized to provide fast transportation between the Atlantic and the Pacific coasts, connecting overland by way of Panama, and the vessels were designed for easy conversion into warships. The Walker Tariff commanded the support of Western Democrats as did the Independent Treasury. An intimate and rather shady connection with Eastern shipowners was created by the subsidies. Eastern merchants were pleased by the Walker Tariff while Whig manufacturers grumbled and bankers were confirmed in their detestation of the party of Jackson. But the grand sectional alliance effected by Jefferson and Jackson was not entirely recreated by Polk, because free-soil Democratic workingmen and reformers of the Northeast were deeply antagonized by the annexation of Texas and the Mexican War.

Compromise on Oregon

Polk was charged with slighting the campaign promises regarding on. In his inaugural address, the President claimed that United title to Oregon was "clear and unquestionable" and called for ex- of American laws to protect American settlers there but did not whether he meant the whole territory. Lord Aberdeen countered

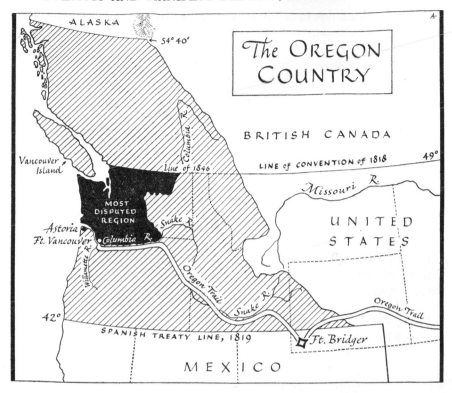

with an assertion that Britain had "clear and unquestionable" rights in Oregon. In both countries war was proposed by excitable elements. During the spring, as Mexico broke diplomatic relations with the United States, Polk decided to retreat in Oregon to the reasonable position of earlier administrations. He offered to divide Oregon at the 49th parallel. Without authority, the British Minister in Washington turned down the offer. When his government repudiated him, Polk nevertheless refused to renew the offer and told Congress in December 1845 that the United States must have the whole of Oregon. He revived the forgotten Monroe Doctrine dictum forbidding further European colonization and recommended that Britain be given the required year's notice ending joint occupation. Southerners in Congress were uninterested in driving to the Northwest now that they had Texas safely in tow. After months of wrangling, the two houses nevertheless passed a joint resolution empowering Polk to end the joint occupation, and he accordingly notice to the British government.

The business-minded government of Great Britain had now and to war with its best customer if that could be decently the the decision of the Hudson's Bay Company to remove northern bank of the Columbia River to Vancouver Island helped the government devise a compromise. Lord Aberdeen offered Polk the 49th parallel on June 6, 1846. By this time war with Mexico had begun. A private visit from a British banker convinced Polk that if he would return to the compromise scheme in Oregon, the British would not use their influence in Mexico in opposition to the United States. Then Polk used an ingenious device to evade responsibility for compromising his campaign commitment: he sent the British offer to the Senate for advice *before* he accepted it. The Senate advised acceptance and on June 15, 1846, the Oregon Treaty was signed. It divided the territory at the 49th parallel except for Vancouver Island which was given to Britain. This and the right to navigate the Columbia River satisfied the Hudson's Bay Company.

Americans had not settled any of the large and rich area between the Columbia River and the 49th parallel, therefore the division may be re-graded as an excellent bargain for the United States. The danger of war with Britain while United States forces were deeply committed in Mexico made it a matter of common sense to accept the bargain without regard to campaign oratory. But a number of Western Senators who had taken "Fifty-four Forty or Fight" seriously voted against the treaty. Thomas H. Benton, the antislavery Senator from Missouri, exclaimed: "Oh! mountain that was delivered of a mouse, thy name shall henceforth be fifty-four forty!"

So, just seventy years after the Declaration of Independence, the United States completed the extension of its northern boundary across the continent to the Pacific. To most observers the feat seemed stupendous. Only thirty-two years had passed since the British government instructed its agents at Ghent to coop up the troublesome Republic east of the Alleghenies. The transformation of its fortunes since that dark day truly merited some other metaphor than Senator Benton's; and in fact much more typical were the exultant recitals by Manifest Destiny orators of expansionist glories already achieved as warrants of more to ome.

HE WAR WITH MEXICO, 1846-1848

Fro the Mexican point of view, the cause of the war with the United States as clear and simple. Americans and their government despoiled Mexico Texas and lusted for California; defensive measures by Mexico e seized upon by the Polk administration as an excuse for a war of on and conquest. Mexicans were confirmed in their position by the of Whigs against their own countrymen, and these Americans the indictment the item of a proslavery conspiracy. It may be in which the United States has engaged has been condemned by so many contemporary and later Americans—statesmen, scholars, and other citizens. But twentieth-century historians tend toward an opinion of the war similar to that finally expressed by James Russell Lowell: "We had as just ground for it as a strong nation ever has against a weak one." The Mexicans, whose thinly-held territories were exposed to the ambitions of land-hungry Americans, command real sympathy; but a review of the actual events shows that the United States government did far more than the Mexican to settle disputes by generous diplomacy rather than by arms.

A condition of virtual anarchy in Mexico, where successive revolutionary chieftains showed interest in little besides cleaning out the national and state treasuries, made regular dealings with foreign governments irresponsible in the extreme. American citizens in Mexico were executed without trials and their property was stolen by government officials. After years of delay, the current government, in 1842, agreed to pay United States claims in the bargain amount of $2 million, then promptly failed to make the promised payments. The French government, treated similarly, in 1838 launched the so-called "Pastry War" to collect its claims. The Tyler administration in 1844 offered to make liberal arrangements in exchange for an agreement on Texas. The Mexican government refused and twisted the offer into an American admission that Mexico still owned Texas. As able a lawyer as Daniel Webster, who opposed annexation, admitted that Mexico had no legal grievance. Mexican leaders declared that annexation would be equivalent to war. The often-discredited Santa Anna rode back to power by whipping up hatred for the United States and promising that he could easily defeat it. Shortly after President Tyler signed the joint resolution of annexation, Mexico broke off diplomatic relations and asserted that war had begun "by act of the United States."

President Polk nevertheless made an earnest effort to avoid war. He refrained from sending troops into the disputed area between the Nueces River and the Rio Grande and appointed John Slidell of Louisiana as envoy to offer Mexico: (1) extinction of American claims in exchange for the Rio Grande as the western boundary of Texas—the United States would not admit that the Rio Grande was not the southern boundary; (2) $5 million if Mexico would sell New Mexico; (3) $25 million if Mexico would sell California. But neither the existing administration nor a new one would even listen to Slidell's proposals. When he learned of his envoy's frustration, Polk in January 1846 ordered General Zachary Taylor to occupy the area between the Nueces and the Rio Grande.

Whigs asserted that this movement was a provocation which justified Mexico in attacking because Texas had never actually established her rule south of the Nueces. From the Mexican point of view, however, there was no boundary dispute because Texas in its entirety had never ceased to be a part of Mexico. Therefore they regarded the annexation itself a sufficient provocation. Some members of Polk's Cabinet were opposed to a war message until news came that Mexicans had crossed the Rio Grande in April and attacked Taylor, killing or wounding sixteen of his soldiers. Then they all supported Polk's statement that war, "notwithstanding all our efforts to avoid it, exists by the act of Mexico herself," since Mexico had "invaded our territory and shed American blood on American soil." Congress also approved it, promptly voting for war on May 13, 1846, by overwhelming majorities.

Soon opposition to the war, particularly among Northerners, was reflected in Congress by mounting antagonism which was climaxed by virtual refusal to make necessary appropriations. The great argument, which was pushed hard and gleefully by a young Whig Representative from Illinois named Abraham Lincoln, was that the Nueces-Rio Grande district was not actually American soil. But this argument seemed convincing to very few who were not opposed to the war on the much more significant ground that it would expand the slavery territory of the Union. An unbroken series of military victories was offset for Polk by sectional disunity at home. "Cotton Whigs" of the South and West joined Southern Democrats in support of the administration and the war effort; Free-Soil Democrats of the North and West joined "Conscience Whigs" and abolitionists in bitter opposition. Polk and the expansionists had hoped that their program would unify the country and silence sectionalism. Never was there a more fateful miscalculation. By 1847, Northerners seemed almost ready to embrace treason. They idolized Senator Thomas Corwin for his famous diatribe: "If I were a Mexican, I would tell you, 'Have you not room in your own country to bury your dead men? If you come into mine, we will greet you with bloody hands and welcome you to hospitable graves.'"

The Invasion of Mexico

It was difficult for the administration to maintain its attitude that the war was defensive while American armies invaded the very heart of Mexico and government agents worked to bring California into the Union. Mexican armies fought bravely, but they were poorly led and badly equipped. The small American Regular Army was rapidly expanded by volunteers and supplemented by militia regiments, particularly from the southern states. Fond of secret intrigue and usually unsuccessful at it, President Polk facilitated the return of Santa Anna from exile on the understanding that he would advocate peace. The slippery Mexican made himself president and took personal command of the army by promising war to the uttermost against the hated Americans. Polk was also unfortunate in that no American general was available for command

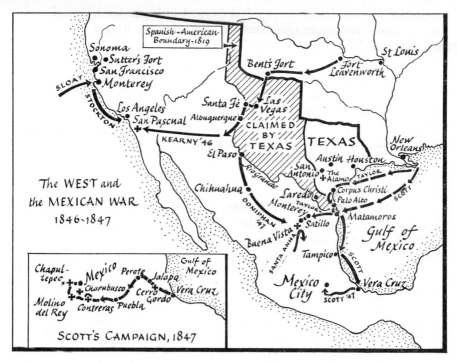

The WEST and the MEXICAN WAR 1846-1847

SCOTT'S CAMPAIGN, 1847

who was not a Whig and likely to conquer votes for the presidency in proportion to his military success. It was charged that Polk's strategy was designed to prevent any one of his generals from bagging too many victories.

This may account for the shift in plan from invasion by land under General Zachary Taylor to invasion by a seaborne expedition to Vera Cruz under General Winfield Scott. Taylor captured Matamoras on the south bank of the Rio Grande without trouble, then pushed into the interior and took Monterey on September 23, 1846, after several days of hard fighting. Santa Anna now came north with an army that out-numbered Taylor's by three to one and attacked him at Buena Vista. Late in February 1847, the Mexicans were defeated and "Old Rough and Ready," was well on the way to the presidency—aided by Whig journalists who glorified his sturdy, homespun ways and unkempt sub-stitutes for a general's uniform. Students of tactics believe that American morale rather than Taylor's generalship accounted for his victories. Polk criticized him for failing to follow them up with annihilating blows.

The President gave over-all command to Scott, who headed an ex-pedition from New Orleans in the spring. He took Vera Cruz and with ten thousand men retraced the path of Cortéz to ancient Tenochtitlan, Mexico City. Santa Anna appeared in the mountains at Jalapa with a new army. He was badly defeated at Cerro Gordo on April 18 and could not reorganize resistance until Scott had reached the final plateau. There the Mexicans fought desperately but in vain at Contreras, Churubusco, Molino del Rey, and, aided by boys of the military school, at Chapultepec. On September 14, 1847, United States Marines who had sung the frontier ballad "Green Grow the Lilacs" (hence "Gringos") all the way, posted guards in the "Halls of Montezuma"—the National Palace of Mexico City. The victory was so complete that only scattered guerrilla bands offered resistance anywhere in Mexico.

California

The extreme wing of American expansionists advocated annexation of all Mexico and Polk pondered the possibility. His minimum terms became clear from events in California. As early as June 1845, Commodore John Drake Sloat on the Pacific station had received secret orders to seize San Francisco if war occurred. The consul at Monterey, Thomas O. Larkin, received broad hints from Washington in October that a revolt against Mexican rule by Americans in California would be welcome. Polk's diary makes clear that when he failed to buy California from Mexico he made up his mind to take it by war, but he preferred to use devious methods. In the spring of 1846, he sent Captain John C. Frémont, "The Pathfinder of the West," in charge of an exploring expedition across the Sierra Nevada. Frémont had no orders to foment rebellion, but he defied the Mexican authorities who ordered him out of California, his presence encouraged American rebels, and he accepted leadership of the "Bear Flag Revolution" of June 14, 1846, the moment he heard that war had been declared. On July 7, Commodore Sloat proclaimed the annexation of California to the United States.

In rapid succession Commodore R. F. Stockton arrived by sea with authority over naval and land forces, and Colonel Stephen W. Kearny came by land claiming authority over Stockton. Kearny marched from Fort Leavenworth, took Santa Fé without a battle, proclaimed New Mexico part of the United States, and arrived in California with five hundred soldiers in time to suppress Mexican resistance. The confusion of authority resulted from Polk's ambiguous orders, but by 1847 California was securely in the hands of American forces. Then began that spectacular process whereby the sleepy Mexican-Indian culture centered around Catholic missions was transformed in three years into a lusty American state attracting gold hunters from all over the world.

But until more was known about the geography of this new Southwest and the discovery of gold had attracted a population to California which was not interested in slavery, it was expected that the region would yield the South an indefinite number of slave states. James Russell Lowell in his *Biglow Papers* saw this as the purpose of the administration's policy:

> They just want this Californy
>   So's to lug new Slave-states in
> To abuse ye, an' to scorn ye,
>   An' to plunder ye like sin.

But Polk himself was motivated by broadly nationalist ambition and appalled by the extremists of both North and South who turned his triumphs into an occasion for sectional fanaticism. He longed to reach out for more of Mexico, but even a "modest" program aroused such fearful clamor that he accepted a peace treaty he had intended to repudiate.

Treaty of Guadalupe Hidalgo

Polk at first labored under the strange conception that the war was merely a means to force the Mexicans to accept the friendly diplomatic overtures of the United States which they had spurned, or as he put it, "to conquer a peace." Therefore, throughout the war he held out money to Mexican leaders in the mistaken belief that because they were often venal they could be bribed into abandoning resistance to invasion. Nicholas P. Trist was sent along with Scott's army to Mexico City as executive agent empowered to conclude a treaty. Scott quarreled with Trist, while the Mexican leaders refused to negotiate and in fact were encouraged by his overtures to believe that the United States was weakening in its war effort. After the capture of Mexico City, Trist could find no officials claiming competence to sign a treaty. In the United States, enthusiasts were crying for the annexation of all Mexico. Polk recalled Trist in October 1847, and thereby opened the door to stiffer peace terms.

Trist, however, refused to be recalled. Finding some Mexican officials who, after Santa Anna's abdication, were willing to accept money in return for a treaty, the agent proceeded to negotiate with them according to his original instructions. As he stated to Polk, the alternative was a prolonged guerrilla campaign. On February 2, 1848, he signed at Guadalupe Hidalgo an agreement which confirmed American title to Texas as far as the Rio Grande, ceded New Mexico and California to the United States and, in return for the latter cession, provided that the United States should assume the old claims of its citizens against Mexico to the amount of $3.25 million and pay Mexico $15 million besides. It is not usual for the victor in a war to pay the vanquished government for peace or territory, and the matter has been explained as a case of "bad conscience" or of "typical American generosity." Actually the Treaty of

Guadalupe Hidalgo represents the accidental projection of Polk's original war aims into a new political situation.

Polk was intensely indignant over Trist's disobedience. When the treaty arrived in Washington, however, it was clear not only that repudiation was impractical but that Northern opponents of the war would very likely refuse further appropriations for the armed forces. James Buchanan, Secretary of State, and Secretary of the Treasury Robert J. Walker advised Polk to reject the treaty because it did not cede enough territory. Polk suspected that Buchanan, who had earlier opposed expansion, wanted to gain Southern support for the Democratic presidential nomination, and he knew that Walker spoke for the extreme proslavery expansionists. On the other hand, the more realistic Calhoun perceived that Mexico was not a promising field for slave labor and had opposed the war in the first place.

The sectional controversy in Congress had focused in the "Wilmot Proviso"—that slavery should not be permitted in any new territory that might be acquired from Mexico. This failed in the Senate but its passage by the House was a storm warning. Polk wisely decided that repudiation of Trist's Treaty in the hope of taking more territory would only intensify the sectional conflict and risk failure as well as disunion, whereas the treaty would isolate extremists of both sides and rally support for moderation. On these statesmanlike grounds he sent it to the Senate. His hopes were borne out and the Senate approved the Treaty of Guadalupe Hidalgo on March 10, 1848, by a vote of 38 to 14. Only diehards who wanted all of Mexico and those who wanted no territory at all voted against it.

The question of organizing the new territories remained. It disrupted Congress and the country during Polk's last months in office. He had refused to stand for renomination, and he attempted to use his position above the battle to make up for the "inadequate" gains of the Treaty by picking up more territory. A petty civil war in Yucatan gave him an opportunity to ask Congress to consider intervention, but the Yucatecans settled their troubles before debate had gone far. Polk offered the Queen of Spain $100 million for Cuba but her minister answered that Spain would rather see the "Pearl of the Antilles" sunk in the ocean. Cuba, where slavery was extremely profitable on the great sugar plantations, was greedily eyed by proslavery expansionists, while its annexation was fiercely opposed by antagonists of slavery. Polk's attempt to buy it argues that his nationalist ambitions were uncowed by the sectionalism the Mexican War had aroused. Exhausted, ill, and discouraged despite his high percentage of domestic and foreign successes, Polk died shortly after he left the White House in the belief that his administration had been a failure.

Modern historians are inclined to regard him on the evidence of his diary as an able and conscientious executive, and as the outstanding President between Jackson and Lincoln. On the domestic side he revived the Jeffersonian policies of low tariffs and refusal to accord federal aid to banks and internal improvements, inaugurating the sixteen-year epoch of laissez faire which was the last in American history. In foreign relations he matched the successes of the negotiators of the Treaty of Paris of 1783 and the Louisiana Purchase Treaty of 1803, adding the last third to the national domain and fixing the continental boundaries in the Northwest (except for Alaska) and the Southwest (except for the bit that Gadsden obtained from Mexico in 1853), boundaries whose "logical" contours on the map have filled and satisfied the eyes of Americans ever since.

But no one can regard the Civil War as other than a tragedy and it remains debatable whether Polk was not right in another sense in saying that his administration was a failure. His bold expansionism precipitated the sectional issues which the wisdom of the next dozen years was incapable of solving peacefully. Polk went home to die, while Lee and Grant, George B. McClellan and Thomas J. Jackson, along with many another young American officer who had served with Scott or Taylor, stored in their memories the military lessons they had learned in Mexico.

CHAPTER 30

Crisis and Compromise
1846-1852

BEHIND THE ISSUES BETWEEN THE POLK ADMINISTRATION and the opposition, between Democrats and Whigs, lay deeper and more dangerous ones between Northerners and Southerners. But the Compromise of 1850 preserved the Union and ushered in a period of apparent domestic peace and unquestionable national prosperity. During the Mexican War the sectional conflict over the future territories found a focus in the Wilmot Proviso, and in the years immediately following the Compromise this was replaced by the Fugitive Slave Law, the most controversial feature of the settlement. At a time of relative political calm, criticism of this law and of the slave system which gave it birth found effective voice in one of the most influential books ever published in the United States, *Uncle Tom's Cabin*. In this a humane romanticist wrote a disruptive epilogue to the great Compromise which statesmen had deemed realistic and had hoped would be enduring.

THE WILMOT PROVISO AND WHAT IT SIGNIFIED

The Wilmot Proviso took its name from a Democratic Congressman from Pennsylvania, David Wilmot, who introduced it in the summer of 1846 as an amendment to a bill appropriating money for negotiations with Mexico. Following the language of the Northwest Ordinance of 1787, it specified that slavery should be prohibited for all time in any territories that might be acquired from Mexico. Wilmot was a Jacksonian and, like many other Northern Democrats, was embarrassed by the Southern leadership of the party after the eclipse of Van Buren. The low-tariff policy, which Wilmot had supported, was becoming a political handicap in Pennsylvania, and throughout the North there was a growing protest against the seeming proslavery trend of the administration. The Proviso was in the first place an expression of Northern independence, and its introduction by a Democrat rather than a Whig clearly indicated that sectional issues were cutting across party lines. The amendment was accepted by the House but failed to pass the Senate. During the rest of Polk's term it was reintroduced repeatedly in one form or another and always met the same fate. Lincoln boasted that as a Congressman he voted for it more than forty times.

The Proviso was based on the assumption that Congress had the right to prohibit slavery in the territories. Southerners had rarely challenged this before now, just as few responsible Northern leaders had questioned the constitutional right of a state to control its domestic institutions. But from this time on Southern leaders increasingly denied Congressional authority to restrict slavery in the territories, and this new doctrine became a test of sectional orthodoxy. When the Proviso was presented a second time, passed by the House, and defeated in the Senate, Calhoun presented (1847) the doctrine in resolutions which he did not expect to be adopted but was sure would be widely promulgated. The territories, he said, belonged to all the states, and there could be no discrimination within them against any state. More specifically, the right of any citizen to carry his slave property into the territories could not be impaired, and any Congressional action to that effect would be a breach of the Constitution and subversion of the Union. On constitutional grounds he regretted the Missouri Compromise, though on practical grounds he would be willing to extend it to the Pacific.

In Alabama the next year, resolutions that were drawn by William L. Yancey and adopted by a state Democratic convention were more strongly phrased and went a step further. Besides repudiating the Missouri Compromise and threatening secession if the Proviso should become law, which Calhoun had not done, these asserted that it was the duty of Congress to *protect* slavery during the territorial stage, although the right of a state to prohibit slavery when it emerged from the territorial stage was not questioned and could not be consistently under the logic of state rights. This position was approved by various Southern legislatures and conventions, but it was generally regarded as extreme and not for some years did Yancey succeed in making it orthodox doctrine in the Lower South.

At the time that the Wilmot Proviso was first introduced, nobody knew for certain what regions would be acquired by war or negotiation. Yet a realistic appraisal of the prospects should have enabled partisans on both sides to perceive the unlikehihood of adding lands suitable to the crops then cultivated by slave labor. Many modern historians have sensed unreality in this heated debate over the extension of the area of slavery, and they have wondered why so many Northerners thought the Wilmot Proviso necessary and so many Southerners found it intolerable. Quite obviously it had become the symbol of the larger conflict between Northern sectionalism, which assumed the mantle of constitutional nationalism, and Southern sectionalism, which had donned for good the constitutional armor of state rights. Criticism of the Proviso in the South lost no votes there, while championship of it lost none in the North. The situation presented large opportunities for the political exploitation of local and sectional patriotism.

The great emphasis that was laid on the Constitution throughout this sectional conflict is a sign of the reverence which all Americans felt for that document, but in view of the strong tendency of constitutional arguments to follow geographical lines it may be safely assumed that the basic disagreement was considerably more than constitutional. To many Northerners whose sincerity cannot be questioned the fundamental issue was moral. If slavery was a sin, as the abolitionists had so long asserted, the federal government should not be a party to its extension. This attitude was accentuated by the interpretation of the war as a slave-owners' conspiracy. But Southerners indignantly repudiated the allegation of sectional immorality; and, for much the same reason, they regarded the Wilmot Proviso as a gratuitous insult.

The struggle for the western lands has often been interpreted in economic terms. Much has been made of the land-hunger of the cotton planters, which was unquestionably real, and of the dynamic character of the plantation system. There was little chance of carrying it into the new Southwest, however, and if the Southern expansionists had that in mind they were chasing a will-o-wisp across the deserts. On the Northen side, there was the desire to have access to fresh lands without fear of slave competition. Northerners wanted to extend the empire of liberty, but most of them did not want free Negroes in it; as their actions showed, most people wanted the territories kept for free *white* people. Under Southern leadership the tariff had been lowered and the Bank defeated, and the administration was indifferent to Northern and Western clamor for cheap or free public lands. The maintenance of a political balance between North and South, when the former was gaining so rapidly in population, seemed inequitable on the one hand while seeming necessary for local safety on the other. Northerners could not forget that the South had more representatives in Congress than the voting population warranted, because of the three-fifths ratio for slaves. In this sense, much of the Southern power was slave power, and this was resented.

Majority rule was basic in the American tradition, and it was to the neutralizing of this by means of devices and interpretations to protect the minority that the powerful mind of Calhoun had turned. With the pessimism which had become so characteristic of him, he predicted that when the balance between the slaveholding and nonslaveholding states was destroyed, "political revolution, anarchy, civil war, and widespread disaster" would follow. He emphasized the importance of the South as the conservative portion of the Union, which it had become since Jefferson's day. But his arguments never strayed far from slavery, which he defended not merely as the inescapabale alternative to social revolution, but also as a positive good. He continued to oppose the disunionist leaders in his own state and section, but by the very aggressiveness of his defense of Southern institutions he ultimately played into their hands, as he now did into those of Northern sectionalists, who could make of antislavery sentiment such an effective weapon.

Southern fears of the results from the loss of political power now seem exaggerated—unless we assume as Calhoun did that the growing Northern majority would be unreasonable and that in the end Southern domestic institutions would be overthrown without consideration of local consequences. On the other hand, Northern fears of Southern aggression seem excessive in view of the practical certainty of Northern political preponderance, barring the actual increase in slavery through the acquisition of such a region as Cuba. If the Union was to be preserved the times called for mutual trust and patience, but the extremists on both sides accentuated the danger by raising the slavery issue on occasions when it was not pertinent.

When the question of organizing Oregon Territory came up in 1847, the slavery issue was injected into the debate, despite the fact that everyone should have known that the climate and the views of the settlers there made slavery virtually impossible. The principle of the Wilmot Proviso was written into the Bill and passed both Houses, further angering Southerners. A little later the Oregon legislature forbade the entrance of free Negroes into this free territory.

Polk wanted the issue settled for all the new territories by extending the Missouri Compromise Line to the Pacific Coast. This arrangement might have prevented the Civil War, but sentiment was rapidly forming around the fateful alternative that slavery was either right everywhere or wrong everywhere. Senator Lewis Cass of Michigan made the ingenious proposal that the settlers in each territory should be allowed to decide for themselves whether to protect or to forbid slavery. This doctrine of popular sovereignty—contemptuously called "squatter sovereignty" by Calhoun—appealed to basic faith in self-government and commanded the support of a majority of the people during the next decade until experience in Kansas showed that it was unworkable. Then advocates of federal protection of slavery in all territories captured the South and advocates of federal prohibition of slavery in all territories captured the North. Civil war followed. Such a tragic outcome came plainly into view during the Mexican War, and some patriotic leaders sought to forestall it.

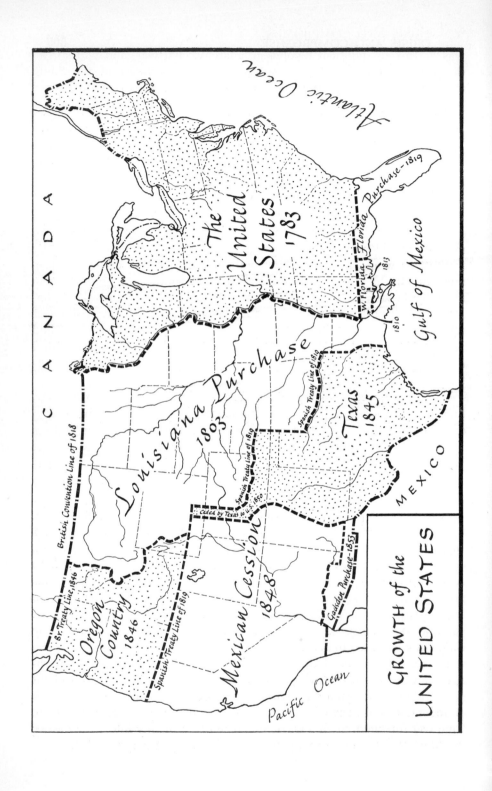

CANADA

Atlantic Ocean

The United States 1783

W. Florida Purchase - 1819

1813

1810

Gulf of Mexico

Louisiana Purchase 1803

Spanish Treaty Line of 1819

Texas 1845

Spanish Treaty Line of 1819

MEXICO

British Convention Line of 1818

Br. Treaty Line, 1846

Oregon Country 1846

Spanish Treaty Line of 1819

Ceded by Texas to U.S. 1850

Mexican Cession 1848

Gadsden Purchase - 1853

Pacific Ocean

GROWTH of the UNITED STATES

THE ELECTION OF 1848 AND ITS AFTERMATH

Far from uniting the country or the party in power, the successful Mexican War served to divide both, and the conclusion inevitably follows that the President lacked the quality of effective popular leadership which Jackson had displayed so conspicuously. Dissension was most pronounced in New York, where the Democrats split into the "Barnburners" (the Van Buren wing, supporting the principle of the Wilmot Proviso) and the administration group known as "Hunkers." The term "doughface" came to be applied in the North to any man charged with being pro-Southern; and, even more than hitherto, the term "free-soiler" was applied to pronounced opponents of the extension of slavery territory, regardless of their political affiliation. The Barnburners and Hunkers sent rival delegations from New York to the Democratic National Convention, and at length the former withdrew. The nomination by the Democrats of Senator Lewis Cass of Michigan, whom the Barnburners regarded as "a Northern man with Southern principles," was objectionable to them, and the end result was the nomination of Van Buren by the Free-Soil Party.

In the division of their foes lay the hope of the Whigs, who had been so often defeated on the historic issues of the Bank, the tariff, and internal improvements. They revived the only political formula on which they had ever gained victory in a presidential election: the nomination of a popular military man whose political sentiments were so vague and uncertain that he excited no opposition because of these. They seized upon General Zachary Taylor, the most popular figure of the war. To old-line leaders of the party like Webster and Clay, who so far surpassed him in political experience, he seemed wholly devoid of qualifications for the highest public office; and the military services of General Winfield Scott had actually been greater. But "Old Fuss and Feathers" could not match the popularity of "Old Rough and Ready," whose sturdy qualities and unpretentious ways had made of him a folk hero. Taylor, a Virginian by birth and technically a resident of Louisiana, had spent most of his mature life on the frontier, and his military record virtually constituted the party platform. To balance the ticket which this Southern slaveowner headed, the Whigs nominated for Vice-President Millard Fillmore of New York, who was regarded as a free-soiler.

No party that was bidding for national support could afford to be aggressively pro-Northern or pro-Southern, and both the Whigs and the Democrats were prudently evasive. The Free-Soil Party was the only positive one, and in the North, the only section where it operated, it drew more votes from the Democrats than from the Whigs. Van Buren carried no state, but in New York he got more votes than Cass, and this Democratic split in New York was decisive. Taylor carried the state for the

Whigs, and its electoral vote represented his margin of victory. Taylor was the victor in a number of southern states, on the other hand, because he was a Southerner. His popular majority was small and he actually carried more slave states than free. In terms of the conflict between North and South, the country as a whole seemed to favor an evasive or compromising policy, but the free-soil group (in or out of the Free-Soil Party) held the balance of power in the North.

To Calhoun the demonstrated influence of this aggressive and wholly Northern group was the main lesson of the election, and his dominant purpose henceforth was to build a Southern party which would disregard Whig and Democratic affiliations and prevent adverse federal action by its cohesiveness. In December 1848, a New York Congressman, a Conscience Whig, presented a resolution against the slave trade in the District of Columbia which irritated even the milder Southerners by its wording, and this led the Representatives from the slave states to set up a Congressional committee of fifteen. Under these auspices Calhoun drafted an address to the Southern people, in which he presented his fears that Northern dominance of the Union would result in Negro dominance of the South. The offensive resolution was blocked and the Southern Address was widely circulated. It framed a sectional platform for the future, and it remained a call for Southern unity. As he had done previously, Calhoun took the position that the federal government had no right either to establish or abolish slavery, no right to distinguish between the domestic institutions of states or sections. Speaking more moderately than a Yancey or Rhett would have done, while buttressing his constitutional position strongly, he said that Southerners insisted, not that slavery be extended, but that slaveowners should not be prohibited from migrating with their property to the territories. He was still speaking to the question raised by the Wilmot Proviso, regarding this as crucial. Meanwhile, the question of slavery and the slave trade in the District of Columbia—which was clearly subject to Congressional action—had been raised.

Certain national leaders in both parties, and especially Henry Clay, saw the central significance of the election in the preference of the large majority of Americans for a policy which would minimize theoretical differences and preserve national unity by evasiveness or compromise. Zachary Taylor, however, seemed oblivious of the peril of the Union; and it soon appeared that he relied most on the New Yorkers who had led the Taylor movement in the East—Senator William H. Seward and that great manipulator, Thurlow Weed. Their free-soil emphasis soon overbore any Southern sympathies the inexperienced President may have had and worked against the more realistic philosophy of the old-time Whig leaders.

The Territorial Crisis

The crisis which the new administration had to face arose from the problem of organizing, at a time when sectional antagonism was acute, the vast region that had been acquired from Mexico. Texas was now fully established as a state and the war had decided once and for all the question of her southern boundary, but her western boundary was disputed by settlers around Santa Fé, and the state was confronted with serious financial problems. North of the lands acquired from Mexico was Oregon. It had been provided with a territorial government in circumstances which had wounded Southern sensibilities without gaining for the North any advantage that section did not have already. The region below the 42nd parallel and extending westward from the boundary of Texas was without political organization.

Part of this was California, though nobody knew just how much, and all the rest was called New Mexico. Under ordinary circumstances, the missions and haciendas that were set down here and there in this huge land of deserts and bare mountains might perhaps have been safely left to slumber in the sun for a while longer; and the vigorous group of Mormons who had established the State of Deseret in the Salt Lake Valley while the ownership of that region was uncertain preferred to escape notice and follow their own political and religious inclinations. But the discovery of gold in California and the unparalleled rapidity of settlement there forced the territorial question onto the center of the stage and made immediate federal action unavoidable.

The discovery of gold at Sutter's mill in the lower Sacramento Valley in late January 1848 antedated by a few days the signing of the Treaty of Guadalupe-Hidalgo, but the Mexicans did not yet realize what riches they were giving up, nor the Americans what they were gaining. News of the discovery was kept quiet at first, and through most of the year the gold rush was a matter for Californians only. But in December 1848 the Director of the United States Mint reported on the high quality of deposits of gold just received from California, and President Polk referred to the discovery in his last annual message to Congress. Then the news became nation-wide and world-wide, and in 1849 the flood began. Prospectors and adventurers and other Forty-niners took the overland route; some went to Chagres by water, crossed the Isthmus to Panama, and then sailed north to the Golden Gate; others made the long voyage around Cape Horn; and nobody got there as soon as he had hoped and expected. With incredible speed the most colorful and fantastic chapter in the whole history of American expansion was being written. San Francisco immediately became a fabulous city as native Californians, Chileans, Hawaiians, and Chinese were joined in its steep streets by every variety of American and many Europeans. Within a few months a town of tents grew into a gaudy metropolis, where gold dust was used for currency and everybody believed that mankind had finally found Eldorado.

In this intoxicating air, excess was inevitable and the need for civil government became imperative. California was ready for statehood before she had had time to become a territory. This polyglot society was incurably individualistic and democratic. Bayard Taylor, correspondent for the *New York Tribune*, summed it up in three words: "Labor is respectable." There was very slight chance that the plantation system of the cotton country would find a replica here. In September 1849, with the blessing of President Taylor though without Congressional authorization, a convention met and it soon framed a constitution which was ratified by popular vote in November. This constitution excluded slavery. Judging from the census returns of the next year, the population was climbing toward 100,000. Obviously, something had to be done about California by the Congress which assembled in December 1849, and the natural thing was to regularize the irregular procedure by formally recognizing the *fait accompli*. The admission of this golden land as a free state could hardly be objected to on state-rights grounds, but it would upset the long-established sectional balance and throw the slave states into the minority in the Senate as they already were in the House of Representatives.

During the year 1849, while Northern legislatures were putting themselves on record in favor of the Wilmot Proviso and urging the abolition of the slave trade in the District of Columbia, Southern groups were passing resolutions requesting state governors to call legislatures in the event of Congressional action on either question, and some of the language was very threatening. These were symbolic issues, but Southerners coupled with them references to Northern obstruction to the recovery of runaway slaves. Even the Virginians were bellicose; and in South Carolina in the spring, Committees of Vigilance and Safety were organized throughout the state. Southern sectional prospects seemed even more clouded in the fall, as the gold rush surged on. It was then that a Mississippi convention, following an earlier suggestion of Calhoun's, issued a call for a convention, to meet at Nashville in June 1850 to consider Southern rights and problems. The prospect of this gathering hung over Congress as a threat when it met in December 1849. By that time the Wilmot Proviso had become a meaningless issue with respect to California, since the people there had spoken for themselves, but the sectional antagonism in Washington was dangerously real. Three weeks were consumed in organizing the House of Representatives. Sixty-three ballots were required for the election of the supposedly moderate Howell Cobb of Georgia as Speaker, and many free-soilers took this as an affront.

The Compromise of 1850

It seemed to President Taylor that territorial questions could be settled piecemeal without regard to other sectional issues. He favored the admission of California on the basis of her new constitution, and this policy had the full support of free-soilers. But representatives of the slave states could object on grounds of constitutional irregularity, and it seemed to them that their section had everything to lose and nothing to gain from this single action. Hence they were disposed to be obstructionist in the absence of compensation elsewhere. The political merit of the proposals of Henry Clay in the Senate early in the year lay in the fact that they added up to a sectional compromise on matters in immediate dispute. In his "package deal," he tried to hold the sectional balance as even as possible, hoping to win over the large body of moderate opinion against the extremists in both sections. Clay, who was now seventy-three, had had himself again elected to the Senate after some years' absence. If the Union was as gravely endangered as he believed it to be, this was probably the greatest service of his long career.

On January 29, 1850, this intensely practical and thoroughly patriotic leader presented eight resolutions which were debated for some weeks before being referred to a committee. They differed somewhat in form and detail, though not in spirit, from the five bills that were passed during the summer and constitute what is known as the Compromise of 1850. In sum, Clay proposed and Congress finally decided: (1) to admit California as a state without reference to slavery—that is, as a free state by her own choice; (2) to provide territorial government for the rest of the acquisition from Mexico, again without reference to slavery—since the institution seemed most unlikely to spread there; (3) to draw the lines of Texas so as to exclude New Mexico, and in return to assume the debts of Texas; (4) to prohibit the slave trade, but not slavery, in the District of Columbia; (5) to strengthen the fugitive slave law. These proposals ruled out the Wilmot Proviso as unnecessary; they originally contained a statement that Congress should not interfere with the domestic slave trade (except in the District of Columbia); and by including the provision about fugitive slaves they met the strongest immediate demand of the slave states. On the other hand, they upset the balance of states in favor of the North while assuming that slavery would not spread in the remaining territories.

The Great Debate and Its Effects

The debate on these resolutions and the bills resulting from them was one of the most impressive in American history. For the last time the trio of Senatorial giants—Clay, Calhoun, and Webster—appeared together. The general alignment was that of the two extremes against the middle. Free-soilers like William H. Seward of New York and Salmon P. Chase of Ohio opposed the Compromise, as did advocates of Southern rights like Calhoun and Jefferson Davis of Mississippi. But the middle group stood for it—led by Clay, Webster, and Stephen A. Douglas. These leaders were supported by Southern Whigs, and by moderate Southern Democrats—such as Henry S. Foote of Mississippi in the Senate, and Speaker Howell Cobb of Georgia in the House. Clay used the language of common sense in the name of common patriotism, but the moral absolutists of the North and the constitutional absolutists of the South were against him.

The most notable Southern speech against the Compromise was that of Calhoun. This was his swan song and his colleague, Senator James M. Mason of Virginia, had to sing it for him while Calhoun sat grim and motionless, knowing that his end was near. He died within the month, and Clay and Webster were among the pallbearers at the funeral in the Senate chamber. Almost his last words were: "The South, the poor South." His final speech followed his characteristic line of pessimism and it was more a discussion of larger sectional grievances than of the specific points at issue. By this time he had written his *Disquisition on Government* and nearly finished his longer *Discourse on the Constitution and Government of the United States*. In these treatises he set down for posterity his doctrine of the "concurrent majority," by means of which the "numerical majority" would be supplemented, and each division or interest within the government be given "either a concurrent voice in making or executing the laws, or a veto on their execution." In practical terms, he was trying to devise a legal mechanism for the protection, not merely of the Southern interest against the growing numerical majority of the North, but also of the right of local self-determination of any part of the Union against the potential tyranny of the rest. In his final speech he referred to the insertion in the Constitution of a provision which would "restore" to the South her power of self-protection, without saying just what this should be. Some supposed he meant a dual executive.

The prevailing opinion since his time has been that such protective devices as he described in his treatises would have rendered the government unworkable. But, divorced from the issue of slavery, his thought has appealed to many later foes of consolidated power and advocates of decentralization. The historic tragedy of Calhoun lay not merely in his inability to adjust himself to the economic and constitutional trends of his time and in his championing of an anachronistic institution to which he could see no alternative. Actually he had attempted what would be impossible in any age: to devise instrumentalities which can *guarantee* that the power of numerical majorities will never be abused. Nonethe-

SAM HOUSTON

1793-1863

The stalwart father of Texas—
president of the short-lived
Republic, first governor of the
Lone Star state.

MEXICAN WAR. General Taylor at the Battle of Buena Vista, February 1847.

SKATING IN CENTRAL PARK, NEW YORK, 1860. *Painting by Winslow Homer.*

*The carefree enjoyment of genteel
Northerners and the security of
Southern plantation owners were soon
to be shattered by the coming of war*

"THE SHADOWS," near NEW IBERIA, LOUISIANA. An example of
neoclassicism in the Deep South, built in 1831.

LINCOLN-DOUGLAS DEBATE, Summer of 1859. This contemporary drawing indicates the intense public interest in the contest between the two leading statesmen of the era.

ADVERTISEMENT FOR

"UNCLE TOM'S CABIN."

That this provocative book was a runaway best seller is verified by the sales figures listed here.

less, the doctrine of the concurrent majority has often been honored in practice while denied in theory, and American history shows many instances where a militant minority has checked the majority will. At this time many thought of him primarily as the voice of such a minority; and to many he sounded like an embittered sectionalist. His colleague Webster saw far more than that in him, however, and that statesman's rejoinder recognized more Southern grievances than free-soilers would admit and won him praise in the South which was denied him in many Northern quarters.

Webster's Seventh-of-March speech is the most famous of all these speeches and was probably the most effective. The greatest of the orators spoke not as a Massachusetts man, not as a Northerner, but as an American, and his main concern was to preserve the Union. He strongly condemned the abolitionists, and saw no need to legislate against slavery in the Southwest, since that region was dedicated to freedom by the ordinance of Nature and the will of God. Unlike the free-soilers and abolitionists, he sedulously avoided the tone of moral superiority and went out of his way to be concilatory—too far, some Northerners thought. He approved the strengthening of the fugitive slave law, as a protection of legal property under constitutional right. Some of his critics overlooked the severity of Webster's condemnation of disunionism and the grandeur of his praise of the Union which gave to his speech its enduring worth. Whittier termed him "Ichabod," Emerson mourned his apostasy, and the abolitionists turned their heaviest artillery on him, but the great middle group in both sections approved. If he erred it was on the side of conciliation, and he believed that the transcendent cause of the Union demanded that.

Jefferson Davis was stiffly uncompromising in the debate. On the other side, Seward was so confident of the triumph of Northern "progress" that he saw no need for concessions; and he referred to a "higher law" than the Constitution, implying that the advocates of a righteous cause need not be deterred by legalities. Senator Stephen A. Douglas invoked the doctrine of "popular sovereignty" which was to excite controversy later in the decade.

The predominant effect of the discussion of compromise was the growth of hope, and this served to restrain the Southern Convention in Nashville in June. Nine slave states were represented, most of these only sparsely, and the current Southern philosophy about the right of access to the territories was asserted in the form which had already become standard. But the tone of the meeting was far more moderate than disunionists like Robert Barnwell Rhett and Edmund Ruffin and Beverly Tucker had expected. The Convention expressed willingness to accept, as an extreme concession, the line of the Missouri Compromise extended to the Pacific, and referred to the disruption of the Union as a shameful climax which it was the paramount duty of Congress to avoid.

The Achievement of Compromise

As summer came on, the chief remaining obstacle to the success of the Compromise was the stubborn opposition of the President, who still wanted to tackle these territorial questions singly and, under Seward's influence, came to an open breach with Clay. Not only had he encouraged the Californians to move toward statehood without Congressional authorization; he was doing the same sort of thing with the much less numerous inhabitants of New Mexico before their boundary dispute with Texas had been disposed of. His lack of foresight was shown by his desire that this sparsely-settled region should skip the territorial stage altogether. At the instance of the commander of the United States forces in New Mexico, a convention was held there in May and it adopted a free-state constitution. Southern Whigs were aghast at this precipitate action, and there was real danger of a shooting war with the Texans, who were trying to extend their authority over the Santa Fé settlement. In a special message to Congress, Taylor expressed the conviction that the United States should maintain possession of the disputed district until the boundary question was settled. Robert Toombs and Alexander H. Stephens, representing the Southern Whigs, threatened the complete withdrawal of their political support if he should use force in these circumstances. The old soldier was unyielding in the face of a virtual ultimatum, and seemed oblivious of the danger that a clash between the irate Texans and United States troops might have been the signal for civil war.

He was preparing a message on this subject and was on the point of reorganizing his Cabinet, which had been shaken by a scandal arising from the generous settlement by the Treasury of certain claims from which the Secretary of War profited, when on July 9 he laid down his arms for good. The President had exposed himself too much in the heat of July 4, and then he had imbibed too freely of iced drinks and eaten cherries. His death was attributed to cholera morbus. The sudden passing of this national military hero was deeply mourned, but he had been clearly inadequate as a statesman and his death at this time was fortunate for his own fame and the country's peace. His successor, Millard Fillmore, had been nominated in the first place as a free-soiler, but he had already announced his support of the Compromise. The reorganization of the Cabinet was made by him, not by Taylor, and his reliance on the old Whigs, rather than Seward and his group, was shown by his appointment of Webster as Secretary of State.

There was no longer any reason why Northern Whigs should oppose

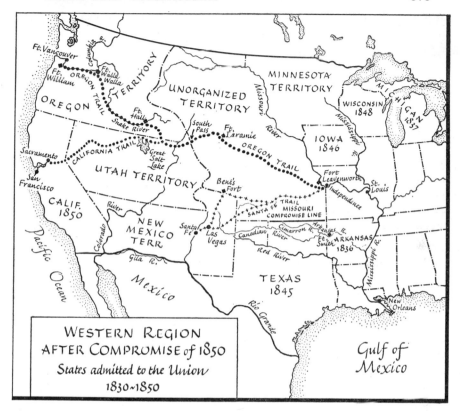

WESTERN REGION
AFTER COMPROMISE of 1850
States admitted to the Union
1830~1850

the Compromise out of deference to the President, hence more of them now swung to its support. The five bills which came to comprise the Compromise were guided through the Senate by Stephen A. Douglas, in Clay's absence for recuperation from an illness. Without much difficulty they went through the House and in September all of them were signed by Fillmore. It had been decided to create two territories in the Southwest instead of one, in order to provide for the Mormon settlements around Great Salt Lake. The region was divided between Utah and New Mexico, and the territorial bills stipulated that when admitted as states they should be received with or without slavery as their constitutions might prescribe. Slavery had disappeared as an American institution long before they reached the stage of statehood. Meanwhile, the boundaries of Texas were drawn as they still are, which are magnificent enough, and that state received $10 million.

The long-range significance of the Compromise, in terms of the sectional controversy, can be clearly seen in the statistics of the decade that followed it. Had a clash between the Texans and the United States army led in 1850 to a shooting war, the advantage on the Northern side would have been considerably less than it was ten years later. In population the free states had an advantage over the slave states of about 4 million in 1850; and in 1860 they were ahead by 7 million. No allowance is made for the border states in this calculation of relative population, but if there was any change in their attitude during the period it was to attach them more closely to the Northern side. Considerations of trade, transportation, and economic developmment lead to similar conclusions about relative growth. The South moved forward in the 1850's but at no such rapid pace as the North. In 1860, Western ties with the North were far stronger than they had been ten years earlier. In retrospect, it seems clear that almost any sort of delay was to the North's advantage, and increased the probability of the endurance of the Union. This in itself was a sufficient warrant for the pragmatism of Clay and Webster and a sufficient answer to the free-soil intransigents.

ACCEPTANCE OF THE COMPROMISE, 1850-1852

Qualified Acceptance in the South

To extremists like Rhett and Yancey it seemed that the South had sealed its own subordination and legalized its own defeat. If the relationship between the sections during these years is thought of as one of rivalry and conflict in which there must be eventual supremacy or subordination, victory or defeat, these men were correct in their judgment. The settlement of the territorial question amounted to little more than a recognition of the actualities of the situation, and it is for just this reason that to relatively dispassionate students of later generations this settlement has seemed largely a matter of common sense. Still it destroyed the equilibrium in the Senate which had been an axiom of Southern policy ever since the Missouri Compromise. There were now sixteen free states and fifteen slave states, and there was little reason to believe that there would be any more of the latter within the continental limits of the country, whatever hopes local politicians might hold out. The removal of the slave-trade depots from the District of Columbia was a genuine relief to many Southern representatives, who themselves preferred to keep the domestic slave trade out of sight, but this could be regarded as a step against the interstate traffic which would be followed by others. The major significance of the entire Compromise was that it preserved the Union as the political framework within which both sections might be prosperous and happy under conditions of greater mutual tolerance and patience. But in strict sectional terms as men commonly used them, the only Southern gain consisted in the new Fugitive Slave Law. At the sparsely attended and little-noted second session of the Nashville Convention in the autumn the settlement was condemned, and there was strong disunionist sentiment in parts of the Lower South during the next few months. But Rhett and Yancey were overborne by more moderate men, the lead being taken by the state of Georgia.

In this important state, Unionist Whigs like Robert Toombs and Alexander H. Stephens combined with Unionist Democrats like Howell Cobb to dominate a state convention that met in December. The resolutions adopted by that body have come to be known as the "Georgia Platform of 1850." These stated that Georgia, while not wholly approving the Compromise, would abide by it as a "permanent adjustment" of the sectional controversy. Similar expressions were being frequently used in the North about this time, but these Georgians left no doubt that their acceptance of the settlement was conditional. They listed a series of possible future actions by Congress which Georgia would resist to a "disruption of every tie" which bound her to the Union. What they meant, in effect, was that there should be no further federal action against slavery—that, so far as Congress was concerned, this settlement must be regarded as final. The concluding resolution voiced Unionist sentiments in what sounded like an ultimatum: it expressed the deliberate opinion of the Convention "that upon the faithful execution of the Fugitive Slave Bill by the proper authorities, depends the preservation of our much loved Union."

It is doubtful that the generality of Georgians were as firm in their opinions as these formal resolutions of their leaders would imply. Like most other Americans at this stage they were riding the tide of prosperity and enjoying the economic benefits of peace within the enduring Union. But they expected the national bargain to be kept on both sides and hoped that slavery would cease to be a national issue. The same attitude was reflected in the North in the announcement by Stephen A. Douglas in the United States Senate that he had resolved never to make another speech on the slavery question, and in the effort of Daniel Webster to read opponents of the Compromise out of the Whig party—an effort which failed in his own Massachusetts. Many of the Northern critics of Compromise believed, in their turn, that it had really given slavery a new lease on life, and they could not reconcile themselves to the Fugitive Slave Law. Thus the Georgia Platform, which was regarded in the Lower South as definitely Unionist, suggested that the country had entered upon a period of truce and that this was not a final settlement.

Southern acceptance of the Compromise was most general in the Upper South. The Virginians were enormously relieved by it, and the Kentuckians tendered Clay a triumphal reception in their legislature. The spirit of disunion was strongest in South Carolina and Mississippi, states which differed greatly in many respects but were alike in that both of them had more slaves than free men, fewer whites than Negroes. In both of them, however, disunionism was defeated. In Calhoun's state this resulted chiefly from the division of secessionists between "immediatists" and "co-operationists"—that is, between those who believed that South Carolina ought to act alone and those who believed that she should not. The latter, with the smaller group of unionists, controlled the state convention of 1851. However, few leaders in South Carolina were willing to be described as "submissionists," and the secessionists there were merely waiting. In Mississippi the conflict was symbolized by the gubernatorial race between Henry S. Foote, who had strongly supported the Compromise in the Senate, and Jefferson Davis, who continued to oppose it, though less violently than John A. Quitman. Quitman had withdrawn from the race in Davis's favor but Davis himself was defeated and retired to private life. Thus Southern objections to the Compromise came to naught, for there was no real weapon against it except secession and relatively few were yet willing to use that.

The North and the Fugitive Slave Law

In the North, meanwhile, the Compromise was very generally approved, and notably so in business circles. But many influential people were assailing the Fugitive Slave Law. The only important concession by the North, and the only apparent gain to Southern slaveowners, ostensibly this became the chief cause of sectional dissension during the next few years.

The basis for the action of Congress was a section in Article IV of the Constitution which provided that any person held to service or labor in one state, under that state's laws, who escaped to another state should be delivered up on claim to the party to whom such service or labor was due. This constitutional provision had been implemented by the Act of 1793, which provided that runaway slaves might be taken before a federal judge or local magistrate. Following a decision of the Supreme Court in 1842, however, this law was considerably nullified. In Prigg vs. Pennsylvania, the Court expressed doubt about the conferring of power on state officials, holding that the latter might act if not forbidden by state law. Northern legislatures, detecting a loophole, proceeded to pass Personal Liberty Laws which forbade state officials, and in some instances private citizens, from assisting in the recovery of runaway slaves. Such laws were contrary to the spirit of the constitutional provision and were deeply resented by slaveowners.

The Act of 1850 sought to satisfy the latter by providing for the appointment of federal commissioners, who were paid a larger fee if they returned a slave than if they did not, and by imposing severe penalties for interference. No jury trials were prescribed in runaway cases, and an affidavit by a claimant was the only necessary evidence. Defenders of the measure said that legal safeguards could be applied in the states whence the slaves had fled, but in those states a Negro's word was not good against a white man's. In short, the Fugitive Slave Act introduced features of the "black codes" of the slave states into federal law. These features of the Act, which Webster had opposed, occasioned special condemnation in the North. There was in the whole situation a conflict between property rights and human rights which baffled the wisdom of that age and which in fact could not be resolved so long as men made property out of human beings.

The new law was objected to in nonslaveholding circles as being contrary to Anglo-Saxon traditional legal process and normal instincts of humanity. In *Uncle Tom's Cabin*, Harriet Beecher Stowe illustrated the situation well. Describing a poor Kentuckian who helped the fugitive Eliza in the hazardous flight that took her across the ice-strewn Ohio River, this author said that he "had not been instructed in his constitutional relations, and consequently was betrayed into acting in a sort of Christianized manner."

Opposition to the law took the form of obstruction. Runaways were taken from jails or captors by Northern well-wishers, as one Shadrach was in Boston; they were speeded to Canada by the Underground Railway; and even when fugitives were recovered the costs to the owners were excessive. Relatively few Northerners actually intervened, however, and one of the anomalies of the situation was that the law was most talked about in regions that were least affected by it. Nowhere was it more strongly objected to than in Massachusetts, a state which made a great deal of a very small number of runaways. On the other side of the fence, the nonenforcement of the law was talked about more violently in Mississippi, which lost relatively few slaves, than in Kentucky, from which flight was much easier. Like the Wilmot Proviso, this was another sectional issue which could be embraced by a politician with local impunity, and extremists played it up for all it was worth. The Fugitive Slave Law became a symbol, but it had vividness and reality far beyond the Wilmot Proviso, and it put the slave states at a moral disadvantage which they were never able to overcome until, years after their defeat, most Americans looked at the "Lost Cause" through the mists of romance and nostalgia.

The Election of 1852

Meanwhile, in the year 1852, when the country was enjoying general prosperity, most people in both North and South wanted to maintain the Compromise of 1850, whether they regarded this as a final settlement or merely as a truce. The victory of the Democrats over the Whigs in the presidential election, when Franklin Pierce of New Hampshire was pitted against General Winfield Scott, can be chiefly attributed to their greater loyalty to the Compromise. Pierce's nomination came about because none of the better-known candidates—Lewis Cass or William L. Marcy or James Buchanan or Stephen A. Douglas—could command a two-thirds vote, and on the forty-ninth ballot the Democratic Convention turned to a "dark horse" who had fewer enemies. Pierce was a party regular, a New Englander who disliked abolitionists, an agreeable and good-looking man. Against him the Whigs, resorting to their only successful formula, nominated a conspicuous soldier without political experience. Winfield Scott deserved honor for his services in Mexico, but he was too fussy and pretentious to be popular. He carried only Massachusetts and Vermont, Kentucky and Tennessee. The Free Soil candidate, John P. Hale, played an insignificant part in the election, showing that the country was in no mood for extremism. Scott was no extremist, but at this particular time almost any Democrat could have defeated almost any Whig.

The continuing objections to the settlement of 1850 by "Conscience Whigs" in the North proved a grave embarrassment to their Southern brethren. The movement of Whig leaders like Robert Toombs and Alexander H. Stephens of Georgia into the Democratic camp provided a striking illustration of the trend in the Lower South. The death of Clay in the spring of 1852 removed the national Whig leader most influential in that region, and the passing of Webster later in the same year signalized the decline of the national spirit among the Northern Whigs. Sectional moderation persisted in the border states among the old followers of Clay, but the moribund party had already ceased to be national and henceforth the opposition to the Democrats was almost wholly Northern.

The Democrats had been far more successful in patching up their quarrels over slavery and they presented a much more united front in the national election. Evasion of the domestic sectional controversy was to their immediate political advantage and they were committed to that policy, but there was no political necessity for them to cater to Southern extremists rather than to moderates. Pierce's Cabinet was headed by William L. Marcy of New York, but the Secretary of War, Jefferson Davis of Mississippi, was probably the most influential member. Friends of the Compromise on both sides of the line were surprised that the President should have appointed this conspicuous opponent of the settlement when strong Southern supporters of it—like Howell Cobb of Georgia—were available. The President was chiefly under Southern influence and this proved politically disastrous to him at a time when the North was increasing its economic ascendancy and moral advantage.

UNCLE TOM'S CABIN

Northern clergymen denounced the Fugitive Slave Law from their pulpits, as politicians did from the platform, but the most effective denunciation it received was literary and dramatic. Students of today pore over statistics of runaway slaves, ponder over the conditions of free Negroes in both North and South, and read comments on slavery by contemporary observers of the actual system. But from 1852 onward, the North got its most vivid impressions of American Negro slavery and the domestic slave trade, as indeed the civilized world did, from *Uncle Tom's Cabin*. Equally important with Northern gains in this decade in the material sphere, and perhaps more important, were the gains that the free states made over the slave in the battle of opinion; and these were in no small part attributable to this moving but unpretentious novel by an author whose only contacts with slavery had been on one brief visit to a Kentucky plantation. Ten years after the publication of *Uncle Tom's Cabin*, President Lincoln greeted Harriet Beecher Stowe by saying: "So you're the little woman who wrote the book that made this great war." He was being both jocular and gallant and was consciously indulging in oversimplification. But it can be safely said that Mrs. Stowe was far more effective than William Lloyd Garrison, more effective even than Theodore Dwight Weld by whom she was so deeply impressed, in convincing the great body of Northerners of the wrongfulness of human slavery.

Harriet Beecher Stowe, daughter of Lyman and sister of Henry Ward Beecher, was the wife of Calvin E. Stowe, a learned and impractical man who was successively a professor in Lane Theological Seminary in Cincinnati, Bowdoin College, and Andover Theological Seminary. It was at the two last seats of learning in New England, and particularly in Brunswick, Maine, that she wrote *Uncle Tom's Cabin, or Life Among the Lowly*. Beginning in June 1851, this appeared as a serial, and in 1852 it was published as a book, achieving success which nobody had anticipated. Besides being a best seller in the United States and being translated into a score of languages, it was an unparalleled success in Northern theatres. The story of poor Uncle Tom, who was sold down the river and finally died under the lash on a Louisiana plantation, of George and Eliza Harris who fled to freedom, of comical Topsy, saintly Little Eva, the officious Miss Ophelia, ineffectual St. Clare, and cruel Simon Legree won the hearts and evoked the tears and groans of countless thousands. It is much too sentimental for the taste of the middle of the twentieth century, but in the middle of the nineteenth, when romance was preferred to realism, it was a gripping story.

Mrs. Stowe intended it to be a fair one. Her main object was to win sympathy for the Negroes, and she was surprised by the chorus of Southern resentment on the one hand and of abolitionist approval on the other. There were nuances in her treatment which escaped the abolitionists. In the angular person of Miss Ophelia she embodied certain limitations of the New England point of view, and suggested to the discerning reader that the reform of social institutions is a slow and discouraging business. The most offensive character in the book, Simon Legree, was a transplanted Yankee. The author avoided the abolitionists' mistake of attacking slaveowners wholesale; she attacked the institution of slavery by arousing sympathy for its individual victims, and, unscientific though her treatment was, few could deny the potentialities of cruelty that lay within the system or the actual cruelties of the domestic slave trade and the Fugitive Slave Law. The most exciting single episode in the book was Eliza's incredible journey across the ice on the Ohio. Bloodhounds on the leash were frequently used in preliminary theater publicity campaigns. In that romantic age the exaggerations of this picture detracted nothing from its appeal to the emotions

No serious student of slavery would now turn to this work as a source-book, and, despite the sympathetic treatment of the Shelby plantation and the St. Clare household, the best of Southern life was not portrayed in it. Mrs. Stowe gave a wholly imaginary picture of the slaves and thus unwittingly created a false impression of the ease of transition from servitude to freedom. That mistake was not made by a realistic observer like Frederick Law Olmsted or a realistic statesman like Lincoln, much as they disliked the peculiar institution. In the end this imaginative representation did a disservice to the slaves themselves, for they shared the vast social injury when too much was expected of them immediately after their emancipation.

There was ill as well as good in this famous book. Mrs. Stowe did not hate Southerners, and with the passing of the years they have granted this humane woman a degree of appreciation which they have generally denied the major abolitionists. The long-range task of removing from the path of freedom's progress the ancient obstacle of human bondage— under the complicated economic, political, and social conditions of the 1850's—was a supreme challenge to statesmanship. The story-teller could not assume that task. Some people now may question, as some people at that time did, the wisdom of the policy of evasion and postponement and local rule which was then recommended by most political leaders in both North and South. But, without much question, the powerful emotional appeal of the novelist rendered many people on both sides of the line impatient of the spirit of compromise, and it strengthened the hands of the extremists in both sections.

CHAPTER 31

The Economy and Society
of the North, 1830-1860

DURING THE YEARS WHEN ANDREW JACKSON WAS THE outstanding personality in American public life, the democratic nationalism of which he was the political embodiment was supported by a burst of economic activity that combined multitudes of individual and group experiments in free enterprise with a strengthening of national ties by means of economic co-operation among the sections. Freedom from foreign threats to their security permitted Americans to give virtually their whole attention to internal development. There followed, besides a prodigious expansion of the farming frontier, a development of internal commerce, transportation facilities, and manufacturing industry that for the first time conspicuously displayed those talents for invention and economic organization which have ever since been regarded as typically American.

Most observers believed that the energy with which Americans now built railroads and factories presaged an easy nationalization of the country's life and loyalties. Divisive East-West forces were no longer a source of national crises. War and diplomacy won a fabulous empire for the farmer and the process was coming to be understood whereby Americans turned each new West—in its American meaning of the frontier of settlement—into a new "East" before its divergent interests could ripen into an ideal and program of separate nationality. North-South fissures seemed manageable by the process of accommodation and compromise. Nothing seemed strong enough to halt the march of nationalism, democracy, and industry.

But within a generation it turned out that all three forces were more narrowly expressive of Northern life than the Jacksonians had realized. The partial defeat of their optimism that reform could quickly abolish all social ills was matched by the temporary defeat of hopes that the South would develop social attitudes and economic activities in sufficient harmony with those of the North to avoid tests of force. Thus we must regard many economic and social phenomena of these years of extraordinary growth, from about 1830 to 1860, as Northern sectional manifestations, though they seemed national developments to most Northerners themselves at the time.

AGRICULTURE

Farming remained the economic pursuit of most Northerners until well after the Civil War. Industry and commerce rapidly expanded the populations of northern cities during the several decades before the War, but the absolute number of farmers increased even though their relative percentage of the total population slowly declined. In the great region now called the Middle West, containing far more "Grade A" soil than any other area in the world, the forests and prairies were converted by 1860 into the farms, towns, and cities of almost half the white population of the Union. The most significant demographic turning-point in American history was reached in the fifties when the center of national population, which had always been below the Mason and Dixon line, simultaneously crossed that line and the Allegheny Mountains into the state of Ohio.

In 1830, Ohio's wheat had only begun to compete with that of New York and Pennsylvania; by 1860, Illinois, Indiana, and Wisconsin were the leading wheat states of the Union. Already in 1850 more wheat was raised west of the mountains than in the Northeast, but during the next decade, while production in the Northeast was stabilized at about 30 million bushels, farmers of the Middle West, their numbers swelled by immigrants and their efficiency increased by McCormick's reaper, more than doubled their wheat production until it reached almost 100 million bushels in 1860. Their production of corn increased at the same dizzying pace, reaching over 400 million bushels in 1860, and hog-raising and meat-packing kept up with corn. By that time frontier settlement had leaped over the High Plains east of the Rockies and produced islands of agriculture on the northern pattern in Oregon, California, and the Mountain States. Californians turned to farming after the Gold Rush and outdid Oregon, multiplying their cattle to 2 million head in 1860 and producing surpluses of grain after 1855. The Mormons in Utah and the Gold Rush of 1859 to Pike's Peak in Colorado initiated similar expansion of farming in the mountains.

Although the Northeast fell behind the West in wheat and corn, its agriculture nevertheless boomed as farmers turned to dairy cattle and grassland farming. From the environs of seaboard cities the dairy region spread northward into Vermont and westward into central New York and Pennsylvania. Milk and cream were converted locally into cheese and butter, accounting by 1860 for well over half of the nation's total of both. In quantity and quality the New York products were supreme, and their consumption marked an improvement in urban diets. The profits from dairies encouraged a great improvement in breeding to differentiate milk producers from beef cattle. The scrubby American cow which had been allowed to stay outdoors all winter gave way to imported Jersey and Guernsey types which were carefully fed and warmly housed. By 1860, the average production of butter per cow had doubled over that of 1800.

The scientific revolution in farming methods affected the North more than the South, despite the fact that Southerners were the first leaders in the movement. Men like Edmund Ruffin, the eminent Virginian agronomist, who preached crop rotation and the use of mineral fertilizers, were heeded in the Northeast more than anywhere else except possibly in the old states of the Upper South. Rotations involving increased use of grass and legumes became popular, and the latter crops in turn produced more animal fertilizers. Legumes such as clover were understood to replace in the soil the nitrogen which grains used up. Clover required lime, and a craze for "gypsum and clover" swept the East. Guano was imported from bird-infested regions of South America. Marl, rich in potash and phosphate, was crushed and worked into the soil. J. J. Mapes of New Jersey invented and patented the first complete chemical fertilizer, a nitrogenous superphosphate comparable to the standard article of modern agriculture.

Because of the supply of fresh land, scientific and soil-conserving methods of farming made slow headway in the country as a whole, and American contributions to agronomy did not match those of Germany and England until the twentieth century. In the North, however, strong foundations were laid for progressive agriculture. The family farm system supported the best agricultural press in the world with hundreds of magazines devoted to farmers' economic, social, and cultural interests. Farmers' organizations flourished, nine hundred of them appearing on a list in 1858. Besides operating fairs, these societies published reports, ran experimental farms, tested machinery, and imported superior seeds and livestock.

The school and the church had much the same value in the Middle West as in New England, and were frequently staffed by teachers and ministers from that region. Wisconsin villages reproduced the trim pattern of New England, but the barns were bigger. Travelers were astonished to find in the pioneers' sod huts, the first structures on prairies where wood was scarce, the same books that New England farmers treasured—always the Bible, often *Pilgrim's Progress,* many tracts and collections of sermons, Webster's speller if not a dictionary, sometimes Shakespeare, Milton, and Pope along with Dickens, Thackeray, Hawthorne, Emerson, and the other contemporary giants. In the Upper Middle West the "old home" now meant the Genessee Valley of New York, or some part of New England, and nostalgia for its culture spurred attention to itinerant lecturers and ambitious literary journals and colleges. In political organization, distances dictated that the Middle West should follow the pattern revolving around the county rather than the town meeting of New England.

Free Soilism became the chief article in the Northern farmers' political faith during the fifties. The Free Soil Party of 1848 expressed Eastern urban rather than Western agrarian interests, but after 1854 the new Republican Party adopted the Free Soil doctrine and program and won the support of farmers as well as workmen. These farmers scorned the abolitionists but nevertheless became bitterly antagonistic to the South and slavery because Southern leaders insisted on a federal land policy which would discourage emigration of Northern small farmers into new areas beyond the Missouri River. A homestead law was not necessary to insure that the Northern system of agriculture would prevail beyond Texas, Missouri, and Iowa. Existing pre-emption laws and sales of family-sized farms at $1.25 an acre would suffice for that. But both Northern farmers and Southern planters took extreme positions, because both sides considered attack to be the best defense of their institutions and the best way to gain control over federal policy. When the question was tested by arms, the agricultural system of the North played a major part in securing the victory for the Union.

TRANSPORTATION AND COMMERCE

The three decades that preceded the Civil War saw the rise of American domestic and foreign commerce to climactic heights and the beginning of its subordination to industry and finance. The development of sailing ships superior in number and speed to those of Great Britain symbolized the climax of the era of merchant capitalism; while the building of a national railroad system symbolized the new age of industry.

The Continuing Mercantile Order

The Jackson era was the heyday of the Yankee peddler—the archetype of the shrewd small businessman who wandered through the country with a wagonload of the lesser manufactures and homely luxuries craved by farmer and villager. The middling sort of merchant continued to operate a network of sea-borne and interstate exchanges with his headquarters in a coastal city or one of the new western centers. At the top of the mercantile ladder, John Jacob Astor emerged with a fortune of $20 million, the largest of the period, which he amassed in the trans-Mississippi fur trade and cannily invested in real estate in New York, where the growth of the city multiplied its value. A German immigrant who had arrived in 1784 with only his clothes and a few flutes that he hoped to trade, Astor provided his descendants with a position of stable wealth from which they dominated Society in New York for almost a century. Popular awe at such a career and many only slightly less astonishing ones explained why "the land of the free" was now called "the land of opportunity." Formerly the most admired Americans were all statesmen or soldiers. Now millionaires began to outshine them, and it became customary to mean dollars when a man's "worth" was mentioned.

Merchants continued until the Civil War to be the chief beneficiaries of the American economy, and most merchants were Northerners or the Southern and Western agents of Northern principals. It was primarily for their operations that governments and private companies hastened to improve transportation by water, road, and rail. Only the largest manufacturer could dominate the merchant and control his own prices and markets. But banking was rapidly differentiated from the merchant's function during this period. The business of receiving funds on deposit and lending them out gave bankers significant control over other business by enabling them to determine what enterprises should be allowed to borrow capital. Yet the infant banking system was riddled with loose practices, especially in the newer regions of settlement, and credit was easy. Businessmen who could not obtain loans from friends or bankers could turn to the public at large and, by issuing stock and promising future profits, sell shares to anyone with idle dollars and a fund of faith. The company form of business organization remained important, especially for the close-held family firm which was most typical of merchant enterprises.

Regional specialization in cash crops required increased capital in the hands of commission merchants, who organized exchanges to buy and sell the ever-increasing produce of the nation. The Cotton Exchange in New Orleans handled a great share of that crop every year. In the Northwest, grain, cattle, and hog exchanges were organized in new cities from Cincinnati to Chicago and Saint Louis. Besides their useful function in providing capital sufficient to move crops, the produce exchanges gave opportunity for speculation in "futures," that is, buying and selling products for future delivery and gambling on the rise and fall of prices.

Transportation in the Jackson Era

Speculation also marked the rise of the transportation industry. Ambitious inhabitants of crossroads, villages, and towns vied to weave webs of roads, canals, and railroads around their future capitals of the universe and to entrap succulent harvests of business. Local groups of "public-spirited citizens" were the usual initiators of transportation projects. If the group had influence in government and a more or less convincing argument that the proposed route would serve the public interest, state or federal aid might be secured. Though the federal government, after Jackson's veto of the Maysville Road Bill in 1830, generally refused to give direct support to new canal and road projects, it turned over money (as in the distribution of the surplus in 1837) and lands to state governments, and these lavishly dispensed subsidies. But most of the capital for the building of transportation routes came from private investors. A significant share of them were English capitalists to whom London investment houses, chiefly Baring Brothers, sold American stocks.

Beginning in the twenties, turnpikes, river steamboats, canals, and railroads were developed with spectacular speed. After the Cumberland-National Road ended short of the goal of Saint Louis, lesser turnpikes were built in many localities, usually by private companies and often to the accompaniment of criticism against their exploitation of the public. No new roads linking East and West were attempted. The development of steamboats on the western rivers promised to make New Orleans and other Gulf ports the permanent outlets of the commerce of the Mississippi Valley. The shallow-draft, low-pressure steamboat of the twenties, forced to putter upstream close inshore at little more than rowboat speed, was transformed by the invention in 1825 of a high-pressure engine which pushed palatial arks upstream at 16 miles per hour. Eastern businessmen, cities, and states turned to the development of canals, Great Lakes steamship lines, and railroads to overcome the advantage of the river steamers. The Erie Canal in New York was followed by a combination of canals and railroad portages over the Alleghenies in Pennsylvania which, however, never overcame the natural advantages of New York's water-level route. All along the eastern seaboard canals were built around the falls of rivers to improve connections with the interior, and in the Old Northwest a comparable network joined the Ohio River and the Mississippi to the Great Lakes.

Turnpikes, steamboats, and canals were all destined to be superseded after brief decades of glory by the railroad. The first American railroad was built in 1827 to transport granite between Quincy, Massachusetts, and the Neponset River. The first passenger railroad was the Baltimore and Ohio, begun on July 4, 1828, and it was closely followed by the Charleston and Hamburg. During the thirties many railroads between pairs of eastern cities were built. These were of little national significance compared with intersectional roads which would traverse the mountains and unite the country. Before this challenge could be met, too-rapid expansion of railroad and other transportation enterprises combined with overexpansion of western land speculation and wild-cat banking methods to produce first a fantastic boom and then, in 1837, a crash followed by years of depression more severe than those after 1819. Individuals lost everything, companies went bankrupt, banks disappeared, and state governments defaulted on transportation bonds. Numerous transportation projects were abandoned. Construction was gradually resumed in the forties and reached boom proportions again in the fifties.

Meanwhile, American inventive talent made great contributions. Although the steam engine was an English invention, and England had built the first railroad in 1825, Americans developed steam power for the special needs of their country. Peter Cooper built the first American locomotive in 1830. The scale of American geography and commerce stimulated the invention of the "cradled" locomotive because it had to be large enough to pull long strings of freight vans and passenger coaches and yet flexible enough to negotiate curves.

Sail and Steam

The Mississippi River steamboat was supreme in its class, but in ocean-going steamship design the British surpassed Americans. Stimulated by government subsidies, they early concentrated on steam for merchantmen and warships, while American shipowners attempted to compete by improving the design of sailing vessels. The result was the beautiful "clipper" design, a triumph of the useful arts, sleek of hull and graceful of bow with towering clouds of sails. It was first developed at Baltimore in the forties and reached perfection in New England yards. The *Flying Cloud* in 1854 sailed from Boston around the Horn to San Francisco in eighty-nine days and eight hours. The clippers for a few years permitted Americans to capture from the British lucrative trades that demanded speed, like that in China tea. Beginning in 1846, the United States government subsidized ocean steamship packet lines, particularly those joining New York and San Francisco to Panama, but these subsidies were abolished under Southern objection in 1858, while British governmental subsidies to steamships increased until they improved sufficiently to outrun the American clippers.

The Telegraph

The electric telegraph, which speeded the transmission of intelligence, was the first important American scientific invention of the Industrial Revolution. Research on electricity had become an American specialty since Franklin flew his famous kite. Joseph Henry, professor in the College of New Jersey (Princeton), made important discoveries, paralleling those of Faraday, regarding self-induction and oscillation in electromagnetism. Samuel F. B. Morse, a noted portrait painter and professor of art in New York University, in 1832 gave up art to pursue his original idea for an electric telegraph. He adopted Joseph Henry's intensity magnet, and invented the "Morse Code" and a system of relays to step up the power of signals over a long distance. Congress in 1843 appropriated $30,000 to help build a line from Washington to Baltimore. On May 24, 1844, Morse transmitted over it the message, "What hath God wrought!"

He offered the federal government a chance to buy his invention, but it refused. Morse and others organized private companies to build telegraph lines. By 1847, Moses Yale Beach, editor of the New York Sun, was able to publish war news from Mexico which came by telegraph from New Orleans. Railroads adopted telegraphic communications for operating purposes, to the great advantage of public safety. The invention made possible prediction of the weather because reports of approaching air movements could be gathered in advance of their arrival. Joseph Henry in 1850 developed a system of weather reporting that provided the basis of the United States Weather Bureau, whose forecasts became of untold value to farmers and others. The telegraph furthermore helped to unify the nation economically as it permitted instantaneous intelligence of crop production and market conditions in the whole country, and politically because it created cohesive consciousness of national and local events by the large-scale transmission of news.

Railroads in the Fifties

Americans built too many miles of railroad too fast to build them well. Inventive skill was concentrated on making them run fast rather than safely. Poor brakes, overworked crews, bad scheduling, shaky bridges, and unsettled roadbeds caused numerous wrecks. A disaster in 1856 made a record of 62 killed, but it did not stand long. The British-built Victoria bridge at Montreal set a standard of building Americans approached only in 1871 with the Eads Bridge at Saint Louis. Railroad building reached a climax in the fifties. When the Mexican War ended in 1848, there were 6000 miles of railroad tracks in the United States. In the next four years the number of miles doubled, by 1860 it more than doubled again, and the nation possessed 30,000 miles. In these years the eastern mountains were conquered and only one major task was left for the future: the building of transcontinental lines to join the Missouri Valley to the Pacific Coast.

Of the five lines that joined the seaboard to the Mississippi Valley in 1860, three were in free states, one was in the slave states, and another, the Baltimore and Ohio, was in both. A sixth sectionally significant line from Chicago to the Gulf of Mexico was not quite finished. The thirty-

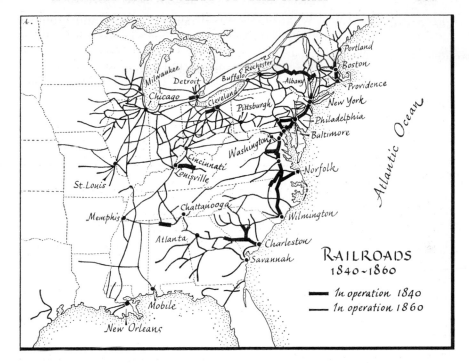

RAILROADS
1840~1860

▬ In operation 1840
— In operation 1860

mile Panama Railroad across the Isthmus, completed in 1856, was built with Northern capial and owned by New York steamship interests. As a link between ship service, it gave the Northeast faster communications with San Francisco than the overland routes from the Middle West and the South.

Dramatic events studded the story of railroad construction. After twenty-five years of effort, climaxed by the employment of a crew of 5000 men and huge expenses that were met by the merchants and bankers of Baltimore, the last spike of the Baltimore and Ohio Railroad to Wheeling was driven on Christmas Eve, 1852. The event was accompanied by celebrations all along the line. From Wheeling the B & O soon struck across southern Ohio, Indiana, and Illinois to Saint Louis, too far north to affect the Southern economy as a whole. The state of Pennsylvania quickly matched Baltimore's connection with the West by eliminating canal and canal-boat portage links and building such marvels as the Horseshoe Curve to give the "Pennsy" an all-rail route. In February 1854, the first through train ran from the city of William Penn to Pittsburgh, the rising metropolis of steel. From there the Pennsylvania made connections with both Chicago and St. Louis. But New York had already consolidated its lead by building two lines, the Erie and the New York Central. The former struck westward from the Hudson opposite New York City directly to Lake Erie, touching no large city. It was bitterly opposed by the "Canal Ring" in Albany, its earning capacity was limited because of its abnormal track gauge and heavy debts, and it was destined to fall victim to financial pirates. Much more useful were the Hudson River Railroad from New York to Albany and the nine roads linking Albany and Buffalo which Cornelius Vanderbilt combined in 1853 into the New York Central. This route competed with river and canal traffic by efficiency and speed which permitted low charges. It is the only route to the West which does not cross high mountains. From Buffalo the New York Central used the Michigan Central tracks to Chicago. Vanderbilt's road maintained and increased the lead of New York in inland and foreign commerce.

By 1855, a passenger could travel from the Atlantic Coast to Chicago or Saint Louis in two days without benefit of river, canal, or horse, at the low fare of $20. All subsequent improvements in American transportation have been minor compared with the accomplishment of the fifties. It was summed up by Senator Lewis Cass at an opening ceremony in Marietta, Ohio. He recalled how in 1799, when he had come out to Ohio a poor boy from New Hampshire, the horseback trip from Baltimore to Marietta took twenty days. The Northwest Territory then contained 30,000 people; now in 1857 it contained 6,000,000, yet the man was still living "whose axe felled the first tree of these forests." He predicted that in another fifty years the population of the United States would reach 100,000,000, and Americans began to believe in such dreams as they saw the railroads daily carry trainloads of immigrants from Atlantic steamships directly to virgin lands in the West.

It was Senator Stephen A. Douglas, the Illinois "steam engine in breeches," who envisioned and promoted a railroad whose sectional significance would be to unite rather than divide the North and the South. This was the Illinois Central Railroad, roughly paralleling the Mississippi River from Chicago to the Gulf. Douglas obtained federal aid for the stretch between Chicago and Cairo, Illinois, by proposing equal land grants for the southern stretch from Cairo to the Gulf. But the southern link between Cairo and the Gulf was not wholly completed before the Civil War. The mid-century high noon of the Mississippi-Ohio-Missouri steamboat era soon passed, eclipsed by the northern railroads to the East.

The railroads nationalized the market for Eastern businessmen and internationalized it for Western farmers. Where freight charges and slow speeds had formerly prohibited the distribution of manufactures and food beyond local markets, a better ratio of cost to speed permitted distribution far and wide. Western wheat and meat now moved to the eastern seaboard and out to the world market, although they did not match cotton exports as yet. In 1850, Cincinnati meat moved chiefly down the Ohio River; by 1860, this first metropolis of the West had reoriented its trade to the East. Chicago soon displaced Cincinnati in both meat and grain, and its lake and rail connections tied it almost exclusively to New York. Besides gaining control over western exports, New York brought in 70 per cent of the nation's imports.

The people were willing to endure many evils for the sake of improved transportation. Only in later decades did the public demand safety measures by governmental authority. Rate wars between competing roads and chaotic rate practices on almost all roads injured investors as well as the public, while experiments with monopolistic agreements between competing roads to jack up the rates were even more injurious. Railroad lobbyists, begging subsidies in the state and national capitols, made corrupt bargains with legislators. The train-riding public not only risked wrecks but suffered from hard benches, missed connections, disregard of stops for food, and abuse from overworked crews. Railroads commonly invaded the main streets of towns and cities, spewing ashes and encouraging the growth of slums. The Illinois Central showed how a company could gouge the public twice by holding federal gifts of land for the rise in values and insiders' profits, instead of selling them to pay for construction. Douglas himself made a practice of obtaining land warrants in new regions which his position as Chairman of the Senate Committee on Territories enabled him to select for government-backed booms. The great array of evils, capped by alliances between promoters and politicians, which made the railroads a public scandal after the Civil War, all came into view during the fifties.

The Panic of 1857 halted railroad construction no more than momentarily. In the last years before the war, eight lines pushed across the Mississippi River like a web fanning out from Chicago into Minnesota, Iowa, and Missouri. Southerners had been insisting that a line from New Orleans to San Diego, California, would serve the nation better than any more northerly route to the Pacific Coast. While some Northerners favored a route from Chicago to St. Paul and thence to Oregon or San Francisco, the majority would settle for a genuinely central route starting from Missouri or Iowa. All parties agreed that federal subsidies would be necessary. Many surveys were made, some at federal expense. Coalitions of promoters were formed and dissolved, and bills of all sorts were offered annually in Congress, but at every crucial juncture Southern Senators prevented action on the only routes that the House, dominated by the North, would support. A major purpose of Stephen A. Douglas in the Kansas-Nebraska Act of 1854 was to facilitate the building of a northern transcontinental railroad, but the law raised such a furor of Northern opposition and Southern counteraction that Congress did not act on the railroad until after Southern Senators left Washington in 1861. So the location of the last major link in the national railroad system was, like so many other issues, thrown into the caldron of civil war for decision.

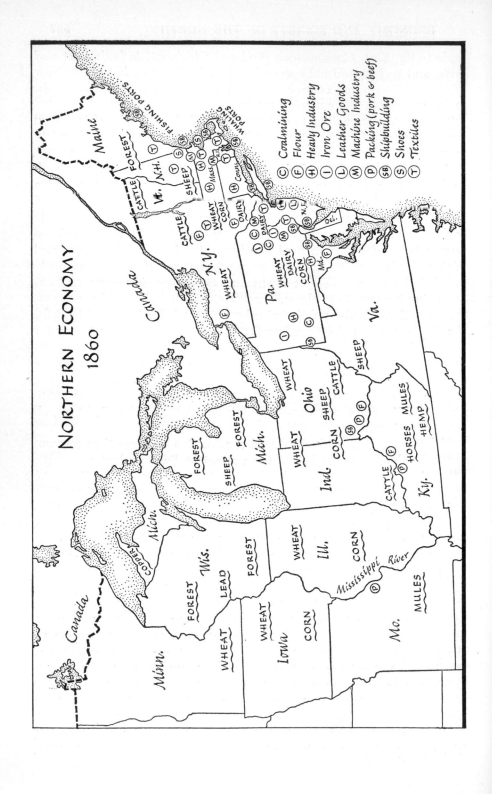

NORTHERN ECONOMY 1860

Legend:
- C — Coalmining
- F — Flour
- H — Heavy Industry
- I — Iron Ore
- L — Leather Goods
- M — Machine Industry
- P — Packing (pork & beef)
- SB — Shipbuilding
- S — Shoes
- T — Textiles

INDUSTRIALISM

The industrial revolution in America placed more emphasis on mass production of machines for consumers than was the case in England, where small-scale production of machines for factory use was the dominant pattern. Much of the textile machinery of the United States was copied from English models; but the United States took the lead in inventing and manufacturing such devices as the reaper and the sewing machine. This difference was owing to the desire of Americans to ease their own labor and to the ability of individual Americans to pay for machine aids; while in England it was chiefly the factory-owner seeking a greater profit who encouraged the improvement of machinery. England was pre-eminent in the manufacture of such minimum necessities of life as cheap textiles; the United States during the pre-Civil War decades became pre-eminent in the manufacture of individually-owned labor-saving devices which were a luxury beyond the means of the mass of consumers everywhere except in America.

Textiles and Iron

In both countries the textile and metallurgical industries remained central in the process of industrialization. In textile manufacturing the chief American contribution occurred in the organization of production rather than in improved machinery. New England capitalists joined in 1813 to form the Boston Manufacturing Company at Waltham, Massachusetts, which was the first in the world to carry on all processes of manufacture from raw cotton to finished cloth under single management. The "Waltham System" was copied at Lowell in 1830 and at Lawrence in 1845 for woolens as well as cotton goods. The manufacture of textile machinery advanced with the establishment of the Merrimac Company (1820) and other specialized factories. Some American improvements occurred—for example, the invention by William Crompton in 1840 of a loom for weaving patterned woolen cloth. Those engaged in the production of textiles regarded the tariff protection as adequate only in the case of cheap cotton cloth, but the rapid development of the industry made the United States relatively independent of imports from England and also caused a decline in household manufacture. It was centralized in eastern Massachusetts and Rhode Island, but the application of steam power to the machines, first at Salem and New Bedford in 1847, made the industry independent of waterfalls and presaged its migration to other areas.

Similar to the Waltham System was the continuous process in iron and steel production with the development (1817) of the puddling and rolling method, which was adopted in Pittsburgh, the center of the industry. By the forties, heavy iron rails and structural beams were being manufactured. Pennsylvania's anthracite coal displaced charcoal and the open forge gave way to the hot-blast furnace. Railroad building provided the chief incentive for speeding up, improving, and expanding the output of ferrous metals. Even without tariff protection, American mills rapidly overtook the British in rails, boiler-plate, and car-wheels. The Cooper-Hewitt Works at Trenton, New Jersey, led the way towards American supremacy in rails, structural beams, and iron for cannon. The Cambria Iron Works at Johnstown, Pennsylvania, inaugurated the "vertical" system which brought raw materials, processing plants, and transportation within its 25,000 acres all under the control of a single corporation. The Baldwin Locomotive Works in Philadelphia turned out ever-larger models of the cradled engine. In fine machinery such as stationary steam engines and textile machines, British makers were still supreme. But Browne and Sharp of Providence began to manufacture vernier calipers in 1851 and Windsor, Vermont, put turret lathes into production in 1854; these were starting points in the history of the American precision machine-tool industry.

The British Bessemer process of steel-making was tried in the United States but was unsuccessful until after the Civil War. An American portent was the development of metal skeletons for buildings. In a country where the abundance of wood had stimulated its use even for elaborate architecture and high labor costs discouraged the wide use of stone, American architects and engineers in the fifties virtually leaped into the age of iron and steel. James Borgardus of New York patented a method of using cast-iron beams for large buildings and erected examples in many cities. Lighter and stronger wrought-iron beams were developed by others and, when structural steel was finally available and cheap, the elevator invented by Elisha G. Otis in 1852 made the skyscraper possible. By 1860, the North produced 14,500,000 tons of coal and the South 500,000 tons; the North 2,500,000 tons of iron, the South 76,000 tons.

Machines for Consumers

On these foundations the northern states erected a program of consumers' machine-goods unmatched in the world. Most significant was the reaper. Cyrus H. McCormick's father had worked on an implement to cut and tie wheat in bundles for twenty years in Virginia when the son in 1832 constructed one that succeeded. It combined a cutter blade with a reel to sweep the stalks into shocks which were tied and dropped back on the field to dry. Horse-drawn and powered by a traction wheel, the weird-looking contraption provoked laughter until its wonderful saving of labor was demonstrated in action. McCormick improved the machine, manufactured it in Virginia until 1847, and then moved north and west to Chicago where his market was assured by the settlement of the premier wheat-growing region of the world. His patent expired in 1848, but business talent enabled him to outdo competitors. The McCormick reaper was a marvel of London's Crystal Palace Exposition in 1851. With great vision the inventor placed his machine in mass production, helped farmers to buy it by offering a deferred-payments plan whereby they could pay for it out of increased crops, and immensely speeded up the production of cheaper food as well as the agricultural conquest of the West.

A consumer's machine of comparable value to the housewife was the sewing machine invented by Elias Howe in 1845. Howe had been an apprentice in a Lowell textile machinery shop. At first he tried to market his invention in England, but returned to America, and, after winning patent suits against Isaac M. Singer, who thereupon paid him royalties sometimes amounting to $4000 a week, he established his own factory at Bridgeport, Connecticut. A Howe or a Singer sewing machine became a most treasured possession of the American housewife, the first of those domestic appliances which have made her the world's greatest mistress of machinery. The Singer firm developed most imaginatively the export potential of the machine: its salesmen invaded even the undeveloped regions of the world and helped tribeswomen make the clothes missionaries were teaching them to wear. Applied to ready-made clothing, the sewing machine drew the industry out of homes and hand-tailoring shops into factories concentrated especially in New York City. Applied to shoemaking, the invention of Lyman R. Blake in 1858 sewed uppers to soles. Gordon McKay, who bought the patent next year, put it to work to complete mechanization of his shoe factory so that leather could be fed into one end of a row of machines and finished footwear emerge at the other. The Blake-McKay machines came into practically universal use.

Samuel Colt invented the revolving pistol in 1835 and put it into production in Connecticut according to Eli Whitney's system of standardized parts. The "six-shooter" was appropriated by the frontiersman, who was able with it to overcome the formidable skill of the Plains Indians in the rapid-firing of arrows from horseback. A little later the Sharps rifle won out in the race to apply the new principle of the rifled barrel to increase range and accuracy. It was the best in the world and gave its name to future "sharpshooters."

In 1839, Charles Goodyear discovered how to vulcanize rubber to make it proof against heat and cold. The typewriter was invented in 1843 by Charles Thurber but further developments were necessary before it was put into production by E. Remington and Sons in 1873. The rotary printing press was invented by Richard M. Hoe in 1846. The first one, which could print 8000 newspapers in an hour, was installed in the plant of the *Philadelphia Public Ledger*. Improvements soon multiplied the output of the Hoe press, lowered the price of some newspapers to one cent and, meeting the challenge of mass literacy in America, introduced the era of mass newspaper circulation.

Sensational demonstrations of American industrial and mechanical progress occurred in London in 1851. The McCormick reaper was ridiculed when it stood idle on the floor of the Crystal Palace Exposition, but a demonstration on an English wheat field produced a different response. A typical advance was demonstrated in lockmaking. Here was a consumer's article, humble but essential, requiring ingenuity and business ability to supersede the laborious contraption of hand-working locksmiths. An American named Alfred Charles Hobbs relegated to antique shops the best that British locksmiths could offer when he demonstrated to a solemn committee how easily he could pick a lock that had been specially made to protect papers of the British government. Americans perfected the principle of revolving cylinders which permits mass production with slight variations to make each lock unique. A visitor to the Crystal Palace listed other examples of American design and production which led the world:

> Our handled axes, hay-rakes, grain cradles, scythes and snathes, three-tined hayforks, solid steel hoes, road scrapers, posthole augers, fan-mills, smut-mills, sausage-cutters, sausage-stuffers, tinman's tools, permutation locks, steel cultivators, carpenter's tools, currycombs, corn-brooms, portmanteaus and trunks, ice-cream freezers, axletrees, paint-mills, and many other things of universal use here, but in the shape and conveniences which we have given them utterly unknown in Europe, established for our industry a character independent of and unlike that of any other nation.

Pre-eminence of Northern Industry

Little wonder that, if the products of Northern industry surprised Europe and sometimes surpassed those of Great Britain, the first home of modern industry, they overwhelmed the Southern states and caused complaint that a Southerner from birth to death was dependent on Northern factories. Northerners by 1860 owned two-thirds of the nation's banking capital, almost all the shipping, and far more farm implements than Southerners. California gold fed the prosperity of the North more than the South. The Southern slaves had an estimated value of $2 billion, but in the North labor required no capital investment, which left all the capital of that region available for improvements in agriculture, transportation, and industry.

Southerners increasingly during the fifties expressed dislike of the manner of life imposed by the new industrialism in the North as well as fear of its economic power. In Cincinnati the gamut of social consequences of the new economic system was early visible. Besides working-class slums, that city developed a forerunner of the "assembly line"—the ultimate in mechanization of labor processes. By the thirties, "Porkopolis" received every fall such abundant shipments of hogs requiring rapid processing that its packing plants developed a line technique. The animal was driven up a ramp to the top floor of the factory, hoisted by its feet to a trolley riding an overhead rail, and moved by gravity past rows of workers, each of whom performed a simple operation until at the lowest level the barrels of meat were loaded onto freight cars or river steamboats. This was a "disassembly" line, but the principle when reversed to *add* a component part at each station until a finished product accumulated was early applied to shoe manufacturing and gradually to many other industries. Under the new method the tempo of production was no longer determined by the worker plying tools but by the mechanism coercing him. Also, skill was devaluated. Anyone could learn one of the simple, repetitive operations in a few minutes. But it was also true that the reduction of labor costs and increase of efficiency contributed to the growth of the American mass market and a rise in the standard of living. The most significant American manufacturers sought prosperity not in high prices and restricted production, but in low unit profits and mass production. This and the hope that labor might gain decent working conditions and a fair share of its product in the form of high wages seemed to justify industrialization even on social grounds.

LABOR AND IMMIGRATION

The American industrial laboring class first took form during the Jackson period. Some industries, notably the railroads and small metallurgical shops of Connecticut, required new skills and drew their labor force chiefly from the sons of old stock. Irish immigrants occupied most of the unskilled pick-and-shovel jobs, especially on railroad construction gangs. The textile mills of Waltham and Lowell were the first large-scale employers of unskilled factory labor. English mills and earlier American ones in Rhode Island used child labor extensively, the employers arguing that work kept children out of mischief, taught them valuable moral discipline, and kept their parents from want. For a time these arguments appealed to the Puritan temper of New England, but when the children's sufferings became widely known protest arose. Children were worked twelve or fourteen hours per day, six days a week. The whipping-room was a standard feature of mill architecture. Blows were used not only to punish laxity but to keep children from falling asleep.

The founders of Waltham and Lowell decided not to employ any children. Instead they recruited unmarried daughters of New England farmers and, like the Puritan divines of old, promised to supervise the conduct of their girl operatives in minutest detail in order to assure parents that factory life would be an ennobling moral experience. Girls of seventeen to twenty flocked to Waltham, Lowell, and other mill towns where the system was copied. They counted on a few years as "Ladies of the Loom" to complete their education, save some money, and with it improve their chances in marriage. The employers required them to live in boarding houses managed by respectable widows who enforced strict rules of conduct much like those of a nunnery. Leisure time was used to attend Lyceum lectures, study French and German, and write and publish their own literary magazine, the *Lowell Offering*. They tacked poems above their looms to memorize while working. With boxes of flowers outside the mill windows, a considerable refinement of manners, clean work that was adjusted to their strength, savings accumulating in the banks, and intellectual activities that surprised English visitors accustomed to the degradation of factory workers, the Lowell girls were a marvel, holding out promise that New England civilization would be proof against industrialism.

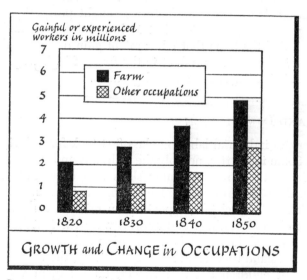

SOURCE: Bureau of the Census.

But the Lowell System was not proof against the depression of 1837. Dwindling markets and falling prices led the companies to cut wages and eliminate the more ornamental features of the girls' life. Cheaper immigrant labor was imported. Supervision of private lives developed into a drastic tyranny. Infractions of the rules of morality or work brought dishonorable discharge, and the placing of names on a blacklist that circulated among other employers. Presently the public which had been convinced that ideal labor conditions prevailed at Lowell was startled by the organization of a spontaneous union, the Lowell Female Labor Reform Association. The girls demanded the ten-hour day, attempted strikes, and paraded in Sunday gloves and hats—carrying banners with highly literary criticisms of their employers.

In the forties, medical investigators found the Lowell mills worse than prisons. An investigation by the state legislature substantiated the justice of workers' complaints but opposed protective laws, because they would place Massachusetts at a disadvantage in competition with other states. The remedy, the investigators' report stated, should rather be sought "in the progressive improvement in art and science, in a higher appreciation of man's destiny, in a less love for money, and a more ardent love for social happiness and intellectual superiority." In short, the employers should restore the paternalism of the original Lowell system.

They did not revive it. Immigrants were too eager to accept low wages and long hours. The ten-hour movement, which swept factory workers into action throughout the Northeast during the forties, was largely a failure. In 1850, the national average of hours of labor in factories was eleven-and-a-half and a decade later it had not much improved. Labor conditions were such that slaveowners could answer Northern abolitionists by asserting with considerable point that the factory workers of the free states were worse off than the slaves of the South. The flaw in the Lowell system was its paternalism. Such experiments have often collapsed under stress of hard times or less justifiable excuse for arbitrarily withdrawing what had been arbitrarily given.

Advocates of labor unions argued that only what workers won by exercising collective bargaining power would be secure against arbitrary employers. Handicapped until after the Massachusetts decision of 1842 in Commonwealth *vs.* Hunt by the common-law rule against unions as conspiracies in restraint of trade, they nevertheless grew fairly strong in northeastern cities in all the leading trades. Boom times in the fifties favored labor's demands. By 1860, the ten-hour day was normal for skilled craftsmen and for common labor outside the factories. The strike was resorted to as the chief weapon in bringing employers to make concessions. The National Trades Union, ancestor of the American Federation of Labor, was not strong enough to survive the Panic of 1857 and the Civil War, but a number of national organizations of particular trades—notably printers, hatters, masons, cigar-makers and iron-molders —emerged by 1860 as powerful and permanent bodies.

The Immigrants and Why They Came

While skilled workers, who were generally of old American stock, slowly learned to use their bargaining power through organization, the market of unskilled labor in the United States was flooded by immigrants who were so eager for jobs that unskilled workers seldom enjoyed much bargaining power. Immigrants numbered fewer than 10,000 per year prior to 1825. By 1832, over 50,000 began to arrive every year, by 1842, over 100,000, and by 1850, almost 400,000. America now became, even more than during the colonial period, a magnet attracting a great folk migration of peoples. American liberty, democracy, and economic opportunity contrasted more sharply than ever with political reaction in Europe after the Congress of Vienna and the economic destitution that followed periodic crop failures in the Old World. All doubt of the ultimate success of the American political experiment vanished, and the new exuberant self-confidence of Americans had its counterpart in a new conviction among the distressed of the Old World that the United States could not fail them.

Englishmen, mostly skilled workers and ambitious farmers, some Scots, and a few Welshmen continued to come, but they were so easily assimilated that they were not much remarked by observers. The most notable feature of the new immigration was the preponderance of Roman Catholic Irishmen and of Germans. The Irish in the thirties amounted to almost half the total number of newcomers, and the Germans almost a third of the total. During the next decade the Irish proportion of the greatly increased totals was still larger.

The peak of pre-Civil War immigration came after 1846. The *Democratic Review,* organ of the political party that most heartily welcomed the newcomers, remarked that there had been nothing like it since "the encampments of the Roman empire, or the tents of the crusaders." In fact the movement meant both empire for the United States as the vast new labor force accelerated agricultural and industrial growth, and new strength in the crusade for liberty because it broke down notions that American institutions would be the exclusive property of Protestant or English-speaking peoples.

Events of 1846 abroad caused hunger to be the chief awakener of dreams of America; and the failure of the European revolutions of 1848 made the yearning for liberty as poignant as the yearning for food. It was that famous gift of the New World to the poor of the Old—the potato—that brought strange disasters to them. The crop of 1845 was injured by a rot disease in the Rhineland all the way from Belgium and The Netherlands to Switzerland, while England and Scotland lost one-sixth of their crop, and Ireland, where the peasants had little else to eat, lost half of it. Charity and government aid prevented actual starvation in Ireland, but many determined to leave the scene of dependence on a crop subject to the mysterious disease. The poorest could not afford to go, but masses of those with small savings used them to escape. In Germany there was less absolute poverty and correspondingly greater capacity to finance emigration. At British ports and at Le Havre, Rotterdam, Amsterdam, Hamburg, and Bremen, emigrants swamped housing facilities and camped out while waiting for empty corners in ships.

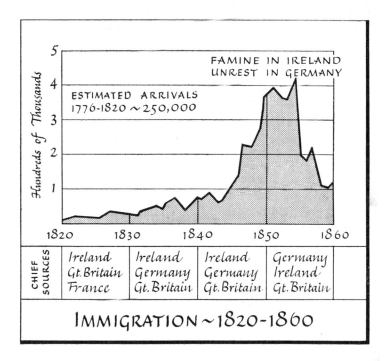

IMMIGRATION ~ 1820-1860

Two crop failures in succession had never occurred before, and in the British Isles great hopes were placed in the Repeal of the Corn Laws in 1846 to replenish food supplies from abroad without paying high duties on them. But disaster struck in July. From Switzerland to Londonderry drought and disease destroyed more crops than in the year before. Lowered tariffs had no immediate effect because an international grain panic led continental countries to forbid exports to Britain. Famine began in Ireland in the fall. Families died in their cottages or wandered half-demented along the roads leaving their dead unburied along the way, and typhus aided by undernourishment took off many. The British government worked belatedly to distribute wheat, and small schooners that had never before gone to sea set out from the United States with cargoes of corn, but the Irish housewife often did not know how to make bread.

After the terrible winter of 1846-1847, even when famine had ended, the Irish felt that a new curse on their land had been added to the age-old one of British misgovernment. "Poor Ireland's done," they said. In the spring of 1847 an exodus to America began that filled the roads, recent arteries of horror, with crowds of desperate, hopeful migrants carrying ragged baggage and clutching a few sovereigns of unpaid rent, charity handouts, or proceeds of a draft from relatives in America. This latter source of funds for passage increased in importance with the years. Whole sections of the land were now deserted; and those who remained felt that the United States had become a happier Ireland.

While in Ireland the poorest braved any hardship in order to go, in Germany the craftsman and the more well-to-do peasant remained the backbone of the horde. On the continent the revolutions of 1848 promised relief to the yearning for liberty but reaction rapidly set in. Disappointed idealists, particularly in Germany where both liberalism and national unity failed, gave up and left for America. A significant element of German liberal intellectuals was added to the "Forty-eighters."

The problems with which the swelling waves of immigrants confronted the United States began at the ports of debarkation. Diseases were carried across the Atlantic; many newcomers arrived too weak to work or deluded by wonderful tales that freedom meant freedom from labor; the sick, the aged, and paupers often became public charges the moment they set foot on shore. The federal government neglected to regulate conditions of entry until state and municipal efforts were swamped by the flood of 1847. In that and following years the federal government enacted legislation to improve sanitary conditions on immigrant ships and confiscate any vessel that subjected passengers to the worst crowding and dietary exploitation. Yet these first attempts at regulation were poorly enforced even in the great ports, and total evasion was easy by landing immigrants at deserted points or at Quebec and letting them filter overland into the United States.

Some European governments, particularly Belgium, some German states, canton authorities in Switzerland, and counties in Great Britain shipped convicts and paupers to the United States to avoid supporting them in their own public institutions. The federal government used diplomatic channels with some success to stop the practice, but even philanthropists in Europe supported it in the hope that criminals and unemployed would respond to American opportunities for honest work. New York and other cities tried to bar the unfit without much result. Americans were appalled to find their poorhouses, hospitals, and jails crowded with foreign inmates. The immigrants were cheated by land sharks and railroad agents, defrauded by confidence men, and corralled by the Tammany type of ward heeler—who, in return for votes, at least provided some genuine assistance.

Fewer Germans than Irish remained in the large eastern cities. They were generally more skilled and often set up their own woodworking, leather-tanning, saddlery, printing, brewery, beer-garden, tailoring, and machine-shop establishments in smaller northern cities and western villages. Many German farmers took up land in the free states from Ohio to Minnesota. In Chicago, Milwaukee, Saint Louis, and the newer farm regions of Wisconsin and Iowa, Germans constituted whole enclaves of settlement. Their musicians transformed the musical life of the North, their educated men edited newspapers, taught school or, in the jest of plain American neighbors, "farmed in Latin." Their reformers staffed many of the labor unions and radical political movements in the cities. Unlike the German immigrants of the eighteenth century in the Pennsylvania Dutch districts, the Forty-eighters were rapidly assimilated into the norms of American life. The Irish showed a notable talent for urban politics. The great majority of both groups were absorbed in useful and sometimes distinguished work that contributed generously to the material and cultural advancement of the country.

Nativist Reaction

But even before the climactic crowds began to arrive in the late forties, Irish immigrants aroused antagonism that took expression ominously in the first organized political movement against aliens. Worried citizens scanned crime reports which showed an excess of Irish names, and wild rumors spread. In a propaganda of fear, Irishmen were said to make up the personnel of gangs who roamed city streets, terrorizing citizens and inadequate police forces and inciting mobs to riot. As Roman Catholics they or their clerical leaders were accused of plotting the perversion of religious freedom in order to subject America to Papal control. Priests and bishops were said to deploy their communicants' votes in perversion of the purposes of Jefferson in founding the Democratic Party and of reformers in extending the franchise to the propertyless. In the early thirties, the painter and inventor, Samuel F. B. Morse, made himself a leading writer and political organizer of "Native Americanism," and the noted minister, Lyman Beecher, called for a Protestant counteroffensive against Catholicism. Morse's book, *Foreign Conspiracy against the Liberties of the United States,* was one of the most effective anti-Catholic attacks.

Germans and smaller Scandinavian groups came in for a share of nativist hatred as a minority of them were Roman Catholics and all of them spoke a strange language and imported strange customs. German athletic clubs, *turner-verein,* were accused of perpetuating Prussian military rites; German labor unions, *arbeiter-verein,* were accused of introducing alien radicalism, including the new "scientific" socialism of Karl Marx. While the Irish were blamed for taking jobs at lower wages than Americans would accept, the very industriousness of the Germans, instead of winning praise, was blamed because it, too, constituted "unfair competition" with Americans.

If immigrants were guilty of social disorder it was not by the incitement of their leaders. The founders of Native Americanism, on the other hand, were guilty of this. Inflamed crowds turned to violence. In

1834 a mob burned the Ursuline Convent in Charlestown, Massachusetts. In 1837, the Native American Association was founded in Washington. Factual consideration of the immigrant problem was submerged in a flood of sensational literature "exposing" the sins and plots of Catholicism. Political action was appealed for by the American Republican Party, founded in New York in 1843 with a platform calling for the disfranchisement of Catholics and the foreign-born. This and other local groups often coalesced with the Whig Party at election time. In May and July 1844, armed conflicts between Protestant and Catholic mobs in Philadelphia resulted in twenty deaths. In the same city the next year the national Native American Party was founded. "The Supreme Order of the Star-Spangled Banner," or "Sons of the Sires of '76," was organized in New York in 1849 as a secret society of descendants of at least two generations of Americans. It gave impetus to the Native American Party under the slogan of "America for Americans" and an oath to vote for none but the native-born in public elections.

In the disruption of the old parties that followed passage of the Kansas-Nebraska Act of 1854, the Native American Party won more political success than any nativist party before or since. Popularly called the "Know-Nothing Party" because its members professed ignorance when asked about it, the organization introduced the twin dangers of racialism and secrecy into American party politics. Tightening up of the naturalization laws was the party's most specific proposal, and nationalism with a racial bias its broadest tendency. The paraphernalia of a secret society fascinated a generation that fed on romanticism in its literature. College students were founding Greek-letter fraternities, elders were flocking into mysterious lodges, and hardly an American lacked a password or ritual costume. Most Northern Know-Nothings were soon attracted to the new Republican Party by its nationalism, although that party rejected racialism and, particularly during the Civil War, welcomed immigrants.

The innumerable social problems presented by the flood of immigrants could therefore be faced without the dangers that permanent political division along racial or religious lines would have brought. Most Irish and Catholic voters adhered to the Democratic Party while most German and Protestant immigrants became Republicans, but neither party made race or religion tests of membership or policy. The Americanization of the new groups was presently indicated by the organization of secret societies for themselves—the "Ancient Order of Hibernians," the "Knights of Columbus," and others—which were of the social rather than political variety. The Catholic Church, which began to be a major religion in America during the fifties, used its influence over immigrants to counsel loyalty to American institutions. It did not advocate any important change in the system of separation of church and state, thereby in the course of time silencing its most virulent critics. The Catholic Church in the United States adopted the American ideal of universal education. It established parochial schools, academies, and colleges and in them developed curricula which duplicated those of non-Catholic institutions with the addition of religious training and more persistent emphasis on classical studies. In charitable as well as educational activities, the progress of Catholicism was remarkable in view of the poverty of most communicants.

LIFE IN THE NORTH ON THE EVE OF CIVIL WAR

All observers agreed that by the 1830's life in America was differentiated from that of the Old World chiefly by exuberance and mobility, and that these phenomena were more characteristic of the North than the South. Economic prosperity that was broken for only a few years after 1837, and hardly at all by the Panic of 1857, joined with the zeal for reform to confirm faith in American institutions as the best in the world. Optimism was not shadowed even by the growth of poverty among factory workers and immigrants which became visible in urban slums. The convictions that a fortune could be made by exceptional talent and a competence by anyone were verified by experience. Poverty was regarded as either a temporary condition, as with immigrants, or a person's own fault. The Gold Rush to California was only an extreme instance of the general situation: not many actually made fortunes but everyone had a fairly equal chance to make one.

The consequence was a crystallization of the peculiar American idea that the "lower" class is a moral category to which only those people belong who are shiftless. All who work hard, live respectably, and try to improve their own or their children's position belong to the "middle" class no matter how poor they may be. The "middle-class mentality" became the pattern in the northeast and it spread westward closely behind the frontiersman. It bound together the laborer, the businessman, and the farmer more tightly than ever even while the actual disparity of wealth increased.

Luxuries and Diversions of a Middle-Class Society

The very wealthy set new standards of urban luxury and sophistication which were admired more than envied. Formerly the Southern gentry had created the most elegant modes of living in America; now the millionaires of New York made Southern standards seem rustic as they built imitations of French châteaux on Fifth Avenue and palatial pleasure houses, romantically called "cottages," at Newport. They acquired steam yachts for jaunts abroad, imported English servants, and lavished money on entertainments. Boston and Philadelphia also began to seem staid alongside the glitter of New York's Astors, Belmonts, and Vanderbilts, as did the old Knickerbocker families of New York itself. In new western cities, particularly Chicago and San Francisco, the wealthy took for their own the "New York" idea that spending money as well as making it is an exciting experience. The North Shore of Chicago, and Nob Hill overlooking the Golden Gate, sprouted fantastic mansions in carpenter-Gothic, Italian villa, and French Second Empire tastes. The owners of these conceded nothing to New York in fine horses, flamboyant equipages, European-imported dress, ornament and works of art, or routs and balls. Grand opera was the prime cultural guerdon of wealth in the West as well as the East, and opera houses were erected before schools in some mining towns. A magazine catering to the rich, like Nathaniel P. Willis's *Home Journal*, sought to bring English aristocratic standards to bear on the habits of the new-rich Americans and urged them to cultivate art, country life, and sports. It was during this period that the New York family of Henry James, senior, made the transition from commercial pursuits to the cultivated leisure which in the next generation produced a great novelist and a great philosopher.

It was remarkable how quickly the fashions and the manners of the wealthiest few spread to the many. Sea-bathing was first a daring diversion at Newport but was soon taken up by everyone who could afford a week at the shore under the new dispensation of the "summer vacation." Lawn tennis was imported from England as a fad of the privileged and was presently universalized. Dancing, that "bodily saltation" abhorred by the Puritans, became the rage with the invasion of the United States by the waltz, the schottische, and the polka. Horse-racing, popular since the late seventeenth century, supported ever-larger tracks. The one at Saratoga Springs, New York, was especially elaborate—with gambling, grandiose hotels, and curative waters as added attractions. Baseball gradually conquered the loyalty of all classes while the English game of cricket began to seem lackadaisical and "upper-class" and was almost forgotten. Sail-boat racing by amateurs became fashionable. American pride was sated when in 1850 an unheralded entry in an English regatta, the *America,* sailed away with "America's Cup" to the United States, where the trophy has remained despite periodic return matches.

When the middle class took up sports they were advocated for moralistic reasons of physical and mental health. These motives opened the way for women to make forays onto the tennis court, the croquet ground, and even the beaches. The dueller's code was still clung to by Southern aristocrats and the eye-gouging match was still practiced in frontier settlements, while the boom in games played for sport was chiefly an index of the rise of the middle class in the North.

The Cult of Nicety

Another index was the spread of "nice" manners. No Northern woman would allow herself to be designated by any name but "lady." Servant-ladies presently followed *Godey's* advice on knitted mittens to the point of wearing them at breakfast. Covering things up, from antimacassars on furniture to euphemisms for the plain realities of life, became a mania sanctioned as highest fashion by the new international arbiter of middle-class standards, Queen Victoria of England. Uneasy Americans studied etiquette books, such as Eliza Leslie's *Behavior Book* (1835) in which she said that listening at doorcracks was not *genteel*. The latter word along with its antonym *vulgar* now became current. Young ladies strove to reproduce the Countess of Blessington's verse-picture of a maiden in her chamber surrounded by dainty volumes, silken embroidery in its frame, an easel, and a harp—

> Here gay and placid speed the hours
> Among her music, books and flowers.

Under the new regime grandparents who were given to the hearty manners and language of the eighteenth century sometimes were hidden away from guests by the new generation, and men were led to refine their behavior and sentiments to a point justifying the title of a recent book— *The Feminine Fifties.*

Middle-class respectability and prosperity frowned on the enthusiasms of the Jacksonian reformers. The search for imminent utopia died out in the North. The last important experiment in socialism was led by the Perfectionist philosopher, John Humphrey Noyes. He was hounded with his followers out of Putney, Vermont, because his unorthodox ideas on love and marriage offended his neighbors. In Oneida, New York, the community presently gave up eccentricity and turned into a respectable business enterprise famous for its silverware. In the North evangelical religion gave way in the fifties to more sedate forms of worship. Cool rationalism in theology penetrated beyond the ranks of Unitarians as clergymen of the Baptist, Methodist, and other formerly volatile groups accepted the ethical approach to Christianity. A prosperous people were losing their sense of sin and damnation and finding emotional fulfillment in the excitements of getting money and the satisfactions of spending it on comforts and luxuries. The abolitionist movement was the last crusade with roots in Jacksonian democracy.

Dependence in Literature

The new middle class of the North rejected the greatest poet to emerge during the last years before the Civil War. Walt Whitman was born in a Long Island Dutch and Yankee farm family of strong Quaker and Jacksonian radical faiths. He educated himself as a journalist, edited the *Brooklyn Eagle* during the Mexican War, then left the Democratic Party to join the Free Soilers, and began work on *Leaves of Grass*. First published in 1855, this catch-all of Whitman's poetry went through nine editions before his death in 1892. The first edition shocked most of its few readers and reviewers. Its author rejected as "class poetry" literature which had celebrated the exceptional man in genteel language and correct form. He celebrated himself as the matrix of the plain people of America, embracing immigrants, prisoners, slaves and all toilers in his "Divine Average," exulting in the new life they were building in their own image, while embodying his vision in their robust language and in verse forms as defiant of tradition as the American experiment itself. He thought of himself as the prophet of democracy and exhorted like a revivalist, glorifying love as the unifier and redeemer of individualist democracy and exalting the life of the senses as the way to human fulfillment.

Emerson hailed Whitman as the author of *the* American poem, but middle-class taste found him vulgar and he acquired notoriety rather than fame. Later editions of *Leaves of Grass* contained lyrics, notably "When Lilacs Last in the Dooryard Bloom'd" on Lincoln's death, which gradually won general appreciation as high points in the history of English poetry. The Preface of the first edition Whitman later expanded into "Democratic Vistas" (1871) which ranks among the greatest assessments of the American experiment. After serving during the Civil War as a devoted volunteer nurse to wounded Union soldiers, the "Good Gray Poet" suffered a paralytic stroke and lived to advanced age in Camden, New Jersey, not so sure as in his youth that the American promise for which he had spoken would be realized in an age of Big Business. His poetry most accurately reflected the mid-century exuberance of Northern and Western life. His intoxication matched continental expansion by and for the average citizen.

The failure of most Americans of that time to accept Whitman as their voice was a failure of self-knowledge. They accepted the use of their own idiom only in writing that poked fun at "literature." Just before and during the Civil War, humorists in the folk tradition of cunning wit and tall tales in the oral "American" language, with garbled grammar and comical misspellings, tickled American risibilities. In newspaper columns were narrated the adventures of Major Jack Downing (Seba Smith), Sam Slick of Onion County, Connecticut (Thomas Chandler Haliburton),

Hosea Biglow (James Russell Lowell), Artemus Ward (Charles Farrar Browne), Petroleum Vesuvius Nasby (David Ross Locke), and tribes of their imitators. Abraham Lincoln loved these grotesques, and himself possessed a wide vein of their sly humor although he knew that, as Mark Twain said, "humor is not enough." In Twain's own work the American version of the English language would be made into a vehicle of mature art, and his humor saved him from Whitman's fate of public neglect.

James Russell Lowell reflected in 1852 that the predicament of America was like that of ancient Rome. The country was supreme in practical politics, aggrandizement, and trade, but in literature and the arts it was dependent on imports. A wide fissure had opened between assurance of the material grandeur of the republic and fear of American inferiority to Europe in all that belonged to culture. The democratic nationalism of the North and the West in the fifties was belied by eager servitude to Old World aristocratic models in manners and the arts. The injunction of Emerson to cultivate American cultural roots went unheeded as the hope of the newly-prosperous that culture could be bought almost always meant the importation of a European article. Francis Parkman concluded that aping John Bull was a Boston disease. The court of Napoleon III glittered more speciously than that of Queen Victoria and its lush styles of architecture, furniture, sculpture, and dress were copied by the American middle class.

The Crystal Palace Exhibition

Self-distrust was the chief meaning of the first American international exhibition, the New York Crystal Palace (1853). As if ashamed of American supremacy in the articles of utility for the many which had been shown at the London Crystal Palace in 1851, Americans copied that building and put on a show aimed at the hopeless goal of matching Europe in articles of luxury for the few. American statuary, furniture, glass, and metalwork were placed side by side with European examples and the results were mortifying. Worse still, the New York structure was only a fifth as large as the one in London! American manufacturers, builders, designers, and artists were merely inspired to more assiduous imitativeness. Uselessness was confused with good taste, trickery with good design. Monti's sculpture, "The Veiled Vestal," whose features were visible through a marble veil, produced soulful awe in American beholders. Stoves of iron acquired culture by being cast in molds of gothic tracery. Dainty chairs grew imitation elk horns, rustic furniture was made of cement to imitate bark and stumps of branches, urban furnishings were garnished with worldly rococo work. Suburban cemeteries were designed as sentimental parks with weeping willows, marble gravestones were shaped like beds, and enclosed family plots were provided with settees of iron ivy for the living. The cheapness of machine-made textiles permitted multiplication of layers of cloth in women's clothes to demonstrate leisure-status by their impracticality. Victorian romanticism produced stuffed ottomans in "oriental cozy corners" inspired by lines in Byron's *Don Juan;* Victorian prudery concealed the legs of pianos in lambrequins. The mania for unnecessary garniture was taken up by men in a sudden sprouting, late in the fifties, of luxuriant beards. When President-elect Lincoln journeyed to Washington in 1861, his shawl and his new beard denoted his efforts to be stylish.

By that time the plain rural ways of the mass of Americans and the classical tastes of the cultivated at the opening of the century had been abandoned in favor of the new middle-class standards of false gentility. Victorianism flourished also in the South, but there it supported agrarian-aristocratic ideals, and these would soon be pitted in battle against the Northern amalgam of romantic sentimentality, industrialism, nationalism, and democracy.

CHAPTER 32

The Ante-Bellum South:
Life and Institutions

In 1850, THERE WERE FIFTEEN STATES IN WHICH SLAVERY was still a legal institution. But the relative size of the slave population greatly increased as one proceeded from Delaware to Florida and from Missouri to Louisiana. Economic and social conditions varied in different parts of the South, and in some places they changed considerably in the last ante-bellum decade. Between 1850 and 1860, the northernmost slave states in varying degrees became more Northern, and the cotton states more Southern. It was in the Lower South that the contrast with the North was greatest, and there the sectional divergence was to prove most fateful. The plantation as an economic institution was most highly developed in the Land of Cotton, and there the Confederacy was to be born.

The plain people of the slave states were more like those of the free states than has often been supposed, but they were more homogeneous and more conservative. Southerners themselves claimed that their civilization followed old American patterns more closely than that of the North did. By comparison, Southern life was unprogressive but, viewed as a whole, it was less dominated by money than Northern life was, and at its best it was marked by a social grace which the old families of the Northeast rarely matched and the newly rich of New York and Chicago had certainly not attained. This was afterwards embodied in a cherished and persistent American tradition. On the other hand, the social philosophy which was evolved in defense of slavery was unacceptable to the vast body of Northerners, and in later years it seemed extreme to most Southerners themselves. Also, time showed unmistakably that slavery threw the economic life of the region out of balance.

SOUTHERN AGRICULTURE

The Southern ante-bellum economy differed from the Northern in that it was less diversified and more agricultural. Despite the growth of the Northwest and the predominance of that region in small grains, the South, in the two decades before the Civil War, was still ahead in agricultural products. It produced all the cotton, rice, and sugar, practically all of the tobacco and hemp, about half of the corn, and more than one-fourth of the wheat. The most significant agricultural invention of the era was the work of a Virginian, Cyrus Hall McCormick, though his reaper was more effective on the western prairies than in the hilly grainfields of his native state. In the older regions, especially in the Upper South, real progress had been made toward diversification of crops and a fair start had been made in industry, but after the troubles of the 1840's, Southern producers of major staple crops (cotton, tobacco, and sugar) came in the 1850's into an era of such prosperity that they were reconciled anew to their predominantly agricultural economy. The system did not escape local criticism, but most people were far more disposed to defend than to change it.

Cotton Expansion in the Gulf States

It was in 1858 that James H. Hammond of South Carolina asserted that no power on earth would dare make war on the chief Southern product. "Cotton is king," he said. The most notable economic development of the two decades before this boast was tested in war was the extension of cotton culture in the Southwest. The crop increased by 60 per cent in the 1840's and in the last ante-bellum decade it doubled, reaching in 1859 the unparalleled total of 4,500,000 bales. In slightly more than half a century the fleecy product had increased thirtyfold.

The swift expansion of cotton culture in the Gulf states was owing to the suitability of the alluvial lands along the Alabama rivers, the Mississippi, the Red River, the Arkansas, the Brazos, and other streams. There was nothing in the South Atlantic states which could be compared to this deep black soil. Some of the best lands required large expenditures for levees, and this fact made it practically inevitable that they should be taken up by men with capital rather than by pioneer farmers. The streams provided easy transportation to the seaports, especially New Orleans. Farmers in the red hills of the Piedmont had no such physical advantages.

The center of cotton culture now lay in the lower Mississippi Valley. In terms of production the order of the leading states in 1849 was Alabama, Georgia, Mississippi, and South Carolina. Ten years later Mississippi, whose crop was nearly tripled, stood first; Alabama was second, being followed by Louisiana with a fourfold increase, and Georgia; then came Texas and Arkansas, while South Carolina was seventh. In the 1850's there was much talk of "Texas fever," which was not a disease but a mania. The population of that state tripled in the decade and its cotton crop increased sevenfold, despite the fact that the black lands of the eastern prairie, later to be white with cotton, were still undeveloped.

Meanwhile, the sugar industry was thriving in Louisiana. It reached a peak in 1858-1859, when the crop had four times the value it had in 1835-1836, the earliest date for which reliable statistics are available. The financial requirements of sugar production were such that this may be described as commercial agriculture *par excellence.* Frederick Law Olmsted, the most careful Northern observer of Southern agriculture in the era, visited one plantation in Louisiana on which the sugar-works were said to have cost $100,000. He commented on the admirable apparatus on many of the plantations, saying that the owners of these were "among the most intelligent, enterprising and wealthy men of business in the United States." Cotton culture on the rich alluvial lands of the Gulf states had also become big business, according to the standards of those times.

Agricultural expansion in the Old Southwest had complicated the economic situation of the Atlantic states. Not only was South Carolina subjected to a drain of population (free and slave) and to the loss of such capital as her emigrant sons carried with them, but also to direct competition in her major crop, which she could not produce as effectively as the planters in the Gulf states. A degree of stability had been given her economy by her minor crops of rice and sea island cotton. In the last ante-bellum decade, furthermore, the foreign and domestic demand for cotton reached such a point that South Carolina could cultivate it advantageously at the current price, even though her profits were much smaller than those in the Southwest. She was never so prosperous as to be content, however, and her economic difficulties continued to be reflected in her political hostility to all things Northern.

The Upper South

A major problem of South Carolina arose from soil depletion, and this was an even greater problem in the old tobacco states, especially in Virginia. The tobacco plant is notoriously exhaustive of the soil, and the red lands of the Piedmont are specially subject to erosion. Until about 1850 the market was unfavorable, because of the tendency of European countries to impose heavy duties on tobacco and encourage their own production of it. Nowhere more than in Virginia was there talk of agricultural readjustment, and in John Taylor of Caroline and Edmund Ruffin she produced two of the best known of Southern agricultural reformers. The former advocated deep plowing, rotation of crops, fertilization by manure, and the restoration of wornout lands by enclosure without grazing. The most influential of ante-bellum agricultural reformers, however, was Ruffin, whose *Essay on Calcareous Manures* was published in 1832 and afterwards expanded. By means of books and numerous articles and his activity in agricultural societies he popularized the use of marl throughout the Southeast while greatly influencing farmers in other regions.

Eventually there were agricultural societies in practically all the southern states. Interest in soil conservation and improvement was naturally greatest, however, where virgin land was not available. There were many agricultural journals, whose life was generally short, and there were agricultural professorships in several educational institutions, though there was no agricultural college. Sale of slaves to the southward was of great economic advantage to the old tobacco states in the thirties and forties, but in the last ante-bellum decade Virginia was faced with a real labor shortage. Contour plowing was considerably employed in the Piedmont and commercial fertilizers began to be used in the 1840's. Guano was then introduced, and it was more used in Maryland and Virginia than anywhere else in the South. Generally it was regarded as too costly.

Because of improved methods, better transportation, and changed external circumstances the agriculture of the old states of the Upper South took a definite turn for the better in the last decade of the era. More reliance was now placed on grain crops. Virginia and Maryland between them produced more than half of the southern wheat and almost half of the oats. The tobacco market was still important, however, and it definitely improved. Export prices became relatively high and the domestic demand expanded. The chief tobacco-producing states were Virginia, Kentucky, and Tennessee in that order. North Carolina had strengthened her economy by developing lumbering and naval stores. The net result of all of this was that, omitting South Carolina, the agricultural prosperity of the old region east of the Blue Ridge was greater in the 1850's than it had been since the beginning of the American Revolution.

The older trans-Appalachian slave states of the Upper South, Kentucky and Tennessee, were spared the agonies of agricultural readjustment because they had long had a mixed economy, and the newer state of Missouri, despite its sentimental and economic ties with the South, was Middle Western in its economic character. Some cotton was raised in southeastern Missouri when the season was long enough, and a great deal in the western counties of Tennessee along the Mississippi, while hemp was produced in Kentucky and Missouri. The bluegrass region of Kentucky and the Nashville basin of Tennessee were the home of blooded horses, and the best-known market for mules was in St. Louis. These were humbler animals—"without pride in ancestry or hope of posterity" as the saying went—but they were indispensable in the cotton fields, and the mule business constituted an important tie between Missouri and the Lower South. These three states were also cattle states but the largest herds roamed the broad plains of Texas.

The Plantation System

The ante-bellum plantation system, considered as an economic form, did not reach its fullest development in the tobacco country, where the trend had long been toward diversified agriculture, but in the cotton and sugar country. Many of the plantations of the Lower South, especially those of medium size, reflected the patriarchal tradition of the older states, but the larger they were the more likely they were to assume the form of a business enterprise rather than a way of life. Under this plantation system agriculture was a large-scale commercial undertaking, carried on in an outdoor factory. The owner of a great plantation did not necessarily live on it. This was a business enterprise, requiring large capital investment, and the test of success was the money income.

The competitive advantage of large enterprises under a system of slave labor was great. The available capital permitted the employment of the best equipment and the most capable overseers; it also enabled owners to take advantage of the market to a degree that was impossible for men with smaller resources. The nature of cotton culture, involving a number of relatively simple operations over a long period of months, lent itself to large-scale management. Frederick Law Olmsted put the matter thus: "Other things being equal, . . . the smaller the estate of slaves, the less is their rate of production per head; and, as a rule, the larger the slave estate the larger is the production per head." It was a matter of good policy to keep the workers well-fed and healthy, but they could be kept at the subsistence level. The price of prime field hands was so high in the last ante-bellum decade as to lead some students to conclude that their employment was ceasing to be economical, and this was a form of competition which no small farmer or small planter could hope to meet.

Some of the cotton plantations on the Mississippi, the Red River, and the Brazos on which Olmsted was told an average of ten bales of cotton to each field hand were raised, provided a picture of the ideal profit situation. The soil was "a perfect garden mould, well-drained and guarded by levees," and he had seen few northern farms that were so well tilled. The laborers worked steadily from dawn till dusk under the direction of skillful and vigilant overseers. They had excellent tools and the best sort of gins and processes, well located for access to steamboats. Olmsted figured that even at seven bales per hand the profits would be enormous, and believed that a return of 15 per cent on the capital investment could easily be gained.

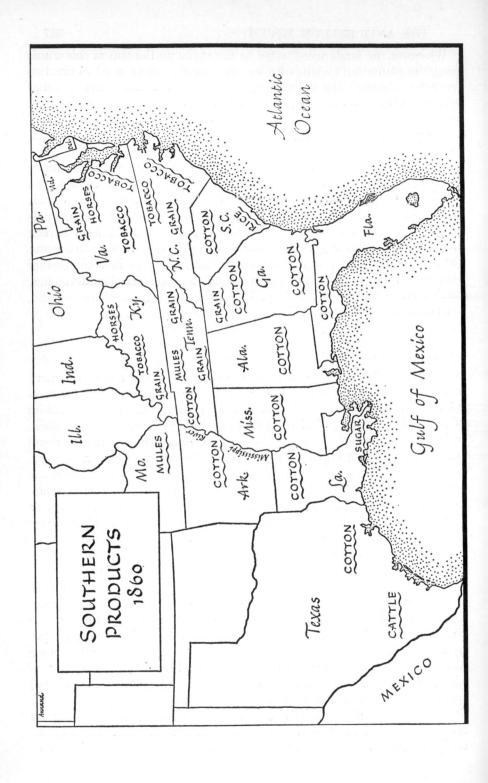

Wherever the lands were suited to the ready production of this staple crop, the plantation system with its advantages of large-scale production tended to supplant the self-sufficient economy of pioneer farmers. Since cotton was the readiest cash crop, most farmers in the proper climate raised some of it, especially when the price was good. The general tendency of the plantation system was to check the movement toward diversification. Owing to their heavy investment and the specialized nature of their operations, the great planters were disposed to increase production in times of low prices, rather than curtail it, hoping to offset the latter by quantity. Thus, while they followed the best methods of the time on their own acres, they tended to hold back the progress of Southern agriculture as a whole. Also, the profits from cotton culture checked the movement toward larger economic diversification by absorbing capital, labor, and capable management in the plantation business. The development of industry was slowed, and commerce and finance remained throughout ante-bellum times the handmaidens of staple agriculture. What is more, a disproportionate share of profits fell into Northern hands.

COMMERCE AND INDUSTRY

Until 1860, the bulk of American exports consisted of southern products. Cotton was much the greatest of these; in 1860, it comprised more than half of the total in value. Yet Southerners played practically no part in carrying these products across the seas to foreign markets. In the course of time they became painfully aware that an excessive share of the profits from this commerce went to the North, especially to New York, but they never succeeded in remedying a situation which continued, actually, into the twentieth century. The result was that the staple-producing South remained in a colonial status. The trend that appeared after the War of 1812 was accentuated by the very success of cotton culture and the improvement in facilities of transportation.

The Course of Trade

The chief port of the Upper South was Baltimore, which handled both grain and tobacco. Tobacco was also shipped from the river port of Richmond—to New York in small-draft boats. The potentialities of Norfolk, which was the nearest physical match of New York as a harbor, were not utilized in this period. In North Carolina, Wilmington at the mouth of the Cape Fear River became an important outlet for naval stores, but only vessels of shallow draft could enter its harbor.

Among the cotton ports Charleston was the early leader. Because of its location on the river of the same name, Savannah could tap the interior more easily, but it never managed to catch up with Charleston.

The chief Gulf ports were Mobile, which did practically no importing business but gradually passed Charleston and Savannah in exports, and New Orleans. The Crescent City, favorably located on the Mississippi, became the greatest of southern ports by far. As the outlet of the richest of all the cotton districts, it took first rank in 1840 in the exports of that commodity. Ten years later it was even further in the lead and had attained a population of 168,000, which was nearly equal to that of Boston. The exports of New Orleans were not limited to cotton. It shipped sugar from the Louisiana canefields and before the railroad age it was the outlet of the entire Mississippi Valley; it even shipped lead from Galena, Illinois, and in the decade beginning in 1834 it surpassed New York in the total value of exports. Toward the end of the ante-bellum era it suffered relatively from the development of through traffic on the northern railroads between West and East, but it remained a seat of lush prosperity. In 1860, it still was second only to New York in exports, and in imports it was exceeded only by New York and Boston.

The commercial predominance of New York can be dated from the establishment of regular packet service with England in the 1820's. Following that, the enterprising New Yorkers (many of whom had come originally from New England) established a coastal packet service with southern ports in order to collect cargoes for their eastbound vessels. The result was that in a period when northern products were little desired by Europe, the chief exports from New York were cotton, rice, naval stores, and other southern products, and the South received most of its imports by way of New York.

This "enslaving of the cotton ports" has been described by Robert G. Albion, historian of the port of New York and of the packet ships, as "one of the most impudent acts in American Commercial history." Both exports and imports traveled several hundreds of miles further than they needed to, costs were increased by loading and unloading in New York, and the commissions, interest, insurance premiums, freight, and profits went chiefly to that city. One Southerner said that of every dollar paid for cotton, forty cents went to Northerners. Southern merchants fell into the practice of going to New York in the summer to purchase stocks of goods, and it is worthy of note that the advertisements in the metropolitan newspapers were addressed to "Southern and Western Merchants." Not until the middle of the 1840's did they begin to be directed to "Western and Southern Merchants."

The direct exportation from southern ports was almost wholly from the Gulf ports, and in that case the trade generally followed what has been called the "cotton triangle." Packet ships from New Orleans and Mobile sailed to Europe, picked up cargoes of manufactured goods and immigrants, carried them to New York, and then sailed to the Gulf coast with the sort of goods the Southerners wanted. The ships themselves were owned by New Yorkers.

The disadvantages to the South arising from the dominance of its commerce by New York were perceived in Charleston in the early 1830's and were talked about in several commercial conventions in the Southeast after the panic of 1837. Direct trade with Europe was then advocated. In 1839, Matthew Fontaine Maury of Virginia, the noted oceanographer, pointed out the real difficulties. New York was closer to Liverpool and Le Havre than any of the southern ports were, and New Yorkers had commercial experience which no other Americans could match. The Southerners lacked capital as well as experience, and in the next two decades the advantages of New York increased rather than diminished. In the era of ocean steamships, which could disregard winds and currents, the shortness of the crossing favored the North Atlantic ports. Meanwhile, the citizens of Charleston and Savannah had turned their attention to railroads, and in the Gulf states cotton culture was sufficiently rewarding to distract attention from Northern control of commerce.

The major physical problem of domestic commerce, as the Southerners saw it until the last decade of the ante-bellum era, was that of facilitating transportation between the seaports and the staple-producing districts. Difficulties were greatest in the Southeast, since rivers could be better relied on in the Gulf States. The process of railroad development was to link the coastal ports with fall-line centers and then to run lateral feeder lines in the cotton-producing country.

Seeking to tap the cotton trade which went to Savannah, the enterprising Charlestonians pushed the Charleston and Hamburg Railroad to the town opposite Augusta on the Savannah River. Put into operation in part in 1830 and completed in 1833 to its full length of 136 miles, this road was then the longest railroad in the world. Soon a road was built from Savannah into the interior, and before the war Georgia possessed with this and other lines the best planned railway system of any southern state. An important link was the state-constructed road (1851) from the junction town of Atlanta to Chattanooga.

Meanwhile, the Charlestonians under the enthusiastic leadership of Robert Y. Hayne had projected a road to the West through the mountains that hemmed their state in and deprived their proud city of Western commerce. This was the Louisville, Cincinnati and Charleston, which was chartered in 1836 and vigorously promoted but had to be abandoned after the panic of 1837. The net result of most of these railroad activities in the Southeast was simply to facilitate the same type of commerce that was already being carried on, and thus to strengthen the hold of cotton on the economy. Little was done to facilitate North-South traffic. In 1860, it was possible, however, to go by rail from Alexandria, Virginia, to Chattanooga; and the line from Chattanooga to Memphis on the Mississippi linked the Southeast with the Gulf states and served to unify the South.

The Factorage System

In marketing their staples the Southern planters relied chiefly on factors. A factor may be described as a commission merchant who acted as agent for the planters, serving as middleman between them and the purchasers. The system represented the development of one that had prevailed in colonial times in plantation districts, when the factors had been English and Scottish, and it was found in all the staple-producing districts, though most notably in connection with cotton. The factor provided credit in nearly all cases and often he acted as purchasing agent for planters. Interest on advances generally ranged from 8 to 12 per cent and purchases were made at credit prices. This was part of the toll which Southern agriculture paid to outside interests, for the factors were generally Northerners or representatives of Northern or English houses. As a rule they made headquarters in the seaport cities but many of them were residents of inland centers and they penetrated the entire plantation country in quest of business. It has been said that they were in the South, not of it.

The custom of making advances on cotton after it had been delivered but before it had been sold was not at all surprising in view of the length of time required for marketing, but factors even made advances on growing crops. These might be for physical improvements or the purchase of slaves; they might be for current supplies. In the case of such advances the planter agreed to market the whole of his crop through the factor, and by means of a penalty clause he promised to pay a certain amount per bale for any shortage below the stipulated quantity. The system accentuated the emphasis on staple crops and tended to fix even the more prosperous planters in a vicious circle of recurrent debt.

It may be asked why there was recourse to factors rather than to banks for credit. The answer lies both in the limitations of Southern resources of capital and in painful past banking experience with agricultural loans. The stronger financial institutions were generally located in the seaport cities, where they were relatively inaccessible to planters, and the most successful of them limited themselves to more conventional commercial banking. They were less disposed to make advances to planters than to factors, and the latter could also get credit in the North and in England. The profits accruing to the total transaction of marketing such a staple crop as cotton were so great that Northern and British houses could afford to take a risk.

The factorage system favored the seaport cities and its services were rendered chiefly to the larger planters. Very similar services were provided, however, by the country stores. These were chiefly in the middling districts and mainly served small planters and farmers who raised other crops besides staples. Nowhere were they more typical than in such a state as Tennessee, where agriculture was relatively diversified. They provided supplies and merchandise on a credit basis, for relatively little actual money was passed in the agricultural South and there was a long time between crops. Credit for a year was the rule rather than the exception, and in turn the storekeepers had to get credit from Northern wholesalers. Thus the vast body of rural Southerners paid credit prices, and profits went chiefly to the region where there was most capital, that is, the Northeast.

Southern Industry

In the series of Southern commercial conventions which began in the late 1840's there was discussion of developing a greater degree of self-sufficiency in industry. More was done to develop manufacturing than has often been supposed, but in comparison with the North the slaveholding states did not hold their own in the two decades, 1840-1860. At the beginning of the period the South had 20 per cent of the capital invested in industry, and at the end it had about 16 per cent. The increase in the value of the Southern industrial output in the last decade, 1850-1860, was more than 75 per cent but that was less than the increase in the whole country and the total Southern output was less than 15 per cent of that of the entire Republic. That is, the North increased the advantage it already had. Furthermore, about three-fourths of the Southern industrial product came from four states of the Upper South—Virginia, Missouri, Maryland, and Kentucky. It was in the borderland, not in the Lower South where the main seats of political dissatisfaction lay, that the movement toward economic reorganization made greatest headway.

The most important Southern industries were processing industries, and of these milling (flour and cornmeal) was much the most important. The chief centers were Richmond, where one mill could produce a thousand barrels of flour per day, and Baltimore. Next came the products of lumbering and sawmills, notably in North Carolina, and tobacco factories. Except for cigars, Virginia and North Carolina by 1860 dominated the tobacco business. They now processed most of their product and had a virtual monopoly on chewing tobacco—the extensive use of which in rural America horrified so many foreign visitors in this period.

With the Tredegar Iron Works (established in 1837), Richmond was also the Southern leader in that industry, employing slave labor extensively. The development of cotton mills near the source of supply was significant, though not yet impressive. The best-known, though not the earliest, of these was the Graniteville Mill (1846) of William Gregg in South Carolina. This was a paternalistic enterprise, employing only white labor. A major purpose of Gregg, who published a series of essays urging the development of domestic industry, was to make provision for poorer white people who were at a disadvantage under the slavery system. Georgia was the leading southern state in cotton mills in 1860, and the war served to set back for several decades the industrial developments which in some southern states were beginning to promise some release from staple agriculture on a long-credit system.

Slavery and the Economy

Slavery was profitable to individual owners under certain conditions. The producer of cotton, sugar, and rice on a large scale gained competitive advantages from the use of slave labor organized in gangs. To Northern observers, however, the Southern slaves generally seemed inefficient except on the great plantations, and this inefficiency put the slave economy at a disadvantage whenever it was in competition with the existing labor of the North. Thus the system tended to discourage the economic diversification that the South needed. Whether rightly or not, most Southerners regarded slave labor as suited to nothing but staple production. Experience with railroad construction in Georgia and in ironworks in Virginia argued otherwise, but the conviction persisted with respect to industry generally and this was an important reason, though not the only one, why Southerners did not promote it more. In the 1850's there was a real labor shortage in Virginia, where industry was being most promoted. Hordes of European immigrants were pouring into the country then, but the existence of slavery was a major reason why very few of them went south. Equally important was the absorption of capital by the slavery system. Thus, without raising the moral or social question, we can safely say on economic grounds alone that slavery was distinctly disadvantageous to the region where it existed.

SOUTHERN SOCIETY

In the two decades before the Civil War, the free population of the fifteen slaveholding states was about two-thirds of the total, and the slave population about one-third. But the proportions varied in the different states, and political and social attitudes varied with them. In Delaware, the slave population was so small that this little commonwealth was a slave state in little more than name; in 1860, the slaves comprised less than a tenth of the total in Missouri and about an eighth in Maryland. The fraction rose to about a fifth in Kentucky, a fourth in Tennessee, and a third in Virginia and North Carolina. In the states of the Lower South, with the single exception of Texas, the proportion was much larger. The average for these states was about 45 per cent, the figure for South Carolina being approximately 57 per cent and that for Mississippi only a little lower. It was in that part of the country, and only in that part, that the people were "half-slave and half-free."

Among the whites in the region as a whole about one-third were members of the slaveholding families. But the percentage of great planters—with fifty slaves or more—was very small and they were largely confined to the Lower South. The term "planter" is generally used for the holder of at least ten slaves. If allowance is made for the children who would normally be included in such a group, no smaller number of slaves would warrant the employment of an overseer. The lesser planters, with from 10 to 49 slaves, were considerably more numerous than the great planters, but most holders of slaves had fewer than nine. The latter, who were farmers under the definition, held about one-fourth of the total of slaves. From these figures it appears that, while most of the slaves were on plantations, most of the individual slaveholders were not even small planters, but were farmers living on their own acres and operating without the help of overseers.

The Plain People

In the border states of Delaware, Missouri, and Maryland the non-slaveholding whites differed little from the inhabitants of the contiguous free states. In the states below the Potomac and the Ohio, they ranged from backward mountaineers and rude herdsmen in the piney woods and "one-horse" farmers to large farmers, with from 300 to 400 acres, who followed agriculture that was largely self-sufficient and often lived in districts where slavery was practically nonexistent. Among such districts were western Virginia, northern Georgia, eastern Tennessee, eastern Mississippi, and western Louisiana. Yeoman farmers were rarely to be found on alluvial lands, but they were intermixed with planters in intermediate counties and they dominated certain districts.

The backcountry of the Gulf states had been opened up within a generation, and the settlers there remained in the frontier stage of society longer than in comparable regions north of the Ohio, because towns did not develop among them to anything like the same degree. But on fresh land in a mild climate they were pretty sure of making a good living, and their social life was much like that of plain farmers elsewhere. They had camp meetings, corn huskings, logrollings, and housewarmings much as people did in Lincoln's Illinois. To be a good rider was a daily necessity and marksmanship with the rifle was highly prized. Out of men like these the Confederate Army was to be largely recruited. Politically, they were often at loggerheads with the plantation districts, but their class consciousness was far more manifest in their attitude toward the Negroes than toward the plantation magnates. These relatively unlettered people, who were emotional and orthodox in religion, were little touched by the ideas of the Enlightenment that had liberalized the social philosophy of the Virginia aristocracy in the eighteenth century, and to them their color seemed a badge of superiority which they shared with the richest planter. On grounds of regional pride they resented attacks on Southern institutions that emanated from the heterogeneous North, and, while slavery was much disliked by farmers in western Virginia and North Carolina and eastern Tennessee, the yeomen of the Lower South accepted it. This was not for economic reasons but on grounds of race relations. Their philosophy was well summed up by an illiterate white man who was discussing the slaves with Frederick Law Olmsted on the Mississippi. "It wouldn't do no good to free 'em and let 'em hang around," he said; "if they was free no man couldn't live." By adding "Taint right to keep 'em as it is" he showed that he perceived the moral dilemma, but he could see no way to resolve it.

The term "poor white," as commonly used, implies degradation which need not be associated with people who are poor in worldly goods. Scholars have generally not applied it to the mountaineers, regarding them as an undeveloped but not a degraded people. In the vastness of the southern Appalachians they lived in suspicious isolation, playing no real part in political life, though they were characteristically hostile to the party and group that chanced to be in power. The designation "poor white" can be applied with more historical justification to certain derelicts in plantation districts and certain rude settlers in the piney woods of the coastal plain that the planters had passed by. These people were described by one observer as "the laziest two-legged animals that walk erect on the fact of the earth"; and by another as the world's "most degraded race of human beings claiming an Anglo-Saxon origin." Because of later medical discoveries, we can now attribute this degeneracy very considerably to physical causes. These people could not avoid the malaria from which the plantation families of the Low Country fled in the summer season; and in their warm climate they went barefoot and became afflicted with hookworm. In a later generation numerous victims of hookworm were found and cured in just the districts where the antebellum "poor whites" dwelt; but the contemporaries of the latter did not have a medical explanation for their pasty faces, their clay-eating habits, and their shiftless ways.

The Slaves

If the "poor whites" were long misunderstood, and the Southern yeomen long ignored, the slaves have rarely been able to appear at the bar of history in their own right because practically all of them were necessarily inarticulate. They had a few spokesmen in persons who escaped from slavery; among these the eloquent Frederick Douglass, who published a noted autobiography, was conspicuous. Those who remained in bondage were not in position to write about themselves, and it was exceedingly difficult for inquiring white men to probe their minds, hence our judgment on slavery as a way of life must be largely external. There are at least two fundamental objections to it which arise in the modern mind. It gave arbitrary power to masters, and that is sufficient ground for condemning the institution, regardless of the way in which that authority may have been exercised. Furthermore, slavery had become a closed system from which there was little or no hope of escape. The system was tightened in the face of external criticism and it was described by leading Southern spokesmen as positively good. The most distressing aspect of the situation was its hopelessness.

The actual conditions of slave life varied with circumstances and masters. Conditions were best among household slaves, who enjoyed a privileged position and were often the objects of genuine affection. The inscription on one slave's tombstone reveals a sentiment that was by no means uncommon: the family that he had served honored him in death, they said, but in life they gave him love, "for he was one of us." The picture of "Mammy," who bossed the children if she did not dominate the household, became a stereotype. The tolerance of masters and mistresses became proverbial and some of them were notoriously indulgent—like "Aunty Betty" Witherspoon of South Carolina who was eventually strangled by slaves whom she had spoiled. But there were few cases of such ill-requited kindness, and never again were personal relations between whites and blacks to be so intimate or affectionate as they were in ante-bellum households. According to the most genteel tradition, domestics were called servants not slaves, and in the best circles it was very bad form to call one of them a "nigger" in his own presence. As late as 1865, Mrs. Mary Boykin Chesnut, whose Diary from Dixie reflects the most aristocratic tradition, could not tolerate that term. Slave domestics in the South were probably as well treated as servants in Northern states in this period, and instead of low wages they had security. The gaiety of the Negroes became a byword, and their humor and homespun philosophy left a perceptible impress on the white people. But even in households there was always the shadow of arbitrary power, and even there whippings were by no means unknown. Furthermore, the old tradition that families should not be broken up by sale had grown weaker as slavery was increasingly commercialized.

Slaves monopolized the field of domestic service in town as well as country and some of them were artisans. They were often hired out, but white artisans resented their competition. Some of them were engaged in industry, but the predominant opinion of white men was that their proper place was on the land, and that is where most of them were.

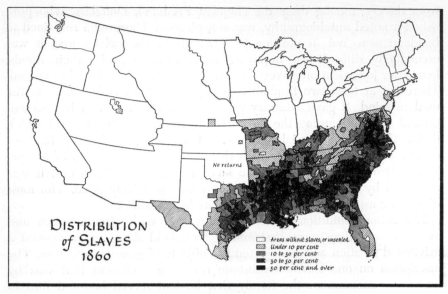

DISTRIBUTION
of SLAVES
1860

Areas without slaves, or unsettled
Under 10 per cent
10 to 30 per cent
30 to 50 per cent
50 per cent and over

No returns

SOURCE: Paullin, *Atlas of the Historical Geography of the United States*

Olmsted confirmed the conventional opinion that the field workers were best treated in small agricultural establishments, and he believed they were better treated in North Carolina and Virginia than in the Lower South. Contacts between masters and field hands became rarer as the size of establishments increased. In the great "outdoor factories," where the owner was only an occasional visitor, the overseers knew little more about them as human beings than their names. The system of plantation slavery was most effective from the economic point of view where it was most impersonal and least humane. The success of an overseer depended on the size of the crop he made. It was not good business to work or beat the slaves to death, and physical conditions tended to be better on great plantations than on small, just as tools did. But whereas the old ideal was that of the patriarchal community, that of the commercialized plantation was the money-making factory. In this the slaves were just so many hands to be exploited and they were defenseless against cruelty. Great inhumanity was to be found in industrial establishments in the Northeast and in England in this period, as apologists for slavery did not fail to point out, but two wrongs did not make a right and these dark-skinned Southern workers did not even have a chance to quit.

The harsh treatment of runaways was one of the most offensive features of Southern life, and along with the domestic slave trade it was the aspect of slavery that was most extensively advertised in the North. The slaves had no status in law in their own right; they were property, not men and women. There were also about a quarter of a million free

Negroes in the South, and their situation can be best described by saying that they were like slaves except that they owed allegiance to no legal master and that, by the same token, they had no guardian. Their position had deteriorated in the North, where they were present in about the same numbers, and cases are on record in the South where free Negroes of their own volition returned to slavery, which would at least provide them with security. No more striking illustration can be given of their plight.

The Ruling Planters

Southern society was much more fluid and mobile than has often been supposed, and in it men could and often did rise to affluence within a generation. The "slave barons" were not necessarily of aristocratic lineage, just as the new merchant princes in New York were not. Frederick Law Olmsted found in the best society of South Carolina "less vulgar display and more intrinsic elegance, and habitual refinement" than in any distinct Northern class, but in newer regions of the Lower South he found many who had the characteristics of the *nouveaux riches*. In the Upper South more than the Lower, and in the seaboard states more than in the Gulf states, the traditions of the landed gentry were maintained. The cotton capitalists were less affected by the spirit of *noblesse oblige*, more by that of the marketplace. Among them, more than any other Southern group, were to be found extreme advocates of the expansion of the area of slavery.

The planters exercised power that was out of all proportion to their numbers. This may be attributed in part to the weight and influence of wealth at a time when, presumably, every white man was free to acquire it. But while there was no more jealousy of rich men as rich men in the South than in the North at this stage, wealth as such carried less prestige in a region where the vast majority of people lived on the land in relative independence and where daily life was marked by little exchange of cash. No Southern taunt of the Yankees was more common than that the latter measured everything by money. The prestige of the planting class was traditional in the older parts of the South, and was similar to that of the country gentry in England to whom the Virginians in particular had looked back for models. The tradition that larger landholders should direct public affairs weakened in the newer regions but it by no means vanished.

To some extent the political dominance of the planters can be attributed to the form of Southern political institutions. In South Carolina, where more power was centered in the legislature than in the other states, representation in that body was still based on property as well as population. In Louisiana, representation was based on population, both slave and free, and this gave a decided advantage to slaveholders in the plantation districts where nonvoting slaves were so numerous. Along with Virginia, where the real seat of power was in the counties, these were the states where the organization of government had been most favorable to control by the planters, but in the Old Dominion the power of the county oligarchies was reduced in the last ante-bellum decade and the most serious inequities in representation were corrected. Everywhere, in the fifties, there was universal suffrage, and it would have been difficult to find in the entire country constitutions that were more democratic in form than those of Mississippi and Alabama. Even in the older states the day had passed when public office went automatically to the sons of great families, and men of humble origin often attained political prominence, though examples were rarer in South Carolina than elsewhere. Baby-kissing politicians appeared in the cotton country as they did in the Middle West. The political power of the planters was in some part the power of wealth and in some degree it rested on tradition, but it was exercised chiefly by means of persuasion. The circumstances of the times played into the hands of men with a vested interest in slavery and permitted them to identify the institution with regional patriotism and white supremacy. The result was to blur the lines of conflict between economic classes among the whites.

The best-known attack on the ruling class in behalf of the nonslaveholding whites was that of Hinton R. Helper in *The Impending Crisis* (1857). Helper, a North Carolinian, painted a vivid picture of Southern economic backwardness and attributed this to the short-sighted selfishness of the master class. Among other bitter things he said: "The lords of the lash are not only absolute masters of the blacks, . . . but they are also the oracles and arbiters of all non-slaveholding whites, whose freedom is purely nominal, and whose unparalleled illiteracy and degradation is purposely and fiendishly perpetuated." This sensational book was received with enthusiasm in the North, where it was widely distributed by the Republican Party in the years 1858-1860, and it was bitterly assailed in the South by proslavery spokesmen. But it did not reach many of the nonslaveholders whom it sought to rally, and the yeomen farmers, if they had read it, would not have liked Helper's identification of them with the "poor whites," who were indeed outcasts. The nonslaveholders constituted no unified group which could be readily mobilized against the planters. As farmers most of them lived independent lives and they did not regard themselves as an exploited class, or even as being in competition with the planters. Social solidarity among the whites was by no means complete, but in the region as a whole there was not much class consciousness. The planters set the political and social pattern, and with relatively slight dissent the plain people accepted it.

Southern Civilization

The social life of the planters has become a national legend, and the historian has difficulty in separating fact from fiction when survey-ing it. As Northerners before the war saw slavery through the eyes of Harriet Beecher Stowe, at a later time they—and most Southerners with them—saw ante-bellum Southern life through the eyes of romancers. It is probable that most Americans still think of that vanished civiliza-tion in terms of its extremes. On the one hand they see the slaves, and on the other rich planters, living in white-columned houses, drinking mint juleps from early morning, racing horses, and fighting duels at the drop of the hat in defense of ladies who were always beautiful.

The Plantation Ideal

The plantation of tradition is most often set in Virginia, though Mrs. Stowe placed it in Kentucky, and in *Gone with the Wind* Americans of the twentieth century saw it in the cotton country of Georgia. Social life was nowhere so luxuriant as in the region tributary to New Orleans, but in the chief southern city it had a Creole flavor, as the cooking did, and this was not country life in the normal Southern sense. Nowhere in the region did aristocracy flourish more than in the low country of South Carolina. Mansions of serene beauty can still be seen there amid the azaleas. Yet the planters left their estates during the malaria season and the glory of the most passionately self-conscious of all the southern states was always Charleston, with its aristocratic town houses. The rich planters of the entire section were much given to travel, going to northern summering places like Newport and to such southern resorts as those at the Virginia Springs—the Hot, the Warm, the Sweet, and the most select and renowned of all, White Sulphur. The traditional planta-tion—as distinguished from the "outdoor factories" of the Lower South —was a home and a way of life; and while in some form it was found throughout the region except in the very newest districts, the romancers have been right in placing it most often in Virginia. That state more than any other fixed the type and set the standard.

Virgina boys were described as "centaurs," and while the Mississippians might not have satisfied a riding master, they sat their horses with grace and careless ease. If planters as a group had been as indolent and unbusinesslike as some Northerners believed them they could hardly have survived, but Edmund Ruffin attributed the agricultural backwardness of the Tidewater country in his own state of Virginia to the excessive exercise of universal hospitality, which left planters time for nothing else. It was not as true in the 1850's as it was in William

Byrd's day that the South was a "silent country," but there was more quiet and leisure than in the bustling North and more genuine grace of living. The virtues most praised were not those of the world of commerce but those of the landed gentry of the Old World and the vanished age of chivalry—not efficiency, shrewdness, and aggressiveness but honor, generosity, and good manners. By and large the leading Southerners found their models in the past, while the Northerners looked forward to a new age of business and boundless progress. There were romantics on both sides of the line, but their romanticism had assumed divergent forms.

Bases of Southernism

There appear to have been two basic causes for the sectional divergence. A generation before the Civil War, Alexis de Tocqueville expressed the opinion that the existence of slavery in the South was the main one. In view of the fact that important differences between Southerners and Northerners existed long after slavery had disappeared, perhaps it would be more precise to say that they arose from the presence of the Negroes, and that as a rule Southerners were most unlike Northerners when they came from districts in which Negroes were most numerous. The determination of the dominant whites—which long outlasted the life of slavery as a legal institution—to keep the Negroes as a subject race deeply colored their political philosophy and created a general attitude of hostility to social change. As Americans went, Southerners were conservative in spirit and defensive in attitude.

Other distinctive characteristics of Southerners reflected the nature of their agricultural society, at a time when in the North agriculture itself was more varied and, with the growth of commerce and industry, the Northern economy was mixed. The South was a region of vast distances, with few urban centers and in comparison with the North few towns. Town promoters, who were omnipresent in the Old Northwest, were rare in the Old Southwest, and in the latter region the forms of business aggressiveness which were coming to be regarded as characteristically American were relatively undeveloped. Also, as a predominantly rural people, Southerners as a whole had much less ready access to the cultural advantages to be found in cities and towns.

Since so few immigrants came south, the white people were much more homogeneous than in the North, most of them being of Old American stock. They showed it in their speech. Many of the forms and expressions commonly described as Southern were simply old-fashioned English, which persisted in the region after fashions elsewhere had changed. Since there were few immigrants among them, the Southerners remained overwhelmingly Protestant in religion. Except in Tidewater and Low

Country and seaport cities they were mostly members of evangelical sects, and they remained emotional longer than the Northerners did, finding in their religion a vent for their romanticism. In theology, as in almost everything else, these Old Americans were conservative, and to restless Northerners it often seemed that they constituted an obstacle to progress in any direction.

Education and the Southern Mind

The worst aspect of Southern ante-bellum life was the backwardness in popular education. The degree of illiteracy among the whites was much higher than in New England, higher than in the recently settled Northwest, and higher in the Lower South than in the Upper. Conditions were no worse than in many countries of the continent of Europe and in certain of the immigrant groups, but *DeBow's Review*, which was noted for its perfervid Southern patriotism, stated in 1850 that for twenty years the situation had become no better. Physical and financial difficulties provide a partial explanation for this state of affairs. About 1850, there were 127 people per square mile in Massachusetts, while there were only 14 in Virginia and 12 in North Carolina. It was far more difficult to establish accessible schools in a southern county than in a New England town, and conditions of transportation were generally worse than in the Northwest. While there was little destitution in the South, there was relatively little money, and taxes for schools were objected to by the class of people who would have paid most of them. Provision was made for the children of the planters in "old-field" schools and academies, which were very numerous, and the poorer people themselves appear to have been indifferent. The churches had laid much less emphasis on the education of all the people than they had in New England, and community spirit was hard to create in a society of individualists.

In the fifties, conditions definitely began to improve. By Virginia law, passed in the previous decade, counties were authorized to establish free schools, supported by local taxes, and some of them did so. There were creditable schools in most of the cities, but the most promising development anywhere was in North Carolina. There, in 1852, Calvin H. Wiley became state superintendent of education, and this far-sighted man created the best system of public schools in the South, though the teachers were paid miserably. The war checked the movement toward public education throughout the Confederacy, and after the conflict the southern states were inevitably at the end of the public-school procession.

Political democracy was not supplemented by the universal education on the elementary level which Jefferson had regarded as essential to its success and which Horace Mann and others were promoting so vigorously in the North. The benefits of higher education were largely restricted to the upper classes. The first state universities in the country had been started in the South, and in the ante-bellum generation the section broke out in a rash of church colleges. The enrollment figures in institutions of higher learning are impressive. In 1857, a higher percentage of the white inhabitants of Virginia than of Massachusetts were in college and the University of Virginia had more students than Harvard. Not every institution calling itself a university or college was one, but according to the standards of the time the South had its quota of notable academic seats. Among these may be mentioned the Universities of Virginia and North Carolina, and South Carolina College. At the University of Virginia the fabulous Basil L. Gildersleeve taught the classics, and William Barton Rogers, afterwards the first president of the Massachusetts Institute of Technology, lectured on chemistry. Francis Lieber, who later became a noted member of the faculty of Columbia University, was for a score of years professor of history and political economy at South Carolina College; and Frederick A. P. Barnard, who became president of Columbia University in 1864, served before the war as professor of natural history in the University of Alabama and the University of Mississippi and as president of the latter. Augustus Baldwin Longstreet, who depicted crude and humorous aspects of Southern life in *Georgia Scenes* (1835), was president at one time or another of Emory College, the University of Mississippi, and South Carolina College. The classics were emphasized in Southern education, but figures on the enrollment in courses show great interest in natural science, which was popular in seminaries for girls as well as in the colleges for men.

The major restrictions on the freedom of the mind in colleges and universities and outside them resulted from inhibitions with respect to the discussion of slavery and the increasing trend towards orthodoxy in political and religious doctrine. In the fifties, the trend toward the insulation of the Southern mind from external influences that were regarded as dangerous was accentuated. There was a strong movement to keep Southern boys out of Northern colleges and to banish textbooks of Northern origin, and scholars of non-Southern birth like Francis Lieber and William Barton Rogers found life increasingly uncomfortable and went north. A professor in the University of North Carolina, Benjamin Sherwood Hedrick, a native, was rendered so unpopular by his advocacy of the election of the Republican Frémont in 1856, that he had to resign; and George Tucker, the economist, who came of a distinguished Virginia family, virtually abandoned in his later writings the opposition to slavery that he had manifested earlier. In the religious field, while there was continued tolerance of Catholics and Jews, there was an increasing hostility to all forms of liberal Protestantism, as there was to almost every variety of "reformism." The Southern mind was closing in on itself and the voice of self-criticism was being silenced.

Part of the reason for the disproportionate influence of the South in the national government until 1860 was that a greater portion of the talent of the region was devoted to public affairs than was generally the case elsewhere. The charge that the region was backward in literature was met by the secessionist William L. Yancey with vainglorious boast: "Our poetry is our lives; our fiction will come when truth has ceased to satisfy; as for history, we have made about all that has glorified the United States." The inhibitions connected with slavery imposed a severe limitation on Southern writers but the literary output was respectable, and if the body of polemical writing in defense of Southern political and social institutions is added to it the total is impressive. In our own day, John C. Calhoun's political philosophy has been a renewed subject of investigation, and the proslavery philosophy which was the work of so many men must be recognized as an intellectual feat. But the Southern intellect wasted itself in defensive measures that were doomed to futility.

At this stage there was genuine need in the United States for conservatism, which could put the brakes on change that was dangerous because of its sheer speed and could apply the critical test to material progress. But Northerners could not agree that the preservation of the values of the past required the indefinite perpetuation of an institution that was anachronistic on economic as well as moral grounds. Nonslaveholding Southerners could be rallied in defense of the civilization of their section, but sooner or later they were sure to find out that slavery was a grievous burden.

CHAPTER 33

Sectionalism and Tropical Imperialism, 1848-1856

JUST AS THE MEXICAN WAR PRECIPITATED SECTIONAL conflict over domestic policy, so it divided the nation on issues of foreign policy. In the latter area the chief problems during the next decade were those of territorial expansion and rivalry with the British. The Democratic Party in general was anti-British and expansionist, and from the 1840's onward it was charged with assuming these positions because of the desire to extend slavery. This was unquestionably the dominant purpose of the extreme Southern imperialists, centering on the port city of New Orleans and the Gulf states of Louisiana and Mississippi, and they gained considerable support from the Northern followers of Stephen A. Douglas until the later 1850's. The Southern Whigs as a rule were rather indifferent to expansion, and as long as they remained in the party they acquiesced in the Northern Whig policy of accommodation with Great Britain for the sake of national commercial interests.

These party attitudes were well illustrated during the administrations of Polk and Taylor in their dealings with the important Isthmian question. It was in the Pierce administration, however, in connection with the far more controversial Cuban question, that the Democrats were most closely identified with the policy of territorial expansion in the interest of slavery. Of all the fears of the extension of the institution that existed in the North during this period, those excited by these imperialistic ambitions were the most justifiable, and it was chiefly because of the disruptive slavery issue that the United States, after the Mexican War, failed to pursue Manifest Destiny to the extremes which external circumstances permitted.

THE ISTHMIAN QUESTION AND ANGLO-AMERICAN RELATIONS

After the Mexican War, Great Britain retreated to a "prepared position" in Central America which, along with Cuba, she was determined to prevent the United States from controlling to the injury of British maritime interests. Since the earliest Spanish explorers, men had dreamed of a canal at one or another of the favorable locations between Mexico and New Granada (Colombia). The overthrow of Spanish rule had left Central America divided among petty and misgoverned states without resources to build a canal. Great Britain saw in an isthmian crossing a link that would bring the Pacific Coast, the burgeoning markets of the Far East, and the increasingly important British positions in Australia, Singapore, and Hong Kong closer by weeks to the mother country.

To Americans the primary meaning of the isthmian question was more intimate and domestic. The trip across the Great Plains and Rockies from the Missouri River to the Pacific Coast took six months—a hazardous term because it could barely be squeezed into the warmer season, and winter froze to death many a party caught in the western mountain passes. The trip by water around the Horn took, in the record time of the clipper ships which during the fifties outran steamships, three months from New York to San Francisco. The trip by steamship from New York to Panama, across the isthmus by mule and Indian dugout or by the Panama Railroad (not completed until 1856), and by steamship to San Francisco, required only one month. Americans regarded the isthmian crossing as essential to their internal communication system. Furthermore, the West Coast was highly vulnerable to attack unless troops could go by way of the Isthmus.

Both Great Britain and the United States therefore took steps before the close of the Mexican War to secure for themselves exclusive isthmian rights. In December 1846, the United States Minister to New Granada signed a treaty in which that government granted the United States transit rights across Panama, and the United States guaranteed the neutrality of the route to prevent any interruptions of free transit. This guarantee of neutrality, which might lead to war, was scored in the Senate, and approval of it was not given until June 1848. Nicaragua, moreover, was thought to offer the easiest passage, because the San Juan River led from the Caribbean shore to the Lake of Nicaragua, from which the land crossing to the Pacific amounted to only twelve miles. The British had developed in the mahogany region north of Nicaragua the crown colony of Belize, or British Honduras. They now decided that a tenuous connection with the Mosquito Indian tribe inhabiting the eastern coast of Nicaragua amounted to a protectorate over their head-

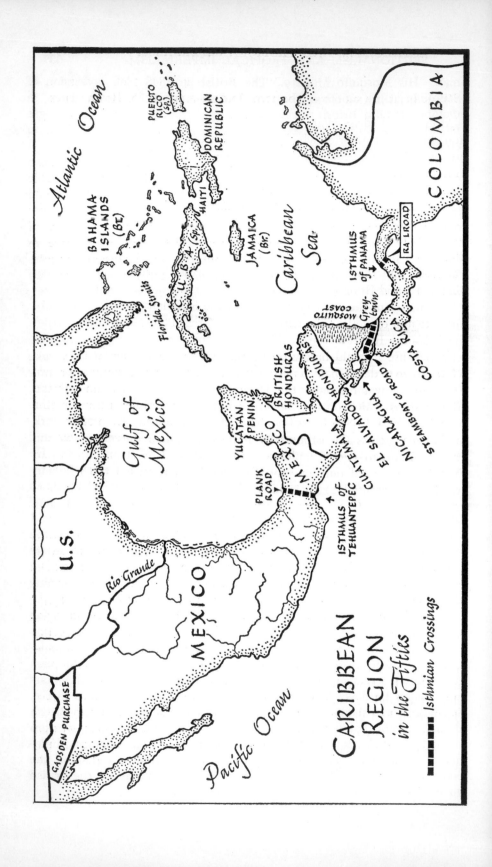

CARIBBEAN REGION in the Fifties

▬▬▬ Isthmian Crossings

man, "His Mosquito Majesty." The British in 1848 took possession of San Juan at the mouth of the river and renamed it Greytown. Then, in October 1849, a British naval officer raised the Union Jack over Tigre Island in the Gulf of Fonseca—a strategic location for a naval base to control a possible western terminus of the Nicaraguan route.

American agents signed several more treaties with Central American governments granting the United States transit rights for any feasible crossing. The one with Nicaragua, whose government feared it would need aid against Britain, gave the United States a virtual protectorate over the republic. The British Foreign Office repudiated the seizure of Tigre Island and the Taylor administration withheld the transit treaties from the Senate, but opinion in both countries was becoming aroused. Secretary of State John M. Clayton wrote that a collision was inevitable unless both sides exercised prudence.

The Clayton-Bulwer Treaty

The Whig administration of President Taylor had no ambition to take territory in Central America or even to assume responsibility for protectorates. Reflecting national sentiment and Northern business interests, it wished only to secure American use of any isthmian crossing in time of war as well as peace. Foreign Secretary Palmerston was more aggressively devoted to exclusive British ambitions, but he sent an able and accommodating minister to the United States, Henry Lytton Bulwer. He and Secretary Clayton drew up (1850) a treaty in which the two governments promised to co-operate in building a canal and to refrain from fortifying or asserting exclusive control over it. This seemed at the time to be a diplomatic victory for the United States, because in Article I both countries promised not to occupy or colonize or exercise dominion over "any part of Central America." Expansionist Democrats in the Senate consented to the Clayton-Bulwer Treaty because they believed it signified a retreat by the British, but the latter interpreted Article I as meaning that they must not assert any *further* territorial claims in the future.

When it developed that the British had no intention of withdrawing from Mosquitia or Greytown, far less from British Honduras, American expansionists were furious. The treaty made excellent campaign material for the Democrats in 1852. The "Young America" followers of Stephen A. Douglas screamed anathemas at Britain, demanded that the Stars and Stripes be flown from Pole to Pole, and voted for Franklin Pierce. In office Pierce showed himself to be more expansionist and anti-British than his Whig predecessors. In July 1854, a United States warship shelled Greytown to punish it for rioting in which an American diplomatic agent had been mildly injured. President Pierce defended the commander's action. If the Crimean War had not preoccupied the British government serious trouble might have resulted.

The story of American relations with Central America after this centered on filibustering activities in violation of neutrality. Expansionists supported with money, arms, and volunteers the extraordinary adventures of the filibuster William Walker of Tennessee, the "grey-eyed man of destiny." Setting out in 1855 with a tiny "American Phalanx," this hundred-pound newspaperman joined one side in a Nicaraguan civil war and made himself dictator of the country. His first official act was to repeal Nicaragua's law against slavery. The Pierce administration recognized Walker's government when the British began arming the Costa Ricans against him, and he was commended in the Democratic platform of 1856. The United States government was lax in preventing aid from going to Walker, but Cornelius Vanderbilt frustrated the prince of filibusters. Vanderbilt had built a lucrative isthmian crossing through Nicaragua, combining steamers on the river and lake with a twelve-mile macadamized road over which fine carriages with Vanderbilt's coat-of-arms rolled passengers for California. He "blockaded" the Walker government and it fell. Walker led two more expeditions to Central America from the United States during the complacent Buchanan administration which followed that of Pierce, and in 1860 he was shot by a Honduran firing squad.

The British government viewed Walker's expeditions as deliberate attempts by the United States government to circumvent the Clayton-Bulwer Treaty. When the Crimean War ended, a showdown was indicated, but surprisingly the British staged a retreat. Besides abandoning their claim of the right to search suspected slave ships flying the American flag, they gave up their Mosquito protectorate and their isthmian designs. So the British government recognized the new power of the United States after the annexation of Texas and the Mexican War. This sensational reversal of British policy, during the administration of Pierce's successor, was chiefly owing to a fuller recognition of the value of commercial and financial relations with the United States on the part of rising Conservative leaders like the young Disraeli. Central America ceased to be a pawn in either the international or the sectional chess-game, and the new British friendliness was distinctly fortunate for the Union when the sectional struggle for advantage turned into war.

The Cuban Question

The Cuban question was the touchstone of sectional conflict over foreign policy between the Mexican and Civil Wars. Americans had long been interested in the "Pearl of the Antilles" for strategic and commercial reasons. There was always the fear that Cuba would slip from the weak hands of Spain into British control, and the desire to safeguard American commercial interests increased as trade did. These national considerations were not without influence after the Mexican War but they were overshadowed by others that were strongly sectional. Among Southern proslavery leaders the conviction grew that the fortunes of the "peculiar institution" in the United States were organically related to its fate in Cuba; and at the same time hope rose, especially in the Gulf states, that the territorial advantages of the North might be offset by the acquisition of a tropical empire. In terms of Southern sectionalism, the movement for the annexation of Cuba was both defensive and offensive in its motives.

The slaves of Haiti had murdered their masters and established a Negro republic which had excited fears in the Southern black belt for half a century; slavery had been abolished in all the Spanish-American countries at the time of their revolutions against Spain; Great Britain had emancipated the slaves in the British West Indies in 1833; France now (1848) freed them in the French West Indies. Only Cuba, Puerto Rico, and Brazil still sustained the institution. Britain and France worked to end slavery in Cuba, where it was fed by notorious illegal importations from Africa. It gave Spain advantages in sugar production over the other West Indies and Louisiana, and was so brutal that liberals the world over and especially in Great Britain cried for international action. Southerners saw close on their horizon the specter of a "Black Cuba" whose half million Negroes would promote servile rebellion on the continent. Meanwhile, Cuban slaveowners supported annexation to the United States as a solution which would give them at one stroke freedom from Spanish despotism and security for their slave property.

Southern expansionists furthermore saw that Cuba was the only remaining territory which would certainly increase and strengthen slavery in the United States. Cuban slave prices were much lower than those in the United States; merging the two markets would reduce prices and increase the American supply. Cuban sugar with the product of Louisiana cane fields could dominate the world market of that commodity. The Cuban population of about one million would add some fifteen proslavery Representatives in the lower house in Washington, with at least two and perhaps more proslavery Senators. The defense, prosperity, and political power of American slavery all dictated the annexation of Cuba. So the Southern expansionists believed, and the more adventurous dreamed of an empire which should comprise the "golden circle" around the Gulf of Mexico and the Caribbean Sea.

In Louisiana there were some who feared the effects that the annexation of Cuba might have on the local sugar industry, but sugar barons could own property in both places, and the expansionists spoke the language of cotton capitalists in the Gulf states who were clamoring for more and cheaper labor. Their arguments were much less appealing in the Upper South, which stood to profit little from a tropical empire and was relatively undisposed to press divisive sectional issues. The aggressive proslavery leaders of the Gulf states found a few conspicuous allies in the North as well as Virginia, and among the firebrands and secessionists of South Carolina.

The López Expeditions and the "Young Americans"

The Whig administration of Presidents Taylor and Fillmore repudiated Polk's attempt to buy Cuba from Spain and tried to draw a line between American commercial and strategic interest in Cuba, which they supported, and proslavery expansionism, which they rejected. Despairing of annexation by purchase, Cuban planters financed filibuster expeditions from the United States. Exiles from the island organized the Cuban Junta on American soil. They found a leader in General Narciso López, who had to escape from the island in 1848 when he was discovered using his office as an official of the Spanish administration to organize rebellion. With other Cuban exiles, and John L. O'Sullivan of New York, author of the phrase "Manifest Destiny," as his chief American organizer, López won the support of many Southern leaders. Frustrated in 1849 by the vigorous action of President Taylor to enforce the neutrality laws, López then established headquarters at New Orleans and organized a large expedition with the connivance of local and federal officials. It captured the town of Cardenas in Cuba in May 1850, but López and his men were forced by Spanish lancers to flee.

The propaganda of the annexationists stressed the motive of Cuban liberation from Spanish despotism, and the fillibusters wore the red shirt of the European liberal revolutionaries of 1848. The Hungarian hero Louis Kossuth, during his famous tour of the United States in 1851, was disillusioned by the attempt to identify liberalism with the cause of slavery and the use of his popularity to support the annexation of Cuba. The confusion of issues became complete when the efforts of the federal government to prevent filibustering were called betrayals of liberty in favor of Spanish despotism. Fearing the political effects of this charge, the federal administrations were henceforth less than vigorous in enforcing the law. Spanish protests were answered by ringing public answers in the spirit of Manifest Destiny.

López again sailed in August 1851 from New Orleans at the head of some 500 armed men. They landed at Bahia Honda, unwisely divided their forces, and were cut to pieces by Spanish troops in prolonged jungle fighting. López himself, the nephew of the Attorney General John J. Crittenden, and some representatives of leading Southern families who were not killed in the fighting were garroted by the Spanish authorities in Havana while others were sent to the Spanish mines in Africa. Many Americans who did not sympathize with the aims of the filibusters were horrified by the revenge against them. Mobs destroyed the Spanish consulate in New Orleans and forced the consul to leave. Secretary of State Webster was constrained to beg Spain to release imprisoned filibusters, but he braved Southern wrath by offering indemnity to Spain and a national salute to the Spanish flag if a consul should be returned to New Orleans. John L. O'Sullivan and other organizers of the filibusters were indicted but juries acquitted them.

In the presidential campaign of 1852, when most people favored sectional compromise, Cuba provided the most exciting topic of debate. "Young Americans," who claimed kinship with the liberal "Young Italy" and "Young Germany" movements abroad, proposed Stephen A. Douglas for the Democratic nomination on a platform of national aid to liberalism in Europe, annexation of Cuba, and sundry other acquisitions. Douglas hoped to combine the votes of Eastern cities, which were interested in trade with a liberalized Europe and in ousting British influence in the West Indies and the Isthmus, with the votes of the South and of his own Middle West. He was defeated in the Democratic Convention, but "Young Cubans" and military formations marched in Pierce demonstrations, and his election was expected to result in the annexation of Cuba as a minimum fulfillment of the Democratic platform.

The British and French governments were aroused by the spectacle of a President supported by filibusters entering the White House. They had asked the Fillmore administration, in April 1852, to join an Anglo-French-American agreement disclaiming all intention to obtain possession of Cuba whether by governmental or private (filibuster) action, but Webster and Fillmore demurred. After Webster's death in October 1852 and Pierce's election in November, Fillmore's interim Secretary of State, Edward Everett of Massachusetts, formally rejected the proposed tripartite agreement. He declared that the President did not covet Cuba for the United States but nevertheless considered this mainly an American question. Then he expounded the special strategic and commercial interest of Cuba to the United States, said that American ownership would be preferable to a Negro republic in the island, and warned of circumstances which might make annexation by the United States necessary for self-preservation. It seemed to Northern opponents of slavery extension that Everett's note was a disgraceful effort to "appease" the South.

Pierce Looks Southward

President Pierce's inaugural address announced that adherence to the Compromise of 1850 and territorial expansion would be the policies of his Administration. He proclaimed that he would not be "controlled by any timid forebodings of evil from expansion," and that the American attitude and position rendered "the acquisition of certain possessions not within our jurisdiction" eminently important for American protection, for commerce, and for the peace of the world. His two policies were actually incompatible because Cuban annexation would inevitably reopen the slavery question. Pierce rewarded his Young-America followers by appointing Caleb Cushing of Massachusetts as Attorney General, with obvious implications of leniency to filibusters; Pierre Soulé of Louisiana, the leading Southern advocate of a combined campaign to free Europe from despots and snatch Cuba during the melée, as minister in Madrid; and a strange assortment of firebrands to lesser diplomatic posts, including the notorious filibuster O'Sullivan to Portugal.

The most extraordinary scenes in American diplomatic history followed. General Quitman organized what promised to be the largest filibuster expedition of the period to descend on Cuba with the blessing of the administration. The frightened Spanish government moved to free and arm the slaves of Cuba, which increased Southern determination to prevent the "Africanization" of the island. Cuban authorities seized the American steamship *Black Warrior* at Havana, and Soulé without authorization issued an ultimatum to Spain. This incredible minister fought a duel with the Duke of Alba, the leading grandee of Spain, and he made the American legation the headquarters of a conspiracy to overthrow the Spanish and French governments. This seemed to him a fair effort to carry out his instructions from Secretary of State Marcy in the spring of 1854 to buy Cuba or, if Spain refused, to "detach" the island from her. Failing in his revolutionary schemes, he then prudently left the country.

The Ostend Manifesto

Few American diplomats have ever been so guilty of high-handed and perilous indiscretion as Soulé was, but the administration was blameable for appointing such an adventurer in the first place and for granting him so much leeway in carrying out what he regarded as proannexation instructions. At home sectional passions had now been aroused by the Kansas-Nebraska Act, and General Quitman's expedition was prudently delayed. Casting about to retrieve something from the imminent disaster to its plans, the administration in the summer of 1854 ordered Soulé to confer with the Minister to Great Britain, James Buchanan, and the Minister to France, John Y. Mason of Virginia, about Spanish relations with special reference to Cuba. Dodging spies of the European governments, these diplomats and lesser Young Americans met at Ostend, then at Aix-la-Chapelle in October 1854, and drew up the "Ostend Manifesto." This document has been aptly called "the *Magnum Opus* of the school of 'Manifest Destiny' and Southern Imperialism." It was intended only for administration eyes but news of it soon leaked out all over the world. It strongly recommended the purchase of Cuba, but the crucial statement in it was that if Spain refused to sell the island, the United

States would be justified in taking it on the principle of self-preservation. Soulé wrote to Secretary Marcy that he favored war with Spain to take Cuba, and a bellicose interpretation was generally placed on the Manifesto, although Buchanan protested that he had only intended peaceful measures of annexation, and Mason suffered a stroke when he heard of Soulé's letter to Marcy.

The Manifesto arrived in Washington at the time of the Congressional elections but was not actually published until the spring of 1855, when it deeply discredited the administration at home and abroad. The Democratic defeat at the polls was chiefly the result of the Kansas-Nebraska Act, but newspaper reports of the activities of the diplomats contributed to it, and actually the attempt to annex Cuba could be described much more accurately as a proslavery move than could the Kansas-Nebraska Act. The administration could not repudiate the latter, but it decided to retreat on the Cuban front. Soulé was told to go back to Madrid and conduct himself with moderation. The passionate chief of the Young American diplomats correctly regarded this as repudiation and resigned. Quitman was called to Washington and talked into resigning as head of the projected expedition to Cuba. Discouraged by such "timidity" and disillusioned by the failure of Quitman to account for some half million dollars of the Junta's money, the Cuban planters and exiles gave up annexationism.

It deserves far more than the Kansas-Nebraska Act ever did to be called a "plot." This sort of an increase in the area of slavery, unlike the gain of permissive rights in the continental territories, would have increased the *number* of slaves. By the same token it would have aggravated the very social difficulties which the Virginians had debated so seriously two decades before, and which they saw no way to escape except by removing the Negroes from their midst. Nonslaveholders in the South as well as free-soilers in the North had good reason to regard such a policy as a thinly veiled design to increase the wealth and power of small groups and particular individuals.

The Young American campaign to dress up proslavery imperialism in the garments of liberalism was a resounding failure before the Pierce administration was two years old. The real meaning that it had in the minds of certain Southern extremists was revealed more frankly after a few years. In 1859, Edward A. Pollard, a Virginia editor, wrote as follows:

> Regarding the magnificent country of tropical America, which lies in the path of our destiny on this continent, we may see an empire as powerful and gorgeous as ever was pictured in our dreams of history. . . . It is an empire founded on military ideas; representing the noble peculiarities of Southern civilization; including within its limits the isthmus of America and the regenerated West Indies; having control of the two dominant staples of the world's commerce—cotton and sugar; possessing the highways of

the world's commerce; surpassing all empires of the age in the strength of its geographical position; and, in short, combining the elements of strength, prosperity, and glory, such as never before in the modern ages have been placed within reach of a single government.

What a splendid vision of empire! How noble and inspiriting the idea, that the destiny of Southern civilization is to be consummated in a glory brighter even than that of old.

THE GADSDEN PURCHASE

Third after the Isthmus and Cuba in interest to expansionist Americans during the fifties was Mexico. The hope that the Treaty of Guadaloupe-Hidalgo of 1848 would be followed by the annexation of "all Mexico" died hard, but Southerners who were interested in railroads to the Pacific were willing to settle for suitable slices of Mexican soil. The Memphis Railroad Convention of 1849, advocating many plans to improve the economic position of the South, recommended that the federal government obtain from the Mexican government the Mesilla Valley near the Gila River. Surveys showed that this pass through the Rockies offered the best chance for a southern transcontinental railroad. At the same time New Orleans business and political groups became interested in a railroad across the Isthmus of Tehuantepec in Mexico. Both of these programs were pushed during the fifties, chiefly by farsighted Southerners who recognized that their section could not compete with the North on a limited diet of agriculture and state rights.

The Tehuantepec plan held the greater danger for Mexico. In 1842, President Santa Anna had granted to Don José de Garay the right to build a transit across Tehuantepec, where the Cordillera drops closer to sea level than anywhere in the hemisphere. One hundred and fifty miles of land on both sides of the route went with the grant. By 1849 it had been acquired by Hargous Brothers of Philadelphia and New York who owned shipping lines to Mexico, engaged in extensive trade there, and acted as Mexican financial agents of the United States government. While the Whig administration of Taylor and Fillmore was favorable to the plans of this Northern firm, and negotiated a convention with Mexico that gave the United States the right to protect the grantees in their operations, Hargous Brothers cannily enlisted the support of Southerners by organizing the New Orleans Tehuantepec Company under the presidency of Judah P. Benjamin. The company started work on the route and boomed colonization of Americans along the right of way.

Mexican patriots took alarm at this new "Texas." In 1851, the government annulled the Garay Grant, refused to ratify the convention with the United States, and expelled the employees of the New Orleans Tehuantepec Company from the Isthmus. Secretary of State Webster wished to adopt a strong policy in defense of the project as a national enterprise, but President Fillmore and other Northern Whigs like William H. Seward would not accept the doctrine that private American interests in a foreign country have a right to the forceful protection of the United States government. The situation was complicated when a Kentucky adventurer, A. G. Sloo, obtained a new grant from the Mexican government to build a route without protectorate features. Early in 1853, another Tehuantepec Company was organized in New Orleans to exploit the Sloo Grant, and the rival companies turned hopefully for a decision to the pro-Southern, expansionist Pierce administration.

Secretary of War Jefferson Davis was more interested in the southern transcontinental route from Texas to California than in the Tehuantepec muddle. He secured the appointment of James Gadsden of Charleston as Minister to Mexico with instructions to buy the Mesilla Valley and settle all outstanding questions in a new treaty. During the forties, Gadsden had settled down in Charleston as a railroad magnate, and his dream was to tie the West to the South. He eagerly accepted the offer of the mission to Mexico and promptly exceeded his instructions by asking Santa Anna, once more the dictator of Mexico, for four entire states near the boundary. It was difficult to dismay the expansionists in Washington. Gadsden soon received secret, unwritten instructions to offer as much as $50 million for a huge cession including all of Lower California or lesser amounts for smaller cessions. It was intended to play upon Santa Anna's greed to induce him to sell a great part of his country.

Scandal dogged the Pierce administration in Mexico, as in its Cuban policy. The secret messenger to Gadsden, Christopher L. Ward, was actually an agent of Hargous Brothers more intent on squeezing a great indemnity out of Mexico for the owners of the nullified Garay Grant than in buying territory. William Walker, heading a filibuster expedition of fifty men from California into Lower California, proclaimed the latter an independent republic in November 1853. This convinced Santa Anna that Mexico was in grievous danger. He tried in vain to get help from Britain or Spain. Desperate, he agreed to a minimum territorial cession of the Mesilla Valley only, in return for $15 million; and Gadsden, fearing that Ward and Walker would ruin everything, agreed. In addition he obligated the United States to pay various claims of Americans against the Mexican government, including damages to Hargous Brothers, to a total of $5 million.

The Gadsden Treaty was thrown into the bitter sectional atmosphere of early 1854 created by the Kansas-Nebraska debate. After being defeated in the Senate, it was amended to reduce the territorial cession slightly, reduce the compensation to Mexico by $5 million, throw out the Garay-Hargous claim, and give the United States the right to intervene in Mexico to protect the Sloo Grantees in building a Tehuantepec route. Sloo lobbyists then added the support of enough Northern Senators to that of Southern Democrats and Whigs to gain the required two-thirds majority. Santa Anna was reluctant to accept the American right of intervention in Tehuantepec but he faced revolution, needed the money, and feared a worse treaty if he rejected this one, so he consented to the amendments. Over bitter opposition, Northern Democrats joined with the Southerners of both parties to pass the appropriation.

The Gadsden Treaty increased Mexican fear and hatred of the United States. It seemed to patriots in Mexico that the weaknesses of their country were deliberately exploited by her stronger neighbor in order to despoil her. Quarrels continued over the carrying out of the Treaty. American bankers and speculators soon obtained for themselves a good share of the money paid to the Mexican government by the United States. Southerners were irritated by Mexicans' aid to slaves who escaped to freedom in their country. The boundary was often violated by raiders from both sides and by a series of American filibuster expeditions. Mexico used trade restrictions to retaliate against the United States. Mexican leaders played on their countrymen's fear of the United States while at the same time selling out its interests to the Americans. Gadsden was criticized for interfering in Mexico's domestic affairs, and was removed as Minister in 1856, partly through the efforts of American speculators whose excesses he had tried to curb. President Pierce before he left office tried to improve relations with Mexico by sending James Forsythe as Minister with assurances that the United States harbored no designs against the unfortunate country. But Secretary of State Marcy spoiled the effect by threatening Mexico with strong measures if her government did not respect American rights. The Gadsden Purchase was the net territorial result of all the efforts of the Pierce administration to continue expansion where Polk had left off, and for this gain it paid heavily in scandalous disrepute and intensification of sectionalism at home and hatred of the United States abroad.

CHAPTER 34

Sectionalism and the West
1853 - 1857

THOUGH CERTAIN FINANCIAL ADVENTURERS AND political leaders in the North shared the enthusiasm of the tropical imperialists of the South, they were a small group in comparison to the Northerners who were interested in the development of the vast western stretches of the continent. The region beyond Missouri and east of the Rockies was without political organization, and a necessary preliminary to its development and the improvement of communications with the Far West was the formation of some sort of territorial government. But Southern leaders were opposed to the development of a region which offered no opportunity to slaveholders, under the terms of the Missouri Compromise, and out of which many free states could be created, increasing Northern political and economic power. The Kansas-Nebraska Act was designed to overcome this hostility. But the measure aroused a storm of indignation in the North because, repealing the Missouri Compromise, it opened to slaveholders and nonslaveholders on equal terms a region which had been regarded for a generation as a preserve for the latter.

The political consequences of the Act were such that it has been described as the most fateful public measure from the beginning of government under the Constitution until the outbreak of the Civil War. Already it was evident that the balance of power was shifting rapidly to the Northern states, and the real danger of the expansion of the slave power was much greater in Cuba than it ever was in Kansas. But on economic, political, and moral grounds a very large number of Northerners regarded the threat there as a mortal challenge. Thus the sectional conflict passed into an acute phase as the struggle for the West was renewed.

Douglas and the Kansas-Nebraska Act

The person most responsible for the highly controversial Kansas-Nebraska Act was Stephen A. Douglas, chairman of the Senate Committee on Territories, who was the most important leader in the Democratic Party in this decade and became the most conspicuous man in public life after the passing of Clay, Calhoun, and Webster. His absurdly short legs prevented him from being physically commanding, but his strong and vigorous personality caused him to be called the "Little Giant." Douglas, who was forty-one in 1854, was born in Vermont but throughout adult life had been identified with Illinois and his career had been that of a self-made man. While he was in Congress and not long before he became a Senator he married a North Carolinian who inherited slaves but she died before Douglas entered upon the stormiest phase of his career. In spirit he was a Western promoter. Soon after his marriage he removed from downstate Illinois, where the life was agricultural and the sentiment pro-Southern, to Chicago, which was distinctly Northern in spirit, and there he invested in real estate and promoted railroad development on a large scale. He was fully sympathetic with plans for a transcontinental road, which he and his constituents naturally wanted to follow a northern or central route.

His vision of physical expansion was broad, and he saw in the increased prosperity which would result from the development of the country the best hope of national unity and sectional peace. He had little or no moral objection to slavery, and his advocacy of the acquisition of Cuba signified his desire that the South and her slaveowners should gain benefits from expansion. But he saw no likelihood that the "slave power" would ever capture the undeveloped Northwest. Nominal concessions to Southern sentiment seemed to him a small price for Western development, and he believed that in the general prosperity the controversy over slavery could be minimized, and perhaps absorbed. The weakness of his position lay in his failure to allow sufficiently for the moral principle of the opponents of the extension of slavery. Besides being broadly nationalistic in spirit, Douglas was democratic, but when he sought to apply to the territories the vague principle of "popular sovereignty" it proved to be unworkable.

It was not to his immediate political advantage to grapple with the controversial territorial question, for his presidential prospects were so good by 1854 that on personal grounds he would have been wise to let well enough alone. But he was convinced of the economic desirability of organizing the undeveloped regions without further delay, and in his position as committee chairman he would have had great difficulty in avoiding the question if he had wanted to. A bill to create a territory

A.

Lake Superior

MINNESOTA
TERRITORY

WIS.

NEBRASKA
TERRITORY

Missouri R.

IOWA

ILL.

SETTLEMENT
LINE

Platte R.

Council
Bluffs

St. Joseph

Atchison
Ft. Leavenworth

St. Louis

KANSAS
TERRITORY

Topeka
Lecompton
Lawrence

Independence

Missouri R.

Osage River

MISSOURI

POTTAWATOMIE
MASSACRE

MISSOURI COMPROMISE LINE ~ 36° 30'

TEXAS

INDIAN
AREA
(Unorganized)

ARKANSAS

Mississippi R.

KANSAS ~ NEBRASKA
1854 ~ 1860

which should be called Nebraska and from which, according to the terms of the Missouri Compromise, slavery would be excluded, had been passed by the House of Representatives of the last Congress by a vote of more than two to one. But it had failed in the Senate, largely because of Southern votes. The attitude of Senator David R. Atchison of Missouri is of special interest in the light of what happened later. As southern states went, there were not many slaves in Missouri, but they were considerably concentrated in the western counties, where he himself lived, and the proslavery faction with which he had allied himself objected to having a free territory next door. Here a move started to repeal the Missouri Compromise.

When the overwhelmingly Democratic Congress that was elected in 1852 assembled in December 1853, a bill for a free territory was introduced by Senator Dodge of the free state of Iowa. This never came to a vote since Douglas, assuming that a bill explicitly forbidding slavery could not win enough votes to pass, presented a bill in behalf of his committee. This developed into a measure that created two territories, Kansas and Nebraska, provided that the decision for or against slavery should be made by the people of the territories, and stated that the prohibition of slavery in the Missouri Compromise was "inoperative and void." The immediate suggestion that this part of the Act of 1820 be explicitly repealed came from Senator Archibald Dixon of Kentucky. President Pierce was consulted and reluctantly approved the proposal, under the influence of Jefferson Davis, his Secretary of War, and Caleb Cushing of Massachusetts, his Attorney General. The measure had the backing of the administration but Douglas was its conspicuous sponsor, and the Southerners who had most to do with it came chiefly from the border states. In most of the South the bill was viewed with general indifference until the opposition to it assumed a violent sectional tone, and then the advocacy of it became spirited.

It was the proposal to repeal the Missouri Compromise that aroused greatest protest in the North. In January 1854, an "appeal of the Independent Democrats in Congress to the People of the United States" was issued. This was drawn by Salmon P. Chase of Ohio and signed by Benjamin F. Wade of that state, Charles Sumner of Massachusetts, and several other active opponents of slavery. They arraigned the bill "as a gross violation of a sacred pledge; as a criminal betrayal of precious rights; as part and parcel of an atrocious plot to exclude from a vast unoccupied region immigrants from the Old World and free laborers from our own States, and convert it into a dreary region of despotism, inhabited by masters and slaves." This extreme statement did violence to the motives of Douglas, who never had any doubt that the region would be settled by free men, but it showed the immediate recognition of the value of this issue, with its powerful moral appeal, in creating a Northern party cutting across old party lines and dedicated to "free soil."

Despite the outcries, the bill passed in the Senate by a large margin. It had great difficulty in the House of Representatives, which contained a much larger proportion of Northerners and was more affected by the swelling chorus of popular disapproval. It finally carried by a small majority which could hardly have been gained without pressure from the administration. Besides speaking incessantly in the Senate, Douglas directed the whole fight. Not without warrant he afterwards said: "I passed the Kansas-Nebraska Act myself. I had the authority and power of a dictator throughout the whole controversy in both houses." He also said afterward that he could travel from Boston to Chicago in the light of his own burning effigies. The bill was signed May 30, 1854, and in September, when he was in Chicago after the adjournment of Congress, he could not get a hearing from his own constituents. For two hours he tried in vain to quiet the mob that howled him down, and finally gave up.

The course of Douglas, as a practical statesman who was trying to organize the territories and made concessions because he believed he had to, can be better understood now than it was in the heat of sectional partisanship a century and more ago. But his failure to sense Northern sentiment about the Missouri Compromise, which had become to so many a sacred symbol, is a serious indictment of his political judgment. Time was to justify his faith in the operations of political democracy, but a major weakness of his plan lay in the uncertainties and difficulties of applying the principle of popular sovereignty. To say that everything should be left to popular vote sounded like good American doctrine, but nobody knew at just what stage a vote should be taken and it might be taken prematurely. Very few slaves ever reached these territories, but in the first years irresponsible proslavery groups in western Missouri caused a lot of trouble across their border. Their actions served to keep alive the charge of a proslavery "plot," and to provide fresh ammunition for Northern extremists.

The Fruits of Popular Sovereignty

The settlement of Nebraska was relatively orderly and that territory was little talked about, while Kansas was settled under conditions of artificiality at first and received more public attention than was good for it or for the country. The best-known Northern organization that stimulated settlement in Kansas was the New England Emigrant Aid Company, organized by Eli Thayer. This sent a number of parties of settlers, supplying them with Bibles and with Sharps rifles (known as "Beecher's Bibles"), but the effects of these activities were probably greater in stimulating antislavery sentiment in the North as a whole than in determining the course of events in Kansas.

During the years 1854-1855, the Company caused the free population to be increased by only a few more than 1200 people. More settlers went to Kansas from New England, however, than from the Lower South. One party of considerable size is known to have gone from Alabama and neighboring states, with the aid of private philanthropy. Though these men were supplied with Bibles by a Baptist church, as if to outdo the New Englanders, they proved fairly belligerent after they arrived in Kansas. But emigrants from the Lower South vastly preferred to go to Texas, where there were plenty of open spaces. The first rush into the new territory of Kansas was naturally from the contiguous counties in Missouri, where proslavery sentiment was strong, but even here there was little disposition to carry slave property into a region where its future status was so uncertain. The bulk of the settlers came from the upper Mississippi Valley, as was to be expected; and, except for the Missourians, Southerners seemed less conscious that a race was on than Northerners. The early proslavery settlers from the state next door particularly resented the group that had been sent by the Emigrant Aid Company, and when voting began, as it soon did, the "border ruffians" brought a large element of fraud and intimidation into the elections. Within two years there were rival governments and the territory was the scene of a small-sized civil war.

The first territorial governor, appointed by the President, was Andrew H. Reeder of Pennsylvania, and the antics and violence of the early proslavery group during his term of less than a year turned him into a free-soiler. The first legislature was chosen in the spring of 1855 under very confused conditions, and because of the proximity of Missouri the proslavery group gained the advantage by illegal voting. A proslavery government was set up at Shawnee against Reeder's will. The legislature requested his removal. He was dismissed by President Pierce, fled the territory, and was afterwards active in the new Republican Party. His successor, Wilson Shannon, was more co-operative with the proslavery faction that had assumed control, but, after serving about a year, he resigned only to learn that he in turn had been dismissed. His successor, John W. Geary, arrived in the late summer of 1856 to find a condition of virtual civil war. By this time the free-state group, who were growing in number, had organized a government of their own, adopting in September 1855 what is known as the Topeka Constitution. In May 1856, a proslavery "posse" attacked Lawrence, which was a center for the Emigrant Aid group, destroying a good deal of property; and soon after that John Brown, who was to become more famous later, took revenge by murdering five innocent proslavery settlers on the Pottawatomie. This violent abolitionist was guided by the philosophy that there can be no remission of sins without the shedding of blood, and people throughout the country were talking of "bleeding Kansas."

Violence appeared on the national legislative stage about the same time, when Senator Charles Sumner pronounced a philippic on the "crime against Kansas," and was the object of physical attack by Congressman Preston S. Brooks of South Carolina. The learned Sumner spoke of the "rape of a virgin territory" and designated this as the "crime of crimes." In his speech and the interchanges that followed he made highly offensive remarks about living persons. Atchison was "Catiline," and Douglas "the noisesome squat and nameless animal"—that is, a skunk. Sumner went out of his way to ridicule the "chivalry" of Senator Andrew Pickens Butler of South Carolina, who had recently made a speech on the Kansas question, and who was now said by Sumner to have made a mistress of "the harlot slavery." Sumner accused Butler of drunkenness on the Senate floor, referring to his incoherent phrases and "the loose expectoration of his speech," and went so far as to charge him with deliberate misrepresentation and untruthfulness.

Senator Lewis Cass, who belonged in the opposite political camp from Sumner, characterized the latter's speech as "the most un-American and unpatriotic that ever grated on the ears of the members of this high body," and Douglas said he deserved to be kicked like a dog. The most effective procedure, perhaps, would have been to leave the speech unanswered and await the natural reaction against such extreme expressions, but young Brooks, a relative of Senator Butler, took vengeance in his own hands, as John Brown had done. A couple of days later, finding Sumner behind his desk writing letters after the Senate had adjourned, the hot-headed young Southerner beat the older man over the head with a cane until Sumner fell unconscious. This brutal attack aroused a storm of indignation in the North. Not for three and a half years did Sumner recover, and inevitably he was viewed as a martyr. The praise which Brooks received in the South was an even more ominous sign of the intensity and irrationality of public sentiment. He resigned his seat in the House and was unanimously re-elected by his constituents, but he died a few months later. The first fruits of popular sovereignty were very bitter.

The Rise of the Republican Party

Since the presidential election of 1852 the party situation had been fluid. The Whig Party was disintegrating. The Native American or Know-Nothing Party was gaining wide support by exploiting prejudice against immigrants, but a major party could not be erected on such a narrow base. The Kansas-Nebraska Act occasioned the rise of the Republican Party, which soon challenged the Democrats. The name "Republican" was first applied to the new party at a state meeting in Jackson, Michigan, in July 1854, and it was employed elsewhere in the next few months, but at the outset the new grouping could be best described as a fusion of opponents of the territorial policies of the administration and could be best designated as the "Anti-Nebraska Party." It was made up of Northern Whigs, Free Soilers, and Know Nothings and Northern Democrats who would not support Pierce and Douglas.

Events in Illinois, the state of Douglas and Abraham Lincoln, illustrate the trend and the new alignment. In the Congressional elections of 1854, Anti-Nebraska candidates carried five of nine districts, and Democratic majorities were reduced in all the others. Early in 1855, the state legislature elected Lyman Trumbull, an Anti-Nebraska Democrat, to the Senate. Lincoln, who ran as a Whig, finally withdrew in favor of Trumbull but not until 1856 would he let himself be labeled as a Republican. Opponents of the territorial policy gained a majority in the federal House of Representatives, and they regarded this issue as the dominant one of the time. Also, it was the most divisive one. The party that grew out of this grouping was new in two important respects. It took a decisive rather than an evasive stand on the question of the extension of slavery. Also, it was wholly sectional in make-up.

In the past, the evasiveness of major parties on questions relating to slavery had been viewed with impatience by Northerners of strong and positive opinions. But it is doubtful if the Union could have been preserved if there had been decisive action against slavery, or even against the extension of it, while the groups supporting and opposing the institution were of comparable strength. National political parties, containing discordant elements within themselves and evading the most divisive sectional issues, had performed an invaluable service in holding the country together. It is a notable fact that national religious organizations split on sectional lines before the major parties did. One reason that the latter maintained geographical unity so long was that, in reality, they were loose organizations with little centralization. A party was a federation of state organizations over which nobody had central authority. But in order to win presidential elections, if for no other reason, it had to minimize divisive issues. Southerners became somewhat less Southern, while Northerners became somewhat less Northern, for the good of the party as a whole. The Democratic Party of Pierce and Douglas was still that sort of party. It was amorphous and opportunistic, but it was national, and its politicians had to consider the Southern as well as the Northern vote.

The Republicans, on the other hand, thrived on sectional controversy. The party absorbed the Northern Whigs but it lacked the conciliatory spirit of Clay and Webster, and the Southern Whigs were impelled into the Democratic camp. Historically, the name "Republican" had been applied to the party of Jefferson, but those who now assumed the name argued that the Democrats, by subservience to the slavery interests, had lost all right to identify themselves with the Jeffersonian lovers of freedom. Certain prominent Democratic politicians by their actions gave real point to this contention. The name had also been used by supporters of Henry Clay, who had called themselves National Republicans. Douglas said that the present Republicans could certainly not call themselves national, "with a platform that cannot cross the Ohio River, and a creed which inevitably brings the North and South into hostile collision." He thought that they should be called "Black Republicans," and they were by Southerners and others, but the allegation that they were abolitionists was untrue. No such charge could be fairly made against Lincoln, who by 1856 was regarded as the leading Republican of Illinois and who consistently urged moderation, or against the vast majority of leaders and supporters of the new party.

It absorbed practically all of the Northern reformers of the time. It had a degree of moral fervor which the Democrats as a group could not match and which Douglas, though a much broader man than his enemies thought him, did not understand. To many men Republicanism was a cloak for Northern sectionalism and a means to power, but to many it was a moral crusade. That was specially true of it in its first stages, from 1854 to 1856.

THE ELECTION OF 1856

The platform adopted by the first national convention of the Republican Party, at Philadelphia in June 1856, was devoted chiefly to the question of the extension of slavery. The Republicans strongly condemned the repeal of the Missouri Compromise, asserted that Congress should prohibit slavery in the territories and admit Kansas as a free state, and denounced the Ostend Manifesto. These resolutions were in the spirit of the Wilmot Proviso and showed a determination that the power of the federal government be employed to confine slavery within the geographical area where it then existed. By favoring federal aid to internal improvements the Republicans associated themselves with the Whig tradition. In taking the position that the newer regions should be the home of a free society they were in the spirit of the Declaration of Independence and the Northwest Ordinance of 1787. The platform was in the best tradition of American freedom and this fact, together with its abandonment of the policy of evasiveness, commended it greatly to moral crusaders.

We cannot justly blame the convention for not taking one more step and urging that the territories be left open to free Negroes. This was not required by sentiment in Northern antislavery circles, and it would have been regarded by Southern slaveowners as an open invitation to slaves to flee. Political circumstances and respect for the constitutional rights of states also made it virtually impossible for the party to propose any constructive solution for the problem of slavery where it existed. If the institution were sharply confined within its present area, presumably it would die out eventually, but even if Northerners had been disposed to anticipate the economic and social difficulties that would then arise in the South, any remedial proposals that they might have made would almost certainly have been resented by Southern leaders, who had persuaded themselves that slavery was a positive good. Republican politicians were little concerned about Southern opinion, but even in the North they had to meet the charge that they were narrow sectionalists and disunionists, and the wisest of them, like Lincoln, denied any intention of interfering in any way with existing Southern institutions. Philosophers and literary men might have viewed the problem as a whole, but in that time when romanticism, idealism, and materialism were so strangely commingled and the sectional conflict had aroused such intense feelings, nobody seemed able to attain the necessary degree of realism and objectivity. Thus the Republican answer to the most difficult domestic problem of the century was simply this: Slavery has gone thus far, but it can go no farther. The tone was positive and it aroused alarm in many Northern and nearly all Southern quarters. Even to Northern sectionalists the political appeal was not yet broad enough, and it lacked the later Republican emphasis on economic factors. Even to become dominant in the North the Republicans needed to build a broader base.

They did not make a happy choice of their first presidential candidate. By unanimous vote the honor went to John C. Frémont, who had captured the public imagination by his exploits as an explorer and soldier in the Far West and was known to be an antislavery man. But his career showed that he lacked the qualities of judgment and self-control that a President should have. He was a glamorous figure and probably he was not expected to be victorious anyway. It was fortunate for his party that he was not. His running mate was Senator William L. Dayton of New Jersey, an old Whig. Abraham Lincoln received a considerable vote in the balloting for the second office and gained prominence. His political availability was already being realized but he was still essentially a local figure and had not yet attained full political stature.

Meanwhile, the Democrats, meeting for the first time west of the mountains at Cincinnati, had faced a more confused situation and had met it in the compromising spirit that had come to characterize them. If the dominant purpose of the Republicans was to prevent the further extension of slavery, that of the Democrats—so they said—was to preserve the Union, and incidentally they wanted to win the election. They kept alive the charge that they were dominated by the "slave power" by advocating the annexation of Cuba, but their condemnation of sectional agitators who were endangering the Union was appealing to many sober citizens. In the platform they explicitly denied the power of Congress to interfere with the domestic institutions of the states, thus giving the slave states an assurance which was not yet forthcoming from the Republicans, and they even cited the Kentucky and Virginia Resolutions. They reaffirmed adherence to the Compromise of 1850 and to the principle of the Kansas-Nebraska Act, claiming that so far as the territories were concerned this was the same. By implication at least they blamed the troubles in Kansas on the antislavery forces when referring to "armed resistance to law." Specifically, they recognized the right of the people in a territory to form at the state level a constitution with or without slavery. No consistent Southern advocate of state-rights doctrines could deny the right of self-determination, including the prohibition of slavery, at the stage of statehood. The crucial constitutional question was that of rights during the territorial stage, and on this point the reference to the application of the "democratic principle" gave ground for different interpretations. Advocates of popular sovereignty and followers of Douglas were saying in the North that settlers could act against slavery before the stage of statehood, while this was denied by many Southern Democrats. There were seeds of future dissension in the ambiguity of the language of the platform and the varying interpretations of it, and the compromising position of the party proved exceedingly difficult to maintain.

The choice of the presidential candidate was determined by the same policy of evasion and was the result of much manipulation by experienced and conservative politicians behind the scenes. Pierce was ruled out because of his lack of success and the unpopularity he had gained from the Kansas-Nebraska Act. Douglas, though a much stronger man, was open to serious objection on the latter grounds. James Buchanan had been Minister to Great Britain amid this turmoil and his long experience in public life commended him to his fellows. He was considerably associated with the Ostend Manifesto and at sixty-five he might have been regarded as overripe, but this plodder seemed the safest man. John C. Breckinridge of Kentucky was his running mate.

The Know-Nothing Party also put up a ticket, headed by former President Millard Fillmore, and he polled a large popular vote, though he carried only the state of Maryland. The appeal of the Democrats in the campaign was made chiefly in the name of the Union and in behalf of conservatism. In general they were successful in retaining the support of business interests in the East, and they spent money very freely in the doubtful states of Pennsylvania and Indiana, both of which they carried. Buchanan ended up with 174 electoral votes, while Frémont got 114, and Fillmore 8, but the winner did not have a popular majority in the total vote. He got 45 per cent to Frémont's 30 per cent and Fillmore's 25 per cent. The distribution of the electoral votes was even more disturbing, because Frémont carried all the free states except New Jersey, Pennsylvania, Indiana, Illinois, and California, and would have won the election if he had carried Pennsylvania and either Illinois or Indiana. It was entirely possible to win the election without any Southern votes, and in the course of the campaign some Southern leaders threatened secession in the case of Republican victory.

THE DRED SCOTT DECISION

The election of 1856 really settled nothing, and it certainly did not answer the disputed question of the constitutional right of the federal government to exclude slaves from the territories, if it should choose to exercise its power. The Republicans assumed that Congress had this right and orthodox Southern constitutionalists denied it, while Douglas and his school sought to avoid the question by invoking the principle of popular sovereignty within the territories. To some well-meaning people it seemed that the air would be cleared by a ruling from the highest constitutional authority, the Supreme Court, and that the country could then proceed peacefully about its business—which was booming in 1856. Such a ruling came very soon after Buchanan's inauguration, in the famous Dred Scott decision (1857), but the effects were very different from what the conciliatory President had expected.

The decision upheld the position which had now become standard in the South and, even if it could have been challenged on no other grounds, the fact was indisputable that seven of the nine Justices were Democrats and that a majority of them came from the slave states. The aged Chief Justice, Roger B. Taney, was from Maryland; Justice James M. Wayne was a Georgian, John Catron came from Tennessee, Peter V. Daniel from Virginia, and John A. Campbell from Alabama. The South had even more disproportionate power in the Supreme Court than in Congress. Justices Samuel Nelson of New York and Robert C. Grier of Pennsylvania were Democrats, and the latter had conspicuously upheld the Fugitive Slave Law. Justice John McLean of Ohio was a Republican, while Benjamin R. Curtis of Massachusetts still clung to the name of Whig. It was not to be expected that these men would view the most controversial issue of the time with complete objectivity, and it was even more unlikely in these excited times that their contemporaries would think them impartial.

Dred Scott, the slave of an army doctor, had been taken from the slave state of Missouri to the free state of Illinois and the territory of Wisconsin, which then included trans-Mississippi territory that was free by virtue of the Congressional act creating it on the terms of the Missouri Compromise. He had then been brought back to the state where the peregrinations started. The suit for freedom that was instituted in Dred Scott's behalf, on the ground that he had been taken to a free state and territory, resulted in an adverse decision in Missouri, on the ground that he was still subject to the law of that commonwealth. A sufficient precedent existed in the Supreme Court decision in the case of Strader vs. Graham (1850). The suit was renewed in 1854, after he had become the property of John A. Sandford of New York, and the case reached the Supreme Court early in 1856. It was pushed by antislavery people as a test case, but it could have been dismissed on the precedent of Strader vs. Graham, without reference to the Missouri Compromise or the power of Congress to forbid slavery in the territories. No just criticism could have been made of the Court for ruling that Dred Scott was still a slave, but ever since that time students and commentators have been wondering why the Court took up the larger controversial questions. Many have regarded their action as one of judicial usurpation, and in the light of later events it was undoubtedly one of extreme unwisdom.

The blame may be divided. In our time many have believed that, after learning that the majority would declare Dred Scott still a slave, McLean and Curtis forced the issue by letting it be known that they would present their free-soil views in dissenting opinions. But certain Southern political leaders were pressing for a full presentation of their constitutional position, and Justice Wayne was particularly insistent on this. Also, it is known that Buchanan himself corresponded with Justice Catron prior to his inauguration and that, in his anxiety to arrive at a nonpolitical settlement of the territorial question, he approached Justice Grier, who was from his own state. These communications with members of the Court and this pressure on them would now be judged improper, and enough was known or suspected at the time to give ground to the charge of collusion. Taney himself was guilty of no impropriety, however, and no one can fairly question either his integrity or his patriotism. He became convinced that a far-reaching decision was called for, and he himself announced it.

Every member of the Court rendered an opinion in this momentous case, thus compounding the confusion. In summary it can be said that: (1) Dred Scott was still a slave, in the opinion of most of the Justices. (2) In the opinion of the majority the Missouri Compromise was unconstitutional and Congress had no authority to exclude slavery from a territory—though the grounds of the judgment were not the same in all cases. (3) In the expressed opinion of three judges, including Taney, no Negro could become a United States citizen, even though freed. (4) In the opinion of two—McLean and Curtis—Dred Scott was a free man and citizen, the Missouri Compromise was constitutional, and Congress had a right to forbid slavery in the territories.

These varying opinions were not immediately published, but the strong dissenting opinion of Curtis was soon widely circulated and certain of Taney's words were widely quoted out of context. He and three other

Justices held that Congress had no right to exclude slaves from the territories on the basis of the Fifth Amendment, which denied Congress the power to deprive any citizen of life, liberty, or property without due process of law. His description of slaves as property was in full accord with current Southern doctrine and was widely accepted in the North, but his emphasis offended the sensibilities of many. His contention that Negroes could not become United States citizens, which he coupled with assertions that the Fathers of the Republic did not expect them to, was even more grievous. It may have been historically true that in 1776 and 1787 Negroes were widely regarded as "beings of an inferior order, and altogether unfit to associate with the white race," and that they then had "no rights which any white man was bound to respect"; but even in that era enlightened liberals like Thomas Jefferson and George Mason, who were themselves slaveowners, would have been shocked by these expressions. Actually, Taney, who had freed his own slaves and was a humane man, did not say that these words applied in 1857, but many people thought he did and were appalled by the harshness of his language.

Curtis, besides producing formidable precedents in support of the right of Congress to legislate against slavery in the territories, pointed out as others did that various states had admitted former slaves to citizenship. The Dred Scott decision aroused strong protests in the name of human rights which did not stop at the color line, but the political repercussions were more violent at the moment. Not since the decision of Marshall in the case of Marbury *vs.* Madison (1803) had the Supreme Court declared an act of Congress unconstitutional, hence the present decision would have been of great constitutional significance even if it had been less provocative. It cut the ground from under the Republican platform. The rejoinder of spokesmen of that rising political group was that no part of the decision except the judgment that Dred Scott was still a slave was binding—everything else being in the nature of an *obiter dictum*. Whether or not Taney and his Court were guilty of judicial usurpation is still a question. John Marshall had built up the authority of the central government by means of *obiter dicta*. But there can be no question of the loss of prestige the highest Court now suffered. Another political embarrassment resulted from the decision: as Lincoln soon pointed out, the reasoning of Taney was difficult to reconcile with Douglas's doctrine of popular sovereignty. The decision was most pleasing to the most extreme Southern defenders of slavery, who could now proceed to demand federal protection for slaves in the territories. By unwisely going beyond the necessities of the case and passing judgment on the most controversial political issue of the time, the Supreme Court served to accentuate that issue; and the storm of Northern indignation that was loosed by this action boded ill for the success of the Buchanan administration.

CHAPTER 35

The Widening Rift, 1857-1860

THE PROBLEMS WHICH PRESIDENT JAMES BUCHANAN had to face would have taxed the powers of the greatest of statesmen, and time was to show that he was quite incapable of coping with them. Six feet tall, white-haired, old-fashioned in dress, and excessively dignified in manner, Buchanan presented to the world an impressive façade; and with the assistance of his niece, Harriet Lane, and an unusually attractive group of Cabinet ladies this bachelor had one of the most pretentious presidential courts on record. But when inaugurated he was nearly sixty-six and not in good health; he was a cold man who did not win personal affection or arouse popular enthusiasm; and he sought to solve great problems of state in the spirit and with the methods of a small-time politician. He regarded the preservation of the Union and the maintenance of Democratic control of the government as virtually indistinguishable, but he was unable to check the forces of disintegration within either his country or his party.

He gave inordinate attention to the patronage but his methods were not conducive to the unity of the party. He had succeeded a Democratic President, but he waged a warfare of extermination on the followers of Pierce. The recent Secretary of State, William L. Marcy, is reported to have said: "Well, they have it that I am the author of the office seeker's doctrine that 'to the victors belong the spoils,' but I should never recommend the policy of pillaging my own camp." Within less than two years, Buchanan was carrying on the same sort of factional warfare against Stephen A. Douglas.

From the Northern point of view he had a disproportionate number of Southerners in his Cabinet—four altogether. The most influential of them, genial Howell Cobb of Georgia, the Secretary of the Treasury, was regarded as a Unionist, but he became more rather than less sectional under the pressure of divisive controversy. John B. Floyd of Virginia, the Secretary of War, a notoriously careless administrator, was destined to

661

prove a heavy liability to the administration. Among the Northerners, Secretary of State Lewis Cass was senile and incompetent; and the only member of the Cabinet capable of standing up against the Southerners was Jeremiah S. Black, the Attorney General. The flavor of the administration proved to be as pro-Southern as that of the Pierce administration; and if this was the price Buchanan paid to preserve the Union, as he believed, it was costly to the Democrats in the North, where the young and vigorous Republican Party had no such handicap.

THE LECOMPTON CONSTITUTION AND THE REVOLT OF DOUGLAS

Buchanan's first moves with respect to Kansas were made in consultation with Douglas, who was far more familiar than he with territorial problems. He decided to appoint a new governor with national prestige, and he hoped to procure the early admission of Kansas as a Democratic state. His choice fell on Robert J. Walker, former Secretary of the Treasury, a noted expansionist now engaged in various promotion schemes who was like Douglas in his enthusiasm to open up and develop the country. Though a native of Pennsylvania, Walker had been identified with the state of Mississippi as a public man and was supposed to be acceptable to the South. His idea was to compose the civil strife in Kansas by holding out bright economic prospects—especially the promise of an unusually large federal grant of land on the attainment of statehood. Like Douglas he hoped that the conflict over slavery in the territory would thus be moderated or absorbed by general prosperity. While in no sense hostile to the proslavery faction then in nominal control of the territorial government, he expected to make an honest application of the doctrine of popular sovereignty and thought the administration would stand behind him.

Arriving in Kansas in May 1857, Walker soon found himself in an intolerable situation. The ruling clique had proceeded with a census, preliminary to the election of delegates to a constitutional convention, but a large segment of the population was not included in this because of the refusal of free-state men to co-operate. Seeking to deter the latter from reviving their own rival government, Walker encouraged them to participate in the election of representatives to the territorial legislature, in which by his orders every actual male resident could vote. When this election was held in the autumn, the vote of certain precincts on the Missouri border was so far in excess of the number of settlers there that he threw out the entire vote of these precincts (largely Democratic) as fraudulent. The free-state faction carried the territorial election and Walker was charged in proslavery circles in Kansas and elsewhere with exceeding his authority. Meanwhile, the constitutional convention, in the choice of whose delegates the free-state settlers had taken virtually no part, met in Lecompton, the temporary capital—a crude village of only one street but with more than ample facilities for drinking and gambling. This unrepresentative convention, consisting chiefly of disreputable adventurers, was wholly dominated by the proslavery faction and it spurned Walker's counsel.

The Lecompton Constitution was its handiwork. No provision was made for the submission of the document as a whole to the electorate. There was opportunity to vote for it "with slavery" or "without slavery," but the slaves already in the territory were to be protected in either case. It was accepted "with slavery" by an overwhelming vote, since the free-state men refrained from voting. The claim of legality could be made for it, but a referendum on the constitution, at the instance of the legislature, led to a considerably larger adverse vote. The conduct of partisans on both sides was open to exception and this was a local factional struggle for power as well as one over slavery, but there could be little doubt that the free-state settlers outnumbered their opponents. Nevertheless, the Lecompton Constitution was transmitted to Washington, and there it became a football of sectional conflict.

Walker, who came east, wanted to dismiss it altogether and start all over again. That would have been the fairest procedure, but Buchanan, still cherishing hopes of speedily adding a Democratic state and unwilling to risk alienating the Southern politicians, most of whom took up the cause of the unworthy proslavery faction in Kansas, was subbornly determined to recognize the *fait accompli*. He recommended the admission of Kansas as a state under the unsavory Lecompton Constitution. Walker had resigned and Douglas, outraged by this travesty of democratic procedure, opposed the bill in the Senate and broke with the administration. He was genuinely devoted to the doctrine of popular sovereignty, and he could hardly have maintained his political position in his own region if he had supported the President, for Northern sentiment was strongly against the Lecompton Constitution. Despite powerful and persistent pressure by the administration, the sentiment in Congress for the resubmission of the Constitution to the electorate of Kansas would not down. Such action would have been regarded as a rebuke to the administration and it was opposed by proslavery Southerners who were sparring for sectional advantage.

The net result of the bitter controversy was the adoption of what was known as the English Bill. This called for the submission to the Kansans of a specific proposition which they were to vote on as a whole: namely, that the territory be admitted immediately as a state on the basis of the Lecompton Constitution and receive a land grant. If the vote should be unfavorable, admission would be delayed until the population of the territory, as shown by a census, had reached the figure required for a Representative in Congress—which would be a matter of several years.

Douglas was opposed to this bill and it was assailed by many as a bribe, though it can also be described as a face-saving subterfuge. The voters of the territory decisively rejected the proposition, preferring delay to immediate admission under the Lecompton Constitution, and this meant that Kansas would be a free state when ultimately admitted— as she was in 1861. Meanwhile, the local action was rightly interpreted as a resounding defeat for the administration and its scheme to add a Democratic state to the Union. Buchanan had catered to proslavery politicians without really helping the South in the struggle for sectional power. Indeed, the moral cause of the South was weakened by this controversy. The President had exhausted his political resources in a vain cause. He had broken with Douglas and widened the gap between that Northern statesman and the Southern extremists. The gap was to be widened further by the powerful blows of Abraham Lincoln of Illinois.

DOUGLAS AND LINCOLN

In the year 1858, when Douglas was seeking re-election to the United States Senate, his political position was anomalous and precarious. His Kansas-Nebraska Act had given rise to the new Republican Party, but now he had broken with the Democratic President over the Lecompton Constitution and had even opposed the English Bill, along with the Republicans. What would be the judgment of his Illinois constituents on his actions? What would be the attitude of the Republicans? An answer to the latter question was given by the Republican state convention in June, when that body nominated their best man, Abraham Lincoln, to oppose him. The campaign which followed, and particularly the public debates between the two candidates, attracted national attention. It has abiding historic interest because the two most important statesmen of the era were pitted against each other. In the end Douglas was re-elected by the legislature, but Lincoln began to reveal his caliber as a statesman and prepared the way for his own far greater victory in the next presidential campaign.

Lincoln towered over his rival in physical stature and, as the saying went, could have held the Little Giant upon his knee; but until this time he had been much less prominent as a public man. Now forty-nine while Douglas was forty-six, he had served inconspicuously as a Whig Representative in Congress for one term (1847-1849) and then had retired from public life for five years, devoting himself to the practice of law in Springfield. Many of the elements which were to make him the most famous of American folk-heroes were visible in him. He already epitomized the American success story. Born obscurely and almost wholly self-educated, he had become a noted lawyer and substantial citizen. Escaping the vices of the frontier, "Honest Abe" embodied its homely virtues, while his feats of strength and robust humor had long since made him a local celebrity. Also, he had shown himself to be an unusually shrewd and ambitious politician. But it was not until the impact of a moral challenge transformed him about the time of the Kansas-Nebraska Act that he began to show signs of greatness.

Lincoln's attitude toward the sectional controversy was never one of self-righteousness, and no Republican leader of his time had a better understanding of the problems of the South. He was a native of Kentucky, as was his wife, Mary Todd, who came of a slaveowning family. He frankly admitted that he had no ready solution for the problem of slavery where it already existed, and he would have no part with the censoriousness of the abolitionists. Of the statesmen of his era he specially admired the great compromiser, Henry Clay. Among statesmen of the more distant past he found his chief inspiration in Jefferson. "I have never had a feeling politically that did not spring from the sentiments of the Declaration of Independence," he said. He believed, as the author of that document did, that all men have fundamental rights, not because of accidents of birth or wealth, but because they are human beings. Thus, inevitably, he was opposed to human bondage. At the same time, he had a healthy respect for the constitutional right of states to determine and control their domestic institutions. Therefore, without attacking local institutions, Lincoln sought to check slavery in the only place where he believed it could be legitimately checked—in the territories.

Though Lincoln intended no direct attack on Southerners as persons or even as slaveowners, the speech in which he accepted the Senatorial nomination could not be expected to appeal to them. "A house divided against itself cannot stand," he said. "I believe this government cannot endure permanently half *slave* and half *free*." Quoted out of context, as it often was in the next few years, this saying gave an impression of impatience which was uncharacteristic of Lincoln and led to misinterpretation of him in the slave states. He was speaking to a local and partisan audience, magnifying the differences between the position of his party and that of its rival in the way that candidates for elective office so often do. In the same partisan spirit he ridiculed Douglas and charged him virtually with being a party to a proslavery conspiracy—along with Pierce, Buchanan, and Chief Justice Taney. Since Douglas had broken with Buchanan and had no possible responsibility for the Dred Scott decision this was manifestly unfair.

The Lincoln-Douglas Debates

Accepting Lincoln's challenge, Douglas joined him in a series of public debates, seven in number, during three months in the late summer and early fall of 1858. These lacked the decorum of the great debates in the

Senate in the heydey of Webster, Calhoun, and Clay, and they reached no such heights of constitutional argument. Addressed to popular audiences in Illinois, they were part of a great political show which included parades, band music, and flag-waving as well as two-hour speeches, and which must also have been a supreme test of endurance on the part of participants and spectators alike. Both men were experienced and skillful debaters, and they stuck closely to the main point of controversy—the question of slavery and its extension into the territories. Each of them described the position of his opponent extremely, trying to put him in a hole, though in terms of public policy the actual differences between them at this stage were slight.

Douglas sought to identify his rival with abolitionism, spoke of the "Black" Republican Party, and charged it with the purpose of interfering with the domestic institutions of the states—repeating these allegations and charges despite denials and refutations. Lincoln said, in a way that should have been convincing, that he had no inclination and believed he had no lawful right to interfere with slavery where it then existed. Also, he denied any purpose "to introduce political and social equality between the white and black races." The main difference between the two men on this point went back to their interpretations of the Declaration of Independence. Like Chief Justice Taney, Douglas denied that the signers of that great charter of liberties intended its wondrous phrases to apply to Negroes. In attacking the Dred Scott decision on this score, Lincoln had already put himself on record in a classic passage.

> . . . I think the authors of that notable instrument intended to include *all* men, but they did not intend to declare all men equal *in all respects.* . . . They defined with tolerable distinctness, in what respects they did consider all men created equal—equal in "certain inalienable rights, among which are life, liberty, and the pursuit of happiness." . . . They meant to set up a standard maxim for free society, which could be familiar to all, and revered by all; constantly looked to, constantly labored for, and even though never perfectly attained, constantly approximated, and thereby constantly spreading and deepening its influence, and augmenting the happiness and value of life to all people of all colors everywhere.

Lincoln was fully as aware as Douglas was of the state of social opinion among the voters in Illinois, and he opposed the counsels of robust common sense to the fears that the abolitionist crusade had aroused there and elsewhere. While chiding the Southern whites for inconsistency in condoning illicit amalgamation under slavery, he sagely said: "There are white men enough to marry all the white women, and black men enough to marry all the black women; and so let them be married." This realistic observer and homespun philosopher took higher moral ground and was more humane than his rival. Douglas callously said: "I do not regard the Negro as my equal, and positively deny

that he is my brother, or any kin to me whatever." Lincoln believed that
the Declaration of Independence "contemplated the progressive improvement in the condition of all men everywhere." Like Jefferson before him,
he had faith in all manner of human beings and left the door of hope
open to them all.

On the crucial question of territorial policy, Lincoln took the position
that Douglas and others had placed the institution of slavery on a new
basis, looking to its *"perpetuation and nationalization,"* and that unless
its spread were checked its advocates would push it forward until it
should become lawful in all the states, North as well as South. In view
of the actualities of the situation, this was a highly partisan assertion;
and his statement that the repeal of the Missouri Compromise could not
be distinguished on moral grounds from the repeal (which had not taken
place) of the law forbidding the importation of slaves from Africa was
extreme. The latter would have led to an actual increase in the number
of slaves in the country, while the former merely permitted the taking
of slaves from one part of the Union to another. He criticized the doctrine of popular sovereignty as now applied, on the ground that, while
permitting the people in a territory to have slaves, it did not permit them
not to have them. This was, indeed, the interpretation towards which
extremists in the Lower South were working, but it was not the interpretation of the doctrine by Douglas.

The Freeport Doctrine

The pronouncement of Douglas came to be known as the Freeport
Doctrine. Pressed by Lincoln, who inquired how a territorial legislature
could forbid slavery in a territory when the Supreme Court had held
in the Dred Scott decision that Congress, which had created that legislature, could not do so, Douglas responded that the local legislature
could refuse to provide the necessary legal safeguards, such as were
found in the slave codes of the southern states, and thus make the
existence of slavery impossible. This Freeport Doctrine was a wedge
driven by Lincoln between Douglas and Southern extremists, and in 1860
this wedge split the Democratic Party, ensuring its defeat and Lincoln's
election as a Republican President of the United States.

Some historians in our own day have expressed deep regret that at
this stage Lincoln and Douglas were rivals and not allies. In the heat of
partisan conflict the differences between them were exaggerated. But it
seemed to Lincoln that Douglas was culpably indifferent to the moral
question of slavery. Douglas said he did not care whether slavery was
voted up or down. Buchanan did not even care whether or not there was a
fair referendum. In any case, it was a reasonable assumption that the Republicans could be better trusted to prevent any future extension of the

area of slavery. The retort of Douglas was that the Democrats could be better trusted to save the Union. That, also, had seemed a fair assumption. By 1858, however, the Democratic Party itself was cracking apart and showing clear signs of incapacity and even of corruption.

POLITICS: NORTH AND SOUTH, 1858-1859

Democratic Disintegration in the North

Among the Democrats in the North a distinction could now be made between the Buchanan men and the anti-Lecomptonites, of whom Douglas was the conspicuous leader. The party as a whole suffered serious reverses in the North in the mid-term Congressional elections of 1858, but in general the anti-Lecomptonites survived the ordeal. In Illinois, for example, the Democrats maintained their strength in the Congressional delegation and Douglas was re-elected by the legislature to the Senate. Democratic casualties were heaviest among the out-and-out supporters of the administration. Buchanan said that the defeat in his own state was so great that it was almost absurd. His party had 15 of 25 representatives from Pennsylvania in the present Congress, but in 1858 only 4 Democrats were elected. Economic factors were important in Pennsylvania, where the Depression of 1857 had been sharply felt and there was a fresh and insistent demand for tariff protection of the iron industry. The President attributed Democratic defeat largely to economic conditions which he regarded as temporary, but the main lesson of the election was the loss of confidence in the administration in the North. This may be attributed in part to a growing awareness of Buchanan's incapacity for leadership, but the chief specific reason for it was his handling of the Kansas question.

Though Douglas had been vindicated in Northern eyes, while Buchanan was being rebuked, he was made the victim of unwarranted and virtually unparalleled punitive action in the final session of the old Congress, which was nominally under Democratic control. By vote of the Democratic caucus, he was removed from the chairmanship of the Committee on Territories which he had held so long. No more striking illustration can be given of the bitter factional spirit within the party. Partisans of Buchanan and Southern extremists united to pull down the Democratic leader who had the largest following in the North. In the absence of effective leadership the Congress itself descended into chaos. Vital appropriation bills were imperiled, and the one for the Post Office Department (the major seat of patronage) actually failed. Half way in the course of the administration the federal government was threatened with paralysis. Buchanan wasted what little political strength he had left in the effort to secure an appropriation for the purchase of Cuba. Since there was no likelihood that Spain would sell Cuba, this move was regarded as a mere political gesture, and if it pleased Southern imperialists it aroused fresh fears in the North.

While the Pennsylvanians were vainly clamoring for a rise in the tariff duties, two other economic measures failed that were generally favored by Northerners and opposed by Southerners. A bill to donate land for agricultural colleges was vetoed by the President on constitutional grounds; and a homestead bill that had passed the House was defeated in the Senate by the vote of the Vice-President. It would have been difficult to pursue a course better calculated to alienate Northern opinion and play into the hands of the Republicans. In the North the conviction became inescapable that the politically-minded President was a captive of Southern proslavery advisers. As a national organization the Democratic Party was disintegrating with appalling rapidity, and it did not even have nominal control of the next Congress, which assembled in December 1859. Two months were required to organize the new House of Representatives. At length a coalition of Republicans, anti-Lecompton Democrats, and men who still called themselves Whigs elected William Pennington as Speaker. He was a Whig from New Jersey. This was the Congress, the Thirty-Sixth, that assembled after John Brown's raid and was in session in 1860-1861 when the cotton states seceded from the Union.

Extremists in the Lower South

In the South in those days, elections occurred in odd rather than even years. Thus the Southerners had time to ponder over events in the North in 1858 before they themselves voted in 1859. From the Southern point of view, the most provocative episode of the Northern campaign was a speech by the Republican leader, William H. Seward, in Rochester, New York (September 25, 1858), in which he used the expression, "irrepressible conflict." While this speech was designed for local consumption and Seward tried to hedge a few days later, news of it traveled fast and far and it gained for him a reputation for radicalism which he did not really deserve. His language was more extreme than that of Lincoln in his "house-divided" speech, and his supposed prophecy of intersectional war was roundly condemned by responsible Northerners. It caused Jefferson Davis to say, in a speech to the Mississippi Legislature a few weeks later, that if an abolitionist were elected President, the only safety for Mississippi would lie outside the Union. To equate Republicanism with abolitionism was unfair, but that was just what Southern politicians did increasingly from this time on. The fact that the Republicans took up Helper's *Impending Crisis*, which was originally intended as an appeal to Southern nonslaveholders, also aroused fresh fears of Northern attacks on Southern institutions. The Republicans circulated in large quantity excerpts from this critique of the slaveholders, though few of these pamphlets got across the border.

The Democratic Party in the South was rent by factions, as the party in the North was, and in some cases there were clearcut Douglas and Buchanan factions. But Buchanan was now discredited in his own section, and the course of events in Kansas had caused extreme proslavery expansionists to regard Douglas as a traitor. The group of men, previously very small, who saw no hope for the South and its institutions except in a separate republic took advantage of these opportune circumstances.

The best-known agitators for Southern independence—Robert Barnwell Rhett of South Carolina, Edmund Ruffin of Virginia, and William L. Yancey of Alabama—were not themselves officeholders, and the only sort of political party they were interested in was a Southern party. Rhett, who had vainly advocated the secession of his state at the time of the Compromise of 1850 and had been beaten by the "co-operationists," spoke chiefly, from 1857 on, through the *Charleston Mercury*, which was edited by his son. This paper nominally supported the Democratic Party while seeking to undermine it. Rhett became convinced that the best hope of secession lay in the success of the Republicans. Edmund Ruffin, who rendered such conspicuous service as an agricultural reformer, was also a secessionist and Southern nationalist by 1858, but he said that the advocacy of his doctrines would be political suicide in Virginia. He exerted far greater influence in the Lower South, through his writings in *DeBow's Review* and other periodicals, and it was he who suggested to William L. Yancey the organization of the League of United Southerners.

As an organization this did not grow fast, but its policies were eloquently proclaimed by Yancey, the most popular Southern orator of his day. These policies were to force the political parties to abandon the "law of compromise" and adopt the "law of the Constitution," and to promote co-operation in support of Southern "rights" and interests. Yancey's uncompromising spirit was wholly incompatible with that of any national party; his interpretation of the Constitution was that of the most extreme Southern sectionalists; and the co-operation he advocated was wholly within the slaveholding region. Indeed, this apostle of disunion was quite willing for the cotton states to secede alone, expecting the states of the Upper South to serve as a barrier between them and the free states at first, and ultimately to join them.

The desirability of slavery was assumed by these agitators, and the effort to gain an actual increase in the number of slaves was a logical corollary. Northern economy had expanded with the aid of European immigrants, and it was being said that Southern expansion required more Africans. At just this period, when the enforcement of the Fugitive Slave Law was being impeded in Northern states, illegal importation of slaves into the South increased. The extent of this cannot be precisely measured, and it was almost certainly exaggerated by Northerners, but it is a fact that the laws against the foreign slave trade were nullified in some quarters. In several notable cases in South Carolina and Georgia, grand juries refused to indict violators of the law or juries acquitted them, and Senator James H. Hammond of South Carolina boasted that his state was invincibly opposed to its enforcement.

There was a definite movement to repeal the legislation and restore the African slave trade to legality. The movement expressed itself in resolutions at the Southern Commercial Convention at Montgomery in 1858. These were defeated, but in 1859 at a similar convention at Vicksburg such resolutions were adopted by an overwhelming vote. This action was not an expression of general opinion, for even its advocates admitted that the great majority of Southerners opposed the reopening of the foreign slave trade and, when the Confederacy was actually set up a couple of years later, it outlawed the traffic. Many Southern leaders opposed the extreme and reckless resolutions in 1859. They were important at the time chiefly because of the effect they had on Northern opinion, and they have abiding historical significance as an illustration of the lengths to which the proslavery philosophy could be stretched.

More fateful than the abortive attempt to reopen the foreign slave trade was the pronouncement at this stage, by Yancey and other extremists, of the constitutional doctrine that the federal government was obligated to *protect* slavery in the territories. This was a reply to the Freeport Doctrine of Douglas that a territorial legislature could prevent slavery by failing to pass the necessary protective legislation. Since several Southern leaders, including Jefferson Davis, took the same position as Yancey and Ruffin about the same time, the charge was made by certain Southern Unionists that these men had conspired to break up the Democratic Party by advancing doctrines which Douglas and his followers could not accept. There does not appear to have been any collusion, but there can be no possible doubt that the desire to stop Douglas was a major purpose in the minds of Southern "fire-eaters."

It was now clear that there was little better prospect of the spread of slavery into the existing territories under popular sovereignty and the Freeport Doctrine than under the Republican policy. Indeed, that had been what Douglas thought all the time, but to many Southerners it now seemed that he had deluded them with false hopes. Even under a system of federal protection during the territorial stage, there would have been little likelihood that many masters would take their slaves into territories which would almost certainly develop into free states, hence the Yancey doctrine was itself a delusion. But in times of excitement men grasp at phantoms, and there were other reasons why the extremists wanted to destroy Douglas as a national Democratic leader. He could not be controlled as Buchanan had been, and his election as President would mean the end of Southern dominance of the party. It now seems that the fire-eaters followed the course of madness, but there was method in it if their main purpose was to prepare the way for a Southern republic.

Moderates in the Upper South

The extremists operated most effectively in the cotton states. Meanwhile, in the Upper South moderate men were making a strong effort to organize a party of opposition to the dominant Democrats. The leadership in this was taken by old Whigs. Perceiving the disunity of the Democrats and realizing that the Republican Party could gain slight following in the Upper South, these advocates of Union sought to provide an acceptable alternative. The threat of this opposition party caused the Democrats to nominate more moderate men in certain states, like Virginia, and the state elections of 1859 in the Upper South were generally favorable to the moderates. The Unionist cause was strongly reinforced, also, by the election of Sam Houston as Governor of Texas. But moderate John Letcher, the Governor-elect of Virginia, had not yet replaced fiery Henry Wise, when John Brown invaded the Old Dominion at Harper's Ferry and aroused in all slaveholding communities the fear of servile insurrection. The grim old warrior of abolition undermined the position of the Southern moderates and played directly into the hands of the fire-eaters, while accentuating antislavery sentiment in the North.

JOHN BROWN'S RAID

Even after a century it is difficult to view John Brown without emotion, and his name still elicits very different emotions in the North and South. Before his famous raid caused Southerners to regard him as a demon, and the circumstances of his death transformed him into a Northern legend, linked with the sacred cause of human freedom, he was recognized by many of his contemporaries as a fanatic. While the very small group who elevated antislavery above all causes, including the preservation of the Union, palliated his excesses, he was generally recognized as a personal failure. He was one of those fanatics who have affected the course of history. He hastened the downfall of slavery as an American institution; but, by fanning emotions into flame on both sides of the line, he enormously reduced the possibility of settling the sectional controversy by any other means than force. He stands in American history as a supreme example of the doctrine that the end justifies the means. But, under different circumstances, his violent means would have been thoroughly discredited in a self-governing society. John Brown was a failure in life but he gained fame by the way he died and as a symbol he went marching on.

Fifty-nine years of age at the time of his raid, weather-beaten and white-bearded, he was regarded by everybody as an old man, and many failures and bloody deeds lay behind him. Born in Connecticut and brought up in Ohio, he came of vigorous Puritan stock on his father's side but was less fortunate in his maternal inheritance. There was insanity in his mother and a number of her relatives, and his contemporaries often described Brown himself as a monomaniac. The term "paranoiac" would probably be applied to him in our own day. In middle life, having failed in everything else, he made a career and crusade of violent abolitionism. He had wandered from place to place—in Ohio, Pennsylvania, New York, and elsewhere—and from one undertaking to another. He could never provide adequately for his large family. Two wives bore him twenty children, and he followed his own sons to Kansas. In the border warfare in Kansas he began to carve out the career for which he is remembered, bringing to the conflicts between proslave and free-state settlers the merciless attitude toward evildoers for which he found warrant in the Old Testament, without being appreciably affected by the merciful spirit of the New. In his eyes, any slaveholder deserved to die.

In 1857, Brown was raising funds in the East for antislavery ventures, ostensibly in Kansas, but he had begun to plan an attack on the very citadel of slavery, and in 1858 his plan matured. The thousand pikes he ordered in New England were intended for the arming of slaves who should be freed in Virginia and states even farther south. By 1858, a secret committee—including Gerrit Smith of New York, the Rev. Thomas Wentworth Higginson, Dr. Samuel G. Howe, Frank B. Sanford, George L. Stearns, and the Rev. Theodore Parker—had been formed to support Brown. Some of these philanthropists and high-minded reformers tried to limit their support to Kansas, but they were aware of Brown's larger and bloodier purposes and some of them hoped that he would create an incident, while others felt powerless to restrain him. Their support, whether active or passive, of Brown's reckless venture is harder to explain than his undertaking it, for they were much more respected and responsible members of society than he.

Before embarking on his most famous raid, Brown returned to Kansas, raided Missouri, and carried a group of freed slaves to Canada—after an innocent Missourian had been killed by a member of his party. His larger purpose was now to attack a point in Virginia, terrify the slaveholders, free the slaves, and erect a standard to which others could repair. He decided on Harper's Ferry, at the junction of the Potomac and the Shenandoah, where there was a federal arsenal. Believing that several hundred slaves would rally to him immediately, he planned next to proceed southward along the mountains. For this ambitious enterprise he collected twenty-one men, including three of his own sons. His followers expected this to be a quick raid like others he had conducted, and, when the plan of attack on Harper's Ferry was revealed, some of them predicted its failure. But Brown's fanaticism bore down all opposition and communicated itself to others.

During the summer of 1859, under an assumed name, he rented the Kennedy farmhouse, on the Maryland side of the Potomac five or six miles away from his objective. On the night of Sunday, October 16, leaving three men behind to guard the farmhouse, Brown and the others seized the bridge across the Potomac. They captured the arsenal and armory on the Potomac and the rifle factory at some distance away on the Shenandoah. Penetrating the countryside, a small band aroused from his bed Colonel Lewis Washington, great-grandnephew of George Washington, and forced him to dress himself and go with them as a prisoner. They also brought along the sword supposed to have been given his great-granduncle by Frederick the Great, and John Brown wore this next day. Other hostages were seized, along with a small group of bewildered slaves. After midnight the raiders stopped a train that was proceeding eastward, and the first fatality occurred when a free Negro, the baggage master in the station, was shot. The train was allowed to proceed after some hours' delay and thus the alarm was carried to Baltimore and Washington. Meanwhile, the townspeople bestirred themselves, further casualties occurred, the alarm spread, militiamen assembled, and before Monday was past Brown and the pitiful remnant of his band were penned with the hostages in an engine-house, a stoutly built brick building. There was no rising of the slaves, and the first of Brown's men to die was another free Negro who had hoped to liberate his own wife and children.

An attack on the engine-house was deferred because of fear of injuring the hostages and the pending arrival of a small detachment of marines from Washington. These were commanded by Colonel Robert E. Lee, who had Lieutenant Jeb Stuart, later the famous Confederate cavalryman, as one of his junior officers. They arrived late Monday night. Early Tuesday morning, when Brown declined to surrender unconditionally, the engine-house was stormed and captured with losses on both sides. Two of Brown's sons had died, only five of his men were left, and he himself was wounded. Had he been killed, he might have aroused little sympathy, for more innocent men than he had died as a result of this mad enterprise. But circumstances conspired to make him into a martyr.

The Trial and Execution of John Brown

The Virginia authorities lost no time in taking legal action against John Brown. Transferred to a jail in Charlestown (now in West Virginia), he was indicted and tried with such speed as to give rise to criticism that he was being railroaded to his death. Under normal circumstances his physical condition would have occasioned delay; during the trial he lay on a cot in the courtroom, though some claimed that he did not really need to. Under modern conditions, he might never have been tried as a criminal, because of the available evidence that he was of unsound mind. He himself indignantly denied the allegation of insanity; he expected to die and already anticipated the glory of martyrdom.

The charges against him were three: treason in making rebellion and levying war against the state of Virginia, conspiring to start a slave insurrection, and the murder of four whites and one Negro. All were capital offenses and the first would have been wisely omitted, since Brown was not a citizen of Virginia. Brown asserted that he could not expect a fair trial. While he had counsel, this was not of his own choosing at first, and insufficient time was given to prepare the defense. In the end, however, he professed that he was entirely satisfied with the treatment he had received. He was convicted on all three counts and, despite his own denial, he clearly deserved to be on the last two of them. It is a great pity, however, that Governor Wise did not commute his sentence on the ground of insanity, or at least grant a stay of execution until that question was explored. He and his outraged fellow Virginians did not realize the truthfulness of the prophecy of Edmund Clarence Stedman:

> And Old Brown,
> Osawatomie Brown,
> May trouble you more than ever,
>   when you've nailed his coffin down.

In his dignified and moving final statement in court the grizzled old warrior denied any sense of guilt and expressed his willingness to forfeit his life in the ends of justice—that is, to release the slaves from bondage. Historians have detected inaccuracies in his final statement, which may be attributed to his self-delusion, but in the North most people were disposed to take all his final words at their face value, and in the weeks between his sentence and his execution on December 2 sympathy for him waxed mightily. His indomitable spirit was revealed in many letters and commented on by all observers. He expressed no regret for the death of his own sons and he left no possible doubt of his own readiness to die. John Brown was hanged within sight of a nation, and an entire people perceived his dauntless courage. Maniacal courage it seemed to those who looked from the South, heroic to those looking from the North. As he departed from his cell to the scaffold he left for his countrymen his final message: "I, John Brown, am now quite *certain* that the crimes of this *guilty land* will never be purged *away* but with blood."

Emotions, Alarms, and Threats, 1859-1860

The initial Northern reaction to the raid itself had been one of incredulity and general condemnation. Among Brown's financial backers there was consternation. Several of them fled the country and Gerrit Smith, who burned incriminating evidence, suffered a collapse and spent a couple of months in a New York asylum. Thomas Wentworth Higginson stood by Brown, but the conduct of most of the others was exceedingly unheroic. Emerson was no party to the raid, though he had made a modest contribution to Brown's work in Kansas. His early comment on the sad "Harper's Ferry business" was that Brown was a hero "but lost his head there." Soon, however, the Sage of Concord was referring to him in public as a saint and predicting that when his martyrdom was perfected he would "make the gallows as glorious as the Cross."

On the day of the execution, bells were tolled in communities from Concord to Chicago, and both houses of the Massachusetts Legislature adjourned. In her diary, Louisa M. Alcott noted the execution of "Saint John the Just;" Thoreau described him as "an angel of light;" and, echoing these sentiments from across the sea, Victor Hugo described him as an apostle and hero, and predicted that the rupture of the Union would "fatally follow" his "assassination." Nobody contributed more to the John Brown legend than Northern literary men, including many, like Longfellow and William Cullen Bryant, who had never identified themselves with the abolitionists. Whittier the Quaker could approve no such violence, and Nathaniel Hawthorne, after he got back from Europe, was appalled by the notion that the "death of this blood-stained fanatic" had made "the gallows as venerable as the cross." He himself believed that "nobody was ever so justly hanged," but among Northern writers his emphasis was exceptional.

In the course of time the leading Northern statesmen condemned Brown's actions. Douglas referred to him as a notorious man who had suffered death for his crimes, and blamed the latest and greatest of these directly on the doctrines of Lincoln's House-Divided Speech and Seward's on "irrepressible conflict." But both of these Republican leaders disowned John Brown. Lincoln compared him to the self-deluded assassins of kings and emperors; and Seward, while more sympathetic with the man, described his act as one of sedition and treason. These party leaders assumed the only possible position, and the Republican platform of 1860 officially denounced "the lawless invasion by armed force of the soil of any State or Territory, no matter under what pretext, as among the gravest of crimes."

The literary men expressed the mood of the Northern people better than the responsible statesmen. This mood was determined not by reason but by emotion, and the picture of John Brown that persisted in the public mind was that of a hero not a criminal. Furthermore, as Charles Eliot Norton believed, the events in which he had been the central figure and the impression of invincible courage that he gave did more to crystallize opposition to slavery than "all the antislavery tracts and novels that were ever written." Harriet Beecher Stowe's *Uncle Tom's Cabin* had warmed hearts toward the hapless slaves, while Brown's fate served to harden Northern hearts against slaveholders. Under these emotional conditions, the difficulties of sectional reconciliation were approaching the insuperable.

The reaction of Southerners was quite otherwise. The raid aroused fears of servile revolt which, as we can now see, were greatly exaggerated. Brown utterly failed of his ostensible purpose, and, as Lincoln pointed out, his plan was so absurd that the slaves themselves saw plainly that it could not succeed and wholly refused to participate in it. The slaves were far more loyal to their masters and less disposed to take advantage of their masters' difficulties than the abolitionists had anticipated. But the "Black Terror" was an emotional reality in the slave country which Northerners rarely perceived, and certain politicians were exploiting it for their own purposes. Erratic Governor Wise of Virginia had increased the alarm, and Edmund Ruffin saw that samples of the pikes with which John Brown would have armed the slaves were displayed in legislative halls throughout the South—to show what the Yankees had been planning. That very few Yankees had any thought of fomenting insurrection made little difference in such a time of perfervid emotion. Brown unquestionably had Northern supporters and the fact that he did was more appalling to Southerners than was the man himself. Most appalling of all were the sentiments of the Northern literary men, which to Southerners seemed quite incredible. The extreme claim that Southern institutions were no longer safe in the Union—that indeed the very lives of white women and children were endangered—could now be supported by an unforgettable illustration.

Thus the Southern mind and heart also hardened, especially against the Republicans, whose protestations fell on deaf ears, but increasingly against Northerners as a group. In this orgy of fear and indignation the enforcement of slave codes became more rigorous. Supposed Northern sympathizers were ostracized and in some instances expelled. In Virginia, where sentiment was still more moderate than in the cotton states, a body of medical students who had withdrawn from Northern institutions were greeted by a cheering crowd in Richmond. Said Governor Wise: "Let Virginia call home her sons!" The spirit of disunion grew and political extremists gained strength almost everywhere.

It is not surprising that, in this atmosphere of intersectional fear and suspicion which was passing into hatred, the new House of Representatives which assembled in December 1859 took two months to elect a speaker. Congress remained a sounding board, a place for rival pronouncements, but it was ceasing to be a place where important questions could be settled, and in the next few months the most fateful political events were to occur outside its halls. In South Carolina in that same month the legislature adopted resolutions calling for a convention of all the southern states to consider concerted measures. The Mississippi Legislature took similar action and the Alabamians were favorable, but this move failed, and opinions differed as to whether the results of such a gathering would have been to promote or to discourage disunion. Some extremists feared the continuing moderation of the Upper South.

The Alabama Platform

The adoption of the Alabama Platform (January 11, 1860) by a convention of that state under the dominance of Yancey pointed in the direction in which the Lower South would travel. Besides affirming that it was the *duty* of the general government to protect slave property in all the territories while these were under its authority, this Platform instructed the Alabama delegates to the Democratic National Convention to withdraw if the principles already stated were not adopted in substance. Thus, three months in advance of the gathering at which the fate of the Democratic Party as a national organization was to be determined, Alabama presented an ultimatum. In the intervening weeks the Southern radicals, exploiting the excitement of the times, put state after state on record—causing doctrines formerly regarded as extreme to be recognized in most of the Lower South as a test of sectional orthodoxy. The six states of South Carolina, Florida, Mississippi, Louisiana, Arkansas, and Texas endorsed the Alabama Platform before the national convention met. Meanwhile, the Alabama Legislature (February 20, 1860) directed the Governor to call a state convention in case a Republican President should be elected.

By springtime, therefore, seven southern states had threatened secession from the Democratic Party if it did not accept the doctrines they now proclaimed, and one had virtually threatened secession from the Union if the Republicans should carry the national election.

CHAPTER 36

The Election of 1860
and Secession

EVER SINCE THE TERRIBLE WAR BETWEEN THE SECTIONS, historians and other interpreters of the American past have been arguing whether this conflict was in fact irrepressible. Only those who regard human society as the helpless victim of external circumstances, without any power to control its destiny, can concede that the conflict was absolutely inevitable at any stage; and all others must believe that at some time in its long course the controversy between the North and South could have been sufficiently resolved to prevent an eventual recourse to arms. With them, therefore, the question is one of relative likelihood.

Looking backward, we can now see that after the actions of the cotton states following John Brown's raid the chance of avoiding an open political breach was slight. The events of the year 1860 provided the occasion for the first acts of secession, but the real causes of these acts antedated the party conventions and the presidential election. On both sides of the line leaders were committed to positions from which it would have been exceedingly difficult to withdraw, and the Southern extremists, now in control of half a dozen states, had presented the Northerners with a virtual ultimatum. The voice of moderation was by no means silenced in these fateful months, and men of good will sought acceptable compromise in a spirit of undying hope. But in 1860-1861 they were trying to reconcile elements which had already become virtually irreconcilable. Wise statesmanship should certainly have prevented a situation where the price of party unity and national union had become surrender or humiliating retreat on one side or the other. Thus the Republic first drifted and then rushed into its greatest historic disaster, impelled by emotions which had been generated by past actions.

THE DEMOCRATIC SPLIT

The Democratic National Convention met toward the end of April 1860, and there was irony in the fact that it did so in Charleston. That lovely city was a capital of Southernism, and the passionately self-conscious state of South Carolina had been conspicuously at odds with the federal government for a generation. It was not merely because of the unseasonably warm weather that the delegates from northern cities did not feel at home. The incongruity of the diverse elements composing the loosely bound party which called itself the "American Democracy" had never been more evident.

The galleries supported the Southern extremists and Buchanan's envoys joined with the latter to discomfit Douglas. That leader had most of the votes, and in the quarrels about the organization of the convention his forces used them highhandedly. They yielded a point, however, by agreeing that the platform should be adopted before the candidates were nominated; and it soon appeared that Douglas would not and could not stand on the broadest one that the delegates from the cotton states would permit him. Even if the Southern ultras had secured the promise of federal protection of slave property in the territories, there would probably have been no enduring enlargement of the area of slavery or any Southern gain of political power in the foreseeable future. To the realistic mind it appears that these men were fighting for an abstraction. The importance of this policy was exaggerated in the North, also, but the acceptance of it there would have amounted to political suicide at this stage. By agreeing to it Douglas would not only have reversed himself; he would also have ruined his chances as a vote-getter in the free states.

In the plank that was finally adopted it was resolved that, inasmuch as there was a difference of opinion about the powers of a territorial legislature and of Congress over the institution of slavery within the territories, the party would abide by the decisions of the Supreme Court on these constitutional questions. This resolution amounted to a surrender of the doctrine of popular sovereignty for which Douglas had so long contended and in Northern opinion it represented a very great concession, but it did not go as far as the Alabama Platform. Accordingly, the adoption of the plank was followed by the withdrawal of all the delegates from the Lower South, except a few from Georgia, along with other delegates from Arkansas and Delaware. It proved impossible to get from the remaining delegates a two-thirds vote of the entire delegation for the nomination of Douglas. So, after a session of ten days, the convention adjourned to meet on June 18 in Baltimore, and the Republicans had met before it reassembled.

In Baltimore the atmosphere was much more favorable to the Douglas faction than it had been in Charleston, but a quarrel immediately arose about representation. Should the Southern bolters be reseated or should they be replaced by contesting delegates who were favorable to Douglas? The Douglas forces were not averse to some compromise, but they followed a punitive policy in certain cases, especially those of Alabama and Louisiana, and thus occasioned another withdrawal in which certain Northern anti-Douglas delegates joined the Southerners. The net result was that Douglas was finally nominated by a two-thirds vote of those remaining. This had become a rump convention: seven states were not represented at all, and seven others by less than half of their delegates. The resolution about slavery in the territories which had been adopted in Charleston remained in the platform. This platform also called for the enforcement of the fugitive slave law, pledged constitutional aid in the construction of a railway to the Pacific, and favored the acquisition of Cuba. Benjamin Fitzpatrick of Alabama was nominated for Vice-President, but when he afterwards declined, Herschel V. Johnson of Georgia was selected by the national committee.

On June 28, the Democratic bolters, meeting in Richmond, adopted a platform which differed little from that of the Douglas group except in the insistence on the protection of slavery in the territories by all departments of the federal government. They nominated John C. Breckinridge of Kentucky for President and Joseph Lane of Oregon for Vice-President, thus seeking to avoid too close identification with the Lower South.

Meanwhile, another convention had been held in Baltimore in May. This group, consisting mostly of old Whigs, was known as the Constitutional Union Party. In this time of divisive sentiments, it recognized no political principle but the Constitution, the Union, and the enforcement of the laws. Its nominees were John Bell of Tennessee for President and Edward Everett of Massachusetts for Vice-President. The latter nomination was a gesture to old Whigs in the North, but the party was in the spirit of the border states and the Upper South, and in the election it took away more votes from Douglas than from the Republicans.

THE NOMINATION AND ELECTION OF LINCOLN

When the Republican National Convention met in Chicago on May 16, 1860, in an immense auditorium that had just been built and was called the Wigwam, the Democratic split had not yet become irrevocable, but all signs pointed toward Democratic disunity and, therefore, toward Republican success. A spirit of boisterous exuberance characterized the meeting in Chicago, but behind the scenes there was incessant maneuvering. At the outset the odds were on William H. Seward for the presidential nomination, but, as is so often the case at national conventions, great prominence was a disadvantage. Seward had powerful enemies, including men in his own state like Horace Greeley, and some of his earlier utterances about the "higher law" and the "irrepressible conflict" had led many to consider him too radical. It seemed politically desirable for the Republicans to play safe; they were chiefly concerned to win the waverers.

These circumstances worked to the advantage of Lincoln, who was widely recognized in the North as a moderate and had gained few enemies. Earlier that year (February 27, 1860) he had made an important speech at Cooper Union in New York City. It was distinctly a partisan speech, but this native of Kentucky was generally conciliatory toward the South; he condemned John Brown's raid, and was adamant only on the question of forbidding the extension of slavery into the territories. His economic views, which were essentially those of an old-line Whig, appealed to Eastern businessmen, and they liked his moderation on the slavery question.

It was to his advantage that the convention was held in his state, and that his chief political strength lay in just the part of the country where Douglas was strongest. The other major candidates were Simon Cameron of Pennsylvania, Salmon P. Chase of Ohio, and Edward Bates of Missouri, but the real contest lay between Lincoln and Seward. Partisans of the "rail-splitter" outshouted those of the New Yorker in the convention, but the success of Lincoln was owing chiefly to his greater political availability and the skillful activities in his behalf behind the scenes—especially those of Judge David Davis. He was established as second choice in delegation after delegation; and, after the complimentary votes for various state favorites, he gained on the second ballot, and then was nominated on the third. Few Republicans may have realized that they had selected their greatest man, but most of them believed that they had nominated the man who stood the best chance of election. To balance the ticket, they chose as their Vice-Presidential candidate Hannibal Hamlin of Maine.

In the face of Democratic dissension, the Republicans laid their emphasis on harmony; and their skillfully worded platform was designed to make a broad appeal. Though it began with a salute to the Declaration of Independence and the Constitution, it did not mention the Negro, nor did it now condemn slavery as a "moral wrong." It took an unequivocal stand against the extension of slavery, asserting that the normal condition of all American territory was that of freedom, and denying the authority of Congress or a territorial legislature to give legal existence to slavery in any territory. This was something of a retreat, however, from the position in 1856 that Congress should forbid slavery in the territories.

The platform laid great emphasis on the Union, asserting that the threats of disunion were Democratic not Republican and that secession was "contemplated treason." It denounced the Democratic Party for the Lecompton Constitution and in effect it challenged the Supreme Court on the Dred Scott decision. It condemned the "reopening" of the African slave trade and urged the immediate admission of Kansas as a state. At the same time, adopting a more moderate tone toward the South, it recognized the rights of the states to control their domestic institutions, and without mentioning John Brown's name condemned his "lawless invasion." Last but by no means least, there were important economic planks. Besides advocating federal aid to a Pacific railroad and the improvement of rivers and harbors, the platform called for homestead legislation and a protective tariff.

Purposely this platform was made broad enough for divergent groups to stand on it—Eastern industrialists and Western farmers most notably. It represented a skillful attempt to effect in politics the union of the East and West to which the economic developments of the past decade had pointed and thus to break up the loose alliance between West and South on which past Democratic success had so often depended. The Republican appeal was couched in positive terms, and vigorous Northerners, annoyed with Democratic incompetence in high places, responded to the call of a vigorous young party which offered positive economic benefits.

The antislavery aspects of Republicanism were played down in the campaign, though extreme language was used by some men of the abolitionist group. Wendell Phillips, far from following the lead of the platform-makers, praised John Brown and described Virginia as a "pirate ship." The Southerners did not believe that the party had repudiated radicalism, and the Breckinridge people kept on attacking the "Black Republicans" even while abolitionist leaders were rejecting Lincoln. Lincoln himself, staying at home, made no speeches, but his nicknames were constantly evoked in a campaign which, in noise and enthusiasm, was comparable to the one in behalf of that other log-cabin candidate, William Henry Harrison. Young men who called themselves "Wide-awakes" carried lighted torches on fence rails in parades, marching in zigzag formations in imitation of rail fences. The qualities of a folk-hero, which were so conspicuous in Lincoln, were fully exploited.

The only presidential candidate who was really active was Douglas. He toured the country in a way that was then unexampled, preaching moderation everywhere while proclaiming his determination to uphold the Union in any and all circumstances. Fate had become unkind to this indomitable little man, who could not match the Breckinridge Democrats or even the Constitutional Unionists in Southernism but was still too Southern in sympathy for most Northerners. He wore himself

ELECTION of 1856

- W WASH. TERR.
- OREGON TERR.
- NEBRASKA TERR.
- UTAH TERR.
- UNORGANIZED TERR.
- KANSAS TERR.
- NEW MEXICO TERR.
- UNORGANIZED TERR.

Frémont - Republican

Buchanan - Democrat

Fillmore - American Party

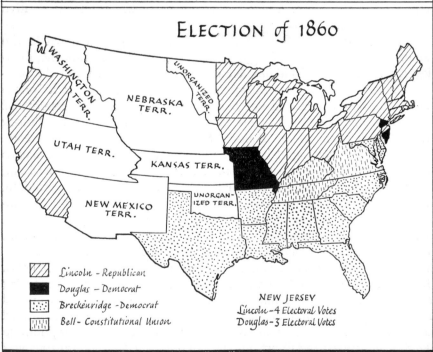

ELECTION of 1860

- W WASHINGTON TERR.
- NEBRASKA TERR.
- UTAH TERR.
- UNORGANIZED TERR.
- KANSAS TERR.
- NEW MEXICO TERR.
- UNORGANIZED TERR.

Lincoln - Republican

Douglas - Democrat

Breckenridge - Democrat

Bell - Constitutional Union

NEW JERSEY
Lincoln - 4 Electoral Votes
Douglas - 3 Electoral Votes

out with speaking while already on the downgrade physically, and he died within a year after the election. Not until another century was he to regain, with the help of historians, the high place among American statesmen to which his political talents, his genuine democracy, and his broad patriotism entitle him.

In the presidential election the Republican victory was decisive. Lincoln carried all of the free states, except for New Jersey which he divided with Douglas, and got 180 electoral votes to 123 for his three opponents. Breckinridge—carrying the Lower South along with North Carolina, Arkansas, Maryland, and Delaware—received 72 electoral votes; while Bell carried Virginia, Kentucky, and Tennessee with 39. Douglas trailed with 12 electoral votes which came from Missouri and New Jersey. In the popular vote, however, Douglas with more than 1,300,000 ran second to Lincoln with some 1,800,000, and had about as many votes as Breckinridge and Bell combined. Lincoln was a minority President so far as popular votes went, since he got about a million fewer than the three others together. His strength was wholly in the free states; he received no votes whatever in ten of the slave states, and only a scattered few in the five others. In the distribution of the votes this election was without parallel in American history. There was no flaw in Lincoln's legal title, however, and actually he would have received an absolute majority in the electoral college even if the votes of his three competitors could have been combined. He would have carried precisely the same states, except for California and Oregon. The Republicans lost ground in the Congressional elections and could not expect to control either the House or the Senate, though this consideration did not encourage the Southerners as much as it should have. Furthermore, the fact that a Breckinridge victory would have been won by a sectional party did not inhibit his supporters from repudiating Lincoln on the ground that his victory was sectional.

Since he had not spoken publicly for so long a time, and so many Southerners did not know how moderate a man he really was, it seems a great pity that, immediately after he got news of his election, Lincoln did not say some of the reassuring things he actually did say four months later in his inaugural. But he still lacked prestige and authority, and he may have anticipated trouble from the radicals in his own party, although Northern extremists had by no means as much political influence in their section as Southern extremists now had in theirs. The abolitionists, too, were disunionists but they had little influence in the North at this stage. It is questionable, of course, whether any sort of assurances of noninterference with Southern domestic institutions would have calmed the fever of fear which had been whipped up. Firebrands like Yancey, Rhett, and Ruffin would certainly not be dissuaded by any words of Lincoln from the disunionist moves for which they could now claim justification. But many moderate Southerners were counseling delay before the taking of any decisive steps, and presidential words might have strengthened them in their position. The supreme tragedy is that more violent men were now able to take advantage of a mood of hopelessness, by translating into precipitate action plans they had already made for just such a contingency.

THE FAILURE OF COMPROMISE

Months before the election the legislature of Alabama authorized a state convention in case of Republican victory, but South Carolina was the first state actually to call one. In South Carolina presidential electors were still chosen by the legislature, and that body, remaining in session until the results of the election were known, then called a convention to meet on December 17. Robert Barnwell Rhett and other avowed secessionists would brook no delay. Throughout the cotton country the ultras were in agreement and they exploited the postelection excitement just as they had the fear that had followed John Brown's raid. On November 18, conventions were called by Georgia, Florida, Mississippi, and Texas; Louisiana took similar action in December, and Alabama in January. The delay in Yancey's state was owing to accidental circumstances and not an indication of lukewarmness. Meanwhile, the legislature of Mississippi recommended (November 30) the secession of the slave states. There were tactical reasons for quick action, before the Republican President should assume office and organize his government, or by moderation disprove the fire-eaters' accusations, and any one of several states could have taken the initiative, but there were historic reasons which made South Carolina the natural leader. Her Senators now resigned, as did prominent federal officials within the state, and it seemed by the month of December that this commonwealth would not be deterred by anything that might happen in Washington.

The message which President Buchanan sent to Congress when it assembled on December 3 reads today like a confession of weakness on the part of a discredited Executive as he neared the end of a disastrous term. Addressing a "lame-duck" Congress, he deplored Northern agitation of the slavery question, as he had so often done before. He asserted that secession was not a constitutional right, as practically all of the Southerners said it was, but revolution. On the other hand, he believed that no power to coerce a state was lodged with the federal government, and that the exercise of such power under these circumstances would be of doubtful wisdom anyway.

This pronouncement has often been contrasted with the forthright proclamation of Andrew Jackson against nullification, but it is only fair to say that the parallel between the two crises is imperfect. Buchanan feared that forceful federal action would precipitate rather than deter secession. He was right in saying that the Union must be one of hearts, and not even now can we be sure that a policy of toughness at that time would have remedied the situation.

Before long the Southern members of the Cabinet, led by the influential Secretary of the Treasury, Howell Cobb of Georgia, resigned, and Buchanan's policy stiffened somewhat. Meanwhile, though the Republicans as a group were unconciliatory, and thirty representatives from the slave states had declared in an address to their constituents (December 14) that the hope of compromise was vain, a serious attempt to preserve the Union peaceably was being made in the Senate. This came too late to affect South Carolina, where secession was voted on December 20, but it antedated the meeting of the other conventions in the Lower South and might conceivably have influenced some of them if it had been successful.

The Crittenden Compromise

The effort in the Senate was centered in the Committee of Thirteen which was appointed on December 20 to consider the crisis, and in the proposals of Senator John J. Crittenden of Kentucky, who had assumed the mantle of the great conciliator, Henry Clay. His plan, consisting of six proposed amendments to the Constitution and four resolutions, generally goes by the name of the Crittenden Compromise. The first and most crucial amendment provided for the extension of the Missouri Compromise line of 36° 30' to the Pacific. In all the region south of that line, slavery should be permitted and protected by the federal government during the territorial stage, and states might be admitted from it with or without slavery as each of them should decide. The other amendments forbade Congress to abolish slavery in places under federal jurisdiction (such as army posts) within slave states, to abolish slavery within the District of Columbia without the consent of Virginia and Maryland, to interfere with the domestic slave trade, or to abolish slavery in any state—all these restrictions being made unamendable. The resolutions called for the enforcement of the fugitive slave law while recommending certain modifications, condemned personal liberty laws, and urged the enforcement of laws against the African slave trade.

Many of these proposals were not unacceptable to Northern moderates like Lincoln, though they might have been objected to as tying things up too tight. But they were defeated in the committee because of the opposition of the Republican members, as they afterwards were when introduced in the Senate itself. The crucial question was the extension of the Missouri Compromise line, and the influence of Lincoln was exerted against this. He believed that if any concession were made with respect to the extension of slavery, all the work of the Republicans would be lost and eventually would have to be done all over again. Room would be left for endless future controversy on a question which should be settled once and for all. He particularly opposed the possibility that Cuba should be annexed and come into the Union as one or more slave states.

The traditional Northern judgment has been that Lincoln was right in concluding that on this issue the time had come to take a stand and run a risk. He was following the logic of his own convictions, without foreknowledge of dreadful events, and he had no assurance that this or any other concession would preserve the Union and prevent war. His fears about the acquisition of Cuba were real enough in view of the two Democratic platforms. A suggestion of Douglas's in the committee is of special interest in this connection. It was that future acquisitions of territory should be made only by treaty or a two-thirds vote of both houses —that is, not by a mere majority on joint resolution as in the case of Texas. A constitutional amendment to the same effect was recommended in February of the next year by the futile Washington Peace Conference which is referred to hereafter. Such a provision would have given the free states an easy veto power and should have been proposed much earlier.

But the abandonment of the principle on which the Republican Party had been founded was too much to ask, even of Lincoln, and he was quite right in supposing that to the Southern fire-eaters no formal compromise would be enough. They were seeking independent control of the future of their own section—if not inside the Union, then outside. There were other efforts to prevent the breakup of the Union, but none was so promising as the one connected with the Crittenden Compromise. No common ground could be found on which moderate men could stand, and they all marched together into supreme tragedy in this era of unreason.

THE SECESSION OF THE LOWER SOUTH

The South Carolina convention which began its sessions in Columbia but soon removed to Charleston, adopted by unanimous vote on December 20, 1860, the Ordinance with which secession started, though actually it did not contain that word. The avowed purpose of this brief and fateful document was "to dissolve the Union between the State of South Carolina and other States united with her under the compact entitled the Constitution of the United States of America"; and, to this end, it declared that the ordinance whereby the state had ratified the Constitution in 1788 was now "repealed." These verbal niceties seemed important to a group of men who took their constitutional doctrines seriously and who believed that they had maintained these in their original purity.

The causes which had led the state to resume her "separate and equal place among nations" were set forth in a declaration which the convention adopted a few days later. This postulated the compact doctrine, which Southerners had talked about since the day of Jefferson and increasingly since that of Calhoun. The declaration asserted, as South Carolinians had so many times before, that the compact had been violated over a long period of years, specific reference being made to the failure of Northerners to deliver up fugitive slaves. It was charged that the nonslaveholding states had "assumed the right of deciding upon the propriety of our domestic institutions"; and it was claimed that for twenty-five years hostile agitation had steadily increased. A geographical line had been drawn across the Union, a "sectional combination for the subversion of the Constitution" had been formed, and, with the accession of this (Republican) Party to power, the destruction of the equal rights of the slave states was to be expected.

In view of Republican losses in the Congressional elections, the clear promises in the Republican platform to respect states' rights over slavery, and Lincoln's moderation, these fears seem excessive. But the South Carolinians did not know Lincoln as well as we do and they were afraid of the Republican radicals. Their fears had been fed for years by the agitation of their own extremists, and they did not perceive, as we can, that the best chance to defeat the radicals was to go along with Lincoln. The frequent references to slavery in the declaration show how important the institution seemed to this group and how determined they were to safeguard it. Since the slaves constituted more than 57 per cent of the total population of South Carolina in 1860, the state had a huge stake in the "peculiar institution." This, however, was not merely a matter of property; it was also a matter of race relations, and, as the events of Reconstruction afterwards proved, South Carolina was one of the states where the ruling whites stood to suffer most from social revolution. South Carolina held like a rock against almost all forms of modernism. Among the southern states she had the most oligarchic political organization, and was least affected by political democracy. The conservative leaders of the most conservative of southern states may well have feared the loss of political as well as economic power under the revolutionary developments which, as they believed, the Republican victory foreshadowed. But they did not take a reluctant citizenry out of the Union. Secession was extremely popular in the state.

The major question was that of the means to be employed to make good the secession program, and it may be asked what grounds there were for what now seems to have been an overweening confidence. One was the assurance that other states in the Lower South would follow. Commissioners from Mississippi and Alabama were present when the convention met and they urged secession. Among the active disunionists of the Lower South there was an expectation that, for a time at least, the states

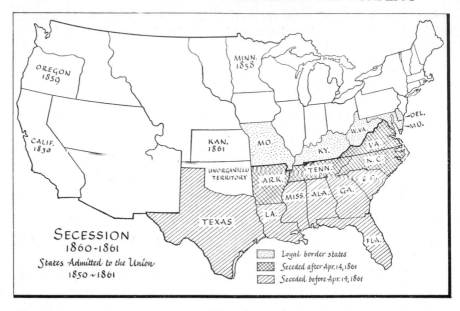

SECESSION
1860-1861
States Admitted to the Union
1850~1861

Loyal border states
Seceded after Apr. 14, 1861
Seceded before Apr. 14, 1861

of the Upper South would remain in the Union. But this was regarded as desirable, since they would serve as a buffer. The ultimate hopes of the South Carolinians, however, were revealed by the banner of the "Southern Republic" which hung behind the president's chair in the convention. This contained the seals of all fifteen of the slave states. South Carolina was the keystone of the arch, but Virginia was at its base and even Delaware and Missouri were included in it. Talk of war was ridiculed. It was a common saying that all the blood that would be shed could be held in a lady's thimble.

So far as the Lower South was concerned, the hopes of the South Carolinians were realized fully and quickly. Between January 9 and February 4, 1861, the six states of Mississippi, Florida, Alabama, Georgia, Louisiana, and Texas seceded in that order. There was greatest doubt in Georgia, where leaders of national caliber like Alexander H. Stephens remained Unionist until after the die was cast. The vote in the convention of that crucial state was 164 to 133. In Texas the cause of the Union was strongly supported by Governor Sam Houston, who had to be removed before a convention could be called and secession voted. Slavery was less important in Texas than elsewhere, and the geographical position of that state was an important reason for its action, but secession began in the part of the South that had most Negroes. It would be a mistake to claim, however, that the movement at this stage was led by the largest planters, for in some states, especially in Louisiana, they were reluctant. By and large, secession was popular. The ground had been well prepared by a decade of agitation, and patriotism now vented itself in

Southern nationalism. There were reluctant Unionists almost everywhere, however, even in South Carolina. "I have seen the last happy day of my life," said James L. Petigru when that state seceded.

Formation of the Confederacy

The new Southern Republic, consisting of seven states and bearing the name Confederate States of America, was organized in Montgomery, Alabama, which became its capital. The first meeting of the delegates, who had been chosen by the various secession conventions, was held on February 4, 1861, a month before Lincoln's inauguration and while a futile conference, instigated by the legislature of Virginia, was assembling in Washington. Howell Cobb of Georgia presided over the sessions in Montgomery and the emphasis there was on unity and moderation. Yancey was not a delegate, and Rhett, much to his chagrin, had slight influence. The day of leadership of these agitators ended when secession had been accomplished. After the adoption of a temporary constitution, provisional officers of the Confederacy were elected on February 9. Jefferson Davis of Mississippi, who was now regarded as a moderate, was elected President. Time was to show that this dignified, sensitive, and high-strung man had serious temperamental limitations as an executive; but, except possibly for Robert Toombs of Georgia, no better qualified man appears to have been available. Alexander H. Stephens of Georgia, a cadaverous little man who never really got over his Unionism, was elected Vice-President. In due course these two high officials were regularly elected (in November 1861) for a six-year term which they never finished.

The "permanent" Constitution, adopted on March 11, a week after Lincoln's inauguration, showed the temper and philosophy of these architects of a new republic. They did not now or ever recognize the designation of themselves as revolutionaries, and they regarded themselves as truly loyal to the old Constitution, which, as they believed, the Northerners had flouted. Some claimed that it was really the Yankees who had seceded from the old Union. These Confederates laid great stress on formal documents, and, in view of the perils their government faced, they spent a disproportionate time in framing their basic law.

Essentially, this short-lived Constitution was the federal Constitution of 1787, slanted in a state-rights direction. In the choice of the President the votes were to be taken by states; and the right of secession, though unmentioned, was implied. In line with the historic position of the section, the Constitution provided that duties on imports should be levied only for revenue and not for the protection of particular branches of industry. The government guaranteed the right of slavery in the territories, but, contrary to the predictions of Northerners, it outlawed the African slave trade. The Bill of Rights, contained in the earliest group of amendments to the federal Constitution, was incorporated in the Confederate document. In their new government these men tried to make some practical improvements on the one they were leaving. Among the most interesting of these were the provisions that the President might veto separate items in appropriation bills, and that members of the Cabinet might appear on the floor of Congress, with the consent of that body, to discuss matters relating to their departments. It was hoped that by means of the latter provision co-operation between the legislative and executive branches would be facilitated.

The "permanent" Confederate Constitution was nowhere submitted to the people, because of the desire for speed and the maintenance of an appearance of unanimity. After its unanimous adoption by the provisional Congress it was ratified by state conventions or legislatures, and little objection was raised to it at the time except on the ground that it too closely followed the federal Constitution.

The Beginnings of Republican Control

The period between the secession of the cotton states and the inauguration of Abraham Lincoln of Illinois constituted a confused and uneasy interim. Legislative control had now come to the Republican Party by default; they gained a clear majority in both houses of Congress when the representatives of the Lower South withdrew. But there was no unity in Republican councils, and leadership had not yet been assumed by Lincoln, who used conciliatory expressions in private letters but refused to make public statements, believing that these would be useless. Whether for good or ill, he kept silent and gave no real inkling of his strength and wisdom. The moderates of the Upper South, who had delayed decisive action in their states, needed his help most, and he failed them if he failed anybody. It would be unjust to say that Lincoln at this stage was thinking more about composing the diverse elements in his own party than of composing the sharply conflicting groups in the whole of the old Union, but he was more a partisan now than he was later.

The Washington Peace Conference, over which ex-President John Tyler presided and on which the moderates of the Upper South had staked their hopes, was not a national convention such as could have and perhaps should have been called several weeks earlier. Thirteen states, including the seven states of the Confederacy and certain unco-operative states of the northern Middle West, were unrepresented. The Republicans who were present were generally obstructive. Secession had strengthened their hand in the continuing Union, and they would be even stronger when they had a Republican President. The amendments to the Constitution which this tragic conference recommended on February 27, a week before the inauguration, were less satisfactory to Southerners than the proposals of Crittenden, which they much resembled, and would have been defeated in the Upper South itself. They got nowhere in a Republican Congress. They were defeated in committee in the Senate and were not even presented in the House.

One amendment to the Constitution, which may be called the Corwin Amendment from the Republican Congressman who presented it, Thomas Corwin of Ohio, did get through both Houses. If adopted by the states it would have been the Thirteenth Amendment, and it was the exact opposite of the one now bearing that number. It provided that the Constitution should never be so altered as to abolish or interfere with the institutions of a state, including slavery. It passed the House on February 28 and the Senate on March 2 by the required two-thirds votes, showing that sentiment among Republicans was definitely against the "abolitionizing" of the slave states. Here was the South's last chance to help defeat radical Republicans and abolitionists, but it was not grasped.

Other actions of this Republican Congress in this confused and contradictory period indicated a surprising retreat from the original position of the party with respect to the prohibition of slavery in the territories. Kansas had been admitted as a free state in January, and the fact that according to the census of 1860 there were only two slaves there, shows that earlier fears of the dominance of this region by the "slave power" had been highly exaggerated. At the very end of the session the territories of Colorado, Nevada, and Dakota were created—without mention of slavery. This action amounted to an admission that the express prohibition of slavery in the western country was unnecessary, and in effect it represented a full vindication of Douglas. By early 1861, many Republicans had strayed from the paths of strict party orthodoxy, but the core of unyielding Northern radicals remained after the most hotheaded Southern radicals had withdrawn, and some of the former were willing that the latter should depart in peace. Moderates like Lincoln felt differently about disunion, but not even he was agreeable to formal recognition of slavery anywhere in the territories.

Also, during this session, the Republicans put through the Morrill Tariff. This bill had been passed by the House in the previous session, and it was passed by the Senate shortly before Lincoln's inauguration. It increased the duties on iron and wool and was more pleasing to Pennsylvania and certain western states than to New England manufacturers. On his way to the national capital, Lincoln made a long, dull speech on the tariff in Pittsburgh. This served a political purpose but his heart was not in it. The Morrill Tariff marked a trend, which became irresistible under the pressure of war and in the continued absence of Southern representatives from Congress.

Lincoln Assumes His Task

On February 7, President-elect Lincoln made a moving little speech of farewell to the citizens of Springfield, where he had lived for a quarter of a century. He said: "I now leave, not knowing when or ever I may return, with a task before me greater than that which rested on Washington." On his journey eastward he had to make many speeches but he discreetly confined himself to generalities. He was an unknown man on exhibition. He did not have a good press, and people in the North as well as the Confederacy applied to him such terms as "ape," "baboon," and "Simple Susan." In Independence Hall, Philadelphia, on Washington's birthday, he made a brief speech which now is deeply moving to those who know him for the man he really was. In it he paid heartfelt tribute to the philosophy of the Declaration of Independence.

For reasons of security he was persuaded to change his plans and pass through Baltimore by night, and he made an unimpressive entrance into Washington in the early morning. He did not really begin to reveal his stature until he spoke his inaugural address from a stand on the east side of the still-uncompleted capitol, after the oath of office had been administered him by the aged Chief Justice, Roger B. Taney, whom so many Republicans had castigated for the Dred Scott decision. Stephen A. Douglas was there, and if he did not hold Lincoln's hat as legend has it, he gave unstinted moral support to a former rival in any and all efforts to support the tottering Union.

Sixty years earlier, President Thomas Jefferson had sought to reassure his recent political foes and to enlist them in common cause in a rising nation. Lincoln, more noted as a speaker, also sought to quiet apprehensions, though under these more difficult circumstances he could hardly have hoped to be equally successful. Again he put himself on record as opposing any interference with slavery where it then existed—he was agreeable to the Corwin Amendment—and as favoring the enforcement of the fugitive slave law with humane safeguards. But he would not concede that the government of the United States or any other country could admit the right of secession. The central idea of secession, he said, was the essence of anarchy, and the rule of a minority was inadmissible. Unlike Jefferson, he did not add that the rule of the majority, to be just, must be reasonable, but he did urge "patient confidence in the ultimate justice of the people." Regarding the Union as unbroken, he expressed his determination to "hold, occupy, and possess the property and places belonging to the government, and to collect the duties and imposts;" but, beyond what might be necessary for those objects, he promised that there would be no invasion.

He was specially effective when speaking of the impracticability and the evil consequences of disunion.

> Physically speaking, we cannot separate. We cannot remove our respective sections from each other, nor build an impassable wall between them. A husband and wife may be divorced, and go out of the presence, and beyond the reach of each other; but the different parts of our country cannot do this. They cannot but remain face to face; and intercourse, either amicable or hostile, must continue between them. Is it possible, then, to make intercourse more advantageous or more satisfactory, *after* separation than *before?* Can aliens make treaties easier than friends can make laws? Can treaties be more faithfully enforced between aliens than laws can among friends?

This passage suggests parts of Washington's Farewell Address, but the final passage, with its references to the "mystic chords of memory" and swelling the "chorus of the Union," was peculiarly in the manner and spirit of Lincoln at his best. In him, as Alexander H. Stephens, the Vice-President of the Confederacy, once said, the sentiment of Union rose to the "sublimity of religious mysticism." This was not the greatest of his speeches, and the Union did not wholly dominate his mind as yet. He was beset with political questions, both large and small, and the most fateful of the large ones was what to do about Fort Sumter.

FORT SUMTER AND THE LAST STAGE OF SECESSION

By the time of Lincoln's inauguration, the Confederate states had already taken over most of the federal forts, navy yards, and custom houses within their borders. Buchanan had permitted this, partly because of his concern not to alienate the remaining southern states, partly because he would have been unable to prevent it with the military force at his disposal, the increase of which would itself have been a provocation. Practically the only forts remaining in Federal hands were Pickens off the Florida coast and Sumter in Charleston harbor. Buchanan had sought to support the small garrison in the latter. He sent the *Star of the West* with men and munitions, and this was fired on by South Carolinians on January 9, 1861, at a time when no other state had seceded. The ship turned back and Buchanan declined to treat this as a provocative incident.

Lincoln's situation would have been less embarrassing if Fort Sumter had given up while Buchanan was President. From reports of Major Robert Anderson, the Kentuckian who was in command at Sumter, Lincoln learned soon after his inauguration that the supplies of the fort would enable it to hold only six weeks and he was thereupon confronted with a dilemma. Sumter had assumed a symbolic importance out of all proportion to its strategic value. To the state of South Carolina and to the newly-formed Confederacy it was a bit of their soil which was now in foreign hands, while to Northerners it signified a remnant of national sovereignty at the very seat of disunion. Despite these sentiments, the Cabinet held almost unanimously the opinion that the fort should be given up. In view of his assertion that the Union was still intact, Lincoln could not concede that the Confederate commissioners who had come to Washington to treat about this matter were official representatives of a foreign government, as they regarded themselves. Secretary of State Seward did not concede it, but he did communicate with them through intermediaries, chiefly Justice Campbell of the Supreme Court, an Alabamian who had been induced by Chief Justice Taney to stay in office. Seward himself was convinced that Sumter must be given up and he let the Confederate emissaries gain the impression that it would be. They regarded this as a pledge and thus another element of confusion was added to a situation which was confused enough already. Seward had overreached himself, but Lincoln had not yet established himself as the master in his own official household.

He wanted to hold the Upper South in the Union, and in order to do this he must avoid even the semblance of coercion of the states which had already seceded. He is reported to have said: "A State for a fort is no bad business." He was in touch with the Virginia Unionists, whether or not he made a bargain with them. Meanwhile, General Winfield Scott was telling him that withdrawal from Sumter was a military necessity at just the time that certain Northerners were saying that this would be treason to the Union.

In his effort to escape this dilemma, Lincoln worked out a double plan which called for careful timing. He would definitely relieve Fort Pickens, hoping that this would arouse little Southern resentment while reassuring the North; and if this expedition succeeded he could then give Sumter up on grounds of military necessity. Meanwhile, an expedition to Sumter was ordered tentatively, and when the Pickens expedition, which was eventually successful, was held up because of misunderstanding and administrative bungling, the Sumter expedition was authorized and set sail. Thus things did not go according to plan, but the crucial fact is that Lincoln finally decided on the Sumter expedition, which was to bear provisions only, and informed the Governor of South Carolina to that effect.

The Confederate authorities, who regarded this as a violation of the pledge they thought they had received indirectly from Seward, now instructed General Pierre G. T. Beauregard, who was in command at Charleston, to demand the evacuation of Sumter and to reduce the fort in case of refusal. Major Anderson agreed to evacuate by April 15, when his supplies would run out, if he did not receive other orders or relief in the meantime. The Confederate officers who were negotiating with him regarded this reply as unsatisfactory, and, after serving notice on Anderson, they gave the order to fire—acting, as they believed, according to the discretion granted them. A momentous act occurred under conditions of great confusion. Firing began at 4:30 A.M. on April 12. On the next day, after thirty hours of bombardment, Anderson agreed to evacuate; and on April 14 he marched out with flags flying and was given the honors of war by the Confederates. Everything was done in good military form and with the best of manners; but it was a fact that the United States flag had been fired upon and that the Confederates had possessed themselves of the fort by force. There is insufficient reason to believe that all this was the result of a maneuver on Lincoln's part to make the Confederates fire the first shot, but he hoped that if a shot was fired his side would not be the one to fire it. The net result was to give the Union the psychological advantage in the North and in the eyes of the outside world.

The Upper South Takes Sides

On receiving news of events in Charleston harbor, Lincoln issued (April 15, 1861) a fateful proclamation. Using the language and the authority of an act of 1795, he declared that in seven states (which he named) the laws were being opposed by "combinations too powerful to be suppressed by the ordinary course of judicial proceedings"; and he called forth the militia from the several states to the aggregate of 75,000 to suppress such "combinations" and to cause the laws to be executed. He stated that the first duty of the troops would probably be to repossess the forts. Congress was called to meet in special session on July 4 and share the responsibility, but before that happened four more states enlarged the combination which Lincoln was trying to disperse.

Within two months of his proclamation the states of Virginia, Arkansas, North Carolina, and Tennessee withdrew from the old Union and joined the new Confederacy. The convention of Virginia, which had been in session for some time, acted immediately (April 17). As one of the sons of this historic commonwealth said: "She turned around, and walked out of the Union, with the step of an old Queen." This was a moment of deep tragedy, for no other state had done so much, perhaps, to create and establish the Union. Some of the inhabitants of small-farming western Virginia remained Unionists, and the vote against secession, though relatively small both in the convention and in the referendum which followed, was larger than in Arkansas, where there was only one adverse vote in the convention (May 6), and in North Carolina where there was none (May 20). In Tennessee there was strong Unionist sentiment, especially in the small-farming east, but secession carried by a large majority. Following the admission of Virginia to the Confederacy, the Congress voted to move the seat of government from Montgomery to Richmond, and the change was made in the summer.

These four accessions completed the Confederate roster of 11 states, though there were 13 stars in the Confederate flag. Kentucky and Missouri were nominally admitted late in 1861, following acts of secession by unauthorized groups in both of them. Many Kentuckians served in the Confederate Army, but Lincoln skillfully restrained his native state, and local victories kept Missouri in the Union. Of the two remaining slave states, Delaware was in no position to secede and never contemplated it, while Maryland had a Unionist Governor, Thomas H. Hicks, and she also was deterred by considerations of military necessity. Lincoln's early war policy was motivated in considerable part by his desire not to alienate these border states and he managed to keep all four of them, although sentiment was sharply divided in most of them.

The reasons for the secession of Virginia, North Carolina, Tennessee, and Arkansas were to some extent practical and political. After the withdrawal of the cotton states from the Union the remaining slave states were in a hopeless minority in it, and their fears for their domestic institutions were accentuated accordingly. Whether these states would have preferred to be the southernmost members of a Northern confederacy or the northernmost members of a Southern, if they had had a free and peaceful choice, is a question which history cannot answer, for the choice was actually made in the certainty of civil conflict. Assuming that they must take sides, the leaders in these states saw no real alternative. "We cannot become partners to the subjugation of our Southern brethren," said a North Carolina paper. "The federal government cannot be maintained by force *applied to sovereign states.*" This was a matter of sentiment, as well as of state-rights doctrines in which they had long been nurtured.

The opposing sentiment of Union, which Lincoln came to personify, was stronger in the Upper South than in the Lower, but now the American experiment in self-government had arrived at a fearful contradiction. Any government has a right to protect itself, as a Virginia paper recognized, but this editor declared at the same time that secession and the formation of the Confederacy was no mere act of insubordination. It was "the protest of one half of a confederation against the other half." The figure was too high, and we cannot be sure that the degree of continuing Unionism in the eleven Confederate states was fully registered in the various votes; but the formation of the Confederacy seemed a clear example of self-determination.

Yet, while the test of the popular will must be applied, so must the test of purpose. One aim of the seceders was to maintain local control of domestic institutions, and, more than anything else, this gave vitality to the Southern cause. Still it is clear that the domestic institution which had been most emphasized during the long years of controversy was slavery. Unlike the revolt of the colonies in 1776, the revolt of 1861 was based on no appeal to the universal rights of man; and its association with an institution which most of the civilized world regarded as anachronistic, and which was potentially if not actually despotic, constituted the fatal historic weakness of the Confederacy.

Perhaps the whole matter can be best summed up by saying that the Southerners sought to get out of the Union because they believed they would be safer, happier, and more prosperous under their own government. In the heat of controversy their leaders had failed to count the whole cost. They did not realize how much they still needed their Northern brethren, how much they stood to lose by leaving them. One of the inner weaknesses of the Confederacy which the next four years was to reveal was that the Southern people could not be fully reconciled to the idea of disunion.

Part VI

THE CIVIL WAR
1861-1865

CHAPTER 37

The Outbreak and Conditions of the War

THERE WAS SOME DISPUTE ABOUT THE EXACT DATE when the war started and the immediate responsibility for it. Most Northerners thought of it as beginning with the firing on Fort Sumter, an overt act which they blamed on the Southerners and which, for a time at least, unified sentiment and opinion in the free states. As a Philadelphia lawyer soon wrote: "There is among us but one thought, one object, one end, one symbol,—the Stars and Stripes." Southerners, especially in the upper and border states, tended to date the beginning of the war with Lincoln's call for the militia, and to lay the chief blame for armed conflict on him. The President's call for state troops was quickly followed (April 19) by his proclamation of blockade of the 7 Confederate states which was soon extended to the seaboard states of Virginia and North Carolina (April 27). By later judgment of the Supreme Court of the United States these two dates marked the actual beginning of the war, so far as those states were concerned. But four of the Justices demurred, preferring the date July 31, 1861, when Congress recognized a state of war. Early official actions on the Union side were presidential, since Congress was not in session until July 4, and that body had little choice but to validate them. Some people charged the President with having exceeded his authority, but by the summer of 1861 there could be no possible doubt that war had started. Nearly everybody expected it to be short but it dragged through four terrible years. What sort of conflict was it, and what should we call it?

THE NATURE OF THE CONFLICT

Lincoln's acts, before Congress met in special session, were based on the assumption that he was facing a domestic insurrection which he, as the Chief Executive, was compelled to put down. Rejecting the Southern interpretation of state sovereignty and regarding the doctrine of secession as "an ingenious sophism," as a sugar-coating for rebellion, he declined to recognize the Confederacy as a government or to deal with the seceded states as states. To him this was a rebellion of individuals against constituted authority. Yet he soon recognized that it was a "giant insurrection," and by the time it was half over Justice Robert C. Grier of the Supreme Court said that it was acknowledged by all the world to be "the greatest civil war known in the history of the human race." Officially, it was designated as the "War of the Rebellion." Technically the Confederates may have been guilty of treason in levying war against the United States, but no one of them was executed as a traitor.

Following Lincoln's proclamation of a blockade, the British government promptly proclaimed its neutrality (May 13, 1861); and, while it did not formally recognize the Confederate government at this or any other time, it did recognize Confederate belligerent rights. So did the Union, to all practical purposes. Prisoners were not shot, and the amenities of war were generally observed. The words "traitorous" and "treasonable" continued to be employed to some extent, especially by the radical Republicans, but in the course of the conflict, Northerners chiefly applied the word "disloyal" to Southern sympathizers in the North. They commonly referred to their Confederate foes as "Rebels."

Though the official Southern position from the first was that secession was a constitutional right, and that war resulted from Northern interference with the peaceful exercise of it, the term Rebel was gaily accepted and was not at all objected to until after the fighting ended. "Johnny Reb" opposed "Billy Yank" and raised the terrifying battle-cry that was called the "rebel yell." Some of the "fire-eaters" described as a revolution the movement they had done so much to accelerate, but after the war, when challenging the charge of treason, Southern spokesmen strongly reasserted their belief in the legality of secession, despite its demonstrated impracticability, while proclaiming loyalty to the "old Union." This line of interpretation was symbolized by the designation of the conflict as the "War between the States." That cumbersome title never gained general acceptance, though it has lasted longer than the "War of the Rebellion," which almost all Southerners came to resent.

In the course of a generation the word "rebellion" virtually disappeared from the history books, and various other names were given the historic conflict. The "War for Southern Independence" is one of the most accurate of these, but the one most generally employed is the "Civil War." This has the merit of brevity and familiarity and is accurate enough, for obviously the conflict was domestic. In its human toll this was the costliest of all American wars, as it was the most tragic, and no other has been so memorialized in song and story. Its poignant and heroic memories are cherished the more because they are peculiarly and distinctively American. The deeds and antics of both Federals and Confederates, the voice of Lincoln and the sword of Lee, the heroism and fortitude of untold thousands—men and women, Northern and Southern—along with some villainy and a vast amount of sheer incompetence on both sides: all these have become the common heritage of an entire people.

Historians have never fully agreed on the fundamental causes of the fratricidal conflict, and these must be sought in the history of the whole ante-bellum generation. Many divisive tendencies had appeared and grown, and in seeking to determine the relative importance of these every interpreter is affected to some degree by the particular tradition which he himself has inherited or adopted. Why did Northerners and Southerners go forth to war in 1861? Even at that time different men answered the question differently, and on both sides the minds of men were clouded by emotions.

On the Northern side the man who was most conspicuously successful in keeping his mind clear and in interpreting the meaning of this conflict was the gaunt and homely giant to whom leadership had fallen. As Lincoln always saw it, the purpose of the war was to preserve the Union. Only a few weeks before the Emancipation Proclamation he wrote Horace Greeley: "What I do about slavery, and the colored race, I do because I believe it helps to save the Union, and what I forbear, I forbear because I do *not* believe it would help to save the Union." Any other definition of the purposes of the war would have alienated powerful groups in the border states, which he was trying to retain in the Union, and would have been incompatible with Lincoln's own constitutional convictions about the right of individual states to control their domestic institutions. At the outset, therefore, he could not identify the Northern cause with that of freedom, and he was in the anomalous position of trying to crush a movement for political independence which its sponsors were seeking to justify on grounds of self-determination. The question naturally arose in many minds whether a Union which had to be pinned together by bayonets had not already failed.

To Lincoln, however, the Union was infinitely more than a framework of government, and he performed perhaps the greatest of all his services to the Union cause in eventually identifying it with that of democracy and the mission of America to establish in the world a freer and more just society than had hitherto existed. At the beginning he said that the struggle was to maintain the sort of government "whose leading object is to elevate the condition of all men." He believed that the plain people understood that the dissolution of the historic Union would mean ill, not good, to them. His vision became clearer and his voice more eloquent as he perceived the costliness of this struggle, and his faith found classic expression in the Gettysburg Address: "that this nation, under God, shall have a new birth of freedom—and that government of the people, by the people, for the people, shall not perish from the earth." There were many who wanted to preserve the Union for more material reasons; and there were some whose hatred grew as the war lengthened and whose dominant purpose was to wreck the South and destroy its civilization; but Lincoln's nobility of democratic spirit awakened an echo in thousands of hearts and served to glorify the Northern cause throughout the world.

Among the Confederates, in their turn, motives were mixed and not always pure. The purpose of the secession movement was to establish a Southern republic and unquestionably a spirit of Southern nationalism had been engendered. The degree of this is difficult to measure, but the predominant Southern mood was defensive and the supreme loyalty of most Southerners was to their respective states. The abiding symbol of the Southern cause came to be, not the fire-eaters, who soon passed into oblivion; not Jefferson Davis, the head of the short-lived Confederacy; but Robert E. Lee, who disliked abolitionists but never defended slavery, who regarded secession as nothing less than revolution, and who was a Virginian from first to last. Before his own commonwealth seceded he said: "If the Union is dissolved . . . I shall return to my native State and share the miseries of my people, and save in defence will draw my sword no more."

At the time Lee was a Colonel in the United States Army, a favorite of Winfield Scott, the General-in-Chief, and on the recommendation of that distinguished old soldier he was informally offered the command of the army which was to be put in the field to enforce the federal laws. This offer Lee felt compelled to decline, because he could not fight against his own kinsmen, and when he learned of the secession of Virginia he sadly resigned his commission and abandoned the service in which he had spent his life. Now fifty-four years old, Lee was described about this time by one observer as "the noblest-looking man I had ever gazed upon." He accepted the command of the military forces of Virginia, more aware of the sorrow than of the glory that awaited him. Later, after this incomparable commander had sheathed his sword, he said: "I did only what my duty demanded. I could have taken no other course without dishonor. And if it were to be done over again, I should act in precisely the same manner."

He was defending his own state, and so most Confederate soldiers were defending their own land without much thought of the Constitution, or the balance of political power, or the mission of America, or slavery as an economic institution. Ostensibly they were defending slavery, which their leaders had been describing for so many years as indispensable, but the chief concern of the nonslaveholders, who were in a very large majority, was to preserve for their respective states control over their own domestic affairs. In this sense most of the Confederates fought chiefly for state rights, as they ever afterward said they did. These men rallied in defense of their way of life and their own soil. Just as the firing on the Stars and Stripes, the symbol of the Union, aroused the Northerners, first the threat and then the reality of invasion aroused the Southerners, and it was in their heroic defense of their own fields and firesides that their glory lay.

In the eyes of Europeans the issues of the war were far from clear at first. The Southern leaders, minimizing slavery, were presenting the cause of the Confederacy to the world as that of liberty against federal tyranny and drawing a parallel with the American Revolution. Meanwhile, Lincoln by his cautious policy with respect to slavery, his emphasis on the Union, and his attempt to restore this by force was confusing foreign friends of freedom. Not until the Emancipation Proclamation, after a year and a half of fighting, did it fully appear to Europeans that the Civil War was a proving ground for democracy in their continent as well as in America. If the South made good its independence, the prestige of aristocracy everywhere would rise; if the North preserved the Union and destroyed slavery, democrats everywhere would take heart. Conservatives and reactionaries in all the European countries despised the American experiment as unholy mob rule, predicted that it must end in disaster, and hoped for Confederate victory. Liberals and radicals fervently hoped for Union victory to prove that democracy could prevail over all its enemies and command the future of humanity. Foreigners could not be expected to understand the local implications of the American domestic conflict, but they eventually saw in it a significance which was not only international but universal.

THE GENERAL CONDITIONS OF THE WAR

"Johnny Reb" was inclined to be a swaggerer, rather given to boasting about his prowess, and in "Billy Yank" he took on an antagonist who was considerably beyond his size. When the lines were drawn there were 23 states against 11. In the decade after the Compromise of 1850, Minnesota and Oregon were added to the free states, and Kansas was admitted early in 1861, increasing the total to 19. The four border slave states remained in the Union, partly because of Lincoln's reassuring policy with respect to slavery and partly because of the actualities of the military situation.

At the outset their status was uncertain. Reporting to Congress on July 4, 1861, the President said that the response of the country to his call for state troops had surpassed expectations, but he candidly admitted that in the border states many were advocating the policy of "armed neutrality." That is, they favored arming their troops so that the forces of neither side could pass over their soil. As Lincoln saw, this would amount to the completion of disunion, for it would set up an impassable wall. Wisely biding his time, he did not press his native state of Kentucky, but he faced an immediate problem in Maryland. Governor Thomas Hicks of that state opposed secession but the legislature and a powerful segment of the population were pro-Southern in sentiment. There the danger of obstructing the movement of Union troops was grave. On April 19, the Sixth Massachusetts regiment had great difficulty in getting through Baltimore, where the soldiers had to transfer from one railroad station to another. Some companies were blocked by barricades, and taunted and stoned by a mob carrying the Confederate flag. They finally forced a passage with fixed bayonets, after some firing and with casualties on both sides. A former citizen of this state was inspired by these events to write "Maryland, My Maryland," which begins with the words: "The despot's heel is on thy shore." A week after this affair the Seventh New York and Eighth Massachusetts went by water from Philadelphia to Annapolis, whence, after considerable difficulty, they proceeded by train to Washington. At first the capital of the country was in danger of being surrounded, but within a few weeks the federal government was keeping the roads open by exercise or threat of force.

The Confederates might have been wise to make a strong military effort at the very start to hold the border slave states, but as things turned out they lost all four of them—except for a good many volunteers, especially from Kentucky and Maryland. Meanwhile, a Unionist movement in the western counties of Virginia, which had opposed secession, led to the establishment of a government at Wheeling in June 1861 and the creation of the state of West Virginia in 1863. The persistence of this government was assured by early military successes in that district. These minor Northern victories served to advertise young Major General George B. McClellan, commander of the Military Department of the Ohio. His star was rising as the Confederacy began to shrink in the very first months of the war.

Comparative Resources

A population of 22,000,000 faced one of 9,000,000. Since 3,500,000 of the latter were slaves, the North had a preponderance in potential fighting men of some 4 to 1. In physical resources, also, the Union was immensely superior. Its advantages were even greater than we have indicated in our account of the ante-bellum economy of the two sections, for in this all the slave states were included in the South. Notable among these Northern advantages were a more diversified and self-sufficient economy, a great superiority in railroads and a greater one in the pro-

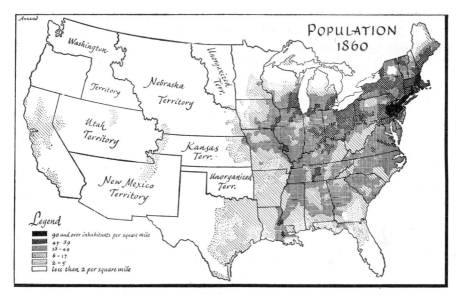

POPULATION
1860

Washington

Territory

Nebraska
Territory

Unorganized
Terr.

Utah
Territory

Kansas
Terr.

New Mexico
Territory

Unorganized
Terr.

Legend
90 and over inhabitants per square mile
45-89
18-44
6-17
2-5
less than 2 per square mile

duction of coal and iron, far more capital and a much more highly
developed financial organization. Important as all these were in peace-
time, they were far more important in time of war. Furthermore, the
Union retained the Navy and, by means of the blockade, increasingly
cut off the Confederacy from foreign markets and sources of supply
to which Northern access continued to be easy. One wonders what the
Confederate leaders were counting on in this unequal contest.

Many of the secessionist leaders had supposed that there would be
no war. This was the first and gravest of their mistakes. The next one,
which was shared by the Northerners, was that the conflict would be
short. In a short war the Union would not have time to realize on its
greater resources. Indeed, the outcome might have been different if the
Confederates had taken the initiative at the very start. They might have
captured Washington. But they were hoping for foreign aid, and they
believed that they would injure their cause in the eyes of the world
by embarking on a career of conquest. Their spirit was predominantly
defensive, and for the defense of their own territories their position was
strong. They had no thought of conquering the North, but they believed
that they could keep the North from conquering them.

The South had few important centers and the conquest of the region
amounted to the conquering of a map. The Southern troops would be
operating on interior lines, and there need not be so many of them.
One initial advantage which Southerners may have exaggerated was
that, by and large, they were a more martial people than the Northerners.
They were more accustomed to horses and firearms and had cherished

a military tradition. They were more addicted to military schools, and in the division of the West Pointers they had the better of the draw. It may have been sheer accident that the South had Lee and Stonewall Jackson, but it is a fact that the greatest of the Northern commanders, especially Grant and Sherman, developed during the conflict, while the Confederates had the better general officers at the beginning. Besides all this, the Southerners had more unity at first, because they were fighting on their own soil against invaders. For many months they thought themselves unconquerable, and this opinion was shared by many of their foes. But in the long war that this one turned out to be, the unmilitary North after much bungling realized on its greatly superior human and physical resources, and the victory of the Union then became inevitable.

The Rival Presidents

In retrospect it is clear that the vision, essential wisdom, and inflexible determination of Lincoln were an indispensable factor in Northern success. But, like the Union itself, he realized on his potentialities slowly. His popularity fluctuated with the fortunes of war, and not until after his death was there general recognition of his greatness. At the beginning many people regarded this strange-looking man, with a propensity for joking, as a mere simpleton. His magnanimity was taken for weakness and his humor for levity. At least two members of his Cabinet were originally regarded by most people as his superiors in ability: William H. Seward, the Secretary of State, and Salmon P. Chase, the Secretary of the Treasury. Both had been strong rivals of his for the presidential nomination, and he appointed them largely for that reason. Each had been Governor of his own state and United States Senator, so both were much more experienced public officials than the President. Between the inauguration and the fall of Sumter, Seward presented an extraordinary memorandum in which he asserted that the administration had no policy and recommended one whereby attention would be distracted from domestic quarrels by means of a vigorous and provocative foreign policy. Only by squelching the Secretary of State was the slow-moving President able to maintain himself as the head of his Cabinet. Seward gave him little more trouble, but Chase, who was the particular favorite of the antislavery group and who was described by Horace Greeley as the ablest living Republican, continued to be hard to handle. Tall, broad-shouldered, carefully dressed, this handsome man looked every inch a statesman; and Lincoln, who honored his ability and character, said that he had been working all his life to become President. A more immediate problem was presented by Simon Cameron, who had been oppointed to the crucially important post of Secretary of War chiefly for political reasons. He had slight competence as an administrator and because of charges of corruption in connection with army contracts he was removed from the scene by a foreign appointment. His successor, Edwin M. Stanton, was a dynamic man but difficult.

Lincoln asserted his leadership when he thought it necessary to do so, but generally left the departments alone. An authority on the presidency, Edward S. Corwin, has said: "A solitary genius who valued the opportunity for reflection above that for counsel, Lincoln came to regard Congress as a more or less necessary nuisance and the Cabinet as a usually unnecessary one." In the restricted sense, he was not a good administrator, and by comparison with the conduct of two world wars in the twentieth century, the conduct of this one was distressingly inefficient. But Lincoln gained and maintained spiritual leadership by his explanations of the purposes of the war, and he exercised unparalleled authority under his interpretation of the war power of the President as Commander in Chief. Many of his actions were sharply challenged, but he maintained his position that the President must wield extraordinary powers in time of national danger. In the matters to which he directed himself he was one of the strongest of the Presidents. Yet he did not crave power for his own sake, and he was wholly swallowed up in the cause of the Union which increasingly he personified.

President Jefferson Davis of the Confederacy had had much more experience in high public office. A graduate of West Point, he had a conspicuous military record, and he had been unusually effective as Secretary of War in the Pierce administration. In the eyes of his contemporaries in 1861 there was more reason to expect great things of him than of Lincoln, but in later years there was an inevitable tendency to make him into a scapegoat. Davis was a notably conscientious administrator, but, by contrast with Lincoln, he immersed himself too deeply in details. His critics, who were many, charged him with imparting a military spirit to the conduct of the government. Actually, this rigid constitutionalist never carried executive authority to the same point as Lincoln, but he had less political skill and did not attain the same degree of spiritual leadership. His popularity also fluctuated with the tides of victory and defeat, but he never commanded the personal devotion that Robert E. Lee inspired. He was high-strung, nervous, and during much of the war in bad health, and he found no such outlet as Lincoln did in humor.

Whether Davis made more and greater mistakes than Lincoln is a question, but the Confederacy could less afford mistakes. In the government itself he did not have the best Southern materials to work with, for the flower of Confederate ability went into the army. The ablest member of his Cabinet was Judah P. Benjamin, successively Attorney General, Secretary of War, and Secretary of State, but this brilliant man became notoriously unpopular. Apart from the fact that in general Davis faced a more difficult task than Lincoln because of smaller resources, he confronted another difficulty in more acute form. The Confederacy had been founded on the philosophy of state rights, while the conduct of a war inevitably requires centralization. Lincoln had plenty of troubles with state officials, but his own hand was not paralyzed by a state-rights philosophy. Before the fighting ended, he had the Northern governors well in hand, while Davis was still being challenged by Southern executives. Under the exigencies of war the Union became a nation, rather than an aggregation of states, in a sense that was never true of the Confederacy.

The First Battle and Its Aftermath

The first major engagement of the war, on July 21, 1861, known in the Union as the First Battle of Bull Run and in the Confederacy as the First Battle of Manassas, has been described as an engagement between armed mobs. Governor Andrew of Massachusetts said that the men from his state thought they were going to a town meeting. Like an athletic event, it attracted a horde of spectators, including Congressmen and ladies from Washington, who afterward went scurrying home in consternation. Yet there were more combatants than in any battle hitherto fought on the North American continent.

The major responsibility for the action lay with the Lincoln administration. The General in Chief, Winfield Scott, was seventy-five years old and unable to mount a horse. This experienced soldier favored what is known as the "Anaconda" policy. He wanted to blockade the Confederacy, seize the Mississippi River from Cairo to the Gulf, and gradually strangle the new Southern Republic. Lincoln rejected this plan, though part of it was revived in the later campaigns for the inland waterways. Throughout the war Lincoln was, as a rule, an advocate of aggressive military action; and during these early months he was subjected to the powerful pressure of public opinion as voiced in the cry, "On to Richmond." The fact that the three-months' terms of the militiamen who had been summoned in April were about to expire was regarded by many as a compelling argument. The major difficulty of the Union, however, was not shortage of men, for more regiments were offered than could yet be accepted. The trouble was that there had not been time to turn these raw recruits into effective soldiers.

Since late May 1861, Union forces had been on the Virginia side of the Potomac, protecting Washington. General Irvin McDowell, who commanded these green troops, was reluctant to assume the offensive as yet; but he and General Scott were overborne, and the latter became optimistic as the army of some 30,000 men moved southward. On July 18, McDowell occupied Centerville, about twenty miles from the Potomac. Between him and Richmond was a smaller army commanded by General Pierre Gustave Toutant Beauregard of New Orleans, the "Great Creole," who had taken a position where he could guard the railroad junction at Manassas. General Joseph E. Johnston, who was senior to Beauregard in rank, commanded a smaller Confederate army in the Shenandoah Valley; and he was opposed by General Robert Patterson with a superior Union force at Harper's Ferry. Johnston's army in the Valley was a threat to Washington which had to be guarded against, while Patterson's at Harper's Ferry was no threat to Richmond. The presumption on which Federal strategy was based was that Patterson would hold Johnston, but the Confederate General slipped away and joined Beauregard, thus making the contesting forces approximately equal.

The Federal forces attacked and had so much the better of it at first that a great victory was reported in Washington. The brigade of General Thomas J. Jackson stood firm. He himself gave God the credit, but then and there he gained the nickname "Stonewall," which he bore ever afterward. The Confederates counterattacked, and, further reinforced by Johnston's men as the day wore on, turned defeat into victory. The contest was close, and if McDowell had had a disciplined army he probably could have staged an orderly withdrawal, but the retreat degenerated into a rout which lasted until the soldiers and bedraggled spectators got back to Washington. To some excited journalists and statesmen it seemed that the fall of the city was inevitable. The failure of the Confederates to follow up their advantage can be explained in part by their own extreme demoralization. As the battle ended President Jefferson Davis arrived and entered into the military counsels. His policy was consistently defensive, and if there was a chance to capture Washington and gain independence by a decisive blow, the Confederates did not seize it.

Actually, this first victory did the Confederate cause more harm than good. It increased the confidence of Davis that the Confederacy could gain recognition by foreign powers merely by holding fast, and it exaggerated in the minds of many Southerners the opinions they already held about their superior military prowess. The boast that one Rebel could whip five Yankees was repeated many times before it was proved to be a dangerous delusion. The international repercussions of the victory were favorable to the Confederacy, but they did not lead to recognition. Within a few months Beauregard was transferred to the western theatre, and the more cautious Johnston remained in command in Virginia.

In the North, there was great discouragement at the outcome of the battle and the unity of sentiment which had marked the weeks just after the fall of Fort Sumter was irretrievably lost, but the Union got down to business, realizing that a long struggle lay ahead. Lincoln did not reproach the unfortunate McDowell, but he did replace him by Major-General George B. McClellan, whose minor successes in western Virginia had been so well advertised and who soon was viewed as "Young Napoleon." Now only thirty-five, this patronizing young man had slight patience with old General Scott, who was retired in the autumn, leaving McClellan wholly free to follow his own ideas in creating a real army. He did marvels in the months of respite that followed the defeat. Washington was safe and all was quiet along the Potomac.

Young Napoleon was to try Lincoln's patience sorely before long, but in the months after Bull Run the harassed President had more trouble with General John C. Frémont. In the summer of 1861, he appointed the "Pathfinder of the West," who had been the first Republican candidate for President, commander of the Department of the West with headquarters at St. Louis. Missouri was then torn by civil strife and Frémont acted presumptuously and recklessly. Toward the end of the summer, without consulting the President or the Department of War, he proclaimed that captives would be tried by court martial and executed if found guilty of rebellion; and he declared the property of Rebels confiscated and their slaves freed. Besides assuming unwarranted political authority, he was pursuing a policy directly contrary to the one Lincoln was following in his effort to retain the border slave states in the Union. At the risk of alienating the antislavery radicals who were making a hero of Frémont, Lincoln removed him in the autumn. The President was leaving no doubt that all other issues must be subordinated to the main one—the saving of the Union.

Armies: North and South

Statistics for the armed forces in the Civil War are so unreliable that all figures must be given as approximations. During the course of the conflict somewhat more than 1,500,000 men were probably enrolled in the Union army and about half that number in the Confederate, though the forces in the field at a particular time represented only a fraction of the totals. The odds lengthened as the conflict wore on, but the over-all ratio of somewhat more than 2 to 1 is borne out by the respective figures for the veterans after the war. Since the advantage of the Union in potential military manpower was about 4 to 1 if the slaves are deducted from the population of the Confederacy, approximately twice as large a proportion of Southerners as Northerners took up arms. The Confederate army was at its peak in the spring of 1863, when some 300,000 men were in the field, and the Union army in the early months of 1865, when it contained approximately 800,000.

In *John Brown's Body*, Stephen Vincent Benét speaks of "the first hot wave of youth, too ready to die," saying that they went to war as if to a ball. But as the ordeal was extended and its horrors were observed, the raising of armies became grim and difficult business on both sides of the line.

ABRAHAM LINCOLN

1809-1865

Photograph by Hesler

The strength and compassion of
the man who was destined to
save the Union is clearly revealed in this photograph taken
just before his nomination.

JEFFERSON DAVIS

1808-1889

Photograph by Matthew Brady

This likeness shows the dignity
and nervous intensity of the
Confederate President.

ULYSSES S. GRANT
1822-1885

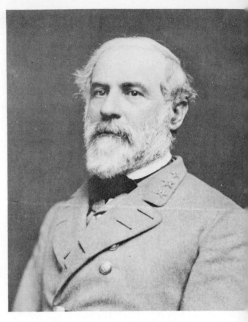

ROBERT E. LEE
1807-1870

The most famous generals of the Civil War

WILLIAM T. SHERMAN
1820-1891

T. J. ("STONEWALL") JACKSON
1824-1863

UNION ATTACK ON THE CONFEDERATE LINES AT VICKSBURG, May 19, 1863. *Modern painting by H. Charles McBarron, Jr., issued by the Department of the Army.* Here is re-created the fierce hand-to-hand conflict between the opposing armies. In this assault the 1st Battalion, 13th Infantry was the only unit to carry its colors to the top of the steep slope.

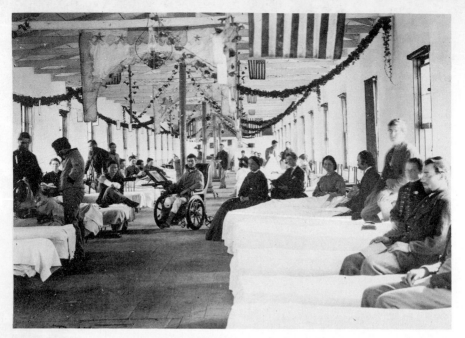

CARVER HOSPITAL near WASHINGTON. *Photograph by Matthew Brady.* The price of battle to the wounded. Few Civil War hospitals were as neat and well-staffed as this one.

FREEDMEN ON THE CANAL BANK AT RICHMOND, April 18 Former slaves just after the cessation of hostilities, surround by the ruins of the Confederate capital.

Soldiers of the Union

In the North there was a regular army to begin with, but, after the withdrawal of Southerners from it, it consisted of only a little more than 13,000 men. In 1861, its authorized strength was increased to 42,000, but this figure was never reached. On the Union side the war was fought at the very first by militiamen and then, increasingly, by United States volunteers, enlisted for a term of three years, to whom eventually were joined a small number of draftees. The act of July 22, 1861, which created a volunteer army of 500,000 men, authorized the President to fix the state quotas but left the recruiting to the states. Also, it recognized the right of companies to elect their officers, and of company officers to elect the regimental officers. The whole procedure was amateurish and often became political. The problems which McClellan faced when trying to weld these volunteer units from an unmilitary society into a disciplined fighting force can easily be imagined. The first equipment of the various units was whatever was available in the locality—with the result that there was a vast variety of uniforms. There was almost as much gray on the Union as on the Confederate side at first.

During the first year of the war the administration simply tried to keep the army of 500,000 men filled up, and in the spring of 1862 Secretary of War Stanton, noting that there were more than 600,000 in service, unwisely ordered that recruiting be stopped. In the summer, faced with serious reverses and responding to an appeal by a group of governors, Lincoln issued a call for 300,000 more volunteers for three years and followed this with a call for an equal number of militia to serve nine months.

Not until March 3, 1863, was a national draft law passed, and modern Americans may wonder if it deserves that description. This act declared that all males from 20 to 45 (20 to 35 if married) were liable to military service and should be enrolled. The draft riots of that summer in New York City were an accompaniment of the enrollment. In practice, drafting was relied on to complete state quotas, and it was possible to hire a substitute or escape service by paying $300 (supposedly the price of a substitute). A number of drafts were made, but it has been estimated that there were only 170,000 conscripts altogether, of whom nearly 120,000 procured substitutes. During the same period there were a million volunteers. Throughout the country there was a horror of the draft, and many thousands enlisted in order to avoid it. The small group of conscripts made good soldiers, and the substitutes—including many of foreign birth and some full-blooded Indians who had never before been fully clothed—appear to have been generally satisfactory. The poorest of all the soldiers were the bounty men.

The offering of bounties was one of the worst aspects of recruiting practice. Certain federal bounties were promised all who enlisted, and in view of the low pay ($11 per month for a private, later increased to $16) this procedure was not unnatural, but a general increase in the pay would have been much fairer. Far worse were the actions of states and cities, which competed with each other in offers, in their anxiety to fill their quotas. It has been estimated that the total cost of the various bounties was nearly $750 million. These practices tended to demoralize the entire recruiting program by injecting into it the factor of competitive bidding, and they led to the abuse of bounty-jumping. An unscrupulous man would enlist, get his bounty, desert, re-enlist under another name, and repeat the process as often as he could get away with it. Old soldiers had no respect for the bounty men, and sometimes said that the government would have been wiser to buy mules. But out of this seeming chaos and these diverse elements—among which thoroughly decent and patriotic volunteers greatly predominated—a powerful citizen army was created in the unfamiliar climate of war.

Confederate Troops

The Confederacy fought the war by means of a provisional army, created by an act of the Confederate Congress on February 28, 1861, authorizing the Government to accept state troops offered by the governors. The service of these state troops was limited to twelve months. Thus the Confederacy, like the Union, was dependent on the militia at first and was plagued by short enlistments. After the firing on Fort Sumter, the Confederate President was authorized to accept volunteers for terms varying from six months to the duration of the war, and he could receive these *without* state consent. One result of the latter provision was to arouse the resentment of governors who cherished their own powers and prerogatives and viewed the conflict from the point of view of local defense rather than unified strategy.

In the first flush of excitement there was a flood of volunteers, speeded by the ladies, who were even more enthusiastic for secession and Southern independence than the men. The flower of Southern aristocracy flocked gaily to the colors at the very start. But during the tedious months following First Manassas (Bull Run), enthusiasm inevitably ebbed and the Provisional Army faced the acute problem of the running out of enlistments. In December 1861, in a mistaken effort to forestall this, the Confederate Congress passed an act granting a sixty-day furlough and small bounty to all twelve-months men who would re-enlist. By dispersing the army this action threatened it with disintegration. Soon thereafter the President was authorized to call upon the governors for more state troops, instead of waiting for these to be offered.

The inadequacy of these measures and the growing consciousness, early in 1862, that the war was going badly in the West, created a strong sentiment for conscription, and on April 16, 1862, the Confederate Congress passed the first general conscription act in American history, being nearly a year ahead of the Union in this matter. By one provision of this act, all soldiers then in the army were required to serve three years or for the duration. The law declared that all male whites between the ages of 18 and 35 (afterwards 18 to 45) and not legally exempt were "members of the Confederate Army" for three years unless the war should end sooner. The drafted men were to be assigned to units from their own states, and if anyone chose to volunteer he might choose his own company. The hiring of substitutes from persons not liable to service was permitted.

In theory this was a selective service system, for those engaged in various occupations supposed to be indispensable were exempted. These exemptions led to grave abuses and loud objections. State officials comprised an exempted class, and certain governors enlarged it by excessively liberal interpretation. The charge that Governor Joseph E. Brown of Georgia exempted 15,000 by this means, and Governor Zebulon Vance of North Carolina 25,000, was doubtless an exaggeration, but it revealed a tendency among the state executives who were least sympathetic with the Davis government. There was strong popular objection to the exemption of overseers on plantations with twenty slaves or more, and the conflict was described by many as "a rich man's war and poor man's fight." The provisions were eventually modified, but by that time the Confederacy was nearing the end of its resources anyway.

A relatively larger number of drafted men served in the Confederate than in the Union Army, but, as in the North, the chief value of the draft was in the stimulus it gave to volunteering. There appears to have been a somewhat smaller relative number of substitutes than in the North, and by common consent they were the poorest of the soldiers. Nothing comparable to the bounties to volunteers developed in the South, and, while the pay was approximately the same as in the North, it never caught up with inflation and often the Confederates did not even get it. More even than in the North, the policy of conscription created ill will and bitterness—of governors against President Davis and of plain citizens against the Confederate government.

In the Confederate Army as in the Union Army, during the early part of the war, company officers were elected by the men, the higher officers in the various state units being generally appointed by the governors. Later, through the operation of efficiency boards, many incompetent officers were dropped. The Confederates were specially fortunate in their general officers, but the most eminent of these, Robert E. Lee, gave his greatest praise to the common soldiers. They were a variegated lot. Gray was the official color for uniforms from an early stage, but Johnny Reb provided his own uniform during the first half of the war, on a commutation basis; he might keep the regimental garb he had come with or wear clothes that came from home or had been captured from the Yankees. In the end he wore whatever was available. He preferred a felt hat to a cap, and would rather be barefoot than bareheaded. He was not very amenable to discipline, being individualistic in spirit and notably informal in manner. He did not look or act like a modern soldier, but if he could not lick five Yankees or his own weight in wildcats, unquestionably he was one of history's most famous fighters. He was at the peak of his powers in the mid-years of the war, while Billy Yank was still maturing as a military man and before Northern strength had grown overwhelming.

Comparative Equipment

The Union Army was superior to the Confederate in practically all articles of equipment, and the advantage of the former grew as the war progressed. There never was any shortage of small arms in the North. The main difficulty lay in their obsolete character. Most of them were muzzle-loaded smoothbores. These were rifled and percussion caps were added, but otherwise they were much the same sort of weapon that had been used in the American Revolution. Breech-loaders, of which the Sharps rifles were the favorite, were well known, but until the last stages of the war the Union largely depended on muzzle-loaders.

The North always had full access to the markets of Europe, and during the first year of the war, especially, it purchased huge quantities of arms abroad. The early purchases, however, consisted largely of weapons which European countries had cast off in the modernization of their arms. The Confederates had even more reason to purchase guns abroad, and they did so as long as they could. In the earlier stages of the war they realized very often on captured Union arms, and if these were no better than their own they knew better how to use them at the beginning.

After the first year, the Union could rely primarily on domestic manufacturing. The Ordnance Bureau long rejected the Spencer rifle, a repeater using copper cartridges which was finally made available to some degree and played an important part in the later victories of Union cavalry. The Confederates then said that the Yankees had made a gun that they could load on Sunday and fire all week; and somebody is reported to have remarked, "It's no use for us to fight you'ens with that kind of gun." Had it been adopted earlier, the war would probably have been far shorter.

Because of their backwardness in heavy industry, the Confederates had no such opportunities to produce modern arms. In the production of cannon and powder, to which Northern industry was effectively converted, they had to start virtually from scratch. In view of the natural difficulties, the achievements of the Confederate Ordnance Bureau were perhaps the most remarkable of the war. Chief credit for these belongs to Josiah Gorgas, a native Pennsylvanian and West Pointer who had married a Southerner and threw in his lot with the South. He has been described as the ablest and most successful organizer in the Confederacy. The Tredegar Iron Works in Richmond became the center for the manufacture of heavy guns and provided an intensely practical reason for the desperate defense of the Confederate capital. The manufacture of powder was one of the greatest achievements of the Ordnance Bureau. This centered on Nashville, Tennessee, until that city fell early in 1862, and in Augusta, Georgia. Practically all the copper came from the mines at Ducktown, Tennessee, and these were lost when Chattanooga was captured. Northern mines and munitions plants, on the other hand, were behind the curtain of war, and they were operated with steadily increasing effectiveness.

THE NAVIES

The Union retained nearly all of the ninety vessels of all classes in the existing Navy. Only about half of these were in commission, however, and most of them were obsolete sailing vessels. Thus the Union had to create virtually a new navy. In Secretary Gideon Welles of Connecticut, known as "Father Welles" because of his luxuriant white whiskers and patriarchal appearance, the Navy had a competent head, and the activities of his department were marked by less bungling and far fewer scandals than those of the Department of War. Unlike most people, Welles expected a long war from the beginning. He himself was more notable for steadiness and persistence than brilliance. The Assistant Secretary, Gustavus V. Fox, a bold and able man on whom he greatly relied, supplemented him admirably. Within the year 1861, the size of the Navy was trebled by the purchase of merchant vessels and the building of warships; and the Northern advantage kept on increasing until it became overwhelming. Compared with the Army, the Navy availed itself more quickly of innovations. Welles was aware of the value of ironclads almost from the first. The *Monitor* type which was first favored by the Navy was more useful on rivers than against fortifications, however, and the capture of Southern seaports was slower than might have been expected in view of Northern naval strength. One of the most important developments was the adoption of turret guns wherever possible, and gunnery was generally better on Union ships than on Confederate.

Except for a few vessels that were seized in southern ports, the Confederacy started without a navy, and it labored under great difficulties in the effort to create one. It retained a couple of navy yards for a time but lost these early in the war. Besides lacking industrial resources, which became increasingly important as ships were increasingly armored, the South had few workmen skilled in ship construction, and as the blockade became tighter it could not meet its needs from abroad. The most spectacular Confederate ships were the commerce raiders, such as the *Alabama*. The most famous of these were built in England and were acquired early in the conflict. The Southerners were pioneers in the effective use of torpedoes or mines and by means of them did their greatest damage to Union warships. Their naval activities, even more than their military operations, were defensive. Under the pressure of necessity, they showed great ingenuity in the use of limited resources, but they could not hope to match the resources and technical skills of the Union and their own government never was navy-minded. Some United States naval officers, including the redoubtable Raphael Semmes of the *Alabama* and the noted oceanographer, Matthew Fontaine Maury, who rendered great service in harbor defense, threw in their lot with the Confederacy, but the proportion was considerably smaller than in the case of Army officers. The most noted Union naval commander in the war, David G. Farragut, was of Southern birth.

Naval preponderance was an indispensable element in Northern success. Besides protecting commerce on the high seas and thus preserving to the North full access to world markets, the Navy blockaded the Confederacy. The arms which the Confederacy got from abroad, especially during the first half of the war, and the articles which slipped through during the very last months, show that the blockade was not completely effective. If it had been, the South would have had to give up much sooner than it did. After the first year, however, Confederate privateers were unable to bring their prizes into their own ports and there was the same difficulty in the case of ships constructed abroad. Furthermore, the blockade brought great hardship on the Southern people.

Early Problems of Diplomacy

There was a real possibility that one or more of the European powers might intervene in the war or grant favors to the Confederacy. Therefore, foreign relations and diplomacy were of the first importance to both the Lincoln and Davis governments. In general, the wealthy and privileged classes of Europe, especially the large landowners, favored the South while the middle and working classes favored the North, though there were many individual exceptions. Some European aristocrats hesitated to support slavery, and liberals who stressed free trade, particularly British liberals, were antagonized by the high tariff laws of the United States after the Republicans took office. The attitudes of the various governments, as distinguished from the sympathies of individuals, were affected by their own international interests. Imperialists in the Spanish and French governments, anticipating the breakup of the Union and the end of the Monroe Doctrine, started to rebuild their American empires. If the British government had taken such a position, it is difficult to imagine that the North could have won the war.

Superficially, Britain would gain in trade and power if the American Republic fell apart, and some British leaders would have been happy to see Confederate sea raiders destroy the Northern merchant fleet, the greatest rival of the British merchant marine. But we have already observed in earlier chapters that important groups of British businessmen and investors had a rich stake in Anglo-American unity, that these groups had powerful spokesmen in both British parties, and that by 1860 this coalition had caused Parliament and the Ministry to accept the idea that Britain should co-operate with United States hegemony in the New World. This significant recent decision was reinforced by the British need for Northern wheat and by the vast expansion of markets for British munitions and manufactures in the war-time North. Thus economic interest offset lingering British jealousy of American power and dislike of Republican tariffs. Furthermore, the middle and lower classes, which sympathized with the Union, were more influential in Britain than in the continental countries, and "Little Englanders" distrusted imperalist adventures such as those of Napoleon III. The policy of the British government toward the Civil War proved to be passive rather than active and was, therefore, a disappointment to both sides, but while it was somewhat injurious to the North it was fatal to the South.

Foreign aid was essential for Confederate success. The Southern leaders knew this and allowed themselves to be intoxicated by an oversimplified calculation of British interest. They accepted the overconfident theory of fire-eating orators that Cotton was King, meaning that the need for Southern cotton by European, and particularly British, textile mills would suffice to force a pro-Confederate policy on the governments. The Confederate government promptly placed an embargo on shipments of the staple abroad, willingly co-operating with the Union blockade to this extent and foregoing money for the purchase of necessities in order to make the British government pay homage to King Cotton. The timing of the action could hardly have been worse. The huge crops of 1859 and 1860 had left a surplus in the hands of British brokers which was a drug on the market until the Confederate embargo came to the rescue. The British mills used this cotton during the early years of the war. After that, the mills that had to close brought some pressure on the government to break the blockade, but unemployed workers were steadfast in friendship towards the Union and the mill owners themselves were mostly unfriendly to the South. Later in the war the cotton famine was relieved by shipments of bales captured by Union troops and by the tapping of new sources in Egypt and India. Furthermore, the British people depended on Northern wheat, and Northern farmers performed the feat of producing enough for foreign markets as well as the Union Army. The defeat of Confederate cotton diplomacy and the triumph of wheat were epitomized when shiploads of breadstuffs were dispatched to hungry, pro-Union mill workers in Britain as the gift of the Northern people. Furthermore, the emancipation policy of the Union government cemented the loyalty of British liberals and working people to the Union cause before the war was half over.

Seward and Charles Francis Adams

Lincoln had faced several diplomatic crises by that time. One of these occurred within the government itself while he was still undecided what to do about Fort Sumter. His Secretary of State and would-be Prime Minister, William H. Seward, wanted to use belligerent talk to prevent European intervention in the affairs of the New World, and by raising the threat of foreign war he hoped to distract attention from the domestic crisis and bring the cotton states back into the Union on a wave of national patriotism. His proposal, made to Lincoln on April 1, 1861, in the presumptuous private paper called, "Some Thoughts for the President's Consideration," has been called Seward's "April Fool's Day Madness," though this is perhaps unfair to Seward. The design of Spain to reconquer Santo Domingo and the scheme of Napoleon III to invade Mexico had not reached a stage where the United States would have been warranted in demanding explanations and threatening war, as Seward seemed to think, but these policies were predicated on the assumption that the Union was breaking up. The Monroe Doctrine could not be preserved without preserving the Union, and it was statesmanlike to emphasize their connection. Furthermore, there was point in Seward's advice to give up federal control of Sumter, which Southerners regarded as a threat to them, and to retain the Gulf forts, which they could regard as a threat to Spain and France. But Lincoln soon concluded that the risk of foreign war was too great to take, and that he could not abandon Sumter. So Seward could only register verbal objections to the designs of Spain and France.

Rumors of his "wrap-the-world-in-fire" policy created great distrust of the Secretary of State in European foreign offices. Fortunately Lincoln sent to Great Britain as Minister Charles Francis Adams, son of John Quincy and grandson of John. Serving there throughout the war, he displayed diplomatic patience, astuteness, unswerving patriotism, and integrity worthy of his eminent ancestors. He won the respect of British officials, toned down the ire in Seward's instructions, and yet yielded nothing when firmness was needed. He had to deal with a bewildering series of crises. On the day he arrived, May 13, 1861, the British government proclaimed neutrality and recognized the Confederate government as a belligerent. This fell short of recognizing the independence of the Confederate states and entering into official relations with them—no government ever did that—but the North and the Lincoln administration felt bitterly injured.

The step was actually justified by Lincoln's own proclamation of a blockade of the South which was incompatible with his view that the Union was merely suppressing an insurrection. Blockade implied the existence of two warring parties and Great Britain recognized their existence as a necessary corollary of her obedience to the proclamation. This was in fact helpful to the North during the early months when the blockade was chiefly paper. On June 1, the British government forbade privateers of both sides to bring prizes into British ports—another "coldly neutral" act which helped the North far more than the South because only the North had a merchant marine worth the attention of privateers. Wanting sympathy rather than neutrality and fearing that Britain would presently recognize the Confederate government, Unionists only later appreciated the correctness of these early British actions.

The Trent Affair

It was not strange that the Union debacle at Bull Run led most Britons, including such a friend of the North as Richard Cobden, to conclude that the South could not be conquered. The Confederate government then decided to strengthen its diplomatic campaign by sending abroad two well-known leaders, James M. Mason of Virginia to Great Britain and John Slidell of Louisiana to France. They ran the blockade to Havana and took passage on the *Trent*, a British mail steamer. In November 1861, Captain Charles Wilkes of the Union sloop-of-war *Jacinto*, acting without orders, stopped the *Trent* with a show of force, took off the diplomats as contraband of war, and caused them to be imprisoned in Boston. But the question whether civilian diplomats were in fact contraband was an unsettled point of international law, while authorities agreed that Wilkes should have taken the *Trent* into port for adjudication of the point by an admiralty court, and that he was judging the point without trial when he took the Confederates to jail in the United States. The Northern public was not interested in these fine distinctions but celebrated Wilkes's exploit as a major victory. The British public regarded the incident as an intolerable insult and talked of war.

The British government sent troops to Canada and the Foreign Secretary, Lord John Russell, wrote a sharp ultimatum, presenting Lincoln and Seward with their gravest diplomatic crisis and a cruel dilemma. If they gave up the prisoners and apologized to Great Britain, the anger of the public and Congress would be politically dangerous; if they refused the ultimatum they faced war over a cause which would virtually guarantee an alliance between the South and Great Britain and Northern defeat. The death of Prince Albert, whose last official act had been to advise Earl Russell to soften his ultimatum, changed the British mood. Lincoln and Seward postponed an answer as long as they could, then agreed to release the prisoners in a masterly note designed to soothe Northern public opinion by pointing out that Britain had now accepted a principle —that civilians cannot be considered as contraband—for which the United States had fought the War of 1812. Northerners were chagrined and demagogues tried to make capital of Lincoln's "craven surrender," but the crisis passed.

The gravest later difficulty centered on the question of building Confederate warships in Great Britain, but before this reached the most dangerous point British sentiment had changed because of the Emancipation Proclamation and the improvement in Northern military fortunes. British neutrality in the first year of the war proved to be decisive. The activities of Napoleon III in Mexico attracted relatively little attention in the North at first. His government, more than any other in Europe, favored the Confederate cause, but he feared war with the Union and could not gain British backing for the mediation which he hoped would lead to a recognition of Southern independence. Circumstances combined to put him in a position of diplomatic isolation. Thus the negative but basically correct British policy was an essential element in eventual Northern victory.

CHAPTER 38

The Height of the Conflict
1862-1863

NOT UNTIL THE LAST YEAR OF THE WAR WAS MILITARY policy really unified in the North. When Winfield Scott retired in the fall of 1861, McClellan became General-in-Chief, but he lost that title when he took the field in the spring of 1862, and he never gained the entire confidence of Lincoln or was able to assume full authority over all the armies. In the summer of 1862, the high-sounding title was passed on to General Henry W. Halleck, but "Old Brains" was essentially a technical adviser to the President, and not until Grant became General-in-Chief early in 1864 was there a supreme military commander. In the first three years of the war Lincoln not only concerned himself with major strategy but also with the movements—at times even with the minor movements— of armies. McClellan, who described him as a "rare bird," regarded him as an incompetent meddler, and it now seems that Lincoln removed and appointed army commanders like so many football coaches.

He joked with generals in their tents but took his responsibilities as Commander-in-Chief with the utmost seriousness. He made grave blunders, but he had sound views about basic strategy. He condoned the appointment of generals for political reasons to a greater degree than Jefferson Davis did, partly because he was less trained in military matters but also because he was seeking the support of all groups—Democrats and Republicans, moderates and radicals, immigrants and native-born. He was under constant pressure from members of his Cabinet and leaders in Congress, especially from the Joint Committee on the Conduct of the War, set up late in 1861. This was controlled by radical Republicans, who wanted to make the war a crusade against slavery from the start and favored generals who agreed with them. Regarding these men as unrealistic extremists, Lincoln yielded to them as little as he could, but he never ceased to be aware of public opinion. Realizing that both the domestic and foreign situation made decisive military victory imperative, he pressed for it unremittingly until finally he got it.

In the matter of major strategy and the larger movements of armies, Jefferson Davis kept things pretty much in his own hands throughout the conflict. The genius of Lee was largely lavished on the Army of Northern Virginia; only at the very end of the war did he become Commander-in-Chief of all the Confederate armies. Meanwhile, there was ill feeling between Davis and other leading generals, especially Joseph E. Johnston, and the Confederate President was charged with playing favorites. Davis made a serious mistake in keeping too many military details in his own hands; one of his successive Secretaries of War said on resigning that the President wanted him to be a mere clerk. The chief military mistakes of Davis, however, lay in the realm of high strategy. Political considerations caused him to assume a completely defensive role at the very beginning, when an offensive policy offered greater military promise, and events proved that he was unwise in minimizing the western theatre while concentrating the best Confederate talent in Virginia.

The prime objective of Union strategy, as Lincoln correctly perceived it, was to put down organized resistance by destroying the Confederate armed forces. The most formidable of these were guarding the northeastern gateway into the Confederacy and the approaches to Richmond, and they constituted a threat to Washington which Lincoln was never willing to disregard. It was natural, therefore, that the eastern theatre should bulk largest in the minds of Americans, both Northern and Southern, and also in the minds of those who followed the war news abroad. In this arena the Confederates could have been awarded the decision on points prior to Gettysburg in July 1863, and they delivered some stunning blows thereafter, but the war was a long series of bouts in far-flung arenas. It was fought in the seaports, while the Union Navy stood silently on guard offshore; and, most decisively of all in the middle years, it was fought on and beside the inland rivers. The Federals began to win the war when they began to gain control of the waterways of the Mississippi Valley, early in 1862. The spotlight was still on McClellan, but we should look first at the West and Ulysses S. Grant, who won the first great Union victory and with whom the future really lay.

The War in 1862: The West

That the northwestern gateway into the Confederacy was easier to force than the northeastern ought to have been obvious to anyone who was at all familiar with geography and topography. The situation was complicated at first by the uncertain status of Kentucky; the military authorities on both sides were reluctant to send troops into the state for fear of arousing local resentment. By the early months of 1862, however, these scruples had been cast aside. In command of the Western Department of the Confederacy by that time was General Albert Sidney Johnston, a Kentuckian by birth but a Texan by adoption. A West Pointer, he was several years older than Lee and ranked him in both the United States and the Confederate Army. Six feet tall, strong and physically commanding, Johnston was regarded by Jefferson Davis as the foremost Southern general. But with forces often armed with flintlocks and squirrel rifles, and much inferior in number to those opposed to them, he was expected to defend a line running most of the length of Kentucky, from Cumberland Gap to the Mississippi. Between his headquarters at Bowling Green and the Mississippi were the Tennessee and Cumberland Rivers, flowing northward to the Ohio. Just below the Tennessee state line the Confederates built Fort Henry on the Tennessee River, which was weak, and Fort Donelson on the Cumberland, which was strong. The latter guarded the waterway to Nashville, the capital of Tennessee, an important railroad center, and the seat of one of the main Confederate powder plants.

The Union command in the western theatre was divided between General Henry W. Halleck, with headquarters in Saint Louis, and General Don C. Buell at Louisville. There was considerable jealousy between these two commanders and their operations were not co-ordinated. In mid-January 1862, troops of Buell under General George H. Thomas defeated at Mill Spring in southeastern Kentucky a detachment from Johnston's army. Southwestern Kentucky was in Halleck's department, and under him was Ulysses S. Grant.

Grant and Fort Donelson

Until this time the career of Grant, who was nearing forty, had not been such as to create great expectations. It seemed that this stubby man with unkempt beard and stooped shoulders had been marked for failure. At West Point he was not notable for anything except his rare knack with horses. He served effectively but obscurely in the Mexican War and was well liked for his simplicity, modesty, and honesty. After that war, when doing lonely military service in the Far West, he took to drinking excessively and was under a cloud when he resigned his commission. His struggles for a livelihood thereafter comprise a pathetic story. He had no gift whatever for making money and really did not know how to do anything well except as a soldier. He was living soberly and respectably but modestly in southern Illinois when the war of his destiny broke out. His wife came of a slaveholding family in Missouri and, though no defender of slavery, he himself was no abolitionist. He was not even a Republican. He had voted for Buchanan in 1856—because he knew Frémont, he said—and he was for Douglas in 1860, though he did not vote.

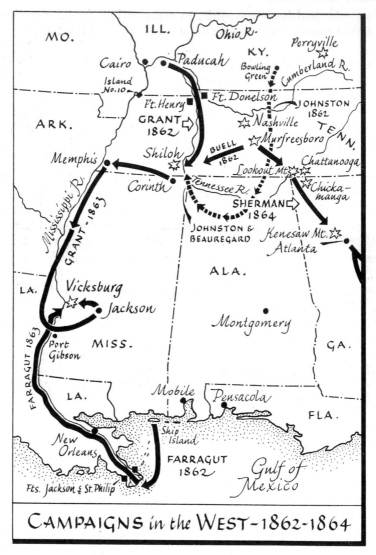

CAMPAIGNS in the WEST - 1862-1864

Politically he was a moderate, and he waged war without vindictiveness, but the loyalty of this simple man to the Union was unquestioning.

Appointed Colonel by the Governor of Illinois, he was shortly appointed Brigadier General of volunteers by Lincoln, on the recommendation of his Congressman. A professional among amateurs, he had already proved an effective organizer when, in the fall of 1861, he was in command at Cairo, Illinois, at the confluence of the Ohio and the Mississippi. Fortunate circumstance caused him to be associated with Commodore Andrew H. Foote, commander of naval operations on the upper Mississippi, who with great vigor and pertinacity had assembled a flotilla of mortars and gunboats. With the co-operation of Foote, Grant occupied Paducah, Kentucky, and the two men explored other possibilities on the rivers.

The capture of Fort Henry on February 6, 1862, was really a naval victory, for Foote's four ironclads and three wooden boats reduced the weak position before Grant's troops could attack. Grant marched overland to Fort Donelson under great physical difficulties, and carried the fort against strong resistance after the gunboats had been beaten back and Foote had been wounded. In the early fighting Grant's right wing crumbled; but he restored order out of chaos, communicated to his troops the inflexible determination which always characterized him as a fighter, and drove back the garrison. Nathan Bedford Forrest escaped with his cavalry by the river road, and the two highest Confederate officers got away by water with a small body of troops, leaving the command to an abler but less fortunate man. It was General Simon B. Buckner who asked for terms and received on February 16 the reply demanding "unconditional surrender" that soon became famous. The 15,000 prisoners were the largest number that had ever been taken in a battle on American soil, and, aided by the happy accident of his initials, the victor was hailed as "Unconditional Surrender" Grant. Though hitherto a pipe smoker, Grant had had a cigar in his mouth throughout this battle. The boxes of cigars that were now bestowed upon him fixed his smoking habits for the rest of life. This unpretentious but hard-hitting soldier captured the imagination of the Union, and he got enough official credit to be appointed a major general of volunteers.

Shiloh and the Mississippi

The cracking of their defense line in the center and the loss of so many men along with valuable supplies at Donelson was a disaster to the Confederates, who had to withdraw all the way across Tennessee. Johnston established his quarters at Corinth, Mississippi, and Union forces under Buell took possession of Nashville. Grant lost touch with Halleck for a time and that fussy General complained of him bitterly to Washington, repeating rumors that Grant had fallen back into his old drinking habits. These were untrue, but Grant was not at his best in the operations that soon followed. At the end of March his army was encamped on the west bank of the Tennessee River at Pittsburg Landing. Halleck, who had now been given supreme command in the West, had ordered Buell's troops to proceed from Nashville and join him.

Union strategy had not allowed for the possibility that Johnston might strike before the two Federal armies were joined. Now reinforced by Beauregard, he had a slight numerical superiority over Grant and on April 6 he struck. Grant and William Tecumseh Sherman, who was with him as a division commander, were caught napping. In the Battle of Shiloh, Johnston had the advantage in the confused fighting of the first morning, but in the early afternoon, when his surgeon was not with him, an artery in his leg was severed and he died within a few minutes. Beauregard succeeded to the command; Grant was somewhat reinforced late that day; and on the next day he threw into action fresh troops of his own, along with large reinforcements from Buell. The numerical advantage had passed to the Union side, and at length Beauregard ordered a withdrawal. This was admirably covered by Forrest, the general officer who came out of this affair most creditably.

The Battle of Shiloh was a Union victory. Never before in American history had there been such casualties. On the Union side these were about 13,000, and on the Confederate side about 11,000. In both armies most of the troops were green and many of them were terrified, but rarely have American soldiers shown equal capacity for taking punishment. By any reckoning, casualties approximating 25 per cent of the number engaged are excessive. A cry of lamentation went through the land, and "Unconditional Surrender" Grant was charged with being a merciless butcher. Lincoln never lost faith in this indomitable fighter, but for many months he was under a cloud.

Halleck arrived and assumed command. Under "Old Brains" the superior Union army proceeded cautiously, step by step, with pick and shovel, finally forcing Beauregard to retire southward from Corinth. The main Confederate army in the West was not crushed as it might have been, and, before going to Washington in the summer to become General-in-Chief, Halleck unwisely caused the Federal armies to be separated. But the Union made important gains on the rivers. On the second day of the Battle of Shiloh, Foote and General John Pope captured Island Number 10 in the Mississippi, and on June 6 Memphis fell to Union gunboats. Before this time, Farragut had captured New Orleans (April 26) in what was perhaps the most daring and brilliant naval exploit of the war.

Farragut and New Orleans

Captain Farragut, who was under suspicion at first because of his Southern birth, had been appointed early in 1862 to command the West Gulf Blockading Squadron with confidential orders to take New Orleans. He had a fleet of seventeen vessels and a flotilla of mortars. New Orleans was defended by Forts Jackson and Philip between the city and the Gulf and some forty miles from the latter. The southernmost of these was bombarded by the mortar flotilla under David D. Porter without considerable effect, and Farragut then reached the daring decision to run by the forts. On April 24, he did so with nearly all of his seventeen ships, passing through dense smoke and blinding fire. Farragut himself afterwards described this as one of the "most awful sights and events" he ever saw or expected to experience. At one time his flagship was run ashore and was all ablaze. He had no great difficulty defeating the Confederate flotilla between the forts and the city, and on April 26 he occupied the latter without bloodshed. Soon thereafter the forts surrendered, now that their line of communication had been severed. New Orleans was the richest prize of the year and one of the very richest of the war. In Farragut, who soon became a Rear Admiral, the Union had found its greatest naval hero. The chief remaining river prize was Vicksburg, and Grant was to be a long time gaining that, but by the middle of 1862 the Union had made immense strides in the West. In the East, progress was so slow that to many it was imperceptible.

THE WAR IN 1862: THE EAST

Until this day George B. McClellan is a controversial figure, but two things about him are generally conceded. He was a great organizer of armies—one high-ranking Confederate afterwards compared him in this respect to Von Moltke. Also, he arrived at the top rank too early for his own good.

Unlike Grant, he seemed fated for success from the very beginning of his professional career. He stood second in his class at West Point and had a distinguished record as an engineer. He had studied the operations of armies abroad, especially in the Crimea, and rendered admirable reports with excellent recommendations. He was a scholar in military affairs, an accomplished linguist, and a highly cultivated man. Though short enough to be called "Little Mac," he was powerfully built and physically impressive. His soldiers adored him, but he could be arrogant and he aroused bitter enemies. His political views were moderate, and he had no patience with antislavery extremists. The Democrats saw him as a political hope, while the radical Republicans tried to drag him down. Lincoln was quite willing to put up with him if he would achieve results.

McClellan was an engineer, seeking to create a perfect machine. He prized and guarded his men and, accentuating the weakness of a very poor intelligence service, he always tended to exaggerate the strength of the enemy. In the winter of 1861-1862, it looked as though he would never begin to fight. So, in late January, Lincoln issued a General War Order, prescribing a general advance on February 22, and soon followed this with a Special War Order requiring the Army of the Potomac to move on Manassas. McClellan disregarded both orders, and in March the Confederates under Joseph E. Johnston withdrew to a position beyond the Rappahannock anyway.

Meanwhile, a long dispute between the President and McClellan over

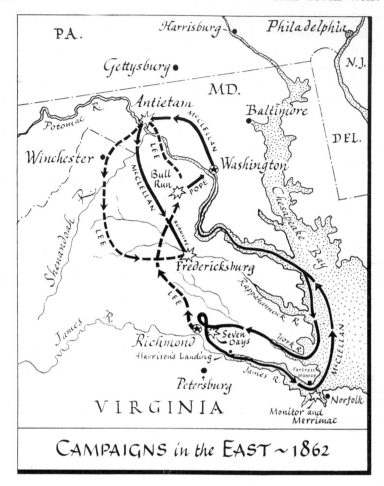

CAMPAIGNS in the EAST ~ 1862

strategy was finally settled by Lincoln's acceptance of the General's plan to attack Richmond from the eastward side. Availing himself of Union naval power, he would proceed by water to the peninsula between the York and James Rivers. The weakness of the plan in Lincoln's eyes was that Washington would be left undefended, so he detached McDowell's corps to protect the capital. But before the Peninsular Campaign got under way there were events in Hampton Roads which for a time cast grave doubts on Northern naval preponderance.

The Merrimac and the Monitor

When the Union abandoned the navy yard at Norfolk, the steam frigate *Merrimac* was abandoned and sunk. The Confederates raised the vessel, converted her into an ironclad, and renamed her the *Virginia*, though she is generally called by the old name. Her engines were inadequate, but when this monster sallied forth on March 8, 1862, she created consternation. The wooden vessels could not stand up to a floating fort from which their own shots bounded off harmlessly; several of them were destroyed and it appeared that the blockade had been broken. Indeed, it was feared that the monster would proceed up the Potomac to Washington and end the war. Some months earlier, however, the Union authorities had started construction of an ironclad following the design of the Swedish-American inventor and engineer, John Ericsson. Finished in the nick of time, this ironclad was towed to Hampton Roads, and on March 9 she engaged her Confederate rival in one of the most renowned of all American naval battles. The *Merrimac* or *Virginia* was a big awkward structure, rather like a box, while the *Monitor* was described as a cheese on a shingle. She was much smaller, more maneuverable, and with her revolving turret had superior firepower. The encounter was indecisive, for neither vessel could injure the other much, but at length the *Merrimac* withdrew and she did little later damage. Within a few weeks, when the Confederates abandoned Norfolk, she was burned. The *Monitor* also disappeared afterward, lost at sea. She was not very seaworthy because of her form, and vessels of her type proved much more useful on rivers, but this conflict left no doubt that a new era in warships had dawned. The Union, with its industrial facilities, was much better able than the Confederacy to adjust itself to this; and in the meantime McClellan's army could be safely transported by water to the Peninsula.

Beginning of the Peninsular Campaign

Early in April, McClellan began the siege of historic Yorktown and this operation consumed a month, permitting Johnston to proceed from his position below the Rappahannock to the defense of Richmond. Yorktown might have been taken by direct assault, but McClellan the engineer preferred a slower and safer procedure. He established headquarters on the Pamunkey River, a tributary of the York, and before the end of May some of his men were only four or five miles from Richmond. His outpost could see the steeples and hear the church bells. In response to his entreaties Lincoln had finally ordered McDowell's corps to reinforce him, and McClellan was waiting for it, convinced that without it he was outnumbered. But Lincoln, revoking his order, despatched McDowell on what proved to be a wild goose chase to the Shenandoah Valley. There Stonewall Jackson, under the supervision of Robert E. Lee, now military adviser to Jefferson Davis, was creating a diversion with the express design of preventing the reinforcement of McClellan. Until this day Jackson's Valley Campaign is regarded as a classic of the art of war.

The Valley Campaign

There were already in or near the Valley two Union armies, each of them equal or superior in size to the entire force available to Jackson. One of these, in what is now West Virginia, was that of Frémont, favorite of the radical Republicans, for whom a Department of the Mountains had been specially created. The other, in the northern part of the Valley, was that of Nathaniel P. Banks, a political general. By rapid marching and countermarching and surprise attacks, Jackson beat up his enemies in detail. He struck a detachment of Frémont's emerging from the mountains, caught a detachment of Banks's in Front Royal, and after sharply defeating Banks himself at Winchester drove him headlong across the Potomac. Lincoln had hoped to trap Jackson between three converging armies, of which that of McDowell was one. But they did not quite catch him as he retreated southward and, before the campaign ended, his command won a couple of further victories—against Frémont at Port Republic and Shields at Cross Keys on the same day. McDowell's corps never got to the Peninsula, and Jackson occupied as many Federal soldiers altogether as Johnston's entire force before Richmond. This was perhaps Jackson's greatest single service to the Confederacy and it gave him undying military fame.

Jackson, who was now thirty-eight, had been in McClellan's class at West Point and by unremitting work this unpromising cadet had finally gained a good ranking. He had been more conspicuous than Grant in the Mexican War, but afterwards had settled into obscurity as a professor at the Virginia Military Institute, at Lexington in the Valley, where he gave the cadets constant occasion for amusement. As one of his officers said, he had peculiarities which would have made a lesser man absurd. One that was frequently commented on by his soldiers was his habit of incessantly sucking a lemon. General Richmond Ewell always thought him crazy and became absolutely sure of it when he heard him soberly declare that he never ate pepper because it "produced a weakness in his left leg." He was indifferent to dress and was perhaps the most awkward officer in the Confederate Army. To him praying and fighting seemed the "whole duty of man." This fantastically devout Presbyterian was utterly brave because he was a complete fatalist, and when the light of battle shone in his eyes he was transformed. Of himself and his men he seemed to demand the impossible, but again and again they virtually achieved it. He conducted his stern life by the Bible, but he got his military principles from Napoleon: to mystify, to mislead, to surprise, and to hurl his forces at the weakest point of the enemy.

Seven Pines and the Seven Days' Battle

McClellan was almost in position to unlimber his siege guns against Richmond when Johnston attacked him. Between the Federal forces and Richmond was the Chickahominy, and McClellan had thrown perhaps a third of his army across it, leaving the rest on the other side, where he could join with such reinforcements as might come from McDowell. On May 31, Johnston struck at the exposed forces while the stream was flooded, and the resulting battle is known as Seven Pines or Fair Oaks. It was indecisive, though it had a bad effect on McClellan's spirits because he did not like to see men dead or wounded. The casualties were actually greater on the Confederate side, and they included Johnston, who was wounded and borne in a litter from the field. Robert E. Lee was then appointed to command what he himself named the Army of Northern Virginia. His ability to command a large army in the field was yet untested, but there was no suspicion between him and Davis, as there had been between Johnston and Davis, and as there was between McClellan and Lincoln and Stanton.

To the cautious McClellan the very fact that the Confederates had attacked was proof positive that they greatly outnumbered him and his conduct throughout the rest of this campaign was based upon that erroneous assumption. The respite which the heavy rains, illness in the Union Army, and McClellan's prudence combined to produce was most welcome to Lee. He set his men to work entrenching Richmond—winning thereby the dubious title of "King of Spades"; he collected reinforcements from points further south and perfected plans whereby Jackson was to bring his army secretly from the Valley. By these means he counted up some 85,000 men altogether. McClellan had perhaps 105,000, along with superior artillery, but it was Lee who took the offensive after nearly a month. His plan was to leave Richmond lightly defended behind the entrenchments on the east and to throw superior forces, including those of Jackson, against the part of McClellan's army north of the Chickahominy and thus to imperil the Federal supply line to the Pamunkey and York.

His strategy was sound, but Jackson was delayed, and on June 26 at Mechanicsville the disjointed Confederate attack was repulsed. This was the beginning of the Seven Days' Battle. At Gaines's Mill on June 27, Lee's forces won a costly victory; and as a result McClellan, abandoning his supply lines, began shifting his base across the Peninsula to the James. It was a skillful operation in a region of swamps and thickets, and the confused Confederates were unable to press their advantage. Their staff work was poor and Jackson, operating on unfamiliar ground and exhausted by lack of sleep, was far below his Valley standard. There was desperate fighting at Savage Station, Frayser's Farm, and Malvern Hill—

where the Confederates were repulsed with great slaughter. McClellan did not counterattack, but by July 2, while the rain was pouring, he was safe at Harrison's Landing on the James.

In the course of his retreat McClellan sent an incredible telegram to Stanton in which he accused the government of sacrificing his army by failing to send reinforcements. In reality, Lee, who had been constantly on the offensive with a smaller army, had suffered the heavier losses; these exceeded 20,000 and comprised almost a fourth of his command. He captured vast quantities of arms, which were a godsend to the Confederates, and the victory was his since he had driven McClellan back. Not until a few weeks later, when McClellan withdrew his powerful army under orders from Lincoln, was it wholly clear that his well-conceived and strongly supported expedition to the Peninsula was a failure, but Lee had already been hailed as the savior of Richmond.

Lee increasingly symbolized and incarnated the Southern cause from this time forward. Tall, well-proportioned, and strikingly handsome, he looked the part of a great commander, and he towered above the petty jealousies and bickerings to which the war gave rise. Rightly regarded as the flower of Southern aristocratic society, he was a man of simple tastes and deep religious faith whose personal austerity was alleviated by his charitable judgment of others. He was not a martinet. "These men are not an army," he said of his soldiers later in the war; "they are citizens defending their country." He could not impose severe discipline upon them, but he demanded of them forced marches and desperate fighting which McClellan would not have thought of asking of his beloved army.

For a military commander, Lee was perhaps too much the gentleman. The greatest military weakness that he had displayed thus far had been his excessive amiability in dealing with opinionated subordinates. Under his theory of command, tactics were largely left to the officers on the field, and Confederate tactics were poor in the Seven Days' Battle. But his confidence in his lieutenants and his respect for his men were rewarded by their faith in him. Jackson said that he would follow him blindfolded, and his soldiers came to believe that to him failure was impossible. As the military leader of a desperate cause he knew that he must take chances, but he had great capacity for taking pains and he calculated risks with care. In the summer of 1862 there were still far more Federals than Confederates in Virginia and his planning revolved around the necessity of preventing their concentration.

Second Bull Run and the Invasion of Maryland

At just this time, military planning on the Union side bogged down in chaos and confusion. Shortly after the Seven Days' Battle, Halleck became General in Chief and during the summer for the first and only time he tried to exercise supreme functions. The remnants of the armies of McDowell, Banks, and Frémont had been brought under one command and assigned to General John Pope, who had won minor successes in the West. He was a big talker and was reputed to be a willing fighter. When he assumed command he issued a bombastic address to his troops, saying that in the West they were accustomed to looking at the backs of their enemies. His forces were below the Rappahannock, considerably southwest of Acquia Creek, where McClellan arrived in late August. Halleck accused the latter of withdrawing the Army of the Potomac from the Peninsula much too slowly, and McClellan's aggrieved state of mind created great psychological complications. Some of his forces had been sent to join Pope, whom he detested, but he was reluctant to send others and Halleck was vacillating in the assertion of his authority. The net result was that the forces of McClellan and Pope were not joined and that Lee struck the smaller army.

Anticipating Federal actions with great acumen, Lee first detached Jackson to block Pope, then proceeded with Longstreet and the rest of the Army of Northern Virginia from Richmond and started a campaign of maneuver. This resulted in the Second Battle of Bull Run (Manassas) on August 29, in which boastful General Pope received a thorough trouncing. In this operation Jackson brilliantly retrieved his lapses in the Peninsular Campaign and made what was perhaps the most spectacular of all his marches. Getting behind Pope, he cut his communications with Washington, then met the attack in a strong position, where Lee and Longstreet joined him. The Confederate strategy was audacious but highly effective, and the results showed that Lee had created a formidable army. At the news of Pope's precipitate retreat, consternation reigned in Washington. Lincoln, much to the disgust of Stanton and Chase, first put McClellan in command of the defenses of the city, and then, removing the blustering Pope, he put McClellan in field command of the united Federal forces. He could not think of anything better to do and he had to do something, for early in September Lee's victorious army had crossed the Potomac into Maryland.

Lee was hoping to draw the Federal forces out of ravaged Virginia, but his decision—to which Jefferson Davis acceded—to take the offensive north of the Potomac was based also on political considerations. Assuming that there were many Confederate sympathizers in Maryland, he wanted to bring succor to them, and he issued at Frederick on September 8 a proclamation written in the spirit of "Maryland, my Maryland." While denying any thought of intimidation, he announced his desire to aid the citizens of the state to throw off the "foreign yoke" which had been imposed upon them and to regain the personal freedom they had previously enjoyed.

But Union sentiment was strong in western Maryland, and the appearance of the ragged Confederate soldiers was no omen of success. These men were lean as wolves, and their shoes, already worn from long marches on the dirt roads of Virginia, could not withstand the hard roads of Maryland. Never before had Lee had such a problem of stragglers. Because of the state of their feet, and because they were uninterested in an invasion of the North while determined to defend their own region, thousands of men dropped out. Also, there was the problem of food. Lee would not let his men forage extensively or take supplies by force, and Confederate money was not generally acceptable. It seemed imperative, therefore, to create a protected supply line southward through the Shenandoah Valley. But the Federal garrison at Harper's Ferry had not been evacuated as he had expected, and he sent Jackson to reduce that post while he and the remnant of the army proceeded in a northwesterly direction, aiming to cut railroad lines in Pennsylvania. He was relying on the dilatoriness of McClellan, but on September 13 in Frederick a copy of his orders was found wrapped around three cigars which had been in some staff officer's pocket, and this was delivered to the Federal Commander. Under these enlightening circumstances McClellan pursued Lee with a speed which for him was unexampled, though it was not quite speed enough.

The Confederates fought a stubborn delaying action at South Mountain, and this was followed by the battle of Antietam (Sharpsburg) on September 17, when more blood was shed than on any other single day in the war. Lee managed to reunite his scattered forces, including Jackson's, but some of them barely got there and the over-all odds were almost 2 to 1. Because of the nature of the terrain, this was in reality three separate battles—on the two wings and in the center—and the Confederates were on the defensive with their backs to the Potomac in a perilously shallow field. Time and again the Federals were on the verge of decisive victory, but Lee, operating on the inner line, shifted his meager forces to the point of greatest immediate danger. The last detachment from Harper's Ferry arrived just in time to stop the final Federal charge against the Confederate right. Lee then had no reserves. McClellan had one corps in reserve, in case of defeat, and if he had thrown it in his victory would probably have been decisive.

He reported it to Lincoln as a complete victory, and Lincoln forthwith announced that on January 1, 1863, he would issue the Emancipation Proclamation—to which McClellan was opposed. The Army of Northern Virginia was on the point of demoralization, but Lee calmly held his ground next day, while tending his wounded and rounding up his stragglers, and without reinforcement McClellan was unwilling to attack. So, on the night of September 18, Lee's ragged army crossed the Potomac and in the next few weeks, on its own soil, it renewed its strength. Counting the large bag of prisoners at Harper's Ferry, the Federals lost twice as many men as the Confederates in this campaign, and Lee never regarded it as a military failure. It was a political failure, however. The Marylanders did not rise up, and the Emancipation Proclamation shortly changed the purpose and character of the war.

From the military point of view, the most important result was to bring to an end Lincoln's patience with McClellan. He is reported to have said that the Army of the Potomac was wrongly named, for it was really only McClellan's bodyguard. On November 7, he removed the idol of that army. The major reason for the action was that McClellan had "the slows," and it is one with which most students of the war fully sympathize. But Lincoln did not have at hand a suitable substitute.

Fredericksburg

General Ambrose E. Burnside was a brave and handsome man who gave the name to a certain style of whiskers, and he had handled himself well in a minor independent command and under his friend McClellan. He had previously declined to assume command of the Army of the Potomac, but Lincoln asked him again, believing that he must get somebody from among the corps commanders and preferring him to Joseph E. Hooker, who was an outspoken anti-McClellan man. Burnside saw no way to escape the responsibility, but it oppressed him after he assumed it. The offensive plan which he devised and which Lincoln accepted with reluctance was to proceed against Richmond by way of Fredericksburg, but there was a misunderstanding with Halleck about the side of the Rappahannock he was to go on. The result was that, proceeding by the north bank, he had to wait on the heights opposite the town for pontoon bridges, and Lee had marshalled his army on the heights on the other side of the river before the Union army began to cross. Here in a strong position the Confederates fought on December 13 a wholly defensive battle. The conflict has little strategic interest and had slight military importance; it was slaughter pure and simple. The horror of the piles of corpses along the incline to Marye's Heights was past description, and was not relieved by the grim humor of the Confederates who robbed the Federal dead of overcoats and other articles of clothing—saying that the former owners did not need them. Union casualties exceeded 12,000, while those of the Confederates were less than half as great, including many men who were only slightly wounded.

Burnside had shown no capacity for high command, and his losses deeply depressed him. The defeat led to a virtual revolt against him among the higher officers, including General Hooker. Lincoln appointed him in place of Burnside, while warning him in a fatherly way of the dangers of jealousy and insubordination. The Christmas season of 1862 was a sad time in the North, but despite defeat Lincoln on January 1, 1863, formally issued the Emancipation Proclamation.

THE EMANCIPATION POLICY AT HOME AND ABROAD

Although the purpose of the war, as stated by Lincoln and affirmed in the first year by resolutions of Congress, was to preserve the Union and not to overthrow the domestic institutions of the rebellious states, the question of slavery would not down. From the moment that Federal troops occupied southern territory, slaves had been coming into the Union lines. General Benjamin F. Butler, at Fortress Monroe in 1861, retained them as "contraband of war," and Congress in the summer provided, rather vaguely, that property used for "insurrectionary purposes" might be seized. Though the actions of military commanders varied, there was a general effort to distinguish between the slaves of loyal and disloyal owners, and Lincoln insisted that there must be no direct attack on the institution of slavery itself. In the fall of 1861, he removed Frémont from his command in Missouri because of that General's precipitate actions, and in May 1862 he overruled General David Hunter in Port Royal, S. C. That officer had declared that all the slaves were free in the so-called Department of the South—consisting of South Carolina, Georgia, and Florida, and still very largely in Confederate hands.

In the summer of that year, Congress, yielding to the pressure of the radicals, passed what is generally known as the Second Confiscation Act (July 17, 1862). This severe law provided for the immediate forfeiture of the property of all Confederate officials and, after sixty days' notice, the forfeiture of the property of all those supporting the rebellion. Lincoln raised strong objections to the measure and signed it reluctantly. Events proved it virtually unenforceable by the courts. The law also had a section about slaves, who were not treated as property—namely, that the escaped or captured slaves of rebel owners should be "forever free." But there were no provisions for making this paper declaration effective.

Congress abolished slavery in the District of Columbia (April 16, 1862) and the territories (July 17, 1862). In the case of the District, provision was made, on the insistence of Lincoln, for compensation to owners and the colonization of freedmen. A fund was provided for the latter and Lincoln interested himself in particular enterprises in the Caribbean and near the Isthmus of Panama which came to nought. His continued belief in colonization is surprising, for it was wholly impracticable and thoroughly unwelcome to the freedmen, but it showed that he saw dangers of social strife after emancipation which no abolitionist would admit. Also, his insistence on compensation showed his realization of the economic difficulties into which individual slaveholders would otherwise be thrown. Lincoln believed that the success of any policy of emancipation was contingent on the consent of the people most directly affected by it. His preferred policy was one of gradualism, and he tried to interest the State of Delaware in a plan of gradual, compensated emancipation but had no success.

It seemed to the antislavery leaders that the President was compromising with the forces of evil. The old abolitionists and the radical Republicans in Congress wanted the war to be a moral crusade against slavery, and they brought increasing pressure to bear on Lincoln. Within the Cabinet the most conspicuous representative of this school of thought was the Secretary of the Treasury, Salmon P. Chase. One of the most vocal advocates of an active emancipation policy was Horace Greeley of the *New York Tribune,* who addressed to the President on August 20, 1862, what that crusading editor called "The Prayer of Twenty Millions." It was this communication which occasioned Lincoln to make the famous statement that his "paramount object" in the conflict was to save the Union. Greeley did not speak for the overwhelming majority of the Northern people, as he claimed, but he voiced the sentiments of many. These became more insistent when the military conflict was going badly, as it certainly seemed to be before Lee was stopped at Antietam Creek. War weariness was already manifest and the Union cause seemed lacking in inspirational appeal. Defined as it had been by Lincoln, it was not yet clearly seen by the world or by the North as a crusade for freedom. Before he heard from Greeley the President had already decided that if he could not save the Union in the way he wanted to he would have to try another.

The Emancipation Proclamation

On July 22, 1862, before McClellan had withdrawn his troops from the Peninsula or the Second Battle of Bull Run had been fought, Lincoln revealed to his Cabinet his purpose to issue a proclamation of emancipation on grounds of military necessity. Seward suggested that the issuance of such a document in a time of defeat would cause it to be regarded as an act of desperation. Agreeing with him, Lincoln put it in storage until after Antietam, issuing it in preliminary form on September 22, when he thought that victory more complete than actually it was. The essence of the document was that on January 1, 1863, the slaves in the areas that were in rebellion against the Union should be free. Lincoln held that the *loyal* slave states retained their full constitutional rights and, accordingly, should continue to control their domestic institutions.

He had not yet given up his hopes of gradual and compensated emancipation. In his message to Congress on December 1, he proposed an amendment to the Constitution providing that any state which should abolish slavery by the year 1900 would receive compensation according

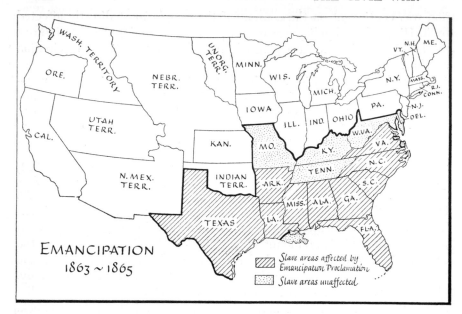

EMANCIPATION
1863 ~ 1865

///// Slave areas affected by
      Emancipation Proclamation
::::: Slave areas unaffected

to a specified procedure. In the fevered emotions of wartime nothing
came of this remarkable proposal, which so generously recognized the
national responsibility for the slavery problem.

As formally issued on January 1, 1863, the Emancipation Proclamation
applied to the seceded states except for Tennessee, which was largely in
Federal hands, and occupied portions of Virginia and Louisiana. That is,
it extended to none of the places where it could have been immediately
enforced, and only to those where it could not yet be put in operation.
Many foreigners commented on this seeming anomaly. Like the blockade,
it existed only on paper at first. To the Confederates it seemed an invitation to slave revolt, and unquestionably it brought hope to any slave who
heard of it. But actually there was no slave insurrection in the South,
and when freedom came it was on the heels of invading armies. In sum,
the famous Proclamation was a dramatic gesture and a declaration of
intention. In itself it struck the shackles from few slaves, and Lincoln
himself wondered if it was strictly legal. But it served its psychological
purpose—less from what it was than from what people thought it was.
In most minds it marked the Northern cause as a crusade for freedom.
Later military victory galvanized the Northern people more than the
Proclamation did, but unquestionably it inspired countless thousands at
home and its effects on foreign opinion were decisive.

British officials wondered about the practical effectiveness of the
Emancipation Proclamation, but it clarified the situation in the minds of
most of the British people. The citizens of Manchester assembled on

New Year's Eve, 1862, and drew up a letter to Lincoln expressing relief and satisfaction. They said:

> We honor your Free States, as a singularly happy abode for the working millions where industry is honored. One thing alone has, in the past, lessened our sympathy with your country and our confidence in it—we mean the ascendancy of politicians who not merely maintained negro slavery, but desired to extend and root it more firmly. Since we have discerned, however, that the victory of the free North . . . will strike off the fetters of the slave, you have attracted our warm and earnest sympathy.

In his turn, Lincoln hailed the workingmen of Britain, and particularly the operatives in the textile mills, as examples of "sublime Christian heroism," giving assurance of "the ultimate and universal triumph of justice, humanity and freedom." Thenceforth no British government dared to favor the South. No less a person than the Confederate Vice-President, Alexander H. Stephens, had said of the new government: "Its foundations are laid, its corner-stone rests, upon the great truth that the negro is not equal to the white man; that slavery—subordination to the superior race—is his natural and moral condition."

The Confederacy had sent abroad contingents of writers and orators who had some success in picturing their cause as a crusade for political freedom. But Lincoln and Seward sent even more effective propagandists, including such a renowned preacher as Henry Ward Beecher and, once they were armed with the Emancipation Proclamation, the Northerners stirred huge audiences to fervent enthusiasm for the cause of the Union. The British people themselves organized numerous societies and mass demonstrations that unmistakably gave the North the victory in the struggle for opinion. Elsewhere in Europe aristocratic governments were also made to understand that a pro-Southern policy might stir revolt at home. Symbolic of Northern success in the diplomacy of opinion was the transformation of foreign attitudes toward Lincoln. At first generally regarded as a backwoods boor, cartooned as a baboon, and described alternatively as a ruthless tyrant and ineffectual shambler, he came to be the synonym of hope "in many a shepherd's lodge in Switzerland—in many a woodman's cabin in the Black Forest—in many a miner's hut in Italy, for there the poor had learned to look upon him as the anointed of God for the redemption of the liberties of mankind." Some appreciation of Lincoln's character finally penetrated even the conservative mind, but this was most strikingly manifested after his assassination sealed his political and military triumph.

THE CLIMAX OF THE WAR, 1863

In the North the winter of 1862-1863 was a winter of discontent. The Republicans suffered a considerable setback in the Congressional elections in the fall, and among the important states carried by Lincoln in 1860 but lost by his party in 1862 was his own Illinois. The pressures of war had created many grievances, but the main one was the lack of military success. The radicals were now gunning for Secretary Seward, whose counsels had generally been moderate. A Republican Senatorial caucus, in which Senator Benjamin F. Wade of Ohio was conspicuous, asked Lincoln to remove the Secretary of State, and Seward himself offered his resignation. But in the midst of the turmoil Secretary Chase, the favorite of the radicals, also offered his resignation, and balancing one against the other Lincoln rode the crisis out. "I have got a pumpkin in each end of my bag," he said. He declined to let either man go and was able to restore a degree of harmony. In a time of declining popularity he showed great political skill, but what he most needed was military victory.

In the West, Halleck had sent General Buell campaigning against Chattanooga, with a view to the "liberation" of East Tennessee where Union sentiment was strong, leaving Grant in West Tennessee with little to do. But Buell, whose slowness exasperated Lincoln, let General Braxton Bragg and a Confederate army elude him and invade Kentucky. Pursuing Bragg, Buell fought an indecisive battle at Perryville in October 1862, after which Bragg withdrew. Then Buell went to Nashville, to start his campaign against Chattanooga all over again. Lincoln removed him, perhaps unjustifiably, and appointed in his stead General William S. Rosecrans. "Old Rosy" finally fought the Battle of Stone's River or Murfreesboro. This began on December 31 and was renewed on January 2, when Bragg attacked and was repulsed. The Confederates then withdrew, but not for a long time was the President to get further action out of Rosecrans. Grant started his difficult and tedious operations against Vicksburg soon after this, but during the spring public attention was centered on the eastern front. In March 1863, Congress passed the Conscription Act, and meanwhile "Fighting Joe" Hooker organized the Army of the Potomac well, restoring its morale.

Chancellorsville

Lee's army at Fredericksburg was now relatively well armed, thanks to captured rifles and artillery pieces. There was beginning to be an ominous scarcity of horses and forage, and even of food for the soldiers, but in morale and organization the Army of Northern Virginia was at or near its peak. In the campaign which began in late April, Lee had slightly more than 62,000 men. Longstreet had been detached to command two divisions below Richmond, where there was a threat from the coast, and the failure to recall him in time to get in the fighting was a Confederate mistake.

Hooker, who had more than twice as many men as Lee, devised an admirable strategical plan to turn his left and threaten his supply lines to the south and southwest. Hooker handled his army well. Leaving a powerful force under Sedgwick to threaten the strongly entrenched Confederate right at Fredericksburg, he threw across the Rappahannock, twenty-odd miles to the west, a force that was larger than Lee's entire army, and it looked as though the Confederates would be either crushed by the pincers or forced to retreat. Lee, leaving a small force on his right, opposed the Federal advance near the crossroads known as Chancellorsville on May 1, and Hooker drew back to a very strong position in this densely wooded country. Thus he lost the initiative, which Lee promptly seized. Lee learned that the Federal right, under the command of General Oliver Otis Howard, was "in the air"—that is, the flank rested on no natural obstacle, and no provision had been made against possible attack from the west. He planned, therefore, a flanking movement to which Jackson contributed the idea that he take his entire corps. The scheme was one of great daring, because Lee would be left to hold the center with only a couple of divisions.

Jackson proceeded by trails and winding roads through the almost impenetrable country, making what speed he could. The Federals believed that the Confederates were retreating in a southwesterly direction. Late in the afternoon of May 2, Jackson hurled his corps at the unsuspecting Union right and threw it back in the utmost confusion, achieving the most spectacular of all his successes before he himself fell wounded by the fire of his own men in the darkness. Next day the Confederate forces, in the center as well as on the left, pressed the attack, bridged the gap in their own lines, and forced a general Federal retreat. But Lee was forced to repair the situation on his own right, where the powerful forces of Sedgwick were overwhelming the weak opposition. Reinforcing that wing, Lee drove the blue-clad forces back in the final fighting, and soon they were again on the north side of the Rappahannock.

With the odds more than 2 to 1 against him, he had won the most brilliant of all his victories, but it cost him Jackson. Learning that Jackson's left arm had been amputated, Lee described him as his right arm, and when the greatest of his lieutenants died of pneumonia after a few days he lost that. Throughout the Confederacy the death of Stonewall was regarded as a supreme misfortune. It is said that no fewer than forty-seven monodies and dirges were written in his honor, and until their dying day Confederate veterans were to assert that with him they lost the war. Beyond a doubt his death marked a turning point in the history of the Army of Northern Virginia, for never again could Lee find another to execute his strategy so unerringly.

The course of events in the two months after Chancellorsville roughly paralleled those after Second Bull Run, for in each case Federal defeat

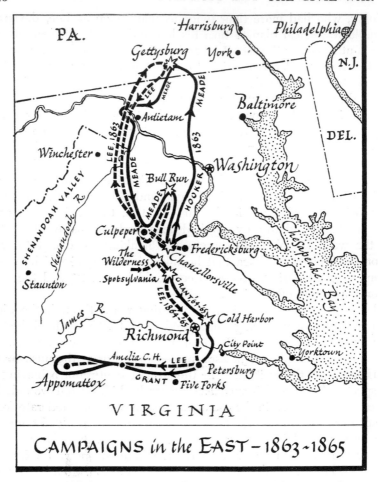

CAMPAIGNS in the EAST - 1863-1865

was followed by an unsuccessful invasion of the North by the Army of
Northern Virginia. Lee was fully aware that the odds against the Confederacy were fast lengthening and was convinced that the only hope
lay in an offensive. Furthermore, in view of the extreme difficulty of
procuring subsistence for his army, the rich grain fields beyond the
Potomac were even more inviting than they had been a year before. In
Pennsylvania he could find food and fat horses. There were political considerations, also; he hoped to strengthen the peace party in the war-
weary North. Finally, he had supreme confidence in his veteran army.
He had reorganized it after the death of Jackson. Previously it had
consisted of two corps, under "Stonewall" and "Old Pete" Longstreet; he
now divided it into three corps, under Longstreet, "Dick" Ewell, and
A. P. Hill, but in reality it was far from a co-ordinated machine when he
started northward. He was overconfident and he underestimated his
opponents.

Gettysburg

In June 1863, the hungry and ill-clad Confederates started northward, with Ewell in the van. Since Lee's army was so widely spread out, Lincoln was convinced that "the animal must be very thin somewhere," and he asked Hooker if he could not break it. It was proceeding through the Shenandoah Valley across Maryland into the Cumberland Valley of Pennsylvania, and Hooker, under Lincoln's pressure, was following it east of the Blue Ridge. There had been many mutterings of discontent against Hooker after Chancellorsville, but Lincoln continued to uphold him until he fell to quarreling with General Halleck about reinforcements. At the very end of July, Hooker offered his resignation and Lincoln accepted it, naming in his place General George Gordon Meade, who had been a corps commander. Meade was not a dramatic soldier or a popular general, but he enjoyed wide respect. He was precipitated into a position of enormous responsibility. Less than a week after his appointment he commanded more than 90,000 men against 70,000 Confederates at Gettysburg, the greatest battle ever fought on the North American continent.

The battle extended through three days, July 1-3, 1863. A few days earlier, Confederate forces under Ewell, who had been collecting supplies, had almost reached Harrisburg, while Hill's corps and Longstreet's were to the southwest. Lee had been deprived of the invaluable services of "Jeb" Stuart, because that dashing cavalry leader, disregarding or misinterpreting his instructions, had ridden around the Union army on a relatively fruitless raid, leaving his Commander virtually without eyes. Not until almost the end of June did Lee realize that the Federals had crossed the Potomac and were near at hand. He then gave orders which led to a concentration at Gettysburg.

The strategic importance of the place had meanwhile been recognized by the Union command, especially by General John F. Reynolds, and advance detachments of the two armies ran into each other on July 1. The Confederates had the advantage in the fighting on that day, on which Reynolds, one of the best of the Union generals, was killed. They gained possession of Seminary Ridge which runs from north to south to the westward of the town. If Jackson had been in command on the Confederate left instead of the less experienced and more indecisive Ewell they might have gained Cemetery Ridge, which was then only lightly held, but which the Federals occupied with steadily increasing forces the next day. In this position of great natural strength, Meade received the attack.

As countless thousands of visitors to this famous battlefield have observed, Seminary Ridge and Cemetery Ridge are roughly parallel, with about a mile of open ground between them. The Union position, including the hills just south of the town (East Cemetery Hill and Culp's Hill), was in the general shape of an inverted fishhook, dominated at the south by Big Round Top and Little Round Top. The Union forces were operating on the interior line, and the vain attempts of the Confederates to take the key hills on the Union right and left flanks marked the fighting on the second day. The slowness of the Confederates in getting their attacks under way has been commonly blamed on the obstinacy of General Longstreet, who did not approve of Lee's plan of battle, preferring to stand on the defensive. The attacks on the two wings were not well correlated, and the Federal concentration was steadily increasing.

On the third day Lee, over Longstreet's protest, ordered an attack on the Federal right center by 15,000 men. This was led by the division of General George E. Pickett, who gave his name to "Pickett's Charge." After a furious artillery duel, three divisions charged over open ground with their colors flying. Some of them reached the crest of Cemetery Ridge and held parts of it briefly, but were forced to retreat. The losses were enormous, including several generals; Pickett himself survived but considerably less than half of his division did. The failure of the charge ended the battle. "It is all my fault," said Lee—not mentioning Longstreet, Ewell, and Stuart, to all of whom he had permitted too great discretion and all of whom had failed him at crucial moments in this campaign. Critics are generally agreed that this was Lee's worst-fought battle, and all have praised the steadfastness of the Army of the Potomac and its skillfull tactics.

Meade did not counterattack on July 3 after Pickett's charge, or on July 4, when the Confederates were waiting. The punishment his army had received is shown by the fact that Federal casualties in the battle as a whole were about 23,000, including prisoners, while the Confederate were nearly 3,000 fewer. He had fought an admirable defensive battle and richly deserved the thanks of the Union, as did General Winfield S. Hancock and others. But Meade was undisposed to assume the offensive against a strong Confederate position; and on the night of July 4 the Confederate retreat began in a heavy rain. This so slowed the movements of Lee's army that he might have been successfully attacked. Nearly all the Union corps commanders thought such action inadvisable, however, and, while Meade was thinking about it, the Confederates crossed the Potomac about the middle of July.

Meade and his magnificent army had driven the redoubtable invader from Northern soil, but the failure to smash the Army of Northern Virginia was a deep disappointment to Abraham Lincoln. A few days after Gettysburg, Lee wrote Jefferson Davis offering to resign his command to a younger and abler man, but the Confederate President recognized that Lee was quite irreplaceable. Lincoln did not replace Meade, but he had a commander in the West who offered more. On the same day that news of Gettysburg reached the President he learned that Vicksburg had surrendered to General Grant. This was a more decisive victory and in the light of history it seems considerably more important.

Vicksburg and Port Hudson

The Gettysburg campaign proved conclusively that the Confederate armed forces could not successfully invade the Union and force a peace, but the most significant demonstration of the ability of the Union to conquer the Confederacy was given when the whole of the Mississippi River was taken, and the three western states—Arkansas, Louisiana, and Texas—were wholly cut off. In the early months of 1863, the Southerners were still in sufficient control of the stretch of some 150 miles between Vicksburg and Port Hudson, just above Baton Rouge. The Confederacy had never availed itself fully of the resources of its Southwest because of inadequate facilities of transportation, but food products and troops could still be taken across the river. Northern gunboats could run by Vicksburg, but the city, set on a high bluff, was virtually impregnable to direct assault and practically unapproachable by land from the north. Originally, Grant tried to approach it that way but attempts by him and Sherman failed. He then conceived the plan of getting past the fortress and approaching it under more favorable physical conditions from the south and east. After wasting weeks in ingenious but vain attempts to cut a canal in a bend of the river, Grant, with the invaluable co-operation of Rear Admiral David D. Porter, ran his transports past the strong Vicksburg batteries to a point far below the city, and at the end of April he ferried his troops across the river to Bruinsburg and high ground on the eastern side. It was an exceedingly difficult operation, performed at a time when Grant's fame was largely in eclipse and when he had practically no friend in high places except Lincoln himself.

In command of Union forces in eastern Louisiana was General Banks, and Grant first hoped to co-operate with him in a move against Port Hudson which would give him a line of supply and communication down the river to New Orleans. But, because of delay on the part of Banks and his own preference for a bolder and more dangerous policy, he determined to live upon the country. He communicated his plan to Halleck too late for the General-in-Chief to make effective protest. Other commanders on both sides had lived upon the country to some extent, but Grant, isolated from his base, did so with unexampled thoroughness. His military operations were marked by bold strategy and skillful tactics. He had to deal with two Confederate armies which jointly exceeded his own in numbers at the outset; he kept them apart and defeated them in detail.

At this point, Confederate strategy bogged down in confusion. General John C. Pemberton was in command of the larger Southern force near

Vicksburg, while Joseph E. Johnston, who had been hastily despatched to this area by President Davis, had a smaller force to the westward near Jackson. Johnston was supposedly in command of the whole area, but Pemberton understood that his orders from Davis required him to hold Vicksburg at any cost. The result was that the armies were not united as Johnston knew they ought to be. Johnston's relatively small army was defeated and driven beyond Jackson, and then Pemberton's was defeated and driven back to Vicksburg. Grant's forces fought five battles altogether but these two were the most important. On May 19, after three weeks of masterly activity, he directly attacked Vicksburg only to be repulsed. He settled down to a siege and within a few days Banks besieged Port Hudson. Vicksburg was invested for nearly seven weeks, while the citizens lived in caves and ran out of food. Grant established supply lines to the North and his forces grew to more than 70,000. Finally, on July 4, the unfortunate Pemberton, who had been an unjust object of suspicion to the Southerners on account of his Northern birth, saw no choice but to surrender the city. With it went nearly 30,000 prisoners, many cannon, and a very large supply of superior small arms that had been imported from Europe. Even in numerical terms, this was by far the greatest Union victory to date, and when the defenders of Port Hudson, bowing to the inevitable, surrendered to Banks five days later, the Father of Waters, as Lincoln said, flowed "unvexed to the sea."

This really meant that the Mississippi Valley, in which Grant and Lincoln had been born, was physically reunited. It was no accident that this result was achieved by a Western General, strongly supported by a Western President, for no one realized more fully than they the enormous importance of the inland waterways. Grant not only lopped three states from the Confederacy; he restored the American heartland to the Union.

Chattanooga

On July 4, 1863, with Gettysburg and Vicksburg, the war passed its climax. There was virtually no action on the eastern front until another spring, but Grant wrote a fitting sequel to his campaign at Chattanooga. This vital railroad center at the southern end of the valley of East Tennessee was second in strategic importance only to Vicksburg in the inland Confederate states.

For six months after the Battle of Stone's River or Murfreesboro the Army of the Cumberland under General Rosecrans was inactive; but, spurred by Lincoln, "Old Rosy" had maneuvered out of Tennessee the Confederate Army under Braxton Bragg by the time that Grant captured Vicksburg. Early in September he occupied Chattanooga. Meanwhile, a small Union army under Burnside had entered East Tennessee from the north, though it did not get close to Rosecrans. In the meantime, also,

Bragg had been reinforced by Longstreet's corps from Lee's army and by other troops. The Confederates now had the numerical advantage, and Rosecrans moved against them unwisely in rough country east of Chattanooga. On September 20, 1863, at Chickamauga the Confederates won a victory, pouring through a gap in the Federal line. Disaster was prevented by the firm stand of the Federal left under Thomas, and it was because of this that he was called the "Rock of Chickamauga." All of the command of Rosecrans retired to Chattanooga, which was virtually besieged.

Lincoln ordered that it be held at all costs. Some 20,000 men under "Fighting Joe" Hooker were sent from Meade's inactive Army of the Potomac to reinforce Rosecrans; and the movement of these troops by a roundabout rail route was perhaps the most striking feat of Federal logistics during the entire war. Furthermore, in October, Lincoln put Grant in command of all the Western armies except those beyond the Mississippi. Grant replaced Rosecrans by Thomas, and on October 23 he himself arrived in Chattanooga to assume full command. Under him, besides Thomas and Hooker, was Sherman with troops from Vicksburg. Bragg, who had dispatched Longstreet against Burnside in East Tennessee, was considerably outnumbered, but he had powerful positions on the heights to the east and south of the city.

The Battle of Chattanooga (November 23-25) was a decisive Federal victory. Sherman met with insurmountable physical difficulties on the Confederate right, where Grant had expected the decisive blow to be delivered, but the Union center under Thomas stormed the Confederate position on Missionary Ridge, taking the heights to the surprise of everybody. Bragg was forced to retreat into Georgia, where he was replaced by Joseph E. Johnston in December. About the same time Longstreet, repulsed at Knoxville, retreated to the northeast, leaving virtually the entire state of Tennessee to Federal occupation.

Disorganized warfare continued in the lower Mississippi Valley, but by the end of 1863 the effective Confederacy was virtually reduced to the South Atlantic states and Alabama. Grant had divided the Southern republic in twain and set the stage for Sherman to quarter it. Northern victory was now practically inevitable. Yet, there was to be desperate fighting for another year and more, along with vast civil confusion and human suffering.

CHAPTER 39

North and South in Wartime

NORTHERNERS AND SOUTHERNERS cherished the same traditions of personal liberty and were alike unprepared for the restrictions and discipline which are inevitable in a long and grueling war. Therefore, Abraham Lincoln and Jefferson Davis faced similar governmental problems and were subjected to the same sort of criticism. The most striking contrast between the warring sections lay in the effects of the conflict on the two economies and societies. Viewed close up the war was not a pretty picture on the side of the civilians any more than it was on the bloody battlefields, in the military prisons, and in the hospitals. But Northern society felt the impetus of increased economic activity and the stimulus of property, while the people of the South came to lack the very necessities of life.

PRESIDENTIAL GOVERNMENT IN THE UNION

Lincoln as President exercised authority which was quite unexampled in the United States before his time, and he differed from his successors in office during the First and Second World Wars in the degree to which he assumed extraordinary power without being authorized to do so by acts of Congress. He based his procedure on the legal ground that he had taken an oath to preserve, protect, and defend the Constitution and that he was Commander-in-Chief; and he justified his actions on considerations of practical necessity. In the course of the war, as his biographer, James G. Randall, has said, he "extended his sphere of activity throughout the whole government—civil and military, state and Federal, legislative and judicial as well as executive." In the Emancipation Proclamation he formulated policy without reference to Congress; he promulgated a code for governing armies in the field without waiting for the legislature to adopt it, and he set up courts in occupied districts in the South on his own authority. This was presidential government such as the country had never known, and it provoked a powerful Congressional reaction on which the radical Republicans capitalized. But Lincoln created the enduring precedent that in time of crisis the President must have power enough to save the country. In two world wars in the next century Congress granted it.

Arbitrary Arrests

Lincoln's curtailment of the rights of individuals, in the name of military necessity, aroused vigorous objection. The most mooted question was that of the suspension of the writ of habeas corpus and arbitrary arrests. The Constitution provides that the privilege of habeas corpus shall not be suspended except when in cases of rebellion or invasion the public safety may require it. On April 27, 1861, Lincoln authorized military commanders to suspend it in order to keep the railroad line open between Philadelphia and Washington at a time when there was strong pro-Southern sentiment in Maryland. The actions of military men under executive sanction in that state were exceedingly high-handed. In September, the Mayor of Baltimore was arrested, as were nine members of the Maryland legislature who were suspected of being disloyal to the Union. Somewhat earlier, the arrest of an obscure man named John Merryman led Chief Justice Taney to declare, while serving on the Circuit Court, that the power to suspend the writ of habeas corpus lay only with Congress. This was not an official pronouncement of the Supreme Court, but it put Lincoln on the defensive. In his message to Congress that summer the harassed President asked this question: "Are all the laws *but one*, to go unexecuted, and the government itself go to pieces lest that one be violated?" In his opinion a perilous situation warranted drastic measures.

The question whether the President or the Congress had the right to decide on the removal of this safeguard of individual liberty was not answered. On September 24, 1862, the day after the preliminary proclamation of emancipation, Lincoln suspended the privilege of the writ of habeas corpus throughout the country. In the following spring, on March 3, 1863, Congress at length passed an act saying that the President was authorized to do this whenever in his judgment the public safety might require it. It is uncertain whether this meant that Congress recognized that Lincoln was already authorized or that Congress now authorized him, but on September 15, 1863, on the eve of important state elections, Lincoln issued another proclamation to the same effect.

He believed that the problem of disloyalty in the Union required executive action, and that speed was imperative where the danger was so immediate. In a conflict like the Civil War, between people of the same blood and tongue, spying was relatively easy on both sides. There were many in the North who were unsympathetic with a war against the Southern states, and some—especially along the border—who were willing to give secret aid to the Confederates. Also, there were critics of the policies of the government who might be deemed subversive.

Political arrests were under the Department of State at first and Seward was so foolish as to question, on hearsay evidence, the loyalty of ex-President Franklin Pierce, who wrote a blistering letter in rejoinder. There was no move to arrest Pierce, but the story went round that Seward could ring a bell and arrest anybody anywhere, while only the President of the United States could release the prisoner. Soon after Stanton became Secretary of War, early in 1862, these operations were transferred to his department, and there were upwards of 13,500 political arrests thereafter. Many prisoners were not long detained and they do not appear to have been harshly treated as a rule. Probably the best known of Lincoln's words on this subject are these: "Must I shoot a simple-minded soldier boy who deserts, while I must not touch a hair of a wily agitator who induces him to desert?" Actually, deserters were not often shot, for there were far too many of them, and Lincoln did his best to make it clear that political arrests were preventive, not punitive. He would leave no stone unturned in his effort to save the Union, but it was not in his nature to be vindictive.

The New York Draft Riot

Opposition to the draft law of 1863 was widespread. It was most strikingly shown in the Draft Riot in the ninth district of New York City on July 13-14 of that year—which was after the victories of Gettysburg and Vicksburg. Enrollment under the act was by house-to-house canvass and it was marked by only slight disturbance. The first day for the drawing of conscripts in New York was Saturday, July 11, and when the names were published in the Sunday papers it appeared that they consisted almost wholly of artisans and laborers. The provisions for relief by paying $300 or hiring a substitute had already aroused indignation among those who could not afford to do either, and a mob stormed the office of the provost marshal at Third Avenue and 46th Street on Monday, driving him away. The place was set on fire, soldiers and policemen were overpowered, and the rioting was even worse on Tuesday. On Wednesday, following the announcement that the draft would be suspended, things quieted down. A large detachment from the Army of the Potomac and the New York National Guard now appeared. Governor Horatio Seymour, who had opposed the law anyway, wanted it to remain suspended until the results of the recruiting of volunteers in New York were known. Lincoln declined to permit this, but he did bring about reductions of quotas in disputed districts and the drawing was peacefully resumed on

August 19. Since Seymour was a Democrat, his attitude in this dispute has often been attributed to political motives, but the sincerity of his devotion to the Union need not be questioned. Lincoln himself made a special point of *not* identifying disloyalty with the Democratic Party, but more extreme Republicans, who were now organizing themselves in Union Leagues, were disposed to do so. Their political line was to claim that only Republicans were true Unionists and that the Democrats were Copperheads.

The Copperheads

Lincoln could not have conducted the war successfully if he had not had the support of the Democrats in crucial matters. In this time of confused party alignment there was, however, a Peace Party with a rather nebulous program and there were antiwar rallies. It was difficult to determine whether or not these went beyond the point of justifiable dissent and became a danger to the Union cause. Some criticism of the conduct of the war was made by Democratic politicians for partisan purposes, and the Peace Party consisted chiefly of Democrats, but a "Peace Democrat" was not the same thing as a Copperhead.

To most people this word suggested a venomous snake, though some sought to identify it with the copper coin, symbolic of the plain people. Passionate Unionists often applied the term to people who were merely expressing discontent. More properly it can be applied to various groups of people who met secretly, discouraged enlistment, encouraged desertion, and even sought to give direct aid to the Confederacy. One group of the sort in the first half of the war was the "Knights of the Golden Circle," an organization which had been active in the "Young America" movement of the previous decade. It was not important in the war years but it was obstructive. Another was the "Order of American Knights," which changed its name to "Sons of Liberty," thus attempting to link itself with the American Revolution. Of this organization the notorious Clement L. Vallandigham of Ohio became the supreme grand commander. He remains until this day the symbol of the Copperheads.

Vallandigham, who was forty-three at the time of his celebrated case in 1863, was born in Ohio but came of Southern stock. A handsome man and an effective speaker, he had long been a prominent local politician; he served in Congress but was defeated for re-election in 1862. Virtually, he was for peace at any price, and he appealed to the war-weary masses by demagogic speeches in which Lincoln and the Republicans were unsparingly denounced. A few weeks before the battle of Gettysburg and the fall of Vicksburg he got into trouble with the Federal military authorities in the Department of the Ohio, commanded by General Burnside after the Battle of Fredericksburg. Burnside in April 1863, without consulting Lincoln, issued General Order Number 38, with a view to preventing disloyal speech and action. On May 1, Vallandigham made a fiery speech to a Democratic mass meeting, and on May 5 Burnside caused him to be arrested. He was tried by a military commission, found guilty of disloyalty and disobedience to the General Order, and sentenced to imprisonment for the rest of the war.

The conviction of a prominent Democratic politician by a military tribunal for disobedience to a military order aroused a storm of protest. Vallandigham was an unworthy symbol of the right of free speech, for he had dangerously abused it, but civilians had no stomach for military rule, and this was not the only instance of Burnside's high-handedness. Soon he suppressed the *Chicago Times* because of its criticisms of him. Lincoln made him revoke the order against this newspaper and greatly regretted his action with respect to Vallandigham, believing that it would have been better to let that fanatical demagogue defeat himself by his own excesses. The President's solution of the difficulty was one of characteristic political adroitness. He commuted the sentence, directing that Vallandigham be sent beyond the Federal military lines. So he was delivered to the surprised Confederates in Tennessee. Soon he made his way to Canada and when he came back to the North in 1864 he was unmolested. In June 1863, the Ohio Democrats were so foolish as to nominate the exile for governor, but in the fall he was decisively defeated.

Loyalty and Politics

Vallandigham imparted to the Democratic Party a stigma of disloyalty which as a whole it clearly did not deserve. Also, his case and the policy it illustrated had real constiutional significance. In effect, the Supreme Court upheld the action of the military commission by declining to review it at the time, but in the famous Milligan case in 1866, after Lincoln was dead and the war was over, the Supreme Court condemned recourse to military tribunals where the civil courts are open. Actually there was little interference with free speech in Lincoln's administration, but it was inevitable that there should have been strong protest against the general policy of arbitrary arrests, and there was constant danger that in the crusade for freedom against the South there would be a loss of freedom in the North. Lincoln himself tempered severity with humor, kindness, and common sense, but in more ruthless and more selfish hands such power as he assumed would have been extremely perilous.

Further illustrations of the effects of wartime policies on the normal liberties of citizens and the normal operations of government can be given from developments in the states. Lincoln's own native commonwealth of Kentucky was under martial law in 1863 when state elections were held, and tests of loyalty were applied to voters by military authorities. The Republican Party had little standing in Kentucky, so the contest was between Union Democrats and Peace Democrats. The victory gained by the former was probably representative of public opinion, but this was the outcome that the Union generals and the President wanted.

In Lincoln's Illinois, and even more notoriously in neighboring Indiana, another sort of abnormality appeared. Both of these states happened to have Republican governors while the Democrats controlled the legislatures. The Republican minorities in the latter, by absenting themselves, made it impossible to gain a quorum; and as a result there was gubernatorial government without a legislature. The President himself made an advance of $250,000 from federal funds at his disposal in support of the state of Indiana, believing that a "loyal" government must be maintained there regardless of irregularity. Scholars of today, removed from the emotions of wartime, wonder if such extreme measures were necessary since the Democrats in Indiana do not appear to have been disloyal.

In his overpowering concern to win the war, Lincoln at times let himself be made an instrument of partisanship. He strengthened his hold on his own party by so doing, and he presented a notable contrast to Jefferson Davis by attaching the governors to him by ties of interest and thus reducing the rivalry between the state and federal governments which was the bane of the Confederacy. His political tactics were not above reproach but his strategy was sound.

The formal test of his own political strength came in the presidential election of 1864, but the year 1863 was crucial in politics as well as on the battlefield, and he gained greatly after the setback in 1862. This was partly because the military tide had turned and partly because of shrewd politics, but there was another important reason. The so-called Peace Party could offer no feasible alternative to his basic policy. Complaint against infringements on personal liberty was natural and proper in a self-governing society and it could have been made in the spirit of complete loyalty. But there was abundant reason to believe that the Confederate authorities would make peace on no other terms except independence, and to have conceded that would have been to make the whole struggle for the Union vain. It is not surprising, therefore, that the year 1863 was marked by a series of victories for the Unionist Party. There were divergent groups within it, and Lincoln had no sympathy with the vindictive spirit toward the South already being manifested by radical Republicans who claimed to have a monopoly on Unionism.

Lincoln's political maneuvers have long since been forgotten by nearly all of his countrymen, but his interpretation of the meaning of the conflict remains. He expressed it in its most moving form in the brief address he delivered on November 19, 1863, at the dedication of the military cemetery at Gettysburg. Edward Everett, who spoke two hours, afterwards remarked that Lincoln said as much in two minutes. Few of the weary thousands who stood through the ceremonies may have really heard what the gaunt and homely President was saying or realized that they were listening to a prose poem that was destined to be graven on stone and immortalized in human hearts. There was no trace of vindictiveness, no shadow of partisanship, no suggestion of arrogance in the matchless words in which he proclaimed the mission of the American Union. To his mind, the war was a supreme test of whether a nation conceived in liberty and dedicated to human equality could endure. Despite the vast authority he had assumed, he wanted this nation to have a new birth of freedom and prayed that democratic government should persist. These were not the words of a demagogue or a dictator, but of a humble man, borne down with almost intolerable responsibility, who meant precisely what he said.

POLITICAL CONFLICT IN THE CONFEDERACY

Presidential government did not go as far in the South as in the North, though the same sort of charges were hurled against Jefferson Davis as against Lincoln. In the midst of the conflict one of his fellow Mississippians described him as a "miserable, stupid, one-eyed, dyspeptic, arrogant tyrant," and his enemies declared that their President was the greatest of the misfortunes of the Confederacy. There was no early prospect of getting anybody else, for he had been elected for a six-year term.

The dislike of Vice-President Stephens for Davis increased as the war went on. This strange little man, who was something of a defeatist from the beginning, absented himself from Richmond for a year and a half in the middle of the war, leaving his duties as presiding officer of the Senate to be performed by another while he nursed his feeble health and constitutional scruples at his home in Georgia. Davis himself had lost the sight of one eye, he suffered from dyspepsia, and his nerves robbed him of sleep. Also, there was a stiffness in his manner which gave color to the charge of arrogance. But despite physical troubles he was an incessant worker, and this stickler for constitutional regularity was not of the stuff from which revolutionary dictators are made.

Unlike Lincoln, he specifically asked the legislative branch of the government to authorize him to suspend the writ of habeas corpus. The successive grants of power by the Confederate Congress were limited in time and scope. During more than half of the war (February 27, 1862 —August 1, 1864) the privilege of the writ was suspended in certain exposed districts, though Davis was denied the necessary authority in the last year, when chaos reigned and he most needed it. Until nearly the end of the war the Congress generally gave Davis the legislation he requested, and during the first half of the conflict the attacks on his appointees were stronger than on himself.

The favorite Congressional target was Judah P. Benjamin, sometimes described as the "Sphinx" of the Confederacy. This brilliant lawyer, a Sephardic Jew who was born in the British West Indies and had been associated in his American career chiefly with New Orleans, always seemed something of an alien to the main body of Southern politicians. He wore a perpetual smile on his inscrutable face and his administrative gifts were great, but he lacked the born politician's sensitivity to popular opinion. Davis relied on him greatly, and when Benjamin as Secretary of War was bitterly but unfairly condemned for the Confederate loss, in 1862, of Fort Donelson and Roanoke Island off the North Carolina coast, the President appointed him Secretary of State. It was a loyal act but hardly good politics. A strong Congressional faction supported General Joseph E. Johnston in his continuing disagreement with Davis, and there was much feeling in Congress against the President's supposed favorite, General Braxton Bragg. On the whole, however, members of the Confederate Congress brought less pressure on Davis in the matter of military appointments and assignments than the Congressional leaders in the North did on Lincoln, and there was nothing in the Confederacy comparable to the Congressional Joint Committee on the Conduct of the War.

The South, like the North, had its problems of disloyalty. In the Union the most disaffected regions were along the border. In the Confederacy, they were in the mountain districts and in the Valley of East Tennessee, which was promptly occupied by Confederate forces and subjected to martial law. Senator Andrew Johnson from this region remained in the United States Congress after secession, gaining much Northern acclaim and Southern abuse for his action. This doughty Unionist, whose concept of the purpose of the war closely coincided with that of Lincoln, was appointed, early in 1862, as Military Governor of his state, though the part of it that was most loyal to the Union and disloyal to the Confederacy was not under Northern military control for another year. Another Unionist from East Tennessee, William G. Brownlow, a one-time Methodist preacher best known as "Parson" Brownlow, provided the closest Southern parallel to Vallandigham. His newspaper, the *Knoxville Whig*, was suspended by Confederate military authority early in the war, and he himself was put through the Confederate lines into the Federal. He made many violent speeches to Northern audiences and ultimately came back to Tennessee to play an important part in the government of his state.

Outspoken opponents of the Confederacy were soon silenced throughout the South, but there was continuing fear of spies and traitors, along with dread of slave revolt. Early in the war Vigilance Committees were organized in towns and counties, and members of these groups searched out persons suspected of disloyalty, often arresting suspicious strangers. Persons of Northern birth were suspect; and admitted Republicans, who were rare birds, were promptly apprehended. After a few months civil and military authorities assumed the place of the Vigilance Committees. Exact figures about political prisoners are not available but there were a good many of them in various prisons, especially in "Castle Thunder" in Richmond.

The suspension of the writ of habeas corpus came later in the South than in the North and was more limited in its geographical scope, but it was objected to by the citizenry in much the same way. Almost as grievous was the conduct of provost marshals, who were originally a sort of military police functioning in the vicinity of armies but whose activities were increasingly extended into the civilian sphere. Passports came to be required of travelers, to the vast annoyance of many civilians, including Congressmen. The greatest of Southern grievances arose, however, from conscription and from the impressment of property. These grievances were directed, not against the army, on which Southern pride always centered, and not against the states, but against the Confederate government. Not only were certain governors opponents of the conscription policy on principle; also, as we have seen, some of them took advantage of the provision exempting state officials to withdraw from the draft a disproportionate number of the residents of their own states, thus assuming the role of protector of their people against a tyrannical government. The Confederate Constitution provided for a Supreme Court but none was ever set up, so there was no appeal from the state supreme courts. The latter generally upheld Confederate laws, but there were eleven separate tribunals and some of them were obstructive. At the very end of the war, certain state courts issued writs of habeas corpus in behalf of conscripts seeking to escape military service.

Governors against President

The conflict between the Confederate government and the officials of individual states was modified or accentuated by military circumstances. Tennessee, which was largely controlled by the Union armies from a relatively early date, soon ceased to have a state government with which Davis could deal; and midway in the war the trans-Mississippi states were cut off. The states of Alabama and Mississippi were generally loyal to Davis until their own governments so deteriorated from 1863 onward that they were incapable of either full co-operation with the Confederacy or strong resistance to it. In the South Atlantic states, Davis had severe newspaper critics in the persons of Edward A. Pollard of Richmond and Robert Barnwell Rhett of the *Charleston Mercury,* but he had relatively slight difficulty with the governments of their respective states. Virginia was always a scene of major fighting and Davis was charged with favoritism to that state, while South Carolina, which had played such a vital part in starting the war, was determined to stake all on the outcome. In 1863, when Rhett offered himself as a candidate for the Confederate House of Representatives he was rejected by the electorate of his own district. Davis had his greatest troubles with the governors of North Carolina and Georgia.

Besides having an unusually large number of nonslaveholders and original opponents of secession, these states had strong champions of their rights in their governors, Zebulon B. Vance and Joseph E. Brown. Vance was elected in 1862 after pledging himself to a vigorous prosecution of the war, and in 1864 he was re-elected, defeating W. W. Holden, an advocate of peace by negotiation. Vance was a great war governor, but there was strong and persistent opposition to conscription in North Carolina and he believed it unwise to enforce the law severely upon an unwilling people. He was generous toward deserters, supported the prerogatives of the state courts against the authority of conscription officials, and upheld writs of habeas corpus. Some of the North Carolina courts were conspicuously obstructive of the war effort of the Confederacy, but many of the differences between Vance and Davis arose from misunderstanding. Governor Joseph E. Brown of Georgia, with the support of Alexander H. Stephens and others, was in sharper conflict with the Confederate government. He was always opposed to the conscription policy; he continued to insist on the right of Georgia troops to select their own officers; and toward the end of the war, after the fall of Atlanta, he openly defied the Davis government, refusing the demand for troops and raising them on his own authority.

From the middle years of the war Southerners were asking an exceedingly difficult question: if they must surrender their rights as individuals and as states to their central government, what were they fighting for? The same sort of question was asked in the North, to be sure, but Lincoln evoked a new vision of the Union and its historic mission. Also, except for an occasional Democrat, he attached the state governors to him by political bonds, while in the South many factors combined to alienate state executives from Davis. Internal political conflict did much to weaken the Confederacy, and from the history of the short-lived Southern Republic important lessons can be learned. One of them is that doctrines of state rights, while protecting citizens against the excesses of centralized power, are divisive in their influence and are in themselves inadequate in any crisis that demands co-operative effort. It is too much to say that the Confederacy "died of state rights," but unquestionably the Southern cause suffered greatly from them in a war which ultimately approached totality.

FINANCES: NORTH AND SOUTH

The Union

Fiscal policies in the North were largely improvised at first and reflected the early belief that the war would be short. The Secretary of the Treasury, Salmon P. Chase, was little experienced in public finance. He had to learn the hard way, and he inherited from the Buchanan administration a chaotic situation. Chase worked incessantly at his particular job, but he was obsessed with presidential ambitions, and nowhere more than in his department can the growth of a federal bureaucracy be seen. There were fewer than 400 clerks in the Treasury in Washington when he became Secretary, but when he left this office in 1864 there were 2000. One of the enduring criticisms of Chase is that he relied too much on loans, and on short-term loans; he did not insist soon enough on taxation. But if such taxes had been recommended at the start as were afterwards imposed, it is highly unlikely that Congress would have agreed to them. Nobody foresaw what huge expenditures would be necessary, and the people were quite unused to taxes.

During the four years of the war the net receipts of the federal government amounted to approximately $3.5 billion, the over-all ratio of loans to taxes being about 4 to 1. In the first year the ratio was about 8½ to 1, and by the last year it was about 3 to 1. The increase in the proportion of taxes may never have been as great as was desirable and it certainly did not come soon enough, but it considerably reflected the change in the total situation. In the first year of the conflict the economy of the North was disrupted and military prospects were discouraging, while in the last year business was booming and eventual military victory seemed inevitable. The issues of paper money known as "Greenbacks" are not included in the foregoing figures and the recourse of the government to them is open to serious criticism.

The Tariff and Excise Taxes

When the war began, the support of the government was dependent on revenue from customs duties, since the unpopular excise taxes had been given up in 1818. Beginning with the internal revenue measure of July 1, 1862, there was increasing reliance on excise taxes, and by the third year of the war receipts from these exceeded those from duties and imports. Nevertheless, considering the four-year period as a whole, customs receipts, which were in gold, comprised almost half (about $305 million) of the total from taxes. This result was attained despite the fact that the war tariff measures increasingly emphasized the principle of protection and were less and less designed with a view to revenue. This part of the wartime financial legislation was destined to be long-lived, for the policy of high protection persisted after the abnormal circumstances that gave rise to it had disappeared.

The Morrill Tariff of March 2, 1861, marked the end of the low-tariff policy which had generally prevailed during the previous generation and which Southern producers of export crops had so strongly espoused. This Act of the last Congress of the Buchanan administration, after the bulk of the Southern Representatives and Senators had withdrawn, was designed to increase revenue, but by raising rates on iron and wool it moved in the protectionist direction and was expected to help the Republicans in the Middle States and the West. Other duties were raised in supplementary measures, but the next Act of major importance was that of July 14, 1862. This followed the Internal Revenue Act of that month, which had imposed new taxes on industry, and higher tariff duties were regarded as compensation. The same argument was applied with increased force in the Tariff of June 30, 1864, at a time when excise taxes were still higher. But for the abnormalities of wartime, such a measure could hardly have been passed, and this Act was passed very hastily.

Meanwhile, various industries were clamoring for more and more protection, and their requests were granted with little discrimination and little thought that such high duties would remain long after the crisis had ended. In the famous compromise Tariff of 1833, the South Carolinians had settled for an average rate of 20 per cent, to be gradually arrived at; in the Tariff of 1862 the average had risen to more than 37 per cent, and in the Act of 1864 it had soared to more than 47 per cent.

An interesting feature of wartime finance was the income tax, which was effective during the last three years of the conflict. In that time it brought in about $55 million, and there were large returns from it until 1872. Then it was dropped—to be revived in 1894, whereupon it was declared unconstitutional. In its final wartime form, it carried an exemption of incomes under $600, and levied taxes from 5 to a maximum of 10 per cent. It was borne cheerfully in the war years and might well have been relied on more.

More vexatious were the internal revenue or excise taxes, imposed in moderate form upon a large number of articles on July 1, 1862. Greatly increased in June 1864, they produced in the last year of the war about twice as much revenue as the tariff. Besides imposing taxes on alcoholic liquors and tobacco of the sort that continued through later generations, these laws taxed virtually everything else that anybody could think of. The list included yachts and carriages, steamboats and railroads, factories and banks, livestock and advertisements, bolts and rivets and steam engines. In the first year after the war, before this list was trimmed down, the returns were greater than during the whole war period and by that time they clearly reflected the unparalleled prosperity of the country.

Loans

The war was financed primarily by loans. Only about 40 per cent of these were long-term loans, to which Secretary Chase was opposed on principle. He was like Jefferson in not wanting to burden the coming generation, and not unlike Andrew Jackson in his distrust of bankers. He wanted interest to be kept low, and although authorized to float bonds at 6 per cent, he held out for 5 per cent. As a result he had difficulty in marketing bonds through ordinary banking channels. In 1863, he employed Jay Cooke as agent with great success and achieved the sort of wide distribution that he himself favored. Cooke, who is sometimes described as the financier of the Civil War, was also used by Chase's successor but William Pitt Fessenden, taking no chances of failure, floated a loan at 6 per cent interest.

Currency

Another consequence of Chase's dislike of long-term loans was that he had to resort to short-term notes at more than 7 per cent interest. Also, he issued "Demand Notes" (within a prescribed limit of $50 million); these did not bear interest and virtually circulated as money. They were receivable for public dues, and were redeemable in gold until the suspension of specie payments at the end of 1861. Most of them were retired before the end of the war, being succeeded by legal tender notes or Greenbacks, which Chase did not favor.

Beginning in February 1862, Greenbacks to the amount of $450 million were authorized by successive acts of Congress and at the end of the war nearly $433 million of these were outstanding, besides some $26 million in fractional currency. These were receivable for public and private debts, except customs duties and interest on bonds (payable in coin). The presumption was that they would ultimately be redeemable in gold, but no time was set and no specific provision was made for their redemption. Thus they amounted to fiat money, and there was considerable question at the time and afterwards about their constitutionality. They depreciated in terms of gold, descending in July 1864 to the low point of 39 cents and rising to about 70 cents at the end of the war. Their effect on prices was unquestionably inflationary. It has been estimated that the cost of the war was increased by about $600 million by the depreciation of the currency.

Specie payments were suspended by the banks at the end of 1861 and the currency fell into confusion. In the year 1862, there were about 1500 banks that issued notes of bewildering variety under divergent state charters and often upon insufficient security. The circulation of bank-notes increased from $130 to $167 million that year, and, while this may not have exceeded the needs of the country for currency, the effects of the increase were inflationary. It was out of this situation that the National Banking System was created and it proved to be Chase's most enduring financial monument. The National Banking Act of February 25, 1863, permitted the formation of national banks which could issue bank notes on United States bonds owned by them and deposited with the Treasury. The limit was 90 per cent of the market value (but not to exceed 90 per cent of par value). These notes were receivable by the government except for customs duties and were payable by the government except for its debt and interest on its bonds. National bank notes were not an obligation of the government, but reliable bank currency was provided for, and a national banking system gradually developed. By later provisions, the government was permitted to deposit in national banks federal funds except receipts from customs; and finally, when the war was nearly over, Congress passed an act taxing state bank notes. When this took effect in the middle of the next year, it forced state bank notes into retirement.

Financial Failure of the Confederacy

The greatest failure of the Confederate government was in the realm of finance, and the main reason for this is clear. Southern capital was tied up in slaves, and the Confederacy had insufficient financial facilities to conduct a long war when cut off from the rest of the world. But the responsible officials made a colossal mistake in checking the shipment of cotton abroad at the very beginning, when the blockade was still ineffective. It would have been much wiser for the government itself to have assumed control of a large share of the most valuable Southern commodity and to have speeded it to Europe in order to gain gold for the coffers of the Treasury and establish credit abroad. The Confederacy was soon receiving cotton from its people in exchange for bonds and it might have taken this at the very start. But nearly everybody was laboring under the delusion that the war would be short, and financial foresight was uncharacteristic of the Confederate officials. The Secretary of the Treasury, Christopher B. Memminger, was neither a trained financier nor a statesman of vision. In 1864, at just about the time that Chase was succeeded by Fessenden in Washington, Memminger was replaced by George A. Trenholm, head of an important exporting firm in Charleston, who is reputed to have controlled fifty blockade runners and was unquestionably a man of boldness. Had he been in office in 1861, the Confederate government might have realized in Europe far more than it did on its financial resources.

The Confederacy could gain little revenue from customs duties, pay-

able in gold, and during its entire life it acquired altogether only about
$27 million in hard money. The South relied much less than the North
on taxation. According to careful estimate, only about 1 per cent of its
entire revenue was derived from that source. The Confederate Treasury
first resorted to bonds, and the first taxes were designed to do little
more than pay the interest on these. Not until April 1863, in the middle
of the war, did the Congress pass a general tax law. It extended to almost
every important commodity and occupation and included an income tax
and a tax on business profits. This complicated law, imposed at a time
when the entire economy was already deteriorating, was widely evaded
and brought disappointing returns. There was no tax on land or slaves
as such, but there was provision that a tenth of the produce of enumerated agricultural commodities and 6 per cent of specified meat products
should be paid the government, along with a small tax on livestock. This
"tax in kind," which was afterwards amended in details, is the most
interesting feature of the bill, and the best hope of successful taxation
probably lay in something of the sort. There was, however, great wastage
of commodities in the course of collection and storage, collections were
uneven, and the agents who roamed the countryside were exceedingly
unpopular. The resentment which they created contributed greatly to
popular discontent with the Davis government. Early in 1864, when affairs
were more desperate, the Congress imposed a direct tax on every kind
of property, but this was equally unpopular and even less successful.
Later actions amounted to little more than gestures.

The Confederacy continued to issue bonds in large quantities throughout the war. The promised interest was higher than in the North, but
the Confederacy could not long hope to pay this in coin, and the value
of the paper declined. The bonds of the states consistently had higher
value. The bond issues were like the 1863 tax law in that they contained
provisions that payment for these might be made in produce or other articles. By these and other means the government came into the possession
of thousands of bales of cotton which would have been much more sale-
able if they had been acquired earlier. Cotton comprised the security for
the only important Confederate loan that was placed abroad—with Er-
langer & Company of France in 1863. The European purchasers of these
bonds got nothing out of them, for the cotton remained on the wrong side
of the Atlantic, and the Confederacy itself got little, perhaps $2.5 million,
on cotton security supposed to be worth nearly twenty times as much.

Confederate Paper

The Confederate Treasury has been described as "the greatest money
factory in the world." At the outset there was extreme scarcity of money
of any sort, but before long Treasury notes were being compared to oak

leaves. It has been estimated that paper money was printed by the Confederacy itself to the amount of $2 billion and that states and other organizations printed $250 million more. This was about five times the amount of the Greenbacks in the North, which were shipped into the South to some extent and were always at a premium over Confederate money. Because of the scarcity of small coins, use was made of all sorts of paper, including the "shinplasters." These were issued by all kinds of businesses and became so common that they were ultimately spurned by beggars. For an American parallel to Confederate paper money one must go back to the era of the American Revolution. Before Gettysburg the Confederate dollar was valued less in gold than the Greenbacks were at their lowest point, and after that the descent was precipitous. The surprising thing is that, despite declining confidence, the people accepted this money so readily. One reason is that they had little choice, but another is that refusal to accept it was regarded everywhere as a mark of disloyalty.

Inflation in the Confederacy made inflation in the Union seem trivial. In the middle of the war flour sold for as much as $500 a barrel, though it fell thereafter. The government tried to reduce the volume of the currency in 1864 but prices continued to be fantastic. In Richmond a ham cost $350, a gentleman's suit $1500, a doctor's visit $45, and it was said that $50 was necessary to get drunk. A diarist quotes this saying: "You take your money to market in a market basket, and bring home what you buy in your pocketbook." Another current joke of the Confederacy was that a hotelkeeper would not allow the Georgia statesman, Robert Toombs, to pay for his room before retiring, since prices might rise before he did. In such times of inflation and fluctuating prices, advantages were gained by unscrupulous speculators, while salaried people in towns were crushed between the upper and nether millstones. The transaction of legitimate business became incredibly difficult, and thousands of country people turned to an economy of barter.

CIVILIAN LIFE: NORTH AND SOUTH

The North

A rough parallel can be drawn between Northern life in the Civil War and that of the American people as a whole during the Second World War. In the 1860's, dead and wounded soldiers were a much more common sight; military events were more fully and more vividly reported by the press, in the absence of effective censorship; and the conflict was personalized to a much greater degree. Yet most Northerners were physically remote from the actual fighting; they lived under conditions of general prosperity, much as Americans did eighty years later; and, despite high prices, the people as a whole had all of the physical requirements of ordinary life. The Confederate privateers took a toll of Northern commerce, but they never blocked the channels of international trade or cut off the Union from foreign markets. The main shortage of raw materials was in cotton, and this was somewhat ameliorated by illicit trade and the spread of Northern conquest.

The economy of the North during the Civil War, like that of the nation in the Second World War, was tremendously stimulated by the war purchases of the government. In the earlier conflict, however, economic life remained highly individualistic, virtually without governmental controls. The profit motive had full play and speculation was rife. There was far less unanimity in support of the war effort than in either of the later world conflicts, and upon the face of the record there was considerably more profiteering and outright corruption. Quite clearly there was more than in the Confederacy, where there was no such opportunity for money-making or such intoxication with prosperity.

Prosperity did not come to the North all at once. In the first year of the war economic life was seriously disrupted. Trade with the South was cut off, the Mississippi was closed, with great injury to the river cities like St. Louis, and debts owed by the South, including state bonds held in the North, were uncollectible. The difficulties of the banks were reflected in the suspension of specie payments at the end of 1861, and there were more business failures in that year than in the panic year of 1857, though the amount involved was smaller. Things got better in 1862, and from that time on they improved with increasing momentum until some observers regarded the prosperity of the country as a positive embarrassment.

Despite the draining of manpower from the farms, there was a sufficient increase in the agricultural output to feed the armies and meet the growing demand for food products abroad. This result was achieved in part by the more extensive use of agricultural machinery, especially the McCormick reaper, in part by the labors of women in the fields—driving harvesters and binding and shocking grain. There was a very considerable increase in the amount of land under cultivation. The passage of the Homestead Act of May 20, 1862, marked the culmination of the long fight for free lands in the West. According to this measure, quarter sections (160 acres) of public land were to be given to those occupying them for five years and paying small fees, and under this law more than two million acres were taken up during the war. In providing good lands for the landless, however, this measure was much less successful than Republican politicians would afterwards admit. Larger tracts were needed in semiarid and arid regions. Furthermore, the best lands were generally taken up by railroads, to which the government made huge grants, and by large operators, who acquired great holdings by purchase. In the same year (1862) Congress passed the Morrill Land Grant Act, granting national public lands to states at the rate of 30,000 acres for each Congressman and Senator, for the support of agricultural and mechanical colleges. This measure was significant in the later development of public education, especially in the West, but it put some of the best lands into the hands of state governments. The general situation was far more advantageous to large holders than to homesteaders or small purchasers, but the net result of all these factors was to expand agriculture.

The war greatly stimulated the exploitation of mineral resources. In the development of oil and steel the period may be regarded as a prelude to the new industrial era which followed it and which made the United States a giant among the nations. The conflict created an increased demand for almost every kind of manufactured product, and virtually any industry could gain high tariff protection. The cotton textile business suffered from the shortage of cotton, but the woolen industry thrived. Meanwhile, railroad building and the consolidation of lines went on. Far from disrupting the economy of the Union, the war accentuated development all along the line, and enterprising men laid massive foundations for the age of big business. The government checked them little if at all, and in many ways it aided them substantially.

It was perhaps inevitable that there should be immense wastage in the war effort, in view of the extent of it and the inexperience of government officials. In its haste and anxiety the government would pay almost any price, and producers were not slow to avail themselves of this golden opportunity. The degree of actual fraud was estimated afterwards by Henry S. Olcott, who had been specifically commissioned by Stanton and Wells to investigate it, as between 20 and 25 per cent of the entire expenditures of the government. Commissions on government contracts were paid to middlemen, and sometimes to public men, while political influence was exerted. Furthermore, the government was supplied with many grossly inferior articles, to the great disadvantage of the army. For example, uniforms were sometimes made of refuse material or "shoddy" which disintegrated in the rain. The term "shoddy" passed into the vernacular, and was applied to certain war millionaires. In the Army, conditions were at their worst during the easy-going, political regime of Cameron. The soldiers also vented their indignation at the transactions in cotton in which certain officers and civilians engaged after the Union had begun to conquer the cotton country. Because of the illicit trading with the enemy that centered on Memphis, that city is said to have served the Confederacy better as a source of supplies after it fell into Federal hands than it ever had previously.

The salaried and laboring classes did not thrive in this period of inflation, but life as a whole was conducted in an atmosphere of extravagance. Crime may not have greatly increased, but intemperance did, while prostitution became a more conspicuous problem, especially in the vicinity of the soldiers. Theaters in New York were filled to overflowing, while college enrollments fell off and the reform spirit, already declining before the war, was largely reduced to hostility to slavery as a Southern institution. Moral indignation was voiced against the horrors of the Confederate prisons, especially Andersonville and Libby, where conditions unquestionably were shocking; and humanitarianism was manifest in the devoted services of women in hospitals. One of the most notable civilian agencies was the United States Sanitary Commission, the forerunner of the American Red Cross. Established in 1861, it brought comfort and cheer to many a camp and hospital and ministered to both Confederates and Federals. Idealism was not dead, but under war conditions it had been driven into a narrower channel. The vast majority of the people and public officials were honest and patriotic, and the war was ennobling to unnumbered individuals, but it had a generally demoralizing effect on public and private character.

The South

The basic fact conditioning Southern life during the war was that an economy which was already far less self-sufficient than that of the North was increasingly cut off from the rest of the world and progressively deprived of resources through loss of territory. Beginning in 1863, the blockade became more and more effective; and in that year, with the fall of Vicksburg and Port Hudson, the trans-Mississippi states were cut off and the Confederacy was denied supplies landed in Mexico and brought across the border into Texas. In 1864, the only ports remaining in Southern hands were Charleston, Mobile, Wilmington, and inaccessible Galveston. Mobile was taken by Farragut that year (August 6, 1864), and the loss of Wilmington early in 1865, along with the abandonment of Fort Sumter in Charleston harbor, put an end to Southern commerce. Except for the Shenandoah Valley, the parts of the South which were most important in the production of grain and the raising of stock were already cut off or overrun by the middle of 1863. The conflict was imposing a much greater drain on Southern than Northern manpower; and the situation worsened with every passing month; in 1864, a Mississippian lamented that there were not enough men left to bury the dead. The story of the Southern economy is not one of development but of progressive deterioration; and, far from being demoralized by abnormal prosperity, the people had a full measure of the discipline of adversity.

Besides the difficulties arising from inadequate industry, the Southerners were confronted, almost from the beginning of the war, with the fact that their cotton and tobacco were inedible and virtually unmarketable. Accordingly, they turned to food crops, especially to corn. The movement to curtail the production of cotton was very successful, and it was accompanied by measures of governmental regulation such as were unknown in the North. Food and equipment were impressed from the first year of the war, and this policy inevitably created discontent, especially since the government was remiss in its payments. It has been estimated that at the end of the war the Confederacy owed its people half a billion dollars for impressed property. There was no real substitute for such imported articles as coffee and tea, and throughout the war there was a painful shortage of salt. This led to all sorts of expedients from the evaporation of seawater to the boiling of the dirt from smokehouse floors. There was, however, plenty of food in the Confederacy as a whole; the main problem was that of transportation. In order to meet military needs, some new links in the inadequate transportation system were built, but there was such a shortage of rails that unimportant lines were dismantled and the rails used elsewhere. Before the war ended, the problem of broken rails had become insoluble and there was always difficulty in keeping locomotives in repair. The final collapse of the railroad system was an important factor in ultimate military failure and in the deprivation of civilians.

Except in regions occupied by Union armies the slave-labor system persisted. The legend of the loyal plantation slave was afterwards embroidered by romantic writers and has been modified by more realistic later historians, but in essence the traditional picture is correct, except for the last year of the war. Some incipient revolts were suppressed and there were inevitable runaways when Union soldiers approached, but there was no servile insurrection. The household servants were instinctively loyal to their "white people," helping the mistresses of plantations in the absence of masters and guarding the children as a sacred trust. The hatred of Southern women for the invaders was commented on by General Sherman among others, and many of the slaves viewed the oncoming Yankees as dread conquerors rather than liberators. Had the vast majority of the bondsmen not performed their allotted tasks faithfully the Confederacy would have fallen much sooner than it did. Many body-servants accompanied the Confederate armies, slaves were used on fortifications and elsewhere in labors connected with defense, and from early 1864 were impressed by the government for labor to some extent. In the last months of the war, the arming of them for actual fighting was authorized, but there was not time enough for the results of this desperate policy to appear.

The business of blockade-running comprised the most conspicuous Southern parallel to Northern profiteering and speculation. The profits from this were enormous, but they were only paper profits unless converted into hard money and they were gained chiefly on luxuries which contributed little to the war effort. The Confederate government itself owned some blockade ruuners, and after the first months of 1864 it sought to maintain complete control of external trade, fixing regulations and requiring permits to a degree which had not been approached in American experience since the last months of Jefferson's Embargo. Some Northerners connived in blockade-running, and trading with the enemy was a joint affair. Because of the value of this in procuring necessities, the Confederate authorities winked at it, and it was a more patriotic exercise on the part of Southerners than Northerners.

The war had far more serious effects on Southern than on Northern education. Besides the lack of teachers, there was a grave shortage of textbooks, which had been so largely procured in the North in peacetime. Some colleges and universities managed to keep open with greatly reduced enrollments, but very many were actually closed. Educational institutions for women suffered least, and the whole course of the war tended to emphasize the importance of women in society. The South produced a striking list of wartime diaries by women. Among these may be mentioned Mary Boykin Chesnut's *A Diary from Dixie,* Julia LeGrand's *Journal,* and Sarah Fowler Morgan's *A Confederate Girl's Diary.* It is also a notable fact that poetry flourished in the embattled South. The poems of Henry Timrod and Paul Hamilton Hayne have never gained such national acclaim as the verse of Walt Whitman, the greatest Northern literary figure of the war, but in their sadness and sentimentality they reflected the spirit of sensitive Southern minds. Even in wartime, Southerners had the saving grace of humor. The waggish and illiterate letters of Bill Arp (Charles Henry Smith) to "Mr. Linkhorn" were published in the newspapers and greatly enjoyed by Father Abraham himself. The South had special need for sentiment and humor; and, along with memories of military glory and heroic women, these were destined to survive political and economic inadequacies in an unequal war.

CHAPTER 40

The End of the War

THE LAST YEAR OF THE WAR WAS BY ALL ODDS THE grimmest. To Confederates the story was one of cumulative failure—on the diplomatic front, on the home front, and on the last battlefronts. At length the superior resources of the Union were sufficiently mobilized to crush the rebellious section. A unified military organization was created; and Union commanders, recognizing the remorseless logic of war more fully and frankly than their predecessors, bore down upon the opposition with a ruthlessness hitherto unknown in American military annals.

Ironical though it was, Northern morale was probably at its lowest point in the summer of 1864, when the fortunes of the Confederacy were in fact irreparable. Lincoln survived the political crisis of that year, emerging with enhanced prestige, but he was slain by a madman soon after he had voiced, in his noble second inaugural, the spirit of human brotherhood and goodwill.

The last phase of the war was one of tragic losses, and only a later generation could count the gains.

THE DIPLOMATIC TRIUMPH OF THE UNION

British Neutrality

The passive policy of the British government with respect to the war was of greater advantage to the Union than to the Confederacy from the beginning, but in one important respect British policy was ambiguous. The contracts made between Confederate agents and British shipyards to build warships for use against Northern merchantmen were an open secret and Minister Adams presented reams of documentary proof to Earl Russell. Warship-building for a belligerent was clearly forbidden to a neutral by international law, but the British Foreign Enlistment Act of 1819 was defective in its requirement that armaments must be found

773

aboard to prove that the ships were in fact intended for war. In that day the design of warships was hardly different from that of merchant vessels, and the Confederates were careful to postpone arming their ships until they had slipped away from British waters. In 1862, the *Florida* was equipped and armed at Nassau, ostensibly as a British vessel, and the more famous *Alabama* was armed off the Azores, where Captain Raphael Semmes took command for the Confederacy. Along with the later *Shenandoah* and lesser vessels, these raiders lighted the oceans with burning Union ships. Charles Francis Adams pointed out that if British domestic law was inadequate, the government was duty-bound to strengthen it, but the Palmerston Ministry was strangely unwilling to ask Parliament to do this.

The issue became more immediate and more acute in connection with the "Laird rams," which were being built by the Laird firm for the Confederacy and were nearing completion in the summer of 1863. These were ironclads with prows designed to wreck the wooden Union blockaders, and they could then attack northern ports. They were readily distinguishable from merchant vessels, but it could be claimed that they were intended for some other government than the Confederacy. The law lords of the British Crown advised the Ministry that it could not legally seize the rams, while Adams addressed a series of notes to Earl Russell that clearly threatened war if the rams were allowed to escape. His note of September 5, 1863, has gained great fame in American diplomatic annals. Already the news of Gettysburg and Vicksburg had helped Russell to make up his mind: he bought the rams for the Royal Navy. This action averted the last possibility of foreign war or decisive foreign aid to the Confederacy. But Northern rancor over the *Alabama* continued after that famous raider was finally sunk (June 19, 1864) by the U. S. S. *Kearsage* in the English Channel, and increased after the Civil War was over. The drawn-out issue of the *Alabama* claims dominated the diplomacy of the Johnson and Grant administrations.

Napoleon III and Maximilian

The French government was as favorable to the Confederacy as circumstances would permit. Napoleon III proposed mediation in January 1863, but the Lincoln administration and Congress firmly refused. Napoleon was afraid of war with the North and did not dare to help the South openly, but he permitted ships to be built in France for the Confederacy and dangled recognition before the eyes of Southern diplomats in return for a free hand in Mexico.

The Mexican government repudiated payments on its foreign debts in July 1861, and a joint expedition on the part of Britain, Spain, and France to collect money due their subjects was projected. Britain and

Spain withdrew when Napoleon's shady deals became too thick for them. He was dreaming of a revival of his uncle's thwarted plans for an American empire. As a first step he provided troops to support the Archduke Maximilian of Austria as Emperor of Mexico. Landowners and clericals of that country, frightened by the social-revolutionary laws of President Benito Juárez, offered Maximilian the throne. Napoleon's troops took Mexico City in June 1863; Juárez retreated to the American border to await Northern victory; and early in 1864, Maximilian took the throne. Napoleon promised him troops for three years in return for a large financial commitment. Maximilian had a tragic awakening when a handful of reactionaries used him and the French troops to plunder the country, while the people showed their hatred in guerrilla fighting.

Here was the realization of the worst prophecies concerning the fate of freedom in America if the Monroe Doctrine should lose its force. Northerners were finally aroused and, with their armies emerging triumphant on Southern battlefields, they demanded action of the Union government. Lincoln and Seward were reluctant to make any move that might bring French aid to the tottering Confederacy. When Maximilian took power Congress passed a resolution of condemnation which Seward felt it necessary to repudiate, and not even after the war ended did he issue any ultimatum. But he left no doubt of American opposition to the presence of French troops in Mexico, and early in 1867 Napoleon found it expedient to withdraw them. Then the Juárez government promptly took over, executing the well-meaning but deluded Maximilian.

The refusal of the British to support Napoleon in his Mexican venture was of immense value to the United States, and the disunity of the European powers helps to explain the success of Union diplomacy. Napoleon III several times told Southern agents that he would recognize the Confederacy only in conjunction with Great Britain. Each government was afraid that if it got involved in the American war the other would gain advantage in Europe. Momentarily in 1863, Britain and France combined in diplomatic support of the Polish rebellion of that year against Russia. Fearing that their fleet would be caught in the Baltic by the British Navy in case of war, the Russians sent their warships to the United States. Northerners concluded that this action presaged Russian help against Britain and France. Overjoyed, they feted the Russian naval officers and spoke of a common crusade against Negro slavery and Russian serfdom. All this was unjustified by the actual motives of the Czar's government, but Northern gratitude to Russia paved the way for the amicable Alaska negotiations after the war. In 1864, a war of Prussia and Austria against Denmark preoccupied European diplomats, and mutual suspicions between Britain and France again came to the fore.

Failure of Confederate Diplomacy

The net result of the Confederate campaign for European recognition
was a letter from the Pope addressed to Jefferson Davis as "President of
the Confederate States of America," and an offer to recognize the Confederacy tendered by three Poles whose own government was unrecog-
nized. In 1863, the Confederate Secretary of State, Judah P. Benjamin,
expelled the British consuls who had remained in the South, though
accredited to the Federal rather than the Confederate government. By
1864, the Southerners' hope for foreign aid turned to bitter disillusionment. Napoleon III refused a gift of 100,000 bales of cotton, offered if he
would break the blockade in order to get it. In Mexico, Confederate
agents formed alliances with bandits to bring supplies across the Rio
Grande, and they did strange things in Canada. In 1864, Jacob Thompson, former Secretary of the Interior, and others were sent to Canada as
secret agents with vague instructions to further the interests of the
Confederacy. These men connived with "Sons of Liberty" in the North
and plotted to release Confederate prisoners who were held near the
border. Thompson denied having any part in the attack on Saint Albans,
Vermont, in October 1864, by a band of escaped prisoners who robbed
three banks of $200,000. Thus the Confederate diplomatic campaign which
had been launched on the high hope of cotton supremacy degenerated
to a low level of desperation.

During the last months of the war, the mood in Richmond varied
between defiance of Europe and hope that some brilliant scheme would
bring last-minute aid. A French-built ram was not ready to sail until after
Appomattox. Belated acknowledgment of the fact that slavery heavily
burdened the Southern cause in foreign countries produced a despairing
offer to Britain, early in 1865, to free the slaves in return for recognition.
Avoiding the words "abolition" and "slavery," James M. Mason offered to
remove the "latent, undisclosed obstacle" to recognition. It was too late,
and everywhere in Europe men now accepted Lincoln's definition of the
conflict as a test whether or not "government of the people, by the people,
for the people" should perish from the earth. The meaning of the war to
the larger cause of freedom and democracy was more clearly perceived
abroad than by many who viewed it from near at hand at home; and,
along with the demonstrated power of Northern arms, this was a major
reason for the cumulative success of Union diplomacy.

THE LAST GREAT CAMPAIGNS, 1864

The military operations of 1864 were unified on the Northern side and
pressed relentlessly. At the end of February, Congress passed an act reviving the rank of Lieutenant General, which everybody knew would

go to Grant, and saying that this officer might be authorized by the President to command all the armies of the United States. There were numerous Lieutenant Generals in the Confederacy and several Generals, like Lee, Joseph E. Johnston, and Beauregard, but the highest rank in the Union Army had been that of Major General. On March 9, Grant received his commission in Washington. Soon thereafter Halleck asked to be relieved as General-in-Chief, which he had been only in name, and Grant assumed the supreme command in fact. The office of Chief-of-Staff was created and given to Halleck, who served thereafter as a sort of liaison officer. The system broke down at times because the General-in-Chief was also with an army in the field and things often got mixed up in Washington, but it was a modern system of command which, as has been claimed, was superior to anything yet achieved in Europe. Meade was continued as the administrative head of the Army of the Potomac and handled details of tactics under Grant.

The over-all strategy, as now devised, called for crushing movements in the two major theatres. The main attack against Lee's army in Virginia was to be delivered by the Army of the Potomac, but simultaneously Benjamin F. Butler was to advance on Richmond from Fortress Monroe and there were supposed to be operations in the Shenandoah Valley. At the same time Sherman, now in command in Chattanooga, was to attack the Confederate army under Joseph E. Johnston in Georgia. Grant's full plan also called for a movement on the part of General Banks from New Orleans against Mobile, but that political general got involved in an expedition up the Red River in Louisiana in conjunction with Admiral David D. Porter. This badly conducted enterprise was checked at Mansfield (Sabine Crossroads) and Pleasant Hill on April 8-9, when the Federal forces were repulsed by Confederates under General Richard Taylor, son of Zachary Taylor. Afterwards, Banks retreated and soon he was superseded in the field. Nothing was done about Mobile until Farragut took the place from the sea in August. Meanwhile, the huge Trans-Mississippi Department of the Confederacy, including Texas, was directed by the redoubtable Edmund Kirby-Smith and known as "Kirby-Smithdom." It was remote from the war and did not affect the course of the major conflicts in Virginia and Georgia.

Grant and Lee in Virginia

On May 3, the Army of the Potomac, more than 100,000 strong, began to cross the Rapidan. The Army of Northern Virginia, to which Longstreet's depleted forces had been returned, consisted of somewhat more than 60,000 men, so the odds were about 5 to 3. Ascertaining that his new opponent was entering the Wilderness of Spotsylvania, where Hooker had been humbled at Chancellorsville, Lee hastened to give battle there, under conditions which would neutralize the Federal advantage in manpower and artillery. In the Battle of the Wilderness (May 5-6) the Federal casualties were nearly 18,000, while those of the Confederates were less than half as great. In this blindfolded fighting in burning undergrowth Grant was punished as severely as Hooker had been, but he did not withdraw as Lee had hoped. Instead, veering to the left, he moved relentlessly toward Richmond, knowing that his antagonist would try to cover the Confederate capital and hoping to catch the "old fox" in the open.

Lee, moving on the inner line, beat him to Spotsylvania Courthouse and quickly established a strong line there—developing field fortifications to a degree that no general had ever done before. The Battle of Spotsylvania Courthouse (May 8-12) was perhaps the most horrible of the war. The heaviest toll was taken at a salient in the Confederate line—called the "Mule Shoe" by the soldiers—at a point known as the "Bloody Angle." Here corpses were piled four or five deep, sometimes with wounded men beneath them. Never before, except in Pickett's charge at Gettysburg, had so many of Lee's soldiers been captured. The severity of the firing was shown by the fact that two great trees, twenty and twenty-two inches in diameter, were cut down by *minié* balls. Lee straightened out the salient and his lines held, while Federal losses exceeded Confederate by about 2 to 1. It was in the midst of this bloody engagement that Grant said that he proposed "to fight it out on this line if it takes all summer." The fighting was taking a heavy toll of Lee's general officers. Longstreet was wounded in the Wilderness, and at a time when the cavalry was greatly weakened because of the condition of the horses, "Jeb" Stuart was killed in the attempt to check a raid of General Philip H. Sheridan, who was in command of all Grant's cavalry.

Withdrawing from before the Confederate lines at Spotsylvania Courthouse, the indomitable Grant resumed his campaign of movement, maintaining the initiative which no other Federal commander had been able to snatch away from Lee for long. Veering again to the left and shielded by the Mattapony River, the Federal commander moved nearer to Richmond. Butler's campaign from the east was badly managed by that politician, but it had forced the Confederates to keep a considerable body of troops, under Beauregard, southeast of Richmond. In the middle of May, Beauregard bottled up Butler in Bermuda Neck, between the James and Appomattox Rivers. Lee, again moving by the inner line, got his forces below the North Anna River, covering the railroad line running westward to the Shenandoah Valley. At this time he was so weakened by illness that he could ride only in a carriage. Strongly fortifying his position, he invited an attack which Grant would not make.

Still shifting to the left, in what his soldiers called the "jug-handle movement," Grant got almost as close to Richmond as McClellan had.

Between the Topotomoy Creek and the Chickahominy River, Lee inter-
posed his defending army and here occurred the Battle of Cold Harbor.
Before the main Federal assault on June 3 the Confederates had dug
in, and the delay was disastrous to the Army of the Potomac. Grant
hurled charges against an entrenched Confederate position which was
far stronger than it appeared to be, exposing his men to murderous fire
and crossfire in open country. This was worse than Pickett's charge at
Gettysburg. Grant lost 7000 men in less than thirty minutes and 13,000
altogether in the entire Cold Harbor operation. This was his most futile
battle and Lee's easiest victory, but it was Lee's last one in the field.

After a month of ceaseless campaigning, it seemed that his rapier
had outmatched Grant's bludgeon, but at no time were the resourceful-
ness and dauntless determination of the Union commander better illustrated than in the operation that followed. In the middle of June, withdrawing his men from the trenches they had dug, he skillfully transferred
his huge army across the James well below Richmond at Wilcox's Landing, by means of ferries and a quickly-built pontoon bridge. Then his
advance forces attacked Petersburg, some twenty miles south of the
Confederate capital and itself an important railroad center. His hope
was to cut communications between Richmond and the southern hinterland, and if staff work and tactics had matched his strategy he might
have succeeded. For a couple of days Lee, who was woefully short of
cavalry, lost touch with Federal movements in a densely wooded country.
Beauregard repulsed the confused and ill-managed attacks on Petersburg, (June 14-17), and on June 18, Lee and virtually his entire army
were on the scene of action. Then, in their respective trenches, the rival
armies settled down to months of siege. After six weeks of incessant
campaigning and Grant's flash of brilliant strategy, stalemate had ensued.

Upon its surface the first phase of the crushing movement, as carried
out in Virginia, was unsuccessful. In six weeks' time the total Federal
losses in this area equalled the whole of Lee's army at the beginning,
and the effects on the soldiers were depressing. Grant himself attributed
the failure of the assault on Petersburg to "the moral condition of the
army," though the soldiers were disposed to blame it on the ineptitude
of their generals. Yet, the campaign was no success for the Confederates.
Lee had maintained his army in the face of great odds, while saving
Richmond from direct attack and even from a siege, which as he recognized would have been the beginning of the end. But he now faced a
siege in Petersburg, which really amounted to the same thing. Meanwhile,
he had been compelled to weaken his already depleted forces by despatch-
ing troops to the Shenandoah Valley, on which Richmond and his army
were so dependent for supplies. If he kept stretching his thin line, eventually it must break.

The most spectacular episode of the summer was the Battle of the

Crater, following the explosion of a mine beneath a Confederate bastion on July 30. The digging of a shaft of more than 500 feet from behind the Union line was a triumph of ingenuity and industry, but the attack by Burnside's corps was incredibly bungled and the net result was the slaughter of nearly 4000 Federals in the pit they had dug with their own powder. Grant had no direct hand in the tactics of this ghastly engagement but its dismal outcome was no credit to his command. Lee restored his line of trenches, but in August the cutting of the Weldon railroad that ran directly southward from Petersburg closed an important channel of communication.

Sheridan, Early, and the Valley

It was partly because of the importance of communications to the westward that Lee sent General Jubal A. Early to the Shenandoah Valley before the siege of Petersburg began. The Union commander in the Valley, General David Hunter, who had burned the buildings at the Virginia Military Institute and the home of the Governor of the state, fled before Early into the mountains of West Virginia, leaving the way open to another raid aross the Potomac. Reaching Harper's Ferry on July 4, "Jube" and his army of perhaps 15,000 men passed over into Maryland. After brushing aside a small Union force at Monocacy River below Frederick, he was on the outskirts of Washington by July 11. The ring of fortifications and trenches that circled the city had been practically denuded of soldiers to swell the Army of the Potomac, but two Federal corps, ordered to Washington by Grant, arrived just in time and Early withdrew. No other Confederate army ever got that close to the seat of government. In the course of his retirement, Early sent a detachment as far north as Chambersburg, Pennsylvania, where demands were made for indemnification for homes recently burned by Federals in Virginia. When these were refused, fire was set to the city (July 30, 1864) on Early's orders.

Grant was determined to dispose of Early and to put the Valley out of the war once and forever. In charge of the operation he placed General Philip H. Sheridan, giving him upwards of 40,000 men, including an unusually large proportion of cavalry. The Federal cavalry, well-mounted at a time when the Confederate horses were giving out, and well-armed with magazine carbines, was now at its peak, and in Sheridan the North had found a fighter as relentless as Grant and with a far greater talent for histrionics. With his greatly superior force he defeated Early at Winchester and Fisher's Hall in September. Then he began to carry out his instructions from Grant to devastate the Confederate grain country, leaving it so bare that a crow flying over it would have to carry its own rations. Before he got through, Sheridan "peeled" the

Valley, burning barns, destroying crops, and seizing stock—all to a total of many millions. Often by accident or design his troops burned private houses; and, while imparting to a smiling landscape the bleakness of a moor, he reduced the civilian population to destitution. This was total war such as the United States had never before witnessed.

Early with his reduced forces turned on the invaders in desperation, surprising them at Cedar Creek (October 19) when Sheridan was absent. After a ride from twenty miles away—which gained ever-increasing fame with the telling of the story—"Little Phil" rallied his retreating troops and defeated Early's force so decisively that it ceased to be effective. Then Sheridan resumed his campaign of destruction. Guerrilla fighting continued in the wasted Valley, on the part of the rangers of Colonel John S. Mosby and others who can be better described as brigands. Not until another spring was Early's army wholly destroyed and the Valley completely sealed off, but never again was it to serve the Army of Northern Virginia as a granary. Meanwhile, Sheridan had done more to restore Northern morale than any other general except William Tecumseh Sherman.

Sherman and Farragut: Atlanta and Mobile

The second phase of the crushing operation of 1864 began at almost the same time as the first. On May 6, Sherman set his army in motion from Chattanooga against Joseph E. Johnston at Dalton, Georgia. The odds were almost the same as in Virginia, for Union forces of nearly 100,000 confronted Confederate troops numbering less than 60,000. In ability the two commanders were comparable, and each of them respected his opponent too much to do anything rash. As a result, the campaign from Chattanooga to Atlanta was one of skillful maneuver and minor engagements. In this rugged country, Johnston confronted his opponent in a succession of powerfully fortified positions which Sherman with his superior forces successively outflanked. As he retired Johnston invariably tore up the tracks of the Western & Atlantic Railroad, and Sherman as regularly rebuilt them. Johnston kept waiting for Sherman to make a mistake, but the Union commander made only one of any importance; on June 27 he attacked the strong Confederate position on Kenesaw Mountain and was repulsed, with losses of 3000 to Johnston's 600. At length Sherman maneuvered Johnston across the Chattahoochee River to the neighborhood of Atlanta, and there on Peach Tree Creek, Johnston intended to make a stand, as he said afterwards. It now seems that his Fabian tactics had served a political purpose: decisive victory had been denied Sherman at a time when the Northern people were deeply discouraged by events in Virginia and the Lincoln administration was facing a presidential election.

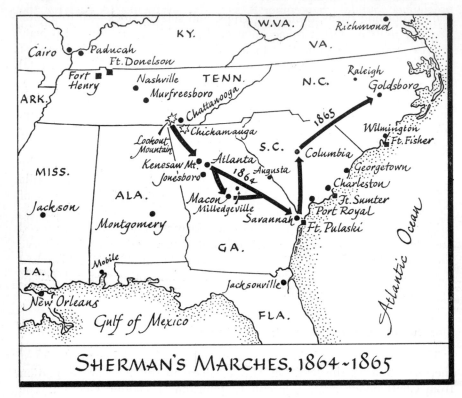

SHERMAN'S MARCHES, 1864~1865

Johnston's retreat, however, created much impatience in high Confederate circles, where his standing was not of the best, and on July 7,
Jefferson Davis unwisely removed him, replacing him by General John
B. Hood whose record was that of a fighter. Lee attested to Hood's
courage and pugnacity but beyond that would not commit himself. The
results were what might have been expected from the attitude of the
Confederate administration and Hood's temperament. Emerging from
his lines before Atlanta while Sherman was spreading a net around
the city, Hood struck the Federals twice at places which seemed weak
but was strongly repulsed in each instance (July 20, 22). Then things
settled down into a virtual siege during which Hood's only unimpaired
communications were on the south. By imperiling these, at the very end
of August, Sherman forced Hood to withdraw from the city, which the
Union forces occupied on September 2.

Sherman had not accomplished his major purpose of destroying the
Confederate Army, but he had greatly weakened it. Meanwhile, he had
attained his secondary object by gaining control of a major railroad
center and further reducing the effective military area of the Confederacy. The capture of Atlanta was glorious news in the North. Lincoln

proclaimed Sunday, September 3, as a day of thanks to God for the victories of Sherman and Farragut, who had taken Mobile on August 5 and deprived the Confederacy of another of its few remaining ports.

The capture of Mobile attracted less public attention than the occupation of Atlanta, but it was an exceedingly important event and Farragut's exploit was one of the most notable in American naval history. His problem was not merely to pass Fort Morgan and Fort Gaines at the entrance of Mobile Bay, but also to escape the mines (then called torpedoes) with which the waters were strewn. His fleet consisted of four ironclads and more than a dozen wooden vessels. It was after the leading ship went down and the others recoiled in confusion that Farragut spoke his most famous words. He said: "Damn the torpedoes, full speed ahead!" He got through, defeated the Confederate flotilla in the bay, and before the month was out had received the surrender of the forts. He had done from the sea what Grant had long wanted to do from the land. Before the end of the year in which he crowned his naval achievements with the capture of Mobile, the grade of Vice-Admiral was created for him and thenceforth he ranked with Grant, being universally recognized as the greatest of the Northern naval heroes.

The capture of Atlanta marked the emergence into the full glare of publicity of Sherman, whose deeds had not been well reported hitherto. This reddish-headed, fiery, and outspoken man had been commonly regarded as erratic, but many were now saying that his military talents exceeded those of Grant. Even better than Grant he personified the logic of war. Generally regarded as an antiabolitionist, he had no sympathy with the radical Republicans and utterly scorned the wiles of politicians. He had been more friendly to Southerners than almost any other prominent Northern general, and he consistently preferred the destruction of property to that of life. But the orders he issued for the evacuation of the civilian population from Atlanta, the verbal controversy with Hood which followed, and the eventual destruction of a large part of the city on his command quickly established him in the public mind, especially in the Southern mind, as the most conspicuous exponent of total war. This title was to be confirmed later in the year by his march to the sea—after the re-election of Lincoln, to which he contributed more perhaps than any other single individual.

RADICAL REPUBLICANS AND THE ELECTION OF 1864

Among the radical Republicans there was strong opposition to the renomination of Lincoln. One of his secretaries, John Hay, termed these men "Jacobins," and in their violence of spirit they presented a sharp contrast to the patient and magnanimous President. To them the conflict was primarily a war against slavery, and their attitude toward the

Southern states and people was such that they have been described as the "vindictives." They emphasized partisan politics to a far greater degree than Lincoln, incessantly attacking Democrats in the government and the army, while seeking to advance the interests of sympathetic statesmen like Secretary of the Treasury Chase and radical generals like Frémont, Burnside, and Butler. The Congressional leaders of this group were: Benjamin F. Wade of Ohio, Zachariah Chandler of Michigan, and Charles Sumner of Massachusetts in the Senate; and Thaddeus Stevens of Pennsylvania, Henry Winter Davis of Maryland, and George W. Julian of Indiana in the House. In part the conflict between them and the President was a phase of the rivalry between the legislative and executive branches of the government which has run through the whole of American national history, and by appealing to Congressional prerogatives and pride they gained legislative support which they would never have won on grounds of policy alone.

Legislative prerogatives had long been proclaimed and effectively exercised by the Joint Committee on the Conduct of the War. Dominated by radicals, especially Senators Wade and Chandler and Representative Julian, this committee provided a conspicuous example of the power than can be wielded by means of legislative investigations. The most flagrant instance of persecution at the hands of this group was the case of General Charles P. Stone, who suffered arrest and imprisonment for six months in connection with the investigation of the minor disaster of Ball's Bluff (October 21, 1861). The charges against Stone were flimsy and he was ultimately vindicated. The committee sought to undermine Democratic and conservative officers like McClellan and Meade, and it repeatedly intervened in military policy. Lincoln's judgment in military matters generally turned out to be better than that of these prejudiced advisers, and it was fortunate for the Union cause that he insisted on his prerogatives as Commander-in-Chief and usually had his way.

When Northern conquest was only in its beginnings, Senator Charles Sumner set forth (in February 1862) what came to be known as the "state-suicide" theory—namely, that the rebellious states had forfeited all their rights. Sumner strongly asserted the authority of Congress over them, while violently opposing the policy of Lincoln to restore the Union with the least possible curtailment of historic rights and the largest possible regard for local sentiment. The policy of the radicals that was embodied in the Second Confiscation Act (July 17, 1862) was opposed to that of Lincoln, and he signed the measure only after Congress had passed an explanatory resolution which met some of his objections. Apart from the serious doubts about the constitutionality of this measure, the sure effect of the indiscriminate attempt to deprive all Confederates of their private property—as one of the opponents of the measure said—would be to make peace and reunion impossible. The actual amount of property confiscated under this extreme measure was slight, and it was most significant as a revelation of the spirit of the radicals and as a threat of punitive measures in the future.

Lincoln's own policy was embodied in a proclamation of amnesty issued by him on December 8, 1863, in which he offered pardon to Southerners who would take an oath of allegiance to the Constitution and the Union, signifying at the same time their acceptance of acts of Congress and presidential proclamations with respect to slavery. He excepted from his offer Confederate officials, high officers of the Confederate Army and Navy, and certain other classes, but obviously he was trying to reduce punitive measures to the minimum, to foster Southern loyalty, and to facilitate the restoration of the Union. He announced that whenever the persons taking the oath in a particular state numbered as many as 10 per cent of the voters there in 1860, a government established by them would be recognized as a true government.

On the basis of this policy he fostered governments in Louisiana, Arkansas, and Tennessee; and as the Executive he sought to extend the operations and protection of the federal laws to these regions. The admission of Representatives to Congress, however, lay within the legislative authority, and the radicals made sure that Congress should not permit this until they themselves could prescribe further and harsher conditions. These self-assertive men resented Lincoln's assumption of leadership, and they saw in his policy a danger that the North and the Republican Party would be denied the full fruits of victory.

The Anti-Lincoln Movement and Its Failure

Other strong antislavery spokesmen like Horace Greeley, while viewing the rebellious Southerners with no such vindictiveness, regarded the administration of Lincoln as a failure and were looking for a better man. To many dissatisfied Republicans this seemed to be Secretary Chase, whose presidential ambition was a perennial plant. His candidacy was urged by a Congressional committee headed by Senator Samuel C. Pomeroy of Kansas, who issued in his behalf, in February 1864, an open letter that was called the "Pomeroy Circular." This asserted that Lincoln could not be re-elected and that Chase had more of the necessary qualifications than any other available candidate. Chase himself assured Lincoln that he knew nothing of this circular and offered his resignation, which Lincoln would not accept. The Chase boom proved abortive, and in March the Secretary of the Treasury announced that he was not a candidate. That he would have been one if conditions had been favorable can hardly be doubted, but the facts were that Lincoln was popular with the people, though not with the radical Congressional politicians, and that he was strongly supported by the state political organizations.

Following the collapse of the movement for Chase, the candidacy of John C. Frémont, long the darling of the extreme antislavery group, was pressed by radical Germans in Missouri and abolitionists like Wendell Phillips. The Congressional politicians held aloof from this movement, but late in May 1864 Frémont was nominated by a third-party convention in Cleveland, on a radical platform calling for the reconstruction of the South under Congressional authority, the confiscation of Rebel lands, and their distribution among soldiers and settlers.

In the meantime, the Lincoln forces had strengthened their grip on the party machinery, and at the regular Republican convention at Baltimore in early June, Lincoln was nominated virtually without dissent. The party called itself the Union Party, and the nomination of Andrew Johnson of Tennessee for Vice-President was hailed as a recognition of War Democrats and Southern Unionists. A few weeks later, after a dispute over patronage, Chase again offered his resignation from the Cabinet, and this time Lincoln accepted it. The ascendancy of Lincoln within his own party and official household now seemed assured, but during the summer a mood of deep despondency was created by the military situation. Grant's costly operations against Lee had settled down into the protracted siege of Petersburg, and General Early threatened Washington in July. At just this time the quarrel between Lincoln and the Congressional radicals over the question of Southern reconstruction became an open breach.

Radical policy at this stage was expressed in the Wade-Davis Bill, which finally got through Congress in July at the very end of the session. Withholding his consent, Lincoln killed it by a pocket veto. This plan did not go as far as the radicals really desired but it differed from Lincoln's in denying to far more Southerners the privilege of taking the oath of allegiance—excluding, among others, all who had voluntarily taken up arms against the United States. Also, it raised to 50 per cent of the voters in 1860 the number necessary to create a state government, while making more specific and more drastic stipulations than Lincoln did about the disfranchisement of Confederate leaders, the abolition of slavery, and the repudiation of state and Confederate debts. Finally, the whole measure implied that Congress not the President should dominate the process of reconstruction.

Lincoln issued a proclamation on July 8 in which he said that he was inflexibly committed to no single plan of restoration and was willing to co-operate with the loyal people of any Southern state who might choose to be restored to the Union on the basis of the Wade-Davis Bill. Quite obviously he preferred his own plan, however, and he was unwilling that the governments already established in occupied Southern states should be set aside. To Thaddeus Stevens the proclamation was "infamous," and on August 5, 1864, Wade and Davis issued a manifesto, charging that Lincoln had rejected the judgment of Congress, "the proper constituted authority," and inaugurated anarchy. "A more studied outrage on the legislative authority of the people has never been perpetrated," they said. They charged him with holding the electoral votes of the Rebel states "at the dictation of his personal ambition," and called upon the country to put an end to this executive usurpation.

Under these circumstances an extraordinary movement got under way —to hold another national convention in late September to consider the state of the Union and select another presidential candidate if necessary. Meetings of the conspirators were held in New York and private calls for a convention went out. Embittered Congressional radicals dominated the movement, but they drew into it others who were disgruntled or frustrated in this time of acute war-weariness. Party morale had sunk to its lowest point, and even Lincoln's managers believed that he had no chance to win the election. Two things saved him: the actions of the Democrats and Union military victory at the eleventh hour.

The Democrats, meeting in convention on August 29, put into their party platform a plank declaring the war a failure and calling for a cessation of hostilities. This was inserted under pressure from the notorious Vallandigham, who favored an armistice; and although it was qualified by expressions of loyalty to the Union, it was naturally termed a Copperhead plank. The convention nominated General McClellan for President and George H. Pendleton of Ohio for Vice-President. The former and his friends believed that he had been badly treated by the administration, chiefly because of the radical Republicans, but McClellan was unwilling to reflect on his old command by describing the war as a failure and he virtually repudiated the peace plank.

Before the Democratic convention, Lincoln drew a private memorandum in which he stated that his own re-election then seemed unlikely. In the case of defeat his duty, as he saw it, would be so to "co-operate with the President-elect as to save the Union between the election and the inauguration; as he will have secured his election on such ground that he cannot save it afterwards." McClellan would hardly have sacrificed the Union, whose armies he had commanded, but the Vallandigham support was a grave embarrassment to him. The combination of McClellan and Vallandigham was too much for the radical Republicans to stomach; they preferred Lincoln, despite the moderation of his views about the restoration of the Southern states. Furthermore, on September 2, Sherman took Atlanta. Sheridan's victories in the Valley followed and Northern morale rose rapidly. Meanwhile, the project of another Republican convention was given up, and on September 22 Frémont retired from the race. This action came about as the result of a deal whereby Postmaster

General Montgomery Blair, a pet abomination of the radicals, was dropped from the Cabinet by way of recompense for the withdrawal of Frémont. The radicals got back on the bandwagon.

In the election that followed, Lincoln carried all the Union states except New Jersey, Delaware, and Kentucky. Also, he carried Louisiana and Tennessee, whose vote was not counted. Nevada had been conveniently admitted to the Union only eight days before the election, but Colorado did not get in quite soon enough to vote. The electoral majority was overwhelming, but the popular majority was only about 400,000 and McClellan had a large vote in crucial states. Under only slightly altered circumstances the outcome might have been very different. Lincoln had again demonstrated his political skill, but the major architects of his victory were Vallandigham on the one hand and Sherman, Sheridan, and Farragut on the other. The Copperhead danger was at an end, but the President still had to reckon with the vindictives in his own party.

THE FINAL MILITARY PHASES, 1864-1865

The final military operations of the war may be roughly divided into two phases. Sherman cut a wide swath from Atlanta through Georgia to the sea and then through the Carolinas. After the effective Confederacy had thus been reduced to a small fraction, Grant was at last able to dislodge Lee from the trenches of Petersburg. It is no reflection on Grant's final tactics as a field commander to say that Northern victory resulted from the successful accomplishment of the larger strategic plan. The precise form which this plan assumed in these final weeks was largely owing to Sherman.

The Marches of Sherman

To Sherman the Confederate cause had seemed hopeless from the fall of Vicksburg and unquestionably lost after the fall of Atlanta. By the time of the latter event a number of realistic Southern leaders agreed with him, but nobody would assume the responsibility of giving up. Jefferson Davis was making a series of patriotic speeches in Georgia at just this stage. Sherman's consuming desire was to end the war as soon as possible. Hood's weakened but undestroyed army had been striking at his communications and constituted a potential peril to the Federal position in Tennessee. But, after calculating this danger, Sherman detached Thomas with forces which he deemed sufficient to meet it, and he gained the consent of Grant and Lincoln to his own plan to take his remaining army of more than 60,000 men to the sea and then northward.

His idea was to lessen the material resources of the Confederacy and cause the civilian population to feel the power of the Union govern-

ment. He wrote Grant: "I can make the march and make Georgia howl!"
Years later (1880), in a public speech, he made a statement which became famous: "There is many a boy here who looks on war as all glory,
but, boys, it is all hell." To his logical mind, war was cruelty which could
not be refined, and he himself was ruthless while he waged it. But he
avoided unnecessary fighting and sought to save lives by destroying
property. The logic of this outspoken commander was not appreciated by
the Georgians and Carolinians whose lands his men ravaged; they hated
him for carrying the war home to helpless civilians. Events were to
show, after the strife had ended, that his attitude toward the defeated
South was as generous as Lincoln's, but the emotions he had aroused
were an obstacle to spiritual reunion.

In the middle of November 1864, about a week after the presidential
election, Sherman set his troops marching toward the sea in four columns,
spread over an area fifty or sixty miles wide. Systematically they destroyed
the railroads, heating the rails and twisting them around trees, and
they foraged thoroughly and freely. They met no organized military
resistance, and by sharp reprisals they punished what organized civilian
resistance there was. The soldiers had a continuous picnic, feeding on
the fat of the land. At Milledgeville, the capital of Georgia, they held
a mock session of the legislature and repealed the ordinance of secession.
Ladies saw their ancestral chests looted and their ballroom dresses
donned by soldiers in gay derision. The march was an unending humilia-
tion to a proud but helpless people. The worst excesses were attributable
to the straggling soldiers, detached from their commands, who were
known as "bummers," but there was practically no rape or other violence
against persons. Sherman discouraged refugees but his columns were
accompanied by throngs of excited Negroes, who thought the Day of
Jubilee had come. His men collected cattle in droves, and they were
instructed to kill horses that they could not use. Sherman himself
estimated the total damage his army did the state of Georgia at $100
million. About a fifth of this was of value to his army, he said, and the
rest total loss.

For about a month the Northern public was without news of Sherman
and the report of his appearance before Savannah in mid-December
was one of the most dramatic stories of the war. Soon the small force
of Confederates in the city were compelled to evacuate it, and Sherman
presented Savannah to Lincoln as a Christmas present.

Meanwhile, Hood had invaded Tennessee, but he was repulsed at
Franklin (Nov. 30, 1864), when he attacked a Federal detachment under
Schofield, and a couple of weeks later (Dec. 15-16) he was overwhelmed at Nashville by Thomas, whom Schofield had rejoined. This
was one of the most decisive Union victories of the war, since it resulted
in the disintegration of Hood's army as a fighting force. With him had

been the redoubtable cavalry leader, General Nathan Bedford Forrest, best remembered for the maxim, "get thar fustest with the mostest." Forrest continued to oppose the Union cavalry, but his native military genius was unavailing against the prevailing odds. Sherman's calculated risk in the West proved a safe one, and more reinforcements from Tennessee were now available to the Union armies in the East than to the Confederate.

In January 1865 the fall of Fort Fisher was followed by the closing of the last Confederate port at Wilmington, N. C., and on February 1 Sherman resumed his itinerary. After covering 425 miles he arrived, on March 23, at Goldsboro, N. C. The march through the middle country of the Carolinas was a greater physical feat than the jaunt through Georgia, and there was more organized opposition, chiefly from cavalry under General Wade Hampton. The Union soldiers, blaming South Carolina for having started the war, were more disposed to "scourge" the state than they had been in Georgia and the stealing was worse. The most notable and controversial incident of the march was the burning of Columbia, the capital of the state (February 17, 1865). This started from burning cotton and appears to have been unintentional, though it was blamed on Wade Hampton by Sherman and on Sherman by virtually all South Carolinians.

President Jefferson Davis, recognizing the extreme gravity of the military situation and yielding to pressure from the Confederate Congress, had finally appointed Lee Commander-in-Chief of all Confederate forces (February 6, 1865). Lee soon restored Joseph E. Johnston to command what was left of his old army and such other troops as could be assembled in North Carolina. There was fighting at Bentonville, N. C. (March 19-20), but Sherman avoided a general engagement, believing that there had been bloodshed enough and that Johnston's retirement was inevitable. At Goldsboro, Sherman received reinforcements that swelled his own forces to 80,000, while Johnston did not have half that number even on paper. The day after his arrival at the place he had aimed at from the beginning, the red-bearded Sherman set out by water for Virginia, for a conference with Lincoln and Grant at City Point, where they talked about peace terms.

The Last of the Confederacy

A few days after Sherman left Savannah, an informal peace conference, known as the Hampton Roads Conference, was held between Lincoln and Seward on the one hand and three Confederate commissioners, including Vice-President Stephens, on the other. The latter were seeking a temporary armistice, which Lincoln would not hear of. He would treat for nothing less than the restoration of the Union, while the Confederates, because of Jefferson Davis, would make no real settlement short of independence. The Thirteenth Amendment, abolishing slavery, had been passed by the Federal Congress on January 31, though not yet ratified by the states, and Lincoln insisted that there should be no halting of the emancipation process, but he himself still favored the compensation of slaveholders. He proposed to his incredulous Cabinet a few days later an offer of compensation, only to find them all opposed. He was willing to offer $400 million, in return for Confederate submission by April.

Jefferson Davis would have served his fellow Southerners well if at this time he had given up the dream of independence, which was now wholly vain, and had come to terms with Lincoln. Instead, he reported to the Confederate Congress that unconditional surrender was demanded, and he launched, in Richmond on February 6, a final patriotic crusade with an unusually moving speech. His passionate appeal was followed by an outburst of patriotism in many of the Southern states. This was very short-lived, however, and the mood of desperation was reflected in the act of the Confederate Congress (March 13, 1865) authorizing the President to call on owners for slaves to perform military service. It was assumed, though not stated, that the emancipation of these Negro soldiers would follow. The action was justified on the ground that the North was using Negro troops. In 1864, there were 150,000 of them in the Federal military service, and in 1865 there were not that many effectives in all the Confederate armies. Most important of all was the fact that Lee had recommended the arming of slaves, though he also recommended definite provision for emancipation. This belated provision amounted to little anyway, and at the end the government had arrived at a state of quarrelsome futility. Throughout the South virtually everybody had lost faith in the politicians.

They had not lost faith in Lee, but in its enfeebled state the Army of Northern Virginia was confronting a task beyond its powers. The line of forts and trenches, extending from a point east and north of Richmond to one south and west of Petersburg, was nearly forty miles long, for by swings to the left Grant had kept on extending it until it was already almost at the breaking point. The only remaining artery of Confederate supply was the Southside Railroad, from Petersburg to Lynchburg, and this did not bring food and forage enough. Meanwhile, at City Point on the James, the Union had created magazines which, it was boasted, could supply 500,000 men if need be. Sheridan had come from the Valley to join Grant. Sherman was marching northward, and the junction of his army with Grant's would seal the doom of the Army of Northern Virginia. The only hope of continued resistance was for Lee to withdraw from his fortified position, join Johnston before Sherman reached him, fall upon Sherman, and then be ready for Grant. It was a forlorn hope but there was no other.

The costly Confederate attack on Fort Steadman (March 25), at a weak point in the Union lines east of Petersburg, was a vain attempt to create a diversion and facilitate a withdrawal, but all the attacking thereafter was done by the Federals. Lee anticipated the blow against the important junction of Five Forks (April 1) to the southwest of Petersburg, but under the vigorous leadership of Sheridan the Federals won a decisive victory, and on the next day they broke through the weakened Confederate line closer to the city. Since there was now no way to prevent them from cutting the vital railroad line, the evacuation of Petersburg and Richmond became imperative. Lee informed Jefferson Davis to that effect, and the Confederate President and his Cabinet proceeded to Danville. Richmond was occupied by Union forces on April 3.

Lee made a skillful withdrawal but the supplies he had ordered sent ahead did not arrive and he lost valuable time seeking food and forage. The story of the next week was that of an unequal race. All the roads to the southward were finally cut off by the well-handled Federals. Meanwhile, Lee's starving army was dwindling as the result of capture and straggling. Grant opened the way by proposing surrender and, after the exchange of several letters, Lee acceded in order to avoid unnecessary bloodshed.

At the McLean house in Appomattox Courthouse on Palm Sunday, April 9, 1865, Grant, in his mud-stained field uniform, was a magnanimous and chivalrous victor. He wore no sword and did not ask for Lee's; he permitted all the Confederate soldiers to be paroled; he allowed the officers and cavalrymen to retain their much-needed horses. Lee surrendered with dignity on honorable terms, and Grant and his officers lifted their hats to the grizzled commander when he mounted Traveller and sadly rode away. Grant ordered rations for the hungry Confederates to the number of 25,000, though in reality only about half that many men were left. Lee issued a final order to the survivors of his command, bidding them an affectionate farewell, and the Army of Northern Virginia passed into history. He himself has remained from that day till this the supreme legendary figure of the South. No one born below the Potomac since George Washington was ever viewed there with such veneration. After seeing him, one daughter of Virginia said: "We had heard of God, but here was General Lee." The "Lost Cause" found in this great gentleman, in this Christian soldier *par excellence*, its purest and noblest symbol.

The surrender of Johnston became inevitable after that of Lee, and Sherman also was magnanimous. Following the wishes of Lincoln, as he had remembered them from their conference at City Point, he offered political assurances as well as a military settlement. But the death of Lincoln intervened and this agreement was repudiated in Washington. The revised terms, which were essentially the same as those Grant gave

Lee, were finally agreed to on April 26. Several more distant minor armies surrendered a little later, and before May had passed the organized resistance to the Union was at an end.

Jefferson Davis made a less dignified exit than Lee and Johnston. From Danville he and the remnants of his government fled to Greensboro, North Carolina, and finally he was captured on May 10 in Georgia in disguise. His fellow Southerners blamed him most for the failure of their cause, and no doubt he would have remained a scapegoat had he not been confined by the United States government in Fortress Monroe in chains. Lincoln, who had hoped that he would get away, would have been too wise to turn him into a martyr, but, unhappily for both North and South, Lincoln had been assassinated.

LINCOLN AND THE PRICE OF VICTORY

Abraham Lincoln was fifty-six years old when inaugurated for his second term on March 4, 1865, and he looked worn and ill. The oath of office was administered by Salmon P. Chase, whom the President had magnanimously appointed Chief Justice in the fall of 1864, after the death of aged Roger B. Taney. Lincoln himself believed that his brief inaugural speech would wear better, perhaps, than anything else he had produced. History has recognized it as a gem of restrained eloquence and bracketed it with the immortal Gettysburg Address. But, as he recognized, it was not immediately popular. Four years of death and destruction had created an emotional atmosphere uncongenial to such judiciousness and magnanimity as he manifested. He reminded his auditors that the Confederates read the same Bible and prayed to the same God that they did; he admonished them to judge not, that they be not judged; and he recognized the terrible war as a sort of divine retribution on both North and South for the offense of slavery. As for the future, he summed up its immediate tasks in his noble concluding words:

> With malice toward none; with charity for all; with firmness in the right, as God gives us to see the right, let us strive on to finish the work we are in; to bind up the nation's wounds; to care for him who shall have borne the battle, and for his widow, and his orphan—to do all which may achieve a just and lasting peace, among ourselves, and with all nations.

Toward the end of March the President visited Grant's headquarters, and he had a conference with Grant and Sherman at City Point. The political settlement which Sherman afterwards offered Johnston was based on a misunderstanding of Lincoln's instructions, but Sherman did not misinterpret Lincoln's desire to restore the Union as quickly as possible on the most generous of terms. Following the evacuation of Richmond by the Confederate government and army, Lincoln visited that late capital, where the Negroes received him joyously and the white people maintained a stunned silence. On Palm Sunday, April 9, he was back in Washington and late that evening he received a telegram from Grant announcing Lee's surrender.

On the night of April 11, he delivered to a crowd of serenaders a speech which proved to be his last. It had none of the mood of exultation which such a crowd expected and Lincoln himself believed that it fell flat. He dealt seriously with the question of Southern restoration, referring specifically to the state of Louisiana, where a government had been set up according to his 10-per-cent plan and this government had prohibited slavery. He was trying to build up support for his own policies of moderation. Slavery was dead or dying, and to his mind the major remaining task was to give practical effect to the restoration of the seceded states, letting bygones be bygones. "Finding themselves safely at home," he said, "it would be utterly immaterial whether they had ever been abroad."

On Good Friday, April 14, while still awaiting from Sherman the news of Johnston's surrender, he had a Cabinet meeting in which the problems of Southern restoration were discussed. Secretary of War Stanton was fearful lest the North should lose the fruits of victory, but Lincoln was more fearful of "feelings of hate and vindictiveness" which were held by some men in Congress and was glad that body was not in session. That night he attended a performance of Laura Keene's *Our American Cousin* at Ford's Theatre, and there in a flag-draped box the victorious Commander-in-Chief of the United States was shot in the head by John Wilkes Booth.

Booth, aged twenty-six, the younger brother of the noted actor, Edwin Booth, was himself a talented actor and he looked rather like Edgar Allan Poe. Whether or not he was technically insane, as his father had been, he was emotionally unbalanced. Though a Southern sympathizer throughout the war, this Marylander had not enlisted in the Confederate Army. He shouted the motto of the state of Virginia, "*Sic Semper Tyrannis!*" on the stage, after jumping from the presidential box, but he was acting independently. The later charge of Confederate complicity was wholly without foundation. Pursued into Virginia and surrounded, he died from a shot, probably his own, soon after he was borne from a burning barn. His accomplices, real and supposed, were afterwards tried before a military commission on the charge of conspiracy with Jefferson Davis to murder the President of the United States. Four were executed. The plot was also directed against the Vice-President and the Secretary of State. Johnson escaped injury because his assailant lost his nerve but Seward, already in bed from a fall, was seriously wounded.

Booth could not have done the South or the Union greater disservice. His mad act created a mood of hysteria in which common sense was stifled. He played directly into the hands of the "irreconcilables" whom Lincoln was trying to block—much as John Brown had played into the hands of the secessionist "fire-eaters." In blind and unreasoning rage he had struck down the South's greatest and most powerful Northern friend and the most conspicuous advocate of spiritual reunion. As Herman Melville put it,

> They have killed him, the forgiver—
> The Avenger takes his place.

Lincoln died a little after seven o'clock on the morning of April 15. The voices of criticism, which he had heard so often, were stilled everywhere, never again to be raised against him. His secretary, John G. Nicolay, soon wrote: "It would seem that Providence had exacted from him the last and only additional service and sacrifice he could give his country—that of dying for her sake." The fact that he was stricken on Good Friday did not go unnoted, and he was hailed as the Saviour of the Union. No President before him had been assassinated; no other had had his career crowned and sanctified by martyrdom. Thus circumstances combined to create the greatest of all American legends centering on a historic person. The most humorous of major American public men now appeared as the supremely tragic figure; already regarded as the personal embodiment of democracy, he now became the enduring symbol of the emancipation of the enslaved, of the preserved Union, of Christlike compassion and vicarious atonement. In death he became a living legend, but many who spoke his name with reverence were unfaithful to him in spirit. His still-divided country needed his wise patience, and in his death it suffered the greatest casualty of the costliest of its wars.

Counting the Costs

Lincoln's statement in his second inaugural, that neither side had expected the war to attain such magnitude or duration or to be so costly, erred on the side of moderation. Neither he nor Jefferson Davis nor anybody else had dreamed of such a conflict. The human costs have never been fully counted and cannot be, but the total casualties in the armed forces of the Union and the Confederacy, including wounded and dead, appear to have been approximately the same as in the American forces in the Second World War, that is, about a million. But there were more than 600,000 deaths in the Civil War, as compared with somewhat more than 400,000 among Americans in the Second World War. In the earlier conflict a higher percentage of wounds proved mortal, and there were more deaths from disease—which exacted a greater toll than the bullets of the enemy. There is no way to measure the suffering, but in an era of amputations without anesthetics unquestionably it was extreme. The relative toll in human life was far greater in the Civil War if we consider the population of the country in the two periods. On that basis, deaths were proportionately seven or eight times as numerous as in the Second World War. To an extent which has not yet been paralleled in its entire history, the country lost the flower of its youth and the potential leaders of the future. This was true of the North and doubly true of the South.

The monetary costs cannot be given with finality, but the estimate that mere war expenses on the two sides amounted to about $5 billion is a convenient approximation. To this may be added the costs of reconstruction, which may be roughly estimated at $3 billion. No allowance is made in these figures for the staggering cost of pensions afterward or for the losses to individuals. The latter were immensely greater in the South, where nearly all the fighting took place and where Sherman and Sheridan carried on their work of systematic devastation. Greatest of all the individual losses were those resulting from the abolition of property in slaves without compensation—some $3 or $4 billion. Nothing in the past history of English-speaking peoples offers a parallel to such deprivation of private property as a result of governmental action. One unquestionable result of the war was the financial ruin of the planter class. This class had passed the point of its greatest fruitfulness but in other times it had produced some of the most eminent leaders of the Republic—such as Washington, Jefferson, and Andrew Jackson.

The dominance of the economy and government of the country by the North was a sure and immediate result of the conflict, but the benefits of victory which bulked largest in the Northern mind, as a justification of the colossal cost in life and fortune, were the preservation of the Union and the disappearance of slavery from the whole land. In the long run the Southerners were glad to be relieved of slavery, and hardly one of them wanted the legal institution back; but emancipation by force of arms brought economic chaos and social revolution to the Confederate states, and the history of the next generation was to show that the war had by no means solved the problems of the relations of white men and Negroes in a democratic society. As for the Union, virtually all Southerners in the course of time came to rejoice that they were still part of it, but out of the war and its immediate aftermath emerged a different sort of Union from the one Lincoln had set out to maintain. His government had triumphed by means of freshly forged power, and the emotions incited by his assassination vastly increased the uncertainty of the wise employment of this new strength. There was all the more question now whether genuine self-government and the true union of hearts could be restored, after an orgy of slaughter and hatred. Dread and terror filled the air as the costliest of American wars ended an era, and the forces of destruction seemed still in the ascendant. There was to be another day, a new South, a genuinely united and fantastically prosperous country, but it was a dark night for all Americans when Lincoln lay dying.

SELECT BIBLIOGRAPHY

General Statement

READING IN MORE DETAILED WORKS CAN ENORMOUSLY ENRICH AND ENLIVEN the story which is inevitably compressed in a book like this; and original sources can provide a vividness of impression that secondary narratives rarely convey. Part of the continuing appeal of historical study arises from the fact that there is always something more which anybody can learn about the past and that the closer one gets to the actual people and events the more vivid and real they become. To some extent every student can become an explorer in his own right, and in the investigation of some appealing topic can taste the joy of discovery.

The purpose of the present bibliography is to acquaint the student and reader with the most useful aids—stress being laid on those that are most accessible—and, without making any pretence of exhaustiveness, to mention selected books which can be read to advantage and sources which can be explored with relative ease. Comments are frequently attached—sometimes as a sort of warning but more often as an invitation to particular items in the historical feast.

First, there is a relatively brief list of works bearing on the whole or most of this volume; then, both general and specific suggestions are given chapter by chapter. These can be richly supplemented from the bibliographical items and suggestions in many of the listed books.

Basic Reference Works

The most important single bibliographical aid is the *Harvard Guide to American History* (1954), edited by Oscar Handlin. Besides excellent chapters on the materials and tools of American history and convenient lists of books in various categories, it contains suggestions for reading on the various periods and topics which go far beyond any that can be given here.

Every historical shelf should have the *Encyclopedia of American History* (1953), edited by R. B. Morris, a handy volume which is invaluable for facts and dates. The arrangement is both chronological and topical.

Among the larger reference works with which students should familiarize themselves is the *Dictionary of American Biography* (20 vols., 1928-36), edited by Allen Johnson and Dumas Malone; supplementary volumes edited by H. E. Starr (1944), and R. L. Schuyler (1958). This co-operative work provides rich personal materials for the whole of American history. A good way to turn mere names into real persons is to look them up in this collection of articles. Those desiring to read further will find suggestions in the bibliographies. (A selected list of biographies is given in the *Harvard Guide*, pp. 190-206).

Excellent examples of large collections of the writings of great Americans are Washington's *Writings*, edited by J. C. Fitzpatrick (39 vols., 1931-44); and

Lincoln's *Collected Works*, edited by R. P. Basler (9 vols., 1953). Among extensive collections now in process the pace-setter is Jefferson's *Papers*, edited by Julian P. Boyd, 15 vols. of which had appeared by 1958. A number of handy one-volume collections are mentioned hereafter.

The *Dictionary of American History* (5 vols., 1940), edited by J. T. Adams, while uneven, is useful in connection with particular topics. The *Encyclopedia of the Social Sciences* (15 vols., 1930-34), edited by E. R. A. Seligman, is a work of much wider scope, but the student should not hesitate to consult it.

Fascinating statistical materials can be found in the publication of the Bureau of the Census, *A Century of Population Growth . . . 1790-1900* (1909). This also contains estimates of population during the colonial and Revolutionary periods. The *Biographical Directory of the American Congress, 1774-1949* (1950), is a big and awkward but useful volume. Besides giving the lists of members of the successive Congresses (and also of executive officers), it contains brief biographical sketches.

Good maps are of the first importance. Two older collections have not yet been excelled for general historical use: W. R. Shepherd, *Historical Atlas* (1911), which deals with Europe as well as America; and *Harper's Atlas of American History* (1920), consisting of maps from the old *American Nation* series. Later school atlases of wide use include: C. E. and E. H. Lord, *Historical Atlas of the United States* (1944); and J. T. Adams, *Atlas of American History* (1943). The fullest and most authoritative work is C. O. Paullin, *Atlas of the Historical Geography of the United States* (1932), edited by J. K. Wright. While too big and cumbersome for frequent use, this is valuable for boundary disputes and other matters of concern to advanced students and specialists.

Much work has been done in making old and recent pictures available. The first extensive modern compilation was *The Pageant of America* (15 vols., 1926-29), edited by R. H. Gabriel. The *Harvard Guide*, pp. 65-66, has a list of later general collections. Some works of special value dealing with particular periods or subjects will be referred to hereafter at appropriate points. Naturally, pictorial records became more accurate as well as more extensive with the development of photography, but the older paintings and prints often convey a delightful sense of their own day.

Convenient Collections of Documents and Readings

The best general collection of documents in convenient form and a strong contender for any historian's bookshelf is *Documents of American History* (6 edn., 1958), edited by H. S. Commager. Besides official documents, this contains party platforms, important speeches, etc. It can be supplemented by L. B. Evans, *Cases on American Constitutional Law*, revised edition by C. G. Fenwick (1948), or by *Cases in Constitutional Law*, by Robert E. and Robert F. Cushman (1958), both of which are fuller in a more limited field. Treaties and diplomatic documents can be best consulted in R. J. Bartlett, ed., *The Record of American Diplomacy* (1950), a book which should stand on the shelf with Commager.

A rich collection of readings bearing especially on social and intellectual matters is *American Issues*, Vol. I, "The Social Record" (rev. edn., 1955), edited by Willard Thorp, Merle Curti, and Carlos Baker. Another good collection, which is more economic and political in emphasis, is *The Shaping of the American Tradition* (1947), edited by L. M. Hacker, whose relatively long introductions are illuminating and provocative. The older and less accessible work, G. S. Callender, ed., *Selections from the Economic History of the United States, 1765-1868* (1909), contains, besides readings, brief but unusually penetrating introductions which comprise a summary of economic history.

The Making of American History (rev. edn., 1954), edited by Donald Sheehan, is an anthology which contains 35 long extracts from historical writers dealing with major topics. Some of these will be specifically referred to hereafter. *Understanding the American Past* (1954), edited by E. N. Saveth, is a similar work.

Problems in American Civilization: Readings Selected by the Department of American Studies, Amherst College (1947-   ) comprise a useful series of paper-bound booklets. Each deals with a particular topic and contains selections from authors with varying views. Somewhat more than a dozen have been issued to date and they offer one of the best methods of studying controversial questions. Individual booklets will be mentioned hereafter.

Larger General Histories

Every student and serious reader should become acquainted with major long histories and series, and should dip into them to some extent. The present list is confined to works or sets covering the whole period of this volume.

Edward Channing, *History of the United States* (6 vols., 1905-25) extends through 1865. To some extent it reflects the author's Northeastern environment and at time his caprices, but generally it is judicious and temperate.

The Chronicles of America (50 vols., 1918-21), edited by Allen Johnson, comprise an unusually readable series of small volumes which inevitably vary in quality.

A History of American Life (13 vols., 1927-48), edited by A. M. Schlesinger and D. R. Fox, is the standard series for social history. The bibliographies are excellent.

The old series, *The American Nation: A History* (26 vols., 1904-08; additional vol., 1918), edited by A. B. Hart, has a distinguished position in American historiography and certain volumes are still of great value. *The New American Nation Series*, edited by H. S. Commager and R. B. Morris, to comprise about 40 vols., is in process. The volumes are of a handy size and contain full and up-to-date bibliographies.

A History of the South, edited by W. H. Stephenson and E. M. Coulter (1947-   ), projected in 10 vols., of which 7 fall in the period to 1865, is an admirable series, now more than half done. The bibliographies are detailed and comprehensive.

Topical Histories

GEOGRAPHY AND ABORIGINES

There is need for a readable work on American historical geography in convenient size. The two following books are useful for reference: J. R. Smith and

M. O. Phillips, *North America* (rev. edn., 1940), a lengthy regional treatment
of the United States, Canada, and Central America; R. H. Brown, *Historical
Geography of the United States* (1948), a sound work, following the order of
settlement. In the field of oceanography, Rachel Carson, *The Sea around Us*
(1951), is fascinating. An excellent account of the Indians, written for the layman, is R. M. Underhill, *Red Man's America* (1953).

SETTLEMENT AND IMMIGRATION

Most general works pay considerable attention to the process of settlement
and there are many specialized studies of particular areas. A comprehensive
but compact book is R. A. Billington, *Westward Expansion; A History of the
American Frontier* (1949), dealing also with transportation and land policies.
The Frontier in America (1921), a collection of essays by F. J. Turner, is a
classic.

   The larger problems of immigration are illuminated by three books by M.
L. Hansen: *The Atlantic Migration, 1607-1860* (1940), and *The Immigrant in
American History* (1941), both edited by A. M. Schlesinger, and *The Mingling
of the Canadian and American Peoples* (1940), completed by J. B. Brebner.
A good general treatment is Carl Wittke, *We Who Built America: The Saga
of the Immigrant* (1939). Works on the Negro and particular ethnic groups
are cited hereafter.

ECONOMIC AND FINANCIAL HISTORY

Among general economic histories in one volume are H. U. Faulkner, *American Economic History* (8 edn., 1959); E. C. Kirkland, *A History of American
Economic Life* (3 edn., 1951); and F. A. Shannon, *America's Economic Growth*
(rev. edn., 1951). The older and more restricted works, D. R. Dewey, *Financial
History of the United States* (12 edn., 1934), and F. W. Taussig, *Tariff History
of the United States* (7 edn., 1923) are still useful handbooks.

AGRICULTURAL HISTORY

The standard works for the period covered by this volume are P. W. Bidwell
and J. I. Falconer, *History of Agriculture in the Northern United States, 1620-
1860* (1925), and L. C. Gray, *History of Agriculture in the Southern United
States to 1860* (2 vols., 1933). While too detailed for general reading, these
books are invaluable to those wishing to explore any part of this vital subject.

INTELLECTUAL HISTORY

Merle Curti, in *The Growth of American Thought* (2 edn., 1951), covers the
whole period systematically and has unusually valuable bibliographies for his
chapters. V. L. Parrington, *Main Currents in American Thought* (3 vols.,
1927-30), is a highly stimulating work and a delight to read, even when one
disputes the author's judgment. R. H. Gabriel, *The Course of American Democratic Thought* (1940), deals admirably with the period after 1815. Harvey

Wish, *Society and Thought in Early America* (1950), covers social as well as intellectual history to 1865.

Literary history

Abundant materials are available in R. E. Spiller and others, *Literary History of the United States* (3 vols., 1948), the third volume of which is an elaborate bibliography; and A. H. Quinn, ed., *The Literature of the American People* (1951).

Labor

F. R. Dulles, *Labor in America* (1949), is a convenient general treatment.

Constitutional History and Parties

For general use the best works on their subject are C. B. Swisher, *American Constitutional Development* (1943); and A. H. Kelly and W. A. Harbison, *The American Constitution: Its Origins and Development* (1948). A. C. McLaughlin, *A Constitutional History of the United States* (1935) becomes less valuable after the early national period. W. E. Binkley, *American Political Parties: Their Natural History* (3 edn., 1958), a good survey, offers a penetrating analysis of the reasons why our political parties are so "illogical."

Diplomacy

General treatments are: J. W. Pratt, *A History of United States Foreign Policy* (1955), a well-proportioned and judicious recent work; the old reliable, S. F. Bemis, *A Diplomatic History of the United States* (rev. edn., 1950); T. A. Bailey, *A Diplomatic History of the American People* (6 edn., 1957). Anyone wishing to inquire into the activities of some particular man will find much information and interpretation in S. F. Bemis, ed., *The American Secretaries of State and Their Diplomacy* (10 vols., 1927-29).

Religion, Science, and Education

General treatments are disappointing, but the following works are useful: W. W. Sweet, *The Story of Religion in America* (rev. edn., 1939); D. J. Struik, *Yankee Science in the Making* (1948); E. P. Cubberly, *Public Education in the United States* (rev. edn., 1934) E. E. Slosson, *The American Spirit in Education* (1921, *Chronicles of America*). M. E. Curti, *Social Ideas of American Educators* (1935), is excellent.

Architecture and Art

The main lines of development are shown in T. F. Hamlin, *The American Spirit in Architecture* (1926); T. F. Tallmadge, *The Story of Architecture in America* (rev. edn., 1936); W. C. Andrews, *Americans, Ambition and Architecture*

(1955); Samuel Isham, *The History of American Painting*, supplemented by Royal Cortissoz (1927).

Military and Naval

The fruitfulness of scholarship in this field is best shown in specialized studies. General works do not yet fully reflect it, but the following are useful: W. A. Ganoe, *A History of the United States Army* (1942); O. L. Spaulding, *The United States Army in War and Peace* (1937); D. W. Knox, *A History of the United States Navy* (rev. edn., 1948); H. H. and Margaret Sprout, *The Rise of American Naval Power, 1776-1918* (1939). The old army textbook, M. F. Steele, *American Campaigns* (2 vols., last edn., 1922), with its maps, is still helpful.

Part I: Colonial Foundations, to 1763

General

A good one-volume history of the entire period is C. P. Nettels, *The Roots of American Civilization* (1938). The most comprehensive general treatment is C. M. Andrews, *The Colonial Period of American History* (4 vols., 1934-38); Vols. I-III are devoted to the settlements, and Vol. IV to the British system. Political institutions are treated exhaustively in H. L. Osgood, *The American Colonies in the Seventeenth Century* (3 vols., 1904-07), and *The American Colonies in the Eighteenth Century* (4 vols., 1924-25), which is not the equal of its predecessor; the style of both works is dull. Social developments are described in early volumes of *A History of American Life*. Literary and intellectual developments are treated in works cited under Topical Histories.

Special

See suggestions under individual chapters. It should be noted that, as the treatment in the text is considerably more compressed in Part I of this work than in the Parts which follow, the bibliography is correspondingly curtailed. Anyone wishing to explore the extensive literature of the colonial period will find abundant suggestions in the *Harvard Guide*, Chs. 6-9.

1. EUROPEAN BACKGROUNDS

General

Since the entire history of western Europe from the late Middle Ages provides backgrounds for American history, students will naturally turn to general works which themselves offer further suggestions for reading. Among these the following are specially helpful: J. W. Thompson, *Economic and Social History of Europe in the Later Middle Ages, 1300-1530* (1931); W. C. Abbott, *The Expansion of Europe* (1938); E. P. Cheyney, *The Dawn of a New Era* (1936); C. H. H. Hayes, *Political and Cultural History of Modern Europe* (1939);

Preserved Smith, *The Age of the Reformation* (1920). The course of thought is dealt with more specifically in J. H. Randall, *The Making of the Modern Mind* (1926); Crane Brinton, *Ideas and Men, The Story of Western Thought* (1950); Preserved Smith, *A History of Modern Culture*, Vols. I, II (1930, 1934); W. C. Dampier-Whetham, *History of Science* (1932).

Special

Pre-Columbian discoveries are described in H. R. Holand, *Westward from Vinland: An Account of Norse Discoveries and Explorations in America* (1940). R. H. Tawney, *Religion and the Rise of Capitalism* (1926), and Max Weber, *The Protestant Ethic and the Spirit of Capitalism* (1930), are stimulating treatments of a pertinent controversial subject. See also E. D. Adams, *The Power of Ideals in American History* (1913).

2. CONTINENTAL POWERS AND THE NEW WORLD

General

Works in European history cited for the previous chapter, especially Abbott, *Expansion of Europe;* Channing, *History of the United States*, Vol. I; J. B. Brebner, *Explorers of North America* (1933); Priestley, *Coming of the White Man (History of American Life)*, Chs. 1-3; H. E. Bolton and T. M. Marshall, *The Colonization of North America, 1492-1783* (1920).

Special

Supplementary reading on this huge topic can be profitably centered on a particular Power or outstanding leader. PORTUGAL: J. P. Oliveira Martins, *Golden Age of Prince Henry the Navigator* (1914). SPAIN: E. G. Bourne, *Spain in America, 1450-1580*, (1905, *American Nation*); C. H. Haring, *Spanish Empire in America* (1952); E. D. Salmon, *Imperial Spain* (1931); H. E. Bolton, *Spanish Borderlands* (1921, *Chronicles of America*), for the North American Southwest. FRANCE: Francis Parkman, *Pioneers of France in the New World* (1885); G. M. Wrong, *Rise and Fall of New France* (1928). DUTCH: E. L. Raesly, *Portrait of New Netherland* (1945).

Those preferring the biographical approach can find fascinating reading in S. E. Morison, *Admiral of the Ocean Sea* (1942), and the same author's briefer book, written for a wider audience, *Christopher Columbus, Mariner* (1955); Germán Arciniegas, *Amerigo and the New World: The Life and Times of Amerigo Vespucci* (1955, trans. from the Spanish); H. E. Bolton, *Coronado* (1949); C. M. Parr, *So Noble a Captain: The Life and Times of Magellan* (1953).

Recent abridgements of classic works are: *The Battle for North America* (1948), edited by John Tebbel from the Works of Francis Parkman; S. E. Morison, ed., *The Parkman Reader* (1955); Prescott's *The Conquest of Mexico, Designed for Modern Reading*, by Marshall McClintock (1948).

3. EARLY ENGLISH SETTLEMENTS:
VIRGINIA AND MARYLAND

General

W. F. Craven, *The Southern Colonies in the Seventeenth Century, 1607-1689* (1949), Chs. 1-6, an admirable account with full bibliography; T. J. Wertenbaker, *The First Americans* (1927, *History of American Life*), Ch. 2, for social history; C. M. Andrews, "Factors Influencing Colonization," in Sheehan, *Making of American History*, pp. 4-30 (from *Colonial Period of American History*).

Special

English Backgrounds

G. M. Trevelyan, *England under the Stuarts* (12 edn., 1927), a brilliant narrative history; Wallace Notestein, *The English People on the Eve of Colonization, 1603-1630* (1954, *New American Nation Series*), an illuminating study of English society; J. A. Williamson, *The Age of Drake* (1938); W. E. Lingelbach, *Merchant Adventures of England* (1902); G. L. Beer, *Origins of the British Colonial System, 1578-1660* (1908), a detailed treatment.

Virginia

T. J. Wertenbaker, in *Virginia under the Stuarts, 1607-1688* (1914), *The Planters of Colonial Virginia* (1922), and other works has freshly interpreted the history and society of the Old Dominion in the seventeenth century, emphasizing the yeoman farmers. The stimulating book of L. B. Wright, *The First Gentlemen of Virginia* (1940), describes the aristocrats, with greater emphasis on the eighteenth century.

Maryland

The best discussion of Maryland's early history is that of C. M. Andrews in *The Colonial Period of American History*, Vol. II, Chs. 8-9. Among special studies of value are C. C. Hall, *The Lords Baltimore and the Maryland Palatinate* (1902); B. C. Steiner, *Beginnings of Maryland, 1631-1639* (1903); N. D. Mereness, *Maryland as a Proprietary Province* (1901). In view of the particular significance of religious developments in Maryland to Catholics, special mention should be made of John G. Shea, *A History of the Catholic Church within the Limits of the United States* (4 vols., 1886-92).

Slaves and Indentured Servants

The beginnings of slavery in the southern colonies are described in general works, such as U. B. Phillips, *American Negro Slavery* (1929), and J. H. Franklin, *From Slavery to Freedom: A History of American Negroes* (1947). A scholarly treatment of bound white labor is A. E. Smith, *Colonists in Bondage: White Servitude and Convict Labor in America, 1607-1776* (1947). R. B.

Morris, *Government and Labor in Early America* (1946) is valuable for both facts and interpretation.

4. THE NEW ENGLAND COLONIES

General

Good narratives are plentiful. C. M. Andrews gives a full story in *Colonial Period of American History*, Vol. I, Chs. 12-22; Vol. II, Chs. 1-4; and a brief one in *Fathers of New England* (1919, *Chronicles of America*). See also Channing, *History*, Vol. I, Chs. 10-14. J. T. Adams, *The Founding of New England* (1921) is good reading but the rather iconoclastic tone which heightened its popularity when the work was published has caused it to be frowned upon by many historians who take a more favorable view of the Puritans. T. J. Wertenbaker, *The Puritan Oligarchy* (1947) is stimulating and readable. For the Pilgrims, see G. F. Willison, *Saints and Strangers* (1945).

Special

William Bradford's classic, *Of Plymouth Plantation, 1620-1647*, has appeared in an edition by S. E. Morison (1953). Along with this may be read Bradford Smith, *Bradford of Plymouth* (1951). Other biographical works are S. E. Morison, *Builders of the Bay Colony* (1930); S. H. Brockunier, *The Irrepressible Democrat: Roger Williams* (1940); D. E. Winslow, *Master Roger Williams* (1957); W. K. Rugg, *Unafraid: A Life of Anne Hutchinson* (1930).

Puritanism is discussed in the general accounts. For able and sympathetic treatment of its theological aspects and intellectual emphasis, see Perry Miller, *Orthodoxy in Massachusetts* (1933), and *The New England Mind* (1939); the introduction to the documentary collection, *The Puritans*, edited by Miller and F. H. Johnson; S. E. Morison, *Founding of Harvard College* (1935); *Puritan Pronaos* (1936); and *Builders of the Bay Colony*. Parrington, in *Main Currents in American Thought*, Vol. I, is less sympathetic. The booklet, *Puritanism in Early America*, in the Amherst *Problems in American Civilization*, offers excellent materials for discussion.

For Witchcraft, see M. L. Starkey, *The Devil in Massachusetts* (1949); G. L. Kittredge, *Witchcraft in Old and New England* (1928). It would be difficult to find in a modern mystery or psychological novel a more engrossing story than that of the actual events in Salem.

5. ORGANIZATION AND DEVELOPMENT OF THE EMPIRE

General

Over-all accounts in Channing, *History*, Vol. II; Nettels, *Roots of American Civilization;* T. J. Wertenbaker, *The Founding of American Civilization: The Middle Colonies* (1938), written in the author's characteristically interesting style; W. F. Craven, *Southern Colonies in the Seventeenth Century*, Chs. 7-11.

Special

British policy, which becomes so important at this time, is ably described and discussed in Andrews, *Colonial Period,* Vol. IV; G. L. Beer, *The Old Colonial System, 1660-1754* (1912); L. A. Harper, *English Navigation Laws* (1939). For the most important non-British group of settlers, see A. B. Faust, *The German Element in the United States* (2 vols., 1909); for the Scotch-Irish and others, see Wittke, *We Who Built America,* and other general accounts of immigration. Other works of special interest are: W. I. Hill, *William Penn* (1937); R. M. Jones, *Quakers in the American Colonies* (1911); T. J. Wertenbaker, *Torchbearer of the Revolution* (1940), an account of Nathaniel Bacon, and W. E. Washburn, *The Governor and the Rebel: A History of Bacon's Rebellion in Virginia* (1957), arriving at different conclusions.

6. COLONIAL LIFE IN THE EIGHTEENTH CENTURY

General

On the process of settlement: R. A. Billington, *Westward Expansion,* Chs. 2-4; F. J. Turner, *Frontier in American History,* Chs. 1, 2; T. P. Abernethy, *Three Virginia Frontiers* (1949). Social, economic, and cultural developments and conditions are described in J. T. Adams, *Provincial Society* (1927, *History of American Life*); C. M. Andrews, *Colonial Folkways* (1919, *Chronicles of America*); T. J. Wertenbaker, *The Golden Age of Colonial Culture* (1942); L. B. Wright, *The Atlantic Frontier* (1947), and *The Cultural Life of the American Colonies, 1607-1763* (1957). Intellectual developments in Curti, *Growth of American Thought,* Part I; Max Savelle, *Seeds of Liberty: The Genesis of the American Mind* (1948); Parrington, *Main Currents in American Thought,* Vol. I. A stimulating fresh study is D. J. Boorstin, *The Americans: The Colonial Experience* (1958).

Special

The following brief list can be readily supplemented from the bibliographies of many of the general works above and from the *Harvard Guide,* pp. 285-289 (sections 103-104); it can cover only a few of the numerous topics of interest and must be merely suggestive: Carl Bridenbaugh, *Cities in the Wilderness: The First Century of Urban Life in America, 1625-1744* (1939), and *Cities in Revolt: Urban Life in America, 1743-1776* (1955); R. G. Albion, *Forests and Sea Power* (1926); V. D. Harrington, *The New York Merchant on the Eve of the Revolution* (1931); R. B. Morris, *Government and Labor in Early America* (1946); L. C. Wroth, *The Colonial Printer* (1938); E. E. Slosson, *The American Spirit in Education* (1921, *Chronicles of America*); O. W. Larkin, *Art and Life in America* (1949); Carl Van Doren, *Benjamin Franklin* (1938), especially Chs. 1-11—an excellent biography of the man who best embodied the diversity of colonial achievement and culture.

7. POLITICS AND WARS

General

Accounts in Channing, *History*, Vol. II; Nettels, *Roots of American Civilization;* E. B. Greene, *Provincial America* (1905, *American Nation*). L. W. Labaree, *Royal Government in America* (1930), well describes the form of government under which most of the colonists lived; it has a full bibliography. The struggle with the French is described briefly by G. M. Wrong in *The Conquest of New France* (1918, *Chronicles of America*), more fully in *The Rise and Fall of New France*. Francis Parkman has written classic works on this topic, reaching the climax in *Montcalm and Wolfe* (2 vols., 1884); in reduced form this comprises Part VI of *The Battle for North America*, ed. by John Tebbel. See also Billington, *Westward Expansion*, Ch. 6; Bolton, *Spanish Borderlands*.

Special

POLITICAL INSTITUTIONS: O. M. Dickerson, *American Colonial Government, 1696-1765* (1912); R. B. Morris, *Studies in the History of American Law* (1930). MERCANTILIST REGULATIONS: G. L. Beer, *British Colonial Policy, 1754-1765* (1937); O. M. Dickerson, *Navigation Acts and the American Revolution* (1951); L. A. Harper, *English Navigation Laws*. INTERNATIONAL STRUGGLE AND COLONIAL WARS: G. S. Graham, *Empire of the North Atlantic: The Maritime Struggle for North America* (1950); L. H. Gipson, *The British Empire before the Revolution* (9 vols., 1936-56), a monumental work, sympathetic with the imperial idea; D. S. Freeman, *George Washington*, Vol. II (1948), giving a detailed and authoritative account of the ill-fated western campaign; Max Savelle, *A Diplomatic History of the Canadian-American Boundary, 1749-1763* (1940), brilliantly summarizing the stakes in the war.

Part II: Beginnings of the Republic, 1763-1789

8. REORGANIZATION OF THE EMPIRE, 1763-1774

General

The story of events in this and the two following chapters is told much more fully in a number of unusually interesting books. These include: C. L. Becker, *The Eve of the Revolution* (1918, in *Chronicles of America*); J. C. Miller, *The Origins of the American Revolution* (1943), and *The Triumph of Freedom, 1775-1783* (1948); L. H. Gipson, *The Coming of the Revolution, 1763-1775* (1954), and J. R. Alden, *The American Revolution, 1775-1783* (1954); J. R. Alden, *The South in the Revolution, 1763-1789* (1957); W. E. H. Lecky, *The American Revolution, 1763-1783* (1898), a temperate English work which retains its value. E. B. Greene, *A Revolutionary Generation, 1763-1790* (1943, in *History of American Life*) provides the social background for the entire period.

Special

Few controversies in American history invite study and stimulate discussion more than that between the colonies and the mother country before the Revolution. Imperial problems at the beginning of the era are treated sympathetically by G. L. Beer in *British Colonial Policy, 1754-1765* (1907). C. M. Andrews views them in the large in *The Colonial Background of the American Revolution* (1924), a brief but illuminating book. The constitutional question within the empire is discussed by C. H. McIlwain in *The American Revolution: A Constitutional Interpretation* (1923), and R. L. Schuyler in *Parliament and the British Empire* (1929), these two eminent scholars arriving at different conclusions. For the ideological conflict see also R. G. Adams, *Political Ideas of the American Revolution, 1763-1783* (1922); Clinton Rossiter, *Seedtime of the Republic* (1953); Philip Davidson, *Propaganda and the American Revolution, 1763-1783* (1941); A. M. Schlesinger, *Prelude to Independence: The Newspaper War on Britain, 1764-1776* (1958). The emphasis is more economic in A. M. Schlesinger, *Colonial Merchants and the American Revolution* (1918); and T. P. Abernethy, *Western Lands and the American Revolution* (1937), a detailed work. The land question is dealt with by C. W. Alvord in *The Mississippi Valley in British Politics* (2 vols., 1917), and by R. A. Billington in his general account, *Westward Expansion*.

Sources and Documents Illustrating the American Revolution, 1764-1788 (1929), edited by S. E. Morison, is a useful collection with excellent comments. The booklet, *The Causes of the American Revolution*, in Amherst *Problems in American Civilization*, provides an admirable basis for discussion.

9. TOWARDS AMERICAN INDEPENDENCE, 1774-1776

General

For the political story see the works referred to in the previous chapter. Early military events are covered in Allen French, *The First Year of the American Revolution* (1934). For other military works see the next chapter. E. C. Burnett, *The Continental Congress* (1941), the standard work on its subject, describes the deliberations and actions of that body.

Special

Interpretative works of interest are: W. A. Brown, *Empire or Independence: A Study in Failure of Reconciliation, 1774-1783* (1941); G. H. Guttridge, *English Whiggism and the American Revolution* (1942); C. H. Van Tyne, *Causes of the War of Independence* (1922).

One of the best ways to gain a vivid view of the course of the revolt is to follow it in a particular locality. Attitudes and developments in Massachussetts are described by Esther Forbes, in *Paul Revere and the World He Lived In* (1942), and Harold Murdock, in *The Nineteenth of April 1775* (1923); and in New York by T. J. Wertenbaker, in *Father Knickerbocker Rebels* (1948). See also A. M. Baldwin, *The New England Clergy and the American Revolution* (1928). H. J. Eckenrode, *The Revolution in Virginia* (1916) is outmoded by recent biographies of leading Virginians but is best in its early chapters.

For the student of political ideas the literature on this era is abundant. Besides the works referred to in the previous chapter, the following are specially commended: A. C. McLaughlin, *The Foundations of American Constitutionalism* (1932); R. B. Perry, *Puritanism and Democracy* (1944), especially Chs. 6-7; Z. S. Fink, *Classical Republicans* (1932); B. F. Wright, *American Interpretations of Natural Law* (1931). Particular thinkers can be looked up in M. C. Tyler, *Literary History of the American Revolution* (2 vols., 1897), an old work which is still valuable. For the attitudes of those who opposed the revolt, see C. H. Van Tyne, *Loyalists in the American Revolution* (1929).

The Declaration of Independence has a literature of its own. A brilliant work on the subject is C. L. Becker, *The Declaration of Independence: A Study in the History of Ideas* (reprinted 1951). Edward Dumbauld, *The Declaration of Independence and What It Means Today* (1951) spells out the terms and charges so as to make them comprehensible to the modern layman. J. H. Hazelton, *The Declaration of Independence: Its History* (1906), is the fullest account of events and a standard work, though too rare a book and too detailed a study for general use. J. P. Boyd, *The Declaration of Independence: The Evolution of the Text* (1945), reproduces the documents in facsimile and discusses them expertly. *The Story of the Declaration of Independence* (1954), text by Dumas Malone, pictures by Hirst Milhollen and Milton Kaplan, is a richly illustrated book; it contains brief sketches of all the Signers.

Biographies of leading men become specially important in this period. Among these may be mentioned: J. C. Miller, *Sam Adams: Pioneer in Propaganda* (1936); Carl Becker, *Benjamin Franklin* (1946), a brilliant sketch originally published in *Dictionary of American Biography;* Carl Van Doren, *Benjamin Franklin*, esp. Chs. 17-18; R. D. Meade, *Patrick Henry: Patriot in the Making* (1957); Catherine Drinker Bowen, *John Adams and the American Revolution* (1950), with fictionalized conversations but fundamentally accurate; D. S. Freeman, *George Washington*, the most detailed study, esp. Vol. III, Chs. 15-18; Dumas Malone, *Jefferson the Virginian* (1948, Vol. I of *Jefferson and His Time*), esp. Chs. 13-16. H. H. Clark, ed., *Thomas Paine: Representative Selections* (1944, *American Writers Series*), is an unusually good one-volume edn.; it contains "Common Sense" and offers an admirable introduction to the most effective popular writer of the day.

10. THE AMERICAN REVOLUTION

General

On the military side, W. M. Wallace, *Appeal to Arms* (1951) is an excellent general account. Christopher Ward, *War of the Revolution* (2 vols., 1952) is fuller. For international relations see, besides the general diplomatic histories, A. B. Darling, *Our Rising Empire, 1763-1803* (1940).

Special Military

Freeman, in *George Washington*, Vol. IV (1951), carries his detailed story through Valley Forge, and in Vol. V (1952) through Yorktown. Bernhard Knollenberg, *Washington and the Revolution* (1940), takes a less favorable view of Washington. See also T. G. Frothingham, *Washington, Commander in Chief* (1930). Particular campaigns, battles, and episodes can be studied in Ward and Freeman, and in specialized works like the following: Hoffman Nickerson, *The Turning Point of the Revolution, or Burgoyne in America* (1928); A. H. Bill, *Valley Forge* (1952); Carl Van Doren, *Secret History of the American Revolution* (1951), giving an account of the conspiracy of Bene- dict Arnold and others. Important aspects of the war are dealt with by Allen Bowman, *The Morale of the American Revolutionary Army* (1943); Herbert Richmond, *Statesmen and Sea Power* (1946). A good view of John Paul Jones can be gained from the article on him in *Dictionary of American Biography*.

Special International

Among studies of value are: S. F. Bemis, *The Diplomacy of the American Revolution* (1935); E. S. Corwin, *French Policy and the American Alliance* (1916); Bernard Faÿ, *The Revolutionary Spirit in France and America* (1927); D. M. Clark, *British Opinion and the American Revolution* (1930). The simplest way to live through the diplomatic problems of the time is to follow the career of Benjamin Franklin, in Van Doren, Chs. 20-23, or elsewhere.

11. THE INTERNAL REVOLUTION

General

Internal developments are treated in varying degree in general accounts of the Revolution, and the larger social background is given in Greene, *Revolutionary Generation*. J. F. Jameson, *The American Revolution as a Social Movement* (1940) is brief and suggestive.

Special

Political developments are emphasized in Allan Nevins, *The American States during and after the Revolution* (1924), which can be supplemented by M. B. Macmillan, *War Governors in the American Revolution* (1943); E. P. Douglass, *Rebels and Democrats: The Struggle for Equal Political Rights and Majority Rule During the American Revolution* (1955); and R. A. Rutland, *The Birth of the Bill of Rights, 1776-1791* (1955). R. A. East, *Business Enterprise in the American Revolutionary Era* (1938) is a stimulating study.

The movement for religious freedom is treated in various monographic works, like H. J. Eckenrode, *Separation of Church and State in Virginia* (1910), and in general works, such as E. B. Greene, *Religion and the State* (1941), and W. W. Sweet, *The Story of Religion in America* (1939). An important biography of a religious leader is P. K. Guilday, *Life and Times of John Carroll* (2 vols., 1922).

For cultural developments, the student will naturally turn first to histories of American thought, literature, architecture, art, etc. To those already listed may be added A. H. Quinn, *A History of the American Drama* (1943).

The important services of Jefferson and Madison to the cause of individual freedom in this period are described in Malone, *Jefferson the Virginian*, Chs. 17-20; Irving Brant, *James Madison* (1948), Vol. II, Ch. 22; Adrienne Koch, *Jefferson and Madison* (1950), Chs. 1-2; and in other biographies of these men. The situation respecting slavery is described briefly in general histories of American slavery, and more specifically in M. S. Locke, *Anti-Slavery Sentiment in America 1619-1808* (1901).

12. THE CONFEDERATION

General

John Fiske, *The Critical Period of American History* (1888), while now recognized as extreme and inaccurate, is still good reading. The Confederation has been most staunchly defended in recent years by Merrill Jensen in *The Articles of Confederation* (1948), and *The New Nation: A History of the United States during the Confederation, 1781-1789* (1950). The volume in the old *American Nation* series, A. C. McLaughlin, *Confederation and Constitution* (1904), still has value; and works very useful for this period are Burnett, *Continental Congress*, and Nettels, *Roots of American Civilization*.

Special

P. J. Treat, *The National Land System* (1910) is full of detailed information. The traditional story of Maryland's refusal to ratify the Articles and of Virginia's cession of western lands has been considerably modified by Abernethy, in *Western Lands and the American Revolution*, by Jensen and others. The documents in the case are in *Papers of Thomas Jefferson* (1950-   ), edited by J. P. Boyd, Vol. III, pp. 625-636; Vol. IV, pp. 386-391; Vol. VI, pp. 571-580, with able and illuminating notes. The lengthy editorial note on Jefferson's plan for the government of the western territory (Vol. VI, pp. 581-600) is the best treatment of this topic in print.

For the events of Shays's Rebellion, see J. T. Adams, *New England in the Republic, 1776-1850* (1926); Jonathan Smith, *Some Features of Shays's Rebellion* (1903; reprinted in *William and Mary Quarterly*, 1948). For the political use of this affair, see R. A. East, "The Massachusetts Conservatives in the Critical Period," in *Era of the American Revolution* (1939), edited by R. B. Morris.

Financial problems are described in Dewey, *Financial History*, and C. L. Ver Steeg, *Robert Morris, Revolutionary Financier* (1954). On trade expansion, see S. E. Morison, *Maritime History of Massachusetts, 1783-1860* (1921), a brilliant book with which all who are sea-going in spirit should become acquainted. International problems are covered by the diplomatic histories already listed. See also: G. S. Graham, *Sea Power and British North America, 1783-1820* (1941); S. F. Bemis, "John Jay," in *American Secretaries of State and Their Diplomacy,* I (1927).

13. THE CONSTITUTION OF 1787

General

Narrative accounts are: Max Farrand, *Framing of the Constitution* (1913); Charles Warren, *The Making of the Constitution* (1928); Carl Van Doren, *The Great Rehearsal* (1948). See also R. L. Schuyler, *The Constitution of the United States* (1923); E. S. Corwin, *The Constitution and What It Means Today* (1954).

Special

On ratification, see O. G. Libby, *Geographical Distribution of the Vote on the Constitution* (1894). C. A. Beard criticizes this in *An Economic Interpretation of the Constitution* (1913), a book which in turn has been subjected to much criticism, as in R. E. Brown, *Charles Beard and the Constitution* (1956), but which every serious student of the Constitution must read.

Irving Brant, *James Madison,* Vol. III (1950), is of the first importance for both the Convention and the ratification fight. Other biographies of special value in this connection are: C. P. Smith, *James Wilson: Founding Father, 1742-1798* (1956); Nathan Schachner, *Alexander Hamilton* (1946); Broadus Mitchell, *Alexander Hamilton: Youth to Maturity, 1755-1788* (1957); D. J. Mays, *Edmund Pendleton,* Vol. II (1952); A. J. Beveridge, *Life of John Marshall,* Vol. I (1916).

Documents are indispensable in any study of the Constitution. The following are standard: Department of State, *Documentary History of the Constitution of the United States* (5 vols., 1894-1905); Max Farrand, ed., *Records of the Federal Convention* (3 vols., 1911); Jonathan Elliott, ed., *Debates in the Several State Conventions on the Adoption of the Federal Constitution* (5 vols., 1861). *The Federalist Papers* of Hamilton, Madison, and John Jay have been published in numerous editions. *The Declaration of Independence and the Constitution* (1949), edited by Earl Lotham, is another booklet in the Amherst *Problems in American Civilization.*

Part III: Establishing the Republic, 1789-1815

14-17. FEDERALIST PERIOD, 1789-1801

General

This list for the period is followed by more specific suggestions for particular chapters.

NARRATIVE HISTORIES

Probably the best in a general history is that of Channing, *History,* Vol. IV, Chs. 1-8; but Ch. 9, describing the election of 1800, is not recommended. The most vivid is C. G. Bowers, *Jefferson and Hamilton* (1936), which accentuates the political duel between the two men and definitely sides with Jefferson. A. J. Beveridge, *Life of John Marshall,* Vol. II (1916), which is virtually a political history of the period, is just as strongly anti-Jeffersonian. Marshall himself belonged at this time to the more moderate Federalist group, to whom Manning Dauer does justice in an important monograph, *The Adams Federalists* (1954). Many of the nineteenth-century histories and biographies that were written in the Federalist tradition reflect the extreme point of view of J. C. Hamilton, *History of the Republic . . . as Traced in the Writings of Alexander Hamilton and His Contemporaries* (6 vols., 1857-60). This was unfair not only to Jefferson but to Adams and even to Washington, whom it tended to minimize.

Biographies

These are of the first importance in this period because of the great influence of a relatively small group of individual leaders on the conduct of public affairs. Biographers of Washington have generally dealt inadequately with his Presidency. D. S. Freeman, in *George Washington,* Vol. VI (1955), which covers the first term, is less penetrating and less convincing than in the earlier and more military volumes. Marcus Cunliffe, *George Washington: Man and Monument* (1958) is a stimulating and witty discussion of the legend and the man. Gilbert Chinard, *Honest John Adams* (1933) is the best general biography of that blunt statesman, but it needs to be supplemented by such works as that of Manning Dauer. Nathan Schachner, *Alexander Hamilton* (1936), is readable and temperate. J. C. Miller, *Alexander Hamilton: Portrait in Paradox* (1959), is a colorful and stimulating recent study. H. S. Randall, *Life of Thomas Jefferson* (3 vols., 1858), has remained a classic, despite its partisanship, because of its scope and its thoroughness within the limits of knowledge available at the time of its writing. Dumas Malone, *Jefferson and the Rights of Man* (1951, Vol. II of *Jefferson and His Time*), extends through the year 1792, and Vol. III of that work (in process) will cover the rest of the Federalist period. A convenient collection of Jefferson's writings is the edition of Adrienne Koch and William Peden (1944) in the Modern Library. Irving Brant, *James Madison* [III]: *Father of the Constitution, 1787-1800* (1948), is invaluable in this period, especially during the first half of it, when Madison was in Congress. The relations between the two men are well treated in Adrienne Koch, *Jefferson and Madison: The Great Collaboration* (1950).

Foreign Affairs

The general diplomatic histories by Bailey, Bemis, and Pratt, can be supplemented by Bemis, *American Secretaries of State,* Vol. II (1927).

Politics and Parties

Binkley, *American Political Parties,* continues to be useful. C. A. Beard, *Economic Origins of Jeffersonian Democracy* (1915), is hard reading but important. Joseph Charles, *Origins of the American Party System* (1956), is brief but challenging. N. E. Cunningham, Jr., *The Jeffersonian Republicans: The Formation of Party Organization, 1789-1801* (1958) is a sound study.

14. LAUNCHING A NEW GOVERNMENT, 1789-1793

Special

COUNTRY AND COURT

Rich information about the national scene can be gained from *A Century of Population Growth,* which says much about the Census of 1790. Washington's "Court" and the personalities of the times are described and commented on in R. W. Griswold, *The Republican Court: or American Society in the Days of Washington* (1855), a strongly Federalist work; Stewart Mitchell, ed., *New Letters of Abigail Adams, 1788-1801* (1947), and other correspondence of that highly articulate lady; *The Journal of William Maclay, United States Senator from Pennsylvania, 1789-1791* (1947), introduction by C. A. Beard, the acidulous and unfailingly interesting diary of the man described as the original Jeffersonian democrat. L. B. Dunbar, *A Study of "Monarchical" Tendencies in the United States, from 1776 to 1801* (1922), is a valuable monograph.

ORGANIZATION AND CONDUCT OF THE GOVERNMENT

L. D. White, *The Federalists: A Study in Administrative History* (1948), covers the entire period and throws fresh light on it. James Hart, *The American Presidency in Action, 1789* (1948), covers the critical first year.

HAMILTON'S POLICIES AND CRITICS: Hamilton's great reports and his opinion on the Bank can be conveniently consulted in Samuel McKee, Jr., ed., *Alexander Hamilton: Papers on Public Credit, Commerce and Finance* (1934). They are decidedly worth reading. His financial policies are described in financial and economic as well as general histories. W. G. Sumner, *Alexander Hamilton* (1890), is good in this connection. Bray Hammond, *Banks and Politics in America, from the Revolution to the Civil War* (1957), is learned and favorable. *Hamilton and the National Debt,* a booklet in the Amherst *Problems in American Civilization,* gives conflicting views. Lewis Leary, *That Rascal Freneau* (1941), is the best account of Hamilton's keenest journalistic critic; D. R. Anderson, *William Branch Giles* (1914), is a scholarly work on one of his most pugnacious Congressional foes.

15. THE NEW REPUBLIC AND THE OLD WORLD, 1789-1793

Special

BRITISH RELATIONS

S. F. Bemis, *Jay's Treaty* (1924), the standard study, is damaging to Hamilton and Jay but the author approves Federalist policies on the whole. The monograph of V. G. Setzer, *The Commercial Reciprocity Policy of the United States, 1774-1829* (1937), presents the policies of Madison and Jefferson more sympathetically. A. L. Burt, *The United States, Great Britain, and British North America* (1940), an able work extending through the War of 1812, is favorable to a pro-British policy and defends Jay. Frank Monaghan, *John Jay* (1935), is a friendly biography.

THE UNITED STATES AND THE FRENCH REVOLUTION

Zoltán Haraszti, *John Adams and the Prophets of Progress* (1952), presents in stimulating form Adams's criticism of French writers. C. D. Hazen, *Contemporary American Opinion of the French Revolution* (1897), frequently cited in this connection, is now largely outmoded. Gilbert Chinard, *Thomas Jefferson: Apostle of Americanism* (1929), a good general biography, is specially good on Jefferson's relations with the French. These are discussed in considerable detail in Malone, *Jefferson and the Rights of Man*. Gouverneur Morris, *A Diary of the French Revolution*, edited by B. C. Davenport (2 vols., 1939), is full of wit and not without wickedness. Paine's "The Rights of Man," in *Representative Selections*, edited by Clark, shows the pamphleteer at his height. R. R. Palmer, in *The Age of the Democratic Revolution*, Vol. I (1959), ably synthesizes developments in the two worlds to 1791.

NEUTRALITY

The monograph of C. M. Thomas, *American Neutrality in 1793* (1931), is the best single study of this important subject. The article on the fiery Genêt by M. H. Woodfin in *Dictionary of American Biography* offers a good shortcut.

The great plague of yellow fever in Philadelphia in 1793 is described in J. H. Powell, *Bring Out Your Dead* (1949). Its hero was the fabulous Dr. Benjamin Rush, whose *Letters*, ably edited by L. H. Butterfield (2 vols., 1951), are full of interest.

16. HAMILTON IN THE ASCENDANT, 1794-1796

Special

FOREIGN AFFAIRS

Important special studies are S. F. Bemis, *Jay's Treaty*, and *Pinckney's Treaty* (1926); A. P. Whitaker, *The Spanish-American Frontier, 1783-1795* (1927), and *The Mississippi Question* (1934). The article of Irving Brant, "Edmund Randolph, Not Guilty!" in *William and Mary Quarterly* (April 1950), is a convincing treatment of a confused and controversial episode. W. P. Cresson, *James Monroe* (1946), is sympathetic.

DOMESTIC DEVELOPMENTS

L. D. Baldwin, *Whiskey Rebels: The Story of a Frontier Uprising* (1939), and E. P. Link, *Democratic-Republican Societies* (1942), are studies of special interest. The attitudes of High Federalists can be seen in the early volumes of C. R. King, *Life and Correspondence of Rufus King* (6 vols., 1894-1900), and George Gibbs, *Memoirs of the Administrations of Washington and Adams* (2 vols., 1846), from the papers of Oliver Wolcott.

V. H. Paltsits, ed., *Washington's Farewell Address* (1935), a full account with documents, is also a moving story. The address itself is in Commager, *Documents,* and should by all means be read.

17. THE END OF FEDERALIST CONTROL, 1797-1801

Special

WAR WITH FRANCE

This is covered by general naval histories and G. W. Allen, *Our Naval War with France* (1909), with good bibliography. See also B. C. Steiner, *James McHenry* (1907).

FEDERALIST REPRESSION

The text of the Alien and Sedition Acts is in Commager, *Documents.* J. M. Smith, *Freedom's Fetters* (1956), and J. C. Miller, *Crisis in Freedom* (1951), give the story; Bernard Faÿ, *The Two Franklins* (1933), tells about the editor, B. F. Bache; Dumas Malone, *Public Life of Thomas Cooper* (1925), Chs. 3-4, covers the trial of one victim; J. F. McLaughlin, *Matthew Lyon* (1901), describes another. Leon Whipple, *The Story of Civil Liberty in the United States* (1927), is a general view.

KENTUCKY AND VIRGINIA RESOLUTIONS

Text in Commager, *Documents.* Koch, *Jefferson and Madison,* Ch. 7, is the best account of the origins of the Resolutions. F. M. Anderson, in *American Historical Review,* Vol. V (Oct. 1899; Jan. 1900), describes contemporary opinion.

POLITICS AND THE ELECTION OF 1800-1801

Dauer, *The Adams Federalists,* and Beard, *Economic Origins of Jeffersonian Democracy,* are specially valuable here. Good use can be made of works on political developments in particular states, such as R. J. Purcell, *Connecticut in Transition, 1775-1818* (1918), and H. M. Tinkcom, *Republicans and Federalists in Pennsylvania* (1950). Morton Borden, *The Federalism of James A. Bayard* (1954), is a good study of a man who played a crucial role in 1801; see especially Ch. 7.

CULTURE

Besides general works on architecture, religion, literature, thought, etc., see H. R. Warfel, *Noah Webster; Schoolmaster of America* (1936); F. L. Mott, *American Journalism* (1950); "The Age of Reason," in Thomas Paine, *Representative Selections;* W. B. Bryan, *History of the National Capital,* Vol. I (1914).

18-19. THE PRESIDENCY OF JEFFERSON

General

This general list for the two chapters is followed by specific suggestions for each of them.

NARRATIVE HISTORIES

Allen Johnson, *Jefferson and His Colleagues* (1921), and E. S. Corwin, *John Marshall and the Constitution* (1919), both in *Chronicles of America,* are excellent within their respective limits. Channing, *History,* Vol. IV, continues to be useful. C. G. Bowers, *Jefferson in Power* (1936), does not come up to *Jefferson and Hamilton* and is equally partisan but is good reading. Henry Adams, *History of the United States* (9 vols., 1889-91), covers the period 1800-1817 elaborately and brilliantly. The work is specially rich on the international side, and the description of the state of the country in Vol. I, Chs. 1-6 is notable. Adams is exceedingly critical of practically everybody.

SOCIAL HISTORY

This topic is covered by Krout and Fox, *Completion of Independence (History of American Life).* A sprightly work showing more liking for the Federalist New Englanders than for anybody else is *Jeffersonian America: Notes . . . Collected in the Years 1805-6-7 and 11-12 by Sir Augustus John Foster, Bart.* (1954), edited by R. B. Davis.

BIOGRAPHIES

Nathan Schachner, *Jefferson, Vol. II* (1951), is the only detailed recent biography of that statesman covering this period. Irving Brant, *James Madison* [IV]: *Secretary of State* (1952) is thorough-going and very critical of Henry Adams. The latter's *Albert Gallatin* (1879) is much more admiring of the Secretary of the Treasury than of the administration as a whole. A good supplement is Raymond Walters, Jr., *Albert Gallatin: Jeffersonian Financier and Diplomat* (1957). Beveridge, *Marshall,* Vol. III, is of the first importance. W. C. Bruce, *John Randolph of Roanoke* (2 vols., 1922), is a comprehensive treatment of that brilliant and erratic Congressional leader. W. E. Dodd, *Life of Nathaniel W. Macon* (1903), is a sympathetic account of a more consistently loyal Jeffersonian. S. E. Morison, *Harrison Gray Otis* (2 vols., 1913), and C. E. Cunningham, *Timothy Dwight, 1752-1817* (1942), are good studies of New England Federalists. William Plumer, *Memorandum of Proceedings in the Senate, 1803-1807,* edited by E. S. Brown (1923), reflects Federalist attitudes. Talbot Hamlin, *Benjamin Henry Latrobe* (1955), is an admirable biography of a major architectural figure.

18. JEFFERSONIAN LIBERALISM, 1801-1805

Special

THE MAN AND HIS MEANING

Jefferson and Jeffersonianism are interpreted variously by Beard, Beveridge, Bowers, Parrington, and others in works already cited. The *Jefferson Reader: A Treasury of Writings about Thomas Jefferson* (1953), edited by F. C. Rosenberger, contains a variety of comments and includes a thoughtful and delightful article, "Thomas Jefferson, Gentle Radical," from Dixon Wecter, *The Hero in America* (1941). See also Richard Hofstadter, "Thomas Jefferson: The Aristocrat as Democrat," in *The American Political Tradition and the Men Who Made It* (1949); C. M. Wiltse, *The Jeffersonian Tradition in American Democracy* (1935). Other aspects of the man are shown in E. T. Martin, *Thomas Jefferson: Scientist* (1952); S. N. Randolph, *Domestic Life of Thomas Jefferson* (1871).

INAUGURATION AND SOCIAL REGIME

The description of the inauguration by Henry Adams is in his *History*, Vol. I, Ch. 7; it is also in Sheehan, *Making of American History*, pp. 149-168. The first inaugural address can be profitably and easily read in Commager, *Documents;* Koch and Peden, *Writings* (Modern Library); and elsewhere. Margaret Bayard Smith gives interesting social description and sympathetic contemporary comments in *The First Forty Years of Washington Society* (1906), edited by Gaillard Hunt. Henry Adams plays up the ludicrous features of the regime in some of the sprightliest of his passages; see especially *History*, Vol. II, Ch. 16.

ADMINISTRATION AND PRESIDENTIAL LEADERSHIP

L. D. White, *The Jeffersonians: A Study in Administrative History* (1951), covers the period to Andrew Jackson. This fresh treatment can be supplemented by the monographs: C. R. Fish, *The Civil Service and the Patronage* (1903); and R. V. Harlow, *History of Legislative methods before 1825* (1917). E. S. Corwin, *The President: Office and Powers* (1948) is a standard general work of great interest.

JUDICIARY FIGHT

Beveridge, in *Marshall*, Vol. III, Chs. 1-4, gives a full and fascinating but biased account. Corwin, *Marshall and the Constitution*, is better balanced. See also Charles Warren, *The Supreme Court in United States History*, Vol. I, Chs. 4-6 (1927); Borden, *Federalism of James A. Bayard*, Ch. 9; general constitutional histories and works on judicial review.

NEW ENGLAND OPPOSITION AND ATTACKS ON JEFFERSON

Theodore Dwight, *The Character of Thomas Jefferson* (1939), is a bitterly hostile view. Henry Adams, *Documents Relating to New England Federalism,*

1800-1815 (1877), is an important collection. J. T. Adams, *New England in the Republic, 1776-1850* (1926), contains a general account. For the Paine episode see Adams, *History*, Vol. I. Ch. 12. F. L. Mott, *Jefferson and the Press* (1943), Ch. 9, shows his disillusionment.

19. EXPANSION AND DOMESTIC FACTION, 1803-1809

Special

WESTERN DEVELOPMENTS

A good over-all account is in Billington, *Westward Expansion*, Chs. 10-13, with bibliographies. See also the narrative of F. A. Ogg, *The Old Northwest* (1921, *Chronicles of America*). P. J. Treat, *The National Land System, 1785-1820* (1910) is a standard work, valuable for details. R. M. Robbins, *Our Landed Heritage: The Public Domain, 1776-1936* (1942), Part I, covers the period to 1850.

LOUISIANA PURCHASE

The best approach is through the general and diplomatic histories. Henry Adams, *History*, Vol. II, Chs. 1-6, has rich materials on this topic. More specialized works are: Whitaker, *Mississippi Question;* E. W. Lyon, *The Man Who Sold Louisiana: The Life of François Barbé-Marbois* (1942); E. S. Brown, *Constitutional History of the Louisiana Purchase* (1920); I. J. Cox, *The West Florida Controversy* (1918).

EXPLORATIONS

Brebner, *Explorers of North America*, Ch. 24, is a general account. The condensed *Journals of Lewis and Clark* (1953), edited by Bernard DeVoto, give a readable first-hand story of a great adventure.

FACTION AND CONSPIRACY

The state of mind of die-hard Federalists in New England is shown in biographies of leaders and in Henry Adams, ed., *Documents Relating to New England Federalism*, pp. 331-381. Nathan Schachner, *Alexander Hamilton*, Ch. 28, is particularly good on the duel with Burr. T. P. Abernethy, *The Burr Conspiracy* (1955) is the latest study of that confused subject. Beveridge, in *Marshall*, Vol. III, Chs. 6-9, describes the conspiracy and is very detailed about the trial; Corwin, in *Marshall and the Constitution* is much more critical of the Chief Justice. R. B. Morris, in *Fair Trial* (1952), Ch. 5, is particularly concerned with procedure and tells a good story.

FOREIGN AFFAIRS AND EMBARGO

R. W. Irwin, *Diplomatic Relations of the United States with the Barbary Powers* (1931) is a monograph with bibliography. L. M. Sears, *Jefferson and the Embargo* (1927) is the fullest study of the subject and more favorable to Jefferson than most; it is particularly good on the effects of the Embargo on different parts of the country. General diplomatic and naval histories can be supplemented by Henry Adams, *History,* Vols, III, IV, and the noted work of A. T. Mahan, *The Influence of Sea Power upon the French Revolution and Empire, 1793-1812* (2 vols., 1892). A fresh and more favorable view of American diplomacy is taken by Brant in *Madison [IV]: Secretary of State.* French Decrees, British Orders in Council, and American Acts for the years 1806-07 are conveniently summed up in Channing, Vol. IV, pp. 375-79, and are given more fully (1806-12) in Bartlett, *Record of American Diplomacy,* Ch. 7.

20. THE WAR OF 1812

General

The story is told in Johnson, *Jefferson and his Colleagues,* and R. D. Paine, *The Fight for a Free Sea* (1920, *Chronicles of America*); Channing, *History, Vol. IV,* Chs. 16-20; F. F. Beirne, *The War of 1812* (1949); and, most fully of all, in Henry Adams, *History,* Vols. VI-IX. Irving Brant, *James Madison, The President, 1809-1812* (1956), deals with the administration to the outbreak of war and provides a modern corrective to Adams.

Special

CAUSES

On the part played by the West, the point of view of J. W. Pratt, in *Expansionists of 1812* (rev. edn., 1949), has been challenged by A. L. Burt, in *The United States, Great Britain, and British America,* Chs. 11-15. For the most conspicuous War Hawk, see Bernard Mayo, *Henry Clay* (1937), Chs. 9-13. See also Billington, *Westward Expansion,* Ch. 13.

OPERATIONS

Anyone wishing to go beyond general histories of the Navy and Army can find abundant materials in A. T. Mahan, *Sea Power in Its Relations to the War of 1812* (2 vols., 1905), and in Marquis James, *Andrew Jackson [I]: The Border Captain* (1933), Chs. 9-20.

NEW ENGLAND OPPOSITION

The best account is in Morison, *Harrison Gray Otis,* Vol. II, Chs. 21-28. For the Report and Resolutions of the Hartford Convention, see Commager, *Documents.*

DIPLOMACY AND PEACE

An excellent account is S. F. Bemis, *John Quincy Adams and the Foundations of American Foreign Policy* (1949), Chs. 9-10.

Part IV: Nationalism, Sectionalism, and Democracy, 1815-1840

21. THE COMPLETION OF INDEPENDENCE: POSTWAR DIPLOMATIC TRIUMPHS, 1815-1823

General

The course of events is described in the general diplomatic histories of Bailey, Bemis, and Pratt, and more fully in Bemis, *John Quincy Adams and the Foundations of American Foreign Policy*, Chs. 11-19; and George Dangerfield, *The Era of Good Feelings* (1952), Part 4.

Special

Dexter Perkins, *The Monroe Doctrine, 1823-1826* (1923) is the standard treatment; this author carries the story through the following century in *Hands Off: A History of the Monroe Doctrine* (1941). Documents, including extracts from Monroe's message of Dec. 2, 1823, to Congress, are in Bartlett, *Record of American Diplomacy*, Ch. 10. Other important works are: A. P. Whitaker, *The United States and the Independence of Latin America* (1941); E. H. Tatum, *The United States and Europe* (1936). See also W. P. Cresson, *James Monroe*.

22-23. ADMINISTRATIONS OF MONROE AND JOHN QUINCY ADAMS

General

NARRATIVES

F. J. Turner, *Rise of the New West, 1819-1828* (1906, *American Nation*), is excellent for sectional developments as well as political events. Turner's famous essay, "The Significance of the Frontier in American History," can be appropriately read at this point. It is in his book, *Frontier in American History*, Ch. 1; and in Sheehan, *Making of American History*, Vol. I, pp. 427-462. George Dangerfield, *The Era of Good Feelings*, is reliable and a pleasure to read. C. S. Sydnor, *The Development of Southern Sectionalism, 1819-1848* (1948, in *History of the South*), Chs. 1-6, is thorough and judicious. Krout and Fox, *The Completion of Independence (History of American Life)*, provides the social background to 1830.

TOPICAL HISTORIES

Dewey, *Financial History*, continues to be useful, and Taussig, *Tariff History*, becomes increasingly so in this period. Attention should again be called to the illuminating editorial introductions in Callender, *Selections from the Economic History of the United States*.

POLITICAL BIOGRAPHIES AND MEMOIRS

Besides Marquis James, *Andrew Jackson* [II]: *Portrait of a President,* and Wiltse, *John C. Calhoun [II]: Nationalist, 1782-1828,* see: M. L. Coit, *John C. Calhoun, American Patriot* (1950), a human and very friendly treatment; G. G. Van Deusen, *The Life of Henry Clay* (1937); Carl Schurz, *The Life of Henry Clay* (2 vols., 1887), old but still interesting; Allan Nevins, ed., *Diary of John Quincy Adams* (rev. edn., 1951), a selection from Adams's famous *Memoirs* (12 vols., 1874-77); C. M. Fuess, *Daniel Webster* (2 vols., 1930).

22. THE "ERA OF GOOD FEELINGS": NATIONS AND SECTIONS

Special

SECTIONALISM

F. J. Turner, *The Significance of Sections in American History,* edited by Max Farrand (1950).

NORTHEAST

Agricultural developments are described in Bidwell and Falconer, *History of Agriculture in the Northern United States;* commercial developments in R. G. Albion, *The Rise of New York Port, 1815-1860* (1939), and Morison, *Maritime History of Massachusetts;* manufacturing in V. S. Clark, *History of Manufacturing in the United States, 1607-1860* (rev. edn., 4 vols., 1929). L. K. Mathews, *The Expansion of New England* (1906) describes New England migrations to the West.

OLDER SOUTH

For agricultural developments of all sorts, see Gray, *History of Agriculture in the Southern United States.* Works more restricted in scope are A. O. Craven, *Soil Exhaustion as a Factor in the Agricultural History of Virginia and Maryland, 1606-1860* (1926); and J. C. Robert, *The Tobacco Kingdom* (1938). The development of cotton culture is described more fully in Ch. 32 of the present work, but the biography, *Eli Whitney* (1952), by Allan Nevins and Jeanette Mirsky, should be mentioned here.

TRANSPORTATION AND WESTERN SETTLEMENT

A. B. Hulbert, *The Paths of Inland Commerce* (1920, *Chronicles of America*) is brief and readable. R. A. Billington, *Westward Expansion,* Chs. 13-17, carries the story to and beyond the limits of the present chapter; the bibliographies give many suggestions for reading about particular localties. Other works of interest are: R. E. Riegel, *America Moves West* (1930); R. C. Buley, *The Old*

Northwest: Pioneer Period, 1815-1840 (2 vols., 1950); Everett Dick, *The Dixie Frontier* (1948).

23. JOHN MARSHALL AND JOHN QUINCY ADAMS

Special

MARSHALL AND HIS DECISIONS

Constitutional histories of McLaughlin, Swisher, Kelly and Harbison; Beveridge, *Marshall*, Vols. III-IV; Corwin, *Marshall and the Constitution;* Warren, *Supreme Court*, Chs. 12-16, 19; C. G. Haines, *The Role of the Supreme Court, 1789-1835* (1944). The major decisions are in Commager, *Documents*. The struggle with Virginia is best described in Warren, Ch. 13, and in Sydnor, *Development of Southern Sectionalism*, Ch. 6. For a brilliant brief description of the "Old Republicans" in the Upper South, see A. M. Schlesinger, Jr., *The Age of Jackson* (1945), Ch. 2. The controversy between the federal government and the state of Georgia, which is referred to again in Ch. 25 of the present work, is described fully in U. B. Phillips, *Georgia and State Rights* (1902; *Annual Report of the American Historical Association* for 1901), Chs. 2-3. D. G. Morgan, *Justice William Johnson, The First Dissenter* (1955), is a good biography of the member of the Court who most opposed Marshall.

POLITICS AND THE TARIFF CONTROVERSY

These are well described in the general works and biographies already cited. Those interested in the rival philosophies of protection and free trade can make a good beginning by reading the articles on these topics in *Encyclopedia of the Social Sciences*. The important American thinkers are described in Joseph Dorfman, *The Economic Mind in American Civilization* (1946), Vol. II; see especially Chs. 28-31. J. A. Garraty, in *Silas Wright* (1949) casts fresh light on the motives of the Jacksonians in the Tariff of Abominations. The activities of an important early opponent of the tariff in South Carolina are described in Malone, *Thomas Cooper*, Chs. 9-10.

24-25. POLITICAL HISTORY OF THE JACKSON ERA

General

NARRATIVES

The posthumous publication of F. J. Turner, *The United States, 1830-1850* (1935), though incomplete, is the best single work on its period. A. M. Schlesinger, Jr., *The Age of Jackson* (1945) goes far beyond party politics and is an unusually stimulating book, though some other scholars do not see so close a parallel with the age of Franklin D. Roosevelt as the author does. C. G. Bowers, *Party Battles of the Jackson Period* (1922) is vivid and partisan.

Sydnor, *Development of Southern Sectionalism,* Chs. 8, 9, continues to be good. An interesting interpretation is that of Richard Hofstadter, "Andrew Jackson and the Rise of Liberal Capitalism," *American Political Tradition,* Ch. 3. C. R. Fish, *The Rise of the Common Man* (1932, *History of American Life*) covers social history.

BIOGRAPHIES

Marquis James, *Andrew Jackson* [II]: *Portrait of a President,* falls in this period, as does Wiltse, *Calhoun* [II]: *Nullifier, 1829-1839* (1949), which is particularly good for national politics, though too favorable to Calhoun and too severe on Jackson and Van Buren for many tastes. There is no good biography of Van Buren but his *Autobiography* is available, edited by J. C. Fitzpatrick (1920: *Annual Report Amer. Hist. Asso.* for 1918, Vol. II). W. E. Smith, in *The Francis Preston Blair Family in Politics,* Vol. I (1933), presents an important member of the "Kitchen Cabinet." Other important biographies, besides those of Clay and Webster already mentioned, are C. B. Swisher, *Roger B. Taney* (1935); T. D. Jervey, *Robert Y. Hayne and His Times* (1909).

Special

JACKSONIAN DEMOCRACY

In its political aspects this is treated in general histories and biographies; in histories of parties, such as Binkley, *American Political Parties,* Chs. 6, 7; and in works on political thought, such as C. E. Merriam, *A History of American Political Theories* (1903), Ch. 5. A recent study of great suggestiveness is Marvin Meyers, *The Jacksonian Persuasion: Politics and Belief* (1957). See also E. M. Carroll, *Origins of the Whig Party* (1923); K. H. Porter, *A History of Suffrage in the United States* (1918); A. B. Darling, "Jacksonian Democracy in Massachusetts," *American Historical Review,* October 1923. A critical view of the "democracy" of Jackson himself is taken by T. P. Abernethy in *From Frontier to Plantation in Tennessee* (1932), Chs. 10-18. J. W. Ward, in *Andrew Jackson: Symbol for an age* (1945), brilliantly argues that his age created him in its own image. The most famous foreign commentator on American democracy in this era, Alexis de Tocqueville, viewed it in the large, not as a party movement. An admirable recent edition of his *Democracy in America,* first published in 1835, is that of Phillips Bradley (2 vols., 1942). Works dealing with expressions of the democratic spirit outside politics are mentioned in the bibliographies for later chapters.

ADMINISTRATION

L. D. White, *The Jacksonians: A Study in Administrative History, 1829-1861* (1954), is a fresh and illuminating study; see esp. Chs. 1, 2, 8. The old work of C. R. Fish, *Civil Service and Patronage* is still useful for the origins and development of the spoils system. For the Presidency under Jackson, see W. E. Binkley, *Powers of the President* (1937), Chs. 4-5; Edward Stanwood, *History of the Presidency* (1921), Vol. I, Ch. 12.

The Bank and Panic

Besides Dewey, *Financial History*, and Hammond, *Banks and Politics in America*, the following more restricted works are suggested: R. C. H. Catterall, *The Second Bank of the United States* (1903); R. C. McGrane, *The Panic of 1837: Some Financial Problems of the Jackson Era* (1924); B. H. Hibbard, *A History of the Public Land Policies* (1939).

Nullification

Special studies are D. F. Houston, *A Critical Study of Nullification in South Carolina* (1906), and C. S. Boucher, *The Nullification Controversy in South Carolina* (1916), giving greater attention to the local fight. Calhoun's Exposition, the South Carolina Ordinance, and Jackson's Proclamation are in Commager, *Documents*.

Indians

Billington, in *Westward Expansion*, Ch. 15, gives a general account of the removal and numerous bibliographical suggestions. Events in Georgia, are well described in Phillips, *Georgia and State Rights*. See also M. L. Starkey, *The Cherokee Nation* (1946).

26. SLAVERY IS ATTACKED AND DEFENDED

General

The abolitionist movement is described in the general histories. It is central in Jesse Macy, *The Anti-Slavery Crusade* (1919, *Chronicles of America*), and bulks large in the old work of A. B. Hart, *Slavery and Abolition* (1900, *American Nation*), both of which are sympathetic. The best modern treatment is G. H. Barnes, *The Anti-Slavery Impulse* (1933), which can be supplemented by D. L. Dumond, *Anti-Slavery Origins of the Civil War* (1939), Chs. 1-4, giving a more favorable interpretation of the movement as a whole. The best general account of developments within the South is in Sydnor, *Development of Southern Sectionalism*, esp. Ch. 10. References to slavery as an economic and social institution are given in the bibliography for Ch. 32 of the present work. In the present chapter, the emphasis is on attitudes and ideas, agitation and repression, but general works on slavery provide a necessary background. Among these are: Phillips, *American Negro Slavery*, based on notable scholarship but reflecting a conservative Southern point of view; K. M. Stampp, *The Peculiar Institution* (1956), emphasizing economics and directly opposing Phillips; Franklin, *From Slavery to Freedom*, the work of an able and conscientious Negro scholar; Gunnar Myrdal, *An American Dilemma* (2 vols., 1944), by a noted sociologist whose major interest was in the contemporary scene and whose chief concern was for the future.

Special

J. C. Robert, *The Road from Monticello: A Study of the Virginia Slavery Debate of 1832* (1941), corrects erroneous impressions of these events and gives significant extracts from speeches. C. H. Ambler, *Sectionalism in Virginia from 1776 to 1861* (1910) gives the background of internal politics. The unhappy position of the Free Negroes is described in Franklin, *Slavery to Freedom*, Ch. 14, and, more specifically, in several treatments of particular states. Among the best of these are J. H. Franklin, *The Free Negro in North Carolina, 1790-1860* (1943), and E. R. Turner, *The Negro in Pennsylvania* (1910). The accounts of the colonization movement in general works can be supplemented by the monograph of E. L. Fox, *The American Colonization Society, 1817-1840* (1919). For the foreign slave trade, see the early monograph of W. E. B. DuBois, *The Suppression of the African Slave Trade* (1896); for the domestic traffic, see W. H. Collins, *The Domestic Slave Trade of the Southern United States* (1904); Frederic Bancroft, *Slave-Trading in the Old South* (1931).

The individual abolitionist most emphasized by Barnes in *Anti-Slavery Impulse* is Theodore Dwight Weld; his article on Weld in *Dictionary of American Biography* offers a convenient shortcut. He is very critical of Garrison. There is no adequate biography of Garrison, since his biographers have largely accepted him at his own valuation. Richard Hofstadter, "Wendell Phillips: The Patrician as Agitator," Ch. 6 of *American Political Tradition*, is excellent. See also works on reform and reformers listed in the following chapter of the present work

The Southern proslavery philosophy is summed up in W. E. Dodd, *The Cotton Kingdom* (1917, *Chronicles of America*), and more fully described in W. S. Jenkins, *Pro-Slavery Thought in the Old South* (1935); see also A. Y. Lloyd, *The Slavery Controversy, 1831-1860* (1934), Chs. 4-7. The "Black Terror" and Southern repression of agitation are well described in the important book of Clement Eaton, *Freedom of Thought in the Old South* (1940), Chs. 4-5. See also R. B. Nye, *Fettered Freedom: Civil Liberties and the Slavery Controversy* (1949); and W. S. Savage, *The Controversy over the Distribution of Abolition Literature, 1830-1860* (1938). J. N. Norwood, *The Schism in the Methodist Episcopal Church, 1844* (1923), gives the details of that fateful occurrence.

27. JACKSONIAN REFORM MOVEMENTS

General

Much that bears on this and the following chapter can be found in Channing, *History*, Vol. V; Fish, *Rise of the Common Man;* Parrington, *Main Currents in American Thought*, Vol. II; Curti, *Growth of American Thought*, esp. Chs. 14-15; Schlesinger, *Age of Jackson*. Other books of general interest are: A. M. Schlesinger, Sr., *The American as Reformer* (1950); Daniel Aaron, *Men of Good Hope: A Story of American Progressives* (1951); A. F. Tyler, *Freedom's Ferment: Phases of American Social History to 1860* (1944). The underlying popular philosophy is nowhere better described than in R. H. Gabriel, *The Course of American Democratic Thought* (1940), Esp. Ch. 2.

Special

The following deal with education in this period and later: Paul Monroe, *The Founding of the American Public School System* (1940), Vol. I; B. A. Hinsdale, *Horace Mann and the Common School Revival in the United States* (1898); D. G. Tewksbury, *The Founding of American Colleges and Universities before the Civil War* (1932); Merle Curti, *Social Ideas of American Educators* (1935). Detailed suggestions for reading on various phases of education and particular institutions are in *Harvard Guide,* sect. 151, p. 350.

In the absence of good accounts of the movement for women's rights, it can be most easily approached, perhaps, by reading in the *Dictionary of American Biography* the articles on Susan B. Anthony, Elizabeth Cady Stanton, and other leaders. Mason Wade, *Margaret Fuller* (1940), is a good biography.

F. R. Dulles, *Labor in America,* Ch. 4, deals with this period. On socialistic experiments, see A. E. Bestor, Jr., *Backwoods Utopias* (1950); J. H. Noyes, *The History of American Socialisms* (1870); R. W. Leopold, *Robert Dale Owen* (1940).

J. A. Krout, *The Origins of Prohibition* (1925) is an excellent account of the temperance movement. On world peace, see Merle Curti, *The American Peace Crusade, 1815-1861* (1929), and *The Learned Blacksmith* (1937). Humanitarianism is well illustrated in Helen Marshall, *Dorothea Dix: Forgotten Samaritan* (1937). Interest in the reformers of this era has produced a luxuriant crop of good biographies. Others of these are: H. S. Commager, *Theodore Parker* (1936); R. V. Harlow, *Gerrit Smith: Philanthropist and Reformer* (1939); A. M. Schlesinger, Jr., *Orestes A. Brownson* (1939); Odell Shepard, *Pedlar's Progress: A Life of Bronson Alcott* (1937); W. R. Waterman, *Frances Wright* (1934).

28. CULTURAL ACHIEVEMENTS IN A DEMOCRATIC ERA

General

Many books dealing with some particular aspect of American cultural history bear on this period without being restricted to it. The growing diversity of American culture is suggested by the following brief list.

RELIGION

W. W. Sweet, *Story of Religion in America;* and *Revivalism in America: Its Origin, Growth and Decline* (1944).

PHILOSOPHY

Curti, *Growth of American Thought,* esp. Ch. 13; H. W. Schneider, *History of American Philosophy* (1946); W. K. Berkmeister, *A History of Philosophical Ideas in America* (1949).

SCIENCE

Struik, *Yankee Science in the Making;* H. E. Siegerist, *American Medicine* (1934); F. R. Packard, *History of Medicine in the United States,* Vol. I (1931).

LITERATURE

Parrington, *Main Currents,* Vol. II; Spiller, *Literary History of the United States,* Vols. I, II; Quinn, *Literature of the American People,* Part Two; F. L. Mott, *A History of American Magazines* (3 vols., 1930-38), esp. Vol. I, and *American Journalism: A History of Newspapers in the United States* (1941)

ARTS

Larkin, *Art and Life in America;* Tallmadge, *Architecture in America;* Virgil Barker, *American Painting* (1950); Lorado Taft, *The History of American Sculpture* (1930); J. T. Howard, *Our American Music* (rev. edn., 1946).

Special

The topics which invite reading and investigation are very numerous, and the richness of the available literature can only be suggested here.

Unitarianism can be most readily viewed, perhaps, in a biography, such as H. S. Commager, *Theodore Parker.* Those wishing to explore evangelicalism further can find abundant materials in W. W. Sweet, *Religion on the American Frontier* (4 vols., 1931-46). For Mormonism see F. M. Brodie, *No Man Knows My History: The Life of Joseph Smith* (1945); and M. R. Werner, *Brigham Young* (1925). Works on various religious groups and denominations are listed in *Harvard Guide,* p. 351.

An excellent approach to the difficult subject of Transcendentalism is provided in *The Transcendentalist Revolt against Materialism* (1949) in the Amherst *Problems in American Civilization.* See also biographies of Margaret Fuller, Bronson Alcott, and Orestes Brownson listed in Ch. 27.

Those wishing to explore works on specific sciences will find references in the bibliography of Curti, Ch. 13, and in *Harvard Guide,* p. 352. For individual scientists, see Bernard Jaffe, *Men of Science in America* (1944); J. F. Fulton and E. H. Thomson, *Benjamin Silliman* (1947); C. L. Lewis, *Matthew Fontaine Maury* (1927); and other biographies.

In literature, there is rich reading in F. O. Matthiessen, *American Renaissance: Art and Expression in the Age of Emerson and Whitman* (1941); great charm in Van Wyck Brooks, *The World of Washington Irving* (1944), and *The Flowering of New England* (1936). Biographies of special worth are: R. L. Rusk, *Emerson* (1949); H. S. Canby, *Thoreau* (1939); S. T. Williams, *Washington Irving* (2 vols., 1935); Newton Arvin, *Hawthorne* (1929), and *Melville* (1950); R. E. Spiller, *Fenimore Cooper* (1931); R. B. Nye, *George Bancroft* (1944). Emerson can be approached delightfully by dipping into *The Heart of Emerson's Journals* (1926), edited by Bliss Perry.

In the arts, a work of special interest is Carl Wittke: *Tambo and Bones: A*

History of the American Minstrel Stage (1930). The stage as a whole is described in the pictorial *Pageant of America*, Vol. XIV.

Part V. Expansion and Sectional Conflict, 1841–1861

29. POLITICS AND MANIFEST DESTINY, 1841-1848

General

There are good general accounts of this period in Channing, *History*, V, Chs. 15-18; Turner, *United States, 1830-1850*, Chs. 11-12; and a brief but interesting volume in the *Chronicles of America*, N. W. Stephenson, *Texas and the Mexican War* (1921). The receding frontier and the process of settlement are treated in Billington, *Westward Expansion*, Chs. 24-28, and *The Far Western Frontier, 1830-1860* (1956, *New American Nation* series). British relations are described in the diplomatic histories of Pratt, Bemis, and Bailey; Bemis, *American Secretaries of State*, Vol. V; Dexter Perkins, *The Monroe Doctrine, 1826-1867* (1933), Ch. 2. See also A. K. Weinberg, *Manifest Destiny: A Study of Nationalist Expansionism in American History* (1935).

Special

PARTIES AND POLITICAL LEADERS

The Whigs are described in Binkley, *American Political Parties*, Ch. 7, and A. C. Cole, *The Whig Party in the South* (1913); important minor groups in T. C. Smith, *The Liberty and Free Soil Parties* (1897). Biographies of Clay, Webster, and Calhoun are important for this period. The *Diary of James K. Polk during His Presidency*, edited by M. M. Quaife (4 vols., 1910), and *Polk: The Diary of a President* (new edn., 1952) in reduced one-volume form by Allan Nevins, reveals the man and statesman as does nothing else. E. I. McCormac has availed himself of it in *James K. Polk: A Political Biography* (1922). C. G. Sellers, *James K. Polk, Jacksonian, 1795-1843* (1957), tells the pre-Presidential story.

THE FAR WEST

The movement to Oregon has received classic treatment in Francis Parkman's *Oregon Trail* (1849 and many later edns.). It is admirably described in the historical novel of A. B. Guthrie, *The Way West* (1949). On California, the widely-read book of R. H. Dana, Jr., *Two Years Before the Mast* (first published, 1840) antedates the American conquest. Bernard DeVoto, *The Year of Decision, 1846* (1942), describes the Far Western frontier in terms of the personal experience of persons who went there. Other works of special interest are Allan Nevins, *Frémont: Pathmaker of the West* (1939); Cardinal Goodwin, *John Charles Frémont* (1930), and *The Trans-Mississippi West* (1922); R. G. Cleland, *From Wilderness to Empire: A History of California* (1944); Nels Anderson, *Desert Saints: The Mormon Frontier in Utah* (1942); L. J. Arrington,

Great Basin Kingdom: An Economic History of the Latter-day Saints 1830-1900 (1958).

TEXAS AND THE MEXICAN WAR

The two most important persons in the early history of Texas have excellent biographies: E. C. Barker, *Life of Stephen F. Austin* (1925); Marquis James, *The Raven: A Biography of Sam Houston* (1929). J. H. Smith, *The Annexation of Texas* (1911), and *The War with Mexico* (2 vols., 1919), have greatly affected all subsequent interpretations of these events by scholars and are generally recognized as standard. Other good books are: W. R. Hogan, *The Texas Republic* (1946); J. F. Rippy, *The United States and Mexico* (1931). Anyone interested in the Mexican experiences of the two most conspicuous military figures in the Civil War will enjoy reading about them in Lloyd Lewis, *Captain Sam Grant* (1950), and D. S. Freeman, *R. E. Lee,* Vol. I (1934).

30. CRISIS AND COMPROMISE, 1846-1852

General

NARRATIVE HISTORIES

Because of the importance of the political events, the sheer interest of the story, and the quality as well as the quantity of available books, this is an excellent period in which to read extensively in narrative history. The most detailed recent work covering the events of the present chapter is Allan Nevins, *The Ordeal of the Union* (2 vols., 1947), esp. Vol. I. The older work of J. F. Rhodes, *History of the United States from the Compromise of 1850* (7 vols., 1893-1906), long regarded as masterly, begins at approximately the same point. Nevins is better for things happening outside Congress, but the modern student can follow the great debate of 1850 advantageously in either work. For Southern attitudes the student should see Sydnor, *Development of Southern Sectionalism,* Ch. 14; and the early chapters of A. O. Craven, *The Growth of Southern Nationalism, 1848-1861* (1954, Vol. VI of *A History of the South*). A good account of these events is in Channing, *History,* Vol. IV, Chs. 3-4.

BIOGRAPHIES

This period has proved fertile to political biographers as well as political historians. C. M. Wiltse, *John C. Calhoun* [III]: *Sectionalist, 1840-1850,* is of particular interest, because of the continuing controversy about Calhoun; see Chs. 25-28 and, especially, Ch. 30. More extreme attitudes can be seen in L. A. White, *Robert Barnwell Rhett: Father of Secession* (1931); and A. O. Craven, *Edmund Ruffin, Southerner* (1932). U. B. Phillips, *Life of Robert Toombs* (1913), is a good account of a Georgian who was a moderate at this time.

Lincoln has not yet emerged at this stage, but Douglas is becoming conspicuous. Allen Johnson, *Stephen A. Douglas* (1908), broke new ground; for a shortcut, see his article in *Dictionary of American Biography*. G. F. Milton, *The Eve of Conflict: Stephen A. Douglas and the Needless War* (1934), is an able and sympathetic treatment. R. F. Nichols, *Franklin Pierce: Young Hickory of the Granite Hills* (1931), bears on this chapter and later ones.

Special

For political conditions and developments in the South, the following studies are valuable: A. C. Cole, *The Whig Party in the South* (1913); R. H. Shryock, *Georgia and the Union in 1850* (1923); J. G. Van Housen, *Economic Bases of Disunion in South Carolina* (1928). The Georgia Platform, the Resolutions of the Nashville Convention, and the compromise measures of 1850 are in Commager *Documents*. Constitutional questions bearing on the Fugitive Slave Law are discussed briefly in the constitutional histories of Kelly and Harbison (in Ch. 14), and Swisher (in Ch. 10); more fully in Warren, *Supreme Court in United States History*, Chs. 25-26. Fugitives are dealt with briefly in the histories of slavery. See also R. B. Nye, *Fettered Freedom*, Ch. 7. There is no good biography of Harriet Beecher Stowe, but Channing, Vol. VI, pp. 116-118, has interesting notes on the Underground Railroad and *Uncle Tom's Cabin*. The famous novel is available in cheap editions and is definitely worth reading because of its historical importance, even though its literary qualities may no longer be appealing.

31. THE NORTH, 1830-1860

General

There are good descriptions of economic and social developments in Turner, *United States, 1830-1850;* Nevins, *Ordeal of the Union*, esp. Vol. II, Chs. 5-8; Channing, *History*, Vol. V; Fish, *Rise of the Common Man;* A. C. Cole, *The Irrepressible Conflict* (1934, *History of American Life*). There are good chapters on the Middle West, the Ohio Valley, and the Mississippi Valley in Turner, *Frontier in American History*, Chs. 4-6. More extended accounts include H. C. Hubbart, *The Older Middle West* (1938); A. L. Kohlmeier, *The Old Northwest* (1938). The economic histories of H. U. Faulkner, E. C. Kirkland, and F. A. Shannon can be advantageously consulted. L. M. Hacker, *The Triumph of American Capitalism* (1940), Chs. 16-20, describes the trend from mercantilist to industrial capitalism; see also Ch. 2. A scholarly work of much statistical interest is W. B. Smith and A. H. Cole, *Fluctuations in American Business, 1790-1865* (1935). Popular books on the last two decades of the era are Meade Minnegerode, *The Fabulous Forties* (1924); E. D. Branch, *The Sentimental Years* (1934).

Special

Some of the titles given here are repeated from Ch. 22, where the emphasis is on the 1820's. Detailed suggestions are given in the *Harvard Guide*, Ch. 14, for the period, 1820-60; see esp. sections 148-150.

AGRICULTURE

The standard work is Bidwell and Falconer, *History of Agriculture in the Northern United States, 1620-1860.* There is a dearth of popular treatments and the best scholarly studies are of particular localities.

COMMERCE

J. H. Frederick, *The Development of American Commerce* (1932), is a general account; Morison, *Maritime History of Massachusetts,* a brilliant story of the far-flung trade of a single state. Ships and foreign trade are admirably described in C. C. Cutler, *Greyhound of the Sea: The Story of the American Clipper Ship* (1930); and R. G. Albion, *Square-Riggers on Schedule: The New York Sailing Packets* (1938).

TRANSPORTATION

G. R. Taylor, *The Transportation Revolution, 1820-1860* (1951) is an excellent account. S. H. Holbrook, *The Story of American Railroads* (1947) is a popular treatment extending into later periods. B. H. Meyer and others, *History of Transportation in the United States before 1860* (1917), is difficult to use but contains valuable materials. Among regional studies, R. E. Riegel, *The Story of Western Railroads* (1926) is of special interest to students of history. R. A. Billington, in *Westward Expansion,* Ch. 19, discusses the relations of railroad developments to sectionalism.

MANUFACTURING AND INVENTION

V. S. Clark, *History of Manufactures in the United States, 1607-1860* (1929) and W. B. Kaempffert, ed., *A Popular History of American Inventions* (2 vols., 1924) are the best works for reference.

LABOR

Dulles, *Labor in America,* Ch. 5, deals with this period. J. R. Commons and others, *History of Labor in the United States,* Vol. I (1918), gives the fullest account of the early labor movement. The best view of working conditions can be had from N. J. Ware, *The Industrial Worker, 1840-1860* (1924), and Edith Abbott, *Women in Industry* (1910), two very interesting books.

IMMIGRATION

Most of the admirable book of M. L. Hansen, *The Atlantic Migration, 1607-1860* (1939), deals with this period. See also Hansen, *The Immigrant in American History* (1941), Chs. 7, 9; Wittke, *We Who Built America,* Part Two. There are special studies of various ethnic groups, such as Faust, *German Element in the United States.* Hansen is particularly good on European backgrounds; see also W. F. Adams, *Ireland and Irish Emigration* (1932). Oscar Handlin, *Boston's*

Immigrants (1941) is a notable special study. An excellent study of Nativism is R. A. Billington, *The Protestant Crusade, 1800-1860* (1938).

SOCIAL LIFE

On recreation, there is fresh and interesting information in F. R. Dulles, *America Learns to Play: A History of Popular Recreation, 1607-1940* (1940); and J. A. Krout, *Annals of American Sport* (1929). Manners were freely commented on by foreign visitors. Two good collections of travel accounts are Allan Nevins, *America through British Eyes* (1948); Oscar Handlin, *This Was America* (1949), giving excerpts from continental travelers. A list of books of travel and description is in *Harvard Guide,* sect. 48.

BIOGRAPHIES

K. W. Porter, *John Jacob Astor: Business Man* (2 vols., 1931); W. T. Hutchinson, *Cyrus Hall McCormick* (2 vols., 1930-35); H. M. Larson, *Jay Cooke: Private Banker* (1936) are among the relatively few good biographies of business leaders.

32. THE ANTE-BELLUM SOUTH

General

Most of the general works cited for the previous chapter give extended treatment to Southern life, especially slavery. A good account is in Nevins, *Ordeal of the Union,* Vol. I, Chs. 13-15. A more compact and rather more sympathetic treatment is in J. G. Randall, *The Civil War and Reconstruction* (1937), Chs. 1-2. In our own day, Northern and Southern scholars alike have striven to be fair-minded in describing this vanished economy and society, and the main difference between them is one of emphasis and shading. The subject is viewed from the Southern side in Sydnor, *Development of Southern Sectionalism,* and Craven, *Growth of Southern Nationalism,* as it is in the briefer works of Clement Eaton, *A History of the Old South* (1949), and F. B. Simkins, *A History of the South* (rev. edn., 1953). All of these books contain good descriptive chapters. The older work of U. B. Phillips, *Life and Labor in the Old South* (1929), a friendly and relatively conservative treatment based on a lifetime's study of plantation records, is still one of the best. W. E. Dodd, *The Cotton Kingdom* (1917, *Chronicles of America*) is more critical of the great planters but this stimulating book is inaccurate in places. W. J. Cash, *The Mind of the South* (1941), a brilliant and impressionistic treatment of social attitudes, should not be missed.

Special

AGRICULTURE

Gray, *History of Agriculture in the Southern United States* is virtually inexhaustible. The account of the spread of cotton into the Gulf states and the attempted adjustment in the older states is in Vol. II, Chs. 27-29. Studies of special interest are J. C. Robert, *The Tobacco Kingdom, 1800-1860* (1938); A. O. Craven, *Soil Exhaustion . . . in . . . Virginia and Maryland*. On agricultural reform the best book to read is Craven, *Edmund Ruffin*. The most famous and most reliable contemporary Northern account of Southern agriculture and slavery is now readily available, F. L. Olmsted, *The Cotton Kingdom* (1953), edited by A. M. Schlesinger; it is interesting as well as valuable. The plantation as an economic institution is discussed in varying degree in the more important works on agriculture and slavery, and in Nevins, *Ordeal*, Vol. I, Ch. 14.

COMMERCE AND INDUSTRY

The "enslavement" of the cotton ports is well described in the works of R. G. Albion: *Square-Riggers on Schedule*, and *Rise of New York Port*. The best work on railroads is U. B. Phillips, *A History of Transportation in the Eastern Cotton Belt to 1860* (1908). The problem of Charleston is personalized in T. D. Jervey, *Robert Y. Hayne*. R. R. Russel, *Economic Aspects of Southern Sectionalism* (1924), and J. G. Van Deusen, *The Ante-Bellum Southern Commercial Conventions* (1926) are valuable. Broadus Mitchell, *William Gregg: Factory Master of the Old South* (1928) deals with early cotton mills; Kathleen Bruce, *Virginia Iron Manufacture in the Slave Era* (1931), with heavy industry.

SLAVERY AND SOCIAL CLASSES

Besides the histories of slavery by Phillips and Franklin, and other works cited for Ch. 26, there are good studies of the actual operations of the system in particular states. Among these are R. B. Flanders, *Plantation Slavery in Georgia* (1933), and C. S. Sydnor, *Slavery in Mississippi* (1933). Contemporary writings of special pertinence include: *The Narrative of the Life of Frederick Douglass, an American Slave* (1845); H. R. Helper, *The Impending Crisis of the South* (1857). L. C. Gray, *Agriculture*, Vol. I, Chs. 21-22, has an admirable discussion of "Economic Types and Social Classes." A good introduction to the nonslaveholding whites is F. L. Owsley, *Plain Folk of the Old South* (1949). Sydnor, *Development of Southern Sectionalism*, Ch. 2, is an illuminating discussion of the "location of political power." Valuable in the same connection are F. M. Green, *Constitutional Development in the South Atlantic States, 1776-1816: A Study in the Evolution of Democracy* (1930); J. T. Carpenter, *The South as a Conscious Minority, 1789-1861* (1930); R. W. Shugg, *Origins of Class Struggle in Louisiana* (1939).

CULTURE

Educational and intellectual conditions and developments are well summed up by Clement Eaton, in *History of the Old South*, and *Freedom of Thought in the Old South*. See also Curti, *Growth of American Thought*, Ch. 17; Nevins, *Ordeal*, Ch. 15. Literature is treated in the various histories of literature; Parrington, *Main Currents*, Vol. II, is especially good on the South. Biographies of important figures in thought and letters are Harvey Wish, *George Fitzhugh* (1943); J. D. Wade, *Augustus Baldwin Longstreet* (1924). F. P. Gaines, *The*

Southern Plantation: A Study in the Development and Accuracy of a Tradition (1925), shows how the romantic picture of Southern civilization was painted. P. H. Buck, in *The Road to Reunion* (1937), shows how it came to be generally accepted.

33. SECTIONALISM AND TROPICAL IMPERIALISM, 1848-1856

General

The international episodes that are grouped here are treated in the diplomatic histories of Bailey, Bemis, and Pratt; and in Bemis, *American Secretaries of State*, Vol. VI. As a rule they have not received sufficient emphasis in general works in connection with the sectional conflict. See, however, Allan Nevins, *Ordeal of the Union*, Vol. II, Ch. 10; and R. F. Nichols, *Franklin Pierce*, Chs. 43-45.

Special

Works bearing on relations with the British are M. W. Williams, *Anglo-American Isthmian Diplomacy, 1815-1915* (1916); J. B. Brebner, *North Atlantic Triangle* (1945), see esp. Ch. 9. Special studies of Spanish relations and developments in Latin-America are: Basil Rauch, *American Interest in Cuba, 1848-1855* (1948), describing events and relating the Cuban question to the Young America movement and national politics; A. A. Ettinger, *The Mission to Spain of Pierre Soulé, 1853-1855* (1932); W. O. Scroggs, *Filibusters and Financiers: The Story of William Walker and His Associates* (1916); P. N. Garber, *The Gadsden Treaty* (1932). For the Ostend Manifesto and other important documents, see Bartlett, *Record of American Diplomacy*.

34-36. POLITICAL HISTORY, 1853-1861

General

General suggestions covering the political history of the administrations of Franklin Pierce and James Buchanan are given here. These will be followed by specific suggestions for the three chapters into which this eventful period has been divided.

NARRATIVE HISTORIES

These are so rich for the period that many students and readers may see no need to go beyond them. Allan Nevins, *Ordeal of the Union* goes through the Pierce administration, and the same author's *Emergence of Lincoln* (2 vols., 1950) continues the story four years longer, being even fuller than its predecessor. Moderate in tone while colorful in detail, it maintains the quality of a narrative and is definitely good reading. So is the older work of J. F. Rhodes, *History*, Vols. I-III. R. F. Nichols, *The Disruption of American Democracy*

(1948) begins with the election of 1856. It is specially good on Democratic politics and on psychology; see Chs. 2, 27. Channing covers the period more briefly in his *History*, Vol. VI, Chs. 5-10. J. G. Randall, in *Civil War and Reconstruction*, sums it up in about the same number of chapters, pp. 128-258, but they are more compact. A. O. Craven interprets Southern attitudes in *Development of Southern Nationalism*, and, even more sympathetically, in *The Coming of the Civil War* (1942).

BIOGRAPHIES

Lincoln has been the favorite biographical subject in the whole of American history. The best one-volume life is B. P. Thomas, *Abraham Lincoln: A Biography* (1952). His account of "Lincoln Literature" (pp. 523ff.) is convenient and dependable. David Donald, *Lincoln Reconsidered: Essays on the Civil War Era* (1956), is fresh and stimulating. Of longer works, the best for this period are J. G. Randall, *Lincoln the President: Springfield to Gettysburg* (2 vols., 1945), which devotes more attention to the prewar years than its title suggests; and A. J. Beveridge, *Abraham Lincoln, 1809-1858* (2 vols., 1928), a work which would have been carried farther had the author lived and which brought Lincoln only to the verge of his greatness. Carl Sandburg, *Abraham Lincoln: The Prairie Years* (2 vols., 1926 and later edns.), is valuable for background and atmosphere. Every serious student or reader of American history should have a one-volume edition of Lincoln's writings. Good selections are R. P. Basler, *Abraham Lincoln: His Speeches and Writings* (1946); Philip Van Doren Stern, *The Life and Writings of Abraham Lincoln* (1940); P. M. Angle and E. S. Miers, *The Living Lincoln . . . Reconstructed from His Own Writings* (1955). Works bearing on particular phases of Lincoln's public life will be mentioned hereafter. Further suggestions for reading on his life before 1854 are given in Thomas, pp. 531-536.

Douglas figures prominently in biographies of Lincoln, especially Beveridge. Johnson, *Douglas*, and Milton, *Eve of Conflict*, continue to be valuable; as does Nichols, *Franklin Pierce*. C. B. Swisher, *Roger B. Taney* (1935) is even more important in the period of the Dred Scott decision than in the Age of Jackson.

34. SECTIONALISM AND THE WEST, 1853-1857

Special

KANSAS

The story of the Kansas-Nebraska Act and of developments in the territories in general histories and biographies is detailed. Among important special studies are P. O. Ray, *Repeal of the Missouri Compromise* (1909); J. C. Malin, *John Brown and the Legend of Fifty-Six* (1942). Riegel, *Western Railroads*, Chs. 2-4, provides good background materials. Sumner's speech on "Bleeding Kansas" and the attack on him by Brooks are vividly described in Rhodes, *History*, Vol. II, pp. 131-150.

REPUBLICAN PARTY AND ELECTION OF 1856

There is a general account in Binkley, *American Political Parties*, Chs. 8-9. Biographical works specially valuable for Republican beginnings are: G. G. Van Deusen, *Thurlow Weed* (1947); J. A. Isely, *Horace Greeley and the Republican Party* (1947); Nevins, *Frémont*. Studies of the "Know-Nothing" movement are too specialized for most readers, but Billington, *Protestant Crusade*, is of wider interest. For the Democrats, Nichols gives a good account of the election in *Disruption of American Democracy;* see also his *Democratic Machine, 1850-1854* (1923).

DRED SCOTT

The famous decision is described briefly in the constitutional histories of Kelly and Harbison, and Swisher; more fully in Warren, *Supreme Court in United States History*, Ch. 26; and Swisher, *Roger B. Taney*, Chs. 23-24. Nevins, availing himself of recent studies, has an excellent account in *Emergence of Lincoln*, Vol. I, Ch. 4. One of the latest detailed treatments is V. C. Hopkins, *Dred Scott's Case* (1951). Extracts from Taney's opinion and from Lincoln's speech of June 17, 1858, in which he commented on it, are in Commager, *Documents*.

35. THE WIDENING RIFT, 1857-1860

Special

LECOMPTON CONSTITUTION AND REVOLT OF DOUGLAS

These are sufficiently covered in Nichols, *Disruption of American Democracy*, Chs. 6-7; Nevins, *Emergence of Lincoln*, Vol. I, Chs. 6, 9-10; and biographies of Douglas.

LINCOLN-DOUGLAS DEBATES

The issues are well discussed in Randall, *Lincoln the President*, Vol. I, Ch. 5; the accounts in Nevins, *Emergence*, Vol. I, Ch. 14, and Beveridge, *Lincoln*, Vol. II, Ch. 10, are graphic. The speeches themselves are in E. E. Sparks, ed., *The Lincoln-Douglas Debates of 1858* (1908); extracts in Commager, *Documents*.

POLITICS, NORTH AND SOUTH

Nichols, Nevins, and Craven in *Growth of Southern Nationalism*, tell a complementary story. At this point, the biographies of the Southern "fire-eaters" become specially important: White, *Robert Barnwell Rhett;* Craven, *Edmund Ruffin*. A fresh biography of Yancey is needed. Useful biographies of Southern leaders not previously mentioned are Elizabeth Merritt, *James Henry Hammond, 1807-1864* (1923); L. A. Kibler, *Benjamin F. Perry* (1946), both South Carolinians and the latter a Unionist. Information about the effort to create a moderate party in the Upper South can be gained from studies of the secession movements in particular states. On the Northern side, there is need for a critical biography of Seward. Financial issues are treated in P. S. Foner, *Business and Slavery* (1941); G. W. Van Vleck, *The Panic of 1857* (1943).

John Brown's Raid and Its Results

Probably the best modern account is in Nevins, *Emergence of Lincoln,* Vol. II, Chs. 3-4; see also Ch. 1. It is more critical than O. G. Villard, *John Brown* (1943), the fullest biography. The Southern reaction is emphasized particularly by Craven. An interesting account of the trial is in R. B. Morris, *Fair Trial* (1952), Ch. 9.

36. THE ELECTION OF 1860 AND SECESSION

Special

Election of 1860

The main events are described in all the general histories and the biographies of Lincoln and Douglas. Conditions in their home state are shown in A. C. Cole, *The Era of the Civil War, 1848-1870* (1922; Vol. III of *Centennial History of Illinois*). Other works bearing directly on Lincoln are: S. D. Wakefield, *How Lincoln Became President* (1936); R. H. Luthin, *The First Lincoln Campaign* (1944). Richard Hofstadter, in *The American Political Tradition and the Men who Made It* (1948), Ch. 5, emphasizes Lincoln's ambition and absorption in politics. The campaign in the South is described in works dealing with secession, but a monograph on the subject is Ollinger Crenshaw, *The Slave States in the Presidential Election of 1860* (1945). The failure of compromise is described in Mary Scrugham, *Peaceable Americans of 1860-1861* (1921).

Secession

The best accounts of events are in E. M. Coulter, *The Confederate States of America* (1950; Vol. VII of *A History of the South*), Chs. 1-3; and D. L. Dumond, *The Secession Movement, 1860-1861* (1931). Among studies of secession in particular states, two good ones, representing respectively the Lower and Upper South, are: P. L. Rainwater, *Mississippi: Storm Center of Secession, 1856-1861* (1938); H. T. Shanks, *The Secession Movement in Virginia, 1847-1861* (1934). Hudson Strode, in *Jefferson Davis: American Patriot, 1808-1861* (1955), draws a picture of a man of cultivation, sincerity, and integrity, and is uncritical of his statesmanship.

Attitudes and Interpretations

Attitudes can be seen in *Southern Editorials on Seccession* (1921), edited by D. L. Dumond; and *Northern Editorials on Secession* (2 vols., 1942), edited by H. C. Perkins. Northern sentiment is well described in K. M. Stamff, *And the War Came* (1950). Northern public policy is considered in the fine study of

D. M. Potter, *Lincoln and His Party in the Secession Crisis* (1942). The conflict in constitutional theory is summed up in C. E. Merriam, *American Political Theories*, Ch. 7. The continuing conflict in interpretation is described by H. K. Beale, "What Historians Have Said about the Causes of the Civil War," an illuminating if perhaps discouraging essay which can be conveniently seen in Donald Sheehan, *The Making of American History*, pp. 314-350. Among many important treatments which can be appropriately mentioned in this connection are D. L. Dumond, *Anti-slavery Origins of the Civil War* (1932); U. B. Phillips, *The Course of the South to Secession* (1939), edited by E. M. Coulter, and A. O. Craven, *The Repressible Conflict, 1830-1861* (1939), both presenting "revisionist" views from the Southern angle; C. A. and Mary Beard, *The Rise of American Civilization*, Vol. II (1927), Chs. 17, 18, viewing the War and Reconstruction as the second American Revolution and emphasizing the economic conflict. The question is argued in the booklet, *Slavery as a Cause of the Civil War*, in the Amherst *Problems in American Civilization*. It would be hard to find a more interesting historical question about which to argue.

Part VI: The Civil War, 1861-1865

CHAPTERS 37-40

General

Probably the most thorough account of the diverse phases of the war in brief compass is Randall, *Civil War and Reconstruction*, Chs. 10-29, but the very compactness of the book makes it hard reading. Channing covers the whole war in *History*, Vol. VI, Chs. 11-20; and, except for the campaigns, N. W. Stephenson does in two small and well-written volumes in the *Chronicles of America: Abraham Lincoln and the Union* (1920), and *The Day of the Confederacy* (1920). J. F. Rhodes, *History of the Civil War* (1917), requires supplementation at many points because of the enormous achievements of specialized scholarship in recent years, but it can be recommended. Allan Nevins, in *The War for the Union*, Vol. I (1959), impressively covers the first year in the first of four projected volumes.

J. G. Randall's *Lincoln the President*—consisting of *From Springfield to Gettysburg* (2 vols., 1945), *Midstream* (1952), and *Last Full Measure* (1955) —a posthumous work ably completed by R. N. Current—is a combination of biography and history, representing the best academic scholarship. This exceedingly important work, crowning a generation of thoughtful study, can be read with profit and pleasure by laymen and specialists alike, and it is indispensable to the serious student of the period.

E. M. Coulter's *Confederate States of America* does not cover military campaigns but is admirable for all other phases of Confederate history; it has a full biography. Clement Eaton, *History of the Southern Confederacy* (1954), a general account, is fresh and reliable. It provides a good introduction, as does R. S. Henry, *The Story of the Confederacy* (1931). Clifford Dowdy, *Experiment in Rebellion* (1946), is centered on Richmond.

There is no better way to catch the spirit of the conflict on both sides than to read and ponder over the war poem of Stephen Vincent Benét, *John Brown's Body* (1928).

Special

THE ARMED CONFLICT

Few wars in history can rival the Civil War in military interest to amateurs as well as professionals. Few have been investigated as fully, and the result is a prodigious body of historical literature. The most notable works dealing with it are lengthy as a rule and gain their rich texture from their myriad details, but the campaigns can be followed in the one-volume history of Rhodes, and in the old West Point textbook, M. F. Steele, *American Campaigns*. There is an admirable brief account of the campaigns, along with an unusually good collection of pictures, in *Divided We Fought* (1952), edited by David Donald. A convenient handbook is J. B. Mitchell, *Decisive Battles of the Civil War* (1955), with brief accounts and good maps. Shelby Foote, in *The Civil War, A Narrative: Fort Sumter to Perryville* (1958), gets half way through the long story.

One of the modern classics consists of a series of three enthralling books by Bruce Catton, which tell the story of the Army of the Potomac: *Mr. Lincoln's Army* (1951); *Glory Road* (1952); and *A Stillness at Appomattox* (1953). On the Confederate side, the history of the Army of Northern Virginia has been written in even greater detail in the magnificent books of D. S. Freeman: *R. E. Lee* (4 vols., 1934-35), and *Lee's Lieutenants* (3 vols., 1942-44).

An illuminating and generally convincing study of strategy and the high command is T. H. Williams, *Lincoln and His Generals* (1952), which emphasizes the military wisdom of the President and assesses the merits and demerits of all the chief commanders. K. P. Williams, in *Lincoln Finds a General* (2 vols., 1949), is definitely anti-McClellan and aggressively pro-Grant; he does full justice to the western theatre of the war.

Military biographies of unusual interest and value are Lloyd Lewis, *Sherman: Fighting Prophet* (1932); G. F. R. Henderson, *Stonewall Jackson and the American Civil War* (1898), an older classic; J. W. Thomason, Jr., *Jeb Stuart* (1930). *The Memoirs of General William T. Sherman* (1957) are specially commended. Studies of particular battles or campaigns include: R. M. Johnston, *Bull Run* (1912), describing the first battle of the name; E. S. Miers and R. A. Brown, eds., *Gettysburg* (1948), a collection of contemporary accounts; E. S. Miers, *Web of Victory* (1954), an account of Grant's Vicksburg campaign.

The lot of the common soldier is depicted by B. I. Wiley, in *The Life of Johnny Reb* (1943), and *The Life of Billy Yank* (1952). One of the darkest aspects of the war is described by W. B. Hesseltine, in *Civil War Prisons* (1930); and in the powerful novel, *Andersonville* (1955), by MacKinlay Kantor. A variety of descriptions from a variety of participants and observers is given in *The Blue and the Gray* (2 vols., 1951), edited by H. S. Commager.

Despite the great importance of the naval operations, they do not lend themselves readily to narrative treatment. They are described briefly in the general and naval histories. Specialized works of interest are: J. D. Hill, *Seadogs of the*

Sixties (1935); W. M. Robinson, *Confederate Privateers* (1928); J. P. Baxter, III, *The Introduction of the Ironclad Warship* (1933). A detailed modern life of a naval hero is C. L. Lewis, *David Glasgow Farragut* (2 vols., 1941-43).

The vital and difficult matter of men and supplies is treated extensively in F. A. Shannon, *The Organization and Administration of the Union Army* (2 vols., 1928). Other important studies are A. H. Meneely, *The War Department, 1861* (1928), covering the Cameron regime; Ella Lonn, *Desertion during the Civil War* (1928), dealing with both sides; A. B. Moore, *Conscription and Conflict in the Confederacy* (1924); F. E. Vandiver, *Ploughshares into Swords: Josiah Gorgas and Confederate Ordnance* (1952).

GOVERNMENT AND POLITICS IN THE UNION

Lincoln himself is naturally emphasized in all treatments of the political history of the period. Carl Sandburg's *Abraham Lincoln: The War Years* (4 vols., 1939) is full of incidents and is incomparable for background. Lincoln's interpretation and exercise of Presidential power are described in the constitutional histories of Kelly and Harbison, Ch. 16; and Swisher, Ch. 14; in W. E. Binkley, *The Powers of the President*, Ch. 16; and in other works on the Presidency. They are discussed in detail in J. G. Randall, *Constitutional Problems under Lincoln* (rev. edn. 1951), the basic work on the subject. The question of arbitrary government, which is of such lively interest to our own generation, is given general treatment in Warren, *Supreme Court in American History*, Ch. 28, and in works on civil liberties. It is treated more specifically in G. F. Milton, *Abraham Lincoln and the Fifth Column* (1942); and Wood Gray, *The Hidden Civil War: The Story of the Copperheads* (1942). E. C. Smith, *The Borderland in the Civil War* (1927) is of interest in this connection, as it is for other reasons. Among special studies of other important executive problems are: H. J. Carman and R. H. Luthin, *Lincoln and the Patronage* (1943); W. B. Hesseltine, *Lincoln and the War Governors* (1948); T. H. Williams, *Lincoln and the Radicals* (1941). These works bear not only on administration and public policy but on politics. The general histories, biographies, and diaries of the era are full of politics. This period is covered by Binkley, *American Political Parties*, Chs. 10-11. E. C. Kirkland, *Peacemakers of 1864* (1927) bears directly on the Presidential election of that war.

A general account of the official family is B. J. Hendrick, *Lincoln's War Cabinet* (1946). Important biographies or personal records of men close to Lincoln include: Helen Nicolay, *Lincoln's Secretary* (1949), an account of John Nicolay; Tyler Dennett, *Lincoln and the Civil War in the Diary and Letters of John Hay* (1939); *Inside Lincoln's Cabinet: The Civil War Diaries of Salmon P. Chase,* edited by David Donald (1954); *Diary of Gideon Welles* (3 vols., 1911), edited by J. T. Morse, Jr.; *Diary of Edward Bates, 1859-1866* (1930), edited by H. K. Beale; *Diary of Orville Hickman Browning* (1927-33), edited by T. C. Pease and J. G. Randall; W. E. Smith, *The Francis Preston Blair Family in Politics* (1933), Vol. II, for Montgomery Blair, the Postmaster General; David Donald, *Lincoln's Herndon* (1948).

The financing of the war is described in Dewey, *Financial History*, Chs. 12-13; and the war tariff in Taussig, *Tariff History*, Part II, Ch. 1. See also

Inside Lincoln's Cabinet; Larson, *Jay Cooke;* E. P. Oberholtzer, *Jay Cooke: Financier of the Civil War* (2 vols., 1907).

GOVERNMENT AND POLITICS IN THE CONFEDERACY

Coulter, in *The Confederate States of America,* describes the government and its operations in numerous chapters, while saying (p. 593) that no adequate study of it has ever been made. The fullest modern biography of the Confederate President is Robert McElroy, *Jefferson Davis: The Unreal and the Real* (2 vols., 1937). The latest is Hudson Strode, *Jefferson Davis: American Patriot, 1808-1861* (1955), carrying him into the Presidency; this is at its best in describing his personal life and military career. Another covering the war period is R. W. Winston, *High Stakes and Hair Trigger: The Life of Jefferson Davis* (1930). A general treatment is B. J. Hendrick, *Statesmen of the Lost Cause* (1939), and a more recent study of value is R. W. Patrick, *Jefferson Davis and His Cabinet* (1944). R. D. Meade, *Judah P. Benjamin* (1943), is a good biography of the person in the government on whom Davis most relied. There is no adequate treatment of Alexander H. Stephens.

F. L. Owsley, in *States Rights in the Confederacy* (1925), presents the thesis that the Confederacy died of that disease, while A. B. Moore, in *Conscription and Conflict in the Confederacy,* describes many difficulties with the states. L. B. Hill, *Joseph E. Brown and the Confederacy* (1939), describes one of Davis's chief gubernatorial foes. W. M. Robinson, Jr., *Justice in Grey: A History of the Judicial System of the Confederate States* (1941), is an excellent study of a subject previously unexplored. J. C. Schwab, *The Confederate States of America, 1861-1865: A Financial and Industrial History* (1913; written earlier), is still valuable, especially for finance, but most readers will probably be content with Coulter's treatment of that depressing subject.

One of the bitterest critics of the Confederate administration, the journalist E. A. Pollard, wrote several books, including *The Lost Cause* (1866), and *Life of Jefferson Davis: With a Secret History of the Southern Confederacy* (1869). Davis presented his own case to posterity in *The Rise and Fall of the Confederate Government* (2 vols., 1881). Modern works on the Confederacy by Southern scholars are far better balanced and more judicious than these old books. Many sympathetic comments on Davis are in Mary B. Chesnut, *A Diary from Dixie* (edn. of 1942 by B. A. Williams). *Inside the Confederate Government: The Diary of Robert Garlick Hill Kean* (1957), edited by Edward Younger, gives illuminating and critical comments on leaders and policies.

DIPLOMACY

This important subject is treated in the general and diplomatic histories, in Bemis, *American Secretaries of State,* Vol. VII (on Seward), and in valuable special studies. Among the latter are: E. D. Adams, *Great Britain and the American Civil War* (2 vols., 1925); Donaldson Jordan and E. J. Pratt, *Europe and the American Civil War* (1931); F. L. Owsley, *King Cotton Diplomacy: Foreign Relations of the Confederate States of America* (1931).

The situation in Great Britain is made vivid in *A Cycle of Adams Letters, 1861-1865* (2 vols., 1920), edited by W. C. Ford; and *The Education of Henry Adams* (1918 and later edns.), Chs. 8-13. Jay Monaghan, *Diplomat in Carpet Slippers* (1945), centers the story on Lincoln. The Mexican episode receives scholarly treatment in Dexter Perkins, *Monroe Doctrine, 1826-1867,* Chs. 5 8.

EMANCIPATION AND THE NEGROES

There is a good general account in Franklin, *From Slavery to Freedom,* Ch. 16, with bibliography citing articles as well as books. The political problems of emancipation are well brought out in the writings of Randall, and in Williams, *Lincoln and the Radicals.* See also works dealing with Chase; Nevins, *Frémont;* and R. N. Current, *Old Thad Stevens* (1941). One of the best books on Negro soldiers is the very old one of T. W. Higginson, *Army Life in a Black Regiment* (1870). On the Confederate side, B. I. Wiley, *Southern Negroes, 1861-1865* (1938) is excellent.

CIVILIAN LIFE

A good picture of life in both North and South is given in Rhodes, *History of the Civil War,* Chs. 11-12. Cole's *Irrepressible Conflict* extends to 1865 and describes economic and social conditions. Many of the selections in Commager, *The Blue and the Gray,* describe civilian life.

Economic conditions and activities in the North are covered in economic and financial histories, and are properly linked with the problems of financing the war and supplying the armies on the one hand, and with postwar developments on the other. A general treatment is E. D. Fite, *Social and Industrial Conditions in the North* (1910). For the Homestead Act and Land Grant Colleges, see Hibbard, *Public Land Policies,* Chs. 17-18, and histories of agriculture and education. Developments in transportation are described in Riegel, *Western Railroads,* and Thomas Weber, *Northern Railroads in the Civil War* (1951). For labor, see N. J. Ware, *The Labor Movement in the United States, 1860-1895* (1929). An interesting account of life in the national capital is Margaret Leech, *Reveille in Washington* (1941).

Descriptions of Southern economic and social life are scattered through various chapters of Coulter's *Confederate States.* Because of the poignancy of the story, many of the special studies have unusual appeal. Among these are: C. H. Wesley, *The Collapse of the Confederacy* (1937); C. W. Ramsdell, *Behind the Lines in the Southern Confederacy* (1944); B. I. Wiley, *The Plain People of the Confederacy* (1943); Ella Lonn, *Foreigners in the Confederacy* (1940), and *Salt as a Factor in the Confederacy* (1933); A. H. Bill, *The Beleaguered City: Richmond, 1861-1865* (1946); R. C. Black, III, *The Railroads of the Confederacy* (1952); F. B. Simkins and J. W. Patton, *The Women of the Confederacy* (1936). A good list of diaries by women is in Simkins, *History of the South,* p. 634. The most famous of these, Mary Boykin Chesnut, *A Diary from Dixie* (edn. of 1950), should not be missed. Also famous is J. B. Jones, *A Rebel War Clerk's Diary* (2 vols., 1866).

THE END OF THE WAR

The dramatic closing scenes of the war are well described in the larger
histories and biographies, especially the biographies of Lincoln and Lee. No
one should fail to read the Second Inaugural. It is in Commager, Documents,
Vol. I, pp. 442-443; for his last address, see Vol. I, pp. 448-450. Jim Bishop,
The Day Lincoln Was Shot (1955), is a vivid account which is also judicious.
The best study of Mrs. Lincoln is Ruth P. Randall, *Mary Lincoln: Biography
of a Marriage* (1953). Two minor works of J. G. Randall, *Lincoln the Liberal
Statesman* (1947), and *Lincoln and the South* (1946), are of great value in the
final summing up. B. F. Thomas, in *Portrait for Posterity: Lincoln and His
Biographers* (1947), virtually traces the history of the Lincoln legend.
Specially good modern statements of it by historians are those of R. H. Gabriel,
Course of American Democratic Thought, pp. 407-13; and David Donald,
Lincoln's Herndon, pp. 368-70. The growing Lee legend can be easily seen
in the later chapters of Freeman, *R. E. Lee*, Vol. IV.

APPENDICES

DECLARATION OF INDEPENDENCE

In Congress, July 4, 1776

A DECLARATION BY THE REPRESENTATIVES OF THE UNITED STATES OF AMERICA, IN CONGRESS ASSEMBLED

When, in the course of human events, it becomes necessary for one people to dissolve the political bands which have connected them with another, and to assume, among the powers of the earth, the separate and equal station to which the laws of nature and of nature's God entitle them, a decent respect to the opinions of mankind requires that they should declare the causes which impel them to the separation.

We hold these truths to be self-evident:—That all men are created equal; that they are endowed by their Creator with certain unalienable rights; that among these are life, liberty, and the pursuit of happiness. That, to secure these rights, governments are instituted among men, deriving their just powers from the consent of the governed; that, whenever any form of government becomes destructive of these ends, it is the right of the people to alter or to abolish it, and to institute a new government, laying its foundation on such principles, and organizing its powers in such form, as to them shall seem most likely to effect their safety and happiness. Prudence, indeed, will dictate, that governments long established should not be changed for light and transient causes; and accordingly all experience hath shown that mankind are more disposed to suffer while evils are sufferable, than to right themselves by abolishing the forms to which they are accustomed. But when a long train of abuses and usurpations, pursuing invariably the same object, evinces a design to reduce them under absolute despotism, it is their right, it is their duty, to throw off such government, and to provide new guards for their future security. Such has been the patient sufferance of these colonies; and such is now the necessity which constrains them to alter their former systems of government. The history of the present King of Great Britain is a history of repeated injuries and usurpations, all having in direct object the establishment of an absolute tyranny over these states. To prove this, let facts be submitted to a candid world.

He has refused his assent to laws the most wholesome and necessary for the public good.

He has forbidden his governors to pass laws of immediate and pressing importance, unless suspended in their operation till his assent should be obtained; and when so suspended, he has utterly neglected to attend to them.

He has refused to pass other laws for the accommodation of large districts of people, unless those people would relinquish the right of representation in the legislature—a right inestimable to them, and formidable to tyrants only.

He has called together legislative bodies at places unusual, uncomfortable, and distant from the depository of their public records, for the sole purpose of fatiguing them into compliance with his measure.

He has dissolved representative houses repeatedly, for opposing, with manly firmness, his invasions on the rights of the people.

He has refused, for a long time after such dissolutions, to cause others to be elected, whereby the legislative powers, incapable of annihilation, have returned to the people at large for their exercise; the State remaining, in the mean time, exposed to all the dangers of invasions from without, and convulsions within.

He has endeavored to prevent the population of these States; for that purpose obstructing the laws for the naturalization of foreigners; refusing to pass others to encourage their migration hither, and raising the conditions of new appropriations of lands.

He has obstructed the administration of justice, by refusing his assent to laws for establishing judiciary powers.

He has made judges dependent on his will alone for the tenure of their offices, and the amount and payment of their salaries.

He has erected a multitude of new offices, and sent hither swarms of officers to harass our people and eat out their substance.

He has kept among us in times of peace, standing armies, without the consent of our legislatures.

He has affected to render the military independent of, and superior to, the civil power.

He has combined with others to subject us to a jurisdiction foreign to our constitutions, and unacknowledged by our laws; giving his assent to their acts of pretended legislation:

For quartering large bodies of armed troops among us;

For protecting them, by a mock trial, from punishment for any murders which they should commit on the inhabitants of these States;

For cutting off our trade with all parts of the world;

For imposing taxes on us without our consent;

For depriving us, in many cases, of the benefits of trial by jury;

For transporting us beyond seas, to be tried for pretended offences;

For abolishing the free system of English laws in a neighboring province, establishing therein an arbitrary government, and enlarging its boundaries, so as to render it at once an example and fit instrument for introducing the same absolute rule into these colonies;

For taking away our charters, abolishing our most valuable laws, and altering, fundamentally, the forms of our governments;

For suspending our own legislatures, and declaring themselves invested with power to legislate for us in all cases whatsoever.

He has abdicated government here, by declaring us out of his protection, and waging war against us.

He has plundered our seas, ravaged our coasts, burned our towns, and destroyed the lives of our people.

He is at this time transporting large armies of foreign mercenaries to complete the works of death, desolation and tyranny, already begun with circumstances of cruelty and perfidy scarcely paralleled in the most barbarous ages, and totally unworthy the head of a civilized nation.

He has constrained our fellow-citizens, taken captive on the high seas, to bear arms against their country, to become the executioners of their friends and brethren, or to fall themselves by their hands.

He has excited domestic insurrection among us, and has endeavored to bring on the inhabitants of our frontiers the merciless Indian savages, whose known rule of warfare is an undistinguished destruction of all ages, sexes, and conditions.

In every stage of these oppressions we have petitioned for redress in the most humble terms; our repeated petitions have been answered only by repeated injury. A prince whose character is thus marked by every act which may define a tyrant, is unfit to be the ruler of a free people.

Nor have we been wanting in our attentions to our British brethren. We have warned them, from time to time, of attempts by their legislature to extend an unwarrantable jurisdiction over us. We have reminded them of the circumstances of our emigration and settlement here. We have appealed to their native justice and magnanimity; and we have conjured them, by the ties of our common kindred, to disavow these usurpations, which would inevitably interrupt our connections and correspondence. They, too, have been deaf to the voice of justice and consanguinity. We must, therefore, acquiesce in the necessity which denounces our separation, and hold them, as we hold the rest of mankind, enemies in war, in peace friends.

We, therefore, the Representatives of the United States of America, in General Congress assembled, appealing to the Supreme Judge of the world for the rectitude of our intentions, do, in the name and by the authority of the good people of these colonies, solemnly publish and declare, That these united Colonies are, and of right ought to be, free and independent states; that they are absolved from all allegiance to the British crown, and that all political connection between them and the state of Great Britain is, and ought to be, totally dissolved; and that, as free and independent states, they have full power to levy war, conclude peace, contract alliances, establish commerce, and do all other acts and things which independent states may of right do. And, for the support of this declaration, with a firm reliance on the protection of Divine Providence, we mutually pledge to each other our lives, our fortunes, and our sacred honor.

The foregoing Declaration was, by order of Congress, engrossed, and signed by the following members:

JOHN HANCOCK

NEW HAMPSHIRE
JOSIAH BARTLETT
WILLIAM WHIPPLE
MATTHEW THORNTON

MASSACHUSETTS BAY
SAMUEL ADAMS
JOHN ADAMS
ROBERT TREAT PAINE
ELBRIDGE GERRY

RHODE ISLAND
STEPHEN HOPKINS
WILLIAM ELLERY

CONNECTICUT
ROGER SHERMAN
SAMUEL HUNTINGTON
WILLIAM WILLIAMS
OLIVER WOLCOTT

NEW YORK
WILLIAM FLOYD
PHILIP LIVINGSTON
FRANCIS LEWIS
LEWIS MORRIS

NEW JERSEY
RICHARD STOCKTON
JOHN WITHERSPOON
FRANCIS HOPKINSON
JOHN HART
ABRAHAM CLARK

PENNSYLVANIA
ROBERT MORRIS
BENJAMIN RUSH
BENJAMIN FRANKLIN
JOHN MORTON
GEORGE CLYMER
JAMES SMITH
GEORGE TAYLOR
JAMES WILSON
GEORGE ROSS

DELAWARE
CAESAR RODNEY
GEORGE READ
THOMAS M'KEAN

MARYLAND
SAMUEL CHASE
WILLIAM PACA
THOMAS STONE

CHARLES CARROLL, of
    Carrollton

VIRGINIA
GEORGE WYTHE
RICHARD HENRY LEE
THOMAS JEFFERSON
BENJAMIN HARRISON
THOMAS NELSON, JR.
FRANCIS LIGHTFOOT LEE
CARTER BRAXTON

NORTH CAROLINA
WILLIAM HOOPER
JOSEPH HEWES
JOHN PENN

SOUTH CAROLINA
EDWARD RUTLEDGE
THOMAS HEYWARD, JR.
THOMAS LYNCH, JR.
ARTHUR MIDDLETON

GEORGIA
BUTTON GWINNETT
LYMAN HALL
GEORGE WALTON

THE
CONSTITUTION
OF THE
UNITED STATES OF AMERICA

WE, THE PEOPLE OF THE UNITED STATES, IN ORDER TO FORM A MORE PERFECT union, establish justice, insure domestic tranquillity, provide for the common defence, promote the general welfare, and secure the blessings of liberty to ourselves and our posterity, do ordain and establish this constitution for the United States of America.

ARTICLE I
SECTION 1

ALL LEGISLATIVE POWERS HEREIN GRANTED SHALL BE VESTED IN A CONGRESS OF the United States, which shall consist of a Senate and a House of Representatives.

SECTION 2

The House of Representatives shall be composed of Members chosen every second Year by the People of the several States, and the Electors in each State shall have the Qualifications requisite for Electors of the most numerous Branch of the State Legislature.

No Person shall be a Representative who shall not have attained to the Age of twenty-five Years, and been seven Years a Citizen of the United States, and who shall not, when elected, be an Inhabitant of that State in which he shall be chosen.

[Representatives and direct Taxes shall be apportioned among the several States which may be included within this Union, according to their respective Numbers, which shall be determined by adding to the whole Number of free Persons, including those bound to Service for a Term of Years, and excluding Indians not taxed, three fifths of all other Persons.]* The actual Enumeration shall be made within three Years after the first Meeting of the Congress of the United States, and within every subsequent Term of ten Years, in such Manner as they shall by Law direct. The Number of Representatives shall not exceed one for every thirty Thousand, but each State shall have at Least one

* Repealed by Section 2 of Amendment XIV.

Representative; and until such enumeration shall be made, the State of New Hampshire shall be entitled to chuse three, Massachusetts eight, Rhode-Island and Providence Plantations one, Connecticut five, New-York six, New Jersey four, Pennsylvania eight, Delaware one, Maryland six, Virginia ten, North Carolina five, South Carolina five, and Georgia three.

When vacancies happen in the Representation from any State, the Executive Authority thereof shall issue Writs of Election to fill such Vacancies.

The House of Representatives shall chuse their Speaker and other Officers; and shall have the sole Power of Impeachment.

Section 3

The Senate of the United States shall be composed of two Senators from each State, [chosen by the Legislature thereof,]* for six Years; and each Senator shall have one Vote.

Immediately after they shall be assembled in Consequence of the first Election, they shall be divided as equally as may be into three Classes. The Seats of the Senators of the first Class shall be vacated at the Expiration of the second Year, of the second Class at the Expiration of the fourth Year, and of the third Class at the Expiration of the sixth Year, so that one-third may be chosen every second Year; [and if Vacancies happen by Resignation, or otherwise, during the Recess of the Legislature of any State, the Executive thereof may make temporary Appointments until the next Meeting of the Legislature, which shall then fill such Vacancies.]†

No person shall be a Senator who shall not have attained to the Age of thirty Years, and been nine Years a Citizen of the United States, and who shall not, when elected, be an Inhabitant of that State for which he shall be chosen.

The Vice President of the United States shall be President of the Senate, but shall have no Vote, unless they be equally divided.

The Senate shall chuse their other Officers, and also a President pro tempore, in the Absence of the Vice President, or when he shall exercise the Office of President of the United States.

The Senate shall have the sole Power to try all Impeachments. When sitting for that Purpose, they shall be an Oath or Affirmation. When the President of the United States is tried, the Chief Justice shall preside: And no Person shall be convicted without the Concurrence of two thirds of the Members present.

Judgment in Cases of Impeachment shall not extend further than to removal from Office, and disqualification to hold and enjoy any Office of honor, Trust or Profit under the United States: but the Party convicted shall nevertheless be liable and subject to Indictment, Trial, Judgment and Punishment, according to Law.

Section 4

The Times, Places and Manner of holding Elections for Senators and Representatives, shall be prescribed in each State by the Legislature thereof; but the Congress may at any time by Law make or alter such Regulations, except as to the Places of chusing Senators.

* Replaced by Section 1 of Amendment XVII.
† Changed by Clause 2 of Amendment XVII.

The Congress shall assemble at least once in every Year, and such Meeting* shall [be on the first Monday in December] unless they shall by Law appoint a different Day.

Section 5

Each House shall be the Judge of the Elections, Returns and Qualifications of its own Members, and a Majority of each shall constitute a Quorum to do Business; but a smaller Number may adjourn from day to day, and may be authorized to compel the Attendance of absent Members, in such Manner, and under such Penalties as each House may provide.

Each House may determine the Rules of its Proceedings, punish its Members for disorderly Behavior, and, with the Concurrence of two thirds, expel a Member.

Each House shall keep a Journal of its Proceedings, and from time to time publish the same, excepting such Parts as may in their Judgment require Secrecy; and the Yeas and Nays of the Members of either House on any question shall, at the Desire of one fifth of those present, be entered on the Journal.

Neither House, during the Session of Congress, shall, without the Consent of the other, adjourn for more than three days, nor to any other Place than that in which the two Houses shall be sitting.

Section 6

The Senators and Representatives shall receive a Compensation for their Services, to be ascertained by Law, and paid out of the Treasury of the United States. They shall in all Cases, except Treason, Felony and Breach of the Peace, be privileged from Arrest during their Attendance at the Session of their respective Houses, and in going to and returning from the same; and for any Speech or Debate in either House, they shall not be questioned in any other Place.

No Senator or Representative shall, during the Time for which he was elected, be appointed to any civil Office under the Authority of the United States, which shall have been created, or the Emoluments whereof shall have been encreased during such time; and no Person holding any Office under the United States, shall be a Member of either House during his Continuance in Office.

Section 7

All Bills for raising Revenue shall originate in the House of Representatives; but the Senate may propose or concur with Amendments as on other Bills.

Every Bill which shall have passed the House of Representatives and the Senate, shall, before it become a Law, be presented to the President of the United States; If he approve he shall sign it, but if not he shall return it, with his Objections to that House in which it shall have originated, who shall enter the Objections at large on their Journal, and proceed to reconsider it. If after such Reconsideration two thirds of that House shall agree to pass the Bill, it shall be sent, together with the Objections, to the other House, by which it shall likewise be reconsidered, and if approved by two thirds of that House, it

* Changed by Section 2 of Amendment XX.

shall become a Law. But in all such Cases the Votes of both Houses shall be determined by Yeas and Nays, and the Names of the Persons voting for and against the Bill shall be entered on the Journal of each House respectively. If any Bill shall not be returned by the President within ten Days (Sundays excepted) after it shall have been presented to him, the Same shall be a Law, in like Manner as if he had signed it, unless the Congress by their Adjournment prevent its Return, in which Case it shall not be a Law.

Every Order, Resolution, or Vote to which the Concurrence of the Senate and House of Representatives may be necessary (except on a question of Adjournment) shall be presented to the President of the United States; and before the Same shall take Effect, shall be approved by him, or being disapproved by him, shall be repassed by two thirds of the Senate and House of Representatives, according to the Rules and Limitations prescribed in the Case of a Bill.

SECTION 8*

The Congress shall have Power To lay and collect Taxes, Duties, Imposts and Excises, to pay the Debts and provide for the common Defence and general Welfare of the United States; but all Duties, Imposts and Excises shall be uniform throughout the United States;

To borrow Money on the credit of the United States;

To regulate Commerce with foreign Nations, and among the several States, and with the Indian Tribes;

To establish an uniform Rule of Naturalization, and uniform Laws on the subject of Bankruptcies throughout the United States;

To coin Money, regulate the Value thereof, and of foreign Coin, and fix the Standard of Weights and Measures;

To provide for the Punishment of counterfeiting the Securities and current Coin of the United States;

To establish Post Offices and post Roads;

To promote the Progress of Science and useful Arts, by securing for limited Times to Authors and Inventors the exclusive Right to their respective Writings and Discoveries;

To constitute Tribunals inferior to the supreme Court;

To define and punish Piracies and Felonies committed on the high Seas, and Offences against the Law of Nations;

To declare War, grant Letters of Marque and Reprisal, and make Rules concerning Captures on Land and Water;

To raise and support Armies, but no Appropriation of Money to that Use shall be for a longer Term than two Years;

To provide and maintain a Navy;

To make Rules for the Government and Regulation of the land and naval Forces;

To provide for calling forth the Militia to execute the Laws of the Union, suppress Insurrections and repel Invasions;

To provide for organizing, arming, and disciplining the Militia, and for governing such Part of them as may be employed in the Service of the United States, reserving to the States respectively, the Appointment of the Officers,

* Paragraphs 1-17 of Section 8 contain the "enumerated powers" of Congress.

and the Authority of training the Militia according to the discipline prescribed by Congress;

To exercise exclusive Legislation in all Cases whatsoever, over such District (not exceeding ten Miles square) as may, by Cession of particular States, and the Acceptance of Congress, become the Seat of the Government of the United States, and to exercise like Authority over all Places purchased by the Consent of the Legislature of the State in which the Same shall be, for the Erection of Forts, Magazines, Arsenals, dock-Yards, and other needful Buildings;—And

To make all Laws which shall be necessary and proper* for carrying into Execution the foregoing Powers, and all other Powers vested by this Constitution in the Government of the United States, or in any Department or Officer thereof.

Section 9†

The Migration or Importation of such Persons as any of the States now existing shall think proper to admit, shall not be prohibited by the Congress prior to the Year one thousand eight hundred and eight, but a Tax or duty may be imposed on such Importation, not exceeding ten dollars for each Person.

The Privilege of the Writ of Habeas Corpus shall not be suspended, unless when in Cases of Rebellion or Invasion the public Safety may require it.

No Bill of Attainder or ex post facto Law shall be passed.

No Capitation, or other direct, tax shall be laid, unless in Proportion to the Census or Enumeration herein before directed to be taken.

No Tax or Duty shall be laid on Articles exported from any State.

No Preference shall be given by any Regulation of Commerce or Revenue to the Ports of one State over those of another: nor shall Vessels bound to, or from, one State, be obliged to enter, clear, or pay Duties in another.

No Money shall be drawn from the Treasury, but in Consequence of Appropriations made by Law; and a regular Statement and Account of the Receipts and Expenditures of all public Money shall be published from time to time.

No Title of Nobility shall be granted by the United States: And no Person holding any Office of Profit or Trust under them, shall, without the Consent of the Congress, accept of any present, Emolument, Office, or Title, of any kind whatever, from any King, Prince, or foreign State.

Section 10‡

No State shall enter into any Treaty, Alliance, or Confederation; grant Letters of Marque and Reprisal; coin Money; emit Bills of Credit; make any Thing but gold and silver Coin a Tender in Payment of Debts; pass any Bill of Attainder, ex post facto Law, or Law impairing the Obligation of Contracts,§ or grant any Title of Nobility.

No State shall, without the Consent of the Congress, lay any Imposts or Duties on Imports or Exports, except what may be absolutely necessary for

* The "coefficient clause" (or "Elastic Clause" or "Necessary and Proper" clause) of the Constitution.
† This section imposes certain limitations on the powers of Congress.
‡ This section imposes certain limitations on the States.
§ The "Obligation of Contract" clause.

executing it's inspection Laws: and the net Produce of all Duties and Imposts, laid by any State on Imports or Exports, shall be for the Use of the Treasury of the United States; and all such Laws shall be subject to the Revision and Control of the Congress.

No State shall, without the Consent of Congress, lay any Duty of Tonnage, keep Troops, or Ships of War in time of Peace, enter into any Agreement or Compact with another State, or with a foreign Power, or engage in War, unless actually invaded, or in such imminent Danger as will not admit of delay.

ARTICLE II

Section 1

The executive Power shall be vested in a President of the United States of America. He shall hold his Office during the Term of four Years, and, together with the Vice President, chosen for the same Term, be elected, as follows:

Each State shall appoint, in such Manner as the Legislature thereof may direct, a Number of Electors, equal to the whole Number of Senators and Representatives to which the State may be entitled in the Congress: but no Senator or Representative, or Person holding an Office of Trust or Profit under the United States, shall be appointed an Elector.

[The electors shall meet in their respective States, and vote by ballot for two Persons, of whom one at least shall not be an Inhabitant of the same State with themselves. And they shall make a List of all the Persons voted for, and of the Number of Votes for each; which List they shall sign and certify, and transmit sealed to the Seat of the Government of the United States, directed to the President of the Senate. The President of the Senate shall, in the Presence of the Senate and House of Representatives, open all the Certificates, and the Votes shall then be counted. The Person having the greatest Number of Votes shall be the President, if such Number be a Majority of the whole Number of Electors appointed; and if there be more than one who have such Majority, and have an equal Number of Votes, then the House of Representatives shall immediately chuse by Ballot one of them for President; and if no Person have a Majority, then from the five highest on the List the said House shall in like Manner chuse the President. But in chusing the President, the Votes shall be taken by States, the Representation from each State having one Vote; A quorum for this Purpose shall consist of a Member or Members from two thirds of the States, and a Majority of all the States shall be necessary to a Choice. In every Case, after the Choice of the President, the Person having the greatest Number of Votes of the Electors shall be the Vice President. But if there should remain two or more who have equal Votes, the Senate shall chuse from them by Ballot the Vice President.]*

The Congress may determine the Time of chusing the Electors, and the Day on which they shall give their Votes; which Day shall be the same throughout the United States.

No Person except a natural born Citizen, or a Citizen of the United States, at the time of the Adoption of this Constitution, shall be eligible to the Office of

---

* Superseded by Amendment XII.

President; neither shall any Person be eligible to that Office who shall not have attained to the Age of thirty five Years, and been fourteen Years a Resident within the United States.

In Case of the Removal of the President from Office, or of his Death, Resignation or Inability to discharge the Powers and Duties of the said Office, the same shall devolve on the Vice President, and the Congress may by Law provide for the Case of Removal, Death, Resignation or Inability, both of the President and Vice President, declaring what Officer shall then act as President, and such Officer shall act accordingly, until the Disability be removed, or a President shall be elected.

The President shall, at stated Times, receive for his Services, a Compensation, which shall neither be encreased nor diminished during the Period for which he shall have been elected, and he shall not receive within that Period any other Emolument from the United States, or any of them.

Before he enter on the Execution of his Office, he shall take the following Oath or Affirmation:—"I do solemnly swear (or affirm) that I will faithfully execute the Office of President of the United States, and will to the best of my Ability, preserve, protect and defend the Constitution of the United States."

SECTION 2

The President shall be Commander in Chief of the Army and Navy of the United States, and of the Militia of the several States, when called into the actual Service of the United States; he may require the Opinion, in writing, of the principal Officer in each of the executive Departments, upon any Subject relating to the Duties of their respective Offices, and he shall have Power to grant Reprieves and Pardons for Offences against the United States, except in Cases of Impeachment.

He shall have Power,* by and with the Advice and Consent of the Senate, to make Treaties, provided two thirds of the Senators present concur; and he shall nominate, and by and with the Advice and Consent of the Senate, shall appoint Ambassadors, other public Ministers and Consuls, Judges of the supreme Court, and all other Officers of the United States, whose Appointments are not herein otherwise provided for, and which shall be established by Law: but the Congress may by Law vest the Appointment of such inferior Officers, as they think proper, in the President alone, in the Courts of Law, or in the Heads of Departments.

The President shall have Power to fill up all Vacancies that may happen during the Recess of the Senate, by granting Commissions which shall expire at the End of their next Session.

SECTION 3

He shall from time to time give to the Congress Information of the State of the Union, and recommend to their Consideration such Measures as he shall judge necessary and expedient; he may, on extraordinary Occasions, convene both Houses, or either of them, and, in Case of Disagreement between them, with Respect to the Time of Adjournment, he may adjourn them to such Time as he shall think proper; he shall receive Ambassadors and other public Min-

* The "Treaty Making Power" is contained in this sentence.

isters; he shall take Care that the Laws be faithfully executed, and shall Commission all the Officers of the United States.

SECTION 4

The President, Vice President and all civil Officers of the United States, shall be removed from Office on Impeachment for, and Conviction of, Treason, Bribery, or other high Crimes and Misdemeanors.

ARTICLE III

SECTION 1

The judicial Power of the United States, shall be vested in one supreme Court, and in such inferior Courts as the Congress may from time to time ordain and establish. The Judges, both of the supreme and inferior Courts, shall hold their Offices during good Behaviour, and shall, at stated Times, receive for their Services, a Compensation, which shall not be diminished during their Continuance in Office.

SECTION 2

The judicial Power shall extend to all Cases, in Law and Equity, arising under this Constitution, the Laws of the United States, and Treaties made, or which shall be made, under their Authority;—to all Cases affecting Ambassadors, other public Ministers and Consuls;—to all Cases of admiralty and maritime Jurisdiction;—to Controversies to which the United States shall be a Party;—to Controversies between two or more States;—between a State and Citizens of another State;—between Citizens of different States,—between Citizens of the same State claiming Lands under Grants of different States, and between a State, or the Citizens thereof, and foreign States, Citizens or Subjects.

In all Cases affecting Ambassadors, other public Ministers and Consuls, and those in which a State shall be Party, the supreme Court shall have original Jurisdiction. In all the other Cases before mentioned, the supreme Court shall have appellate Jurisdiction, both as to Law and Fact, with such Exceptions, and under such Regulations as the Congress shall make.

The Trial of all Crimes, except in Cases of Impeachment, shall be by Jury; and such Trial shall be held in the State where the said Crimes shall have been committed; but when not committed within any State, the Trial shall be at such Place or Places as the Congress may by Law have directed.

SECTION 3

Treason against the United States, shall consist only in levying War against them, or in adhering to their Enemies, giving them Aid and Comfort. No Person shall be convicted of Treason unless on the Testimony of two Witnesses to the same overt Act, or on Confession in open Court.

The Congress shall have Power to declare the Punishment of Treason, but no Attainder of Treason shall work Corruption of Blood, or Forfeiture except during the Life of the Person attainted.

ARTICLE IV

Section 1

Full Faith and Credit shall be given in each State to the public Acts, Records, and judicial Proceedings of every other State. And the Congress may by general Laws prescribe the Manner in which such Acts, Records and Proceedings shall be proved, and the Effect thereof.

Section 2

The Citizens of each State shall be entitled to all Privileges and Immunities of Citizens in the several States.

A person charged in any State with Treason, Felony, or other Crime, who shall flee from Justice, and be found in another State, shall on Demand of the executive Authority of the State from which he fled, be delivered up, to be removed to the State having Jurisdiction of the Crime.

No Person held to Service or Labour in one State, under the Laws thereof, escaping into another, shall, in Consequence of any Law or Regulation therein, be discharged from such Service or Labour, but shall be delivered up on Claim of the Party to whom such Service or Labour may be due.

Section 3

New States may be admitted by the Congress into this Union; but no new State shall be formed or erected within the Jurisdiction of any other State; nor any State be formed by the Junction of two or more States, or Parts of States, without the Consent of the Legislatures of the States concerned as well as of the Congress.

The Congress shall have Power to dispose of and make all needful Rules and Regulations respecting the Territory or other Property belonging to the United States; and nothing in this Constitution shall be so construed as to Prejudice any Claims of the United States, or of any particular State.

Section 4

The United States shall guarantee to every State in this Union a Republican Form of Government, and shall protect each of them against Invasion; and on Application of the Legislature, or of the Executive (when the Legislature cannot be convened) against domestic Violence.

ARTICLE V

The Congress, whenever two thirds of both Houses shall deem it necessary, shall propose Amendments to this Constitution,* or, on the Application of the Legislatures of two thirds of the several States, shall call a Convention for proposing Amendments, which, in either Case, shall be valid to all Intents and Purposes, as Part of this Constitution, when ratified by the Legislatures of three fourths of the several States, or by Conventions in three fourths thereof, as the one or the other Mode of Ratification may be proposed by the Congress; Provided that no Amendment which may be made prior to the Year One thousand eight hundred and eight shall in any Manner affect the first and fourth

* The Amending power.

Clauses in the Ninth Section of the first Article; and that no State, without its Consent, shall be deprived of its equal Suffrage in the Senate.

ARTICLE VI

All Debts contracted and Engagements entered into, before the Adoption of this Constitution, shall be as valid against the United States under this Constitution, as under the Confederation.

This Constitution, and the Laws of the United States which shall be made in Pursuance thereof; and all Treaties made, or which shall be made, under the Authority of the United States, shall be the supreme Law of the Land; and the Judges in every State shall be bound thereby, any Thing in the Constitution or Laws of any State to the Contrary notwithstanding.

The Senators and Representatives before mentioned, and the Members of the several State Legislatures, and all executive and judicial Officers, both of the United States and of the several States, shall be bound by Oath or Affirmation, to support this Constitution; but no religious Test shall ever be required as a Qualification to any Office or public Trust under the United States.

ARTICLE VII

The Ratification of the Conventions of nine States, shall be sufficient for the Establishment of this Constitution between the States so ratifying the Same.

DONE in Convention by the Unanimous Consent of the States present the Seventeenth Day of September in the Year of our Lord one thousand seven hundred and Eighty seven and of the Independence of the United States of America the Twelfth. IN WITNESS whereof We have hereunto subscribed our Names.

G° WASHINGTON
Presid' and deputy from Virginia

NEW HAMPSHIRE	JOHN LANGDON NICHOLAS GILMAN
MASSACHUSETTS	NATHANIEL GORHAM RUFUS KING
CONNECTICUT	WM. SAML. JOHNSON ROGER SHERMAN
NEW YORK	ALEXANDER HAMILTON
NEW JERSEY	WIL: LIVINGSTON DAVID BREARLEY WM. PATERSON JONA: DAYTON
PENNSYLVANIA	B FRANKLIN THOMAS MIFFLIN ROBT. MORRIS GEO. CLYMER THOS. FITZSIMONS JARED INGERSOLL JAMES WILSON GOUV MORRIS

DELAWARE	GEO: READ GUNNING BEDFORD jun JOHN DICKINSON RICHARD BASSETT JACO: BROOM
MARYLAND	JAMES McHENRY DAN OF ST. THOS. JENIFER DANL. CARROLL
VIRGINIA	JOHN BLAIR — JAMES MADISON JR.
NORTH CAROLINA	WM. BLOUNT RICHD. DOBBS SPAIGHT HU WILLIAMSON
SOUTH CAROLINA	J. RUTLEDGE CHARLES COTESWORTH PINCKNEY CHARLES PINCKNEY PIERCE BUTLER
GEORGIA	WILLIAM FEW ABR BALDWIN

Attest WILLIAM JACKSON *Secretary*

AMENDMENTS

ARTICLE I

Congress shall make no law respecting an establishment of religion, or pro-hibiting the free exercise thereof; or abridging the freedom of speech, or of the press; or the right of the people peaceably to assemble, and to petition the Government for a redress of grievances.

ARTICLE II

A well regulated Militia, being necessary to the security of a free State, the right of the people to keep and bear Arms, shall not be infringed.

ARTICLE III

No Soldier shall, in time of peace, be quartered in any house, without the consent of the Owner, nor in time of war, but in a manner to be prescribed by law.

ARTICLE IV

The right of the people to be secure in their persons, houses, papers, and effects, against unreasonable searches and seizures, shall not be violated, and no Warrants shall issue, but upon probable cause, supported by Oath or affirma-tion, and particularly describing the place to be searched, and the persons or things to be seized.

ARTICLE V

No person shall be held to answer for a capital, or otherwise infamous crime, unless on a presentment or indictment of a Grand Jury, except in cases arising in the land or naval forces, or in the Militia, when in actual service in time of War or public danger; nor shall any person be subject for the same offence to be twice put in jeopardy of life or limb; nor shall be compelled in any Criminal Case to be a witness against himself, nor be deprived of life, liberty, or property, without due process of law; nor shall private property be taken for public use, without just compensation.

ARTICLE VI

In all criminal prosecutions, the accused shall enjoy the right to a speedy and public trial, by an impartial jury of the State and district wherein the crime shall have been committed, which district shall have been previously ascertained by law, and to be informed of the nature and cause of the accusa-tion; to be confronted with the witnesses against him; to have compulsory process for obtaining Witnesses in his favor, and to have the Assistance of Coun-sel for his defence.

ARTICLE VII

In suits at common law, where the value in controversy shall exceed twenty dollars, the right of trial by jury shall be preserved, and no fact tried by a jury shall be otherwise re-examined in any Court of the United States, than according to the rules of the common law.

ARTICLE VIII

Excessive bail shall not be required, nor excessive fines imposed, nor cruel and unusual punishments inflicted.

ARTICLE IX

The enumeration in the Constitution, of certain rights, shall not be construed to deny or disparage others retained by the people.

ARTICLE X

The powers not delegated to the United States by the Constitution, nor prohibited by it to the States, are reserved to the States respectively, or to the people.

[THE FIRST TEN ARTICLES PROPOSED 25 SEPTEMBER 1789; DECLARED IN FORCE 15 DECEMBER 1791]*

ARTICLE XI
[DECLARED RATIFIED 8 JANUARY 1798]

The Judicial power of the United States shall not be contrued to extend to any suit in law or equity, commenced or prosecuted against one of the United States by Citizens of another State, or by Citizens or Subjects of any Foreign State.

ARTICLE XII
[DECLARED RATIFIED 25 SEPTEMBER 1804]

The Electors shall meet in their respective states, and vote by ballot for President and Vice-President, one of whom, at least, shall not be an inhabitant of the same state with themselves; they shall name in their ballots the person voted for as President, and in distinct ballots the person voted for as Vice-President, and they shall make distinct lists of all persons voted for as President, and of all persons voted for as Vice-President, and of the number of votes for each, which lists they shall sign and certify, and transmit sealed to the seat of the Government of the United States, directed to the President of the Senate;— The President of the Senate shall, in the presence of the Senate and House of Representatives, open all the certificates and the votes shall then be counted;— The person having the greatest number of votes for President, shall be the President, if such number be a majority of the whole number of Electors appointed; and if no person have such majority, then from the persons having the highest numbers not exceeding three on the list of those voted for as President, the House of Representatives shall choose immediately, by ballot, the President. But in choosing the President, the votes shall be taken by states, the representation from each state having one vote; a quorum for this purpose shall consist of

* These amendments bind only the National Government, but these rights are not infrequently binding against State authority because of the Court's interpretation of the "due process clause" of Amendment XIV.

a member or members from two-thirds of the states, and a majority of all the states shall be necessary to a choice. And if the House of Representatives shall not choose a President whenever the right of choice shall devolve upon them, before the fourth day of March next following, then the Vice-President shall act as President, as in the case of the death or other constitutional disability of the President. The person having the greatest number of votes as Vice-President, shall be the Vice-President, if such number be a majority of the whole number of Electors appointed, and if no person have a majority, then from the two highest numbers on the list, the Senate shall choose the Vice-President; a quorum for the purpose shall consist of two-thirds of the whole number of Senators, and a majority of the whole number shall be necessary to a choice. But no person constitutionally ineligible to the office of President shall be eligible to that of Vice-President of the United States.

ARTICLE XIII

[DECLARED RATIFIED 18 DECEMBER 1865]

SECTION 1

Neither slavery nor involuntary servitude, except as a punishment for crime whereof the party shall have been duly convicted, shall exist within the United States, or any place subject to their jurisdiction.

SECTION 2

Congress shall have power to enforce this article by appropriate legislation.

ARTICLE XIV

[DECLARED RATIFIED 28 JULY 1868]*

SECTION 1

All persons born or naturalized in the United States, and subject to the jurisdiction thereof, are citizens of the United States and of the State wherein they reside. No State shall make or enforce any law which shall abridge the privileges or immunities of citizens of the United States; nor shall any State deprive any person of life, liberty, or property, without due process of law; nor deny to any person within its jurisdiction the equal protection of the law.

SECTION 2

Representatives shall be apportioned among the several States according to their respective numbers, counting the whole number of persons in each State, excluding Indians not taxed. But when the right to vote at any election for the choice of electors for President and Vice-President of the United States, Representatives in Congress, the Executive and Judicial officers of a State, or the members of the Legislature thereof, is denied to any of the male inhabitants of such State, being twenty-one years of age, and citizens of the United States, or in any way abridged, except for participation in rebellion, or other crime, the basis of representation therein shall be reduced in the proportion which the

---

* Prior to date of ratification of the twenty-eighth state, Ohio and New Jersey "withdrew" their earlier assents to the amendment. Congress passed a joint resolution on July 21, 1868 declaring the amendment a part of the Constitution and directing the Secretary of State to promulgate it as such. On July 13th South Carolina ratified and on July 21 Georgia added its ratification.

number of such male citizens shall bear to the whole number of male citizens twenty-one years of age in such State.

Section 3

No person shall be a Senator or Representative in Congress, or elector of President and Vice-President, or hold any office, civil, or military, under the United States, or under any State, who, having previously taken an oath, as a member of Congress, or as an officer of the United States, or as a member of any State legislature, or as an executive or judicial officer of any State, to support the Constitution of the United States, shall have engaged in insurrection or rebellion against the same, or given aid or comfort to the enemies thereof. But Congress may by a vote of two-thirds of each House, remove such disability.

Section 4

The validity of the public debt of the United States, authorized by law, including debts incurred for payment of pensions and bounties for services in suppressing insurrection or rebellion, shall not be questioned. But neither the United States nor any State shall assume or pay any debt or obligation incurred in aid of insurrection or rebellion against the United States, or any claim for the loss or emancipation of any slave; but all such debts, obligations and claims shall be held illegal and void.

Section 5

The Congress shall have power to enforce, by appropriate legislation, the provisions of this article.

ARTICLE XV

[DECLARED RATIFIED 30 MARCH 1870]

Section 1

The right of citizens of the United States to vote shall not be denied or abridged by the United States or by any State on account of race, color, or previous condition of servitude.

Section 2

The Congress shall have power to enforce this article by appropriate legislation.

ARTICLE XVI

[PROPOSED 12 JULY 1909; DECLARED RATIFIED 25 FEBRUARY 1913]

The Congress shall have power to lay and collect taxes on incomes, from whatever source derived, without apportionment among the several States, and without regard to any census or enumeration.

ARTICLE XVII

[DECLARED RATIFIED 31 MAY 1913]

The Senate of the United States shall be composed of two senators from each State, elected by the people thereof, for six years; and each Senator shall have one vote. The electors in each State shall have the qualifications requisite for electors of the most numerous branch of the State legislature.

When vacancies happen in the representation of any State in the Senate, the executive authority of such State shall issue writs of election to fill such vacancies: PROVIDED, That the legislature of any State may empower the executive thereof to make temporary appointments until the people fill the vacancies by election as the legislature may direct.

This amendment shall not be so construed as to affect the election or term of any senator chosen before it becomes valid as part of the Constitution.

ARTICLE XVIII*

[DECLARED RATIFIED 29 JANUARY 1919]

After one year from the ratification of this article, the manufacture, sale, or transportation of intoxicating liquors within, the importation thereof into, or the exportation thereof from the United States and all territory subject to the jurisdiction thereof for beverage purposes is hereby prohibited.

The Congress and the several States shall have concurrent power to enforce this article by appropriate legislation.

This article shall be inoperative unless it shall have been ratified as an amendment to the Constitution by the legislatures of the several States, as provided in the Constitution, within seven years from the date of the submission hereof to the States by the Congress.

ARTICLE XIX

[PROPOSED 4 JUNE 1919; DECLARED RATIFIED 26 AUGUST 1920]

The right of citizens of the United States to vote shall not be denied or abridged by the United States or by any States on account of sex.

The Congress shall have power, by appropriate legislation, to enforce the provisions of this article.

ARTICLE XX

[DECLARED RATIFIED 6 FEBRUARY 1933]

SECTION 1

The terms of the President and Vice-President shall end at noon on the twentieth day of January, and the terms of Senators and Representatives at noon on the third day of January, of the years in which such terms would have ended if this article had not been ratified; and the terms of their successors shall then begin.

SECTION 2

The Congress shall assemble at least once in every year, and such meeting shall begin at noon on the third day of January, unless they shall by law appoint a different day.

SECTION 3

If, at the time fixed for the beginning of the term of the President, the President-elect shall have died, the Vice-President-elect shall become President. If a President shall not have been choosen before the time fixed for the beginning of his term, or if the President-elect shall have failed to qualify, then the Vice-President-elect shall act as President until a President shall have qualified;

* Repealed by section 1 of Amendment XXI.

and the Congress may by law provide for the case wherein neither a President-elect nor a Vice-President-elect shall have qualified, declaring who shall then act as President, or the manner in which one who is to act shall be selected, and such person shall act accordingly until a President or Vice-President shall have qualified.

Section 4

The Congress may by law provide for the case of the death of any of the persons from whom the House of Representatives may choose a President whenever the right of choice shall have devolved upon them, and for the case of the death of any of the persons from whom the Senate may choose a Vice-President whenever the right of choice shall have devolved upon them.

Section 5

Sections 1 and 2 shall take effect on the 15th day of October following the ratification of this article.

Section 6

This article shall be inoperative unless it shall have been ratified as an amendment to the Constitution by the legislatures of three-fourths of the several States within seven years from the date of its submission.

ARTICLE XXI

[DECLARED RATIFIED 5 DECEMBER 1933]

Section 1

The eighteenth article of amendment to the Constitution of the United States is hereby repealed.

Section 2

The transportation or importation into any State, Territory or possession of the United States for delivery or use therein of intoxicating liquors, in violation of the laws thereof, is hereby prohibited.

Section 3

This article shall be inoperative unless it shall have been ratified as an amendment to the Constitution by convention in the several States, as provided in the Constitution, within seven years from the date of the submission hereof to the States by the Congress.

ARTICLE XXII

[DECLARED RATIFIED 1 MARCH 1951]

Section 1

No person shall be elected to the office of President more than twice, and no person who has held the office of President, or acted as President, for more than two years of a term to which some other person was elected President shall be elected to the office of the President more than once. But this article shall not apply to any person holding the office of President when this article was proposed by the Congress, and shall not prevent any person who may be holding the office of President, or acting as President, during the term within which this Article becomes operative from holding the office of President or acting as President during the remainder of such term.

SECTION 2

This Article shall be inoperative unless it shall have been ratified as an amendment to the Constitution by the legislatures of three-fourths of the several States within seven years from the date of its submission to the States by the Congress.

UNRATIFIED AMENDMENTS

Twenty-two Amendments have been ratified by the required three-fourths of the states, 5 others have been submitted to the States but have not been ratified.

In *Coleman vs Miller*, 307 U.S. 433, (1939) the U.S. Supreme Court ruled that the reasonableness of time for ratification was a political question to be determined by Congress.

The Two Unratified Amendments of the Proposed Bill of Rights (1789)

ARTICLE I

After the first enumeration required by the first article of the Constitution, there shall be one Representative for every thirty thousand, until the number shall amount to one hundred, after which the proportion shall be so regulated by Congress, that there shall be no less than one hundred Representatives, nor less than one Representative for every forty thousand persons, until the number of Representatives shall amount to two hundred; after which the proportion shall be so regulated by Congress, that there shall not be less than two hundred Representatives for every fifty thousand persons.

ARTICLE II

No law varying the compensation for the services of the Senators and Representatives shall take effect, until an election of Representatives shall have intervened.

The Unratified Amendment Relating to Titles of Nobility of Foreign Governments
(proposed by 2nd Session of the 11th Congress)

Resolved by the Senate and House of Representatives of the United States of America in Congress assembled (two-thirds of both Houses concurring), That the following section be submitted to the legislatures of the several states, which, when ratified by the legislatures of three-fourths of the states, shall be valid and binding, as a part of the constitution of the United States.

If any citizen of the United States shall accept, claim, receive or retain any title of nobility or honour, or shall, without the consent of Congress, accept and retain any present, pension, office of emolument of any kind whatever, from any emperor, king, prince or foreign power, such person shall cease to be a citizen of the United States, and shall be incapable of holding any office of trust or profit under them, or either of them.

THE UNRATIFIED 13TH AMENDMENT (proposed by the 36th Congress, March 2, 1861)

This was signed by President Lincoln the day after the seizure of Fort Sumter. This is the only proposed amendment ever signed by the President. The President's signature is not considered necessary because of the constitutional provision that two-thirds of both Houses of Congress must concur before the amendment can be submitted to the States for ratification.

Resolved by the Senate and House of Representatives of the United States of America in Congress assembled, That the following article be proposed to the Legislatures of the several States as an amendment to the Constitution of the United States, which, when ratified by three-fourths of said Legislatures, shall be valid, to all intents and purposes, as part of the said Constitution, viz:

ARTICLE XIII

No amendment shall be made to the Constitution which will authorize or give to Congress the power to abolish or interfere, within any State, with the domestic institutions thereof, including that of persons held to labor or service by the laws of said State.

THE UNRATIFIED CHILD-LABOR AMENDMENT (proposed by the 1st Session of the 68th Congress in June 1924)

Resolved by the Senate and House of Representatives of the United States of America in Congress assembled (two-thirds of each House concurring therein), That the following article is proposed as an amendment to the Constitution of the United States, which, when ratified by the legislatures of three-fourths of the several States, shall be valid to all intents and purposes as a part of the Constitution:

ARTICLE ——

SECTION 1. The Congress shall have power to limit, regulate, and prohibit the labor of persons under 18 years of age.

SECTION 2. The power of the several States is unimpaired by this article except that the operation of State laws shall be suspended to the extent necessary to give effect to legislation enacted by the Congress.

STATES OF THE UNION, 1787–1865

State	Date Admitted		Rank in Population 1790	1820	1850
THE ORIGINAL THIRTEEN*					
Delaware	1787		13	22	30
Pennsylvania	1787		3	3	2
New Jersey	1787		9	13	19
Georgia	1788		11	11	9
Connecticut	1788		8	14	21
Massachusetts	1788	(& Maine)→	2	7	6
Maryland	1788		6	10	17
South Carolina	1788		7	8	14
New Hampshire	1788		10	15	22
Virginia	1788		1	2	4
New York	1788		5	1	1
North Carolina	1789		4	4	10
Rhode Island	1790		12	20	28
Vermont	1791			16	23
Kentucky	1792			6	8
Tennessee	1796			9	5
Ohio	1803			5	3
Louisiana	1812			17	18
Indiana	1816			18	7
Mississippi	1817			21	15
Illinois	1818			24	11
Alabama	1819			19	12
Maine	1820			12	16
Missouri	1821			23	13
Arkansas	1836				26
Michigan	1837				20
Florida	1845				31
Texas	1845				25
Iowa	1846				27
Wisconsin	1848				24
California	1850				29
Minnesota	1858				
Oregon	1859				
Kansas	1861				
West Virginia	1863				
Nevada	1864				

* Arranged in the order of their ratification of the Constitution.

POLITICAL PARTIES, 1796-1860

	FEDERALIST		REPUBLICAN
1796	J. Adams (1797-1801)		
1800			Jefferson (1801-09)
1804			
1808			Madison (1809-17)
1812			
1816			Monroe (1817-25)
1820			
1824			

J. Q. Adams (1825-29)
Jackson-candidate

	NATIONAL-REPUBLICAN	DEMOCRATIC-REPUBLICAN
1828	Adams-candidate	Jackson (1829-37)
		DEMOCRATIC
1832	Clay-candidate	Jackson elected again 1832
	WHIG	
1836	Coalition candidates in 1836	Van Buren (1837-41)
1840	Harrison (1841) Tyler (1841-45)	
1844		Polk (1845-49)
1848	Taylor (1849-50) Fillmore (1850-53)	
1852		Pierce (1853-57)

	REPUBLICAN	AMERICAN	
1856	Frémont candidate	Fillmore candidate	Buchanan (1857-61)

		CONSTITUTION-UNION	NORTHERN DEMOCRATS	SOUTHERN DEMOCRATS
1860	Lincoln (1861-65)	Bell candidate	Douglas candidate	Breckinridge candidate

MAJOR EXECUTIVE OFFICERS
OF THE
UNITED STATES, 1789-1865

President		Term
GEORGE WASHINGTON of Virginia		1789-97
Vice-President	John Adams of Mass.	1789-97
Secretary of State	Thomas Jefferson of Va.	1790-93
	Edmund Randolph of Va.	1794-95
	Timothy Pickering of Pa.	1795-97
Secretary of the Treasury	Alexander Hamilton of N.Y.	1789-95
	Oliver Wolcott of Conn.	1795-97
Secretary of War	Henry Knox of Mass.	1789-95
	Timothy Pickering of Pa.	1795
	James McHenry of Md.	1796-97
Attorney General	Edmund Randolph of Va.	1789-94
	William Bradford of Pa.	1794-95
	Charles Lee of Va.	1795-97
Postmaster General	Samuel Osgood of Mass.	1789-91
	Timothy Pickering of Pa.	1791-95
	Joseph Habersham of Ga.	1795-97
JOHN ADAMS of Massachusetts		1797-1801
Vice-President	Thomas Jefferson of Va.	1797-1801
Secretary of State	Timothy Pickering of Pa.	1797-1800
	John Marshall of Va.	1800-01

873

Secretary of the Treasury	Oliver Wolcott of Conn.	1797-1801
	Samuel Dexter of Mass.	1801
Secretary of War	James McHenry of Md.	1797-1800
	Samuel Dexter of Mass.	1800-01
Attorney General	Charles Lee of Va.	1797-1801
Postmaster General	Joseph Habersham of Ga.	1797-1801
Secretary of the Navy	Benjamin Stoddert of Md.	1798-1801

THOMAS JEFFERSON of Virginia   1801-09

Vice-President	Aaron Burr of N.Y.	1801-05
	George Clinton of N.Y.	1805-09
Secretary of State	James Madison of Va.	1801-09
Secretary of the Treasury	Albert Gallatin of Pa.	1801-09
Secretary of War	Henry Dearborn of Mass.	1801-09
Attorney General	Levi Lincoln of Mass.	1801-05
	John Breckinridge of Ky.	1805-07
	Caesar Rodney of Del.	1807-09
Postmaster General	Gideon Granger of Conn.	1801-09
Secretary of the Navy	Robert Smith of Md.	1801-05
	Jacob Crowninshield of Mass.,	1805-09

JAMES MADISON of Virginia   1809-17

Vice-President	George Clinton* of N.Y.	1809-12
	Elbridge Gerry† of Mass.	1813-14

* Died 1812.
† Died 1814.

Secretary of State	Robert Smith of Md.	1809-11
	James Monroe of Va.	1811-17
Secretary of the Treasury	Albert Gallatin of Pa.	1809-14
	George Campbell of Tenn.	1814
	Alexander Dallas of Pa.	1814-16
	William H. Crawford of Ga.	1816-17
Secretary of War	William Eustis of Mass.	1809-13
	John Armstrong of N.Y.	1813-14
	James Monroe of Va.	1814-15
	William H. Crawford of Ga.	1815-17
Attorney General	Caesar Rodney of Del.	1809-11
	William Pinckney of Md.	1811-14
	Richard Rush of Pa.	1814-17
Postmaster General	Gideon Granger of Conn.	1809-14
	Return J. Meigs of Ohio	1814-17
Secretary of the Navy	Paul Hamilton of S.C.	1809-13
	William Jones of Pa.	1813-14
	Benjamin Crowninshield of Mass.	1814-17

JAMES MONROE of Virginia   1817-25

Vice-President	Daniel D. Tompkins of N.Y.	1817-25
Secretary of State	John Quincy Adams of Mass.	1817-25
Secretary of the Treasury	William H. Crawford of Ga.	1817-25
Secretary of War	John C. Calhoun of S.C.	1817-25
Attorney General	Richard Rush of Pa.	1817
	William Wirt of Va.	1817-25
Postmaster General	Return J. Meigs of Ohio	1817-23
	John McLean of Ohio	1823-25
Secretary of the Navy	Benjamin Crowninshield of Mass.	1817-18
	Smith Thompson of N.Y.	1818-23
	Samuel L. Southard of N.J.	1823-25

JOHN QUINCY ADAMS of Massachusetts		1825-29
Vice-President	John C. Calhoun of S.C.	1825-29
Secretary of State	Henry Clay of Ky.	1825-29
Secretary of the Treasury	Richard Rush of Pa.	1825-29
Secretary of War	James Barbour of Va.	1825-28
	Peter B. Porter of N.Y.	1828-29
Attorney General	William Wirt of Va.	1825-29
Postmaster General	John McLean of Ohio	1825-29
Secretary of the Navy	Samuel L. Southard of N.J.	1825-29

ANDREW JACKSON of Tennessee		1829-37
Vice-President	John C. Calhoun* of S.C.	1829-32
	Martin Van Buren of N.Y.	1833-37
Secretary of State	Martin Van Buren of N. Y.	1829-31
	Edward Livingston of N.Y.	1831-33
	Louis McLane of Del.	1833-34
	John Forsyth of Ga.	1834-37
Secretary of the Treasury	Samuel Ingham of Pa.	1829-31
	Louis McLane of Del.	1831-33
	William Duane of Pa.	1833
	Roger B. Taney of Md.	1833-34
	Levi Woodbury of N.H.	1834-37
Secretary of War	John H. Eaton of Tenn.	1829-31
	Lewis Cass of Ohio	1831-37
Attorney General	John M. Berrien of Ga.	1829-31
	Roger B. Taney of Md.	1831-33
	Benjamin F. Butler of N.Y.	1833-37
Postmaster General	William Barry of Ky.	1829-35
	Amos Kendall of Ky.	1835-37

* Resigned in Dec. 1832.

Secretary of the Navy	John Branch of N.C.	1829-31
	Levi Woodbury of N.H.	1831-34
	Mahlon Dickerson of N.J.	1834-37

MARTIN VAN BUREN of New York		1837-41
Vice-President	Richard M. Johnson of Ky.	1837-41
Secretary of State	John Forsyth of Ga.	1837-41
Secretary of the Treasury	Levi Woodbury of N.H.	1837-41
Secretary of War	Joel R. Poinsett of S.C.	1837-41
Attorney General	Benjamin F. Butler of N.Y.	1837-38
	Felix Grundy of Tenn.	1838-40
	Henry D. Gilpin of Pa.	1840-41
Postmaster General	Amos Kendall of Ky.	1837-40
	John M. Niles of Conn.	1840-41
Secretary of the Navy	Mahlon Dickerson of N.J.	1837-38
	James K. Paulding of N.Y.	1838-41

WILLIAM HENRY HARRISON* of Ohio		1841
Vice-President	John Tyler of Va.	1841
Secretary of State	Daniel Webster of Mass.	1841
Secretary of the Treasury	Thomas Ewing of Ohio	1841
Secretary of War	John Bell of Tenn.	1841
Attorney General	John J. Crittenden of Ky.	1841
Postmaster General	Francis Granger of N.Y.	1841
Secretary of the Navy	George E. Badger of N.C.	1841

* Died one month after taking office.

JOHN TYLER of Virginia   1841-45

Secretary of State	Daniel Webster of Mass.	1841-43
	Abel P. Upshur of Va.	1843-44
	John C. Calhoun of S.C.	1844-45
Secretary of the Treasury	Thomas Ewing of Ohio	1841
	Walter Forward of Pa.	1841-43
	John C. Spencer of N.Y.	1843-44
	George M. Bibb of Ky.	1844-45
Secretary of War	John Bell of Tenn.	1841
	John C. Spencer of N.Y.	1841-43
	James M. Porter of Pa.	1843-44
	William Wilkins of Pa.	1844-45
Attorney General	John J. Crittenden of Ky.	1841
	Hugh S. Legare of S.C.	1841-43
	John Nelson of Md.	1843-45
Postmaster General	Francis Granger of N.Y.	1841
	Charles A. Wicliffe of Ky.	1841-45
Secretary of the Navy	George E. Badger of N.C.	1841
	Abel P. Upshur of Va.	1841-43
	David Henshaw of Mass.	1843-44
	Thomas Gilmer of Va.	1844
	John Y. Mason of Va.	1844-45

JAMES K. POLK of Tennessee   1845-49

Vice-President	George M. Dallas of Pa.	1845-49
Secretary of State	James Buchanan of Pa.	1845-49
Secretary of the Treasury	Robert J. Walker of Miss.	1845-49
Secretary of War	William L. Marcy of N.Y.	1845-49
Attorney General	John Y. Mason of Va.	1845-46
	Nathan Clifford of Me.	1846-48
	Isaac Toucey of Conn.	1848-49

Postmaster General	Cave Johnson of Tenn.	1845-49
Secretary of the Navy	George Bancroft of Mass.	1845-46
	John Y. Mason of Va.	1846-49

ZACHARY TAYLOR* of Louisiana 1849-50

Vice-President	Millard Fillmore of N.Y.	1849-50
Secretary of State	John M. Clayton of Del.	1849-50
Secretary of the Treasury	William M. Meredith of Pa.	1849-50
Secretary of War	George W. Crawford of Ga.	1849-50
Attorney General	Reverdy Johnson of Md.	1849-50
Postmaster General	Jacob Collamer of Vt.	1849-50
Secretary of the Navy	William R. Preston of Va.	1849-50
Secretary of the Interior	Thomas Ewing of Ohio	1849-50

MILLARD FILLMORE of New York 1850-53

Secretary of State	Daniel Webster of Mass.	1850-52
	Edward Everett of Mass.	1852-53
Secretary of the Treasury	Thomas Corwin of Ohio	1850-53
Secretary of War	Charles M. Conrad of La.	1850-53
Attorney General	John J. Crittenden of Ky.	1850-53
Postmaster General	Nathan K. Hall of N.Y.	1850-52
	Sam D. Hubbard of Conn.	1852-53

* Died in office July 9, 1850.

Secretary of the Navy	William A. Graham of N.C.	1850-52
	John P. Kennedy of Md.	1852-53
Secretary of the Interior	Alexander H. H. Stuart of Va.	1852-53

FRANKLIN PIERCE of New Hampshire   1853-57

Vice-President	William R. D. King* of Ala.	1853
Secretary of State	William R. Marcy of N.Y.	1853-57
Secretary of the Treasury	James Guthrie of Ky.	1853-57
Secretary of War	Jefferson Davis of Miss.	1853-57
Attorney General	Caleb Cushing of Mass.	1853-57
Postmaster General	James Campbell of Pa.	1853-57
Secretary of the Navy	James C. Dobbin of N.C.	1853-57
Secretary of the Interior	Jacob Thompson of Miss.	1853-57

JAMES BUCHANAN of Pennsylvania   1857-61

Vice-President	John C. Breckinridge of Ky.	1857-61
Secretary of State	Lewis Cass of Mich.	1857-60
	Jeremiah S. Black of Pa.	1860-61
Secretary of the Treasury	Howell Cobb of Ga.	1857-60
	Philip F. Thomas of Md.	1860-61
	John A. Dix of N.Y.	1861
Secretary of War	John B. Floyd of Va.	1857-61
	Joseph Holt of Ky.	1861
Attorney General	Jeremiah S. Black of Pa.	1857-60
	Edwin M. Stanton of Pa.	1860-61

* Died 1853.

Postmaster General	Aaron V. Brown of Tenn.	1857-59
	Joseph Holt of Ky.	1859-61
Secretary of the Navy	Isaac Toucey of Conn.	1857-61
Secretary of the Interior	Jacob Thompson of Miss.	1857-61

ABRAHAM LINCOLN* of Illinois		1861-65
Vice-President	Hannibal Hamlin of Me.	1861-65
	Andrew Johnson of Tenn.	1865
Secretary of State	William H. Seward of N.Y.	1861-65
Secretary of the Treasury	Salmon P. Chase of Ohio	1861-64
	William P. Fessenden of Me.	1864-65
	Hugh McCulloch of Ind.	1865
Secretary of War	Simon Cameron of Pa.	1861-62
	Edwin M. Stanton of Pa.	1862-65
Attorney General	Edward Bates of Mo.	1861-63
	James Speed of Ky.	1864-65
Postmaster General	Montgomery Blair of Md.	1861-64
	William Dennison of Ohio	1864-65
Secretary of the Navy	Gideon Welles of Conn.	1861-65
Secretary of the Interior	Caleb B. Smith of Ind.	1861-63
	John P. Usher of Ind.	1863-65

* Died April 15, 1865 from assassin's bullet.

JUSTICES OF THE UNITED STATES SUPREME COURT, 1789-1865

Name

John Jay of N.Y. (CHIEF JUSTICE)	1789-95
John Rutledge of S.C.	1789-91
William Cushing of Mass.	1789-1810
James Wilson of Pa.	1789-98
John Blair of Va.	1789-96
James Iredell of N.C.	1790-99
Thomas Johnson of Md.	1791-93
William Paterson of N.J.	1793-1806
John Rutledge of S.C. (CHIEF JUSTICE)	1795
Samuel Chase of Md.	1796-1811
Oliver Ellsworth of Conn. (CHIEF JUSTICE)	1796-99
Bushrod Washington of Va.	1798-1829
Alfred Moore of N.C.	1799-1804
John Marshall of Va. (CHIEF JUSTICE)	1801-35
William Johnson of S.C.	1804-34
Henry B. Livingston of N.Y.	1806-23
Thomas Todd of Ky.	1807-26
Joseph Story of Mass.	1811-45
Gabriel Duval of Md.	1812-35
Smith Thompson of N.Y.	1823-43
Robert Trimble of Ky.	1826-28
John McLean of Ohio	1829-61
Henry Baldwin of Pa.	1830-44
James M. Wayne of Ga.	1835-67
Roger B. Taney of Md. (CHIEF JUSTICE)	1836-64
Philip P. Barbour of Va.	1836-41
John Catron of Tenn.	1837-52
John McKinley of Ala.	1837-52
Peter V. Daniel of Va.	1841-60
Samuel Nelson of N.Y.	1845-72
Levi Woodbury of N.H.	1845-51
Robert C. Grier of Pa.	1846-70
Benj. R. Curtis of Mass.	1851-57
John A. Campbell of Ala.	1853-61
Nathan Clifford of Me.	1858-81
Noah H. Swayne of Ohio	1862-81
Samuel F. Miller of Iowa	1862-90
David Davis of Ill.	1862-77
Stephen J. Field of Cal.	1863-97
Salmon P. Chase (CHIEF JUSTICE)	1864-73

INDEX

DATE DUE